A SELECT LIBRARY

OF

NICENE AND POST-NICENE FATHERS

OF

THE CHRISTIAN CHURCH

Second Series

TRANSLATED INTO ENGLISH WITH PROLEGOMENA AND EXPLANATORY NOTES.

UNDER THE EDITORIAL SUPERVISION OF

PHILIP SCHAFF, D.D., LL.D.,   AND   HENRY WACE, D.D.,

Professor of Church History in the
Union Theological Seminary, New York.

Principal of King's College,
London.

IN CONNECTION WITH A NUMBER OF PATRISTIC SCHOLARS OF EUROPE
AND AMERICA.

VOLUME XI

SULPITIUS SEVERUS

VINCENT OF LERINS

JOHN CASSIAN

T&T CLARK
EDINBURGH

WM. B. EERDMANS PUBLISHING COMPANY
GRAND RAPIDS, MICHIGAN

British Library Cataloguing in Publication Data

Nicene & Post-Nicene Fathers. — 2nd series
1. Fathers of the church
I. Schaff, Philip   II. Mace, Henry
230'.11   BR60.A62

T&T Clark ISBN 0 567 09420 0

Eerdmans ISBN 0-8028-8125-4

Reprinted, June 1991

CONTENTS OF VOLUME XI.

THE WORKS OF SULPITIUS SEVERUS.

TRANSLATED,

WITH PREFACE, AND NOTES,

BY

REV. ALEXANDER ROBERTS, D. D.,

PROFESSOR OF HUMANITY, UNIVERSITY OF ST. ANDREWS, SCOTLAND.

LIFE AND WRITINGS OF SULPITIUS SEVERUS.

SULPITIUS (or Sulpicius) SEVERUS was born in Aquitania about A.D. 363, and died, as is generally supposed, in A.D. 420. He was thus a contemporary of the two great Fathers of the Church,
St. Jerome and St. Augustine. The former refers to him in his Commentary on the 36th chapter
of Ezekiel as "our friend Severus." St. Augustine, again, having occasion to allude to him in
his 205th letter, describes him as "a man excelling in learning and wisdom." Sulpitius belonged
to an illustrious family. He was very carefully educated, and devoted himself in his early years
to the practice of oratory. He acquired a high reputation at the bar; but, while yet in the
prime of life, he resolved to leave it, and seek, in company with some pious friends, contentment
and peace in a life of retirement and religious exercises. The immediate occasion of this resolution was the premature death of his wife, whom he had married at an early age, and to whom he
was deeply attached. His abandonment of the pleasures and pursuits of the world took place
about A.D. 392; and, notwithstanding all the entreaties and expostulations of his father, he
continued, from that date to his death, to lead a life of the strictest seclusion. Becoming a
Presbyter of the Church, he attached himself to St. Martin of Tours, for whom he ever afterwards cherished the profoundest admiration and affection, and whose extraordinary career he has
traced with a loving pen in by far the most interesting of his works.

It is stated by some ancient writers that Sulpitius ultimately incurred the charge of heresy,
having, to some extent, embraced Pelagian opinions. And there have not been wanting those in
modern times who thought they could detect traces of such errors in his works. But it seems to
us that there is no ground for any such conclusion. Sulpitius constantly presents himself to us
as a most strenuous upholder of "catholic" or "orthodox" doctrines. It is evident that his
whole heart was engaged in the love and maintenance of these doctrines: he counts as his
"friends" those only who consistently adhered to them; and, while by no means in favor of
bitterly prosecuting or severely punishing "heretics," he shrunk with abhorrence from all thought
of communion with them. Perhaps the most striking impression we receive from a perusal of
his writings is his *sincerity*. We may often feel that he is over-credulous in his acceptance of the
miraculous; and we may lament his narrowness in clinging so tenaciously to mere ecclesiastical
formulæ; but we are always impressed with the genuineness of his convictions, and with his
fervent desire to bring what he believed to be truth under the attention of his readers.

The style of Sulpitius is, upon the whole, marked by a considerable degree of classical purity
and clearness. He has been called "the Christian Sallust," and there are not a few obvious
resemblances between the two writers. But some passages occur in Sulpitius which are almost,
if not entirely, unintelligible. This is owing partly to the uncertainty of the text, and partly to
the use of terms which had sprung up since classical times, and the exact import of which it is
impossible to determine. In executing our version of this author (now for the first time, we
believe, translated into English), we have had constantly before us the editions of Sigonius
(1609), of Hornius (1664), of Vorstius (1709), and of Halm (1866). We have also consulted
a very old French translation of the *Historia Sacra*, published at Rouen in 1580.

The order in which we have arranged the writings of Sulpitius is as follows : —

1. Life of St. Martin.
2. Letters (undoubted).
3. Dialogues.
4. Letters (doubtful).
5. Sacred History.

By far the most attractive of these works are those bearing on the life and achievements of St. Martin. Sulpitius delights to return again and again to this wonderful man, and cannot find language sufficiently strong in which to extol his merits. Hence, not only in the professed *Life*, but also in the *Letters* and *Dialogues*, we have him brought very fully before us. The reader will find near the beginning of the *Vita* as translated by us, a note bearing upon the solemn asseverations of Sulpitius as to the reality of the miracles which Martin performed.

Most of the *Letters* here given are deemed spurious by Halm, the latest editor of our author. He has, nevertheless, included the whole of them in his edition, and we have thought it desirable to follow his example in our translation.

The *Sacred History* of Sulpitius has for its object to present a compendious history of the world from the Creation down to the year A.D. 400. The first and longer portion of the work is simply an abridgment of the Scripture narrative. The latter part is more interesting and valuable, as it deals with events lying outside of Scripture, and respecting which we are glad to obtain information from all available sources. Unfortunately, however, Sulpitius is not always a trustworthy authority. His inaccuracies in the first part of his work are very numerous, and will be found pointed out in our version.

The following are some of the *Estimates* which have been formed of our author.

Paulinus, a contemporary of Sulpitius, and bishop of Nola, addressed to him about fifty letters, in the fifth of which he thus writes : " It certainly would not have been given to thee to draw up an account of Martin, unless by a pure heart thou hadst rendered thy mouth worthy of uttering his sacred praises. Thou art blessed, therefore, of the Lord, inasmuch as thou hast been able, in worthy style, and with proper feeling, to complete the history of so great a priest, and so illustrious a confessor. Blessed, too, is he, in accordance with his merits, who has obtained a historian worthy of his faith and of his life ; and who has become consecrated to the Divine glory by his own virtues, and to human memory by thy narrative regarding him."

Gennadius (died A.D. 496), in his " Catalogue of illustrious men," says : " The Presbyter Severus, whose cognomen was Sulpitius, belonged to the province of Aquitania. He was a man distinguished both for his family and learning, and was remarkable for his love of poverty and humility. He was also a great friend of some holy men, such as Martin, bishop of Tours, and Paulinus, bishop of Nola ; and his works are by no means to be neglected."

In modern times, J. J. Scaliger has said of Sulpitius, " He is the purest of all the ecclesiastical writers." And Vossius, referring to some remarks of Baronius on Sulpitius, says : " I differ from him (Baronius) in this, that, without sufficient care, he calls Gennadius the contemporary of Severus, since Gennadius flourished seventy years, more or less, after Severus. For he dedicated his book ' On Faith ' (as he himself tells us) to Pope Gelasius, who became bishop of Rome in A.D. 492. But he greatly extols the holiness of Sulpitius ; and in the Roman martyrology his memory (i.e. of Sulpitius) is celebrated on the 29th of January."

Archdeacon Farrar has recently remarked concerning Martin and Sulpitius, " Owing partly to the eloquent and facile style of his (Martin's) biographer, Sulpicius Severus, his name was known from Armenia to Egypt more widely than that of any other monk or bishop of his day." — *Lives of the Fathers*, i. 628.

SULPITIUS SEVERUS ON THE LIFE OF ST. MARTIN.

PREFACE TO DESIDERIUS.

SEVERUS to his dearest brother Desiderius sendeth greeting. I had determined, my like-minded brother, to keep private, and confine within the walls of my own house, the little treatise which I had written concerning the life of St. Martin. I did so, as I am not gifted with much talent, and shrank from the criticisms of the world, lest (as I think will be the case) my somewhat unpolished style should displease my readers, and I should be deemed highly worthy of general reprehension for having too boldly laid hold of a subject which ought to have been reserved for truly eloquent writers. But I have not been able to refuse your request again and again presented. For what could there be which I would not grant in deference to your love, even at the expense of my own modesty? However, I have submitted the work to you on the sure understanding that you will reveal it to no other, having received your promise to that effect. Nevertheless, I have my fears that you will become the means of its publication to the world; and I well know that, once issued, it can never[1] be recalled. If this shall happen, and you come to know that it is read by some others, you will, I trust, kindly ask the readers to attend to the facts related, rather than the language in which they are set forth. You will beg them not to be offended if the style chances unpleasantly to affect their ears, because the kingdom of God consists not of eloquence, but faith. Let them also bear in mind that salvation was preached to the world, not by orators, but by fishermen, although God could certainly have adopted the other course, had it been advantageous. For my part, indeed, when I first applied my mind to writing what follows, because I thought it disgraceful that the excellences of so great a man should remain concealed, I resolved with myself not to feel ashamed on account of solecisms of language. This I did because I had never attained to any great knowledge of such things; or, if I had formerly some taste of

---

[1]   " Delere licebit
Quod non edideris: nescit vox missa reverti."
             —Hor. *Art Poet.* 389-90.

studies of the kind, I had lost the whole of that, through having neglected these matters for so long a course of time. But, after all, that I may not have in future to adopt such an irksome mode of self-defense, the best way will be that the book should be published, if you think right, with the author's name suppressed. In order that this may be done, kindly erase the title which the book bears on its front, so that the page may be silent; and (what is quite enough) let the book proclaim its subject-matter, while it tells nothing of the author.

CHAPTER I.

Reasons for writing the Life of St. Martin.

MOST men being vainly devoted to the pursuit of worldly glory, have, as they imagined, acquired a memorial of their own names from this source; viz. devoting their pens to the embellishment of the lives of famous men. This course, although it did not secure for them a lasting reputation, still has undoubtedly brought them some fulfilment of the hope they cherished. It has done so, both by preserving their own memory, though to no purpose, and because, through their having presented to the world the examples of great men, no small emulation has been excited in the bosoms of their readers. Yet, notwithstanding these things, their labors have in no degree borne upon the blessed and never-ending life to which we look forward. For what has a glory, destined to perish with the world, profited those men themselves who have written on mere secular matters? Or what benefit has posterity derived from reading of Hector as a warrior, or Socrates as an expounder of philosophy? There can be no profit in such things, since it is not only folly to imitate the persons referred to, but absolute madness not to assail them with the utmost severity. For, in truth, those persons who estimate human life only by present actions, have consigned their hopes to fables, and their souls to the tomb. In fact, they gave themselves up to be perpetuated simply in the memory of mortals, whereas it is the duty of man rather to seek after eternal life than an eternal memorial, and that, not by writing, or fighting, or philosophizing, but by living a pious, holy, and religious life. This erroneous conduct of mankind, being enshrined in literature, has prevailed to such an extent that it has found many who have been emulous either of the vain philosophy or the foolish excellence which has been celebrated. For this reason, I think I will accomplish something well worth the necessary pains, if I write the life of a most holy man, which shall serve in future as an example to others ; by which, indeed, the readers shall be roused to the pursuit of true knowledge, and heavenly warfare, and divine virtue. In so doing, we have regard also to our own advantage, so that we may look for, not a vain remembrance among men, but an eternal reward from God. For, although we ourselves have not lived in such a manner that we can serve for an example to others, nevertheless, we have made it our endeavor that he should not remain unknown who was a man worthy of imitation. I shall therefore set about writing the life of St. Martin, and shall narrate both what he did previous to his episcopate, and what he performed as a bishop. At the same time, I cannot hope to set forth all that he was or did. Those excellences of which he alone was conscious are completely unknown, because, as he did not seek for honor from men, he desired, as much as he could accomplish it, that his virtues should be concealed. And even of those which had become known to us, we have omitted a great number, because we have judged it enough if only the more striking and eminent should be recorded. At the same time, I had in the interests of readers to see to it that, no undue amount of instances being set before them should make them weary of the subject. But I implore those who are to read what follows to give full faith to the things narrated, and to believe that I have written nothing of which I had not certain knowledge and evidence. I should, in fact, have preferred to be silent rather than to narrate things which are false.[1]

---

1 This is a remarkable asseveration in view of the many miraculous accounts which follow. When we remember, on the one hand, how intimate Sulpitius was with St. Martin, and how strongly, as in this passage, he avouches the truth of all he narrates, it is extremely difficult to decide as to the real value of his narrative. It has been said (Smith's *Dict.* II. 967) that Sulpitius' Life of St. Martinus is "filled with the most puerile fables," and undoubtedly many of the stories recorded are of that character. But whether, considering the close relation in which the two men stood to each other, *all* the miraculous accounts are to be discredited, must be left to the judgment of the reader. The following valuable remarks may be quoted on this interesting question. "Some forty years ago," writes Dr. Cazenove, "an audience in Oxford was listening to a professor of modern history (Dr. Arnold of Rugby), who discussed this subject. After pointing out the difference between the Gospel miracles and those recorded by ecclesiastical historians, the lecturer proceeded as follows: 'Some appear to be unable to conceive of belief or unbelief, except as having some ulterior object: "We believe this because we love it; we disbelieve it because we wish it to be disproved." There is, however, in minds more healthfully constituted a belief and a disbelief, founded solely upon the evidence of the case, arising neither out of partiality, nor out of prejudice against the supposed conclusions, which may result from

CHAPTER II.

Military Service of St. Martin.

MARTIN, then, was born at Sabaria[1] in Pannonia, but was brought up at Ticinum,[2] which is situated in Italy. His parents were, according to the judgment of the world, of no mean rank, but were heathens. His father was at first simply a soldier, but afterwards a military tribune. He himself in his youth following military pursuits was enrolled in the imperial guard, first under king Constantine, and then under Julian Cæsar. This, however, was not done of his own free will, for, almost from his earliest years, the holy infancy of the illustrious boy aspired rather to the service of God.[3] For, when he was of the age of ten years, he betook himself, against the wish of his parents, to the Church, and begged that he might become a catechumen. Soon afterwards, becoming in a wonderful manner completely devoted to the service of God, when he was twelve years old, he desired to enter on the life of a hermit ; and he would have followed up that desire with the necessary vows, had not his as yet too youthful age prevented. His mind, however, being always engaged on matters pertaining to the monasteries or the Church, already meditated in his boyish years what he afterwards, as a professed servant of

---

its truth or falsehood. And in such a spirit the historical student will consider the case of Bede's and other historians' miracles. He will, I think, as a general rule, disbelieve them; for the immense multitude which he finds recorded, and which, I suppose, no credulity could believe in, shows sufficiently that on this point there was a total want of judgment and a blindness of belief generally existing which make the testimony wholly insufficient; and, while the external evidence in favor of these alleged miracles is so unsatisfactory, there are, for the most part, strong internal evidence against them. But with regard to some miracles, he will see that there is no strong *à priori* improbability in their occurrence, but rather the contrary; as, for instance, when the first missionaries of the Gospel in a barbarous country are said to have been assisted by a manifestation of the spirit of power; and, if the evidence appears to warrant his belief, he will readily and gladly yield it. And in doing so he will have the countenance of a great man (Burke) who in his fragment of English history has not hesitated to express the same sentiments. Nor will he be unwilling, but most thankful, to find sufficient grounds for believing that not only at the beginning of the Gospel, but in ages long afterwards, believing prayer has received extraordinary answers; that it has been heard even in more than it might have dared to ask for. Yet, again, if the gift of faith — the gift as distinguished from the grace — of the faith which removes mountains, has been given to any in later times in remarkable measure, the mighty works which such faith may have wrought cannot be incredible in themselves to those who remember our Lord's promise, and if it appears from satisfactory evidence that they were wrought actually, we shall believe them, — and believe with joy. Only as it is in most cases impossible to admit the trustworthiness of the evidence, our minds must remain at the most in a state of suspense; and I do not know why it is necessary to come to any positive decision.'" — "The Fathers for English Readers": *St. Hilary of Poitiers and St. Martin of Tours*, p. 191.

On this subject it has lately been said: "Most, if not all, of the so-called miracles which were supposed to surround Martin with a blaze of glory were either absolutely and on the face of them false; or were gross exaggerations of natural events; or were subjective impressions clothed in objective images; or were the distortions of credulous rumor; or at the best cannot claim in their favor a single particle of trustworthy evidence. They cannot be narrated as though they were actual events. Martin was an eminent bishop, but half of the wonderful deeds attributed to him are unworthy and absurd." — Farrar's *Lives of the Fathers*, I. 644.

1 Sarwar. 　　　　2 Pavia.

3 The text is here corrupt and uncertain, but the general meaning is plain to the above effect. Hahn has adopted "divinam servitutem," instead of the common "divina servitute."

Christ, fulfilled. But when an edict was issued by the ruling powers[4] in the state, that the sons of veterans should be enrolled for military service, and he, on the information furnished by his father, (who looked with an evil eye on his blessed actions) having been seized and put in chains, when he was fifteen years old, was compelled to take the military oath, then showed himself content with only one servant as his attendant. And even to him, changing places as it were, he often acted as though, while really master, he had been inferior; to such a degree that, for the most part, he drew off his [servant's] boots and cleaned them with his own hand; while they took their meals together, the real master, however, generally acting the part of servant. During nearly three years before his baptism, he was engaged in the profession of arms, but he kept completely free from those vices in which that class of men become too frequently involved. He showed exceeding kindness towards his fellow-soldiers, and held them in wonderful affection; while his patience and humility surpassed what seemed possible to human nature. There is no need to praise the self-denial which he displayed: it was so great that, even at that date, he was regarded not so much as being a soldier as a monk. By all these qualities he had so endeared himself to the whole body of his comrades, that they esteemed him while they marvelously loved him. Although not yet made a new creature[5] in Christ, he, by his good works, acted the part of a candidate for baptism. This he did, for instance, by aiding those who were in trouble, by furnishing assistance to the wretched, by supporting the needy, by clothing the naked, while he reserved nothing for himself from his military pay except what was necessary for his daily sustenance. Even then, far from being a senseless hearer of the Gospel, he so far complied with its precepts as to take no thought about the morrow.

CHAPTER III.

Christ appears to St. Martin.

ACCORDINGLY, at a certain period, when he had nothing except his arms and his simple military dress, in the middle of winter, a winter which had shown itself more severe than ordinary, so that the extreme cold was proving fatal to many, he happened to meet at the gate of the city of Amiens[1] a poor man destitute of clothing. He was entreating those that passed by to have compassion upon him, but all passed the wretched man without notice, when Martin, that man full of God, recognized that a being to whom others showed no pity, was, in that respect, left to him. Yet, what should he do? He had nothing except the cloak in which he was clad, for he had already parted with the rest of his garments for similar purposes. Taking, therefore, his sword with which he was girt, he divided his cloak into two equal parts, and gave one part to the poor man, while he again clothed himself with the remainder. Upon this, some of the by-standers laughed, because he was now an unsightly object, and stood out as but partly dressed. Many, however, who were of sounder understanding, groaned deeply because they themselves had done nothing similar. They especially felt this, because, being possessed of more than Martin, they could have clothed the poor man without reducing themselves to nakedness. In the following night, when Martin had resigned himself to sleep, he had a vision of Christ arrayed in that part of his cloak with which he had clothed the poor man. He contemplated the Lord with the greatest attention, and was told to own as his the robe which he had given. Ere long, he heard Jesus saying with a clear voice to the multitude of angels standing round — "Martin, who is still but a catechumen, clothed[2] me with this robe." The Lord, truly mindful of his own words (who had said when on earth — "Inasmuch[3] as ye have done these things to one of the least of these, ye have done them unto me), declared that he himself had been clothed in that poor man; and to confirm the testimony he bore to so good a deed, he condescended to show him himself in that very dress which the poor man had received. After this vision the sainted man was not puffed up with human glory, but, acknowledging the goodness of God in what had been done, and being now of the age of twenty years, he hastened to receive baptism. He did not, however, all at once, retire from military service, yielding to the entreaties of his tribune, whom he admitted to be his familiar tent-companion.[4] For the tribune promised that, after the period of his office had expired, he too would retire from the world. Martin, kept back by the expectation of this event, continued, although but in name, to act the part of a soldier, for nearly two years after he had received baptism.

---

[4] Sulpitius uses *reges* instead of the more common expression *imperatores*.
[5] Sulpitius manifestly refers to baptism in these words. However mistakenly, several others of the early Fathers held that regeneration does not take place before baptism, and that baptism is, in fact, absolutely necessary to regeneration. St. Ambrose has the following strong statement on the subject: "Credit catechumenus; sed nisi baptizetur, remissionem peccatorum non potest obtinere." — *Libri de his, qui initiantur mysteriis*, chap. 4.

[1] The place here called by Sulpitius "Ambianensium civitas" was also known as "Samarobriva," and is supposed to be the modern *Amiens*. [2] St. Matt. xxv. 40.
[3] There is a peculiar use of *quamdiu* in the old Latin rendering of the passage here quoted. It is used as an equivalent for the Greek ἐφ' ὅσον, no doubt with the meaning "inasmuch as."
[4] Comp. *Tacitus, Agric.* chap. 5, "electus, quem contubernio æstimaret."

CHAPTER IV.

Martin retires from Military Service.

IN the meantime, as the barbarians were rushing within the two divisions of Gaul, Julian Cæsar,[1] bringing an army together at the city[2] of the Vaugiones, began to distribute a donative to the soldiers. As was the custom in such a case, they were called forward, one by one, until it came to the turn of Martin. Then, indeed, judging it a suitable opportunity for seeking his discharge — for he did not think it would be proper for him, if he were not to continue in the service, to receive a donative — he said to Cæsar, "Hitherto I have served *you* as a soldier : allow me now to become a soldier to God : let the man who is to serve thee receive thy donative : I am the soldier of Christ : it is not lawful for me to fight." Then truly the tyrant stormed on hearing such words, declaring that, from fear of the battle, which was to take place on the morrow, and not from any religious feeling, Martin withdrew from the service. But Martin, full of courage, yea all the more resolute from the danger that had been set before him, exclaims, "If this conduct of mine is ascribed to cowardice, and not to faith, I will take my stand unarmed before the line of battle to-morrow, and in the name of the Lord Jesus, protected by the sign of the cross, and not by shield or helmet, I will safely penetrate the ranks of the enemy." He is ordered, therefore, to be thrust back into prison, determined on proving his words true by exposing himself unarmed to the barbarians. But, on the following day, the enemy sent ambassadors to treat about peace and surrendered both themselves and all their possessions. In these circumstances who can doubt that this victory was due to the saintly man? It was granted him that he should not be sent unarmed to the fight. And although the good Lord could have preserved his own soldier, even amid the swords and darts of the enemy, yet that his blessed eyes might not be pained by witnessing the death of others, he removed all necessity for fighting. For Christ did not require to secure any other victory in behalf of his own soldier, than that, the enemy being subdued without bloodshed, no one should suffer death.

CHAPTER V.

Martin converts a Robber to the Faith.

FROM that time quitting military service, Martin earnestly sought after the society of Hilarius, bishop of the city Pictava,[1] whose faith in the things of God was then regarded as of high renown, and in universal esteem. For some time Martin made his abode with him. Now, this same Hilarius, having instituted him in the office of the diaconate, endeavored still more closely to attach him to himself, and to bind him by leading him to take part in Divine service. But when he constantly refused, crying out that he was unworthy, Hilarius, as being a man of deep penetration, perceived that he could only be constrained in this way, if he should lay that sort of office upon him, in discharging which there should seem to be a kind of injury done him. He therefore appointed him to be an exorcist. Martin did not refuse this appointment, from the fear that he might seem to have looked down upon it as somewhat humble. Not long after this, he was warned in a dream that he should visit his native land, and more particularly his parents, who were still involved in heathenism, with a regard for their religious interests. He set forth in accordance with the expressed wish of the holy Hilarius, and, after being adjured by him with many prayers and tears, that he would in due time return. According to report Martin entered on that journey in a melancholy frame of mind, after calling the brethren to witness that many sufferings lay before him. The result fully justified this prediction. For, first of all, having followed some devious paths among the Alps, he fell into the hands of robbers. And when one of them lifted up his axe and poised it above Martin's head, another of them met with his right hand the blow as it fell ; nevertheless, having had his hands bound behind his back, he was handed over to one of them to be guarded and stripped. The robber, having led him to a private place apart from the rest, began to enquire of him who he was. Upon this, Martin replied that he was a Christian. The robber next asked him whether he was afraid. Then indeed Martin most courageously replied that he never before had felt so safe, because he knew that the mercy of the Lord would be especially present with him in the midst of trials. He added that he grieved rather for the man in whose hands he was, because, by living a life of robbery, he was showing himself unworthy of the mercy of Christ. And then entering on a discourse concerning Evangelical truth, he preached the word of God to the robber. Why should I delay stating the result? The robber believed ; and, after expressing his respect for Martin, he restored him to the way, entreating him to pray the Lord for him. That same robber was after-

---

[1] Commonly known as Julian the Apostate.
[2] This city was called Borbetomagus, and is represented by the modern *Worms*.

[1] This was a city of the Pictones (or Pictavi) who are mentioned by Cæsar, *Bell Gall.* iii 11. Their territory corresponded to the modern diocese of Poitiers.

wards seen leading a religious life ; so that, in fact, the narrative I have given above is based upon an account furnished by himself.

CHAPTER VI.

The Devil throws himself in the Way of Martin.

MARTIN, then, having gone on from thence, after he had passed Milan, the devil met him in the way, having assumed the form of a man. The devil first asked him to what place he was going. Martin having answered him to the effect that he was minded to go whithersoever the Lord called him, the devil said to him, "Wherever you go, or whatever you attempt, the devil will resist you." Then Martin, replying to him in the prophetical word, said, "The Lord is my helper ; I will not fear what man can do unto me."[1] Upon this, his enemy immediately vanished out of his sight ; and thus, as he had intended in his heart and mind, he set free his mother from the errors of heathenism, though his father continued to cleave to its evils. However, he saved many by his example.

After this, when the Arian heresy had spread through the whole world, and was especially powerful in Illyria, and when he, almost single-handed, was fighting most strenuously against the treachery of the priests, and had been subjected to many punishments (for he was publicly scourged, and at last was compelled to leave the city), again betaking himself to Italy, and having found the Church in the two divisions of Gaul in a distracted condition through the departure also of the holy Hilarius, whom the violence of the heretics had driven into exile, he established a monastery for himself at Milan. There, too, Auxentius, the originator and leader of the Arians, bitterly persecuted him ; and, after he had assailed him with many injuries, violently expelled him from the city. Thinking, therefore, that it was necessary to yield to circumstances, he withdrew to the island Gallinaria,[2] with a certain presbyter as his companion, a man of distinguished excellences. Here he subsisted for some time on the roots of plants ; and, while doing so, he took for food hellebore, which is, as people say, a poisonous kind of grass. But when he perceived the strength of the poison increasing within him, and death now nearly at hand, he warded off the imminent danger by means of prayer, and immediately all his pains were put to flight. And not long after having discovered that, through penitence on the part of the king, permission to return had been granted

to holy Hilarius, he made an effort to meet him at Rome, and, with this view, set out for that city.

CHAPTER VII.

Martin restores a Catechumen to Life.

As Hilarius had already gone away, so Martin followed in his footsteps ; and having been most joyously welcomed by him, he established for himself a monastery not far from the town. At this time a certain catechumen joined him, being desirous of becoming instructed in the doctrines[1] and habits of the most holy man. But, after the lapse only of a few days, the catechumen, seized with a languor, began to suffer from a violent fever. It so happened that Martin had then left home, and having remained away three days, he found on his return that life had departed from the catechumen ; and so suddenly had death occurred, that he had left this world without receiving baptism. The body being laid out in public was being honored by the last sad offices on the part of the mourning brethren, when Martin hurries up to them with tears and lamentations. But then laying hold, as it were, of the Holy Spirit, with the whole powers of his mind, he orders the others to quit the cell in which the body was lying ; and bolting the door, he stretches himself at full length on the dead limbs of the departed brother. Having given himself for some time to earnest prayer, and perceiving by means of the Spirit of God that power was present,[2] he then rose up for a little, and gazing on the countenance of the deceased, he waited without misgiving for the result of his prayer and of the mercy of the Lord. And scarcely had the space of two hours elapsed, when he saw the dead man begin to move a little in all his members, and to tremble with his eyes opened for the practice of sight. Then indeed, turning to the Lord with a loud voice and giving thanks, he filled the cell with his ejaculations. Hearing the noise, those who had been standing at the door immediately rush inside. And truly a marvelous spectacle met them, for they beheld the man alive whom they had formerly left dead. Thus being restored to life, and having immediately obtained baptism, he lived for many years afterwards ; and he was the first who offered himself to us both as a subject that had experienced the virtues[3] of Martin, and as a witness to their existence. The same man was wont to relate that, when he left the body, he was brought before the tribunal of the Judge, and being assigned to gloomy regions and vulgar crowds, he

---

[1] Comp. Ps. cxviii. 6.
[2] An island near Albium Ingaunum — the modern Allenga, on the Gulf of Genoa. The island was so named from abounding in fowls in a half-tamed state. It still bears the name of Gallinaria.

[1] All this seems to be implied in the words " institui disciplinis."
[2] " adesse virtutem."
[3] Or " powers " according to the use of the Greek word δύναμις in St. Luke viii. 46.

received a severe[4] sentence. Then, however, he added, it was suggested by two angels of the Judge that he was the man for whom Martin was praying; and that, on this account, he was ordered to be led back by the same angels, and given up to Martin, and restored to his former life. From this time forward, the name of the sainted man became illustrious, so that, as being reckoned holy by all, he was also deemed powerful and truly apostolical.

CHAPTER VIII.

Martin restores one that had been strangled.

NOT long after these events, while Martin was passing by the estate of a certain man named Lupicinus, who was held in high esteem according to the judgment of the world, he was received with shouting and the lamentations of a wailing crowd. Having, in an anxious state of mind, gone up to that multitude, and enquired what such weeping meant, he was told that one of the slaves of the family had put an end to his life by hanging. Hearing this, Martin entered the cell in which the body was lying, and, excluding all the multitude, he stretched himself upon the body, and spent some little time in prayer. Ere long, the deceased, with life beaming in his countenance, and with his drooping eyes fixed on Martin's face, is aroused; and with a gentle effort attempting to rise, he laid hold of the right hand of the saintly man, and by this means stood upon his feet. In this manner, while the whole multitude looked on, he walked along with Martin to the porch of the house.

CHAPTER IX.

High Esteem in which Martin was held.

NEARLY about the same time, Martin was called upon to undertake the episcopate of the church at Tours;[1] but when he could not easily be drawn forth from his monastery, a certain Ruricius, one of the citizens, pretending that his wife was ill, and casting himself down at his knees, prevailed on him to go forth. Multitudes of the citizens having previously been posted by the road on which he traveled, he is thus under a kind of guard escorted to the city. An incredible number of people not only from that town, but also from the neighboring cities, had, in a wonderful manner, assembled to give

their votes.[2] There was but one wish among all, there were the same prayers, and there was the same fixed opinion to the effect that Martin was most worthy of the episcopate, and that the church would be happy with such a priest. A few persons, however, and among these some of the bishops, who had been summoned to appoint a chief priest, were impiously offering resistance, asserting forsooth that Martin's person was contemptible, that he was unworthy of the episcopate, that he was a man despicable in countenance, that his clothing was mean, and his hair disgusting. This madness of theirs was ridiculed by the people of sounder judgment, inasmuch as such objectors only proclaimed the illustrious character of the man, while they sought to slander him. Nor truly was it allowed them to do anything else, than what the people, following the Divine will, desired[3] to be accomplished. Among the bishops, however, who had been present, a certain one of the name Defensor is said to have specially offered opposition; and on this account it was observed that he was at the time severely censured in the reading from the prophets. For when it so happened that the reader, whose duty it was to read in public that day, being blocked out by the people, failed to appear, the officials falling into confusion, while they waited for him who never came, one of those standing by, laying hold of the Psalter, seized upon the first verse which presented itself to him. Now, the Psalm ran thus: "Out of the mouth of babes and sucklings thou hast perfected praise because of thine enemies, that thou mightest destroy the enemy and the avenger."[4] On these words being read, a shout was raised by the people, and the opposite party were confounded. It was believed that this Psalm had been chosen by Divine ordination, that Defensor[5] might hear a testimony to his own work, because the praise of the Lord was perfected out of the mouth of babes and sucklings in the case of Martin, while the enemy was at the same time both pointed out and destroyed.

CHAPTER X.

Martin as Bishop of Tours.

AND now having entered on the episcopal office, it is beyond my power fully to set forth how Martin distinguished himself in the discharge of its duties. For he remained with the utmost constancy, the same as he had been

---

[2] It is clear from this passage that the people at large were accustomed in ancient times to give their votes on the appointment of a bishop.
[3] We here adopt Halm's reading "cogitabat," in preference to the usual "cogebat." [4] Ps. viii. 3.
[5] The word translated "avenger" in the English A. V. is "defensor" in the Vulgate, and thus the man referred to would have seemed to be expressly named.

before. There was the same humility in his heart, and the same homeliness in his garments. Full alike of dignity and courtesy, he kept up the position of a bishop properly, yet in such a way as not to lay aside the objects and virtues of a monk. Accordingly he made use, for some time, of the cell connected with the church; but afterwards, when he felt it impossible to tolerate the disturbance caused by the numbers of those visiting it, he established a monastery for himself about two miles outside the city. This spot was so secret and retired that he enjoyed in it the solitude of a hermit. For, on one side, it was surrounded by a precipitous rock of a lofty mountain, while the river Loire had shut in the rest of the plain by a bay extending back for a little distance; and the place could be approached only by one, and that a very narrow passage. Here, then, he possessed a cell constructed of wood. Many also of the brethren had, in the same manner, fashioned retreats for themselves, but most of them had formed these out of the rock of the overhanging mountain, hollowed into caves. There were altogether eighty disciples, who were being disciplined after the example of the saintly master. No one there had anything which was called his own; all things were possessed in common. It was not allowed either to buy or to sell anything, as is the custom among most monks. No art was practiced there, except that of transcribers, and even this was assigned to the brethren of younger years, while the elders spent their time in prayer. Rarely did any one of them go beyond the cell, unless when they assembled at the place of prayer. They all took their food together, after the hour of fasting was past. No one used wine, except when illness compelled them to do so. Most of them were clothed in garments of camels' hair.[1] Any dress approaching to softness[2] was there deemed criminal, and this must be thought the more remarkable, because many among them were such as are deemed of noble rank. These, though far differently brought up, had forced themselves down to this degree of humility and patient endurance, and we have seen numbers of these afterwards made bishops. For what city or church would there be that would not desire to have its priests from among those in the monastery of Martin?

CHAPTER XI.

Martin demolishes an Altar consecrated to a Robber.

BUT let me proceed to a description of other

excellences which Martin displayed as a bishop. There was, not far from the town, a place very close to the monastery, which a false human opinion had consecrated, on the supposition that some martyrs had been buried together there. For it was also believed that an altar had been placed there by former bishops. But Martin, not inclined to give a hasty belief to things uncertain, often asked from those who were his elders, whether among the presbyters or clerics, that the name of the martyr, or the time when he suffered, should be made known to him. He did so, he said, because he had great scruples on these points, inasmuch as no steady tradition respecting them had come down from antiquity. Having, therefore, for a time kept away from the place, by no means wishing to lessen the religious veneration with which it was regarded, because he was as yet uncertain, but, at the same time not lending his authority to the opinion of the multitude, lest a mere superstition should obtain a firmer footing, he one day went out to the place, taking a few brethren with him as companions. There standing above the very sepulchre, Martin prayed to the Lord that he would reveal who the man in question was, and what was his character or desert. Next turning to the left-hand side, he sees standing very near a shade of a mean and cruel appearance. Martin commands him to tell his name and character. Upon this, he declares his name, and confesses his guilt. He says that he had been a robber, and that he was beheaded on account of his crimes; that he had been honored simply by an error of the multitude; that he had nothing in common with the martyrs, since glory was their portion, while punishment exacted its penalties from him. Those who stood by heard, in a wonderful way, the voice of the speaker, but they beheld no person. Then Martin made known what he had seen, and ordered the altar which had been there to be removed, and thus he delivered the people from the error of that superstition.

CHAPTER XII.

Martin causes the Bearers of a Dead Body to stop.

Now, it came to pass some time after the above, that while Martin was going a journey, he met the body of a certain heathen, which was being carried to the tomb with superstitious funeral rites. Perceiving from a distance the crowd that was approaching, and being ignorant as to what was going on, he stood still for a little while. For there was a distance of nearly half a mile between him and the crowd, so that it

---

[1] Cf. St. Matt. iii. 4.
[2] In St. Matt. xi. 8, there is a reference to those " that wear soft clothing,"—οἱ τὰ μαλακὰ φοροῦντες.

was difficult to discover what the spectacle he beheld really was. Nevertheless, because he saw it was a rustic gathering, and when the linen clothes spread over the body were blown about by the action of the wind, he believed that some profane rites of sacrifice were being performed. This thought occurred to him, because it was the custom of the Gallic rustics in their wretched folly to carry about through the fields the images of demons veiled with a white covering. Lifting up, therefore, the sign of the cross opposite to them, he commanded the crowd not to move from the place in which they were, and to set down the burden. Upon this, the miserable creatures might have been seen at first to become stiff like rocks. Next, as they endeavored, with every possible effort, to move forward, but were not able to take a step farther, they began to whirl themselves about in the most ridiculous fashion, until, not able any longer to sustain the weight, they set down the dead body. Thunderstruck, and gazing in bewilderment at each other, as not knowing what had happened to them, they remained sunk in silent thought. But when the saintly man discovered that they were simply a band of peasants celebrating funeral rites, and not sacrifices to the gods, again raising his hand, he gave them the power of going away, and of lifting up the body. Thus he both compelled them to stand when he pleased, and permitted them to depart when he thought good.

CHAPTER XIII.

Martin escapes from a Falling Pine-tree.

AGAIN, when in a certain village he had demolished a very ancient temple, and had set about cutting down a pine-tree, which stood close to the temple, the chief priest of that place, and a crowd of other heathens began to oppose him. And these people, though, under the influence of the Lord, they had been quiet while the temple was being overthrown, could not patiently allow the tree to be cut down. Martin carefully instructed them that there was nothing sacred in the trunk of a tree, and urged them rather to honor God whom he himself served. He added that there was a moral necessity why that tree should be cut down, because it had been dedicated to a demon. Then one of them who was bolder than the others says, " If you have any trust in thy God, whom you say you worship, we ourselves will cut down this tree, and be it your part to receive it when falling; for if, as you declare, your Lord is with you, you will escape all injury." Then Martin, courageously trusting in the Lord, promises that he would do what had been asked. Upon this, all

that crowd of heathen agreed to the condition named ; for they held the loss of their tree a small matter, if only they got the enemy of their religion buried beneath its fall. Accordingly, since that pine-tree was hanging over in one direction, so that there was no doubt to what side it would fall on being cut, Martin, having been bound, is, in accordance with the decision of these pagans, placed in that spot where, as no one doubted, the tree was about to fall. They began, therefore, to cut down their own tree, with great glee and joyfulness, while there was at some distance a great multitude of wondering spectators. And now the pine-tree began to totter, and to threaten its [1] own ruin by falling. The monks at a distance grew pale, and, terrified by the danger ever coming nearer, had lost all hope and confidence, expecting only the death of Martin. But he, trusting in the Lord, and waiting courageously, when now the falling pine had uttered its expiring crash, while it was now falling, while it was just rushing upon him, simply holding up his hand against it, he put in its way the sign of salvation. Then, indeed, after the manner of a spinning-top (one might have thought it driven[2] back), it swept round to the opposite side, to such a degree that it almost crushed the rustics, who had taken their places there in what was deemed a safe spot. Then truly, a shout being raised to heaven, the heathen were amazed by the miracle, while the monks wept for joy ; and the name of Christ was in common extolled by all. The well-known result was that on that day salvation came to that region. For there was hardly one of that immense multitude of heathens who did not express a desire for the imposition of hands, and abandoning his impious errors, made a profession of faith in the Lord Jesus. Certainly, before the times of Martin, very few, nay, almost none, in those regions had received the name of Christ ; but through his virtues and example that name has prevailed to such an extent, that now there is no place thereabouts which is not filled either with very crowded churches or monasteries. For wherever he destroyed heathen temples, there he used immediately to build either churches or monasteries.

CHAPTER XIV.

Martin destroys Heathen Temples and Altars.

NOR did he show less eminence, much about the same time, in other transactions of a like

---

[1] Perhaps " suam " here stands for " ejus," as in other passages of our author. The meaning will then be, " and to threaten his (Martin's) destruction by falling."

[2] It seems better to preserve the parenthesis than to translate the words as they stand in Halm's text, " tum vero — velut turbinis modo retro actam putares — diversam in partem ruit."

kind. For, having in a certain village set fire to a very ancient and celebrated temple, the circle of flames was carried by the action of the wind upon a house which was very close to, yea, connected with, the temple. When Martin perceived this, he climbed by rapid ascent to the roof of the house, presenting himself in front of the advancing flames. Then indeed might the fire have been seen thrust back in a wonderful manner against the force of the wind, so that there appeared a sort of conflict of the two elements fighting together. Thus, by the influence of Martin, the fire only acted in the place where it was ordered to do so. But in a village which was named Leprosum, when he too wished to overthrow a temple which had acquired great wealth through the superstitious ideas entertained of its sanctity, a multitude of the heathen resisted him to such a degree that he was driven back not without bodily injury. He, therefore, withdrew to a place in the vicinity, and there for three days, clothed in sackcloth[1] and ashes, fasting and praying the whole time, he besought the Lord, that, as he had not been able to overthrow that temple by human effort, Divine power might be exerted to destroy it. Then two angels, with spears and shields after the manner of heavenly warriors, suddenly presented themselves to him, saying that they were sent by the Lord to put to flight the rustic multitude, and to furnish protection to Martin, lest, while the temple was being destroyed, any one should offer resistance. They told him therefore to return, and complete the blessed work which he had begun. Accordingly Martin returned to the village; and while the crowds of heathen looked on in perfect quiet as he razed the pagan temple even to the foundations, he also reduced all the altars and images to dust. At this sight the rustics, when they perceived that they had been so astounded and terrified by an intervention of the Divine will, that they might not be found fighting against the bishop, almost all believed in the Lord Jesus. They then began to cry out openly and to confess that the God of Martin ought to be worshiped, and that the idols should be despised, which were not able to help them.

CHAPTER XV.

Martin offers his Neck to an Assassin.

I SHALL also relate what took place in the village of the Ædui. When Martin was there overthrowing a temple, a multitude of rustic heathen rushed upon him in a frenzy of rage. And when one of them, bolder than the rest, made an attack upon him with a drawn sword, Martin, throwing back his cloak, offered his bare neck to the assassin. Nor did the heathen delay to strike, but in the very act of lifting up his right arm, he fell to the ground on his back, and being overwhelmed by the fear of God, he entreated for pardon. Not unlike this was that other event which happened to Martin, that when a certain man had resolved to wound him with a knife as he was destroying some idols, at the very moment of fetching the blow, the weapon was struck out of his hands and disappeared. Very frequently, too, when the pagans were addressing him to the effect that he would not overthrow their temples, he so soothed and conciliated the minds of the heathen by his holy discourse that, the light of truth having been revealed to them, they themselves overthrew their own temples.

CHAPTER XVI.

Cures effected by St. Martin.

MOREOVER, the gift[1] of accomplishing cures was so largely possessed by Martin, that scarcely any sick person came to him for assistance without being at once restored to health. This will clearly appear from the following example. A certain girl at Treves[2] was so completely prostrated by a terrible paralysis that for a long time she had been quite unable to make use of her body for any purpose, and being, as it were, already dead, only the smallest breath of life seemed still to remain in her. Her afflicted relatives were standing by, expecting nothing but her death, when it was suddenly announced that Martin had come to that city. When the father of the girl found that such was the case, he ran to make a request in behalf of his all but lifeless child. It happened that Martin had already entered the church. There, while the people were looking on, and in the presence of many other bishops, the old man, uttering a cry of grief, embraced the saint's knees and said: "My daughter is dying of a miserable kind of infirmity; and, what is more dreadful than death itself, she is now alive only in the spirit, her flesh being already dead before the time. I beseech thee to go to her, and give her thy blessing; for I believe that through you she will be restored to health." Martin, troubled by such an address, was bewildered, and shrank back, saying that this was a matter not in his own hands; that the old man was mistaken in the judgment he

---

[1] Literally "a covering made of Cilician goats' hair." It was called *Cilicium*, and was worn by soldiers and others.

[1] The Latin word *gratia* here corresponds to the Greek χάρισμα. St. Paul says much respecting the various χαρίσματα in 1 Cor. xii., and speaks, among others, of χαρίσματα ἰαμάτων (v. 9).
[2] The name *Treveri* at first denoted the people (as often in Cæsar, *Bell. Gall.* i. 37. &c.), and was afterwards applied to their chief city, the modern Treves.

had formed; and that he was not worthy to be the instrument through whom the Lord should make a display of his power. The father, in tears, persevered in still more earnestly pressing the case, and entreated Martin to visit the dying girl. At last, constrained by the bishops standing by to go as requested, he went down to the home of the girl. An immense crowd was waiting at the doors, to see what the servant of the Lord would do. And first, betaking himself to his familiar arms in affairs of that kind, he cast himself down on the ground and prayed. Then gazing earnestly upon the ailing girl, he requests that oil should be given him. After he had received and blessed this, he poured the powerful sacred liquid into the mouth of the girl, and immediately her voice returned to her. Then gradually, through contact with him, her limbs began, one by one, to recover life, till, at last, in the presence of the people, she arose with firm steps.

the family, who was staying in the inner part of the house; and the poor wretch began at once to rage with his teeth, and to lacerate whomsoever he met. The house was thrown into disorder; the family was in confusion; and the people present took to flight. Martin threw himself in the way of the frenzied creature, and first of all commanded him to stand still. But when he continued to gnash with his teeth, and, with gaping mouth, was threatening to bite, Martin inserted his fingers into his mouth, and said, "If you possess any power, devour these." But then, as if red-hot iron had entered his jaws, drawing his teeth far away he took care not to touch the fingers of the saintly man; and when he was compelled by punishments and tortures, to flee out of the possessed body, while he had no power of escaping by the mouth, he was cast out by means of a defluxion of the belly, leaving disgusting traces behind him.

CHAPTER XVII.

Martin casts out Several Devils.

AT the same time the servant of one Tetradius, a man of proconsular rank, having been laid hold of by a demon, was tormented with the most miserable results. Martin, therefore, having been asked to lay his hands on him, ordered the servant to be brought to him; but the evil spirit could, in no way, be brought forth from the cell in which he was: he showed himself so fearful, with ferocious teeth, to those who attempted to draw near. Then Tetradius throws himself at the feet of the saintly man, imploring that he himself would go down to the house in which the possessed of the devil was kept. But Martin then declared that he could not visit the house of an unconverted heathen. For Tetradius, at that time, was still involved in the errors of heathenism. He, therefore, pledges his word that if the demon were driven out of the boy, he would become a Christian. Martin, then, laying his hand upon the boy, cast the evil spirit out of him. On seeing this, Tetradius believed in the Lord Jesus, and immediately became a catechumen, while, not long after, he was baptized; and he always regarded Martin with extraordinary affection, as having been the author of his salvation.

About the same time, having entered the dwelling of a certain householder in the same town, he stopped short at the very threshold, and said, that he perceived a horrible demon in the court-yard of the house. When Martin ordered it to depart, it laid hold of a certain member of

CHAPTER XVIII.

Martin performs Various Miracles.

IN the meanwhile, as a sudden report had troubled the city as to the movement and inroad of the barbarians, Martin orders a possessed person to be set before him, and commanded him to declare whether this message was true or not. Then he confessed that there were sixteen demons who had spread this report among the people, in order that by the fear thus excited, Martin might have to flee from the city, but that, in fact, nothing was less in the minds of the barbarians than to make any inroad. When the unclean spirit thus acknowledged these things in the midst of the church, the city was set free from the fear and tumult which had at the time been felt.

At Paris, again, when Martin was entering the gate of the city, with large crowds attending him, he gave a kiss to a leper, of miserable appearance, while all shuddered at seeing him do so; and Martin blessed him, with the result that he was instantly cleansed from all his misery. On the following day, the man appearing in the church with a healthy skin, gave thanks for the soundness of body which he had recovered. This fact, too, ought not to be passed over in silence, that threads from Martin's garment, or such as had been plucked from the sackcloth which he wore, wrought frequent miracles upon those who were sick. For, by either being tied round the fingers or placed about the neck, they very often drove away diseases from the afflicted.

CHAPTER XIX.

A Letter of Martin effects a Cure, with Other Miracles.

FURTHER, Arborius, an ex-prefect, and a man of a very holy and faithful character, while his daughter was in agony from the burning fever of a quartan ague, inserted in the bosom of the girl, at the very paroxysm of the heat, a letter of Martin which happened to have been brought to him, and immediately the fever was dispelled. This event had such an influence upon Arborius, that he at once consecrated the girl to God, and devoted her to perpetual virginity. Then, proceeding to Martin, he presented the girl to him, as an obvious living example of his power of working miracles, inasmuch as she had been cured by him though absent; and he would not suffer her to be consecrated by any other than Martin, through his placing upon her the dress characteristic of virginity.

Paulinus, too, a man who was afterwards to furnish a striking example of the age, having begun to suffer grievously in one of his eyes, and when a pretty thick skin [1] having grown over it had already covered up its pupil, Martin touched his eye with a painter's brush, and, all pain being removed, thus restored it to its former soundness. He himself also, when, by a certain accident, he had fallen out of an upper room, and tumbling down a broken, uneven stair, had received many wounds, as he lay in his cell at the point of death, and was tortured with grievous sufferings, saw in the night an angel appear to him, who washed his wounds, and applied healing ointment to the bruised members of his body. As the effect of this, he found himself on the morrow restored to soundness of health, so that he was not thought to have suffered any harm. But because it would be tedious to go through everything of this kind, let these examples suffice, as a few out of a multitude; and let it be enough that we do not in striking cases [of miraculous interposition] detract from the truth, while, having so many to choose from, we avoid exciting weariness in the reader.

CHAPTER XX.

How Martin acted towards the Emperor Maximus.

AND here to insert some smaller matters among things so great (although such is the nature of our times in which all things have fallen into decay and corruption, it is almost a pre-eminent virtue for priestly firmness not to have yielded to royal flattery), when a number of bishops from various parts had assembled to the Emperor Maximus, a man of fierce character, and at that time elated with the victory he had won in the civil wars, and when the disgraceful flattery of all around the emperor was generally remarked, while the priestly dignity had, with degenerate submissiveness, taken a second place to the royal retinue, in Martin alone, apostolic authority continued to assert itself. For even if he had to make suit to the sovereign for some things, he commanded rather than entreated him; and although often invited, he kept away from his entertainments, saying that he could not take a place at the table of one who, out of two emperors, had deprived one of his kingdom, and the other of his life. At last, when Maximus maintained that he had not of his own accord assumed the sovereignty, but that he had simply defended by arms the necessary requirements [1] of the empire, regard to which had been imposed upon him by the soldiers, according to the Divine appointment, and that the favor of God did not seem wanting to him who, by an event seemingly so incredible, had secured the victory, adding to that the statement that none of his adversaries had been slain except in the open field of battle, at length, Martin, overcome either by his reasoning or his entreaties, came to the royal banquet. The king was wonderfully pleased because he had gained this point. Moreover, there were guests present who had been invited as if to a festival; men of the highest and most illustrious rank,— the prefect, who was also consul, named Evodius, one of the most righteous men that ever lived; two courtiers possessed of the greatest power, the brother and uncle of the king, while between these two, the presbyter of Martin had taken his place; but he himself occupied a seat which was set quite close to the king. About the middle of the banquet, according to custom, one of the servants presented a goblet to the king. He orders it rather to be given to the very holy bishop, expecting and hoping that he should then receive the cup from his right hand. But Martin, when he had drunk, handed the goblet to his own presbyter, as thinking no one worthier to drink next to himself, and holding that it would not be right for him to prefer either the king himself, or those who were next the king, to the presbyter. And the emperor, as well as all those who were then present, admired this conduct so much, that this very thing, by which they had been undervalued, gave them pleasure. The report then ran through the whole palace that Martin had done, at the king's dinner, what no bishop had dared to do

---

[1] "Nubes," lit. "a cloud."

[1] "Regni necessitatem" — an awkward expression.

at the banquets of the lowest judges. And Martin predicted to the same Maximus long before, that if he went into Italy to which he then desired to go, waging war, against the Emperor Valentinianus, it would come to pass that he should know he would[2] indeed be victorious in the first attack, but would perish a short time afterwards. And we have seen that this did in fact take place. For, on his first arrival, Valentinianus had to betake himself to flight; but recovering his strength about a year afterwards, Maximus was taken and slain by him within the walls of Aquileia.

CHAPTER XXI.

Martin has to do both with Angels and Devils.

It is also well known that angels were very often' seen by him, so that they spoke in turns with him in set speech. As to the devil, Martin held him so visible and ever under the power of his eyes, that whether he kept himself in his proper form, or changed himself into different shapes of spiritual wickedness, he was perceived by Martin, under whatever guise he appeared. The devil knew well that he could not escape discovery, and therefore frequently heaped insults upon Martin, being unable to beguile him by trickery. On one occasion the devil, holding in his hand the bloody horn of an ox, rushed into Martin's cell with great noise, and holding out to him his bloody right hand, while at the same time he exulted in the crime he had committed, said : " Where, O Martin, is thy power? I have just slain one of your people." Then Martin assembled the brethren, and related to them what the devil had disclosed, while he ordered them carefully to search the several cells in order to discover who had been visited with this calamity. They report that no one of the monks was missing, but that one peasant, hired by them, had gone to the forest to bring home wood in his wagon. Upon hearing this, Martin instructs some of them to go and meet him. On their doing so, the man was found almost dead at no great distance from the monastery. Nevertheless, although just drawing his last breath, he made known to the brethren the cause of his wound and death. He said that, while he was drawing tighter the thongs which had got loose on the oxen yoked together, one of the oxen, throwing his head free, had wounded him with his horn in the groin. And not long after the man expired. You[1] see with what judgment of the Lord this power was given to the devil. This was a marvelous feature in

Martin that not only on this occasion to which I have specially referred, but on many occasions of the same kind, in fact as often as such things occurred, he perceived them long beforehand, and[2] disclosed the things which had been revealed to him to the brethren.

CHAPTER XXII.

Martin preaches Repentance even to the Devil.

Now, the devil, while he tried to impose upon the holy man by a thousand injurious arts, often thrust himself upon him in a visible form, but in very various shapes. For sometimes he presented himself to his view changed into the person of Jupiter, often into that of Mercury and Minerva. Often, too, were heard words of reproach, in which the crowd of demons assailed Martin with scurrilous expressions. But knowing that all were false and groundless, he was not affected by the charges brought against him. Moreover, some of the brethren bore witness that they had heard a demon reproaching Martin in abusive terms, and asking why he had taken back, on their subsequent repentance, certain of the brethren who had, some time previously, lost their baptism by falling into various errors. The demon set forth the crimes of each of them ; but they added that Martin, resisting the devil firmly, answered him, that by-past sins are cleansed away by the leading of a better life, and that through the mercy of God, those are to be absolved from their sins who have given up their evil ways. The devil saying in opposition to this that such guilty men as those referred to did not come within the pale of pardon, and that no mercy was extended by the Lord to those who had once fallen away, Martin is said to have cried out in words to the following effect : " If thou, thyself, wretched being, wouldst but desist from attacking mankind, and even, at this period, when the day of judgment is at hand, wouldst only repent of your deeds, I, with a true confidence in the Lord, would promise you the mercy of Christ."[1] O what a holy boldness with respect to the lovingkindness of the Lord, in which, although he could not assert authority, he nevertheless showed the feelings dwelling within him ! And since our discourse has here sprung up concerning the devil and his devices, it does not seem away from the point, although the matter does not

---

[2] There is considerable confusion in this sentence.
[1] Halm reads the imperative " videris," " consider."

[2] Halm reads " aut sibi nuntiata fratribus indicabat."
[1] This is a truly noteworthy passage. It anticipates a well-known sentiment of Burns, the national bard of Scotland. In his *Address to the Deil*, Burns has said that if the great enemy would only " tak a thocht an' men'," he might still have a chance of safety, and this idea seems very much in accordance with the opinion of St. Martin as expressed above. Hornius, however, is very indignant on account of it, and exclaims: " Intolerabilis hic Martini error. Nec Sulpicius excusatione sua demit, sed auget. Origenes primus ejus erroris author."

bear immediately upon Martin, to relate what took place ; both because the virtues of Martin do, to some extent, appear in the transaction, and the incident, which was worthy of a miracle, will properly be put on record, with the view of furnishing a caution, should anything of a similar character subsequently occur.

CHAPTER XXIII.

A Case of Diabolic Deception.

THERE was a certain man, Clarus by name, a most noble youth, who afterwards became a presbyter, and who is now, through his happy departure from this world, numbered among the saints. He, leaving all others, betook himself to Martin, and in a short time became distinguished for the most exalted faith, and for all sorts of excellence. Now, it came to pass that, when he had erected an abode for himself not far from the monastery of the bishop, and many brethren were staying with him, a certain youth, Anatolius by name, having, under the profession of a monk, falsely assumed every appearance of humility and innocence, came to him, and lived for some time on the common store along with the rest. Then, as time went on, he began to affirm that angels were in the habit of talking with him. As no one gave any credit to his words, he urged a number of the brethren to believe by certain signs. At length he went to such a length as to declare that angels passed between him and God ; and now he wished that he should be regarded as one of the prophets. Clarus, however, could by no means be induced to believe. He then began to threaten Clarus with the anger of God and present afflictions, because he did not believe one of the saints. At the last, he is related to have burst forth with the following declaration : " Behold, the Lord will this night give me a white robe out of heaven, clothed in which, I will dwell in the midst of you ; and that will be to you a sign that I am the Power of God, inasmuch as I have been presented with the garment of God." Then truly the expectation of all was highly raised by this profession. Accordingly, about the middle of the night, it was seen, by the noise of people moving eagerly about, that the whole monastery in the place was excited. It might be seen, too, that the cell in which the young man referred to lived was glittering with numerous lights ; and the whisperings of those moving about in it, as well as a kind of murmur of many voices, could be heard. Then, on silence being secured, the youth coming forth calls one of the brethren, Sabatius by name, to himself, and shows him the robe in which he had been clothed. He

again, filled with amazement, gathers the rest together, and Clarus himself also runs up ; and a light being obtained, they all carefully inspect the garment. Now, it was of the utmost softness, of marvelous brightness, and of glittering purple, and yet no one could discover what was its nature, or of what sort of fleece it had been formed. However, when it was more minutely examined by the eyes or fingers, it seemed nothing else than a garment. In the meantime, Clarus urges upon the brethren to be earnest in prayer, that the Lord would show them more clearly what it really was. Accordingly, the rest of the night was spent in singing hymns and psalms. But when day broke, Clarus wished to take the young man by the hand, and bring him to Martin, being well aware that he could not be deceived by any arts of the devil. Then, indeed, the miserable man began to resist and refuse, and affirmed that he had been forbidden to show himself to Martin. And when they compelled him to go against his will, the garment vanished from among the hands of those who were conducting him. Wherefore, who can doubt that this, too, was an illustration of the power of Martin, so that the devil could no longer dissemble or conceal his own deception, when it was to be submitted to the eyes of Martin?

CHAPTER XXIV.

Martin is tempted by the Wiles of the Devil.

IT was found, again, that about the same time there was a young man in Spain, who, having by many signs obtained for himself authority among the people, was puffed up to such a pitch that he gave himself out as being Elias. And when multitudes had too readily believed this, he went on to say that he was actually Christ ; and he succeeded so well even in this delusion that a certain bishop named Rufus worshiped him as being the Lord. For so doing, we have seen this bishop at a later date deprived of his office. Many of the brethren have also informed me that at the same time one arose in the East, who boasted that he was John. We may infer from this, since false prophets of such a kind have appeared, that the coming of Antichrist is at hand ; for he is already practicing in these persons the mystery of iniquity. And truly I think this point should not be passed over, with what arts the devil about this very time tempted Martin. For, on a certain day, prayer[1] having been previously offered, and the fiend himself being surrounded by a purple light, in order that he might the more easily deceive people by the brilliance of the splendor assumed, clothed also

---

[1] " Prece " for the usual reading " prae se."

in a royal robe, and with a crown of precious stones and gold encircling his head, his shoes too being inlaid with gold, while he presented a tranquil countenance, and a generally rejoicing aspect, so that no such thought as that he was the devil might be entertained — he stood by the side of Martin as he was praying in his cell. The saint being dazzled by his first appearance, both preserved a long and deep silence. This was first broken by the devil, who said : " Acknowledge, Martin, who it is that you behold. I am Christ ; and being just about to descend to earth, I wished first to manifest myself to thee." When Martin kept silence on hearing these words, and gave no answer whatever, the devil dared to repeat his audacious declaration : " Martin, why do you hesitate to believe, when you see ? I am Christ." Then Martin, the Spirit revealing the truth to him, that he might understand it was the devil, and not God, replied as follows : " The Lord Jesus did not predict that he would come clothed in purple, and with a glittering crown upon his head. I will not believe that Christ has come, unless he appears with that appearance and form in which he suffered, and openly displaying the marks of his wounds upon the cross." On hearing these words, the devil vanished like smoke, and filled the cell with such a disgusting smell, that he left unmistakable evidences of his real character. This event, as I have just related, took place in the way which I have stated, and my information regarding it was derived from the lips of Martin himself ; therefore let no one regard it as fabulous.[2]

CHAPTER XXV.

Intercourse of Sulpitius with Martin.

For since I, having long heard accounts of his faith, life and virtues, burned with a desire of knowing him, I undertook what was to me a pleasant journey for the purpose of seeing him. At the same time, because already my mind was inflamed with the desire of writing his life, I obtained my information partly from himself, in so far as I could venture to question him, and partly from those who had lived with him, or well knew the facts of the case. And at this time it is scarcely credible with what humility and with what kindness he received me ; while he cordially wished me joy, and rejoiced in the Lord that he had been held in such high estimation by me that I had undertaken a journey owing to my desire of seeing him. Unworthy me ! (in fact, I hardly dare acknowledge it), that

he should have deigned to admit me to fellowship with him ! He went so far as in person to present me with water to wash my hands, and at eventide he himself washed my feet ; nor had I sufficient courage to resist or oppose his doing so. In fact, I felt so overcome by the authority he unconsciously exerted, that I deemed it unlawful to do anything but acquiesce in his arrangements. His conversation with me was all directed to such points as the following : that the allurements of this world and secular burdens were to be abandoned in order that we might be free and unencumbered in following the Lord Jesus ; and he pressed upon me as an admirable example in present circumstances the conduct of that distinguished man Paulinus, of whom I have made mention above. Martin declared of him that, by parting with his great possessions and following Christ, as he did, he showed himself almost the only one who in these times had fully obeyed the precepts of the Gospel. He insisted strongly that that was the man who should be made the object of our imitation, adding that the present age was fortunate in possessing such a model of faith and virtue. For Paulinus, being rich and having many possessions, by selling them all and giving them to the poor according to the expressed will of the Lord, had, he said, made possible by actual proof what appeared impossible of accomplishment. What power and dignity there were in Martin's words and conversation ! How active he was, how practical, and how prompt and ready in solving questions connected with Scripture ! And because I know that many are incredulous on this point, — for indeed I have met with persons who did not believe me when I related such things, — I call to witness Jesus, and our common hope as Christians, that I never heard from any other lips than those of Martin such exhibitions of knowledge and genius, or such specimens of good and pure speech. But yet, how insignificant is all such praise when compared with the virtues which he possessed ! Still, it is remarkable that in a man who had no claim to be called learned, even this attribute [of high intelligence] was not wanting.

CHAPTER XXVI.

Words cannot describe the Excellences of Martin.

But now my book must be brought to an end, and my discourse finished. This is not because all that was worthy of being said concerning Martin is now exhausted, but because I, just as sluggish poets grow less careful towards the end of their work, give over, being baffled by the immensity of the matter. For, although his

---

[2] In spite of the combined testimony of Martin and Sulpitius here referred to, few will have any doubt as to the real character of this narrative.

outward deeds could in some sort of way be set forth in words, no language, I truly own, can ever be capable of describing his inner life and daily conduct, and his mind always bent upon the things of heaven. No one can adequately make known his perseverance and self-mastery in abstinence and fastings, or his power in watchings and prayers, along with the nights, as well as days, which were spent by him, while not a moment was separated from the service of God, either for indulging in ease, or engaging in business. But, in fact, he did not indulge either in food or sleep, except in so far as the necessities of nature required. I freely confess that, if, as the saying is, Homer himself were to ascend from the shades below, he could not do justice to this subject in words; to such an extent did all excellences surpass in Martin the possibility of being embodied in language. Never did a single hour or moment pass in which he was not either actually engaged in prayer; or, if it happened that he was occupied with something else, still he never let his mind loose from prayer. In truth, just as it is the custom of blacksmiths, in the midst of their work to beat their own anvil as a sort of relief to the laborer, so Martin even when he appeared to be doing something else, was still engaged in prayer. O truly blessed man in whom there was no guile — judging no man, condemning no man, returning evil for evil to no man! He displayed indeed such marvelous patience in the endurance of injuries, that even when he was chief[1] priest, he allowed himself to be wronged by the lowest clerics with impunity; nor did he either remove them from the office on account of such conduct, or, as far as in him lay, repel them from a place in his affection.

CHAPTER XXVII.

Wonderful Piety of Martin.

No one ever saw him enraged, or excited, or lamenting, or laughing; he was always one and the same: displaying a kind of heavenly happiness in his countenance, he seemed to have passed the ordinary limits of human nature. Never was there any word on his lips but Christ,

and never was there a feeling in his heart except piety, peace, and tender mercy. Frequently, too, he used to weep for the sins of those who showed themselves his revilers — those who, as he led his retired and tranquil life, slandered him with poisoned tongue and a viper's mouth. And truly we have had experience of some who were envious of his virtues and his life — who really hated in him what they did not see in themselves, and what they had not power to imitate. And — O wickedness worthy of deepest grief and groans! — some of his calumniators, although very few, some of his maligners, I say, were reported to be no others than bishops! Here, however, it is not necessary to name any one, although a good many of these people are still venting[1] their spleen against myself. I shall deem it sufficient that, if any one of them reads this account, and perceives that he is himself pointed at, he may have the grace to blush. But if, on the other hand, he shows anger, he will, by that very fact, own that he is among those spoken of, though all the time perhaps I have been thinking of some other person. I shall, however, by no means feel ashamed if any people of that sort include myself in their hatred along with such a man as Martin. I am quite persuaded of this, that the present little work will give pleasure to all truly good men. And I shall only say further that, if any one read this narrative in an unbelieving spirit, he himself will fall into sin. I am conscious to myself that I have been induced by belief in the facts, and by the love of Christ, to write these things; and that, in doing so, I have set forth what is well known, and recorded what is true; and, as I trust, that man will have a reward prepared by God, not who shall read these things, but who shall believe them.[2]

---

1 "Summus sacerdos": "that is," remarks Hornius, "bishop. They were also in those ages styled Popes (Papæ). This is clear from Cyprian, Jerome, and others of a much later age."

1 Lit. "are barking round about."

2 It seems extremely difficult (to recur to the point once more), after reading this account of St. Martin by Sulpitius, to form any certain conclusion regarding it. The writer so frequently and solemnly assures us of his good faith, and there is such a verisimilitude about the style, that it appears impossible to accept the theory of willful deception on the part of the writer. And then, he was so intimately acquainted with the subject of his narrative, that he could hardly have accepted fictions for facts, or failed in his estimate of the friend he so much admired and loved. Altogether, this *Life of St. Martin* seems to bring before us one of the puzzles of history. The saint himself must evidently have been a very extraordinary man, to impress one of the talents and learning of Sulpitius so remarkably as he did; but it is extremely hard to say how far the miraculous narratives, which enter so largely into the account before us, were due to pure invention, or unconscious hallucination. Milner remarks (*Church History*, II. 193), "I should be ashamed, as well as think the labor ill spent, to recite the stories at length which Sulpitius gives us." See, on the other side, Cardinal Newman's *Essays on Miracles*, p. 127, 209, &c.

THE LETTERS OF SULPITIUS SEVERUS.

———o⋅ᵒ⋅ᵒ⋅oo———

LETTER I.

TO EUSEBIUS.

Against Some Envious Assailants of Martin.

YESTERDAY a number of monks having come to me, it happened that amid endless fables, and much tiresome discourse, mention was made of the little work which I published concerning the life of that saintly man Martin, and I was most happy to hear that it was being eagerly and carefully read by multitudes. In the meantime, however, I was told that a certain person, under the influence of an evil spirit, had asked why Martin, who was said to have raised the dead and to have rescued houses from the flames, had himself recently become subject to the power of fire, and thus been exposed to suffering of a dangerous character. Wretched man, whoever he is, that expressed himself thus! We recognize his perfidious talk in the words of the Jews of old, who reviled the Lord, when hanging upon the cross, in the following terms : "He saved others ; himself he cannot save."[1] Truly it is clear that, whoever be the person referred to, if he had lived in those times, he would have been quite prepared to speak against the Lord in these terms, inasmuch as he blasphemes a saint of the Lord, after a like fashion. How then, I ask thee, whosoever thou art, how does the case stand? Was Martin really not possessed of power, and not a partaker of holiness, because he became exposed to danger from fire? O thou blessed man, and in all things like to the Apostles, even in the reproaches which are thus heaped upon thee! Assuredly those Gentiles are reported to have entertained the same sort of thought respecting Paul also, when the viper had bitten him, for they said, "This man must be a murderer, whom, although saved from the sea, the fates do not permit to live."[2] But he, shaking off the viper into the fire, suffered no harm. They, however, imagined that he would suddenly fall down, and speedily die ; but when they saw that no harm befell him, changing their minds, they said that he was a God. But, O thou most miserable of men, you ought, even from that example to have yourself been convinced of your falsity ; so that, if it had proved a stumbling-block to thee that Martin appeared touched by the flame of fire, you should, on the other hand, have ascribed his being merely touched to his merits and power, because, though surrounded by flames, he did not perish. For acknowledge, thou miserable man, acknowledge what you seem ignorant of, that almost all the saints have been more remarkable for[3] the dangers they encountered, than even for the virtues they displayed. I see, indeed, Peter strong in faith, walking over the waves of the sea, in opposition to the nature of things, and that he pressed the unstable waters with his footprints. But not on that account does the preacher of the Gentiles[4] seem to me a smaller man, whom the waves swallowed up ; and, after three days[5] and three nights, the water restored him emerging from the deep. Nay, I am almost inclined to think that it was a greater thing to have lived in the deep, than to have walked along the depths of the sea. But, thou foolish man, you had not, I suppose, read these things ; or, having read them, had not understood them. For the blessed Evangelist would not have recorded in holy writ an incident of that kind—under divine guidance—(except that, from such cases, the human mind might be instructed as to the dangers connected with shipwrecks and serpents!) and, as the Apostle relates, who gloried in his nakedness, and hunger, and perils from robbers, all these things are indeed to be endured in common by holy men, but that it has always been the chief excellence of the righteous in enduring and conquering such things, while amid all their trials, being patient and ever unconquerable, they overcame them all the more courageously, the heavier was the burden which they had to bear. Hence this event which is ascribed to the infirmity of Martin is, in reality, full of dignity and glory, since indeed, being tried

---

[1] St. Matt. xxvii. 42.　　[2] Acts xxviii. 4.

[3] "magis insignes periculorum suorum" : such is the construction of *insignis* with later writers.
[4] This refers to St. Paul, being an echo of the Apostle's own words in Rom. xi. 13—ἐγὼ ἐθνῶν ἀπόστολος.
[5] The writer here supposes that St. Paul was sunk for three days and three nights in the sea—a mistaken inference from 2 Cor. xi. 25. The construction of the very long sentence which soon follows is very confused, and has not been rigidly followed in our translation.

by a most dangerous calamity, he came forth a conqueror. But let no one wonder that the incident referred to was omitted by me in that treatise which I wrote concerning his life, since in that very work I openly acknowledged that I had not embraced all his acts; and that for the good reason that, if I had been minded to narrate them all, I must have presented an enormous volume to my readers. And indeed, his achievments were not of so limited a number that they could all be comprehended in a book. Nevertheless, I shall not leave this incident, about which a question has arisen, to remain in obscurity, but shall relate the whole affair as it occurred, lest I should appear perchance to have intentionally passed over that which might be put forward in calumniation of the saintly man.

Martin having, about the middle of winter, come to a certain parish,[6] according to the usual custom for the bishops to visit the churches in the diocese, the clerics had prepared an abode for him in the private[7] part of the church, and had kindled a large fire beneath the floor which was decayed and very thin.[8] They also erected for him a couch consisting of a large amount of straw. Then, when Martin betook himself to rest, he was annoyed with the softness of the too luxurious bed, inasmuch as he had been accustomed to lie on the bare ground with only a piece of sackcloth stretched over him. Accordingly, influenced by the injury which had, as it were, been done him, he threw aside the whole of the straw. Now, it so happened that part of the straw which he had thus removed fell upon the stove. He himself, in the meantime, rested, as was his wont, upon the bare ground, tired out by his long journey. About midnight, the fire bursting up through the stove which, as I have said, was far from sound, laid hold of the dry straw. Martin, being wakened out of sleep by this unexpected occurrence, and being prevented by the pressing danger, but chiefly, as he afterwards related, by the snares and urgency of the devil, was longer than he ought to have been in having recourse to the aid of prayer. For, desiring to get outside, he struggled long and laboriously with the bolt by which he had secured the door. Ere long he perceived that he was surrounded by a fearful conflagration; and the fire had even laid hold of the garment with which he was clothed. At length recovering his habitual conviction that his safety lay not in flight, but in the Lord, and seizing the shield of faith and prayer,

committing himself entirely to the Lord, he lay down in the midst of the flames. Then truly, the fire having been removed by divine interposition, he continued to pray amid a circle of flames that did him no harm. But the monks, who were before the door, hearing the sound of the crackling and struggling fire, broke open the barred door; and, the fire being extinguished, they brought forth Martin from the midst of the flames, all the time supposing that he must ere then have been burnt to ashes by a fire of so long continuance. Now, as the Lord is my witness, he himself related to me, and not without groans, confessed that he was in this matter beguiled by the arts of the devil; in that, when roused from sleep, he did not take the wise course of repelling the danger by means of faith and prayer. He also added that the flames raged around him all the time that, with a distempered mind, he strove to throw open the door. But he declared that as soon as he again sought assistance from the cross, and tried the weapons of prayer, the central flames gave way, and that he then felt them shedding a dewy refreshment over him, after having just experienced how cruelly they burned him. Considering all which, let every one who reads this letter understand that Martin was indeed tried by that danger, but passed through it with true acceptance.[9]

LETTER II.

TO THE DEACON AURELIUS.

Sulpitius has a Vision of St. Martin.

SULPITIUS SEVERUS to Aurelius the Deacon sendeth greeting, —[1]

After you had departed from me in the morning, I was sitting alone in my cell; and there occurred to me, as often happens, that hope of the future which I cherish, along with a weariness of the present world, a terror of judgment, a fear of punishment, and, as a consequence, indeed as the source from which the whole train of thought had flowed, a remembrance of my sins, which had rendered me worn and miserable. Then, after I had placed on my couch my limbs fatigued with the anguish of my mind, sleep crept upon me, as frequently happens from melancholy; and such sleep, as it is always somewhat light and uncertain in the morning hours, so it pervaded my members only in a hovering and doubtful manner. Thus it happens, what does not occur in a different kind of slumber, that one can feel he is dreaming while almost awake. In these circumstances, I seemed suddenly to see St. Martin appear to me in the character of

---

6 "ad diœcesim quandam": it seems certain that *diocesis* has here the meaning of "parish."
7 "in secretario ecclesiæ": it is very difficult to say what is here meant by "secretarium." It appears from *Dial.* II. 1, that there might be two or more *secretaria* in one church.
8 "pavimento": this word usually means "a floor," or "pavement," but some take it here to be the same as *fornax*. This, however, can hardly be the case; and the meaning probably is that the church was heated, as the baths were, by means of a *hypocaustum*, or flue running below the pavement.

9 Halm here inserts, "vere."
1 This salutation is omitted by Halm.

a bishop, clothed in a white robe, with a countenance as of fire, with eyes like stars, and with purple hair.[2] He thus appeared to me with that aspect and form of body which I had known, so that I find it almost difficult to say what I mean — he could not be steadfastly beheld, though he could be clearly recognized. Well, directing a gentle smile towards me, he held out in his right hand the small treatise which I had written concerning his life. I, for my part, embraced his sacred knees, and begged for his blessing according to custom. Upon this, I felt his hand placed on my head with the sweetest touch, while, amid the solemn words of benediction, he repeated again and again the name of the cross so familiar to his lips. Ere long, while my eyes were earnestly fixed upon him, and when I could not satisfy myself with gazing upon his countenance, he was suddenly taken away from me and raised on high. At last, having passed through the vast expanse of the air, while my straining eyes followed him ascending in a rapidly moving cloud, he could no longer be seen by me gazing after him. And not long after, I saw the holy presbyter Clarus, a disciple of Martin's who had lately died, ascend in the same way as I had seen his master. I, impudently desiring to follow, while I aim at and strive after such lofty steps, suddenly wake up ; and, being roused from sleep, I had begun to rejoice over the vision, when a boy, a servant in the family, enters to me with a countenance sadder than is usual with one who gives utterance to his grief in words. "What," I enquire of him, "do you wish to tell me with so melancholy an aspect?" "Two monks," he replied, "have just been here from Tours, and they have brought word that Martin is dead." I confess that I was cut to the heart ; and bursting into tears, I wept most abundantly. Nay, even now, as I write these things to you, brother, my tears are flowing, and I find no consolation for my all but unbearable sorrow. And I should wish you, when this news reaches you, to be a partaker in my grief, as you were a sharer with me in his love. Come then, I beg of you, to me without delay, that we may mourn in common him whom in common we love. And yet I am well aware that such a man ought not to be mourned over, to whom, after his victory and triumph over the world, there has now at last been given the crown of righteousness. Nevertheless, I cannot so command myself as to keep from grieving. I have, no doubt, sent on before me one who will plead my cause in heaven, but I have, at the same time, lost my great source of consolation in this present life ; yet if grief would yield to the influence of reason, I certainly ought

to rejoice. For he is now mingling among the Apostles and Prophets, and (with all respect for the saints on high be it said) he is second to no one in that assembly of the righteous as I firmly hope, believe, and trust, being joined especially to those who washed their robes in the blood of the[3] Lamb. He now follows the Lamb as his guide, free from all spot of defilement. For although the character[4] of our times could not ensure him the honor of martyrdom, yet he will not remain destitute of the glory of a martyr, because both by vow and virtues he was alike able and willing to be a martyr. But if he had been permitted, in the times of Nero and of Decius,[5] to take part in the struggle which then went on, I take to witness the God of heaven and earth that he would freely have submitted[6] to the rack of torture, and readily surrendered himself to the flames : yea, worthy of being compared to the illustrious Hebrew youths, amid circling flames, and though in the very midst of the furnace, he would have sung a hymn of the Lord. But if perchance it had pleased the persecutor to inflict upon him the punishment which Isaiah endured, he would never have shown himself inferior to the prophet, nor would have shrunk from having his members torn in pieces by saws and swords. And if impious fury had preferred to drive the blessed man over precipitous rocks or steep mountains, I maintain that, clinging[7] to the testimony of truth he would willingly have fallen. But if, after the example of the teacher of the Gentiles,[8] as indeed often happened, he had been included among other victims who were condemned[9] to die by the sword, he would have been foremost to urge on the executioner to his work that he might obtain the crown[10] of blood. And, in truth, far from shrinking from a confession of the Lord, in the face of all those penalties and punishments, which frequently prove too much for human infirmity, he would have stood so immovable as to have smiled with joy and gladness over the sufferings and torments he endured, whatever might have been the tortures inflicted upon him. But although he did in fact suffer none of these things, yet he fully attained to the honor of martyrdom without shedding his blood. For what agonies of human sufferings did he not endure in behalf of the hope of eternal life, in hunger, in watchings, in nakedness, in fastings,

---

2 "crine purpureo" : it is impossible to tell the exact color which is intended.

3 Compare Rev. vii. 14.
4 As being peaceful, the imperial power having now passed into the hands of Christians.
5 Roman emperor, A.D. 249–251; his full name was C. Messius Quintus Trajanus Decius.
6 "equileum ascendisset": lit. "would have mounted the wooden horse," an instrument of torture.
7 Some read "perhibeo confisus testimonium veritati," and others "veritatis"; in either case, the construction is confused and irregular.
8 St. Paul is referred to: tradition bears that he was beheaded.
9 A late use of the verb *deputare*.
10 *i.e.* martyrdom, "palmam sanguinis."

in reproachings of the malignant, in persecutions of the wicked, in care for the weak, in anxiety for those in danger? For who ever suffered but Martin suffered along with him? Who was made to stumble and he burnt not? Who perished, and he did not mourn deeply? Besides those daily struggles which he carried on against the various conflicts with human and spiritual wickedness, while invariably, as he was assailed with divers temptations, there prevailed in his case fortitude in conquering, patience in waiting, and placidity in enduring. O man, truly indescribable in piety, mercy, love, which daily grows cold even in holy men through the coldness of the world, but which in his case increased onwards to the end, and endured from day to day! I, for my part, had the happiness of enjoying this grace in him even in an eminent degree, for he loved me in a special manner, though I was far from meriting such affection. And, on the remembrance, yet again my tears burst forth, while groans issue from the bottom of my heart. In what man shall I for the future find such repose for my spirit as I did in him? and in whose love shall I enjoy like consolation? Wretched being that I am, sunk in affliction, can I ever, if life be spared me, cease to lament that I have survived Martin? Shall there in future be to me any pleasure in life, or any day or hour free from tears; or can I ever, my dearest brother, make mention of him to you without lamentation? And yet, in conversing with you, can I ever talk of any other subject than him? But why do I stir you up to tears and lamentations? So I now desire you to be comforted, although I am unable to console myself. He will not be absent from us; believe me, he will never, never forsake us, but will be present with us as we discourse regarding him, and will be near to us as we pray; and the happiness which he has even to-day deigned to bestow, even that of seeing him in his glory, he will frequently in future afford; and he will protect us, as he did but a little while ago, with his unceasing benediction. Then again, according to the arrangement of the vision, he showed that heaven was open to those following him, and taught us to what we ought to follow him; he instructed us to what objects our hope should be directed, and to what attainment our mind should be turned. Yet, my brother, what is to be done? For, as I am myself well aware, I shall never be able to climb that difficult ascent, and penetrate into those blessed regions. To such a degree does a miserable burden press me down; and while I cannot, through the load of sin which overwhelms me, secure an ascent to heaven, the cruel pressure rather sinks me in my misery to the place of despair.[11] Nevertheless, hope remains, one last and solitary hope, that, what I cannot obtain of myself, I may, at any rate, be thought worthy of, through the prayers of Martin in my behalf. But why, brother, should I longer occupy your time with a letter which has turned out so garrulous, and thus delay you from coming to me? At the same time, my page being now filled, can admit no more. This, however, was my object in prolonging my discourse to a somewhat undue extent, that, since this letter conveys to you a message of sorrow, it might also furnish you with consolation, through my sort of friendly conversation with you.

LETTER III.

TO BASSULA, HIS MOTHER-IN-LAW.

How St. Martin passed from this Life to Life Eternal.

Sulpitius Severus to Bassula, his venerable parent, sendeth greeting.

If it were lawful that parents should be summoned to court by their children, clearly I might drag you with a righteous thong[1] before the tribunal of the prætor, on a charge of robbery and plunder. For why should I not complain of the injury which I have suffered at your hands? You have left me no little bit of writing at home, no book, not even a letter — to such a degree do you play the thief with all such things and publish them to the world. If I write anything in familiar style to a friend; if, as I amuse myself I dictate anything with the wish at the same time that it should be kept private, all such things seem to reach you almost before they have been written or spoken. Surely you have my secretaries[2] in your[3] debt, since through them any trifles I compose are made known to you. And yet I cannot be moved with anger against them if they really obey you, and have invaded my rights under the special influence of your generosity to them, and ever bear in mind that they belong to you rather than to me. Yes, thou alone art the culprit — thou alone art to blame — inasmuch as you both lay your snares for me, and cajole them with your trickery, so that without making any[4] selection, pieces written familiarly, or let out of hand without care, are sent to thee quite unelaborated and unpolished. For, to say nothing about other writings, I beg to ask how that letter could reach you so speedily, which I recently wrote to Aurelius the Deacon. For,

---

11 " in tartara."

1 Instead of " justo loro," Halm reads, " justo dolore," *i.e.* " with just resentment."
2 " notarios ": shorthand writers, who wrote from dictation.
3 Halm here reads " obarratos," with what sense I know not: the reading " obæratos," followed in the text seems to yield a very good meaning.
4 The reading " sine dilectu ullo," adopted by Halm, seems preferable to the old reading, " sine delicto ullo."

as I was situated at Toulouse,[5] while you were dwelling at Treves, and were so far distant from your native land, owing to the anxiety felt on account of your son, what opportunity, I should like to know, did you avail yourself of, to get hold of that familiar[6] epistle? For I have received your letter in which you write that I ought in the same epistle in which I made mention of the death of our master, Martin, to have described the manner in which that saintly man left this world. As if, indeed, I had either given forth that epistle with the view of its being read by any other except him to whom it purported to be sent; or as if I were fated to undertake so great a work as that all things which should be known respecting Martin are to be made public through me particularly as the writer. Therefore, if you desire to learn anything concerning the end of the saintly bishop, you should direct your enquiries rather to those who were present when his death occurred. I for my part have resolved to write nothing to you lest you publish me[7] everywhere. Nevertheless if you pledge your word that you will read to no one what I send you, I shall satisfy your desire in a few words. Accordingly I shall communicate[8] to you the following particulars which are comprised within my own knowledge.

I have to state, then, that Martin was aware of the period of his own death long before it occurred, and told the brethren that his departure from the body was at hand. In the meantime, a reason sprang up which led him to visit the church at Condate.[9] For, as the clerics of that church were at variance among themselves, Martin, wishing to restore peace, although he well knew that the end of his own days was at hand, yet he did not shrink from undertaking the journey, with such an object in view. He did, in fact, think that this would be an excellent crown to set upon his virtues, if he should leave behind him peace restored to a church. Thus, then, having set out with that very numerous and holy crowd of disciples who usually accompanied him, he perceives in a river a number of water-fowl busy in capturing fishes, and notices that a voracious appetite was urging them on to frequent seizures of their prey. "This," exclaimed he, "is a picture of how the demons act: they lie in wait for the unwary and capture them before they know it: they devour their victims when taken, and they can never be satisfied with what they have devoured." Then Martin, with a miraculous[10] power in his words, commands the birds to leave the pool in which they were swimming, and to betake themselves to dry and desert regions; using with respect to those birds that very same authority with which he had been accustomed to put demons to flight. Accordingly, gathering themselves together, all those birds formed a single body, and leaving the river, they made for the mountains and woods, to no small wonder of many who perceived such power in Martin that he could even rule the birds. Having then delayed some time in that village or church to which he had gone, and peace having been restored among the clerics, when he was now meditating a return to his monastery, he began suddenly to fail in bodily strength, and, assembling the brethren, he told them that he was on the point of dissolution. Then indeed, sorrow and grief took possession of all, and there was but one voice of them lamenting, and saying: "Why, dear father, will you leave us? Or to whom can you commit us in our desolation? Fierce wolves will speedily attack thy flock, and who, when the shepherd has been smitten, will save us[11] from their bites? We know, indeed, that you desire to be with Christ; but thy reward above is safe, and will not be diminished by being delayed; rather have pity upon us, whom you are leaving desolate." Then Martin, affected by these lamentations, as he was always, in truth, full[12] of compassion, is said to have burst into tears; and, turning to the Lord, he replied to those weeping round him only in the following words, "O Lord, if I am still necessary to thy people, I do not shrink from toil: thy will be done." Thus hovering as he did between[13] desire and love, he almost doubted which he preferred; for he neither wished to leave us, nor to be longer separated from Christ. However, he placed no weight upon his own wishes, nor reserved anything to his own will, but committed himself wholly to the will and power of the Lord. Do you not think you hear him speaking in the following few words which I repeat? "Terrible, indeed, Lord, is the struggle of bodily warfare, and surely it is now enough that I have continued the fight till now; but, if thou dost command me still to persevere in the same toil for the defense[14] of thy flock, I do not refuse, nor do I plead against such an appoint-

---

[5] The identity of Tolosa, mentioned in the text with the modern Toulouse, is uncertain.

[6] Of course, this is all jocular, and shows the best relations as existing between Sulpitius and his mother-in-law.

[7] There is clearly some affectation in the horror which Sulpitius expresses in this and other passages at the thought of his writings being published. It is obvious that he derived gratification from the fact of their being widely read.

[8] " præstabo his participem ": the construction is peculiar, but the meaning is obvious.

[9] There were several towns of this name in Gaul. The one probably here referred to was on the road from Augustodunum (Autun) to Paris. It corresponds to the modern Cosne, at the junction of the stream Nonain with the river Loire.

[10] " potenti virtute verborum ": Halm reads simply " potenti verbo."

[11] A singular and obviously corrupt reading is " quis eos a morsibus nostris prohibebit ?" Halm's reading has been followed in the text.

[12] Lit. " as he always flowed with bowels of mercy in the Lord."

[13] " spes " seems here to mean " longing of heart."

[14] " pro castris tuorum."

ment my declining years. Wholly given to thee, I will fulfill whatever duties thou dost assign me, and I will serve under thy standard as long as thou shalt prescribe. Yea, although release is sweet to an old man after lengthened toil, yet my mind is a conqueror over my years, and I have no desire [15] to yield to old age. But if now thou art merciful to my many years, good, O Lord, is thy will to me; and thou thyself wilt guard over those for whose safety I fear." O man, whom no language can describe, unconquered by toil, and unconquerable even by death, who didst show no personal preference for either alternative, and who didst neither fear to die nor refuse to live! Accordingly, though he was for some days under the influence of a strong fever, he nevertheless did not abandon the work of God. Continuing in supplications and watchings through whole nights, he compelled his worn-out limbs to do service to his spirit as he lay on his glorious [16] couch upon sackcloth and ashes. And when his disciples begged of him that at least he should allow some common straw to be placed beneath him, he replied: "It is not fitting that a Christian should die except among ashes; and I have sinned if I leave you a different example." However, with his hands and eyes steadfastly directed towards heaven, he never released his unconquerable spirit from prayer. And on being asked by the presbyters who had then gathered round him, to relieve his body a little by a change of side, he exclaimed: "Allow me, dear brother, to fix my looks rather on heaven than on earth, so that my spirit which is just about to depart on its own journey may be directed towards the Lord." Having spoken these words, he saw the devil standing close at hand, and exclaimed: "Why do you stand here, thou bloody monster? Thou shalt find nothing in me, thou deadly one: Abraham's bosom is about to receive me."

As he uttered these words, his spirit fled; and those who were there present have testified to us that they saw his face as if it had been the face [17] of an angel. His limbs too appeared white as snow, so that people exclaimed, "Who would ever believe that man to be clothed in sackcloth, or who would imagine that he was enveloped with ashes?" For even then he presented such an appearance, as if he had been manifested in the glory of the future resurrection, and with the nature of a body which had been changed. But it is hardly credible what a multitude of human beings assembled at the performance of his funeral rites: the whole city poured forth to meet his body; all the inhabitants of the district and villages, along with many also from the neighboring cities, attended. O how great was the grief of all! how deep the lamentations in particular of the sorrowing monks! They are said to have assembled on that day almost to the number of two thousand, — a special glory of Martin, — through his example so numerous plants had sprung up for the service of the Lord. Undoubtedly the shepherd was then driving his own flocks before him — the pale crowds of that saintly multitude — bands arrayed in cloaks, either old men whose life-labor was finished, or young soldiers who had just taken the oath of allegiance to Christ. Then, too, there was the choir of virgins, abstaining out of modesty from weeping; and with what holy joy did they conceal the fact of their affliction! No doubt faith would prevent the shedding of tears, yet affection forced out groans. For there was as sacred an exultation over the glory to which he had attained, as there was a pious sorrow on account of his death. One would have been inclined to pardon those who wept, as well as to congratulate those who rejoiced, while each single person preferred that he himself should grieve, but that another should rejoice. Thus then this multitude, singing hymns of heaven, attended the body of the sainted man onwards to the place of sepulture. Let there be compared with this spectacle, I will not say the worldly [18] pomp of a funeral, but even of a triumph; and what can be reckoned similar to the obsequies of Martin? Let your worldly great men lead before their chariots captives with their hands bound behind their backs. Those accompanied the body of Martin who, under his guidance, had overcome the world. Let madness honor these earthly warriors with the united praises of nations. Martin is praised with the divine psalms, Martin is honored in heavenly hymns. Those worldly men, after their triumphs here are over, shall be thrust into cruel Tartarus, while Martin is joyfully received into the bosom of Abraham. Martin, poor and insignificant on earth, has a rich entrance granted him into heaven. From that blessed region, as I trust, he looks upon me, as my guardian, while I am writing these things, and upon you while you read them. [19]

---

15 Or, "I am not one to yield," *nescius cedere*.
16 "nobili illo strato suo"; *nobilis* in one sense, though so humble in another.
17 There is a great variety of readings here; Halm has been followed in the text.

18 Or, "the pomp of a worldly funeral."
19 Halm inserts this last sentence in brackets.

THE DIALOGUES OF SULPITIUS SEVERUS.

—◦○◌○◦—

DIALOGUE I.

CONCERNING THE VIRTUES OF THE MONKS OF THE EAST.

CHAPTER I.

WHEN I and a Gallic friend had assembled in one place, this Gaul being a man very dear to me, both on account of his remembrance of Martin (for he had been one of his disciples), and on account of his own merits, my friend Postumianus joined us. He had just, on my account, returned from the East, to which, leaving his native country, he had gone three years before. Having embraced this most affectionate friend, and kissed both his knees and his feet, we were for a moment or two, as it were, astounded; and, shedding mutual tears of joy, we walked about a good deal. But by and by we sat down on our garments of sackcloth laid upon the ground. Then Postumianus, directing his looks towards me is the first to speak, and says, —

"When I was in the remote parts of Egypt, I felt a desire to go on as far as the sea. I there met with a merchant vessel, which was ready to set sail with the view of making for Narbonne.[1] The same night you seemed in a dream to stand beside me, and laying hold of me with your hand, to lead me away that I should go on board that ship. Ere long, when the dawn dispersed the darkness, and when I rose up in the place in which I had been resting, as I revolved my dream in my mind, I was suddenly seized with such a longing after you, that without delay I went on board the ship. Landing on the thirtieth day at Marseilles, I came on from that and arrived here on the tenth day — so prosperous a voyage was granted to my dutiful desire of seeing you. Do thou only, for whose sake I have sailed over so many seas, and have traversed such an extent of land, yield yourself over to me to be embraced and enjoyed apart from all others."

"I truly," said I, "while you were still stay-

ing in Egypt, was ever holding fellowship with you in my mind and thoughts, and affection for you had full possession of me as I meditated upon you day and night. Surely then, you cannot imagine that I will now fail for a single moment to gaze with delight upon you, as I hang upon your lips. I will listen to you, I will converse with you, while no one at all is admitted to our retirement, which this remote cell of mine furnishes to us. For, as I suppose, you will not take amiss the presence of this friend of ours, the Gaul, who, as you perceive, rejoices with his whole heart over this arrival of yours, even as I do myself."

"Quite right," said Postumianus, "that Gaul will certainly be retained in our company; who, although I am but little acquainted with him, yet for this very reason that he is greatly beloved by you, cannot fail also to be dear to me. This must especially be the case, since he is of the school of Martin; nor will I grudge, as you desire, to talk with you in connected discourse, since I came hither for this very purpose, that I should, even at the risk of being tedious, respond to the desire of my dear Sulpitius" — and in so speaking he affectionately took hold of me with both his hands.

CHAPTER II.

"TRULY," said I, "you have clearly proved how much a sincere love can accomplish, inasmuch as, for my sake, you have traveled over so many seas, and such an extent of land, journeying, so to speak, from the rising of the sun in the East to where he sets in the West. Come, then, because we are here in a retired spot by ourselves, and not being otherwise occupied, feel it our duty to attend to your discourse, come, I pray thee, relate to us the whole history of your wanderings. Tell us, if you please, how the faith of Christ is flourishing in the East; what peace the saints enjoy; what are the customs of the monks; and with what signs and miracles Christ is working in his servants. For assuredly, because in this region of ours and amid the circumstances in which we are placed,

---

[1] Narbona, more commonly called Narbo Martius; the modern Narbonne.

life itself has become a weariness to us, we shall gladly hear from you, if life is permitted to Christians even in the desert."

In reply to these words, Postumianus declares, "I shall do as I see you desire. But I beg you first to tell me, whether all those persons whom I left here as priests, continue the same as I knew them before taking my departure."

Then I exclaim, "Forbear, I beseech thee, to make any enquiry on such points, which you either, I think, know as well as I do, or if you are ignorant of them, it is better that you should hear nothing regarding them. I cannot, however, help saying, that not only are those, of whom you enquire, no better than they were when you knew them, but even that one man, who was formerly a great friend of mine, and in whose affection I was wont to find some consolation from the persecutions of the rest, has shown himself more unkind towards me than he ought to have been. However, I shall not say anything harsher regarding him, both because I once esteemed him as a friend, and loved him even when he was deemed my enemy. I shall only add that while I was silently meditating on these things in my thoughts, this source of grief deeply afflicted me, that I had almost lost the friendship of one who was both a wise and a religious man. But let us turn away from these topics which are full of sorrow, and let us rather listen to you, according to the promise which you gave some time ago."

"Let it be so," exclaimed Postumianus. And on his saying this, we all kept silence, while, moving his robe of sackcloth, on which he had sat down, a little nearer me, he thus began.

CHAPTER III.

"THREE years ago, Sulpitius, at which time, leaving this neighborhood, I bade thee farewell, after setting sail from Narbonne, on the fifth day we entered a port of Africa: so prosperous, by the will of God, had been the voyage. I had in my mind a great desire to go to Carthage, to visit those localities connected with the saints, and, above all, to worship at the tomb[1] of the martyr Cyprian. On the fifth day we returned to the harbor, and launched forth into the deep. Our destination was Alexandria; but as the south wind was against us, we were almost driven upon the Syrtis;[2] the cautious sailors, however, guarding against this, stopped the ship by casting anchor. The continent of Africa then lay

before our eyes; and, landing on it in boats, when we perceived that the whole country round was destitute of human cultivation, I penetrated farther inland, for the purpose of more carefully exploring the locality. About three miles from the sea-coast, I beheld a small hut in the midst of the sand, the roof of which, to use the expression[3] of Sallust, was like the keel of a ship. It was close to[4] the earth, and was floored with good strong boards, not because any very heavy rains are there feared (for, in fact, such a thing as rain has there never even been heard of), but because, such is the strength of the winds in that district, that, if at any time only a little breath of air begins there to be felt, even when the weather is pretty mild, a greater wreckage takes place in those lands than on any sea. No plants are there, and no seeds ever spring up, since, in such shifting soil, the dry sand is swept along with every motion of the winds. But where some promontories, back from the sea, act as a check to the winds, the soil, being somewhat more firm, produces here and there some prickly grass, and that furnishes fair pasturage for sheep. The inhabitants live on milk, while those of them that are more skillful, or, so to speak, more wealthy, make use of barley bread. That is the only kind of grain which flourishes there, for barley, by the quickness of its growth in that sort of soil, generally escapes the destruction caused by the fierce winds. So rapid is its growth that we are told it is ripe on the thirtieth day after the sowing of the seed. But there is no reason why men should settle there, except that all are free from the payment of taxes. The sea-coast of the Cyrenians is indeed the most remote, bordering upon that desert which lies between Egypt and Africa,[5] and through which Cato formerly, when fleeing from Cæsar, led an army.[6]

CHAPTER IV.

I THEREFORE bent my steps toward the hut which I had beheld from a distance. There I find an old man, in a garment made of skins, turning a mill with his hand. He saluted and received us kindly. We explain to him that we had been forced to land on that coast, and were prevented by the continued raging of the sea[1] from being able at once to pursue our voyage; that, having made our way on shore, we had desired, as is in keeping with ordinary human

---

1 "Ad sepulchrum Cypriani martyris adorare."
2 This was probably the Syrtis Minor, a dangerous sandbank in the sea on the northern coast of Africa; it is now known as the Gulf of Cabes. The Syrtis Major lay farther to the east, and now bears the name of the Gulf of Sidra.

3 "Ædificia Numidarum agrestium, quæ mapalia illi vocant, oblonga, incurvis lateribus tecta, quasi navium carinæ sunt."— Sall. *Jug*. XVIII. 8.
4 The hut was perhaps built on piles rising slightly above the ground.
5 The term Africa is here used in its more restricted sense to denote the territory of Carthage.
6 This took place in the spring of the year B.C. 47.
1 "maris mollitie."

nature, to become acquainted with the character of the locality, and the manners of the inhabitants. We added that we were Christians, and that the principal object of our enquiry was whether there were any Christians amid these solitudes. Then, indeed, he, weeping for joy, throws himself at our feet; and, kissing us over and over again, invites us to prayer, while, spreading on the ground the skins of sheep, he makes us sit down upon them. He then serves up a breakfast truly luxurious,[2] consisting of the half of a barley cake. Now, we were four, while he himself constituted the fifth. He also brought in a bundle of herbs, of which I forget the name, but they were like mint, were rich in leaves, and yielded a taste like honey. We were delighted with the exceedingly sweet taste of this plant, and our hunger was fully satisfied."

Upon this I smiled, and said to my friend the Gaul, "What, Gaul, do you think of this? Are you pleased with a bundle of herbs and half a barley cake as a breakfast for five men?"

Then he, being an exceedingly modest person, and blushing somewhat, while he takes my[3] joke in good part, says, "You act, Sulpitius, in a way like yourself, for you never miss any opportunity which is offered you of joking us on the subject of our fondness for eating. But it is unkind of you to try to force us Gauls to live after the fashion of angels; and yet, through my own liking for eating, I could believe that even the angels are in the habit of eating; for such is my appetite that I would be afraid even singly to attack that half barley cake. However, let that man of Cyrene be satisfied with it, to whom it is either a matter of necessity or nature always to feel hungry; or, again, let those be content with it from whom, I suppose, their tossing at sea had taken away all desire for food. We, on the other hand, are at a distance from the sea; and, as I have often testified to you, we are, in one word, Gauls. But instead of wasting time over such matters, let our friend here rather go on to complete his account of the Cyrenian."

CHAPTER V.

"Assuredly," continues Postumianus, "I shall take care in future not to mention the abstinence of any one, in case the difficult example should quite offend our friends the Gauls. I had intended, however, to give an account also of the dinner of that man of Cyrene — for we were seven days with him — or some of the subsequent feasts; but these things had better be passed over, lest the Gaul should think that

he was jeered at. However, on the following day, when some of the natives had come together to visit us, we discovered that that host of ours was a Presbyter — a fact which he had concealed from us with the greatest care. We then went with him to the church, which was about two miles distant, and was concealed from our view by an intervening mountain. We found that it was constructed of common and worthless trees, and was not much more imposing than the hut of our host, in which one could not stand without stooping. On enquiring into the customs of the men of the district, we found that they were not in the habit of either buying or selling anything. They knew not the meaning of either fraud or theft. As to gold and silver, which mankind generally deem the most desirable of all things, they neither possess them, nor do they desire to possess them. For when I offered that Presbyter ten gold coins, he refused them, declaring, with profound wisdom, that the church was not benefited but rather[1] injured by gold. We presented him, however, with some pieces of clothing.

CHAPTER VI.

"After he had kindly accepted our gifts, on the sailors calling us back to the sea, we departed; and after a favorable passage, we arrived at Alexandria on the seventh day. There we found a disgraceful strife raging between the bishops and monks, the cause or occasion of which was that the priests were known when assembled together often to have passed decrees in crowded synods to the effect that no one should read or possess the books of Origen. He was, no doubt, regarded as a most able disputant on the sacred Scriptures. But the bishops maintained that there were certain things in his books of an unsound character; and his supporters, not being bold enough to defend these, rather took the line of declaring that they had been inserted by the heretics. They affirmed, therefore, that the other portions of his writings were not to be condemned on account of those things which justly fell under censure, since the faith of readers could easily make a distinction, so that they should not follow what had been forged, and yet should keep hold of those points which were handled in accordance with the Catholic faith. They remarked that there was nothing wonderful if, in modern and recent writings, heretical guile had been at work; since it had not feared in certain places to attack even Gospel truth. The bishops, struggling against these positions

---

[2] "Prandium sane locupletissimum": of course, there is a friendly irony in the words.
[3] "fatigationem," a late sense of the word.

[1] "non instrui, sed potius destrui."

to the utmost extent of their power, insisted that what was quite correct in the writings of Origen should, along with the author himself, and even his whole works, be condemned, because those books were more than sufficient which the church had received. They also said that the reading was to be avoided of such works as would do more harm to the unwise than they would benefit the wise. For my part, on being led by curiosity to investigate some portions of these writings, I found very many things which pleased me, but some that were to be blamed. I think it is clear that the author himself really entertained these impious opinions, though his defenders maintain that the passages have been forged. I truly wonder that one and the same man could have been so different from himself as that, in the portion which is approved, he has no equal since the times of the Apostles, while in that which is justly condemned, no one can be shown to have erred more egregiously.

CHAPTER VII.

For while many things in his books which were extracted from them by the bishops were read to show that they were written in opposition to the Catholic faith, that passage especially excited bad feeling against him, in which we read in his published works that the Lord Jesus, as he had come in the flesh for the redemption of mankind, and suffering upon the cross for the salvation of man, had tasted death to procure eternal life for the human race, so he was, by the same course of suffering, even to render the devil a partaker of redemption. He maintained this on the ground that such a thing would be in harmony with his goodness and beneficence, inasmuch as he who had restored fallen and ruined man, would thus also set free an angel who had previously fallen. When these and other things of a like nature were brought forward by the bishops, a tumult arose owing to the zeal of the different parties; and when this could not be quelled by the authority of the priests, the governor of the city was called upon to regulate the discipline of the church by a perverse precedent; and through the terror which he inspired, the brethren were dispersed, while the monks took to flight in different directions; so that, on the decrees being published, they were not permitted to find lasting acceptance[1] in any place. This fact influenced me greatly, that Hieronymus, a man truly Catholic and most skillful in the holy law, was thought at first to have been a follower of Origen, yet now, above most others, went the length of condemning the whole of his writings. Assuredly, I am

not inclined to judge rashly in regard to any one; but even the most learned men were said to hold different opinions in this controversy. However, whether that opinion of Origen was simply an error, as I think, or whether it was a heresy, as is generally supposed, it not only could not be suppressed by multitudes of censures on the part of the priests, but it never could have spread itself so far and wide, had it not gathered strength from their contentions. Accordingly, when I came to Alexandria, I found that city in a ferment from disturbances connected with the matter in question. The Bishop, indeed, of that place received me very kindly, and in a better spirit than I expected, and even endeavored to retain me with him. But I was not at all inclined to settle there, where a recent outbreak of ill-will had resulted in a destruction of the brethren. For, although perhaps it may seem that they ought to have obeyed the bishops, yet such a multitude of persons, all living in an open confession of Christ, ought not for that reason to have been persecuted, especially by bishops.

CHAPTER VIII.

Accordingly, setting out from that place, I made for the town of Bethlehem, which is six miles distant from Jerusalem, but requires sixteen stoppages[1] on the part of one journeying from Alexandria. The presbyter Jerome[2] rules the church of this place; for it is a parish of the bishop who has possession of Jerusalem. Having already in my former journey become acquainted with Hieronymus, he had easily brought it about that I with good reason deemed no one more worthy of my regard and love. For, besides the merit due to him on account of his faith, and the possession of many virtues, he is a man learned not only in Latin and Greek, but also Hebrew, to such a degree that no one dare venture to compare himself with him in all knowledge. I shall indeed be surprised if he is not well known to you also through means of the works which he has written, since he is, in fact, read the whole world over."

"Well," says the Gaul at this point, "he is, in truth, but too well known to us. For, some five years ago, I read a certain book of his, in which the whole tribe of our monks is most vehemently assaulted and reviled by him. For this reason, our Belgian friend is accustomed to be very angry, because he has said that we are in the habit of cramming ourselves even to repletion. But I, for my part, pardon the eminent man; and am of opinion that he had made the remark rather about Eastern than Western monks. For

---

[1] "in nulla consistere sede sinerentur."

[1] "mansionibus."   [2] Otherwise, "Hieronymus."

the love of eating is gluttony in the case of the Greeks, whereas among the Gauls it is owing to the nature they possess."

Then exclaimed I, "You defend your nation, my Gallic friend, by means of rhetoric; but I beg to ask whether that book condemns only this vice in the case of the monks?"

"No indeed," replies he; "the writer passed nothing over, which he did not blame, scourge, and expose: in particular, he inveighed against avarice and no less against arrogance. He discoursed much respecting·pride, and not a little about superstition; and I will freely own that he seemed to me to draw a true picture of the vices of multitudes."

CHAPTER IX.

"BUT as to familiarities which take place between virgins and monks, or even clerics, how true and how courageous were his words! And, on account of these, he is said not to stand high in favor with certain people whom I am unwilling to name. For, as our Belgian friend is angry that we were accused of too great fondness for eating, so those people, again, are said to express their rage when they find it written in that little work, — 'The virgin despises her true unmarried brother, and seeks a stranger.'"

Upon this I exclaim, "You are going too far, my Gallic friend: take heed lest some one who perhaps owns to these things, hear what you are saying, and begin to hold you, along with Hieronymus, in no great affection. For, since you are a learned[1] man, not unreasonably will I admonish you in the verse of that comic poet who says, — 'Submission procures friends, while truth gives rise to hatred.' Let rather, Postumianus, your discourse to us about the East, so well begun, now be resumed."

"Well," says he, "as I had commenced to relate, I stayed with Hieronymus six months, who carried on an unceasing warfare against the wicked, and a perpetual struggle in opposition to the deadly hatred of ungodly men. The heretics hate him, because he never desists from attacking them; the clerics hate him, because he assails their life and crimes. But beyond doubt, all the good admire and love him; for those people are out of their senses, who suppose that he is a heretic. Let me tell the truth on this point, which is that the knowledge of the man is Catholic, and that his doctrine is sound. He is always occupied in reading, always at his books with his whole heart: he takes no rest day or night; he is perpetually either reading or writing something. In fact, had I not been resolved in mind, and had promised

to God first to visit[2] the desert previously referred to, I should have grudged to depart even for the shortest time from so great a man. Handing over, then, and entrusting to him all my possessions and my whole family, which having followed me against my own inclination, kept me in a state of embarrassment, and thus being in a sort of way delivered from a heavy burden, and restored to freedom of action, I returned to Alexandria, and having visited the brethren there I set out from the place for upper Thebais, that is for the farthest off confines of Egypt. For a great multitude of monks were said to inhabit the widely extending solitudes of that wilderness. But here it would be tedious, were I to seek to narrate all the things which I witnessed: I shall only touch lightly on a few points.

CHAPTER X.

"NOT far from the desert, and close to the Nile, there are numerous monasteries. For the most part, the monks there dwell together in companies of a hundred; and their highest rule is to live under the orders of their Abbot, to do nothing by their own inclination, but to depend in all things on his will and authority. If it so happens that any of them form in their minds a lofty ideal of virtue, so as to wish to betake themselves to the desert to live a solitary life, they do not venture to act on this desire except with the permission of the Abbot. In fact, this is the first of virtues in their estimation, — to live in obedience to the will of another. To those who betake themselves to the desert, bread or some other kind of food is furnished by the command of that Abbot. Now, it so happened that, in those days during which I had come thither, the Abbot had sent bread to a certain person who had withdrawn to the desert, and had erected a tent for himself not more than six miles from the monastery. This bread was sent by the hands of two boys, the elder of whom was fifteen, and the younger twelve years of age. As these boys were returning home, an asp of remarkable size encountered them, but they were not the least afraid on meeting it; and moving up to their very feet, as if charmed by some melody, it laid down its dark-green neck before them. The younger of the boys laid hold of it with his hand, and, wrapping it in his dress, went on his way with it. Then, entering the monastery with the air of a conqueror, and meeting with the brethren, while all looked on, he opened out his dress, and set down the imprisoned beast, not without some appearance of boastfulness. But while the rest of the spectators extolled the faith and virtue of the chil-

---

[1] "scholasticus."

[2] "propositam eremum."

dren, the Abbot, with deeper insight, and to prevent them at such a tender age from being puffed up with pride, subjected both to punishment. This he did after blaming them much for having publicly revealed what the Lord had wrought through their instrumentality. He declared that that was not to be attributed to their faith, but to the Divine power; and added that they should rather learn to serve God in humility, and not to glory in signs and wonders; for that a sense of their own weakness was better than any vainglorious exhibition of power.

CHAPTER XI.

"WHEN the monk whom I have mentioned heard of this, — when he learned both that the children had encountered danger through meeting the snake, and that moreover, having got the better of the serpent, they had received a sound beating, — he implored the Abbot that henceforth no bread or food of any kind should be sent to him. And now the eighth day had passed since that man of Christ had exposed himself to the danger of perishing from hunger; his limbs were growing dry with fasting, but his mind fixed upon heaven could not fail; his body was wearing away with abstinence, but his faith remained firm. In the meantime, the Abbot was admonished by the Spirit to visit that disciple. Under the influence of a pious solicitude, he was eager to learn by what means of preserving life that faithful man was supported, since he had declined any human aid in ministering to his necessities. Accordingly, he sets out in person to satisfy himself on the subject. When the recluse saw from a distance the old man coming to him, he ran to meet him: he thanks him for the visit, and conducts him to his cell. As they enter the cell together, they behold a basket of palm branches, full of hot bread, hanging fixed at the door-post. And first the smell of the hot bread is perceived; but on touching it, it appears as if just a little before it had been taken from the oven. At the same time, they do not recognize the bread as being of the shape common in Egypt. Both are filled with amazement, and acknowledge the gift as being from heaven. On the one side, the recluse declared that this event was due to the arrival of the Abbot; while, on the other side, the Abbot ascribed it rather to the faith and virtue of the recluse; but both broke the heaven-sent bread with exceeding joy. And when, on his return to the monastery, the old man reported to the brethren what had occurred, such enthusiasm seized the minds of all of them, that they vied with each other in their haste to betake themselves to the desert, and its sacred seclusion; while they declared themselves miserable in having made their abode only too long amid a multitude, where human fellowship had to be carried on and endured.

CHAPTER XII.

"IN this monastery I saw two old men who were said to have already lived there for forty years, and in fact never to have departed from it. I do not think that I should pass by all mention of these men, since, indeed, I heard the following statement made regarding their virtues on the testimony of the Abbot himself, and all the brethren, that in the case of one of them, the sun never beheld him feasting, and in the case of the other, the sun never saw him angry."

Upon this, the Gaul looking at me exclaims: "Would that a friend of yours — I do not wish to mention his name — were now present; I should greatly like him to hear of that example, since we have had too much experience of his bitter anger in the persons of a great many people. Nevertheless, as I hear, he has lately forgiven his enemies; and, in these circumstances, were he to hear of the conduct of that man, he would be more and more strengthened in his forgiving course by the example thus set before him, and would feel that it is an admirable virtue not to fall under the influence of anger. I will not indeed deny that he had just reasons for his wrath; but where the battle is hard, the crown of victory is all the more glorious. For this reason, I think, if you will allow me to say so, that a certain man was justly to be praised, because when an ungrateful freedman abandoned him he rather pitied than inveighed against the fugitive. And, indeed, he was not even angry with the man by whom he seems to have been carried off." [1]

Upon this I remarked: "Unless Postumianus had given us that example of overcoming anger, I would have been very angry on account of the departure of the fugitive; but since it is not lawful to be angry, all remembrance of such things, as it annoys us, ought to be blotted from our minds. Let us rather, Postumianus, listen to what you have got to say."

"I will do," says he, "Sulpitius, what you request, as I see you are all so desirous of hearing me. But remember that I do not address my speech to you without hope of a larger recompense; I shall gladly perform what you require, provided that, when ere long my turn comes, you do not refuse what I ask."

"We indeed," said I, "have nothing by

---

[1] It appears impossible to give a certain rendering of these words — "a quo videtur abductus."

means of which we can return the obligation we shall lie under to you even without a larger return.[2] However, command us as to anything you have thought about, provided you satisfy our desires, as you have already begun to do, for your speech conveys to us true delight."

"I will stint nothing," said Postumianus, "of your desires ; and inasmuch as you have recognized the virtue of one recluse, I shall go on to relate to you some few things about more such persons.

CHAPTER XIII.

"WELL then, when I entered upon the nearest parts of the desert, about twelve miles from the Nile, having as my guide one of the brethren who was well acquainted with the localities, we arrived at the residence of a certain old monk who dwelt at the foot of a mountain. In that place there was a well, which is a very rare thing in these regions. The monk had one ox, the whole labor of which consisted in drawing water by moving a machine worked with a wheel. This was the only way of getting at the water, for the well was said to be a thousand or more feet deep. There was also a garden there full of a variety of vegetables. This, too, was contrary to what might have been expected in the desert where, all things being dry and burnt up by the fierce rays of the sun produce not even the slenderest root of any plant. But the labor which in common with his ox, the monk performed, as well as his own special industry, produced such a happy state of things to the holy man ; for the frequent irrigation in which he engaged imparted such a fertility to the sand that we saw the vegetables in his garden flourishing and coming to maturity in a wonderful manner. On these, then, the ox lived as well as its master ; and from the abundance thus supplied, the holy man provided us also with a dinner. There I saw what ye Gauls, perchance, may not believe — a pot boiling without fire[1] with the vegetables which were being got ready for our dinner : such is the power of the sun in that place that it is sufficient for any cooks, even for preparing the dainties of the Gauls. Then after dinner, when the evening was coming on, our host invites us to a palm-tree, the fruit of which he was accustomed to use, and which was at a distance of about two miles. For that is the only kind of tree found in the desert, and even these are rare, though they do occur. I am not sure whether this is owing to the wise foresight of former ages, or whether the soil naturally produces them. It may indeed be that God, knowing beforehand that the desert was one day to be inhabited by the saints, prepared these things for his servants. For those who settle within these solitudes live for the most part on the fruit of such trees, since no other kinds of plants thrive in these quarters. Well, when we came up to that tree to which the kindness of our host conducted us, we there met with a lion ; and on seeing it, both my guide and myself began to tremble ; but the holy man went up to it without delay, while we, though in great terror, followed him. As if commanded by God, the beast modestly withdrew and stood gazing at us, while our friend, the monk, plucked some fruit hanging within easy reach on the lower branches. And, on his holding out his hand filled with dates, the monster ran up to him and received them as readily as any domestic animal could have done ; and having eaten them, it departed. We, beholding these things, and being still under the influence of fear, could not but perceive how great was the power of faith in his case, and how weak it was in ourselves.

CHAPTER XIV.

"WE found another equally remarkable man living in a small hut, capable only of containing a single person. Concerning him we were told that a she-wolf was accustomed to stand near him at dinner; and that the beast could by no means be easily deceived so as to fail to be with him at the regular hour when he took refreshment. It was also said that the wolf waited at the door until he offered her the bread which remained over his own humble dinner ; that she was accustomed to lick his hand, and then, her duty being, as it were, fulfilled, and her respects paid to him, she took her departure. But it so happened that that holy man, while he escorted a brother who had paid him a visit, on his way home, was a pretty long time away, and only returned under night.[1] In the meanwhile, the beast made its appearance at the usual dinner time. Having entered the vacant cell and perceived that its benefactor was absent, it began to search round the hut with some curiosity to discover, if possible, the inhabitant. Now it so happened that a basket of palm-twigs was hanging close at hand with five loaves of bread in it. Taking one of these, the beast devoured it, and then, having committed this evil deed, went its way. The recluse on his return found the basket in a state of disorder, and the number of loaves less than it should have been.

---

2 " vel sine fænore."

1 Hornius strangely remarks on this, " Frequens id in Africa. Quin et ferrum nimio solis ardore mollescere scribunt qui interiorem Libyam perlustrarunt."

1 " sub nocte " : this may be used for the usual classical form " sub noctem," *towards evening.*

He is aware of the loss of his household goods, and observes near the threshold some fragments of the loaf which had been stolen. Considering all this, he had little doubt as to the author of the theft. Accordingly, when on the following days the beast did not, in its usual way, make its appearance (undoubtedly hesitating from a consciousness of its audacious deed to come to him on whom it had inflicted injury), the recluse was deeply grieved at being deprived of the happiness he had enjoyed in its society. At last, being brought back through his prayers, it appeared to him as usual at dinner time, after the lapse of seven days. But to make clear to every one the shame it felt, through regret for what had been done, not daring to draw very near, and with its eyes, from profound self-abasement, cast upon the earth, it seemed, as was plain to the intelligence of every one, to beg in a sort of way, for pardon. The recluse, pitying its confusion, bade it come close to him, and then, with a kindly hand, stroked its head; while, by giving it two loaves instead of the usual one, he restored the guilty creature to its former position; and, laying aside its misery on thus having obtained forgiveness, it betook itself anew to its former habits. Behold, I beg of you, even in this case, the power of Christ, to whom all is wise that is irrational, and to whom all is mild that is by nature savage. A wolf discharges duty; a wolf acknowledges the crime of theft; a wolf is confounded with a sense of shame: when called for, it presents itself; it offers its head to be stroked; and it has a perception of the pardon granted to it, just as if it had a feeling of shame on account of its misconduct, — this is thy power, O Christ — these, O Christ, are thy marvelous works. For in truth, whatever things thy servants do in thy name are thy doings; and in this only we find cause for deepest grief that, while wild beasts acknowledge thy majesty, intelligent beings fail to do thee reverence.

CHAPTER XV.

"BUT lest this should perchance seem incredible to any one, I shall mention still greater things. I call Christ[1] to witness that I invent nothing, nor will I relate things published by uncertain authors, but will set forth facts which have been vouched for to me by trustworthy men.

"Numbers of those persons live in the desert without any roofs over their heads, whom people call anchorites.[2] They subsist on the roots of plants; they settle nowhere in any fixed place, lest they should frequently have men visiting them; wherever night compels them they choose their abode. Well, two monks from Nitria directed their steps towards a certain man living in this style, and under these conditions. They did so, although they were from a very different quarter, because they had heard of his virtues, and because he had formerly been their dear and intimate friend, while a member of the same monastery. They sought after him long and much; and at length, in the seventh month, they found him staying in that far-distant wilderness which borders upon Memphis. He was said already to have dwelt in these solitudes for twelve years; but although he shunned intercourse with all men, yet he did not shrink from meeting these friends; on the contrary, he yielded himself to their affection for a period of three days. On the fourth day, when he had gone some distance escorting them in their return journey, they beheld a lioness of remarkable size coming towards them. The animal, although meeting with three persons, showed no uncertainty as to the one she made for, but threw herself down at the feet of the anchorite : and, lying there with a kind of weeping and lamentation, she manifested mingled feelings of sorrow and supplication. The sight affected all, and especially him who perceived that he was sought for: he therefore sets out, and the others follow him. For the beast stopping from time to time, and, from time to time looking back, clearly wished it to be understood that the anchorite should follow wherever she led. What need is there of many words? We arrived at the den of the animal, where she, the unfortunate mother, was nourishing five whelps already grown up, which, as they had come forth with closed eyes from the womb of their dam, so they had continued in persistent blindness. Bringing them out, one by one, from the hollow of the rock, she laid them down at the feet of the anchorite. Then at length the holy man perceived what the creature desired ; and having called upon the name of God, he touched with his hand the closed eyes of the whelps; and immediately their blindness ceased, while light, so long denied them, streamed upon the open eyes of the animals. Thus, those brethren, having visited the anchorite whom they were desirous of seeing, returned with a very precious reward for their labor, inasmuch as, having been permitted to be eye-witnesses of such power, they had beheld the faith of the saint, and the glory of Christ, to which they will in future bear testimony. But I have still more marvels to tell: the lioness, after five days, returned to the man who had done her so great a kindness, and brought him, as a gift, the skin of an un-

---

[1] " Fides Christi adest ": lit. " the faith of Christ is present."
[2] Also spelt " anchoret ": it means " one who has retired from the world " (ἀναχωρέω).

common animal. Frequently clad in this, as if it were a cloak, that holy man did not disdain to receive that gift through the instrumentality of the beast; while, all the time, he rather regarded Another as being the giver.

CHAPTER XVI.

"THERE was also an illustrious name of another anchorite in those regions, a man who dwelt in that part of the desert which is about Syene. This man, when first he betook himself to the wilderness, intended to live on the roots of plants which the sand here and there produces, of a very sweet and delicious flavor; but being ignorant of the nature of the herbs, he often gathered those which were of a deadly character. And, indeed, it was not easy to discriminate between the kind of the roots by the mere taste, since all were equally sweet, but many of them, of a less known nature, contained within them a deadly poison. When, therefore, the poison within tormented him on eating these, and all his vitals were tortured with terrific pains, while frequent vomitings, attended by excruciating agonies, were shattering the very citadel of life, his stomach being completely exhausted, he was in utter terror of all that had to be eaten for sustaining existence. Having thus fasted for seven days, he was almost at the point of death, when a wild animal called an Ibex came up to him. To this creature standing by him, he offered a bundle of plants which he had collected on the previous day, yet had not ventured to touch; but the beast, casting aside with its mouth those which were poisonous, picked out such as it knew to be harmless. In this way, that holy man, taught by its conduct what he ought to eat, and what to reject, both escaped the danger of dying of hunger and of being poisoned by the plants. But it would be tedious to relate all the facts which we have either had personal knowledge of, or have heard from others, respecting those who inhabit the desert. I spent a whole year, and nearly seven months more, of set purpose, within these solitudes, being, however, rather an admirer of the virtues of others, than myself making any attempt to manifest the extraordinary endurance which they displayed. For the greater part of the time I lived with the old man whom I have mentioned, who possessed the well and the ox.

CHAPTER XVII.

"I VISITED two monasteries of St. Anthony, which are at the present day occupied by his disciples. I also went to that place in which

the most blessed Paul, the first of the eremites, had his abode. I saw the Red Sea and the ridges of Mount Sinai, the top of which almost touches heaven, and cannot, by any human effort, be reached. An anchorite was said to live somewhere within its recesses: and I sought long and much to see him, but was unable to do so. He had for nearly fifty years been removed from all human fellowship, and used no clothes, but was covered with bristles growing on his own body, while, by Divine gift, he knew not of his own nakedness. As often as any pious men desired to visit him, making hastily for the pathless wilderness, he shunned all meeting with his kind. To one man only, about five years before my visit, he was said to have granted an interview; and I believe that man obtained the favor through the power of his faith. Amid much talk which the two had together, the recluse is said to have replied to the question why he shunned so assiduously all human beings, that the man who was frequently visited by mortals like himself, could not often be visited by angels. From this, not without reason, the report had spread, and was accepted by multitudes, that that holy man enjoyed angelic fellowship. Be this as it may, I, for my part, departed from Mount Sinai, and returned to the river Nile, the banks of which, on both sides, I beheld dotted over with numerous monasteries. I saw that, for the most part, as I have already said, the monks resided together in companies of a hundred; but it was well known that so many as two or three thousand sometimes had their abode in the same villages. Nor indeed would one have any reason to think that the virtue of the monks there dwelling together in great numbers, was less than that of those was known to be, who kept themselves apart from human fellowship. The chief and foremost virtue in these places, as I have already said, is obedience. In fact, any one applying for admission is not received by the Abbot of the monastery on any other condition than that he be first tried and proved; it being understood that he will never afterwards decline to submit to any injunction of the Abbot, however arduous and difficult, and though it may seem something unworthy to be endured.

CHAPTER XVIII.

"I WILL relate two wonderful examples of almost incredible obedience, and two only, although many present themselves to my recollection; but if, in any case, a few instances do not suffice to rouse readers to an imitation of the like virtues, many would be of no advantage. Well then, when a certain man having laid aside all worldly business, and having entered a monastery of very[1] strict discipline, begged that he might be accepted as a member, the Abbot began to place many considerations before him, — that the toils of that order were severe; that his own requirements were heavy, and such as no one's endurance could easily comply with; that he should rather enquire after another monastery where life was carried on under easier conditions; and that he should not try to attempt that which he was unable to accomplish. But he was in no degree moved by these terrors; on the contrary, he all the more promised obedience, saying that if the Abbot should order him to walk into the fire, he would not refuse to enter it. The Master then, having accepted that profession of his, did not delay putting it to the test. It so happened that an iron vessel was close at hand, very hot, as it was being got ready by a powerful fire for cooking some loaves of bread: the flames were bursting forth from the oven broken open, and fire raged without restraint within the hollows of that furnace. The Master, at this stage of affairs, ordered the stranger to enter it, nor did he hesitate to obey the command. Without a moment's delay he entered into the midst of the flames, which, conquered at once by so bold a display of faith, subsided at his approach, as happened of old to the well-known Hebrew children. Nature was overcome, and the fire gave way; so that he, of whom it was thought that he would be burned to death, had reason to marvel at himself, besprinkled, as it were, with a cooling dew. But what wonder is it, O Christ, that that fire did not touch thy youthful soldier? The result was that, neither did the Abbot regret having issued such harsh commands, nor did the disciple repent having obeyed the orders received. He, indeed, on the very day on which he came, being tried in his weakness, was found perfect; deservedly happy, deservedly glorious, having been tested in obedience, he was glorified through suffering.

CHAPTER XIX.

"In the same monastery, the fact which I am about to narrate was said to have occurred within recent memory. A certain man had come to the same Abbot in like manner with the former, in order to obtain admission. When the first law of obedience was placed before him, and he promised an unfailing patience for the endurance of all things however extreme, it so happened that the Abbot was holding in his hand a twig of storax already withered. This

the Abbot fixed in the ground, and imposed this work upon the visitor, that he should continue to water the twig, until (what was against every natural result) that dry piece of wood should grow green in the sandy soil. Well, the stranger, being placed under the authority of unbending law, conveyed water every day on his own shoulders — water which had to be taken from the river Nile, at almost two miles' distance. And now, after a year had run its course, the labor of that workman had not yet ceased, but there could be no hope of the good success of his undertaking. However, the grace of obedience continued to be shown in his labor. The following year also mocked the vain labor of the (by this time) weakened brother. At length, as the third annual circle was gliding by, while the workman ceased not, night or day, his labor in watering, the twig began to show signs of life. I have myself seen a small tree sprung from that little rod, which, standing at the present day with green branches in the court of the monastery, as if for a witness of what has been stated, shows what a reward obedience received, and what a power faith can exert. But the day would fail me before I could fully enumerate the many different miracles which have become known to me in connection with the virtues of the saints.

CHAPTER XX.

"I will, however, still further give you an account of two extraordinary marvels. The one of these will be a notable warning against the inflation of wretched vanity, and the other will serve as no mean guard against the display of a spurious righteousness.

"A certain saint, then, endowed with almost incredible power in casting out demons from the bodies of those possessed by them, was, day by day, performing unheard-of miracles. For, not only when present, and not merely by his word, but while absent also, he, from time to time, cured possessed bodies, by some threads taken from his garment, or by letters which he sent. He, therefore, was to a wonderful degree visited by people who came to him from every part of the world. I say nothing about those of humbler rank; but prefects, courtiers, and judges of various ranks often lay at his doors. Most holy bishops also, laying aside their priestly dignity, and humbly imploring him to touch and bless them, believed with good reason that they were sanctified, and illumined with a divine gift, as often as they touched his hand and garment. He was reported to abstain always and utterly from every kind of drink, and for food (I will whisper this, Sulpitius, into your ear lest our friend the Gaul hear it), to subsist upon only six dried figs. But in the meantime, just as honor accrued to the holy man from his excellence,[1] so vanity began to steal upon him from the honor which was paid him. When first he perceived that this evil was growing upon him, he struggled long and earnestly to shake it off, but it could not be thoroughly got rid of by all his efforts, since he still had a secret consciousness of being under the influence of vanity. Everywhere did the demons acknowledge his name, while he was not able to exclude from his presence the number of people who flocked to him. The hidden poison was, in the meantime, working in his breast, and he, at whose beck demons were expelled from the bodies of others, was quite unable to cleanse himself from the hidden thoughts of vanity. Betaking himself, therefore, with fervent supplication to God, he is said to have prayed that, power being given to the devil over him for five months, he might become like to those whom he himself had cured. Why should I delay with many words? That most powerful man, — he, renowned for his miracles and virtues through all the East, he, to whose threshold multitudes had gathered, and at whose door the highest dignitaries of that age had prostrated themselves — laid hold of by a demon, was kept fast in chains. It was only after having suffered all those things which the possessed are wont to endure, that at length in the fifth month he was delivered, not only from the demon, but (what was to him more useful and desirable) from the vanity which had dwelt within him.

CHAPTER XXI.

"But to me reflecting on these things, there occurs the thought of our own unhappiness and our own infirmity. For who is there of us, whom if one despicable creature of a man has humbly saluted, or one woman has praised with foolish and flattering words, is not at once elated with pride and puffed up with vanity? This will bring it about that even though one does not possess a consciousness of sanctity, yet, because through the flattery, or, it may be, the mistake of fools, he is said to be a holy man, he will, in fact, deem himself most holy! And then, if frequent gifts are sent to him, he will maintain that he is so honored by the munificence of God, inasmuch as all necessary things are bestowed upon him when sleeping and at rest. But further, if some signs of any kind of power fall to him even in a low degree, he

will think himself no less than an angel. And even if he is not marked out from others either by acts or excellence, but is simply made a cleric, he instantly enlarges the fringes of his dress, delights in salutations, is puffed up by people visiting him, and himself gads about everywhere. Nay, the man who had been previously accustomed to travel on foot, or at most to ride on the back of an ass, must needs now ride proudly on frothing steeds ; formerly content to dwell in a small and humble cell, he now builds a lofty fretted ceiling ; he constructs many rooms ; he cuts and carves doors ; he paints wardrobes ; he rejects the coarser kind of clothing, and demands soft garments ; and he gives such orders as the following to dear widows and friendly virgins, that the one class weave for him an embroidered cloak, and the other a flowing robe. But let us leave all these things to be described more pungently by that blessed man Hieronymus ; and let us return to the object more immediately in view."

"Well," says our Gallic friend upon this, "I know not indeed what you have left to be said by Hieronymus ; you have within such brief compass comprehended all our practices, that I think these few words of yours, if they are taken in good part, and patiently considered, will greatly benefit those in question, so that they will not require in future to be kept in order by the books of Hieronymus. But do thou rather go on with what you had begun, and bring forward an example, as you said you would do, against spurious righteousness ; for to tell you the truth, we are subject to no more destructive evil than this within the wide boundaries of Gaul."

"I will do so," replied Postumianus, "nor will I any longer keep you in a state of expectation.

CHAPTER XXII.

"A certain young man from Asia, exceedingly wealthy, of distinguished family, and having a wife and little son, happening to have been a tribune in Egypt, and in frequent campaigns against the Blembi to have touched on some parts of the desert, and having also seen several tents of the saints, heard the word of salvation from the blessed John. And he did not then delay to show his contempt for an unprofitable military life with its vain honor. Bravely entering into the wilderness, he in a short time became distinguished as being perfect in every kind of virtue. Capable of lengthened fasting, conspicuous for humility, and steadfast in faith, he had easily obtained a reputation in the pur-

---

[1] "virtute," perhaps *power*, as in many other places.

suit of virtue equal to that of the monks of old. But by and by, the thought (proceeding from the devil) entered his mind that it would be more proper for him to return to his native land and be the means of saving his only son and his family along with his wife; which surely would be more acceptable to God than if he, content with only rescuing himself from the world, should, not without impiety, neglect the salvation of his friends. Overcome by the plausible appearance of that kind of spurious righteousness, the recluse, after a period of nearly four years, forsook his cell and the end to which he had devoted his life. But on arriving at the nearest monastery, which was inhabited by many brethren, he made known to them, in reply to their questionings, the reason of his departure and the object he had in view. All of them, and especially the Abbot of that place, sought to keep him back; but the intention he had unfortunately formed could not be rooted out of his mind. Accordingly with an unhappy obstinacy he went forth, and, to the grief of all, departed from the brethren. But scarcely had he vanished from their sight, when he was taken possession of by a demon, and vomiting bloody froth from his mouth, he began to lacerate himself with his own teeth. Then, having been carried back to the same monastery on the shoulders of the brethren, when the unclean spirit could not be restrained within its walls, he was, from dire necessity, loaded with iron fetters, being bound both in hands and feet — a punishment not undeserved by a fugitive, inasmuch as chains now restrained him whom faith had not restrained. At length, after two years, having been set free from the unclean spirit by the prayers of the saints, he immediately returned to the desert from which he had departed. In this way he was both himself corrected and was rendered a warning to others, that the shadow of a spurious righteousness might neither delude any one, nor a shifting fickleness of character induce any one, with unprofitable inconstancy, to forsake the course on which he has once entered. And now let it suffice for you to learn these things respecting the various operations of the Lord which he has carried on in the persons of his servants; with the view either of stimulating others to a like kind of conduct, or of deterring them from particular actions. But since I have by this time fully satisfied your ears — have, in fact, been more lengthy than I ought to have been — do you now (upon this he addressed himself to me) — pay me the recompense you owe, by letting us hear you, after your usual fashion, discoursing about your friend Martin, for my longings after this have already for a long time been strongly excited."

CHAPTER XXIII.

"WHAT," replied I, "is there not enough about my friend Martin in that book of mine which you know that I published respecting his life and virtues?"

"I own it," said Postumianus, "and that book of yours is never far from my right hand. For if you recognize it, look here — (and so saying he displayed the book which was concealed in his dress) — here it is. This book," added he, "is my companion both by land and sea: it has been my friend and comforter in all my wanderings. But I will relate to you to what places that book has penetrated, and how there is almost no spot upon earth in which the subject of so happy a history is not possessed as a well-known narrative. Paulinus, a man who has the strongest regard for you, was the first to bring it to the city of Rome; and then, as it was greedily laid hold of by the whole city, I saw the booksellers rejoicing over it, inasmuch as nothing was a source of greater gain to them, for nothing commanded a readier sale, or fetched a higher price. This same book, having got a long way before me in the course of my traveling, was already generally read through all Carthage, when I came into Africa. Only that presbyter of Cyrene whom I mentioned did not possess it; but he wrote down its contents from my description. And why should I speak about Alexandria? for there it is almost better known to all than it is to yourself. It has passed through Egypt, Nitria, the Thebaid, and the whole of the regions of Memphis. I found it being read by a certain old man in the desert; and, after I told him that I was your intimate friend, this commission was given me both by him and many other brethren, that, if I should ever again visit this country, and find you well, I should constrain you to supply those particulars which you stated in your book you had passed over respecting the virtues of the sainted man. Come then, as I do not desire you to repeat to me those things which are already sufficiently known from what you have written, let those other points, at my request and that of many others, be fully set forth, which at the time of your writing you passed over, to prevent, as I believe, any feeling of weariness on the part of your readers."

CHAPTER XXIV.

"INDEED, Postumianus," replied I, "while I was listening attentively, all this time, to you talking about the excellences of the saints, in my secret thoughts I had my mind turned to my friend Martin, observing on the best of grounds that all those things which different individuals had done separately, were easily and entirely accomplished by that one man alone. For, although you certainly related lofty deeds, I really heard nothing from your lips (may I say it, without offence to these holy men), in which Martin was inferior to any one of them. And while I hold that the excellence of no one of these is ever to be compared with the merits of that man, still this point ought to be attended to, that it is unfair he should be compared, on the same terms, with the recluses of the desert, or even with the anchorites. For they, at freedom from every hindrance, with heaven only and the angels as witnesses, were clearly instructed to perform admirable deeds; he, on the other hand, in the midst of crowds and intercourse with human beings — among quarrelsome clerics, and among furious bishops, while he was harassed with almost daily scandals on all sides, nevertheless stood absolutely firm with unconquerable virtue against all these things, and performed such wonders as not even those accomplished of whom we have heard that they are, or at one time were, in the wilderness. But even had they done things equal to his, what judge would be so unjust as not, on good grounds, to decide that he was the more powerful? For put the case that he was a soldier who fought on unfavorable ground, and yet turned out a conqueror, and compare them, in like manner, to soldiers, who, however, contended on equal terms, or even on favorable terms, with the enemy. What then? Although the victory of all is one and the same, the glory of all certainly cannot be equal. And even though you have narrated marvelous things, still you have not stated that a dead man was recalled to life by any one. In this one particular undoubtedly, it must be owned that no one is to be compared with Martin.

CHAPTER XXV.

"FOR, if it is worthy of admiration that the flames did not touch that Egyptian of whom you have spoken, Martin also not infrequently proved his power over fire. If you remind us that the savagery of wild beasts was conquered by, and yielded to, the anchorites, Martin, for his part, was accustomed to keep in check both the fury of wild beasts and the poison of serpents. But, if you bring forward for comparison him who cured those possessed of unclean spirits, by the authority of his word, or even through the instrumentality of threads from his dress, there are many proofs that Martin was not, even in this respect, inferior. Nay, should you have recourse to him, who, covered with his own hair instead of a garment, was thought to

be visited by angels, with Martin angels were wont to hold daily discourse. Moreover, he bore so unconquerable a spirit against vanity and boastfulness, that no one more determinedly disdained these vices, and that, although he often, while absent, cured those who were filled with unclean spirits, and issued his commands not only to courtiers or prefects, but also to kings themselves. This was indeed a very small thing amid his other virtues, but I should wish you to believe that no one ever contended more earnestly than he did against not only vanity, but also the causes and the occasions of vanity. I shall also mention what is indeed a small point, but should not be passed over, because it is to the credit of a man who, being possessed of the highest power, manifested such a pious desire to show his regard for the blessed Martin. I remember, then, that Vincentius the prefect, an illustrious man, and one of the most eminent in all Gaul for every kind of virtue, when he had occasion to be in the vicinity of Tours, often begged of Martin that he would allow him to stay with him in the monastery. In making this request, he brought forward the example of Saint Ambrose, the bishop, who was generally spoken of at that time as being in the habit of entertaining both consuls and prefects. But Martin, with deeper judgment, refused so to act, lest by so doing some vanity and inflation of spirit might steal upon him. You, therefore, must acknowledge that there existed in Martin the virtues of all those men whom you have mentioned, but there were not found in all of them the virtues by which Martin was distinguished."

CHAPTER XXVI.

"WHY do you," here exclaimed Postumianus, "speak to me in such a manner? As if I did not hold the same opinion as yourself, and had not always been of the same mind. I, indeed, as long as I live, and retain my senses, will ever celebrate the monks of Egypt: I will praise the anchorites; I will admire the eremites; but I will place Martin in a position of his own: I do not venture to compare to him any one of the monks, far less any of the bishops. Egypt owns this: Syria and Æthiopia have discovered this: India has heard this; Parthia and Persia have known this; not even Armenia is ignorant of it; the remote Bosphorus is aware of it; and in a word, those are acquainted with it who visit the Fortunate Islands or the Arctic Ocean. All the more wretched on this account is this country of ours, which has not been found worthy to be acquainted with so great a man, although he was in its immediate vicinity. However, I will not include the people at large in this censure: only the clerics, only the priests know nothing of him; and not without reason were they, in their ill-will, disinclined to know him, inasmuch as, had they become acquainted with his virtues, they must have recognized their own vices. I shudder to state what I have lately heard, that a miserable man (I know him not), has said that you have told many lies in that book of yours. This is not the voice of a man, but of the devil; and it is not Martin who is, in this way, injured, but faith is taken from the Gospels themselves. For, since the Lord himself testified of works of the kind which Martin accomplished, that they were to be performed by all the faithful, he who does not believe that Martin accomplished such deeds, simply does not believe that Christ uttered such words. But the miserable, the degenerate, the somnolent, are put to shame, that the things which themselves cannot do, were done by him, and prefer rather to deny his virtues than to confess their own inertness. But let us, as we hasten on to other matters, let go all remembrance of such persons: and do you rather, as I have for a long time desired, proceed to narrate the still untold deeds of Martin."

"Well," said I, "I think that your request would more properly be directed to our friend the Gaul, since he is acquainted with more of Martin's doings than I am — for a disciple could not be ignorant of the deeds of his master — and who certainly owes a return of kindness, not only to Martin, but to both of us, inasmuch as I have already published my book, and you have, so far, related to us the doings of our brethren in the East. Let then, our friend the Gaul commence that detailed account which is due from him: because, as I have said, he both owes us a return in the way of speaking, and will, I believe, do this much for his friend Martin — that he shall, not unwillingly, give a narrative of his deeds."

CHAPTER XXVII.

"Well," said the Gaul, "I, for my part, though I am unequal to so great a task, feel constrained by those examples of obedience which have been related above by Postumianus, not to refuse that duty which you impose upon me. But when I reflect that I, a man of Gaul,[1] am about to speak in the presence of natives of Aquitania, I fear lest my somewhat rude form of speech should offend your too delicate ears.

However, you will listen to me as a foolish sort[2] of man, who says nothing in an affected or stilted fashion. For if you have conceded to me that I was a disciple of Martin, grant me this also that I be allowed, under the shelter of his example, to despise the vain trappings of speech and ornaments of words."

"Certainly," replied Postumianus, "speak either in Celtic, or in Gaulish, if you prefer it, provided only you speak of Martin. But for my part, I believe, that, even though you were dumb, words would not be wanting to you, in which you might speak of Martin with eloquent lips, just as the tongue of Zacharias was loosed at the naming of John. But as you are, in fact, an orator,[3] you craftily, like an orator, begin by begging us to excuse your unskillfulness, because you really excel in eloquence. But it is not fitting either that a monk should show such cunning, or that a Gaul should be so artful. But to work rather, and set forth what you have still got to say, for we have wasted too much time already in dealing with other matters; and the lengthening shadow of the declining sun warns us that no long portion of day remains till night be upon us. Then, after we had all kept silence for a little, the Gaul thus begins — "I think I must take care in the first place not to repeat those particulars about the virtues of Martin, which our friend Sulpitius there has related in his book. For this reason, I shall pass over his early achievements, when he was a soldier; nor will I touch on those things which he did as a layman and a monk. At the same time, I shall relate nothing which I simply heard from others, but only events of which I myself was an eye-witness."

DIALOGUE II.

CONCERNING THE VIRTUES OF ST. MARTIN.

CHAPTER I.

"Well then, when first, having left the schools, I attached myself to the blessed man, a few days after doing so, we followed him on his way to the church. In the way, a poor man, half-naked in these winter-months, met him, and begged that some clothing might be given him. Then Martin, calling for the chief-deacon, gave orders that the shivering creature should be clothed without delay. After that, entering a private apartment, and sitting down by himself, as his custom was — for he secured for himself this retirement even in the church, liberty being

---

[1] The word *Gaul* must here be taken in its more limited sense as denoting only the country of the Celtae. See the well-known first sentence of Cæsar's Gallic War.

[2] "Gurdonicus": a word said to have been derived from the name of a people in Spain noted for their stolidity.

[3] "Scholasticus."

granted to the clerics, since indeed the presbyters were seated in another apartment, either spending their time in mutual[1] courtesies, or occupied in listening to affairs of business. But Martin kept himself in his own seclusion up to the hour at which custom required that the sacred rites should be dispensed to the people. And I will not pass by this point that, when sitting in his retirement, he never used a chair; and, as to the church, no one ever saw him sitting there, as I recently saw a certain man (God is my witness), not without a feeling of shame at the spectacle, seated on a lofty throne, yea, in its elevation, a kind of royal tribunal; but Martin might be seen sitting on a rude little stool, such as those in use by the lowest of servants, which we Gallic country-people call *tripets*,[2] and which you men of learning, or those at least who are from Greece, call *tripods*. Well, that poor man who had been chanced upon, as the chief-deacon delayed to give him the garment, rushed into this private apartment of the blessed man, complaining that he had not been attended to by the cleric, and bitterly mourning over the cold he suffered. No delay took place: the holy man, while the other did not observe, secretly drew off his tunic which was below his outer[3] garment, and clothing the poor man with this, told him to go on his way. Then, a little after, the chief-deacon coming in informs him, according to custom, that the people were waiting in the church, and that it was incumbent on him to proceed to the performance of the sacred rites. Martin said to him in reply that it was necessary that the poor man — referring to himself — should be clothed, and that he could not possibly proceed to the church, unless the poor man received a garment. But the deacon, not understanding the true state of the case — that Martin, while outwardly clad with a cloak, was not seen by him to be naked underneath, at last begins to complain that the poor man does not make his appearance. 'Let the garment which has been got ready,' said Martin, 'be brought to me; there will not be wanting the poor man requiring to be clothed.' Then, at length, the cleric, constrained by necessity, and now in not the sweetest temper, hurriedly procures a rough[4] garment out of the nearest shop, short and shaggy, and costing only five pieces of silver, and lays it, in wrath. at the feet of Martin. 'See,' cries he, 'there is the garment, but the poor man is not here.' Martin, nothing moved, bids him go to the door for a little, thus obtaining secrecy, while, in his nakedness, he clothes himself with the garment, striving with all his might to keep secret what he had done. But when do such things remain concealed in the case of the saints desiring that they should be so? Whether they will or not, all are brought to light.

CHAPTER II.

" MARTIN, then, clothed in this garment, proceeds to offer the sacrifice[1] to God. And then on that very day — I am about to narrate something wonderful — when he was engaged in blessing the altar, as is usual, we beheld a globe of fire dart from his head, so that, as it rose on high, the flame produced a hair of extraordinary length. And, although we saw this take place on a very famous day in the midst of a great multitude of people, only one of the virgins, one of the presbyters, and only three of the monks, witnessed the sight: but why the others did not behold it is a matter not to be decided by our judgment.

"About the same time, when my uncle Evanthius, a highly Christian man, although occupied in the affairs of this world, had begun to be afflicted with a very serious illness, to the extreme danger of his life, he sent for Martin. And, without any delay, Martin hastened towards him; but, before the blessed man had completed the half of the distance between them, the sick man experienced the power of him that was coming; and, being immediately restored to health, he himself met us as we were approaching. With many entreaties, he detained Martin, who wished to return home on the following day; for, in the meantime, a serpent had struck with a deadly blow a boy belonging to my uncle's family; and Evanthius himself, on his own shoulders, carried him all but lifeless through the force of the poison, and laid him at the feet of the holy man, believing that nothing was impossible to him. By this time, the serpent had diffused its poison through all the members of the boy: one could see his skin swollen in all his veins, and his vitals strung up like a leather-bottle. Martin stretched forth his hand, felt all the limbs of the boy, and placed his finger close to the little wound, at which the animal had instilled the poison. Then in truth — I am going to tell things wonderful — we saw the whole poison, drawn from every part of the body, gather quickly together to Martin's finger; and next, we beheld the poison mixed with blood press through the small puncture of the wound, just as a long line

---

[1] " salutationibus vacantes ": this is, in the original, a very confused and obscure sentence.
[2] Halm edits " tripeccias," which may have been the local *patois* for " tripetias " (ter-pes), corresponding to the Greek τρίπους, and meaning " a three-legged stool."
[3] " Amphibalum ": a late Latin word corresponding to the more classical *toga*.
[4] " bigerricam vestem."

[1] " oblaturus sacrificium."

of abundant milk is wont to flow forth from the teats of goats or sheep, when these are squeezed by the hand of shepherds. The boy rose up quite well. We were amazed by so striking a miracle; and we acknowledged — as, indeed, truth compelled us to do — that there was no one under heaven who could equal the deeds of Martin.

CHAPTER III.

" In the same way, some time afterwards, we made a journey with him while he visited the various parishes in his diocese. He had gone forward a little by himself, some necessity or other, I know not what, compelling us to keep behind. In the meantime, a state-conveyance, full of military men, was coming along the public highway. But when the animals near the side beheld Martin in his shaggy garment, with a long black cloak over it, being alarmed, they swerved a little in the opposite direction. Then, the reins getting entangled, they threw into confusion those extended lines in which, as you have often seen, those wretched creatures are held together; and as they were with difficulty rearranged, delay, of course, was caused to those people hastening forward. Enraged by this injury, the soldiers, with hasty leaps, made for the ground. And then they began to belabor Martin with whips and staves; and as he, in silence and with incredible patience, submitted his back to them smiting him, this roused the greater fury in these wretches, for they became all the more violent from the fact, that he, as if he did not feel the blows showered upon him, seemed to despise them. He fell almost lifeless to the earth; and we, ere long, found him covered with blood, and wounded in every part of his body. Lifting him up without delay, and placing him upon his own ass, while we execrated the place of that cruel bloodshed, we hastened off as speedily as possible. In the meantime, the soldiers having returned to their conveyance, after their fury was satisfied, urge the beasts to proceed in the direction in which they had been going. But they all remained fixed to the spot, as stiff as if they had been brazen statues, and although their masters shouted at them, and the sound of their whips echoed on every side, still the animals never moved. These men next all fall to with lashes; in fact, while punishing the mules, they waste all the Gallic whips they had. The whole of the neighboring wood is laid hold of, and the beasts are beaten with enormous cudgels; but these cruel hands still effected nothing: the animals continued to stand in one and the same place like fixed effigies. The wretched men knew not what to do, and they could no longer conceal from themselves that,

in some way or other, there was a higher power at work in the bosoms of these brutes, so that they were, in fact, restrained by the interposition of a deity. At length, therefore, returning to themselves, they began to enquire who he was whom but a little before they had scourged at the same place; and when, on pursuing the investigation, they ascertained from those on the way that it was Martin who had been so cruelly beaten by them, then, indeed, the cause of their misfortune appeared manifest to all; and they could no longer doubt that they were kept back on account of the injury done to that man. Accordingly, they all rush after us at full speed, and, conscious of what they had done and deserved, overwhelmed with shame, weeping, and having their heads and faces smeared with the dust with which they themselves had besprinkled their bodies, they cast themselves at Martin's feet, imploring his pardon, and begging that he would allow them to proceed. They added that they had been sufficiently punished by their conscience alone, and that they deeply felt that the earth might swallow them alive in that very spot, or that rather, they, losing all sense, might justly be stiffened into immovable rocks, just as they had seen their beasts of burden fixed to the places in which they stood; but they begged and entreated him to extend to them pardon for their crime, and to allow them to go on their way. The blessed man had been aware, before they came up to us, that they were in a state of detention, and had already informed us of the fact; however, he kindly granted them forgiveness; and, restoring their animals, permitted them to pursue their journey.

CHAPTER IV.

" I have often noticed this, Sulpitius, that Martin was accustomed to say to you, that such an abundance[1] of power was by no means granted him while he was a bishop, as he remembered to have possessed before he obtained that office. Now, if this be true, or rather since it is true, we may imagine how great those things were which, while still a monk, he accomplished, and which, without any witness, he effected apart by himself; since we have seen that, while a bishop, he performed so great wonders before the eyes of all. Many, no doubt, of his former achievements were known to the world, and could not be hid, but those are said to have been innumerable which, while he avoided boastfulness, he kept concealed and did not allow to come to the knowledge of mankind; for, inasmuch as he transcended the capa-

---

[1] " eam virtutum gratiam."

bilities of mere man, in a consciousness of his own eminence, and trampling upon worldly glory, he was content simply to have heaven as a witness of his deeds. That this is true we can judge even from these things which are well known to us, and could not be hid; since e.g. before he became a bishop he restored two dead men to life, facts of which your book has treated pretty fully, but, while he was bishop, he raised up only one, a point which I am surprised you have not noticed. I myself am a witness to this latter occurrence; but, probably, you have no doubts about the matter being duly testified. At any rate, I will set before you the affair as it happened. For some reason, I know not what, we were on our way to the town of the Carnutes.[2] In the meantime, as we pass by a certain village most populous in inhabitants, an enormous crowd went forth to meet us, consisting entirely of heathen; for no one in that village was acquainted with a Christian. Nevertheless, owing to the report of the approach of so great a man, a multitude of those streaming to one point had filled all the widely spreading plains. Martin felt that some work was to be performed; and as the spirit within' him was thus moving him, he was deeply excited. He at once began to preach to the heathen the word of God, so utterly different from that of man, often groaning that so great a crowd should be ignorant of the Lord the Saviour. In the meantime, while an incredible multitude had surrounded us, a certain woman, whose son had recently died, began to present, with outstretched hands, the lifeless body to the blessed man, saying, "We know that you are a friend of God: restore me my son, who is my only one." The rest of the multitude joined her, and added their entreaties to those of the mother. Martin perceiving, as he afterwards told us, that he could manifest power, in order to the salvation of those waiting for its display, received the body of the deceased into his own hands; and when, in the sight of all, he had fallen on his knees, and then arose, after his prayer was finished, he restored to its mother the child brought back to life. Then, truly, the whole multitude, raising a shout to heaven, acknowledged Christ as God, and finally began to rush in crowds to the knees of the blessed man, sincerely imploring that he would make them Christians. Nor did he delay to do so. As they were in the middle of the plain, he made them all catechumens, by placing his hand upon the whole of them; while, at the same time, turning to us, he said that, not without reason, were these made catechumens in that plain where the martyrs were wont to be consecrated."

CHAPTER V.

"You have conquered, O Gaul," said Postumianus, "you have conquered, although certainly not me, who am, on the contrary, an upholder of Martin, and who have always known and believed all these things about that man; but you have conquered all the eremites and anchorites. For no one of them, like your friend, or rather our friend, Martin, ruled over deaths of all[1] kinds. And Sulpitius there justly compared him to the apostles and prophets, inasmuch as the power of his faith, and the works accomplished by his power, bear witness that he was, in all points, like them. But go on, I beg of you, although we can hear nothing more striking than we have heard — still, go on, O Gaul, to set forth what still remains of what you have to say concerning Martin. For the mind is eager to know even the least and commonest of his doings, since there is no doubt that the least of his actions surpass the greatest deeds of others."

"I will do so," replies the Gaul, "but I did not myself witness what I am about to relate, for it took place before I became an associate of Martin's; still, the fact is well known, having been spread through the world by the accounts given by faithful brethren, who were present on the occasion. Well, just about the time when he first became a bishop, a necessity arose for his visiting the imperial[2] court. Valentinian, the elder, then was at the head of affairs. When he came to know that Martin was asking for things which he did not incline to grant, he ordered him to be kept from entering the doors of the palace. Besides his own unkind and haughty temper, his wife Arriana had urged him to this course, and had wholly alienated him from the holy man, so that he should not show him the regard which was due to him. Martin, accordingly, when he had once and again endeavored to procure an interview with the haughty prince, had recourse to his well-known weapons — he clothes himself in sackcloth, scatters ashes upon his person, abstains from food and drink, and gives himself, night and day, to continuous prayer. On the seventh day, an angel appeared to him, and tells him to go with confidence to the palace, for that the royal doors, although closed against him, would open of their own accord, and that the haughty spirit of the emperor would be softened. Martin, therefore, being encouraged by the address of the angel who thus appeared to him, and trusting to his assistance, went to the palace. The doors stood open, and no one opposed his

---

1 "mortibus."
2 "adire comitatum": this is a common meaning of *comitatus* in writers of the period.

entrance ; so that, going in, he came at last into the presence of the king, without any one seeking to hinder him. The king, however, seeing him at a distance as he approached, and gnashing his teeth that he had been admitted, did not, by any means, condescend to rise up as Martin advanced, until fire covered the royal seat, and until the flames seized on a part of the royal person. In this way the haughty monarch is driven from his throne, and, much against his will, rises up to receive Martin. He even gave many embraces to the man whom he had formerly determined to despise, and, coming to a better frame of mind, he confessed that he perceived the exercise of Divine power ; without waiting even to listen to the requests of Martin, he granted all he desired before being asked. Afterwards the king often invited the holy man both to conferences and entertainments ; and, in the end, when he was about to depart, offered him many presents, which, however, the blessed man, jealously maintaining his own poverty, totally refused, as he did on all similar occasions.

CHAPTER VI.

"AND as we have, once for all, entered the palace, I shall string together events which there took place, although they happened at different times. And, indeed, it does not seem to me right that I should pass unmentioned the example of admiration for Martin which was shown by a faithful queen. Maximus then ruled the state, a man worthy of being extolled in[1] his whole life, if only he had been permitted to reject a crown thrust upon him by the soldiery in an illegal tumult, or had been able to keep out of civil war. But the fact is, that a great empire can neither be refused without danger, nor can be preserved without war. He frequently sent for Martin, received him into the palace, and treated him with honor ; his whole speech with him was concerning things present, things to come, the glory of the faithful, and the immortality of the saints ; while, in the meantime, the queen hung upon the lips of Martin, and not inferior to her mentioned in the Gospel, washed the feet of the holy man with tears and wiped them with the hairs of her head. Martin, though no woman had hitherto touched him, could not escape her assiduity, or rather her servile attentions. She did not think of the wealth of the kingdom, the dignity of the empire, the crown, or the purple ; only stretched upon the ground, she could not be torn away from the feet of Martin. At last she begs of

her husband (saying that both of them should constrain Martin to agree) that all other attendants should be removed from the holy man, and that she alone should wait upon him at meals. Nor could the blessed man refuse too obstinately. His modest entertainment is got up by the hands of the queen ; she herself arranges his seat for him ; places his table ; furnishes him with water for his hands ; and serves up the food which she had herself cooked. While he was eating, she, with her eyes fixed on the ground, stood motionless at a distance, after the fashion of servants, displaying in all points the modesty and humility of a ministering servant. She herself mixed for him his drink and presented it. When the meal was over, she collected the fragments and crumbs of the bread that had been used, preferring with true faithfulness these remains to imperial banquets. Blessed woman ! worthy, by the display of so great piety, of being compared to her who came from the ends of the earth to hear Solomon, if we merely regard the plain letter of the history. But the faith of the two queens is to be compared (and let it be granted me to say this, setting aside the majesty of the secret[2] truth implied): the one obtained her desire to hear a wise man ; the other was thought worthy not only to hear a wise man, but to wait upon him."

CHAPTER VII.

To these sayings Postumianus replies : "While listening to you, O Gaul, I have for a long time been admiring the faith of the queen ; but to what does that statement of yours lead, that no woman was ever said to have stood more close to Martin? For let us consider that that queen not only stood near him, but even ministered unto him. I really fear lest those persons who freely mingle among women should to some extent defend themselves by that example."

Then said the Gaul : "Why do you not notice, as grammarians are wont to teach us, the place, the time, and the person? For only set before your eyes the picture of one kept in the palace of the emperor importuned by prayers, constrained by the faith of the queen, and bound by the necessities of the time, to do his utmost that he might set free those shut up in prison, might restore those who had been sent into exile, and might recover goods that had been taken away, — of how much importance do you think that these things should have appeared to a bishop, so as to lead him, in order to the accomplishment of them all, to abate not a little of the rigor of his general scheme of life?

---

[1] Halm's text is here followed. The older texts, which read "vir omni vitæ merito prædicandus," seem hardly intelligible.

[2] " Quod mihi liceat separata mysterii majestate dixisse."

However, as you think that some will make a bad use of the example thus furnished them, I shall only say that those will be truly happy if they do not fall short of the excellence of the example in question. For let them consider that the facts of the case are these: once in his life only, and that when in his seventieth year, was Martin served and waited upon at his meals, *not* by a free sort of widow, nor by a wanton virgin, but by a queen, who lived under the authority of a husband, and who was supported in her conduct by the entreaties of her husband, that she might be allowed so to act. It is further to be observed that she did not recline with Martin at the entertainment, nor did she venture even to partake in the feast, but simply gave her services in waiting upon him. Learn, therefore, the proper course; let a matron serve thee, and not rule thee; and let her serve, but not recline along with thee; just as Martha, of whom we read, waited upon the Lord without being called to partake in the feast: nay, she who chose rather simply to hear the word was preferred to her that served. But in the case of Martin, the queen spoken of fulfilled both parts: she both served like Martha, and listened like Mary. If any one, then, desires to make use of this example, let him keep to it in all particulars; let the cause be the same, the person the same, the service the same, and the entertainment the same, — and let the thing occur once only in one's whole life."

CHAPTER VIII.

"Admirably," exclaimed Postumianus, "does your speech bind those friends of ours from going beyond the example of Martin; but I own to you my belief that these remarks of yours will fall upon deaf ears. For if we were to follow the ways of Martin, we should never need to defend ourselves in the case of kissing, and we should be free from all the reproaches of sinister opinion. But as you are wont to say, when you are accused of being too fond of eating, 'We are Gauls,' so we, for our part, who dwell in this district, will never be reformed either by the example of Martin, or by your dissertations. But while we have been discussing these points at so great length, why do you, Sulpitius, preserve such an obstinate silence?"

"Well, for my part," replied I, "I not only keep silence, but for a long time past I have determined to be silent upon such points. For, because I rebuked a certain spruce gadding-about widow, who dressed expensively, and lived in a somewhat loose manner, and also a virgin, who was following somewhat indecently a certain young man who was dear to me, — al-though, to be sure, I had often heard her blaming others who acted in such a manner, — I raised up against me such a degree of hatred on the part of all the women and all the monks, that both bands entered upon sworn war against me. Wherefore, be quiet, I beg of you, lest even what we are saying should tend to increase their animosity towards me. Let us entirely blot out these people from our memory, and let us rather return to Martin. Do thou, friend Gaul, as you have begun, carry out the work you have taken in hand."

Then says he: "I have really related already so many things to you, that my speech ought to have satisfied your desires; but, because I am not at liberty to refuse compliance with your wishes, I shall continue to speak as long as the day lasts. For, in truth, when I glance at that straw, which is being prepared for our beds, there comes into my mind a recollection respecting the straw on which Martin had lain, that a miracle was wrought in connection with it. The affair took place as follows. Claudiomagus is a village on the confines of the Bituriges and the Turoni. The church there is celebrated for the piety of the saints, and is not less illustrious for the multitude of the holy virgins. Well, Martin, being in the habit of passing that way, had an apartment in the private part of the church. After he left, all the virgins used to rush into that retirement: they kiss[1] every place where the blessed man had either sat or stood, and distribute among themselves the very straw on which he had lain. One of them, a few days afterwards, took a part of the straw which she had collected for a blessing to herself, and hung it from the neck of a possessed person, whom a spirit of error was troubling. There was no delay; but sooner than one could speak the demon was cast out, and the person was cured.

CHAPTER IX.

"About the same time, a cow which a demon harassed met Martin as he was returning from Treves. That cow, leaving its proper herd, was accustomed to attack human beings, and had already seriously gored many with its horns. Now, when she was coming near us, those who followed her from a distance began to warn us, with a loud voice, to beware of her. But after she had in great fury come pretty near to us, with rage in her eyes, Martin, lifting up his hand, ordered the animal to halt, and she immediately stood stock-still at his word. Upon this, Martin perceived a demon sitting upon her back, and reproving it, he exclaimed, 'Begone,

---

1 " adlambunt ": perhaps only " touch."

thou deadly being ; leave the innocent beast, and cease any longer to torment it.' The evil spirit obeyed and departed. And the heifer had sense enough to understand that she was set free ; for, peace being restored to her, she fell at the feet of the holy man ; and on Martin directing her, she made for her own herd, and, quieter than any sheep, she joined the rest of the band. This also was the time at which he had no sensation of being burnt, although placed in the midst of the flames ; but I do not think it necessary for me to give an account of this, because Sulpitius there, though passing over it in his book, has nevertheless pretty fully narrated it in the epistle which he sent to Eusebius, who was then a presbyter, and is now a bishop. I believe, Postumianus, you have either read this letter, or, if it is still unknown to you, you may easily obtain it, when you please, from the bookcase. I shall simply narrate particulars which he has omitted.

"Well, on a certain occasion, when he was going round the various parishes, we came upon a band of huntsmen. The dogs were pursuing a hare, and the little animal was already much exhausted by the long run it had had. When it perceived no means of escape in the plains spreading far on every side, and was several times just on the point of being captured, it tried to delay the threatened death by frequent doublings. Now the blessed man pitied the danger of the creature with pious feelings, and commanded the dogs to give up following it, and to permit it to get safe away. Instantly, at the first command they heard, they stood quite still : one might have thought them bound, or rather arrested, so as to stand immovable in their own footprints. In this way, through her pursuers being stopped as if tied together, the hare got safe away.

CHAPTER X.

"MOREOVER, it will be worth while to relate also some of his familiar sayings, since they were all salted with spiritual instruction. He happened to see a sheep[1] that had recently been sheared ; and, 'See,' says he, 'she has fulfilled the precept of the Gospel : she had two coats, and one of them she has given to him who had none : thus, therefore, ye ought also to do.' Also, when he perceived a swineherd in a garment of skin, cold and, in fact, all but naked, he exclaimed : ' Look at Adam, cast out of Paradise, how he feeds his swine in a garment of skin ; but let us, laying aside that old Adam, who still remains in that man, rather put

on the new Adam.' Oxen had, in one part, eaten up the grass of the meadows ; pigs also had dug up some portions of them with their snouts ; while the remaining portion, which continued uninjured, flourished, as if painted with variously tinted flowers. 'That part,' said he, 'which has been eaten down by cattle, although it has not altogether lost the beauty of grass, yet retains no grandeur of flowers, conveys to us a representation of marriage ; that part, again, which the pigs, unclean animals, had dug up, presents a loathsome picture of fornication ; while the remaining portion, which had sustained no injury, sets forth the glory of virginity ; — it flourishes with abundance of grass ; the fruits of the field abound in it ; and, decked with flowers to the very extreme of beauty, it shines as if adorned with glittering gems. Blessed is such beauty and worthy of God ; for nothing is to be compared with virginity. Thus, then, those who set marriage side by side with fornication grievously err ; and those who think that marriage is to be placed on an equal footing with virginity are utterly wretched and foolish. But this distinction must be maintained by wise people, that marriage belongs to those things which may be excused, while virginity points to glory, and fornication must incur punishment unless its guilt is purged away through atonement.'

CHAPTER XI.

"A CERTAIN soldier had renounced the military[1] life in the Church, having professed himself a monk, and had erected a cell for himself at a distance in the desert, as if with the purpose of leading the life of an eremite. But in course of time the crafty adversary harassed his unspiritual[2] nature with various thoughts, to the effect that, changing his mind, he should express a desire that his wife, whom Martin had ordered to have a place in the nunnery[3] of the young women, should rather dwell along with him. The courageous eremite, therefore, visits Martin, and makes known to him what he had in his mind. But Martin denied very strongly that a woman could, in inconsistent fashion, be joined again to a man who was now a monk, and not a husband. At last, when the soldier was insisting on the point in question ; asserting that no evil would follow from carrying out his purpose ; that he simply desired to possess the solace of his wife's company ; and that there was no fear of his again returning to his own

---

[1] Halm has here an unintelligible reading, probably a misprint — " quem recens tonsam forte conspexerat."

[1] "cingulum": lit. a girdle, or sword-belt, and then put for military service.
[2] "brutum pectus": the words seem to refer to the man as ψυχικὸς, in opposition to πνευματικὸς.
[3] "monasterio."

pursuits; adding that he was a soldier of Christ, and that she also had taken the oath of allegiance in the same service; and that the bishop therefore should allow to serve as soldiers together people who were saints, and who, in virtue of their faith, totally ignored the question of sex, — then Martin (I am going to repeat his very words to you) exclaimed: 'Tell me if you have ever been in war, and if you have ever stood in the line of battle?' In answer he said, 'Frequently; I have often stood in line of battle, and been present in war.' On this Martin replies: 'Well, then, tell me, did you ever in a line which was prepared with arms for battle, or, having already advanced near, was fighting against a hostile army with drawn sword — did you ever see any woman standing there, or fighting?' Then at length the soldier became confused and blushed, while he gave thanks that he had not been permitted to follow his own evil counsel, and at the same time had not been put right by the use of any harsh language, but by a true and rational analogy, connected with the person of a soldier. Martin, for his part, turning to us (for a great crowd of brethren had surrounded him), said: 'Let not a woman enter the camp of men, but let the line of soldiers remain separate, and let the females, dwelling in their own tent, be remote from that of men. For this renders an army ridiculous, if a female crowd is mixed with the regiments of men. Let the soldier occupy the line, let the soldier fight in the plain, but let the woman keep herself within the protection of the walls. She, too, certainly has her own glory, if, when her husband is absent, she maintains her chastity; and the first excellence, as well as completed victory of that, is, that she should not be seen.'

CHAPTER XII.

"I BELIEVE, my dear Sulpitius, that you remember with what emphasis he extolled to us (when you too were present) that virgin who had so completely withdrawn herself from the eyes of all men, that she did not admit to her presence Martin himself, when he wished to visit her in the discharge of duty. For when he was passing by the little property, within which for several years she had chastely confined herself, having heard of her faith and excellence, he turned out of his way that, as a bishop, he might honor, with pious respect, a girl of such eminent merit. We who journeyed with him thought that that virgin would rejoice, inasmuch as she was to obtain such a testimony to her virtue, while a priest of so great reputation, departing from his usual rigor of conduct, paid her a visit.

But she did not relax those bonds of a most severe method of life, which she had imposed upon herself, even by allowing herself to see Martin. And thus the blessed man, having received, through another woman, her praiseworthy apology, joyfully departed from the doors of her who had not permitted herself to be seen or saluted. O glorious virgin, who did not allow herself to be looked upon even by Martin! O blessed Martin, who did not regard that repulse as being any insult to himself, but, extolling with exultant heart her excellence, rejoiced in an example only too rare in that locality! Well, when approaching night had compelled us to stay at no great distance from her humble dwelling, that same virgin sent a present to the blessed man; and Martin did what he had never done before (for he accepted a present or gift from nobody), he refused none of those things which the estimable virgin had sent him, declaring that her blessing was by no means to be rejected by a priest, since she was indeed to be placed before many priests. Let, I beg, virgins listen to that example, so that they shall, if they desire to close their doors to the wicked, even shut them against the good; and that the ill-disposed may have no free access to them, they shall not fear even to exclude priests from their society. Let the whole world listen attentively to this: a virgin did not permit herself to be looked upon by Martin. And it was no common[1] priest whom she repulsed, but the girl refused to come under the eyes of a man whom it was the salvation of onlookers to behold. But what priest, besides Martin, would not have regarded this as doing an injury to him? What irritation and fury would he have conceived in his mind against that virgin? He would have deemed her a heretic; and would have resolved that she should be laid under an anathema. And how surely would such a man have preferred to that blessed soul those virgins who are always throwing themselves in the way of the priest, who get up sumptuous entertainments, and who recline at table with the rest! But whither is my speech carrying me? That somewhat too free manner of speaking must be checked, lest perchance it may give offense to some; for words of reproach will not profit the unfaithful, while the example quoted will be enough for the faithful. At the same time, I wish so to extol the virtue of this virgin, as nevertheless to think that no deduction is to be made from the excellence of those others, who often came from remote regions for the purpose of seeing Martin, since indeed, with the same object in view, even angels ofttimes visited the blessed man.

---

[1] " quemcumque," in the sense of *qualemcumque*, which is, in fact, found in some of the MSS.

CHAPTER XIII.

"But in what I am now about to narrate, I possess you, Sulpitius" (here he looked at me) "as a fellow-witness. One day, I and Sulpitius there were watching before Martin's door, and had already sat in silence for several hours. We did so with deep reverence and awe, as if we were carrying out a watch prescribed to us before the tent of an angel; while, all the time, the door of his cell being closed, he did not know that we were there. Meanwhile, we heard the sound of people conversing, and by and by we were filled with a kind of awe and amazement, for we could not help perceiving that something divine was going on. After nearly two hours, Martin comes out to us; and then our friend Sulpitius (for no one was accustomed to speak to him more familiarly) began to entreat him to make known to us, piously enquiring on the subject, what meant that sort of Divine awe which we confessed we had both felt, and with whom he had been conversing in his cell. We added that, as we stood before the door, we had undoubtedly heard a feeble sound of people talking, but had scarcely understood it. Then he after a long delay (but there was really nothing which Sulpitius could not extort from him even against his will: I am about to relate things somewhat difficult of belief, but, as Christ is my witness, I lie not, unless any one is so impious as to think that Martin himself lied) said: 'I will tell *you*, but I beg you will not speak of it to any one else. Agnes, Thecla, and Mary were there with me.' He proceeded to describe to us the face and general aspect of each. And he acknowledged that, not merely on that day, but frequently, he received visits from them. Nor did he deny that Peter also and Paul, the Apostles, were pretty frequently seen by him. Moreover, he was in the habit of rebuking the demons by their special names, according as they severally came to him. He found Mercury a cause of special annoyance, while he said that Jupiter was stupid and doltish. I am aware that these things seemed incredible even to many who dwelt in the same monastery; and far less can I expect that all who simply hear of them will believe them. For unless Martin had lived such an inestimable life, and displayed such excellence, he would by no means be regarded among us as having been endowed with so great glory. And yet it is not at all wonderful that human infirmity doubted concerning the works of Martin, when we see that many at the present day do not even believe the Gospels. But we have ourselves had personal knowledge and experience, that angels often appeared and spoke familiarly with Martin. As bearing upon this, I am to narrate a matter, of small importance indeed, but still I will state it. A synod, composed of bishops, was held at Nemausus, and while he had refused to attend it, he was nevertheless desirous of knowing what was done at it. It so happened that our friend Sulpitius was then on board ship with him, but, as was his custom, he kept his place at a distance from the rest, in a retired part of the vessel. There an angel announced to him what had taken place in the synod. And when, afterwards, we carefully enquired into the time at which the council was held, we found, beyond all doubt, that that was the very day of the council, and that those things were there decreed by the bishops which the angel had announced to Martin.

CHAPTER XIV.

"But when we questioned him concerning the end of the world, he said to us that Nero and Antichrist have first to come; that Nero will rule in the Western portion of the world, after having subdued ten kings; and that a persecution will be carried on by him, with the view of compelling men to worship the idols of the Gentiles. He also said that Antichrist, on the other hand, would first seize upon the empire of the East, having his seat and the capital of his kingdom at Jerusalem; while both the city and the temple would be restored by him. He added that his persecution would have for its object to compel men to deny Christ as God, while he maintained rather that he himself was Christ, and ordered all men to be circumcised, according to the law. He further said that Nero was to be destroyed by Antichrist, and that the whole world, and all nations, were to be reduced under the power of Antichrist, until that impious one should be overthrown by the coming of Christ. He told us, too, that there was no doubt but that Antichrist, having been conceived by an evil spirit, was already born, and had, by this time, reached the years of boyhood, while he would assume power as soon as he reached the proper age. Now, this is the eighth year since we heard these words from his lips: you may conjecture, then, how nearly about to happen are those things which are feared in the future."

As our friend the Gaul was emphatically speaking thus, and had not yet finished what he intended to relate, a boy of the family entered with the announcement that the presbyter Refrigerius was standing at the door. We began to doubt whether it would be better to hear the Gaul further, or to go and welcome that man whom we so greatly loved, and who had come to pay his respects to us, when our friend the Gaul remarked: "Even although this most holy priest had not arrived, this talk of ours would have had to be cut short, for the approach of night was itself urging us to finish the discourse which has been so far continued. But inasmuch as all things bearing upon the excellences of Martin have by no means yet been mentioned, let what you have heard suffice for to-day: to-morrow we shall proceed to what remains." This promise of our Gallic friend being equally acceptable to us all, we rose up.

DIALOGUE III.

THE VIRTUES OF MARTIN CONTINUED.

CHAPTER I.

"It is daylight, our Gallic friend, and you must get up. For, as you see, both Postumianus is urgent, and this presbyter, who was yesterday admitted to hear what was going on, expects that what you put off narrating with regard to our beloved Martin till to-day, you should now, in fulfillment of your promise, proceed to tell. He is not, indeed, ignorant of all the things which are to be related, but knowledge is sweet and pleasant even to one who goes over again things already known to him; since, indeed, it has been so arranged by nature that one rejoices with a better conscience in his knowledge of things which he is sure, through the testimony borne to them by many, are not in any degree uncertain. For this man, too, having been a follower of Martin from his early youth, has indeed been acquainted with all his doings; but he gladly hears over again things already known. And I will confess to thee, O Gaul, that the virtues of Martin have often been heard of by me, since, in fact, I have committed to writing many things regarding him; but through the admiration I feel for his deeds, those things are always new to me which, although I have already heard them, are, over and over again, repeated concerning him. Wherefore, we congratulate you that Refrigerius has been added to us as a hearer, all the[1] more earnestly that Postumianus is manifesting such eagerness, because he hastens, as it were, to convey a knowledge of these things to the East, and is now to hear the truth from you confirmed, so to speak, by witnesses."

As I was saying these words, and as the Gaul was now ready to resume his narrative, there rushes in upon us a crowd of monks, Evagrius the presbyter, Aper, Sabbatius, Agricola; and, a little after, there enters the presbyter Ætherius, with Calupio the deacon, and Amator the subdeacon; lastly, Aurelius the presbyter, a very dear friend of mine, who came from a longer distance, rushes up out of breath. "Why," I enquire, "do you so suddenly and unexpectedly run together to us from so many different quarters, and at so early an hour in the morning?" "We," they reply, "heard yesterday that your friend the Gaul spent the whole day in narrating the virtues of Martin, and, as night overtook him, put off the rest until to-day: wherefore, we have made haste to furnish him with a crowded audience, as he speaks about such interesting matters." In the meantime, we are informed that a multitude of lay people are standing at the door, not venturing to enter, but begging, nevertheless, that they might be admitted. Then Aper declares, "It is by no means proper that these people should be mixed up with us, for they have come to hear, rather from curiosity than piety." I was grieved for the sake of those who ought not, as he thought, to be admitted, but all that I could obtain, and with difficulty, was that they should admit Eucherius from among the lieutenants,[2] and Celsus, a man of consular rank, while the rest were kept back. We then place the Gaul in the middle seat; and he, after long keeping silence, in harmony with his well-known modesty, at length began as follows.

CHAPTER II.

"You have assembled, my pious and eloquent friends, to hear me; but, as I presume, you have brought to the task religious rather than learned ears; for you are to listen to me simply as a witness to the faith, and not as speaking with the fluency of an orator. Now, I shall not repeat the things which were spoken yesterday: those who did not hear them can become acquainted with them by means of the written records. Postumianus expects something new, intending to make known what he hears to the East, that it may not, when Martin is brought into comparison, esteem itself above the West. And first, my mind inclines to set forth an incident respecting which Refrigerius has just whispered in my ear: the affair took place in the city of Carnutes. A certain father of a family ventured to bring to Martin his daughter of twelve years old, who had been dumb from her birth, begging that the blessed man would loose, by his pious merits, her tongue, which was thus tied. He, giving way to the bishops Valentinus and Victricius, who then happened to be by his

---

[1] The original is here very obscure.

[2] "ex vicariis."

side, declared that he was unequal to so great an undertaking, but that nothing was impossible to them, as if holier than himself. But they, adding their pious entreaties, with suppliant voices, to those of the father, begged Martin to accomplish what was hoped for. He made no further delay, — being admirable in both respects, in the display, first of all, of humility, and then in not putting off a pious duty, — but orders the crowd of people standing round to be removed; and while the bishops only, and the father of the girl, were present, he prostrates himself in prayer, after his usual fashion. He then blesses a little oil, while he utters the formula of exorcism; and holding the tongue of the girl with his fingers, he thus pours the consecrated liquid into her mouth. Nor did the result of the power thus exerted disappoint the holy man. He asks her the name of her father, and she instantly replied. The father cries out, embracing the knees of Martin, with a mixture of joy and tears; and while all around are amazed, he confesses that then for the first time he listened to the voice of his daughter. And that this may not appear incredible to any one, let Evagrius, who is here, furnish you with a testimony of its truth; for the thing took place in his very presence.

CHAPTER III.

"THE following is a small matter which I learned lately from the narration of Arpagius the presbyter, but I do not think it ought to be passed over. The wife of the courtier Avitianus had sent some oil to Martin, that he might bless it (such is the custom) so as to be ready when needful to meet different causes of disease. It was contained in a glass jar of a shape which, round throughout, gradually bulges[1] out towards the middle, with a long neck; but the hollow of the extended neck was not filled, because it is the custom to fill vessels of the kind in such a way that the top may be left free for the knobs which stop up the jar. The presbyter testified that he saw the oil increase under the blessing of Martin, so much that, the abundance of it overflowing the jar, it ran down from the top in every direction. He added that it bubbled up with the same[2] effect, while the vessel was being carried back to the mistress of the household; for the oil so steadily flowed over in the hands of the boy carrying it, that the abundance of the liquid, thus pouring down, covered all his garment. He said, moreover, that the lady received the vessel so full even to the brim,

that (as the same presbyter tells[3] us at the present day) there was no room in that jar for inserting the stopper by which people are accustomed to close those vessels, the contents of which are to be preserved with special care. That, too, was a remarkable thing that happened to this man." Here he looked at me. "He had set down a glass vessel containing oil blessed by Martin in a pretty high window; and a boy of the family, not knowing that a jar was there, drew towards him the cloth covering it, with rather much violence. The vessel, in consequence, fell down on the marble pavement. Upon this, all were filled with dread lest the blessing of God, bestowed on the vessel by Martin, had been lost; but the jar was found as safe as ever, just as if it had fallen on the softest feathers. Now, this result should be ascribed, not so much to chance, as to the power of Martin, whose blessing could not possibly perish.

"There is this, too, which was effected by a certain person, whose name, because he is present, and has forbidden it to be mentioned, shall be suppressed: Saturninus too, who is now with us, was present on the occasion referred to. A dog was barking at us in a somewhat disagreeable manner. 'I command thee,' said the person in question, 'in the name of Martin, to be quiet.' The dog — his barking seemed to stick in his throat, and one might have thought that his tongue had been cut out — was silent. Thus it is really a small matter that Martin himself performed miracles: believe me that other people also have accomplished many things in his name.

CHAPTER IV.

"YOU knew the too barbarous and, beyond measure, bloody ferocity of Avitianus, a former courtier. He enters the city of the Turones with a furious spirit, while rows of people, laden with chains, followed him with melancholy looks, orders various kinds of punishments to be got ready for slaying them; and to the grave amazement of the city, he arranges them for the sad work on the following day. When this became known to Martin, he set out all alone, a little before midnight, for the palace of that beast. But when, in the silence of the depths of the night, and as all were at rest, no entrance was possible through the bolted doors, he lays himself down before that cruel threshold. In the meantime, Avitianus, buried in deep sleep, is smitten by an assailing angel, who says to him, 'Does the servant of God lie at your threshold, and do you continue sleeping?' He, on listening to these words, rises, in much disturbance, from his bed; and calling his servants, he ex-

---

[1] The text of this sentence is very uncertain, and the meaning somewhat obscure.
[2] Here, again, the text is in confusion.

[3] Text and meaning both very obscure.

claims in terror, 'Martin is at the door: go immediately, and undo the bolts, that the servant of God may suffer no harm.' But they, in accordance with the tendency of all servants, having scarcely stepped beyond the first threshold, and laughing at their master as having been mocked by a dream, affirm that there was no one at the door. This they did as simply inferring from their own disposition, that no one could be keeping watch through the night, while far less did they believe that a priest was lying at the threshold of another man during the horror of that night. Well, they easily persuaded Avitianus of the truth of their story. He again sinks into sleep; but, being ere long struck with greater violence than before, he exclaimed that Martin *was* standing at the door, and that, therefore, no rest either of mind or body was allowed him. As the servants delayed, he himself went forward to the outer threshold; and there he found Martin, as he had thought he would. The wretched man, struck by the display of so great excellence, exclaimed, 'Why, sir, have you done this to me? There is no need for you to speak: I know what you wish: I see what you require: depart as quickly as possible, lest the anger of heaven consume me on account of the injury done you: I have already suffered sufficient punishment. Believe me, that I have firmly determined in my own mind how I should now proceed.' So then, after the departure of the holy man, he calls for his officials and orders all the prisoners to be set free, while presently he himself went his way. Thus Avitianus being put to flight, the city rejoiced, and felt at liberty.

CHAPTER V.

"WHILE these are certain facts, since Avitianus related them to many persons, they are further confirmed on this ground that Refrigerius the presbyter, whom you see here present, lately had them narrated to him, under an appeal to the Divine majesty, by Dagridus, a faithful man among the tribunes, who swore that the account was given him by Avitianus himself. But I do not wish you to wonder that I do to-day what I did not do yesterday; viz. that I subjoin to the mention of every individual wonder the names of witnesses, and mention persons to whom, if any one is inclined to disbelieve, he may have recourse, because they are still in the body. The unbelief of very many has compelled that; for they are said to hesitate about some things which were related yesterday. Let these people, then, accept as witnesses persons who are still alive and well, and let them give more credit to such, inasmuch as they doubt our good faith.

But really, if they are so unbelieving, I give it as my opinion that they will not believe even the witnesses named. And yet I am surprised that any one, who has even the least sense of religion, can venture on such wickedness as to think that any one could tell lies concerning Martin. Be that far from every one who lives in obedience to God; for, indeed, Martin does not require to be defended by falsehoods. But, O Christ, we lay the truth of our whole discourse before thee, to the effect that we neither have said, nor will say, anything else than what either we ourselves have witnessed, or have learned from undoubted authorities, and, indeed, very frequently from Martin himself. But although we have adopted the form of a dialogue, in order that the style might be varied to prevent weariness, still we affirm that we are really setting forth [1] a true history in a dutiful spirit. The unbelief of some has compelled me, to my great regret, to insert in my narrative these remarks which are apart from the subject in hand. But let the discourse now return to our assembly; in which since I saw that I was listened to so eagerly, I found it necessary to acknowledge that Aper acted properly in keeping back the unbelieving, under the conviction he had that those only ought to be allowed to hear who were of a believing spirit.

CHAPTER VI.

"I AM enraged in heart, believe me, and, through vexation, I seem to lose my senses: do Christian men not believe in the miraculous powers of Martin, which the demons acknowledged?

"The monastery of the blessed man was at two miles' distance from the city; but if, as often as he was to come to the church, he only had set his foot outside the threshold of his cell, one could perceive the possessed roaring through the whole church, and the bands of guilty [1] ones trembling as if their judge were coming, so that the groanings of the demons announced the approach of the bishop to the clerics, who were not previously aware that he was coming. I saw a certain man snatched up into the air on the approach of Martin, and suspended there with his hands stretched upwards, so that he could in no way touch the ground with his feet. But if at any time Martin undertook the duty of exorcising the demons, he touched no one with his hands, and reproached no one in words, as a multitude of expressions is generally rolled forth by the clerics; but the possessed, being brought up to

---

[1] " nos pie præstruere profitemur historiæ veritatem."
[1] " agmina damnanda."

him, he ordered all others to depart, and the doors being bolted, clothed in sackcloth and sprinkled with ashes, he stretched himself on the ground in the midst of the church, and turned to prayer. Then truly might one behold the wretched beings tortured with various results — some hanging, as it were, from a cloud, with their feet turned upwards, and yet their garments did not fall down over their faces, lest the part of their body which was exposed should give rise to shame; while in another part of the church one could see them tortured without any question being addressed to them, and confessing their crimes. They revealed their names, too, of their own accord; one acknowledged that he was Jupiter, and another that he was Mercury. Finally, one could see all the servants of the devil suffering agony, along with their master, so that we could not help acknowledging that in Martin there was fulfilled that which is written that 'the saints shall judge angels.'

CHAPTER VII.

"THERE was a certain village in the country of the Senones which was every year annoyed with hail. The inhabitants, constrained by an extreme of suffering, sought help from Martin. A highly respectable embassy was sent to him by Auspicius, a man of the rank of prefect, whose fields the storm had been wont to smite more severely than it did those of others. But Martin, having there offered up prayer, so completely freed the whole district from the prevailing plague, that for twenty years, in which he afterwards remained in the body, no one in those places suffered from hail. And that this may not be thought to be accidental, but rather effected by Martin, the tempest, returning afresh, once more fell upon the district in the year in which he died. The world thus felt the departure of a believing man to such a degree, that, as it justly rejoiced in his life, so it also bewailed his death. But if any hearer, weak in faith, demands also witnesses to prove those things which we have said, I will bring forward, not one man, but many thousands, and will even summon the whole region of the Senones to bear witness to the power which was experienced. But not to speak of this, you, presbyter Refrigerius, remember, I believe, that we lately had a conversation, concerning the matter referred to, with Romulus, the son of that Auspicius I mentioned, an honored and religious man. He related the points in question to us, as if they had not been previously known; and as he was afraid of constant losses in future harvests, he did, as you yourself beheld, regret, with much lamentation, that Martin was not preserved up to this time.

CHAPTER VIII.

"BUT to return to Avitianus: while at every other place, and in all other cities, he displayed marks of horrible cruelty, at Tours alone he did no harm. Yes, that beast, which was nourished by human blood, and by the slaughter of unfortunate creatures, showed himself meek and peaceable in the presence of the blessed man. I remember that Martin one day came to him, and having entered his private apartment, he saw a demon of marvelous size sitting behind his back. Blowing upon him from a distance (if I may, as a matter of necessity, make use of a word which is hardly Latin[1]), Avitianus thought that he was blowing at *him*, and exclaimed, 'Why, thou holy man, dost thou treat me thus?' But then Martin said, 'It is not at you, but at him who, in all his terribleness, leans over your neck.' The devil gave way, and left his familiar seat; and it is well known that, ever after that day, Avitianus was milder, whether because he now understood that he had always been doing the will of the devil sitting by him, or because the unclean spirit, driven from his seat by Martin, was deprived of the power of attacking him; while the servant was ashamed of his master, and the master did not force on his servant.

"In a village of the Ambatienses, that is in an old stronghold, which is now largely inhabited by brethren, you know there is a great idol-temple built up with labor. The building had been constructed of the most polished stones and furnished with turrets; and, rising on high in the form of a cone, it preserved the superstition of the place by the majesty of the work. The blessed man had often enjoined its destruction on Marcellus, who was there settled as presbyter. Returning after the lapse of some time, he reproved the presbyter, because the edifice of the idol-temple was still standing. He pleaded in excuse that such an immense structure could with difficulty be thrown down by a band of soldiers, or by the strength of a large body of the public, and far less should Martin think it easy for that to be effected by means of weak clerics or helpless monks. Then Martin, having recourse to his well-known auxiliaries, spent the whole night in watching and prayer — with the result that, in the morning, a storm arose, and cast down even to its foundations the idol-temple. Now let this narrative rest on the testimony of Marcellus.

---

[1] "exsufflans."

CHAPTER IX.

" I WILL make use of another not dissimilar marvel in a like kind of work, having the concurrence of Refrigerius in doing so. Martin was prepared to throw down a pillar of immense size, on the top of which an idol stood, but there was no means by which effect could be given to his design. Well, according to his usual practice, he betakes himself to prayer. It is undoubted that then a column, to a certain degree like the other, rushed down from heaven, and falling upon the idol, it crushed to powder the whole of the seemingly indestructible mass : this would have been a small matter, had he only in an invisible way made use of the powers of heaven, but these very powers were beheld by human eyes serving Martin in a visible manner.

" Again, the same Refrigerius is my witness that a woman, suffering from an issue of blood, when she had touched the garment of Martin, after the example of the woman mentioned in the Gospel, was cured in a moment of time.

" A serpent, cutting its way through a river, was swimming towards the bank on which we had taken our stand. ' In the name of the Lord,' said Martin, ' I command thee to return.' Instantly, at the word of the holy man, the venomous beast turned round, and while we looked on, swam across to the farther bank. As we all perceived that this had not happened without a miracle; he groaned deeply, and exclaimed, 'Serpents hear me, but men will not hear.'

CHAPTER X.

" BEING accustomed to eat fish at the time of Easter, he enquired a little before the hour for refreshment, whether it was in readiness. Then Cato, the deacon, to whom the outward management of the monastery belonged, and who was himself a skillful fisher, tells him that no capture had fallen to his lot the whole day, and that other fishers, who used to sell what they caught, had also been able to do nothing. ' Go,' said he, ' let down your line, and a capture will follow.' As Sulpitius there has already described, we had our dwelling close to the river. We all went, then, as these were holidays, to see our friend fishing, with the hopes of all on the stretch, that the efforts would not be in vain by which, under the advice of Martin himself, it was sought to obtain fish for his use. At the first throw the deacon drew out, in a very small net, an enormous pike, and ran joyfully back to the monastery, with the feeling un-

doubtedly to which some poet gave utterance (for we use a learned verse, inasmuch as we are conversing with learned people) —

' And brought his captive boar[1] to wondering Argos.'

" Truly that disciple of Christ, imitating the miracles performed by the Saviour, and which he, by way of example, set before the view of his saints, showed Christ also working in him, who, glorifying his own holy follower everywhere, conferred upon that one man the gifts of various graces. Arborius, of the imperial body-guard, testifies that he saw the hand of Martin as he was offering sacrifice, clothed, as it seemed, with the noblest gems, while it glittered with a purple light ; and that, when his right hand was moved, he heard the clash of the gems, as they struck together.

CHAPTER XI.

" I WILL now come to an event which he always concealed, owing to the character of the times, but which he could not conceal from us. In the matter referred to, there is this of a miraculous nature, that an angel conversed, face to face, with him. The Emperor Maximus, while in other respects doubtless a good man, was led astray by the advices of some priests after Priscillian had been put to death. He, therefore, protected by his royal power Ithacius the bishop, who had been the accuser of Priscillian, and others of his confederates, whom it is not necessary to name. The emperor thus prevented every one from bringing it as a charge against Ithacius, that, by his instrumentality, a man of any sort had been condemned to death. Now Martin, constrained to go to the court by many serious causes of people involved in suffering, incurred the whole force of the storm which was there raging. The bishops who had assembled at Treves were retained in that city, and daily communicating with Ithacius, they had made common cause with him. When it was announced to them expecting no such information, that Martin was coming, completely losing courage, they began to mutter and tremble among themselves. And it so happened that already, under their influence, the emperor had determined to 'send some tribunes armed with absolute power into the two Spains, to search out heretics, and, when found, to deprive them of their life or goods. Now there was no doubt that that tempest would also make havoc of multitudes of the real saints, little distinction being made between the various classes of in-

---

[1] " captivum suem." Probably there is here an allusion to the capture of the Erymanthian boa. by Hercules, with a punning reference to a secondary meaning of *sus* as a kind of fish.

dividuals. For in such circumstances, a judgment was formed simply by appearances, so that one was deemed a heretic rather on his turning pale from fear, or wearing a particular garment, than by the faith which he professed. And the bishops were well aware that such proceedings would by no means please Martin; but, conscious of evil as they were, this was a subject of deep anxiety to them, lest when he came, he should keep from communion with them; knowing well as they did, that others would not be wanting who, with his example to guide them, would follow the bold course adopted by so great a man. They therefore form a plan with the emperor, to this effect, that, officials of the court being sent on to meet him, Martin should be forbidden to come any nearer to that city, unless he should declare that he would maintain peace with the bishops who were living there. But he skillfully frustrated their object, by declaring that he would come among them with the peace of Christ. And at last, having entered during the night, he went to the church, simply for the purpose of prayer. On the following day he betakes himself to the palace. Besides many other petitions which he had to present, and which it would be tedious to describe, the following were the principal: entreaties in behalf of the courtier Narses, and the president Leucadius, both of whom had belonged to the party of Gratianus, and that, with more than ordinary zeal, upon which this is not the time to dilate, and who had thus incurred the anger of the conqueror; but his chief request was, that tribunes, with the power of life and death, should not be sent into the Spains. For Martin felt a pious solicitude not only to save from danger the true Christians in these regions, who were to be persecuted in connection with that expedition, but to protect even heretics themselves. But on the first and second day the wily emperor kept the holy man in suspense, whether that he might impress on him the importance of the affair, or because, being obnoxious to the bishops, he could not be reconciled to them, or because, as most people thought at the time, the emperor opposed his wishes from avarice, having cast a longing eye on the property of the persons in question. For we are told that he was really a man distinguished by many excellent actions, but that he was not successful in contending against avarice. This may, however, have been due to the necessities of the empire at the time, for the treasury of the state had been exhausted by former rulers; and he, being almost constantly in the expectation of civil wars, or in a state of preparation for them, may easily be excused for having, by all sorts of expedients, sought resources for the defense of the empire.

CHAPTER XII.

"In the meantime, those bishops with whom Martin would not hold communion went in terror to the king, complaining that they had been condemned beforehand; that it was all over with them as respected the *status* of every one of them, if the authority of Martin was now to uphold the pertinacity of Theognitus, who alone had as yet condemned them by a sentence publicly pronounced; that the man ought not to have been received within the walls; that he was now not merely the defender of heretics, but their vindicator; and that nothing had really been accomplished by the death of Priscillian, if Martin were to act the part of his avenger. Finally, prostrating themselves with weeping and lamentation, they implored the emperor[1] to put forth his power against this one man. And the emperor was not far from being compelled to assign to Martin, too, the doom of heretics. But after all, although he was disposed to look upon the bishops with too great favor, he was not ignorant that Martin excelled all other mortals in faith, sanctity, and excellence: he therefore tries another way of getting the better of the holy man. And first he sends for him privately, and addresses him in the kindest fashion, assuring him that the heretics were condemned in the regular course of public trials, rather than by the persecutions of the priests; and that there was no reason why he should think that communion with Ithacius and the rest of that party was a thing to be condemned. He added that Theognitus had created disunion, rather by personal hatred, than by the cause he supported; and that, in fact, he was the only person who, in the meantime, had separated himself from communion: while no innovation had been made by the rest. He remarked further that a synod, held a few days previously, had decreed that Ithacius was not chargeable with any fault. When Martin was but little impressed by these statements, the king then became inflamed with anger, and hurried out of his presence; while, without delay, executioners are appointed for those in whose behalf Martin had made supplication.

CHAPTER XIII.

"When this became known to Martin, he rushed to the palace, though it was now night. He pledges himself that, if these people were spared, he would communicate; only let the tribunes, who had already been sent to the Spains for the destruction of the churches, be

---

[1] "potestatem regiam."

recalled. There is no delay: Maximus grants all his requests. On the following day, the ordination of Felix as bishop was being arranged, a man undoubtedly of great sanctity, and truly worthy of being made a priest in happier times. Martin took part in the communion of that day, judging it better to yield for the moment, than to disregard the safety of those over whose heads a sword was hanging. Nevertheless, although the bishops strove to the uttermost to get him to confirm the fact of his communicating by signing his name, he could not be induced to do so. On the following day, hurrying away from that place, as he was on the way returning, he was filled with mourning and lamentation that he had even for an hour been mixed up with the evil communion, and, not far from a village named Andethanna, where remote woods stretch[1] far and wide with profound solitude, he sat down while his companions went on a little before him. There he became involved in deep thought, alternately accusing and defending the cause of his grief and conduct. Suddenly, an angel stood by him and said, 'Justly, O Martin, do you feel compunction, but you could not otherwise get out of your difficulty. Renew your virtue, resume your courage, lest you not only now expose your fame, but your very salvation, to danger.' Therefore, from that time forward, he carefully guarded against being mixed up in communion with the party of Ithacius. But when it happened that he cured some of the possessed more slowly and with less grace than usual, he at once confessed to us with tears that he felt a diminution of his power on account of the evil of that communion in which he had taken part for a moment, through necessity, and not with a cordial spirit. He lived sixteen years after this, but never again did he attend a synod, and kept carefully aloof from all assemblies of bishops.

CHAPTER XIV.

" But very clearly, as we experienced, he repaired, with manifold interest, his grace, which had been diminished for a time. I saw afterwards a possessed person brought to him at the gate[1] of the monastery; and that, before the man touched the threshold, he was cured.

" I lately heard one testifying that, when he was sailing on the Tuscan Sea, following that course which leads to Rome, whirlwinds having suddenly arisen, all on board were in extreme peril of their lives. In these circumstances, a certain Egyptian merchant, who was not yet a Christian, cried out, 'Save us, O God of Martin,' upon which the tempest was immediately stilled, and they held their desired course, while the pacified ocean continued in perfect tranquillity.

" Lycontius, a believing man belonging to the lieutenants, when a violent disease was afflicting his family, and sick bodies were lying all through his house in sad proof of unheard-of calamity, implored the help of Martin by a letter. At this time the blessed man declared that the thing asked was difficult to be obtained, for he knew in his spirit that that house was then being scourged by Divine appointment. Yet he did not give up an unbroken course of prayer and fasting for seven whole days and as many nights, so that he at last obtained that which he aimed at in his supplications. Speedily, Lycontius, having experienced the Divine kindness, flew to him, at once reporting the fact and giving thanks, that his house had been delivered from all danger. He also offered a hundred pounds of silver, which the blessed man neither rejected nor accepted; but before the amount of money touched the threshold of the monastery, he had, without hesitation, destined it for the redemption of captives. And when it was suggested to him by the brethren, that some portion of it should be reserved for the expenses of the monastery, since it was difficult for all of them to obtain necessary food, while many of them were sorely in need of clothing, he replied, ' Let the church both feed and clothe us, as long as we do not appear to have provided, in any way, for our own wants.'

" There occur to my mind at this point many miracles of that illustrious man, which it is more easy for us to admire than to narrate. You all doubtless recognize the truth of what I say: there are many doings of his which cannot be set forth in words. For instance, there is the following, which I rather think cannot be related by us just as it took place. A certain one of the brethren (you are not ignorant of his name, but his person must be concealed, lest we should cause shame to a godly man), — a certain one, I say, having found abundance of coals for his stove, drew a stool to himself, and was sitting, with outspread legs and exposed person, beside that fire, when Martin at once perceived that an improper thing was done under the sacred roof, and cried out with a loud voice, 'Who, by exposing his person, is dishonoring our habitation?' When our brother heard this, and felt from his own conscience, that it was he who was rebuked, he immediately ran to us almost in a fainting condition, and acknowledged his shame; which was done, how-

---

[1] The text is here very corrupt: we have followed a conjecture of Halm's.
[1] " Pseudothyrum ": Halm prefers the form " pseudoforum," but the meaning is the same.

ever, only through the forth-putting of the power of Martin.

CHAPTER XV.

" AGAIN, on a certain day, after he had sat down on that wooden seat of his (which you all know), placed in the small open court which surrounded his abode, he perceived two demons sitting on the lofty rock which overhangs the monastery. He then heard them, in eager and gladsome tones, utter the following invitation, 'Come hither, Brictio, come hither, Brictio.' I believe they perceived the miserable man approaching from a distance, being conscious how great frenzy of spirit they had excited within him. Nor is there any delay: Brictio rushes in in absolute fury; and there, full of madness, he vomits forth a thousand reproaches against Martin. For he had been reproved by him on the previous day, because he who had possessed nothing before he entered the clerical office, having, in fact, been brought up in the monastery by Martin himself, was now keeping horses and purchasing slaves. For at that time, he was accused by many of not only having bought boys belonging to barbarous nations, but girls also of a comely appearance. The miserable man, moved with bitter rage on account of these things, and, as I believe, chiefly instigated by the impulse received from those demons, made such an onset upon Martin as scarcely to refrain from laying hands upon him. The holy man, on his part, with a placid countenance and a tranquil mind, endeavored by gentle words to restrain the madness of the unhappy wretch. But the spirit of wickedness so prevailed within him, that not even his own mind, at best a very vain one, was under his control. With trembling lips, and a changing countenance, pale with rage, he rolled forth the words of sin, asserting that he was a holier man than Martin who had brought him up, inasmuch as from his earliest years he had grown up in the monastery amid the sacred institutions of the Church, while Martin had at first, as he could not deny, been tarnished with the life of a soldier, and had now entirely sunk into dotage by means of his baseless superstitions, and ridiculous fancies about visions. After he had uttered many things like these, and others of a still more bitter nature, which it is better not to mention, going out, at length, when his rage was satisfied, he seemed to feel as if he had completely vindicated his conduct. But with rapid steps he rushed back by the way he had gone out, the demons having, I believe, been, in the meantime, driven from his heart by the prayers of Martin, and he was now brought back to re-

pentance. Speedily, then, he returns, and throws himself at the feet of Martin, begging for pardon and confessing his error, while, at length, restored to a better mind, he acknowledges that he had been under the influence of a demon. It was no difficult business for Martin to forgive the suppliant. And then the holy man explained both to him and to us all, how he had seen him driven on by demons, and declared that he was not moved by the reproaches which had been heaped upon him; for they had, in fact, rather injured the man who uttered them. And subsequently, when this same Brictio was often accused before him of many and great crimes, Martin could not be induced to remove him from the presbyterate, lest he should be suspected of revenging the injury done to himself, while he often repeated this saying: ' If Christ bore with Judas, why should not I bear with Brictio?'"

CHAPTER XVI.

UPON this, Postumianus exclaims, "Let that well-known man in our immediate neighborhood, listen to that example, who, when he is wise, takes no notice either of things present or future, but if he has been offended, falls into utter fury, having no control over himself. He then rages against the clerics, and makes bitter attacks upon the laity, while he stirs up the whole world for his own revenge. He will continue in this state of contention for three years without intermission, and refuse to be mollified either by time or reason. The condition of the man is to be lamented and pitied, even if this were the only incurable evil by which he is afflicted. But you ought, my Gallic friend, to have frequently recalled to his mind such examples of patience and tranquillity, that he might know both how to be angry and how to forgive. And if he happens to hear of this speech of mine which has been briefly interpolated into our discourse, and directed against himself, let him know that I spoke, not more with the lips of an enemy than the mind of a friend; because I should wish, if the thing were possible, that he should be spoken of rather as being like the bishop Martin, than the tyrant Phalaris. But let us pass away from him, since the mention of him is far from pleasant, and let us return, O Gaul, to our friend Martin."

CHAPTER XVII.

THEN said I, since I perceived by the setting sun that evening was at hand: "The day is gone, Postumianus; we must rise up; and at the same time some refreshment is due to these so zealous listeners. And as to Martin, you ought not to expect that there is any limit to one talking about him : he extends too far to be comprised fully in any conversation. In the meantime, you will convey to the East the things you have now heard about that famous man ; and as you retrace your steps to your former haunts, and pass along by various coasts, places, harbors, islands, and seas, see that you spread among the peoples the name and glory of Martin. Especially remember that you do not omit Campania ; and although your route will take you far off the beaten track, still any expenditure from delay will not be to you of so much importance as to keep you from visiting in that quarter Paulinus, a man renowned and praised throughout the whole world. I beg you first to unroll to him the volume of discourse which we either completed yesterday, or have said to-day. You will relate all to him ; you will repeat all to him ; that in due time, by his means, Rome may learn the sacred merits of this man, just as he spread that first little book of ours not only through Italy, but even through the whole of Illyria. He, not jealous of the glories of Martin, and being a most pious admirer of his saintly excellences in Christ, will not refuse to compare our leading man with his own friend Felix. Next, if you happen to cross over to Africa, you will relate what you have heard to Carthage ; and, although, as you yourself have said, it already knows the man, yet now pre-eminently it will learn more respecting him, that it may not admire its own martyr Cyprian alone, although consecrated by his sacred blood. And then, if carried down a little to the left, you enter the gulf of Achaia, let Corinth know, and let Athens know, that Plato in the academy was not wiser, and that Socrates in the prison was not braver, than Martin. You will say to them that Greece was indeed happy which was thought worthy to listen to an apostle pleading, but that Christ has by no means forsaken Gaul, since he has granted it to possess such a man as Martin. But when you have come as far as Egypt, although it is justly proud of the numbers and virtues of its own saints, yet let it not disdain to hear how Europe will not yield to it, or to all Asia, in having only Martin.

CHAPTER XVIII.

" But when you have again set sail from that place with the view of making for Jerusalem, I enjoin upon you a duty connected with our grief, that, if you ever come to the shore of renowned Ptolemais, you enquire most carefully where Pomponius, that friend of ours, is buried, and that you do not refuse to visit his remains on that foreign soil. There shed many tears, as much from the working of your own feelings, as from our tender affection ; and although it is but a worthless gift, scatter the ground there with purple flowers and sweet-smelling grass. And you will say to him, but not roughly, and not harshly, — with the address of one who sympathizes, and not with the tone of one who reproaches, — that if he had only been willing to listen to you at one time, or to me constantly, and if he had invited Martin rather than that man whom I am unwilling to name, he would never have been so cruelly separated from me, or covered by a heap of unknown dust, having suffered death in the midst of the sea with the lot of a ship-wrecked pirate, and with difficulty securing burial on a far-distant shore. Let those behold this as their own work, who, in seeking to revenge him, have wished to injure me, let them behold their own glory, and being avenged, let them henceforth cease to make any attacks upon me."

Having uttered these sad words in a very mournful voice, and while the tears of all the others were drawn forth by our laments, we at length departed, certainly with a profound admiration for Martin, but with no less sorrow from our own lamentations.

THE DOUBTFUL LETTERS OF SULPITIUS SEVERUS.

———⊶⊷⊷⊶———

LETTER I.

A LETTER OF THE HOLY PRESBYTER SEVERUS TO HIS SISTER CLAUDIA CONCERNING THE LAST JUDGMENT.

CHAPTER I.

ON reading your letters, my feelings were, in many ways, deeply moved, and I could not refrain from tears. For I both wept for joy because I could perceive from the very language of your letters, that you were living according to the precepts of the Lord God, and out of my exceeding desire after you, I could not help lamenting that, without any fault on my part, I was parted from you; and I would have felt this still more strongly had you not sent me a letter. Should I not, then, enjoy the company of such a sister? But I call your salvation to witness, that I have very often wished to come to you, but have up till now been prevented, through the opposition of him [1] who is accustomed to hinder us. For, in my eager desire, I was both urgent to satisfy my wishes by seeing you; and we seemed, if we should meet, likely to accomplish more effectually the work of the Lord, since by comforting one another we should live with the heavy load of this world trodden under our feet. But I do not now fix the day or time of visiting you, because, as often as I have done so, I have not been able to fulfil my purpose. I shall wait on the will of the Lord, and hope that, by my supplications and your prayers, he may bring it about that we reap some advantage from our perseverance.[2]

CHAPTER II.

BUT because you have desired from me in all my letters which I had sent to you precepts to nourish your life and faith, it has come to pass that, through the frequency of my writings to you, I have now exhausted language of that kind; and I can really write nothing new to you, so as to avoid what I have written before. And in truth, through the goodness of God, you do not now need to be exhorted, inasmuch as, perfecting your faith at the very beginning of your saintly life, you display a devoted love in Christ. One thing, however, I do press upon you, that you do not go back on things you have already passed away from, that you do not long again for things you have already scorned, and that, having put your hand to the plow, you do not look back [1] again, retracing your steps; for, undoubtedly, by falling into this fault, your furrow will lose its straightness, and the cultivator will not receive his own proper reward. Moreover, he does not secure even a measure of the reward, if he has, in a measure, failed. For, as we must flee from sin to righteousness, so he who has entered on the practice of righteousness must beware lest he lay himself open to sin. For it is written that "his righteousness shall not profit the righteous on the day on which he has gone astray." [2] For this, then, we must take our stand, for this we must labor, that we, who have escaped from sins, do not lose the prepared rewards. For the enemy stands ready against us, that he may at once strike the man who has been stripped of the shield of faith. Our shield, therefore, is not to be cast aside, lest our side be exposed to attack; and our sword is not to be put away, lest the enemy then begin to give up all fear: moreover, we know that if he sees a man fully armed, he will retreat. Nor are we ignorant that it is a hard and difficult thing daily to fight against the flesh and the world. But if you reflect upon eternity, and if you consider the kingdom of heaven, which undoubtedly the Lord will condescend to bestow upon us although we are sinners, what suffering, I ask, is sufficiently great, by which we may merit such things? And besides, our struggle in this world is but for a short time; for although death do not speedily overtake us, old

---

[1] It is obvious that, in this whole passage, Sulpitius has in his mind the language of St. Paul, Rom. i. 9-12.
[2] Halm reads *præsentia*, instead of the old reading *perseverantia*, but apparently without good grounds.

[1] Luke ix. 62.
[2] Ezek. xviii. 24.

age will come. The years flow on, and time glides by; while, as I hope, the Lord Jesus will speedily call us to himself, as being dear to his heart.

CHAPTER III.

O how happy shall be that departure of ours, when Christ shall receive us into his own abode after we have been purged[1] from the stains of sin through the experience[2] of a better life! Martyrs and prophets will meet with us, apostles will join themselves to us, angels will be glad, archangels will rejoice, and Satan, being conquered, will look pale, though still retaining his cruel countenance, inasmuch as he will lose all[3] advantage from our sins which he had secured for himself in us. He will see glory granted us through mercy, and merits honored by means of glory. We shall triumph over our conquered foe. Where shall now the wise men of the world appear? Where shall the covetous man, where shall the adulterer, where shall the irreligious, where shall the drunkard, where shall the evil-speaker be recognized? What shall these wretched beings say in their own defense? "We did not know thee, Lord; we did not see that thou wast in the world: thou didst not send the prophets: thou didst not give the law to the world: we did not see the patriarchs: we did not read the lives of the saints. Thy Christ never was upon the earth: Peter was silent: Paul refused to preach: no Evangelist taught. There were no martyrs whose example we should follow: no one predicted thy future judgment: no one commanded us to clothe the poor: no one enjoined us to restrain lust: no one persuaded us to fight against covetousness: we fell through ignorance, not knowing what we did."

CHAPTER IV.

Against these, from among the company of the saints, righteous Noah shall first proclaim, "I, Lord, predicted that a deluge was about to come on account of the sins of men, and after the deluge I set an example to the good in my own person; since I did not perish with the wicked who perished, that they might know both what was the salvation of the innocent, and what the punishment of sinners." After him, faithful Abraham will say in opposition to them, "I,

Lord, about the mid-time[1] of the age of the world, laid the foundation of the faith by which the human race should believe in thee; I was chosen as the father of the nations, that they might follow my example; I did not hesitate, Lord, to offer Isaac, while yet a youth, as a sacrifice to thee, that they might understand that there is nothing which ought not to be presented to the Lord, when they perceived that I did not spare even my only son: I left, Lord, my country, and my family, at thy command, that they also might have an example teaching them to leave the wickedness of the world and the age: I, Lord, was the first to recognize thee, though under a corporeal[2] form, nor did I hesitate to believe who it was that I beheld, although thou didst appear to me in a different form from thine own, that these might learn to judge, not according to the flesh, but according to the spirit." Him the blessed Moses will support in his pleadings, saying: "I Lord, delivered the law to all these, at thy command, that those whom a free[3] faith did not influence, the spoken law at least might restrain: I said, 'Thou shalt not[4] commit adultery,' in order that I might prevent the licentiousness of fornication: I said, 'Thou shalt love[5] thy neighbor,' that affection might abound; I said, 'Thou shalt worship the Lord alone,'[7] in order that these might not sacrifice to idols, or allow temples to exist; I commanded that false witness should not be spoken, that I might shut the lips of these people against all falsehood. I set forth the things which had been done and said from the beginning of the world, through the working within me of the spirit of thy power, that a knowledge of things past might convey to these people instruction about things to come. I predicted, O Lord Jesus, thy coming, that it might not be an unexpected thing to these people, when they were called to acknowledge him whom I had before announced as about to come."

CHAPTER V.

After him, there will stand up David worthy of his descendant the Lord, and declare: "I, Lord, proclaimed thee by every means; I set forth that only thy name was to be worshiped; I said, 'Blessed is the man[1] who fears the Lord'; I said too, 'The saints shall[2] be joyful in glory'; and I said, 'The desire of the

---

[1] Clericus here remarks that "these words clearly teach us that Severus knew of no other purgation than that by which we are cleansed in this life from sin by a change of character, and which change if we steadily maintain, then, when life is ended, we are received into the abode of Christ, without any dread of the fire of purgatory."
[2] "conversatione."
[3] Having led us into sin that we might be condemned along with himself. The meaning, however, is obscure.

[1] Abraham lived (in round numbers) about 2000 years B.C., and assuming the beginning of the world to have been about 4000 years B.C., he may thus be said to have lived about "the mid-time." The note of Clericus which refers the words to the *end* of the world seems quite mistaken.
[2] The reference is to Gen. xviii.
[3] A faith having no regard to either rewards or punishments.
[4] Ex. xx. 14.   [7] Ex. xx. 3, &c.
[5] Lev. xix. 18.   [1] Ps. cxi. 1.
[6] Deut. vi. 13.   [2] Ps. cxlix. 5.

wicked[3] shall perish,' that these people might acknowledge thee and cease to sin. I, when I had become possessed of royal power, clothed in sackcloth, with dust spread beneath me, and with the emblems of my greatness laid aside, lay down in my clothes, that an example might be given to these people of gentleness and humility. I spared my enemies who desired to slay me, that these people might approve of my mercifulness, as worthy of being imitated." After him, Isaiah, who was worthy of the Spirit of God, will not be silent; but will say: "I, Lord, whilst thou wast speaking through my mouth, gave this warning, — 'Woe to those[4] who join house to house,' that I might set a limit to covetousness. I bore witness that thine anger came upon the wicked, that at any rate fear of punishment, if not hope of reward, might keep back these people from their evil deeds."

CHAPTER VI.

AFTER these, and several others who have discharged for us the duties of instruction, the Son of God himself will speak thus: "I, certainly, exalted on a lofty seat, holding heaven in my hand, and the earth in my fist, extended within and without, in the inside of all things which are produced, and on the outside of all[1] things that move, inconceivable, infinite in the power[2] of nature, invisible to sight, inaccessible to touch, in order that I might exist as the least of you (for the purpose of subduing the hardness of your heart and for softening your faithlessness by sound doctrines), condescended to be born in flesh, and, having laid aside the glory of God, I assumed the form of a servant, so that, sharing with you in bodily infirmity, I might in turn bring you to a participation in my glory, through obedience to the precept of salvation. I restored health to the sick and infirm, hearing to the deaf, sight to the blind, the power of speech to the dumb, and the use of their feet to the lame; that I might influence you, by heavenly signs, all the more easily to believe in me, and in those things which I had announced, I promised you the kingdom of heaven; I also, in order that you might have an example of escape from punishment, placed in Paradise the robber who acknowledged me almost at the moment of his death, that ye might follow even the faith of him who had been thought worthy of having his sins forgiven him. And that by my example in your behalf, ye yourselves also might be able to suffer; I suffered for you, that

no man might hesitate to suffer for himself what God[3] had endured for man. I showed myself after my resurrection, in order that your faith might not be overthrown. I admonished the Jews in the person of Peter; I preached to the Gentiles in the person of Paul; and I do not regret doing so, for good results followed. The good have understood my work; the faithful have perfected it; the righteous have completed it; the merciful have consummated it: there have been a large number of martyrs, and a large number of saints. Those to whom I thus refer were undoubtedly in the same body and in the same world as you. Why, then, do I find no good work in you, ye descendants of vipers? Ye have shown no repentance for your wicked deeds, even at the very end of your earthly course. And what does it profit that ye honor me with your lips, when you deny me by your deeds and works? Where are now your riches, where your honors, where your powers, and where your pleasures? I pronounce no new sentence over you: you simply incur the judgment which I formerly predicted."

CHAPTER VII.

THEN will the Evangelist repeat this to the wretched beings, "Go ye[1] into outer darkness, where shall be weeping and gnashing of teeth." O ye miserable men, whom these words do not now impress! They shall then see their own punishment, and the glory of others. Let them use this present world, provided they do not enjoy that eternity which is prepared for the saints. Let them abound in riches: let them rest on gold; provided that there they be found needy and destitute. Let them be wealthy in this world, provided they be poor in eternity, for it is written regarding them, " The rich were in[2] want, and suffered hunger." But the Scripture has added what follows respecting the good, — " but those who seek the Lord shall not want any good thing."

Therefore, my sister, although those people mock at us, and although they call us foolish and unhappy, let us all the more joyfully exult in such reproaches, by which glory is heaped up for us, and punishment for them. And do not let us laugh at their folly, but rather grieve over their unhappiness; because there is among them a large number of our own people, whom if we win over, our glory shall be increased. But however they may conduct themselves, let

---

[3] Ps. cxii. 10.   [4] Isa. v. 8.
[1] The divine omnipresence is here denoted.
[2] Or, according to another punctuation, "inconceivable in nature, infinite in power."

[3] Clericus thinks this expression unscriptural, and fitted to support heresy. But it may be justified by such a passage as Acts xx. 28, if θεοῦ be accepted as the correct reading, which is now generally agreed upon.
[1] St. Matt. xxii. 13.
[2] Ps. xxxiv. 10: the above rendering entirely departs from the Hebrew text.

them be to us as Gentiles and publicans; but let us keep ourselves safe and sound. If they rejoice now over us lamenting, it will be our turn afterwards to rejoice over their suffering. Farewell, dearest sister, and tenderly beloved in Christ.

LETTER II.

A LETTER OF SULPITIUS SEVERUS TO HIS SISTER CLAUDIA CONCERNING VIRGINITY.

CHAPTER I.

How great blessedness, among heavenly gifts, belongs to holy virginity, besides the testimonies of the Scriptures, we learn also from the practice of the Church, by which we are taught that a peculiar merit belongs to those who have devoted themselves to it by special consecration. For while the whole multitude of those that believe receive equal gifts of grace, and all rejoice in the same blessings of the sacraments, those who are virgins possess something above the rest, since, out of the holy and unstained company of the Church, they are chosen by the Holy Spirit, and are presented by the bishop[1] at the altar of God, as if being more holy and pure sacrifices, on account of the merits of their voluntary dedication. This is truly a sacrifice worthy of God, inasmuch as it is the offering of so precious a being, and none will please him more than the sacrifice of his own image. For I think that the Apostle especially referred to a sacrifice of this kind, when he said, " Now, I beseech you, brethren, by the mercy of God, that you present your bodies a living sacrifice, holy and acceptable[2] to God." Virginity, therefore, possesses both that which others have, and that which others have not; while it obtains both common and special grace, and rejoices (so to speak) in its own peculiar privilege of consecration. For ecclesiastical authority permits us to style virgins also the brides of Christ; while, after the manner of brides, it veils those whom it consecrates to the Lord, openly exhibiting those as very especially about to possess spiritual marriage who have fled away from carnal fellowship. And those are worthily united, after a spiritual manner, to God, in accordance with the analogy of marriage, who, from love to him, have set at nought human alliances. In their case, that saying of the apostle finds its fullest possible fulfillment, " He who is joined to the Lord,[3] is one spirit."

CHAPTER II.

FOR it is a great and a divine thing, almost beyond a corporeal nature, to lay aside[1] luxury, and to extinguish, by strength of mind, the flame of concupiscence, kindled by the torch of youth; to put down by spiritual effort the force of natural delight; to live in opposition to the practice of the human race; to despise the comforts of wedlock; to disdain the sweet enjoyments derived from children; and to regard as nothing, in the hope of future blessedness, everything that is reckoned among the advantages of this present life. This is, as I have said, a great and admirable virtue, and is not undeservedly destined to a vast reward, in proportion to the greatness of its labor. The Scripture says, " I will give to the eunuchs, saith the Lord, a place in my house and within my walls, a place counted better than[2] sons and daughters; I will give them an eternal name, and it shall not[3] fail." The Lord again speaks concerning such eunuchs in the Gospel, saying, " For there are eunuchs who have made themselves eunuchs for the kingdom of heaven's sake."[4] Great, indeed, is the struggle connected with chastity, but greater is the reward; the restraint is temporal, but the reward will be eternal. For the blessed Apostle John also speaks concerning these, saying that " they follow the Lamb whithersoever he goeth."[5] This, I think, is to be understood to the following effect, that there will be no place in the court of heaven closed against them, but that all the habitations of the divine mansions will be thrown open before them.

CHAPTER III.

BUT that the merit of virginity may shine forth more clearly, and that there may be a better understanding as to how worthy it is of God, let this be considered, that the Lord God, our Saviour, when, for the salvation of the human race, he condescended to assume mankind, chose no other than a virgin's womb, that he might show how virtue of this kind especially pleased him; and that he might point out the blessedness of chastity to both sexes, he had a virgin mother, while he himself was ever to remain in a like condition. He thus furnished in his own person to men, and in the person of his mother to women, an example of virginity, by which it might be proved, with respect to both sexes, that the blessed state of purity possessed the

---

1 " per summum sacerdotem."
2 Rom. xii. 1.
3 1 Cor. vi. 17.

1 " sopire luxuriam," lit. to put to sleep.
2 " a filiis et filiabus ": a mistaken rendering of the Hebrew text.
3 Isa. lvi. 5.   4 Matt. xix. 12.   5 Rev. xiv. 4.

fullness of divinity,[1] for whatever dwelt in the Son was also wholly in the mother. But why should I take pains to make known the excellent and surpassing merit of chastity, and to set forth the glorious good of virginity, when I am not ignorant that many have discoursed on this subject, and have proved its blessedness by most conclusive reasons, and since it can never be a matter of doubt to any reflecting mind, that a thing has all the more merit, the more difficult it is of accomplishment? For if any one judges chastity to be of no moment or only of small consequence, it is certain that he is either ignorant of the matter, or is not willing to incur the trouble it implies. Hence it comes to pass that those always derogate from the importance of chastity, who either do not possess it, or who are unwillingly compelled to maintain it.

CHAPTER IV.

Now, therefore, since we have set forth, although in few words, both the difficulty and the merit of purity, great care must be taken lest a matter which in itself implies great virtue, and is also destined to a vast reward, should fail to produce its proper fruits. For the more precious every sort of thing is, the more it is guarded with anxious solicitude. And since there are many things which fail to secure their proper excellence, unless they are assisted by the aid of other things, as is, for instance, the case with honey, which, unless it is preserved by the protection of wax, and by the cells of the honeycombs, and is indeed, to state the matter more truly, sustained by these, loses its deliciousness and cannot exist apart by itself; and again as it is with wine, which, unless it be kept in vessels of a pleasant odor, and with the pitch frequently renewed, loses the power of its natural sweetness; so, great care must be taken lest perchance some things may be necessary also to virginity, without which it can by no means produce its proper fruits, and thus a matter of so great difficulty may be of no advantage (while all the time it is believed to be of advantage), because it is possessed without the other necessary adjuncts. For unless I am mistaken, chastity is preserved in its entirety, for the sake of the reward to be obtained in the kingdom of heaven, which it is perfectly certain no one can obtain who does[1] not deserve eternal life. But that eternal life cannot be merited except by the keeping of all the divine commandments, the Scripture testifies, saying, "If thou wilt enter into life, keep the command-

ments."[2] Therefore no one has that life, except the man who has kept all the precepts of the law, and he who has not such life cannot be a possessor of the kingdom of heaven, in which it is not the dead, but the living who shall reign. Therefore virginity, which hopes for the glory of the kingdom of heaven, will profit nothing by itself, unless it also possess that to which eternal life is promised, by means of which the reward of the kingdom of heaven is possessed. Above all things, therefore, the commandments which have been enjoined upon us must be kept by those who preserve chastity in its entireness, and who are hoping for its reward from the justice of God, lest otherwise the pains taken to maintain a glorious chastity and continence come to nothing. No one acquainted with the law does not know that virginity is above[3] the commandment or precept, as the Apostle says, "Now, as to virgins, I have no precept of the Lord, but I give my advice."[4] When, therefore, he simply gives advice about maintaining virginity, and lays down no precept, he acknowledges that it is above the commandment. Those, therefore, who preserve virginity, do more than the commandment requires. But it will then only profit you to have done more than was commanded, if you also do that which *is* commanded. For how can you boast that you have done more, if, in respect to some point, you do less? Desiring to fulfill the Divine counsel, see that, above all things, you keep the commandment: wishing to attain to the reward of virginity, see that you keep fast hold of what is necessary to merit life, that your chastity may be such as can receive a recompense. For as the observance of the commandments ensures life, so, on the other hand, does the violation give rise to death. And he who through disobedience has been doomed to death cannot hope for the crown pertaining to virginity; nor, when really handed over to punishment, can he expect the reward promised to chastity.

CHAPTER V.

Now, there are three kinds of virtue, by means of which the possession of the kingdom of heaven is secured. The first is chastity, the second, contempt of the world, and the third, righteousness, which, as when joined together, they very greatly benefit their possessors, so, when separated, they can hardly be of any advantage, since every one of them is required, not for its own sake only, but for the sake of another. First of all, then, chastity is demanded,

---

1 The text is here most uncertain; that adopted by Halm seems unintelligible.

1 "quod sine æternæ vitæ merito neminem consequi posse satis certum est."

2 Matt. xix. 17.

3 "supra mandatum": Clericus remarks on this, "Non *supra*, sed *præter*, nam ea de re nihil præcepit Christus."

4 1 Cor. vii. 25.

that contempt of the world may more easily follow, because the world can be more easily despised by those who are not held fast in the bonds of matrimony. Contempt of the world, again, is required, in order that righteousness may be maintained, which those can with difficulty fully preserve who are involved in desires after worldly advantages, and in the pursuit of mundane pleasures. Whosoever, therefore, possesses the first kind of virtue, chastity, but does not, at the same time, have the second, which is contempt of the world, possesses the first almost to no purpose, since he does not have the second, for the sake of which the first was required. And if any one possesses the first and second, but is destitute of the third which is righteousness, he labors in vain, since the former two are principally required for the sake of the third. For what profits it to possess chastity in order to contempt of the world, and yet not to have that on account of which you have the other? Or why should you despise the things of the world, if you do not observe righteousness, for the sake of which it is fitting that you should possess chastity, as well as contempt for the world? For as the first kind of virtue is on account of the second, and the second on account of the third, so the first and the second are on account of the third ; and if it does not exist, neither the first nor the second will prove of any advantage.

CHAPTER VI.

But you perhaps say here, "Teach me, then, what righteousness is, so that knowing it, I may be able more easily to fully practice it." Well, I shall briefly explain it to you, as I am able, and shall use the simplicity of common words, seeing that the subject of which we treat is such as ought by no means to be obscured by attempts at eloquent description, but should be opened up by the simplest forms of expression. For a matter which is necessary to all in common ought to be set forth in a common sort of speech. Righteousness, then, is nothing else than not to commit sin ; and not to commit sin is just to keep the precepts of the law. Now, the observance of these precepts is maintained in a two-fold way — thus, that one do none of those things which are forbidden, and that he strive to fulfill the things which are commanded. This is the meaning of the following statement : " Depart from evil, and do[1] good." For I do not wish you to think that righteousness consists simply in not doing evil, since not to do good is also evil, and a transgression of the law takes place in both, since he who said, " Depart from evil " said also, " and do good." If you depart

from evil, and do not do good, you are a transgressor of the law, which is fulfilled, not simply by abhorring all evil deeds, but also by the performance of good works. For, indeed, you have not merely received this commandment, that you should not deprive one who is clothed of his garments, but that you should cover with your own the man who has been deprived of his ; nor that you should not take away bread of his own from one who has it, but that you should willingly impart of your bread to him who has none ; nor that you should not simply not drive away a poor man from a shelter of his own, but that you should receive him when he has been driven out, and has no shelter, into your own. For the precept which has been given us is " to weep with them that[2] weep." But how can we weep with them, if we share in none of their necessities, and afford no help to them in those matters on account of which they lament? For God does not call for the fruitless moisture of our tears ; but, because tears are an indication of grief, he wishes you to feel the distresses of another as if they were your own. And just as you would wish aid to be given you if you were in such tribulation, so should you help another in accordance with the statement, " Whatsoever ye would that men should do unto you, do ye even so[3] to them." For to weep with one that weeps, and at the same time to refuse to help, when you can, him that weeps, is a proof of mockery, and not of piety. In short, our Saviour wept with Mary and Martha, the sisters of Lazarus, and proved the feeling of infinite compassion within him by the witness of his tears. But works, as the proofs of true affection soon followed, when Lazarus, for whose sake the tears were shed, was raised up and restored to his sisters. This was sincerely to weep with those who wept, when the occasion of the weeping was removed. But he did it, you will say, as having the power. Well, nothing is demanded of you which it is impossible for you to perform : he has fulfilled his entire duty who has done what he could.

CHAPTER VII.

But (as we had begun to remark) it is not sufficient for a Christian to keep himself from wickedness, unless he also has fulfilled the duties implied in good works, as is very distinctly proved by that statement in which the Lord threatened that those will be doomed to eternal fire, who, although they have done no evil, have not done all that is good, declaring " Then will the king say to those who are on his right hand : depart from me, ye cursed, into eternal

---

[1] Ps. xxxiv. 14.   [2] Rom. xii. 15.   [3] Matt. vii. 12.

fire, which my Father has prepared for the devil and his angels; for I was hungry, and ye gave me not to eat; I was thirsty, and ye gave me no [1] drink," with what follows. He did not say, "Depart from me, ye cursed, because ye have committed murder, or adultery, or theft"; for it is not because they had done evil, but because they had not done good, that they are condemned, and doomed to the punishments of the eternal Gehenna; nor because they had committed things which were forbidden, but because they had not been willing to do those things which had been commanded. And from this it is to be observed what hope those can have, who, in addition, do some of those things which are forbidden, when even such are doomed to eternal fire as have simply not done the things which are commanded. For I do not wish you to flatter yourself in this way, — if you have not done certain things, because you have done certain other things, since it is written, "Whosoever shall keep the whole law, and yet offend in one point, has become guilty of all." [2] For Adam sinned once, and died; and do you think that you can live, when you are often doing that which killed another person, when he had only done it once? Or do you imagine that he committed a great crime, and was therefore justly condemned to a severer punishment? Let us consider, then, what it was he really did. He ate of the fruit of the tree, contrary to the commandment. What then? Did God punish man with death for the sake of the fruit of a tree? No: not on account of the fruit of the tree, but on account of the contempt of the commandment. The question, therefore, is not about the nature of the offense, but about the transgression of the commandment. And the same being who told Adam not to eat of the fruit of the tree, has commanded you not to speak evil, not to lie, not to detract, not to listen to a detractor, to swear not at all, not to covet, not to envy, not to be drunken, not to be greedy, not to render evil for evil to any one, to love your enemies, to bless them that curse you, to pray for them that malign and persecute you, to turn the other cheek to one smiting you, and not to go to law before a worldly tribunal, so that, if any one seeks to take away your goods, you should joyfully lose them, to flee from the charge of avarice, to beware of the sin of all pride and boastfulness, and live, humble and meek, after the example of Christ, avoiding fellowship with the wicked so completely that you will not even eat with fornicators, or covetous persons, or those that speak evil of others, or the envious, or detractors, or the drunken, or the rapacious. Now, if you despise him in any such matter,

then, if he spared Adam, he will also spare you. Yea, he might have been spared with better reason than you, inasmuch as he was still ignorant and inexperienced, and was restrained by the example of no one who had previously sinned, and who had died on account of his sin. But after such examples as you possess, after the law, after the prophets, after the gospels, and after the apostles, if you still set your mind on transgressing, I see not in what way pardon can be extended to you.

CHAPTER VIII.

Do you flatter yourself on account of the attribute of virginity? Remember Adam and Eve fell when they were virgins, and that the perfect purity of their bodies did not profit them when they sinned. The virgin who sins is to be compared to Eve, and not to Mary. We do not deny that, in the present life, there is the remedy of repentance, but we remind you rather to hope for reward, than to look for pardon. For it is disgraceful that those should ask for indulgence who are expecting the crown of virginity, and that those should commit anything unlawful who have even cut themselves off from things lawful; for it must be remembered that it is lawful to contract an alliance by marriage. And as those are to be praised who, from love to Christ, and for the glory of the kingdom of heaven, have despised the tie of wedlock, so those are to be condemned who, through pleasure of incontinence, after they have vowed themselves to God, have recourse to the Apostolic remedy. Therefore, as we have said, those who decline marriage despise not things unlawful, but things lawful. And if that class of people swear, if they speak evil of others, if they are detractors, or if they patiently listen to detractors, if they return evil for evil, if they incur the charge of covetousness with respect to other people's property, or of avarice in regard to their own, if they cherish the poison of revenge or envy, if they either say or think anything unbefitting against the institutions of the law or the Apostles, if with a desire of pleasing in the flesh, they exhibit themselves dressed up and adorned, if they do any other unlawful things, as is only too common, what will it profit them to have spurned what is lawful, while they practice what is not lawful? If you wish it to be of advantage to you, that you have despised things lawful, take care that you do not any of those things which are not lawful. For, it is foolish to have dreaded that which is in its nature less, and not to dread that which is intrinsically more [or not to avoid those things [1] which are inter-

---

[1] Matt. xxv. 41. [2] James ii. 10.

[1] The genuineness of this clause is very doubtful, and the text is, at best, exceedingly corrupt.

dicted, while such things as are permitted meet with contempt]. For the Apostle says, "She that is unmarried careth for the things of the Lord, how she may please God, that she may be holy both in body and spirit; but she who is married careth for the things of this world, how she may please[2] her husband." He thus affirms that the married woman pleases her husband by thinking of worldly things, while the unmarried woman pleases God, inasmuch as she has no anxiety about the things of the world. Let him tell me, then, whom *she* desires to please, who has no husband, and yet cares for the things of the world? Shall not the married woman, in such a case, be preferred to her? Yes, since she by caring for the things of the world pleases at least her husband, but the other neither pleases her husband, since she does not have one, nor can she please God.[3] But it is not fitting that we should pass over in silence that which he said: "The unmarried woman careth for the things of the Lord, how she may please God, that she may be holy both in body and spirit" [she careth, he says, for the things of the Lord; she does not care for the things of the world, or of men, but for the things of God]. What, then, *are* the things of the Lord? Let the Apostle tell: "Whatsoever[4] things are holy, whatsoever things are just, whatsoever things are lovely, whatsoever things are of good report, if there be any virtue, and if there be any praise of doctrine": these are the things of the Lord, which holy and truly apostolic virgins meditate upon, and think of, day and night, without any interval of time. Of the Lord is the resurrection of the dead, of the Lord is immortality, of the Lord is incorruption, of the Lord is that splendor of the sun which is promised to the saints, as it is written in the Gospel, "Then shall the righteous shine forth as the sun in the kingdom of their Father":[5] of the Lord are the many mansions of the righteous in the heavens, of the Lord is the fruit which is produced, whether thirty fold, or sixty fold, or an hundred fold. Those virgins who think on these things, and by what works they may be able to merit them, think of the things of the Lord. Of the Lord, too, is the law of the new and old testament, in which shine forth the holy utterances of his lips; and if any virgins meditate without intermission on these things, they think of the things of the Lord. In that case, there is fulfilled in them the saying of the prophet: "The eternal[6] foundations are upon a solid rock, and the commands of God are in the heart of the holy woman."

CHAPTER IX.

THERE follows the clause "how she may please God,"—God, I say, not men,—"that she may be holy both in body and spirit." He does not say that she may be holy only in a member or in the body, but that she may be holy in body and spirit. For a member is only one part of the body, but the body is a union of all the members. When, therefore, he says that she may be holy in the body, he testifies that she ought to be sanctified in all her members, because the sanctification of the other members will not avail, if corruption be found remaining in one. Also, *she* will not be holy in body (which consists of all the members), who is defiled by the pollution of even one of them. But in order that what I say may be made more obvious and clear, suppose the case of a woman who is purified by the sanctification of all her other members, and sins only with her tongue, inasmuch as she either speaks evil[1] of people or bears false testimony, will all her other members secure the acquittal of one, or will all the rest be judged on account of the one? If, therefore, the sanctification of the other members will not avail, even when one only is at fault, how much more, if all are corrupted by the guilt of various sins, will the perfection of one be of no avail?

CHAPTER X.

WHEREFORE, I beseech you, O virgin, do not flatter yourself on the ground of your purity alone, and do not trust in the perfection of one member; but according to the Apostle, maintain the sanctity of your body throughout. Cleanse thy head from all defilement, because it is a disgrace that it, after the sanctifying oil has been applied to it, should be polluted with the juice or powder of either crocus, or any other pigment, or should be adorned with gold or gems or any other earthly ornament, because it already shines with the radiance of heavenly adornment. It is undoubtedly a grave insult to Divine grace to prefer to it any mundane and worldly ornament. And next, cleanse thy forehead, that it may blush at human, and not at Divine works, and may display that shame which gives rise not to sin, but to the favor of God, as the sacred Scripture declares, "There is a shame that causes sin, and there is a shame that brings with it the favor[1] of God." Cleanse, too, thy neck, that it may not carry thy[2] locks in a golden net and necklaces hung round it,

---

[2] 1 Cor. vii. 34.
[3] The text is here very uncertain; we have followed that of Halm, but with hesitation.
[4] Phil. iv. 8, with the addition of ἐπιστήμης.
[5] Matt. xiii. 43.   [6] Eccl. xxvi. 24.

[1] "Blasphemet."
[1] Eccl. iv. 21.
[2] The text is here most uncertain; Halm's "ut non aurea reticula capillus portet" is "that thy hair may not carry golden nets."

but may rather bear about it those ornaments of which the Scripture says, "Let not [3] mercy and faith depart from thee," and hang them upon thy heart as upon thy neck. Cleanse thine eyes, whilst thou dost withdraw them from all concupiscence, and dost never turn them away from the sight of the poor, and dost keep them from all dyes, in that purity in which they were made by God. Cleanse thy tongue from falsehood, because "a mouth [4] which tells lies destroys the soul": cleanse it from detraction, from swearing, and from perjury. I beg you not to think it is an inverted order that I have said the tongue should be cleansed from swearing before perjury, for one will then the more easily escape perjury, if he swears not at all, so that there may be fulfilled in him that statement, "Keep [5] thy tongue from evil, and thy lips from speaking guile." And be mindful of the Apostle who says, "Bless, and [6] curse not." But often call to mind the following words, "See that no one render evil for evil to any man, or cursing for cursing, but on the contrary, do ye bless them, because to this ye have been called, that ye should possess a blessing [7] by inheritance"; and this other passage, "If any [8] one offend not in tongue, he is a perfect man." For it is shameful that those lips, by which you confess God, pray to him, bless him, and praise him, should be defiled by the pollution of any sin. I know not with what conscience any one can pray to God with that tongue with which he either speaks falsehood, or calumniates, or detracts. God listens to holy lips, and speedily answers those prayers which an unpolluted tongue pours forth. Cleanse also thine ears, so that they may not listen except to holy and true discourse, that they never admit into them obscene, or infamous, or worldly words, or tolerate any one detracting from another, on account of that which is written, "Hedge up [9] thine ears with thorns, and do not listen to a wicked tongue, that you may have your part with him, of whom it is said, that he was [10] righteous in hearing and seeing; i.e. he sinned neither with his eyes nor his ears. Cleanse, too, thy hands, "that they [11] be not stretched out to receive, but shut against giving," and that they be not prompt to strike, but ever ready for all the works of mercy and piety. In fine, cleanse thy feet, that they follow not the broad and ample way which leads to grand and costly worldly banquets, but that they tread rather the difficult and narrow path, which guides to heaven, for it is written, "Make a [12] straight path for your feet." Acknowledge that your members were formed for you by God the Maker, not for vices, but for virtues; and, when you have cleansed the whole of your limbs from every stain of sin, and they have become sanctified throughout your whole body, then understand that this purity will profit you, and look forward with all confidence to the prize of virginity.

CHAPTER XI.

I BELIEVE that I have now set forth, briefly indeed, but, at the same time, fully, what is implied in a woman's purity of body: it remains that we should learn what it is to be pure also in spirit; i.e. that what it is unlawful for one to do in act, it is also unlawful for one even to imagine in thought. For she is holy, alike in body and in spirit, who sins neither in mind nor heart, knowing that God is one who examines also the heart; and, therefore, she takes every pains to possess a mind as well as a body free from sin. Such a person is aware that it is written, "Keep thy [1] heart with all diligence"; and again, "God loveth [2] holy hearts, and all the undefiled are acceptable to him"; and elsewhere, "Blessed [3] are those of a pure heart; for they shall see God." I think that this last statement is made regarding those whom conscience accuses of the guilt of no sin; concerning whom I think that John also spoke in his Epistle when he said, "If our heart [4] condemn us not, then have we confidence towards God, and whatsoever we ask we shall receive from him." I do not wish you to think that you have escaped the accusation of sin, although act does not follow desire, since it is written, "Whosoever [5] looketh on a woman to lust after her, hath already committed adultery with her in his heart." And do not say, "I had the thought, indeed, but I did not carry it out in act"; for it is unlawful even to desire that which it is unlawful to do. Wherefore also blessed Peter issues a precept to this effect: "purify your [6] souls"; and if he had not been aware of such a thing as defilement of the soul, he would not have expressed a desire that it should be purified. But we should also very carefully consider that passage which says, "These [7] are they who did not defile themselves with women, for they remained virgins, and they follow the Lamb whithersoever he goeth"; and should reflect whether, if these are joined to the Divine retinue, and traverse all the regions of the heavens, through the merit of chastity and purity alone, there may be also other means by which virginity being assisted may attain to the

[3] Prov. iii. 3.
[4] Wisd. i. 11.
[5] Ps. xxxiv. 13.
[6] Rom. xii. 14.
[7] 1 Thess. v. 15; 1 Pet. iii. 9.

[8] James iii. 2.
[9] Eccl. xxviii. 24.
[10] 2 Pet. ii. 8.
[11] Eccles. iv. 31.
[12] Prov. iv. 26.

[1] Prov. iv. 23.
[2] Prov. xvii. 3; xi. 20.
[3] Matt. v. 8.
[4] 1 John iii. 21.

[5] Matt. v. 28.
[6] 1 Pet. i. 22.
[7] Rev. xiv. 4.

glory of so great blessedness. But whence shall we be able to know this? From the following passages (if I mistake not) in which it is written, "These were[8] purchased from among men as the first fruits to God and the Lamb, and in their mouth there was found no falsehood, for they are without spot before the throne of God." You see, then, that they are spoken of as closely following in the footsteps of the Lord, not in virtue of one member only, but those are said to do so, who, besides virginity, had passed a life freed from all the pollution of sin. Wherefore, let the virgin especially despise marriage on this account, that, while she is safer than others, she may the more easily accomplish what is also required from those who are married; viz. keep herself from all sin, and obey all the commandments of the law. For if she does not marry, and nevertheless indulges in those things from which even married women are enjoined to keep themselves free, what will it profit her not to have married? For although it is not allowed to any Christian to commit sin, and it befits all without exception who are purified through the sanctification of the spiritual bath, to lead an unstained life, that they may be thoroughly identified[9] with the Church, which is described as being "without[10] spot, or wrinkle, or any such thing," much more is it requisite that a virgin should reach this standard, whom neither the existence of a husband, nor of sons, nor of any other necessity, prevents from fully carrying out the demands of holy Scripture; nor shall she be able, if she fail, to defend herself by any sort of excuse.

CHAPTER XII.

O VIRGIN, maintain thy purpose which is destined for a great reward. Eminent with the Lord is the virtue of virginity and purity, if it be not disfigured by other kinds of lapses into sins and wickedness. Realize your state, realize your position, realize your purpose. You are called the bride of Christ; see that you commit no act which is unworthy of him to whom you profess to be betrothed. He will quickly write a bill of divorcement, if he perceive in you even one act of unfaithfulness. Accordingly, whosoever receives those gifts which, as an earnest, are bestowed in the case of human betrothals, immediately begins earnestly and diligently to enquire of domestics, intimates, and friends, what is the character of the young man, what he especially loves, what he receives, in what style he lives, what habits he practices, what luxuries he indulges in, and in what pursuits he

finds his chief pleasure and delight. And when she has learned these things, she so conducts herself, in all respects, that her service, her cheerfulness, her diligence, and her whole mode of life, may be in harmony with the character of her betrothed. And do thou, who hast Christ as thy bridegroom, enquire from the domestics and intimates of that bridegroom of thine what is his character; yes, do thou zealously and skillfully enquire in what things he specially delights, what sort of arrangement he loves in thy dress, and what kind of adornment he desires. Let his most intimate associate Peter tell thee, who does not allow personal adorning even to married women, as he has written in his epistle, "Let wives,[1] in like manner, be subject to their own husbands. so that, if any believe not the word, they may, without the word, be won over by the conduct of their wives, contemplating their chaste behavior in the fear of God; and let theirs not be an outward adornment of the hair, or the putting on of gold, or elegance in the apparel which is adopted, but let there be the hidden man of the heart in the stainlessness[2] of a peaceful and modest spirit, which is in the sight of God of great price." Let another apostle also tell thee, the blessed Paul, who, writing to Timothy, gives his approval to the same things in regard to the conduct of believing women: "Let wives[3] in like manner adorn themselves with the ornament of a habit of modesty and sobriety, not with curled hair, or gold, or pearls, or costly array, but as becomes women that profess chastity, with good and upright behavior."

CHAPTER XIII.

BUT perhaps you say, "Why did not the Apostles enjoin these things on virgins?" Because they did not think that necessary, lest such an exhortation, if given to them, might rather seem an insult than a means of edification. Nor, in fact, would they have believed that virgins could ever proceed to such an extreme of hardihood, as to claim for themselves carnal and worldly ornaments, not permitted even to married women. Undoubtedly, the virgin ought to adorn and array herself; for how can she be able to please her betrothed, if she does not come forth in a neat and ornamental form? Let her be adorned by all means, but let her ornaments be of an internal and spiritual kind, and not of a carnal nature; for God desires in her a beauty not of the body, but of the soul. Do thou, therefore, who desirest that thy soul

---

[8] Rev. xiv. 4 ff.
[9] "visceribus intimari."

[10] Eph. v. 27.

[1] 1 Pet. iii. 1 ff.
[2] "incorruptibilitate."
[3] 1 Tim. ii. 9, 10; *chastity* is here unwarrantably read in place of *godliness*.

should be loved and dwelt in by God, array it with all diligence, and adorn it with spiritual garments. Let nothing unbecoming, nothing repulsive, be seen in it. Let it shine with the gold of righteousness, and gleam with the gems of holiness, and glitter with the most precious pearl of purity ; instead of fine linen and silk, let it be arrayed in the robe of mercifulness and piety, according to what is written, " Put ye[1] on, therefore, as the elect of God, holy and beloved, bowels of mercy, kindness, humility," and so forth. And let the virgin not ask for the beauty due to ceruse,[2] or any other pigment, but let her have the brightness of innocence and simplicity, the rosy hue of modesty, and the purple glow of honorable shamefacedness. Let her be washed with the nitre of heavenly doctrine, and purified by all spiritual lavements.[3] Let no stain of malice or sin be left in her. And lest, at any time, she should give forth the evil odor of sin, let her be imbued, through and through, with the most pleasant ointment of wisdom and knowledge.

CHAPTER XIV.

God seeks for adornment of this kind, and desires a soul arrayed in such a manner. Remember that you are called the daughter of God, according to what he says, " Hearken,[1] O daughter, and consider." But you yourself also, as often as you call God your Father, bear witness that you are the daughter of God. Wherefore, if you are the daughter of God, take care that you do none of those things which are unworthy of God, your Father ; but do all things as being the daughter of God. Reflect how the daughters of nobles in this world conduct themselves, to what habits they are accustomed and by what exercises they train themselves. In some of them, there is so great modesty, so great dignity, so great self-restraint, that they excel the habits of other human beings in regard to human nobleness, and, lest they should attach any mark of disgrace on their honorable parents by their failure, they strive to acquire another[2] nature for themselves by the mode of their acting in the world. And do you, therefore, have regard to your origin, consider your descent, attend to the glory of your nobility. Acknowledge that you are not merely the daughter of man, but of God, and adorned with the nobility of a divine birth. So present yourself to the world that your heavenly birth be

seen in you, and your divine nobleness shine clearly forth. Let there be in you a new dignity, an admirable virtue, a notable modesty, a marvelous patience, a gait becoming a virgin with a bearing of true shamefacedness, speech always modest, and such as is uttered only at the proper time, so that whosoever beholds you may admiringly exclaim : " What is this exhibition of new dignity among men? What is this striking modesty, what this well-balanced excellence, what this ripeness of wisdom? This is not the outcome of human training or of mere human discipline. Something heavenly sheds its fragrance on me in that earthly body. I really believe that God does reside in some human beings." And when he comes to know that you are a handmaid of Christ, he will be seized with the greater amazement, and will reflect how marvelous must be the Master, when his handmaid manifests such excellence.

CHAPTER XV.

If you wish, then, to be with Christ, you must live according to the example of Christ, who was so far removed from all evil and wickedness, that he did not render a recompense even to his enemies, but rather even prayed for them. For I do not wish you to reckon those souls Christian, who (I do not say) hate either their brothers or sisters, but who do not, before God as a witness, love their neighbors with their whole heart and conscience, since it is a bounden duty for Christians, after the example of Christ himself, even to love their enemies. If you desire to possess fellowship with the saints, cleanse your heart from the thought of malice and sin. Let no one circumvent you ; let no one delude you by beguiling speech. The court of heaven will admit none except the holy, and righteous, and simple, and innocent, and pure. Evil has no place in the presence of God. It is necessary that he who desires to reign with Christ should be free from all wickedness and guile. Nothing is so offensive, and nothing so detestable to God, as to hate any one, to wish to harm any one ; while nothing is so acceptable to him as to love all men. The prophet knowing this bears witness to it when he teaches, " Ye who[1] love the Lord, hate evil."

CHAPTER XVI.

Take heed that ye love not human glory in any respect, lest your portion also be reckoned among those to whom it was said, " How[1] can ye believe, who seek glory, one from another?"

---

[1] Col. iii. 12.
[2] "cerussæ": *white lead*, used by women to whiten their skins.
[3] "lomentis": a mixture of bean-meal and rice, used as a lotion to preserve the smoothness of the skin.
[1] Ps. xlv. 10.
[2] Only a guess can here be made at the meaning; the text is in utter confusion.

[1] Ps. xcvii. 10.   [1] John v. 44.

and of whom it is said through the prophet, " Increase [2] evils to them ; increase evils to the boastful of the earth " ; and elsewhere, " Ye are confounded [3] from your boasting, from your re-proaching in the sight of the Lord." For I do not wish you to have regard to those, who are virgins of the world, and not of Christ ; who un-mindful of their purpose and profession, rejoice in delicacies, are delighted with riches, and boast of their descent from a merely carnal nobility ; who, if they assuredly believed themselves to be the daughters of God, would never, after their divine ancestry, admire mere human nobility, nor glory in any honored earthly father : if they felt that they had God as their Father, they would not love any nobility connected with the flesh. Why, thou foolish woman, dost thou flatter thyself about the nobleness of thy descent, and take delight in it? God, at the beginning, created two human beings, from whom the whole multitude of the human race has descended ; and thus it is not the equity of nature, but the ambition of evil desire, which has given rise to worldly nobility. Unquestionably, we are all rendered equal by the grace of the divine [4] bath, and there can be no difference among those, whom the second birth has generated, by means of which alike the rich man and the poor man, the free man and the slave, the nobly born and the lowly born, is rendered a son of God. Thus mere earthly rank is overshadowed by the bril-liance of heavenly glory, and henceforth is taken no account of, while those who formerly had been unequal in worldly honors are now equally arrayed in the glory of a heavenly and divine nobility. There is now among such no place for lowness of birth ; nor is any one inferior to another whom the majesty of the divine birth adorns ; except in the estimation of those who do not think that the things of heaven are to be preferred to those of earth. There can be no worldly boasting among them, if they reflect how vain a thing it is that they should, in smaller mat-ters, prefer themselves to those whom they know to be equal to themselves in greater matters, and should regard, as placed below themselves on earth, those whom they believe to be equal to themselves in what relates to heaven. But do thou, who art a virgin of Christ, and not of the world, flee from all the glory of this present life, that thou mayest attain to the glory which is promised in the world to come.

CHAPTER XVII.

AVOID words of contention and causes of ani-mosity : flee also from all occasions of discord and strife. For if, according to the doctrine of the Apostle " the servant [1] of the Lord must not strive," how much more does this become the handmaid of the Lord, whose mind ought to be more gentle, as her sex is more bashful and retiring. Restrain thy tongue from evil speak-ing, and put the bridle of the law upon thy mouth ; so that you shall speak, if you speak at all, only when it would be a sin to be silent. Beware lest you utter anything which might be justly found fault with. A word once spoken is like a stone which has been thrown : wherefore it should be long thought over before it is uttered. Blessed, assuredly, are the lips, which never utter what they would wish to recall. The talk of a chaste mind ought itself also to be chaste, such as may always rather edify than injure the hearers, according to that command-ment of the Apostle when he says, " Let no [2] corrupt communications proceed out of your mouth, but that which is good for the edification of faith, that it may convey grace to them that hear." Precious to God is that tongue which knows not to form words except about divine things, and holy is that mouth from which heavenly utterances continually flow forth. Put down by the authority of Scripture calumniators of those who are absent, as being evil-minded persons, because the prophet mentions this also as among the virtues of a perfect man, if, in the presence of the righteous an evil-minded man, who brings forward things against his neighbor which cannot be proved, is brought down to nothing. For it is not lawful for you patiently to listen to evil-speaking against another, inas-much as you would not wish that to be done by others when directed against yourself. Certainly, everything is unrighteous which goes against the Gospel of Christ, and that is the case, if you quietly permit anything to be done to another, which you would feel painful, if done by any one to yourself. Accustom your tongue always to speak about those who are good, and lend your ears rather to listen to the praises of good men than to the condemnation of such as are wicked. Take heed that all the good actions you perform are done for the sake of God, knowing that for every such deed you will only receive a reward, so far as you have done it out of regard to his fear and love. Study rather to be holy than to appear so, because it is of no avail to be reckoned what you are not ; and the guilt of a twofold sin is contracted when you do not have what you are credited with having, and when you pretend to possess what you do not possess.

---

[1] 2 Tim. ii. 24. [2] Eph. iv. 29.

---

[2] Isa. xxvi. 15, after the LXX.
[3] Jer. xii. 13, after the LXX.
[4] " divini lavacri ": referring to baptism.

CHAPTER XVIII.

DELIGHT thyself rather in fastings than in feastings, mindful of that widow who did not depart from the temple, but served God with fastings and prayers day and night. Now, if she who was a widow, and a Jewish widow, proved herself such, what is it fitting that a virgin of Christ should now attain to? Love more than any other thing the feast of the divine word, and desire that you be filled with spiritual dainties, while you seek for such food as refreshes the soul, rather than for that which only pleases the body. Flee from all kinds of flesh and wine, as being the sources of heat and provocatives to lust. And only then, if need be, use a little wine, when the stomach's uneasiness, or great infirmity of body, requires you to do so. Subdue anger, restrain enmity, and whatever there may be which gives rise to remorse when it is done, avoid as an abomination giving rise[1] to immediate sin. It is fitting that that mind should be very tranquil and quiet, as well as free from all the tumults of anger, which desires to be the dwelling-place of God, as he testifies through the prophet, saying, "Upon[2] what other man shall I rest than upon him who is humble and quiet, and who trembleth at my words?" Believe that God is a witness of all thy deeds and thoughts, and take good heed lest you either do or think anything which is unworthy of the divine eyesight. When you desire to engage in prayer, show yourself in such a frame of mind as becomes one who is to speak with the Lord.

CHAPTER XIX.

WHEN you repeat[1] a psalm, consider whose words you are repeating and delight yourself more with true contrition of soul, than with the pleasantness of a trilling voice. For God sets a higher value on the tears of one thus praising[2] him, than on the beauty of his voice; as the prophet says, "Serve[3] the Lord with fear, and rejoice with trembling." Now, where there are fear and trembling, there is no lifting up of the voice, but humility of mind with lamentation and tears. Display diligence in all thy doings; for it is written, "Cursed[4] is the man who carelessly performs the work of the Lord." Let grace grow in you with years; let righteousness increase with age; and let your faith appear the more perfect the older you become;

for Jesus, who has left us an example how to live, increased not only in years as respected his body, but in wisdom and spiritual grace before God and men. Reckon all the time in which you do not perceive yourself growing better as positively lost. Maintain to the last that purpose of virginity which you have formed; for it is the part of virtue not merely to begin, but to finish, as the Lord says in the Gospel, "Whosoever[5] shall endure to the end, the same shall be saved." Beware, therefore, lest you furnish to any one an occasion even of evil desire, because thy God, betrothed to thee, is jealous; for an adulteress against Christ is more guilty than one against her husband. Be thou, therefore, a model of life to all; be an example; and excel in actual conduct those whom you precede in your consecration[6] to chastity. Show thyself in all respects a virgin; and let no stain of corruption be brought as a charge against thy person. And let one whose body is perfect in its purity be also irreproachable in conduct. Now, as we said in the beginning of this letter, that you have become a sacrifice pertaining to God, such a sacrifice as undoubtedly imparts its own sanctity also to others, that, as every one worthily receives from it, he himself also may be a partaker of sanctification, so then, let the other virgins also be sanctified through you, as by means of a divine offering. Show yourself to them so holy in all things, that, whosoever comes in contact with thy life, whether by hearing or seeing, may experience the power of sanctification, and may feel that such an amount of grace passes to him from your manner of acting, that, while he desires to imitate thee, he himself becomes worthy of being a sacrifice devoted to God.

LETTER III.

A LETTER OF SEVERUS TO HOLY PAUL THE BISHOP.

AFTER I learned that all thy cooks had given[1] up thy kitchen (I believe because they felt indignant at having to fulfill the duty towards cheap dishes of pulse[2]), I sent a little boy to you out of our own workshop. He is quite skillful enough to cook pale beans and to pickle homely beetroot, with vinegar and sauce, as well as to prepare cheap porridge for the jaws of the hungry monks. He knows nothing, however, of pepper or of laser,[3] but he is quite at home with cumin,

---

1 "velut proximi criminis abominationem declina": the text and construction are both very uncertain, so that we can only make a guess at the meaning.
2 Isa. lxvi. 2.
1 "dicis": the reference seems to be to singing or chanting.
2 "psallentis."   3 Ps. ii. 11.   4 Jer. xlviii. 10.

5 Matt. x. 22.
6 The text and meaning are here somewhat uncertain.
1 "renuntiasse."
2 "pulmentariis": this word generally means some sort of relish, but here it seems to denote a kind of pottage.
3 *Laser* was the juice of a plant called *laserpitium*.

and is especially clever in plying the noisy mortar with sweetly smelling plants. He has one fault, that he is no kindly foe to admit to any garden ; for if let in, he will mow down with a sword all things within his reach, and he will never be satisfied with the slaughter simply of mallows. However, in furnishing himself with fuel he will not swindle you. He will burn whatever comes in his way ; he will cut down and not hesitate to lay hands upon buildings, and to carry off old beams from the household. We present him, then, to you, with this character and these virtues ; and we wish you to regard him not as a servant, but as a son, because you are not ashamed to be the father of very small creatures. I myself would have wished to serve you instead of him ; but if good-will may be taken as in some measure standing for the deed, do you only, in return, take care to remember me amid your breakfasts and delightful dinners, because it is more proper to be your slave, than the master of others. Pray for me.[4]

LETTER IV.

TO THE SAME, ON HIS WISDOM AND GENTLENESS.

The faithful exponent of our holy religion so arranges all things that no place be found in future for transgressors : for what else do you, for instance, promise us by so great sanctity of character, than that, all errors being laid aside, we should lead a blessed life? In this matter, I see that the greatest praise befits thy virtues, because you have changed even an uninstructed mind by your exhortations, and drawn it over to an excellent condition. But it would not seem so wonderful, if you had simply strengthened educated minds by instilling wisdom into them ; for intelligent men have a sort of relationship to devotion, but rustic natures are not easily won over to the side of severity.[1] Just as those who shape the forms of animals out of stone, undertake a business of a pretty difficult kind, when they strike very hard rocks with their chisels, while those who make their attempts on substances of a softer nature feel that their hands are aided by the ease of fashioning these materials, and it is deemed proper that the labor of the workman, when difficult, should be held in the highest honor, so, Sir, singular commendation ought so be given to you, because you have made unpolished and rustic minds, set free from the darkness of sin, both to think what is human, and to understand what is divine.

No less is Xenocrates, by far the most learned of the philosophers, held in estimation, who succeeded by severe exhortations in having luxury conquered. For when a certain Polemo, heavy with wine, staggered openly out of a nocturnal revel at the time when his hearers were flocking to the school of Xenocrates, he, too, entered the place, and impudently took his seat among the crowd of disciples, in that dress in which he had come forth from the banquet. A chaplet of flowers covered his head, and yet he did not feel ashamed that he would seem unlike all the others, because, in truth, indulgence in a long drinking-bout had upset his brains, which are the seat of reason. As the rest of those there present began to murmur grievously, because so unsuitable a hearer had found his way in among a multitude of men of letters, the master himself was not in the slightest degree disturbed, but, on the contrary, began to discourse on the science of morals, and the laws of moderation. And so powerful proved the influence of the teacher that the mind of that impudent intruder was persuaded to the love of modesty. First of all, then, Polemo, in utter confusion, took off the chaplet from his head, and professed himself a disciple. And in course of time he conformed himself so thoroughly to the duties implied in dignity, and surrendered himself so entirely to the exhibition of modesty, that a glorious amendment of character threw a cloak over the habits of his former life. Now we admire this very thing in your instructions, that, without the use of any threats, and without having recourse to terrors of any kind, you have turned infatuated minds to the worship of God ; so that even a badly ordered intellect should believe it preferable[2] to live well and happily with all, rather than to hold unrighteous opinions with a few.

LETTER V.

TO AN UNKNOWN PERSON, ENTREATING HIM TO DEAL GENTLY WITH HIS BROTHER.

Although my lord and brother has already begged of your nobleness that you would see that Tutus should be most[1] safe, yet it has been allowed to me to commend the same person in a letter, in order that, by the petition being doubled, he may be held all the safer. For let it be granted that a youthful fault and error of a yet unsettled age has injured him, so as to inflict a stain on his early years ; still one, who did not yet know what was due to right conduct,

---

[4] Clericus remarks, " Jocosa haec est epistola," but the fun is certainly of a very ponderous kind. We are, by no means, sure of the sense in some parts of the letter.
[1] " crudelitati," which, as Clericus remarks, must here be equivalent to *severitati*.

[2] " rectissimum," where *rectius* might have been expected.
[1] There is a play upon the words — " Tutum esse tutissimum."

has gone wrong almost without contracting blame. For when he came to a right state of mind and to reflection, he understood on better thoughts that a theatrical life was to be condemned. However, he could not be completely cleared of his fault, unless he should wash its guilt away by the aid[2] of Deity, since, by the remedy obtained through the Catholic religion, changing his views, he has denied himself the enjoyment of a less honorable place, and has withdrawn himself from the eyes of the people.

OF THE MASTER AS ABOVE.[3]

Since, therefore, both divine and state laws do not permit a faithful body and sanctified minds to exhibit disgraceful though pleasing spectacles, and to set forth vulgar means of enjoyment, especially since an injury seems in some degree to accrue to the chaste dedication of one's self, in case any one who has been renewed by holy baptism should fall back upon his old licentiousness, it behooves your Excellency to show favor to good intentions, so that he who, by the goodness of God, has entered on a pious duty, should not be forced to sink into the pitfall of the theatre. He does not, however, refuse compliance with the judgment of you all, if you enjoin other fitting actions on his part in behalf of the requirements of our common country.[4]

LETTER VI.

TO SALVIUS: A COMPLAINT THAT THE COUNTRY PEOPLE WERE HARASSED, AND THEIR POSSESSIONS PLUNDERED.

Forensic excitement ought to be at full heat during the time of business in the law-courts; for it is fitting that the arms of industry, as it struggles daily, should display energetic movements. But when loud-toned eloquence has sounded a retreat, and has retired to peaceful groves and pleasant dwelling-places, it is right that one lay aside idle murmurs, and cease to utter ineffectual threats. For we know that palm-bearing steeds, when they have retired from the circus, rest with the utmost quietness in their stables. Neither constant fear nor doubtful palms of victory distress them, but at length, haltered to the peaceful cribs, they now no longer stand in awe of the master urging them on, enjoying sweet oblivion of the restless rivalry

which had prevailed. In like manner, let it delight the boastful soldier after his term of service is completed, to hang up his trophies, and patiently to bear the burden of age.

But I do not quite understand why you should take a delight in terrifying miserable husbandmen; and I do not comprehend why you wish to harass my rustics with the fear of want of sustenance;[1] as if, indeed, I did not know how to console them, and to deliver them from fear, and to show them that there is not so great a reason to fear as you pretend. I confess that, while we were occupied in the plain, I was often frightened by the arms of your eloquence, but frequently I returned you corresponding blows, as far as I was able. I certainly learned along with you, by what right, and in what order, the husbandmen are demanded back, to whom a legal process is competent, and to whom the issue of a process is not competent. You say that the Volusians wished you brought back, and frequently, in your wrath, you repeat that you will withdraw the country people from my little keep; and you, the very man, as I hope and desire, bound to me by the ties of old relationship, now rashly threaten that, casting our agreement to the winds, you will lay hold upon my men. I ask of your illustrious knowledge, whether there is one law for advocates, and another for private persons, whether one thing is just at Rome, and quite another thing at Matarum.

In the meantime, I do not know that you were ever lord of the Volusian property, since Dionysius is said to have preserved the right of possession to it, and he never wanted heirs; who, while he lived, was accustomed to hurl the envenomed jibes of his low language upon a multitude of individuals.[2] There was, at that time, one Porphyrius, the son of Zibberinus, and yet he was not properly named the son of Zibberinus. He kept hidden, by military service, the question as to his birth, and, that he might dispel the cloud from his forehead, he took part in officious services and willing acts of submission. He was much with me both at home and in the forum, having often employed me as his defender with my father, and as his advocate before the judge. Sometimes I even kept back Dionysius, feeling that he ought not, for the sake of twenty acres to discharge vulgar abuse upon Porphyrius.

See, here is the reason why thy remarkable prudence threatened my agents, so that, though you are not the owner of the place, you everywhere make mention of my husbandmen. But if you give yourself out as the successor of Porphyrius, you must know that the narrow

---

[2] " divinitatis accessu ": the context is almost unintelligible.
[3] This probably denotes that what follows is the substance of the Master's petition.
[4] Clericus, while accepting most of the letters with which we are now dealing, doubts, from the difference of style, whether this is an epistle of Sulpitius. It is certainly very different from his usual clearness and correctness.

[1] " exhibitionis formidine " — a strange phrase.
[2] The text is uncertain, and the meaning very obscure.

space of twenty acres cannot certainly be managed by one cultivator, or, if mindful of your
proper dignity and determined to maintain it,
you shrink from naming yourself the heir of
Porphyrius, it is certain and obvious that he can
commence proceedings,[3] to whom the right of
doing so belongs, so as to go to law with those
who have no property in that land. But if you
diligently look into the matter, you will see that
the endeavor to recover it most especially de-
volves on me. Wherefore, my much esteemed
lord and brother, it behooves you to be at peace,
and to return to friendship with me, while you
condescend to come to a private conference.
Cease, I pray you, to disturb inactive and
easily frightened persons, and utter your boastful
words at a distance. Believe me, however, that
I am delighted with your high spirit, and by no
means offended ; for we are neither of a harsh

---

[3] " posse proponere."
[4] We thoroughly agree with Clericus that this letter is, in style,
more alien even than the preceding from the genuine epistles of
Sulpitius. It is barbarous as regards composition, and in several
places not intelligible.

disposition, nor destitute of learning,   Let Maximinus at least render you gentle.[4]

LETTER VII.

TO AN UNKNOWN PERSON, BEGGING THE FAVOR OF A LETTER.

THE faith and piety of souls, no doubt, remain, but this should be made known by the
evidence of a letter, in order that an increase of
affection may be gained by such mutual courtesy. For just as a fertile field cannot bring
forth abundant fruits, if its cultivation has been
neglected, and the good qualities of soil are lost
through the indolence of one who rests, instead
of working, so I think that the love and kindly
feelings of the mind grow ·feeble, unless those
who are absent are visited, as if present, by
means of a letter.[1]

---

[1] Most editions add " Deo gratias, Amen."

THE SACRED HISTORY OF SULPITIUS SEVERUS.

—oo:o:oo—

BOOK I.

CHAPTER I.

I ADDRESS myself to give a condensed account of those things which are set forth in the sacred Scriptures from the beginning of the world, and to tell of them, with distinction of dates, and according to[1] their importance, down to a period within our own remembrance. Many who were anxious to become acquainted with divine things by means of a compendious treatise, have eagerly entreated me to undertake this work. I, seeking to carry out their wish, have not spared my labor, and have thus succeeded in comprising in two short books things which elsewhere filled many volumes. At the same time, in studying brevity, I have omitted hardly any of the facts. Moreover, it seemed to me not out of place that, after I had run through the sacred history down to the crucifixion of Christ, and the doings of the Apostles, I should add an account of events which subsequently took place. I am, therefore, to tell of the destruction of Jerusalem, the persecutions of the Christian people, the times of peace which followed, and of all things again thrown into confusion by the intestine dangers of the churches. But I will not shrink from confessing that, wherever reason required, I have made use of profane historians to fix dates and preserve the series of events unbroken, and have taken out of these what was wanting to a complete knowledge of the facts, that I might both instruct the ignorant and carry conviction to the learned. Nevertheless, as to those things which I have condensed from the sacred books, I do not wish so to present myself as an author to my readers, that they, neglecting the source from which my materials have been derived, should be satisfied with what I have written. My aim is that one who is already familiar with the original should recognize here what he has read there ; for all the mysteries of divine things cannot be brought out except from the fountain-head itself. I shall now enter upon my narrative.

CHAPTER II.

THE world was created by God nearly six[1] thousand years ago, as we shall set forth in the course of this book ; although those who have entered upon and published a calculation of the dates, but little agree among themselves. As, however, this disagreement is due either to the will of God or to the fault of antiquity, it ought not to be a matter of censure. After the formation of the world man was created, the male being named Adam, and the female Eve. Having been placed in Paradise, they ate of the tree from which they were interdicted, and therefore were cast forth as exiles into our earth.[2] To them were born Cain and Abel ; but Cain, being an impious man, slew his brother. He had a son called Enoch, by whom a city was first built,[3] and was called after the name of its founder. From him Irad, and from him again Maüiahel was descended. He had a son called Mathusalam, and he, in turn, begat Lamech, by whom a young man is said to have been slain, without, however, the name of the slain man being mentioned—a fact which is thought by the wise to have presaged a future mystery. Adam, then, after the death of his younger son, begat another son called Seth, when he was now two hundred and thirty years old : he lived altogether eight hundred and thirty years. Seth begat Enos, Enos Cainan, Cainan Malaleel, Malaleel Jared, and Jared Enoch, who on account of his righteousness is said to have been translated by God. His son was called Mathusalam who begat Lamech ; from whom Noah was descended, remarkable for his righteousness, and above all other mortals dear and acceptable to God. When by this time the human race had increased to a great multitude, certain angels, whose habitation was in heaven, were captivated by the appearance of some beautiful virgins, and cherished illicit desires after them, so much so, that falling beneath their own proper nature and origin, they left the higher regions of which they

---

[1] " carptim " : such seems to be the meaning of the word here, as Sigonius has noted. His words are " Carptim — profecto innuit se non singulas res eodem modo persecuturum, sed quæ memoratu digniores visæ fuerint, selecturum."

[1] Sulpitius follows the Greek version, which ascribes many more years to the fathers of mankind than does the original Hebrew.
[2] Many of the ancients (among whom our author is apparently to be reckoned) believed that Paradise was situated outside our world altogether.
[3] An obvious mistake. The first city was built, not by Enoch, but by Cain. Gen. iv. 17.

were inhabitants, and allied themselves in earthly marriages. These angels gradually spreading wicked habits, corrupted the human family, and from their alliance giants are said to have sprung, for the mixture with them of beings of a different nature, as a matter of course, gave birth to monsters.

CHAPTER III.

GOD being offended by these things, and especially by the wickedness of mankind, which had gone beyond measure, had determined to destroy the whole human race. But he exempted Noah, a righteous man and of blameless life, from the destined doom. He being warned by God that a flood was coming upon the earth, built an ark of wood of immense size, and covered it with pitch so as to render it impervious to water. He was shut into it along with his wife, and his three sons and his three daughters-in-law. Pairs of birds also and of the different kinds of beasts were likewise received into it, while all the rest were cut off by a flood. Noah then, when he understood that the violence of the rain had ceased, and that the ark was quietly floating on the deep, thinking (as really was the case) that the waters were decreasing, sent forth first a raven for the purpose of enquiring into the matter, and on its not returning, having settled, as I conjecture, on the dead bodies, he then sent forth a dove. It, not finding a place of rest, returned to him, and being again sent out, it brought back an olive leaf, in manifest proof that the tops of the trees were now to be seen. Then being sent forth a third time, it returned no more, from which it was understood that the waters had subsided ; and Noah accordingly went out from the ark. This was done, as I reckon, two thousand two hundred[1] and forty-two years after the beginning of the world.

CHAPTER IV.

THEN Noah first of all erected an altar to God, and offered sacrifices from among the birds.[1] Immediately afterwards he was blessed by God along with his sons, and received a command that he should not eat blood, or shed the blood of any human being, because Cain, having no such precept, had stained the first age of the world. Accordingly, the sons of Noah were alone left in the then vacant world ; for he had three, Shem, Ham, and Japhet. But Ham, because he had mocked his father when

senseless with wine, incurred his father's curse. His son, Chas by name, begat the giant Nebroth,[2] by whom the city of Babylon is said to have been built. Many other towns are related to have been founded at that time, which I do not here intend to name one by one. But although the human race was now multiplied, and men occupied different places and islands, nevertheless all made use of one tongue, as long as the multitude, afterwards to be scattered through the whole world, kept itself in one body. These, after the manner of human nature, formed the design of obtaining a great name by constructing some great work before they should be separated from one another. They therefore attempted to build a tower which should reach up to heaven. But by the ordination of God, in order that the labors of those engaged in the work might be hindered, they began to speak in a kind of languages very different from their accustomed form of speech, while no one understood the others. This led to their being all the more readily dispersed, because, regarding each other as foreigners, they were easily induced to separate. And the world was so divided to the sons of Noah, that Shem occupied the East, Japhet the West, and Ham the intermediate parts. After this, till the time of Abraham,[3] their genealogy presented nothing very remarkable or worthy of record.

CHAPTER V.

ABRAHAM, whose father was Thara, was born in the one thousand and seventeenth year after the deluge. His wife was called Sara, and his dwelling-place was at first in the country[1] of the Chaldæans. He then dwelt along with his father at Charræ. Being at this time spoken to by God, he left his country and his father, and taking with him Lot, the son of his brother, he came into the country of the Canaanites, and settled at a place named Sychem. Ere long, owing to the want of corn, he went into Egypt, and again returned. Lot, owing to the size of the household, parted from his uncle, that he might take advantage of more spacious territories in what was then a vacant region, and settled at Sodom. That town was infamous on account of its inhabitants, males forcing themselves upon males, and it is said on that account to have been hateful to God. At that period the kings of the neighboring peoples were in arms, though previously there had been no[2] war among man-

---

[1] After the LXX, as usual.
[1] Not of *birds* only, but other animals also. Gen. viii. 20.

[2] This is the *Nimrod* of the A. V.; he is called *Nebrod* by the LXX. We have, for the most part, given the proper names as they appear in the edition of Halm.
[3] Such is the form of the name as given by Halm, though *Abram* would be expected.
[1] The LXX has χώρᾳ, instead of *Ur*.
[2] A most improbable statement.

kind. But the kings of Sodom and Gomorrah and of the adjacent territories went forth to battle against those who were making war upon the regions round about, and being routed at the first onset, yielded the victory to the opposite side. Then Sodom was plundered and made a spoil of by the victorious enemy, while Lot was led into captivity. When Abraham heard of this, he speedily armed his servants, to the number of three hundred and eighteen, and, stripping of their spoils and arms the kings flushed with victory, he put them to flight. Then he was blessed by Melchisedech the priest, and gave him tithes of the spoil. He restored the remainder to those from whom it had been taken.

CHAPTER VI.

At the same time God spoke to Abraham, and promised that his seed was to be multiplied as the sand of the sea; and that his predicted seed would live in a land not his own, while his posterity would endure slavery in a hostile country for four hundred years, but would afterwards be restored to liberty. Then his name was changed, as well as that of his wife, by the addition of one letter; so that instead of Abram [1] he was called Abraham, and, instead of Sara, she was called Sarra. The mystery involved in this is by no means trifling, but it is not the part of this work to treat of it. At the same time, the law of circumcision was enjoined on Abraham, and he had by a maid-servant a son called Ishmael. Moreover, when he himself was a hundred years old, and his wife ninety, God promised that they should have a son Isaac, the Lord having come to him along with two angels. Then the angels being sent to Sodom, found Lot sitting in the gate of the city. He supposed them to be human beings, and welcomed them to share in his hospitality, and provided an entertainment for them in his house, but the wicked youth of the town demanded the new arrivals for impure purposes. Lot offered them his daughters in place of his guests, but they did not accept the offer, having a desire rather for things forbidden, and then Lot himself was laid hold of with vile designs. The angels, however, speedily rescued him from danger, by causing blindness to fall upon the eyes of these unchaste sinners. Then Lot, being informed by his guests that the town was to be destroyed, went away from it with his wife and daughters; but they were commanded not to look back upon it. His wife, however, not obeying this precept (in accordance with that evil tendency of human nature which renders it difficult to abstain from

things forbidden), turned back her eyes, and is said to have been at once changed into a monument. As for Sodom, it was burned to ashes by fire from heaven. And the daughters of Lot, imagining that the whole human race had perished, sought a union with their father while he was intoxicated, and hence sprung the race of Moab and Ammon.

CHAPTER VII.

Almost at the same time, when Abraham was now a hundred years old, his son Isaac was born. Then Sara expelled the maid-servant by whom Abraham had had a son; and she is said to have dwelt in the desert along with her son, and defended by the help of God. Not long after this, God tried the faith of Abraham, and required that his son Isaac should be sacrificed to him by his father. Abraham did not hesitate to offer him, and had already laid the lad upon the altar, and was drawing the sword to slay him, when a voice came from heaven commanding him to spare the young man; and a ram was found at hand to be for a victim. When the sacrifice was offered, God spoke to Abraham, and promised him those things which he had already said he would bestow. But Sara died in her one hundred and twenty-seventh year, and her body was, through the care of her husband, buried in Hebron, a town of the Canaanites, for Abraham was staying in that place. Then Abraham, seeing that his son Isaac was now of youthful [1] age, for he was, in fact, in his fortieth year, enjoined his servant to seek a wife for him, but only from that tribe and territory from which he himself was known to be descended. He was instructed, however, on finding the girl, to bring her into the land of the Canaanites, and not to suppose that Isaac would return into the country of his father for the purpose of obtaining a wife. In order that the servant might carry out those instructions zealously, Abraham administered an oath to him, while his hand rested on the thigh of his master. The servant accordingly set out for Mesopotamia, and came to the town of Nachor, the brother of Abraham. He entered into the house of Bathuel, the Syrian, son of Nachor; and having seen Rebecca, a beautiful virgin, the daughter of Nachor, he asked for her, and brought her to his master. After this, Abraham took a wife named Kethurah, who is called in the Chronicles his concubine, and begat children by her. But he left his possessions to Isaac, the son of Sara, while, at the same time, he distributed gifts to those whom he had begotten by his concubines; and thus they were separated from Isaac. Abraham

---

[1] In the Greek of the LXX. the name appears as *Abraam*, so that, as our author says, there is only a change of one letter.

[1] "juvenilis ætatis": the meaning is that he had ceased to be a mere *adolescens*, and had reached the flower of his age.

died after a life of a hundred and seventy-five years; and his body was laid in the tomb of Sara his wife.

CHAPTER VIII.

Now, Rebecca, having long been barren, at length, through the unceasing prayers of her husband to the Lord, brought forth twins about twenty years after the time of her marriage. These are said to have often leaped[1] in the womb of their mother; and it was announced by the answer of the Lord on this subject, that two peoples were foretold in these children, and that the elder would, in rank, be inferior to the younger. Well, the first that was born, bristling over with hair, was called Esau, while Jacob was the name given to the younger. At that time, a grievous famine had taken place. Under the pressure of this necessity, Isaac went to Gerar, to King Abimelech, having been warned by the Lord not to go down into Egypt. There he is promised the possession of the whole land, and is blessed, and having been greatly increased in cattle and every kind of substance, he is, under the influence of envy, driven out by the inhabitants. Thus expelled from that region, he sojourned by the well, known as "the well[2] of the oath." By and by, being advanced in years, and his eyesight being gone, as he made ready to bless his son Esau, Jacob through the counsel of his mother, Rebecca, presented himself to be blessed in the place of his brother. Thus Jacob is set before his brother as the one to be honored by the princes and the peoples. Esau, enraged by these occurrences, plotted the death of his brother. Jacob, owing to the fear thus excited, and by the advice of his mother, fled into Mesopotamia, having been urged by his father to take a wife of the house of Laban, Rebecca's brother: so great was their care, while they dwelt in a strange country, that their children should marry within their own kindred. Thus Jacob, setting out for Mesopotamia, is said in sleep to have had a vision of the Lord; and on that account regarding the place of his dream as sacred, he took a stone from it; and he vowed that, if he returned in prosperity, the name[3] of the pillar should be the "house of the Lord," and that he would devote to God the tithes of all the possessions he had gained. Then he betook himself to Laban, his mother's brother, and was kindly received by him to share in his hospitality as the acknowledged son of his sister.

___
[1] So in LXX.
[2] This is the meaning of the Hebrew word, *Beersheba*.
[3] "Titulum sibi domus Dei futurum": the rendering of the Hebrew original is here obviously faulty, and the words, as they stand, are scarcely intelligible.

CHAPTER IX.

LABAN had two daughters, Leah and Rachel; but Leah had tender eyes, while Rachel is said to have been beautiful. Jacob, captivated by her beauty, burned with love for the virgin, and, asking her in marriage from the father, gave himself up to a servitude of seven years. But when the time was fulfilled, Leah was foisted upon him, and he was subjected to another servitude of seven years, after which Rachel was given him. But we are told that she was long barren, while Leah was fruitful. Of the sons whom Jacob had by Leah, the following are the names: Reuben, Symeon, Levi, Judah, Issachar, Zebulon, and a daughter Dinah; while there were born to him by the handmaid of Leah, Gad and Asher, and by the handmaid of Rachel, Dan and Naphtali. But Rachel, after she had despaired of offspring, bare Joseph. Then Jacob, being desirous of returning to his father, when Laban his father-in-law had given him a portion of the flock as a reward for his service, and Jacob the son-in-law, thinking him not to be acting justly in that matter, while he [also] suspected deceit on his part, privately departed about the thirtieth year after his arrival. Rachel, without the knowledge of her husband, stole the idols[1] of her father, and on account of this injury Laban followed his son-in-law, but not finding his idols, returned, after being reconciled, having straitly charged his son-in-law not to take other wives in addition to his daughters. Then Jacob, going on his way, is said to have had a vision of angels and of the army[2] of the Lord. But, as he directed his journey past the region of Edom, which his brother Esau inhabited, suspecting the temper of Esau, he first sent messengers and gifts to try him. Then he went to meet his brother, but Jacob took care not to trust him beyond what he could help. On the day before the brothers were to meet, God, taking a human form, is said to have wrestled with Jacob. And when he had prevailed with God, still he was not ignorant that his adversary was no mere mortal; and therefore begged to be blessed by him. Then his name was changed by God, so that from Jacob he was called Israel. But when he, in turn, inquired of God the name of God, he was told that that should not be asked after because it was wonderful.[3] Moreover, from that wrestling, the breadth[4] of Jacob's thigh shrank.

___
[1] εἴδωλα is the Septuagint rendering of the Hebrew *Teraphim*. Perhaps the original word should simply be transliterated into English as has been done in the Revised Version.
[2] The rendering of the LXX.
[3] "Admirabile."
[4] "Latitudo": Vorstius says this refers to the broad bone, or broad nerve of the thigh.

CHAPTER X.

ISRAEL, therefore, avoiding the house of his brother, sent forward his company to Salem, a town of the Shechemites, and there he pitched his tent on a spot which he had purchased. Emor, a Chorræan prince, was the ruler of that town. His son Sychem defiled Dinah, the daughter of Jacob by Leah. Symeon and Levi, the brothers of Dinah, discovering this, cut off by a stratagem all those of the male sex in the town, and thus terribly avenged the injury done to their sister. The town was plundered by the sons of Jacob, and all the spoil carried off. Jacob is said to have been much displeased with these proceedings. Soon after being instructed by God, he went to Bethel, and there erected an altar to God. Then he fixed his tent in a part of the territory belonging to the tower[1] Gader. Rachel died in childbirth: the boy she bore was called Benjamin. Israel died at the age of one hundred and eighty years. Now, Esau was mighty in wealth, and had taken to himself wives of the nation of the Canaanites. I do not think that, in a work so concise as the present, I am called upon to mention his descendants, and, if any one is curious on the subject, he may turn to the original. After the death of his father, Jacob stayed on in the place where Isaac had lived. His other sons occasionally left him along with the flocks, for the sake of pasturage, but Joseph and the little Benjamin remained at home. Joseph was much beloved by his father, and on that account was hated by his brethren. There was this further cause for their aversion, that by frequent dreams of his it seemed to be indicated that he would be greater than all of them. Accordingly, having been sent by his father to inspect the flocks and pay a visit to his brothers, there seemed to them a fitting opportunity for doing him harm. For, on seeing their brother, they took counsel to slay him. But Reuben, whose mind shuddered at the contemplation of such a crime, opposing their plan, Joseph was let down into a well.[2] Afterwards, by the persuasions of Judah, they were brought to milder measures, and sold him to merchants, who were on their way to Egypt. And by them he was delivered to Petifra, a governor of Pharaoh.

CHAPTER XI.

ABOUT this same time, Judah, the son of Jacob, took in marriage Sava,[1] a woman of Canaan. By her he had three sons, — Her, Onan, and Sela. Her was allied by concubinage[2] to Thamar. On his death, Onan took his brother's wife ; and he is related to have been destroyed by God, because he spilled his seed upon the earth. Then Thamar, assuming the garb of a harlot, united with her brother-in-law, and bore him two sons. But when she brought them forth, there was this remarkable fact, that, when on one of the boys being born, the midwife had bound his hand with a scarlet thread to indicate which of them was born first, he, drawing back again into the womb of his mother, was born[3] the last boy of the two. The names of Fares and Zarah were given to the children. But Joseph, being kindly treated by the royal governor who had obtained him for a sum of money, and having been made manager of his house and family, had drawn the eyes of his master's wife upon himself through his remarkable beauty. And as she was madly laboring under that base passion, she made advances to him oftener than once, and when he would not yield to her desires, she disgraced him by the imputation of a false crime, and complained to her husband that he had made an attempt upon her virtue. Accordingly, Joseph was thrown into prison. There were in the same place of confinement two of the king's servants, who made known their dreams to Joseph, and he, interpreting these as bearing upon the future, declared that one of them would be put to death, and the other would be pardoned. And so it came to pass. Well, after the lapse of two years, the king also had a dream. And when this could not be explained by the wise men among the Egyptians, that servant of the king who was liberated from prison informs the king that Joseph was a wonderful interpreter of dreams. Accordingly, Joseph was brought out of prison, and interpreted to the king his dream, to this effect, that, for the next seven years, there would be the greatest fertility in the land ; but in those that followed, famine. The king being alarmed by this terror, and seeing that there was a divine spirit in Joseph, set him over the department of food-supply, and made him equal with himself in the government. Then Joseph, while corn was abundant throughout all Egypt, gathered together an immense quantity, and, by increasing the number of granaries, took measures against the future famine. At that time, the hope and safety of Egypt were placed in him alone. About the same period, Aseneh bore him two sons, Manasseh and Ephraim. He himself, when he received the chief power from the king, was thirty years old ; for he was sold by his brothers when he was seventeen years of age.

---

1 "In parte turris Gadir": this is a strange rendering of the Hebrew. The LXX has "beyond the tower Gader"; while the Revised English Version has "beyond the tower of Eder."
2 "Lacum."
1 Called *Shuah* in A. V.

2 Or perhaps, rather, *marriage* of a sort, as appears from what follows.
3 A different reading gives, "was born on the following day."

CHAPTER XII.

In the mean time, affairs having been well settled in Egypt to meet the famine, a grievous want of corn began to distress the world. Jacob, constrained by this necessity, sent his sons into Egypt, keeping only Benjamin with himself at home. Joseph, then, being at the head of affairs, and having complete power over the corn-supplies, his brothers come to him, and pay the same honor to him as to a king. He, when he saw them, craftily concealed his recognition of them, and accused them of having come as enemies, subtly to spy out the land. But he was annoyed that he did not see among them his brother Benjamin. Matters, then, are brought to this point, that they promised he should be present, specially that he might be asked whether they had entered Egypt for the purpose of spying out the land. In order to secure the fulfillment of this promise, Symeon was retained as hostage, while to them corn was given freely. Accordingly, they returned, bringing Benjamin with them as had been arranged. Then Joseph made himself known to his brothers, to the shame of these evil-deservers. Thus, he sent them home again, laden with corn, and presented with many gifts, forewarning them that there were still five years of famine to come, and advising them to come down with their father, their children, and their whole connections to Egypt. So Jacob went down to Egypt, to the great joy of the Egyptians and of the king himself, while he was tenderly welcomed by his son. That took place in the hundred and thirtieth year of the life of Jacob, and one thousand three hundred and sixty years [1] after the deluge. But from the time when Abraham settled in the land of the Canaanites, to that when Jacob entered Egypt, there are to be reckoned two hundred and fifteen years. After this, Jacob, in the seventeenth year of his residence in Egypt, suffering severely from illness, entreated Joseph to see his remains placed in the tomb. Then Joseph presented his sons to be blessed; [2] and when this had been done, but so that he set the younger before the elder as to the value of the blessing given, Jacob then blessed all his sons in order. He died at the age of one hundred and forty-seven years. His funeral was of a most imposing character, and Joseph laid his remains in the tomb of his fathers. He continued to treat his brothers with kindness, although, after the death of their father, they felt alarmed from a consciousness of the wrong they had done. Joseph himself died in his one hundred and tenth year.

CHAPTER XIII.

It is almost incredible to relate how the Hebrews who had come down into Egypt so soon increased in numbers, and filled Egypt with their numerous descendants. But on the death of the king, who kindly cherished them on account of the services of Joseph, they were kept down by the government of the succeeding kings. For both the heavy labor of building cities was laid upon them, and because their abounding numbers were now feared, lest some day they should secure their independence by arms, they were compelled by a royal edict to drown their newly-born male children. And no permission was granted to evade this cruel order. Well, at that time, the daughter of Pharaoh found an infant in the river, and caused it to be brought up as her own son, giving the boy the name of Moses. This Moses, when he had come to manhood, saw a Hebrew being assaulted by an Egyptian; and, filled with sorrow at the sight, he delivered his brother from injury, and killed the Egyptian with a stone. Soon after, fearing punishment on account of what he had done, he fled into the land of Midian, and, taking up his abode with Jothor the priest of that district, he received his daughter Sepphora in marriage, who bore him two sons, Gersam and Eliezer. At this epoch lived Job, who had acquired both the knowledge of God and all righteousness simply from the law [1] of nature. He was exceedingly rich, and on that account all the more illustrious, because he was neither corrupted by that wealth while it remained entire, nor perverted by it when it was lost. For, when, through the agency of the devil, he was stripped of his goods, deprived of his children, and finally covered in his own person with terrible boils, he could not be broken down, so as, from impatience of his sufferings, in any way, to commit sin. At length he obtained the reward of the divine approval, and being restored to health, he got back doubled all that he had lost.

CHAPTER XIV.

But the Hebrews, oppressed by the multiplied evils of slavery, directed their complaints to heaven, and cherished the hope of assistance from God. Then, as Moses was feeding his sheep, suddenly a bush appeared to him burning, but, what was surprising, the flames did it no harm. Astonished at such an extraordinary sight, he drew nearer to the bush, and immedi-

---

[1] The chronology of the LXX is, as usual, here followed.
[2] The original is, " quibus benedictis, cum tamen benedictionis merito majori minorem præposuisset, filios omnes benedictione lustravit."

[1] This somewhat remarkable statement is supported by the text of Halm, who reads, " lege naturæ." But other editions have " legem naturæ," and the meaning will then be " who had learned the law of nature, and the knowledge of God," &c.

ately God spoke to him in words to this effect, that he was the Lord of Abraham, Isaac, and Jacob, and that he desired that their descendants, who were kept down under the tyranny of the Egyptians, should be delivered from their sufferings, and that he, therefore, should go to the king of Egypt, and present himself as a leader for restoring them to liberty. When he hesitated, God strengthened him with power, and imparted to him the gift of working miracles. Thus Moses, going into Egypt, after he had first performed miracles in the presence of his own people, and having associated his brother Aaron with him, went to the king, declaring that he had been sent by God, and that he now told him in the words of God to let the Hebrew people go. But the king, affirming that he did not know the Lord, refused to obey the command addressed to him. And when Moses, in proof that the orders he issued were from God, changed his rod into a serpent,[1] and soon after converted all the water into blood, while he filled the whole land with frogs, as the Chaldæans were doing similar things, the king declared that the wonders performed by Moses were simply due to the arts of magic, and not to the power of God, until the land was covered with stinging insects brought over it, when the Chaldæans confessed that this was done by the divine majesty. Then the king, constrained by his sufferings, called to him Moses and Aaron, and gave the people liberty to depart, provided that the calamity brought upon the kingdom were removed. But, after the suffering was put an end to, his mind, having no control over itself, returned to its former state, and did not allow the Israelites to depart, as had been agreed upon. Finally, however, he was broken down and conquered by the ten plagues which were sent upon his person and his kingdom.

CHAPTER XV.

But on the day[1] before the people went out of Egypt, being as yet unacquainted with · dates, they were instructed by the command of God to acknowledge that month which was then passing by as the first of all months; and were told that the sacrifice of the day was to be solemnly and regularly offered in coming ages, so that, on the fourteenth day of the month, a lamb without blemish, one year old, should be slain as a victim, and that the door-posts should be sprinkled with its blood; that its flesh was wholly to be eaten, but not a bone of it was to be broken; that they should abstain from what was leavened for seven days, using only un-

leavened bread; and that they should hand down the observance to their posterity. Thus the people went forth rich, both by their own wealth, and still more by the spoils of Egypt. Their number had grown from those seventy-five[2] Hebrews, who had first gone down into Egypt, to six hundred thousand men. Now, there had elapsed from the time when Abraham first reached the land of the Canaanites a period of four hundred and thirty years, but from the deluge a period of five hundred and seventy-five[3] years. Well, as they went forth in haste, a pillar of cloud by day, and a pillar of fire by night, marched before them. But since, owing to the fact that the gulf of the Red Sea lay between, the way led by[4] the land of the Philistines, in order that an opportunity might not afterwards be offered to the Hebrews, shrinking from the desert, of returning into Egypt by a well-known road through a continuous land-journey, by the command of God they turned aside, and journeyed towards the Red Sea, where they stopped and pitched their camp. When it was announced to the king that the Hebrew people, through mistaking the road, had come to have the sea right before them, and that they had no means of escape since the deep would prevent them, vexed and furious that so many thousand men should escape from his kingdom and power, he hastily led forth his army. And already the arms, and standards, and the lines drawn up in the widespreading plains were visible, when, as the Hebrews were in a state of terror, and gazing up to heaven, Moses being so instructed by God, struck the sea with his rod, and divided it. Thus a road was opened to the people as on firm land, the waters giving way on both sides. Nor did the king of Egypt hesitate to follow the Israelites going forward, for he entered the sea where it had opened; and, as the waters speedily came together again, he, with all his host, was destroyed.

CHAPTER XVI.

Then Moses, exulting in the safety of his own people, and in the destruction of the enemy, by such a miracle,[1] sang a song of praise to God, and the whole multitude, both of males and females, took part in it. But, after they had entered the desert, and advanced a journey of three days, want of water distressed them; and, when it was found, it proved of no use on

---

[2] The Hebrew text has "seventy," but our author, as usual, follows the LXX.
[3] Again after the LXX.
[4] The text here is uncertain and obscure.
[1] "Virtute."

---

[1] "Draconem."
[1] Such is Halm's reading; another is simply "before."

account of its bitterness. And then for the first time the stubbornness of the impatient people showed itself, and burst forth against Moses; when, as instructed by God, he cast some wood into the waters, and its power was such that it rendered the taste of the fluid sweet. Thence advancing, the multitude found at Elim twelve fountains of waters, with seventy palm-trees, and there they encamped. Again the people, complaining of famine, heaped reproaches upon Moses, and longed for the slavery of Egypt, accompanied as it was with abundance to please their appetite, when a flock of quails was divinely sent, and filled the camp. Besides, on the following day, those who had gone forth from the camp perceived that the ground was covered with a sort of pods,[2] the appearance of which was like a coriander-seed of snowy whiteness, as we often see the earth in the winter months covered with the hoar-frost that has been spread over it. Then the people were informed, through Moses, that this bread had been sent them by the gift of God; that every one should gather in vessels prepared for the purpose only so much of it as would be sufficient for each, according to their number, during one day; but that on the sixth day they should gather double, because it was not lawful to collect it on the Sabbath. The people, however, as they were never prone to obedience, did not, in accordance with human nature, restrain their desires, providing in their stores not merely for one, but also for the following day. But that which was thus laid up swarmed with worms, while its fetid odor was dreadful, yet that which was laid up on the sixth day with a view to the Sabbath remained quite untainted. The Hebrews made use of this food for forty years; its taste was very like that of honey; and its name is handed down as being *manna.* Moreover, as an abiding witness to the divine gift, Moses is related to have laid up a full gomer of it in a golden vessel.

CHAPTER XVII.

THE people going on from thence, and being again tried with want of water, hardly restrained themselves from destroying their leader. Then Moses, under divine orders, striking with his rod the rock at the place which is called Horeb, brought forth an abundant supply of water. But when they came to Raphidin, the Amalekites destroyed numbers of the people by their attacks. Moses, leading out his men to battle, placed Joshua at the head of the army; and, in

company with Aaron and Hur, was himself simply to be a spectator of the fight, while, at the same time, for the purpose of praying to the Lord, he went up to the top of a mountain. But when the armies had met with doubtful issue, through the prayers of Moses, Joshua slew the enemy until nightfall. At the same time, Jothor, Moses' father-in-law, with his daughter Sepphora (who, having been married to Moses, had remained at home when her husband went into Egypt), and his children, having learned the things which were being done by Moses, came to him. By his advice Moses divided the people into various ranks; and, setting tribunes, centurions, and decurions[1] over them, thus furnished a mode of discipline and order to posterity. Jothor then returned to his own country, while the Israelites came on to Mount Sinai. There Moses was admonished by the Lord that the people should be sanctified, since they were to hearken to the words of God; and that was carefully seen to. But when God rested on the mountain, the air was shaken with the loud sounds of trumpets, and thick clouds rolled around with frequent flashes of lightning. But Moses and Aaron were on the top of the mountain beside the Lord, while the people stood around the bottom of the mountain. Thus a law was given, manifold and full of the words of God, and frequently repeated; but if any one is desirous of knowing particulars regarding it, he must consult the original, as we here only briefly touch upon it. "There shall not be," said God, "any strange gods among you, but ye shall worship me alone; thou shalt not make to thee any idol; thou shalt not take the name of thy God in vain; thou shalt do no work upon the Sabbath; honor thy father and thy mother; thou shalt not kill; thou shalt not commit adultery; thou shalt not steal; thou shalt not bear false witness against thy neighbor; thou shalt not covet anything belonging to thy neighbor."

CHAPTER XVIII.

THESE things being said by God, while the trumpets uttered their voices, the lamps blazed, and smoke covered the mountain, the people trembled from terror; and begged of Moses that God should speak to him alone, and that he would report to the people what he thus heard. Now, the commandments of God to Moses were as follows: A Hebrew servant purchased with money shall serve six years, and after that he shall be free; but his ear shall be bored, should he willingly remain in slavery. Whosoever slays a man shall be put to death;

---

[2] This is a somewhat strange description of the manna. Hornius remarks upon it that there may be a reference to the dew in which the Hebrews believed the manna to have been enveloped, but that seems a far-fetched explanation.

[1] These words denote what is expressed in the Greek, "rulers of thousands, of hundreds, and of tens."

he who does so unwittingly shall in due form be banished. Whosoever shall beat his father or his mother, and utter evil sayings against them, shall suffer death. If any one sell a Hebrew who has been stolen, he shall be put to death. If any one strike his own man-servant or maid-servant, and he or she die of the blow, he shall be put on his trial for doing so. If any one cause a woman[1] to miscarry, he shall be put to death. If any one knock out the eye or the tooth of his servant, that servant shall receive his liberty in due form. If a bull kill a man, it shall be stoned ; and if its master, knowing the vicious temper of the animal, did not take precautions in connection with it, he also shall be stoned, or shall redeem himself by a price as large as the accuser shall demand. If a bull kill a servant, money to the amount of thirty double-drachmas shall be paid to his master. If any one does not cover up a pit which has been dug, and an animal fall into that pit, he shall pay the price of the animal to its master. If a bull kill the bull of another man, the animal shall be sold, and the two masters shall share the price ; they shall also divide the animal that has been killed. But if a master, knowing the vicious temper of the bull, did not take precautions in connection with it, he shall give up the bull. If any one steals a calf, he shall restore five ; if he steals a sheep, the penalty shall be fourfold ; and if the animals be found alive in the hands of him who drove them off, he shall restore double. It shall be lawful to kill a thief by night, but not one by day. If the cattle of any one has eaten up the corn of another, the master of the cattle shall restore what has been destroyed. If a deposit disappears, he, in whose hands it was deposited, shall swear that he has not been guilty of any deceit. A thief who is caught shall pay double. An animal given in trust, if devoured by a wild beast, shall not be made good. If any one defile a virgin not yet be-trothed, he shall bestow a dowry on the girl, and thus take her to wife ; but, if the father of the girl shall refuse to give her in marriage, then the ravisher shall give her a dowry. If any one shall join himself to a beast, he shall be put to death. Let him who sacrifices to idols perish. The widow and orphan are not to be oppressed ; the poor debtor is not to be hardly treated, nor is usury to be demanded : the garment of the poor is not to be taken as a pledge. A ruler of the people is not to be evil spoken of. All the first-born are to be offered to God. Flesh taken from a wild beast is not to be eaten. Agreements to bear false witness, or for any evil purpose, are not to be made. Thou shalt not pass by any animal of thine enemy which has

strayed, but shalt bring it back. If you find an animal of your enemy fallen down under a burden, it will be your duty to raise it up. Thou shalt not slay the innocent and the righteous. Thou shalt not justify the wicked for rewards. Gifts are not to be accepted. A stranger is to be kindly treated. Work is to be done on six days : rest is to be taken on the Sabbath. The crops of the seventh year are not to be reaped, but are to be left for the poor and needy.

CHAPTER XIX.

MOSES reported these words of God to the people, and placed an altar of twelve stones at the foot of the mountain. Then he again as-cended the mountain on which the Lord had taken his place, bringing with him Aaron, Nabad, and seventy of the elders. But these were not able to look upon the Lord ; nevertheless, they saw the place[1] in which God stood, whose form is related to have been wonderful, and his splen-dor glorious. Now, Moses, having been called by God, entered the inner cloud which had gathered round about God, and is related to have remained there forty days and forty nights. During this time, he was taught in the words of God about building the tabernacle and the ark, and about the ritual of sacrifice — things which I, as they were obviously told at great length, have not thought proper to be in-serted in such a concise work as the present. But as Moses stayed away a long time, since he spent forty days in the presence of the Lord, the people, despairing of his return, compelled Aaron to construct images. Then, out of metals which had been melted together, there came forth the head of a calf. The people, unmindful of God, having offered sacrifices to this, and given themselves up to eating and drinking, God, looking upon these things, would in his righteous indignation, have destroyed the wicked people, had he not been entreated by Moses not to do so. But Moses, on his return, bringing down the two tables of stone which had been written by the hand of God, and seeing the people devoted to luxury and sacrilege, broke the tables, thinking the nation unworthy of having the law of the Lord delivered to them. He then called around himself the Levites, who had been assailed with many insults, and commanded them to smite the people with drawn swords. In this onset twenty-three thousand[2] men are said to have been slain. Then Moses set up the tabernacle outside the camp ; and, as often

---

[1] Some words seem to have been lost here.

[1] The Hebrew text is here different.
[2] Curiously enough, our author here reads, "twenty-three thou-sand," in opposition alike to the Greek and Hebrew text, both of which have "three thousand."

as he entered it, the pillar of cloud was observed to stand before the door; and God spoke, face to face, with Moses. But when Moses entreated that he might see the Lord in his peculiar majesty, he was answered that the form of God could not be seen by mortal eyes; yet it was allowed to see his back parts; and the tables which Moses had formerly broken were constructed afresh. And Moses is reported, during this conference with God, to have stayed forty days with the Lord. Moreover, when he descended from the mountain, bringing with him the tables, his face shone with so great brightness, that the people were not able to look upon him. It was arranged, therefore, that when he was to make known to them the commands of God, he covered his face with a veil, and thus spoke to the people in the words of God. In this part of the history an account is given [3] of the tabernacle, and the building of its inner parts. Which having been finished, the cloud descended from above, and so overshadowed the tabernacle that it prevented Moses himself from entering. These are the principal matters contained in the two books of Genesis and Exodus.

CHAPTER XX.

THEN follows the book of Leviticus, in which the precepts bearing upon sacrifice are set forth; commandments also are added to the law formerly given; and almost the whole is full of instructions connected with the priests. If any one wishes to become acquainted with these, he will obtain fuller information from that source. For we, keeping within the limits of the work undertaken, touch upon the history only. The tribe of Levi, then, being set apart for the priesthood, the rest of the tribes were numbered, and were found to amount to six hundred and three thousand five hundred persons.[1] When, therefore, the people made use of the manna for food, as we have related above, even amid so many and so great kindnesses of God, showing themselves, as ever, ungrateful, they longed after the worthless viands to which they had been accustomed in Egypt. Then the Lord brought an enormous supply of quails into the camp; and as they were eagerly tearing these to pieces, as soon as their lips touched the flesh, they perished. There was indeed on that day a great destruction in the camp, so that twenty and three thousand men are said to have died. Thus the people were punished by the very food which they desired. Thence the company went forward, and came to Faran; and Moses was

instructed by the Lord that the land was now near, the possession of which the Lord had promised them. Spies, accordingly, having been sent into it, they report that it was a land blessed with all abundance, but that the nations were powerful, and the towns fortified with immense walls. When this was made known to the people, fear seized the minds of all; and to such a pitch of wickedness did they come, that, despising the authority of Moses, they prepared to appoint for themselves a leader, under whose guidance they might return to Egypt. Then Joshua and Caleb, who had been of the number of the spies, rent their garments with tears, and implored the people not to believe the spies relating such terrors; for that they themselves had been with them, and had found nothing dreadful in that country; and that it behooved them to trust the promises of God, that these enemies would rather become their prey than prove their destruction. But that stiff-necked race, setting themselves against every good advice, rushed upon them to destroy them. And the Lord, angry on account of these things, exposed a part of the people to be slain by the enemy, while the spies were slain for having excited fear among the people.

CHAPTER XXI.

THERE followed the revolt of those, who, with Dathan and Abiron as leaders, endeavored to set themselves up against Moses and Aaron; but the earth, opening, swallowed them alive. And not long after, a revolt of the whole people arose against Moses and Aaron, so that they rushed into the tabernacle, which it was not lawful for any but the priests to enter. Then truly death mowed them down in heaps; and all would have perished in a moment, had not the Lord, appeased by the prayers of Moses, turned aside the disaster. Nevertheless, the number of those slain amounted to seven hundred and fourteen thousand.[1] And not long after, as had already often happened, a revolt of the people arose on account of the want of water. Then Moses, instructed by God to strike the rock with his rod, with a kind of trial now familiar to him, since he had already done that before, struck the rock once and again, and thus water flowed out of it. In regard, however, to this point, Moses is said to have been reproved by God, that, through want of faith, he did not bring out the water except by repeated blows; in fact, on account of this transgression, he did not enter the land promised to him, as I shall show farther on. Moses, then, moving away from that place, as he was preparing to lead his

---

[3] Halm here reads "referetur," but "refertur," another reading, seems preferable.
[1] The text here varies: we have followed Halm.

[1] "septingenti et xiiii milia."

company along by the borders of Edom, sent ambassadors to the king to beg liberty to pass by; for he thought it right to abstain from war on account of the connection by blood; for that nation was descended from Esau. But the king despised the suppliants, and refused them liberty to pass by, being ready to contend in arms. Then Moses directed his march towards the mountain, Or, keeping clear of the forbidden road, that he might not furnish any cause of war between those related by blood, and on that route he destroyed the king of the nation of the Canaanites. He smote also Seon the king of the Amorites, and possessed himself of all their towns: he conquered, too, Basan and Balac. He pitched his camp beyond Jordan, not far from Jericho. Then a battle took place against the Midianites, and they were conquered and subdued. Moses died, after he had ruled the people forty years in the wilderness. But the Hebrews are said to have remained in the wilderness for so long a time, with this view, until all those who had not believed the words of God perished. For, except Joshua and Caleb, not one of those who were more than twenty years old on leaving Egypt passed over Jordan. That Moses himself only saw the promised land, and did not reach it, is ascribed to his sin, because, at that time when he was ordered to strike the rock, and bring forth water, he doubted, even after so many proofs of his miraculous power. He died in the one hundred and twentieth year of his age. Nothing is known concerning the place of his burial.

CHAPTER XXII.

AFTER the death of Moses, the chief power passed into the hands of Joshua the son of Nun, for Moses had appointed him his successor, being a man very like himself in the good qualities which he displayed. Now, at the commencement of his rule, he sent messengers through the camp to instruct the people to make ready supplies of corn, and announces that they should march on the third day. But the river Jordan, a very powerful stream, hindered their crossing, because they did not have a supply of vessels for the occasion, and the stream could not be crossed by fords, as it was then rushing on in full flood. He, therefore, orders the ark to be carried forward by the priests, and that they should take their stand against the current of the river. On this being done, Jordan is said to have been divided, and thus the army was led over on dry ground. There was in these places a town called Jericho, fortified with very strong walls, and not easy to be taken, either by storm or blockade. But Joshua, putting his

trust in God, did not attack the city either by arms or force; he simply ordered the ark of God to be carried round the walls, while the priests walked before the ark, and sounded trumpets. But when the ark had been carried round seven times, the walls and the towers fell; and the city was plundered and burnt. Then Joshua is said to have addressed the Lord, and[1] to have called down a curse upon any one who should attempt to restore the town which had thus by divine help been demolished. Next, the army was led against Geth, and an ambuscade having been placed behind the city, Joshua, pretending fear, fled before the enemy. On seeing this, those who were in the town, opening the gates, began to press upon the enemy giving way. Thus, the men who were in ambush took the city, and all the inhabitants were slain, without one escaping: the king also was taken, and suffered capital punishment.

CHAPTER XXIII.

WHEN this became known to the kings of the neighboring nations, they made a warlike alliance to put down the Hebrews by arms. But the Gibeonites, a powerful nation with a wealthy city, spontaneously yielded to the Hebrews, promising to do what they were ordered, and were received under protection, while they were told to bring in wood and water. But their surrender had roused the resentment of the kings of the nearest cities. Accordingly, moving up their troops, they surround with a blockade their town, which was called Gabaoth. The townspeople, therefore, in their distress, send messengers to Joshua, that he would help them in their state of siege. Accordingly, he by a forced march came upon the enemy at unawares, and many thousands of them were completely destroyed. When day failed the victors, and it seemed that night would furnish protection to the vanquished, the Hebrew general, through the power of his faith, kept off the night, and the day continued, so that there was no means of escape for the enemy. Five kings who were taken suffered death. By the same attack, neighboring cities also were brought under the power of Joshua, and their kings were cut off. But as it was not my design, studious as I am of brevity, to follow out all these things in order, I only carefully observe this, that twenty-nine kingdoms were brought under the yoke of the Hebrews, and that their territory was distributed among eleven tribes, to man after man. For to the Levites, who had been set apart for the priesthood, no portion was given, in order that

[1] Some words have here been lost, but are conjecturally supplied in the text.

they might the more freely serve God. I desire not, in silence, to pass over the example thus set, but I would earnestly bring it forward as well worthy of being read by the ministers of the Church. For these seem to me not only unmindful of this precept, but even utterly ignorant of it — such a lust for possessing has, in this age, seized, like an incurable disease, upon their minds. They gape upon possessions; they cultivate estates; they repose upon gold; they buy and sell; they study gain by every possible means. And even, if any of them seem to have a better aim in life, neither possessing nor trading, still (what is much more disgraceful) remaining inactive, they look for gifts, and have corrupted the whole glory of life by their mercenary dispositions, while they present an appearance of sanctity, as if even that might be made a source of gain. But I have gone farther than I intended in expressing my loathing and disgust over the character of our times; and I hasten to return to the subject in hand. The vanquished territory, then, as I have already said, having been divided among the tribes, the Hebrews enjoyed profound peace; their neighbors, being terrified by war, did not venture to attempt hostilities against those distinguished by so many victories. At the same period died Joshua in the hundred and tenth year of his age. I do not express any definite opinion as to the length of time he ruled: the prevalent view, however, is, that he was at the head of the Hebrew affairs during twenty-seven years. If this were so, then three thousand eight hundred and eighty-four years had elapsed from the beginning of the world to his death.

CHAPTER XXIV.

AFTER the death of Joshua, the people acted without a leader. But a necessity of making war with the Canaanites having arisen, Judah was appointed as general in the war. Under his guidance, matters were successfully conducted: there was the greatest tranquillity both at home and abroad: the people ruled over the nations which had either been subdued or received under terms of surrender. Then, as almost always happens in a time of prosperity, becoming unmindful of morals and discipline, they began to contract marriages from among the conquered, and by and by to adopt foreign customs, yea, even in a sacrilegious manner to offer sacrifice to idols: so pernicious is all alliance with foreigners. God, foreseeing these things long before, had, by a wholesome precept enjoined upon the Hebrews to give over the conquered nations to utter destruction. But

the people, through lust for power, preferred (to their own ruin) to rule over those who were conquered. Accordingly, when, forsaking God, they worshiped idols, they were deprived of the divine assistance, and, being vanquished and subdued by the king of Mesopotamia, they paid the penalty of eight years' captivity, until, with Gothoniel as their leader, they were restored to liberty, and enjoyed independence for fifty years. Then again, corrupted by the evil effect of a lengthened peace, they began to sacrifice to idols. And speedily did retribution fall upon them thus sinning. Conquered by Eglon, king of the Moabites, they served him eighteen years, until, by a divine impulse, Aod slew the enemies' king by a stratagem, and, gathering together a hasty army, restored them to liberty by force of arms. The same man ruled the Hebrews in peace for forty years. To him Semigar succeeded, and he, engaging in battle with the Philistines,[1] secured a decisive victory. But again, the king of the Canaanites, Jabin by name, subdued the Hebrews who were once more serving idols, and exercised over them a grievous tyranny for twenty years, until Deborah, a woman, restored them to their former condition. They had to such a degree lost confidence in their generals, that they were now protected by means of a woman. But it is worthy of notice, that this form of deliverance was arranged beforehand, as a type of the Church, by whose aid captivity to the devil is escaped. The Hebrews were forty years under this leader or judge. And being again delivered over to the Midianites for their sins, they were kept under hard rule; and, being afflicted by the evils of slavery, they implored the divine help. Thus always when in prosperity they were unmindful of the kindnesses of heaven, and prayed to idols; but in adversity they cried to God. Wherefore, as often as I reflect that those people who lay under so many obligations to the goodness of God, being chastised with so many disasters when they sinned, and experiencing both the mercy and the severity of God, yet were by no means rendered better, and that, though they always obtained pardon for their transgressions, yet they as constantly sinned again after being pardoned, it can appear nothing wonderful that Christ when he came was not received by them, since already, from the beginning, they were found so often rebelling against the Lord. It is, in fact, far more wonderful that the clemency of God never failed them when they sinned, if only they called upon his name.[2]

---

[1] "Allophylos": lit. strangers.
[2] Many of the proper names occurring in this and other chapters are very different in form from those with which we are familiar in the O. T. But they have generally been given as they stand in the text of our author, and they can easily be identified by any readers who think it worth while to do so.

CHAPTER XXV.

ACCORDINGLY, when the Midianites, as we have related above, ruled over them, they turned to the Lord, imploring his wonted tender mercy, and obtained it. There was then among the Hebrews one Gideon by name, a righteous man, who was dear and acceptable to God. The angel stood by him as he was returning home from the harvest-field, and said unto him, "The Lord is with thee, thou mighty man of valor." But he in a humble voice complained that the Lord was not[1] with him, because captivity pressed sore upon his people, and he remembered with tears the miracles wrought by the Lord, who had brought them out of the land of Egypt. Then the angel said, "Go, in this spirit in which you have spoken, and deliver the people from captivity." But he declared that he could not, with his[2] feeble strength, since he was a man of very small importance, undertake such a heavy task. The angel, however, persisted in urging him not to doubt that those things could be done which the Lord said. So then, having offered sacrifice, and overthrown the altar which the Midianites had consecrated to the image of Baal, he went to his own people, and pitched his camp near the camp of the enemy. But the nation of the Amalekites had also joined themselves to the Midianites, while Gideon had not gathered more than an army of thirty-two thousand men. But before the battle began, God said to him that this was a larger number than he wished him to lead forth to the conflict; that, if he did make use of so many, the Hebrews would, in accordance with their usual wickedness, ascribe the result of the fight, not to God, but to their own bravery; he should therefore furnish an opportunity of leaving to those who desired to do so. When this was made known to the people, twenty and two thousand left the camp. But of the ten thousand who had remained, Gideon, as instructed by God, did not retain more than three hundred: the rest he dismissed from the field. Thus, entering the camp of the enemy in the middle watch of the night, and having ordered all his men to sound their trumpets, he caused great terror to the enemy; and no one had courage to resist; but they made off in a disgraceful flight wherever they could. The Hebrews, however, meeting them in every direction, cut the fugitives to pieces. Gideon pursued the kings beyond Jordan, and having captured them, gave them over to death. In that battle, a hundred and twenty thousand of the enemy are said to have been slain, and fifteen thousand captured. Then, by universal con-

sent, a proposal was made to Gideon that he should be king of the people. But he rejected this proposal, and preferred rather to live on equal terms with his fellow-citizens than to be their ruler. Having, therefore, escaped from their captivity, which had pressed upon the people for seven years, they now enjoyed peace for a period of forty years.

CHAPTER XXVI.

BUT on the death of Gideon, his son Abimelech, whose mother was a concubine, having slain his brothers with the concurrence of a multitude of wicked men, and especially by the help of the chief men among the Shechemites, took possession of the kingdom. And he, being harassed by civil strife, while he pressed hard upon his people by war, attempted to storm a certain tower, into which they, after losing the town, had betaken themselves by flight. But, as he approached the place without sufficient caution, he was slain by a stone which a woman threw, after holding the government for three years. To him succeeded Thola, who reigned two and twenty years. After him came Jair; and after he had held the chief place for a like period of twenty-two years, the people, forsaking God, gave themselves up to idols. On this account, the Israelites were subdued by the Philistines and Ammonites, and remained under their power for eighteen years. At the end of this period, they began to call upon God; but the divine answer to them was that they should rather invoke the aid of their images, for that he would no longer extend his mercy to those who had been so ungrateful. But they with tears confessed their fault, and implored forgiveness; while, throwing away their idols, and earnestly calling upon God, they obtained the divine compassion, though it had been at first refused. Accordingly, under Jephtha as general, they assembled in great numbers for the purpose of recovering their liberty by arms, having first sent ambassadors to King Ammon, begging that, content with his own territories, he should keep from warring against them. But he, far from declining battle, at once drew up his army. Then Jephtha, before the signal for battle was given, is said to have vowed that, if he obtained the victory, the person who first met him as he returned home, should be offered to God as a sacrifice. Accordingly, on the enemy being defeated, as Jephtha was returning home, his daughter met him, having joyfully gone forth with drums and dances to receive her father as a conqueror. Then Jephtha, being overwhelmed with sorrow, rent his clothes in his affliction, and made known to his daughter the stringent

---

1 " Non esse in se."
2 " Infractis viribus": Vorstius well remarks that " infractis " is here used with the sense of the simple " fractis."

obligation of his vow. But she, with a courage not to be expected from a woman, did not refuse to die; she only begged that her life might be spared for two months, that she might before dying have the opportunity of seeing the friends of her own age. This being done, she willingly returned to her father, and fulfilled the vow to God. Jephtha held the chief power for six years. To him Esebon succeeded, and having ruled in tranquillity for seven years, then died. After him, Elon the Zebulonite ruled for ten years, and Abdon also for eight years; but, as their rule was peaceful, they performed nothing which history might record.

CHAPTER XXVII.

THE Israelites yet again turned to idols; and, being deprived of the divine protection, were subdued by the Philistines, and paid the penalty of their unfaithfulness by forty years of captivity. At that time, Samson is related to have been born. His mother, after being long barren, had a vision of an angel, and was told to abstain from wine, and strong drink, and everything unclean; for that she should bear a son who would be the restorer of liberty to the Israelites, and their avenger upon their enemies. He, with unshorn locks, is said to have been possessed of marvelous strength, so much so that he tore to pieces with his hands a lion which met him in the way. He had a wife from the Philistines, and when she, in the absence of her husband, had entered into marriage with another, he, through indignation on account of his wife being thus taken from him, wrought destruction to her nation. Trusting in God and his own strength, he openly brought disaster on those hitherto victors. For, catching three hundred foxes, he tied burning torches to their tails, and sent them into the fields of the enemy. It so happened that at the time the harvest was ripe, and thus the fire easily caught, while the vines and olive-trees were burnt to ashes. He was thus seen to have avenged the injury done him in taking away his wife, by a great loss inflicted on the Philistines. And they, enraged at this disaster, destroyed by fire the woman who had been the cause of so great a calamity, along with her house and her father. But Samson, thinking himself as yet but poorly avenged, ceased not to harass the heathen race with all sorts of evil devices. Then the Jews, being compelled to it, handed him over as a prisoner to the Philistines; but, when thus handed over, he burst his bonds, and seizing the jaw-bone [1] of an ass, which chance offered him as a weapon, he slew a thousand of his enemies. And, as the heat of the day grew

violent, and he began to suffer from thirst, he called upon God, and water flowed forth from [2] the bone which he held in his hand.

CHAPTER XXVIII.

AT that time Samson ruled over the Hebrews, the Philistines having been subdued by the prowess of a single individual. They, therefore, sought his life by stratagem, not daring to assail him openly, and with this view they bribe his wife (whom he had received after what has been stated took place) to betray to them wherein the strength of her husband lay. She attacked him with female blandishments; and, after he had deceived her, and staved off her purpose for a long time, she persuaded him to tell that his strength was situated in his hair. Presently she cut off his hair stealthily while he was asleep, and thus delivered him up to the Philistines; for although he had often before been given up to them, they had not been able to hold him fast. Then they, having put out his eyes, bound him with fetters, and cast him into prison. But, in course of time, his hair which had been cut off began to grow again, and his strength to return with it. And now Samson, conscious of his recovered strength, was only waiting for an opportunity of righteous revenge. The Philistines had a custom on their festival days of producing Samson as if to make a public spectacle of him, while they mocked their illustrious captive. Accordingly, on a certain day, when they were making a feast in honor of their idol, they ordered Samson to be exhibited. Now, the temple, in which all the people and all the princes of the Philistines feasted, rested on two pillars of remarkable size; and Samson, when brought out, was placed between these pillars. Then he, having first called upon the Lord, seized his opportunity, and threw down the pillars. The whole multitude was overwhelmed in the ruins of the building, and Samson himself died along with his enemies, not without having avenged himself upon them, after he had ruled the Hebrews twenty years. To him Simmichar succeeded, of whom Scripture relates nothing more than that simple fact. For I do not find that even the time when his rule came to an end is mentioned, and I see that the people was for some time without a leader. Accordingly, when civil war arose against the tribe of Benjamin, Judah was chosen as a temporary leader in the war. But most of those who have written about these times note that his rule was only for a single year. On this account, many

---

[1] Simply "osse asini" in text.

[2] This is clearly the meaning, and Halm's punctuation, "invocato Deo ex osse, quod manu tenebat, aqua fluxit," is obviously wrong.

pass him by altogether, and place Eli, the priest, immediately after Samson. We shall leave that point doubtful, as one not positively ascertained.

CHAPTER XXIX.

ABOUT these times, civil war, as we have said, had broken out; and the following was the cause of the tumult. A certain Levite was on a journey along with his concubine, and, constrained by the approach of night, he took up his abode in the town of Gabaa, which was inhabited by men of Benjamin. A certain old man having kindly admitted him to hospitality, the young men of the town surrounded the guest, with the view of subjecting him to improper treatment. After being much chidden by the old man, and with difficulty dissuaded from their purpose, they at length received for their wanton sport the person of his concubine as a substitute for his own; and they thus spared the stranger, but abused her through the whole night, and only restored her on the following day. But she (whether from the injury their vile conduct had inflicted on her, or from shame, I do not venture to assert) died on again seeing[1] her husband. Then the Levite, in testimony of the horrible deed, divided her members into twelve parts, and distributed them among the twelve tribes, that indignation at such conduct might the more readily be excited in them all. And when this became known to all of them, the other eleven tribes entered into a warlike confederacy against Benjamin. In this war, Judah, as we have said, was the general. But they had bad success in the first two battles. At length, however, in the third, the Benjamites were conquered, and cut off to a man; thus the crime of a few was punished by the destruction of a multitude. These things also are contained in the Book of Judges: the Books of Kings follow. But to me who am following the succession of the years, and the order of the dates, the history does not appear marked by strict chronological accuracy. For, since after Samson as judge, there came Semigar, and a little later the history certifies that the people lived without judges, Eli the priest is related in the Books of Kings to have also been a judge,[2] but the Scripture has not stated how many years there were between Eli and Samson. I see that there was some portion of time between these two, which is left in obscurity. But, from the day of the death of Joshua up to the time at which Samson died, there are reckoned four hundred and eighteen years, and from the beginning of the world, four thousand

three hundred and three. Nevertheless, I am not ignorant that others differ from this reckoning of ours; but I am at the same time conscious that I have, not without some care, set forth the order of events in the successive years (a thing hitherto left in obscurity), until I have fallen upon these times, concerning which I confess that I have my doubts. Now I shall go on to what remains.

CHAPTER XXX.

THE Hebrews, then, as I have narrated above, were living according to their own will, without any judge or general. Eli was priest; and in his days Samuel was born. His father's name was Elchana, and his mother's, Anna. She having long been barren, is said, when she asked a child from God, to have vowed that, if it were a boy, it should be dedicated to God. Accordingly, having brought forth a boy, she delivered him to Eli the priest. By and by, when he had grown up, God spoke to him. He denounced wrath against Eli the priest on account of the life of his sons, who had made the priesthood of their father a means of gain to themselves, and exacted gifts from those who came to sacrifice; and, although their father is related to have often reproved them, yet his reproofs were too gentle to serve the purpose of discipline. Well, the Philistines made an incursion into Judæa, and were met by the Israelites. But the Hebrews, being beaten, prepare to renew the contest: they carry the ark of the Lord with them into battle, and the sons of the priests go forth with it, because he himself, being burdened with years, and afflicted with blindness, could not discharge that duty. But, when the ark was brought within sight of the enemy, terrified as if by the majesty of God's presence, they were ready to take to flight. But again recovering courage, and changing their minds (not without a divine impulse), they rush into battle with their whole strength. The Hebrews were conquered; the ark was taken; the sons of the priest fell. Eli, when the news of the calamity was brought to him, being overwhelmed with grief, breathed his last, after he had held the priesthood for twenty[1] years.

CHAPTER XXXI.

THE Philistines, victorious in this prosperous battle, brought the ark of God, which had fallen into their hands, into the temple of Dagon in the town of Azotus. But the image, dedicated to a demon, fell down when the ark was brought in there; and, on their setting the idol up again

---

[1] A clear mistake of memory in our author. The whole narrative is confused.
[2] The meaning is here doubtful.

[1] The Hebrew text has *forty* years.

in its place, in the following night it was torn in pieces. Then mice, springing up throughout all the country, caused by their venomous bites the death of many thousand persons.[1] The men of Azotus, constrained by this source of suffering, in order to escape the calamity, removed the ark to Gath. But the people there being afflicted with the same evils, conveyed the ark to Ascalon. The inhabitants, however, of that place, the chief men of the nation having been called together, formed the design of sending back the ark to the Hebrews. Thus, in accordance with the opinion of the chiefs, and augurs, and priests, it was placed upon a cart, and sent back with many gifts. This remarkable thing then happened, that when they had yoked heifers to the conveyance, and had retained their calves at home, these cattle took their course, without any guide, towards Judæa, and showed no desire of returning, from affection toward their young left behind. The rulers of the Philistines, who had followed the ark into the territory of the Hebrews, were so struck by the marvelousness of this occurrence that they performed a religious service. But the Jews, when they saw the ark brought back, vied with each other in joyously rushing forth from the town of Betsamis to meet it, and in hurrying, exulting, and returning thanks to God. Presently, the Levites, whose business it was, perform a sacrifice to God, and offer those heifers which had brought the ark. But the ark could not be kept in the town which I have named above, and thus severe illness fell, by the appointment of God, upon the whole city. The ark was then transferred to the town of Cariathiarim,[2] and there it remained twenty years.

CHAPTER XXXII.

At this time, Samuel the priest[1] ruled over the Hebrews; and there being a cessation of all war, the people lived in peace. But this tranquillity was disturbed by an invasion of the Philistines, and all ranks were in a state of terror from their consciousness of guilt. Samuel, having first offered sacrifice, and trusting in God, led his men out to battle, and the enemy being routed at the first onset, victory declared for the Hebrews. But when the fear of the enemy was thus removed, and affairs were now prosperous and peaceful, the people, changing their views for the worse, after the manner of the mob, who are always weary of what they have, and long for things of which they have had no experience, expressed a desire for the kingly name — a name greatly disliked by almost all free nations. Yes, with an example of madness certainly very remarkable, they now preferred to exchange liberty for slavery. They, therefore, come in great numbers to Samuel, in order that, as he himself was now an old man, he might make for them a king. But he endeavored in a useful address, quietly to deter the people from their insane desire; he set forth the tyranny and haughty rule of kings, while he extolled liberty, and denounced slavery; finally, he threatened them with the divine wrath, if they should show themselves men so corrupt in mind as that, when having God as their king, they should demand for themselves a king from among men. Having spoken these and other words of a like nature to no purpose, finding that the people persisted in the determination, he consulted God. And God, moved by the madness of that insane nation, replied that nothing was to be refused to them asking against their own interests.

CHAPTER XXXIII.

Accordingly, Saul, having been first anointed by Samuel with the sacerdotal oil, was appointed king. He was of the tribe of Benjamin, and his father's name was Kish. He was modest in mind, and of a singularly handsome figure, so that the dignity of his person worthily corresponded to the royal dignity. But in the beginning of his reign, some portion of the people had revolted from him, refusing to acknowledge his authority, and had joined themselves to the Ammonites. Saul, however, energetically wreaked his vengeance on these people; the enemy were conquered, and pardon was granted to the Hebrews. Then Saul is said to have been anointed by Samuel a second time. Next, a bloody war arose by an invasion of the Philistines; and Saul had appointed Gilgal as the place where his army was to assemble. As they waited there seven days for Samuel, that he might offer sacrifice to God, the people gradually dropped away owing to his delay, and the king, with unlawful presumption, presented a burnt-offering, thus taking upon him the duty of a priest. For this he was severely rebuked by Samuel, and acknowledged his sin with a penitence that was too late. For, as a result of the king's sin, fear had pervaded the whole army. The camp of the enemy lying at no great distance showed them how actual the danger was, and no one had the courage to think of going forth to battle: most had betaken themselves to the marshes.[1] For besides the want of courage on the part of those who

---

[1] No reference to this occurs in the Hebrew text, but it is found in the Greek, and is also noticed by Josephus. See the LXX. 1 Sam. v. 6, and Josephus, *Antiq.* vi. 1.
[2] Called *Kirjath-jearim* in the English version.
[1] Samuel was a Levite, but not a priest.

[1] The text here is very uncertain; we have followed the reading of Halm, "lamas," but others have "lacrimas" or "latebras."

felt that God was alienated from them on account of the king's sin, the army was in the greatest want of iron weapons; so much so that nobody, except Saul and Jonathan his son, is said to have possessed either sword or spear. For the Philistines, as conquerors in the former wars, had deprived the Hebrews of the use of arms,[2] and no one had had the power of forging any weapon of war, or even making any implement for rural purposes. In these circumstances, Jonathan, with an audacious design, and with his armor-bearer as his only companion, entered the camp of the enemy, and having slain about twenty of them, spread a terror throughout the whole army. And then, through the appointment of God, betaking themselves to flight, they neither carried out orders nor kept their ranks, but placed all the hope of safety in flight. Saul, perceiving this, hastily drew forth his men, and pursuing the fugitives, obtained a victory. The king is said on that day to have issued a proclamation that no one should help himself to food until the enemy were destroyed. But Jonathan, knowing nothing of this prohibition, found a honey-comb, and, dipping the point of his weapon in it, ate up the honey. When that became known to the king through the anger of God which followed, he ordered his son to be put to death. But by the help of the people, he was saved from destruction. At that time, Samuel, being instructed by God, went to the king, and told him in the words of God to make war on the nation of the Amalekites, who had of old hindered the Hebrews when they were coming out of Egypt; and the prohibition was added that they should not covet any of the spoils of the conquered. Accordingly, an army was led into the territory of the enemy, the king was taken, and the nation subdued. But Saul, unable to resist the magnitude of the spoil, and unmindful of the divine injunctions, ordered the booty to be saved and gathered together.

CHAPTER XXXIV.

GOD, displeased with what had been done, spoke to Samuel, saying that he repented that he had made Saul king. The priest reports what he had heard to the king. And ere long, being instructed by God, he anointed David with the royal oil, while he was as yet only a little boy[1] living under the care of his father, and acting as a shepherd, while he was accustomed often to play upon the harp. For this reason, he was taken afterwards by Saul, and

reckoned among the servants of the king. And the Philistines and Hebrews being at this time hotly engaged in war, as the armies were stationed opposite to each other, a certain man of the Philistines named Goliath, a man of marvelous size and strength, passing along the ranks of his countrymen, cast insults, in the fiercest terms, upon the enemy, and challenged any one to engage in single combat with him. Then the king promised a great reward and his daughter in marriage to any one who should bring home the spoils of that boaster; but no one out of so great a multitude ventured to make the attempt. In these circumstances, though still a youth,[2] David offered himself for the contest, and rejecting the arms by which his yet tender age was weighed down, simply with a staff and five stones which he had taken, advanced to the battle. And by the first blow, having discharged one of the stones from a sling, he overthrew the Philistine; then he cut off the head of his conquered foe, carried off his spoils, and afterwards laid up his sword in the temple. In the meanwhile, all the Philistines, turning to flight, yielded the victory to the Hebrews. But the great favor shown to David as they were returning from the battle excited the envy of the king. Fearing, however, that if he put to death one so beloved by all, that might give rise to hatred against himself and prove disastrous, he resolved, under an appearance of doing him honor, to expose him to danger. First then he made him a captain, that he might be charged with the affairs of war; and next, although he had promised him his daughter, he broke his word, and gave her to another. Ere long, a younger daughter of the king, Melchol by name, fell violently in love with David. Accordingly, Saul sets before David as the condition of obtaining her in marriage the following proposal: that if he should bring in a hundred foreskins of the enemy, the royal maiden would be given him in marriage; for he hoped that the youth, venturing on so great dangers, would probably perish. But the result proved very different from what he imagined, for David, according to the proposal made to him, speedily brought in a hundred foreskins of the Philistines; and thus he obtained the daughter of the king in marriage.

CHAPTER XXXV.

THE hatred of the king towards him increased daily, under the influence of jealousy, for the wicked always persecute the good. He, therefore, commanded his servants and Jonathan his son, to prepare snares against his life. But Jonathan had even from the first had a great

---

[2] " Armorum " is here supplied, but some prefer " cotis," according to 1 Sam. xiii. 20.

[1] This is a mistake: David was undoubtedly then a grown-up young man.

[2] " Puer ": another mistake.

regard and affection for David ; and therefore the king, being taken to task by his son, suppressed the cruel order he had given. But the wicked are not long good. For, when Saul was afflicted by a spirit of error, and David stood by him, soothing him with the harp under his trouble, Saul tried to pierce him with a spear, and would have done so, had not he rapidly evaded the deadly blow. From this time forth, the king no longer secretly but openly sought to compass his death ; and David no longer trusted himself in his power. He fled, and first betook himself to Samuel, then to Abimelech, and finally fled to the king of Moab. By-and-by, under the instructions of the prophet Gad, he returned into the land of Judah, and there ran in danger of his life. At that time, Saul slew Abimelech the priest because he had received David ; and when none of the king's servants ventured to lay hands upon the priest, Doeg, the Syrian, fulfilled the cruel duty. After that, David made for the desert. Thither Saul also followed him, but his efforts at his destruction were in vain, for God protected him. There was a cave in the desert, opening with a vast recess. David had thrown himself into the inner parts of this cave. Saul, not knowing that he was there, had gone into it for the purpose of taking[1] bodily refreshment, and there, overcome by sleep, he was resting. When David perceived this, although all urged him to avail himself of the opportunity, he abstained from slaying the king, and simply took away his mantle. Presently going out, he addressed the king from a safe position behind, recounting the services he had done him, how often he had exposed his life to peril for the sake of the kingdom, and how last of all, he had not, on the present occasion, sought to kill him when he was given over to him by God. Upon hearing these things, Saul confessed his fault, entreated pardon, shed tears, extolled the piety of David, and blamed his own wickedness, while he addressed David as king and son. He was so much changed from his former ferocious character, that no one could now have thought he would make any further attempt against his son-in-law. But David, who had thoroughly[2] tested and known his evil disposition, did not think it safe to put himself in the power of the king, and kept himself within the desert. Saul, almost mad with rage, because he was unable to capture his son-in-law, gave in marriage to one Faltim his daughter Melchol, who, as we have related above, had been married to David. David fled to the Philistines.

---

[1] " Reficiendi corporis gratia " : different from the Hebrew text.
[2] The text is uncertain, but the meaning is clear.

CHAPTER XXXVI.

At that time Samuel died. Saul, when the Philistines made war upon him, consulted God, and no answer was returned to him. Then, by means of a woman whose entrails a spirit of error[1] had filled, he called up and consulted Samuel. Saul was informed by him that on the following day he with his sons, being overcome by the Philistines, would fall in the battle. The Philistines, accordingly, having pitched their camp on the enemy's territory, drew up their army in battle array on the following day, David, however, being sent away from the camp, because they did not believe that he would be faithful to them against his own people. But the battle taking place, the Hebrews were routed and the sons of the king fell ; Saul, having sunk down from his horse, that he might not be taken alive by the enemy, fell on his own sword. We do not find any certain statements as to the length of his reign, unless that he is said in the Acts of the Apostles to have reigned forty years. As to this, however, I am inclined to think that Paul, who made the statement in his preaching, then meant to include also the years of Samuel under the length of that king's reign.[2] Most of those, however, who have written about these times, remark that he reigned thirty years. I can, by no means, agree with this opinion, for at the time when the ark of God was transferred to the town of Cariathiarim, Saul had not yet begun to reign, and it is related that the ark was removed by David the king out of that town after it had been there twenty years. Therefore, since Saul reigned and died within that period, he must have held the government only for a very brief space of time. We find the same obscurity concerning the times of Samuel, who, having been born under the priesthood of Eli, is related, when very old, to have fulfilled the duties of a priest. By some, however, who have written about these times (for the sacred history has recorded almost nothing about his years),[3] but by most he is said to have ruled the people seventy years. I have, however, been unable to discover what authority there is for this assumption. Amid such variety of error, we have followed the account of the Chronicles,[4] because we think that it was taken (as said above) from the Acts of the Apostles, and we repeat that Samuel and Saul together held the government for forty years.

---

[1] The witch of Endor seems here to be referred to as if she had practised ventriloquism, this being regarded as a form of demoniacal possession.
[2] See Alford on Acts xiii. 21.
[3] Halm here inserts the usual mark of a *lacuna* in the text : others omit the words " a plerisque autem."
[4] He here specially refers to the well-known *Chronicles* of Eusebius, which were translated into Latin, and supplemented by Saint Jerome.

CHAPTER XXXVII.

SAUL having thus been cut off, David, when the news of his death was brought to him in the land of the Philistines, is related to have wept, and to have given a marvelous proof of his affection. He then betook himself to Hebron, a town of Judæa ; and, being there again anointed with the royal oil, received the title of king. But Abenner, who had been master of the host of King Saul, despised David, and made Isbaal king, the son of King Saul. Various battles then took place between the generals of the kings. Abenner was generally routed ; yet in his flight he cut off the brother of Joab, who had the command of the army on the side of David. Joab, on account of the sorrow he felt for this, afterwards, when Abenner had surrendered to King David, ordered him to be murdered, not without regret on the part of the king, whose honor he had thus tarnished. At the same time, almost all the older men of the Hebrews conferred on him by public consent the sovereignty of the whole nation ; for during seven years he had reigned only in Hebron. Thus, he was anointed king for the third time, being about thirty years of age. He repulsed in successful battles the Philistines making inroads upon his kingdom. And at that time, he transferred to Zion the ark of God, which, as I have said above, was in the town of Cariathiarim. And when he had formed the intention of building a temple to God, the divine answer was given him to the effect, that that was reserved for his son. He then conquered the Philistines in war, subjugated the Moabites, and subdued Syria, imposing tribute upon it. He brought back with him an enormous amount of booty in gold and brass. Next, a war arose against the Ammonites on account of the injury which had been done by their king, Annon. And when the Syrians again rebelled, having formed a confederacy for war with the Ammonites, David intrusted the chief command of the war to Joab, the master of his host, and he himself remained in Jerusalem far from the scene of strife.

CHAPTER XXXVIII.

AT this time, he knew in a guilty way Bersabe, a woman of remarkable beauty. She is said to have been the wife of a certain man called Uriah, who was then in the camp. David caused him to be slain by exposing him to the enemy at a dangerous place in the battle. In this way, he added to the number of his wives the woman who was now free from the bond of marriage, but who was already pregnant through adultery.

Then David, after being severely reproved by Nathan the prophet, although he confessed his sin, did not escape the punishment of God. For he lost in a few days the son who was born from the clandestine connection, and many terrible things happened in respect to his house and family. At last his son Absalom lifted impious arms against his father, with the desire of driving him from the throne. Joab encountered him in the field of battle, and the king entreated him to spare the young man when conquered ; but he, disregarding this command, avenged with the sword his parricidal attempts. That victory is said to have been a mournful one to the king : so great was his natural affection that he wished even his parricidal son to be forgiven. This war seemed hardly finished when another arose, under a certain general called Sabæa, who had stirred up all the wicked to arms. But the whole commotion was speedily checked by the death of the leader. David then engaged in several battles against the Philistines with favorable results ; and all being subdued by war, both foreign and home disturbances having been brought to accord, he possessed in peace a most flourishing kingdom. Then a sudden desire seized him of numbering the people, in order to ascertain the strength of his empire ; and accordingly they were numbered by Joab, the master of the host, and were found to amount to one million three hundred thousand [1] citizens. David soon regretted and repented of this proceeding, and implored pardon of God for having lifted up his thoughts to this, that he should reckon the power of his kingdom rather by the multitude of his subjects than by the divine favor. Accordingly, an angel was sent to him to reveal to him a threefold punishment, and to give him the power of choosing either one or another. Well, when a famine for three years was set before him, and flight before his enemies for three months, and a pestilence for three days, shunning both flight and famine, he made choice of pestilence, and, almost in a moment of time, seventy thousand men perished. Then David, beholding the angel by whose right hand the people were overthrown, implored pardon, and offered himself singly to punishment instead of all, saying that he deserved destruction inasmuch as it was he who had sinned. Thus, the punishment of the people was turned aside ; and David built an altar to God on the spot where he had beheld the angel. After this, having become infirm through years and illness, he appointed Solomon, who had been born to him by Bersabe, the wife of Uriah, his successor in the kingdom. He, having been anointed with the royal oil by

---

[1] As is often the case with respect to numbers, there are discrepancies in the various accounts given of this census.

Sadoc the priest, received the title of king, while his father was still alive. David died, after he had reigned forty years.

CHAPTER XXXIX.

SOLOMON in the beginning of his reign surrounded the city with a wall. To him while asleep God appeared standing by him, and gave him the choice of whatever things he desired. But he asked that nothing more than wisdom should be granted him, deeming all other things of little value. Accordingly, when he arose from sleep, taking his stand before the sanctuary of God, he gave a proof of the wisdom which had been bestowed upon him by God. For two women who dwelt in one house, having given birth to male children at the same time, and one of these having died in the night three days afterwards, the mother of the dead child, while the other woman slept, insidiously substituted her child, and took away the living one. Then there arose an altercation between them, and the matter was at length brought before the king. As no witness was forthcoming, it was a difficult matter to give a judgment between both denying guilt. Then Solomon, in the exercise of his gift of divine wisdom, ordered the child to be slain, and its body to be divided between the two doubtful claimants. Well, when one of them acquiesced in this judgment, but the other wished rather to give up the boy than that he should be cut in pieces, Solomon, concluding from the feeling displayed by this woman that she was the true mother, adjudged the child to her. The bystanders could not repress their admiration at this decision, since he had in such a way brought out the hidden truth by his sagacity. Accordingly, the kings of the neighboring nations, out of admiration for his ability and wisdom, courted his friendship and alliance, being prepared to carry out his commands.

CHAPTER XL.

TRUSTING in these resources, Solomon set about erecting a temple of immense size to God, funds for the purpose having been got together during three years, and laid the foundation of it about the fourth year of his reign. This was about the five hundred and eighty-eighth year after the departure of the Hebrews from Egypt, although in the third Book of Kings the years are reckoned at four hundred and forty.[1] This is by no means accurate ; for it would have been more likely that, in the order of dates I have given above, I should perhaps reckon fewer years than more. But I do not doubt that the truth had been falsified by the carelessness of copyists, especially since so many ages intervened, rather than that the sacred[2] writer erred. In the same way, in the case of this little work of ours, we believe it will happen that, through the negligence of transcribers, those things which have been put together, not without care on our part, should be corrupted. Well, then, Solomon finished his work of building the temple in the twentieth year from its commencement. Then, having offered sacrifice in that place, as well as uttered a prayer, by which he blessed the people and the temple, God spoke to him, declaring that, if at any time they should sin and forsake God, their temple should be razed to the ground. We see that this has a long time ago been fulfilled, and in due time we shall set forth the connected order of events. In the meantime, Solomon abounded in wealth, and was, in fact, the richest of all the kings that ever lived. But, as always takes place in such circumstances, he sunk from wealth into luxury and vice, forming marriages (in spite of the prohibition of God) with foreign women, until he had seven hundred wives, and three hundred concubines. As a consequence, he set up idols for them, after the manner of their nations, to which they might offer sacrifice. God, turned away from him by such doings, reproved him sharply, and made known to him as a punishment, that the greater part of his kingdom would be taken from his son, and given to a servant. And that happened accordingly.

CHAPTER XLI.

FOR, on the death of Solomon in the fortieth year of his reign, Roboam his son having succeeded to the throne of his father in the sixteenth year of his age, a portion of the people, taking offense, revolted from him. For, having asked that the very heavy tribute which Solomon had imposed upon them might be lessened, he rejected the entreaties of these suppliants, and thus alienated from him the favor of the whole people. Accordingly, by universal consent, the government was bestowed on Jeroboam. He, sprung from a family of middle rank, had for some time been in the service of Solomon. But when the king found that the sovereignty of the Hebrews had been promised to him by a response of the prophet Achia, he had resolved privately to cut him off. Jeroboam, under the influence of this fear, fled into Egypt, and there married a wife of the royal family. But, when at length he heard of the death of Solomon, he

---

[1] Here, again, there is much discrepancy in the accounts.

[2] " Propheta."

returned to his native land, and, by the wish of the people, as we have said above, he assumed the government. Two tribes, however, Judah and Benjamin, had remained under the sway of Roboam; and from these he got ready an army of thirty thousand men. But when the two hosts advanced, the people were instructed by the words of God to abstain from fighting, for that Jeroboam had received the kingdom by divine appointment. Thus the army disdained the command of the king, and dispersed, while the power of Jeroboam was increased. But, since Roboam held Jerusalem, where the people had been accustomed to offer sacrifice to God in the temple built by Solomon, Jeroboam, fearing lest their religious feelings might alienate the people from him, resolved to fill their minds with superstition. Accordingly, he set up one golden calf at Bethel, and another at Dan, to which the people might offer sacrifice; and, passing by the tribe of Levi, he appointed priests from among the people. But censure followed this guilt so hateful to God. Frequent battles then took place between the kings, and so they retained their respective kingdoms on doubtful conditions. Roboam died at the close of the seventeenth year of his reign.

CHAPTER XLII.

In his room Abiud his son held the kingdom at Jerusalem for six years, although he is said in the Chronicles[1] to have reigned three years. Asab his son succeeded him, being the fifth from David, as he was his great-great-grandson. He was a pious worshiper of God; for, destroying the altars and the groves of the idols, he removed the traces of his father's faithlessness. He formed an alliance with the king of Syria, and by his help inflicted much loss on the kingdom of Jeroboam, which was then held by his son, and often, after conquering the enemy, carried off spoil as the result of victory. After forty-one years he died, afflicted with disease in his feet. To him sin of a three-fold kind is ascribed; first, that he trusted too much to his alliance with the king of Syria; secondly, that he cast into prison a prophet of God who rebuked him for this; and thirdly, that, when suffering from disease in his feet, he sought a remedy, not from God, but from the physicians. In the beginning of his reign died Jeroboam, king of the ten tribes, and left his throne to his son Nabath. He, from his wicked works, and, both by his own and his[2] father's doings, hateful to God, did not possess the kingdom more than two years, and his children, as being unworthy,

were deprived[3] of the government. He had for his successor Baasa, the son of Achia, and he proved himself equally estranged from God. He died in the twenty-sixth year of his reign: and his power passed to Ela his son, but was not retained more than two years. For Zambri, leader of his cavalry, killed him at a banquet, and seized the kingdom, — a man equally odious to God and men. A portion of the people revolted from him, and the royal power was conferred on one Thamnis. But Zambri reigned before him seven years, and at the same time with him twelve years. And, on the death of Asab, Josaphat his son began to reign over part of the tribe of Judah, a man deservedly famous for his pious virtues. He lived at peace with Zambri; and he died, after a reign of twenty-five years.

CHAPTER XLIII.

In the time of his reign, Ahab, the son of Ambri, was king of the ten tribes, impious above all against God. For having taken in marriage Jezebel, the daughter of Basa, king of Sidon, he erected an altar and groves to the idol Bahal, and slew the prophets of God. At this time, Elijah the prophet by prayer shut up heaven, that it should not give any rain to the earth, and revealed that to the king, in order that he, in his impiety, might know himself to be the cause of the evil. The waters of heaven, therefore, being restrained, and since the whole country, burned up by the heat of the sun, did not furnish food either for man or beast, the prophet had even exposed himself to the side of perishing from hunger. At that time, when he betook himself to the desert, he depended for life on the ravens furnishing him with food, while a neighboring rivulet furnished him with water, until it was dried up. Then, being instructed by God, he went to the town of Saraptæ, and turned aside to lodge with a widow-woman. And when, in his hunger, he begged food from her, she complained that she had only a handful of meal and a little oil, on the consumption of which she expected death along with her children.[1] But when Elijah promised in the words of God that neither should the meal lessen in the barrel nor the oil in the vessel, the woman did not hesitate to believe the prophet demanding faith, and obtained[2] the fulfillment of what was promised, since by daily increase as much

---

[1] The *Chronicon* of Eusebius is referred to.
[2] Many editors here read "maternis," instead of "paternis."

[3] It is remarkable, as Hornius has observed after Ligonius, that, while in the kingdom of Judah the sovereignty remained in the same family, in the kingdom of Ephraim the scepter was hardly ever transmitted to son or grandson.
[1] "Cum filiis": after the Greek; the Hebrew text speaks of only one son.
[2] Such seems clearly to be the meaning of the somewhat strange phrase, "promissorum fidem consecuta est."

was added as was day by day taken away. At the same time, Elijah restored to life the dead son of the same widow. Then, by the command of God, he went to the king, and having reproved his impiety, he ordered all the people to be gathered together to himself. When these had hastily assembled, the priests of the idols and of the groves to the number of about four hundred and fifty, were also summoned. Then there arose a dispute between them, Elijah setting forth the honor of God, while they upheld their own superstitions. At length they agreed that a trial should be made to this effect, that, if fire sent down from heaven should consume the slain victim of either of them, that religion should be accepted as the true one which performed the miracle. Accordingly, the priests, having slain a calf, began to call upon the idol Bahal ; and, after wasting their invocations to no purpose, they tacitly acknowledged the helplessness of their God. Then Elijah mocked them and said, " Cry aloud more vehemently, lest perchance he sleeps, and that thus you may rouse him from the slumber in which he is sunk." The wretched men could do nothing but shudder and mutter to themselves, but still they waited to see what Elijah would do. Well, he slew a calf and laid it upon the altar, having first of all filled the sacred place with water ; and then, calling upon the name of the Lord, fire fell from heaven in the sight of all, and consumed alike the water and the victim. Then truly the people, casting themselves upon the earth, confessed God and execrated the idols ; while finally, by the command of Elijah, the impious priests were seized, and, being brought down to the brook, were there slain. The prophet followed the king as he returned from that place ; but as Jezebel, the wife of the king, was devising means for taking his life, he retired to a more remote spot. There God addressed him, telling him that there were still seven thousand men who had not given themselves up to idols. That was to Elijah a marvelous statement, for he had supposed that he himself was the only one who had kept free from impiety.

CHAPTER XLIV.

At that time, Ahab, king of Samaria, coveted the vineyard of Naboth, which was adjacent to his own. And as Naboth was unwilling to sell it to him, he was cut off by the wiles of Jezebel. Thus Ahab got possession of the vineyard, though he is said at the same time to have regretted the death of Naboth. Acknowledging his crime, he is related to have done[1] penance clothed in sackcloth ; and in this way he turned

---

[1] " Egisse pænitentiam."

aside threatening punishment. For the king of Syria with a great army, having formed a military confederacy with thirty-two kings, entered the territories of Samaria, and began to besiege the city with its king. The affairs of the besieged being then in a state of great distress, the Syrian king offers these conditions in the war, — if they should give up their gold and silver and women, he would spare their lives. But, with such iniquitous conditions offered, it seemed better to suffer the greatest extremities. And now when the safety of all was despaired of, a prophet sent by God went to the king, encouraged him to go forth to battle, and when he hesitated, strengthened his confidence in many ways. Accordingly making a sally, the enemy were routed, and an abundant store of booty was secured. But, after a year, the Syrian king returned with recruited strength into Samaria, burning to avenge the defeat he had received, but was again overthrown. In that battle one hundred and twenty thousand of the Syrians perished ; the king was pardoned, and his kingdom and former position were granted him. Then Ahab was reproved by the prophet in the words of God, for having abused the divine kindness, and spared the enemy delivered up to him. The Syrian king, therefore, after three years, made war upon the Hebrews. Against him Ahab, under the advice of some false prophet, went forth to battle, having spurned the words of Michea the prophet and cast him into prison, because the prophet had warned him that the fight would prove disastrous to him. Thus, then, Ahab, being slain in that battle, left the kingdom to his son Ochozia.

CHAPTER XLV.

He being sick in body, and having sent some of his servants to consult an idol about his recovery, Elijah, as instructed by God, met them in the way, and, after rebuking them ordered them to inform the king that his death would follow from that disease. Then the king ordered him to be seized and brought into his presence, but those who were sent for this purpose were consumed by fire from heaven. The king died, as the prophet had predicted. To him there succeeded his brother Joram ; and he held the government for the space of twelve years. But on the side of the two tribes, Josaphat the king having died, Joram his son possessed the kingdom for eighteen years. He had the daughter of Ahab to wife, and proved himself more like his father-in-law than his father. After him, Ochozias his son obtained the kingdom. During his reign, Elijah is related to have been taken up to heaven. At the same time,

Elisha his disciple showed himself powerful by working many miracles, which are all too well known to need any description from my pen. By him the son of a widow was restored to life, a leper of Syria was cleansed, at a time of famine abundance of all things was brought into the city by the enemy having been put to flight, water was furnished for the use of three armies, and from a little oil the debt of a woman was paid by the oil being immensely multiplied, and sufficient means for a livelihood was provided for herself. In his times, as we have said, Ochozia was king of the two tribes, while Joram, as we have related above, ruled over the ten; and an alliance was formed between them. For war was carried on by them with combined forces both against the Syrians, and against Jeu, who had been anointed by the prophet as king of the ten tribes; and having gone forth to battle in company, they both perished in the same fight.

CHAPTER XLVI.

BUT Jeu possessed the kingdom of Joram. After the death of Ochozia in Judæa, when he had reigned one year, his mother, Gotholiah, seized the supreme power, having deprived her grandson (whose name was Joas) of the government, he being at the time but a little child. But the power thus snatched from him by his grandmother was, after eight years, restored to him through means of the priests and people, while his grandmother was driven into exile. He, at the beginning of his reign, was most devoted to the divine worship, and embellished the temple at great expense; afterwards, however, being corrupted by the flattery of the chief men, and unduly honored by them, he incurred wrath. For Azahel, king of Syria, made war upon him; and, as things went badly with him, he purchased peace with the gold of the temple. He did not, however, obtain it; but through resentment for what he had done, he was slain by his own people in the fortieth year of his reign. He was succeeded by his son Amassia. But, on the side of the ten tribes, Jeu having died, Joachas his son began to reign, displeasing to God on account of his wicked works, in punishment of which his kingdom was ravaged by the Syrians, until, through the mercy of God, the enemy was driven back, and the inhabitants of the land began to occupy their former position. Joachas, having ended his days, left the kingdom to his son Joa. He raised civil war against Amassia, king of the two tribes; and, having obtained the victory, conveyed much spoil into his own kingdom. That is related to have occurred to Amassia as a

punishment of his sin, for, having entered as a conqueror the territories of the Idumæans, he had adopted the idols of that nation. He is described as having reigned nine years, so far as I find it stated in the Books of Kings. But in the Chronicles [1] of Scripture, as well as in the Chronicles [2] of Eusebius, he is affirmed to have held the government twenty-nine years; and the mode of reckoning which may easily be perceived in these Books of Kings undoubtedly leads to that conclusion. For Jeroboam is said to have begun to reign as king of the ten tribes in the eighth year of the reign of Amassia, and to have held the government forty-one years, and to have at length died in the fourth year of the reign of Ozia, son of Amassia. By this mode of reckoning, the reign of Amassia is made to extend over twenty-eight years. Accordingly, we, following out this, inasmuch as it is our purpose to adhere in this work to the dates in their proper order, have accepted the authority of the Chronicles.[3]

CHAPTER XLVII.

OZIAS, then, the son of Amassia, succeeded to him. For, on the side of the ten tribes, Joas, reaching the end of his days, had given place to his son Jeroboa, and after him, again, his son Zacharias began to reign. Of these kings, and of all who ruled over Samaria on the side of the ten tribes, we have not thought it necessary to note the dates, because, aiming at brevity, we have omitted everything superfluous; and we have thought that the years should be carefully traced for a knowledge especially of the times of that portion [1] of the Jews, which being carried into captivity at a later period than the other, passed through a longer time as a kingdom. Ozias, then, having obtained the kingdom of Judah, gave his principal care to knowing the Lord, making great use of Zachariah the prophet (Isaiah, too, is said to have first prophesied under this king); and, on this account, he carried on war against his neighbors with deservedly prosperous results, while he also conquered the Arabians. And already he had shaken Egypt with the terror of his name; but, being elated by prosperity, he ventured on what was forbidden, and offered incense to God, a thing which it was the established custom for the priests alone to do. Being, then, rebuked by Azaria the priest, and compelled to leave the sacred place, he burst out into a rage, but was, when he finally withdrew, covered with leprosy. Under the influence of this disease he ended his

---

[1] "Paralipomenis."
[2] "Chronicis," *i.e.* of Eusebius.
[3] "Chronicorum," *i.e.* of Eusebius.
[1] There is a reference in these words to the two tribes, or kingdom of Judah.

days, after having reigned fifty-two years. Then tne kingdom was given to Joathas his son ; and he is related to have been very pious, and carried on the government with success : he subdued in war the nation of the Ammonites, and compelled them to pay tribute. He reigned sixteen years, and his son Achaz succeeded him.

CHAPTER XLVIII.

THE remarkable faith of the Ninevites is related to have been manifested about these times. That town, founded of old by Assure, the son of Sem, was the capital of the kingdom of the Assyrians. It was then full of a multitude of inhabitants, sustaining one hundred and twenty thousand men, and abounding in wickedness, as is usually the case among a vast concourse of people. God, moved by their sinfulness, commanded the prophet Jonah to go from Judæa, and denounce destruction upon the city, as Sodom and Gomorrah had of old been consumed by fire from heaven. But the prophet declined that office of preaching, not out of contumacy, but from foresight, which enabled him to behold God reconciled through the repentance of the people ; and he embarked on board a ship which was bound for Tharsus, in a very different direction. But, after they had gone forth into the deep, the sailors, constrained by the violence of the sea, inquired by means of the lot who was the cause of that suffering. And when the lot fell upon Jonah, he was cast into the sea, to be, as it were, a sacrifice for stilling the tempest, and he was seized and swallowed by a whale — a monster of the deep. Cast out three days afterwards on the shores of the [1] Ninevites, he preached as he had been commanded, namely that the city would be destroyed in three [2] days, as a punishment for the sins of the people. The voice of the prophet was listened to, not in a hypocritical fashion, as at Sodom of old ; and immediately by the order, and after the example, of the king, the whole people, and even those infants newly born, are commanded to abstain from meat and drink : the very beasts of burden in the place, and animals of different kinds, being forced by hunger and thirst, presented an appearance of those who lamented along with the human inhabitants. In this way, the threatened evil was averted. To Jonah, complaining to God, that his words had not been fulfilled, it was answered that pardon could never be denied to the penitent.

---

[1] Surely a blunder; for, as has been well asked, how could Jonah, who was swallowed by a whale in the Mediterranean, have been cast out by the fish on the shores of the Ninevites? The Hebrew text has simply " the dryland."
[2] After the Greek; the Hebrew has " forty days."

CHAPTER XLIX.

BUT in Samaria, Zacharia the king, who was very wicked, and whom we have spoken of above as occupying the throne, was slain by a certain Sella, who seized the kingdom. He, in turn, perished by the treachery of Mane, who simply repeated the conduct of his predecessor. Mane held the government which he had taken from Sella, and left it to his son Pache. But a certain person of the same name slew Pache, and seized the kingdom. Ere long being cut off by Osee, he lost the sovereignty by the same crime by which he had received it. This man, being ungodly beyond all the kings who had preceded him, brought punishment upon himself from God, and a perpetual captivity on his nation. For Salmanasar, king of the Assyrians, made war with him, and when conquered rendered him tributary. But when, with secret plans, he was preparing for rebellion, and had asked the king of the Ethiopians, who then had possession of Egypt for his assistance, Salmanasar, on discovering that, cast him into prison with fetters never taken off, while he destroyed the city, and carried off the whole people into his own kingdom, Assyrians being placed in the enemy's country to guard it. Hence that district was called Samaria, because in the language of the Assyrians guards are called Samaritæ.[1] Very many of their settlers accepted the divine rites of the Jewish religion, while others remained in the errors of heathenism. In this war, Tobias was carried into captivity. But on the side of the two tribes, Achaz, who was displeasing to God on account of his impiety, finding he had frequently the worst of it in wars with his neighbors, resolved to worship the gods of the heathen, undoubtedly because by their help his enemies had proved victorious in frequent battles. He ended his days with this crime [2] in his wicked mind, after a reign of sixteen years.

CHAPTER L.

TO him succeeded Ezekias his son, a man very unlike his father in character. For, in the beginning of his reign, urging the people and the priests to the worship of God, he discoursed to them in many words, showing how often, after being chastened by the Lord, they had obtained mercy, and how the ten tribes, having been at last carried away into captivity, as had lately happened, were now paying the penalty of their impiety. He added that their duty was carefully to be on their guard lest they should deserve to suffer the same things. Thus, the

---

[1] Vorstius remarks that this is a totally erroneous statement.
[2] " Piaculo ": a very old meaning is here attached to the word.

minds of all being turned to religion, he appointed the Levites and all the priests to offer sacrifices according to the law, and arranged that the Passover, which had for a long time been neglected, should be celebrated. And when the holy day was at hand, he proclaimed the special day of assembly by messengers sent throughout all the land, so that, if any had remained in Samaria, after the removal of the ten tribes, they might gather together for the sacred observance. Thus, in a very full assemblage, the sacred day was spent with public rejoicing, and, after a long interval, the proper religious rites were restored by means of Ezekias. He then carried on military affairs with the same diligence with which he had attended to divine things, and defeated the Philistines in frequent battles; until Sennacherim, king of the Assyrians, made war against him, having entered his territories with a large army; and then, when the country had been laid waste without any opposition, he laid siege to the city. For Ezekias, being inferior in numbers, did not venture to come to an engagement with him, but kept himself safe within the walls. The king of Assyria, thundering at the gates, threatened destruction, and demanded surrender, exclaiming that in vain did Ezekias put his trust in God, for that he rather had taken up arms by the appointment of God; and that the conqueror of all nations, as well as the overthrower of Samaria, could not be escaped, unless the king secured his own safety by a speedy surrender. In this state of affairs, Ezekias, trusting in God, consulted the prophet Isaiah, and from his answer he learned that there would be no danger from the enemy, and that the divine assistance would not fail him. And, in fact, not long after, Tarraca, king of Ethiopia, invaded the kingdom of the Assyrians.

CHAPTER LI.

By this news Sennacherim was led to return in order to defend his own territories, and he gave up the war, at the same time murmuring and crying out that victory was snatched from him the victor. He also sent letters to Ezekias, declaring, with many insulting words, that he, after settling his own affairs, would speedily return for the destruction of Judæa. But Ezekias, in no wise disturbed by these threats, is said to have prayed to God that he would not allow the so great insolence of this man to pass unavenged. Accordingly, in the same night, an angel attacking the camp of the Assyrians, caused[1] the death of many thousand men. The

king in terror fled to the town of Nineveh, and being there slain by his sons, met with an end worthy of himself. At the same time, Ezekias, sick in body, lay suffering from disease. And when Isaiah had announced to him in the words of the Lord that the end of his life was at hand, the king is related to have wept; and thus he got fifteen years added to his life. These coming to an end, he died in the twenty-ninth year of his reign, and left the kingdom to his son Manasse. He, degenerating much from his father, forsook God, and took to the practice of impious worship; and being, as a punishment for this, delivered into the power of the Assyrians, he was by his sufferings constrained to acknowledge his error, and exhorted the people that, forsaking their idols, they should worship God. He accomplished nothing worthy of special mention, but reigned for fifty-five years. Then Amos his son obtained the kingdom, but possessed it only two years. He was the heir of his father's impiety, and showed himself regardless of God: being entrapped by some stratagems of his friends, he perished.

CHAPTER LII.

THE government then passed to his son Josia. He is related to have been very pious, and to have attended to divine things with the utmost care, profiting largely by the aid of the priest Helchia. Having read a book written with the words of God, and which had been found in the temple by the priest, in which it was stated that the Hebrew nation would be destroyed on account of their frequent acts of impiety and sacrilege, by his pious supplications to God, and constant tears, he averted the impending overthrow. When he learned through Olda the prophetess that this favor was granted him, he then with still greater care set himself to practice the worship of God, inasmuch as he was now under obligation to the divine goodness. Accordingly, he burned all the vessels which had by the superstitions of former kings been consecrated to idols. For to such a height had profane observances prevailed, that they used to pay divine honors to the sun and moon, and even erected shrines made of metal to these fancied deities. Josia reduced these to powder, and also slew the priests of the profane temples. He did not even spare the tombs of the impious; and it was observed that thus was fulfilled what had of old been predicted by the prophet. In the eighteenth year of his reign, the Passover was celebrated. And about three years afterwards, having gone forth to battle against Nechao, king of Egypt, who was making war upon the Assyrians, before the armies prop-

---

[1] Our author is here guilty of omission and consequent inaccuracy. Comp. Isa. chap. 37.

erly engaged, he was wounded by an arrow. And being carried back to the city, he died of that wound, after he had reigned twenty and one years.

CHAPTER LIII.

JOACHAS, his son, having then obtained the kingdom, held it for three months, being doomed to captivity on account of his impiety. For Nechao, king of Egypt, bound him and led him away captive, and not long after, while still a prisoner, he ended his days. An annual tribute was demanded of the Jews, and a king was given them at the will of the victor. His name was Eliakim, but he afterwards changed it to Joachim. He was the brother of Joacha, and the son of Josia, but liker his brother than his father, displeasing God by his impiety. Accordingly, while he was in subjection to the king of Egypt, and in token thereof paid him tribute, Nabuchodonosor, the king of Babylon, seized the land of Judæa, and as victor held it by the right of war for three years. For the king of Egypt now giving way, and the boundaries of their empire being fixed between them, it had been agreed that the Jews should belong to Babylon. Thus after Joachim, having finished his reign of eleven years, had given place to his son of the same name, and he had excited against himself the wrath of the king of Babylon (God undoubtedly overruling everything, having resolved to give the nation of the Jews up to captivity and destruction), Nabuchodonosor entered Jerusalem with an army, and leveled the walls and the temple to the ground. He also carried off an immense amount of gold, with sacred ornaments either public or private, and all of mature age both of the male and female sex, those only being left behind whose weakness or age caused trouble to the conquerors. This useless crowd had the task assigned them of working and cultivating the fields in slavery, in order that the soil might not be neglected. Over them a king called Sedechias was appointed; but while the empty shadow of the name of king was allowed him, all real power was taken away. Joachim, for his part, possessed the sovereignty only for three months. He was carried away, along with the people, to Babylon, and was there thrown into prison; but being, after a period of thirty years released, while he was admitted by the king to his friendship, and made a partaker with him at his table and in his counsels, he died at last, not without some consolation in that his misfortunes had been removed.

CHAPTER LIV.

MEANWHILE Sedechias, the king of the useless multitude, although without power, being of an unfaithful disposition and neglectful of God, and not understanding that captivity had been brought upon them on account of the sins of the nation, becoming at length ripe for suffering the last evils he could endure, offended the mind of the king. Accordingly, after a period of nine years, Nabuchodonosor made war against him, and having forced him to flee within the walls, besieged him for three years. At this time, he consulted Jeremia the prophet, who had already often proclaimed that captivity impended over the city, to discover if perhaps there might still be some hope. But he, not ignorant of the anger of heaven, having frequently had the same question put to him, at length gave an answer, denouncing special punishment upon the king. Then Sedechias, roused to resentment, ordered the prophet to be thrust into prison. Ere long, however, he regretted this cruel act, but, as the chief men of the Jews (whose practice it had been even from the beginning to afflict the righteous) opposed him, he did not venture to release the innocent man. Under coercion from the same persons, the prophet was let down into a pit[1] of great depth, and which was disgusting from its filth and squalor, while a deadly stench issued from it. This was done that he might not simply die by a common death. But the king, impious though he was, yet showed himself somewhat more merciful than the priests, and ordered the prophet to be taken out of the pit, and restored to the safekeeping of the prison. In the meantime the force of the enemy and want began to press the besieged hard, and everything being consumed that could be eaten, famine took a firm hold of them. Thus, its defenders being worn out with want of food, the town was taken and burnt. The king, as the prophet had declared, had his eyes put out, and was carried away to Babylon, while Jeremia, through the mercy of the enemy, was taken out of his prison. When Nabuzardan, one of the royal princes, was leading him away captive with the rest, the choice was granted by him to the prophet, either to remain in his deserted and desolated native country, or to go along with him in the possession of the highest honors; and Jeremia preferred to abide in his native land. Nabuchodonosor, having carried away the people, appointed as governor over those left behind by the conquerors (either from the circumstances attending the war, or from an absolute weariness of accumulating spoil) Godolia, who belonged to the same nation. He gave

---

[1] "Lacum," as once before.

him, however, no royal ensign, or even the name of governor, because there was really no honor in ruling over these few wretched persons.

BOOK II.

CHAPTER I.

THE times of the captivity have been rendered illustrious by the predictions and deeds of the prophets, and especially by the remarkable persistency of Daniel in upholding the law, and by the deliverance of Susanna through the divine wisdom, as well as by the other things which it accomplished, and which we shall now relate in their order. Daniel was made a prisoner under King Joachim, and was brought to Babylon, while still a very little child. Afterwards, on account of the beauty of his countenance, he had a place given him among the king's servants, and along with him, Annanias, Misael, and Azarias. But, when the king had ordered them to be supplied with the finer kinds of food, and had imposed it as a duty on Asphane the eunuch to attend to that matter, Daniel, mindful of the traditions of his fathers which forbade him to partake of food from the table of a king of the Gentiles, begged of the eunuch to be allowed to use a diet of pulse only. Asphane objected that the leanness which would follow might reveal the fact that the king's commandment had been disobeyed; but Daniel, putting his trust in God, promised that he would have greater beauty of countenance from living on pulse than from the use of the king's dainties. And his words were made good, so that the faces of those who were cared for at the public expense were regarded as by no means comparable to those of Daniel and his friends. Accordingly, being promoted by the king to honor and favor, they were, in a short time, by their prudence and wise conduct, preferred to all those that stood nearest to the king. About the same time, Susanna, the wife of a certain man called Joachis, a woman of remarkable beauty, was desired by two elders, and, when she would not listen to their unchaste proposals, was assailed by a false accusation. These elders reported that a young man was found with her in a retired place, but escaped their hands by his youthful nimbleness, while they were enfeebled with age. Credit, accordingly, was given to these elders, and Susanna was condemned by the sentence of the people. And, as she was being led away to punishment according to the law, Daniel, who was then twelve years old, after having rebuked the Jews for delivering the innocent to death, demanded that she should be brought back to trial, and

that her cause should be heard afresh. For the multitude of the Jews who were then present, thought that a boy of an age so little commanding respect, had not ventured to take such a bold step without a divine impulse, and, granting him the favor which was asked, returned anew to council. The trial, then, is entered upon once more; and Daniel was allowed to take his place among the elders. Upon this, he orders the two accusers to be separated from each other, and inquires of each of them in turn, under what kind of a tree he had discovered the adulteress. From the difference of answers which they gave, their falsehood was detected: Susanna was acquitted; and the elders, who had brought the innocent into danger, were condemned to death.

CHAPTER II.

AT that time, Nabuchodonosor had a dream marvelous for that insight[1] into the future which it implied. As he could not of himself bring out its interpretation, he sent for the Chaldæans who were supposed by magic arts and by the entrails of victims to know secret things, and to predict the future, in order to its interpretation. Presently becoming apprehensive lest, in the usual manner of men, they should extract from the dream not what was true, but what would be acceptable to the king, he suppresses the things he had seen, and demands of them that, if a real power of divination was in them, they should relate to him the dream itself; saying that he would then believe their interpretation, if they should first make proof of their skill by relating the dream. But they declined attempting so great a difficulty, and confessed that such a thing was not within the reach of human power. The king, enraged because, under a false profession of divination, they were mocking men with their errors, while they were compelled by the present case to acknowledge that they had no such knowledge as was pretended, made an exposure of them by means of a royal edict; and all the men professing that art were publicly put to death. When Daniel heard of that, he spoke to one of those nearest to the king, and promised to give an account of the dream, as well as supply its interpretation. The thing is reported to the king, and Daniel is sent for. The mystery had already been revealed to him by God; and so he relates the vision of the king, as well as interprets it. But this matter demands that we set forth the dream of the king and its interpretation, along with the fulfillment of his words by what followed. The king,

[1] "mysterio futurorum mirabile."

then, had seen in his sleep an image with a head of gold, with a breast and arms of silver, with a belly and thighs of brass, with legs of iron, and which in its feet ended partly with iron, and partly with clay. But the iron and the clay when blended together could not adhere to each other. At last, a stone cut out without hands broke the image to pieces, and the whole, being reduced to dust, was carried away by the wind.

CHAPTER III.

ACCORDINGLY, as the prophet interpreted the matter, the image which was seen furnished a representation of the world. The golden head is the empire of the Chaldæans; for we have understood that it was the first and wealthiest. The breast and the arms of silver represent the second kingdom; for Cyrus, after the Chaldæans and the Medes were conquered, conferred the empire on the Persians. In the brazen belly it is said that the third sovereignty was indicated; and we see that this was fulfilled, for Alexander took the empire from the Persians, and won the sovereignty for the Macedonians. The iron legs point to a fourth power, and that is understood of the Roman empire, which is more powerful[1] than all the kingdoms which were before it. But the fact that the feet were partly of iron and partly clay, indicates that the Roman empire is to be divided, so as never to be united. This, too, has been fulfilled, for the Roman state is ruled not by one emperor but by several, and these are always quarreling among themselves, either in actual warfare or by factions. Finally, by the clay and the iron being mixed together, yet never in their substance thoroughly uniting, are shadowed forth those future mixtures of the human race which disagree among themselves, though apparently combined. For it is obvious that the Roman territory is occupied by foreign nations, or rebels, or that it has been given over to those who have surrendered themselves under an appearance[2] of peace. And it is also evident that barbarous nations, and especially Jews, have been commingled with our armies, cities, and provinces; and we thus behold them living among us, yet by no means agreeing to adopt our customs. And the prophets declare that these are the last times. But in the stone cut out without hands, which broke to pieces the gold, silver, brass, iron, and clay, there is a figure of Christ. For he, not born under human conditions (since he was born not of the will of man, but of the will of God), will reduce to

nothing that world in which exist earthly kingdoms, and will establish another kingdom, incorruptible and everlasting, that is, the future world, which is prepared for the saints. The faith of some still hesitates about this point only, while they do not believe about things yet to come, though they are convinced of the things that are past. Daniel, then, was presented with many gifts by the king, was set over Babylon and the whole empire, and was held in the highest honor. By his influence, Annanias, Azarias, and Misael, were also advanced to the highest dignity and power. About the same time, the remarkable prophecies of Ezekiel came out, the mystery of future things and of the resurrection[3] having been revealed to him. His book is one of great weight, and deserves to be read with care.

CHAPTER IV.

BUT in Judæa, over which, as we have related above, Godolia was set after the destruction of Jerusalem, the Jews taking it very ill that a ruler not of the royal race had been assigned them by the mere will of the conqueror, with a certain Ismael as their leader and instigator of the execrable conspiracy, cut off Godolia by means of treachery while he was at a banquet. Those, however, who had no part in the plot, wishing to take steps for avenging the deed, hastily take up arms against Ismael. But when he learned that destruction threatened him, leaving the army which he had collected, and with not more than eight companions he fled to the Ammonites. Fear, therefore, fell upon the whole people, lest the king of Babylon should avenge the guilt of a few by the destruction of all; for, in addition to Godolia, they had slain many of the Chaldæans along with him. They, therefore, form a plan of fleeing into Egypt, but they first go in a body to Jeremia, requesting of him divine counsel. He then exhorted them all in the words of God to remain in their native country, telling them that if they did so, they would be protected by the power of God, and that no danger would accrue from the Babylonians, but that, if they went into Egypt, they would all perish there by sword, and famine, and different kinds of death. The rabble, however, with the usual evil tendency they show, being unaccustomed to yield to useful advice and the divine power, did go into Egypt. The sacred Scriptures are silent as to their future fate; and I have not been able to discover anything regarding it.

---

[1] Such is clearly the meaning, but it is strangely expressed by the words "omnibus ante regnis validissimum."

[2] The text is here very uncertain and obscure.

[3] "resurrectionis," referring probably not to the rising again of the dead, but to the restoration of the Jews. See Ezek. chap. 37.

CHAPTER V.

At this period of time, Nabuchodonosor, elated with prosperity, erected a golden statue to himself of enormous size, and ordered it to be worshiped as a sacred image. And when this was zealously gone about by all, inasmuch as their minds had been corrupted by the universal flattery which prevailed, Annanias, Azarias, and Misael kept aloof from the profane observance, being well aware that that honor was due to God alone. They were therefore, according to an edict of the king, regarded as criminals, and there was set before them, as the means of punishment, a fiery furnace, in order that, by present terror, they might be compelled to worship the statue. But they preferred to be swallowed up by the flames rather than to commit such a sin. Accordingly, they were bound, and cast into the midst of the fire. But the flames laid hold of the agents in this execrable work, as they were forcing, with all eagerness, the victims into the fire ; while — wonderful to say, and indeed incredible to all but eye-witnesses — the fire did not touch the Hebrews at all. They were seen by the spectators walking in the midst of the furnace, and singing a song of praise to God, while there was also beheld along with them a fourth person having the appearance of an angel, and whom Nabuchodonosor, on obtaining a nearer view of him, acknowledged to be the[1] Son of God. Then the king having no doubt that the divine power was present in the event which had taken place, sent proclamations throughout his whole kingdom making known the miracle which had taken place, and confessing that honor was to be paid to God alone. Not long after, being instructed by a vision which presented itself to him, and presently also by a voice which reached him from heaven, he is said to have done penance by laying aside his kingly power, retiring from all intercourse with mankind, and to have sustained life by herbs alone. However, his empire was kept for him by the will of God, until the time was fulfilled, and at length duly acknowledging God, he was, after seven years, restored to his kingdom and former position. He is related, after having conquered Sedechia (whom he carried away captive to Babylon), as we have said above, to have reigned twenty-six years, although I do not find that recorded in the sacred history. But it has perhaps happened that, while I was engaged in searching out many points, I found this remark in the work of some anonymous author which had become interpolated in course of time, and in which the dates of the Babylonish kings were contained. I did not think it right to pass the remark unnoticed, since it does in fact harmonize with the Chronicles, and thus its account agrees with us, to the effect that, through the succession of the kings, whose dates the record contained, it completed seventy years up to the first year of king Cyrus, and such in fact is the number of years which is stated in the sacred history to have elapsed from the captivity up to the time of Cyrus.

CHAPTER VI.

After Nabuchodonosor, the kingdom fell to his son, whom I find called Euilmarodac in the Chronicles. He died in the twelfth year of his reign, and made room for his younger brother, who was called Balthasar. He, when in the fourteenth year he gave a public feast to his chief men and rulers, ordered the sacred vessels (which had been taken away by Nabuchodonosor from the temple at Jerusalem, yet had not been employed for any uses of the king, but were kept laid up in the treasury) to be brought forth. And when all persons, both of the male and female sex, with his wives and concubines, were using these amid the luxury and licentiousness of a royal banquet, suddenly the king observed fingers writing upon the wall, and the letters were perceived to be formed into words.[1] But no one could be found who was able to read the writing. The king, therefore, in perturbation called for the magi and the Chaldæans. When these simply muttered among themselves and answered nothing, the queen reminded the king that there was a certain Hebrew, Daniel by name, who had formerly revealed to Nabuchodonosor a dream containing a secret mystery, and had then, on account of his remarkable wisdom, been promoted to the highest honors. Accordingly, he, being sent for, read and interpreted the writing, to the effect that, on account of the sin of the king, who had profaned vessels sacred to God, destruction impended over him, and that his kingdom was given to the Medes and Persians. And this presently took place. For, on the same night, Balthasar perished, and Darius, a Mede by nation, took possession of his kingdom. He again, finding that Daniel was held in the highest reputation, placed him at the head of the whole empire, in this following the judgment of the kings who had preceded him. For Nabuchodonosor had also set him over the kidgdom, and Balthasar had presented him with a purple robe and a golden chain, while he also constituted him the third ruler in the kingdom.

---

[1] Or, " confessed that he had seen a son of God."

[1] " in versum ductae literae ": various emendations have been proposed, but the text may stand. The meaning appears to be that the letters were not thrown together at random, but so placed as to form words.

CHAPTER VII.

THOSE, therefore, who were possessed of power along with him, stimulated by envy, because a foreigner belonging to a captive nation had been placed on a footing of equality with them, constrain the king, who had been corrupted by flattery, to enact that divine honors should be paid to him for the next thirty days, and that it should not be lawful for any one to pray to a god except the king. Darius was easily persuaded to that, through the folly of all kings who claim for themselves divine honors. In these circumstances, Daniel being not unacquainted with what had happened, and not being ignorant that prayer ought to be addressed to God, and not to man, is accused of not having obeyed the king's commandment. And much against the will of Darius, to whom he had always been dear and acceptable, the rulers prevailed that he should be let down into a den.[1] But no harm came to him when thus exposed to the wild beasts. And on the king discovering this, he ordered his accusers to be given over to the lions. They, however, did not pass through a similar experience, for they were instantly devoured to satisfy the hunger of the savage beasts. Daniel, who had been famous before, was now esteemed still more famous; and the king, repealing his former edict, issued a new one to the effect that, all errors and superstitions being abandoned, the God of Daniel was to be worshiped. There exists also a record of visions of Daniel, in which he revealed the order of events in coming ages, embracing in them also the number of the years, within which he announced that Christ would descend to earth (as has taken place), and clearly set forth the future coming of Antichrist. If any one is eager to inquire into these points, he will find them more fully treated of in the book of Daniel: our design is simply to present a connected statement of events. Darius is related to have reigned eighteen years; after which date Astyages began to rule over the Medes.

CHAPTER VIII.

HIM Cyrus, his grandson by his daughter, expelled from the kingdom, having used the arms of the Persians for the purpose; and hence the chief power was transferred to the Persians. The Babylonians also fell under his power and government. It happened at the beginning of his reign that, by the issue of public edicts, he gave permission to the Jews to return into their own country; and he also restored the sacred vessels which Nabuchodonosor had carried away from the temple at Jerusalem. Accordingly, a few then returned into Judæa; as to the others, we have not been able to discover whether the desire of returning, or the power of doing so, was wanting. There was at that time among the Babylonians a brazen image of Belus, a very ancient king, whom Virgil also has mentioned.[1] This having been deemed sacred by the superstition of the people, Cyrus also had been accustomed to worship, being deceived by the trickery of its priests. They affirmed that the image ate and drank, while they themselves secretly carried off the daily portion which was offered to the idol. Cyrus, then, being on intimate terms with Daniel, asked him why he did not worship the image, since it was a manifest symbol of the living God, as consuming those things which were offered to it. Daniel, laughing at the mistake of the man, replied that it could not possibly be the case, that that work of brass — mere insensate matter — could use either meat or drink. The king, therefore, ordered the priests to be called (they were about seventy in number); and, bringing terror to bear upon them, he reprovingly asked them who was in the way of consuming what was offered, since Daniel, a man distinguished for his wisdom, maintained that that could not be done by an insensate image. Then they, trusting in their ready-made trick, ordered the usual offering to be made, and the temple to be sealed up by the king, on the understanding that, unless on the following day the whole offering were found to have been consumed, they should suffer death, while, on the opposite being discovered, the same fate awaited Daniel. Accordingly, the temple was sealed up by the signet of the king; but Daniel had previously, without the knowledge of the priests, covered the floor of it with ashes, so that their footprints might betray the clandestine approaches of those who entered. The king, then, having entered the temple on the following day, perceived that those things had been taken away, which he had ordered to be served up to the idol. Then Daniel lays open the secret fraud by the betraying footprints, showing that the priests, with their wives and children, had entered the temple by a hole opened from below, and had devoured those things which were served up to the idol. Accordingly, all of them were put to death by the order of the king, while the temple and image were submitted to the power of Daniel, and were destroyed at his command.

---

[1] The reference is to *Æn.* I. 729, but Sigonius and others have suspected the words as being a gloss. They are, however, probably genuine. Virgil's words are, —

" Hic regina gravem gemmis auroque poposcit
Implevitque mero paternam, quam Belus et omnes
A Belo soliti; tum facta silentia tectis."

---

[1] " lacum ": twice used before in the sense of *pit.*

CHAPTER IX.

IN the meantime, those Jews, who, as we have said above, returned into their native land by the permission of Cyrus, attempted to restore their city and temple. But, being few and poor, they made but little progress, until, at last, after the lapse of about a hundred years, while Artaxerxes the king ruled over the Persians, they were absolutely deterred from building by those who had local authority. For, at that time, Syria and all Judæa was ruled under the empire of the Persians by magistrates and governors. Accordingly, these took counsel to write to king Artaxerxes, that it was not fitting that opportunity should be granted to the Jews of rebuilding their city, lest, in accordance with their stubborn character, and being accustomed to rule over other nations, they should, on recovering their strength, not submit to live under the sway of a foreign power. Thus, the plan of the rulers being approved of by the king, the building of the city was put a stop to, and delayed until the second year of Darius the king. But, who were kings of Persia throughout this period of time, we shall here insert, in order that the succession of the dates may be set forth in a regular and fixed order. Well, then, after Darius the Mede, who, as we have said above, reigned eighteen years, Cyrus held the supreme power for thirty-one years. While making war upon the Scythians, he fell in battle, in the second year after Tarquinius Superbus began to reign at Rome. To Cyrus succeeded his son Cambyses, and reigned eight years. He, after harassing with war Egypt and Ethiopia, and subduing these countries, returned as victor to Persia, but accidentally hurt himself, and died from that wound. After his death, two brothers, who were magi, and Medes by nation, held rule over the Persians for seven months. To slay these, seven of the most noble of the Persians formed a conspiracy, of whom the leader was Darius, the son of Hystaspes, who was a cousin of Cyrus, and by unanimous consent the kingdom was bestowed on him : he reigned thirty and six years. He, four years before his death, fought at Marathon, in a battle greatly celebrated both in Greek and Roman history. That took place about the two hundred and sixtieth year after the founding of Rome, while Macerinus and Augurinus were consuls, that is, eight hundred and eighty-eight years ago, provided the research I have made into the succession of Roman consuls does not deceive me ; for I have made the entire reckoning down to the time of Stilico.[1] After Darius came Xerxes, and he is said to have reigned twenty-one years, although I have found that the length of his rule is, in most copies,[2] set down at twenty and five years. To him succeeded Artaxerxes, of whom we have made mention above. Since he ordered the building of the Jewish city and temple to be stopped, the work was suspended to the second year of king Darius. But that the succession of dates may be completed up to him, I have to state that Artaxerxes reigned forty-one years, Xerxes two months, and that, after him, Sucdianus ruled for seven months.

CHAPTER X.

NEXT, Darius, under whom the temple was restored, obtained the kingdom, his name being at that time Ochus. He had three Hebrew youths of tried fidelity as his body-guard, and one of these had, from the proof of his prudence which he had given, attracted towards himself the admiration of the king. The choice, then, being given him of asking for anything which he had formed a desire for in his heart, groaning over the ruins of his country, he begged permission to restore the city, and obtained an order from the king to urge the lieutenants and rulers to hurry forward the building of the holy temple, and furnish the expense needful to that end. Accordingly, the temple was completed in four years ; that is, in the sixth year after Darius began to reign, and that seemed, for the time, enough to the people of the Jews. For, as it was a work of great labor to restore the city, distrusting their own resources, they did not venture at the time to begin an undertaking of so great difficulty, but were content with having rebuilt the temple. At the same time, Esdras the scribe, who was skilled in the law, about twenty years after the temple had been completed (Darius being now dead who had possessed the sovereignty for nineteen years), by the permission of Artaxerxes the second (not he who had a place between the two Xerxes, but he who had succeeded to Darius Ochus), set out from Babylon with many following him, and they carried to Jerusalem the vessels of various workmanship, as well as the gifts which the king had sent for the temple of God. Along with them were but twelve Levites ; for with difficulty that number of the tribe is related then to have been found. He, having found that the Jews had united in marriage with the Gentiles, rebuked them severely on that account, and ordered them to renounce all connections of that kind, as well as to put away the children which had been the issue of such marriages ; and all yielded obedience to his word. The people, then, being

---

[1] Stilico was consul during the lifetime of Sulpitius.

[2] "in plerisque exemplaribus" : the MSS. varying, as they so often do, with respect to numbers.

sanctified, performed the rites sanctioned by the ancient law. But I do not find that Esdras did anything with the view of restoring the city; because he thought, as I imagine, that a more urgent duty was to reform the people from the corrupt habits which they had contracted.

CHAPTER XI.

THERE was at that time at Babylon one Nehemiah, a servant of the king, a Jew by birth, and very much beloved by Artaxerxes on account of the services he had rendered. He, having inquired of his fellow-countrymen the Jews, what was the condition of their ancestral city; and having learned that his native land remained in the same fallen condition as before, is said to have been disturbed with all his heart, and to have prayed to God with groans and many tears. He also called to mind the sins of his nation, and urgently entreated the divine compassion. Accordingly, the king noticing that he, while waiting at table, seemed more sorrowful than usual, asked him to explain the reasons of his grief. Then he began to bewail the misfortunes of his nation, and the ruin of his ancestral city, which now, for almost two hundred and fifty years, being leveled with the ground, furnished a proof of the evils which had been endured, and a gazing-stock to their enemies. He therefore begged the king to grant him the liberty of going and restoring it. The king yielded to these dutiful entreaties, and immediately sent him away with a guard of cavalry, that he might the more safely accomplish his journey, giving him, at the same time, letters to the rulers requesting them to furnish him with all that was necessary. When he arrived at Jerusalem, he distributed the work connected with the city to the people, man by man; and all vied with each other in carrying out the orders which they received. And already the work of rebuilding[1] had been half accomplished, when the jealousy of the surrounding heathen burst out, and the neighboring cities conspired to interrupt the works, and to deter the Jews from building. But Nehemiah, having stationed guards against those making assaults upon the people, was in no degree alarmed, and carried out what he had begun. And thus, after the wall was completed, and the entrances of the gates finished, he measured out the city for the construction by families of houses within it. He reckoned, also, that the people were not adequate in numbers to the size of the city; for there were not more of them than fifty thousand of both sexes

and of all ranks — to such an extent had their formerly enormous numbers been reduced by frequent wars, and by the multitude kept in captivity. For, of old, those two tribes, of whom the remaining people were all that survived, had, when the ten tribes were separated from them, been able to furnish three hundred and twenty thousand armed men. But being given up by God, on account of their sin, to death and captivity, they had sunk down to the miserably small number which they now presented. This company, however, as I have said, consisted only of the two tribes: the ten[2] which had previously been carried away being scattered among the Parthians, Medes, Indians, and Ethiopians never returned to their native country, and are to this day held under the sway of barbarous nations. But the completion of the restored city is related to have been effected in the thirty-second year of the reign of Artaxerxes. From that time to the crucifixion of Christ; that is, to the time when Fufius Geminus and Rubellius were consuls, there elapsed three hundred and ninety and eight years. But from the restoration of the temple to its destruction, which was completed by Titus under Vespasian, when Augustus was consul, there was a period of four hundred and eighty-three years. That was formerly predicted by Daniel, who announced that from the restoration of the temple to its overthrow there would elapse seventy and nine weeks. Now, from the date of the captivity of the Jews until the time of the restoration of the city, there were two hundred and sixty years.

CHAPTER XII.

AT this period of time we think Esther and Judith lived, but I confess that I cannot easily perceive with what kings especially I should connect the actions of their lives. For, while Esther is said to have lived under King Artaxerxes, I find that there were two Persian kings of that name, and there is much hesitation in concluding to which of these her date is to be assigned. However, it has seemed preferable to me to connect the history of Esther with that Artaxerxes under whom Jerusalem was restored, because it is not likely that, if she had lived under the former Artaxerxes, whose times Esdras has given an account of, he would have made no mention of such an illustrious woman. This is all the more convincing since we know

---

[1] "jamque ad medium machinæ processerant."

[2] Our author here touches upon a most interesting question—the ultimate destiny of the ten tribes. He seems to imply that none of them returned to Palestine, but were wholly absorbed among the Gentile nations. That, however, cannot be correct, for it was still possible, in the time of Christ, to speak of some as connected with the tribe of Asher, one of the ten tribes. See Luke ii. 36.

that the building of the temple was (as we have related above) prohibited by that Artaxerxes, and Esther would not have allowed that had she then been united with him in marriage. But I will now repeat what things she accomplished. There was at that time a certain Vastis connected with the king in marriage, a woman of marvelous beauty. Being accustomed to extol her loveliness to all, he one day, when he was giving a public entertainment, ordered the queen to attend for the purpose of exhibiting her beauty. But she, more prudent than the foolish king, and being too modest to make a show of her person before the eyes of men, refused compliance with his orders. His savage mind was enraged by this insult, and he drove her forth, both from her condition of marriage with him and from the palace. Consequently, when a young woman was sought after to take her place as the wife of the king, Esther was found to excel all others in beauty. She being a Jewess of the tribe of Benjamin, and an orphan, without father or mother, had been brought up by her cousin-german,[1] Mardochæus. On being espoused to the king, she, by the instructions of him who had brought her up, concealed her nation and fatherland, and was also admonished by him not to become forgetful of her ancestral traditions, nor, though as a captive she had entered into marriage with a foreigner, to take part in the food of the heathen. Thus, then, being united to the king, she, in a short time, as was to be expected, easily captivated his whole mind by the power of her beauty, so that, equalizing her with himself in the emblem of sovereign power, he presented her with a purple robe.

CHAPTER XIII.

At this time, Mardochæus was among those nearest to the king, having entirely under his charge the affairs of the household. He had made known to the king a plot which had been formed by two eunuchs, and, on that account, had become a greater favorite, while he was presented with the highest honors. There was at that period one Haman, a very confidential friend of the king, whom he had made equal to himself and, after the manner of sovereign rulers, had ordered to be worshiped. Mardochæus being the one man among all who refused to do that, had greatly kindled the wrath of the Persian against himself. Accordingly, Haman setting his mind to work the ruin of the Hebrew, went to the king, and affirmed that there was in

his kingdom a race of men of wicked superstitions, and hateful alike to God and men. He said that, as they lived according to foreign laws, they deserved to be destroyed; and that it was a righteous thing to hand over the whole of this nation to death. At the same time, he promised the king immense wealth out of their possessions. The barbarous prince was easily persuaded, and an edict was issued for the slaughter of the Jews, while men were at once sent out to publish it through the whole kingdom from India even to Ethiopia. When Mardochæus heard of this, he rent his clothes, clothed himself in sackcloth, scattered ashes upon his head, and, going to the palace, he there made the whole place resound with his wailing and complaints, crying out that it was an unworthy thing that an innocent nation should perish, while there existed no ground for its destruction. Esther's attention was attracted by the voice of lamentation, and she learned how the case really stood. But she was then at a loss what step she should take (for, according to the custom of the Persians, the queen is not permitted access to the king, unless she has been sent for, and indeed is not admitted at any time the king may please, but only at a fixed period); and it happened at the time, that by this rule, Esther was held as separated from the presence of the king for the next thirty days. However, thinking that she ought to run some risk in behalf of her fellow-countrymen, even should sure destruction await her, she was prepared to encounter death in such a noble cause, and, after having called upon God, she entered the court of the king. But the barbarian, though at first amazed at this unusual occurrence, was gradually won over by female blandishments, and at length went so far as to accompany the queen to a banquet which she had prepared. Along with him also went Haman, the favorite of the king, but a deadly enemy of the nation of the Jews. Well, when after the feasting the banquet began to become jovial through the many cups which were drank, Esther cast herself down at the knees of the king, and implored him to stay the destruction which threatened her nation. Then the king promised to refuse nothing to her entreaties, if she had any further request to make. Esther at once seized the opportunity, and demanded the death of Haman as a satisfaction to her nation, which he had desired to see destroyed. But the king could not forget his friend, and hesitating a little, he withdrew for a short time for the purpose of considering the matter. He then returned, and when he saw Haman grasping the knees of the queen, excited with rage, and, crying out that violence was being applied to the queen, he ordered him to be put to death. It then came to the knowl-

---

[1] " patruele patre ": words which have much perplexed the editors.

edge of the king that a cross[1] had been got ready by Haman on which Mardochæus was to suffer. Thus, Haman was fixed to that very cross, and all his goods were handed over to Mardochæus, while the Jews at large were set free. Artaxerxes reigned sixty and two years, and was succeeded by Ochus.

CHAPTER XIV.

To this series of events it will be right that I should append an account of the doings of Judith; for she is related to have lived after the captivity, but the sacred history has not revealed who was king of the Persians in her day. It, however, calls the king under whom her exploits were performed by the name of Nabuchodonosor, and that was certainly not the one who took Jerusalem. But I do not find that any one of that name reigned over the Persians after the captivity, unless it be that, on account of the[1] wrath and like endeavors which he manifested, any king acting so was styled Nabuchodonosor by the Jews. Most persons, however, think that it was Cambyses, the son of Cyrus, on this ground that he, as a conqueror, penetrated into Egypt and Ethiopia. But the sacred history is opposed to this opinion; for Judith is described as having lived in the twelfth year of the king in question. Now, Cambyses did not possess the supreme power for more than eight years. Wherefore, if it is allowable to make a conjecture on a point of history, I should be inclined to believe that her exploits were performed under king Ochus, who came after the second Artaxerxes. I found this conjecture on the fact that (as I have read in profane histories) he is related to have been by nature cruel and fond of war. For he both engaged in hostilities with his neighbors, and recovered by wars Egypt, which had revolted many years before. At that time, also, he is related to have ridiculed the sacred rites of the Egyptians and Apis, who was regarded by them as a god; a thing which Baguas, one of his eunuchs, an Egyptian by nation, and indignant at the king's conduct, afterwards avenged by the death of the king, considering that the king had insulted the race to which he belonged. Now, the inspired[2] history makes mention of this Baguas; for, when Holofernes by the order of the king led an army against the Jews, it has related that Baguas was among the host. Wherefore, not without reason may I bring it forward in proof of the opinion I have expressed that that king who was named Nabuchodonosor was really Ochus, since profane historians have related that Baguas lived in his reign. But this ought not to be felt at all remarkable by any one, that mere worldly writers have not touched on any of those points which are recorded in the sacred writings. The spirit of God thus took care that the history should be strictly confined within its own mysteries, unpolluted by any corrupt mouth, or that which mingled truth with fiction. That history being, in fact, separated from the affairs of the world, and of a kind to be expressed only in sacred words, clearly ought not to have been mixed up with other histories, as being on a footing of equality with them. For it would have been most unbecoming that this history should be commingled with others treating of other things, or pursuing different inquiries. But I will now proceed to what remains, and will narrate in as few words as I can the acts performed by Judith.

CHAPTER XV.

THE Jews, then, having returned, as we have narrated above, to their native land, and the condition of their affairs and of their city being not yet properly settled, the king of the Persians made war on the Medes, and engaged in a successful battle against their king, who was named Arphaxad. That monarch being slain, he added the nation to his empire. He did the same to other nations, having sent before him Holofernes whom he had appointed master of his host, with a hundred and twenty thousand foot-soldiers, and twelve thousand cavalry. He, after having ravaged in war, Cilicia and Arabia, took many cities by force, or compelled them through fear to surrender. And now the army, having moved on to Damascus, had struck the Jews with great terror. But as they were unable to resist, and as, at the same time, they could not bring their minds to acquiesce in the thought of surrender, since they had previously known from experience the miseries of slavery, they betook themselves in crowds to the temple. There, with a general groaning and commingled wailing, they implored the divine assistance; saying that they had been sufficiently punished by God for their sins and offenses; and begging him to spare the remnant of them who had recently been delivered from slavery. In the meantime, Holofernes had admitted the Moabites to surrender, and joined them to himself as allies in the war against the Jews. He inquired of their chief men what was the power on which the Hebrews relied in not bringing their minds to submit to the thought of submission. In reply, a certain

---

[1] "pœnam crucis": after the Greek.
[1] The text is here uncertain.
[2] "historia divina": the writer applies these words to the book of Judith.

man called Achior stated to him the facts, viz. : that the Jews being worshipers of God, and trained by their fathers to pious observances, had formerly passed through a period of slavery in Egypt, and that, brought out from that country by the divine aid, and having passed over on foot the sea which was dried up before them, they had at last conquered all the opposing nations, and recovered the territory inhabited by their ancestors. That subsequently, with various fluctuations in their affairs, they had either prospered or the reverse, that, when they did sink into adversity, they had again escaped from their sufferings, finding that God was, in turn, either angry against them, or reconciled towards them, according to their deserts, so that, when they sinned, they were chastised by the attacks of enemies or by being sent into captivity, but were always unconquerable when they enjoyed the divine favor. So then, if at the present time they are free from guilt, they cannot possibly be subdued ; but if they are otherwise situated, they will easily be conquered. Upon this, Holofernes, flushed with many victories, and thinking that everything must give way before him, was roused to wrath, because victory on his part was regarded as principally depending on the sin of the Jews, and ordered Achior to be pushed forward into the camp of the Hebrews, that he might perish in company with those who he had affirmed could not be conquered. Now, the Jews had then made for the mountains ; and those to whom the business had been assigned, proceeded to the foot of the mountains, and there left Achior in chains. When the Jews perceived that, they freed him from his bonds and conducted him up the hill. On their inquiring the reason of what had happened, he explained it to them, and, being received in peace, awaited the result. I may add that, after the victory, he was circumcised and became a Jew. Well, Holofernes, perceiving the difficulty of the localities, because he could not reach the heights, surrounded the mountains with soldiers, and took the greatest pains to cut off the Hebrews from all water supplies. On that account, they felt all the sooner the misery of a siege. Being therefore overcome through want of water, they went in a company to Ozias, their leader, all inclined to make a surrender. But he replied that they should wait a little, and look for the divine assistance, so that the time of surrender was fixed for the fifth day afterwards.

CHAPTER XVI.

WHEN this became known to Judith (a widow woman of great wealth, and remarkable for beauty, but still more distinguished for her virtue than her beauty), who was then in the camp, she thought that, in the distressed circumstances of her people, some bold effort ought to be made by her, even though it should lead to her own destruction. She therefore decks her head and beautifies her countenance, and then, attended by a single maid-servant, she enters the camp of the enemy. She was immediately conducted to Holofernes, and tells him that the affairs of her countrymen were desperate, so that she had taken precautions for her life by flight. Then she begs of the general the right of a free egress from the camp during night, for the purpose of saying her prayers. That order was accordingly given to the sentinels and keepers of the gates. But when by the practice of three days she had established for herself the habit of going out and returning, and had also in this way inspired belief in her into the barbarians, the desire took possession of Holofernes of abusing the person of his captive ; for, being of surpassing beauty, she had easily impressed the Persian. Accordingly, she was conducted to the tent of the general by Baguas, the eunuch ; and, commencing a banquet, the barbarian stupefied himself with a great deal of wine. Then, when the servants withdrew, before he offered violence to the woman, he fell asleep. Judith, seizing the opportunity, cut off the head of the enemy and carried it away with her. Being regarded as simply going out of the camp according to her usual custom, she returned to her own people in safety. On the following day the Hebrews held forth for show the head of Holofernes from the heights ; and, making a sally, marched upon the camp of the enemy. And then the barbarians assemble in crowds at the tent of their general, waiting for the signal of battle. When his mutilated body was discovered, they turned to flight under the influence of a disgraceful panic, and fled before the enemy. The Jews, for their part, pursued the fugitives, and after slaying many thousands, took possession of the camp and the booty within it. Judith was extolled with the loftiest praises, and is said to have lived one hundred and five years. If these things took place, as we believe, under king Ochus, in the twelfth year of his reign, then from the date of the restoration of Jerusalem up to that war there elapsed two and twenty years. Now Ochus reigned in all twenty-three years. And he was beyond all others cruel, and more than of a barbarous disposition. Baguas, the eunuch, took him off by poison on an occasion of his suffering from illness. After him, Arses his son held the government for three years, and Darius for four.

CHAPTER XVII.

AGAINST him Alexander of Macedon engaged in war. And on his being conquered, the sovereign power was taken from the Persians, after having lasted, from the time of its establishment by Cyrus, two hundred and fifty years. Alexander, the conqueror of almost all nations, is said to have visited the temple at Jerusalem, and to have conveyed gifts into it ; and he proclaimed throughout the whole territory which he had reduced under his sway that it should be free to the Jews living in it to return to their own country. At the end of the twelfth year of his reign, and seven years after he had conquered Darius, he died at Babylon. His friends who, along with him, had carried on those very important wars, divided his empire among themselves. For some time they administered the charges they had undertaken without making use of the name of king, while a certain Arridæus Philippus, the brother of Alexander, reigned, to whom, being of a very weak character, the sovereignty was nominally and in appearance given, but the real power was in the hands of those who had divided among themselves the army and the provinces. And indeed this state of things did not long continue, but all preferred that they should be called by the name of kings. In Syria Seleucus was the first king after Alexander, Persia and Babylon being also subject to his sway. At that time the Jews paid an annual tribute of three hundred talents of silver to the king ; but they were governed not by foreign magistrates but by their own priests. And they lived according to the fashions of their ancestors until very many of them, again corrupted by a long peace, began to mingle all things with seditions, and to create disturbances, while they aimed at the high-priesthood under the influence of lust, avarice, and the desire of power.

CHAPTER XVIII.

FOR, first of all, under king Seleucus, the son of Antiochus the great, a certain man called Simon accused to the king on false charges Onias the priest, a holy and uncorrupted man, and thus tried, but in vain, to overthrow him. Then, after an interval of time, Jason, the brother of Onias, went to Antiochus the king, who had succeeded his brother Seleucus, and promised him an increase of tribute, if the high-priesthood were transferred to him. And although it was an unusual, and indeed, until now, an unpermitted thing for a man to enjoy the high-priesthood year after year, still the eager mind of the king, diseased with avarice, was easily persuaded. Accordingly, Onias was driven from office, and the priesthood bestowed on Jason. He harassed his countrymen and his country in the most shameful manner. Then, as he had sent through a certain Menelaus (the brother of that Simon who has been mentioned) the money he had promised to the king, a way being once laid open to his ambition, Menelaus obtained the priesthood by the same arts which Jason had employed before. But not long after, as he had not furnished the promised amount of money, he was driven from his position, and Lysimachus substituted in his stead. Then there arose disgraceful conflicts between Jason and Menelaus, until Jason, as an exile, left the country. By examples like these, the morals of the people became corrupted to such an extent, that numbers of the natives begged permission from Antiochus to live after the fashion of the Gentiles. And when the king granted their request, all the most worthless vied with each other in their endeavors to construct temples, to sacrifice to idols, and to profane the law. In the meantime, Antiochus returned from Alexandria (for he had then made war upon the king of Egypt, which, however, he gave up by the orders of the senate and Roman people, when Paulus and Crassus were consuls), and went to Jerusalem. Finding the people at variance from the diverse superstitions they had adopted, he destroyed the law of God, and showed favor to those who followed impious courses, while he carried off all the ornaments of the temple, and wasted it with much destruction. That came to pass in the hundred and fiftieth year after the death of Alexander, Paulus and Crassus being, as we have said, consuls, about five years after Antiochus began to reign.

CHAPTER XIX.

BUT that the order of the dates may be correctly preserved, and that it may appear more clearly who this Antiochus was, we shall enumerate both the names and times of the kings who came after Alexander in Syria. Well, then, king Alexander having died, as we have related above, his whole empire was portioned out by his friends, and was governed for some time by them under the name of the king.[1] Seleucus, after the lapse of nine years, was himself styled king in Syria, and reigned thirty-two years. After him came Antiochus, his son, with a reign of twenty-one years. Then came Antiochus, the son of Antiochus, who was surnamed Theus, and he reigned fifteen years. After him, his son

---

[1] They did not themselves, for a time, assume the name of king, but, as said above, professed to rule under the authority of king Arridæus, brother of Alexander.

Seleucus, surnamed Callinicus, reigned twenty-one years. Another Seleucus, the son of Callinicus, reigned three years. After his death, Antiochus, the brother of Callinicus, held Asia and Syria for thirty-seven years. This is the Antiochus against whom Lucius Scipio Asiaticus made war ; and he, being worsted in the war, was stripped of a part of his empire. He had two sons, Seleucus and Antiochus, the latter of whom he had given as a hostage to the Romans. Thus, then, Antiochus the great having died, his younger son Seleucus obtained the kingdom, under whom, as we have said, Onias the priest had an accusation brought against him by Simon. Then Antiochus was set free by the Romans, and there was given in his place as hostage Demetrius, the son of Seleucus, who was at that time reigning. Seleucus dying in the twelfth year of his reign, his brother Antiochus, who had been a hostage at Rome, seized the kingdom. He, five years after the beginning of his reign, did, as we have shown above, lay waste Jerusalem. For, as he had to pay a heavy tribute to the Romans, he was almost of necessity compelled, in order to meet that enormous expense, to provide himself with money by rapine, and to neglect no opportunity of plundering. Then, after two years, the Jews being again visited by a similar disaster to that which they had suffered before, lest it should happen that, driven on by their numerous miseries, they should commence war, he placed a garrison in the citadel. Next, with the view of overturning the holy law, he published an edict, that all, forsaking the traditions of their ancestors, should live after the manner of the Gentiles. And there were not wanting those who readily obeyed this profane enactment. Then truly there was a horrible spectacle presented ; through all the cities sacrifices were publicly offered in the streets, while the sacred volumes of the law and the prophets were consumed with fire.

CHAPTER XX.

AT that time, Matthathias, the son of John, was high-priest. When he was being forced by the servants of the king to obey the edict, with marvelous courage he set at naught the profane enactments, and slew, in the presence of all, a Hebrew who was publicly performing profane acts. A leader having thus been found, rebellion at once took place. Matthathias left the town ; and as many flocked to him, he got up the appearance of a regular army. The object of every man in that host was to defend himself by arms against a profane government, and rather even to fall in war than to take part in impious ceremonies. In the meantime, Anti-ochus was compelling those Jews who were found in the Greek cities in his dominions to offer sacrifice, and was visiting with unheard-of torments those who refused. At this time, there occurred that well-known and remarkable suffering of the seven brothers and their mother. All of the brothers, when they were being forced to violate the law of God, and the customs of their ancestors, preferred rather to die. At last, their mother, too, accompanied them both in their sufferings and death.

CHAPTER XXI.

IN the meantime, Matthathias dies, having appointed in his own place his son Judah, as general of the army which he had brought together. Under his leadership, several successful battles took place against the royal forces. For first of all, he destroyed, along with his whole army, Apollonius, the enemy's general, who had entered on the conflict with a large number of troops. When a certain man, named Seron, who was then the ruler of Syria, heard of this, he increased his forces, and attacked Judah with much spirit as being superior in numbers, but when a battle took place, he was routed and put to flight ; and with the loss of nearly eight hundred men, he returned to Syria. On this becoming known to Antiochus, he was filled with rage and regret, inasmuch as it vexed him that his generals had been conquered, notwithstanding their large armies. He therefore gathers aid from his whole empire, and bestows a donative on the soldiers, almost to the exhaustion of his treasury. For he was then suffering in a very special manner from the want of money. The reason of this was, on the one side, that the Jews, who had been accustomed to pay him an annual tribute of more than three hundred talents of silver, were now in a state of rebellion against him ; and on the other side, that many of the Greek cities and countries were unsettled by the evil of persecution. For Antiochus had not spared even the Gentiles, whom he had sought to persuade to abandon their long-established superstitions, and to draw over to one kind of religious observance. And no doubt, those of them who regarded nothing as sacred, easily were induced to give up their ancient forms of worship, but at the same time all were in a state of alarm and disaster. For these reasons, then, the taxes had ceased to be paid. Boiling with wrath on these grounds (for he who had of old been the richest of kings now deeply felt the poverty due to his own wickedness), he divided his forces with Lysias, and committed to him Syria and the war against the Jews, while he himself set out against the Persians, to collect the taxes among them. Lysias, then, selected Ptolemy, Gorgias, Doro, and Nicanor, as generals in the war; and to these he gave forty thousand infantry, and seven thousand cavalry. At the first onset, these caused great alarm among the Jews. Then Judah, when all were in despair, exhorted his men to go with courageous hearts to battle — that, if they put their trust in God, everything would give way before them; for that often before then the victory had been won by a few fighting against many. A fast was proclaimed, and sacrifice was offered, after which they went down to battle. The result was that the forces of the enemy were scattered, and Judah, taking possession of their camp, found in it both much gold and Tyrian treasures. For merchants from Syria, having no doubt as to victory, had followed the king's army with the hope of purchasing prisoners, and now were themselves spoiled. When these things were reported to Lysias by messengers, he got together troops with still greater efforts, and in a year after again attacked the Jews with an enormous army; but being defeated, he retreated to Antioch.

CHAPTER XXII.

JUDAH, on the defeat of the enemy, returned to Jerusalem, and bent his mind on the purification and restoration of the temple, which having been overthrown by Antiochus, and profaned by the Gentiles, presented a melancholy spectacle. But as the Syrians held the citadel, which being connected with the temple, but standing above it in position, was really impregnable, the lower parts proved inaccessible, as frequent sallies from above prevented persons from approaching them. But Judah placed against these assailants a very powerful body of his men. Thus the work of the sacred building was protected, and the temple was surrounded with a wall, while armed men were appointed to maintain a perpetual defence. And Lysias, having again returned into Judæa with increased forces, was once more defeated with a great loss both of his own army and of the auxiliaries, which being sent to him by various states had combined with him in the war. In the meantime, Antiochus, who, as we have said above, had marched into Persia, endeavored to plunder the town of Elymus, the wealthiest in the country, and a temple situated there which was filled with gold; but, as a multitude flocked together from all sides for the defense of the place, he was put to flight. Moreover, he received news of the want of success which had attended the

efforts of Lysias.[1] Thus, from distress of mind, he fell into bodily disease. But as he was then tormented with internal sufferings, he remembered the miseries which he had inflicted on the people of God, and acknowledged that these evils had deservedly been sent upon him. Then, after a few days, he died, having reigned eleven years. He left the kingdom to his son Antiochus, to whom the name of Eupator was given.

CHAPTER XXIII.

AT that time Judah besieged the Syrians who were posted in the citadel. They, being sore pressed with famine and want of all things, sent messengers to the king to implore assistance. Accordingly, Eupator came to their aid with a hundred thousand infantry and twenty thousand cavalry, while elephants marched in front of his line, causing immense terror to the onlookers. Then Judah, abandoning the siege, went to meet the king, and routed the Syrians in the first battle. The king begged for peace, which, because[1] he, with his treacherous disposition, made a bad use of, vengeance followed his treachery. For Demetrius, the son of Seleucus, who, we have said above, was handed over as a hostage to the Romans, when he heard that Antiochus had departed, begged that they would send him to take possession of the kingdom. And when this was refused to him, he secretly fled from Rome, came into Syria, and seized the supreme power, having slain the son of Antiochus, who had reigned one year and six months. It was during his reign that the Jews first begged the friendship of the Roman people, and alliance with them; and the embassy to this effect having been kindly received, they were, by a decree of the senate, styled allies and friends. In the meantime Demetrius was, by means of his generals, carrying on war against Judah. And first the army was led by a certain man named Bacchides, and by Alcimus, a Jew; Nicanor, being afterwards placed at the head of the war, fell in battle. Then Bacchides and Alcimus, recovering power, and having increased their forces, fought against Judah. The Syrians, turning out victorious in that battle, cruelly abused their victory. The Hebrews elect Jonathan, the brother of Judah, in his place. In the meantime, Alcimus, after he had fearfully desolated Jerusalem, dies; Bacchides, being thus deprived of his ally, returns to the king. Then, after an interval of two years, Bacchides again made war upon the Jews, and being beaten, he

---

[1] Some add the words, "or of Lysimachus," but this appears to have been a gloss.
[1] The text is here in utter confusion; we have followed that suggested by Vorstius.

begged for peace. This was granted him on certain conditions, to the effect that he should give up the deserters and prisoners, along with all that he had taken in war.

CHAPTER XXIV.

WHILE these things are going on in Judæa, a certain young man educated at Rhodes, by name Alexander, gave himself out as being the son of Antiochus (which was false), and assisted by the power of Ptolemy, king of Alexandria, came into Syria with an army. He conquered Demetrius in war, and slew him after he had reigned twelve years. This Alexander, before he made war against Demetrius, had formed an alliance with Jonathan, and had presented him with a purple robe and royal ensigns. For this reason Jonathan had assisted him with auxiliary forces; and on the defeat of Demetrius, had been the very first to meet him with congratulations. Nor did Alexander afterwards violate the faith which he had pledged. Accordingly, in the five years during which he held the chief power, the affairs of the Jews were peaceful. In these circumstances, Demetrius, the son of Demetrius, who, after the death of his father, had betaken himself to Crete, at the instigation of Lasthenes, general of the Cretans, tried by war to recover the kingdom of his father, but finding his power unequal to the task, he implored Ptolemy Philometor, king of Egypt, the father-in-law of Alexander, but who was then on bad terms with his son-in-law, to give him assistance. But he, induced not so much by the entreaties of the suppliant as by the hope of seizing Syria, joined his forces with those of Demetrius, and gives him his daughter, who had been married to Alexander. Against these two Alexander fought a pitched battle. Ptolemy fell in the fight, but Alexander was defeated; and he was soon afterwards slain, after he had reigned five, or as I find it stated in many authors, nine years.

CHAPTER XXV.

DEMETRIUS, having thus obtained the kingdom, treated Jonathan with kindness, made a treaty with him, and restored the Jews to their own laws. In the meantime, Tryphon, who had belonged to the party of Alexander, was appointed[1] governor of Syria, to keep him in check by war. Jonathan,[2] on the other hand,

descended to battle, formidable with an army of forty thousand men. Tryphon, when he saw himself unequal to the contest, pretended a desire for peace, and slew Ptolemais who had been received and invited into friendship with him. After Jonathan, the chief power was conferred on his brother Simon. He celebrated the funeral of his brother with great pomp, and built those well-known seven pyramids of most noble workmanship, in which he buried the remains both of his brothers and of his father. Then Demetrius renewed his treaty with the Jews; and in consideration of the loss caused to them by Tryphon (for after the death of Jonathan he had wasted by war their cities and territories), he remitted to them their annual tribute forever; for up to that time, they had paid tribute to the kings of Syria, except when they resisted by force of arms. That took place in the second year of king Demetrius; and we have noted that, because up to this year we have run through the times of the Asiatic kings, that the series of dates being given in order might be perfectly clear. But now we shall arrange the order of events through the times of those, who were either high-priests or kings among the Jews, up to the period of the birth of Christ.

CHAPTER XXVI.

WELL, then, after Jonathan, his brother Simon, as has been said above, ruled over the Hebrews with the power of high-priest. For that honor was then bestowed upon him both by his own countrymen and by the Roman people. He began to rule over his countrymen in the second year of king Demetrius, but eight years afterwards, being deceived by a plot of Ptolemy, he met his death. He was succeeded by his son John. And he, on the ground that he had fought with distinction against the Hyrcani, a very powerful nation, received the surname of Hyrcanus. He died, after having held the supreme power for twenty-six years. After him, Aristobulus being appointed high-priest, was the first of all living after the captivity to assume the name of king, and to have a crown placed upon his head. At the close of a year, he died. Then Alexander, his son, who was both king and high-priest, reigned twenty-seven years; but I have found nothing in his doings worthy of mention, except his cruelty. He having left two young sons named Aristobulus and Hyrcanus, Salina or Alexandra, his wife, held the sovereignty for three years. After his decease, frightful conflicts about the supreme power arose between the two brothers. And first of all, Hyrcanus held the government; but being by and by defeated by his brother Aristobulus, he

---

[1] Some words have here been lost, but the critics are not agreed as to what should be supplied.
[2] As Vorstius suggests, we have here taken Jonathan as a nominative, but the passage is very obscure.

fled to Pompey. That Roman general, having finished the war with Mithridates, and settled Armenia and Pontus, being, in fact, the conqueror of all the nations which he had visited, desired to march inwards,[1] and to add all the neighboring regions to the Roman empire. He therefore inquired into the causes of the war, and the means of obtaining[2] the mastery. Accordingly he readily received Hyrcanus, and, under his guidance, attacked the Jews; but when the city was taken and destroyed, he spared the temple. He sent Aristobulus in chains to Rome, and restored the right of the high-priesthood to Hyrcanus. Settling the tribute to be paid by the Jews, he placed over them as governor a certain Antipater of Askelon. Hyrcanus held the chief power for thirty-four years; but while he carried on war against the Parthians, he was taken prisoner.

CHAPTER XXVII.

THEN Herod, a foreigner, the son of Antipater of Askelon, asked and received the sovereignty of Judæa from the senate and people of Rome. Under him, the Jews began for the first time to have a foreigner as king. For as now the advent of Christ was at hand, it was necessary, according to the predictions of the prophets, that they should be deprived of their own rulers, that they might not look for anything beyond Christ. Under this Herod, in the thirty-third year of his reign, CHRIST was born on the twenty-fifth of December in the consulship of Sabinus and Rufinus. But we do not venture to touch on these things which are contained in the Gospels, and subsequently in the Acts of the Apostles, lest the character of our condensed work should, in any measure, detract from the dignity of the events; and I shall proceed to what remains. Herod reigned four years after the birth of the Lord; for the whole period of his reign comprised thirty-seven years. After him, came Archelaus the tetrarch, for eight years, and Herod for twenty-four years. Under him, in the eighteenth year of his reign, the Lord was crucified, Fufius Geminus and Rubellius Geminus being consuls; from which date up to the consulship of Stilico, there have elapsed three hundred and seventy-two years.

CHAPTER XXVIII.

LUKE made known the doings of the apostles up to the time when Paul was brought to Rome under the emperor Nero. As to Nero, I shall not say that he was the worst of kings, but that he was worthily held the basest of all men, and even of wild beasts. It was he who first began a persecution; and I am not sure but he will be the last also to carry it on, if, indeed, we admit, as many are inclined to believe, that he will yet appear immediately before the coming of Antichrist. Our subject would induce me to set forth his vices at some length, if it were not inconsistent with the purpose of this work to enter upon so vast a topic. I content myself with the remark, that he showed himself in every way most abominable and cruel, and at length even went so far as to be the murderer of his own mother. After this, he also married a certain Pythagoras in the style of solemn alliances, the bridal veil being put upon the emperor, while the usual dowry, and the marriage couch, and wedding torches, and, in short, all the other observances were forthcoming — things which even in the case of women are not looked upon without some feeling of modesty. But as to his other actions, I doubt whether the description of them would excite greater shame or sorrow. He first attempted to abolish the name of Christian, in accordance with the fact that vices are always inimical to virtues, and that all good men are ever regarded by the wicked as casting reproach upon them. For, at that time, our divine religion had obtained a wide prevalence in the city. Peter was there executing the office of bishop, and Paul, too, after he had been brought to Rome, on appealing to Cæsar from the unjust judgment of the governor. Multitudes then came together to hear Paul, and these, influenced by the truth which they were given to know, and by the miracles[1] of the apostles, which they then so frequently performed, turned to the worship of God. For then took place the well-known and celebrated encounter of Peter and Paul with Simon.[2] He, after he had flown up into the air by his magical arts, and supported by two demons (with the view of proving that he was a god), the demons being put to flight by the prayers of the apostles, fell to the earth in the sight of all the people, and was dashed to pieces.

CHAPTER XXIX.

IN the meantime, the number of the Christians being now very large, it happened that Rome was destroyed by fire, while Nero was stationed at Antium. But the opinion of all cast the odium of causing the fire upon the emperor, and he was believed in this way to have sought for the glory of building a new city. And in fact, Nero could not by any means he tried

---

[1] "Introrsum," *towards home*; another reading is "ultrorsum," *farther onwards.*
[2] "vincendi": others read "incendii."

[1] "virtutibus."
[2] Generally spoken of as Simon Magus

escape from the charge that the fire had been caused by his orders. He therefore turned the accusation against the Christians, and the most cruel tortures were accordingly inflicted upon the innocent. Nay, even new kinds of death were invented, so that, being covered in the skins of wild beasts, they perished by being devoured by dogs, while many were crucified or slain by fire, and not a few were set apart for this purpose, that, when the day came to a close, they should be consumed to serve for light during the night. In this way, cruelty first began to be manifested against the Christians. Afterwards, too, their religion was prohibited by laws which were enacted; and by edicts openly set forth it was proclaimed unlawful to be a Christian. At that time Paul and Peter were condemned to death, the former being beheaded with a sword, while Peter suffered crucifixion. And while these things went on at Rome, the Jews, not able to endure the injuries they suffered under the rule of Festus Florus, began to rebel. Vespasian, being sent by Nero against them, with proconsular power, defeated them in numerous important battles, and compelled them to flee within the walls of Jerusalem. In the meanwhile Nero, now hateful even to himself from a consciousness of his crimes, disappears from among[1] men, leaving it uncertain whether or not he had laid violent hands upon himself: certainly his body was never found. It was accordingly believed that, even if he did put an end to himself with a sword, his wound was cured, and his life preserved, according to that which was written regarding him, — "And his mortal[2] wound was healed," — to be sent forth again near the end of the world, in order that he may practice the mystery of iniquity.

CHAPTER XXX.

So then, after the departure of Nero, Galba seized the government; and ere long, on Galba being slain, Otho secured it. Then Vitellius from Gaul, trusting to the armies which he commanded, entered the city, and having killed Otho, assumed the sovereignty. This afterwards passed to Vespasian, and although that was accomplished by evil means, yet it had the good effect of rescuing the state from the hands of the wicked. While Vespasian was besieging Jerusalem, he took possession of the imperial power; and as the fashion is, he was saluted as emperor by the army, with a diadem placed upon his head. He made his son Titus, Cæsar; and assigned him a portion of the forces, along with the task of continuing the siege of Jerusalem. Vespasian set out for Rome, and was re-

ceived with the greatest favor by the senate and people; and Vitellius having killed himself, his hold of the sovereign power was fully confirmed. The Jews, meanwhile, being closely besieged, as no chance either of peace or surrender was allowed them, were at length perishing from famine, and the streets began everywhere to be filled with dead bodies, for the duty of burying them could no longer be performed. Moreover, they ventured on eating all things of the most abominable nature, and did not even abstain from human bodies, except those which putrefaction had already laid hold of and thus excluded from use as food. The Romans, accordingly, rushed in upon the exhausted defenders of the city. And it so happened that the whole multitude from the country, and from other towns of Judæa, had then assembled for the day of the Passover: doubtless, because it pleased God that the impious race should be given over to destruction at the very time of the year at which they had crucified the Lord. The Pharisees for a time maintained their ground most boldly in defense of the temple, and at length, with minds obstinately bent on death, they, of their own accord, committed themselves to the flames. The number of those who suffered death is related to have been eleven hundred thousand, and one hundred thousand were taken captive and sold. Titus is said, after calling a council, to have first deliberated whether he should destroy the temple, a structure of such extraordinary work. For it seemed good to some that a sacred edifice, distinguished above all human achievements, ought not to be destroyed, inasmuch as, if preserved, it would furnish an evidence of Roman moderation, but, if destroyed, would serve for a perpetual proof of Roman cruelty. But on the opposite side, others and Titus himself thought that the temple ought specially to be overthrown, in order that the religion of the Jews and of the Christians might more thoroughly be subverted; for that these religions, although contrary to each other, had nevertheless proceeded from the same authors; that Christians had sprung up from among the Jews; and that, if the root were extirpated, the offshoot would speedily perish. Thus, according to the divine will, the minds of all being inflamed, the temple was destroyed, three hundred and thirty-one years ago. And this last overthrow of the temple, and final captivity of the Jews, by which, being exiles from their native land, they are beheld scattered through the whole world, furnish a daily demonstration to the world, that they have been punished on no other account than for the impious hands which they laid upon Christ. For though on other occasions they were often given over to captivity

---

[1] " humanis rebus eximitur."   [2] Rev. xiii. 3.

on account of their sins, yet they never paid the penalty of slavery beyond a period of seventy years.

CHAPTER XXXI.

THEN, after an interval, Domitian, the son of Vespasian, persecuted the Christians. At this date, he banished John the Apostle and Evangelist to the island of Patmos. There he, secret mysteries having been revealed to him, wrote and published his book of the holy Revelation, which indeed is either foolishly or impiously not accepted by many. And with no great interval there then occurred the third persecution under Trajan. But he, when after torture and racking he found nothing in the Christians worthy of death or punishment, forbade any further cruelty to be put forth against them. Then under Adrian the Jews attempted to rebel, and endeavored to plunder both Syria and Palestine ; but on an army being sent against them, they were subdued. At this time Adrian, thinking that he would destroy the Christian faith by inflicting an injury upon the place, set up the images of demons both in the temple and in the place where the Lord suffered. And because the Christians were thought principally to consist of Jews (for the church at Jerusalem did not then have a priest except of the circumcision), he ordered a cohort of soldiers to keep constant guard in order to prevent all Jews from approaching to Jerusalem. This, however, rather benefited[1] the Christian faith, because almost all then believed in Christ as God while continuing[2] in the observance of the law. Undoubtedly that was arranged by the over-ruling care of the Lord, in order that the slavery of the law might be taken away from the liberty of the faith and of the church. In this way, Mark from among the Gentiles was then, first of all, bishop at Jerusalem. A fourth persecution is reckoned as having taken place under Adrian, which, however, he afterwards forbade to be carried on, declaring it to be unjust that any one should be put on his trial without a charge being specified against him.

CHAPTER XXXII.

AFTER Adrian, the churches had peace under the rule of Antoninus Pius. Then the fifth persecution began under Aurelius, the son of Antoninus. And then, for the first time, mar-

[1] How so? Because, according to Drusius, the Christian Jews were thus first taught to cast off the yoke of the law, which they had observed up to this time.
[2] These were half-Jews and half-Christians, and were known at a later date under the name of Nazarites. They made use of what was called the Gospel according to the Hebrews.

tyrdoms were seen taking place in Gaul, for the religion of God had been accepted somewhat late beyond the Alps. Then the sixth persecution of the Christians took place under the emperor Severus. At this time Leonida, the father of Origen, poured forth his sacred blood in martyrdom. Then, during an interval of thirty-eight years, the Christians enjoyed peace, except that at the middle of that time Maximinus persecuted the clerics of some churches. Ere long, under Decius as emperor, the seventh bloody persecution broke out against the Christians. Next, Valerian proved himself the eighth enemy of the saints. After him, with an interval of about fifty years, there arose, under the emperors Diocletian and Maximian, a most bitter persecution which, for ten continuous years, wasted the people of God. At this period, almost the whole world was stained with the sacred blood of the martyrs. In fact, they vied with each other in rushing upon these glorious struggles, and martyrdom by glorious deaths was then much more keenly sought after than bishoprics are now attempted to be got by wicked ambition. Never more than at that time was the world exhausted by wars, nor did we ever achieve victory with a greater triumph than when we showed that we could not be conquered by the slaughters of ten long years. There survive also accounts of the sufferings of the martyrs at that time which were committed to writing ; but I do not think it suitable to subjoin these lest I should exceed the limits prescribed to this work.

CHAPTER XXXIII.

WELL, the end of the persecutions was reached eighty-eight years ago, at which date the emperors began to be Christians. For Constantine then obtained the sovereignty, and he was the first Christian of all the Roman rulers. At that time, it is true, Licinius, who was a rival of Constantine for the empire, had commanded his soldiers to sacrifice, and was expelling from the service those who refused to do so. But that is not reckoned among the persecutions ; it was an affair of too little moment to be able to inflict any wound upon the churches. From that time, we have continued to enjoy tranquillity ; nor do I believe that there will be any further persecutions, except that which Antichrist will carry on just before the end of the world. For it has been proclaimed in divine words, that the world was to be visited by ten afflictions ;[1] and since nine of these have already been endured, the one which remains must be

[1] "decem plagis."

the last. During this period of time, it is marvelous how the Christian religion has prevailed. For Jerusalem which had presented a horrible mass of ruins was then adorned with most numerous and magnificent churches. And Helena, the mother of the emperor Constantine (who reigned along with her son as Augusta), having a strong desire to behold Jerusalem, cast down the idols and the temples which were found there; and in course of time, through the exercise of her royal powers, she erected churches[2] on the site of the Lord's passion, resurrection, and ascension. It is a remarkable fact that the spot on which the divine footprints had last been left, when the Lord was carried up in a cloud to heaven, could not be joined by a pavement with the remaining part of the street. For the earth, unaccustomed to mere human contact, rejected all the appliances laid upon it, and often threw back the blocks of marble in the faces of those who were seeking to place them. Moreover, it is an enduring proof of the soil of that place having been trodden by God, that the footprints are still to be seen; and although the faith of those who daily flock to that place, leads them to vie with each other in seeking to carry away what had been trodden by the feet of the Lord, yet the sand of the place suffers no injury; and the earth still preserves the same appearance which it presented of old, as if it had been sealed by the footprints impressed upon it.

CHAPTER XXXIV.

THROUGH the kind efforts of the same queen, the cross of the Lord was then found. It could not, of course, be consecrated at the beginning, owing to the opposition of the Jews, and afterwards it had been covered over by the rubbish of the ruined city. And now, it would never have been revealed except to one seeking for it in such a believing spirit. Accordingly, Helena having first got information about the place of our Lord's passion, caused a band of soldiers to be brought[1] up to it, while the whole multitude of the inhabitants of the locality vied with each other in seeking to gratify the desires of the queen, and ordered the earth to be dug up, and all the adjacent most extensive ruins to be cleared out. Ere long, as the reward of her faith and labor, three crosses (as of old they had been fixed for the Lord and the two robbers) were discovered. But upon this, the greater difficulty of distinguishing the gibbet on which the Lord had hung, disturbed the minds and thoughts of all, lest by a mistake, likely

enough to be committed by mere mortals, they might perhaps consecrate as the cross of the Lord, that which belonged to one of the robbers. They form then the plan of placing one who had recently died in contact with the crosses. Nor is there any delay in carrying out this purpose; for just as if by the appointment of God, the funeral of a dead man was then being conducted with the usual ceremonies, and all rushing up took the body from the bier. It was applied in vain to the first two crosses, but when it touched that of Christ, wonderful to tell, while all stood trembling, the dead body was[2] shaken off, and stood up in the midst of those looking at it. The cross was thus discovered, and was consecrated with all due ceremony.[3]

CHAPTER XXXV.

SUCH were the things accomplished by Helena, while, under a Christian prince, the world had both attained to liberty, and possessed in him an exemplar of faith. But a far more dreadful danger than all that had preceded fell upon all the churches from that state of tranquillity. For then the Arian heresy burst forth, and disturbed the whole world by the error which it instilled. For by means of the two[1] Ariuses, who were the most active originators of this unfaithfulness, the emperor himself was led astray; and while he seemed to himself to fulfill a religious duty, he proceeded to a violent exercise of persecution. The bishops were driven into exile: cruelty was exerted against the clerics; and even the laity were punished, who had separated from the communion of the Arians. Now, the doctrines which the Arians proclaimed were of the following nature, — that God the Father had begotten his Son for the purpose of creating the world; and that, by his power, he had made[2] out of nothing into a new and second substance, a new and second God; and that there was a time when the Son had no existence. To meet this evil, a synod was convened from the whole world to meet at Nicæa. Three hundred and eighteen bishops were there assembled: the faith was fully set forth in writing; the Arian heresy was condemned; and the emperor confirmed the whole by an imperial decree. The Arians, then, not daring to make any further attempt against the orthodox faith, mixed themselves among the churches, as if they acquiesced in the conclusions which had been reached, and did not hold any different opinions.

---

2 "funus excussum": a singular expression.
3 "ambitu": apparently used here with the meaning which sometimes belongs to "ambitione."
1 The one of these was Arius, the author of the heresy, and the other a presbyter of Alexandria bearing the same name.
2 Both the text and meaning are here obscure. We have read, with Halm, "fecisse" for the usual "factum."

2 "basilicas": edifices, which, in size and grandeur, had some resemblance to a royal palace.
1 "admota militari manu atque omnium provincialium multitudine in studia reginæ certantium."

There remained, however, in their hearts, a deep-seated hatred against the Catholics, and they assailed, with suborned accusers and trumped-up charges, those with whom they could not contend in argument on matters of faith.

CHAPTER XXXVI.

ACCORDINGLY, they first attack and condemn in his absence Athanasius, bishop of Alexandria, a holy man, who had been present as deacon at the Synod of Nicæa. For they added to the charges which false witnesses had heaped up against him, this one, that, with wicked intentions, he had receiv·d[1] Marcellus and Photinus, heretical priests who had been condemned by a sentence of the Synod. Now, it was not doubtful as to Photinus that he had been justly condemned. But in the case of Marcellus, it seemed that nothing had then been found worthy of condemnation, and[2] a belief in his innocence was above all strengthened by the *animus* of that party, inasmuch as no one doubted that those same judges were heretical by whom he had been condemned. But the Arians did not so much desire to get these persons out of the way as Athanasius himself. Accordingly, they constrain the emperor to go so far as this, that Athanasius should be sent as an exile into Gaul. But ere long, eighty bishops, assembling together in Egypt, declare that Athanasius had been unjustly condemned. The matter is referred to Constantine: he orders[3] bishops from the whole world to assemble at Sardes, and that the entire process by which Athanasius had been condemned, should be reconsidered by the council. In the meantime, Constantine dies, but the Synod, called together while he was yet emperor, acquits Athanasius. Marcellus, too, is restored to his bishopric, but the sentence on Photinus, bishop of Sirmion, was not rescinded; for even[4] in the judgment of our friends, he is regarded as a heretic. However, even this result chagrined Marcellus, because Photinus was known to have been his disciple in his youth. But this, too, tended to secure an acquittal for Athanasius, that Ursatius and Valens, leading men among the Arians, when they were openly separated from the communion of the Church after the Synod at Sardes, entering into the presence of

Julius, bishop of Rome, asked pardon of him for having condemned the innocent, and publicly declared that he had been justly acquitted by the decree of the Council of Sardes.

CHAPTER XXXVII.

WHEN, after an interval of some time had elapsed, Athanasius, finding that Marcellus was by no means sound in the faith, suspended him from communion. And he had this degree of modesty, that, being censured by the judgment of so great a man, he voluntarily gave way. But though at a former period innocent, yet confessedly afterwards becoming heretical, it may be allowed to conclude that he was really then guilty when judgment was pronounced regarding him. The Arians, then, finding an opportunity of that kind, conspire to subvert altogether the decrees of the Synod of Sardes. For a certain coloring of right seemed to be furnished them in this fact, that a favorable judgment had as unjustly been formed on the side of Athanasius, as Marcellus had been improperly acquitted, since now, even in the opinion of Athanasius himself, he was deemed a heretic. For Marcellus had stood forward as an upholder of the Sabellian heresy.[1] But Photinus had already brought forward a new heresy, differing indeed from Sabellius with respect to the union of the divine persons, but proclaiming that Christ had his beginning in Mary. The Arians, therefore, with cunning design, mix up what was harmless with what was blameworthy, and embrace, under the same judgment, the condemnation of Photinus, and Marcellus, and Athanasius. They undoubtedly did this with the view of leading the minds of the ignorant to conclude, that those had not judged incorrectly regarding Athanasius, who, it was admitted, had expressed a well-based opinion respecting Marcellus and Photinus. At that time, however, the Arians concealed their treachery; and not daring openly to proclaim their erroneous doctrines, they professed themselves Catholics. They thought that their first great object should be to get Athanasius turned out of the church, who had always presented a wall of opposition to their endeavors, and they hoped that, if he were removed, the rest would pass over to their evil[2] opinion. Now, that part of the bishops which followed the Arians accepted the condemnation of Athanasius with delight. Another part, constrained by fear and faction, yielded to the wish of the Arian party; and only a few, to

---

[1] Different periods and events are here mixed up by our author.
[2] The text is in utter confusion, and we can only make a probable guess at the meaning.
[3] It has been remarked that Sulpitius is in error in ascribing the summoning of this council to Constantine the Great, instead of his son Constantine II. The curious thing is that he should have made a mistake regarding an event so near his own time.
[4] " qui etiam nostrorum judicio hæreticus probatur."

[1] As Epiphanius remarks, Sabellius taught that the Father, Son, and Holy Ghost were all the same person, only under different appellations.
[2] " libidinem."

whom the true faith was dearer than any other consideration, refused to accept their unjust judgment. Among these was Paulinus, the bishop of Treves. It is related that he, when a letter on the subject was placed before him, thus wrote, that he gave his consent to the condemnation of Photinus and Marcellus, but did not approve that of Athanasius.

CHAPTER XXXVIII.

BUT then the Arians, seeing that stratagem did not succeed, determined to proceed by force. For it was easy for those to attempt and carry out anything who were supported by the favor of the monarch, whom they had thoroughly won over to themselves by wicked flatteries. Moreover, they were by the consent of all unconquerable; for almost all the bishops of the two Pannonias, and many of the Eastern bishops, and those throughout all Asia, had joined in their unfaithfulness. But the chief men in that evil company were Ursatius of Singidunum, Valens of Mursa, Theodorus of Heraclia, Stephanus of Antioch, Acatius of Cæsarea, Menofantus of Ephesus, Georgius of Laodicia, and Narcissus of Neronopolis. These had got possession of the palace to such an extent that the emperor did nothing without their concurrence. He was indeed at the beck of all of them, but was especially under the influence of Valens. For at that time, when a battle was fought at Mursa against Magnentius, Constantius had not the courage to go down to witness for himself the conflict, but took up his abode in a church of the martyrs which stood outside the town, Valens who was then the bishop of the place being with him to keep up his courage. But Valens had cunningly arranged, through means of his agents, that he should be the first to be made acquainted with the result of the battle. He did this either to gain the favor of the king, if he should be the first to convey to him good news, or with a view to saving his own life, since he would obtain time for flight, should the issue prove unfortunate. Accordingly, the few persons who were with the king being in a state of alarm, and the emperor himself being a prey to anxiety, Valens was the first to announce to them the flight of the enemy. When Constantius requested that the person who had brought the news should be introduced to his presence, Valens, to increase the reverence felt for himself, said that an angel was the messenger who had come to him. The emperor, who was easy of belief, was accustomed afterwards openly to declare that he had won the victory through the merits of Valens, and not by the valor of his army.

CHAPTER XXXIX.

FROM this first proof that the prince had been won over to their side, the Arians plucked up their courage, knowing that they could make use of the power of the king, when they could make little impression by their own authority. Accordingly, when our friends did not accept of the judgment which they had pronounced in regard to Athanasius, an edict was issued by the emperor to the effect that those who did not subscribe to the condemnation of Athanasius should be sent into banishment. But, at that time, councils of bishops were held by our friends at Arles and Bitteræ, towns situated in Gaul. They requested that before any were compelled to subscribe against Athanasius, they should rather enter on a discussion as to the true faith; and maintained that only then was a decision to be come to respecting the point in question, when they had agreed as to the person of the judges.[1] But Valens and his confederates not venturing on a discussion respecting the faith, first desired to secure by force the condemnation of Athanasius. Owing to this conflict of parties, Paulinus was driven into banishment. In the meantime, an assembly was held at Milan, where the emperor then was; but the same controversy was there continued without any relaxation of its bitterness. Then Eusebius, bishop of the Vercellenses, and Lucifer, bishop of Caralis[2] in Sardinia, were exiled. Dionysius, however, priest of Milan, subscribed to the condemnation of Athanasius, on the condition that there should be an investigation among the bishops as to the true faith. But Valens and Ursatius, with the rest of that party, through fear of the people, who maintained the Catholic faith with extraordinary enthusiasm, did not venture to set forth in public their monstrous[3] doctrines, but assembled within the palace. From that place, and under the name of the emperor, they issued a letter full[4] of all sorts of wickedness, with this purpose, no doubt, that, if the people gave it a favorable hearing, they should then bring forward, under public authority, the things which they desired; but if it should be received otherwise, that all the ill feeling might be directed against the king, while his mistake might be regarded as excusable, because being then only a catechumen, he might readily be supposed to have erred concerning the mysteries of the faith. Well, when the letter was read in the church, the people expressed their aversion to it. And Dionysius, because he did not concur with them, was banished from the city, while Auxentius was immediately chosen as

---

[1] The text is here in utter confusion and uncertainty. Some for " ac tum " read " nec tum," and some, instead of " judicum " read "judicium." The meaning therefore can only be guessed at.
[2] The modern *Cagliari*. [3] " Piacula profiteri."
[4] Instead of " refertam," some read " infectam."

bishop in his place.   Liberius, too, bishop of the city of Rome, and Hilarius, bishop of Poictiers, were driven into exile.   Rhodanius, also, bishop of Toulouse (who, being by nature of a softer disposition, had resisted the Arians, not so much from his own powers as from his fellowship with Hilarius) was involved in the same punishment.   All these persons, however, were prepared to suspend Athanasius from communion, only in order that an inquiry might be instituted among the bishops as to the true faith. But it seemed best to the Arians to withdraw the most celebrated men from the controversy.   Accordingly, those whom we have mentioned above were driven into exile, forty-five years ago, when Arbitio and Lollianus were consuls.   Liberius, however, was, a little afterwards, restored to the city, in consequence of the disturbances at Rome.   But it is well known that the persons exiled were celebrated by the admiration of the whole world, and that abundant supplies of money were collected to meet their wants, while they were visited by deputies of the Catholic people from almost all the provinces.

CHAPTER XL.

In the meantime, the Arians, not secretly, as before, but openly and publicly proclaimed their monstrous heretical doctrines.   Moreover, they interpreted after their own views the Synod of Nicæa, and by the addition of one letter to its finding, threw a sort of obscurity over the truth. For where the expression *Homoousion* had been written, which denotes " of one substance," they maintained that it was written *Homoiousion*, which simply means " of like substance."   They thus granted a likeness, but took away unity ; for likeness is very different from unity ; just as, for illustration's sake, a picture of a human body might be like a man, and yet possess nothing of the reality of a man.   But some of them went even farther, and maintained *Anomoiousia*, that is, an unlike substance.   And to such a pitch did these controversies extend, that the wide world was involved in these monstrous errors. For Valens and Ursatius, with their supporters, whose names we have stated, infected Italy, Illyria, and the East with these opinions.   Saturninus, bishop of Arles, a violent and factious man, harassed our country of Gaul in like manner.   There was also a prevalent belief that Osius from Spain had gone over to the same unfaithful party, which appears all the more wonderful and incredible on this account, that he had been, almost during his whole life, the most determined upholder of our views, and the Synod of Nice was regarded as having been held at his instigation.   If he did go over, the reason

may have been that in his extreme old age (for he was then more than a centenarian, as St. Hilarius relates in his epistles) he had fallen into dotage.   While the world was disturbed by these things, and the churches were languishing as if from a sort of disease, an anxiety, less exciting indeed, but no less serious, pressed upon the emperor, that although the Arians, whom he favored, appeared the stronger, yet there was still no agreement among the bishops concerning the faith.

CHAPTER XLI.

Accordingly, the emperor orders a Synod to assemble at Ariminum, a city of Italy, and instructs Taurus the prefect, not to let them separate, after they were once assembled, until they should agree as to one faith, at the same time promising him the consulship, if he carried the affair to a successful termination.   Imperial[1] officers, therefore, being sent through Illyria, Italy, Africa, and the two Gauls, four hundred and rather more Western bishops were summoned or compelled to assemble at Ariminum ; and for all of these the emperor had ordered provisions[2] and lodgings to be provided.   But that appeared unseemly to the men of our part of the world, that is, to the Aquitanians, the Gauls, and Britons, so that refusing the public supplies, they preferred to live at their own expense.   Three only of those from Britain, through want of means of their own, made use of the public bounty, after having refused contributions offered by the rest ; for they thought it more dutiful to burden the public treasury than individuals.   I have heard that Gavidius, our bishop, was accustomed to refer to this conduct in a censuring sort of way, but I would be inclined to judge far otherwise ; and I hold it matter of admiration that the bishops had nothing of their own, while they did not accept assistance from others rather than from the public treasury, so that they burdened nobody. In both points, they thus furnished us with a noble example.   Nothing worthy of mention is recorded of the others ; but I return to the subject in hand.   After all the bishops had been collected together, as we have said, a separation of parties took place.   Our friends[3] take possession of the church, while the Arians select, as a place for prayer, a temple which was then intentionally standing empty.   But these did not amount to more than eighty persons : the rest belonged to our party.   Well, after frequent meetings had been held, nothing was really

---

[1] " magistris officialibus ": Halm reads " magistri."
[2] " annonas et cellaria."
[3] Of course, the Catholics, or orthodox.

accomplished, our friends continuing in the faith, and the others not abandoning their un-faithfulness. At length it was resolved to send ten deputies to the emperor, that he might learn what was the faith or opinion of the parties, and might know that there could be no peace with heretics. The Arians do the same thing, and send a like number of deputies, who should con-tend with our friends in the presence of the emperor. But on the part of our people, young men of but little learning and little prudence had been selected; while, on the side of the Arians, old men were sent, skillful and abounding in talent, thoroughly imbued, too, with their old unfaithful doctrines; and these easily got the upper hand with the prince. But our friends had been specially charged not to enter into any kind of communion with the Arians, and to reserve every point, in its entirety, for discussion in a Synod.

CHAPTER XLII.

In the meantime in the East, after the example of the West, the emperor ordered almost all the bishops to assemble at Seleucia, a town of Isauria. At that time, Hilarius, who was now spending the fourth year of his exile in Phrygia, is compelled to be present among the other bishops, the means of a public conveyance being furnished to him by the lieutenant[1] and governor. As, however, the emperor had given no special orders regarding him, the judges, simply following the general order by which they were commanded to gather all bishops to the council, sent him also among the rest who were willing to go. This was done, as I imagine, by the special ordination of God, in order that a man who was most deeply instructed in divine things, might be present when a discussion was to be carried on respecting the faith. He, on arriving at Seleucia, was received with great favor, and drew the minds and affections of all towards himself. His first inquiry was as to the real faith of the Gauls, because at that time the Arians had spread evil reports regarding us, and we were held suspected by the Easterns as hav-ing embraced the belief of Sabellius, to the effect that the unity of the one God was simply distinguished[2] by a threefold name. But after he had set forth his faith in harmony with those conclusions which had been reached by the fathers at Nicæa, he bore his testimony in favor of the Westerns. Thus the minds of all having been satisfied, he was admitted to com-

munion, and being also received into alliance, was added to the council. They then pro-ceeded to actual work, and the originators of the wicked heresy being discovered, were sepa-rated from the body of the Church. In that number were Georgius of Alexandria, Acacius, Eudoxius, Vranius, Leontius, Theodosius, Eva-grius, Theodulus. But when the Synod was over, an embassy was appointed to go to the emperor and make him acquainted with what had been done. Those who had been con-demned also went to the prince, relying upon the power of their confederates, and a common cause with the monarch.

CHAPTER XLIII.

In the meantime, the emperor compels those deputies of our party who had been sent from the council at Ariminum to join in communion with the heretics. At the same time, he hands them a confession of faith which had been drawn up by these wicked men, and which, being expressed in deceptive terms, seemed to exhibit the Catholic faith, while unfaithfulness secretly lay hid in it. For under an appearance of false reasoning, it abolished the use of the word *Ousia* as being ambiguous, and as having been too hastily adopted by the fathers, while it rested upon no Scriptural authority. The object of this was that the Son might not be believed to be of one substance with the Father. The same confession of faith acknowledged that the Son was *like* the Father. But deception was carefully prepared within the words, in order that he might be like, but not equal. Thus, the deputies being sent away, orders were given to the prefect that he should not dissolve the Synod, until all professed by their subscriptions their agreement to the declaration of faith which had been drawn up; and if any should hold back with excessive obstinacy, they should be driven into banishment, provided their number did not amount to fifteen. But when the depu-ties returned, they were refused communion, although they pleaded the force which had been brought to bear upon them by the king. For when it was discovered what had been decreed, greater disturbance arose in their affairs and purposes. Then by degrees numbers of our people, partly overcome through the weakness of their character, and partly influenced by the thought of a weary journeying into foreign lands, surrendered to the opposite party. These were now, on the return of the deputies, the stronger of the two bodies, and had taken possession of the church, our friends being driven out of it. And when the minds of our people once began to incline in that direction, they rushed

---

[1] " per vicarium ac præsidem ": as Vorstius remarks, these were the two magistrates of Phrygia.
[2] " trionymam solitarii Dei unionem ": Hornius here remarks that " Sabellius believed that the Father, the Son, and the Holy Spirit were the same, and differed among themselves only in name."

in flocks over to the other side, until the number of our friends was diminished down to twenty.

CHAPTER XLIV.

BUT these, the fewer they became, showed themselves all the more powerful; as the most steadfast among them was to be reckoned our friend Fœgadius, and Servatio, bishop of the Tungri. As these had not yielded to threats and terrors, Taurus assails them with entreaties, and beseeches them with tears to adopt milder counsels. He argued that the bishops were now in the seventh month since they had been shut up within one city — that no hope of returning home presented itself to them, worn out by the inclemency of winter and positive want; and what then would be the end? He urged them to follow the example of the majority, and to derive authority for so doing at least from the numbers who had preceded them. For Fœgadius openly declared that he was prepared for banishment, and for every kind of punishment that might be assigned him, but would not accept that confession of faith which had been drawn up by the Arians. Thus several days passed in this sort of discussion. And when they made little progress towards a pacification, by degrees Fœgadius began to yield, and at the last was overcome by a proposal which was made to him. For Valens and Ursatius affirmed that the present confession of faith was drawn up on the lines of Catholic doctrine, and having been brought forward by the Easterns at the instigation of the emperor, could not be rejected without impiety; and what possible end of strife could there be if a confession which satisfied the Easterns was rejected by those of the West? Finally, if there appeared anything less fully stated in the present confession than was desirable, they themselves should add what they thought ought to be added, and that they, for their part, would acquiesce in those things which might be added. This friendly profession was received with favorable minds by all. Nor did our people venture any longer to make opposition, desiring as they did in some way or other now to put an end to the business. Then confessions drawn up by Fœgadius and Servatio began to be published; and in these first Arius and his whole unfaithful scheme was condemned, while the Son of God also was[1] pronounced equal to the Father, and without beginning, [that is] without any commencement[2] in time. Then

Valens, as if assisting our friends, subjoined the statement (in which there lurked a secret guile) that the Son of God was not a creature like the other creatures; and the deceit involved in this declaration escaped the notice of the hearers. For in these words, in which the Son was denied to be like the other creatures, he was nevertheless pronounced a creature, only superior to the rest. Thus neither party could hold that it had wholly conquered or had wholly been conquered, since the confession itself was in favor of the Arians, but the declarations afterwards added were in favor of our friends. That one, however, must be excepted which Valens had subjoined, and which, not being at the time understood, was at length comprehended when it was too late. In this way, at any rate, the council was brought to an end, a council which had a good beginning but a disgraceful conclusion.

CHAPTER XLV.

THUS, then, the Arians, with their affairs in a very flourishing condition, and everything turning out according to their wishes, go in a body to Constantinople where the emperor was. There they found the deputies from the Synod of Seleucia, and compel them by an exercise of the royal power to follow the example of the Westerns, and accept that heretical confession of faith. Numbers who refused were tortured with painful imprisonment and hunger, so that at length they yielded their conscience captive. But many who resisted more courageously, being deprived of their bishoprics, were driven into exile, and others substituted in their place. Thus, the best priests being either terrified by threats, or driven into exile, all gave way before the unfaithfulness of a few. Hilarius was there at the time, having followed the deputies from Seleucia; and as no certain orders had been given regarding him, he was waiting on the will of the emperor to see whether perchance he should be ordered to return into banishment. When he perceived the extreme danger into which the faith had been brought, inasmuch as the Westerns had been beguiled, and the Easterns were being overcome by means of wickedness, he, in three papers publicly presented, begged an audience of the king, in order that he might debate on points of faith in the presence of his adversaries. But the Arians opposed that to the utmost extent of their ability. Finally, Hilarius was ordered to return to Gaul, as being a sower[1] of discord, and a troubler of the East, while the sentence of exile against him remained uncanceled. But when he had wandered over almost the whole earth which was in-

---

[1] The text is very uncertain; we have followed that of Halm, but the common text inserts a "non," and reads thus: "but the Son of God is not pronounced equal to the Father, and without beginning," etc.
[2] "sine tempore."

[1] "seminarium": lit. seed-plot.

fected with the evil of unfaithfulness, his mind was full of doubt and deeply agitated with the mighty burden of cares which pressed upon it. Perceiving that it seemed good to many not to enter into communion with those who had acknowledged the Synod of Ariminum, he thought the best thing he could do was to bring back all to repentance and reformation. In frequent councils within Gaul, and while almost all the bishops publicly owned the error that had been committed, he condemns the proceedings at Ariminum, and frames anew the faith of the churches after its pristine form. Saturninus, however, bishop of Arles, who was, in truth, a very bad man, of an evil and corrupt character, resisted these sound measures. He was, in fact, a man who, besides the infamy of being a heretic, was convicted of many unspeakable crimes, and cast out of the Church. Thus, having lost its leader, the strength of the party opposed to Hilarius was broken. Paternus also of Petrocorii,[2] equally infatuated, and not shrinking from openly professing unfaithfulness, was expelled from the priesthood: pardon was extended to the others. This fact is admitted by all, that our regions of Gaul were set free from the guilt of heresy through the kind efforts of Hilarius alone. But Lucifer, who was then at Antioch, held a very different opinion. For he condemned those who assembled at Ariminum to such an extent, that he even separated himself from the communion of those who had received them as friends, after they had made satisfaction or exhibited penitence. Whether this resolution of his was right or wrong, I will not take upon me to say. Paulinus and Rhodanius died in Phrygia; Hilarius died in his native country in the sixth year after his return.

CHAPTER XLVI.

THERE follow the times of our own day, both difficult and dangerous. In these the churches have been defiled with no ordinary evil, and all things thrown into confusion. For then, for the first time, the infamous heresy of the Gnostics was detected in Spain — a deadly[1] superstition which concealed itself under mystic[2] rites. The birthplace of that mischief was the East, and specially Egypt, but from what beginnings it there sprang up and increased is not easy to explain. Marcus was the first to introduce it into Spain, having set out from Egypt, his birthplace being Memphis. His pupils were a certain Agape, a woman of no mean origin, and a

rhetorician named Helpidius. By these again Priscillian was instructed, a man of noble birth, of great riches, bold, restless, eloquent, learned through much reading, very ready at debate and discussion — in fact, altogether a happy man, if he had not ruined an excellent intellect by wicked studies. Undoubtedly, there were to be seen in him many admirable qualities both of mind and body. He was able to spend much time in watchfulness, and to endure both hunger and thirst; he had little desire for amassing wealth, and he was most economical in the use of it. But at the same time he was a very vain man, and was much more puffed up than he ought to have been with the knowledge of mere earthly[3] things: moreover, it was believed that he had practised magical arts from his boyhood. He, after having himself adopted the pernicious system referred to, drew into its acceptance many persons of noble rank and multitudes of the common people by the arts of persuasion and flattery which he possessed. Besides this, women who were fond of novelties and of unstable faith, as well as of a prurient curiosity in all things, flocked to him in crowds. It increased this tendency that he exhibited, a kind of humility in his countenance and manner, and thus excited in all a greater honor and respect for himself. And now by degrees the wasting disorder of that heresy[4] had pervaded the most of Spain, and even some of the bishops came under its depraving influence. Among these, Instantius and Salvianus had taken up the cause of Priscillian, not only by expressing their concurrence in his views, but even by binding themselves to him with a kind of oath. This went on until Hyginus, bishop of Cordova, who dwelt in the vicinity, found out how matters stood, and reported the whole to Ydacius, priest of Emerita. But he, by harassing Instantius and his confederates without measure, and beyond what the occasion called for, applied, as it were, a torch to the growing conflagration, so that he rather exasperated than suppressed these evil men.

CHAPTER XLVII.

So, then, after many controversies among them, which are not worthy of mention, a Synod was assembled at Saragossa, at which even the Aquitanian bishops were present. But the heretics did not venture to submit themselves to the judgment of the council; sentence, however, was passed against them in their absence, and Instantius and Salivanus, bishops, with Helpidius and Priscillian, laymen, were condemned. It was also added that if any one should admit the

---

[2] The modern *Perigueux*.

[1] " superstitio exitiabilis ": the very words which Tacitus employs, when speaking of Christianity itself (*Annal.* xv. 44).

[2] " arcanis occultata secretis ": it is impossible to say what is the exact meaning of these words.

[3] " profanarum rerum. "   [4] " perfidiæ istius. "

condemned persons to communion, he should understand that the same sentence would be pronounced against himself. And the duty was entrusted to Ithacius, bishop of Sossuba, of seeing that the decree of the bishops was brought to the knowledge of all, and that Hyginus especially should be excluded from communion, who, though he had been the first to commence open proceedings against the heretics, had afterwards fallen away shamefully and admitted them to communion. In the meantime, Instantius and Salvianus, having been condemned by the judgment of the priests, appoint as bishop in the town of Arles, Priscillian, a layman indeed, but the leader in all these troubles, and who had been condemned along with themselves in the Synod at Saragossa. This they did with the view of adding to their strength, doubtless imagining that, if they armed with sacerdotal authority a man of bold and subtle character, they would find themselves in a safer position. But then Ydacius and Ithacius pressed forward their measures more ardently, in the belief that the mischief might be suppressed at its beginning. With unwise counsels, however, they applied to secular judges, that by their decrees and prosecutions the heretics might be expelled from the cities. Accordingly, after many disgraceful squabbles, a rescript was, on the entreaty of Ydacius, obtained from Gratianus, who was then emperor, in virtue of which all heretics were enjoined not only to leave churches or cities, but to be driven forth beyond all the territory under[1] his jurisdiction. When this edict became known, the Gnostics, distrusting their own affairs, did not venture to oppose the judgment, but those of them who bore the name of bishops gave way of their own accord, while fear scattered the rest.

CHAPTER XLVIII.

AND then Instantius, Salvianus, and Priscillian set out for Rome, in order that before Damasus, who was at that time the bishop of the city, they might clear themselves of the charges brought against them. Well, their journey led them through the heart of Aquitania, and being there received with great pomp by such as knew no better, they spread the seeds of their heresy. Above all, they perverted by their evil teachings the people of Elusa, who were then of a good and religious disposition. They were driven forth from Bordeaux by Delfinus, yet lingering for a little while in the territory of Euchrotia,[1] they infected some with their errors. They then pursued the journey on which they had entered, attended by a base and shameful company, among whom were their wives and even strange women. In the number of these was Euchrotia and her daughter Procula, of the latter of whom there was a common report that, when pregnant through adultery with Priscillian, she procured abortion by the use of certain plants. When they reached Rome with the wish of clearing themselves before Damasus, they were not even admitted to his presence. Returning to Milan, they found that Ambrose was equally opposed to them. Then they changed their plans, with the view that, as they had not got the better of the two bishops, who were at that time possessed of the highest authority, they might, by bribery and flattery, obtain what they desired from the emperor. Accordingly, having won over Macedonius, who was the master[2] of public services, they procured a rescript, by which, those decrees which had formerly been made being trampled under foot, they were ordered to be restored to their churches. Relying upon this, Instantius and Priscillian made their way back to Spain (for Salvianus had died in the city); and they then, without any struggle, recovered the churches over which they had ruled.

CHAPTER XLIX.

BUT the power, not the will, to resist, failed Ithacius; for the heretics had won over by bribes Voluentius, the proconsul, and thus consolidated their own power. Moreover, Ithacius was put on his trial, by these men as being a disturber of the churches, and he having been ordered as the result of a fierce prosecution, to be carried off[1] as a prisoner, fled in terror into Gaul, where he betook himself to Gregory the prefect. He, after he learned what had taken place, orders the authors of these tumults to be brought before himself, and makes a report on all that had occurred to the emperor, in order that he might close against the heretics every means of flattery or bribery. But that was done in vain; because, through the licentiousness and power of a few, all things were there to be purchased. Accordingly, the heretics by their artifices, having presented Macedonius with a large sum of money, secure that, by the imperial authority, the hearing of the trial was taken from the prefect, and transferred to the lieutenant in Spain. By that time, the Spaniards had ceased to have a proconsul as ruler, and officials were sent by the Master to bring back to Spain Ithacius who was then living at Treves. He, however, craftily escaped them, and being subsequently defended by the bishop Pritannius, he set them at

---

[1] The text has merely " extra omnes terras."
[2] Some read *Euchrocia,* and so afterwards.

[2] " magistro officiorum."
[1] This appears to be the meaning, but the text is obscure.

defiance. Then, too, a faint[2] rumor had spread that Maximus had assumed imperial power in Britain, and would, in a short time, make an incursion into Gaul. Accordingly, Ithacius then resolved, although his affairs were in a ticklish state, to wait the arrival of the new emperor; and that, in the meantime, no step should on his part be taken. When therefore Maximus, as victor, entered the town of the Treveri, he poured forth entreaties full of ill-will and accusations against Priscillian and his confederates. The emperor influenced by these statements, sent letters to the prefeet of Gaul and to the lieutenant in Spain, ordering that all whom that disgraceful[3] heresy had affected should be brought to a Synod at Bordeaux. Accordingly, Instantius and Priscillian were escorted thither, and, of these, Instantius was enjoined to plead his cause; and after he was found unable to clear himself, he was pronounced unworthy of the office of a bishop. But Priscillian, in order that he might avoid being heard by the bishops, appealed to the emperor. And that was permitted to be done through the want of resolution on the part of our friends, who ought either to have passed a sentence even against one who resisted it, or, if they were regarded as themselves suspicious persons, should have reserved the hearing for other bishops, and should not have transferred to the emperor a cause involving such manifest offences.

that he should give up his accusations, or to implore Maximus that he should not shed the blood of the unhappy persons in question. He maintained that it was quite sufficient punishment that, having been declared heretics by a sentence of the bishops, they should have been expelled from the churches; and that it was, besides, a foul and unheard-of indignity, that a secular ruler should be judge in an ecclesiastical cause. And, in fact, as long as Martin survived, the trial was put off; while, when he was about to leave this world, he, by his remarkable influence, obtained a promise from Maximus, that no cruel measure would be resolved on with respect to the guilty persons. But subsequently, the emperor being led astray by Magnus and Rufus, and turned from the milder course which Martin had counseled, entrusted the case to prefect Evodius, a man of stern and severe character. He tried Priscillian in two assemblies, and convicted him of evil conduct. In fact, Priscillian did not deny that he had given himself up to lewd doctrines; had been accustomed to hold, by night, gatherings of vile women, and to pray in a state of nudity. Accordingly, Evodius pronounced him guilty, and sent him back to prison, until he had time to consult the emperor. The matter, then, in all its details, was reported to the palace, and the emperor decreed that Priscillian and his friends should be put to death.

CHAPTER L.

THUS, then, all whom the process embraced were brought before the king. The bishops Ydacius and Ithacius followed as accusers; and I would by no means blame their zeal in overthrowing heretics, if they had not contended for victory with greater keenness than was fitting. And my feeling indeed is, that the accusers were as distasteful to me as the accused. I certainly hold that Ithacius had no worth or holiness about him. For he was a bold, loquacious, impudent, and extravagant man; excessively devoted to the pleasures of sensuality. He proceeded even to such a pitch of folly as to charge all those men, however holy, who either took delight in reading, or made it their object to vie with each other in the practice of fasting, with being friends or disciples of Priscillian. The miserable wretch even ventured publicly to bring forward a disgraceful charge of heresy against Martin, who was at that time a bishop, and a man clearly worthy of being compared to the Apostles. For Martin, being then settled at Treves, did not cease to importune Ithacius,

CHAPTER LI.

BUT Ithacius, seeing how much ill-will it would excite against him among the bishops, if he should stand forth as accuser also at the last trial on a capital charge (for it was requisite that the trial should be repeated), withdrew from the prosecution. His cunning, however, in thus acting was in vain, as the mischief was already accomplished. Well, a certain Patricius, an advocate connected with the treasury, was then appointed accuser by Maximus. Accordingly, under him as prosecutor, Priscillian was condemned to death, and along with him, Felicissimus and Armenius, who, when they were clerics, had lately adopted the cause of Priscillian, and revolted from the Catholics. Latronianus, too, and Euchrotia were beheaded. Instantius, who, as we have said above, had been condemned by the bishops, was transported to the island of Sylina[1] which lies beyond Britain. A process was then instituted against the others in trials which followed, and Asarivus, and Aurelius the deacon, were condemned to be beheaded, while Tiberianus was deprived of his goods, and ban-

---

[2] "clemens": some read "Clementen," and join it with "Maximum." [3] "labes illa."

[1] Halm prefers the form "Sylinancim" to "Sylinam." The reference is probably to the Scilly Isles.

ished to the island of Sylina. Tertullus, Potamius, and Joannes, as being persons of less consideration, and worthy of some merciful treatment, inasmuch as before the trial they had made a confession, both as to themselves and their confederates, were sentenced to a temporary banishment into Gaul. In this sort of way, men who were most unworthy of the light of day, were, in order that they might serve as a terrible example to others, either put to death or punished with exile. That conduct[2] which he had at first defended by his right of appeal to the tribunals, and by regard to the public good, Ithacius, harassed[3] with invectives, and at last overcome, threw the blame of upon those, by whose direction and counsels he had effected his object. Yet he was the only one of all of them who was thrust out of the episcopate. For Ydacius, although less guilty, had voluntarily resigned his bishopric: that was wisely and respectfully done, had he not afterward spoiled the credit of such a step by endeavoring to recover the position which had been lost. Well, after the death of Priscillian, not only was the heresy not suppressed, which, under him, as its author, had burst forth, but acquiring strength, it became more widely spread. For his followers who had previously honored him as a saint, subsequently began to reverence him as a martyr. The bodies of those who had been put to death were conveyed to Spain, and their funerals were celebrated with great pomp. Nay, it came to be thought the highest exercise of religion to swear by Priscillian. But between them and our friends, a perpetual war of quarreling has been kept up. And that conflict, after being sustained for fifteen years with horrible dissension, could not by any means be set at rest. And now all things were seen to be disturbed and confused by the discord, especially of the bishops, while everything was corrupted by them through their hatred, partiality, fear, faithlessness, envy, factiousness, lust, avarice, pride, sleepiness, and inactivity. In a word, a large number were striving with insane plans and obstinate inclinations against a few giving wise counsel: while, in the meantime, the people of God, and all the excellent of the earth were exposed to mockery and insult.

---

[2] The meaning seems to be, that Ithacius being blamed for bringing accusations against his brethren, at first defended his conduct by an appeal to the laws and the public weal, both of which justified the prosecution of heretics; but being at last driven from this position, he turned round and cast the blame upon those for whom he had acted.

[3] Some read " solitus," instead of " sollicitus."

THE COMMONITORY

OF

VINCENT OF LÉRINS,

FOR THE ANTIQUITY AND UNIVERSALITY OF THE CATHOLIC FAITH
AGAINST THE PROFANE NOVELTIES OF ALL HERESIES:

TRANSLATED BY

THE REV. C. A. HEURTLEY, D.D.,

THE LADY MARGARET'S PROFESSOR OF DIVINITY IN THE UNIVERSITY OF OXFORD,
AND CANON OF CHRIST CHURCH.

CONTENTS.

INTRODUCTION.

VERY little is known of the author of the following Treatise. He writes under the assumed name of Peregrinus, but Gennadius of Marseilles,[1] who flourished A.D. 495, some sixty years after its date, ascribes it to Vincentius, an inmate of the famous monastery of Lérins, in the island of that name,[2] and his ascription has been universally accepted.

Vincentius was of Gallic nationality. In earlier life he had been engaged in secular pursuits, whether civil or military is not clear, though the term he uses, "secularis militia," might possibly imply the latter. He refers to the Council of Ephesus, held in the summer and early autumn of 431, as having been held some three years previously to the time at which he was writing "ante triennium ferme."[3] This gives the date of the Commonitory 434. Cyril, bishop of Alexandria, was still living.[4] Sixtus the Third had succeeded to the See of Rome;[5] his predecessor, Celestine, having died in 432. Gennadius says that Vincentius died, "Theodosio et Valentiniano regnantibus."[6] Theodosius died, leaving Valentinian still reigning, in July, 450. Vincentius' death, therefore, must have occurred in or before that year.

Baronius places his name in the Roman Martyrology, Tillemont doubts whether with sufficient reason.[7] He is commemorated on the 24th of May.

Vincentius has been charged with Semipelagianism. Whether he actually held the doctrine which was afterwards called by that name is not clear. Certainly the express enunciation of it is nowhere to be found in the Commonitory. But it is extremely probable that at least his sympathies were with those who held it. For not only does he omit the name of St. Augustine, who was especially obnoxious to them, when making honorable mention at any time of the champions of the faith, but he denounces his doctrine, though under a misrepresentation of it, as one of the forms of that novel error which he reprobates.[8] Indeed, whoever will compare what he says in § 70 of the heresy which he describes but forbears to name, with Prosper's account of the charges brought against Augustine by certain Semipelagian clergymen of Marseilles,[9] will have little doubt that Vincentius and they had the same teacher in view, and were of the same mind with regard to his teaching.

---

[1] *De Scriptoribus Ecclesiasticis.* Gennadius's work is to be found at the end of the second volume of Vallarsius's edition of St. Jerome's works.

[2] Now St. Honorat, so called from St. Honoratus, the founder of the monastery.

The monastery seems at first to have consisted of an aggregation of separate cells, each of which, according to the usage of that time, would be called a "monasterium." "Tota ubique insula, exstructis cellulis, unum velut monasterium evasit."—CARDINAL NORIS, *Histor. Pelag.* p. 251. "Monasterium potest unius monachi habitaculum nominari."—CASSIAN. *Collat.* xvii. 18.

Among its more prominent members, contemporary with Vincentius, were Honoratus and Hilary, afterwards successively bishops of Arles, and Faustus, afterwards bishop of Riez, all of them in sympathy with the neighbouring clergy of Marseilles, opposed to St. Augustine's later teaching, and holding what was afterwards called Semipelagian doctrine.

The adjoining islet of St. Marguérite, one of the Lérins group, has acquired notoriety of late, from having been the place to which Marshal Bazaine, the betrayer of Metz, was banished in 1873.

[3] § 79.   [4] § 80.   [5] § 85.   [6] De Illustr. Eccles. Scrip. c. 84.   [7] xv. p. 146.

[8] Cardinal Noris does not hesitate to say of him, "Non modo Semipelagianum se prodit, sed disertis verbis Augustini discipulos tanquam hæreticos traducit."—*Historia Pelagiana*, p. 245. See below, Appendix II.

[9] See Prosper's letter to Augustine in Augustine's works, Ep. 225, Tom. ii. Ed. Paris, 1836, etc.

Be this however as it may, when it is considered that the monks of Lérins, in common with the general body of the churchmen of Southern Gaul, were strenuous upholders of Semipelagianism, it will not be thought surprising that Vincentius should have been suspected of at least a leaning in that direction. Tillemont, who forbears to express himself decidedly, but evidently inclines to that view, says "L'opinion qui le condamne et l'abandonne aux Semipelagiens passe aujourd'hui pour la plus commune parmi les savans." [1]

It has been matter of question whether Vincentius is to be credited with the authorship of the "Objectiones Vincentianæ," a collection of Sixteen Inferences alleged to be deducible from St. Augustine's writings, which has come down to us in Prosper's Reply.

Its date coincides so nearly with that of the Commonitory as to preclude all doubt as to the identity of authorship on that score, [2] and it must be confessed that its animus and that of the 70th and 86th sections of the Commonitory are too much in keeping to make it difficult to believe that both are from the same pen.

VINCENTIUS'S object in the following treatise is to provide himself, as he states, with a general rule whereby to distinguish Catholic truth from heresy; and he commits what he has learnt, he adds, to writing, that he may have it by him for reference as a Commonitory, or Remembrancer, to refresh his memory.

This rule, in brief, is the authority of Holy Scripture. By that all questions must be tried in the first instance. And it would be abundantly sufficient, but that, unfortunately, men differ in the interpretation of Holy Scripture. The rule, therefore, must be supplemented by an appeal to that sense of Holy Scripture which is supported by universality, antiquity, and consent: by universality, when it is the faith of the whole Church; by antiquity, when it is that which has been held from the earliest times; by consent, when it has been the acknowledged belief of all, or of almost all, whose office and character gave authority to their determinations. This is the famous "Quod ubique, quod semper, quod ab omnibus," with which Vincentius's name is associated." [3] The body of the work is taken up with its illustration and application.

The work consisted originally of two books; but unfortunately the second was lost, or rather, as Gennadius says, was stolen, while the author was still alive; and there remains to us nothing but a recapitulation of its contents, which the authour, unwilling to encounter the labour of re-writing the whole, has drawn up. [4]

In prosecution of his purpose Vincentius proceeds to show how his rule applies for the detection of error in the instances of some of the more notorious heretics and schismatics who up to his time had made havoc of the Church,—the Donatists and the Arians, for instance, and the maintainers of the iteration of Baptism; and how the great defenders of the Faith were guided in their maintenance of the truth by its observance. [5]

But the perplexing question occurs: Wherefore, in God's providence, were persons, eminent for their attainments and their piety, such as Photinus, Apollinaris, and Nestorius, permitted to fall into heresy? [6] To which the answer is, For the Church's trial. And Vincentius proceeds to show, in the case of each of these, how great a trial to the Church his fall was. This leads him to give an account of their erroneous teaching severally, [7] from which he turns aside for a while to expound the Catholic doctrine of the Trinity as opposed to the heresy of Photinus, and of the Incarnation as opposed to the heresies of Apollinaris and Nestorius, in an exposition remarkable for its clearness and precision. [8] It contains so much in common with the so-called Athanasian Creed, both as to the sentiments and the

---

[1] T. xv. p. 146.

[2] The Objectiones Vincentianæ must have been published at some time between the publication of St. Augustine's Antipelagian Treatises and the death of Prosper. They are to be found in Prosper's Reply, contained in St. Augustine's works, Appendix, Tom. x. coll. 2535 *et seq.* Paris, 1836, etc.

[3] § 6.   [4] §§ 77–88.   [5] §§ 9 *sqq.*   [6] §§ 27 *sqq.*   [7] §§ 32 *sqq.*   [8] §§ 36 *sqq.*

language, that some have inferred from it, that Vincentius was the author of that Formulary.[1]

Returning from this digression, Vincentius proceeds, after promising to deal with these subjects more fully on a future occasion,[2] to two other very signal instances of heretical defection caused by the disregard of antiquity and universality; those of Origen[3] and Tertullian,[4] of both of whom he draws a vivid picture, contrasting them, such as they were before their fall with what they became afterwards, and enlarging on the grievous injury to the Church generally, and the distressing trial to individuals in particular, consequent upon their defection.

But it will be asked, Is Christian doctrine to remain at a standstill? Is there to be no progresss, as in other sciences?[5] Undoubtedly there is to be progress; but it must be real progress, analogous, for instance, to the growth of the human body from infancy to childhood, from childhood to mature age; or to the development of a plant from the seed to the full-grown vegetable or tree; it must be such as the elucidation of what was before obscure, the following out into detail of what was before expressed only in general terms,[6] not the addition of new doctrine, not the rejection of old.

One difficulty which is not unlikely to perplex a simple Christian is the readiness with which heretics appeal to Scripture, following therein the example of their arch-leader, who, in his temptation of our Lord, dared to make use of arms drawn from that armoury.[7] This leads to the question, How are we to ascertain the true sense of Scripture? And, in the answer to it, to a more detailed exposition of the general rule given at the outset.

Scripture, then, must be interpreted in accordance with the tradition of the Catholic Church, our guide being antiquity, universality, consent.

With regard to antiquity, that interpretation must be held to which has been handed down from the earliest times; with regard to universality, that which has always been held, if not by all, at least by the most part, in preference to that which has been held only by a few; with regard to consent, the determination of a General Council on any point will of course be of summary authority, and will hold the first place; next to this, the interpretation which has been held uniformly and persistently by all those Fathers, or by a majority of them, who have lived and died in the communion of the Catholic Church. Accordingly, whatsoever interpretation of Holy Scripture is opposed to an interpretation thus authenticated, even though supported by the authority of one or another individual teacher, however eminent, whether by his position, or his attainments, or his piety, or by all of these together, must be rejected as novel and unsound.

Here the first Commonitory ends; but it ends with a promise of a still further and more detailed inquiry, to be prosecuted in the Commonitory which is to follow, into the way in which the opinions of the ancient Fathers are to be collected, and the rule of faith determined in accordance with them.

Unfortunately that promise, however fulfilled according to the author's intention, has been frustrated to his readers. The second Commonitory, as was said above, was lost, or rather stolen, and all that remains to us is a brief and apparently partial recapitulation of its contents and of the contents of the preceding.

---

[1] ANTELMI, *Nova de Symbolo Athanasiano Disquisitio.* See the note on § 42, Appendix I.

[2] 42. [3] §§ 44–46. [4] § 47. [5] § 55.

[6] §§ 55–60. For instances in point, he might have referred to the enlargement and expansion of the earlier Creed, first in the Nicene, afterward in the Constantinopolitan Formulary. Thus, in the Definition of the Faith of the Council of Chalcedon, the Fathers are careful to explain that they are making no addition to the original deposit, but simply unfolding and rendering more intelligible what before had been less distinctly set forth: "Teaching in its fulness the doctrine which from the beginning hath remained unshaken, it decrees, in the first place, that the Creed of the 318 (the original Nicene Creed) remain untouched; and on account of those who impugn the Holy Spirit, it ratifies and confirms the doctrine subsequently delivered, concerning the essence of the Holy Spirit, by the hundred and fifty holy Fathers, (the Constantinopolitan Creed), which they promulgated for universal acceptance, not as though they were supplying some omission of their predecessors, but testifying in express words in writing their own minds concerning the Holy Spirit."

[7] §§ 65 *sqq.*

In this Vincentius repeats the rule for ascertaining the Catholic doctrine which he had laid down at the outset, enlarging especially upon the way in which the consent of the Fathers is to be arrived at, and illustrating what he says by the course pursued by the Council of Ephesus in the matter of Nestorius, — how the Fathers of the Council, instead of resting upon their own judgment, eminent as many of them were, collected together the opinions of the most illustrious of their predecessors, and following their consentient belief, determined the question before them.   To this most noteworthy example he adds the authority of two bishops of Rome, Sixtus III., then occupying the Papal Chair, and Celestine, his immediate predecessor, — the gist of the whole being the confirmation of the rule which it had been his object to enforce throughout the Treatise — that profane novelties must be rejected, and that faith alone adhered to which the universal Church has held consentiently from the earliest times, QUOD UBIQUE, QUOD SEMPER, QUOD AB OMNIBUS.

A COMMONITORY[1]

FOR THE ANTIQUITY AND UNIVERSALITY OF THE CATHOLIC FAITH AGAINST THE PROFANE NOVELTIES OF ALL HERESIES.

CHAPTER I.

The Object of the Following Treatise.

[1.] I, PEREGRINUS,[2] who am the least of all the servants of God, remembering the admonition of Scripture, "Ask thy fathers and they will tell thee, thine elders and they will declare unto thee,"[3] and again, "Bow down thine ear to the words of the wise,"[4] and once more, "My son, forget not these instructions, but let thy heart keep my words:"[5] remembering these admonitions, I say, I, Peregrinus, am persuaded, that, the Lord helping me, it will be of no little use and certainly as regards my own feeble powers, it is most necessary, that I should put down in writing the things which I have truthfully received from the holy Fathers, since I shall then have ready at hand wherewith by constant reading to make amends for the weakness of my memory.

[2.] To this I am incited not only by regard to the fruit to be expected from my labour but also by the consideration of time and the opportuneness of place:—

By the consideration of time,—for seeing that time seizes upon all things human, we also in turn ought to snatch from it something which may profit us to eternal life,

especially since a certain awful expectation of the approach of the divine judgment importunately demands increased earnestness in religion, while the subtle craftiness of new heretics calls for no ordinary care and attention.

I am incited also by the opportuneness of place, in that, avoiding the concourse and crowds of cities, I am dwelling in the seclusion of a Monastery, situated in a remote grange,[6] where, I can follow without distraction the Psalmist's[7] admonition, "Be still, and know that I am God."

Moreover, it suits well with my purpose in adopting this life; for, whereas I was at one time involved in the manifold and deplorable tempests of secular warfare, I have now at length, under Christ's auspices, cast anchor in the harbour of religion, a harbour to all always most safe, in order that, having there been freed from the blasts of vanity and pride, and propitiating God by the sacrifice of Christian humility, I may be able to escape not only the shipwrecks of the present life, but also the flames of the world to come.

[3.] But now, in the Lord's name, I will set about the object I have in view; that is to say, to record with the fidelity of a narrator rather than the presumption of an author, the things which our forefathers have handed down to us and committed to our keeping, yet observing this rule in what I write, that I

---

[1] COMMONITORY. I have retained the original title in its anglicised form, already familiar to English ears in connection with the name of Vincentius. Its meaning, as he uses it, is indicated sufficiently, in § 3, "An aid to memory." Technically, it meant a Paper of Instructions given to a person charged with a commission, to assist his memory as to its details.

[2] *Peregrinus*. It does not appear why Vincentius writes under an assumed name. Vossius, with whom Cardinal Noris evidently agrees, supposes that his object was to avoid openly avowing himself the author of a work which covertly attacked St. Augustine. Vossius, *Histor. Pelag.* p. 40. Ego quidem ad Vossii sententiam plane accessissem, nisi tot delatæ a sapientissimis Scriptoribus Commonitorio laudes religionem mihi pene injecissent.— NORIS, *Histor. Pelag.* p. 246.

[3] Deut. xxxii. 7.

[4] Prov. xxii. 17.

[5] Prov. iii. 1.

[6] Noris, from this word, "villula," a grange or country house, concludes that Vincentius, at the time of writing, though a monk, was not a monk of Lérins, for there could be no "villula" there then, Honoratus having found the island desolate and without inhabitant, when he settled on it but a few years previously, "vacantem insulam ob nimicitatem squaloris, et inaccessam venenatorum animalium metu." *Histor. Pelag.* p. 251. Why, however, may not the "villula" have been built subsequently to Honoratus's settlement, and indeed, as a part of it? Whether Vincentius was an inmate of the monastery of Lérins at the time of writing the Commonitory or not, he was so eventually, and died there.

[7] Ps. xlvi. 10.

shall by no means touch upon everything that might be said, but only upon what is necessary; nor yet in an ornate and exact style, but in simple and ordinary language,[1] so that the most part may seem to be intimated, rather than set forth in detail. Let those cultivate elegance and exactness who are confident of their ability or are moved by a sense of duty. For me it will be enough to have provided a COMMONITORY (or Remembrancer) for myself, such as may aid my memory, or rather, provide against my forgetfulness: which same Commonitory however, I shall endeavor, the Lord helping me, to amend and make more complete by little and little, day by day, by recalling to mind what I have learnt. I mention this at the outset, that if by chance what I write should slip out of my possession and come into the hands of holy men, they may forbear to blame anything therein hastily, when they see that there is a promise that it will yet be amended and made more complete.

CHAPTER II.

A General Rule for distinguishing the Truth of the Catholic Faith from the Falsehood of Heretical Pravity.

[4.] I HAVE often then inquired earnestly and attentively of very many men eminent for sanctity and learning, how and by what sure and so to speak universal rule I may be able to distinguish the truth of Catholic faith from the falsehood of heretical pravity; and I have always, and in almost every instance, received an answer to this effect: That whether I or any one else should wish to detect the frauds and avoid the snares of heretics as they rise, and to continue sound and complete in the Catholic faith, we must, the Lord helping, fortify our own belief in two ways; first, by the authority of the Divine Law, and then, by the Tradition of the Catholic Church.

[5.] But here some one perhaps will ask, Since the canon of Scripture is complete, and sufficient of itself for everything, and more than sufficient, what need is there to join with it the authority of the Church's interpretation? For this reason, — because, owing to the depth of Holy Scripture, all do not accept it in one and the same sense, but one understands its words in one way, another in another; so that it seems to be capable of as many interpretations as there are interpreters. For Novatian expounds it one way, Sabellius another, Donatus another, Arius, Eunomius, Macedonius,

another, Photinus, Apollinaris, Priscillian, another, Iovinian, Pelagius, Celestius, another, lastly, Nestorius another. Therefore, it is very necessary, on account of so great intricacies of such various error, that the rule for the right understanding of the prophets and apostles should be framed in accordance with the standard of Ecclesiastical and Catholic interpretation.

[6.] Moreover, in the Catholic Church itself, all possible care must be taken, that we hold that faith which has been believed everywhere, always, by all. For that is truly and in the strictest sense "Catholic," which, as the name itself and the reason of the thing declare, comprehends all universally. This rule we shall observe if we follow universality, antiquity, consent. We shall follow universality if we confess that one faith to be true, which the whole Church throughout the world confesses; antiquity, if we in no wise depart from those interpretations which it is manifest were notoriously held by our holy ancestors and fathers; consent, in like manner, if in antiquity itself we adhere to the consentient definitions and determinations of all, or at the least of almost all priests and doctors.

CHAPTER III.

What is to be done if one or more dissent from the rest.

[7.] WHAT then will a Catholic Christian do, if a small portion of the Church have cut itself off from the communion of the universal faith? What, surely, but prefer the soundness of the whole body to the unsoundness of a pestilent and corrupt member? What, if some novel contagion seek to infect not merely an insignificant portion of the Church, but the whole? Then it will be his care to cleave to antiquity, which at this day cannot possibly be seduced by any fraud of novelty.

[8.] But what, if in antiquity itself there be found error on the part of two or three men, or at any rate of a city or even of a province? Then it will be his care by all means, to prefer the decrees, if such there be, of an ancient General Council to the rashness and ignorance of a few. But what, if some error should spring up on which no such decree is found to bear? Then he must collate and consult and interrogate the opinions of the ancients, of those, namely, who, though living in divers times and places, yet continuing in the communion and faith of the one Catholic Church, stand forth acknowledged and approved authorities: and whatsoever he shall ascertain to have been held, written, taught, not by one or two of these only, but

---

[1] "Il dit qu'il l'a voulu écrire d'un style facile et commun, sans le vouloir orner et polir; et je voudrois que les ouvrages qu'on a pris le plus de peine à polir dans ce siècle (le 4me) et dans le suivant, ressemblassent à celui-ci." — *Tillemont*, T. xv. p. 144.

by all, equally, with one consent, openly, frequently, persistently, that he must understand that he himself also is to believe without any doubt or hesitation.

CHAPTER IV.

The evil resulting from the bringing in of Novel Doctrine shown in the instances of the Donatists and Arians.

[9.] BUT that we may make what we say more intelligible, we must illustrate it by individual examples, and enlarge upon it somewhat more fully, lest by aiming at too great brevity important matters be hurried over and lost sight of.

In the time of Donatus,[1] from whom his followers were called Donatists, when great numbers in Africa were rushing headlong into their own mad error, and unmindful of their name, their religion, their profession, were preferring the sacrilegious temerity of one man before the Church of Christ, then they alone throughout Africa were safe within the sacred precincts of the Catholic faith, who, detesting the profane schism, continued in communion with the universal Church, leaving to posterity an illustrious example, how, and how well in future the soundness of the whole body should be preferred before the madness of one, or at most of a few.

[10.] So also when the Arian poison had infected not an insignificant portion of the Church but almost the whole world,[2] so that a sort of blindness had fallen upon almost all the bishops[3] of the Latin tongue, circumvented partly by force partly by fraud, and was preventing them from seeing what was most expedient to be done in the midst of so much confusion, then whoever was a true lover and worshipper of Christ, preferring the ancient belief to the novel misbelief, escaped the pestilent infection.

[11.] By the peril of which time was abundantly shown how great a calamity the introduction of a novel doctrine causes. For then truly not only interests of small account, but others of the very gravest importance, were subverted. For not only affinities, relationships, friendships, families, but moreover, cities, peoples, provinces, nations, at last the whole Roman Empire, were shaken to their foundation and ruined.

For when this same profane Arian novelty, like a Bellona or a Fury, had first taken captive the Emperor,[4] and had then subjected all the principal persons of the palace to new laws, from that time it never ceased to involve everything in confusion, disturbing all things, public and private, sacred and profane, paying no regard to what was good and true, but, as though holding a position of authority, smiting whomsoever it pleased. Then wives were violated, widows ravished, virgins profaned, monasteries demolished, clergymen ejected, the inferior clergy scourged, priests driven into exile, jails, prisons, mines, filled with saints, of whom the greater part, forbidden to enter into cities, thrust forth from their homes to wander in deserts and caves, among rocks and the haunts of wild beasts, exposed to nakedness, hunger, thirst, were worn out and consumed. Of all of which was there any other cause than that, while

---

[1] There were two persons of this name, both intimately connected with the schism, — the earlier one, bishop of Casa Nigra in Numidia, the other the successor of Majorinus, whom in the year 311 the party had elected to be bishop of Carthage in opposition to Cecilian, the Catholic bishop, the ground of the opposition being that the principal among Cecilian's consecrators lay under the charge of having delivered up the sacred books to the heathen magistrates in the Dioclesian persecution, and of having thereby rendered his ministerial acts invalid. It was from the last-mentioned probably that the sect was called.

The Donatists affected great strictness of life, and ignoring the plain declarations of Scripture, and notably the prophetic representations contained in our Lord's parables of the Tares, the Draw-net, and others, they held that no church could be a true church which endured the presence of evil men in its society. Accordingly they broke off communion with the rest of the African Church and with all who held communion with it, which was in effect the rest of Christendom, denying the validity of their sacraments, rebaptizing those who came over to them from other Christian bodies, and reordaining their clergy.

The sect became so powerful that for some time it formed the stronger party in the church of North Western Africa, its bishops exceeding four hundred in number; but partly checked through the exertions of Augustine in the first years of the fifth century, and of Pope Gregory the Great at the close of the sixth, and partly weakened by divisions among themselves, they dwindled away and became extinct.

[2] The rise of Arianism was nearly contemporaneous with that of Donatism. It originated with Arius, a presbyter of Alexandria, a man of a subtle wit and a fluent tongue. He began by calling in question the teaching of his bishop, when discoursing on a certain occasion on the subject of the Trinity. For himself he denied our blessed Lord's coeternity and consubstantiality with the Father, which was in effect to deny that He is God in any true sense, though he made no scruple of giving Him the name. His doctrine may be best inferred from the anathema directed against it, appended to the original Nicene Creed: "Those who say, that once the Son of God did not exist, and that before He was begotten He did not exist, or who affirm that He is of a different substance or essence (from that of the Father), or that His Nature is mutable or alterable, those the Catholic and Apostolic Church anathematises."

[3] Arianism spread with great rapidity; and though condemned by the Council of Nicæa in 325, it gained fresh strength on the death of Constantine and the accession of Constantius, so that for many years thenceforward the history of the Church is occupied with nothing so much as with accounts of its struggle for supremacy.

"Arians and Donatists began both about one time, which heresies, according to the different strength of their own sinews, wrought, as the hope of success led them, the one with the choicest wits, the other with the multitude, so far, that after long and troublesome experience, the perfectest view that men could take of both was hardly able to induce any certain determinate resolution, whether error may do more by the curious subtlety of sharp discourse, or else by the mere appearance of zeal and devout affection."—*Hooker*, Eccles. Pol. v. 62. § 8.

[3] The Catholic bishops, in number more than four hundred, who at Ariminum, in 359, after having subscribed the Creed of Nicæa, were induced, partly by fraud, partly by threats, to repudiate its crucial terms and sign an Arian Formulary. It was in reference to this that St. Jerome wrote, "Ingemuit orbis, et Arium se esse miratus est." "The world groaned and marvelled to find itself Arian." He continues, "The vessel of the apostles was in extreme danger. The storm raged, the waves beat upon the ship, all hope was gone. The Lord awakes, rebukes the tempest, the monster (Constantius) dies, tranquillity is restored. The bishops who had been thrust out from their sees return, through the clemency of the new emperor. Then did Egypt receive Athanasius in triumph, then did the Church of Gaul receive Hilary returning from battle, then did Italy put off her mourning garments at the return of Eusebius (of Vercellæ)."—*Advers. Luciferianos*, § 10.

[4] Constantius, the Emperor of the West.

human superstitions are being brought in to supplant heavenly doctrine, while well established antiquity is being subverted by wicked novelty, while the institutions of former ages are being set at naught, while the decrees of our fathers are being rescinded, while the determinations of our ancestors are being torn in pieces, the lust of profane and novel curiosity refuses to restrict itself within the most chaste limits of hallowed and uncorrupt antiquity? [1]

CHAPTER V.

The Example set us by the Martyrs, whom no force could hinder from defending the Faith of their Predecessors.

[12.] BUT it may be, we invent these charges out of hatred to novelty and zeal for antiquity. Whoever is disposed to listen to such an insinuation, let him at least believe the blessed Ambrose, who, deploring the acerbity of the time, says, in the second book of his work addressed to the Emperor Gratian: [2] "Enough now, O God Almighty! have we expiated with our own ruin, with our own blood, the slaughter of Confessors, the banishment of priests, and the wickedness of such extreme impiety. It is clear, beyond question, that they who have violated the faith cannot remain in safety."

And again in the third book of the same work, [3] "Let us observe the precepts of our predecessors, and not transgress with rude rashness the landmarks which we have inherited from them. That sealed Book of Prophecy no Elders, no Powers, no Angels, no Archangels, dared to open. To Christ alone was reserved the prerogative of explaining it. [4] Who of us may dare to unseal the Sacerdotal Book sealed by Confessors, and consecrated already by the martyrdom of numbers, which they who had been compelled by force to unseal afterwards resealed, condemning the fraud which had been practised

upon them; while they who had not ventured to tamper with it proved themselves Confessors and martyrs? How can we deny the faith of those whose victory we proclaim?"

[13.] We proclaim it truly, O venerable Ambrose, we proclaim it, and applaud and admire. For who is there so demented, who, though not able to overtake, does not at least earnestly desire to follow those whom no force could deter from defending the faith of their ancestors, no threats, no blandishments, not life, not death, not the palace, not the Imperial Guards, not the Emperor, not the empire itself, not men, not demons? — whom, I say, as a recompense for their steadfastness in adhering to religious antiquity, the Lord counted worthy of so great a reward, that by their instrumentality He restored churches which had been destroyed, quickened with new life peoples who were spiritually dead, replaced on the heads of priests the crowns which had been torn from them, washed out those abominable, I will not say letters, but blotches (*non literas, sed lituras*) of novel impiety, with a fountain of believing tears, which God opened in the hearts of the bishops? — lastly, when almost the whole world was overwhelmed by a ruthless tempest of unlooked for heresy, recalled it from novel misbelief to the ancient faith, from the madness of novelty to the soundness of antiquity, from the blindness of novelty to pristine light?

[14.] But in this divine virtue, as we may call it, exhibited by these Confessors, we must note especially that the defence which they then undertook in appealing to the Ancient Church, was the defence, not of a part, but of the whole body. For it was not right that men of such eminence should uphold with so huge an effort the vague and conflicting notions of one or two men, or should exert themselves in the defence of some ill-advised combination of some petty province; but adhering to the decrees and definitions of the universal priesthood of Holy Church, the heirs of Apostolic and Catholic truth, they chose rather to deliver up themselves than to betray the faith of universality and antiquity. For which cause they were deemed worthy of so great glory as not only to be accounted Confessors, but rightly and deservedly to be accounted foremost among Confessors.

CHAPTER VI.

The example of Pope Stephen in resisting the Iteration of Baptism.

[15.] GREAT then is the example of these same blessed men, an example plainly divine, and worthy to be called to mind, and medi-

---

[1] Though Vincentius' account of the Arian persecutions refers to those under the Arian emperors, Constantius and Valens, the former especially, yet he could not but have had in mind the atrocious cruelties which were being perpetrated, at the time when he was writing, by the Arian Vandals in Africa. Possidius, in his life of St. Augustine, who lay on his death-bed in Hippo while the fierce Vandal host was encamped round the city (c. xxviii.), gives a detailed account of them, belonging to a date some four years earlier, entirely of a piece with Vincentius' description in the text. Victor, bishop of Vite, himself a sufferer, has left a still ampler relation, *De Persecutione Vandalorum.*
[2] St. Ambrose. *De Fide,* l. 2, c. 15, § 141. See also *St. Jerome* adv. *Luciferianos,* § 19.
[3] *Ibid.* l. 3, § 128, St. Ambrose speaks of the Gothic war as a judgment upon Valens, both for his Arianism and for his persecution of the Catholics. He had permitted the Goths to cross the Danube, and settle in Thrace and the adjoining parts, with the understanding that they should embrace Christianity in its Arian form. They had now turned against him, and Gratian was on the eve of setting out to carry aid to him. St. Ambrose's book, *De Fide,* was written to confirm Gratian in the Catholic faith, in view especially of the Arian influence to which he might be subjected in his intercourse with Valens. Valens was killed the following year, 378, at the battle of Adrianople.
[4] Rev. v. 1-5.

tated upon continually by every true Catholic, who, like the seven-branched candlestick, shining with the sevenfold light of the Holy Spirit, showed to posterity how thenceforward the audaciousness of profane novelty, in all the several rantings of error, might be crushed by the authority of hallowed antiquity.

Nor is there anything new in this? For it has always been the case in the Church, that the more a man is under the influence of religion, so much the more prompt is he to oppose innovations. Examples there are without number: but to be brief, we will take one, and that, in preference to others, from the Apostolic See,[1] so that it may be clearer than day to every one with how great energy, with how great zeal, with how great earnestness, the blessed successors of the blessed apostles have constantly defended the integrity of the religion which they have once received.

[16.] Once on a time then, Agrippinus,[2] bishop of Carthage, of venerable memory, held the doctrine — and he was the first who held it — that Baptism ought to be repeated, contrary to the divine canon, contrary to the rule of the universal Church, contrary to the customs and institutions of our ancestors. This innovation drew after it such an amount of evil, that it not only gave an example of sacrilege to heretics of all sorts, but proved an occasion of error to certain Catholics even.

When then all men protested against the novelty, and the priesthood everywhere, each as his zeal prompted him, opposed it, Pope Stephen of blessed memory, Prelate of the Apostolic See, in conjunction indeed with his colleagues but yet himself the foremost, withstood it, thinking it right, I doubt not, that as he exceeded all others in the authority of his place, so he should also in the devotion of his faith. In fine, in an epistle sent at the time to Africa, he laid down this rule: "Let there be no innovation — nothing but what has been handed down."[3] For that

holy and prudent man well knew that true piety admits no other rule than that whatsoever things have been faithfully received from our fathers the same are to be faithfully consigned to our children; and that it is our duty, not to lead religion whither we would, but rather to follow religion whither it leads; and that it is the part of Christian modesty and gravity not to hand down our own beliefs or observances to those who come after us, but to preserve and keep what we have received from those who went before us. What then was the issue of the whole matter? What but the usual and customary one? Antiquity was retained, novelty was rejected.

[17.] But it may be, the cause of innovation at that time lacked patronage. On the contrary, it had in its favor such powerful talent, such copious eloquence, such a number of partisans, so much resemblance to truth, such weighty support in Scripture (only interpreted in a novel and perverse sense), that it seems to me that that whole conspiracy could not possibly have been defeated, unless the sole cause of this extraordinary stir, the very novelty of what was so undertaken, so defended, so belauded, had proved wanting to it. In the end, what result, under God, had that same African Council or decree?[4] None whatever. The whole affair, as though a dream, a fable, a thing of no possible account, was annulled, cancelled, and trodden underfoot.

[18.] And O marvellous revolution! The authors of this same doctrine are judged Catholics, the followers heretics; the teachers are absolved, the disciples condemned; the writers of the books will be children of the Kingdom, the defenders of them will have their portion in Hell. For who is so demented as to doubt that that blessed light among all holy bishops and martyrs, Cyprian, together with the rest of his colleagues, will reign with Christ; or, who on the other hand so sacrilegious as to deny that the Donatists and those other pests, who boast the authority of that council for their iteration of baptism, will be consigned to eternal fire with the devil?[5]

---

[1] "The Apostolic see" (Sedes Apostolica) here means Rome of course. But the title was not restricted to Rome. It was common to all sees which could claim an apostle as their Founder. Thus St. Augustine, suggesting a rule for determining what books are to be regarded as Canonical, says, "In Canonicis Scripturis Ecclesiarum Catholicarum quamplurium auctoritatem sequatur, inter quas sane illæ sint quæ Apostolicas Sedes habere et Epistolas accipere meruerunt." "Let him follow the authority of those Catholic Churches which have been counted worthy to have Apostolic Sees; *i.e.*, to have been founded by Apostles, and to have been the recipients of Apostolic Epistles." — *De Doctr. Christiana*, II. § 13. But the title, even in St. Augustine's time, had even a wider meaning. "Anciently every bishop's see was dignified with the title of Sedes Apostolica, which in those days was no peculiar title of the bishop of Rome, but given to all bishops in general, as deriving their origin and counting their succession from the apostles." — *Bingham, Antiq.* II., c. 2, § 3.

[2] Agrippinus. See note 4, below.

[3] Stephen's letter has not come down to us, happily perhaps for

his credit, judging by the terms in which Cyprian speaks of it in the letter in which he quotes the passage in the text. — *Ad Pompeian*, Ep. 74.

[4] The Council held under the presidency of Cyprian in 256. Its acts are contained in Cyprian's works, Ed. Fell. pp. 158, etc. An earlier council had been held in the same city in the beginning of the century under Agrippinus. Both had affirmed the necessity of rebaptizing heretics, or, as they would rather have said, of baptizing them. The controversy was set at rest by a decision of the council of Arles, in 314, which ordered, in its Eighth Canon, that if the baptism had been administered in the name of the Trinity, converts should be admitted simply by the imposition of hands that they might receive the Holy Ghost.

[5] See Hooker's reference to this passage. — *Eccles. Pol.* v, 62, § 9.

CHAPTER VII.

How Heretics, craftily cite obscure passages in ancient writers in support of their own novelties.

[19.] THIS condemnation, indeed,[1] seems to have been providentially promulgated as though with a special view to the fraud of those who, contriving to dress up a heresy under a name other than its own, get hold often of the works of some ancient writer, not very clearly expressed, which, owing to the very obscurity of their own doctrine, have the appearance of agreeing with it, so that they get the credit of being neither the first nor the only persons who have held it. This wickedness of theirs, in my judgment, is doubly hateful: first, because they are not afraid to invite others to drink of the poison of heresy; and secondly, because with profane breath, as though fanning smouldering embers into flame, they blow upon the memory of each holy man, and spread an evil report of what ought to be buried in silence by bringing it again under notice, thus treading in the footsteps of their father Ham, who not only forebore to cover the nakedness of the venerable Noah, but told it to the others that they might laugh at it, offending thereby so grievously against the duty of filial piety, that even his descendants were involved with him in the curse which he drew down, widely differing from those blessed brothers of his, who would neither pollute their own eyes by looking upon the nakedness of their revered father, nor would suffer others to do so, but went backwards, as the Scripture says, and covered him, that is, they neither approved nor betrayed the fault of the holy man, for which cause they were rewarded with a benediction on themselves and their posterity.[2]

[20.] But to return to the matter in hand: It behoves us then to have a great dread of the crime of perverting the faith and adulterating religion, a crime from which we are deterred not only by the Church's discipline, but also by the censure of apostolical authority. For every one knows how gravely, how severely, how vehemently, the blessed apostle Paul inveighs against certain, who, with marvellous levity, had "been so soon removed from him who had called them to the grace of Christ to another Gospel, which was not another;"[3] "who had heaped to themselves teachers after their own lusts, turning away their ears from the truth, and being turned aside unto fables;"[4] "having damnation because they

had cast off their first faith;"[5] who had been deceived by those of whom the same apostle writes to the Roman Christians, "Now, I beseech you, brethren, mark them which cause divisions and offences, contrary to the doctrine which ye have learned, and avoid them. For they that are such serve not the Lord Christ, but their own belly, and by good words and fair speeches deceive the hearts of the simple;"[6] "who enter into houses, and lead captive silly women laden with sins, led away with diverse lusts, ever learning and never able to come to the knowledge of the truth;"[7] "vain talkers and deceivers, who subvert whole houses, teaching things which they ought not, for filthy lucre's sake;"[8] "men of corrupt minds, reprobate concerning the faith;"[9] "proud knowing nothing, but doting about questions and strifes of words, destitute of the truth, supposing that godliness is gain,"[10] "withal learning to be idle, wandering about from house to house, and not only idle, but tattlers also and busybodies, speaking things which they ought not,"[11] "who having put away a good conscience have made shipwreck concerning the faith;"[12] "whose profane and vain babblings increase unto more ungodliness, and their word doth eat as doth a cancer."[13] Well, also, is it written of them: "But they shall proceed no further: for their folly shall be manifest unto all men, as their's also was."[14]

CHAPTER VIII.

Exposition of St. Paul's Words, *Gal.* i. 8.

[21.] WHEN therefore certain of this sort wandering about provinces and cities, and carrying with them their venal errors, had found their way to Galatia, and when the Galatians, on hearing them, nauseating the truth, and vomiting up the manna of Apostolic and Catholic doctrine, were delighted with the garbage of heretical novelty, the apostle putting in exercise the authority of his office, delivered his sentence with the utmost severity, "Though we," he says, "or an angel from heaven, preach any other Gospel unto you than that which we have preached unto you, let him be accursed."[15]

[22.] Why does he say "Though we"? why not rather "though I"? He means, "though Peter, though Andrew, though John,

---

[1] The condemnation of St. Cyprian's practice of rebaptism.
[2] Gen. ix. 22.
[3] Gal. i. 6.

[4] 2 Tim. iv. 3, 4.
[5] 1 Tim. v. 12.
[6] Rom. xvi. 17, 18.
[7] 2 Tim. iii. 6.
[8] Tit. i. 10.
[9] 2 Tim. iii. 8.
[10] 1 Tim. vi. 4.
[11] 1 Tim. v. 13.
[12] 1 Tim. i. 19.
[13] 2 Tim. ii. 16, 17.
[14] 2 Tim. iii. 9.
[15] Gal. i. 8.

in a word, though the whole company of apostles, preach unto you other than we have preached unto you, let him be accursed." Tremendous severity! He spares neither himself nor his fellow apostles, so he may preserve unaltered the faith which was at first delivered. Nay, this is not all. He goes on: "Even though an angel from heaven preach unto you any other Gospel than that which we have preached unto you, let him be accursed." It was not enough for the preservation of the faith once delivered to have referred to man; he must needs comprehend angels also. "Though we," he says, "or an angel from heaven." Not that the holy angels of heaven are now capable of sinning. But what he means is: Even if that were to happen which cannot happen,— if any one, be he who he may, attempt to alter the faith once for all delivered, let him be accursed.

[23.] But it may be, he spoke thus in the first instance inconsiderately, giving vent to human impetuosity rather than expressing himself under divine guidance. Far from it. He follows up what he had said, and urges it with intense reiterated earnestness, "As we said before, so say I now again, If any man preach any other Gospel to you than that ye have received, let him be accursed." He does not say, "If any man deliver to you another message than that you have received, let him be blessed, praised, welcomed," — no; but "let him be accursed," [anathema] i.e., separated, segregated, excluded, lest the dire contagion of a single sheep contaminate the guiltless flock of Christ by his poisonous intermixture with them.

CHAPTER IX.

His warning to the Galatians a warning to all.

[24.] But, possibly, this warning was intended for the Galatians only. Be it so; then those other exhortations which follow in the same Epistle were intended for the Galatians only, such as, "If we live in the Spirit, let us also walk in the Spirit; let us not be desirous of vain glory, provoking one another, envying one another," etc.;[1] which alternative if it be absurd, and the injunctions were meant equally for all, then it follows, that as these injunctions which relate to morals, so those warnings which relate to faith are meant equally for all; and just as it is unlawful for all to provoke one another, or to envy one another, so, likewise, it is ·unlawful

for all to receive any other Gospel than that which the Catholic Church preaches everywhere.

[25.] Or perhaps the anathema pronounced on any one who should preach another Gospel than that which had been preached was meant for those times, not for the present. Then, also, the exhortation, "Walk in the Spirit and ye shall not fulfil the lust of the flesh,"[2] was meant for those times, not for the present. But if it be both impious and pernicious to believe this, then it follows necessarily, that as these injunctions are to be observed by all ages, so those warnings also which forbid alteration of the faith are warnings intended for all ages. To preach any doctrine therefore to Catholic Christians other than what they have received never was lawful, never is lawful, never will be lawful: and to anathematize those who preach anything other than what has once been received, always was a duty, always is a duty, always will be a duty.

[26.] Which being the case, is there any one either so audacious as to preach any other doctrine than that which the Church preaches, or so inconstant as to receive any other doctrine than that which he has received from the Church? That elect vessel, that teacher of the Gentiles, that trumpet of the apostles, that preacher whose commission was to the whole earth, that man who was caught up to heaven,[3] cries and cries again in his Epistles to all, always, in all places, "If any man preach any new doctrine, let him be accursed." On the other hand, an ephemeral, moribund set of frogs, fleas, and flies, such as the Pelagians, call out in opposition, and that to Catholics, "Take our word, follow our lead, accept our exposition, condemn what you used to hold, hold what you used to condemn, cast aside the ancient faith, the institutes of your fathers, the trusts left for you by your ancestors and receive instead, — what? I tremble to utter it: for it is so full of arrogance and self-conceit, that it seems to me that not only to affirm it, but even to refute it, cannot be done without guilt in some sort.

CHAPTER X.

Why Eminent Men are permitted by God to become Authors of Novelties in the Church.

[27.] But some one will ask, How is it then, that certain excellent persons, and of position in the Church, are often permitted by God to preach novel doctrines to Catholics? A proper question, certainly,

---

[1] Gal. v. 25.   [2] Gal. v. 16.   [3] 2 Cor. xii. 2.

and one which ought to be very carefully and fully dealt with, but answered at the same time, not in reliance upon one's own ability, but by the authority of the divine Law, and by appeal to the Church's determination.

Let us listen, then, to Holy Moses, and let him teach us why learned men, and such as because of their knowledge are even called Prophets by the apostle, are sometimes permitted to put forth novel doctrines, which the Old Testament is wont, by way of allegory, to call " strange gods," forasmuch as heretics pay the same sort of reverence to their notions that the Gentiles do to their gods.

[28.] Blessed Moses, then, writes thus in Deuteronomy: [1] "If there arise among you a prophet or a dreamer of dreams," that is, one holding office as a Doctor in the Church, who is believed by his disciples or auditors to teach by revelation: well, — what follows? "and giveth thee a sign or a wonder, and the sign or the wonder come to pass whereof he spake," — he is pointing to some eminent doctor, whose learning is such that his followers believe him not only to know things human, but, moreover, to foreknow things superhuman, such as, their disciples commonly boast, were Valentinus, Donatus, Photinus, Apollinaris, and the rest of that sort! What next? "And shall say to thee, Let us go after other gods, whom thou knowest not, and serve them." What are those other gods but strange errors which thou knowest not, that is, new and such as were never heard of before? "And let us serve them;" that is, "Let us believe them, follow them." What last? "Thou shalt not hearken to the words of that prophet or dreamer of dreams." And why, I pray thee, does not God forbid to be taught what God forbids to be heard? "For the Lord, your God, trieth you, to know whether you love Him with all your heart and with all your soul." The reason is clearer than day why Divine Providence sometimes permits certain doctors of the Churches to preach new doctrines — "That the Lord your God may try you," he says. And assuredly it is a great trial when one whom thou believest to be a prophet, a disciple of prophets, a doctor and defender of the truth, whom thou hast folded to thy breast with the utmost veneration and love, when such a one of a sudden secretly and furtively brings in noxious errrors, which thou canst neither quickly detect, being held by the prestige of former authority, nor lightly think it right to condemn, being prevented by affection for thine old master.

[1] Deut. xiii. 1. etc.

CHAPTER XI.

Examples from Church History, confirming the words of Moses, — Nestorius, Photinus, Apollinaris.

[29.] HERE, perhaps, some one will require us to illustrate the words of holy Moses by examples from Church History. The demand is a fair one, nor shall it wait long for satisfaction.

For to take first a very recent and very plain case: what sort of trial, think we, was that which the Church had experience of the other day, when that unhappy Nestorius,[2] all at once metamorphosed from a sheep into a wolf, began to make havoc of the flock of Christ, while as yet a large proportion of those whom he was devouring believed him to be a sheep, and consequently were the more exposed to his attacks? For who would readily suppose him to be in error, who was known to have been elected by the high choice of the Emperor, and to be held in the greatest esteem by the priesthood? who would readily suppose him to be in error, who, greatly beloved by the holy brethren, and in high favor with the populace, expounded the Scriptures in public daily, and confuted the pestilent errors both of Jews and Heathens? Who could choose but believe that his teaching was Orthodox, his preaching Orthodox, his belief Orthodox, who, that he might open the way to one heresy of his own, was zealously inveighing against the blasphemies of all heresies? But this was the very thing which Moses says: "The Lord your God doth try you that He may know whether you love Him or not."

[30.] Leaving Nestorius, in whom there was always more that men admired than they were profited by, more of show than of reality, whom natural ability, rather than divine grace, magnified for a time in the opinion of the common people, let us pass on to speak of those who, being persons of great attainments and of much industry, proved no small trial to Catholics. Such, for instance, was Photinus, in Pannonia,[3] who, in the memory

[2] Nestorius was a native of Germanicia, a town in the patriarchate of Antioch, of which Church he became a Presbyter. On the See of Constantinople becoming vacant by the death of Sisinnius, the Emperor Theodosius sent for him and caused him to be consecrated Archbishop. He was at first extremely popular, and so eloquent that people said of him (what was much to be said of a successor of Chrysostom), that there had never before been such a bishop. He was condemned by the Council of Ephesus, in 431. The emperor, after ordering him to return to the monastery to which he formally belonged, eventually banished him to the great Oasis, whence he was harried from place to place till death put an end to his sufferings, in 440. *Evagrius*, i. 7.
[3] Photinus, bishop of Sirmium in Pannonia, was a native of Galatia, and a disciple of Marcellus of Ancyra. Bishop Pearson (on the Creed, Art. 11) has an elaborate note, in which he collects together many notices of him left by the ancients. These agree with Vincentius in representing him as a man of extraordinary ability and of consummate eloquence. His heresy consisted in the denial of

of our fathers, is said to have been a trial to the Church of Sirmium, where, when he had been raised to the priesthood with universal approbation, and had discharged the office for some time as a Catholic, all of a sudden, like that evil prophet or dreamer of dreams whom Moses refers to, he began to persuade the people whom God had intrusted to his charge, to follow "strange gods," that is, strange errors, which before they knew not. But there was nothing unusual in this: the mischief of the matter was, that for the perpetration of so great wickedness he availed himself of no ordinary helps. For he was of great natural ability and of powerful eloquence, and had a wealth of learning, disputing and writing copiously and forcibly in both languages, as his books which remain, composed partly in Greek, partly in Latin, testify. But happily the sheep of Christ committed to him, vigilant and wary for the Catholic faith, quickly turned their eyes to the premonitory words of Moses, and, though admiring the eloquence of their prophet and pastor, were not blind to the trial. For from thenceforward they began to flee from him as a wolf, whom formerly they had followed as the ram of the flock.

[31.] Nor is it only in the instance of Photinus that we learn the danger of this trial to the Church, and are admonished withal of the need of double diligence in guarding the faith. Apollinaris[1] holds out a like warning. For he gave rise to great burning questions and sore peplexities among his disciples, the Church's authority drawing them one way, their Master's influence the opposite; so that, wavering and tossed hither and thither between the two, they were at a loss what course to take.

But perhaps he was a person of no weight of character. On the contrary, he was so eminent and so highly esteemed that his word would only too readily be taken on whatsoever subject. For what could exceed his acute-

ness, his adroitness, his learning? How many heresies did he, in many volumes, annihilate! How many errors, hostile to the faith, did he confute! A proof of which is that most noble and vast work, of not less than thirty books, in which, with a great mass of arguments, he repelled the insane calumnies of Porphyry.[2] It would take a long time to enumerate all his works, which assuredly would have placed him on a level with the very chief of the Church's builders, if that profane lust of heretical curiosity had not led him to devise I know not what novelty which as though through the contagion of a sort of leprosy both defiled all his labours, and caused his teachings to be pronounced the Church's trial instead of the Church's edification.

CHAPTER XII.

A fuller account of the Errors of Photinus, Apollinaris and Nestorius.

[32.] HERE, possibly, I may be asked for some account of the above mentioned heresies; those, namely, of Nestorius, Apollinaris, and Photinus. This, indeed, does not belong to the matter in hand: for our object is not to enlarge upon the errors of individuals, but to produce instances of a few, in whom the applicability of Moses' words may be evidently and clearly seen; that is to say, that if at any time some Master in the Church, himself also a prophet in interpreting the mysteries of the prophets, should attempt to introduce some novel doctrine into the Church of God, Divine Providence permits this to happen in order to try us. It will be useful, therefore, by way of digression, to give a brief account of the opinions of the above-named heretics, Photinus, Apollinaris, Nestorius.

[33.] The heresy of Photinus, then, is as follows: He says that God is singular and sole, and is to be regarded as the Jews regarded Him. He denies the completeness of the Trinity, and does not believe that there is any Person of God the Word, or any Person of the Holy Ghost. Christ he affirms to be a mere man, whose original was from Mary. Hence he insists with the utmost obstinacy that we are to render worship only to the Person of God the Father, and that we are to honour Christ as man only. This is the doctrine of Photinus.

[34.] Apollinaris, affecting to agree with the Church as to the unity of the Trinity, though

---

our blessed Lord's divine nature, whom he regarded as man, and nothing more, ψιλὸς ἄνθρωπος, and as having had no existence before his birth of the Virgin. He was condemned in several synods, the fifth of which, a Council of the Western bishops, held at Sirmium, in 350, deposed him. But in spite of the deposition, so great was his popularity, that he could not even yet be removed. The following year however he was by another council, held at the same place, again condemned, and sent into banishment. He died in Galatia, in 377. See Cave, *Hist. Lit.*, who refers with praise to a learned dissertation on Photinus by Larroque.

[1] Apollinaris the younger (a contemporary of Photinus), bishop of Laodicea in Syria, was one of the most distinguished men of the age in which he lived. Epiphanius (*Hær.* lxxvii. 2), referring to his fall into heresy, says that when it first began to be spoken of, people would hardly credit it, so great was the estimation in which he was held. His heresy, which consisted in the denial of the verity of our Lord's human nature, the Divine WORD supplying the place of the rational soul, and in the assertion that his flesh was not derived from the Virgin, but was brought down from heaven, was condemned by the Council of Constantinople, in 381 (Canon I.). It was in reference to the latter form of it that the clause "of the Holy Ghost and the Virgin Mary" was inserted in the Nicene Creed.

[2] This work, of which St. Jerome speaks in high terms (*de Viris Illustr.*, c. 104), has not come down to us, nor indeed have his other writings, except in fragments.

not this even with entire soundness of belief,[1] as to the Incarnation of the Lord, blasphemes openly. For he says that the flesh of our Saviour was either altogether devoid of a human soul, or, at all events, was devoid of a rational soul. Moreover, he says that this same flesh of the Lord was not received from the flesh of the holy Virgin Mary, but came down from heaven into the Virgin; and, ever wavering and undecided, he preaches one while that it was co-eternal with God the Word, another that it was made of the divine nature of the Word. For, denying that there are two substances in Christ, one divine, the other human, one from the Father, the other from his mother, he holds that the very nature of the Word was divided, as though one part of it remained in God, the other was converted into flesh: so that whereas the truth says that of two substances there is one Christ, he affirms, contrary to the truth, that of the one divinity of Christ there are become two substances. This, then, is the doctrine of Apollinaris.

[35.] Nestorius, whose disease is of an opposite kind, while pretending that he holds two distinct substances in Christ, brings in of a sudden two Persons, and with unheard of wickedness would have two sons of God, two Christs, — one, God, the other, man, one, begotten of his Father, the other, born of his mother. For which reason he maintains that Saint Mary ought to be called, not *Theotocos* (the mother of God), but *Christotocos* (the mother of Christ), seeing that she gave birth not to the Christ who is God, but to the Christ who is man. But if any one supposes that in his writings he speaks of one Christ, and preaches one Person of Christ, let him not lightly credit it. For either this is a crafty device, that by means of good he may the more easily persuade evil, according to that of the apostle, "That which is good was made death to me,"[2] — either, I say, he craftily affects in some places in his writings to believe one Christ and one Person of Christ, or else he says that after the Virgin had brought forth, the two Persons were united into one Christ, though at the time of her conception or parturition, and for some short time afterwards, there were two Christs; so that forsooth, though Christ was born at first an ordinary man and nothing more, and not as yet associated in unity of Person with the Word of God, yet afterwards the Person of the Word assuming descended upon Him; and though now the Person assumed remains

in the glory of God, yet once there would seem to have been no difference between Him and all other men.

CHAPTER XIII.

The Catholic Doctrine of the Trinity and the Incarnation explained.

[36.] IN these ways then do these rabid dogs, Nestorius, Apollinaris, and Photinus, bark against the Catholic faith: Photinus, by denying the Trinity; Apollinaris, by teaching that the nature of the Word is mutable, and refusing to acknowledge that there are two substances in Christ, denying moreover either that Christ had a soul at all, or, at all events, that he had a rational soul, and asserting that the Word of God supplied the place of the rational soul; Nestorius, by affirming that there were always or at any rate that once there were two Christs. But the Catholic Church, holding the right faith both concerning God and concerning our Saviour, is guilty of blasphemy neither in the mystery of the Trinity, nor in that of the Incarnation of Christ. For she worships both one Godhead in the plenitude of the Trinity, and the equality of the Trinity in one and the same majesty, and she confesses one Christ Jesus, not two; the same both God and man, the one as truly as the other.[3] One Person indeed she believes in Him, but two substances; two substances but one Person: Two substances, because the Word of God is not mutable, so as to be convertible into flesh; one Person, lest by acknowledging two sons she should seem to worship not a Trinity, but a Quaternity.

[37.] But it will be well to unfold this same doctrine more distinctly and explicitly again and again.

In God there is one substance, but three Persons; in Christ two substances, but one Person. In the Trinity, another and another Person, not another and another substance (distinct Persons, not distinct substances);[4] in the Saviour another and another substance, not another and another Person, (distinct substances, not distinct Persons). How in the Trinity another and another Person (distinct Persons) not another and another substance (distinct substances)?[5] Because there is one Person of the Father, another

---

[1] "Et hoc ipsum non plena fidei sanitate." — The Cambridge Ed., 1687, with Baluzius's notes appended, reads, "et hoc ipsum plena fidei sanctitate."

[2] Rom. vii. 13.

[3] Unum Christum Jesum non duos, eundemque Deum pariter atque Hominem confitetur. Compare the Athanasian Creed, "Est ergo fides recta et credamus et confiteamur, quia Dominus Noster Jesus Christus. Dei Filius, Deus pariter et Homo est."

[4] In Trinitate alius atque alius, non aliud atque aliud. In Salvatore aliud atque aliud, non alius atque alius.

[5] Aliud atque aliud, non alius atque alius.

of the Son, another of the Holy Ghost;[1] but yet there is not another and another nature (distinct natures) but one and the same nature. How in the Saviour another and another substance, not another and another Person (two distinct substances, not two distinct Persons)? Because there is one substance of the Godhead, another of the manhood. But yet the Godhead and the manhood are not another and another Person (two distinct Persons), but one and the same Christ, one and the same Son of God, and one and the same Person of one and the same Christ and Son of God, in like manner as in man the flesh is one thing and the soul another, but one and the same man, both soul and flesh. In Peter and Paul the soul is one thing, the flesh another; yet there are not two Peters, — one soul, the other flesh, or two Pauls, one soul, the other flesh,— but one and the same Peter, and one and the same Paul, consisting each of two diverse natures, soul and body. Thus, then, in one and the same Christ there are two substances, one divine, the other human; one of (ex) God the Father, the other of (ex) the Virgin Mother; one co-eternal with and co-equal with the Father, the other temporal and inferior to the Father; one consubstantial with his Father, the other consubstantial with his Mother, but one and the same Christ in both substances. There is not, therefore, one Christ God, the other man, not one uncreated, the other created; not one impassible, the other passible; not one equal to the Father, the other inferior to the Father; not one of his Father (ex), the other of his Mother (ex), but one and the same Christ, God and man, the same uncreated and created, the same unchangeable and incapable of suffering, the same acquainted by experience with both change and suffering, the same equal to the Father and inferior to the Father, the same begotten of the Father before time, ("before the world"), the same born of his mother in time ("in the world"),[2] perfect God, perfect Man. In God supreme divinity, in man perfect humanity. Perfect humanity, I say, forasmuch as it hath both soul and flesh; the flesh, very flesh; our flesh, his mother's flesh; the soul, intellectual, endowed with mind and reason. There is then in Christ the Word, the soul, the flesh; but the whole is one Christ, one Son of God, and

one our Saviour and Redeemer: One, not by I know not what corruptible confusion of Godhead and manhood, but by a certain entire and singular unity of Person. For the conjunction hath not converted and changed the one nature into the other, (which is the characteristic error of the Arians), but rather hath in such wise compacted both into one, that while there always remains in Christ the singularity of one and the self-same Person, there abides eternally withal the characteristic property of each nature; whence it follows, that neither doth God (i.e., the divine nature) ever begin to be body, nor doth the body ever cease to be body. The which may be illustrated in human nature: for not only in the present life, but in the future also, each individual man will consist of soul and body; nor will his body ever be converted into soul, or his soul into body; but while each individual man will live for ever, the distinction between the two substances will continue in each individual man for ever. So likewise in Christ each substance will for ever retain its own characteristic property, yet without prejudice to the unity of Person.

CHAPTER XIV.

Jesus Christ Man in Truth, not in Semblance.

[38.] But when we use the word "Person," and say that God became man by means of a Person, there is reason to fear that our meaning may be taken to be, that God the Word assumed our nature merely in imitation, and peformed the actions of man, being man not in reality, but only in semblance, just as in a theatre, one man within a brief space represents several persons, not one of whom himself is. For when one undertakes to sustain the part of another, he performs the offices, or does the acts, of the person whose part he sustains, but he is not himself that person. So, to take an illustration from secular life and one in high favour with the Manichees, when a tragedian represents a priest or a king, he is not really a priest or a king. For, as soon as the play is over, the person or character whom he represented ceases to be. God forbid that we should have anything to do with such nefarious and wicked mockery. Be it the infatuation of the Manichees, those preachers of hallucination, who say that the Son of God, God, was not a human person really and truly, but that He counterfeited the person of a man in feigned conversation and manner of life.

[39.] But the Catholic Faith teaches that the Word of God became man in such wise, that He took upon Him our nature, not feign-

[1] Quia scilicet alia est Persona Patris, alia Filii, alia Spiritus Sancti sed tamen Patris et Filii et Spiritus Sancti non alia et alia sed una cadunque natura. So the Athanasian Creed, "Alia est enim Persona Patris, alia Filii, alia Spiritus Sancti, sed Patris et Filii et Spiritus Sancti una est Divinitas, etc." The coincidence between the whole of this context and the Athanasian Creed is very observable, though the agreement is not always exact to the very letter.
[2] Idem ex Patre ante sæcula genitus, Idem in sæculo ex matre generatus. Compare the Athanasian Creed, "Deus est ex substantia Patris ante sæcula genitus; Homo ex substantia Matris in sæculo natus." See Appendix I.

edly and in semblance, but in reality and truth, and performed human actions, not as though He were imitating the actions of another, but as performing His own, and as being in reality the person whose part He sustained. Just as we ourselves also, when we speak, reason, live, subsist, do not imitate men, but are men. Peter and John, for instance, were men, not by imitation, but by being men in reality. Paul did not counterfeit an apostle, or feign himself to be Paul, but was an apostle, was Paul. So, also, that which God the Word did, in His condescension, in assuming and having flesh, in speaking, acting, and suffering, through the instrumentality of flesh, yet without any marring of His own divine nature, came in one word to this: — He did not imitate or feign Himself to be perfect man, but He shewed Himself to be very man in reality and truth. Therefore, as the soul united to the flesh, but yet not changed into flesh, does not imitate man, but is man, and man not feignedly but substantially, so also God the Word, without any conversion of Himself, in uniting Himself to man, became man, not by confusion, not by imitation, but by actually being and subsisting. Away then, once and for all, with the notion of His Person as of an assumed fictitious character, where always what is is one thing, what is counterfeited another, where the man who acts never is the man whose part he acts. God forbid that we should believe God the Word to have taken upon Himself the person of a man in this illusory way. Rather let us acknowledge that while His own unchangeable substance remained, and while He took upon Himself the nature of perfect man, Himself actually was flesh, Himself actually was man, Himself actually was personally man; not feignedly, but in truth, not in imitation, but in substance; not, finally, so as to cease to be when the performance was over, but so as to be, and continue to be substantially and permanently.[1]

CHAPTER XV.

The Union of the Divine with the Human Nature took place in the very Conception of the Virgin. The appellation "The Mother of God."

[40.] This unity of Person, then, in Christ was not effected after His birth of the Virgin, but was compacted and perfected in her very womb. For we must take most especial heed that we confess Christ not only one, but always one. For it were intolerable blasphemy, if while thou dost confess Him one now, thou shouldst maintain that once He was not one, but two; one forsooth since His baptism, but two at His birth. Which monstrous sacrilege we shall assuredly in no wise avoid unless we acknowledge the manhood united to the Godhead (but by unity of Person), not from the ascension, or the resurrection, or the baptism, but even in His mother, even in the womb, even in the Virgin's very conception.[2] In consequence of which unity of Person, both those attributes which are proper to God are ascribed to man, and those which are proper to the flesh to God, indifferently and promiscuously.[3] For hence it is written by divine guidance, on the one hand, that the Son of man came down from heaven;[4] and on the other, that the Lord of glory was crucified on earth.[5] Hence it is also that since the Lord's flesh was made, since the Lord's flesh was created, the very Word of God is said to have been made, the very omniscient Wisdom of God to have been created, just as prophetically His hands and His feet are described as having been pierced.[6] From this unity of Person it follows, by reason of a like mystery, that, since the flesh of the Word was born of an undefiled mother, God the Word Himself is most Catholicly believed, most impiously denied, to have been born of the Virgin; which being the case, God forbid that any one should seek to defraud Holy Mary of her prerogative of divine grace and her special glory. For by the singular gift of Him who is our Lord and God, and withal, her own son, she is to be confessed most truly and most blessedly — The mother of God

---

ambiguity which is not continued in our derived word *Person*. *Persona* signifies not only *Person*, in our sense of the word, but also an *assumed character*. Though however we have not this sense in *Person*, we have it in *Personate*.

[2] If the Son of God had taken to Himself a man now made and already perfected, it would of necessity follow that there are in Christ two persons, the one assuming and the other assumed; whereas, the Son of God did not assume a man's *person* unto His own, but a man's *nature* to His own person, and therefore took *semen*, the seed of Abraham, the very first original element of our nature, before it was come to have any personal human subsistence. The flesh, and the conjunction of the flesh with God, began both in one instant. His making and taking to Himself our flesh was but one act, so that in Christ there is no personal subsistence but one, and that from everlasting. By taking only the nature of man He still continueth one person, and changeth but the manner of His subsisting, which was before in the mere glory of the Son of God, and is now in the habit of our flesh. — *Hooker, Eccl. Pol.* v. 52, § 3.

[3] "A kind of mutual commutation there is, whereby those concrete names, God and man, when we speak of Christ, do take interchangeably one another's room, so that for truth of speech, it skilleth not, whether we say that the Son of God hath created the world, and the Son of man by His death hath saved it, or else, that the Son of man did create, and the Son of God die to save the world. Howbeit, as oft as we attribute to God what the manhood of Christ claimeth, or to man what His Deity hath right unto, we understand by the name of God and the name of man neither the one nor the other nature, but the whole person of Christ, in whom both natures are." — *Hooker, Eccl. Polity*, v. 53, § 4. This is technically called "The Communication of Properties," *Communicatio idiomatum.*

[4] St. John iii. 13.   [5] 1 Cor. ii. 8.   [6] Ps. xxii. 16.

---

[1] The word "Person" is used in this and the preceding section in a way which might seem at variance with Catholic truth. Christ did not assume the Person of a man; but, being God, He united in his one divine Person, the Godhead and the Manhood. This Vincentius himself teaches most explicitly. But his object here is to show that our blessed Lord, while conversant among us as man, and being to all appearance man, did not *personate* man, but was man in deed and in truth. The misconception against which Vincentius seeks to guard arises from the ambiguity of the Latin *Persona*, an

"Theotocos," but not in the sense in which it is imagined by a certain impious heresy which maintains, that she is to be called the Mother of God for no other reason than because she gave birth to that man who afterwards became God, just as we speak of a woman as the mother of a priest, or the mother of a bishop, meaning that she was such, not by giving birth to one already a priest or a bishop, but by giving birth to one who afterwards became a priest or a bishop. Not thus, I say, was the holy Mary "Theotocos," the mother of God, but rather, as was said before, because in her sacred womb was wrought that most sacred mystery whereby, on account of the singular and unique unity of Person, as the Word in flesh is flesh, so Man in God is God.[1]

CHAPTER XVI.

Recapitulation of what was said of the Catholic Faith and of divers Heresies, Chapters xi–xv.

[41.] But now that we may refresh our remembrance of what has been briefly said concerning either the afore-mentioned heresies or the Catholic Faith, let us go over it again more briefly and concisely, that being repeated it may be more thoroughly understood, and being pressed home more firmly held.

Accursed then be Photinus, who does not receive the Trinity complete, but asserts that Christ is mere man.

Accursed be Apollinaris, who affirms that the Godhead of Christ is marred by conversion, and defrauds Him of the property of perfect humanity.

Accursed be Nestorius, who denies that God was born of the Virgin, affirms two Christs, and rejecting the belief of the Trinity, brings in a Quaternity.

But blessed be the Catholic Church, which worships one God in the completeness of the Trinity, and at the same time adores the equality of the Trinity in the unity of the Godhead, so that neither the singularity of substance confounds the propriety of the Persons, not the distinction of the Persons in the Trinity separates the unity of the Godhead.

Blessed, I say, be the Church, which believes that in Christ there are two true and perfect substances but one Person, so that neither doth the distinction of natures divide the unity of Person, nor the unity of Person confound the distinction of substances.

Blessed, I say, be the Church, which understands God to have become Man, not by conversion of nature, but by reason of a Person, but of a Person not feigned and transient, but substantial and permanent.

Blessed, I say, be the Church, which declares this unity of Person to be so real and effectual, that because of it, in a marvellous and ineffable mystery, she ascribes divine attributes to man, and human to God; because of it, on the one hand, she does not deny that Man, as God, came down from heaven, on the other, she believes that God, as Man, was created, suffered, and was crucified on earth; because of it, finally, she confesses Man the Son of God, and God the Son of the Virgin.

Blessed, then, and venerable, blessed and most sacred, and altogether worthy to be compared with those celestial praises of the Angelic Host, be the confession which ascribes glory to the one Lord God with a threefold ascription of holiness. For this reason moreover she insists emphatically upon the oneness of the Person of Christ, that she may not go beyond the mystery of the Trinity (that is by making in effect a Quaternity.)

Thus much by way of digression. On another occasion, please God, we will deal with the subject and unfold it more fully.[2] Now let us return to the matter in hand.

CHAPTER XVII.

The Error of Origen a great Trial to the Church.

[42.] We said above that in the Church of God the teacher's error is the people's trial, a trial by so much the greater in proportion to the greater learning of the erring teacher. This we showed first by the authority of Scripture, and then by instances from Church History, of persons who having at one time had the reputation of being sound in the faith, eventually either fell away to some sect already in existence, or else founded a heresy of their own. An important fact truly, useful to be learnt, and necessary to be remembered, and to be illustrated and enforced again and again, by example upon example, in order that all true Catholics may understand that it behoves them with the Church to receive Teachers, not with Teachers to desert the faith of the Church.

[43.] My belief is, that among many instances of this sort of trial which might be produced, there is not one to be compared with that of Origen,[3] in whom there were

---

[1] Sicut Verbum in carne caro, ita Homo in Deo Deus est. Compare the Athanasian Creed, v. 33, in what is probably the true reading, "Unus autem, non conversione Divinitatis in carne, sed assumptione Humanitatis in Deo."

[2] Anrtelmi, who ascribed the Athanasian Creed to Vincentius, thought that document a fulfilment of the promise here made. *Nova de Symbolo Athanasiano Disquisitio.* — See Appendix I.

[3] Origen was born of Christian parents, at Alexandria, about the year 186. His father, Leonidas, suffered martyrdom in the persecution under Severus, in 202; and the family estate having been confiscated, his mother, with six younger children, became dependent upon him for her support. At the age of eighteen he was appointed by the bishop Demetrius over the Catechetical School of Alexandria,

many things so excellent, so unique, so admirable, that antecedently any one would readily deem that implicit faith was to be placed in all his assertions. For if the conversation and manner of life carry authority, great was his industry, great his modesty, his patience, his endurance; if his descent or his erudition, what more noble than his birth of a house rendered illustrious by martyrdom? Afterwards, when in the cause of Christ he had been deprived not only of his father, but also of all his property, he attained so high a standard in the midst of the straits of holy poverty, that he suffered several times, it is said, as a Confessor. Nor were these the only circumstances connected with him, all of which afterwards proved an occasion of trial. He had a genius so powerful, so profound, so acute, so elegant, that there was hardly any one whom he did not very far surpass. The splendour of his learning, and of his erudition generally, was such that there were few points of divine philosophy, hardly any of human, which he did not thoroughly master. When Greek had yielded to his industry, he made himself a proficient in Hebrew. What shall I say of his eloquence, the style of which was so charming, so soft, so sweet, that honey rather than words seemed to flow from his mouth! What subjects were there, however difficult, which he did not render clear and perspicuous by the force of his reasoning? What undertakings, however hard to accomplish, which he did not make to appear most easy? But perhaps his assertions rested simply on ingeniously woven argumentation? On the contrary, no teacher ever used more proofs drawn from Scripture. Then I suppose he wrote little? No man more, so that, if I mistake not, his writings not only cannot all be read through, they cannot all be found;[1] for that nothing might be wanting to his opportunities of obtaining knowledge, he had the additional advantage of a life greatly prolonged.[2] But perhaps he was not particularly happy in his disciples? Who ever more so? From his school came forth doctors, priests, confessors,

martyrs, without number.[3] Then who can express how much he was admired by all, how great his renown, how wide his influence? Who was there whose religion was at all above the common standard that did not hasten to him from the ends of the earth? What Christian did not reverence him almost as a prophet; what philosopher as a master? How great was the veneration with which he was regarded, not only by private persons, but also by the Court, is declared by the histories which relate how he was sent for by the mother of the Emperor Alexander,[4] moved by the heavenly wisdom with the love of which she, as he, was inflamed. To this also his letters bear witness, which, with the authority which he assumed as a Christian Teacher, he wrote to the Emperor Philip,[5] the first Roman prince that was a Christian. As to his incredible learning, if any one is unwilling to receive the testimony of Christians at our hands, let him at least accept that of heathens at the hands of philosophers. For that impious Porphyry says that when he was little more than a boy, incited by his fame, he went to Alexandria, and there saw him, then an old man, but a man evidently of so great attainments, that he had reached the summit of universal knowledge.

[44.] Time would fail me to recount, even in a very small measure, the excellencies of this man, all of which, nevertheless, not only contributed to the glory of religion, but also increased the magnitude of the trial. For who in the world would lightly desert a man of so great genius, so great learning, so great influence, and would not rather adopt that saying, That he would rather be wrong with Origen, than be right with others.[6]

What shall I say more? The result was that very many were led astray from the integrity of the faith, not by any human excellencies of this so great man, this so great doctor, this so great prophet, but, as the event showed, by the too perilous trial which he proved to be. Hence it came to pass, that this Origen, such and so great as he was, wantonly abusing the grace of God, rashly following the bent of his own genius, and placing overmuch confidence in himself, making light account of the ancient simplicity of the Christian religion, presuming that he knew more than all the world besides, de-

---

the duties of which place he discharged with eminent ability and success. He remained a layman till the age of forty-three, when he was admitted to priest's orders at Cæsarea, greatly to the displeasure of Demetrius, by whose hand, according to the Church's rule, the office ought to have been conferred, and he was in consequence banished from Alexandria. Returning to Cæsarea, he taught there with great reputation, and had many eminent persons among his disciples. He suffered much in the Decian persecution in 250, when he was thrown into prison and subjected to severe tortures. His works, as Vincentius says, were very numerous, including among them the Hexapla, a revised edition of the Hebrew Scriptures and of the Septuagint version, together with three other versions, the Hebrew being set forth in both Hebrew and Greek characters. His writings were corrupted in many instances, so that, as Vincentius says, opinions were often imputed to him which he would not have acknowledged. He died in his sixty-ninth year at Tyre, and was buried there.

[1] "Quis nostrum," says St. Jerome, "potest tanta legere quanta ille conscripsit." — *Hieron. ad Pam. et Occan.*

[2] He died, as was said in the preceding note, in his sixty-ninth year.

[3] Among these were Gregory Thaumaturgus, Bishop of Neo-Cæsarea in Pontus, and Firmilian, Bishop of Cæsarea in Cappadocia.

[4] Mammea.

[5] These are St. Jerome's words, from whose book, *De Viris illustribus* c. 54, Vincentius's account of Origen is taken. The vexed question of Philip's claim to be ranked as a Christian is discussed by Tillemont. — *Histoire des Empereurs*, T. iii. pp. 494 *sqq.*

[6] Errare malo cum Platone quam cum istis vera sentire. — Cicero, *Tuscul. Quæst.* 1.

spising the traditions of the Church and the determinations of the ancients, and interpreting certain passages of Scripture in a novel way, deserved for himself the warning given to the Church of God, as applicable in his case as in that of others, "If there arise a prophet in the midst of thee," . . . "thou shalt not hearken to the words of that prophet," . . . "because the Lord your God doth make trial of you, whether you love Him or not."[1] Truly, thus of a sudden to seduce the Church which was devoted to him, and hung upon him through admiration of his genius, his learning, his eloquence, his manner of life and influence, while she had no fear, no suspicion for herself, — thus, I say, to seduce the Church, slowly and little by little, from the old religion to a new profaneness, was not only a trial, but a great trial.[2]

[45.] But some one will say, Origen's books have been corrupted. I do not deny it; nay, I grant it readily. For that such is the case has been handed down both orally and in writing, not only by Catholics, but by heretics as well. But the point is, that though himself be not, yet books published under his name are, a great trial, which, abounding in many hurtful blasphemies, are both read and delighted in, not as being some one else's, but as being believed to be his, so that, although there was no error in Origen's original meaning, yet Origen's authority appears to be an effectual cause in leading people to embrace error.

CHAPTER XVIII.

Tertullian a great Trial to the Church.

[46.] THE case is the same with Tertullian.[3] For as Origen holds by far the first place

among the Greeks, so does Tertullian among the Latins. For who more learned than he, who more versed in knowledge whether divine or human? With marvellous capacity of mind he comprehended all philosophy, and had a knowledge of all schools of philosophers, and of the founders and upholders of schools, and was acquainted with all their rules and observances, and with their various histories and studies. Was not his genius of such unrivalled strength and vehemence that there was scarcely any obstacle which he proposed to himself to overcome, that he did not penetrate by acuteness, or crush by weight? As to his style, who can sufficiently set forth its praise? It was knit together with so much cogency of argument that it compelled assent, even where it failed to persuade. Every word almost was a sentence; every sentence a victory. This know the Marcions, the Apelleses, the Praxeases, the Hermogeneses, the Jews, the Heathens, the Gnostics, and the rest, whose blasphemies he overthrew by the force of his many and ponderous volumes, as with so many thunderbolts. Yet this man also, notwithstanding all that I have mentioned, this Tertullian, I say, too little tenacious of Catholic doctrine, that is, of the universal and ancient faith, more eloquent by far than faithful,[4] changed his belief, and justified what the blessed Confessor, Hilary, writes of him, namely, that "by his subsequent error he detracted from the authority of his approved writings."[5] He also was a great trial in the Church. But of Tertullian I am unwilling to say more. This only I will add, that, contrary to the injunction of Moses, by asserting the novel furies of Montanus[6] which arose in the Church, and those mad dreams of new doctrine dreamed by mad women, to be true prophecies, he deservedly made both himself and his writings obnoxious to the words, "If there arise a prophet in the midst of thee," . . . "thou shalt not hearken to the words of that prophet." For why? "Because the Lord your God doth make trial of you, whether you love Him or not."

CHAPTER XIX.

What we ought to learn from these Examples.

[47.] IT behoves us, then, to give heed to these instances from Church History, so many and so great, and others of the same

---

[1] Deuteronomy xiii. 1.
[2] "The great Origen died after his many labors in peace. His immediate pupils were saints and rulers in the Church. He has the praise of St. Athanasius, St. Basil, and St. Gregory Nazianzen, and furnishes materials to St. Ambrose and St. Hilary; yet, as time proceeded, a definite heterodoxy was the growing result of his theology, and at length, three hundred years after his death, he was condemned, and, as has generally been considered, in an Œcumenical Council." — NEWMAN on *Development*, p. 85, First Edition.
[3] Hardly anything is known of Tertullian, besides what may be gathered from his works, in addition to the following account given by St. Jerome (*De Viris Illustribus*), which I quote from Bishop Kaye's work on Tertullian and his writings: "Tertullian, a presbyter, the first Latin writer after Victor and Apollonius, was a native of the province of Africa and city of Carthage, the son of a proconsular centurion. He was a man of a sharp and vehement temper, flourished under Severus and Caracalla, and wrote numerous works, which, as they are generally known, I think it unnecessary to particularize. I saw at Concordia, in Italy, an old man named Paulus, who said that, when young, he had met at Rome with an aged amanuensis of the blessed Cyprian, who told him that Cyprian never passed a day without reading some portion of Tertullian's works, and used frequently to say, 'Give me my master,' meaning Tertullian. After remaining a presbyter of the Church till he had attained the middle of life, Tertullian was by the cruel and contumelious treatment of the Roman clergy driven to embrace the opinions of Montanus, which he has mentioned in several of his works, under the title of 'The New Prophecy.' He is reported to have lived to a very advanced age." He was born about the middle of the second century, and flourished, according to the dates indicated above, between the years 190 and 216.

[4] Fidelior, Baluz, Felicior, others.   [5] In Mat. v.
[6] Montanus, with his two prophetesses, professed that he was intrusted with a new dispensation, — a dispensation in advance of the Gospel, as the Gospel was in advance of the Law. His system was a protest against the laxity which had grown up in the Church, as has repeatedly been the case after revivals of religious fervor, verifying Tertullian's apophthegm, "Christiani fiunt, non nascuntur" (men become Christians, they are not born such). Its characteristics

description, and to understand distinctly, in accordance with the rule laid down in Deuteronomy, that if at any time a Doctor in the Church have erred from the faith, Divine Providence permits it in order to make trial of us, whether or not we love God with all our heart and with all our mind.

CHAPTER XX.

The Notes of a true Catholic.

[48.] THIS being the case, he is the true and genuine Catholic who loves the truth of God, who loves the Church, who loves the Body of Christ, who esteems divine religion and the Catholic Faith above every thing, above the authority, above the regard, above the genius, above the eloquence, above the philosophy, of every man whatsoever; who sets light by all of these, and continuing steadfast and established in the faith, resolves that he will believe that, and that only, which he is sure the Catholic Church has held universally and from ancient time; but that whatsoever new and unheard-of doctrine he shall find to have been furtively introduced by some one or another, besides that of all, or contrary to that of all the saints, this, he will understand, does not pertain to religion, but is permitted as a trial, being instructed especially by the words of the blessed Apostle Paul, who writes thus in his first Epistle to the Corinthians, "There must needs be heresies, that they who are approved may be made manifest among you:"[1] as though he should say, This is the reason why the authors of Heresies are not forthwith rooted up by God, namely, that they who are approved may be made manifest; that is, that it may be apparent of each individual, how tenacious and faithful and steadfast he is in his love of the Catholic faith.

[49.] And in truth, as each novelty springs up incontinently is discerned the difference between the weight of the wheat and the lightness of the chaff. Then that which had no weight to keep it on the floor is without difficulty blown away. For some at once fly off entirely; others having been only shaken out, afraid of perishing, wounded, half alive, half dead, are ashamed to return. They have, in fact swallowed a quantity of poison — not enough to kill, yet more than can be got rid of; it neither causes death, nor suffers to live. O wretched condition! With what

surging tempestuous cares are they tossed about! One while, the error being set in motion, they are hurried whithersoever the wind drives them; another, returning upon themselves like refluent waves, they are dashed back: one while, with rash presumption, they give their approval to what seems uncertain; another, with irrational fear, they are frightened out of their wits at what is certain, in doubt whither to go, whither to return, what to seek, what to shun, what to keep, what to throw away.

[50.] This affliction, indeed, of a hesitating and miserably vacillating mind is, if they are wise, a medicine intended for them by God's compassion. For therefore it is that outside the most secure harbour of the Catholic Faith, they are tossed about, beaten, and almost killed, by divers tempestuous cogitations, in order that they may take in the sails of self-conceit, which, they had with ill advice unfurled to the blasts of novelty, and may betake themselves again to, and remain stationary within, the most secure harbour of their placid and good mother, and may begin by vomiting up those bitter and turbid floods of error which they had swallowed, that thenceforward they may be able to drink the streams of fresh and living water. Let them unlearn well what they had learnt not well, and let them receive so much of the entire doctrine of the Church as they can understand: what they cannot understand let them believe.

CHAPTER XXI.

Exposition of St. Paul's Words. — 1 Tim. vi. 20.

[51.] SUCH being the case, when I think over these things, and revolve them in my mind again and again, I cannot sufficiently wonder at the madness of certain men, at the impiety of their blinded understanding, at their lust of error, such that, not content with the rule of faith delivered once for all, and received from the times of old, they are every day seeking one novelty after another, and are constantly longing to add, change, take away, in religion, as though the doctrine, "Let what has once for all been revealed suffice," were not a heavenly but an earthly rule, — a rule which could not be complied with except by continual emendation, nay, rather by continual fault-finding; whereas the divine Oracles cry aloud, "Remove not the landmarks, which thy fathers have set,"[2] and "Go not to law with a Judge,"[3] and "Whoso breaketh through a fence a serpent shall bite him,"[4] and that saying of the Apostle where-

---

were extreme asceticism, rigorous fasting, the exaltation of celibacy, the absolute prohibition of second marriage, the expectation of our Lord's second advent as near at hand, the disparagement of the clergy in comparison with its own Paraclete-inspired teachers. It had its rise in Phrygia, and from thence spread throughout Asia Minor, thence it found its way to Southern Gaul, to Rome, to North Western Africa, in which last for a time it had many followers.

[1] 1 Cor. ii. 9.

[2] Prov. xxii. 28.   [3] Ecclus. viii. 14.   [4] Eccles. x. 8.

with, as with a spiritual sword, all the wicked novelties of all heresies often have been, and will always have to be, decapitated, "O Timothy, keep the deposit, shunning profane novelties of words and oppositions of the knowledge falsely so called, which some professing have erred concerning the faith." [1]

[52.] After words such as these, is there any one of so hardened a front, such anvil-like impudence, such adamantine pertinacity, as not to succumb to so huge a mass, not to be crushed by so ponderous a weight, not to be shaken in pieces by such heavy blows, not to be annihilated by such dreadful thunderbolts of divine eloquence? "Shun profane novelties," he says. He does not say shun "antiquity." But he plainly points to what ought to follow by the rule of contrary. For if novelty is to be shunned, antiquity is to be held fast; if novelty is profane, antiquity is sacred. He adds, "And oppositions of science falsely so called." "Falsely called" indeed, as applied to the doctrines of heretics, where ignorance is disguised under the name of knowledge, fog of sunshine, darkness of light. "Which some professing have erred concerning the faith." Professing what? What but some (I know not what) new and unheard-of doctrine. For thou mayest hear some of these same doctors say, "Come, O silly wretches, who go by the name of Catholics, come and learn the true faith, which no one but ourselves is acquainted with, which same has lain hid these many ages, but has recently been revealed and made manifest. But learn it by stealth and in secret, for you will be delighted with it. Moreover, when you have learnt it, teach it furtively, that the world may not hear, that the Church may not know. For there are but few to whom it is granted to receive the secret of so great a mystery." Are not these the words of that harlot who, in the proverbs of Solomon, calls to the passengers who go right on their ways, "Whoso is simple let him turn in hither." And as for them that are void of understanding, she exhorts them saying: "Drink stolen waters, for they are sweet, and eat bread in secret for it is pleasant." What next? "But he knoweth not that the sons of earth perish in her house." [1] Who are those "sons of earth"? Let the apostle explain: "Those who have erred concerning the faith."

CHAPTER XXII.

A more particular Exposition of 1 Tim. vi. 20.

[53.] BUT it is worth while to expound the whole of that passage of the apostle more fully, "O Timothy, keep the deposit, avoiding profane novelties of words."

"O!" The exclamation implies fore-knowledge as well as charity. For he mourned in anticipation over the errors which he foresaw. Who is the Timothy of to-day, but either generally the Universal Church, or in particular, the whole body of The Prelacy, whom it behoves either themselves to possess or to communicate to others a complete knowledge of religion? What is "Keep the deposit"? "Keep it," because of thieves, because of adversaries, lest, while men sleep, they sow tares over that good wheat which the Son of Man had sown in his field. "Keep the deposit." What is "The deposit"? That which has been intrusted to thee, not that which thou hast thyself devised: a matter not of wit, but of learning; not of private adoption, but of public tradition; a matter brought to thee, not put forth by thee, wherein thou art bound to be not an author but a keeper, not a teacher but a disciple, not a leader but a follower. "Keep the deposit." Preserve the talent of Catholic Faith inviolate, unadulterate. That which has been intrusted to thee, let it continue in thy possession, let it be handed on by thee. Thou hast received gold; give gold in turn. Do not substitute one thing for another. Do not for gold impudently substitute lead or brass. Give real gold, not counterfeit.

O Timothy! O Priest! O Expositor! O Doctor! if the divine gift hath qualified thee by wit, by skill, by learning, be thou a Bazaleel of the spiritual tabernacle, [3] engrave the precious gems of divine doctrine, fit them in accurately, adorn them skilfully, add splendor, grace, beauty. Let that which formerly was believed, though imperfectly apprehended, as expounded by thee be clearly understood. Let posterity welcome, understood through thy exposition, what antiquity venerated without understanding. Yet teach still the same truths which thou hast learnt, so that though thou speakest after a new fashion, what thou speakest may not be new.

CHAPTER XXIII.

On Development in Religious Knowledge.

[54.] BUT some one will say perhaps, Shall there, then, be no progress in Christ's Church? Certainly; all possible progress. For what being is there, so envious of men, so full of hatred to God, who would seek to forbid it? Yet on condition that it be real

---

[1] 1 Tim. vi. 20. [2] Prov. ix. 16-18. [3] Exod. xxxi. 1, etc.

progress, not alteration of the faith. For progress requires that the subject be enlarged in itself, alteration, that it be transformed into something else. The intelligence, then, the knowledge, the wisdom, as well of individuals as of all, as well of one man as of the whole Church, ought, in the course of ages and centuries, to increase and make much and vigorous progress; but yet only in its own kind; that is to say, in the same doctrine, in the same sense, and in the same meaning.

[55.] The growth of religion in the soul must be analogous to the growth of the body, which, though in process of years it is developed and attains its full size, yet remains still the same. There is a wide difference between the flower of youth and the maturity of age; yet they who were once young are still the same now that they have become old, insomuch that though the stature and outward form of the individual are changed, yet his nature is one and the same, his person is one and the same. An infant's limbs are small, a young man's large, yet the infant and the young man are the same. Men when full grown have the same number of joints that they had when children; and if there be any to which maturer age has given birth, these were already present in embryo, so that nothing new is produced in them when old which was not already latent in them when children. This, then, is undoubtedly the true and legitimate rule of progress, this the established and most beautiful order of growth, that mature age ever develops in the man those parts and forms which the wisdom of the Creator had already framed beforehand in the infant. Whereas, if the human form were changed into some shape belonging to another kind, or at any rate, if the number of its limbs were increased or diminished, the result would be that the whole body would become either a wreck or a monster, or, at the least, would be impaired and enfeebled.

[56.] In like manner, it behoves Christian doctrine to follow the same laws of progress, so as to be consolidated by years, enlarged by time, refined by age, and yet, withal, to continue uncorrupt and unadulterate, complete and perfect in all the measurement of its parts, and, so to speak, in all its proper members and senses, admitting no change, no waste of its distinctive property, no variation in its limits.

[57.] For example: Our forefathers in the old time sowed wheat in the Church's field. It would be most unmeet and iniquitous if we, their descendants, instead of the genuine truth of corn, should reap the counterfeit error of tares. This rather should be the result, — there should be no discrepancy between the first and the last. From doctrine which was sown as wheat, we should reap, in the increase, doctrine of the same kind — wheat also; so that when in process of time any of the original seed is developed, and now flourishes under cultivation, no change may ensue in the character of the plant. There may supervene shape, form, variation in outward appearance, but the nature of each kind must remain the same. God forbid that those rose-beds of Catholic interpretation should be converted into thorns and thistles. God forbid that in that spiritual paradise from plants of cinnamon and balsam darnel and wolfsbane should of a sudden shoot forth.

Therefore, whatever has been sown by the fidelity of the Fathers in this husbandry of God's Church, the same ought to be cultivated and taken care of by the industry of their children, the same ought to flourish and ripen, the same ought to advance and go forward to perfection. For it is right that those ancient doctrines of heavenly philosophy should, as time goes on, be cared for, smoothed, polished; but not that they should be changed, not that they should be maimed, not that they should be mutilated. They may receive proof, illustration, definiteness; but they must retain withal their completeness, their integrity, their characteristic properties.

[58.] For if once this license of impious fraud be admitted, I dread to say in how great danger religion will be of being utterly destroyed and annihilated. For if any one part of Catholic truth be given up, another, and another, and another will thenceforward be given up as a matter of course, and the several individual portions having been rejected, what will follow in the end but the rejection of the whole? On the other hand, if what is new begins to be mingled with what is old, foreign with domestic, profane with sacred, the custom will of necessity creep on universally, till at last the Church will have nothing left untampered with, nothing unadulterated, nothing sound, nothing pure; but where formerly there was a sanctuary of chaste and undefiled truth, thenceforward there will be a brothel of impious and base errors. May God's mercy avert this wickedness from the minds of his servants; be it rather the frenzy of the ungodly.

[59.] But the Church of Christ, the careful and watchful guardian of the doctrines deposited in her charge, never changes anything in them, never diminishes, never adds, does not cut off what is necessary, does not add what is superfluous, does not lose her own, does not appropriate what is another's, but while dealing faithfully and judiciously with ancient doctrine, keeps this one object carefully in view, — if there be anything which antiquity has left shapeless and rudimentary, to fashion and polish it, if anything already reduced to shape and developed, to consolidate and strengthen it, if any already ratified and defined to keep and guard it. Finally, what other object have Councils ever aimed at in their decrees, than to provide that what was before believed in simplicity should in future be believed intelligently, that what was before preached coldly should in future be preached earnestly, that what was before practised negligently should thenceforward be practised with double solicitude? This, I say, is what the Catholic Church, roused by the novelties of heretics, has accomplished by the decrees of her Councils, — this, and nothing else, — she has thenceforward consigned to posterity in writing what she had received from those of olden times only by tradition, comprising a great amount of matter in a few words, and often, for the better understanding, designating an old article of the faith by the characteristic of a new name.[1]

CHAPTER XXIV.

Continuation of the Exposition of 1 Tim. vi. 20.

[60.] BUT let us return to the apostle. "O Timothy," he says, "Guard the deposit, shunning profane novelties of words." "Shun them as you would a viper, as you would a scorpion, as you would a basilisk, lest they smite you not only with their touch, but even with their eyes and breath." What is "to shun"? Not even to eat[2] with a person of this sort. What is "shun"? "If anyone," says St. John, "come to you and bring not this doctrine." What doctrine? What but the Catholic and universal doctrine, which has continued one and the same through the several successions of ages by the uncorrupt tradition of the truth, and so will continue for ever— "Receive him not into your house, neither bid him Godspeed, for he that biddeth him Godspeed communicates with him in his evil deeds."[3]

[61.] "Profane novelties of words." What words are these? Such as have nothing sacred, nothing religious, words utterly remote from the inmost sanctuary of the Church, which is the temple of God. "Profane novelties of words," that is, of doctrines,

subjects, opinions, such as are contrary to antiquity and the faith of the olden time. Which if they be received, it follows necessarily that the faith of the blessed fathers is violated either in whole, or at all events in great part; it follows necessarily that all the faithful of all ages, all the saints, the chaste, the continent, the virgins, all the clergy, Deacons and Priests, so many thousands of Confessors, so vast an army of martyrs, such multitudes of cities and of peoples, so many islands, provinces, kings, tribes, kingdoms, nations, in a word, almost the whole earth, incorporated in Christ the Head, through the Catholic faith, have been ignorant for so long a tract of time, have been mistaken, have blasphemed, have not known what to believe, what to confess.

[62.] "Shun profane novelties of words," which to receive and follow was never the part of Catholics; of heretics always was. In sooth, what heresy ever burst forth save under a definite name, at a definite place, at a definite time? Who ever originated a heresy that did not first dissever himself from the consentient agreement of the universality and antiquity of the Catholic Church? That this is so is demonstrated in the clearest way by examples. For who ever before that profane Pelagius[4] attributed so much antecedent strength to Free-will, as to deny the necessity of God's grace to aid it towards good in every

---

[1] For instance, the proper Deity of our Blessed Lord by the word "Homousios," consubstantial, of one substance, essence, nature.
[2] Cor. v. 11.
[3] 2 John 10.

[4] Pelagius, a monk, a Briton by birth, but resident in Rome, where by the strictness of his life he had acquired a high reputation for sanctity, was led, partly perhaps by opposition to St. Augustine's teaching on the subject of election and predestination, partly by indignation at the laxity of professing Christians, who pleaded, in excuse for their low standard, the weakness of human nature, to insist upon man's natural power, and to deny his need of divine grace.
Pelagius was joined by another monk, Cœlestius, a younger man, with whom about the year 410, the year in which Rome was taken by the Goths, he began to teach openly and in public what before he had held and taught in private. After the sack of Rome, the two friends passed over into Africa, and from thence Pelagius proceeded to Palestine, where he was in two separate synods acquitted of the charge of heresy, which had been brought against him by Orosius, a Spanish monk, whom Augustine had sent for that purpose. But in 416, two African synods condemned his doctrine, and Zosimus, bishop of Rome, whom he had appealed to, though he had set aside their decision, was eventually obliged to yield to the firmness with which they held their ground, and not only to condemn Pelagius, but to take stringent measures against his adherents. "In 418, another African synod of two hundred and fourteen bishops passed nine canons, which were afterwards generally accepted throughout the Church, and came to be regarded as the most important bulwark against Pelagianism." The heresy was formally condemned, in 431, by the General Council of Ephesus. Canons 2 and 4.
The Pelagians denied the corruption of man's nature, and the necessity of divine grace. They held that infants new-born are in the same state in which Adam was before his fall; that Adam's sin injured no one but himself, and affected his posterity no other wise than by the evil example which it afforded; they held also that men may live without sin if they will, and that some have so lived.
Those who were afterwards called semi-Pelagians (they belonged chiefly to the churches of Southern Gaul) were orthodox except in one particular: In their anxiety to justify, as they thought, God's dealings with man, they held that the first step in the way of salvation must be from ourselves: we must ask that we may receive, seek that we may find, knock that it may be opened to us; thenceforward in every stage of the road, our strenuous efforts must be aided by divine grace. They did not understand, or did not grant, that to that same grace must be referred even the disposition to ask, to seek, to knock. See Prosper's letter to Augustine, August. Opera, Tom. x.
The semi-Pelagian doctrine was condemned in the second Council of Orange (A.D. 529), the third and fifth canons of which are directed against it.

single act? Who ever before his monstrous disciple Cœlestius denied that the whole human race is involved in the guilt of Adam's sin? Who ever before sacrilegious Arius dared to rend asunder the unity of the Trinity? Who before impious Sabellius was so audacious as to confound the Trinity of the Unity? Who before cruellest Novatian represented God as cruel in that He had rather the wicked should die than that he should be converted and live? Who before Simon Magus, who was smitten by the apostle's rebuke, and from whom that ancient sink of every thing vile has flowed by a secret continuous succession even to Priscillian of our own time, — who, I say, before this Simon Magus, dared to say that God, the Creator, is the author of evil, that is, of our wickednesses, impieties, flagitiousnesses, inasmuch as he asserts that He created with His own hands a human nature of such a description, that of its own motion, and by the impulse of its necessity-constrained will, it can do nothing else, can will nothing else, but sin, seeing that tossed to and fro, and set on fire by the furies of all sorts of vices, it is hurried away by unquenchable lust into the utmost extremes of baseness?

[63.] There are innumerable instances of this kind, which for brevity's sake, pass over; by all of which, however, it is manifestly and clearly shown, that it is an established law, in the case of almost all heresies, that they evermore delight in profane novelties, scorn the decisions of antiquity, and, through oppositions of science falsely so called, make shipwreck of the faith. On the other hand, it is the sure characteristic of Catholics to keep that which has been committed to their trust by the holy Fathers, to condemn profane novelties, and, in the apostle's words, once and again repeated, to anathematize every one who preaches any other doctrine than that which has been received.[1]

CHAPTER XXV.

Heretics appeal to Scripture that they may more easily succeed in deceiving.

[64.] HERE, possibly, some one may ask, Do heretics also appeal to Scripture? They do indeed, and with a vengeance; for you may see them scamper through every single book of Holy Scripture, — through the books of Moses, the books of Kings, the Psalms, the Epistles, the Gospels, the Prophets. Whether among their own people, or among strangers, in private or in public, in speaking or in writing, at convivial meetings, or in the streets, hardly ever do they bring forward anything of their own which they do not endeavour to shelter under words of Scripture. Read the works of Paul of Samosata, of Priscillian, of Eunomius, of Jovinian, and the rest of those pests, and you will see an infinite heap of instances, hardly a single page, which does not bristle with plausible quotations from the New Testment or the Old.

[65.] But the more secretly they conceal themselves under shelter of the Divine Law, so much the more are they to be feared and guarded against. For they know that the evil stench of their doctrine will hardly find acceptance with any one if it be exhaled pure and simple. They sprinkle it over, therefore, with the perfume of heavenly language, in order that one who would be ready to despise human error, may hesitate to condemn divine words. They do, in fact, what nurses do when they would prepare some bitter draught for children; they smear the edge of the cup all round with honey, that the unsuspecting child, having first tasted the sweet, may have no fear of the bitter. So too do these act, who disguise poisonous herbs and noxious juices under the names of medicines, so that no one almost, when he reads the label, suspects the poison.

[66.] It was for this reason that the Saviour cried, "Beware of false prophets who come to you in sheep's clothing, but inwardly they are ravening wolves."[2] What is meant by "sheep's clothing"? What but the words which prophets and apostles with the guilelessness of sheep wove beforehand as fleeces, for that immaculate Lamb which taketh away the sin of the world? What are the ravening wolves? What but the savage and rabid glosses of heretics, who continually infest the Church's folds, and tear in pieces the flock of Christ wherever they are able? But that they may with more successful guile steal upon the unsuspecting sheep, retaining the ferocity of the wolf, they put off his appearance, and wrap themselves, so to say, in the language of the Divine Law, as in a fleece, so that one, having felt the softness of wool, may have no dread of the wolf's fangs. But what saith the Saviour? "By their fruits ye shall know them;" that is, when they have begun not only to quote those divine words, but also to expound them, not as yet only to make a boast of them as on their side, but also to interpret them, then will that bitterness, that acerbity, that rage, be understood; then will the ill-savour of that novel

---

[1] Gal. ii. 9.

[2] Matt. vii. 15.

poison be perceived, then will those profane novelties be disclosed, then may you see first the hedge broken through, then the landmarks of the Fathers removed, then the Catholic faith assailed, then the doctrine of the Church torn in pieces.

[67.] Such were they whom the Apostle Paul rebukes in his Second Epistle to the Corinthians, when he says, "For of this sort are false apostles, deceitful workers, transforming themselves into apostles of Christ."[1] The apostles brought forward instances from Holy Scripture; these men did the same. The apostles cited the authority of the Psalms; these men did so likewise. The apostles brought forward passages from the prophets; these men still did the same. But when they began to interpret in different senses the passages which both had agreed in appealing to, then were discerned the guileless from the crafty, the genuine from the counterfeit, the straight from the crooked, then, in one word, the true apostles from the false apostles. "And no wonder," he says, "for Satan himself transforms himself into an angel of light. It is no marvel then if his servants are transformed as the servants of righteousness." Therefore, according to the authority of the Apostle Paul, as often as either false apostles or false teachers cite passages from the Divine Law, by means of which, misinterpreted, they seek to prop up their own errors, there is no doubt that they are following the cunning devices of their father, which assuredly he would never have devised, but that he knew that where he could fraudulently and by stealth introduce error, there is no easier way of effecting his impious purpose than by pretending the authority of Holy Scripture.

CHAPTER XXVI.

Heretics, in quoting Scripture, follow the example of the Devil.

[68.] BUT some one will say, What proof have we that the Devil is wont to appeal to Holy Scripture? Let him read the Gospels wherein it is written, "Then the Devil took Him (the Lord the Saviour) and set Him upon a pinnacle of the Temple, and said unto Him: If thou be the Son of God, cast thyself down, for it is written, He shall give His angels charge concerning thee, that they may keep thee in all thy ways: In their hands they shall bear thee up, lest perchance thou dash thy foot against a stone."[2] What sort of treatment must men, insignificant wretches that they are, look for at the hands of him who assailed even the Lord of Glory with quotations from Scripture? "If thou be the Son of God," saith he, "cast thyself down." Wherefore? "For," saith he, "it is written." It behoves us to pay special attention to this passage and bear it in mind, that, warned by so important an instance of Evangelical authority, we may be assured beyond doubt, when we find people alleging passages from the Apostles or Prophets against the Catholic Faith, that the Devil speaks through their mouths. For as then the Head spoke to the Head, so now also the members speak to the members, the members of the Devil to the members of Christ, misbelievers to believers, sacrilegious to religious, in one word, Heretics to Catholics.

[69.] But what do they say? "If thou be the Son of God, cast thyself down;" that is, If thou wouldst be a son of God, and wouldst receive the inheritance of the Kingdom of Heaven, cast thyself down; that is, cast thyself down from the doctrine and tradition of that sublime Church, which is imagined to be nothing less than the very temple of God. And if one should ask one of the heretics who gives this advice, How do you prove? What ground have you, for saying, that I ought to cast away the universal and ancient faith of the Catholic Church? he has the answer ready, "For it is written;" and forthwith he produces a thousand testimonies, a thousand examples, a thousand authorities from the Law, from the Psalms, from the apostles, from the Prophets, by means of which, interpreted on a new and wrong principle, the unhappy soul may be precipitated from the height of Catholic truth to the lowest abyss of heresy. Then, with the accompanying promises, the heretics are wont marvellously to beguile the incautious. For they dare to teach and promise, that in their church, that is, in the conventicle of their communion, there is a certain great and special and altogether personal grace of God, so that whosoever pertain to their number, without any labour, without any effort, without any industry, even though they neither ask, nor seek, nor knock, have such a dispensation from God, that, borne up by angel hands, that is, preserved by the protection of angels, it is impossible they should ever dash their feet against a stone, that is, that they should ever be offended.[3]

---

[1] 2 Cor. xi. 12.

[2] Matt. iv. 5, etc.
[3] See Appendix II.

CHAPTER XXVII.

What Rule is to be observed in the Interpretation of Scripture.

[70.] BUT it will be said, If the words, the sentiments, the promises of Scripture, are appealed to by the Devil and his disciples, of whom some are false apostles, some false prophets and false teachers, and all without exception heretics, what are Catholics and the sons of Mother Church to do? How are they to distinguish truth from falsehood in the sacred Scriptures? They must be very careful to pursue that course which, in the beginning of this Commonitory, we said that holy and learned men had commended to us, that is to say, they must interpret the sacred Canon according to the traditions of the Universal Church and in keeping with the rules of Catholic doctrine, in which Catholic and Universal Church, moreover, they must follow universality, antiquity, consent. And if at any time a part opposes itself to the whole, novelty to antiquity, the dissent of one or a few who are in error to the consent of all or at all events of the great majority of Catholics, then they must prefer the soundness of the whole to the corruption of a part; in which same whole they must prefer the religion of antiquity to the profaneness of novelty; and in antiquity itself in like manner, to the temerity of one or of a very few they must prefer, first of all, the general decrees, if such there be, of a Universal Council, or if there be no such, then, what is next best, they must follow the consentient belief of many and great masters. Which rule having been faithfully, soberly, and scrupulously observed, we shall with little difficulty detect the noxious errors of heretics as they arise.

CHAPTER XXVIII.

In what Way, on collating the consentient opinions of the Ancient Masters, the Novelties of Heretics may be detected and condemned.

[71.] AND here I perceive that, as a necessary sequel to the foregoing, I ought to show by examples in what way, by collating the consentient opinions of the ancient masters, the profane novelties of heretics may be detected and condemned. Yet in the investigation of this ancient consent of the holy Fathers we are to bestow our pains not on every minor question of the Divine Law, but only, at all events especially, where the Rule of Faith is concerned. Nor is this way of dealing with heresy to be resorted to always, or in every instance, but only in the case of those heresies which are new and recent, and that on their first arising, before they have had time to deprave the Rules of the Ancient Faith, and before they endeavour, while the poison spreads and diffuses itself, to corrupt the writings of the ancients. But heresies already widely diffused and of old standing are by no means to be thus dealt with, seeing that through lapse of time they have long had opportunity of corrupting the truth. And therefore, as to the more ancient schisms or heresies, we ought either to confute them, if need be, by the sole authority of the Scriptures, or at any rate, to shun them as having been already of old convicted and condemned by universal councils of the Catholic Priesthood.

[72.] Therefore, as soon as the corruption of each mischievous error begins to break forth, and to defend itself by filching certain passages of Scripture, and expounding them fraudulently and deceitfully, forthwith, the opinions of the ancients in the interpretation of the Canon are to be collected, whereby the novelty, and consequently the profaneness, whatever it may be, that arises, may both without any doubt be exposed, and without any tergiversation be condemned. But the opinions of those Fathers only are to be used for comparison, who living and teaching, holily, wisely, and with constancy, in the Catholic faith and communion, were counted worthy either to die in the faith of Christ, or to suffer death happily for Christ. Whom yet we are to believe on this condition, that that only is to be accounted indubitable, certain, established, which either all, or the more part, have supported and confirmed manifestly, frequently, persistently, in one and the same sense, forming, as it were, a consentient council of doctors, all receiving, holding, handing on the same doctrine. But whatsoever a teacher holds, other than all, or contrary to all, be he holy and learned, be he a bishop, be he a Confessor, be he a martyr, let that be regarded as a private fancy of his own, and be separated from the authority of common, public, general persuasion, lest, after the sacrilegious custom of heretics and schismatics, rejecting the ancient truth of the universal Creed, we follow, at the utmost peril of our eternal salvation, the newly devised error of one man.

[73.] Lest any one perchance should rashly think the holy and Catholic consent of these blessed fathers to be despised, the Apostle says, in the First Epistle to the Corinthians, "God hath placed some in the

Church, first Apostles,"[1] of whom himself was one; "secondly Prophets,'' such as Agabus, of whom we read in the Acts of the Apostles;[2] "then doctors," who are now called Homilists, Expositors,[3] whom the same apostle sometimes calls also "Prophets," because by them the mysteries of the Prophets are opened to the people. Whosoever, therefore, shall despise these, who had their appointment of God in His Church in their several times and places, when they are unanimous in Christ, in the interpretation of some one point of Catholic doctrine, despises not man, but God, from whose unity in the truth, lest any one should vary, the same Apostle earnestly protests, "I beseech you, brethren, that ye all speak the same thing, and that there be no divisions among you, but that ye be perfectly joined together in the same mind and in the same judgment."[4] But if any one dissent from their unanimous decision, let him listen to the words of the same apostle," "God is not the God of dissension but of peace;"[5] that is, not of him who departs from the unity of consent, but of those who remain steadfast in the peace of consent; "as," he continues, "I teach in all Churches of the saints," that is, of Catholics, which churches are therefore churches of the saints, because they continue steadfast in the communion of the faith.

[74.] And lest any one, disregarding every one else, should arrogantly claim to be listened to himself alone, himself alone to be believed, the Apostle goes on to say, "Did the word of God proceed from you, or did it come to you only?" And, lest this should be thought lightly spoken, he continues, "If any man seem to be a prophet or a spiritual person, let him acknowledge that the things which I write unto you are the Lord's commands." As to which, unless a man be a prophet or a spiritual person, that is, a master in spiritual matters, let him be as observant as possible of impartiality and unity, so as neither to prefer his own opinions to those of every one besides, nor to recede from the belief of the whole body. Which injunction, whoso ignores, shall be himself ignored;[6] that is, he who either does not learn what he does not know, or treats with contempt what he knows, shall be ignored, that is, shall be deemed unworthy to be ranked of God with those who are united to each other by faith, and equalled with each other by humility, than which I cannot imagine a more terrible evil. This it is however which, according to

the Apostle's threatening, we see to have befallen Julian the Pelagian,[7] who either neglected to associate himself with the belief of his fellow Christians, or presumed to dissociate himself from it.

[75.] But it is now time to bring forward the exemplification which we promised, where and how the sentences of the holy Fathers have been collected together, so that in accordance with them, by the decree and authority of a council, the rule of the Church's faith may be settled. Which that it may be done the more conveniently, let this present Commonitory end here, so that the remainder which is to follow may be begun from a fresh beginning.

[The Second Book of the Commonitory is lost. Nothing of it remains but the conclusion : in other words, the recapitulation which follows.]

CHAPTER XXIX.

Recapitulation.

[76.] THIS being the case, it is now time that we should recapitulate, at the close of this second Commonitory, what was said in that and in the preceding.

We said above, that it has always been the custom of Catholics, and still is, to prove the true faith in these two ways; first by the authority of the Divine Canon, and next by the tradition of the Catholic Chnrch. Not that the Canon alone does not of itself suffice for every question, but seeing that the more part, interpreting the divine words according to their own persuasion, take up various erroneous opinions, it is therefore necessary that the interpretation of divine Scripture should be ruled according to the one standard of the Church's belief, especially in those articles on which the foundations of all Catholic doctrine rest.

[77.] We said likewise, that in the Church itself regard must be had to the consentient voice of universality equally with that of antiquity, lest we either be torn from the integrity of unity and carried away to schism, or be precipitated from the religion of antiquity into heretical novelties. We said, further, that in this same ecclesiastical antiquity two points are very carefully and earnestly to be held in view by those who

---

[1] 1 Cor. xii. 27, 28.   [2] Acts xi. 28.
[3] " Tractatores." St. Augustine's Expository Lectures on St. John's Gospel are entitled "Tractatus."
[4] 1 Cor. i. 10.   [5] 1 Cor. xiv. 33.   [6] 1 Cor. xiv. 33.

[7] Julian, bishop of Eclanum, a small town in Apulia or Campania, was one of nineteen bishops, who, having espoused the cause of Pelagius, and having refused to subscribe a circular letter issued by Zosimus, now adopting the decisions of the African Council (see above note p. 147) were deposed and banished. St. Augustine at his death left a work against Julian unfinished, " Opus imperfectum contra Julianum," in which he had been engaged till the sickness of which he died put an end to his labours.

would keep clear of heresy: first, they should ascertain whether any decision has been given in ancient times as to the matter in question by the whole priesthood of the Catholic Church, with the authority of a General Council: and, secondly, if some new question should arise on which no such decision has been given, they should then have recourse to the opinions of the holy Fathers, of those at least, who, each in his own time and place, remaining in the unity of communion and of the faith, were accepted as approved masters; and whatsoever these may be found to have held, with one mind and with one consent, this ought to be accounted the true and Catholic doctrine of the Church, without any doubt or scruple.

[78.] Which lest we should seem to allege presumptuously on our own warrant rather than on the authority of the Church, we appealed to the example of the holy council which some three years ago was held at Ephesus[1] in Asia, in the consulship of Bassus and Antiochus, where, when question was raised as to the authoritative determining of rules of faith, lest, perchance, any profane novelty should creep in, as did the perversion of the truth at Ariminum,[2] the whole body of priests there assembled, nearly two hundred in number, approved of this as the most Catholic, the most trustworthy, and the best course, viz., to bring forth into the midst the sentiments of the holy Fathers, some of whom it was well known had been martyrs, some Confessors, but all had been, and continued to the end to be, Catholic priests, in order that by their consentient determination the reverence due to ancient truth might be duly and solemnly confirmed, and the blasphemy of profane novelty condemned. Which having been done, that impious Nestorius was lawfully and deservedly adjudged to be opposed to Catholic antiquity, and contrariwise blessed Cyril to be in agreement with it. And that nothing might be wanting to the credibility of the matter, we recorded the names and the number (though we had forgotten the order) of the Fathers, according to whose consentient and unanimous judgment, both the sacred preliminaries of judicial procedure were expounded, and the rule of divine truth established. Whom, that we may strengthen our memory, it will be no superfluous labour to mention again here also.

CHAPTR XXX.

The Council of Ephesus.

[79.] These then are the men whose writings, whether as judges or as witnesses, were recited in the Council: St. Peter, bishop of Alexandria, a most excellent Doctor and most blessed martyr, Saint Athanasius, bishop of the same city, a most faithful Teacher, and most eminent Confessor, Saint Theophilus, also bishop of the same city, a man illustrious for his faith, his life, his knowledge, whose successor, the revered Cyril, now[3] adorns the Alexandrian Church. And lest perchance the doctrine ratified by the Council should be thought peculiar to one city and province, there were added also those lights of Cappadocia, St. Gregory of Nazianzus, bishop and Confessor, St. Basil of Cæsarea in Cappadocia, bishop and Confessor, and the other St. Gregory, St. Gregory of Nyssa, for his faith, his conversation, his integrity, and his wisdom, most worthy to be the brother of Basil. And lest Greece or the East should seem to stand alone, to prove that the Western and Latin world also have always held the same belief, there were read in the Council certain Epistles of St. Felix, martyr, and St. Julius, both bishops of Rome. And that not only the Head, but the other parts, of the world also might bear witness to the judgment of the council, there was added from the South the most blessed Cyprian, bishop of Carthage and martyr, and from the North St. Ambrose, bishop of Milan.

[80.] These all then, to the sacred number of the decalogue,[4] were produced at Eph-

---

[1] The Council of Ephesus, summoned by the Emperor Theodosius to meet at Whitsuntide, 431 (June 7), held its first sitting on June 22, in the Church of St. Mary, where the blessed Virgin was believed to have been buried.
[2] See note above, p. 131, n. 3.

[3] This marks Vincentius's date within very narrow limits, viz. after the Council of Ephesus, and before Cyril's death. Cyril died in 444.
[4] Vincentius's copy of the acts of the Council appears to have contained extracts from no more than ten Fathers. But the Fathers from whose writings extracts were read were twelve in number; the two omitted by Vincentius being Atticus, bishop of Constantinople, and Amphilochius, bishop of Iconium. In Labbe's *Concilia*, where the whole are given, it is remarked that in one manuscript the two last mentioned occupy a different place from the others.

Dean Milman (*Latin Christianity*, vol. 1, p. 164) speaks of the passages read, "as of very doubtful bearing on the question raised by Nestorius." It is true only two, those from Athanasius and Gregory Nazianzen, contain the crucial term "Theotocos" but all express the truth which "Theotocos" symbolizes. That the word was not of recent introduction, Bishop Pearson (*Creed*, Art. 3) shows by quotations from other writers besides those produced at the Council, going back as far as to Origen.

The Fathers cited may certainly be said to fulfil to some extent Vincentius's requirement of universality. They represent the teaching of Alexandria, Rome, Carthage, Milan, Constantinople, and Asia Minor; but his appeal would have been more to his purpose if antiquity had been more expressly represented. With the exception of Cyprian, all the passages cited were from writers of comparatively recent date at the time, though, as Vincentius truly remarks, others might have been produced.

Petavius (*De Incarn.* l. xiv. c. 15), in defending the *cultus* of the blessed Virgin and of the saints generally, lays much stress on this omission of citations from earlier Fathers at the Council, as he does also on similar omissions in the case of the fourth, fifth, and sixth

esus as doctors, councillors, witnesses, judges. And that blessed council holding their doctrine, following their counsel, believing their witness, submitting to their judgment without haste, without foregone conclusion, without partiality, gave their determination concerning the Rules of Faith. A much greater number of the ancients might have been adduced; but it was needless, because neither was it fit that the time should be occupied by a multitude of witnesses, nor does any one suppose that those ten were really of a different mind from the rest of their colleagues.

CHAPTER XXXI.

The Constancy of the Ephesine Fathers in driving away Novelty and maintaining Antiquity.

[81.] AFTER the preceding we added also the sentence of blessed Cyril, which is contained in these same Ecclesiastical Proceedings. For when the Epistle of Capreolus,[1] bishop of Carthage, had been read, wherein he earnestly intreats that novelty may be driven away and antiquity maintained, Cyril made and carried the proposal, which it may not be out of place to insert here: For says he, at the close of the proceedings, " Let the Epistle of Capreolus also, the reverend and very religious bishop of Carthage, which has been read, be inserted in the acts. His mind is obvious, for he intreats that the doctrines of the ancient faith be confirmed, such as are novel, wantonly devised, and impiously promulgated, reprobated and condemned." All the bishops cried out, "These are the words of all; this we all say, this we all desire." What mean "the words of all," what mean "the desires of all," but that what has been handed down from antiquity should be retained, what has been newly devised, rejected with disdain?

[82.] Next we expressed our admiration of the humility and sanctity of that Council,

such that, though the number of priests was so great, almost the more part of them metropolitans, so erudite, so learned, that almost all were capable of taking part in doctrinal discussions, whom the very circumstance of their being assembled for the purpose, might seem to embolden to make some determination on their own authority, yet they innovated nothing, presumed nothing, arrogated to themselves absolutely nothing, but used all possible care to hand down nothing to posterity but what they had themselves received from their Fathers. And not only did they dispose satisfactorily of the matter presently in hand, but they also set an example to those who should come after them, how they also should adhere to the determinations of sacred antiquity, and condemn the devices of profane novelty.

[83.] We inveighed also against the wicked presumption of Nestorius in boasting that he was the first and the only one who understood holy Scripture, and that all those teachers were ignorant, who before him had expounded the sacred oracles, forsooth, the whole body of priests, the whole body of Confessors and martyrs, of whom some had published commentaries upon the Law of God, others had agreed with them in their comments, or had acquiesced in them. In a word, he confidently asserted that the whole Church was even now in error, and always had been in error, in that, as it seemed to him, it had followed, and was following, ignorant and misguided teachers.

CHAPTER XXXII.

The zeal of Celestine and Sixtus, bishops of Rome, in opposing Novelty.

[84.] THE foregoing would be enough and very much more than enough, to crush and annihilate every profane novelty. But yet that nothing might be wanting to such completeness of proof, we added, at the close, the twofold authority of the Apostolic See, first, that of holy Pope Sixtus, the venerable prelate who now adorns the Roman Church; and secondly that of his predecessor, Pope Celestine of blessed memory, which same we think it necessary to insert here also.

Holy Pope Sixtus[2] then says in an Epistle which he wrote on Nestorius's matter to the bishop of Antioch, "Therefore, because, as the Apostle says, the faith is one, — evidently the faith which has obtained hitherto, — let

---

Councils, with what object is sufficiently obvious. Bishop Bull points out Petavius's disposition to disparage or misrepresent the teaching of the earlier Fathers, in another and still more important instance. (*Defens. Fid. Nic.*) *Introd.* § 8.

[1] The letter of Capreolus is given in Labbe's *Concilia*, vol. 3, col. 529 *sqq.* The Emperor Theodosius had written to Augustine, requiring his presence at the Council which he had summoned to meet at Ephesus in the matter of Nestorius. But Augustine having died while the letter was on its way, it was brought to Capreolus, bishop of Carthage and Metropolitan. Capreolus would have summoned a meeting of the African bishops, that they might appoint a delegate to represent them at the Council; but the presence of the hostile Vandals, who were laying waste the country in all directions, made it impossible for the bishops to travel to any place of meeting. Capreolus therefore could do no more than send his deacon Besula to represent him and the African Church, bearing with him the letter referred to in the text. The letter, after having been read before the Council, both in the original Latin and in a Greek translation, was, on the motion of Cyril, inserted in the acts.

[2] Sixtus III. See the Epistle in Labbe's *Concilia*, T. iii. Col. 1262.

us believe the things that are to be said, and say the things that are to be held." What are the things that are to be believed and to be said? He goes on: "Let no license be allowed to novelty, because it is not fit that any addition should be made to antiquity. Let not the clear faith and belief of our fore-fathers be fouled by any muddy admixture." A truly apostolic sentiment! He enhances the belief of the Fathers by the epithet of clearness; profane novelties he calls muddy.

[85.] Holy Pope Celestine also expresses himself in like manner and to the same effect. For in the Epistle which he wrote to the priests of Gaul, charging them with con-nivance with error, in that by their silence they failed in their duty to the ancient faith, and allowed profane novelties to spring up, he says: "We are deservedly to blame if we encourage error by silence. Therefore rebuke these people. Restrain their liberty of preaching." But here some one may doubt who they are whose liberty to preach as they list he forbids, — the preachers of antiquity or the devisers of novelty. Let himself tell us; let himself resolve the reader's doubt. For he goes on: "If the case be so (that is, if the case be so as certain persons complain to me touching your cities and provinces, that by your hurtful dissimulation you cause them to consent to certain novelties), if the case be so, let novelty cease to assail antiquity." This, then, was the sentence of blessed Celestine, not that antiquity should cease to subvert nov-elty, but that novelty should cease to assail antiquity.[2]

CHAPTER XXXIII.

The Children of the Catholic Church ought to adhere to the Faith of their Fathers and die for it.

[86.] WHOEVER then gainsays these Apos-tolic and Catholic determinations, first of all necessarily insults the memory of holy Celes-tine, who decreed that novelty should cease to assail antiquity; and in the next place sets at naught the decision of holy Sixtus, whose sentence was, "Let no license be allowed to novelty, since it is not fit that any addition be made to antiquity;" moreover, he con-temns the determination of blessed Cyril, who extolled with high praise the zeal of

the venerable Capreolus, in that he would fain have the ancient doctrines of the faith con-firmed, and novel inventions condemned; yet more, he tramples upon the Council of Ephesus, that is, on the decisions of the holy bishops of almost the whole East, who de-creed, under divine guidance, that nothing ought to be believed by posterity save what the sacred antiquity of the holy Fathers, consentient in Christ, had held, who with one voice, and with loud acclaim, testified that these were the words of all, this was the wish of all, this was the sentence of all, that as almost all heretics before Nestorius, despising antiquity and upholding novelty, had been condemned, so Nestorius, the author of novelty and the assailant of antiq-uity, should be condemned also. Whose consentient determination, inspired by the gift of sacred and celestial grace, whoever disapproves must needs hold the profaneness of Nestorius to have been condemned un-justly; finally, he despises as vile and worthless the whole Church of Christ, and its doctors, apostles, and prophets, and especially the blessed Apostle Paul: he despises the Church, in that she hath never failed in loyalty to the duty of cherishing and preserv-ing the faith once for all delivered to her; he despises St. Paul, who wrote, "O Timothy, guard the deposit intrusted to thee, shunning profane novelties of words;"[2] and again, "If any man preach unto you other than ye have received, let him be accursed."[3] But if neither apostolical injunctions nor ecclesias-tical decrees may be violated, by which, in accordance with the sacred consent of univer-sality and antiquity, all heretics always, and, last of all, Pelagius, Cœlestius, and Nestorius have been rightly and deservedly condemned, then assuredly it is incumbent on all Catho-lics who are anxious to approve themselves genuine sons of Mother Church, to adhere henceforward to the holy faith of the holy Fathers, to be wedded to it, to die in it; but as to the profane novelties of profane men — to detest them, abhor them, oppose them, give them no quarter.

[87.] These matters, handled more at large in the two preceding Commonitories, I have now put together more briefly by way of recapitulation, in order that my memory, to aid which I composed them, may, on the one hand, be refreshed by frequent reference, and, on the other, may avoid being wearied by prolixity.

---

[1] Celestine's letter will be found in the appendix to Vol. x., Part II., of St. Augustine's Works, col. 2403, Paris, 1838. See the remarks on Vincentius's mode of dealing with Celestine's letter, Appendix III.

[2] Tim. vi. 20.   [3] Gal. i. 9.

APPENDIX I.

THERE is so close an agreement, both in substance and often in the form of expression, between the preceding sections (36–42) and the so-called Athanasian Creed, that it led Antelmi (*Nova de Symb. Athanas. Disquisitio,*) to ascribe that document to Vincentius as its author, and to suppose that in it we have the fulfilment of the promise here referred to. If, however, the Creed was the work of Vincentius, it cannot well be the work promised at the close of § 41, for Vincentius's words point to a fuller and more explicit treatment of the subjects referred to, whereas in the Athanasian Creed, though the subjects are the same, the treatment of them is very much briefer and more concise.

Whoever was the author however, if it was not Vincentius, he must at least, as the subjoined extracts seem to prove, have been familiar with the Commonitory, as also with St. Augustine's writings, of which, as well as of the Commonitory, the Creed bears evident traces.

I subjoin the following instances of agreement between the Commonitory and the Creed: Antelmi gives several others.

COMMONITORY.	ATHANASIAN CREED.
Unum Christum Jesum, non duos, eumdemque Deum pariter atque Hominem confitetur. § 36.	Est ergo Fides recta, ut credamus et confiteamur, quia Dominus noster Jesus Christus, Dei Filius, Deus pariter et Homo est. v. 28.
Alia est Persona Patris, alia Filii, alia Spiritus Sancti. § 37.	Alia est Persona Patris, alia Filii, alia Spiritus Sancti. v. 5.
Unus idemque Christus, Deus et Homo, Idem Patri et æqualis et minor, Idem ex Patre ante sæcula genitus, Idem in sæculo ex Matre generatus, perfectus Deus, perfectus Homo. § 37.	Deus ex substantia Patris, ante sæcula genitus, Homo ex substantia Matris, in sæculo natus; perfectus Deus perfectus Homo. vv. 29, 30.
Unus, non corruptibili nescio qua Divinitatis et Humanitatis confusione, sed integra et singulari quadam unitate Personæ. § 37.	Unus omnino, non conversione substantiæ, sed unitate Personæ. v. 34.
Sicut Verbum in carne caro, ita Homo in Deo Deus est. § 40.	Unus, non conversione Divinitatis in carne, sed Adsumptione Humanitatis in Deo.[1] v. 33.

[1] This is probably the true reading.

APPENDIX II.

NOTE ON SECTION 69, PAGE 149.

That Vincentius had Augustine and his adherents in view in this description will hardly be doubted by any one who will compare it with the following extracts, the first from Prosper's letter to Augustine,[1] giving him an account of the complaints made against his doctrine by the Massilian clergy; the second from St. Augustine's treatise, " De dono Perseveranti "[2] written in consequence of it.

COMMONITORY, § 69.

"Si quis interroget quempiam hæreticorum sibi talia persuadentem, Unde probas, unde doces quod Ecclesiæ Catholicæ universalem et antiquam fidem dimittere debeam? Statim ille, '*Scriptum est enim,*' et continuo *mille testimonia, mille exempla, mille auctoritates parat de Lege, de Psalmis, de Apostolis, de Prophetis,* quibus, novo et malo more interpretatis, ex arce Catholica in hæreseos barathrum infelix anima præcipitetur. Audent enim polliceri et docere, quod in Ecclesia sua, id est, in communionis suæ conventiculo, *magna et specialis ac plane personalis* quædam sit Dei gratia, adeo ut *sine ullo labore, sine ullo studio, sine ulla industria, etiamsi nec petant, nec quærant, nec pulsent,* quicunque illi ad numerum suum pertinent, tamen ita divinitus dispensentur, ut, angelicis evecti manibus, id est, angelica protectione servati, nunquam possint offendere ad lapidem pedem suum, id est, nunquam scandalizari."

PROSPER TO AUGUSTINE.

"The Massilian clergy complain," he says, " *Romoveri omnem industriam,* tollique virtutes, si Dei constitutio humanus præveniat voluntates." § 3.

Then referring to the teaching of the Massilians themselves, Prosper continues,

" Ad conditionem hanc velint uniuscujusque hominis pertinere, ut ad cognitionem Dei et ad obedientiam mandatorum Ejus possit suam dirigere voluntatem, et ad hanc gratiam qua in Christo renascimur pervenire, per naturalem scilicet facultatem, *petendo, quærendo, pulsando.*"

Referring to the line of argument pursued by himself and others of Augustine's friends and the Massilian way of dealing with it, he says, "Et cum contra eos Scripta Beatitudinis tuæ *validissimis et innumeris testimoniis Divinarum Scripturarum instructa* proferimus, . . . *obstinationem suam vetustate defendunt.*" § 3.

St. Augustine replies to Prosper not in an ordinary letter, but in two short Treatises, which must have been written immediately after its receipt, for he died in August 430, the first entitled " De Prædestinatione Sanctorum," the second " De Dono Perseverantiæ."

The following extract is from the latter:

" Attendant ergo quomodo falluntur qui putant *Esse a nobis, non dari nobis, ut petamus, quæramus, pulsemus.* Et hoc esse, dicunt, quod gratia præceditur merito nostro, ut sequatur illa cum *accipimus petentes, et invenimus quærentes, aperiturque pulsantibus.* Nec volunt intelligere etiam hoc divini muneris esse ut oremus, hoc est, *petamus, quæramus, atque pulsamus.*"— *De Dono Persev.* c. 23, § 64.

Vincentius's language is in keeping with that of others of St. Augustine's opponents, as Cassian and Faustus, extracts from whom are given by Noris; only, as he observes, while Vincentius uses the term "heresy" of the doctrine impugned, — they are content to use the milder term "error." — *Histor. Pelag.* p. 246.

---

[1] Inter Epistolas S. August. Ep. 225. Tom. ii. and again Tom. x. col. 1327.   [2] Opera ix. col. 1833.

APPENDIX III.

Note on Section 85, Page 156.

Celestine's letter was addressed to certain Bishops of Southern Gaul, who are particularized by name.

It appears that Prosper and Hilary had made a journey to Rome, where they then were, for the purpose of complaining to Celestine of the connivance of certain bishops of Southern Gaul with the unsound teaching of their clergy. They complained too of the disrespectful manner in which these same clergy treated the memory of Augustine, then recently deceased.

Celestine writes to these bishops: blames their connivance with a fault, which, says he, by their silence they make their own, and then proceeds to charge them, as in the passage quoted in the text, "Rebuke these people: restrain their liberty of preaching. If the case be so, let novelty cease to assail antiquity, let restlessness cease to disturb the Church's peace." Then, after some further exhortation, he adds, "We cannot wonder at their thus assailing the living, when they do not shrink from seeking to asperse the memory of the departed. With Augustine, whom all men everywhere loved and honoured, we ever held communion. Let a stop be put to this spirit of disparagement, which unhappily is on the increase."

The manner in which Vincentius deals with this letter has been very commonly thought, and with reason, to indicate a Semipelagian leaning.[1] His "si ita est," "if the case be so," emphasized by being repeated again and again, quite in an excited manner, as we should say, shows an evident wish to shift the charge of novelty from those against whom it had been brought, and fix it upon the opposite party. "Who are the introducers of novelty? The Massilians, as Prosper represents them, or their calumniators? Not the Massilians: they notoriously appeal to antiquity, — not the Massilians, but Prosper and the rest of Augustine's followers."

The feeling with regard to Augustine, on the part of the Massilian clergy, as indicated in Celestine's letter, is quite in accordance with the animus of § 69 above. See the note on that place, and see Noris's remarks, pp. 246-248.

---

[1] *E. g.* "Hunc locum Vincentius Lirinensis sic a vero sensu contra Prosperum et Hilarium detorquet, ut ipse haud injuria in erroris Semipelagiani suspicionem veniat." The Benedictine editor of St. Augustine's works on Celestine's letter, Tom. x. col. 2403. To the same purpose, among others, Card. Norris, *Histor. Pelag.*, 246. Vossius, *Histor. Pelag.* Tillemont, T. xv. pp. 145, 862. Neander, *Church History*, iv. p. 388.

THE WORKS OF JOHN CASSIAN.

TRANSLATED,

WITH PROLEGOMENA, PREFACES, AND NOTES,

BY

REV. EDGAR C. S. GIBSON, M.A.,

PRINCIPAL OF THE THEOLOGICAL COLLEGE, WELLS, SOMERSET.

CONTENTS.

THE INSTITUTES OF THE CŒNOBIA.

BOOK I.

OF THE DRESS OF THE MONKS.

BOOK II.

OF THE CANONICAL SYSTEM OF THE NOCTURNAL PRAYERS AND PSALMS.

BOOK III.

OF THE CANONICAL SYSTEM OF THE DAILY PRAYERS AND PSALMS.

BOOK IV.

OF THE INSTITUTES OF THE RENUNCIANTS.

BOOK V.

OF THE SPIRIT OF GLUTTONY.

BOOK VI.

ON THE SPIRIT OF FORNICATION.[1]

BOOK VII.

OF THE SPIRIT OF COVETOUSNESS.

[1] Omitted in the translation.

<hr style="width:20%" />

BOOK VIII.

OF THE SPIRIT OF ANGER.

<hr style="width:20%" />

BOOK IX.

OF THE SPIRIT OF DEJECTION.

BOOK X.

OF THE SPIRIT OF ACCIDIE.

BOOK XI.

OF THE SPIRIT OF VAIN-GLORY.

BOOK XII.

OF THE SPIRIT OF PRIDE.

THE FIRST PART OF THE CONFERENCES OF JOHN CASSIAN, CONTAINING CONFERENCES
I-X. PREFACE.

I. — FIRST CONFERENCE OF ABBOT MOSES; ON THE GOAL OR AIM OF THE MONK.

II. — THE SECOND CONFERENCE OF ABBOT MOSES; ON DISCRETION.

III. — CONFERENCE OF ABBOT PAPHNUTIUS; ON THE THREE SORTS OF RENUNCIATIONS.

IV. — Conference of Abbot Daniel; on the Lust of the Flesh and of the Spirit.

V. — Conference of Abbot Serapion; on the Eight Principal Faults.

X. — The Second Conference of Abbot Isaac; on Prayer.

THE SECOND PART OF THE CONFERENCES OF JOHN CASSIAN, CONTAINING XI.–XVII. PREFACE.

XI. — The First Conference of Abbot Chœremon; on Perfection.

XII. — The Second Conference of Abbot Chœremon; on Chastity.[1]

XIII. — The Third Conference of Abbot Chœremon; on the Protection of God.

[1] Omitted in the translation.

XVII. — THE SECOND CONFERENCE OF ABBOT JOSEPH; ON MAKING PROMISES.

THE THIRD PART OF THE CONFERENCES OF JOHN CASSIAN, CONTAINING XVIII.-XXIV.
PREFACE.

XXII. — THE SECOND CONFERENCE OF ABBOT THEONAS; ON NOCTURNAL ILLUSIONS.[1]

XXIII. — THE THIRD CONFERENCE OF ABBOT THEONAS; ON SINLESSNESS.

[1] Omitted in the translation.

THE SEVEN BOOKS OF JOHN CASSIAN ON THE INCARNATION OF THE LORD AGAINST NESTORIUS. PREFACE.

BOOK I.

BOOK II.

BOOK III.

BOOK IV.

BOOK V.

PROLEGOMENA.

CHAPTER I.

The Life of Cassian.

"Cassianus natione Scytha" is the description given by Gennadius[1] of the writer whose works are now for the first time translated into English. In spite, however, of the precision of this statement, considerable doubt hangs over Cassian's nationality, and it is hard to believe that he was in reality a Scythian. Not only is his language and style free from all trace of barbarism, but as a boy he certainly received a liberal education; for in his Conferences he laments that the exertions of his tutor and his own attention to continual study had so weakened him that his mind was so filled with songs of the poets that even at the hour of prayer it was thinking of those trifling fables and stories of battles with which it had from earliest infancy been stored; "and," he adds, "when singing Psalms or asking forgiveness of sins, some wanton recollection of the poems intrudes itself or the image of heroes fighting presents itself before the eyes; and an imagination of such phantoms is always haunting me."[2] Further evidence of the character of his education is also supplied by the fact that in his work on the Incarnation against Nestorius he manifests an acquaintance not only with the works of earlier Christian Fathers, but also with those of such writers as Cicero and Persius.[3]

These considerations are sufficient to make us hesitate before accepting the statement of Gennadius in what would at first sight be its natural meaning; although from the fact of his connection with Marseilles, where so much of Cassian's life was spent, as well as the early date at which he wrote (A.D. 495), it is dangerous to reject his authority altogether. It is, however, possible that the term "Scytha" is not really intended to denote a Scythian, but to refer to the desert of Scete, or Scitis,[4] in Egypt, where Cassian passed many years of his life, and with which his fame was closely associated; and, therefore, without going to the length of rejecting the authority of Gennadius altogether, we are free to look for some other country as the birthplace of our author. But little light is thrown on this subject by the statements of other writers. Photius[5] (A.D. 800) calls him ʽΡωμαῖος, which need mean no more than born within the Roman Empire; while Honorius of Autun (A.D. 1130) speaks of him as Afer. The last-mentioned writer is, however, of too late a date to be of any authority; and it is just possible that the term "Afer," like the "Scytha" of Gennadius, may be owing to his lengthy residence in Egypt. [6] In the writings of Cassian himself there is nothing to enable us to identify the country of his birth with certainty; but, in describing the situation of his ancestral home, he speaks of the delightful pleasantness of the neighbourhood, and the recesses of the woods, which would not only delight the heart of a monk but would also furnish him with a plentiful supply of food;[7] while in a later passage he says that in his own country it was impossible to find any one who had adopted the monastic life.[8] From these notices, compared with a passage in the Preface to the Institutes, where

---

[1] Gennadius Catalogus, c. lxii.
[2] Conference XIV. xii.
[3] On the Incarnation, VI. ix., x.
[4] Σκιαθίς, and Σκιαθική (v. l. Σκιθιακή) χώρα are the forms of the name given by Ptolemy. The Greek Fathers speak of the district as Σκῆτις, while in Latin writers the name appears as Scythia, or Scythis; and, though the printed texts of Cassian give the form as Scitium, heremus Scitii, and heremus Scitiotica, yet we learn from Petschenig that in the MSS. of his works it is not seldom written as Scythium. It should be added that in the text of Gennadius the reading is not absolutely free from doubt, as there is some slight authority for reading "natus Serta."
[5] Bibliotheca, cod. cxcvii.
[6] Dr. Gregory Smith (*Dictionary of Christian Biography*, art. Cassian) thinks that 'Cassianus' possibly points to Casius, a small town in Syria; but, apart from the fact that the name was not uncommon in the West as well as in the East, the description of his home as being in a country where there were no monasteries is quite fatal to this idea.
[7] Conference XXIV. i.
[8] c. xviii.

the diocese of Apta Julia in Gallia Narbonensis is spoken of as still without monasteries, some ground is given for the conjecture that Cassian was really a native of Gaul, whither he returned in mature age after his wanderings were ended, and where most of his friends of whom we have any knowledge were settled. On the whole, then, it appears to the present writer to be the most probable view that Cassian was of Western origin, and, perhaps, a native of Provence, although it must be freely acknowledged that it is impossible to speak with certainty on this subject.[1]

Once more: not only is there this doubt about his nationality, but questions have also been raised concerning his original name. Gennadius and Cassiodorus[2] speak of him simply as Cassianus. In his own writings he represents himself as addressed by the monks in Egypt more than once by the name of John.[3] Prosper of Aquitaine (his contemporary and antagonist) combines both names, and speaks of him as "Joannes cognomento Cassianus."[4] In the titles of the majority of the MSS. of his own writing he is merely "Cassianus," though in one case the work is entitled "Beatissimi Joannis qui et Cassiani."[5] Are we, then, with the writer of the last-mentioned MS., to suppose that the names John and Cassian are alternatives; or, with Prosper, that John was his nomen and Cassianus his cognomen, or, more strictly, agnomen? The former view is, perhaps, the more probable, as he may well have taken the name of John at his baptism or at his admission to the monastic life. The theory which has sometimes been advocated — that he received it at his ordination by S. John Chrysostom — falls to the ground when we notice that he represents himself as called John during his residence in Egypt, several years before his ordination and intercourse with S. Chrysostom.

To pass now from the question of his name and nationality to the narrative of Cassian's life. Various considerations point to the date of his birth as about the year 360. Of his family we know nothing, except that in one passage of his writings he incidentally makes mention of a sister;[6] while the language which he uses of his parents would imply that they were well-to-do and pious.[7] As we have already seen, he received a liberal education as a boy, but while still young forsook the world, and was received, together with his friend Germanus, into a monastery at Bethlehem,[8] where he spent several years and became thoroughly familiar with the customs and traditions of the monasteries of Syria. Eager, however, to make further progress in the perfect life, the two friends finally determined to visit Egypt,[9] where, as it was the country in which the monastic life originated, the most famous monasteries existed, and the most illustrious Anchorites were to be found. Permission to undertake the journey was sought and obtained from their superiors, a pledge being required of a speedy return when the object of their visit was gained.[10] Sailing from some port of Syria, perhaps Joppa, the friends arrived at Thennesus, a town at the mouth of the Tanitic branch of the Nile, near Lake Menzaleh. Here they fell in with a celebrated Anchorite named Archebius, bishop of the neighbouring town of Panephysis, who had come to Thennesus on business connected with the election of a bishop. He, on hearing the object of their visit to Egypt, at once offered them an introduction to some celebrated Anchorites in his own neighbourhood. The offer was gladly accepted, and under his guidance they made their way through a dreary district of salt marshes, many of the villages being in ruins and deserted by their inhabitants owing to the floods which had inundated the country and turned the rising grounds into islands, "and thus afforded the desired solitudes to the holy Anchorites, among whom three old men— Chæremon, Nesteros, and Joseph— were famed as the Anchorites of the longest standing."[11] Archebius brought them first to Chæremon, who had already passed his hundredth year, and was so far bent with age and constant prayer that he could no longer walk upright, but crawled upon his hands and knees. The saint's hesitation at allowing himself to be thus interviewed by strangers was soon overcome, and he finally

---

[1] No difficulty need be felt on the score of his thorough knowledge of Greek, for this could easily be accounted for by his education at Bethlehem, and prolonged residence in the East.

[2] De Div. Lect. Pref., and c. xxix.

[3] Conference XIV. ix.; Institute V. xxxv.

[4] Chronicle.

[5] Parisinus. *Nouv. acquis. Lat.* 260, of the eighth or ninth century.

[6] Institutes XI. xviii.

[7] Conference XXIV. i.

[8] See the Institutes III. iv.; IV. xix.-xxi., xxxi. Conferences I. i.; XI. i. v.; XIX. i.; XX. i. The date is too early for this to have been S. Jerome's famous monastery, as that father only settled at Bethlehem towards the close of 386, by which time Cassian himself must have been already in Egypt; nor does he anywhere in his writings make any allusion to Jerome as his teacher, although he mentions him with great respect in his work on the Incarnation, Book VII. c. xxvi.

[9] Conference XI. i. A good account of Cassian's visits to Egypt is given in Fleury's *Ecclesiastical History*, Book XX., c. iii.-vii.

[10] Conference XVII. ii.

[11] Conference XI. i.-iii., and compare VII. xxvi. for another description of the same district.

gratified their curiosity by delivering three discourses, on the subjects of Perfection, Chastity, and the Protection of God.[1] From the cell of Chæremon Cassian and his companion proceeded to that of Abbot Nesteros, who honoured them with two discourses, on Spiritual Knowledge, and Divine Gifts;[2] and from him they repaired to Joseph, who belonged to a noble family, and before his renunciation of the world had been "primarius" of his native city, Thmuis. He was naturally better educated than the others, and was able to converse with them in Greek instead of being obliged to have recourse to the help of an interpreter, as had been the case with Chæremon and Nesteros.[3] His first question referred to the relationship between Cassian and Germanus: were they brothers? And their reply — that the brotherhood was spiritual and not carnal — furnished the old man with a text for his first discourse, which was on Friendship, and which was followed up on the next day by one on the Obligation of Promises,[4] called forth by the perplexity in which the travellers found themselves owing to their promise to return to Bethlehem, — a promise which they were loth to break, and which yet they could not fulfil without losing a grand opportunity of making progress in the spiritual life. In their difficulty they consulted Joseph; and, fortified by his authority and advice, they determined to break the letter of their promise and make a longer stay in Egypt, where they accordingly remained for seven years in spite of their brethren at Bethlehem, whose displeasure at their conduct, Cassian tells us, was not removed by their frequent letters home.[5]

It was while Cassian and his fellow-traveller were still in the neighbourhood of Panephysis that these energetic precursors of the modern "interviewers" paid a visit to Abbot Pinufius, a priest who presided over a large monastery. This man was an old friend of theirs, whose acquaintance they had previously made at Bethlehem, whither (after an ineffectual attempt to conceal himself in a monastery in the island of Tabenna) he had fled in order to escape the responsibilities of his office. There he had been received as a novice, and had been assigned by the abbot as an inmate of Cassian's cell, until he was recognized by a visitor from Egypt and brought back in triumph to his own monastery.[6] To him, therefore, Cassian and Germanus made their way; and by him they were warmly welcomed; the old man repaying their former hospitality by giving them quarters in his own cell. While staying in this monastery they were so fortunate as to be present at the admission of a novice, and heard the charge which Pinufius made to the new-comer on the occasion;[7] and afterwards the abbot favoured them with a discourse "on the end of penitence and the marks of satisfaction."[8] After this, resisting his pressing invitation to remain with him in the monastery, they proceeded once more on their travels, and, crossing the river, came to Diolcos, a town hard by the Sebennytic mouth of the Nile. Here was a barren tract of land between the river and the sea, rendered unfit for cultivation by the saltness of the soil and the dryness of the sand. It was, therefore, eagerly seized upon by the monks, who congregated here in great numbers in spite of the absence of water; the river from which it had to be fetched being some three miles distant.[9] In this neighbourhood they made the acquaintance of Abbot Piamun, a most celebrated Anchorite, who explained to them with great care the characteristics of the three kinds of monks; viz., the Cœnobites, the Anchorites, and the Sarabaites.[10] This discourse had the effect of exciting their desire more keenly than ever for the Anchorites' life in preference to that of the Cœnobite, — a desire which was afterwards confirmed by what they saw and heard in the desert of Scete. They next visited a large monastery in the same neighbourhood, which was governed by the Abbot Paul, and which ordinarily accommodated two hundred monks, but was at that moment filled with a much larger number, who had come from the surrounding monasteries to celebrate the "depositio" of the late abbot.[11] Here they met a certain Abbot John, whose humility had led him to give up the life of an Anchorite for that of a Cœnobite, in order that he might have the opportunity of practising the virtues of obedience and subjection, which seemed out of the reach of the solitary. He was accordingly well qualified to speak of the subject which he selected for his discourse; viz., the aims of the Anchorite and Cœnobite life.[12] Another well-known abbot, whose acquaintance they now made, was Theonas, who, when quite a young man, had been married by his parents, and later on, on failing to obtain the consent of his wife to a separation, in

---

[1] Conferences XI., XII., XIII.
[2] Conferences XIV., XV.
[3] Conference XVI. i.
[4] Conferences XVI., XVII.
[5] See Conference XVII. i.–v. and xxx.
[6] Conference XX. i., ii. The story is also told in the Institutes, IV. xxx.
[7] Institute V. xxxii.–xlii.
[8] Conference XX.
[9] Institute V. xxxvi.
[10] Conference XVIII. On the Sarabaites, see the note on c. vii.
[11] Conference XIX. i.
[12] Conference XIX. i.

order that they might devote themselves to the monastic life, had deserted her and fled away into a monastery, where after a time he had been promoted to the office of almoner. From him they heard a discourse on the relaxation of the fast during Easter-tide and Pentecost,[1] and, later on, one concerning Nocturnal Illusions,[2] and another on Sinlessness.[3] By these various discourses the two friends were rendered more desirous than ever of adopting the Anchorite life, and less inclined than before to return to the subjection of the monastery at Bethlehem. A far better course seemed to them to return to their own home, probably (as we have seen) in Gaul, where they would be free to practice what austerities they pleased without let or hindrance.[4] In their perplexity they consulted Abbot Abraham, who threw cold water on their plan in a discourse on Mortification,[5] which was entirely successful in persuading them to relinquish their half-formed intention. They, therefore, remained in Egypt for some years longer; and it is to the time of their stay in the neighbourhood of Diolcos that their acquaintance with Abbot Archebius must be assigned. This man, so Cassian tells us,[6] having discovered their desire to make some stay in the place, offered them the use of his cell, pretending that he was about to go off on a journey. They gladly accepted his offer. He went away for a few days, collected materials, and then returned and proceeded to build a new cell for himself. Shortly afterwards some more brethren came. He at once gave up to them his newly built cell, and once more set to work to build another for himself.

It is difficult to determine whether a stay in the desert of Scete was comprised in the seven years which the two friends now spent in Egypt, or whether they visited it for the first time during their second tour, after their return from Bethlehem. On the one hand, the language used in Conference XVIII. cc. i. and xvi. would almost suggest that they made their way into this remote district during their first sojourn in Egypt; and, on the other hand, that employed in Conference I. c. i. might imply a distinct journey to Egypt for the sake of visiting this region: and in XVII. xxx. Cassian distinctly asserts that they *did* visit Scete after their return to Bethlehem in fulfilment of their promise. On the whole, it appears the more natural view to suppose that their first tour was not extended beyond the Delta, more distant expeditions being reserved for a future occasion. Adopting, then, this view, we follow the travellers, after a seven years' absence, back to the monastery at Bethlehem, where they managed to pacify the irate brethren, and, strange to say, obtained leave to return to Egypt a second time.[7] On this occasion they penetrated farther into the country than they had previously done. The region which they now visited was the desert of Scete, or Scitis; that is, the southern part of the famous Nitrian Valley, a name which is well known to all students from the rich treasure of Syrian MSS. brought home from thence by the Hon. Robert Curzon and Archdeacon Tattam now more than forty years ago. The district lies "to the northwest of Cairo, three days' journey in the Libyan desert,"[8] and gains its name of Nitria from the salt lakes which still furnish abundance of nitre, which has been worked for fully two thousand years. The valley has some claims to be considered the original home of monasticism. Some have thought that a colony of Therapeutæ was settled here in the earliest days; and hither S. Frontonius is said to have retired with seventy brethren, to lead the life of ascetics, about the middle of the second century.[9] Less doubtful is the fact that S. Ammon, a contemporary and friend of S. Antony, organized the monastic system here in the fourth century, and "filled the same place in lower Egypt as Antony in the Thebaid."[10] Towards the close of the fourth century the valley was crowded with cells and monasteries. Rufinus, who visited it about 372, mentions fifty monasteries;[11] and the same number is given by Sozomen, who says that "some were inhabited by monks who live together in society, others by monks who have adopted a solitary mode of existence."[12] About twenty years later Palladius passed a considerable time here, and reckons the total number of monks and ascetics at five thousand.[13] They were also visited by S. Jerome about the same time, and various details of the life of the monks are given by him in his Epistles.[14] Some few monks still linger on to the present day to keep up the traditions of nearly eighteen centuries. They were visited (among others) by the Hon. Robert Curzon in 1833; and an interesting account of them is given by him in his volume on "the monasteries of the Levant:"[15] but the latest and best account of them is that given by Mr. A. J. Butler, who

[1] Conference XXI. [2] Conference XXII. [3] Conference XXIII.
[4] Conference XXIV. i. [5] Conference XXIV. [6] Institute V. xxxvi. *sq.*
[7] Conference XVII. xxx. [8] Butler's *Coptic Churches*, Vol. I., p. 287.
[9] Rosweyd, *Vitae Patrum;* and the Bollandist *Acta Sanctorum*, 14 April, Vol. II., 201-3.
[10] *Dictionary of Christian Biography*, art. Ammon; cf. Rufinus, Hist.: Monach, xxx.; and Palladius, Hist.: Lausiaca, viii.
[11] *Hist.*, Monach, c. xxi. [12] Sozomen, H. E. VI. xxxi. [13] *Hist.*, Laus., c. vii.
[14] Epp.: ad Eustochium, ad Rustic. [15] Part I., cc. vii., viii.

succeeded in gaining permission to visit them in 1883, and has described his journey in his excellent work on "the ancient Coptic Churches of Egypt."[1] Four monasteries alone remain,• known as Dair Abu Makâr, Dair Anba Bishôi, Dair es Sûrianî, and Dair al Baramûs; but the ruins of many others may still be traced in the desert tracts on the west side of the Natron lakes, and the valley of the waterless river which at some very remote period is supposed to have formed the bed of one of the branches of the Nile."[2] The monasteries are all built on the same general plan, so that, as Mr. Butler tells us, a description of one will more or less accurately describe the others. Dair Abu Makâr (the monastery of S. Macarius), the first which he visited, which lies strictly within the desert of Scete, is spoken of as "a veritable fortress, standing about one hundred and fifty yards square, with blind, lofty walls rising sheer out of the sand." "Each monastery has also, either detached or not, a large keep, or tower, standing four-square, and approached only by a draw-bridge. The tower contains the library, store-rooms for the vestments and sacred vessels, cellars for oil and corn, and many strange holes and hiding-places of the monks in the last resort, if their citadel should be taken by the enemy. Within the monastery in enclosed one principal and one or two smaller court-yards, around which stand the cells of the monks, domestic buildings, such as the mill-room, the oven, the refectory, and the like, and the churches."[3] The outward aspect can have changed but little since the fourth century. The buildings are perhaps stronger and more adapted to resist hostile attacks, but the general plan is probably identical with that adopted in the earliest monasteries erected in this remote region. Such, then, was the district to which Cassian and Germanus now made their way. Here they first sought and obtained an interview with Abbot Moses, who had formerly dwelt in the Thebaid near S. Antony, and was now living at a spot in the desert of Scete known as Calamus,[4] and was famous not only for practical goodness but also for contemplative excellence. After much persuasion he yielded to their entreaties and discoursed to them "on the goal or aim of a monk,"[5] and, on the following day, on Discretion.[6] They next visited Abbot Paphnutius, or "the Buffalo," as he was named, from his love of solitude. He was an aged priest who had lived for years the life of an Anchorite, only leaving his cell for the purpose of going to the church, which was five miles off, on Saturday and Sunday, and returning with a large bucket of water on his shoulders to last him for the week. From him they heard of the "three kinds of renunciation" necessary for a monk.[7] They also visited his disciple Daniel, who had been ordained priest through the instrumentality of Paphnutius, but was so humble that he would never perform priestly functions in the presence of his master. The subject of his discourse in answer to the inquiry of the two friends was "the lust of the flesh and the spirit."[8] The next ascetic interviewed was Serapion, who spoke of the "eight principal faults" to which a monk was exposed; viz., gluttony, fornication, covetousness, anger, dejection, "accidie," vain glory, and pride.[9] After this they proceeded on a journey of some eighty miles to Cellæ, a place that lay between the desert of Scete (properly so called) and the Nitrian Valley, in order to consult Abbot Theodore on a difficulty which the recent massacre of a number of monks in Palestine by the Saracens had brought forcibly before them; viz., why was it that men of such illustrious merits and so great virtues should be slain by robbers, and why should God permit so great a crime to be committed? The difficulty was solved by Abbot Theodore in a discourse on "the death of the saints;"[10] and thus the journey was not taken in vain. Two other celebrated monks were also visited by the friends, whose discourses are recorded by Cassian: viz., Abbot Serenus, who spoke of "Inconstancy of mind, and Spiritual wickedness,"[11] as well as of the nature of evil spirits, in a Conference on "Principalities;"[12] and Abbot Isaac, who delivered two discourses on the subject of Prayer.[13] A few days after the first of these was delivered there arrived in the desert the "festal letters" of Theophilus, Bishop of Alexandria, in which he denounced the heresy of the Anthropomorphites. This caused a great commotion among the monks of Scete; and Abbot Paphnutius, who presided over the monastery where Cassian was staying, was the only one who would allow the letters to be publicly read in the congregation. Finally, however, owing to the conciliatory firmness of Paphnutius, the great body of the monks was won over to a sounder and less materialistic view of the nature of the Godhead than had hitherto been prevalent among them.[14]

[1] *The Ancient Coptic Churches of Egypt*, by Alfred J. Butler. 2 vols. (Oxford, 1884).
[2] Curzon, p. 79.
[3] Butler, Vol. I., pp. 295, 6, 7.
[4] Conference II. ii.; III. v.
[5] Conference I.
[6] Conference II.
[7] Conference III.
[8] Conference IV.
[9] Conference V.
[10] Conference VI.
[11] Conference VII.
[12] Conference VIII.
[13] Conference IX. x.
[14] See Conference X. cc. i-iii.

These are all the details that can be gathered from Cassian's writings of his stay in Scete, further than which he does not appear to have penetrated, as, when he speaks of the Thebaid and the monasteries there, it is only from hearsay and not from personal knowledge, although his original intention had certainly been to visit this district among others.[1]

In considering the date of Cassian's visit to Egypt there are various indications to guide us. In Conference XVIII. c. xiv., S. Athanasius is spoken of by Abbot Piamun as "of blessed memory;" and the language used of the Emperor Valens in c. vii. is such as to imply that he was already dead. The former died in 373, and the latter in 378. Again, in Conference XXIV. c. xxvi. Abbot Abraham is made to speak of John of Lycopolis as so famous that he was consulted by the very lords of creation, who sought his advice, and entrusted to his prayers and merits the crown of their empire and the fortunes of war. These expressions evidently allude to John's announcement to Theodosius of his victory over Maxentius in 388, and his success against Eugenius in 395.[2] If they stood alone, we could scarcely rely on these indications of date with any great confidence because the Conferences were not written till many years later, and it is impossible to determine with certainty how far they really represent the discourses actually spoken by the Egyptian Fathers, or how far they are the ideal compositions of Cassian himself. But, as we have seen, it is certain that Cassian was actually in Egypt at the time of the Anthropomorphite controversy raised by the letters of Theophilus in 399; and, as the other notices of events previously mentioned coincide very fairly with this, we cannot be far wrong in placing the two visits to Egypt between 380 and 400. About the last-named date Cassian must have finally left the country; and we next hear of him in Constantinople, where he was ordained deacon by S. Chrysostom,[3] and, together with his friend Germanus, put in charge of the treasury, the only part of the Cathedral which escaped the flames in the terrible conflagration of 404. Thus Cassian was, a witness of all the troublous scenes which attended the persecution of S. Chrysostom, whose side he warmly espoused in the controversy which rent the East asunder. And when the Saint was violently deposed and removed from Constantinople, the two friends — Germanus, who was by this time raised to the priesthood, and Cassian, who was still in deacon's orders — were chosen as the bearers of a letter to Pope Innocent I. from the clergy who adhered to Chrysostom, detailing the scandalous scenes that had taken place, and the trials to which they had been exposed.[4] Of the length of Cassian's stay in Rome we have no information, but it is likely that it was of some considerable duration; and it may have been at this time that he was ordained priest by Innocent. Possibly, also, it was now that he made the acquaintance of one who was then quite young, but was destined afterwards to become famous as Pope Leo the Great; for some years afterwards (A.D. 430) it was at the request of Leo, then Archdeacon of Rome, that Cassian wrote his work on the Incarnation against Nestorius. Leaving Rome, Cassian is next found in Gaul,[5] which (if we are right in the supposition that it was his birthplace) he must have quitted when scarcely more than a child. When he left it monasticism was a thing almost if not quite unknown there, but during his absence in the East a few monasteries had been founded in the district of the Loire by S. Martin and S. Hilary of Poictiers. Ligugé was founded shortly after 360, and Marmoutier rather later, after 371; and about the time of his return similar institutions were beginning to spring up in Provence. In 410 S. Honoratus founded the monastery which will ever be associated with his name, in the island of Lérins, and, in the eloquent words of the historian of the monks of the West, "opened the arms of his love to the sons of all countries who desired to love Christ. A multitude of disciples of all nations joined him. The West could no longer envy the East; and shortly that retreat, destined in the intentions of its founder to renew upon the coasts of Provence the austerities of the Thebaid, became a celebrated school of theology and Christian philosophy, a citadel inaccessible to the waves of barbarian invasion, an asylum for literature and science, which had fled from Italy invaded by the Goths; — in short, a nursery of bishops and saints, who were destined to spread over the whole of Gaul the knowledge of the gospel and the glory of Lérins."[6]

It must have been about the same time — a little earlier or a little later — that Cassian settled at Marseilles; and there, "in the midst of those great forests which had supplied the

---

[1] See Conference XI. i.   [2] Compare the Institutes, IV. xxiii.   [3] On the Incarnation, VII. xxxi.
[4] Palladius Dial. iii.; Sozomen, H. E. VIII. xxvi.
[5] It is highly precarious to infer from the language used in the Institutes, III. that Cassian visited Mesopotamia before settling in Gaul. His departure from Rome may perhaps have been occasioned by the Gothic invasion of Italy and Alaric's sieges of Rome, 408–410.
[6] Montalembert's *Monks of the West*, Vol. I. p. 464 (Eng. Translation). The names of Hilary of Arles, Vincent of Lérins, Salvian, Eucherius of Lyons, Lupus of Troyes, and Cæsarius of Arles, are alone sufficient to render the monastery of Lérins illustrious in the annals of the Church of Gaul.

Phœnician navy, which in the time of Cæsar reached as far as the sea-coast, and the mysterious obscurity of which had so terrified the Roman soldiers that the conqueror, to embolden them, had himself taken an axe and struck down an old oak,"[1] two monasteries were now established, — one for men, built it is said over the tomb of S. Victor, a martyr in the persecution of Diocletian,[2] and the other for women. Cassian's long residence in the East and his intimate knowledge of the monastic system in vogue in Egypt made him at once looked up to as an authority, and practically as the head of the movement which was so rapidly taking root in Provence; and, although his fame has been overshadowed by that of the greatest of Western monks, S. Benedict of Nursia, yet his is really the credit of being, not indeed the actual founder, but the first organizer and systematizer, of Western monachism: and it is hoped that the copious illustrations from the Benedictine rule given in the notes to the first four books of the Institutes will serve to show how much the founder of the greatest order in the West was really indebted to his less-known predecessor. " He brought to bear upon the organization of Gallic monasteries lessons learnt in the East. Although S. Martin and others were before him, yet his life must be regarded as a new departure for monasticism in the land. The religious communities of S. Martin and S. Victricius in the centre of France were doubtless rudimentary and half-developed in discipline when compared with that established by Cassian at Marseilles, and with the many others which speedily arose modelled upon his elaborate rules."[3] The high estimation in which his work was held throughout the Middle Ages is shown not only by the immense number of MSS. of the Institutes and Conferences which still remain scattered throughout the libraries of Europe, but also by the recommendation of them by Cassiodorus, and by S. Benedict himself, who enjoins that the Conferences should be read daily by the monks of his order.

At Marseilles, then, Cassian settled; and here it was that he wrote his three great works, — the Institutes, the Conferences, and On the Incarnation against Nestorius; the two former being written for the express purpose of encouraging and developing the monastic life. Of these the Institutes was the earliest, being composed in "twelve books on the institutes of the monasteries and the remedies for the eight principal faults,"[4] at the request of Castor, Bishop of Apta Julia, some forty miles due north of Marseilles, who was desirous of introducing the monastic life into his diocese, where it was still a thing unknown.[5] As Castor died in 426,[6] and the work is dedicated to him, it must have been written some time between the years 419 and 426. When it was first undertaken Cassian's design already was to follow it up by a second treatise containing the Conferences of the Fathers, to which he several times alludes in the Institutes as a forthcoming work,[7] and which, like the companion volume, was undertaken at Castor's instigation. But, before even the first part of it was ready for publication, the Bishop of Apta was dead; and thus, to Cassian's sorrow, he was unable to dedicate it to him, as he had hoped to do. He therefore dedicated Conferences I.–X. (the first portion of the work) to Leontius, Bishop (probably) of Fréjus, and Helladius, who is termed "frater" in the Preface to this work, though, as we see from the Preface to Conference XVIII., he was afterwards raised to the episcopate.[8]

This portion of Cassian's work must have been completed shortly after the death of Castor in 426. It was speedily followed by Part II., containing Conferences XI. to XVII. This is dedicated to Honoratus and Eucherius, who are styled "fratres." Eucherius did not become Bishop of Lyons till 434; but, as Honoratus was raised to the see of Arles in 426, the volume must have been published not later than that year, or he would have been termed "Episcopus," as he is in the Preface to Conference XVIII., instead of "frater."

The third and last part of the work, containing Conferences XVIII. to XXIV., is dedicated to Jovinian, Minervius, Leontius, and Theodore, who are collectively styled "fratres." Leontius must, therefore, be a different person from the bishop to whom Conferences I.–X. were dedicated; and nothing further is known of him, or of Minervius and Jovinian. Theodore was afterwards raised to the Episcopate, and succeeded Leontius in the see of Fréjus in 432. This third part of Cassian's work was ready before the death of Honoratus, Bishop of

---

[1] Montalembert, l. c.
[2] The Acts of S. Victor's martyrdom given by Ruinart, *Acta Sincera*, p. 225, have been attributed by Tillemont and others to Cassian, but without sufficient reason.
[3] *The Church in Roman Gaul*, by R. Travers Smith, p. 245.
[4] This is the title which Cassian himself gives to the work in his Preface to the Conferences.
[5] Institutes, Preface.
[6] Castor is commemorated on the twenty-first of September. See the Bollandist *Acta Sanctorum*, Sept. VI. 249.
[7] See the Institutes II. i., ix., xviii.; V. iv.
[8] With *Papa Leonti et Sancte frater Helladi*, in the Preface to Conference I., compare *beatissimis Episcopis Helladio ac Leontio*, in the Preface to Conference XVIII.

Arles, who is spoken of in the Preface as if still living; and, therefore, its publication cannot be later than 428, as Honoratus died in January, 429.

Thus the whole work was completed between the years 426 and 428; and now Cassian, who was growing old, was desirous of rest, feeling as if his life's work was nearly over.[1] But the repose which he sought was not to be granted to him, for the remaining years of his life were troubled by two controversies, — the Nestorian, and the Pelagian, — or, rather, its offshoot, the Semi-Pelagian. Into the history of the former of these there is no need to enter here in detail. It broke out at Constantinople, where Nestorius had become bishop in succession to Sisinnius, in 428. The immediate occasion which gave rise to the controversy was a sermon by Anastasius, the Bishop's chaplain, in which he inveighed against the title Theotocos, as given to the Blessed Virgin Mary. This at once created a great sensation, as Nestorius warmly supported his chaplain, and proceeded to develop the heresy connected with his name, in a course of sermons. News of the controversy was brought to Egypt, and Cyril of Alexandria at once entered into the fray. After some correspondence between the two bishops, both parties endeavoured to gain the adherence of the Church of Rome early in the year 430; and now it was that Cassian became mixed up with the dispute. Greek learning was evidently at a low ebb in the Roman Church at this time;[2] and it was, perhaps, partly owing to Cassian's familiar acquaintance with this language, as well as owing to his connexion with Constantinople, where the trouble had now arisen, that Celestine's Archdeacon Leo turned to him at this crisis for help. Anyhow, whatever was the reason, an earnest appeal from Rome reached him, begging him to write a refutation of the new heresy. After some hesitation he consented, and the result of his labours is seen in the seven books on the Incarnation against Nestorius. The work was evidently done in haste, and published in 430, before the Council of Ephesus (for Cassian speaks of Nestorius throughout as still Bishop of Constantinople), and, judging from the way in which Augustine is spoken of in VII. xxvii., before the death of that Father, which took place in August, 430. A great part of the work is occupied with Scripture proof of our Lord's Divinity and unity of Person; but, taken as a whole, the treatise is distinctly of less value than Cassian's earlier writings, and betrays the haste in which it was composed by the occasional use of inaccurate language on the subject of the Incarnation, and of terms and phrases which the mature judgment of the Church has rejected. But the writer's keen penetration is seen by the quickness with which he connects the new heresy with the teaching of Pelagius, the connecting link between the two being found in the errors of Leporius of Trêves, who, in propagating Pelagian views of man's sufficiency and strength, had applied them to the case of our Lord, not shrinking from the conclusion that He was a mere man who had used his free will so well as to have lived without sin, and had only been made Christ in virtue of His baptism, whereby the Divine and human were associated in such manner that virtually there were *two* Christs.[3] The connexion between Nestorianism and Pelagianism has often been noticed by later writers, but to Cassian belongs the credit of having been the first to point it out. Of the impression produced by his book we have no record. He appears to have taken no further part in the controversy, which, indeed, must have been to him an episode, coming in the midst of that other controversy with which his name is inseparably associated; viz., that on Semi-Pelagianism, on which something must now be said.

The controversy arose in the following way. During the struggle with Pelagianism between the years 410 and 420, Augustine's views on the absolute need of grace were gradually hardening into a theory that grace was irresistible and therefore indefectible. "Intent above all things on magnifying the Divine Sovereignty, he practically forgot the complexity of the problem in hand and failed to do justice to the human element in the mysterious process of man's salvation."[4] The view of an absolute predestination irrespective of foreseen character, and of the irresistible and indefectible character of grace, was put forward by him, in a letter to a Roman priest, Sixtus, in the year 418.[5] Some years afterwards this letter fell into the hands of the monks of Adrumetum, some of whom were puzzled by its teaching; and, in order to allay the disputes among them, the matter was referred to Augustine himself. Thinking that the monks had misunderstood his teaching, he not only explained the letter but also wrote a fresh treatise, — "De Gratia et Libero Arbitrio" (426); and, when that failed

---

[1] See the Preface to the work *On the Incarnation against Nestorius.*
[2] See the Epistle of Celestine to Nestorius in Mansi IV. 1026, in which he apologizes for delay by saying that the letter and other documents sent by Nestorius had had to be translated into Latin.
[3] See *On the Incarnation*, Book I. c. ii. *sq.*
[4] *The Anti-Pelagian Treatises of S. Augustine;* with an Introduction by William Bright, D.D. (Oxford), 1889, p. 1.
[5] Epistle xciv.

to satisfy the malcontents, he followed it up with his work "De Correptione et Gratia" (426), which, so far as the monks of Adrumetum were concerned, seems to have ended the controversy. Elsewhere, however, hesitation was felt in going the full length of Augustine's teaching; and, in the South of Gaul especially, many were seriously disturbed at the turn which the controversy had lately taken, and were prepared to reject Augustine's teaching, as not merely novel, but also practically dangerous. "They said, in effect," to quote Canon Bright's lucid summary of their position, "to treat predestination as irrespective of foreseen conduct, and to limit the Divine good-will to a fixed number of persons thus selected, who, as such, are assured of perseverance, is not only to depart from the older theology, and from the earlier teaching of the Bishop of Hippo himself, but to cut at the root of religious effort, and to encourage either negligence or despair. They insisted that whatever theories might be devised concerning this mystery, which was not a fit subject for popular discussion, the door of salvation should be regarded as open to all, because the Saviour ' died for all.' To explain away the Scriptural assurance was, they maintained, to falsify the Divine promise and to nullify human responsibility. They believed in the doctrine of the Fall; they acknowledged the necessity of real grace in order to man's restoration; they even admitted that this grace must be 'prevenient' to such acts of will as resulted in Christian good works: but some of them thought — and herein consisted the error called Semi-Pelagian — that nature, unaided, could take the first step towards its recovery, by desiring to be healed through faith in Christ. If it could not, — if the very beginning of all good were strictly a Divine act, — exhortations seemed to them to be idle, and censure unjust, in regard to those on whom no such act had been wrought, and who, therefore, until it should be wrought, were helpless, and so far guiltless, in the matter." [1] Of the party which took up this position Cassian was the recognized head. True, he did not directly enter into the controversy himself, nor is he the author of any polemical works upon the subject; but it is impossible to doubt that the thirteenth Conference, containing the teaching of Abbot Chæremon on the Protection of God, was intended to meet what he evidently regarded as a serious error; viz., the implicit denial by the Augustinians of the need of *effort* on man's part.

Augustine was informed of the teaching of the School of Marseilles, as it was called, by one Hilary (a layman, not to be confounded with his namesake, the Bishop of Arles), who wrote to him two letters, of which the former is lost. The latter is still existing, and contains a careful account of what was maintained at Marseilles. Towards the close of it Hilary says that, as he was pressed for time, he had prevailed upon a friend to write as well, and would attach his letter to his own. This friend was Prosper of Aquitaine, also a layman and an ardent Augustinian, whose epistle has been preserved as well as Hilary's. [2] From these letters, and from the works which Augustine wrote in reply, we learn that the "Massilians" had been first disturbed by some of Augustine's earlier writings, as the Epistle to Paulinus; and that their distrust of his teaching on the subjects of Grace, Predestination, and Freewill had been increased by the receipt of his work "De Correptione et Gratia," although in other matters they agreed with him entirely, and were great admirers of his. [3] Personally, they are spoken of with great respect as men of no common virtue, and of wide influence; and, though Cassian's name is never mentioned in the correspondence, yet it is easy to read between the lines and see that he is referred to. [4]

Augustine replied to his correspondents by writing what proved to be almost his latest works, — the treatises "De Prædestinatione Sanctorum" and "De dono Perseverantiæ." In these volumes Augustine, while freely acknowledging the great difference between his opponents and the Pelagians, yet maintained as strongly as ever his own position, and "did not abate an iota of the contention that election and rejection were arbitrary, and that salvation was not really within the reach of all Christians." [5] Thus the books naturally failed to satisfy the recalcitrant party, or to convince those who thought that the denial of the freedom of the will tended to destroy man's responsibility. Prosper, however, was delighted with the treatises, and proceeded to follow them up with a work of his own, a poem of a thousand lines,

[1] *Anti-Pelagian Treatises*, p. liv., lv.
[2] Epp. ccxxv., ccxxvi., in the correspondence of S. Augustine. *Works*, Vol. II. 820, in the Benedictine Edition.
[3] Cassian himself quotes Augustine as an authority for the Catholic doctrine of the Incarnation in his work against Nestorius, VII. xxvii. But it is remarkable that, whereas on all the other authorities quoted (Hilary, Ambrose, Jerome, Rufinus, Gregory, Nazianzen, Athanasius, and Chrysostom) a high encomium is passed, Augustine alone is alluded to with no words of praise, being simply spoken of as priest (sacerdos) of Hippo Regius. There is no authority for the reading " magnus sacerdos," found in the editions of Cuyck and Gazet, which misled Neander. Ch. *Hist*. Vol. IV. p. 376, E. T.
[4] The only person referred to by name is Hilary, who had just succeeded Honoratus as Bishop of Arles. This fixes the date of the correspondence as 429.
[5] Bright's *Anti-Pelagian Treatises*, l. c.

"De Ingratis," by which he designates the Pelagians and Semi-Pelagians, whose opinions he speaks of as spreading with alarming rapidity. The date of this publication was probably the early part of 430. It was certainly written before the death of Augustine, which took place on August 28 of the same year. The removal from this life of the great champion of Grace did not bring to an end the controversy to which his writings had given birth. The school of Marseilles continued to propagate its views with unabated vigour, in spite of the protests of Prosper and Hilary, who finally took the important step of appealing to Pope Celestine, from whom they succeeded in obtaining a letter addressed to the Gallican Bishops, Venerius of Marseilles, Leontius of Fréjus, Marinus, Auxonius, Arcadius, Filtanius, and the rest.[1] Celestine speaks strongly of their negligence in not having suppressed what he regarded as a public scandal, and says that "priests ought not to teach so as to invade the episcopal prerogative," an expression in which we may well see an allusion to Cassian, the leading presbyter, of the diocese of Marseilles, whose Bishop is named first in the opening salutation; and the letter concludes with some words of eulogium on Augustine "of holy memory." Never, perhaps, was Gallican independence shown in a more striking manner than in the sturdy way in which the Massilians clung to their views in spite of the authority of the Pope now brought to bear upon them. Prosper and Hilary on their return found the obnoxious teaching daily spreading, so that the former of them finally determined to put down, if possible, the upholders of the objectionable tenets by a direct criticism of Cassian's Conferences. This was the origin of Prosper's work "Contra Collatorem," against the author of the Conferences, a treatise of considerable power and force, although not scrupulously fair.[2] The respect in which Cassian was held is strikingly shown by the fact that his antagonist never once names him directly, but merely speaks of him as a man of priestly rank who surpassed all his companions in power of arguing. The work consists of an examination of the thirteenth Conference, that of Abbot Chæremon, on the Protection of God, from which Prosper extracts twelve propositions, the first of which he says is orthodox while all the others are erroneous[3]. He concludes

---

[1] The letter is given in full in Gazet's edition of Cassian, with certain doctrinal articles appended, which really belong to a later date. See Dr. Newman's note to the English translation of Fleury, Book XXVI. c. xi.

[2] The treatise is given in Gazet's edition of Cassian.

[3] The propositions extracted by Prosper are the following : —

(1) That the initiative not only of our actions but also of our good thoughts comes from God, who inspires us with a good will to begin with, and supplies us with the opportunity of carrying out what we rightly desire; for "every good gift and every perfect gift cometh down from above, from the Father of light," who both begins what is good, and continues it and completes it in us. c. iii. This proposition Prosper allows to be catholic and orthodox.

(2) The Divine protection is inseparably present with us, and so great is the kindness of the Creator towards His creatures that His Providence not only accompanies it, but even constantly precedes it, as the prophet experienced and plainly confessed, saying, "My God will prevent me with His mercy." And when He sees in us some beginnings of a good will, He at once enlightens and strengthens it, and urges it on towards salvation, increasing that which He Himself implanted, or which He sees to have arisen from our own efforts. c. viii.

(3) Only in all these there is a declaration of the grace of God *and* the freedom of the will, because even of his own motion a man can be led to the quest of virtue, but always stands in need of the help of the Lord. For neither does any one enjoy good health whenever he likes, nor is he of his own will and pleasure set free from disease and sickness. c. ix.

(4) That it may be still clearer that, through the excellence of nature, which is granted by the goodness of the Creator, sometimes the first beginnings of a good will arise, which, however, cannot attain to the complete performance of what is good unless they are guided by the Lord, the apostle bears witness, and says, "For to will is present with me, but to perform what is good I find not." *Ib.*

(5) And so these are somehow mixed up and indiscriminately confused, so that, among many persons, the question which depends upon the other is involved in great difficulty; i.e., does God have compassion upon us because we have shown the beginning of a good will, or does the beginning of a good will follow because God has had compassion upon us? For many, believing each of these alternatives, and asserting them more broadly than is right, are entangled in all kinds of opposite errors. For if we say that the beginning of free will is in our own power, what about Paul the persecutor, what about Matthew the publican, of whom the one was drawn to salvation while eager for bloodshed and the punishment of the innocent, the other while eager for violence and rapine? But, if we say that the beginning of our free will is always due to the inspiration of the grace of God, what about the faith of Zacchæus, or what are we to say of the goodness of the thief on the cross, who by their own desires brought violence to bear on the kingdom of heaven, and prevented the special leadings of their vocation? c. xi.

(6) These two, then, viz., the grace of God and Free-will, seem opposed to each other, but really are in harmony; and we gather from natural piety that we ought to have both alike, lest if we withdraw one of them from men we should seem to have broken the rule of the Church's faith. *Ib.*

(7) Adam, therefore, after the fall, conceived a knowledge of evil which he had not previously, but did not lose the knowledge of good which he already possessed. c. xii.

(8) Wherefore we must take care not to refer all the merits of the saints to the Lord in such a way as to ascribe nothing but what is evil and perverse to human nature. *Ib.*

(9) It cannot be doubted that there are by nature some seeds of goodness implanted by the kindness of the Creator, but unless they are quickened by the assistance of God they cannot attain an increase of perfection. *Ib.*

(10) And for this, too, we read that in the case of Job, his well-tried athlete, when the Devil had challenged him to single combat, the Divine righteousness had made provision. For, if he had advanced against his foe not with his own strength, but solely with the protection of God's grace, and, supported only by Divine aid, without any virtue of patience on his own part, had borne that manifold weight of temptations and losses, contrived with all the cruelty of his foe might not the Devil have repeated with some justice that slanderous speech which he had previously uttered, "Doth Job serve God for nought? Hast Thou not hedged him in, and all his substance round about? But take away thine hand," ie., allow him to fight with me in his own strength, "and he will curse Thee to Thy face." But, as after the struggle the slanderous foe dared not give vent to any such murmur as this, he admitted that he was vanquished by his (i.e., Job's) strength, and not by that of God: although, too, we must not hold that the grace of God was altogether wanting to him, which gave to the tempter a power of tempting in proportion to that which he had of resisting. c. xiv.

(11) The Lord marvelled at him (viz., the centurion), and praised him, and put him before all those of the people of Israel who had believed, saying, "Verily, I say unto you, I have not found so great faith in Israel." For there would have been no ground for praise or merit if Christ had only preferred in him what He Himself had given. *Ib.*

(12) Hence it comes that in our prayers we proclaim God as not only our protector and Saviour, but actually as our helper and sponsor. For whereas He first calls us to Him, and while we are still ignorant and unwilling draws us towards salvation, He is our protector and

by warning his antagonist of the danger of Pelagianism, and expresses a hope that his doctrine may be condemned by Pope Sixtus as it had been by Celestine and his predecessors. The last statement fixes the date of the book as not earlier than 432; for Celestine only died in April in that year.

Cassian was evidently still living when this attack upon him was made; but, so far as we know, he made no reply to it. Its publication is the last event in his life of which we have any knowledge. He probably died shortly afterwards, as the expression used by Gennadius in speaking of his work against Nestorius would seem to imply that it preceded his death by no long interval; for he says that with this he brought to a close his literary labours and his life in the reign of Theodosius and Valentinian.[1]

The controversy on Grace and Freewill lingered on for nearly a century longer, and was only finally disposed of by the wise moderation shown by Cæsarius of Arles and those who acted with him at the Council of Orange (Arausio), in the year 529.[2]

While it cannot be denied that the teaching of Cassian and his school in denying the *necessity* of initial and prevenient grace is erroneous and opens a door at which Pelagianism may easily creep in, yet it was an honest attempt to vindicate human responsibility; and it must be frankly admitted that the teaching of Augustine was one-sided and required to be balanced: nor would the question have ever been brought into prominence had it not been for the hard and rigorous way in which the doctrine of Predestination was taught, and the denial that the possibility of salvation lay within the reach of all men. While, then, it is granted that a verdict of guilty must be returned on the charge of Semi-Pelagianism in Cassian's case, we are surely justified in claiming that a recommendation to mercy be attached to it on the plea of extenuating circumstances. Since his death Cassian has ever occupied a somewhat ambiguous position in the mind of the Church. Never formally canonized, his name is not found in the Calendars of the West; nor is he honoured with the title of "Saint." He is, however, generally spoken of as "the blessed Cassian," holding in this respect the same position as Theodoret, of whom Dr. Newman says that, though he "has the responsibility of acts which have forfeited to him that œcumenical dignity," yet he is "not without honorary title in the Church's hagiology; for he has ever been known as the ' blessed Theodoret.' "[3] In the East Cassian's position is somewhat better. He is there regarded as a saint, and may possibly be intended by the Cassian who is commemorated on February 29.[4] It is only natural that this difference should be made, for the Eastern Church has always held a milder view of the effect of the Fall than that which has been current in the West since the days of Augustine; and, indeed, Cassian, in making his protest againt the rising tide of Augustinianism, was in the main only handing on the teaching which he had received from his Eastern instructors.

CHAPTER II.

THE HISTORY OF CASSIAN'S WRITINGS, MSS., AND EDITIONS.

THE literary history of Cassian's works is not without an interest of its own. We have already seen the estimation in which they were held in spite of their Semi-Pelagian doctrines. These were naturally accounted a blemish, and it is not surprising that those who most admired their excellences were anxious to avoid propagating their errors. Hence they were often "expurgated," and in many MSS. the text has suffered considerably from the changes made by copyists in the interests of orthodoxy. As early as the fifth century we find two revised versions of portions of his works existing. His friend Eucherius, Bishop of Lyons,

---

Saviour; but whereas, when we are already striving, He is wont to bring us help, and to receive and defend those who fly to Him for refuge, He is deemed our sponsor and refuge. c. xvii.

This last extract is in itself perfectly orthodox, and might be thought merely to express the distinction between " preventing " and " co-operating " grace; but the context makes it clear that Cassian means that in some cases grace " prevents," while in others the initial movement towards salvation comes from man, and grace is only needed to " co-operate."

[1] Gennadius, in *Catal.*, c. lxii. Ad extremum rogatus a Leone Archidiacono, postea urbis Romæ Episcopo, scripsit adversus Nestorium " De Incarnatione Domini " libros septem, et in his scribendi apud Massiliam et vivendi finem fecit Theodosio et Valentiniano regnantibus. The local commemoration of Cassian is on July 23.

[2] On the history of Semi-Pelagianism see Bright's *Anti-Pelagian Treatises of S. Augustine*, Introd., pp. xlix.–lxviii., and the *Christian Remembrancer*, Vol. XXXI. pp. 155–162.

[3] *Historical Sketches*, Vol. III., p. 307.

[4] The identification is anything but certain, for though there is no difficulty in the term 'Ρωμαῖος, as that is also applied to our author by Photius, yet the additional statement made in the Horologion, that he was originally στρατιωτικὸς τὴν τάξιν, suggests that a different person is alluded to, possibly the same as the Cassian commemorated in the Roman martyrology on August 13.

A list of some twenty-five churches where Cassian is honoured as a saint is given in Guesnay's *Cassianus Illustratus*.

was the author of an epitome of the Institutes, which still exists;[1] and although this was compiled for convenience' sake because of the length of the original work, rather than from any suspicion of his teaching, the case is different with a recension made for use in Africa by Victor, Bishop of Martyrites. This is no longer extant, but Cassiodorus distinctly tells us that it was made in the interests of orthodoxy by means of expurgation as well as addition of what was wanting.[2] Yet another epitome of three of the Conferences (I., II., VII.) was made at some time before the tenth century. It was translated into Greek, and known to Photius, who speaks[3] of three works of Cassian as translated into Greek: viz., (1) an Epitome of the Institutes, Books I.–IV.; (2) Epitome of the Institutes, Books V.–XII.; and (3) one of the Conferences I., II., VII.

Thus in very early days the fashion was set of expurgating and emending the writings of Cassian; and Leuwis de Ryckel, better known as Dionysius Carthusianus, might have quoted several precedents for his method of dealing with the text. This famous divine, — the *doctor exstaticus* of the fifteenth century, — shocked as others had been before him at the Semi-Pelagianism of the Conferences, and yet sensible of their real value in spite of sundry blemishes, took in hand to correct them, and gave to the world a free paraphrase both of the Institutes and of the Conferences, in a somewhat simple style and one more easy to be understood than the original. The greatest alterations, as might be expected, are visible in the thirteenth Conference; as Dionysius, in his endeavour to make Cassian orthodox, omits all that savours of Semi-Pelagianism; and from c. viii. onward there are large omissions and various suggestive alterations in the text.[4]

Incidental mention has been already made of the esteem in which the Institutes and Conferences were held by S. Benedict and Cassiodorus. In the Rule of the former (c. xlii.) it is ordered that after supper the brethren should assemble together, and one of them should read the Conferences, or Lives of the Fathers, or any other book calculated to edify. And again, in the closing chapter of the same rule, the study of them is recommended to those who are desirous of perfection; for "what are the Conferences of the Fathers, the Institutes, and the lives of them; what, too, the Rule of our holy father, S. Basil, but examples of virtuous and obedient monks, and helps to the attainment of virtue?" Equally strong is the recommendation of Cassiodorus: "Sedulo legite, frequenter audite;" but at the same time he reminds his readers that Cassian was very properly censured by Prosper for his teaching on Freewill, and that, therefore, he is to be read with caution whenever he touches on this subject. With testimonies such as these to their value it is no wonder that copies were rapidly multiplied, so that scarcely a monastery was without a copy of some part of them; and existing MSS. of the Institutes and Conferences are very numerous. But none of the oldest MSS. contain the complete work. The Institutes were often regarded as made up of two separate treatises, — (1) the Institutes of the Cœnobia, containing Books I.–IV., and (2) On the Eight Principal Faults, comprising Books V.–XII. So, too, with the Conferences, and their three divisions: they are often found separately in different MSS.

The MSS. being so numerous, it was found impossible to collate them all for the latest edition of Cassian's works; viz., that edited by Petschenig for the Vienna Corpus Scriptorum Ecclesiasticorum Latinorum. The Editor therefore confined his attention to a limited number, of which the following is the list.

I. THE INSTITUTES.

1. Codex Casinensis Rescriptus, 295. A Palimpsest with the Epistles of S. Jerome written over Cassian's work. The date of this MS. is the seventh or eighth century, and it contains portions only of the Institutes, nothing remaining of Books I.–IV., or of VIII. and IX.
2. Codex Majoris Seminarii Œduensis (Autun), 24. Seventh century, containing portions of Books V.–XII.
3. Caroliruhensis, 87. Eighth century, containing all twelve books.
4. Sangallensis, 183. Ninth century.
5. Parisinus, 12292. Tenth century.
6. Laudunensis (Laon), 328 bis. Ninth century.
7. Caroliruhensis, 164. Ninth century.

---

[1] Gennadius, *Catal.* lxiv. In the *Dictionary of Christian Antiquities*, art. Eucherius, this is said to be lost. But see Migne, Vol. L. p. 867 *sq*; and cf. Petschenig's *Introduction to Cassian*, p. xcvi.
[2] *Div. Lect.* c. xxix. Cujus (Cassiani) dicta Victor Mattaritanus Episcopus Afer ita Domino juvante purgavit et quæ minus erant addidit ut ei rerum istarum palma merito conferatur: quem inter alios de Africa partibus cito nobis credimus esse dirigendum.
[3] Biblioth, Cod. 197.
[4] The "Doctrina Catholica Beati Dionysii Richelii Carthusiani precedenti Collationi ab ipso substituta," given in Gazet's edition, and hence in Migne's, as c. xix., is only the *latter* part of the paraphrase of this Conference, beginning in c. viii., with the words, "Adest igitur inseparabiliter nobis," etc.
The paraphrase may be found in Vol. III. of the edition of the works of Dionysius, published at Cologne in 1540. Of this there is a copy in the British Museum which was formerly in the possession of Archbishop Cranmer, and which still contains his autograph.

II. CONFERENCES I.–X.

 1. Vaticanus, 5766. Eighth century.
 2. Parisinus, Bibl. Nat., 13384. Ninth century.
 3. Vercellensis (Chapter Library), 187, 44. Cent. 8–10.
 4. Parisinus. Bibl. Nat. nouv. fonds, 2170. Ninth century. This (with a few lacunæ) contains *all* the Conferences, being the only one of Petschenig's MSS. of which this can be said.
 5. Vaticanus, Bibl. Palat., 560. Tenth century.
 6. Sangallensis, 574. Cent. 9–10.
Of these MSS. the last two contain many errors and interpolations, some of which are followed in the editions of Cassian published at Basle, 1485–1495.

III. CONFERENCES XI.–XVII.

 1. Sessorianus (Rome), 55. Cent. 7–8.
 2. Petropolitanus, Bibl. Imp. O. 1, 4. Seventh or eighth century.
 3. Sangallensis, 576. Ninth century.
 4. Parisinus, Bibl. Nat. nouv. fonds., 2170 (as above).
 5. Vindobonensis, 397. Tenth century. This Vienna MS. contains Prosper's work *Contra Collatorem*, the passages of Cassian being written in the margin.

IV. CONFERENCES XVIII.–XXIV.

 1. Monacensis, 4549. Cent. 8–9.
 2. Monacensis, 6343. Ninth century.
 3. Parisinus, Bibl. Nat. nouv. fonds., 2170 (as above).
 4. Vaticanus, Bibl. Reginæ Sueciæ, 140. Cent. 9–10.
 5. Caroliruhensis, 92. Ninth century.
 6. Sangallensis, 575. Ninth century.

Passing now from the Institutes and Conferences to the work "On the Incarnation against Nestorius," we are no longer encumbered by the number of MSS. There was not the same reason for the multiplication of copies of it as there was in the case of those writings which bore on the monastic life. It appears never to have obtained any special popularity, and, so far as is known, only seven MSS. of it are still in existence. The following are those of which Petschenig made use for his edition : —

 1. Codex Bibl. Armentarii Parisiensis (Bibl. de l'Arsenal), 483. Cent. 10–11.
 2. British Museum addl., 16414. Cent. 11–12.
 3. Parisinus, Bibl. Nat., 14860. Thirteenth cen tury.
 4. Bibl. Coloniensium Augustinianorum. This MS. is now lost, but was used by Cuyck for his **edition** of Cassian, and from this Petschenig is able to give selected readings.

The remaining MSS. known to exist, but not used by Petschenig, are these : —

Matritensis, Bibl. Nat., Q. 106. Twelfth century.
Laurentianus (Laurentian Library at Florence), XXVI., 13. Fifteenth century.
Bibl. Leop. Medici Fœsulanæ (also at Florence), 48. Fifteenth century.
Parisinus, 2143. Fourteenth century.[1]

It only remains to give some account of the various editions of the printed text.

It has generally been stated that the earliest edition of the Institutes was that printed at Venice in 1481, of which only a single copy is known to exist, viz., in the Laurentian Library at Florence; and that the first edition which included the Conferences was that published by Amerbach at Basle in 1485. This statement, however, appears to be erroneous, as there still exists in the British Museum a single copy of a very early black-letter edition of the Conferences. The title-page is gone, and there is no colophon; and, therefore, the date cannot be given with certainty, but the work is assigned by the authorities of the Museum to the year 1476, and is thought to have proceeded from the press of the Brothers of the Common life at Brussels. The first page of the work begins as follows: "Ut Valeas cōr in opere isto citius invenire qd requiris hæc tibi concapitulatio breviter demōstrabit quis unde in singulis collationibus disputaverit." Then follows a list of the twenty-four Conferences with their authors, and the page ends with these words: "Prologus cassiani sup. collationes patrū ad leontiū et elladiū epos. In nomine Domini īhu cristi dei nostri feliciter."

This, then, in all probability was the first edition of the Latin text of the Conferences. But it is a curious fact that at a still earlier date a free German translation or paraphrase of them had already been published. This, like the work just mentioned, has been overlooked by all the editors of Cassian, but two copies of it still remain in the British Museum, beginning as follow: "Hic liber a quodam egregio sacrarum literarum professore magistro Johañe Nide ordīs p̄dicatorum fratre de latino in vulgarem Nuremberge translatus est." The colophon

---

[1] On all these MSS. see Petschenig's introduction, *Cassian*, Vol. I. pp. xiv.-lxxviii.

in one copy gives the date as 1472, and the place at which it was printed as Augsberg. The other copy has no date but is assigned by the authorities of the Museum to a still earlier year; viz., 1470.

The Basle edition of 1485 was reprinted at the press of Amerbach in 1497; and at Venice there was issued a second edition of the Institutes, to which the Conferences were added, in 1491.[1] Subsequent early editions are those of Lyons, in 1516 and 1525, and Bologna 1521. But not till 1534 were the seven books on the Incarnation against Nestorius published. They appear for the first time in the edition which was issued in this year from the press of Cratander at Basle.

Far superior to all these early editions, which were very faulty, was that published by Christopher Plantin at Antwerp in 1578, edited by H. Cuyck, Professor at Louvain and afterward Bishop of Ruremonde. It was undertaken at the suggestion of Cardinal Carafa, and its full title is the following: "D. Ioannis Cassiani Eremitæ Monasticarum Institutionum libri IIII. De Capitalibus vitiis libri VIII. Collationes SS. Patrum XXIIII. De Verbi Incarnatione libri VII. Nunc demum post varias editiones ad complurium MS. fidem a non pancis mendarum milibus incredibili labore expurgati: id quod ex subiectis ad calcem castigationibus facile cognosci poterit: additis etiam ad quædam loca censoriis notationibus, et obscurarum vocum ac sententiarun elucidatione, un a cum duobus Indicibus locupletissimis. Accesserunt quoque Regulæ SS. Patrum ex antiquissimo Affliginiensis monasterii MS. codice desumptæ. Opera et studio Henrici Cuyckii Sacræ Theologiæ Licentiati."

Cuyck's work was supplemented, also at Carafa's desire, by Petrus Ciacconius, a priest of Toledo, who died in 1581, before it was ready for the press. A new edition was, however, published at Rome in 1588 "ex Edibus Dominicæ Basæ," in which the notes and emendations of Ciacconius were embodied. Unfortunately this edition does not contain the books on the Incarnation. Its full title is as follows: "Ioannis Cassiani Eremitæ de institutis renuntiantium Libri XII. Collationes Sanctorum Patrum XXIIII. Adiectæ sunt quarundam obscurarum dictionum interpretationes ordine alphabeti dispositæ: et observationes in loca ambigua et minus tuta. Præterea Indices duo testimoniorum sacræ Scripturæ, quæ a Cassiano vel explicantur, vel aliter quam vulgata editio habet, citantur: ac postremo verum memorabilium Index copiosissimus. Accedit Regula S. Pachomii, quæ a S. Hieronymo in Latinum sermonem conversa est: Omnia multo quam antehac, auxilio vetustissimorum codicum, emendatiora, et ad suam integritatem restituta." This edition, as well as the previous one, contained a dissertation on a number of passages (some thirty in all) of doubtful orthodoxy, in order to put the reader on his guard against following Cassian in his errors.

In 1616 there was published at Douay in two volumes what has remained until the present day the standard edition of Cassian's works, prepared with loving care by a Benedictine monk of the Abbey of St. Vaast at Arras, named Gazet. This edition is enriched throughout with copious annotations, containing an immense amount of illustrative matter; and besides the text of Cassian's works it contains several other documents of importance for a right understanding of them. The full title is this: "Ioannis Cassiani presbyteri, quem alii eremitam, alii abbatem nuncupant, opera omnia. Novissime recognita, repurgata et notis amplissimis illustrata. Quibus accessere alia ejusdem argumenti opuscula, quorum elenchum sequens pagina exhibebit. Studio et opera D. Alardi Gazæi cœnobitæ Vedastini ord. Benedicti."

Besides the Institutes, Conferences, and the work on the Incarnation against Nestorius, these volumes contained the following among other material: —

The Rule of St. Pachomius.

The Catholic doctrine substituted for the latter part of Conference XIII. by Dionysius Carthusianus.

Prosper "Contra Collatorem."

This edition has been frequently reprinted,[2] some of the later reprints containing still more illustrative material. It still remains indispensable to the student of Cassian's works by reason of the valuable commentary with which it is throughout enriched. But for the mere *text* it is now altogether superseded by the fine edition prepared by Petschenig for the Vienna Corpus Scriptorum Ecclesiasticorum Latinorum, in two volumes.

Vol. I. — Ioannis Cassiani De Institutis Cœnobiorum et de octo Principalium Vitiorum Remediis Libri XII. De Incarnatione Domini Contra Nestorium Libri VII. recensuit et commentario critico instruxit Michael Petschenig. Accedunt Prolegomena et Indices (Vindobonæ, 1888).

---

[1] Of this edition there is a copy in the British Museum which formerly belonged to the Convent of S. Mark at Florence, and is enriched with marginal notes in the handwriting of Girolamo Savonarola.

[2] Gazet himself prepared a revised edition, which was brought out after his death, at Arras, in 1628.

Vol. II. — Ioannis Cassiani Conlationes XXIIII. (Vindobonæ, 1886). Petschenig's work is admirably done, and the text of this edition is vastly superior to that of all its predecessors. In the present translation it has been used throughout the Conferences. The volume containing the Institutes and the work on the Incarnation unfortunately appeared too late for the translation to be made from it. It has, however, been carefully compared with the text of Ciacconius, which Gazet merely repeats,[1] and attention is called to the chief variations in the notes.

Mention has already been made of the early German paraphrase or translation, dating from 1470 or 1472; and the popularity of the Cassian's works is evinced by the number of other early translations made into the various languages of Europe. Of these next in order of time is one in Flemish. In the copy of this in the British Museum the title is wanting, the book beginning as follows: "Hier beghint der ouder vader collacie. Hi hyetede Ioannes Cassianus die dese vierētwintich navolgende vad, collacien ghemaect hevet." The colophon is this: "Hier eyndet een seer goede eñ profitelike leeringhe. Eñ is ghenoemt der ouder vaders collacien. Michiel hiller van Hoochstraten. Tantwerpen 1506. fol."

Very little later is the first of several French translations, with the following curious title: "Les Collacions des sains Peres anciens translateez de Grec en latin. Par Cassiodorus tres sainct docteur en theologie et translateez de latin en francoys par maistre iehā gosein aussy docteur en theologie de l'ordre des freres de la Montaigne du carme et imprimees nouvellement a paris." No date is given, but the work is assigned by the Museum authorities to the year 1510.

Later French translations are the following: —

Paris. Chez Charles Savreux. 8° les Conférences de Cassien traduites en françois par De Saligny. 1663. (This edition altogether omits the thirteenth Conference.)

Paris Chez Charles Savreux. 8° les Institutions de Cassien traduites en françois par De Saligny. 1667.

Institutions de Cassien traduites par E. Cartier. Paris, Tours, 1872.

There are also two Italian translations, one as early as 1563 (Opera. Tradotta per B. Buffi. Venetia. 1563. 4°), and one of the present century, — Volgarizzamento delle collazioni dei SS. Padri del venerabile G. C. [By Bartolommeo da San Concordio?] Testo di lingua in edito [edited by T. Bini]. Lucca. 1854. 8°.

It is remarkable that England has till now stood almost alone in possessing no translation, Cassian's works having never yet appeared in an English press. It is hoped that the version now offered to the reader may do something to make the works of this interesting and most instructive writer more widely known than they appear to be at present.

---

[1] The edition used is that published at Leipsic in 1733. It cannot, however, be recommended, as it is full of misprints.

PREFACE.

THE history of the Old Testament tells us that the most wise Solomon received from heaven "wisdom and understanding exceeding much, and largeness of heart even as the sand that is on the seashore that cannot be counted;"[1] so that by the Lord's testimony we may say that no one either has arisen in time past equal to him or will arise after him: and afterward, when wishing to raise that magnificent temple to the Lord, we are told that he asked the help of a foreigner, the king of Tyre. And when there was sent to him one Hiram, the son of a widow woman,[2] it was by his means and ministration that he executed all the glorious things which he devised by the suggestion of the Divine wisdom either for the temple of the Lord or for the sacred vessels. If, then, that power that was higher than all the kingdoms of the earth, and that noble and illustrious scion of the race of Israel, and that divinely inspired wisdom which excelled the training and customs of all the Easterns and Egyptians, by no means disdained the advice of a poor man and a foreigner, rightly also do you, most blessed Pope[3] Castor, taught by these examples, deign to call in me, a worthless creature though I am, and in every respect as poor as possible, to a share in so great a work. When you are planning to build a true and reasonable temple for God, not with inanimate stones but with a congregation of saints, and no temporal or corruptible building, but one that is eternal and cannot be shaken; and desiring also to consecrate to the Lord most precious vessels not forged of dumb[4] metal, of gold or silver, which a Babylonish monarch may afterwards take and devote to the pleasures of his concubines and princes,[5] but fashioned of holy souls which shine with the uprightness of innocence, righteousness, and purity, and bear about Christ abiding in themselves as King;—since, then, you are anxious that the institutions of the East and especially of Egypt should be established in your province, which is at present without monasteries,[6] although you are yourself perfect in all virtues and knowledge and so filled with all spiritual riches that not only your talk but even your life alone is amply sufficient for an example to those who are seeking perfection, — yet you ask me, not knowing what to say, and feeble in speech and knowledge, to contribute something from the scanty supply of my thoughts toward the satisfaction of your desire; and you charge me to declare, although with inexpert pen, the customs of the monasteries which we have seen observed throughout Egypt and Palestine, as they were there delivered to us by the Fathers; not looking for graceful speech, in which you yourself are especially skilled, but wanting the simple life of holy men to be told in simple language to the brethren in your new monastery. But in proportion as a dutiful desire of granting your request urges me to obey, so do manifold difficulties and embarrassments deter me when wishing to comply. First, because my merits are not so proportioned to my age as for me to trust that I can worthily comprehend with my mind and heart matters so difficult, so obscure, and so sacred. Secondly, because that which we either tried to do or learnt or saw when from our earliest youth we lived among them and were urged on by their daily exhortations and examples, — this we can scarcely retain in its entirety when we have been for so many years withdrawn from intercourse with them and from following their mode of life; especially as the method of these things cannot possibly be taught or understood or kept in the memory by idle meditation and verbal teaching, for it depends entirely upon experience and practice. And, as these things cannot be taught save by one

---

[1] Kings iv. 29. [2] *Ib.* vii. 13.
[3] *Papa.* The title was at an early period confined to bishops in the West, but was not limited to the Bishop of Rome till a later date.
[4] Petschenig's text reads *muto.* Another reading is *multo.*
[5] Cf. Dan. v. 2.
[6] Castor, at whose request this work was written, was Bishop of Apta Julia in Gallia Narbonensis.

who has had experience of them, so they cannot even be learnt or understood except by one who has tried with equal care and pains to grasp them; while, unless they are often discussed and well worn in frequent conferences with spiritual men, they quickly fade away through carelessness of mind. Thirdly, because a discourse that is lacking in skill cannot properly expound those things which we can recall to mind, not as the things themselves deserve, but as our condition allows us. To this it must be added that on this very subject men who were noble in life and eminent for speech and knowledge have already put forth several little books, I mean Basil and Jerome, and some others, the former of whom, when the brethren asked about various rules and questions, replied in language that was not only eloquent but rich in testimonies from Holy Scripture; while the latter not only published works that were the offspring of his own genius, but also translated into Latin works that had been written in Greek.[1] And, after such abundant streams of eloquence, I might not unfairly be accused of presumption for trying to produce this feeble rill, were it not that the confidence of your holiness encouraged me, and the assurance that these trifles would be acceptable to you, whatever they were like, and that you would send them to the congregation of the brethren dwelling in your newly founded monastery. And if by chance I have said anything without sufficient care, may they kindly overlook it and endure it with a somewhat indulgent pardon, asking rather for trustworthiness of speech than for grace of style on my part. Wherefore, most blessed Pope, remarkable example of religion and humility, encouraged by your prayers, I will to the best of my ability approach the work which you enjoin; and those matters which were altogether left untouched by those who preceded us, since they endeavoured to describe what they had heard rather than what they had experienced, these things I will tell as to an inexperienced monastery, and to men who are indeed[2] athirst. Nor certainly shall I try to weave a tale of God's miracles and signs, although we have not only heard of many such among our elders, and those past belief, but have also seen them fulfilled under our very eyes; yet, leaving out all these things which minister to the reader nothing but astonishment and no instruction in the perfect life, I shall try, so far as I can, with the help of God, faithfully to explain only their institutions and the rules of their monasteries, and especially the origin and causes of the principal faults, of which they reckon eight, and the remedies for them according to their traditions, — since my purpose is to say a few words not about God's miracles, but about the way to improve our character, and the attainment of the perfect life, in accordance with that which we received from our elders. In this, too, I will try to satisfy your directions, so that, if I happen to find that anything has been either withdrawn or added in those countries not in accordance with the example of the elders established by ancient custom, but according to the fancy of any one who has founded a monastery, I will faithfully add it or omit it, in accordance with the rule which I have seen followed in the monasteries anciently founded throughout Egypt and Palestine, as I do not believe that a new establishment in the West, in the parts of Gaul could find anything more reasonable or more perfect than are those customs, in the observance of which the monasteries that have been founded by holy and spiritually minded fathers since the rise of apostolic preaching endure even to our own times. I shall, however, venture to exercise this discretion in my work, — that where I find anything in the rule of the Egyptians which, either because of the severity of the climate, or owing to some difficulty or diversity of habits, is impossible in these countries, or hard and difficult, I shall to some extent balance it by the customs of the monasteries which are found throughout Pontus and Mesopotamia; because, if due regard be paid to what things are possible, there is the same perfection in the observance although the power may be unequal.

---

[1] The reference is to Basil's ὅροι κατὰ πλάτος (the greater monastic rules), and ὅροι κατὰ ἐπιτομήν (the lesser rules), written in the form of answers to questions of the monks. Jerome translated the rule of Pachomius, besides writing the lives of the hermits Paul, Malchus, and Hilarion.

[2] *in veritate.* Another reading is *veritatem.*

THE TWELVE BOOKS OF JOHN CASSIAN

ON THE

INSTITUTES OF THE CŒNOBIA,

AND THE

REMEDIES FOR THE EIGHT PRINCIPAL FAULTS.

BOOK I.

OF THE DRESS OF THE MONKS.

CHAPTER I.

Of the Monk's Girdle.

As we are going to speak of the customs and rules of the monasteries, how by God's grace can we better begin than with the actual dress of the monks, for we shall then be able to expound in due course their interior life when we have set their outward man before your eyes. A monk, then, as a soldier of Christ ever ready for battle, ought always to walk with his loins girded. For in this fashion, too, the authority of Holy Scripture shows that they walked who in the Old Testament started the original of this life, — I mean Elijah and Elisha; and, moreover, we know that the leaders and authors of the New Testament, viz., John, Peter, and Paul, and the others of the same rank, walked in the same manner. And of these the first-mentioned, who even in the Old Testament displayed the flowers of a virgin life and an example of chastity and continence, when he had been sent by the Lord to rebuke the messengers of Ahaziah, the wicked king of Israel, because when confined by sickness he had intended to consult Beelzebub, the god of Ekron, on the state of his health, and thereupon the said prophet had met them and said that he should not come down from the bed on which he lay, — this man was made known to the bed-ridden king by the description of the character of his clothing. For when the messengers returned to him and brought back the prophet's message, he asked what the man who had met them and spoken such words was like and how he was dressed. "An hairy man," they said, "and girt with a girdle of leather about his loins;" and by this dress the king at once saw that it was the man of God, and said: "It is Elijah the Tishbite:"[1] i.e., by the evidence of the girdle and the look of the hairy and unkempt body he recognized without the slightest doubt the man of God, because this was always attached to him as he dwelt among so many thousands of Israelites, as if it were impressed as some special sign of his own particular style. Of John also, who came as a sort of sacred boundary between the Old and New Testament, being both a beginning and an ending, we know by the testimony of the Evangelist that "the same John had his raiment of camel's hair and a girdle of skin about his loins."[2] When Peter also had been put in prison by Herod and was to be brought forth to be slain on the next day, when the angel stood by him he was charged: "Gird thyself and put on thy shoes."[3] And the angel of the Lord would certainly not have charged him to do this had he not seen that for the sake of his night's rest he had for a while freed his wearied limbs from the girdle usually tied round them. Paul also, going up to Jerusalem and soon to be put in chains by the Jews, was met at Cæsarea by the prophet Agabus, who took his girdle and bound his hands and feet

---

[1] Cf. Basil's Greater Monastic Rules, Q. xxii., from which a considerable portion of this chapter is taken.

[1] 2 Kings i. 1.–8. [2] S. Matt. iii. 4. [3] Acts xii. 8.

to show by his bodily actions the injuries which he was to suffer, and said: "So shall the Jews in Jerusalem bind the man whose girdle this is, and deliver him into the hands of the Gentiles." [1] And surely the prophet would never have brought this forward, or have said "the man whose girdle this is," unless Paul had always been accustomed to fasten it round his loins.

CHAPTER II.

Of the Monk's Robe.

LET the robe also of the monk be such as may merely cover the body and prevent the disgrace of nudity, and keep off harm from cold, not such as may foster the seeds of vanity and pride; for the same apostle tells us: "Having food and covering, with these let us be content." [2] "Covering," he says, not "raiment," as is wrongly found in some Latin copies: that is, what may merely cover the body, not what may please the fancy by the splendour of the attire; commonplace, so that it may not be thought remarkable for novelty of colour or fashion among other men of the same profession; and quite free from anxious carefulness, yet not discoloured by stains acquired through neglect. Lastly, let them be so far removed from this world's fashions as to remain altogether common property for the use of the servants of God. For whatever is claimed by one or a few among the servants of God and is not the common property of the whole body of the brethren alike is either superfluous or vain, and for that reason to be considered harmful, and affording an appearance of vanity rather than virtue. And, therefore, whatever models we see were not taught either by the saints of old who laid the foundations of the monastic life, or by the fathers of our own time who in their turn keep up at the present day their customs, these we also should reject as superfluous and useless: wherefore they utterly disapproved of a robe of sackcloth as being visible to all and conspicuous, and what from this very fact will not only confer no benefit on the soul but rather minister to vanity and pride, and as being inconvenient and unsuitable for the performance of necessary work for which a monk ought always to go ready and unimpeded. But even if we hear of some respectable persons who have been dressed in this garb, a rule for the monasteries is not, therefore, to be passed by us, nor should the ancient decrees of the holy fathers be upset because we do not think that a few men, presuming on the possession of other virtues, are to be blamed even in regard of those things which they have practised not in accordance with the Catholic rule. For the opinion of a few ought not to be preferred to or to interfere with the general rule for all. For we ought to give unhesitating allegiance and unquestioning obedience, not to those customs and rules which the will of a few have introduced, but to those which a long standing antiquity and numbers of the holy fathers have passed on by an unanimous decision to those that come after. Nor, indeed, ought this to influence us as a precedent for our daily life, that Joram, the wicked king of Israel, when surrounded by bands of his foes, rent his clothes, and is said to have had sackcloth inside them; [3] or that the Ninevites, in order to mitigate the sentence of God, which had been pronounced against them by the prophet, were clothed in rough sackcloth. [4] The former is shown to have been clothed with it secretly underneath, so that unless the upper garment had been rent it could not possibly have been known by any one, and the latter tolerated a covering of sackcloth at a time when, since all were mourning over the approaching destruction of the city and were clothed with the same garments, none could be accused of ostentation. For where there is no special difference and all are alike no harm is done. [5]

CHAPTER III.

Of the Hoods of the Egyptians.

THERE are some things besides in the dress of the Egyptians which concern not the care of the body so much as the regulation of the character, that the observance of simplicity and innocence may be preserved by the very character of the clothing. For they constantly use both by day and by night very small hoods coming down to the end of the neck and shoulders, which only cover the head, in order that they may constantly be moved to preserve the simplicity and innocence of little children by imitating their actual dress. [6] And

---

[1] Acts xxi. 11.
[2] 1 Tim. vi. 8. The Greek is σκεπάσματα, for which Jerome's version has "quibus tegamur." Sabbatier gives "victum et vestitum" as the rendering of the old Latin, but it is often quoted as "victus et tegumentum" by Augustine. "Alimenta et operimenta" must be Cassian's own rendering from the Greek. "Vestimenta," which he speaks of as being found in some Latin copies, is not given by Sabbatier at all, though Jerome quotes the text with "vestimentum" in Ep. ad Titum, III.

[3] 2 Kings vi. 30.   [4] Jonah iii. 8.
[5] Quia nisi insolens sit diversitas, non offendit æqualitas (Petschenig). The text of Gazæus has inæqualitas.
[6] The hood, or cowl (cuculla), was anciently worn by children and peasants, and thus was said to symbolize humility. Compare the account of the Egyptian monks given by Sozomen, Hist. III. xiv.: "They wore a covering on their heads called a cowl, to show that they ought to live with the same innocence and purity as infants who are nourished with milk and wear a covering of the same form."

these men have returned to childhood in Christ and sing at all hours with heart and soul: "Lord, my heart is not exalted nor are mine eyes lofty. Neither have I walked in great matters nor in wonderful things above me. If I was not humbly minded, but exalted my soul: as a child that is weaned is towards his mother."[1]

CHAPTER IV.

Of the Tunics of the Egyptians.

THEY wear also linen tunics[2] which scarcely reach to the elbows, and for the rest leave their hands bare, that the cutting off of the sleeves may suggest that they have cut off all the deeds and works of this world, and the garment of linen teach that they are dead to all earthly conversation, and that hereby they may hear the Apostle saying day by day to them: "Mortify your members which are upon the earth;" their very dress also declaring this: "For ye are dead, and your life is hid with Christ in God;" and again: "And I live, yet now not I but Christ liveth in me. To me indeed the world is crucified, and I to the world."[3]

CHAPTER V.

Of their Cords.[4]

THEY also wear double scarves[5] woven of woollen yarn which the Greeks call ἀνάλαβοι, but which we should name girdles[6] or strings,[7] or more properly cords.[8] These falling down over the top of the neck and divided on either side of the throat go round the folds (of the robe) at the armpits and gather them up on either side, so that they can draw up and tuck in close to the body the wide folds of the dress, and so with their arms girt they are made active and ready for all kinds of work, endeavouring with all their might to fulfil the Apostle's charge: "For these hands have ministered not only to me but to those also who are with me," "Neither have we eaten any man's bread for

nought, but with labour and toil working night and day that we should not be burdensome to any of you." And: "If any will not work neither let him eat."[9]

CHAPTER VI.

Of their Capes.[10]

NEXT they cover their necks and shoulders with a narrow cape, aiming at modesty of dress as well as cheapness and economy; and this is called in our language as well as theirs *mafors*; and so they avoid both the expense and the display of cloaks and great coats.

CHAPTER VII.

Of the Sheepskin and the Goatskin.[11]

THE last article of their dress is the goatskin, which is called *melotes*, or *pera*,[12] and a staff, which they carry in imitation of those who foreshadowed the lines of the monastic life in the Old Testament, of whom the Apostle says: "They wandered about in sheepskins and goatskins, being in want, distressed, afflicted; of whom the world was not worthy; wandering in deserts, and in mountains, and in dens, and in caves of the earth."[13] And this garment of goatskin signifies that having destroyed all wantonness of carnal passions they ought to continue in the utmost sobriety of virtue, and that nothing of the wantonness or heat of youth, or of their old lightmindedness, should remain in their bodies.

CHAPTER VIII.

Of the Staff of the Egyptians.

FOR Elisha, himself one of them, teaches that the same men used to carry a staff; as he says to Gehazi, his servant, when sending him to raise the woman's son to life: "Take my staff and run and go and place it on the lad's face that he may live."[14] And the prophet

---

[1] Ps. cxxx. (cxxxi.) 1, 2.
[2] Colobium (κολόβιον), a tunic with very short sleeves. Cf. Dorotheus (Migne, Patrol. Græca lxxxviii. 1631). Τὸ σχῆμα ὁ φοροῦμεν κολόβιόν ἐστι, μὴ ἔχον χειρίδια, καὶ ζώνη δερματίνη καὶ ἀνάλαβος καὶ κουκούλιον.
[3] Col. iii. 5, 3. Gal. ii. 20; vi. 14. Cf. Sozomen l. c.: "They wore their tunics without sleeves in order to teach that the hands ought not to be ready to do evil."
[4] Rebracchiatoria. The whole passage is somewhat obscure, and the various synonyms do not help us much in the elucidation of it. Ἀνάλαβοι is given in Petschenig's text, but ἀναβολάι has some MS. authority. Ἀναβολεύς is the word used by Sozomen, who also mentions this cord. "Their girdle also and cord, the former girding the loins, the latter going round the shoulders and arms, admonish them that they ought always to be ready for the service of God and their work."
[5] Resticulæ.
[6] Succinctoria.
[7] Redimicula.
[8] Rebracchiatoria.

[9] Acts xx. 34; 2 Thess. iii. 8, 10.
[10] The mafors (μαφώριον or μαφόριον) is the monkish scapular, or working-dress. Cf. the Rule of S. Benedict, c. 55: "Scapulare propter opera." In form it was a large, coarse cape, or hood.
[11] The melotes (μηλωτής), a sheepskin garment hanging down on one side, was the usual dress of monks. S. Anthony bequeathed his, at his death, to S. Athanasius. Ath. Vita Anton, 91.
[12] Pera can hardly be used here in its ordinary sense of scrip or wallet πήρα. Gazæus suggests that it may be a transcriber's error for pœnula, while Ducange would read, "quæ melotes appellatur, vel pera, et baculus." Mr. Sinker, in the *Dictionary of Christian Antiquities* (Vol. II. p. 1619), suggests that possibly the word may be Egyptian.
[13] Heb. xi. 37, 38.
[14] 2 Kings iv. 29.

would certainly not have given it to him to take unless he had been in the habit of constantly carrying it about in his hand. And the carrying of the staff spiritually teaches that they ought never to walk unarmed among so many barking dogs of faults and invisible beasts of spiritual wickedness (from which the blessed David, in his longing to be free, says: "Deliver not, O Lord, to the beasts the soul that trusteth in Thee "),[1] but when they attack them they ought to beat them off with the sign of the cross and drive them far away; and when they rage furiously against them they should annihilate them by the constant recollection of the Lord's passion and by following the example of His mortified life.

CHAPTER IX.

Of their Shoes.

But refusing shoes, as forbidden by the command of the gospel, if bodily weakness or the morning cold in winter or the scorching heat of midday compels them, they merely protect their feet with sandals, explaining that by the use of them and the Lord's permission it is implied that if, while we are still in this world we cannot be completely set free from care and anxiety about the flesh, nor can we be altogether released from it, we should at least provide for the wants of the body with as little fuss and as slight an entanglement as possible: and as for the feet of our soul which ought to be ready for our spiritual race and always prepared for preaching the peace of the gospel (with which feet we run after the odour of the ointments of Christ, and of which David says: "I ran in thirst," and Jeremiah: "But I am not troubled, following Thee "),[2] we ought not to suffer them to be entangled in the deadly cares of this world, filling our thoughts with those things which concern not the supply of the wants of nature, but unnecessary and harmful pleasures. And this we shall thus fulfil if, as the Apostle advises, we "make not provision for the flesh with its lusts."[3] But though lawfully enough they make use of these sandals, as permitted by the Lord's command, yet they never suffer them to remain on their feet when they approach to celebrate or to receive the holy mysteries, as they think that they ought to observe in the letter that which was said to Moses and to Joshua, the son of Nun: "Loose the latchet of thy shoe: for the place whereon thou standest is holy ground."[4]

CHAPTER X.

Of the modification in the observances which may be permitted in accordance with the character of the climate or the custom of the district.

So much may be said, that we may not appear to have left out any article of the dress of the Egyptians. But we need only keep to those which the situation of the place and the customs of the district permit. For the severity of the winter does not allow us to be satisfied with slippers [6] or tunics or a single frock; and the covering of tiny hoods or the wearing of a sheepskin would afford a subject for derision instead of edifying the spectators. Wherefore we hold that we ought to introduce only those things which we have described above, and which are adapted to the humble character of our profession and the nature of the climate, that the chief thing about our dress may be not the novelty of the garb, which might give some offence to men of the world, but its honourable simplicity.

CHAPTER XI.

Of the Spiritual Girdle and its Mystical Meaning.[7]

Clad, therefore, in these vestments, the soldier of Christ should know first of all that he is protected by the girdle tied round him, not only that he may be ready in mind for all the work and business of the monastery, but also that he may always go without being hindered by his dress. For he will be proved to be the more ardent in purity of heart for spiritual progress and the knowledge of Divine things in proportion as he is the more earnest in his zeal for obedience and work. Secondly, he should realize that in the actual wearing of the girdle there is no small mystery declaring what is demanded of him. For the girding of the loins and binding them round with a dead skin signifies that he bears about the mortification of those members in which are contained the seeds of lust and lasciviousness, always knowing that the command of the gospel, which says, "Let your loins be girt about,"[8] is applied to him by the Apostle's interpretation; to wit, "Mortify your members which are upon the earth; fornication, uncleanness, lust, evil concupiscence."[9] And so we find in Holy Scripture that only those were girt with the girdle in whom the seeds of carnal lust are found to

---

[1] Ps. lxxiii. (lxxiv.) 19.
[2] Ps. lxi. (lxii.) 5; Jer. xvii. 16 (lxx.).
[3] Rom. xiii. 14.
[4] Exod. iii. 5; Josh. v. 16.

[5] This and the following chapter are altogether omitted in the edition of Gazæus.
[6] Gallica.
[7] Sacramentum.
[8] S. Luke xii. 35.
[9] Col. iii. 5.

be destroyed, and who sing with might and main this utterance of the blessed David: "For I am become like a bottle in the frost,"[1] because when the sinful flesh is destroyed in the inmost parts they can distend by the power of the spirit the dead skin of the outward man. And therefore he significantly adds "in the frost," because they are never satisfied merely with the mortification of the heart, but also have the motions of the outward man and the incentives of nature itself frozen by the ap-

proach of the frost of continence from without, if only, as the Apostle says, they no longer allow any reign of sin in their mortal body, nor wear a flesh that resists the spirit."[2]

---

[1] Ps. cxviii. (cxix.) 83.

[2] Cf. Rom. vi. 12; Gal. v. 17. S. Benedict's rule about the dress of the monks is as follows: "Let the dress of the brethren be adapted to the character of the place or climate in which they live, as more clothing is required in cold than in hot countries. Hence we leave this to the abbot to determine. However, in temperate climates we are of opinion that it will be enough for each monk to have a hood and a frock, a rough one for the winter, and in the summer a simple or old one; a scapular also for work; and the covering of the feet, shoes and socks. And the monks are not to complain of the colour or size of these articles, but to be satisfied with whatever can be found or got cheapest in the country where they live." Regula S. Bened. c. lv.

BOOK II.

OF THE CANONICAL SYSTEM OF THE NOCTURNAL PRAYERS AND PSALMS.

CHAPTER I.

Of the Canonical System of the Nocturnal Prayers and Psalms.

GIRT, therefore, with this twofold girdle of which we have spoken,[3] the soldier of Christ should next learn the system of the canonical prayers and Psalms which was long ago arranged by the holy fathers in the East. Of their character, however, and of the way in which we can pray, as the Apostle directs, "without ceasing,"[4] we shall treat, as the Lord may enable us, in the proper place, when we begin to relate the Conferences of the Elders.

CHAPTER II.

Of the difference of the number of Psalms appointed to be sung in all the provinces.

FOR we have found that many in different countries, according to the fancy of their mind (having, indeed, as the Apostle says, "a zeal for God but not according to knowledge"[5]), have made for themselves different rules and arrangements in this matter. For some have appointed that each night twenty or thirty Psalms should be said, and that these should be prolonged by the music of antiphonal singing,[6] and by the addition of some modulations

as well. Others have even tried to go beyond this number. Some use eighteen. And in this way we have found different rules appointed in different places, and the system and regulations that we have seen are almost as many in number as the monasteries and cells which we have visited. There are some, too, to whom it has seemed good that in the day offices of prayer, viz., Tierce, Sext, and Nones,[7] the number of Psalms and prayers should be made to correspond exactly to the number of the hours at which the services are offered up to the Lord.[8] Some have thought fit that six Psalms should be assigned to each service of the day. And so I think it best to set forth the most ancient system of the fathers which is still observed by the servants of God throughout the whole of Egypt, so that your new monastery in its untrained infancy in Christ[9] may be instructed in the most ancient institutions of the earliest fathers.

CHAPTER III.

Of the observance of one uniform rule throughout the whole of Egypt, and of the election of those who are set over the brethren.

AND so throughout the whole of Egypt and the Thebaid, where monasteries are not founded at the fancy of every man who renounces

---

[3] See Book I. c. xi.
[4] 1 Thess. v. 17.
[5] Rom. x. 2.
[6] *Antiphona.* In this passage the word appears to mean the actual Psalms sung antiphonally, rather than what is generally meant in later writings by the term. Cf. the Rule of Aurelian, "Dicite matutinarios, i.e., primo canticum in antiphona, deinde directaneum, judica me Deus . . . in antiphona dicite hymnum, splendor patudæ gloriæ." And see the use of the word later on by Cassian himself, c. vii.

[7] The third, sixth, and ninth hours were observed as hours of prayer from the earliest days. Cf. Tertullian De Oratione, c. 25; Clem. Alex. Stromata, VII., c. 7, § 40.
[8] I.e., that at Tierce there should be three Psalms, at Sext six, and at Nones nine.
[9] Castor had founded a monastery about the year 420.

the world, but through a succession of fathers and their traditions last even to the present day, or are founded so to last, in these we have noticed that a prescribed system of prayers is observed in their evening assemblies and nocturnal vigils. For no one is allowed to preside over the assembly of the brethren, or even over himself, before he has not only deprived himself of all his property but has also learnt the fact that he is not his own maker and has no authority over his own actions. For one who renounces the world, whatever property or riches he may possess, must seek the common dwelling of a Cœnobium, that he may not flatter himself in any way with what he has forsaken or what he has brought into the monastery. He must also be obedient to all, so as to learn that he must, as the Lord says,[1] become again a little child, arrogating nothing to himself on the score of his age and the number of the years which he now counts as lost while they were spent to no purpose in the world; and, as he is only a beginner, and because of the novelty of the apprenticeship, which he knows he is serving in Christ's service, he should not hesitate to submit himself even to his juniors. Further, he is obliged to habituate himself to work and toil, so as to prepare with his own hands, in accordance with the Apostle's command,[2] a daily supply of food, either for his own use or for the wants of strangers; and that he may also forget the pride and luxury of his past life, and gain by grinding toil humility of heart. And so no one is chosen to be set over a congregation of brethren before that he who is to be placed in authority has learnt by obedience what he ought to enjoin on those who are to submit to him, and has discovered from the rules of the Elders what he ought to teach to his juniors. For they say that to rule or to be ruled well needs a wise man, and they call it the greatest gift and grace of the Holy Spirit, since no one can enjoin salutary precepts on those who submit to him but one who has previously been trained in all the rules of virtue; nor can any one obey an Elder but one who has been filled with the love of God and perfected in the virtue of humility. And so we see that there is a variety of rules and regulations in use throughout other districts, because we often have the audacity to preside over a monastery without even having learnt the system of the Elders, and appoint ourselves Abbots before we have, as we ought, professed ourselves disciples, and are readier to require the observance of our own inventions than to preserve the well-tried teaching of our predecessors. But, while we meant to explain the best system of prayers to be observed, we have in our eagerness for the institutions of the fathers anticipated by a hasty digression the account which we were keeping back for its proper place. And so let us now return to the subject before us.

CHAPTER IV.

How throughout the whole of Egypt and the Thebaid the number of Psalms is fixed at twelve.

So, as we said, throughout the whole of Egypt and the Thebaid the number of Psalms is fixed at twelve both at Vespers and in the office of Nocturns,[3] in such a way that at the close two lessons follow, one from the Old and the other from the New Testament.[4] And this arrangement, fixed ever so long ago, has continued unbroken to the present day throughout so many ages, in all the monasteries of those districts, because it is said that it was no appointment of man's invention, but was brought down from heaven to the fathers by the ministry of an angel.

CHAPTER V.

How the fact that the number of the Psalms was to be twelve was received from the teaching of an angel.

FOR in the early days of the faith when only a few, and those the best of men, were known by the name of monks, who, as they received that mode of life from the Evangelist Mark of blessed memory, the first to preside over the Church of Alexandria as Bishop, not only preserved those grand characteristics for which we read, in the Acts of the Apostles, that the Church and multitude of believers in primitive times was famous ("The multitude of believers had one heart and one soul. Nor did any of them say that any of the things which he possessed was his own: but they had all things common; for as many as were owners of lands or houses sold them, and brought the price of the things which they sold, and laid it at the feet of the Apostles, and distribution was made to every man as he had need"),[5] but they added to these characteristics others still more sublime. For withdrawing into more secluded spots outside the cities they led a life marked by such rigorous abstinence

---

[1] Cf. S. Matt. xviii. 3.
[2] Cf. 1 Thess. iv. 11.

[3] The rule of Cæsarius also prescribes twelve Psalms on every Sabbath, Lord's day, and festival (c. 25); so also, according to the Benedictine rule, there are twelve Psalms at mattins, besides the fixed ones, iii. and xcv. (see c. 9 and 10), as there are still in the Roman Breviary on ordinary week-days.
[4] The custom of having *two* lessons only appears to have been peculiar to Egypt. Most of the early Western rules give *three*, e.g., those of Cæsarius and Benedict, while in the Eastern daily offices there are no lections from Holy Scripture.
[5] Acts iv. 32–34.

that even to those of another creed the exalted character of their life was a standing marvel. For they gave themselves up to the reading of Holy Scripture and to prayers and to manual labour night and day with such fervour that they had no desire or thoughts of food — unless on the second or third day bodily hunger [1] reminded them, and they took their meat and drink not so much because they wished for it as because it was necessary for life; and even then they took it not before sunset, in order that they might connect the hours of daylight with the practice of spiritual meditations, and the care of the body with the night, and might perform other things much more exalted than these. And about these matters, one who has never heard anything from one who is at home in such things, may learn from ecclesiastical history.[2] At that time, therefore, when the perfection of the primitive Church remained unbroken, and was still preserved fresh in the memory by their followers and successors, and when the fervent faith of the few had not yet grown lukewarm by being dispersed among the many, the venerable fathers with watchful care made provision for those to come after them, and met together to discuss what plan should be adopted for the daily worship throughout the whole body of the brethren; that they might hand on to those who should succeed them a legacy of piety and peace that was free from all dispute and dissension, for they were afraid that in regard of the daily services some difference or dispute might arise among those who joined together in the same worship, and at some time or other it might send forth a poisonous root of error or jealousy or schism among those who came after. And when each man in proportion to his own fervour — and unmindful of the weakness of others — thought that *that* should be appointed which he judged was quite easy by considering his own faith and strength, taking too little account of what would be possible for the great mass of the brethren in general (wherein a very large proportion of weak ones is sure to be found); and when in different degrees they strove, each according to his own powers, to fix an enormous number of Psalms, and some were for fifty, others sixty, and some, not content with this number, thought that they actually ought to go beyond it, — there was such a holy difference of opinion in their pious discussion on the rule of their religion that the time for their Vesper office came before the sacred question was decided; and, as they were going to celebrate their daily rites and prayers, one rose

up in the midst to chant the Psalms to the Lord. And while they were all sitting (as is still the custom in Egypt[3]), with their minds intently fixed on the words of the chanter, when he had sung eleven Psalms, separated by prayers introduced between them, verse after verse being evenly enunciated,[4] he finished the twelfth with a response of Alleluia,[5] and then, by his sudden disappearance from the eyes of all, put an end at once to their discussion and their service.[6]

CHAPTER VI.

Of the Custom of having Twelve Prayers.

WHEREUPON the venerable assembly of the Fathers understood that by Divine Providence a general rule had been fixed for the congregations of the brethren through the angel's direction, and so decreed that this number should be preserved both in their evening and in their nocturnal services; and when they added to these two lessons, one from the Old and one from the New Testament, they added them simply as extras and of their own appointment, only for those who liked, and who were eager to gain by constant study a mind well stored with Holy Scripture. But on Saturday and Sunday they read them both from the New Testament; viz., one from the Epistles[7] or the Acts of the Apostles, and one from the Gospel.[8] And this also those do whose concern is the reading and the recollection of the Scriptures, from Easter to Whitsuntide.[9]

CHAPTER VII.

Of their Method of Praying.

THESE aforesaid prayers, then, they begin and finish in such a way that when the Psalm is ended they do not hurry at once to kneel down, as some of us do in this country, who, before

---

[1] Petschenig's text has *inedia*, others *inediam*.
[2] Cf. Eusebius, Book II. c. xv., xvi. Sozomen, Book I. c. xii., xiii.

[3] Cf. below, c. xii.
[4] Cumque . . . undecim Psalmos orationum interjectione distinctos contiguis versibus parili pronunciatione cantassat.
[5] So, according to the Benedictine rule, the Psalms at mattins are ended with Alleluia (c. ix.): "After these three lessons with their responds there shall follow the remaining six Psalms with the Alleluia." Cf. c. xi. and xv.
[6] This story is referred to in the Eighteenth Canon of the Second Council of Tours, A.D. 567. "The statutes of the Fathers have prescribed that twelve Psalms be said at the Twelfth (i.e., Vespers), with Alleluia, which, moreover, they learnt from the showing of an angel."
[7] *Apostolus*, the regular name for the book of the Epistles.
[8] Cf. the note above on c. v.
[9] *Totis Quinquagessimæ diebus;* i.e., the whole period of fifty days between Easter and Whitsuntide (cf. c. xviii. and the Conferences XXI. viii., xi., xx.). This is the usual meaning of the term Pentecost in early writers, though it is also used more strictly for the actual festival of Whitsunday. Cf. the Twentieth Canon of the Council of Nicæa, and see Canon Bright's *Notes on the Canons*, p. 72, for other instances.

the Psalm is fairly ended, make haste to prostrate themselves for prayer, in their hurry to finish the service[1] as quickly as possible. For though we have chosen to exceed the limit which was anciently fixed by our predecessors, supplying the number of the remaining Psalms, we are anxious to get to the end of the service, thinking of the refreshment of the wearied body rather than looking for profit and benefit from the prayer. Among them, therefore, it is not so, but before they bend their knees they pray for a few moments, and while they are standing up spend the greater part of the time in prayer. And so after this, for the briefest space of time, they prostrate themselves to the ground, as if but adoring the Divine Mercy, and as soon as possible rise up, and again standing erect with outspread hands — just as they had been standing to pray before — remain with thoughts intent upon their prayers. For when you lie prostrate for any length of time upon the ground you are more open to an attack, they say, not only of wandering thoughts but also of slumber. And would that we too did not know the truth of this by experience and daily practice — we who when prostrating ourselves on the ground too often wish for this attitude to be prolonged for some time, not for the sake of our prayer so much as for the sake of resting. But when he who is to "collect" the prayer[2] rises from the ground they all start up at once, so that no one would venture to bend the knee before *he* bows down, nor to delay when *he* has risen from the ground, lest it should be thought that he has offered his own prayer independently instead of following the leader to the close.

CHAPTER VIII.

Of the Prayer which follows the Psalm.

THAT practice too which we have observed in this country — viz., that while one sings to the end of the Psalm, all standing up sing together with a loud voice, "Glory be to the Father and to the Son and to the Holy Ghost" — we have never heard anywhere throughout the East, but there, while all keep silence when

the Psalm is finished, the prayer that follows is offered up by the singer. But with this hymn in honour of the Trinity only the whole Psalmody[3] is usually ended.[4]

CHAPTER IX.

Of the characteristics of the prayer, the fuller treatment of which is reserved for the Conferences of the Elders.

AND as the plan of these Institutes leads us to the system of the canonical prayers, the fuller treatment of which we will however reserve for the Conferences of the Elders (where we shall speak of them at greater length when we have begun to tell in their own words of the character of their prayers, and how continuous they are), still I think it well, as far as the place and my narrative permit, as the occasion offers itself, to glance briefly for the present at a few points, so that by picturing in the meanwhile the movements of the outer man, and by now laying the foundations, as it were, of the prayer, we may afterwards, when we come to speak of the inner man, with less labour build up the complete edifice of his prayers; providing, above all for this, that if the end of life should overtake us and cut us off from finishing the narration which we are anxious (D.V.) fitly to compose, we may at least leave in this work the *beginnings* of so necessary a matter to you, to whom everything seems a delay, by reason of the fervour of your desire: so that, if a few more years of life are granted to us, we may at least mark out for you some outlines of their prayers, that those above all who live in monasteries may have some information about them; providing also, at the same time, that those who perhaps may meet only with this book, and be unable to procure the other, may find that they are supplied with some sort of information about the nature of their prayers; and as they are instructed about the dress and clothing of the outer man, so too they may not be ignorant what his behaviour ought to be in offering spiritual sacrifices.

---

[1] *Ad celeritatem missæ.* The word "missa" is here used for the breaking up of the congregation after service, as it is again in Book III. c. vii., where Cassian says that one who came late for prayer had to wait, standing before the door, for the "missa" of the whole assembly. Cf. III. c. viii., "post vigiliarum missam," and the rule of S. Benedict (c. xvii.): "After the three Psalms are finished, let one lesson be read, a verse, and Kyrie Eleison: *et missæ fiant.*" A full account of the various meanings given to the word will be found in the *Dictionary of Christian Antiquities*, Vol. II. p. 1193 *sq.*

[2] *Colligere orationem.* The phrase corresponds to the Greek συνάπτειν, but Ducange gives but few instances of its use in Latin. It is found, however, in Canon xxx. of the Council of Agde. "Plebs *collecta oratione* ad vesperam ab Episcopo cum benedictione dimittatur."

[3] *Antiphona.* The word must certainly be used here not in the later sense of "antiphon," but as descriptive of the whole of the Psalmody of the office. Cf. note on c. i.

[4] In the Eastern offices the Psalter is divided into twenty sections called καθίσματα, each of which is subdivided into three στάσεις, at the close of each of which the Gloria is said, and not, as in the West, after every Psalm. This Western custom which Cassian here notices seems to have originated in Gaul, and thence spread to other churches, as, according to Walafrid Strabo, at Rome it was used but rarely after the Psalms in the ninth century. See Walafrid Strabo, c. xxv. ap. Hittorp. 688. The earliest certain indications of the use of the hymn itself are found in the fourth century. See S. Basil, *De Spiritu Sancto*, c. xxix.; Theodoret, *Eccl. Hist.*, II. xxiv.; Sozomen, *Eccl. Hist.*, III. xx. The Greek form is Δόξα πατρὶ καὶ υἱῷ καὶ ἁγίῳ πνευμάτι καὶ νῦν καὶ ἀεὶ καὶ εἰς τοὺς αἰῶνας τῶν αἰωνῶν, ἀμήν. The additional words in use in the West, "sicut erat in principio," were first adopted in the sixth century, being ordered by the Council of Vaison, A.D. 529, "after the example of the apostolic see."

Since, though *these* books, which we are now arranging with the Lord's help to write, are mainly taken up with what belongs to the outer man and the customs of the Cœnobia, yet *those* will rather be concerned with the training of the inner man and the perfection of the heart, and the life and doctrine of the Anchorites.

CHAPTER X.

Of the silence and conciseness with which the Collects are offered up by the Egyptians.

WHEN, then, they meet together to celebrate the aforementioned rites, which they term *synaxes*,[1] they are all so perfectly silent that, though so large a number of the brethren is assembled together, you would not think a single person was present except the one who stands up and chants the Psalm in the midst; and especially is this the case when the prayer is offered up,[2] for then there is no spitting, no clearing of the throat, or noise of coughing, no sleepy yawning with open mouths, and gaping, and no groans or sighs are uttered, likely to distract those standing near. No voice is heard save that of the priest concluding the prayer, except perhaps one that escapes the lips through aberration of mind and unconsciously takes the heart by surprise, inflamed as it is with an uncontrollable and irrepressible fervour of spirit, while that which the glowing mind is unable to keep to itself strives through a sort of unutterable groaning to make its escape from the inmost chambers of the breast. But if any one infected with coldness of mind prays out loud or emits any of those sounds we have mentioned, or is overcome by a fit of yawning, they declare that he is guilty of a double fault. He is blameworthy, first, as regards his own prayer because he offers it to God in a careless way; and, secondly, because by his unmannerly noise he disturbs the thoughts of another who would otherwise perhaps have been able to pray with greater attention. And so their rule is that the prayer ought to be brought to an end with a speedy conclusion, lest while we are lingering over it some superfluity of spittle or phlegm should interfere with the close of our prayer. And, therefore, while it is still glowing the prayer is to be snatched as speedily as possible out of the jaws of the enemy, who, although he is indeed always hostile to us, is yet never more hostile than when he sees that we are anxious to offer up prayers to God against his attacks; and by exciting wandering thoughts and all sorts of rheums he endeavours to distract our minds from attending to our prayers, and by this means tries to make it grow cold, though begun with fervour. Wherefore they think it best for the prayers to be short and offered up very frequently:[3] on the one hand that by so often praying to the Lord we may be able to cleave to Him continually; on the other, that when the devil is lying in wait for us, we may by their terse brevity avoid the darts with which he endeavours to wound us especially when we are saying our prayers.

CHAPTER XI.

Of the system according to which the Psalms are said among the Egyptians.

AND, therefore, they do not even attempt to finish the Psalms, which they sing in the service, by an unbroken and continuous recitation. But they repeat them separately and bit by bit, divided into two or three sections, according to the number of verses, with prayers in between.[4] For they do not care about the quantity of verses, but about the intelligence of the mind; aiming with all their might at this: "I will sing with the spirit: I will sing also with the understanding."[5] And so they consider it better for ten verses to be sung with understanding and thought[6] than for a whole Psalm to be poured forth with a bewildered mind. And this is sometimes caused by the hurry of the speaker, when, thinking of the character and number of the remaining Psalms to be sung, he takes no pains to make the meaning clear to his hearers, but hastens on to get to the end of the service. Lastly, if any of the younger monks, either through fervour of spirit or because he has not yet been properly

---

[3] Cf. Augustine, *Ep.* cxxx., § 20 (Vol. II. 389): "Dicuntur fratres in Ægypto crebras quidem habere orationes, sed eas tamen brevissimas, et raptim quodammodo jaculatas, ne illa vigilantes erecta, quæ oranti plurimum necessaria est, per productiores moras evanescat atque hebetetur intentio;" and Hooker, *Eccl. Polity*, Book V. c. xxxiii.: "The brethren in Egypt (saith S. Augustine) are reported to have many prayers, but every of them very short, as if they were darts thrown out with a kind of sudden quickness, lest that vigilant and erect attention of mind which in prayer is very necessary should be wasted or dulled through continuance, if their prayers were few and long. . . . Those prayers whereunto devout minds have added a piercing kind of brevity, as well in that respect which we have already mentioned, as also thereby the better to express that quick and speedy expedition wherewith ardent affections, the very wings of prayer, are delighted to present our suits in heaven, even sooner than our tongues can devise to utter them," etc.

[4] This plan of dividing some of the longer Psalms (as is still done with the 119th in the English Psalter) was adopted sometimes in the West also. Cf. the Rule of S. Benedict, c. xviii., and the Third Council of Narbonne (A.D. 589), Canon 2 : " Ut in psallendis ordinibus per quemque Psalmum *Gloria* dicatur Omnipotenti Deo, per majores vero Psalmos, prout fuerint prolixius, pausationes fiant, et per quamque pausationem *Gloria Trinitatis* Domino decantetur." Further, the rule that prayers should be intermingled with Psalms, which was perhaps introduced into the West by Cassian, was widely adopted both in Gaul and in Spain.

[5] 1 Cor. xiv. 15.

[6] Cum rationabili assignatione.

---

[1] *Synaxis* (σύναξις), a general name for the course of the ecclesiastical offices.

[2] *Consummatur.*

taught, goes beyond the proper limit of what is to be sung, the one who is singing the Psalm is stopped by the senior clapping his hands where he sits in his stall, and making them all rise for prayer. Thus they take every possible care that no weariness may creep in among them as they sit through the length of the Psalms, as thereby not only would the singer himself lose the fruits of understanding, but also loss would be incurred by those whom he made to feel the service a weariness by going on so long. They also observe this with the greatest care; viz., that no Psalm should be said with the response of Alleluia except those which are marked with the inscription of Alleluia in their title.[1] But the aforesaid number of twelve Psalms they divide in such a way that if there are two brethren they each sing six; if there are three, then four; and if four, three each. A smaller number than this they never sing in the congregation, and accordingly, however large a congregation is assembled, not more than four brethren sing in the service.[2]

CHAPTER XII.

Of the reason why while one sings the Psalms the rest sit down during the service ; and of the zeal with which they afterwards prolong their vigils in their cells till daybreak.

THIS canonical system of twelve Psalms, of which we have spoken, they render easier by such bodily rest that when, after their custom, they celebrate these services, they all, except the one who stands up in the midst to recite the Psalms, sit in very low stalls and follow the voice of the singer with the utmost attention of heart. For they are so worn out with fasting and working all day and night that, unless they were helped by some such indulgence, they could not possibly get through this number standing up. For they allow no time to pass idly without the performance of some work, because not only do they strive with all earnestness to do with their hands those things which can be done in daylight, but also with anxious minds they examine into those sorts of work which not even the darkness of night can put a stop to, as they hold that they will gain a far deeper insight into subjects of spiritual contemplation with purity of heart, the more earnestly that they devote themselves to work and labour. And therefore they consider that a moderate allowance of canonical prayers was divinely arranged in order that for those

who are very ardent in faith room might be left in which their never-tiring flow of virtue might spend itself, and notwithstanding no loathing arise in their wearied and weak bodies from too large a quantity. And so, when the offices of the canonical prayers have been duly finished, every one returns to his own cell (which he inhabits alone, or is allowed to share with only one other whom partnership in work or training in discipleship and learning has joined with him, or perhaps similarity of character has made his companion), and again they offer with greater earnestness the same service of prayer, as their special private sacrifice, as it were; nor do any of them give themselves up any further to rest and sleep till when the brightness of day comes on the labours of the day succeed the labours and meditations of the night.

CHAPTER XIII.

The reason why they are not allowed to go to sleep after the night service.[3]

AND these labours they keep up for two reasons, besides this consideration, — that they believe that when they are diligently exerting themselves they are offering to God a sacrifice of the fruit of their hands. And, if we are aiming at perfection, we also ought to observe this with the same diligence. First, lest our envious adversary, jealous of our purity against which he is always plotting, and ceaselessly hostile to us, should by some illusion in a dream pollute the purity which has been gained by the Psalms and prayers of the night: for after that satisfaction which we have offered for our negligence and ignorance, and the absolution implored with profuse sighs in our confession, he anxiously tries, if he finds some time given to repose, to defile us; then above all endeavouring to overthrow and weaken our trust in God when he sees by the purity of our prayers that we are making most fervent efforts towards God: so that sometimes, when he has been unable to injure some the whole night long, he does his utmost to disgrace them in that short hour. Secondly, because, even if no such dreaded illusion of the devil arises, even a pure sleep in the interval produces laziness in the case of the monk who ought soon to wake up; and, bringing on a sluggish torpor in the mind, it dulls his vigour throughout the whole day, and deadens that keenness

---

[1] Viz.: Pss. civ., cv., cvi., cx., cxi., cxii., cxiii., cxiv., cxv., cxvi., cxvii., cxviii., cxxxiv., cxxxv., cxlv., cxlvi., cxlvii., cxlviii., cxlix., cl., in the LXX. and the Latin.
[2] This arrangement by which the Psalm was sung by a single voice, while the rest of the congregation listened, is that which was afterwards known by the name of *Tractus.*

[3] *Missæ.* The use of this word for the offices of the Canonical Hours, though not common, is found also in the Thirtieth Canon of the Council of Agde, A.D. 506. " At the end of the morning and evening *missæ*, after the hymns, let the little chapters from the Psalms be said."

of perception and exhausts that energy[1] of heart which would be capable of keeping us all day long more watchful against all the snares of the enemy and more robust. Wherefore to the Canonical Vigils there are added these private watchings, and they submit to them with the greater care, both in order that the purity which has been gained by Psalms and prayers may not be lost, and also that a more intense carefulness to guard us diligently through the day may be secured beforehand by the meditation of the night.

CHAPTER XIV.

Of the way in which they devote themselves in their cells equally to manual labour and to prayer.

AND therefore they supplement their prayer by the addition of labour, lest slumber might steal upon them as idlers. For as they scarcely enjoy any time of leisure, so there is no limit put to their spiritual meditations. For practising equally the virtues of the body and of the soul, they balance what is due to the outer by what is profitable to the inner man;[2] steadying the slippery motions of the heart and the shifting fluctuations of the thoughts by the weight of *labour*, like some strong and immoveable anchor, by which the changeableness and wanderings of the heart, fastened within the barriers of the cell, may be shut up in some perfectly secure harbour, and so, intent only on spiritual meditation and watchfulness over the thoughts, may not only forbid the watchful mind to give a hasty consent to any evil suggestions, but may also keep it safe from any unnecessary and idle thoughts: so that it is not easy to say which depends on the other — I mean, whether they practise their incessant manual labour for the sake of spiritual meditation, or whether it is for the sake of their continuous labours that they acquire such remarkable spiritual proficiency and light of knowledge.

CHAPTER XV.

Of the discreet rule by which every one must retire to his cell after the close of the prayers; and[3] of the rebuke to which any one who does otherwise is subject.

AND so, when the Psalms are finished, and the daily assembly, as we said above, is broken up, none of them dares to loiter ever so little or to gossip with another: nor does he presume even to leave his cell throughout the whole day, or to forsake the work which he is wont to carry on in it, except when they happen to be called out for the performance of some necessary duty, which they fulfil by going out of doors so that there may not be any chattering at all among them. But every one does the work assigned to him in such a way that, by repeating by heart some Psalm or passage of Scripture, he gives no opportunity or time for dangerous schemes or evil designs, or even for idle talk, as both mouth and heart are incessantly taken up with spiritual meditations. For they are most particular in observing this rule, that none of them, and especially of the younger ones, may be caught stopping even for a moment or going anywhere together with another, or holding his hands in his. But, if they discover any who in defiance of the discipline of this rule have perpetrated any of these forbidden things, they pronounce them guilty of no slight fault, as contumacious and disobedient to the rules; nor are they free from suspicion of plotting and nefarious designs. And, unless they expiate their fault by public penance when all the brethren are gathered together, none of them is allowed to be present at the prayers of the brethren.

CHAPTER XVI.

How no one is allowed to pray with one who has been suspended from prayer.

FURTHER, if one of them has been suspended from prayer for some fault which he has committed, no one has any liberty of praying with him before he performs his penance on the ground,[4] and reconciliation and pardon for his offence has been publicly granted to him by the Abbot before all the brethren. For by a plan of this kind they separate and cut themselves off from fellowship with him in prayer for this reason — because they believe that one who is suspended from prayer is, as the Apostle says, "delivered unto Satan:"[5] and if any one, moved by an ill-considered affection, dares to hold communion with him in prayer before he has been received by the Elder, he makes himself partaker of his damnation, and delivers himself up of his own free will to Satan, to whom the other had been consigned for the correction of his guilt. And in this he falls into a more grievous offence because, by uniting with him in fellowship either in talk or in prayer, he gives him grounds for still greater arrogance, and only encourages and makes worse the obstinacy of the offender. For, by

---

[1] *Pinguetudo.*
[2] *Exterioris hominis stipendia cum emolumentis interioris exæquant.*
[3] *Post orationum missam.* See note on c. vii.

[4] Cf. III. vii., and the description of this penance in IV. xvi.
[5] 1 Cor. v. 5; 1 Tim. i. 20.

giving him a consolation that is only hurtful, he will make his heart still harder, and not let him humble himself for the fault for which he was excommunicated; and through this he will make him hold the Elder's rebuke as of no consequence, and harbour deceitful thoughts about satisfaction and absolution.

CHAPTER XVII.

How he who rouses them for prayer ought to call them at the usual time.

BUT he who has been entrusted with the office of summoning the religious assembly and with the care of the service should not presume to rouse the brethren for their daily vigils irregularly, as he pleases, or as he may wake up in the night, or as the accident of his own sleep or sleeplessness may incline him. But, although daily habit may constrain him to wake at the usual hour, yet by often and anxiously ascertaining by the course of the stars the right hour for service, he should summon them to the office of prayer, lest he be found careless in one of two ways: either if, overcome with sleep, he lets the proper hour of the night go by, or if, wanting to go to bed and impatient for his sleep, he anticipates it, and so may be thought to have secured his own repose instead of attending to the spiritual office and the rest of all the others.[1]

CHAPTER XVIII.

How they do not kneel from the evening of Saturday till the evening of Sunday.

THIS, too, we ought to know, — that from the evening of Saturday which precedes the Sunday,[2] up to the following evening, among the Egyptians they never kneel, nor from Easter to Whitsuntide;[3] nor do they at these times observe a rule of fasting,[4] the reason for which shall be explained in its proper place in the Conferences of the Elders,[5] if the Lord permits. At present we only propose to run through the causes very briefly, lest our book exceed its due limits and prove tiresome or burdensome to the reader.

BOOK III.

OF THE CANONICAL SYSTEM OF THE DAILY PRAYERS AND PSALMS.

CHAPTER I.

Of the services of the third, sixth, and ninth hours, which are observed in the regions of Syria.

THE nocturnal system of prayers and Psalms as observed throughout Egypt has been, I think, by God's help, explained so far as our slender ability was able; and now we must speak of the services of Tierce, Sext, and None, according to the rule of the monasteries of Palestine and Mesopotamia,[6] as we said in the Preface, and must moderate by the customs of these the perfection and inimitable rigour of the discipline of the Egyptians.

CHAPTER II.

How among the Egyptians they apply themselves all day long to prayer and Psalms continually, with the addition of work, without distinction of hours.

FOR among them (viz., the Egyptians) these offices which we are taught to render to the Lord at separate hours and at intervals of time, with a reminder from the convener, are celebrated continuously throughout the whole

in a fragment of Irenæus, there is a mention of the fact that Christians abstained from kneeling on Sunday in token of the resurrection. For later testimonies see Ambrose, *Ep.* 119, *ad Januarium.* Epiphanius, *on Heresies*, Book III. (Vol. III. p. 583, ed. Dindorf). Jerome, *Dial: Adv. Lucif.* c. iv.; and the Twentieth Canon of the Council of Nicæa, with Canon Bright's notes (*Notes on the Canons of the First Four General Councils*, p. 72).
    [5] Cf. the Conferences XXI. xi.
    [6] According to S. Jerome, Hilarion was the first to introduce the monastic life into Palestine (*Vita Hilar.*). His work was carried on by his companion and pupil Hesycas, and Epiphanius, afterwards Bishop of Salamis in Cyprus. In Asia Minor S. Basil was the greater organizer of monasticism, though, as he tells us, there were already many monks, not only in Egypt, but also in Palestine, Cœlosyria, and Mesopotamia (Ep. ccxxiii.). See also on the early monks of Palestine and the East, Sozomen, H. E., Book VI., cc. xxxii.-xxxv.

    [1] The rule of S. Benedict is similarly careful that the brethren may not oversleep themselves. See c. xi. and xlvii.
    [2] *Quæ lucescit inm die dominicum.* The phrase is borrowed by Cassian from the Latin of S. Matt. xxviii. i.
    [3] *Totis Quinquagesimæ diebus.* See above on c. vi.
    [4] That this was the rule of the primitive Church is shown by Tertullian, *De Corona Militis*, c. iii. "We count fasting or kneeling in worship on the Lord's day to be unlawful. We rejoice in the same privilege, also, from Easter to Whitsunday." And even earlier,

day, with the addition of work, and that of their own free will. For manual labour is incessantly practised by them in their cells in such a way that meditation on the Psalms and the rest of the Scriptures is never entirely omitted. And as with it at every moment they mingle suffrages and prayers, they spend the whole day in those offices which we celebrate at fixed times. Wherefore, except Vespers and Nocturns, there are no public services among them in the day except on Saturday and Sunday, when they meet together at the third hour for the purpose of Holy Communion.[1] For that which is continuously offered is more than what is rendered at intervals of time; and more acceptable as a free gift than the duties which are performed by the compulsion of a rule: as David for this rejoices somewhat exultingly when he says, "Freely will I sacrifice unto Thee;" and, "Let the free will offerings of my mouth be pleasing to Thee, O Lord." [2]

CHAPTER III.

How throughout all the East the services of Tierce, Sext, and None are ended with only three Psalms and prayers each; and the reason why these spiritual offices are assigned more particularly to those hours.

AND so in the monasteries of Palestine and Mesopotamia and all the East the services of the above-mentioned hours are ended each day with three Psalms apiece, so that constant prayers may be offered to God at the appointed times, and yet, the spiritual duties being completed with due moderation, the necessary offices of work may not be in any way interfered with: for at these three seasons we know that Daniel the prophet also poured forth his prayers to God day by day in his chamber with the windows open.[3] Nor is it without good reasons that these times are more particularly assigned to religious offices, since at them what completed the promises and summed up our salvation was fulfilled. For we can show that at the third hour the Holy Spirit, who had been of old promised by the prophets, descended in the first instance on the Apostles assembled together for prayer. For when in their astonishment at the speaking with tongues, which proceeded from them through

the outpouring of the Holy Ghost upon them, the unbelieving people of the Jews mocked and said that they were full of new wine, then Peter, standing up in the midst of them, said: "Men of Israel, and all ye who dwell at Jerusalem, let this be known unto you, and consider my words. For these men are not, as ye imagine, drunk, since it is the third hour of the day; but this is that which was spoken by the prophet Joel: and it shall come to pass in the last days, saith the Lord, I will pour out of my Spirit upon all flesh, and your sons and your daughters shall prophesy, and your young men shall see visions and your old men shall dream dreams. And indeed upon my servants and my handmaids in those days I will pour out of my Spirit, and they shall prophesy." [4] And all of this was fulfilled at the third hour, when the Holy Spirit, announced before by the prophets, came at that hour and abode upon the Apostles. But at the sixth hour the spotless Sacrifice, our Lord and Saviour, was offered up to the Father, and, ascending the cross for the salvation of the whole world, made atonement for the sins of mankind, and, despoiling principalities and powers, led them away openly; and all of us who were liable to death and bound by the debt of the handwriting that could not be paid, He freed, by taking it away out of the midst and affixing it to His cross for a trophy.[5] At the same hour, too, to Peter, in an ecstasy of mind, there was divinely revealed both the calling of the Gentiles by the letting down of the Gospel vessel from heaven, and also the cleansing of all the living creatures contained in it, when a voice came to him and said to him: "Rise, Peter; kill and eat;" [6] which vessel, let down from heaven by the four corners, is plainly seen to signify nothing else than the Gospel. For although, as it is divided by the fourfold narrative of the Evangelists, it seems to have "four corners" (or beginnings), yet the body of the Gospel is but one; embracing, as it does, the birth as well as the Godhead, and the miracles as well as the passion of one and the same Christ. Excellently, too, it says not "of linen" but "as if of linen." For linen signifies death. Since, then, our Lord's death and passion were not undergone by the law of human nature, but of His own free will, it says "as if of linen." For when dead according to the flesh He was not dead according to the spirit, because "His soul was not left in hell, neither

---

[1] The *Saturday* Communion (in addition to that of Wednesday and Friday, as well as Sunday) is also mentioned by S. Basil (*Ep.* xciii.), and cf. the Forty-ninth Canon of the Council of Laodicæa (circa 360 A.D.): "During Lent the bread shall not be offered except on Saturday and Sunday." In the West there is no trace of a special Saturday celebration of the Holy Communion.

The third hour was the ordinary time for Holy Communion, as may be seen from the decree (falsely) ascribed to Pope Telesphorus (A.D. 127-138), in the *Liber Pontificalis:* "Ut nullus ante horam tertiam sacrificium offerre præsumeret," and many other testimonies.

[2] Ps. liii. (liv.) 8; cxviii. (cxix.) 108.
[3] Cf. Daniel vi. 10.

[4] Acts ii. 14-18.
[5] The whole passage is alluding to Col. ii. 14, 15, which runs as follows in the Vulgate: "Delens quod adversum nos erat chirografum decretis, quod erat contrarium nobis, et ipse tulit de medio, affigens illud cruci, expolians principatus et potestates traduxit confidenter, palam triumphans illos in semet ipso."
[6] Acts x. 11 *sq.*

did His flesh see corruption."[1] And again He says: "No man taketh My life from Me : but I lay it down of Myself. I have power to lay it down, and I have power to take it again."[2] And so in this vessel of the Gospels let down from heaven, that is written by the Holy Ghost, all the nations which were formerly outside the observance of the law and reckoned as unclean now flow together through belief in the faith that they may to their salvation be turned away from the worship of idols and be serviceable for health-giving food, and are brought to Peter and cleansed by the voice of the Lord. But at the ninth hour, penetrating to hades, He there by the brightness of His splendour extinguished the indescribable darkness of hell, and, bursting its brazen gates and breaking the iron bars, brought away with Him to the skies the captive band of saints which was there shut up and detained in the darkness of inexorable hell,[3] and, by taking away the fiery sword, restored to paradise its original inhabitants by his pious confession. At the same hour, too, Cornelius, the centurion, continuing with his customary devotion in his prayers, is made aware through the converse of the angel with him that his prayers and alms are remembered before the Lord, and at the ninth hour the mystery[4] of the calling of the Gentiles is clearly shown to him, which had been revealed to Peter in his ecstasy of mind at the sixth hour. In another passage, too, in the Acts of the Apostles, we are told as follows about the same time: "But Peter and John went up into the temple at the hour of prayer, the ninth hour."[5] And by these notices it is clearly proved that these hours were not without good reason consecrated with religious services by holy and apostolic men, and ought to be observed in like manner by us, who, unless we are compelled, as it were, by some rule to discharge these pious offices at least at stated times, either through sloth or through forgetfulness, or being absorbed in business, spend the whole day without engaging in prayer. But concerning the evening sacrifices what is to be said, since even in the Old Testament these are

ordered to be offered continually by the law of Moses? For that the morning whole-burnt offerings and evening sacrifices were offered every day continually in the temple, although with figurative offerings, we can show from that which is sung by David: "Let my prayer be set forth in Thy sight as the incense, and let the lifting up of my hands be an evening sacrifice,"[6] in which place we can understand it in a still higher sense of that true evening sacrifice which was given by the Lord our Saviour in the evening to the Apostles at the Supper, when He instituted the holy mysteries of the Church, and of that evening sacrifice which He Himself, on the following day, in the end of the ages, offered up to fhe Father by the lifting up of His hands for the salvation of the whole world; which spreading forth of His hands on the Cross is quite correctly called a "lifting up." For when we were all lying in hades He raised us to heaven, according to the word of His own promise when He says: "When I am lifted up from the earth, I will draw all men unto Me."[7] But concerning Mattins, that also teaches us which it is customary every day to sing at it: "O God, my God, to Thee do I watch at break of day;" and "I will meditate on Thee in the morning;" and "I prevented the dawning of the day and cried;" and again, "Mine eyes to Thee have prevented the morning, that I might meditate on Thy words."[8] At these hours too that householder in the Gospel hired labourers into his vineyard. For thus also is he described as having hired them in the early morning, which time denotes the Mattin office; then at the third hour; then at the sixth; after this, at the ninth; and last of all, at the eleventh,[9] by which the hour of the lamps[10] is denoted.[11]

---

[6] Ps. cxl. (cxli.) 2.
[7] S. John xii. 32.
[8] Pss. lxii. (lxiii.) 2, 7; cxviii. (cxix.) 147, 8. In both East and West Ps. lxii. (lxiii.) has from very early times been used as a morning hymn. See the Apost. Constitutions II. lix., VIII. xxxvii. In the East it is still one of the fixed Psalms at Lauds, as it is also in the West, according to the Roman use. But in Cassian's time it had apparently been transferred from Lauds to Prime. See below, c. vi.
[9] S. Matt. xx. 1-6.
[10] *Lucernaris hora;* i.e., the hour for Vespers, which is sometimes called lucernarium or lucernalis. S. Jerome *in Ps. cxix.* S. Augustine, *Sermo i ad fratres in er.*
[11] It will be noticed that in this chapter Cassian alludes to five offices: (1) A morning office; (2) the third hour; (3) the sixth; (4) the ninth; and (5) Vespers; and gives the grounds for their observance. Similar grounds are given by Cyprian, *De Orat. Dominica sub fine:* "For upon the disciples, at the third hour, the Holy Spirit descended, who fulfilled the grace of the Lord's promise. Moreover, at the sixth hour, Peter, going up to the housetop, was instructed as well by the sign as by the word of God, admonishing him to receive all to the grace of salvation, whereas he was previously doubtful of the receiving of the Gentiles to baptism. And from the sixth hour to the ninth the Lord, being crucified, washed away our sins by His blood; and that He might redeem and quicken us, He then accomplished His victory by His passion. But for us, beloved brethren, besides the hours of prayer observed of old, both the times and the sacraments have now increased in number. For we must also pray in the morning, that the Lord's resurrection may be celebrated by morning prayer. . . . Also at the sun-setting and decline of day we

---

[1] Ps. xv. (xvi.) 10.
[2] S. John x. 18.
[3] The belief that by the descent into hell our Lord released some who were there detained was almost, if not quite, universal in the early ages, and is recognized by a large number of the Fathers. It is alluded to by so early a writer as Ignatius (*Ad Magn.* ix.), and appears in Irenæus (IV. c. xlii.) as a tradition of those who had seen the Apostles. See also Tertullian, *De Anima,* c. lv., and a host of later writers.
[4] *Sacramentum.* This word is used by Cassian, as by other Latin writers, as the regular equivalent of the Greek μυστήριον, and as such is applied to sacred *truths* equally with sacred *rites.* See Book V. xxxiv.: "Sacramenta scriptorum:" Conferences IX. xxxiv.: "Sacramentum resurrectionis Dominicæ." And again and again the word is used of the mystery of the Incarnation in the books against Nestorius.
[5] Acts iii. 1.

CHAPTER IV.

How the Mattin office was not appointed by an ancient tradition but was started in our own day for a definite reason.

But you must know that this Mattins, which is now very generally observed in Western countries, was appointed as a canonical office in our own day, and also in our own monastery, where our Lord Jesus Christ was born of a Virgin and deigned to submit to growth in infancy as man, and where by His Grace He supported our own infancy, still tender in religion, and, as it were, fed with milk.[1] For up till that time we find that when this office of Mattins (which is generally celebrated after a short interval after the Psalms and prayers of Nocturns in the monasteries of Gaul) was finished, together with the daily vigils, the remaining hours were assigned by our Elders to bodily refreshment. But when some rather carelessly abused this indulgence and prolonged their time for sleep too long, as they were not obliged by the requirements of any service to leave their cells or rise from their beds till the third hour; and when, as well as losing their labour, they were drowsy from excess of sleep in the daytime, when they ought to have been applying themselves to some duties, (especially on those days when an unusually oppressive weariness was caused by their keeping watch from the evening till the approach of morning), a complaint was brought to the Elders by some of the brethren who were ardent in spirit and in no slight measure disturbed by this carelessness, and it was determined by them after long discussion and anxious consideration that up till sunrise, when they could without harm be ready to read or to undertake manual labour, time for rest should be given to their wearied bodies, and after this they should all be summoned to the observance of this service and should rise from their beds, and by reciting three Psalms and prayers (after the order anciently fixed for the

observance of Tierce and Sext, to signify the confession of the Trinity)[2] should at the same time by an uniform arrangement put an end to their sleep and make a beginning to their work. And this form, although it may seem to have arisen out of an accident and to have been appointed within recent memory for the reason given above, yet it clearly makes up according to the letter that number which the blessed David indicates (although it can be taken spiritually): "Seven times a day do I praise Thee because of Thy righteous judgments."[3] For by the addition of this service we certainly hold these spiritual assemblies seven times a day, and are shown to sing praises to God seven times in it.[4] Lastly, though this same form, starting from the East, has most beneficially spread to these parts, yet still in some long-established monasteries in the East, which will not brook the slightest violation of the old rules of the Fathers, it seems never to have been introduced.[5]

CHAPTER V.

How they ought not to go back to bed again after the Mattin prayers.

But some in this province, not knowing the reason why this office was appointed and introduced, go back again to bed after their Mattin prayers are finished, and in spite of it fall into that very habit to check which our Elders instituted this service. For they are eager to finish it at that hour, that an opportunity may be given, to those who are inclined to be indifferent and not careful enough, to go back to bed again, which most certainly ought not to be done (as we showed more fully in the previous book when describing the service of the Egyptians),[6] for fear least the force of

---

must pray again. For since Christ is the true Sun and the true Day, as the worldly sun and day depart, when we pray and ask that light may return to us again, we pray for the advent of Christ, which shall give us the grace of everlasting light." Cf. also S. Basil, *The Greater Monastic Rules*, Q. xxxvii., where the same subject is discussed, and *Apost. Const.* Book VIII. c. xxxiv. In later times the Seven Canonical Hours were all connected with the events of our Lord's Passion, and supposed to commemorate His sufferings, as the following stanzas show: —

At *Mattins* bound, at *Prime* reviled,
  Condemned to death at *Tierce*,
Nailed to the Cross at *Sext*, at *Nones*
  His blessed side tﬂey pierce.

They take Him down at *Vesper-tide*,
  In grave at *Compline* lay;
Who thenceforth bids His Church observe
  Her sevenfold hours alway.

[1] The allusion is to the monastery at Bethlehem, where Cassian had himself been educated. See the Introduction.

[2] *Trinæ confessionis exemplo.* The words appear to mean that the three Psalms used at these offices are significant of the Persons of the Holy Trinity. So somewhat similarly Cyprian (on the Lord's Prayer) speaks of the third, sixth, and ninth hours being observed as a sacrament of the Trinity.

[3] Ps. cxviii. (cxix.) 164.

[4] This second "Mattins" of which Cassian has been speaking is the service which the later Church called Prime, Cassian's first Mattins corresponding to Lauds, and his Nocturns, or "Vigiliæ," to Mattins. Thus the "seven hours" are made up as follows: (1) Nocturns or Mattins, (2) Lauds, (3) Prime, (4) Tierce, (5) Sext, (6) None, (7) Vespers. Compline, it will be noticed, had not yet been introduced. This appears for the first time in the Rule of S. Benedict (c. xvi.), a century later. By its introduction the "day hours" were made up to seven, Nocturns belonging strictly to the night, and answering to the Psalmist's words, "At *midnight* will I rise to give thanks to Thee." Ps. cxix. 62.

[5] The introduction of Prime appears to have been very gradual, even in the West; for, though an office for it is prescribed in S. Benedict (c. xix.), yet there is no mention of it in the Rule of Cæsarius of Arles for monks, nor in that of Isidore of Seville, and it is omitted by Cassiodorus in his enumeration of the seven hours observed by the monks. After Benedict the next to mention it appears to be Aurelius, a successor of Cæsarius at Arles, and by degrees it made its way to universal adoption in the West. In the Greek Church the office for it is said continuously with Lauds (τὸ ὄρθρον).

[6] Book II. c. xiii.

our natural passions should be aroused and stain that purity of ours which was gained by humble confession and prayers before the dawn, or some illusion of the enemy pollute us, or even the repose of a pure and natural sleep interfere with the fervour of our spirit and make us lazy and slothful throughout the whole day, as we are chilled by the sluggishness caused by sleep. And to avoid this the Egyptians, and especially as they are in the habit of rising at fixed times even before the cock-crow, when the canonical office [1] has been celebrated, afterwards prolong their vigils even to daylight, that the morning light when it comes on them may find them established in fervour of spirit, and keep them still more careful and fervent all through the day, as it has found them prepared for the conflict and strengthened against their daily struggle with the devil by the practice of nocturnal vigils and spiritual meditation.

CHAPTER VI.

How no change was made by the Elders in the ancient system of Psalms when the Mattin office was instituted.

BUT this too we ought to know, viz., that no change was made in the ancient arrangement of Psalms by our Elders who decided that this Mattin service should be added; [2] but that office [3] was always celebrated in their nocturnal assemblies according to the same order as it had been before. For the hymns which in this country they used at the Mattin service at the close of the nocturnal vigils, which they are accustomed to finish after the cock-crowing and before dawn, these they still sing in like manner; viz., Ps. 148, beginning "O praise the Lord from heaven," and the rest which follow; but the 50th Psalm and the 62nd, and the 89th have, we know, been

---

[1] *Missa.*
[2] I.e., Prime. Some confusion is likely to be caused by the fact that Cassian speaks of both "Lauds" and "Prime" by the same title of Mattins. Immediately below, where he speaks of the "Mattin service at the close of the nocturnal vigils" he is referring to Lauds, which always followed immediately (or after a very short interval) after Nocturns, or Mattins. At this service Pss. cxlviii.–cl. have always been sung; indeed, they form the characteristic feature which gives the service its name of "Lauds" (οἱ αἶνοι). Of the other three Psalms, l. (li.), lxii. (lxiii.), and lxxxix. (xc.), which Cassian says had been transferred from Lauds to the newly instituted service of Prime, lxii. has been already spoken of as a morning hymn of the early Church (see the notes on c. iii.), and we learn from S. Basil that in his day Ps. l. (ὁ τῆς ἐξομολογήσεως ψαλμός) was regularly sung after Mattins when the day began to break (*Ep. ccvii. ad clericos Neo-Cæs.*), and it is still a Lauds Psalm in both East and West. lxxxix. (xc.) is now one of the fixed Psalms at Prime in the East, but in the West it is, according to the Roman rule, sung at Lauds on Thursdays only. Thus it would appear that the transfer of these three Psalms from Lauds to Prime, of which Cassian speaks, never obtained widely, but that the older arrangement, whereby, at any rate, l. and lxii. were assigned to Lauds, has generally been adhered to both in the East and West. Cf. the Rule of S. Benedict, according to which Ps. l. is sung daily at Lauds, and lxii. as well on Sundays (c. xii., xiii.).
[3] *Missa.*

---

assigned to this new service. Lastly, throughout Italy at this day, when the Mattin hymns are ended, the 50th Psalm is sung in all the churches, which I have no doubt can only have been derived from this source.

CHAPTER VII.

How one who does not come to the daily prayer before the end of the first Psalm is not allowed to enter the Oratory; but at Nocturns a late arrival up to the end of the second Psalm can be overlooked.

BUT one who at Tierce, Sext, or None has not come to prayer before the Psalm is begun and finished does not venture further to enter the Oratory nor to join himself to those singing the Psalms; but, standing outside, he awaits the breaking-up of the congregation,[4] and while they are all coming out does penance lying on the ground, and obtains absolution for his carelessness and lateness, knowing that he can in no other way expiate the fault of his sloth, nor can ever be admitted to the service which will follow three hours later, unless he has been quick to make satisfaction at once for his present negligence by the help of true humility. But in the nocturnal assemblies a late arrival up to the *second* Psalm is allowed, provided that before the Psalm is finished and the brethren bow down in prayer he makes haste to take his place in the congregation and join them; but he will most certainly be subjected to the same blame and penance which we mentioned before if he has delayed ever so little beyond the hour permitted for a late arrival.[5]

CHAPTER VIII.

Of the Vigil service which is celebrated on the evening preceding the Sabbath; of its length, and the manner in which it is observed.

IN the winter time, however, when the nights are longer, the Vigils,[6] which are celebrated every week on the evening at the commencing the Sabbath, are arranged by the elders in the monasteries to last till the fourth cock-crow-

---

[4] *Congregationis missam.*
[5] The Rule of S. Benedict has similar provisions, allowing a late arrival at Mattins till the Gloria after the Venite (the second Psalm, as it is preceded by Ps. iii.), and at the other services till the Gloria after the first Psalm. "If any come later than this, he is not to take his usual place in the choir, but stand last of all, or take whatever place the Abbot may have appointed for those who are guilty of a similar neglect, so that he may be seen of all; and in this place he is to remain until he shall have made public satisfaction, at the end of the office. We deem it necessary," the Rule proceeds, "to place such offenders thus apart, that, being thus exposed to the view of all their brethren, they may be shamed into a sense of duty. Moreover, if such were allowed to remain outside the church, they might either sit down at their ease, or while away their time in chatting, or perhaps return to the dormitory and compose themselves to sleep, and thus expose themselves to the temptations of the enemy." Rule of S. Benedict, c. xliii.
[6] *Vigiliæ* is here used as the equivalent of Nocturns.

ing, for this reason, viz., that after the watch through the whole night they may, by resting their bodies for the remaining time of nearly two hours, avoid flagging through drowsiness the whole day long, and be content with repose for this short time instead of resting the whole night. And it is proper for us, too, to observe this with the utmost care, that we may be content with the sleep which is allowed us after the office of Vigils up to daybreak, — i.e., till the Mattin Psalms,[1] — and afterwards spend the whole day in work and necessary duties, lest through weariness from the Vigils, and feebleness, we might be forced to take by day the sleep which we cut off from the night, and so be thought not to have cut short our bodily rest so much as to have changed our time for repose and nightly retirement. For our feeble flesh could not possibly be defrauded of the whole night's rest and yet keep its vigour unshaken throughout the following day without sleepiness of mind and heaviness of spirit, as it will be hindered rather than helped by this unless after Vigils are over it enjoys a short slumber. And, therefore, if, as we have suggested, at least an hour's sleep is snatched before daybreak, we shall save all the hours of Vigils which we have spent all through the night in prayer, granting to nature what is due to it, and having no necessity of taking back by day what we have cut off from the night. For a man will certainly have to give up everything to this flesh if he tries, not in a rational manner to withhold a part only, but to refuse the whole, and (to speak candidly) is anxious to cut off not what is superfluous but what is necessary. Wherefore Vigils have to be made up for with greater interest if they are prolonged with ill-considered and unreasonable length till daybreak. And so they divide them into an office in three parts, that by this variety the effort may be distributed and the exhaustion of the body relieved by some agreeable relaxation. For when standing they have sung three Psalms antiphonally,[2] after this, sitting on the ground or in very low stalls, one of them repeats three Psalms, while the rest respond, each Psalm being assigned to one of the brethren, who succeed each other in turn; and to these they add three lessons while still sitting quietly. And so, by lessening their bodily exertion, they manage to observe their Vigils with greater attention of mind.[3]

CHAPTER IX.

The reason why a Vigil is appointed as the Sabbath day dawns, and why a dispensation from fasting is enjoyed on the Sabbath all through the East.

AND throughout the whole of the East it has been settled, ever since the time of the preaching of the Apostles, when the Christian faith and religion was founded, that these Vigils should be celebrated as the Sabbath dawns,[4] for this reason, — because, when our Lord and Saviour had been crucified on the sixth day of the week, the disciples, overwhelmed by the freshness of His sufferings, remained watching throughout the whole night, giving no rest or sleep to their eyes. Wherefore, since that time, a service of Vigils has been appointed for this night, and is stillt observed in the same way up to the presene day all through the East. And so, after the exertion of the Vigil, a dispensation from fasting, appointed in like manner for the Sabbath by apostolic men,[5] is not without reason enjoined in all the churches of the East, in accordance with that saying of Ecclesiastes, which, although it has another and a mystical sense, is not misapplied to this, by which we are charged to give to both days — that is, to the seventh and eighth equally — the same share of the service, as it says: "Give a portion to these seven and also to these eight."[6] For this dispensation from fasting must not be understood as a participation in the Jewish festival by those above all who are shown to be free from all Jewish superstition, but as contributing to that rest of the wearied body of which we have spoken; which, as it fasts continually for five days in the week all through the year, would easily be worn out and fail, unless it were revived by an interval of at least two days.

---

[1] I.e., the office of Lauds.
[2] *Tria Antiphona.* The word is here used (as above, II. c. ii.), not in the modern sense of antiphon, but to denote a Psalm or Psalms sung antiphonally.
[3] In this chapter Cassian describes two of the different methods of Psalmody employed in the ancient Church: (1) Antiphonal singing, where the congregation was divided into two parts, or choirs, which sang alternate verses; (2) the method according to which one

voice alone sang the first part of the verse, and the rest of the congregation joined in at the close. Both methods are described in a well-known passage in an Epistle of S. Basil (*Ep. ccvii. ad clericos Neocæs*), where he tells us that in the morning service, at one time, the people divide themselves into two parties, and sing antiphonally to each other (ἀντιψάλλουσιν ἀλλήλοις), while at another time they entrust to one person the duty of beginning the strain, and the rest respond (ὑπηχοῦσι). This latter method seems to have been a very favourite one, the Psalms which were thus sung being called *Responsoria*. See Isidore, *De Offic.*, i. 8; and compare the *Dictionary of Christian Antiquities*, Vol. II. p. 1745; and Bingham, *Antiquities*, Book XIV. c. i. A third method has been already described by Cassian in Book II. c. xi.; viz., that called *Tractus*, where the Psalm was executed by a single voice, while all the rest of the congregation listened.
[4] The observance of a vigil for the whole or greater part of the night was a regular part of the preparation for the greater festivals, and as such was usual in the East before the Sabbath (Saturday) and Lord's Day, as well as Pentecost and Easter. See Socrates, H. E., VI. viii., where there is an allusion to this.
[5] Saturday, as well as Sunday, was long regarded as a festival in the East, and, indeed, originally in most churches of the West as well. See the *Apost. Const.* II. lix. 1; VIII. xxxiii. 1. *Apost. Canons* lxvi.; Council of Laodicæa, Canons xvi., xlix., li.
[6] Eccl. xi. 2.

CHAPTER X.

How it was brought about that they fast on the Sabbath in the city.

BUT some people in some countries of the West, and especially in the city,[1] not knowing the reason of this indulgence, think that a dispensation from fasting ought certainly not to be allowed on the Sabbath, because they say that on this day the Apostle Peter fasted before his encounter with Simon.[2] But from this it is quite clear that he did this not in accordance with a canonical rule, but rather through the needs of his impending struggle. Since there, too, for the same purpose, Peter seems to have imposed on his disciples not a general but a special fast, which he certainly would not have done if he had known that it was wont to be observed by canonical rule; just as he would surely have been ready to appoint it even on Sunday, if the occasion of his struggle had fallen upon it: but no canonical rule of fasting would have been made general from this, because it was no general observance that led to it, but a matter of necessity, which forced it to be observed on a single occasion.

CHAPTER XI.

Of the points in which the service held on Sunday differs from what is customary on other days.

BUT we ought to know this, too, that on Sunday only one office[3] is celebrated before dinner, at which, out of regard for the actual service[4] and the Lord's communion, they use

a more solemn and a longer service of Psalms and prayers and lessons, and so consider that Tierce and Sext are included in it. And hence it results that, owing to the addition of the lessons, there is no diminution of the amount of their devotions, and yet some difference is made, and an indulgence over other times seems to be granted to the brethren out of reverence for the Lord's resurrection; and this seems to lighten the observance all through the week, and, by reason of the difference which is interposed, it makes the day to be looked forward to more solemnly as a festival, and owing to the anticipation of it the fasts of the coming week are less felt. For any weariness is always borne with greater equanimity, and labour undertaken without aversion, if some variety is interposed or change of work succeeds.

CHAPTER XII.

Of the days on which, when supper is provided for the brethren, a Psalm is not said as they assemble for the meal, as is usual at dinner.

LASTLY, also, on those days,— i. e., on Saturday and Sunday, — and on holy days, on which it is usual for both dinner and supper to be provided for the brethren, a Psalm is not said in the evening, either when they come to supper or when they rise from it, as is usual at their ordinary dinner[5] and the canonical refreshment on fast days, which the customary Psalms usually precede and follow. But they simply make a plain prayer and come to supper, and again, when they rise from it, conclude with prayer alone; because this repast is something special among the monks: nor are they all obliged to come to it, but it is only for strangers who have come to see the brethren, and those whom bodily weakness or their own inclination invites to it.

---

[1] Viz., Rome.

[2] The Saturday fast was observed at Rome in very early days, being noticed by Tertullian, who seems to suggest that it originated in the prolongation of the Friday fast (*on Fasting*, c. xiv). But it seems to have been almost peculiar to Rome, and at Milan, in the time of S. Ambrose, the Eastern custom prevailed. See the important letter of Augustine to Casulanus (*Ep.* xxxvi.), where the whole subject of the difference of usage on this matter is fully discussed. The reason here given by Cassian for the origin of the local Roman custom (viz., that S. Peter's traditional encounter with Simon Magus took place on Sunday, and was prepared for by the apostle with a Saturday fast) is also there alluded to by Augustine as being the opinion of very many, though he tells us candidly that most of the Romans thought it false. "Est quidem et hæc opinio plurimorum, quamvis eam perhibeant esse falsam plerique Romani, quod Apostolus Petrus cum Simone Mago die dominico certaturo, propter ipsum magnæ tentationis periculum, pridie cum ejusdem urbis ecclesia jejunaverit, et consecuto tam prospero gloriosoque successu, eundem morem tenuerit, eumque imitatæ sunt nonnullæ Occidentis ecclesiæ." Cf. also Augustine, *Ep. ad Januarium*, liv.

[3] *Missa.*

[4] *Collecta.* This word, from which our word "Collect" is possibly derived, is used for an assembly for worship in the Vulgate in Lev. xxiii. 36; Deut. xvi. 8; 2 Chron. vii. 9; Neh. viii. 18: and compare the phrase, "Ad Collectam," in the Sacramentary of Gregory for the Feast of the Purification.

[5] In *sollemnibus prandiis.* The phrase must here refer to their dinner on ordinary days (cf. solemnitatem ciborum, "their usual food," Book IV. c. xxi.). Among the early monks it was the custom ordinarily to have but one meal a day on the fast days (viz., Wednesday and Friday); this was at the ninth hour; on other days, at the sixth (i.e., midday). Cf. the Conferences XXI. c. xxiii. On festivals (viz., Saturday, Sunday, and holy days), beside the midday meal, a supper was allowed as well. And on these days, as we learn from the passage before us, the ordinary grace before and after meat was shortened by the omission of the customary Psalms at other times included in it. On the meals of the monks, cf. S. Jerome's Preface to the Rule of Pachomius and the Rule of S. Benedict, cc. xxxix.-xli., the former of which tells us that, except on Wednesday and Friday, dinner was at midday, and a table was also set for labourers, old men, and children, and (apparently) for all, in the height of summer. For the use of Psalms at grace, see Clement of Alexandria, *Pædag.* II. iv. 44; *Stromateis* VII. vii. 49.

BOOK IV.

OF THE INSTITUTES OF THE RENUNCIANTS.

CHAPTER I.

Of the training of those who renounce this world, and of the way in which those are taught among the monks of Tabenna and the Egyptians who are received into the monasteries.

FROM the canonical system of Psalms and prayers which ought to be observed in the daily services throughout the monasteries, we pass, in the due course of our narrative, to the training of one who renounces this world; endeavouring first, as well as we can, to embrace, in a short account, the terms on which those who desire to turn to the Lord can be received in the monasteries; adding some things from the rule of the Egyptians, some from that of the monks of Tabenna,[1] whose monastery in the Thebaid is better filled as regards numbers, as it is stricter in the rigour of its system, than all others, for there are in it more than five thousand brethren under the rule of one Abbot; and the obedience with which the whole number of monks is at all times subject to one Elder is what no one among us would render to another even for a short time, or would demand from him.

CHAPTER II.

Of the way in which among them men remain in the monasteries even to extreme old age.

AND I think that before anything else we ought to touch on their untiring perseverance and humility and subjection,— how it lasts for so long, and by what system it is formed, through which they remain in the monasteries till they are bent double with old age; for it is so great that we cannot recollect any one who joined our monasteries keeping it up unbroken even for a year: so that when we have seen the beginning of their renunciation of the world, we shall understand how it came about that, starting from such a commencement, they reached such a height of perfection.

CHAPTER III.

Of the ordeal by which one who is to be received in the monastery is tested.

ONE, then, who seeks to be admitted to the discipline of the monastery is never received before he gives, by lying outside the doors for ten days or even longer, an evidence of his perseverance and desire, as well as of humility and patience. And when, prostrate at the feet of all the brethren that pass by, and of set purpose repelled and scorned by all of them, as if he was wanting to enter the monastery not for the sake of religion but because he was obliged; and when, too, covered with many insults and affronts, he has given a practical proof of his steadfastness, and has shown what he will be like in temptations by the way he has borne the disgrace; and when, with the ardour of his soul thus ascertained, he is admitted, then they enquire with the utmost care whether he is contaminated by a single coin from his former possessions clinging to him. For they know that he cannot stay for long under the discipline of the monastery, nor ever learn the virtue of humility and obedience, nor be content with the poverty and difficult life of the monastery, if he knows that ever so small a sum of money has been kept hid; but, as soon as ever a disturbance arises on some occasion or other, he will at once dart off from the monastery like a stone from a sling, impelled to this by trusting in that sum of money.[2]

CHAPTER IV.

The reason why those who are received in the monastery are not allowed to bring anything in with them.

AND for these reasons they do not agree to take from him money to be used even for the

---

[1] Tabenna, or Tabennæ, was an island in the Nile, where was founded a flourishing monastery by Pachomius c. 330 A.D. Of Pachomius there is a notice in Sozomen H. E., Book III. c. xiv., and his Rule was translated into Latin, with a preface by S. Jerome, who mentions his fame in *Ep.* cxxvii. There is a Life of Pachomius given by Rosweyde (*Vitae Patrum*), which is said to be a translation of a work by a contemporary of his.

[2] Cf. the Rule of Pachomius, c. xxvi.: "If any one comes to the door of the monastery wanting to renounce the world, and to join the number of the brethren, he shall not be allowed to enter, but the Abbot of the monastery must first be told, and he shall stay for a few days outside before the gate, and shall be taught the Lord's Prayer, and as many Psalms as he can learn, and shall diligently give proof of himself that he has not done any thing wrong and fled in trouble for the time, and that he is not in any one's power, and that he can forsake his relations and disregard his property. And if they see that he is apt for everything, then he shall be taught the rest of the rules of the monastery,— what he ought to do, whom he is to obey," etc.; and, finally, he is to be admitted, See also the Rule of S. Benedict, c. lviii., which is to much the same effect; and S. Basil's *Longer Monastic Rules*, Q. x.

good of the monastery: First, in case he may be puffed up with arrogance, owing to this offering, and so not deign to put himself on a level with the poorer brethren; and next, lest he fail through this pride of his to stoop to the humility of Christ, and so, when he cannot hold out under the discipline of the monastery, leave it, and afterwards, when he has cooled down, want in a bad spirit to receive and get back — not without loss to the monastery — what he had contributed in the early days of his renunciation, when he was aglow with spiritual fervour. And that this rule should always be kept they have been frequently taught by many instances. For in some monasteries where they are not so careful some who have been received unreservedly have afterwards tried most sacrilegiously to demand a return of that which they had contributed and which had been spent on God's work.

CHAPTER V.

The reason why those who give up the world, when they are received in the monasteries, must lay aside their own clothes and be clothed in others by the Abbot.

WHEREFORE each one on his admission is stripped of all his former possessions, so that he is not allowed any longer to keep even the clothes which he has on his back: but in the council of the brethren he is brought forward into the midst and stripped of his own clothes, and clad by the Abbot's hands in the dress of the monastery, so that by this he may know not only that he has been despoiled of all his old things, but also that he has laid aside all worldly pride, and come down to the want and poverty of Christ, and that he is now to be supported not by wealth sought for by the world's arts, nor by anything reserved from his former state of unbelief, but that he is to receive out of the holy and sacred funds of the monastery his rations for his service; and that, as he knows that he is thence to be clothed and fed and that he has nothing of his own, he may learn, nevertheless, not to be anxious about the morrow, according to the saying of the Gospel, and may not be ashamed to be on a level with the poor, that is with the body of the brethren, with whom Christ was not ashamed to be numbered, and to call himself their brother, but that rather he may glory that he has been made to share the lot of his own servants.[1]

---

[1] So the Rule of Pachomius (c. xxvi.) orders that on the admission of a monk "they shall strip him of his secular dress, and put on him the garb of the monks;" and that of S. Benedict (c. lviii.), "He shall then be clothed in the religious habit, and his secular clothes deposited in the wardrobe, that if, at the instigation of the devil, he should ever leave the monastery, they may be given back to him, and the religious dress be taken from him."

CHAPTER VI.

The reason why the clothes of the renunciants with which they joined the monastery are preserved by the steward.

BUT those clothes, which he laid aside, are consigned to the care of the steward and kept until by different sorts of temptations and trials they can recognize the excellence of his progress and life and endurance. And if they see that he can continue therein as time goes on, and remain in that fervour with which he began, they give them away to the poor. But if they find that he has been guilty of any fault of murmuring, or of even the smallest piece of disobedience, then they strip off from him the dress of the monastery in which he had been clad, and reclothe him in his old garments which had been confiscated, and send him away.[2] For it is not right for him to go away with those which he had received, nor do they allow any one to be any longer dressed in them if they have seen him once grow cold in regard to the rule of their institution. Wherefore, also, the opportunity of going out openly is not given to any one, unless he escapes like a runaway slave by taking advantage of the thickest shades of night, or is judged unworthy of this order and profession and lays aside the dress of the monastery and is expelled with shame and disgrace before all the brethren.

CHAPTER VII.

The reason why those who are admitted to a monastery are not permitted to mix at once with the congregation of the brethren, but are first committed to the guest house.

WHEN, then, any one has been received and proved by that persistence of which we have spoken, and, laying aside his own garments, has been clad in those of the monastery, he is not allowed to mix at once with the congregation of the brethren, but is given into the charge of an Elder, who lodges apart not far from the entrance of the monastery, and is entrusted with the care of strangers and guests, and bestows all his diligence in receiving them kindly. And when he has served there for a whole year without any complaint, and has given evidence of service towards strangers,[3] being thus initiated in the first rudiments

---

[2] See the quotation from the Rule of S. Benedict in the note on the last chapter.

[3] In the same way the Rule of S. Benedict (c. lviii.) directs that the novice is to be placed in the guest house for a few days, while that of S. Isidore is more precise in ordering him to be placed there "for three months," and to wait on the guests there. Two months is the period fixed by other rules, but a few days was all that was ultimately required, and Cassian stands alone in mentioning a full year as the duration of this service, though Sozomen speaks of the monks of Tabenna as having to undergo a probation of three years. H. E., III. xiv.

of humility and patience, and by long practice in it acknowledged, when he is to be admitted from this into the congregation of the brethren he is handed over to another Elder, who is placed over ten of the juniors, who are entrusted to him by the Abbot, and whom he both teaches and governs in accordance with the arrangement which we read of in Exodus as made by Moses.[1]

CHAPTER VIII.

Of the practices in which the juniors are first exercised that they may become proficient in overcoming all their desires.

AND his anxiety and the chief part of his instruction — through which the juniors brought to him may be able in due course to mount to the greatest heights of perfection — will be to teach him first to conquer his own wishes; and, anxiously and diligently practising him in this, he will of set purpose contrive to give him such orders as he knows to be contrary to his liking; for, taught by many examples, they say that a monk, and especially the younger ones, cannot bridle the desire of his concupiscence unless he has first learnt by obedience to mortify his wishes. And so they lay it down that the man who has not first learnt to overcome his desires cannot possibly stamp out anger or sulkiness, or the spirit of fornication; nor can he preserve true humility of heart, or lasting unity with the brethren, or a stable and continuous concord; nor remain for any length of time in the monastery.

CHAPTER IX.

The reason why the juniors are enjoined not to keep back any of their thoughts from the senior.

BY these practices, then, they hasten to impress and instruct those whom they are training with the alphabet, as it were, and first syllables in the direction of perfection, as they can clearly see by these whether they are grounded in a false and imaginary or in a true humility. And, that they may easily arrive at this, they are next taught not to conceal by a false shame any itching thoughts in their hearts, but, as soon as ever such arise, to lay them bare to the senior, and, in forming a judgment about them, not to trust anything to their own discretion, but to take it on trust that that is good or bad which is considered

and pronounced so by the examination of the senior. Thus it results that our cunning adversary cannot in any way circumvent a young and inexperienced monk, or get the better of his ignorance, or by any craft deceive one whom he sees to be protected not by his own discretion but by that of his senior, and who cannot be persuaded to hide from his senior those suggestions of his which like fiery darts he has shot into his heart; since the devil, subtle as he is, cannot ruin or destroy a junior unless he has enticed him either through pride or through shame to conceal his thoughts. For they lay it down as an universal and clear proof that a thought is from the devil if we are ashamed to disclose it to the senior.[2]

CHAPTER X.

How thorough is the obedience of the juniors even in those things which are matters of common necessity.

NEXT, the rule is kept with such strict obedience that, without the knowledge and permission of their superior, the juniors not only do not dare to leave their cell but on their own authority do not venture to satisfy their common and natural needs. And so they are quick to fulfil without any discussion all those things that are ordered by him, as if they were commanded by God from heaven;[3] so that sometimes, when impossibilities are commanded them, they undertake them with such faith and devotion as to strive with all their powers and without the slightest hesitation to fulfil them and carry them out; and out of reverence for their senior they do not even consider whether a command is an impossibility.[4] But of their obedience I omit at present to speak more particularly, for we propose to speak of it in the proper place a little later on, with instances of it, if through your prayers the Lord carry us safely through. We now proceed to the other regulations, passing over all account of those which cannot be imposed on

---

[1] Cf. Exod. xviii. 25. The office of "Dean" (Decanus), which is here spoken of by Cassian, is also referred to by Augustine (*De Mor. Eccl.* xxxi.) and Jerome (*Ep.* xxii. *ad Eustoch.*), and recognized by the Rule of S. Benedict, c. xxi., where directions for his appointment are given.

[2] Compare the Conferences, Book II. c. x., where Cassian returns to the same subject. A similar rule that the brethren are to lay bare all the secrets of their hearts to their superior is given by S. Basil in the Longer Monastic Rules, Q. xxvi., and in the Rule of S. Isaiah (cc. vi., xliii.), printed in Holsten's *Codex Regularum*, Vol. I.
[3] Cf. the Rule of S. Benedict, c. v., where it is said that "the first degree of humility is ready obedience. This is peculiar to those who . . . prefer nothing to Christ, and fulfil the injunctions of their superiors as promptly as if God Himself had given them the command," etc.
[4] The Rule of S. Benedict has a chapter to explain what is to be done if a brother is commanded to perform impossibilities (c. lxviii.). "If a brother is commanded to do anything that is difficult, or even impossible, let him receive the command with all meekness and obedience; meanwhile, should he see that he is utterly unequal to the task laid upon him, let him represent the matter to his superior calmly and respectfully, without pride, resistance, or contradiction. If the superior, after hearing what he has to say, still insists on the execution of the command, let the junior be persuaded that it is for his spiritual good, and accordingly, trusting in God's assistance, let him for His love undertake the work."

or kept in the monasteries in this country, as we promised to do in our Preface; for instance, how they never use woollen garments, but only cotton, and these not double, changes of which each superior gives out to the ten monks under his care when he sees that those which they are wearing are dirty.

CHAPTER XI.

The kind of food which is considered the greatest delicacy by them.

I PASS over, too, that difficult and sublime sort of self-control, through which it is considered the greatest luxury if the plant called cherlock,[1] prepared with salt and steeped in water, is set on the table for the repast of the brethren; and many other things like this, which in this country neither the climate nor the weakness of our constitution would permit. And I shall only follow up those matters which cannot be interfered with by any weakness of the flesh or local situation, if only no weakness of mind or coldness of spirit gets rid of them.

CHAPTER XII.

How they leave off every kind of work at the sound of some one knocking at the door, in their eagerness to answer at once.

AND SO, sitting in their cells and devoting their energies equally to work and to meditation, when they hear the sound of some one knocking at the door and striking on the cells of each, summoning them to prayer or some work, every one eagerly dashes out from his cell, so that one who is practising the writer's art, although he may have just begun to form a letter, does not venture to finish it, but runs out with the utmost speed, at the very moment when the sound of the knocking reaches his ears, without even waiting to finish the letter he has begun; but, leaving the lines of the letter incomplete, he aims not at abridging and saving his labour, but rather hastens with the utmost earnestness and zeal to attain the virtue of obedience, which they put not merely before manual labour and reading and silence and quietness in the cell, but even before all virtues, so that they consider that everything should be postponed to it, and are content to undergo any amount of inconvenience if only it may be seen that they have in no way neglected this virtue.[2]

CHAPTER XIII.

How wrong it is considered for any one to say that anything, however trifling, is his own.

AMONG their other practices I fancy that it is unnecessary even to mention this virtue, viz., that no one is allowed to possess a box or basket as his special property, nor any such thing which he could keep as his own and secure with his own seal, as we are well aware that they are in all respects stripped so bare that they have nothing whatever except their shirt, cloak, shoes, sheepskin, and rush mat;[3] for in other monasteries as well, where some indulgence and relaxation is granted, we see that this rule is still most strictly kept, so that no one ventures to say even in word that anything is his own: and it is a great offence if there drops from the mouth of a monk such an expression as "my book," "my tablets," "my pen," "my coat," or "my shoes;" and for this he would have to make satisfaction by a proper penance, if by accident some such expression escaped his lips through thoughtlessness or ignorance.

CHAPTER XIV.

How, even if a large sum of money is amassed by the labour of each, still no one may venture to exceed the moderate limit of what is appointed as adequate.

AND although each one of them may bring in daily by his work and labour so great a return to the monastery that he could out of it not only satisfy his own moderate demands but could also abundantly supply the wants of many, yet he is no way puffed up, nor does he flatter himself on account of his toil and this large gain from his labour, but, except two biscuits,[4] which are sold there for scarcely threepence, no one thinks that he has a right to anything further. And among them there is nothing (and I am ashamed to say this, and heartily wish it was unknown in our own monasteries) which is claimed by any of them, I will not say in deed but even in thought, as

---

[1] *Labsanion.* Cf. below, c. xxiii., where cherlock is mentioned again, together with other delicacies (!) of the Egyptians.

[2] Cf. the Rule of S. Benedict, c. v.: "Those who choose to tread the path that leads to life eternal immediately quit their private occupations at the call of obedience, and, renouncing their own will so far as to cast away unfinished out of their hands whatever they may be occupied with, hasten to execute the orders of their superiors," etc.

[3] *Psiathium.* The rush mats which served as a seat by day and a bed by night for the monks. See Book V. xxxv., and the Conferences I. xxiii.; XV. i.; XVII. iii.; XVIII. xi. S. Jerome mentions it in his preface to the Rule of Pachomius as one of the very few articles contained in the cells of the monks of Tabenna. "They have nothing in their cells except a mat and what is described below: two 'lebitonaria,' a kind of garment without sleeves which the Egyptian monks use (the colobium, or shirt), one old one for sleeping or working, a linen garment and two hoods, a sheepskin, a linen girdle, shoes, and a staff."

[4] *Paxamatium,* a biscuit. The word comes from the Greek παξαμάδιον, and is said to be derived from the name of a baker, Παξαμός (see Liddell and Scott, c. v.). These biscuits formed an important part of the diet of the Egyptian monks, as we see from the Conferences, where they are often mentioned; e.g., II. xi., xix., xxiv., xxvi.; XII. xv.; XIX. iv.

his special property. And though he believes that the whole granary of the monastery forms his substance, and, as lord of all, devotes his whole care and energy to it all, yet nevertheless, in order to maintain that excellent state of want and poverty which he has secured and which he strives to preserve to the very last in unbroken perfection, he regards himself as a foreigner and an alien to them all, so that he conducts himself as a stranger and a sojourner in this world, and considers himself a pupil of the monastery and a servant instead of imagining that he is lord and master of anything.

CHAPTER XV.

Of the excessive desire of possession among us.

To this what shall we wretched creatures say, who though living in Cœnobia and established under the government and care of an Abbot yet carry about our own keys, and trampling under foot all feeling of shame and disgrace which should spring from our profession, are not ashamed actually to wear openly upon our fingers rings with which to seal what we have stored up; and in whose case not merely boxes and baskets, but not even chests and closets are sufficient for those things which we collect or which we reserved when we forsook the world; and who sometimes get so angry over trifles and mere nothings (to which however we lay claim as if they were our own) that if any one dares to lay a finger on any of them, we are so filled with rage against him that we cannot keep the wrath of our heart from being expressed on our lips and in bodily excitement. But, passing by our faults and treating with silence those things of which it is a shame even to speak, according to this saying: " My mouth shall not speak the deeds of men," [1] let us in accordance with the method of our narration which we have begun proceed to those virtues which are practised among them, and which we ought to aim at with all earnestness; and let us briefly and hastily set down the actual rules and systems that afterwards, coming to some of the deeds and acts of the elders which we propose carefully to preserve for recollection, we may support by the strongest testimonies what we have set forth in our treatise, and still further confirm everything that we have said by examples and instances from life.

CHAPTER XVI.

On the rules for various rebukes.

IF then any one by accident breaks an earthenware jar (which they call " baucalis "), he can only expiate his carelessness by public penance; and when all the brethren are assembled for service he must lie on the ground and ask for absolution until the service of the prayers is finished; and will obtain it when by the Abbot's command he is bidden to rise from the ground. The same satisfaction must be given by one who when summoned to some work or to the usual service comes rather late, or who when singing a Psalm hesitates ever so little. Similarly if he answers unnecessarily or roughly or impertinently, if he is careless in carrying out the services enjoined to him, if he makes a slight complaint, if preferring reading to work or obedience he is slow in performing his appointed duties, if when service is over he does not make haste to go back at once to his cell, if he stops for ever so short a time with some one else, if he goes anywhere else even for a moment, if he takes any one else by the hand, if he ventures to discuss anything however small with one who is not the joint-occupant of his cell, [2] if he prays with one who is suspended from prayer, if he sees any of his relations or friends in the world and talks with them without his senior, if he tries to receive a letter from any one or to write back without his Abbot's leave. [3] To such an extent does spiritual censure proceed and in such matters and faults like these. But as for other things which when indiscriminately committed among us are treated by us too as blameworthy, viz. : open wrangling, manifest contempt, arrogant contradictions, going out from the monastery freely and without check, familiarity with women, wrath, quarrelling, jealousies, disputes, claiming something as

---

[1] Ps. xvi. (xvii.) 4.
[2] From this passage we gather that in Egypt *two monks* were often the joint occupants of a single cell. Cf. II. xii. and Conference XX. i., ii.

[3] Many of these faults are noticed in the Rule of Pachomius as deserving censure e.g., unpunctuality at or carelessness in service (c. viii. ix.), breaking anything (c. cxxv.), murmuring (lxxxvii.), taking the hand of another (xliv.). So also in the Rule of S. Benedict (cc. xliii.–xlvi.) similar directions are given, while in c. xliv. the nature of the penance is more fully described. He who in punishment of a grievous fault has been excluded from the Refectory and the Church, shall lie prostrate at the door of the latter at the end of each office, and shall there remain in silence with his forehead touching the ground, until the brethren retiring from church have all walked over him. This penance he shall continue to perform till it be commanded by the Abbot to appear before him, he shall go and cast himself at his feet and then at the feet of all the brethren, begging of them to pray for him. He shall then be admitted to the choir, if the Abbot so order, and shall take there whatever place he may assign him : but let him not presume to intone a Psalm, read a lesson or perform any similar duty, without the special permission of the Abbot. He shall, moreover, prostrate himself in his place in choir at the end of every office, until the Abbot tells him to discontinue this penance. Those who for light faults are excluded merely from the common table, shall make satisfaction in the church according as the Abbot shall direct, and shall continue to do so until he gives them his blessing and tells them that they have made sufficient atonement.

one's own property, the infection of covetousness, the desire and acquisition of unnecessary things which are not possessed by the rest of the brethren, taking food between meals and by stealth, and things like these — they are dealt with not by that spiritual censure of which we spoke, but by stripes; or are atoned for by expulsion.

CHAPTER XVII.

Of those who introduced the plan that the holy Lessons should be read in the Cœnobia while the brethren are eating, and of the strict silence which is kept among the Egyptians.

BUT we have been informed that the plan that, while the brethren are eating, the holy lessons should be read in the Cœnobia did not originate in the Egyptian system but in the Cappadocian. And there is no doubt that they meant to establish it not so much for the sake of the spiritual exercise as for the sake of putting a stop to unnecessary and idle conversation, and especially discussions, which so often arise at meals; since they saw that these could not be prevented among them in any other way.[1] For among the Egyptians and especially those of Tabenna so strict a silence is observed by all that when so large a number of the brethren has sat down together to a meal, no one ventures to talk even in a low tone except the dean, who however if he sees that anything is wanted to be put on or taken off the table, signifies it by a sign rather than a word. And while they are eating, the rule of this silence is so strictly kept that with their hoods drawn down over their eyelids (to prevent their roving looks having the opportunity of wandering inquisitively) they can see nothing except the table, and the food that is put on it, and which they take from it; so that no one notices what another is eating.[2]

CHAPTER XVIII.

How it is against the rule for any one to take anything to eat or drink except at the common table.

IN between their regular meals in common they are especially careful that no one should presume to gratify his palate with any food:[3] so that when they are walking casually through gardens or orchards, when the fruit hanging enticingly on the trees not only knocks against their breasts as they pass through, but is also lying on the ground and offering itself to be trampled under foot, and (as it is all ready to be gathered) would easily be able to entice those who see it to gratify their appetite, and by the chance offered to them and the quantity of the fruit, to excite even the most severe and abstemious to long for it; still they consider it wrong not merely to taste a single fruit, but even to touch one with the hand, except what is put on the table openly for the common meal of all, and supplied publicly by the steward's catering through the service of the brethren, for their enjoyment.

CHAPTER XIX.

How throughout Palestine and Mesopotamia a daily service is undertaken by the brethren.

IN order that we may not appear to omit any of the Institutes of the Cœnobia I think that it should be briefly mentioned that in other countries as well there is a daily service undertaken by the brethren. For throughout the whole of Mesopotamia, Palestine, and Cappadocia and all the East the brethren succeed one another in turn every week for the performance of certain duties, so that the number serving is told off according to the whole number of monks in the Cœnobium. And they hasten to fulfil these duties with a zeal and humility such as no slave bestows on his service even to a most harsh and powerful master; so that not satisfied only with these services which are rendered by canonical rule, they actually rise by night in their zeal and relieve those whose special duty this is; and secretly anticipating them try to finish those duties which these others would have to do. But each one who undertakes these weeks is on duty and has to serve until supper on

---

[1] It is quite in keeping with what is here said by Cassian that in the Rule of Pachomius there is no mention of reading at meals, but only of the strict silence observed, so that anything wanted might not be asked for but only indicated by a sign (cc. xxxi., xxxiii.), while in the shorter Monastic Rules of S. Basil the custom of reading at meals is distinctly alluded to (Q. clxxx.). It is of course also ordered in most of the later monastic rules, e.g. that of Cesarius of Arles "ad Monachos" c. xlix., "ad Virgines" c. xvi.; that of S. Aurelian, c. xlix.; S. Isidore, c. x., and S. Benedict, c. xxxviii. The regulations in the last mentioned are as follows: — "A book should be read in the Refectory while the brethren are at meals. Let no one presume to read of his own accord; but let there be one appointed to perform that duty, who, commencing on Sunday, will read during the entire week. . . Profound silence shall be observed during meals, so that no voice save that of the reader may be heard. The brethren will so help each other to what is necessary as regards food and drink that no one may have occasion to ask for anything; should, however, anything be wanted, let it be asked for by sign rather than word. Let no one presume to make any observation either on what is being read or on any other subject, lest occasion be given to the enemy. The Prior, however, should he think fit, may say a few words to edify the brethren."
[2] So Pachomius (c. xxix.). While they are eating they shall sit in their right places and shall cover their heads.

[3] Similarly we find in the Rule of Pachomius that no one is allowed to keep any food in his cell besides what he receives from the steward (c. lxxix.); and the Benedictine Rule also says: "Let no one presume to take any food or drink out of the regular hours of meals" (c. xliii). Cf. also the Rule of Pachomius cc. lxxv. and lxxviii., S. Basil's longer Monastic Rules Q. xv., Ἅψατο βρωμάτων παρὰ καιρόν; ἐπὶ πλεῖστον τῆς ἡμέρας ἀπόσιτος ἔστω, the Rule of Aurelian (c. lii.), that of Isidore (c. xiii.), etc.

Sunday, and when this is done, his duty for the whole week is finished, so that, when all the brethren come together to chant the Psalms (which according to custom they sing before going to bed) those whose turn is over wash the feet of all in turn, seeking faithfully from them the reward of this blessing for their work during the whole week, that the prayers offered up by all the brethren together may accompany them as they fulfil the command of Christ, the prayer, to wit, that intercedes for their ignorances and for their sins committed through human frailty, and may commend to God the complete service of their devotion like some rich offering. And so on Monday after the Mattin hymns they hand over to others who take their place the vessels and utensils with which they have ministered, which these receive and keep with the utmost care and anxiety, that none of them may be injured or destroyed, as they believe that even for the smallest vessels they must give an account, as sacred things, not only to a present steward, but to the Lord, if by chance any of them is injured through their carelessness. And what limit there is to this discipline, and what fidelity and care there is in keeping it up, you may see from one instance which I will give as an example. For while we are anxious to satisfy that fervour of yours through which you ask for a full account of everything, and want even what you know perfectly well to be repeated to you in this treatise, we are also afraid of exceeding the limits of brevity.[1]

CHAPTER XX.

Of the three lentil beans which the Steward found.

DURING the week of a certain brother the steward passing by saw lying on the ground three lentil beans which had slipped out of the hand of the monk on duty for the week[2] as he was hastily preparing them for cooking, together with the water in which he was washing them; and immediately he consulted the Abbot on the subject; and by him the monk was adjudged a pilferer and careless about sacred property, and so was suspended from

prayer. And the offence of his negligence was only pardoned when he had atoned for it by public penance. For they believe not only that they themselves are not their own, but also that everything that they possess is consecrated to the Lord. Wherefore if anything whatever has once been brought into the monastery they hold that it ought to be treated with the utmost reverence as an holy thing. And they attend to and arrange everything with great fidelity, even in the case of things which are considered unimportant or regarded as common and paltry, so that if they change their position and put them in a better place, or if they fill a bottle with water, or give anybody something to drink out of it, or if they remove a little dust from the oratory or from their cell they believe with implicit faith that they will receive a reward from the Lord.

CHAPTER XXI.

Of the spontaneous service of some of the brethren.

WE have been told of brethren in whose week there was such a scarcity of wood that they had not enough to prepare the usual food for the brethren; and when it had been ordered by the Abbot's authority that until more could be brought and fetched, they should content themselves with dried food,[3] though this was agreed to by all and no one could expect any cooked food; still these men as if they were cheated of the fruit and reward of their labour and service, if they did not prepare the food for their brethren according to custom in the order of their turn — imposed upon themselves such uncalled-for labour and care that in those dry and sterile regions where wood cannot possibly be procured unless it is cut from the fruit trees (for there are no wild shrubs found there as with us), they wander about through the wide deserts, and traversing the wilderness which stretches towards the Dead Sea,[4] collect in their lap and the folds of their dress the scanty stubble and brambles which the wind carries hither and thither, and so by their voluntary service prepare all their usual food for the brethren, so that they suffer nothing to be diminished of the ordinary supply; discharging these duties of theirs towards their brethren with such fidelity that though the scarcity of wood and the

---

[1] The weekly officers here spoken of were termed "Hebdomadarii" (see the next chapter). According to most rules their duties included cooking, serving, and reading at meals. They are mentioned in S. Jerome's preface to the Rule of Pachomius (cf. also Ep. xxii. ad Eustochium), but it would appear from what Cassian says below in c. xxii. that in Egypt the office of cook was assigned to some one brother and not undertaken by all in turn. According to Cassian they entered upon office on Monday morning, but the Benedictine (c. xxxv.) and other rules speak of them as beginning their duties on Sunday morning. The custom of washing the feet of the brethren, which Cassian here describes, is also mentioned by S. Benedict. l. c.

[2] *Hebdomadarius.*

[3] *Xerophagia* (ξηροφαγία), "dried food," distinguished from what is raw (*omophagia*) in the next chapter. Cf. for the word, Tertullian on Fasting c. i. and xvii.
[4] This shows that Cassian is here writing about the monks of Palestine, *not* those of Egypt, who (according to the next chapter) had a permanent cook. There is a further allusion to and description of this desert in the Conference VI. i.

Abbot's order would be a fair excuse for them, yet still out of regard for their profit and reward they will not take advantage of this liberty.

CHAPTER XXII.

Of the system of the Egyptians, which is appointed for the daily service of the brethren.

THESE things have been told in accordance with the system, as we remarked before, of the whole East, which also we say should be observed as a matter of course in our own country. But among the Egyptians whose chief care is for work there is not the mutual change of weekly service, for fear lest owing to the requirements of office they might all be hindered from keeping the rule of work. But one of the most approved brethren is given the care of the larder and kitchen, and he takes charge of that office for good and all as long as his strength and years permit. For he is exhausted by no great bodily labour, because no great care is expended among them in preparing food or in cooking, as they so largely make use of dried and uncooked food,[1] and among them the leaves of leeks cut each month, and cherlock, table salt,[2] olives, tiny little salt fish which they call sardines,[3] form the greatest delicacy.

CHAPTER XXIII.

Of the obedience of Abbot John by which he was exalted even to the grace of prophecy.

AND since this book is about the training of one who renounces this world, whereby, making a beginning of true humility and perfect obedience, he may be enabled to ascend the heights of the other virtues as well, I think it well to set down just by way of specimen, as we promised, some of the deeds of the elders whereby they excelled in this virtue, selecting a few only out of many instances, that, if any are anxious to aim at still greater heights, they may not only receive from these an incitement towards the perfect life, but may also be furnished with a model of what they pur-

pose. Wherefore, to make this book as short as possible we will produce and set down two or three out of the whole number of the Fathers; and first of all Abbot John who lived near Lycon[4] which is a town in the Thebaid; and who was exalted even to the grace of prophecy for his admirable obedience, and was so celebrated all the world over that he was by his merits rendered famous even among kings of this world. For though, as we said, he lived in the most remote parts of the Thebaid, still the Emperor Theodosius did not venture to declare war against the most powerful tyrants before he was encouraged by his utterances and replies: trusting in which as if they had been brought to him from heaven he gained victories over his foes in battles which seemed hopeless.[5]

CHAPTER XXIV.

Of the dry stick which, at the bidding of his senior, Abbot John kept on watering as if it would grow.

AND so this blessed John from his youth up even to a full and ripe age of manhood was subject to his senior as long as he continued living in this world, and carried out his commands with such humility that his senior himself was utterly astounded at his obedience; and as he wanted to make sure whether this virtue came from genuine faith and profound simplicity of heart, or whether it was put on and as it were constrained and only shown in the presence of the bidder, he often laid upon him many superfluous and almost unnecessary or even impossible commands. From which I will select three to show to those who wish to know how perfect was his disposition and subjection. For the old man took from his woodstack a stick which had previously been cut and got ready to make the fire with, and which, as no opportunity for cooking had come, was lying not merely dry but even mouldy from the lapse of time. And when he had stuck it into the ground before his very eyes, he ordered him to fetch water and to

---

[1] The distinction between the xerophagia and omophagia is shown by the following passage from S. Jerome's Life of Hilarion, describing his food: "From his twenty-first year to his twenty-seventh for three years . . . . his food was dry bread and water (xerophagia). Further from his twenty-seventh to his thirtieth year he supported himself on herbs, and the raw roots of certain plants (omophagia)."

[2] *Sal frictum*, "rubbed salt," i.e., table salt as distinct from rough or block salt.

[3] *Mænomenia* (Petschenig) or *Mœnidia* (Gazæus). The word comes from the Greek μαινόμενα or μαινίδιον, dimin. from μαίνη, a small salted fish.

[4] Lycon or Lycopolis in the Thebaid is the modern El Syout on the west banks of the Nile, S.E. of Hermopolis (= Minieh).

[5] This John of Lycopolis was one of the most celebrated hermits of the fourth century. Originally a carpenter, he retired at the age of twenty-five into the wilderness, and after the death of his instructor settled near Lycopolis. Here, as Cassian tells us, he received as a reward for his obedience the gift of prophecy; and was consulted by crowds who came to him for this purpose and among others by the Emperor Theodosius, to whom he foretold (1) his victory over the usurper Maximus (A.D. 388), and (2) his success against Eugenius in A.D. 395. He is mentioned again by Cassian in the Conferences I. xxi., XXIV. xxvi., etc. A full account of him is given by Rufinus in his history of the monks c. i., and by Palladius in the Lausiac History 43–60; he is also mentioned by Augustine De Civitate Dei, Book V. c. xxvi; De Cura pro mortuis gerenda, c. xvii., and Jerome Ep. cxxxiii. ad Ctesiphontem, as well as by Theodoret H.E. V. xxiv. and Sozomen H.E. VI. xxviii.

water it twice a day that by this daily watering it might strike roots and be restored to life as a tree, as it was before, and spread out its branches and afford a pleasant sight to the eyes as well as a shade for those who sat under it in the heat of summer. And this order the lad received with his customary veneration, never considering its impossibility, and day by day carried it out so that he constantly carried water for nearly two miles and never ceased to water the stick; and for a whole year no bodily infirmity, no festival services, no necessary business (which might fairly have excused him from carrying out the command), and lastly no severity of winter could interfere and hinder him from obeying this order. And when the old man had watched this zeal of his on the sly without saying anything for several days and had seen that he kept this command of his with simple willingness of heart, as if it had come from heaven, without any change of countenance or consideration of its reasonableness — approving the unfeigned obedience of his humility and at the same time commiserating his tedious labour which in the zeal of his devotion he had continued for a whole year — he came to the dry stick, and, "John," said he, "has this tree put forth roots or no?" And when the other said that he did not know, then the old man as if seeking the truth of the matter and trying whether it was yet depending on its roots, pulled up the stick before him with a slight disturbance of the earth, and throwing it away told him that for the future he might stop watering it.[1]

CHAPTER XXV.

Of the unique vase of oil thrown away by Abbot John at his senior's command.

THUS the youth, trained up by exercises of this sort, daily increased in this virtue of obedience, and shone forth more and more with the grace of humility; and when the sweet odour of his obedience spread throughout all the monasteries, some of the brethren, coming to the elder for the sake of testing him or rather of being edified by him, marvelled at his obedience of which they had heard; and so the elder called him suddenly, and said, "Go up and take this cruse of oil"[2] (which was the only one in the desert and which furnished

a very scanty supply of the rich liquid for their own use and for that of strangers) "and throw it down out of window." And he flew up stairs when summoned and threw it out of window and cast it down to the ground and broke it in pieces without any thought or consideration of the folly of the command, or their daily wants, and bodily infirmity, or of their poverty, and the trials and difficulties of the wretched desert in which, even if they had got the money for it, oil of that quality, once lost, could not be procured or replaced.

CHAPTER XXVI.

How Abbot John obeyed his senior by trying to roll a huge stone, which a large number of men were unable to move.

AGAIN, when some others were anxious to be edified by the example of his obedience, the elder called him and said: "John, run and roll that stone hither as quickly as possible;" and he forthwith, applying now his neck, and now his whole body, tried with all his might and main to roll an enormous stone which a great crowd of men would not be able to move, so that not only were his clothes saturated with sweat from his limbs, but the stone itself was wetted by his neck; in this too never weighing the impossibility of the command and deed, out of reverence for the old man and the unfeigned simplicity of his service, as he believed implicitly that the old man could not command him to do anything vain or without reason.

CHAPTER XXVII.

Of the humility and obedience of Abbot Patermucius,[3] which he did not hesitate to make perfect by throwing his little boy into the river at the command of his senior.

So far let it suffice for me to have told a few things out of many concerning Abbot John: now I will relate a memorable deed of Abbot Patermucius. For he, when anxious to renounce the world, remained lying before the doors of the monastery for a long time until by his dogged persistence he induced them — contrary to all the rules of the Cœnobia — to receive him together with his little boy who was about eight years old. And when they were at last admitted they were at once not

---

[1] A somewhat similar story is told by Sulpitius Severus (Dialogi I. c. xiii.) of an Egyptian monk, only in that case the story terminates in a more satisfactory manner, as in the third year the stick took root and sprouted!

[2] *Lenticula;* the word is used for a cruse of oil in the Vulgate. i Sam. x. 1; 2 Kings ix. 1, 3.

[3] *Patermucius* (Petschenig) or *Mucius* (Gazæus); probably a different person from the man of this name of whom we read in Rufinus, History of the Monks, c. ix.; as there is no allusion there to the narrative which Cassian gives here, nor any hint that that Patermucius had a son.

only committed to the care of different superiors, but also put to live in separate cells that the father might not be reminded by the constant sight of the little one that out of all his possessions and carnal treasures, which he had cast off and renounced, at least his son remained to him; and that as he was already taught that he was no longer a rich man, so he might also forget the fact that he was a father. And that it might be more thoroughly tested whether he would make affection and love[1] for his own flesh and blood of more account than obedience and Christian mortification (which all who renounce the world ought out of love to Christ to prefer), the child was on purpose neglected and dressed in rags instead of proper clothes; and so covered and disfigured with dirt that he would rather disgust than delight the eyes of his father whenever he saw him. And further, he was exposed to blows and slaps from different people, which the father often saw inflicted without the slightest reason on his innocent child under his very eyes, so that he never saw his cheeks without their being stained with the dirty marks of tears. And though the child was treated thus day after day before his eyes, yet still out of love for Christ and the virtue of obedience the father's heart stood firm and unmoved. For he no longer regarded him as his own son, as he had offered him equally with himself to Christ; nor was he concerned about his present injuries, but rather rejoiced because he saw that they were endured, not without profit; thinking little of his son's tears, but anxious about his own humility and perfection. And when the Superior of the Cœnobium saw his steadfastness of mind and immovable inflexibility, in order thoroughly to prove the constancy of his purpose, one day when he had seen the child crying, he pretended that he was annoyed with him and told the father to throw him into the river. Then he, as if this had been commanded him by the Lord, at once snatched up the child as quickly as possible, and carried him in his arms to the river's bank to throw him in. And straightway in the fervour of his faith and obedience this would have been carried out in act, had not some of the brethren been purposely set to watch the banks of the river very carefully, and when the child was thrown in, had somehow snatched him from the bed of the stream, and prevented the command, which was really fulfilled by the obedience and devotion of the father, from being consummated in act and result.

---

[1] *Affectionem . . . . charitatem.*— Petschenig. The text of Gazæus reads the ablative.

CHAPTER XXVIII.

Of how it was revealed to the Abbot concerning Patermucius that he had done the deed of Abraham; and how when the same Abbot died, Patermucius succeeded to the charge of the monastery.

AND this man's faith and devotion was so acceptable to God that it was immediately approved by a divine testimony. For it was forthwith revealed to the Superior that by this obedience of his he had copied the deed of the patriarch Abraham. And when shortly afterwards the same Abbot of the monastery departed out of this life to Christ, he preferred him to all the brethren, and left him as his successor and as Abbot to the monastery.

CHAPTER XXIX.

Of the obedience of a brother who at the Abbot's bidding carried about in public ten baskets and sold them by retail.

WE will also not be silent about a brother whom we knew, who belonged to a high family according to the rank of this world, for he was sprung from a father who was a count and extremely wealthy, and had been well brought up with a liberal education. This man, when he had left his parents and fled to the monastery, in order to prove the humility of his disposition and the ardour of his faith was at once ordered by his superior to load his shoulders with ten baskets (which there was no need to sell publicly), and to hawk them about through the streets for sale: this condition being attached, so that he might be kept longer at the work, viz.: that if any one should chance to want to buy them all together, he was not to allow it, but was to sell them to purchasers separately. And this he carried out with the utmost zeal, and trampling under foot all shame and confusion, out of love for Christ, and for His Name's sake, he put the baskets on his shoulders and sold them by retail at the price fixed and brought back the money to the monastery; not in the least upset by the novelty of so mean and unusual a duty, and paying no attention to the indignity of the thing and the splendour of his birth, and the disgrace of the sale, as he was aiming at gaining through the grace of obedience that humility of Christ which is the true nobility.

CHAPTER XXX.

Of the humility of Abbot Pinufius, who left a very famous Cœnobium over which he presided as Presbyter, and out of the love of subjection sought a distant monastery where he could be received as a novice.

THE limits of the book compel us to draw to a close; but the virtue of obedience, which holds the first place among other good qualities, will not allow us altogether to pass over in silence the deeds of those who have excelled by it. Wherefore aptly combining these two together, I mean, consulting brevity as well as the wishes and profit of those who are in earnest, we will only add one example of humility, which, as it was shown by no novice but one already perfect and an Abbot, may not only instruct the younger, but also incite the elders to the perfect virtue of humility, as they read it. Thus we saw Abbot Pinufius [1] who when he was presbyter of a huge Cœnobium which is in Egypt not far from the city of Panephysis,[2] was held in honour and respect by all men out of reverence either for his life or for his age or for his priesthood; and when he saw that for this reason he could not practise that humility which he longed for with all the ardour of his disposition, and had no opportunity of exercising the virtue of subjection which he desired, he fled secretly from the Cœnobium and withdrew alone into the furthest parts of the Thebaid, and there laid aside the habit of the monks and assumed a secular dress, and thus sought the Cœnobium of Tabenna, which he knew to be the strictest of all, and in which he fancied that he would not be known owing to the distance of the spot, or else that he could easily lie hid there in consequence of the size of the monastery and the number of brethren. There he remained for a long time at the entrance, and as a suppliant at the knees of the brethren sought with most earnest prayers to gain admission. And when he was at last with much scorn admitted as a feeble old man who had lived all his life in the world, and had asked in his old age to be allowed to enter a Cœnobium when he could no longer gratify his passions,— as they said that he was seeking this not for the sake of religion but because he was compelled by hunger and want, they gave him the care and management of the garden, as he seemed an old man and not specially fitted for any particular work. And this he performed under another and a younger brother who kept him by him as intrusted to him, and he was so subordinate to him, and cultivated the desired virtue of humility so obediently that he daily performed with the utmost diligence not only everything that had to do with the care and management of the garden, but also all those duties which were

looked on by the other as hard and degrading, and disagreeable. Rising also by night he did many things secretly, without any one looking on or knowing it, when darkness concealed him so that no one could discover the author of the deed. And when he had hidden himself there for three years and had been sought for high and low by the brethren all through Egypt, he was at last seen by one who had come from the parts of Egypt, but could scarcely be recognized owing to the meanness of his dress and the humble character of the duty he was performing. For he was stooping down and hoeing the ground for vegetables and bringing dung on his shoulders and laying it about their roots. And seeing this the brother for a long time hesitated about recognizing him, but at last he came nearer, and taking careful note not only of his looks but also of the tone of his voice, straightway fell at his feet: and at first all who saw it were struck with the greatest astonishment why he should do this to one who was looked upon by them as the lowest of all, as being a novice and one who had but lately forsaken the world: but afterwards they were struck with still greater wonder when he forthwith announced his name, which was one that had been well known amongst them also by repute. And all the brethren asking his pardon for their former ignorance because they had for so long classed him with the juniors and children, brought him back to his own Cœnobium, against his will and in tears because by the envy of the devil he had been cheated out of a worthy mode of life and the humility which he was rejoicing in having discovered after his long search, and because he had not succeeded in ending his life in that state of subjection which he had secured. And so they guarded him with the utmost care lest he should slip away again in the same sort of way and escape from them also.

CHAPTER XXXI.

How when Abbot Pinufius was brought back to his monastery he stayed there for a little while and then fled again into the regions of Syrian Palestine.

And when he had stopped there for a little while, again he was seized with a longing and desire for humility, and, taking advantage of the silence of night, made his escape in such a way that this time he sought no neighbouring district, but regions which were unknown and strange and separated by a wide distance. For embarking in a ship he managed to travel to Palestine, believing that he would more

---

[1] Cassian repeats this story in the Conferences XX. c. i., as an introduction to the Conference " On the End of Penitence and the Marks of Satisfaction," which he gives as the work of the said Abbot Pinufius.

[2] Panephysis is more fully described in the Conferences VII. xxvi.; XI. iii. It is mentioned by Ptolemy (IV. v. § 52), but not by many other ancient writers. It was situated in the Delta between the Tanitic and Mendesian arms of the Nile, and was identified by Champollion with the modern Menzaleh.

securely lie hid if he betook himself to those places in which his name had never been heard. And when he had come thither, at once he sought out our own monastery [1] which was at no great distance from the cave [2] in which our Lord vouchsafed to be born of a virgin. And though he concealed himself here for some time, yet like "a city set on an hill" [3] (to use our Lord's expression) he could not long be hid. For presently some of the brethren who had come to the holy places from Egypt to pray there recognized him and recalled him with most fervent prayers to his own Cœnobium.

CHAPTER XXXII.

The charge which the same Abbot Pinufius gave to a brother whom he admitted into his monastery in our presence.

THIS old man, then, we afterwards diligently sought out in Egypt because we had been intimate with him in our own monastery; and I propose to insert in this work of mine an exhortation which he gave in our presence to a brother whom he admitted into the monastery, because I think that it may be useful. You know, said he, that after lying for so many days at the entrance you are to-day to be admitted. And to begin with you ought to know the reason of the difficulty put in your way. For it may be of great service to you in this road on which you are desirous to enter, if you understand the method of it and approach the service of Christ accordingly, and as you ought.

CHAPTER XXXIII.

How it is that, just as a great reward is due to the monk who labours according to the regulations of the fathers, so likewise punishment must be inflicted on an idle one; and therefore no one should be admitted into a monastery too easily.

FOR as unbounded glory hereafter is promised to those who faithfully serve God and cleave to Him according to the rule of this system; so the severest penalties are in store for those who have carried it out carelessly and coldly, and have failed to show to Him fruits of holiness corresponding to what they professed or what they were believed by men to be. For "it is better," as Scripture says, "that a man should not vow rather than that he should vow and not pay;" and "Cursed is he that doeth the work of the Lord care-

lessly." [4] Therefore you were for a long while declined by us, not as if we did not desire with all our hearts to secure your salvation and the salvation of all, nor as if we did not care to go to meet even afar off those who are longing to be converted to Christ; but for fear lest if we received you rashly we might make ourselves guilty in the sight of God of levity, and make you incur a yet heavier punishment, if, when you had been too easily admitted by us without realizing the responsibility of this profession, you had afterwards turned out a deserter or lukewarm. Wherefore you ought in the first instance to learn the actual reason for the renunciation of the world, and when you have seen this, you can be taught more plainly what you ought to do, from the reason for it.

CHAPTER XXXIV.

Of the way in which our renunciation is nothing but mortification and the image of the Crucified.

RENUNCIATION is nothing but the evidence of the cross and of mortification. And so you must know that to-day you are dead to this world and its deeds and desires, and that, as the Apostle says, you are crucified to this world and this world to you. [5] Consider therefore the demands of the cross under the sign [6] of which you ought henceforward to live in this life; because *you* no longer live but *He* lives in you who was crucified for you. [7] We must therefore pass our time in this life in that fashion and form in which He was crucified for us on the cross so that (as David says) piercing our flesh with the fear of the Lord, [8] we may have all our wishes and desires not subservient to our own lusts but fastened to His mortification. For so shall we fulfil the command of the Lord which says: "He that taketh not up his cross and followeth me is not worthy of me." [9] But perhaps you will say: How can a man carry his cross continually? or how can any one who is alive be crucified? Hear briefly how this is.

CHAPTER XXXV.

How the fear of the Lord is our cross.

THE fear of the Lord is our cross. As then one who is crucified no longer has the power of moving or turning his limbs in any direc-

---

[1] On Cassian's connection with the monastery at Bethlehem, see the Introduction.
[2] On the Cave of the Nativity, see Justin Martyr Dialogue with Trypho, c. lxxviii. Origen against Celsus, I. c. li.
[3] S. Matt. v. 14.

[4] Eccl. v. 4 (LXX.); Jer. xlviii. 10 (LXX.).
[5] Cf. Gal. vi. 14.
[6] *Sacramentum.*
[7] Cf. Gal. ii. 20.
[8] Cf. Ps. cxviii. (cxix.) 120, where the Gallican Psalter has "Confige timore tuo carnes meas."
[9] S. Matt. x. 38.

tion as he pleases, so we also ought to affix our wishes and desires — not in accordance with what is pleasant and delightful to us now, but in accordance with the law of the Lord, where it constrains us.   And as he who is fastened to the wood of the cross no longer considers things present, nor thinks about his likings, nor is perplexed by anxiety and care for the morrow, nor disturbed by any desire of possession, nor inflamed by any pride or strife or rivalry, grieves not at present injuries, remembers not past ones, and while he is still breathing in the body considers that he is dead to all earthly things,[1] sending the thoughts of his heart on before to that place whither he doubts not that he is shortly to come: so we also, when crucified by the fear of the Lord ought to be dead indeed to all these things, i.e. not only to carnal vices but also to all earthly things,[1] having the eye of our minds fixed there whither we hope at each moment that we are soon to pass.   For in this way we can have all our desires and carnal affections mortified.

CHAPTER XXXVI.

How our renunciation of the world is of no use if we are again entangled in those things which we have renounced.

BEWARE therefore lest at any time you take again any of those things which you renounced and forsook, and, contrary to the Lord's command, return from the field of evangelical work, and be found to have clothed yourself again in your coat which you had stripped off;[2] neither sink back to the low and earthly lusts and desires of this world, and in defiance of Christ's word come down from the roof of perfection and dare to take up again any of those things which you have renounced and forsaken.   Beware that you remember nothing of your kinsfolk or of your former affections, and that you are not called back to the cares and anxieties of this world, and (as our Lord says) putting your hand to the plough and looking back be found unfit for the kingdom of heaven.[3]   Beware lest at any time, when you have begun to dip into the knowledge of the Psalms and of this life, you be little by little puffed up and think of reviving that pride which now at your beginning you have trampled under foot in the ardour of faith and in fullest humility; and thus (as the Apostle says) building again those things which you had destroyed, you make yourself a backslider.[4]   But rather take heed to con-

tinue even to the end in that state of nakedness of which you made profession in the sight of God and of his angels.   In this humility too and patience, with which you persevered for ten days before the doors and entreated with many tears to be admitted into the monastery, you should not only continue but also increase and go forward.   For it is too bad that when you ought to be carried on from the rudiments and beginnings, and go forward to perfection, you should begin to fall back from these to worse things.   For not he who begins these things, but he who endures in them to the end, shall be saved.[5]

CHAPTER XXXVII.

How the devil always lies in wait for our end, and how we ought continually to watch his head.[6]

FOR the subtle serpent is ever "watching our heel," that is, is lying in wait for the close, and endeavouring to trip us up right to the end of our life.   And therefore it will not be of any use to have made a good beginning and to have eagerly taken the first step towards renouncing the world with all fervour, if a corresponding end does not likewise set it off and conclude it, and if the humility and poverty of Christ, of which you have now made profession in His sight, are not preserved by you even to the close of your life, as they were first secured.   And that you may succeed in doing this, do you ever "watch his head," i.e. the first rise of thoughts, by bringing them at once to your superior.   For thus you will learn to "bruise" his dangerous beginnings, if you are not ashamed to disclose any of them to your superior.

CHAPTER XXXVIII.

Of the renunciant's preparation against temptation, and of the few who are worthy of imitation.

WHEREFORE, as Scripture says, "when you go forth to serve the Lord stand in the fear of the Lord, and prepare your mind"[7] not for repose or carelessness or delights, but for temptations and troubles.   For "through much tribulation we must enter into the kingdom of God."   For "strait is the gate and narrow is the way which leadeth unto life, and

---

1 *Elementa.*
2 Cf. S. Matt. xxiv. 18.
3 S. Luke ix. 62.
4 Cf. Gal. ii. 18.

---

5 Cf. S. Matt. xxiv. 13.
6 All through this chapter Cassian is alluding to Gen. iii. 15: " I will put enmity between thee and the woman and between thy seed and her seed; it shalt bruise thy head and thou shalt bruise his heel:" the last clause of which is rendered by the LXX. αὐτός σου τηρήσει κεφαλὴν καὶ σὺ τηρήσεις αὐτοῦ πτέρναν, where the Vulgate has " Ipsa conteret caput tuum et tu insidiaberis calcaneo ejus."
7 Ecclus. ii. 1.

few there be which find it."[1] Consider therefore that you belong to the few and elect; and
do not grow cold after the examples of the
lukewarmness of many: but live as the few,
that with the few you may be worthy of a
place in the kingdom of God: for "many are
called, but few chosen," and it is a "little
flock to which it is the Father's good pleasure
to give"[2] an inheritance. You should therefore realize that it is no light sin for one who
has made profession of perfection to follow
after what is imperfect. And to this state of
perfection you may attain by the following
steps and in the following way.

CHAPTER XXXIX.

Of the way in which we shall mount towards perfection, whereby we may afterwards ascend from the fear of God up to
love.

"The beginning" of our salvation and the
safeguard of it is, as I said, "the fear of the
Lord."[3] For through this those who are
trained in the way of perfection can gain a
start in, conversion as well as purification
from vices and security in virtue. And when
this has gained an entrance into a man's heart
it produces contempt of all things, and begets
a forgetfulness of kinsfolk and a horror of the
world itself. But by the contempt for the
loss of all possessions humility is gained.
And humility is attested by these signs: First
of all if a man has all his desires mortified;
secondly, if he conceals none of his actions
or even of his thoughts from his superior;
thirdly, if he puts no trust in his own opinion,
but all in the judgment of his superior, and
listens eagerly and willingly to his directions;
fourthly, if he maintains in everything obedience and gentleness and constant patience;
fifthly, if he not only hurts nobody else, but
also is not annoyed or vexed at wrongs done
to himself; sixthly, if he does nothing and
ventures on nothing to which he is not urged
by the Common Rule or by the example of
our elders; seventhly, if he is contented with
the lowest possible position, and considers
himself as a bad workman and unworthy in
the case of everything enjoined to him;
eighthly, if he does not only outwardly profess with his lips that he is inferior to all, but
really believes it in the inmost thoughts of his
heart; ninthly, if he governs his tongue, and
is not over talkative; tenthly, if he is not
easily moved or too ready to laugh. For by
such signs and the like is true humility recog-
nised. And when this has once been genu-

inely secured, then at once it leads you on by
a still higher step to love which knows no fear;[4]
and through this you begin, without any effort
and as it were naturally, to keep up everything
that you formerly observed not without fear
of punishment; no longer now from regard of
punishment or fear of it but from love of goodness itself, and delight in virtue.[5]

CHAPTER XL.

That the monk should seek for examples of perfection not
from many instances but from one or a very few.

And that you may the more easily arrive at
this, the examples of the perfect life of one
dwelling in the congregation, which you may
imitate, should be sought from a very few or
indeed from one or two only and not from too
many. For apart from the fact that a life
which is tested and refined and purified is only
to be found in a few, there is this also to be
gained, viz.: that a man is more thoroughly
instructed and formed by the example of some
one, towards the perfection which he sets before
him, viz.: that of the Cœnobite life.

CHAPTER XLI.

The appearance of what infirmities one who lives in a Cœnobium ought to exhibit.[6]

And that you may be able to attain all this,
and continually remain subject to this spiritual
rule, you must observe these three things in
the congregation: viz.: that as the Psalmist
says: "I was like a deaf man and heard not
and as one that is dumb who doth not open
his mouth; and I became as a man that heareth not, and in whose mouth there are no
reproofs,"[7] so you also should walk as one that
is deaf and dumb and blind, so that — putting
aside the contemplation of him who has been
rightly chosen by you as your model of perfection — you should be like a blind man and
not see any of those things which you find
to be unedifying, nor[8] be influenced by the
authority or fashion of those who do these
things, and give yourself up to what is worse
and what you formerly condemned. If you
hear any one disobedient or insubordinate or
disparaging another or doing anything different from what was taught to you, you should
not go wrong and be led astray by such an

---

1 Acts xiv. 22; S. Matt. vii. 14.
2 S. Matt. xx. 16; S. Luke xii. 32.
3 Prov. ix. 10.

4 Cf. 1 John iv. 18.
5 With this chapter there should be compared the Rule of S.
Benedict c. vii., where a very similar description is given of twelve
grades "on the mystic ladder [of humility] which Jacob saw,"
evidently suggested by the chapter before us.
6 *Quarum debilitatum similitudinem suscipere debeat qui in
cœnobio commoratur.* — Petschenig. The text of Gazæus gives as the
title of this chapter: "*In congregatione cœnobitica constituti quid
tolerare ac sustinere debeant.*"
7 Ps. xxxvii. (xxxviii.) 14, 15.
8 *Nec* (Petschenig). Gazæus reads *ne.*

example to imitate him ; but, "like a deaf man," as if you had never heard it, you should pass it all by. If insults are offered to you or to any one else, or wrongs done, be immovable, and as far as an answer in retaliation is concerned be silent "as one that is dumb," always singing in your heart this verse of the Psalmist: "I said I will take heed to my ways that I offend not with my tongue. I set a guard to my mouth when the sinner stood before me. I was dumb and was humbled and kept silence from good things." [1] But cultivate above everything this fourth thing which adorns and graces those three of which we have spoken above; viz.: make yourself, as the Apostle directs,[2] a fool in this world that you may become wise, exercising no discrimination and judgment of your own on any of those matters which are commanded to you, but always showing obedience with all simplicity and faith, judging that alone to be holy, useful, and wise which God's law or the decision of your superior declares to you to be such. For built up on such a system of instruction you may continue forever under this discipline, and not fall away from the monastery in consequence of any temptations or devices of the enemy.

CHAPTER XLII.

How a monk should not look for the blessing of patience in his own case as a result of the virtue of others, but rather as a consequence of his own longsuffering.

You should therefore not look for patience in your own case from the virtue of others, thinking that then only can you secure it when you are not irritated by any (for it is not in your own power to prevent this from happening); but rather you should look for it as the consequence of your own humility and long-suffering which *does* depend on your own will.

CHAPTER XLIII.

Recapitulation of the explanation how a monk can mount up towards perfection.

And in order that all these things which have been set forth in a somewhat lengthy discourse may be more easily stamped on your heart and may stick in your thoughts with all tenacity, I will make a summary of them so that you may be able to learn all the changes by heart by reason of their brevity and conciseness. Hear then in few words how you can mount up to the heights of perfection without any effort or difficulty. "The beginning" of our salvation and "of wisdom" is, according to Scripture, "the fear of the Lord." [3] From the fear of the Lord arises salutary compunction. From compunction of heart springs renunciation, i.e. nakedness and contempt of all possessions. From nakedness is begotten humility; from humility the mortification of desires. Through mortification of desires all faults are extirpated and decay. By driving out faults virtues shoot up and increase. By the budding of virtues purity of heart is gained. By purity of heart the perfection of apostolic love is acquired.

BOOK V.

OF THE SPIRIT OF GLUTTONY.

CHAPTER I.

The transition from the Institutes of the monks to the struggle against the eight principal faults.

This fifth book of ours is now by the help of God to be produced. For after the four books which have been composed on the customs of the monasteries, we now propose, being strengthened by God through your prayers, to approach the struggle against the eight prin-cipal faults, i.e. first, Gluttony or the pleasures of the palate; secondly, Fornication; thirdly, Covetousness, which means Avarice, or, as it may more properly be called, the love of money, fourthly, Anger; fifthly, Dejection; sixthly, "Accidie," [4] which is heaviness or

---

[1] Ps. xxxviii. (xxxix.) 2, 3.   [2] Cf. 1 Cor. iii. 18.

[3] Ps. cxi. 10.
[4] *Acedia.* It is much to be regretted that the old English word "Accidie" has entirely dropped out of use. It is used by Chaucer and other early writers for the sin of spiritual sloth or sluggishness. See "The Persone's Tale," where it is thus described: "After the sinne of wrath, now wol I speke of the sinne of accidie or slouth: for envie blindeth the herte of a man, and ire troubleth a man, and accidie maketh him hevy, thoughtful, and wrawe. Envie and ire

weariness of heart; seventhly, κενοδοξία which means foolish or vain glory; eighthly, pride. And on entering upon this difficult task we need your prayers, O most blessed Pope Castor, more than ever; that we may be enabled in the first place worthily to investigate the nature of these in all points however trifling or hidden or obscure: and next to explain with sufficient clearness the causes of them; and thirdly to bring forward fitly the cures and remedies for them.

CHAPTER II.

How the occasions of these faults, being found in everybody, are ignored by everybody; and how we need the Lord's help to make them plain.

AND of these passions as the occasions are recognized by everybody as soon as they are laid open by the teaching of the elders, so before they are revealed, although we are all overcome by them, and they exist in every one, yet nobody knows of them. But we trust that we shall be able in some measure to explain them, if by your prayers that word of the Lord, which was announced by Isaiah, may apply to us also — "I will go before thee, and bring low the mighty ones of the land, I will break the gates of brass, and cut asunder the iron bars, and I will open to thee concealed treasures and hidden secrets "[1] — so that the word of the Lord may go before us also, and first may bring low the mighty ones of our land, i.e. these same evil passions which we are desirous to overcome, and which claim for themselves dominion and a most horrible tyranny in our mortal body; and may make them yield to our investigation and explanation, and thus breaking the gates of our ignorance, and cutting asunder the bars of vices which shut us out from true knowledge, may lead to the hidden things of our secrets, and reveal to us who have been illuminated, according to the Apostle's word, "the hidden things of darkness, and may make manifest

the counsels of the hearts," [2] that thus penetrating with pure eyes of the mind to the foul darkness of vices, we may be able to disclose them and drag them forth to light; and may succeed in explaining their occasions and natures to those who are either free from them, or are still tied and bound by them, and so passing as the prophet says,[3] through the fire of vices which terribly inflame our minds, we may be able forthwith to pass also through the water of virtues which extinguish them unharmed, and being bedewed (as it were) with spiritual remedies may be found worthy to be brought in purity of heart to the consolations of perfection.

CHAPTER III.

How our first struggle must be against the spirit of gluttony, i.e. the pleasures of the palate.

AND so the first conflict we must enter upon is that against gluttony, which we have explained as the pleasures of the palate: and in the first place as we are going to speak of the system of fasts, and the quality of food, we must again recur to the traditions and customs of the Egyptians, as everybody knows that they contain a more advanced discipline in the matter of self-control, and a perfect method of discrimination.

CHAPTER IV.

The testimony of Abbot Antony in which he teaches that each virtue ought to be sought for from him who professes it in a special degree.

FOR it is an ancient and excellent saying of the blessed Antony [4] that when a monk is endeavouring after the plan of the monastic life to reach the heights of a more advanced perfection, and, having learned the consideration of discretion, is able now to stand in his own judgment, and to arrive at the very summit of the anchorite's life, he ought by no means to seek for all kinds of virtues from one man however excellent. For one is adorned with flowers of knowledge, another is more strongly fortified with methods of discretion, another is established in the dignity of patience, another excels in the virtue of humility, another in that of continence, another is decked with the grace of simplicity.

---

maken bitternesse in herte, which bitternesse is mother of accidie, and benimeth him the love of alle goodnesse; than is accidie the anguish of a troubled herte." The English word lingered on till the seventeenth century, as it is used by Bishop Hall (Serm. V. 140), in the form "Acedy," which is etymologically more correct as being nearer the Latin *Acedia* and the Greek Ἀκηδία, a word which occurs in the LXX. version of the Old Testament in Isaiah lxi. 3; Ps. cxviii. (cxix.) 28; Baruch iii. 1; Ecclus. xxix. 6 (cf. the use of the verb ἀκηδιάζω in Ps. lx. (lxi.) 2; ci. (cii.) 1; cxlii. (cxliii.) 4; Ecclus. xxii. 14). In ecclesiastical writers the term Acedia is a favourite one to denote primarily the mental prostitution induced by fasting and other physical causes, and afterwards spiritual sloth and sluggishness in general. It forms the subject of the tenth book of the Institutes, and is treated of again by Cassian in the Conferences V. iii. sq.; cf. also the "Summa" of S. Thomas, II. ii. q. xxxv., where there is a full discussion of its nature and character. — cf. Dr. Paget's essay "Concerning Accidie" in "The Spirit of Discipline."
[1] Isa. xlv. 2, 3.

[2] 1 Cor. iv. 5.
[3] Ps. lxv. (lxvi.) 12.
[4] S. Antony, the "founder of asceticism" and one of the most famous of the early monks, was born about 250 A.D. at Coma, on the borders of Egypt, and died about 355, at the great age of 105. He is frequently mentioned by Cassian in the Conferences.

This one excels all others in magnanimity, that one in pity, another in vigils, another in silence, another in earnestness of work. And therefore the monk who desires to gather spiritual honey, ought like a most careful bee, to suck out virtue from those who specially possess it, and should diligently store it up in the vessel of his own breast: nor should he investigate what any one is lacking in, but only regard and gather whatever virtue he has. For if we want to gain all virtues from some one person, we shall with great difficulty or perhaps never at all find suitable examples for us to imitate. For though we do not as yet see that even Christ is made "all things in all," as the Apostle says;[1] still in this way we can find Him bit by bit in all. For it is said of Him, "Who was made of God to you wisdom and righteousness and sanctification and redemption."[2] While then in one there is found wisdom, in another righteousness, in another sanctification, in another kindness, in another chastity, in another humility, in another patience, Christ is at the present time divided, member by member, among all of the saints. But when all come together into the unity of the faith and virtue, He is formed into the "perfect man,"[3] completing the fulness of His body, in the joints and properties of all His members. Until then that time arrives when God will be "all in all," for the present God can in the way of which we have spoken be "in all," through particular virtues, although He is not yet "all in all" through the fulness of them. For although our religion has but one end and aim, yet there are different ways by which we approach God, as will be more fully shown in the Conferences of the Elders.[4] And so we must seek a model of discretion and continence more particularly from those from whom we see that those virtues flow forth more abundantly through the grace of the Holy Spirit; not that any one can alone acquire those things which are divided among many, but in order that in those good qualities of which we are capable we may advance towards the imitation of those who especially have acquired them.

CHAPTER V.

That one and the same rule of fasting cannot be observed by everybody.

AND so on the manner of fasting a uniform rule cannot easily be observed, because everybody has not the same strength; nor is it like the rest of the virtues, acquired by steadfastness of mind alone. And therefore, because it does not depend only on mental firmness, since it has to do with the possibilities of the body, we have received this explanation concerning it which has been handed down to us, viz.: that there is a difference of time, manner, and quality of the refreshment in proportion to the difference of condition of the body, the age, and sex: but that there is one and the same rule of restraint to everybody as regards continence of mind, and the virtue of the spirit. For it is impossible for every one to prolong his fast for a week, or to postpone taking refreshment during a two or three days' abstinence. By many people also who are worn out with sickness and especially with old age, a fast even up to sunset cannot be endured without suffering. The sickly food of moistened beans does not agree with everybody: nor does a sparing diet of fresh vegetables suit all, nor is a scanty meal of dry bread permitted to all alike. One man does not feel satisfied with two pounds, for another a meal of one pound, or six ounces, is too much; but there is one aim and object of continence in the case of all of these, viz.: that no one may be overburdened beyond the measure of his appetite, by gluttony. For it is not only the quality, but also the quantity of food taken which dulls the keenness of the mind, and when the soul as well as the flesh is surfeited, kindles the baneful and fiery incentive to vice.

CHAPTER VI.

That the mind is not intoxicated by wine alone.

THE belly when filled with all kinds of food gives birth to seeds of wantonness, nor can the mind, when choked with the weight of food, keep the guidance and government of the thoughts. For not only is drunkenness with wine wont to intoxicate the mind, but excess of all kinds of food makes it weak and uncertain, and robs it of all its power of pure and clear contemplation. The cause of the overthrow and wantonness of Sodom was not drunkenness through wine, but fulness of bread. Hear the Lord rebuking Jerusalem through the prophet. "For how did thy sister Sodom sin, except in that she ate her bread in fulness and abundance?"[5] And because through fulness of bread they were inflamed with uncontrollable lust of the flesh, they were burnt up by the judgment of God with fire and brimstone from heaven. But if excess of bread alone

---

[1] 1 Cor. xv. 28.   [2] 1 Cor. i. 30.   [3] Eph. iv. 13.
[4] See especially Conferences XVIII. and XIX.

[5] Ezek. xvi. 49.

drove them to such a headlong downfall into sin through the vice of satiety, what shall we think of those who with a vigorous body dare to partake of meat and wine with unbounded licence, taking not just what their bodily frailty demands, but what the eager desire of the mind suggests.

CHAPTER VII.

How bodily weakness need not interfere with purity of heart.

BODILY weakness is no hindrance to purity of heart, if only so much food is taken as the bodily weakness requires, and not what pleasure asks for. It is easier to find men who altogether abstain from the more fattening kinds of foods than men who make a moderate use of what is allowed to our necessities; and men who deny themselves everything out of love of continence than men who taking food on the plea of weakness preserve the due measure of what is sufficient.[1] For bodily weakness has its glory of self-restraint, where though food is permitted to the failing body, a man deprives himself of his refreshment, although he needs it, and only indulges in just so much food as the strict judgment of temperance decides to be sufficient for the necessities of life, and not what the longing appetite asks for. The more delicate foods, as they conduce to bodily health, so they need not destroy the purity of chastity, if they are taken in moderation. For whatever strength[2] is gained by partaking of them is used up in the toil and waste of care. Wherefore as no state of life can be deprived of the virtue of abstinence, so to none is the crown of perfection denied.

CHAPTER VIII.

How food should be taken with regard to the aim at perfect continence.[3]

AND so it is a very true and most excellent saying of the Fathers that the right method of fasting and abstinence lies in the measure of moderation and bodily chastening; and that this is the aim of perfect virtue for all alike, viz.: that though we are still forced to desire it, yet we should exercise self-restraint in the matter of the food, which we are obliged to take owing to the necessity of supporting the body. For even if one is weak in body, he can attain to a perfect virtue and one equal to that of those who are thoroughly strong and healthy, if with firmness of mind he keeps a check upon the desires and lusts which are not due to weakness of the flesh. For the Apostle says: "And take not care for the flesh in its lusts."[4] He does not forbid care for it in every respect: but says that care is not to be taken in regard to its desires and lusts. He cuts away the luxurious fondness for the flesh: he does not exclude the control necessary for life: he does the former, lest through pampering the flesh we should be involved in dangerous entanglements of the desires; the latter lest the body should be injured by our fault and unable to fulfil its spiritual and necessary duties.

CHAPTER IX.

Of the measure of the chastisment to be undertaken, and the remedy of fasting.

THE perfection then of abstinence is not to be gathered from calculations of time alone, nor only from the quality of the food; but beyond everything from the judgment of conscience. For each one should impose such a sparing diet on himself as the battle of his bodily struggle may require. The canonical observance of fasts is indeed valuable and by all means to be kept. But unless this is followed by a temperate partaking of food, one will not be able to arrive at the goal of perfection. For the abstinence of prolonged fasts — where repletion of body follows — produces weariness for a time rather than purity and chastity. Perfection of mind indeed depends upon the abstinence of the belly. He has no lasting purity and chastity, who is not contented always to keep to a well-balanced and temperate diet. Fasting, although severe, yet if unnecessary relaxation follows, is rendered useless, and presently leads to the vice of gluttony. A reasonable supply of food partaken of daily with moderation, is better than a severe and long fast at intervals. Excessive fasting has been known not only to undermine the constancy of the mind, but also to weaken the power of prayers through sheer weariness of body.

---

1 Petschenig's text in this passage is as follows: "Facilius vidimus viros qui ab escis corpulentioribus omnimodis temperarent, quam moderate usos pro necessitate concessis, et qui totum sibi pro amore continentiæ denegarent, quam qui eas sub infirmitatis occasione sumentes mensuram sufficientiæ custodirent." Gazæus gives something quite different: "Facilius vidimus victos qui ab escis corpulentioribus omnimodis temperarent, quas moderate usus pro necessitate concedit, et qui totum sibi pro continentiæ amore denegarent; quam qui eas sub infirmitatis occasione sumentes mensuram sufficientiæ custodirent."

2 *Quidquid enim fortitudinis.* — Petschenig. Gazæus has "*Quid quid enim fortitudinis causa.*"

3 *Quod pro perfectæ continentiæ fine esca sumenda sit.* — Petschenig. *Quomodo cibum appetere, ac sumere liceat* is the title as given by Gazæus.

4 Rom. xiii. 14.

CHAPTER X.

That abstinence from food is not of itself sufficient for preservation of bodily and mental purity.

In order to preserve the mind and body in a perfect condition abstinence from food is not alone sufficient: unless the other virtues of the mind as well are joined to it. And so humility must first be learned by the virtue of obedience, and grinding toil [1] and bodily exhaustion. The possession of money must not only be avoided, but the desire for it must be utterly rooted out. For it is not enough not to possess it, — a thing which comes to many as a matter of necessity: but we ought, if by chance it is offered, not even to admit the *wish* to have it. The madness of anger should be controlled; the downcast look of dejection be overcome; vainglory should be despised, the disdainfulness of pride trampled under foot, and the shifting and wandering thoughts of the mind restrained by continual recollection of God. And the slippery wanderings of our heart should be brought back again to the contemplation of God as often as our crafty enemy, in his endeavour to lead away the mind a captive from this consideration, creeps into the innermost recesses of the heart.

CHAPTER XI.

That bodily lusts are not extinguished except by the entire rooting out of vice.

For it is an impossibility that the fiery motions of the body can be extinguished, before the incentives of the other chief vices are utterly rooted out: concerning which we will speak in their proper place, if God permits, separately, in different books. But now we have to deal with Gluttony, that is the desire of the palate, against which our first battle is. He then will never be able to check the motions of a burning lust, who cannot restrain the desires of the appetite. The chastity of the inner man is shown by the perfection of this virtue. For you will never feel sure that he can strive against the opposition of a stronger enemy, whom you have seen overcome by weaker ones in a higher conflict. For of all virtues the nature is but one and the same, although they appear to be divided into many different kinds and names: just as there is but one substance of gold, although it may

seem to be distributed through many different kinds of jewelry according to the skill of the goldsmith. And so he is proved to possess no virtue perfectly, who is known to have broken down in some part of them. For how can we believe that that man has extinguished the burning heats of concupiscence (which are kindled not only by bodily incitement but by vice of the mind), who could not assuage the sharp stings of anger which break out from intemperance of heart alone? Or how can we think that he has repressed the wanton desires of the flesh and spirit, who has not been able to conquer the simple fault of pride? Or how can we believe that one has trampled under foot a wantonness which is ingrained in the flesh, who has not been able to disown the love of money, which is something external and outside our own substance? In what way will he triumph in the war of flesh and spirit, who has not been man enough to cure the disease of dejection? However great a city may be protected by the height of its walls and the strength of its closed gates, yet it is laid waste by the giving up of one postern however small. For what difference does it make whether a dangerous foe makes his way into the heart of the city over high walls, and through the wide spaces of the gate, or through secret and narrow passages?

CHAPTER XII.

That in our spiritual contest we ought to draw an example from the carnal contests.

"One who strives in the games is not crowned unless he has contended lawfully." [2] One who wants to extinguish the natural desires of the flesh, should first hasten to overcome those vices whose seat is outside our nature. For if we desire to make trial of the force of the Apostle's saying, we ought first to learn what are the laws and what the discipline of the world's contest, so that finally by a comparison with these, we may be able to know what the blessed Apostle meant to teach to us who are striving in a spiritual contest by this illustration. For in these conflicts, which, as the same Apostle says, hold out "a corruptible crown" [3] to the victors, this rule is kept, that he who aims at preparing himself for the crown of glory, which is embellished with the privilege of exemption, and who is anxious to enter the highest struggle in the

---

[1] *Operis contritione* (Petschenig): *cordis contritione* (Gazæus).   [2] 2 Tim. ii. 5.   [3] 1 Cor. ix. 25.

contest, should first in the Olympic and Pythian games give evidence of his abilities as a youth, and his strength in its first beginnings; since in these the younger men who want to practise this training are tested as to whether they deserve or ought to be admitted to it, by the judgment both of the president of the games and of the whole multitude. And when any one has been carefully tested, and has first been proved to be stained by no infamy of life, and then has been adjudged not ignoble through the yoke of slavery, and for this reason unworthy to be admitted to this training and to the company of those who practise it, and when thirdly he produces sufficient evidence of his ability and prowess and by striving with the younger men and his own compeers has shown both his skill and valour as a youth, and going forward from the contests of boys has been by the scrutiny of the president permitted to mix with full-grown men and those of approved experience, and has not only shown himself their equal in valour by constant striving with them, but has also many a time carried off the prize of victory among them, then at last he is allowed to approach the most illustrious conflict of the games, permission to contend in which is granted to none but victors and those who are decked with many crowns and prizes. If we understand this illustration from a carnal contest, we ought by a comparison with it to know what is the system and method of our spiritual conflict as well.

CHAPTER XIII.

That we cannot enter the battle of the inner man unless we have been set free from the vice of gluttony.

WE also ought first to give evidence of our freedom from subjection to the flesh. For "of whom a man is overcome, of the same is he the slave."[1] And "every one that doeth sin is the slave of sin."[2] And when the scrutiny of the president of the contest finds that we are stained by no infamy of disgraceful lust, and when we are judged by him not to be slaves of the flesh, and ignoble and unworthy of the Olympic struggle against our vices, then we shall be able to enter the lists against our equals, that is the lusts of the flesh and the motions and disturbances of the soul. For it is impossible for a full belly to make trial of the combat of the inner man: nor is he worthy to be tried in harder battles, who can be overcome in a slight skirmish.

CHAPTER XIV.

How gluttonous desires can be overcome.

FIRST then we must trample under foot gluttonous desires, and to this end the mind must be reduced not only by fasting, but also by vigils, by reading, and by frequent compunction of heart for those things in which perhaps it recollects that it has been deceived or overcome, sighing at one time with horror at sin, at another time inflamed with the desire of perfection and saintliness: until it is fully occupied and possessed by such cares and meditations, and recognizes the participation of food to be not so much a concession to pleasure, as a burden laid upon it; and considers it to be rather a necessity for the body than anything desirable for the soul. And, preserved by this zeal of ·mind and continual compunction, we shall beat down the wantonness of the flesh (which becomes more proud and haughty by being fomented with food) and its dangerous incitement, and so by the copiousness of our tears and the weeping of our heart we shall succeed in extinguishing the fiery furnace of our body, which is kindled by the Babylonish king[3] who continually furnishes us with opportunities for sin, and vices with which we burn more fiercely, instead of naphtha and pitch — until, through the grace of God, instilled like dew by His Spirit in our hearts, the heats of fleshly lusts can be altogether deadened. This then is our first contest, this is as it were our first trial in the Olympic games, to extinguish the desires of the palate and the belly by the longing for perfection. On which account we must not only trample down all unnecessary desire for food by the contemplation of the virtues, but also must take what is necessary for the support of nature, not without anxiety of heart, as if it were opposed to chastity. And so at length we may enter on the course of our life, so that there may be no time in which we feel that we are recalled from our spiritual studies, further than when we are obliged by the weakness of the body to descend for the needful care of it. And when we are subjected to this necessity — of attending to the wants of life rather than the desires of the soul — we should hasten to withdraw as quickly as possible from it, as if it kept us back from really health-giving studies. For we cannot possibly scorn the gratification of food presented to us, unless the mind is fixed on the contemplation of divine things, and is the rather

---

[1] 2 Pet. ii. 19.   [2] John viii. 34.

[3] Cf. Dan. iii. 6; and see below Book VI. c. xvii. where Cassian once more speaks of the devil as the Babylonish king.

entranced with the love of virtue and the delight of things celestial. And so a man will despise all things present as transitory, when he has securely fixed his mental gaze on those things which are immovable and eternal, and already contemplates in heart — though still in the flesh — the blessedness of his future life.

CHAPTER XV.

How a monk must always be eager to preserve his purity of heart.

IT is like the case when one endeavours to strike some mighty prize of virtue on high pointed out by some very small mark; with the keenest eyesight he points the aim of his dart, knowing that large rewards of glory and prizes depend on his hitting it; and he turns away his gaze from every other consideration, and must direct it thither, where he sees that the reward and prize is placed, because he would be sure to lose the prize of his skill and the reward of his prowess if the keenness of his gaze should be diverted ever so little.[1]

CHAPTER XVI.

How, after the fashion of the Olympic games, a monk should not attempt spiritual conflicts unless he has won battles over the flesh.

AND so when the desires of the belly and of the palate have been by these considerations overcome, and when we have been declared, as in the Olympic contests, neither slaves of the flesh nor infamous through the brand of sin, we shall be adjudged to be worthy of the contest in higher struggles as well, and, leaving behind lessons of this kind, may be believed capable of entering the lists against spiritual wickednesses, against which only victors and those who are allowed to contend in a spiritual conflict are deemed worthy to struggle. For this is so to speak a most solid foundation of all the conflicts, viz.: that in the first instance the impulses of carnal desires should be destroyed. For no one can lawfully strive unless his own flesh has been overcome. And one who does not strive lawfully certainly cannot take a share in the contest, nor win a crown of glory and the grace of victory. But if we have been overcome in this battle, having been proved as it were slaves of carnal lusts, and thus displaying the tokens neither of freedom nor of strength, we shall be straightway repulsed from the conflicts with spiritual hosts, as unworthy and as slaves, with every mark of confusion. For "every one that doeth sin is the servant of sin."[2] And this will be addressed to us by the blessed Apostle, together with those among whom fornication is named. "Temptation does not overtake you, except such as is human."[3] For if we do not seek for strength of mind[4] we shall not deserve to make trial of severer contest against wickedness on high, if we have been unable to subdue our weak flesh which resists the spirit. And some not understanding this testimony of the Apostle, have read the subjunctive instead of the indicative mood, i.e., "Let no temptation overcome you, except such as is human."[5] But it is clear that it is rather said by him with the meaning not of a wish but of a declaration or rebuke.

CHAPTER XVII.

That the foundation and basis of the spiritual combat must be laid in the struggle against gluttony.

WOULD you like to hear a true athlete of Christ striving according to the rules and laws of the conflict? "I," said he, "so run, not as uncertainly; I so fight, not as one that beateth the air: but I chastise my body and bring it into subjection, lest by any means when I have preached to others I myself should be a castaway."[6] You see how he made the chief part of the struggle depend upon himself, that is upon his flesh, as if on a most sure foundation, and placed the result of the battle simply in the chastisement of the flesh and the subjection of his body. "I then so run not as uncertainly." He does not run uncertainly, because,[7] looking to the heavenly Jerusalem, he has a mark set, towards which his heart is swiftly directed without swerving. He does not run uncertainly, because, "forgetting those things which are behind, he reaches forth to those that are before, pressing towards the mark for the prize of the high calling of God in Christ Jesus,"[8] whither he ever directs his mental gaze, and hastening towards it with all speed[9] of heart, proclaims with confidence, "I have fought a good fight, I have finished

---

1 Compare a similar illustration in the Conferences I. v.

2 S. John viii. 34.
3 1 Cor. x. 13.
4 *Mentis robore non quæsito.* — Petschenig. Gazæus omits the negative and reads *conquisito.*
5 S. Jerome's version, which was certainly known to Cassian (cf. Conferences XXIII. viii.) has "Temptatio vos non apprehendat nisi humana."
6 1 Cor. ix. 26, 27.
7 *Quia* (Petschenig): *Qui* (Gazæus).
8 Phil. iii. 13, 14.
9 *Properatione,* others *Præparatione.*

my course, I have kept the faith."[1] And because he knows he has run unweariedly "after the odour of the ointment"[2] of Christ with ready devotion of heart, and has won the battle of the spiritual combat by the chastisement of the flesh, he boldly concludes and says, "Henceforth there is laid up for me a crown of righteousness, which the Lord, the righteous judge, will give to me in that day." And that he might open up to us also a like hope of reward, if we desire to imitate him in the struggle of his course, he added: "But not to me only, but to all also who love His coming;"[3] declaring that we shall be sharers of his crown in the day of judgment, if we love the coming of Christ — not that one only which will be manifest to men even against their will; but also this one which daily comes to pass in holy souls — and if we gain the victory in the fight by chastising the body. And of this coming it is that the Lord speaks in the Gospel. "I," says He, "and my Father will come to him, and will make our abode with him."[4] And again: "Behold, I stand at the door and knock: if any man hear my voice and open the gate, I will come in to him and will sup with him, and he with me."[5]

CHAPTER XVIII.

Of the number of different conflicts and victories through which the blessed Apostle ascended to the crown of the highest combat.

BUT he does not mean that he has only finished the contest of a race when he says "I so run, not as uncertainly" (a phrase which has more particularly to do with the intention of the mind and fervour of his spirit, in which he followed Christ with all zeal, crying out with the Bride, "We will run after thee for the odour of thine ointments;"[6] and again, "My soul cleaveth unto thee:"[7] but he also testifies that he has conquered in another kind of contest, saying, "So fight I, not as one that beateth the air, but I chastise my body and bring it into subjection." And this properly has to do with the pains of abstinence, and bodily fasting and affliction of the flesh: as he means by this that he is a vigorous bruiser of his own flesh, and points out that not in vain has he planted his blows of continence against it; but that he has gained a battle triumph by mortifying his own body; for when it is chastised with the blows of continence and struck down with the boxing-gloves of fasting, he has

secured for his victorious spirit the crown of immortality and the prize of incorruption. You see the orthodox method of the contest, and consider the issue of spiritual combats: how the athlete of Christ having gained a victory over the rebellious flesh, having cast it as it were under his feet, is carried forward as triumphing on high. And therefore "he does not run uncertainly," because he trusts that he will forthwith enter the holy city, the heavenly Jerusalem. He "so fights," that is with fasts and humiliation of the flesh, "not as one that beateth the air," that is, striking into space with blows of continence, through which he struck not the empty air, but those spirits who inhabit it, by the chastisement of his body. For one who says "not as one that beateth the air," shows that he strikes — not empty and void air, but certain beings in the air. And because he had overcome in this kind of contest, and marched on enriched with the rewards of many crowns, not undeservedly does he begin to enter the lists against still more powerful foes, and having triumphed over his former rivals, he boldly makes proclamation and says, "Now our striving is not against flesh and blood, but against principalities, against powers, against world-rulers of this darkness, against spiritual wickedness in heavenly places."[8]

CHAPTER XIX.

That the athlete of Christ, so long as he is in the body, is never without a battle.

THE athlete of Christ, as long as he is in the body, is never in want of a victory to be gained in contests: but in proportion as he grows by triumphant successes, so does a severer kind of struggle confront him. For when the flesh is subdued and conquered, what swarms of foes, what hosts of enemies are incited by his triumphs and rise up against the victorious soldier of Christ! for fear lest in the ease of peace the soldier of Christ might relax his efforts and begin to forget the glorious struggles of his contests, and be rendered slack through the idleness which is caused by immunity from danger, and be cheated of the reward of his prizes and the recompense of his triumphs. And so if we want to rise with ever-growing virtue to these stages of triumph we ought also in the same way to enter the lists of battle and begin by saying with the Apostle: "I so fight, not as one that beateth the air, but I chastise my body and bring it into sub-

---

1 2 Tim. iv. 7.
2 Cant. i. 3.
3 2 Tim. iv. 8.
4 John xiv. 23.

5 Rev. iii. 20.
6 Cant. i. 3.
7 Ps. lxii. (lxiii.) 9.

8 Eph. vi. 12.

jection," [1] that when this conflict is ended we may once more be able to say with him: "we wrestle not against flesh and blood, but against principalities, against powers, against world-rulers of this darkness, against spiritual wickedness in heavenly places." [2] For otherwise we cannot possibly join battle with them nor deserve to make trial of spiritual combats if we are baffled in a carnal contest, and smitten down in a struggle with the belly: and deservedly will it be said of us by the Apostle in the language of blame: "Temptation does not overtake you, except what is common to man." [3]

CHAPTER XX.

How a monk should not overstep the proper hours for taking food, if he wants to proceed to the struggle of interior conflicts.

A MONK therefore who wants to proceed to the struggle of interior conflicts should lay down this as a precaution for himself to begin with: viz.: that he will not in any case allow himself to be overcome by any delicacies, or take anything to eat or drink before the fast [4] is over and the proper hour for refreshment has come, outside meal times; [5] nor, when the meal is over, will he allow himself to take a morsel however small; and likewise that he will observe the canonical time and measure of sleep. For that self-indulgence must be cut off in the same way that the sin of unchastity has to be rooted out. For if a man is unable to check the unnecessary desires of the appetite how will he be able to extinguish the fire of carnal lust? And if a man is not able to control passions, which are openly manifest and are but small, how will he be able with temperate discretion to fight against those which are secret, and excite him, when none are there to see? And therefore strength of mind is tested in separate impulses and in any sort of passion: and if it is overcome in the case of very small and manifest desires, how it will endure in those that are really great and powerful and hidden, each man's conscience must witness for himself.

[1] 1 Cor. ix. 26, 27.
[2] Eph. vi. 12.
[3] 1 Cor. x. 13.
[4] *Statio.* This is properly the term for the weekly fasts on Wednesday and Friday, observed by the early Church in memory of our Lord's betrayal and crucifixion. See Tertullian on Prayer c. xix.; on Fasting c. i. x. In this place the word appears to be used by Cassian for the close of the fast; while elsewhere he uses it for fasting generally (not specially on Wednesday and Friday,) as in c. xxiv. of the present Book, and in the Conferences, II. xxv.; XXI. xxi. The origin of the word is somewhat uncertain (a) because the fast was observed on stated days (*statis diebus*); or (b), as S. Ambrose suggests, because "our fasts are our encampments which protect us from the devil's attacks: in short, they are called *stationes*, because standing (*stantes*) and staying in them we repel our plotting foe" (Serm. 25). See Dictionary of Christian Antiquities, vol. ii. p. 1928.
[5] *Extra mensam.*

CHAPTER XXI.

Of the inward peace of a monk, and of spiritual abstinence.

FOR it is not an external enemy whom we have to dread. Our foe is shut up within ourselves: an internal warfare is daily waged by us: and if we are victorious in this, all external things will be made weak, and everything will be made peaceful and subdued for the soldier of Christ. We shall have no external enemy to fear, if what is within is overcome and subdued to the spirit. And let us not believe that that external fast from visible food alone can possibly be sufficient for perfection of heart and purity of body unless with it there has also been united a fast of the soul. For the soul also has its foods which are harmful, fattened on which, even without superfluity of meats, it is involved in a downfall of wantonness. Slander is its food, and indeed one that is very dear to it. A burst of anger also is its food, even if it be a very slight one; yet supplying it with miserable food for an hour, and destroying it as well with its deadly savour. Envy is a food of the mind, corrupting it with its poisonous juices and never ceasing to make it wretched and miserable at the prosperity and success of another. Kenodoxia, i.e., vainglory is its food, which gratifies it with a delicious meal for a time; but afterwards strips it clear and bare of all virtue, and dismisses it barren and void of all spiritual fruit, so that it makes it not only lose the rewards of huge labours, but also makes it incur heavier punishments. All lust and shifty wanderings of heart are a sort of food for the soul, nourishing it on harmful meats, but leaving it afterwards without share of the heavenly bread and of really solid food. If then, with all the powers we have, we abstain from these in a most holy fast, our observance of the bodily fast will be both useful and profitable. For labour of the flesh, when joined with contrition of the spirit, will produce a sacrifice that is most acceptable to God, and a worthy shrine of holiness in the pure and undefiled inmost chambers of the heart. But if, while fasting as far as the body is concerned, we are entangled in the most dangerous vices of the soul, our humiliation of the flesh will do us no good whatever, while the most precious part of us is defiled: since we go wrong through that substance by virtue of which we are made a shrine of the Holy Ghost. For it is not so much the corruptible flesh as the clean heart, which is made a shrine for God, and a temple of the Holy Ghost. We ought therefore, whenever the outward man fasts, to restrain the inner man as well from food which is bad for him: that inner man, namely, which the blessed Apostle above all urges us to present pure before God, that it may be found worthy to receive Christ as a guest within, saying "that in the inner man Christ may dwell in your hearts through faith." [1]

CHAPTER XXII.

That we should for this reason practise bodily abstinence that we may by it attain to a spiritual fast.

AND so we know that we ought therefore to bestow attention on bodily abstinence, that we may by this fasting attain to purity of heart. Otherwise our labours will be spent in vain, if we endure this without weariness, in contemplating the end, but are unable to reach the end for which we have endured such trials; and it would have been better to have abstained from the forbidden foods of the soul, than to have fasted with the body from things indifferent and harmless, for in the case of these latter there is a simple and harmless reception of a creature of God, which in itself has nothing wrong about it: but in the case of the former there is at the very first a dangerous tendency to devour the brethren; of which it is said, "Do not love backbiting lest thou be rooted out." [2] And concerning anger and jealousy the blessed Job says: "For anger slayeth a fool, and envy killeth a child." [3] And at the same time it should be noticed that he who is angered is set down as a fool; and he who is jealous, as a child. For the former is not undeservedly considered a fool, since of his own accord he brings death upon himself, being goaded by the stings of anger; and the latter, while he is envious, proves that he is a child and a minor, for while he envies another he shows that the one at whose prosperity he is vexed, is greater than he.

CHAPTER XXIII.

What should be the character of the monk's food.

WE should then choose for our food, not only that which moderates the heat of burning lust, and avoids kindling it; but what is easily got ready, and what is recommended by its cheapness, and is suitable to the life of the brethren and their common use. For the nature of gluttony is threefold: first, there is that which forces us to anticipate the proper hour for a meal, next that which delights in stuffing the stomach, and gorging all kinds of food; thirdly, that which takes pleasure in more refined and delicate feasting. And so against it a monk should observe a threefold watch: first, he should wait till the proper time for breaking the fast; secondly, he should not give way to gorging; thirdly, he should be contented with any of the commoner sorts of food. For anything that is taken over and above what is customary and the common use of all, is branded by the ancient tradition of the fathers as defiled with the sin of vanity and glorying and ostentation. Nor of those whom we have seen to be deservedly eminent for learning and discretion, or whom the grace of Christ has singled out as shining lights for every one to imitate, have we known any who have abstained from eating bread which is accounted cheap and easily to be obtained among them; nor have we seen that any one who has rejected this rule and given up the use of bread and taken to a diet of beans or herbs or fruits, has been reckoned among the most esteemed, or even acquired the grace of knowledge and discretion. For not only do they lay it down that a monk ought not to ask for foods which are not customary for others, lest his mode of life should be exposed publicly to all and rendered vain and idle and so be destroyed by the disease of vanity; but they insist that the common chastening discipline of fasts ought not lightly to be disclosed to any one, but as far as possible concealed and kept secret. But when any of the brethren arrive they rule that we ought to show the virtues of kindness and charity instead of observing a severe abstinence and our strict daily rule: nor should we consider what our own wishes and profit or the ardour of our desires may require, but set before us and gladly fulfil whatever the refreshment of the guest, or his weakness may demand from us.

CHAPTER XXIV.

How in Egypt we saw that the daily fast was broken without scruple on our arrival.

WHEN we had come from the region of Syria and had sought the province of Egypt, in our desire to learn the rules of the Elders, we were astonished at the alacrity of heart with which we were there received so that no rule forbidding refreshment till the appointed hour of the fast was over was observed, such as we had been brought up to observe in the monasteries of Palestine; but except in the case of the regular days, Wednesdays and Fridays,

---

[1] Eph. iii. 16, 17. [2] Prov. xx. 13. (LXX.). [3] Job v. 2.

wherever we went the daily fast[1] was broken:[2] and when we asked why the daily fast was thus ignored by them without scruple one of the elders replied: "The opportunity for fasting is always with me. But as I am going to conduct you on your way, I cannot always keep you with me. And a fast, although it is useful and advisable, is yet a free-will offering. But the exigencies of a command require the fulfilment of a work of charity. And so receiving Christ in you I ought to refresh Him: but when I have sent you on your way I shall be able to balance the hospitality offered for His sake by a stricter fast on my own account. For 'the children of the bridegroom cannot fast while the bridegroom is with them:'[3] but when he has departed, then they will rightly fast."

CHAPTER XXV.

Of the abstinence of one old man who took food six times so sparingly that he was still hungry.

WHEN one of the elders was pressing me to eat a little more as I was taking refreshment, and I said that I could not, he replied: "I have already laid my table six times for different brethren who had arrived, and, pressing each of them, I partook of food with him, and am still hungry, and do you, who now partake of refreshment for the first time, say that you cannot eat any more?"

CHAPTER XXVI.

Of another old man, who never partook of food alone in his cell.

WE have seen another who lived alone, who declared that he had never enjoyed food by himself alone, but that even if for five days running none of the brethren came to his cell he constantly put off taking food until on Saturday or Sunday he went to church for service and found some stranger whom he brought home at once to his cell, and together with him partook of refreshment for the body not so much by reason of his own needs, as for the sake of kindness and on his brother's account. And so as they know that the daily fast is broken without scruple on the arrival of brethren, when they leave, they compensate for the refreshment which has been enjoyed on their account by a greater abstinence, and sternly make up for the reception of even a very little food by a severer chastisement not only as regards bread, but also by lessening their usual amount of sleep.

CHAPTER XXVII.

What the two Abbots Pæsius and John said of the fruits of their zeal.

WHEN the aged John, who was superior of a large monastery and of a quantity of brethren, had come to visit the aged Pæsius, who was living in a vast desert, and had been asked of him as of a very old friend, what he had done in all the forty years in which he had been separated from him and had scarcely ever been disturbed in his solitude by the brethren: "Never," said he, "has the sun seen me eating," "nor me angry," said the other.[4]

CHAPTER XXVIII.

The lesson and example which Abbot John when dying left to his disciples.

WHEN the same old man, as one who was readily going to depart to his own, was lying at his last gasp, and the brethren were standing round, they implored and intreated that he would leave them, as a sort of legacy, some special charge by which they could attain to the height of perfection, the more easily from the brevity of the charge: he sighed and said, "I never did my own will, nor taught any one what I had not first done myself."

CHAPTER XXIX.

Of Abbot Machetes, who never slept during the spiritual conferences, but always went to sleep during earthly tales.

WE knew an old man, Machetes by name, who lived at a distance from the crowds of the brethren, and obtained by his daily prayers

---

1 *Statio.*
2 The allusion is here to the sparing diet and voluntary fasts of the monks, among whom but one meal a day was usual (see the note on III. xiii.); and though this was ordinarily taken at midday, yet many of the more celebrated anchorites never broke their fast till the evening; e.g. S. Antony is said never to have eaten till sunset (Vita Anton.), and S. Jerome gives a similar account of Hilarion (Vita Hil. § 4), while other instances of voluntary fasts are given by Cassian in the following chapters, xxv.-xxvii. The "station" days, however, viz., Wednesday and Friday, being of ecclesiastical authority, were strictly observed as a matter of rule, but these other voluntary fasts at other times were to be freely broken through on account of the arrival of visitors. See the Conferences II. xxvi., XXI. xiv., XXIV. xxi., and cf. Rufinus, History of the Monks II. vii., Palladius, the Lausiac History, c. lii. So the Rule of S. Benedict (c. liii.) orders that on the arrival of visitors the Superior is to sit at table with them and break his fast, unless it be a special fast day which may not be broken; but the brethren are to observe the regular fasts.
3 S. Matt. ix. 15. The Latin has *sponsus* in each clause.

4 There is a Pæsius mentioned by Palladius in the Lausiac History, but it is not clear whether he is the same man whom Cassian mentions. John is a different person from the one already mentioned in Book IV. xxiii. He is mentioned again below in xl., and the Nineteenth Conference is assigned to him.

this grace from the Lord, that as often as a spiritual conference was held, whether by day or by night, he never was at all overcome by sleep: but if any one tried to introduce a word of detraction, or idle talk, he dropped off to sleep at once as if the poison of slander could not possibly penetrate to pollute his ears.

CHAPTER XXX.

A saying of the same old man about not judging any one.

THE same old man, when he was teaching us that no one ought to judge another, remarked that there were three points on which he had charged and rebuked the brethren, viz.: because some allowed their uvula to be cut off, or kept a cloak in their cell, or blessed oil and gave it to those dwelling in the world who asked for it: and he said that he had done all these things himself. For having contracted some malady of the uvula, I wasted away, said he, for so long, through its weakness, that at last I was driven by stress of the pain, and by the persuasion of all the elders, to allow it to be cut off. And I was forced too by reason of this illness, to keep a cloak. And I was also compelled to bless oil and give it to those who prayed for it — a thing which I execrated above everything, since that I thought that it proceeded from great presumption of heart — when suddenly many who were living in the world surrounded me, so that I could not possibly escape them in any other way, had they not extorted from me with no small violence, and entreaties that I would lay my hand on a vessel offered by them, and sign it with the sign of the cross: and so believing that they had secured blessed oil, at last they let me go. And by these things I plainly discovered that a monk was in the same case and entangled in the same faults for which he had ventured to judge others. Each one therefore ought only to judge himself, and to be on the watch, with care and circumspection in all things not to judge the life and conduct of others in accordance with the Apostle's charge, "But thou, why dost thou judge thy brother? to his own master he standeth or falleth." And this: "Judge not, that ye be not judged. For with what judgment ye judge, ye shall be judged." [1] For besides the reason of which we have spoken, it is for this cause also dangerous to judge concerning others because in those matters in which we are offended — as we do not know the need or the reason for which they are really acting either rightly in the

---

1 Rom. xiv. 10, 4; S. Matt. vii. 1, 2.

sight of God, or at any rate in a pardonable manner — we are found to have judged them rashly and in this commit no light sin, by forming an opinion of our brethren different from what we ought.

CHAPTER XXXI.

The same old man's rebuke when he saw how the brethren went to sleep during the spiritual conferences, and woke up when some idle story was told.

THE same old man made clear by this proof that it was the devil who encouraged idle tales, and showed himself always as the enemy of spiritual conferences. For when he was discoursing to some of the brethren on necessary matters and spiritual things, and saw that they were weighed down with a sound slumber, and could not drive away the weight of sleep from their eyes, he suddenly introduced an idle tale. And when he saw that at once they woke up, delighted with it, and pricked up their ears, he groaned and said, "Up till now we were speaking of celestial things and all your eyes were overpowered with a sound slumber; but as soon as an idle tale was introduced, we all woke up and shook off the drowsiness of sleep which had overcome us. And from this therefore consider who is the enemy of that spiritual conference, and who has shown himself the suggester of that useless and carnal talk. For it is most evidently shown that it is he who, rejoicing in evil, never ceases to encourage the latter and to oppose the former."

CHAPTER XXXII.

Of the letters which were burnt without being read.

NOR do I think it less needful to relate this act of a brother who was intent on purity of heart, and extremely anxious with regard to the contemplation of things divine. When after an interval of fifteen years a large number of letters had been brought to him from his father and mother and many friends in the province of Pontus, he received the huge packet of letters, and turning over the matter in his own mind for some time, "What thoughts," said he, "will the reading of these suggest to me, which will incite me either to senseless joy or to useless sadness! for how many days will they draw off the attention of my heart from the contemplation I have set before me, by the recollection of those who wrote them! How long will it take for the disturbance of mind thus created to be calmed, and what an effort will it cost for that former state of peacefulness to be restored, if the mind is once moved by the sympathy of the letters, and by recalling the words and looks of those whom it has left for so long begins once more in thought and spirit to revisit them, to dwell among them and to be with them. And it will be of no use to have forsaken them in the body, if one begins to look on them with the heart, and readmits and revives that memory which on renouncing this world every one gave up, as if he were dead. Turning this over in his mind, he determined not only not to read a single letter, but not even to open the packet, for fear lest, at the sight of the names of the writers, or on recalling their appearance, the purpose of his spirit might give way. And so he threw it into the fire to be burnt, all tied up just as he had received it, crying, "Away, O ye thoughts of my home, be ye burnt up, and try no further to recall me to those things from which I have fled."

CHAPTER XXXIII.

Of the solution of a question which Abbot Theodore obtained by prayer.

WE knew also Abbot Theodore,[1] a man gifted with the utmost holiness and with perfect knowledge not only in practical life, but also in understanding the Scriptures, which he had not acquired so much by study and reading, or worldly education, as by purity of heart alone: since he could with difficulty understand and speak but a very few words of the Greek language. This man when he was seeking an explanation of some most difficult question, continued without ceasing for seven days and nights in prayer until he discovered by a revelation from the Lord the solution of the question propounded.

CHAPTER XXXIV.

Of the saying of the same old man, through which he taught by what efforts a monk can acquire a knowledge of the Scriptures.

THIS man therefore, when some of the brethren were wondering at the splendid light of his knowledge and were asking of him some meanings of Scripture, said that a monk who wanted to acquire a knowledge of the Scriptures ought not to spend his labour on the

works of commentators, but rather to keep all the efforts of his mind and intentions of his heart set on purifying himself from carnal vices: for when these are driven out, at once the eyes of the heart, as if the veil of the passions were removed, will begin as it were naturally to gaze on the mysteries [2] of Scripture: since they were not declared to us by the grace of the Holy Spirit in order that they should remain unknown and obscure; but they are rendered obscure by our fault, as the veil of our sins covers the eyes of the heart, and when these are restored to their natural state of health, the mere reading of Holy Scripture is by itself amply sufficient for beholding the true knowledge, nor do they need the aid of commentators, just as these eyes of flesh need no man's teaching how to see, provided that they are free from dimness or the darkness of blindness. For this reason there have arisen so great differences and mistakes among commentators because most of them, paying no sort of attention towards purifying the mind, rush into the work of interpreting the Scriptures, and in proportion to the density or impurity of their heart form opinions that are at variance with and contrary to each other's and to the faith, and so are unable to take in the light of truth.

CHAPTER XXXV.

A rebuke of the same old man, when he had come to my cell in the middle of the night.

THE same Theodore came unexpectedly to my cell in the dead of night, with paternal inquisitiveness seeking what I — an unformed anchorite as I was — might be doing by myself; and when he had found me there already, as I had finished my vesper office, beginning to refresh my wearied body, and lying down on a mat, he sighed from the bottom of his heart, and calling me by name, said, "How many, O John, are at this hour communing with God, and embracing Him, and detaining Him with them, while you are deprived of so great light, enfeebled as you are with lazy sleep!"

And since the virtues of the fathers and the grace given to them have tempted us to turn aside to a story like this, I think it well to record in this volume a noteworthy deed of charity, which we experienced from the kindness of that most excellent man Archebius, that the purity of continence grafted on to a work of charity may more readily shine forth, being embellished with a pleasing variety.

---

1 Nothing further is known for certain of this Theodore. He may be the author of the VIth of the Conferences; but must be carefully distinguished from his more celebrated namesake, the friend of Pachomius, and third Abbot of Tabenna, who died before Cassian's visit to Egypt.

2 *Sacramenta.*

For the duty of fasting is then rendered acceptable to God, when it is made perfect by the fruits of charity.

CHAPTER XXXVI.

A description of the desert in Diolcos, where the anchorites live.

AND so when we had come, while still beginners, from the monasteries of Palestine, to a city of Egypt called Diolcos,[1] and were contemplating a large number of monks bound by the discipline of the Cœnobium, and trained in that excellent system of monasteries, which is also the earliest, we were also eager to see with all wisdom of heart another system as well which is still better, viz. : that of the anchorites, as we were incited thereto by the praises of it by everybody. For these men, having first lived for a very long time in Cœnobia, and having diligently learnt all the rules of patience and discretion, and acquired the virtues of humility and renunciation, and having perfectly overcome all their faults, in order to engage in most fearful conflicts with devils, penetrate the deepest recesses of the desert. Finding then that men of this sort were living near the river Nile in a place which is surrounded on one side by the same river, on the other by the expanse of the sea, and forms an island, habitable by none but monks seeking such recesses, since the saltness of the soil and dryness of the sand make it unfit for any cultivation — to these men, I say, we eagerly hastened, and were beyond measure astonished at their labours which they endure in the contemplation of the virtues and their love of solitude. For they are hampered by such a scarcity even of water that the care and exactness with which they portion it out is such as no miser would bestow in preserving and hoarding the most precious kind of wine. For they carry it three miles or even further from the bed of the above-mentioned river, for all necessary purposes; and the distance, great as it is, with sandy mountains in between, is doubled by the very great difficulty of the task.

CHAPTER XXXVII.

Of the cells which Abbot Archebius gave up to us with their furniture.

HAVING then seen this, as we were inflamed with the desire of imitating them, the aforesaid Archebius, the most famous among them

for the grace of kindness, drew us into his cell, and having discovered our desire, pretended that he wanted to leave the place, and to offer his cell to us, as if he were going away, declaring that he would have done it, even if we had not come. And we, inflamed with the desire of remaining there, and putting unhesitating faith in the assertions of so great a man, willingly agreed to this, and took over his cell with all its furniture and belongings. And so having succeeded in his pious fraud, he left the place for a few days in which to procure the means for constructing a cell, and after this returned, and with the utmost labour built another cell for himself. And after some little time, when some other brethren came inflamed with the same desire to stay there, he deceived them by a similar charitable falsehood, and gave this one up with everything pertaining to it. But he, unweariedly persevering in his act of charity, built for himself a third cell to dwell in.[2]

CHAPTER XXXVIII.

The same Archebius paid a debt of his mother's by the labour of his own hands.

IT seems to me worth while to hand down another charitable act of the same man, that the monks of our land may be taught by the example of one and the same man to maintain not only a rigorous continence, but also the most unfeigned affection of love. For he, sprung from no ignoble family, while yet a child, scorning the love of this world and of his kinsfolk, fled to the monastery which is nearly four miles distant from the aforementioned town, where he so passed all his life, that never once throughout the whole of fifty years did he enter or see the village from which he had come, nor even look upon the face of any woman, not even his own mother. In the mean while his father was overtaken by death, and left a debt of a hundred solidi. And though he himself was entirely free from all annoyances, since he had been disinherited of all his father's property, yet he found that his mother was excessively annoyed by the creditors. Then he through consideration of duty somewhat moderated that gospel severity through which formerly, while his parents were prosperous, he did not recognize that he possessed a father or mother on earth; and acknowledged that he had a mother, and hastened to relieve her in her distress, without relaxing anything of the austerity he had set

---

[1] Diolcos is mentioned again in the Conferences XVIII. i. Sozomen (VI. xxix.) speaks of two celebrated monasteries near there presided over by Piamun and John.

[2] Somewhat similar stories are told of others by Palladius, (Lausiac History, cc. ii. 1, lxx.); and Rufinus, History of the Monks, I. xxiii.

himself. For remaining within the cloister of the monastery he asked that the task of his usual work might be trebled. And there for a whole year toiling night and day alike he paid to the creditors the due measure of the debt secured by his toil and labour, and relieved his mother from all annoyance and anxiety; ridding her of the burden of the debt in such a way as not to suffer aught of the severity he had set himself to be diminished, on plea of duteous necessity. Thus did he preserve his wonted austerities, without ever denying to his mother's heart the work which duty demanded, as, though he had formerly disregarded her for the love of Christ, he now acknowledged her again out of consideration of duty.

CHAPTER XXXIX.

Of the device of a certain old man by which some work was found for Abbot Simeon when he had nothing to do.

WHEN a brother who was very dear to us, Simeon by name, a man utterly ignorant of Greek, had come from the region of Italy, one of the elders, anxious to show to him, as he was a stranger, a work of charity, with some pretence of the benefit being mutual, asked him why he sat doing nothing in his cell, guessing from this that he would not be able to stay much longer in it both because of the roving thoughts which idleness produces and because of his want of the necessities of life; well knowing that no one can endure the assaults made in solitude, but one who is contented to procure food for himself by the labour of his hands. And when the other replied that he could not do or manage any of the things which were usually done by the brethren there, except write a good hand, if any one in Egypt wanted a Latin book for his use, then he at length seized the opportunity to secure the long wished for work of charity, under colour of its being a mutual benefit; and said, "From God this opportunity comes, for I was just looking for some one to write out for me the Epistles[1] in Latin; for I have a brother who is bound in the chains of military service, and is a good Latin scholar, to whom I want to send something from Scripture for him to read for his edification." And so when Simeon gratefully took this as an opportunity offered to him by God, the old man also gladly seized the pretext, under colour of which he could freely carry out his work of charity, and at once not only brought him as a matter of business everything he could want for a whole

year, but also conveyed to him parchment and everything requisite for writing, and received afterwards the manuscript, which was not of the slightest use (since in those parts they were all utterly ignorant of this language), and did no good to anybody except that which resulted from this device and large outlay, as the one, without shame or confusion, procured his necessary food and sustenance by the reward of his work and labour, and the other carried out his kindness and bounty as it were by the compulsion of a debt: securing for himself a more abundant reward proportioned to the zeal with which he procured for his foreign brother not only his necessary food, but als materials for writing, and an opportunity of work.

CHAPTER XL.

Of the boys who when bringing to a sick man some figs, died in the desert from hunger, without having tasted them.

BUT since in the section in which we proposed to say something about the strictness of fasting and abstinence, kindly acts and deeds of charity seem to have been intermingled, again returning to our design we will insert in this little book a noteworthy deed of some who were boys in years though not in their feelings. For when, to their great surprise, some one had brought to Abbot John, the steward in the desert of Scete, some figs from Libya Mareotis,[2] as being a thing never before seen in those districts,— (John) who had the management of the church in the days of the blessed Presbyter Paphnutius,[3] by whom it had been intrusted to him, at once sent them by the hands of two lads to an old man who was laid up in ill health in the further parts of the desert, and who lived about eighteen miles from the church. And when they had received the fruit, and set off for the cell of the above-mentioned old man, they lost the right path altogether — a thing which there easily happens even to elders — as a thick fog suddenly came on. And when all day and night they had wandered about the trackless waste of the desert, and could not possibly find the sick man's cell, worn out at last both by weariness from their journey, and from hunger and thirst, they bent their knees and gave up their souls to God in the very act of prayer. And afterwards, when they had been for a

---

[1] *Apostolus.*

[2] The Mareotic nome is the district round Lake Mareotis, a lake in the north of the delta bordering upon the Libyan desert (the modern *Birket el Mariout*), and running parallel to the Mediterranean, from which it is separated by a long and narrow ridge of sand.
[3] On Paphnutius see the note on the Conference III. i.

long while sought for by the marks of their footsteps which in those sandy regions are impressed as if on snow, until a thin coating of sand blown about even by a slight breeze covers them up again, it was found that they had preserved the figs untouched, just as they had received them; choosing rather to give up their lives, than their fidelity to their charge, and to lose their life on earth than to violate the commands of their senior.

CHAPTER XLI.

The saying of Abbot Macarius of the behaviour of a monk as one who was to live for a long while, and as one who was daily at the point of death.

THERE is still one valuable charge of the blessed Macarius to be brought forward by us, so that a saying of so great a man may close this book of fasts and abstinence. He said then that a monk ought to bestow attention on his fasts, just as if he were going to remain in the flesh for a hundred years; and to curb the motions of the soul, and to forget injuries, and to loathe sadness, and despise sorrows and losses, as if he were daily at the point of death. For in the former case discretion is useful and proper as it causes a monk always to walk with well-balanced care, and does not suffer him by reason of a weakened body to fall from the heights over most dangerous precipices: in the other high-mindedness is most valuable as it will enable him not only to despise the seeming prosperity of this present world, but also not to be crushed by adversity and sorrow, and to despise them as small and paltry matters, since he has the gaze of his mind continually fixed there, whither daily at each moment he believes that he is soon to be summoned.[1]

BOOK VI.

ON THE SPIRIT OF FORNICATION.

WE have thought best to omit altogether the translation of this book.

BOOK VII.

OF THE SPIRIT OF COVETOUSNESS.

CHAPTER I.

How our warfare with covetousness is a foreign one, and how this fault is not a natural one in man, as the other faults are.

OUR third conflict is against covetousness which we can describe as the love of money; a foreign warfare, and one outside of our nature, and in the case of a monk originating only from the state of a corrupt and sluggish mind, and often from the beginning of his renunciation being unsatisfactory, and his love towards God being lukewarm at its foundation. For the rest of the incitements to sin planted in human nature seem to have their commencement as it were congenital with us, and somehow being deeply rooted in our flesh, and almost coeval with our birth, anticipate our powers of discerning good and evil, and although in very early days they attack a man, yet they are overcome with a long struggle.

CHAPTER II.

How dangerous is the disease of covetousness.

BUT this disease coming upon us at a later period, and approaching the soul from with-

---

[1] Socrates (H.E. Book IV. c. xxiii.) gives an account of two monks of the name of Macarius, one of whom was from Upper Egypt, and the other from Alexandria. Compare also Rufinus, History of the Monks, cc. xxviii., xxix. It is not certain to which of them Cassian's stories refer, here and in the Conferences V. xii., VII. xxvii., XXIV. xiii. The story told in Conference XV. iii. refers to the "Egyptian" Macarius (cf. Sozomen H. E. III. xiv., where the miracle is expressly assigned to him): that in XIV. iv. evidently belongs to the "Alexandrian" Macarius. The two are mentioned together in Conference XIX. ix., and by various other writers.

out, as it can be the more easily guarded against and resisted, so, if it is disregarded and once allowed to gain an entrance into the heart, is the more dangerous to every one, and with the greater difficulty expelled. For it becomes "a root of all evils,"[1] and gives rise to a multiplicity of incitements to sin.

CHAPTER III.

What is the usefulness of those vices which are natural to us.

For example, do not we see those natural impulses of the flesh not only in boys in whom innocence still anticipates the discernment of good and evil, but even in little children and infants, who although they have not even the slightest approach to lust within them, yet show that the impulses of the flesh exist in them and are naturally excited? Do not we also see that the deadly pricks of anger already exist in full vigour likewise in little children? and before they have learnt the virtue of patience, we see that they are disturbed by wrongs, and feel affronts offered to them even by way of a joke; and sometimes, although strength is lacking to them, the desire to avenge themselves is not wanting, when anger excites them. Nor do I say this to lay the blame on their natural state, but to point out that of these impulses which proceed from us, some are implanted in us for a useful purpose, while some are introduced from without, through the fault of carelessness and the desire of an evil will. For these carnal impulses, of which we spoke above, were with a useful purpose implanted in our bodies by the providence of the Creator, viz.: for perpetuating the race, and raising up children for posterity: and not for committing adulteries and debaucheries, which the authority of the law also condemns. The pricks of anger too, do we not see that they have been most wisely given to us, that being enraged at our sins and mistakes, we may apply ourselves the rather to virtues and spiritual exercises, showing forth all love towards God, and patience towards our brethren? We know too how great is the use of sorrow, which is reckoned among the other vices, when it is turned to an opposite use. For on the one hand, when it is in accordance with the fear of God it is most needful, and on the other, when it is in accordance with the world, most pernicious; as the Apostle teaches us when he says that "the sorrow which is according to God worketh repentance that is steadfast unto salvation, but the sorrow of the world worketh death."[2]

---

[1] 1 Tim. vi. 10. [2] 2 Cor. vii. 10.

CHAPTER IV.

That we can say that there exist in us some natural faults, without wronging the Creator.

If then we say that these impulses were implanted in us by the Creator, He will not on that account seem blameworthy, if we choose wrongly to abuse them, and to pervert them to harmful purposes, and are ready to be made sorry by means of the useless Cains of this world, and not by means of showing penitence and the correction of our faults: or at least if we are angry not with ourselves (which would be profitable) but with our brethren in defiance of God's command. For in the case of iron, which is given us for good and useful purposes, if any one should pervert it for murdering the innocent, one would not therefore blame the maker of the metal because man had used to injure others that which he had provided for good and useful purposes of living happily.

CHAPTER V.

Of the faults which are contracted through our own fault, without natural impulses.

But we affirm that some faults grow up without any natural occasion giving birth to them, but simply from the free choice of a corrupt and evil will, as envy and this very sin of covetousness; which are caught (so to speak) from without, having no origination in us from natural instincts. But these, in proportion as they are easily guarded against and readily avoided, just so do they make wretched the mind that they have got hold of and seized, and hardly do they suffer it to get at the remedies which would cure it: either because these who are wounded by persons whom they might either have ignored, or avoided, or easily overcome, do not deserve to be healed by a speedy cure, or else because, having laid the foundations badly, they are unworthy to raise an edifice of virtue and reach the summit of perfection.

CHAPTER VI.

How difficult the evil of covetousness is to drive away when once it has been admitted.

Wherefore let not this evil seem of no account or unimportant to anybody: for as it can easily be avoided, so if it has once got hold of any one, it scarcely suffers him to get at the remedies for curing it. For it is a regular nest of sins, and a "root of all kinds of evil," and becomes a hopeless incitement to wickedness, as the Apostle says, "Covetousness," i.e. the love of money, "is a root of all kinds of evil."[1]

CHAPTER VII.

Of the source from which covetousness springs, and of the evils of which it is itself the mother.

WHEN then this vice has got hold of the slack and lukewarm soul of some monk, it begins by tempting him in regard of a small sum of money, giving him excellent and almost reasonable excuses why he ought to retain some money for himself. For he complains that what is provided in the monastery is not sufficient, and can scarcely be endured by a sound and sturdy body. What is he to do if ill health comes on, and he has no special store of his own to support him in his weakness? He says that the allowance of the monastery is but meagre, and that there is the greatest carelessness about the sick: and if he has not something of his own so that he can look after the wants of his body, he will perish miserably. The dress which is allowed him is insufficient, unless he has provided something with which to procure another. Lastly, he says that he cannot possibly remain for long in the same place and monastery, and that unless he has secured the money for his journey, and the cost of his removal over the sea, he cannot move when he wants to, and, detained by the compulsion of want, will henceforth drag out a wretched and wearisome existence without making the slightest advance: that he cannot without indignity be supported by another's substance, as a pauper and one in want. And so when he has bamboozled himself with such thoughts as these, he racks his brains to think how he can acquire at least one penny. Then he anxiously searches for some special work which he can do without the Abbot knowing anything about it. And selling it secretly, and so securing the coveted coin, he torments himself worse and worse in thinking how he can double it: puzzled as to where to deposit it, or to whom to intrust it. Then he is oppressed with a still weightier care as to what to buy with it, or by what transaction he can double it. And when this has turned out as he wished, a still more greedy craving for gold springs up, and is more and more keenly excited, as his store of money grows larger and larger. For with the

increase of wealth the mania of covetousness increases. Then next he has forebodings of a long life, and an enfeebled old age, and infirmities of all sorts, and long drawn out, which will be insupportable in old age, unless a large store of money has been laid by in youth. And so the wretched soul is agitated, and held fast, as it were, in a serpent's toils, while it endeavours to add to that heap which it has unlawfully secured, by still more unlawful care, and itself gives birth to plagues which inflame it more sorely, and being entirely absorbed in the quest of gain, pays attention to nothing but how to get money with which to fly[2] as quickly as possible from the discipline of the monastery, never keeping faith where there is a gleam of hope of money to be got. For this it shrinks not from the crime of lying, perjury, and theft, of breaking a promise, of giving way to injurious bursts of passion. If the man has dropped away at all from the hope of gain, he has no scruples about transgressing the bounds of humility, and through it all gold and the love of gain become to him his god, as the belly does to others. Wherefore the blessed Apostle, looking out on the deadly poison of this pest, not only says that it is a root of all kinds of evil, but also calls it the worship of idols, saying "And covetousness (which in Greek is called φιλαργυρία) which is the worship of idols."[3] You see then to what a downfall this madness step by step leads, so that by the voice of the Apostle it is actually declared to be the worship of idols and false gods, because passing over the image and likeness of God (which one who serves God with devotion ought to preserve undefiled in himself), it chooses to love and care for images stamped on gold instead of God.

CHAPTER VIII.

How covetousness is a hindrance to all virtues.

WITH such strides then in a downward direction he goes from bad to worse, and at last cares not to retain I will not say the virtue but even the shadow of humility, charity, and obedience; and is displeased with everything, and murmurs and groans over every work; and now having cast off all reverence, like a bad-tempered horse, dashes off headlong and unbridled: and discontented with his daily food and usual clothing, announces that he will not put

---

[1] 1 Tim. vi. 10.

[2] The same danger is strongly spoken of by S. Basil in the "Monastic Constitutions" c. xxxiv., a passage which should be compared with the one above.
[3] Col. iii. 5.

up with it any longer. He declares that God is not only there, and that his salvation is not confined to that place, where, if he does not take himself off pretty quickly from it, he deeply laments that he will soon die.

CHAPTER IX.

How a monk who has money cannot stay in the monastery.

And so having money to provide for his wanderings, with the assistance of which he has fitted himself as it were with wings, and now being quite ready for his move, he answers impertinently to all commands, and behaves himself like a stranger and a visitor, and whatever he sees needing improvement, he despises and treats with contempt. And though he has a supply of money secretly hidden, yet he complains that he has neither shoes nor clothes, and is indignant that they are given out to him so slowly. And if it happens that through the management of the superior some of these are given first to one who is known to have nothing whatever, he is still more inflamed with burning rage, and thinks that he is despised as a stranger; nor is he contented to turn his hand to any work, but finds fault with everything which the needs of the monastery require to be done. Then of set purpose he looks out for opportunities of being offended and angry, lest he might seem to have gone forth from the discipline of the monastery for a trivial reason. And not content to take his departure by himself alone, lest it should be thought that he has left as it were from his own fault, he never stops corrupting as many as he can by clandestine conferences. But if the severity of the weather interferes with his journey and travels, he remains all the time in suspense and anxiety of heart, and never stops sowing and exciting discontent; as he thinks that he will only find consolation for his departure and an excuse for his fickleness in the bad character and defects of the monastery.

CHAPTER X.

Of the toils which a deserter from a monastery must undergo through covetousness, though he used formerly to murmur at the very slightest tasks.

And so he is driven about, and more and more inflamed with the love of his money, which when it is acquired, never allows a monk either to remain in a monastery or to live under the discipline of a rule. And when separating him like some wild beast from the rest of the herd, it has made him through want of companions an animal fit for prey, and caused him to be easily eaten up, as he is deprived of fellow lodgers, it forces him, who once thought it beneath him to perform the slight duties of the monastery, to labour without stopping night and day, through hope of gain; it suffers him to keep no services of prayer, no system of fasting, no rule of vigils; it does not allow him to fulfil the duties of seemly intercession, if only he can satisfy the madness of avarice, and supply his daily wants; inflaming the more the fire of covetousness, while believing that it will be extinguished by getting.

CHAPTER XI.

That under pretence of keeping the purse women have to be sought to dwell with them.

Hence many are led on over an abrupt precipice, and by an irrevocable fall, to death, and not content to possess by themselves that money which they either never had before, or which by a bad beginning they kept back, they seek for women to dwell with them, to preserve what they have unjustifiably amassed or retained. And they implicate themselves in so many harmful and dangerous occupations, that they are cast down even to the depths of hell, while they refuse to acquiesce in that saying of the Apostle, that "having food and clothing they should be content" with that which the thrift of the monastery supplied, but "wishing to become rich they fall into temptation and the snare of the devil, and many unprofitable and hurtful desires, which drown men in destruction and perdition. For the love of money," i.e. covetousness, "is a root of all kinds of evil, which some coveting have erred from the faith, and have entangled themselves in many sorrows."[1]

CHAPTER XII.

An instance of a lukewarm monk caught in the snares of covetousness.

I know of one, who thinks himself a monk, and what is worse flatters himself on his perfection, who had been received into a monastery, and when charged by his Abbot not to turn his thoughts back to those things which he had given up and renounced, but to free himself from covetousness, the root of all kinds of evil, and from earthly snares; and

---

[1] 1 Tim. vi. 8-10.

when told that if he wished to be cleansed from his former passions, by which he saw that he was from time to time grievously oppressed, he should cease from caring about those things which even formerly were not his own, entangled in the chains of which he certainly could not make progress towards purifying himself of his faults: with an angry expression he did not hesitate to answer, "If you have that with which you can support others, why do you forbid me to have it as well?"[1]

CHAPTER XIII.

What the elders relate to the juniors in the matter of stripping off sins.

BUT let not this seem superfluous or objectionable to any one. For unless the different kinds of sins are first explained, and the origin and causes of diseases traced out, the proper healing remedies cannot be applied to the sick, nor can the preservation of perfect health be secured by the strong. For both these matters and many others besides these are generally put forward for the instruction of the younger brethren by the elders in their conferences, as they have had experience of numberless falls and the ruin of all sorts of people. And often recognizing in ourselves many of these things, when the elders explained and showed them, as men who were themselves disquieted[2] by the same passions, we were cured without any shame or confusion on our part, since without saying anything we learnt both the remedies and the causes of the sins which beset us, which we have passed over and said nothing about, not from fear of the brethren, but lest our book should chance to fall into the hands of some who have had no instruction in this way of life, and might disclose to inexperienced persons what ought to be known only to those who are toiling and striving to reach the heights of perfection.

CHAPTER XIV.

Instances to show that the disease of covetousness is threefold.

AND so this disease and unhealthy state is threefold, and is condemned with equal abhorrence by all the fathers. One feature is this, of which we described the taint above, which by deceiving wretched folk persuades them to hoard though they never had anything of their own when they lived in the world. Another,

which forces men afterwards to resume and once more desire those things which in the early days of their renunciation of the world they gave up. A third, which springing from a faulty and hurtful beginning and making a bad start, does not suffer those whom it has once infected with this lukewarmness of mind to strip themselves of all their worldly goods, through fear of poverty and want of faith; and those who keep back money and property which they certainly ought to have renounced and forsaken, it never allows to arrive at the perfection of the gospel. And we find in Holy Scripture instances of these three catastrophes which were visited with no light punishment. For when Gehazi wished to acquire what he had never had before, not only did he fail to obtain the gift of prophecy which it would have been his to receive from his master by hereditary succession, but on the contrary he was covered by the curse of the holy Elisha with a perpetual leprosy: while Judas, wanting to resume the possession of the wealth which he had formerly cast away when he followed Christ, not only fell into betraying the Lord, and lost his apostolic rank, but also was not allowed to close his life with the common lot of all but ended it by a violent death. But Ananias and Sapphira, keeping back a part of that which was formerly their own, were at the Apostle's word punished with death.

CHAPTER XV.

Of the difference between one who renounces the world badly and one who does not renounce it at all.

OF those then who say that they have renounced this world, and afterwards being overcome by want of faith are afraid of losing their worldly goods, a charge is given mystically in Deuteronomy. "If any man is afraid and of a fearful heart let him not go forth to war: let him go back and return home, lest he make the hearts of his brethren to fear as he himself is timid and frightened."[3] What can one want plainer than this testimony? Does not Scripture clearly prefer that they should not take on them even the earliest stages of this profession and its name, rather than by their persuasion and bad example turn others back from the perfection of the gospel, and weaken them by their faithless terror. And so they are bidden to withdraw from the battle and return to their homes, because a man cannot fight the Lord's battle with a double heart. For "a double-minded man is unstable in all his ways."[4] And thinking, according to that

---

1 *Cur prohibes* (Petschenig). Gazæus omits *Cur.*
2 *Pulsarentur* (Petschenig). The text of Gazæus has *pulsaremur.*

3 Deut. xx. 8.　　4 S. James i. 8.

Parable in the Gospel,[1] that he who goes forth with ten thousand men against a king who comes with twenty thousand, cannot possibly fight, they should, while he is yet a great way off, ask for peace; that is, it is better for them not even to take the first step towards renunciation, rather than afterwards following it up coldly, to involve themselves in still greater dangers. For "it is better not to vow, than to vow and not pay."[2] But finely is the one described as coming with ten thousand and the other with twenty. For the number of sins which attack us is far larger than that of the virtues which fight for us. But "no man can serve God and Mammon."[3] And "no man putting his hand to the plough and looking back is fit for the kingdom of God."[4]

CHAPTER XVI.

Of the authority under which those shelter themselves who object to stripping themselves of their goods.

THESE then try to make out a case for their original avarice, by some authority from Holy Scripture, which they interpret with base ingenuity, in their desire to wrest and pervert to their own purposes a saying of the Apostle or rather of the Lord Himself: and, not adapting their own life or understanding to the meaning of the Scripture, but making the meaning of Scripture bend to the desires of their own lust, they try to make it to correspond to their own views, and say that it is written, "It is more blessed to give than to receive."[5] And by an entirely wrong interpretation of this they think that they can weaken the force of that saying of the Lord in which he says: "If thou wilt be perfect, go sell all that thou hast and give to the poor, and thou shalt have treasure in heaven; and come, follow me."[6] And they think that under colour of this they need not deprive themselves of their riches: declaring indeed that they are more blessed if, supported by that which originally belonged to them, they give to others also out of their superabundance. And while they are shy of embracing with the Apostle that glorious state of abnegation for Christ's sake, they will not be content either with manual labour or the sparing diet of the monastery. And the only thing is that these must either know that they are deceiving themselves, and have not really renounced the world while they are clinging to their former riches; or, if they really and truly

want to make trial of the monastic life, they must give up and forsake all these things and keep back nothing of that which they have renounced, and, with the Apostle, glory "in hunger and thirst, in cold and nakedness."[7]

CHAPTER XVII.

Of the renunciation of the apostles and the primitive church.

As if he (who, by his assertion that he was endowed with the privileges of a Roman citizen from his birth, testifies that he was no mean person according to this world's rank) might not likewise have been supported by the property which formerly belonged to him! And as if those men who were possessors of lands and houses in Jerusalem and sold everything and kept back nothing whatever for themselves, and brought the price of them and laid it at the feet of the apostles, might not have supplied their bodily necessities from their own property, had this been considered the best plan by the apostles, or had they themselves deemed it preferable! But they gave up all their property at once, and preferred to be supported by their own labour, and by the contributions of the Gentiles, of whose collection the holy Apostle speaks in writing to the Romans, and declaring his own office in this matter to them, and urging them on likewise to make this collection: "But now I go to Jerusalem to minister to the saints. For it has pleased them of Macedonia and Achaia to make a certain contribution for the poor saints who are at Jerusalem: it has pleased them indeed, and their debtors they are. For if the Gentiles are made partakers of their spiritual things, they ought also to minister to them in carnal things."[8] To the Corinthians also he shows the same anxiety about this, and urges them the more diligently to prepare before his arrival a collection, which he was intending to send for their needs. "But concerning the collection for the saints, as I appointed to the churches of Galatia, so also do ye. Let each one of you on the first day of the week put apart with himself, laying up what it shall well please him, that when I come the collections be not then to be made. But when I come whomsoever you shall approve by your letters, them I will send to carry your grace to Jerusalem." And that he may stimulate them to make a larger collection, he adds, "But if it be meet that I also go, they shall go with me:"[9] meaning if your offering is of such a character as

---

[1] S. Luke xiv. 31, 32. [4] S. Luke ix. 62.
[2] Eccl. v. 4 (LXX.). [5] Acts xx. 35.
[3] S. Matt. vi. 24. [6] S. Matt. xix. 21.

[7] 2 Cor. ii. 27. [8] Rom. xv. 25-27. [9] 1 Cor. xvi. 1-4.

to deserve to be taken there by my ministration. To the Galatians too, he testifies that when he was settling the division of the ministry of preaching with the apostles, he had arranged this with James, Peter, and John: that he should undertake the preaching to the Gentiles, but should never repudiate care and anxious thought for the poor who were at Jerusalem, who for Christ's sake gave up all their goods, and submitted to voluntary poverty. "And when they saw," said he, "the grace of God which was given to me, James and Cephas and John, who seemed to be pillars, gave to me and to Barnabas the right hand of fellowship, that we should preach to the Gentiles, but they to those of the circumcision: only they would that we should be mindful of the poor." A matter which he testifies that he attended to most carefully, saying, "which also I was anxious of myself to do."[1] Who then are the more blessed, those who but lately were gathered out of the number of the heathen, and being unable to climb to the heights of the perfection of the gospel, clung to their own property, in whose case it was considered a great thing by the Apostle if at least they were restrained from the worship of idols, and from fornication, and from things strangled, and from blood,[2] and had embraced the faith of Christ, with their goods and all: or those who live up to the demands of the gospel, and carry the Lord's cross daily, and want nothing out of their property to remain for their own use? And if the blessed Apostle himself, bound with chains and fetters, or hampered by the difficulties of travelling, and for these reasons not being able to provide with his hands, as he generally did, for the supply of his food, declares that he received that which supplied his wants from the brethren who came from Macedonia; "For that which was lacking to me," he says, "the brethren who came from Macedonia supplied:"[3] and to the Philippians he says: "For ye Philippians know also that in the beginning of the gospel, when I came from Macedonia, no church communicated with me in the matter of giving and receiving, except you only; because even in Thessalonica once and again you sent to supply my needs:"[4] (if this was so) then, according to the notion of these men, which they have formed in the coldness of their heart, will those men really be more blessed than the Apostle, because it is found that they have ministered to him of their substance? But this no one will venture to assert, however big a fool he may be.

CHAPTER XVIII.

That if we want to imitate the apostles we ought not to live according to our own prescriptions, but to follow their example.

WHEREFORE if we want to obey the gospel precept, and to show ourselves the followers of the Apostle and the whole primitive church, or of the fathers who in our own days succeeded to their virtues and perfection, we should not acquiesce in our own prescriptions, promising ourselves perfection from this wretched and lukewarm condition of ours: but following their footsteps, we should by no means aim at looking after our own interests, but should seek out the discipline and system of a monastery, that we may in very truth renounce this world; preserving nothing of those things which we have despised through the temptation of want of faith; and should look for our daily food, not from any store of money of our own, but from our own labours.

CHAPTER XIX.

A saying of S. Basil, the Bishop, directed against Syncletius.[5]

THERE is current a saying of S. Basil, Bishop of Cæsarea, directed against a certain Syncletius, who was growing indifferent with the sort of lukewarmness of which we have spoken; who, though he professed to have renounced this world, had yet kept back for himself some of his property, not liking to be supported by the labour of his own hands, and to acquire true humility by stripping himself and by grinding toil, and the subjection of the monastery: "You have," said he, "spoilt Syncletius, and not made a monk."

CHAPTER XX.

How contemptible it is to be overcome by covetousness.

AND so if we want to strive lawfully in our spiritual combat, let us expel this dangerous enemy also from our hearts. For to overcome him does not so much show great virtue, as to be beaten by him is shameful and disgraceful. For when you are overpowered by a strong man, though there is grief in being overthrown, and distress at the loss of victory, yet some consolation may be derived by the vanquished

---

1 Gal. ii. 9, 10.   3 2 Cor. xi. 9.
2 Acts xv. 20.   4 Phil. iv. 15, 16.

5 Petschenig's text has *Syncletium* as a proper name. Gazæus, however, thinks that it should be *Syncleticum*; i.e. Συγκλητικός or Senator: and in the saying of S. Basil at the close of the chapter actually reads (apparently without any MS. authority), *Et Senatorem*, inquit, perdidisti.

from the strength of their opponent. But if the enemy is a poor creature, and the struggle a feeble one, besides the grief for defeat there is confusion of a more disgraceful character, and a shame which is worse than loss.

CHAPTER XXI.

How covetousness can be conquered.

AND in this case it will be the greatest victory and a lasting triumph, if, as is said, the conscience of the monk is not defiled by the possession of the smallest coin. For it is an impossibility for him who, overcome in the matter of a small possession, has once admitted into his heart a root of evil desire, not to be inflamed presently with the heat of a still greater desire. For the soldier of Christ will be victorious and in safety, and free from all the attacks of desire, so long as this most evil spirit does not implant in his heart a seed of this desire. Wherefore, though in the matter of all kinds of sins we ought ordinarily to watch the serpent's head,[1] yet in this above all we should be more keenly on our guard. For if it has been admitted it will grow by feeding on itself, and will kindle for itself a worse fire. And so we must not only guard against the *possession* of money, but also must expel from our souls the *desire* for it. For we should not so much avoid the results of covetousness, as cut off by the roots all disposition towards it. For it will do no good not to possess money, if there exists in us the desire for getting it.

CHAPTER XXII.

That one who actually has no money may still be deemed covetous.

FOR it is possible even for one who has no money to be by no means free from the malady of covetousness, and for the blessing of penury to do him no good, because he has not been able to root out the sin of cupidity: delighting in the advantages of poverty, not in the merit of the virtue, and satisfied with the burden of necessity, not without coldness of heart. For just as the word of the gospel declares of those who are not defiled in body, that they are adulterers in heart;[2] so it is possible that those who are in no way pressed down with the weight of money may be condemned with the covetous in disposition and intent. For it was the opportunity of possess-

ing which was wanting in their case, and not the will for it: which latter is always crowned by God, rather than compulsion. And so we must use all diligence lest the fruits of our labours should be destroyed to no purpose. For it is a wretched thing to have endured the effects of poverty and want, but to have lost their fruits, through the fault of a shattered will.

CHAPTER XXIII.

An example drawn from the case of Judas.

WOULD you like to know how dangerously and harmfully that incitement, unless it has been carefully eradicated, will shoot up for the destruction of its owner, and put forth all sorts of branches of different sins? Look at Judas, reckoned among the number of the apostles, and see how because he would not bruise the deadly head of this serpent it destroyed him with its poison, and how when he was caught in the snares of concupiscence, it drove him into sin and a headlong downfall, so that he was persuaded to sell the Redeemer of the world and the author of man's salvation for thirty pieces of silver. And he could never have been impelled to this heinous sin of the betrayal if he had not been contaminated by the sin of covetousness: nor would he have made himself wickedly guilty of betraying[3] the Lord, unless he had first accustomed himself to rob the bag intrusted to him.

CHAPTER XXIV.

That covetousness cannot be overcome except by stripping one's self of everything.

THIS is a sufficiently dreadful and clear instance of this tyranny, which, when once the mind is taken prisoner by it, allows it to keep to no rules of honesty, nor to be satisfied with any additions to its gains. For we must seek to put an end to this madness, not by riches, but by stripping ourselves of them. Lastly, when he (viz. Judas) had received the bag set apart for the distribution to the poor, and intrusted to his care for this purpose, that he might at least satisfy himself with plenty of money, and set a limit to his avarice, yet his plentiful supply only broke out into a still greedier incitement of desire, so that he was ready no longer secretly to rob the bag, but actually to sell the Lord Himself. For the madness of this avarice is not satisfied with any amount of riches.

---

[1] Gen. iii. 15.   [2] S. Matt. v. 28.   [3] *Negationis* (Petschenig). Another reading is *necationis*.

CHAPTER XXV.

Of the deaths of Ananias and Sapphira, and Judas, which they underwent through the impulse of covetousness.

LASTLY, the chief of the apostles, taught by these instances, and knowing that one who has any avarice cannot bridle it, and that it cannot be put an end to by a large or small sum of money, but only by the virtue of renunciation of everything, punished with death Ananias and Sapphira, who were mentioned before, because they had kept back something out of their property, that that death which Judas had voluntarily met with for the sin of betraying the Lord, they might also undergo for their lying avarice.[1] How closely do the sin and punishment correspond in each case! In the one case treachery, in the other falsehood, was the result of covetousness. In the one case the truth is betrayed, in the other the sin of lying is committed. For though the issues of their deeds may appear different, yet they coincide in having one and the same aim. For the one, in order to escape poverty, desired to take back what he had forsaken; the others, for fear lest they might become poor, tried to keep back something out of their property, which they should have either offered to the Apostle in good faith, or have given entirely to the brethren. And so in each case there follows the judgment of death; because each sin sprang from the root of covetousness. And so if against those who did not covet other persons' goods, but tried to be sparing of their own, and had no desire to *acquire*, but only the wish to *retain*, there went forth so severe a sentence, what should we think of those who desire to amass wealth, without ever having had any of their own, and, making a show of poverty before men, are before God convicted of being rich, through the passion of avarice?

CHAPTER XXVI.

That covetousness brings upon the soul a spiritual leprosy.

AND such are seen to be lepers in spirit and heart, after the likeness of Gehazi, who, desiring the uncertain riches of this world, was covered with the taint of foul leprosy, through which he left us a clear example that every soul which is defiled with the stain of cupidity is covered with the spiritual leprosy of sin, and is counted as unclean before God with a perpetual curse.

CHAPTER XXVII.

Scripture proofs by which one who is aiming at perfection is taught not to take back again what he has given up and renounced.

IF then through the desire of perfection you have forsaken all things and followed Christ who says to thee, "Go sell all that thou hast, and give to the poor, and thou shalt have treasure in heaven: and come follow me,"[2] why, having put your hand to the plough, do you look back, so that you will be declared by the voice of the same Lord not to be fit for the kingdom of heaven?[3] When secure on the top of the gospel roof, why do you descend to carry away something from the house, from those things, namely, which beforetime you despised? When you are out in the field and working at the virtues, why do you run back and try to clothe yourself again with what belongs to this world, which you stripped off when you renounced it?[4] But if you were hindered by poverty from having anything to give up, still less ought you to amass what you never had before. For by the grace of the Lord you were for this purpose made ready that you might hasten to the more readily, being hampered by no snares of wealth. But let no one who is wanting in this be disappointed; for there is no one who has not something to give up. He has renounced all the possessions of this world, whoever has thoroughly eradicated the desire to possess them.

CHAPTER XXVIII.

That the victory over covetousness can only be gained by stripping one's self bare of everything.

THIS then is the perfect victory over covetousness: not to allow a gleam from the very smallest scrap of it to remain in our heart, as we know that we shall have no further power of quenching it, if we cherish even the tiniest bit of a spark of it in us.

CHAPTER XXIX.

How a monk can retain his poverty.

AND we can only preserve this virtue unimpaired if we remain in a monastery, and as the Apostle says, having food and clothing, are therewith content.[5]

---

[1] Cf. Acts v.

[2] Matt. xix. 21. [4] Cf. S. Luke xvii. 31.
[3] Cf. S. Luke ix. 62. [5] 1 Tim. vi. 8.

CHAPTER XXX.

The remedies against the disease of covetousness.

KEEPING then in mind the judgment of Ananias and Sapphira let us dread keeping back any of those things which we gave up and vowed utterly to forsake. Let us also fear the example of Gehazi, who for the sin of covetousness was chastised with the punishment of perpetual leprosy. From this let us beware of acquiring that wealth which we never formerly possessed. Moreover also dreading both the fault and the death of Judas, let us with all the power that we have avoid taking back any of that wealth which once we cast away from us. Above all, considering the state of our weak and shifty nature, let us beware lest the day of the Lord come upon us as a thief in the night,[1] and find our conscience defiled even by a single penny; for this would make void all the fruits of our renunciation of the world, and cause that which was said

to the rich man in the gospel to be directed towards us also by the voice of the Lord: "Thou fool, this night thy soul shall be required of thee: then whose shall those things be which thou hast prepared?"[4] And taking no thought for the morrow, let us never allow ourselves to be enticed away from the rule of the Cœnobium.

CHAPTER XXXI.

That no one can get the better of covetousness unless he stays in the Cœnobium: and how one can remain there.

BUT we shall certainly not be suffered to do this, ·nor even to remain under the rule of a system, unless the virtue of patience, which can only spring from humility as its source, is first securely fixed and established in us. For the one teaches us not to trouble any one else; the other, to endure with magnanimity wrongs offered to us.

BOOK VIII.

OF THE SPIRIT OF ANGER.

CHAPTER I.

How our fourth conflict is against the sin of anger, and how many evils this passion produces.

IN our fourth combat the deadly poison of anger has to be utterly rooted out from the inmost corners of our soul. For as long as this remains in our hearts, and blinds with its hurtful darkness the eye of the soul, we can neither acquire right judgment and discretion, nor gain the insight which springs from an honest gaze, or ripeness of counsel, nor can we be partakers of life, or retentive of righteousness, or even have the capacity for spiritual and true light: "for," says one, "mine eye is disturbed by reason of anger."[2] Nor can we become partakers of wisdom, even though we are considered wise by universal consent, for "anger rests in the bosom of fools."[3] Nor can we even attain immortal

life, although we are accounted prudent in the opinion of everybody, for "anger destroys even the prudent."[5] Nor shall we be able with clear judgment of heart to secure the controlling power of righteousness, even though we are reckoned perfect and holy in the estimation of all men, for "the wrath of man worketh not the righteousness of God."[6] Nor can we by any possibility acquire that esteem and honour which is so frequently seen even in worldlings, even though we are thought noble and honourable through the privileges of birth, because "an angry man is dishonoured."[7] Nor again can we secure any ripeness of counsel, even though we appear to be weighty, and endowed with the utmost knowledge; because "an angry man acts without counsel."[8] Nor can we be free from dangerous disturbances, nor be without sin, even though no sort of disturbances be brought upon us by others;

---

1 1 Thess. v. 4.   2 Ps. xxx. (xxxi.) 10.   3 Eccl. vii. 10 (LXX.).

4 S. Luke xii. 20.   7 Prov. xi. 25 (LXX.).
5 Prov. xv. 1 (LXX.).   8 Prov. xiv. 17 (LXX.).
6 S. James i. 20.

because "a passionate man engenders quarrels, but an angry man digs up sins."[1]

CHAPTER II.

Of those who say that anger is not injurious, if we are angry with those who do wrong, since God Himself is said to be angry.

WE have heard some people trying to excuse this most pernicious disease of the soul, in such a way as to endeavour to extenuate it by a rather shocking way of interpreting Scripture: as they say that it is not injurious if we are angry with the brethren who do wrong, since, say they, God Himself is said to rage and to be angry with those who either will not know Him, or, knowing Him, spurn Him, as here: "And the anger of the Lord was kindled against His people;"[2] or where the prophet prays and says, "O Lord, rebuke me not in thine anger, neither chasten me in thy displeasure;"[3] not understanding that, while they want to open to men an excuse for a most pestilent sin, they are ascribing to the Divine Infinity and Fountain of all purity a taint of human passion.

CHAPTER III.

Of those things which are spoken of God anthropomorphically.

FOR if when these things are said of God they are to be understood literally in a material and gross signification, then also He *sleeps*, as it is said, "Arise, wherefore sleepest thou, O Lord?"[4] though it is elsewhere said of Him: "Behold he that keepeth Israel shall neither slumber nor sleep."[5] And He *stands* and *sits*, since He says, "Heaven is my seat, and earth the footstool for my feet:"[6] though He "measure out the heaven with his hand, and holdeth the earth in his fist."[7] And He is "drunken with wine" as it is said, "The Lord awoke like a sleeper, a mighty man, drunken with wine;"[8] He "who only hath immortality and dwelleth in the light which no man can approach unto:"[9] not to say anything of the "ignorance" and "forgetfulness,"

of which we often find mention in Holy Scripture: nor lastly of the outline of His limbs, which are spoken of as arranged and ordered like a man's; e.g., the hair, head, nostrils, eyes, face, hands, arms, fingers, belly, and feet: if we are willing to take all of which according to the bare literal sense, we must think of God as in fashion with the outline of limbs, and a bodily form; which indeed is shocking even to speak of, and must be far from our thoughts.

CHAPTER IV.

In what sense we should understand the passions and human parts which are ascribed to the unchanging and incorporeal God.

AND so as without horrible profanity these things cannot be understood literally of Him who is declared by the authority of Holy Scripture to be invisible, ineffable, incomprehensible, inestimable, simple, and uncompounded, so neither can the passion of anger and wrath be attributed to that unchangeable nature without fearful blasphemy. For we ought to see that the limbs signify the divine powers and boundless operations of God, which can only be represented to us by the familiar expression of limbs: by the mouth we should understand that His utterances are meant, which are of His mercy continually poured into the secret senses of the soul, or which He spoke among our fathers and the prophets: by the eyes we can understand the boundless character of His sight with which He sees and looks through all things, and so nothing is hidden from Him of what is done or can be done by us, or even thought. By the expression "hands," we understand His providence and work, by which He is the creator and author of all things; the arms are the emblems of His might and government, with which He upholds, rules and controls all things. And not to speak of other things, what else does the hoary hair of His head signify but the eternity and perpetuity of Deity, through which He is without any beginning, and before all times, and excels all creatures? So then also when we read of the anger or fury of the Lord, we should take it not ἀνθρωποπαθῶς; i.e., according to an unworthy meaning of human passion,[10] but in a sense worthy of God, who is free from all passion; so that by this we should understand that He is the judge and avenger of all the unjust things which are done in this world; and by reason of these

---

1 Prov. xxix. 22 (LXX.) Ἀνὴρ θυμώδης ἐγείρει νεῖκος, ἀνὴρ δὲ ὀργίλος ἐξώρυξεν ἁμαρτιαν. The old Latin as given by Sabatier has "Vir animosus parit zixas: vir autem iracundus effodit peccata." The verse is quoted by Gregory the Great in a passage which seems a reminiscence of Cassian's words, with the reading *effundit* for *effodit* (Moral V. xxxi.) Jerome's rendering in the Vulgate is quite different: "Vir iracundus provocat zixas: et qui ad indignandum facilis est erit ad peccandum proclivior."
2 Ps. cv. (cvi.) 40.
3 Ps. vi. 2.
4 Ps. xliii. (xliv.) 23.
5 Ps. cxx. (cxxi.) 4.
6 Isa. lxvi. 1.
7 Isa. xl. 12.
8 Ps. lxxvii. (lxxviii.) 65.
9 1 Tim. vi. 16.

10 On the heresy of the Anthropomorphites see the notes on Conference X. c. ii.

terms and their meaning we should dread Him as the terrible rewarder of our deeds, and fear to do anything against His will. For human nature is wont to fear those whom it knows to be indignant, and is afraid of offending: as in the case of some most just judges, avenging wrath is usually feared by those who are tormented by some accusation of their conscience; not indeed that this passion exists in the minds of those who are going to judge with perfect equity, but that, while they so fear, the disposition of the judge towards them is that which is the precursor of a just and impartial execution of the law. And this, with whatever kindness and gentleness it may be conducted, is deemed by those who are justly to be punished to be the most savage wrath and vehement anger. It would be tedious and outside the scope of the present work were we to explain all the things which are spoken metaphorically of God in Holy Scripture, with human figures. Let it be enough for our present purpose, which is aimed against the sin of wrath, to have said this that no one may through ignorance draw down upon himself a cause of this evil and of eternal death, out of those Scriptures in which he should seek for saintliness and immortality as the remedies to bring life and salvation.

CHAPTER V.

How calm a monk ought to be.

AND so a monk aiming at perfection, and desiring to strive lawfully in his spiritual combat, should be free from all sin of anger and wrath, and should listen to the charge which the "chosen vessel" gives him. "Let all anger," says he, and wrath, and clamour, and evil speaking, be taken away from among you, with all malice." [1] When he says, "Let all anger be taken away from you," he excepts none whatever as necessary or useful for us. And if need be, he should at once treat an erring brother in such a way that, while he manages to apply a remedy to one afflicted with perhaps a slight fever, he may not by his wrath involve himself in a more dangerous malady of blindness. For he who wants to heal another's wound ought to be in good health and free from every affection of weakness himself, lest that saying of the gospel should be used to him, "Physician, first heal thyself;" [2] and lest, seeing a mote in his brother's eye, he see not the beam in his own eye, for how will he see to cast out the mote from his brother's eye, who has the beam of anger in his own eye? [3]

CHAPTER VI.

Of the righteous and unrighteous passion of wrath.

FROM almost every cause the emotion of wrath boils over, and blinds the eyes of the soul, and, bringing the deadly beam of a worse disease over the keenness of our sight, prevents us from seeing the sun of righteousness. It makes no difference whether gold plates, or lead, or what metal you please, are placed over our eyelids, the value of the metal makes no difference in our blindness.

CHAPTER VII.

Of the only case in which anger is useful to us.

WE have, it must be admitted, a use for anger excellently implanted in us for which alone it is useful and profitable for us to admit it, viz., when we are indignant and rage against the lustful emotions of our heart, and are vexed that the things which we are ashamed to do or say before men have risen up in the lurking places of our heart, as we tremble at the presence of the angels, and of God Himself, who pervades all things everywhere, and fear with the utmost dread the eye of Him from whom the secrets of our hearts cannot possibly be hid.

CHAPTER VIII.

Instances from the life of the blessed David in which anger was rightly felt.

AND at any rate (this is the case), when we are agitated against this very anger, because it has stolen on us against our brother, and when in wrath we expel its deadly incitements, nor suffer it to have a dangerous lurking place in the recesses of our heart. To be angry in this fashion even that prophet teaches us who had so completely expelled it from his own feelings that he would not retaliate even on his enemies and those delivered by God into his hands: when he says "Be ye angry and sin not." [4] For he, when he had longed for water from the well of Bethlehem, and had been given it by his mighty men, who had brought it through the midst of the hosts of the enemy, at once poured it out on the ground: and thus in his anger extinguished the delicious feeling of his desire, and poured it out to the Lord, without satisfying the longing that he had expressed, saying: "That be

---

1 Eph. iv. 31.   2 S. Luke iv. 23.   3 Cf. S. Matt. vii. 3-5.   4 Ps. iv. 5.

far from me that I should do this! Shall I drink the blood of those men who went forth, on the danger of their souls?"[1] And when Shimei threw stones at King David and cursed him, in his hearing, before everybody, and Abishai, the son of Zeruiah, the captain of the host, wished to cut off his head and avenge the insult to the king, the blessed David, moved with pious wrath against this dreadful suggestion of his, and keeping the due measure of humility and a strict patience, said with imperturbable gentleness, "What have I to do with you, ye sons of Zeruiah? Let him alone that he may curse. For the Lord hath commanded him to curse David. And who is he who shall dare to say, Why hast thou done this? Behold my son, who came forth from my loins, seeks my life, and how much more this son of Benjamin? Let him alone, that he may curse, according to the command of the Lord. It may be the Lord will look upon my affliction, and return to me good for this cursing to-day."[2]

CHAPTER IX.

Of the anger which should be directed against ourselves.

AND some are commanded to "be angry" after a wholesome fashion, but with our own selves, and with evil thoughts that arise, and "not to sin," viz., by bringing them to a bad issue. Finally, the next verse explains this to be the meaning more clearly: "The things you say in your hearts, be sorry for them on your beds:"[3] i.e., whatever you think of in your hearts when sudden and nervous excitements rush in on you, correct and amend with wholesome sorrow, lying as it were on a bed of rest, and removing by the moderating influence of counsel all noise and disturbance of wrath. Lastly, the blessed Apostle, when he made use of the testimony of this verse, and said, "Be ye angry and sin not," added, "Let not the sun go down upon your wrath, neither give place to the devil."[4] If it is dangerous for the sun of righteousness to go down upon our wrath, and if when we are angry we straightway give place to the devil in our hearts, how is it that above he charges us to be angry, saying, "Be ye angry, and sin not"? Does he not evidently mean this: be ye angry with your faults and your tempers, lest, if you acquiesce in them, Christ, the sun of righteousness, may on account of your anger begin to go down on your darkened minds, and when He departs you may furnish a place for the devil in your hearts?

CHAPTER X.

Of the sun, of which it is said that it should not go down upon your wrath.

AND of this sun God clearly makes mention by the prophet, when He says, "But to those that fear my name the sun of righteousness shall arise with healing in His wings."[5] And this again is said to "go down" at midday on sinners and false prophets, and those who are angry, when the prophet says, "Their sun is gone down at noon."[6] And at any rate "tropically"[7] the mind, that is the $\nu o\tilde{\upsilon}_s$ or reason, which is fairly called the sun because it looks over all the thoughts and discernings of the heart, should not be put out by the sin of anger: lest when it "goes down" the shadows of disturbance, together with the devil their author, fill all the feelings of our hearts, and, overwhelmed by the shadows of wrath, as in a murky night, we know not what we ought to do. In this sense it is that we have brought forward this passage of the Apostle, handed down to us by the teaching of the elders, because it was needful, even at the risk of a somewhat lengthy discourse, to show how they felt with regard to anger, for they do not permit it even for a moment to effect an entrance into our heart: observing with the utmost care that saying of the gospel: "Whosoever is angry with his brother is in danger of the judgment."[8] But if it be lawful to be angry up till sunset, the surfeit of our wrath and the vengeance of our anger will be able to give full play to passion and dangerous excitement before that sun inclines towards its setting.[9]

CHAPTER XI.

Of those to whose wrath even the going down of the sun sets no limit.

BUT what am I to say of those (and I cannot say it without shame on my own part) to whose implacability even the going down of the sun sets no bound: but prolonging it for several days, and nourishing rancorous feelings against those against whom they have been excited, they say in words that they are not angry, but in fact and deed they show that

---

1 2 Sam. xxiii. 17.
2 2 Sam. xvi. 10–12.
3 Ps. iv. 5.
4 Eph. iv. 26.

5 Mal. iv. 2.
6 Amos viii. 9.
7 On the different senses of Scripture see the note on Conference XIV. viii.
8 S. Matt. v. 22.
9 Petschenig's text is as follows: *Ceterum si usque ad occasum solis licitur sit irasci, ante furoris satietas et ultrices iræ commotionem poterunt noxiæ perturbationis explere, quam sol iste ad locum sui vergat occasus.* That of Gazæus has "*ante perturbationes noxiæ poterunt furoris satietatem et ultricis iræ commotionem explere, etc.*"

they are extremely disturbed? For they do not speak to them pleasantly, nor address them with ordinary civility, and they think that they are not doing wrong in this, because they do not seek to avenge themselves for their upset. But since they either do not dare, or at any rate are not able to show their anger openly, and give place to it, they drive in, to their own detriment, the poison of anger, and secretly cherish it in their hearts, and silently feed on it in themselves; without shaking off by an effort of mind their sulky disposition, but digesting it as the days go by, and somewhat mitigating it after a while.

CHAPTER XII.

How this is the end of temper and anger when a man carries it into act as far as he can.

BUT it looks as if even this was not the end of vengeance to every one, but some can only completely satisfy their wrath or sulkiness if they carry out the impulse of anger as far as they are able; and this we know to be the case with those who restrain their feelings, not from desire of calming them, but simply from want of opportunity of revenge. For they can do nothing more to those with whom they are angry, except speak to them without ordinary civility: or it looks as if anger was to be moderated only in action, and not to be altogether rooted out from its hiding place in our bosom: so that, overwhelmed by its shadows, we are unable not only to admit the light of wholesome counsel and of knowledge, but also to be a temple of the Holy Spirit, so long as the spirit of anger dwells in us. For wrath that is nursed in the heart, although it may not injure men who stand by, yet excludes the splendour of the radiance of the Holy Ghost, equally with wrath that is openly manifested.

CHAPTER XIII.

That we should not retain our anger even for an instant.

OR how can we think that the Lord would have it retained even for an instant, since He does not permit us to offer the spiritual sacrifices of our prayers, if we are aware that another has any bitterness against us: saying, " If then thou bringest thy gift to the altar and there rememberest that thy brother hath aught against thee, leave there thy gift at the altar and go thy way; first be reconciled to thy brother, and then come and offer thy gift."[1] How then may we retain displeasure against

our brother, I will not say for several days, but even till the going down of the sun, if we are not allowed to offer our prayers to God while he has anything against us? And yet we are commanded by the Apostle: "Pray without ceasing;"[2] and "in every place lifting up holy hands without wrath and disputing."[3] It remains then either that we never pray at all, retaining this poison in our hearts, and become guilty in regard of this apostolic or evangelic charge, in which we are bidden to pray everywhere and without ceasing; or else if, deceiving ourselves, we venture to pour forth our prayers, contrary to His command, we must know that we are offering to God no prayer, but an obstinate temper with a rebellious spirit.

CHAPTER XIV.

Of reconciliation with our brother.

AND because we often spurn the brethren who are injured and saddened, and despise them, and say that they were not hurt by any fault of ours, the Healer of souls, who knows all secrets, wishing utterly to eradicate all opportunities of anger from our hearts, not only commands us to forgive if we have been wronged, and to be reconciled with our brothers, and keep no recollection of wrong or injuries against them, but He also gives a similar charge, that in case we are aware that they have anything against us, whether justly or unjustly, we should leave our gift, that is, postpone our prayers, and hasten first to offer satisfaction to them; and so when our brother's cure is first effected, we may bring the offering of our prayers without blemish. For the common Lord of all does not care so much for our homage as to lose in one what He gains in another, through displeasure being allowed to reign in us. For in any one's loss He suffers some loss, who desires and looks for the salvation of all His servants in one and the same way. And therefore our prayer will lose its effect, if our brother has anything against us, just as much as if we were cherishing feelings of bitterness against him in a swelling and wrathful spirit.

CHAPTER XV.

How the Old Law would root out anger not only from the actions but from the thoughts.

BUT why should we spend any more time over evangelic and apostolic precepts, when even the old law, which is thought to be some-

---

[1] S. Matt. v. 23, 24.

[2] 1 Thess. v. 17. [3] 1 Tim. ii. 8.

what slack, guards against the same thing, when it says, "Thou shalt not hate thy brother in thine heart;" and again, "Be not mindful of the injury of thy citizens;"[1] and again, "The ways of those who preserve the recollection of wrongs are towards death"?[2] You see there too that wickedness is restrained not only in action, but also in the secret thoughts, since it is commanded that hatred be utterly rooted out from the heart, and not merely retaliation for, but the very recollection of, a wrong done.

CHAPTER XVI.

How useless is the retirement of those who do not give up their bad manners.

SOMETIMES when we have been overcome by pride or impatience, and we want to improve our rough and bearish manners, we complain that we require solitude, as if we should find the virtue of patience there where nobody provokes us: and we apologize for our carelessness, and say that the reason of our disturbance does not spring from our own impatience, but from the fault of our brethren. And while we lay the blame of our fault on others, we shall never be able to reach the goal of patience and perfection.

CHAPTER XVII.

That the peace of our heart does not depend on another's will, but lies in our own control.

THE chief part then of our improvement and peace of mind must not be made to depend on another's will, which cannot possibly be subject to our authority, but it lies rather in our own control. And so the fact that we are not angry ought not to result from another's perfection, but from our own virtue, which is acquired, not by somebody else's patience, but by our own long-suffering.

CHAPTER XVIII.

Of the zeal with which we should seek the desert, and of the things in which we make progress there.

FURTHER, it is those who are perfect and purified from all faults who ought to seek the desert, and when they have thoroughly exterminated all their faults amid the assembly of the brethren, they should enter it not by way of cowardly flight, but for the purpose of divine contemplation, and with the desire of deeper insight into heavenly things, which can only be gained in solitude by those who are perfect. For whatever faults we bring with us uncured into the desert, we shall find to remain concealed in us and not to be got rid of. For just as when the character has been improved, solitude can lay open to it the purest contemplation, and reveal the knowledge of spiritual mysteries to its clear gaze, so it generally not only preserves but intensifies the faults of those who have undergone no correction. For a man appears to himself to be patient and humble, just as long as he comes across nobody in intercourse; but he will presently revert to his former nature, whenever the chance of any sort of passion occurs: I mean that those faults will at once appear on the surface which were lying hid, and, like unbridled horses diligently fed up during too long a time of idleness, dash forth from the barriers the more eagerly and fiercely, to the destruction of their charioteer. For when the opportunity for practising them among men is removed, our faults will more and more increase in us, unless we have first been purified from them. And the mere shadow of patience, which, when we mixed with our brethren, we seemed fancifully to possess, at least out of respect for them and publicity, we lose altogether through sloth and carelessness.

CHAPTER XIX.

An illustration to help in forming an opinion on those who are only patient when they are not tried by any one.

BUT it is like all poisonous kinds of serpents or of wild beasts, which, while they remain in solitude and their own lairs, are still not harmless;[3] for they cannot really be said to be harmless, because they are not actually hurting anybody. For this results in their case, not from any feeling of goodness, but from the exigencies of solitude, and when they have secured an opportunity of hurting some one, at once they produce the poison stored up in them, and show the ferocity of their nature. And so in the case of men who are aiming at perfection, it is not enough not to be angry with *men*. For we recollect that when we were living in solitude a feeling of irritation would creep over us against our pen because it was too large or too small; against our penknife when it cut badly and with a blunt edge what we wanted cut; and against a flint if by chance when we were rather late and hurrying to the reading, a spark of fire flashed out, so that we could not remove

---

[1] Lev. xix. 17, 18.   [2] Prov. xii. 28 (LXX.).   [3] Reading *non innoxia* (Petschenig).

and get rid of our perturbation of mind except by cursing the senseless matter, or at least the devil. Wherefore for a method of perfection it will not be of any use for there to be a dearth of men against whom our anger might be roused: since, if patience has not already been acquired, the feelings of passion which still dwell in our hearts can equally well spend themselves on dumb things and paltry objects, and not allow us to gain a continuous state of peacefulness, or to be free from our remaining faults: unless perhaps we think that some advantage and a sort of cure may be gained for our passion from the fact that inanimate and speechless things cannot possibly reply to our curses and rage, nor provoke our ungovernable temper to break out into a worse madness of passion.

CHAPTER XX.

Of the way in which anger should be banished according to the gospel.

WHEREFORE if we wish to gain the substance of that divine reward of which it is said, "Blessed are the pure in heart, for they shall see God,"[1] we ought not only to banish it from our actions, but entirely to root it out from our inmost soul. For it will not be of any good to have checked anger in words, and not to have shown it in deeds, if God, from whom the secrets of the heart are not hid, sees that it remains in the secret recesses of our bosom. For the word of the gospel bids us destroy the roots of our faults rather than the fruits; for these, when the incitements are all removed, will certainly not put forth shoots any more; and so the mind will be able to continue in all patience and holiness, when this anger has been removed, not from the surface of acts and deeds, but from the very innermost thoughts. And, therefore to avoid the commission of murder, anger and hatred are cut off, without which the crime of murder cannot possibly be committed. For "whosoever is angry with his brother, is in danger of the judgment;"[2] and "whosoever hateth his brother is a murderer;"[3] viz., because in his heart he desires to kill him, whose blood we know that he has certainly not shed among men with his own hand or with a weapon; yet, owing to his burst of anger, he is declared to be a murderer by God, who renders to each man, not merely for the result of his actions, but for his purpose and desires and wishes, either a reward or a punishment; according to that which He Himself says through the prophet: "But I come that I may gather them together with all nations and tongues;"[4] and again:[5] "Their thoughts between themselves accusing or also defending one another, in the day when God shall judge the secrets of men."[6]

CHAPTER XXI.

Whether we ought to admit the addition of "without a cause," in that which is written in the Gospel, "whosoever is angry with his brother," etc.

BUT you should know that in this, which is found in many copies, "Whosoever is angry with his brother without a cause, is in danger of the judgment,"[7] the words "without a cause" are superfluous, and were added by those who did not think that anger for just causes was to be banished: since certainly nobody, however unreasonably he is disturbed, would say that he was angry without a cause. Wherefore it appears to have been added by those who did not understand the drift of Scripture, which intended altogether to banish the incentive to anger, and to reserve no occasion whatever for indignation; lest while we were commanded to be angry with a cause, an opportunity for being angry without a cause might occur to us. For the end and aim of patience consists, not in being angry with a good reason, but in not being angry at all. Although I know that by some this very expression, "without a cause," is taken to mean that he is angry without a cause who when he is angered is not allowed to seek for vengeance. But it is better so to take it as we find it written in many modern copies and all the ancient ones.

CHAPTER XXII.

The remedies by which we can root out anger from our hearts.

WHEREFORE the athlete of Christ who strives lawfully ought thoroughly to root out the feeling of wrath. And it will be a sure remedy for this disease, if in the first place we make up our mind that we ought never to be angry at all, whether for good or bad reasons: as we know that we shall at once lose the light of discernment, and the security of good counsel, and our very uprightness, and the temperate character of righteousness, if the

---

[1] S. Matt. v. 8. [2] Ib. ver. 22. [3] 1 John iii. 15.

[4] Isaiah lxvi. 18.
[5] *Et rursum* (Petschenig): *et Apostolus* (Gazæus).
[6] Rom. ii. 15, 16.
[7] S. Matt. v. 22. The word εἰκῆ is said by Westcott and Host to be "Western and Syrian." It is wanting in א, B, Origen, and was not admitted by Jerome in the Vulgate.

main light of our heart has been darkened by its shadows: next, that the purity of our soul will presently be clouded, and that it cannot possibly be made a temple for the Holy Ghost while the spirit of anger resides in us; lastly, that we should consider that we ought never to pray, nor pour out our prayer to God, while we are angry. And above all, having before our eyes the uncertain condition of mankind, we should realize daily that we are soon to depart from the body, and that our continence and chastity, our renunciation of all our possessions, our contempt of wealth, our efforts in fastings and vigils will not help us at all, if solely on account of anger and hatred eternal punishments are awarded to us by the judge of the world.

BOOK IX.

OF THE SPIRIT OF DEJECTION.

CHAPTER I.

How our fifth combat is against the spirit of dejection, and of the harm which it inflicts upon the soul.

IN our fifth combat we have to resist the pangs of gnawing dejection: for if this, through separate attacks made at random, and by haphazard and casual changes, has secured an opportunity of gaining possession of our mind, it keeps us back at all times from all insight in divine contemplation, and utterly ruins and depresses the mind that has fallen away from its complete state of purity. It does not allow it to say its prayers with its usual gladness of heart, nor permit it to rely on the comfort of reading the sacred writings, nor suffer it to be quiet and gentle with the brethren; it makes it impatient and rough in all the duties of work and devotion: and, as all wholesome counsel is lost, and steadfastness of heart destroyed, it makes the feelings almost mad and drunk, and crushes and overwhelms them with penal despair.

CHAPTER II.

Of the care with which the malady of dejection must be healed.

WHEREFORE if we are anxious to exert ourselves lawfully in the struggle of our spiritual combat we ought with no less care to set about healing this malady also. For "as the moth injures the garment, and the worm the wood, so dejection the heart of man."[1] With sufficient clearness and appropriateness has the Divine Spirit expressed the force of this dangerous and most injurious fault.

CHAPTER III.

To what the soul may be compared which is a prey to the attacks of dejection.

FOR the garment that is moth-eaten has no longer any commercial value or good use to which it can be put; and in the same way[2] the wood that is worm-eaten is no longer worth anything for ornamenting even an ordinary building, but is destined to be burnt in the fire. So therefore the soul also which is a prey to the attacks of gnawing dejection will be useless for that priestly garment which, according to the prophecy of the holy David, the ointment of the Holy Spirit coming down from heaven, first on Aaron's beard, then on his skirts, is wont to assume: as it is said, "It is like the ointment upon the head which ran down upon Aaron's beard, which ran down to the skirts of his clothing.[3] Nor can it have anything to do with the building or ornamentation of that spiritual temple of which Paul as a wise master builder laid the foundations, saying, "Ye are the temple of God, and the Spirit of God dwelleth in you:"[4] and what the beams of this are like the bride tells us in the Song of Songs: "Our rafters are of cypress: the beams of our houses are of cedar."[5] And therefore those sorts of wood are chosen for the temple of God which are fragrant and not liable to rot, and which are not subject to decay from age nor to be worm-eaten.

---

1 Prov. xxv. 20 (LXX.).

2 *Totidem* is used here by Cassian for *itidem*, as in III. ix.
3 Ps. cxxxii. (cxxxiii.) 2.
4 1 Cor. iii. 16; vi. 16.
5 Cant. i. 16 (LXX.).

CHAPTER IV.

Whence and in what way dejection arises.

BUT sometimes it is found to result from the fault of previous anger, or to spring from the desire of some gain which has not been realized, when a man has found that he has failed in his hope of securing those things which he had planned. But sometimes without any apparent reason for our being driven to fall into this misfortune, we are by the instigation of our crafty enemy suddenly depressed with so great a gloom that we cannot receive with ordinary civility the visits of those who are near and dear to us; and whatever subject of conversation is started by them, we regard it as ill-timed and out of place; and we can give them no civil answer, as the gall of bitterness is in possession of every corner of our heart.

CHAPTER V.

That disturbances are caused in us not by the faults of other people, but by our own.

WHENCE it is clearly proved that the pains of disturbances are not always caused in us by other people's faults, but rather by our own, as we have stored up in ourselves the causes of offence, and the seeds of faults, which, as soon as a shower of temptation waters our soul, at once burst forth into shoots and fruits.

CHAPTER VI.

That no one comes to grief by a sudden fall, but is destroyed by falling through a long course of carelessness.[1]

FOR no one is ever driven to sin by being provoked through another's fault, unless he has the fuel of evil stored up in his own heart. Nor should we imagine that a man has been deceived suddenly when he has looked on a woman and fallen into the abyss of shameful lust: but rather that, owing to the opportunity of looking on her, the symptoms of disease which were hidden and concealed in his inmost soul have been brought to the surface.

CHAPTER VII.

That we ought not to give up intercourse with our brethren in order to seek after perfection, but should rather constantly cultivate the virtue of patience.

AND so God, the creator of all things, having regard above everything to the amendment of His own work, and because the roots and causes of our falls are found not in others, but in ourselves, commands that we should not give up intercourse with our brethren, nor avoid those who we think have been hurt by us, or by whom we have been offended, but bids us pacify them, knowing that perfection of heart is not secured by separating from men so much as by the virtue of patience. Which when it is securely held, as it can keep us at peace even with those who hate peace, so, if it has not been acquired, it makes us perpetually differ from those who are perfect and better than we are: for opportunities for disturbance, on account of which we are eager to get away from those with whom we are connected, will not be wanting so long as we are living among men; and therefore we shall not escape altogether, but only change the causes of dejection on account of which we separated from our former friends.

CHAPTER VIII.

That if we have improved our character it is possible for us to get on with everybody.

WE must then do our best to endeavour to amend our faults and correct our manners. And if we succeed in correcting them we shall certainly be at peace, I will not say with men, but even with beasts and the brute creation, according to what is said in the book of the blessed Job: "For the beasts of the field will be at peace with thee;"[2] for we shall not fear offences coming from without, nor will any occasion of falling trouble us from outside, if the roots of such are not admitted and implanted within in our own selves: for "they have great peace who love thy law, O God; and they have no occasion of falling."[3]

CHAPTER IX.

Of another sort of dejection which produces despair of salvation.

THERE is, too, another still more objectionable sort of dejection, which produces in the guilty soul no amendment of life or correction of faults, but the most destructive despair: which did not make Cain repent after the murder of his brother, or Judas, after the betrayal, hasten to relieve himself by making amends, but drove him to hang himself in despair.

CHAPTER X.

Of the only thing in which dejection is useful to us.

AND so we must see that dejection is only useful to us in one case, when we yield to it either in penitence for sin, or through being inflamed with the desire of perfection, or the contemplation of future blessedness. And of this the blessed Apostle says: "The sorrow which is according to God worketh repentance steadfast unto salvation: but the sorrow of the world worketh death."[1]

CHAPTER XI.

How we can decide what is useful and the sorrow according to God, and what is devilish and deadly.

BUT that dejection and sorrow which "worketh repentance steadfast unto salvation" is obedient, civil, humble, kindly, gentle, and patient, as it springs from the love of God, and unweariedly extends itself from desire of perfection to every bodily grief and sorrow of spirit; and somehow or other rejoicing and feeding on hope of its own profit preserves all the gentleness of courtesy and forbearance, as it has in itself all the fruits of the Holy Spirit of which the same Apostle gives the list: "But the fruit of the Spirit is love, joy, peace, forbearance, goodness, benignity, faith, mildness, modesty."[2]. But the other kind is rough, impatient, hard, full of rancour and useless grief and penal despair, and breaks down the man on whom it has fastened, and hinders him from energy and wholesome sorrow, as it is unreasonable, and not only hampers the efficacy of his prayers, but actually destroys all those fruits of the Spirit of which we spoke, which that other sorrow knows how to produce.

CHAPTER XII.

That except that wholesome sorrow, which springs up in three ways, all sorrow and dejection should be resisted as hurtful.

WHEREFORE except that sorrow which is endured either for the sake of saving penitence, or for the sake of aiming at perfection, or for the desire of the future, all sorrow and dejection must equally be resisted, as belonging to this world, and being that which "worketh death," and must be entirely expelled from our hearts like the spirit of fornication and covetousness and anger.

CHAPTER XIII.

The means by which we can root out dejection from our hearts.

WE should then be able to expel this most injurious passion from our hearts, so that by spiritual meditation we may keep our mind constantly occupied with hope of the future and contemplation of the promised blessedness. For in this way we shall be able to get the better of all those sorts of dejection, whether those which flow from previous anger or those which come to us from disappointment of gain, or from some loss, or those which spring from a wrong done to us, or those which arise from an unreasonable disturbance of mind, or those which bring on us a deadly despair, if, ever joyful with an insight into things eternal and future, and continuing immovable, we are not depressed by present accidents, or over-elated by prosperity, but look on each condition as uncertain and likely soon to pass away.

BOOK X.

OF THE SPIRIT OF ACCIDIE.[3]

CHAPTER I.

How our sixth combat is against the spirit of accidie, and what its character is.

OUR sixth combat is with what the Greeks call ἀκηδία, which we may term weariness or distress of heart. This is akin to dejection, and is especially trying to solitaries, and a dangerous and frequent foe to dwellers in the desert; and especially disturbing to a monk about the sixth hour, like some fever which seizes him at stated times, bringing the burning heat of its attacks on the sick man at usual and regular hours. Lastly, there are some of the elders who declare that this is the "midday demon" spoken of in the ninetieth Psalm.[4]

---

[1] 2 Cor. vii. 10.   [2] Gal. v. 22, 23.   [3] See the note on Bk. V. c. i.

[4] Ps. xc. (xci.) 6., where the Latin "et dæmonio meridiano" follows the LXX. καὶ δαιμονίου μεσημβρινοῦ, instead of "the destruction that wasteth at noonday."

CHAPTER II.

A description of accidie, and the way in which it creeps over the heart of a monk, and the injury it inflicts on the soul.

AND when this has taken possession of some unhappy soul, it produces dislike of the place, disgust with the cell, and disdain and contempt of the brethren who dwell with him or at a little distance, as if they were careless or unspiritual. It also makes the man lazy and sluggish about all manner of work which has to be done within the enclosure of his dormitory. It does not suffer him to stay in his cell, or to take any pains about reading, and he often groans because he can do no good while he stays there, and complains and sighs because he can bear no spiritual fruit so long as he is joined to that society; and he complains that he is cut off from spiritual gain, and is of no use in the place, as if he were one who, though he could govern others and be useful to a great number of people, yet was edifying none, nor profiting any one by his teaching and doctrine. He cries up distant monasteries and those which are a long way off, and describes such places as more profitable and better suited for salvation; and besides this he paints the intercourse with the brethren there as sweet and full of spiritual life. On the other hand, he says that everything about him is rough, and not only that there is nothing edifying among the brethren who are stopping there, but also that even food for the body cannot be procured without great difficulty. Lastly he fancies that he will never be well while he stays in that place, unless he leaves his cell (in which he is sure to die if he stops in it any longer) and takes himself off from thence as quickly as possible. Then the fifth or sixth hour brings him such bodily weariness and longing for food that he seems to himself worn out and wearied as if with a long journey, or some very heavy work, or as if he had put off taking food during a fast of two or three days. Then besides this he looks about anxiously this way and that, and sighs that none of the brethren come to see him, and often goes in and out of his cell, and frequently gazes up at the sun, as if it was too slow in setting, and so a kind of unreasonable confusion of mind takes possession of him like some foul darkness,[1] and makes him idle and useless for every spiritual work, so that he imagines that no cure for so terrible an attack can be found in anything except visiting some one of the brethren, or in the solace of sleep alone. Then the disease suggests that he ought to show courteous and friendly hospitalities to the brethren, and pay visits to the sick, whether near at hand or far off. He talks too about some dutiful and religious offices; that those kinsfolk ought to be inquired after, and that he ought to go and see them oftener; that it would be a real work of piety to go more frequently to visit that religious woman, devoted to the service of God, who is deprived of all support of kindred; and that it would be a most excellent thing to get what is needful for her who is neglected and despised by her own kinsfolk; and that he ought piously to devote his time to these things instead of staying uselessly and with no profit in his cell.

CHAPTER III.

Of the different ways in which accidie overcomes a monk.

AND so the wretched soul, embarrassed by such contrivances of the enemy, is disturbed, until, worn out by the spirit of accidie, as by some strong battering ram, it either learns to sink into slumber, or, driven out from the confinement of its cell, accustoms itself to seek for consolation under these attacks in visiting some brother, only to be afterwards weakened the more by this remedy which it seeks for the present. For more frequently and more severely will the enemy attack one who, when the battle is joined, will as he well knows immediately turn his back, and whom he sees to look for safety neither in victory nor in fighting but in flight: until little by little he is drawn away from his cell, and begins to forget the object of his profession, which is nothing but meditation and contemplation of that divine purity which excels all things, and which can only be gained by silence and continually remaining in the cell, and by meditation, and so the soldier of Christ becomes a runaway from His service, and a deserter, and "entangles himself in secular business," without at all pleasing Him to whom he engaged himself.[2]

CHAPTER IV.

How accidie hinders the mind from all contemplation of the virtues.

ALL the inconveniences of this disease are admirably expressed by David in a single verse, where he says, "My soul slept from weariness,"[3] that is, from accidie. Quite

---

[1] *Velut tætra suppletur caligine* (Petschenig); the text of Gazæus reads *terra* for *tætra*.

[2] 2 Tim. ii. 4.
[3] Ps. cxviii. (cxix.) 28, where the LXX. has ἐνύσταξεν ἡ ψυχή μου ἀπὸ ἀκηδίας.

rightly does he say, not that his body, but that his soul slept. For in truth the soul which is wounded by the shaft of this passion does sleep, as regards all contemplation of the virtues and insight of the spiritual senses.

CHAPTER V.

How the attack of accidie is twofold.

AND so the true Christian athlete who desires to strive lawfully in the lists of perfection, should hasten to expel this disease also from the recesses of his soul; and should strive against this most evil spirit of accidie in both directions, so that he may neither fall stricken through by the shaft of slumber, nor be driven out from the monastic cloister, even though under some pious excuse or pretext, and depart as a runaway.

CHAPTER VI.

How injurious are the effects of accidie.

AND whenever it begins in any degree to overcome any one, it either makes him stay in his cell idle and lazy, without making any spiritual progress, or it drives him out from thence and makes him restless and a wanderer, and indolent in the matter of all kinds of work, and it makes him continually go round the cells of the brethren and the monasteries, with an eye to nothing but this; viz., where or with what excuse he can presently procure some refreshment. For the mind of an idler cannot think of anything but food and the belly, until the society of some man or woman, equally cold and indifferent, is secured, and it loses itself in their affairs and business, and is thus little by little ensnared by dangerous occupations, so that, just as if it were bound up in the coils of a serpent, it can never disentangle itself again and return to the perfection of its former profession.

CHAPTER VII.

Testimonies from the Apostle concerning the spirit of accidie.

THE blessed Apostle, like a true and spiritual physician, either seeing this disease, which springs from the spirit of accidie, already creeping in, or foreseeing, through the revelation of the Holy Spirit, that it would arise among monks, is quick to anticipate it by the healing medicines of his directions.

For in writing to the Thessalonians, and at first, like a skilful and excellent physician, applying to the infirmity of his patients the soothing and gentle remedy of his words, and beginning with charity, and praising them in that point, that[1] this deadly wound, having been treated with a milder remedy, might lose its angry festering and more easily bear severer treatment, he says: "But concerning brotherly charity ye have no need that I write to you: for you yourselves are taught of God to love one another. For this ye do toward all the brethren in the whole of Macedonia."[2] He first began with the soothing application of praise, and made their ears submissive and ready for the remedy of the healing words. Then he proceeds: "But we ask you, brethren, to abound more." Thus far he soothes them with kind and gentle words; for fear lest he should find them not yet prepared to receive their perfect cure. Why is it that you ask, O Apostle, that they may abound more in charity, of which you had said above, "But concerning brotherly charity we have no need to write to you"? And why is it necessary that you should say to them: "But we ask you to abound more," when they did not need to be written to at all on this matter? especially as you add the reason why they do not need it, saying, "For you yourselves have been taught of God to love one another." And you add a third thing still more important: that not only have they been taught of God, but also that they fulfil in deed that which they are taught. "For ye do this," he says, not to one or two, but "to all the brethren;" and not to your own citizens and friends only, but "in the whole of Macedonia." Tell us then, I pray, why it is that you so particularly begin with this. Again he proceeds, "But we ask you, brethren, to abound the more." And with difficulty at last he breaks out into that at which he was driving before: "and that ye take pains to be quiet." He gave the first aim. Then he adds a second, "and to do your own business;" and a third as well: "and work with your own hands, as we commanded you;" a fourth: "and to walk honestly towards those that are without;" a fifth: "and to covet no man's goods." Lo, we can see through that hesitation, which made him with these preludes put off uttering what his mind was full of: "And that ye take pains to be quiet;" i.e., that you stop in your cells, and be not disturbed by rumours, which generally spring from the wishes and gossip of idle persons, and so yourselves disturb others.

---

[1] *Quousque* is used as equivalent to *donec*, again in Conf. XXIII. xii.

[2] 1 Thess. iv. 9, 10.

And, "to do your own business," you should not want to inquire curiously of the world's actions, or, examining the lives of others, want to spend your strength, not on bettering yourselves and aiming at virtue, but on depreciating your brethren. "And work with your own hands, as we charged you;" to secure that which he had warned them above not to do; i.e., that they should not be restless and anxious about other people's affairs, nor walk dishonestly towards those without, nor covet another man's goods, he now adds and says, "and work with your own hands, as we charged you." For he has clearly shown that leisure is the reason why those things were done which he blamed above. For no one can be restless or anxious about other people's affairs, but one who is not satisfied to apply himself to the work of his own hands. He adds also a fourth evil, which springs also from this leisure, i.e., that they should not walk dishonestly: when he says: "And that ye walk honestly towards those without." He cannot possibly walk honestly, even among those who are men of this world, who is not content to cling to the seclusion of his cell and the work of his own hands; but he is sure to be dishonest, while he seeks his needful food; and to take pains to flatter, to follow up news and gossip, to seek for opportunities for chattering and stories by means of which he may gain a footing and obtain an entrance into the houses of others. "And that you should not covet another man's goods." He is sure to look with envious eyes on another's gifts and boons, who does not care to secure sufficient for his daily food by the dutiful and peaceful labour of his hands. You see what conditions, and how serious and shameful ones, spring solely from the malady of leisure. Lastly, those very people, whom in his first Epistle he had treated with the gentle application of his words, in his second Epistle he endeavours to heal with severer and sterner remedies, as those who had not profited by more gentle treatment; and he no longer applies the treatment of gentle words, no mild and kindly expressions, as these, "But we ask you, brethren," but "We adjure you, brethren, in the name of our Lord Jesus Christ, that ye withdraw from every brother that walketh disorderly."[1] There he asks; here he adjures. There is the kindness of one who is persuading; here the sternness of one protesting and threatening. "We adjure you, brethren:" because, when we first *asked* you, you scorned to listen; now at least obey our threats. And this adjuration he renders terrible, not by his bare word, but by the imprecation of the name of our Lord Jesus Christ: for fear lest they might again scorn it, as merely man's word, and think that it was not of much importance. And forthwith, like a well-skilled physician with festering limbs, to which he could not apply the remedy of a mild treatment, he tries to cure by an incision with a spiritual knife, saying, "that ye withdraw yourselves from every brother that walketh disorderly, and not according to the tradition which ye received of us." And so he bids them withdraw from those who will not make time for work, and to cut them off like limbs tainted with the festering sores of leisure: lest the malady of idleness, like some deadly contagion, might infect even the healthy portion of their limbs, by the gradual advance of infection. And when he is going to speak of those who will not work with their own hands and eat their bread in quietness, from whom he urges them to withdraw, hear with what reproaches he brands them at starting. First he calls them "disorderly," and "not walking according to the tradition." In other words, he stigmatizes them as obstinate, since they will not walk according to his appointment; and "dishonest," i.e., not keeping to the right and proper times for going out, and visiting, and talking. For a disorderly person is sure to be subject to all those faults. "And not according to the tradition which they received from us." And in this he stamps them as in some sort rebellious, and despisers, who scorned to keep the tradition which they had received from him, and would not follow that which they not only remembered that the master had taught in word, but which they knew that he had performed in deed. "For you yourselves know how ye ought to be followers of us." He heaps up an immense pile of censure when he asserts that they did not observe that which was still in their memory, and which not only had they learned by verbal instruction, but also had received by the incitement of his example in working.

CHAPTER VIII.

That he is sure to be restless who will not be content with the work of his own hands.

"BECAUSE we were not restless among you." When he wants to prove by the practice of work that he was not restless among them, he fully shows that those who will not work are always restless, owing to the fault of idleness. "Nor did we eat any man's bread for nought." By each expression the teacher of the Gentiles

---

[1] 2 Thess. iii. 6.

advances a step in the rebuke.[1] The preacher of the gospel says that he has not eaten any man's bread for nought, as he knows that the Lord commanded that "they who preach the gospel should live of the gospel:"[2] and again, "The labourer is worthy of his meat."[3] And so if he who preached the gospel, performing a work so lofty and spiritual, did not venture in reliance on the Lord's command to eat his bread for nought, what shall we do to whom not merely is there no preaching of the word intrusted, but no cure of souls except our own committed? with what confidence shall we dare with idle hands to eat our bread for nought, when the "chosen vessel," constrained by his anxiety for the gospel and his work of preaching, did not venture to eat without labouring with his own hands? "But in labour," he says, "and weariness, working night and day lest we should be burdensome to any of you."[4] Up to this point he amplifies and adds to his rebuke. For he did not simply say, "We did not eat bread for nought from any of you," and then stop short. For it might have been thought that he was supported by his own private means, and by money which he had saved, or by other people's, though not by *their* collections and gifts. "But in labour," he says, "and weariness, working night and day;" that is, being specially supported by our own labour. And this, he says, we did not of our own wish, and for our own pleasure, as rest and bodily exercise suggested, but as our necessities and the want of food compelled us to do, and that not without great bodily weariness. For not only throughout the whole day, but also by night, which seems to be granted for bodily rest, I was continually plying the work of my hands, through anxiety for food.

CHAPTER IX.

That not the Apostle only, but those two who were with him laboured with their own hands.

AND he testifies that it was not he alone who so lived among them, lest haply this method might not seem important or general if he depended only on his example. But he declares that all those who were appointed with him for the ministry of the gospel, i.e., Silvanus and Timothy, who wrote this with him, worked in the same fashion. For by saying, "lest we should be burdensome to any of you," he covers them with great shame. For if he who preached the gospel and com-

mended it by signs and mighty works, did not dare to eat bread for nought, lest he should be burdensome to any, how can those men help thinking that they are burdensome who take it every day in idleness and at their leisure?

CHAPTER X.

That for this reason the Apostle laboured with his own hands, that he might set us an example of work.

"NOT as if we had not power; but that we might give ourselves a pattern to you to imitate us." He lays bare the reason why he imposed such labour on himself: "that we might," says he, "give a pattern to you to imitate us," that if by chance you become forgetful of the teaching of our words which so often passes through your ears, you may at least keep in your recollection the example of my manner of life given to you by ocular demonstration. There is here too no slight reproof of them, where he says that he has gone through this labour and weariness by night and day, for no other reason but to set an example, and that nevertheless they would not be instructed, for whose sakes he, although not obliged to do it, yet imposed on himself such toil. "And indeed," he says, "though we had the power, and opportunities were open to us of using all your goods and substance, and I knew that I had the permission[5] of our Lord to use them: yet I did not use this power, lest what was rightly and lawfully done on my part might set an example of dangerous idleness to others. And therefore when preaching the gospel, I preferred to be supported by my own hands and work, that I might open up the way of perfection to you who wish to walk in the path of virtue, and might set an example of good life by my work."

CHAPTER XI.

That he preached and taught men to work not only by his example, but also by his words.

BUT lest haply it might be thought that, while he worked in silence and tried to teach them by example, he had not instructed them by precepts and warnings, he proceeds to say: "For when we were with you, this we declared to you, that if a man will not work neither should he eat." Still greater does he make their idleness appear, for, though they knew that he, like a good master, worked with his hands for the sake of his teaching and in order to instruct them, yet they were ashamed to

---

1 *Increpationis* (Petschenig). *Interpretationis* (Gazæus).
2 1 Cor. ix. 14.
3 S. Matt. x. 10.
4 2 Thess. iii. 8.

5 *Permissum* (Petschenig). *Promissum* (Gazæus).

imitate him; and he emphasizes our diligence and care by saying that he did not only give them this for an example when present, but that he also proclaimed it continually in words; saying that if any one would not work, neither should he eat.

CHAPTER XII.

Of his saying: "If any will not work, neither shall he eat."

AND now he no longer addresses to them the advice of a teacher or physician, but proceeds with the severity of a judicial sentence, and, resuming his apostolic authority, pronounces sentence on his despisers as if from the judgment seat: with that power, I mean, which, when writing with threats to the Corinthians, he declared was given him of the Lord, when he charged those taken in sin, that they should make haste and amend their lives before his coming: thus charging them, "I beseech you that I may not be bold when I am present, against some, with that power which is given to me over you." And again: "For if I also should boast somewhat of the power which the Lord has given me unto edification, and not for your destruction, I shall not be ashamed."[1] With that power, I say, he declares, "If a man will not work, neither let him eat." Not punishing them with a carnal sword, but with the power of the Holy Ghost forbidding them the goods of this life, that if by chance, thinking but little of the punishment of future death, they still should remain obstinate through love of ease, they may at last, forced by the requirements of nature and the fear of immediate death, be compelled to obey his salutary charge.

CHAPTER XIII.

Of his saying: "We have heard that some among you walk disorderly."

THEN after all this rigour of gospel severity, he now lays bare the reason why he put forward all these matters. "For we have heard that some among you walk disorderly, working not at all, but curiously meddling." He is nowhere satisfied to speak of those who will not give themselves up to work, as if they were victims of but a single malady. For in his first Epistle[2] he speaks of them as "disorderly," and not walking according to the traditions which they had received from him: and he

also asserts that they were restless, and ate their bread for nought. Again he says here, "We have heard that there are some among you who walk disorderly." And at once he subjoins a second weakness, which is the root of this restlessness, and says, "working not at all;" a third malady as well he adds, which springs from this last like some shoot: "but curiously meddling."

CHAPTER XIV.

How manual labour[3] prevents many faults.

AND so he loses no time in at once applying a suitable remedy to the incentive to so many faults, and laying aside that apostolic power of his which he had made use of a little before, he adopts once more the tender character of a good father, or of a kind physician, and, as if they were his children or his patients, applies by his healing counsel remedies to cure them, saying: "Now we charge them that are such, and beseech them by the Lord Jesus, that working with silence they would eat their own bread." The cause of all these ulcers, which spring from the root of idleness, he heals like some well-skilled physician by a single salutary charge to work; as he knows that all the other bad symptoms, which spring as it were from the same clump, will at once diappear when the cause of the chief malady has been removed.

CHAPTER XV.

How kindness should be shown even to the idle and careless.

NEVERTHELESS, like a far-sighted and careful physician, he is not only anxious to heal the wounds of the sick, but gives suitable directions as well to the whole, that their health may be preserved continually, and says: "But be not ye weary in well doing:" ye who following us, i.e., our ways, copy the example given to you by imitating us in work, and do not follow their sloth and laziness: "Do not be weary in well doing;" i.e., do you likewise show kindness towards them if by chance they have failed to observe what we said. As then he was severe with those who were weak, for fear lest being enervated by laziness they might yield to restlessness and inquisitiveness, so he admonishes those who are in good health neither to restrain that kindness

---

[1] Cor. x. 2, 8.
[2] A mistake on Cassian's part: the reference being to 2 Thess. iii. 6.

[3] The text of Gazæus has *oratio*, but the reading which Petschenig gives, *operatio manuum*, is clearly so.

which the Lord's command bids us show to the good and evil,[1] even if some bad men will not turn to sound doctrine; nor to desist from doing good and encouraging them both by words of consolation and by rebuke as well as by ordinary kindness and civility.

CHAPTER XVI.

How we ought to admonish those who go wrong, not out of hatred, but out of love.

BUT again in case some might be encouraged by this gentleness, and scorn to obey his commands, he proceeds with the severity of an apostle: "But if any man obey not our word by this Epistle, note that man and do not keep company with him that he may be ashamed." And in warning them of what they ought to observe out of regard for him and for the good of all, and of the care with which they should keep the apostolic commands, at once he joins to the warning the kindness of a most indulgent father; and teaches them as well, as if they were his children, what a brotherly disposition they should cultivate towards those mentioned above, out of love. "Yet do not esteem him as an enemy, but admonish him as a brother." With the severity of a judge he combines the affection of a father, and tempers with kindness and gentleness the sentence delivered with apostolic sternness. For he commands them to note that man who scorns to obey his commands, and not to keep company with him; and yet he does not bid them do this from a wrong feeling of dislike, but from brotherly affection and out of consideration for their amendment. "Do not keep company," he says, "with him that he may be ashamed;" so that, even if he is not made better by my mild charges, he may at last be brought to shame by being publicly separated from all of you, and so may some day begin to be restored to the way of salvation.

CHAPTER XVII.

Different passages in which the Apostle declares that we ought to work, or in which it is shown that he himself worked.

IN the Epistle to the Ephesians also he thus gives a charge on this subject of work, saying: "He that stole, let him now steal no more, but rather let him labour, working with his hands the thing that is good, that he may have something to give to him that suffereth need."[2] And in the Acts of the Apostles too we find that he not only taught this, but actually practised it himself. For when he had come to Corinth, he did not permit himself to lodge anywhere except with Aquila and Priscilla, because they were of the same trade which he himself was accustomed to practise. For we thus read: "After this, Paul departing from Athens came to Corinth; and finding a certain Jew named Aquila, born in Pontus, and Priscilla his wife, he came to them because they were of the same trade; and abode with them, and worked: for they were tent-makers by trade."[3]

CHAPTER XVIII.

That the Apostle wrought what he thought would be sufficient for him and for others who were with him.

THEN going to Miletus, and from thence sending to Ephesus, and summoning to him the elders of the church of Ephesus, he charged them how they ought to rule the church of God in his absence, and said: "I have not coveted any man's silver and gold; you yourselves know how for such things as were needful for me and them that are with me these hands have ministered. I have showed you all things, how that so labouring you ought to support the weak, and to remember the words of the Lord Jesus, how he said: It is more blessed to give than to receive."[4] He left us a weighty example in his manner of life, as he testifies that he not only wrought what would supply his own bodily wants alone, but also what would be sufficient for the needs of those who were with him: those, I mean, who, being taken up with necessary duties, had no chance of procuring food for themselves with their own hands. And as he tells the Thessalonians that he had worked to give them an example that they might imitate him, so here too he implies something of the same sort when he says: "I have showed you all things, how that so labouring you ought to support the weak," viz., whether in mind or body; i.e., that we should be diligent in supplying their needs, not from the store of our abundance, or money laid by, or from another's generosity and substance, but rather by securing the necessary sum by our own labour and toil.

CHAPTER XIX.

How we should understand these words: "It is more blessed to give than to receive."

AND he says that this is a command of the Lord: "For He Himself," namely the Lord

---

[1] S. Matt. v. 43-45.   [2] Eph. iv. 28.   [3] Acts xviii. 1-3.   [4] Acts xx. 33-35.

Jesus, said he, "said it is more blessed to give than to receive." That is, the bounty of the giver is more blessed than the need of the receiver, where the gift is not supplied from money that has been kept back through unbelief or faithlessness, nor from the stored-up treasures of avarice, but is produced from the fruits of our own labour and honest toil. And so "it is more blessed to give than to receive," because while the giver shares the poverty of the receiver, yet still he is diligent in providing with pious care by his own toil, not merely enough for his own needs, but also what he can give to one in want; and so he is adorned with a double grace, since by giving away all his goods he secures the perfect abnegation of Christ, and yet by his labour and thought displays the generosity of the rich; thus honouring God by his honest labours, and plucking for him the fruits of his righteousness, while another, enervated by sloth and indolent laziness, proves himself by the saying of the Apostle unworthy of food, as in defiance of his command he takes it in idleness, not without the guilt of sin and of obstinacy.

CHAPTER XX.

Of a lazy brother who tried to persuade others to leave the monastery.

WE know a brother, whose name we would give if it would do any good, who, although he was remaining in the monastery and compelled to deliver to the steward his fixed task daily, yet for fear lest he might be led on to some larger portion of work, or put to shame by the example of one labouring more zealously, when he had seen some brother admitted into the monastery, who in the ardour of his faith wanted to make up the sale of a larger piece of work, if he found that he could not by secret persuasion check him from carrying out his purpose, he would by bad advice and whisperings persuade him to depart thence. And in order to get rid of him more easily he would pretend that he also had already been for many reasons offended, and wanted to leave, if only he could find a companion and support for the journey. And when by secretly running down the monastery he had wheedled him into consenting, and arranged with him the time at which to leave the monastery, and the place to which he should go before, and where he should wait for him, he himself, pretending that he would follow, stopped where he was. And when the other out of shame for his flight did not dare to return again to the monastery from which he had run away, the miserable author of his

flight stopped behind in the monastery. It will be enough to have given this single instance of this sort of men in order to put beginners on their guard, and to show clearly what evils idleness, as Scripture says,[1] can produce in the mind of a monk, and how "evil communications corrupt good manners."[2]

CHAPTER XXI.

Different passages from the writings of Solomon against accidie.

AND Solomon, the wisest of men, clearly points to this fault of idleness in many passages, as he says: "He that followeth idleness shall be filled with poverty,"[3] either visible or invisible, in which an idle person and one entangled with different faults is sure to be involved, and he will always be a stranger to the contemplation of God, and to spiritual riches, of which the blessed Apostle says: "For in all things ye were enriched in him, in all utterance and in all knowledge."[4] But concerning this poverty of the idler elsewhere he also writes thus: "Every sluggard shall be clothed in torn garments and rags."[5] For certainly he will not merit to be adorned with that garment of incorruption (of which the Apostle says, "Put ye on the Lord Jesus Christ,"[6] and again: "Being clothed in the breastplate of righteousness and charity,"[7] concerning which the Lord Himself also speaks to Jerusalem by the prophet: "Arise, arise, O Jerusalem, put on the garments of thy glory,'"[8] whoever, overpowered by lazy slumber or by accidie, prefers to be clothed, not by his labour and industry, but in the rags of idleness, which he tears off from the solid piece and body of the Scriptures, and fits on to his sloth no garment of glory and honour, but an ignominious cloak and excuse. For those, who are affected by this laziness, and do not like to support themselves by the labour of their own hands, as the Apostle continually did and charged us to do, are wont to make use of certain Scripture proofs by which they try to cloak their idleness, saying that it is written, "Labour not for the meat that perisheth, but for that which remains to life eternal;"[9] and "My meat is to do the will of my Father."[10] But these proofs are (as it were) rags, from the

---

[1] The reference is probably to Ecclus. xxiii. 29, "Idleness hath taught much evil."
[2] 1 Cor. xv. 33.
[3] Prov. xxviii. 19.
[4] 1 Cor. i. 5.
[5] Prov. xxiii. 21 (LXX.).
[6] Rom. xiii. 14.
[7] 1 Thess. v. 8.
[8] Is. lii. 1.
[9] S. John vi. 27.
[10] S. John iv. 34.

solid piece of the gospel, which are adopted for this purpose, viz., to cover the disgrace of our idleness and shame rather than to keep us warm, and adorn us with that costly and splendid garment of virtue which that wise woman in the Proverbs, who was clothed with strength and beauty, is said to have made either for herself or for her husband; of which presently it is said: "Strength and beauty are her clothing, and she rejoices in the latter days."[1] Of this evil of idleness Solomon thus makes mention again: "The ways of the idlers are strown with thorns;"[2] i.e., with these and similar faults, which the Apostle above declared to spring from idleness. And again: "Every sluggard is always in want."[3] And of these the Apostle makes mention when he says, "And that you want nothing of any man's."[4] And finally: "For idleness has been the teacher of many evils:"[5] which the Apostle has clearly enumerated in the passage which he expounded above: "Working not at all, but curiously meddling." To this fault also he joins another: "And that ye study to be quiet;" and then, "that ye should do your own business and walk honestly towards them that are without, and that you want nothing of any man's." Those also whom he notes as disorderly and rebellious, from these he charges those who are earnest to separate themselves: "That ye withdraw yourselves," says he, "from every brother that walketh disorderly and not according to the tradition which they received from us."[6]

CHAPTER XXII.

How the brethren in Egypt work with their hands, not only to supply their own needs, but also to minister to those who are in prison.

AND so taught by these examples the Fathers in Egypt never allow monks, and especially the younger ones, to be idle,[7] estimating the purpose of their hearts and their growth in

patience and humility by their diligence in work; and they not only do not allow them to receive anything from another to supply their own wants, but further, they not merely refresh pilgrims and brethren who come to visit them by means of their labours, but actually collect an enormous store of provisions and food, and distribute it in the parts of Libya which suffer from famine and barrenness, and also in the cities, to those who are pining away in the squalor of prison; as they believe that by such an offering of the fruit of their hands they offer a reasonable and true sacrifice to the Lord.

CHAPTER XXIII.

That idleness is the reason why there are not monasteries for monks in the West.

HENCE it is that in these countries we see no monasteries found with such numbers of brethren: for they are not supported by the resources of their own labour in such a way that they can remain in them continually; and if in some way or other, through the liberality of another, there should be a sufficient provision to supply them, yet love of ease and restlessness of heart does not suffer them to continue long in the place. Whence this saying has been handed down from the old fathers in Egypt: that a monk who works is attacked by but one devil; but an idler is tormented by countless spirits.

CHAPTER XXIV.

Of Abbot Paul[8] who every year burnt with fire all the works of his hands.

LASTLY, Abbot Paul, one of the greatest of the Fathers, while he was living in a vast desert which is called the Porphyrian desert,[9] and being relieved from anxiety by the date palms and a small garden, had plenty to support himself, and an ample supply of food, and could not find any other work to do, which would support him, because his dwelling was separated from towns and inhabited districts by seven days'journey,[10] or even more, through the desert, and more would be asked for the carriage of the goods than the price of the work would be worth; he collected the leaves of the palms, and regularly exacted of himself his daily task, as if he was to be sup-

---

1 Prov. xxxi. 25 (LXX.).
2 Prov. xv. 19 (LXX.).
3 Prov. xiii. 4 (LXX.).
4 1 Thess. iv. 11.
5 Ecclus. xxxiii. 29.
6 2 Thess. iii. 11; 6; 1 Thess. iv. 11.
7 The monks of Egypt were famous for their labours, and Cassian's language might be illustrated from many passages in the Fathers; e.g., Epiphanius, in his third book against heresies, compares the monks, and especially those in Egypt, to bees, because of their diligence. So S. Jerome, writing to Rusticus (Ep. cxxv.), says that no one is received in a monastery in Egypt unless he will work, and that this rule is made for the good of the soul rather than for the sake of providing food. Compare also Sozomen H. E. VI. xxviii., where it is said of Serapion and his followers in the neighbourhood of Arsinoë that "they lived on the produce of their labour and provided for the poor. During harvest-time they busied themselves in reaping: they set aside sufficient corn for their own use, and furnished grain gratuitously for the other monks." S. Basil also, in his Monastic Constitutions cc. iv. and v., speaks strongly of the value of labour; and the Rule of S. Benedict (c. xlviii.) enjoins that "as idleness is the enemy of the soul, the brethren are to be employed alternately in manual labour and pious reading."

8 This Paul is perhaps the same as the one mentioned in connection with Abbot Moses in Conference VII. xxvi. As he was a contemporary of Cassian he must be carefully distinguished from his more illustrious namesakes, the first hermit and the disciple of S. Antony.
9 Also called the desert of Calamus, Conference XXIV. iv., but its position has not been ascertained.
10 *Mansio* used here and again in Conference XXIV. iv. for the stage of a day's journey.

ported by it. And when his cave had been filled with a whole year's work, each year he would burn with fire that at which he had so diligently laboured: thus proving that without manual labour a monk cannot stop in a place nor rise to the heights of perfection: so that, though the need for food did not require this to be done, yet he performed it simply for the sake of purifying his heart, and strengthening his thoughts, and persisting in his cell, and gaining a victory over accidie and driving it away.

CHAPTER XXV.

The words of Abbot Moses which he said to me about the cure of accidie.

WHEN I was beginning my stay in the desert, and had said to Abbot Moses, the chief of all the saints, that I had been terribly troubled yesterday by an attack of accidie, and that I could only be freed from it by running at once to Abbot Paul, he said, "You have not freed yourself from it, but rather have given yourself up to it as its slave and subject. For the enemy will henceforth attack you more strongly as a deserter and runaway, since it has seen that you fled at once when overcome in the conflict: unless on a second occasion when you join battle with it you make up your mind not to dispel its attacks and heats for the moment by deserting your cell, or by the inactivity of sleep, but rather learn to triumph over it by endurance and conflict." Whence it is proved by experience that a fit of accidie should not be evaded by running away from it, but overcome by resisting it.[1]

BOOK XI.

OF THE SPIRIT OF VAINGLORY.

CHAPTER I.

How our seventh combat is against the spirit of vainglory, and what its nature is.

OUR seventh combat is against the spirit of κενοδοξία, which we may term vain or idle glory: a spirit that takes many shapes, and is changeable and subtle, so that it can with difficulty, I will not say be guarded against, but be seen through and discovered even by the keenest eyes.

CHAPTER II.

How vainglory attacks a monk not only on his carnal, but also on his spiritual side.

FOR not only does this, like the rest of his faults, attack a monk on his carnal side, but on his spiritual side as well, insinuating itself by craft and guile into his mind: so that those who cannot be deceived by carnal vices are more grievously wounded through their spiritual proficiency; and it is so much the worse to fight against, as it is harder to guard against. For the attack of all other vices is more open and straightforward, and in the case of each of them, when he who stirs them up is met by a determined refusal, he will go away the weaker for it, and the adversary who has been beaten will on the next occasion attack his victim with less vigour. But this malady when it has attacked the mind by means of carnal pride, and has been repulsed by the shield of reply, again, like some wickedness that takes many shapes, changes its former guise and character, and under the appearance of the virtues tries to strike down and destroy its conqueror.

CHAPTER III.

How many forms and shapes vainglory takes.

FOR our other faults and passions may be said to be simpler and of but one form: but this takes many forms and shapes, and changes about and assails the man who stands up against it from every quarter, and assaults its conqueror on all sides. For it tries to injure the soldier of Christ in his dress, in his manner, his walk, his voice, his work, his vigils, his fasts, his prayers, when he withdraws, when he reads, in his knowledge, his silence, his obedience, his humility, his patience; and like some most dangerous rock hidden by surging waves, it causes an unforeseen and miserable shipwreck to those who are sailing with a fair breeze, while they are not on the lookout for it or guarding against it.

---

[1] This Abbot Moses is probably the one to whom the first two Conferences are attributed (cf. also Conference VII. xxvi.); and possibly the second of this name (Moses the Libyan) mentioned by Sozomen, H. E. VI. xxix. Cf. also Palladius, the Lausiac History, c. xxii.

CHAPTER IV.

How vainglory attacks a monk on the right hand and on the left.

AND SO one who wishes to go along the King's highway by means of the "arms of righteousness which are on the right hand and on the left," ought by the teaching of the Apostle to pass through "honour and dishonour, evil report and good report,"[1] and with such care to direct his virtuous course amid the swelling waves of temptation, with discretion at the helm, and the Spirit of the Lord breathing on us, since we know that if we deviate ever so little to the right hand or to the left, we shall presently be dashed against most dangerous crags. And so we are warned by Solomon, the wisest of men: "Turn not aside to the right hand or to the left;"[2] i.e., do not flatter yourself on your virtues and be puffed up by your spiritual achievements on the right hand; nor, swerving to the path of vices on the left hand, seek from them for yourself (to use the words of the Apostle) "glory in your shame."[3] For where the devil cannot create vainglory in a man by means of his well-fitting and neat dress, he tries to introduce it by means of a dirty, cheap, and uncared-for style. If he cannot drag a man down by honour, he overthrows him by humility. If he cannot make him puffed up by the grace of knowledge and eloquence, he pulls him down by the weight of silence. If a man fasts openly, he is attacked by the pride of vanity. If he conceals it for the sake of despising the glory of it, he is assailed by the same sin of pride. In order that he may not be defiled by the stains of vainglory he avoids making long prayers in the sight of the brethren; and yet because he offers them secretly and has no one who is conscious of it, he does not escape the pride of vanity.

CHAPTER V.

A comparison which shows the nature of vainglory.

OUR elders admirably describe the nature of this malady as like that of an onion, and of those bulbs which when stripped of one covering you find to be sheathed in another; and as often as you strip them, you find them still protected.

CHAPTER VI.

That vainglory is not altogther got rid of by the advantages of solitude.

IN solitude also it does not cease from pursuing him who has for the sake of glory fled from intercourse with all men. And the more thoroughly a man has shunned the whole world, so much the more keenly does it pursue him. It tries to lift up with pride one man because of his great endurance of work and labour, another because of his extreme readiness to obey, another because he outstrips other men in humility. One man is tempted through the extent of his knowledge, another through the extent of his reading, another through the length of his vigils. Nor does this malady endeavour to wound a man except through his virtues; introducing hindrances which lead to death by means of those very things through which the supplies of life are sought. For when men are anxious to walk in the path of holiness and perfection, the enemies do not lay their snares to deceive them anywhere except in the way along which they walk, in accordance with that saying of the blessed David: "In the way wherein I walked have they laid a snare for me;"[4] that in this very way of virtue along which we are walking, when pressing on to "the prize of our high calling,"[5] we may be elated by our successes, and so sink down, and fall with the feet of our soul entangled and caught in the snares of vainglory. And so it results that those of us who could not be vanquished in the conflict with the foe are overcome by the very greatness of our triumph, or else (which is another kind of deception) that, overstraining the limits of that self-restraint which is possible to us, we fail of perseverance in our course on account of bodily weakness.

CHAPTER VII.

How vainglory, when it has been overcome, rises again keener than ever for the fight.

ALL vices when overcome grow feeble, and when beaten are day by day rendered weaker, and both in regard to place and time grow less and subside, or at any rate, as they are unlike the opposite virtues, are more easily shunned and avoided: but this one when it is beaten rises again keener than ever for the struggle; and when we think that it is destroyed, it revives again, the stronger for its

---

[1] 2 Cor. vi. 7, 8.
[2] Prov. iv. 27 (LXX.).
[3] Phil. iii. 19.

[4] Ps. cxli. (cxlii.) 4.
[5] Phil. iii. 14.

death. The other kinds of vices usually only attack those whom they have overcome in the conflict; but this one pursues its victors only the more keenly; and the more thoroughly it has been resisted, so much the more vigorously does it attack the man who is elated by his victory over it. And herein lies the crafty cunning of our adversary, namely, in the fact that, where he cannot overcome the soldier of Christ by the weapons of the foe, he lays him low by his own spear.

CHAPTER VIII.

How vainglory is not allayed either in the desert or through advancing years.

OTHER vices, as we said, are sometimes allayed by the advantages of position, and when the matter of the sin and the occasion and opportunity for it are removed, grow slack, and are diminished: but this one penetrates the deserts with the man who is flying from it, nor can it be shut out from any place, nor when outward material for it is removed does it fail. For it is simply encouraged by the achievements of the virtues of the man whom it attacks. For all other vices, as we said above, are sometimes diminished by the lapse of time, and disappear: to this one length of life, unless it is supported by skilful diligence and prudent discretion, is no hindrance, but actually supplies it with new fuel for vanity.

CHAPTER IX.

That vainglory is the more dangerous through being mixed up with virtues.

LASTLY, other passions which are entirely different from the virtues which are their opposites, and which attack us openly and as it were in broad daylight, are more easily overcome and guarded against: but this being interwoven with our virtues and entangled in the battle, fighting as it were under cover of the darkness of night, deceives the more dangerously those who are off their guard and not on the lookout.

CHAPTER X.

An instance showing how King Hezekiah was overthrown by the dart of vainglory.

FOR so we read that Hezekiah, King of Judah, a man of most perfect righteousness in all things, and one approved by the witness of Holy Scripture, after unnumbered commendations for his virtues, was overthrown by a single dart of vainglory. And he who by a single prayer of his was able to procure the

death of a hundred and eighty-five thousand of the army of the Assyrians, whom the angel destroyed in one night, is overcome by boasting and vanity. Of whom — to pass over the long list of his virtues, which it would take a long time to unfold — I will say but this one thing. He was a man who, after the close of his life had been decreed and the day of his death determined by the Lord's sentence, prevailed by a single prayer to extend the limits set to his life by fifteen years, the sun returning by ten steps, on which it had already shone in its course towards its setting, and by its return dispersing those lines which the shadow that followed its course had already marked, and by this giving two days in one to the whole world, by a stupendous miracle contrary to the fixed laws of nature.[1] Yet after signs so great and so incredible, after such immense proofs of his goodness, hear the Scripture tell how he was destroyed by his very successes. "In those days," we are told, "Hezekiah was sick unto death: and he prayed to the Lord, and He heard him and gave him a sign," that, namely of which we read in the fourth book of the kingdoms, which was given by Isaiah the prophet through the going back of the sun. "But," it says, "he did not render again according to the benefits which he had received, for his heart was lifted up; and wrath was kindled against him and against Judah and Jerusalem: and he humbled himself afterwards because his heart had been lifted up, both he and the inhabitants of Jerusalem, and therefore the wrath of the Lord came not upon them in the days of Hezekiah."[2] How dangerous, how terrible is the malady of vanity! So much goodness, so many virtues, faith and devotion, great enough to prevail to change nature itself and the laws of the whole world, perish by a single act of pride! So that all his good deeds would have been forgotten as if they had never been, and he would at once have been subject to the wrath of the Lord unless he had appeased Him by recovering his humility: so that he who, at the suggestion of pride, had fallen from so great a height of excellence, could only mount again to the height he had lost by the same steps of humility. Do you want to see another instance of a similar downfall?

CHAPTER XI.

The instance of King Uzziah who was overcome by the taint of the same malady.

OF Uzziah, the ancestor of this king of whom we have been speaking, himself also praised in all things by the witness of the

---

[1] Cf. 2 Kings xx.   [2] 2 Chron. xxxii. 24-26.

Scripture, after great commendation for his virtue, after countless triumphs which he achieved by the merit of his devotion and faith, learn how he was cast down by the pride of vainglory. "And," we are told, "the name of Uzziah went forth, for the Lord helped him and had strengthened him. But when he was made strong, his heart was lifted up to his destruction, and he neglected the Lord his God."[1] You behold another instance of a most terrible downfall, and see how two men so upright and excellent were undone by their very triumphs and victories. Whence you see how dangerous the successes of prosperity generally are, so that those who could not be injured by adversity are ruined, unless they are careful, by prosperity; and those who in the conflict of battle have escaped the danger of death fall before their own trophies and triumphs.

CHAPTER XII.

Several testimonies against vainglory.

AND so the Apostle warns us: "Be not desirous of vainglory."[2] And the Lord, rebuking the Pharisees, says, "How can ye believe, who receive glory from one another, and seek not the glory which comes from God alone?"[3] Of these too the blessed David speaks with a threat: "For God hath scattered the bones of them that please men."[4]

CHAPTER XIII.

Of the ways in which vainglory attacks a monk.

IN the case also of beginners and of those who have as yet made but little progress either in powers of mind or in knowledge it usually puffs up their minds, either because of the quality of their voice because they can sing well, or because their bodies are emaciated,[5] or because they are of a good figure, or because they have rich and noble kinsfolk, or because they have despised a military life and honours. Sometimes too it persuades a man that if he had remained in the world he would easily have obtained honours and riches, which perhaps could not possibly have been secured, and inflates him with a vain hope of uncertain things; and in the case of those things which he never possessed, puffs him up with pride and vanity, as if he were one who had despised them.

CHAPTER XIV.

How it suggests that a man may seek to take holy orders.

BUT sometimes it creates a wish to take holy orders, and a desire for the priesthood or diaconate. And it represents that if a man has even against his will received this office, he will fulfil it with such sanctity and strictness that he will be able to set an example of saintliness even to other priests; and that he will win over many people, not only by his manner of life, but also by his teaching and preaching. It makes a man, even when alone and sitting in his cell, to go round in mind and imagination to the dwellings and monasteries of others, and to make many conversions under the inducements of imaginary exultatio

CHAPTER XV.

How vainglory intoxicates the mind.

AND so the miserable soul is affected by such vanity — as if it were deluded by a profound slumber — that it is often led away by the pleasure of such thoughts, and filled with such imaginations, so that it cannot even look at things present, or the brethren, while it enjoys dwelling upon these things, of which with its wandering thoughts it has waking dreams, as if they were true.

CHAPTER XVI.

Of him whom the superior came upon and found in his cell, deluded by idle vainglory.

I REMEMBER an elder, when I was staying in the desert of Scete, who went to the cell of a certain brother to pay him a visit, and when he had reached the door heard him muttering inside, and stood still for a little while, wanting to know what it was that he was reading from the Bible or repeating by heart (as is customary) while he was at work. And when this most excellent eavesdropper diligently applied his ear and listened with some curiosity, he found that the man was induced by an attack of this spirit to fancy that he was delivering a stirring sermon to the people. And when the elder, as he stood still, heard him finish his discourse and return again to his office, and give out the dismissal of the catechumens, as the deacon does,[6] then at last he

---

[1] 2 Chron. xxvi. 15, 16.
[2] Gal. v. 26.
[3] S. John v. 44.

[4] Ps. lii. (liii.) 6.
[5] viz., by fasting.

[6] *Celebrare velut diaconum catechumenis missam. Missa* is here used for the dismissal of the catechumens, which it was the deacon's office to proclaim. The whole service was divided into two parts, (1) the mass of the catechumens, containing the Scrip-

knocked at the door, and the man came out, and met the elder with the customary reverence, and brought him in and (for his knowledge of what had been his thoughts made him uneasy) asked him when he had arrived, for fear lest he might have taken some harm from standing too long at the door: and the old man joking pleasantly replied, "I only got here while you were giving out the dismissal of the catechumens."

CHAPTER XVII.

How faults cannot be cured unless their roots and causes have been discovered.

I THOUGHT it well to insert these things in this little work of mine, that we might learn, not only by reason, but also by examples, about the force of temptations and the order of the sins which hurt an unfortunate soul, and so might be more careful in avoiding the snares and manifold deceits of the enemy. For these things are indiscriminately brought forward by the Egyptian fathers, that by telling them, as those who are still enduring them, they may disclose and lay bare the combats with all the vices, which they actually do suffer; and those which the younger ones are sure to suffer; so that, when they explain the illusions arising from all the passions, those who are but beginners and fervent in spirit may know the secret of their struggles, and seeing them as in a glass, may learn both the causes of the sins by which they are troubled, and the remedies for them, and instructed beforehand concerning the approach of future struggles, may be taught how they ought to guard against them, or to meet them and to fight with them. As clever physicians are accustomed not only to heal already existing diseases, but also by a wise skill to seek to obviate future ones, and to prevent them by their prescriptions and healing draughts, so these true physicians of the soul, by means of spiritual conferences, like some celestial antidote, destroy beforehand those maladies of the soul which would arise, and do not allow them to gain a footing in the minds of the juniors, as they unfold to them the causes of the passions

which threaten them, and the remedies which will heal them.

CHAPTER XVIII.

How a monk ought to avoid women and bishops.

WHEREFORE this is an old maxim of the Fathers that is still current, — though I cannot produce it without shame on my own part, since I could not avoid my own sister, nor escape the hands of the bishop, — viz., that a monk ought by all means to fly from women and bishops. For neither of them will allow him who has once been joined in close intercourse any longer to care for the quiet of his cell, or to continue with pure eyes in divine contemplation through his insight into holy things.

CHAPTER XIX.

Remedies by which we can overcome vainglory.

AND so the athlete of Christ who desires to strive lawfully in this true and spiritual combat, should strive by all means to overcome this changeable monster of many shapes, which, as it attacks us on every side like some manifold wickedness, we can escape by such a remedy as this; viz., thinking on that saying of David: "The Lord hath scattered the bones of those who please men."[1] To begin with we should not allow ourselves to do anything at the suggestion of vanity, and for the sake of obtaining vainglory. Next, when we have begun a thing well, we should endeavour to maintain it with just the same care, for fear lest afterwards the malady of vainglory should creep in and make void all the fruits of our labours. And anything which is of very little use or value in the common life of the brethren, we should avoid as leading to boasting; and whatever would render us remarkable amongst the others, and for which credit would be gained among men, as if we were the only people who could do it, this should be shunned by us. For by these signs the deadly taint of vainglory will be shown to cling to us: which we shall most easily escape if we consider that we shall not merely lose the fruits of those labours of ours which we have performed at the suggestion of vainglory, but that we shall also be guilty of a great sin, and as impious persons undergo eternal punishments, inasmuch as we have wronged God by doing for the favour of men what we ought to have done for His sake, and are convicted by Him who knows all secrets of having preferred men to God, and the praise of the world to the praise of the Lord.

ture lessons, sermon, and prayers for the catechumens; and (2) the mass of the faithful, or the Eucharist proper. At the end of the first part the deacon warned the catechumens to depart, in words varying slightly in different churches, but substantially the same in all, both east and west: e.g. in the Liturgy of S. Chrysostom the form is "Let all the catechumens depart: let not any of the catechumens — Let all the faithful — "; in that of S. Mark it is still briefer: "Look lest any of the catechumens." The Roman missal does not now contain this feature, but it was certainly originally found in it, for it is alluded to by Gregory the Great (Dial. Book II. c. xxiii.), who gives the form as follows: "Si quis non communicat det locum." It was also customary in Spain and Gaul, as well as in Africa, being alluded to by Augustine in Sermon xlix.: "Ecce post sermonen fit missa catechumenis: manebunt fideles, venietur ad locum orationis."

[1] Ps. lii. (liii.) 6.

BOOK XII..

OF THE SPIRIT OF PRIDE.

CHAPTER I.

How our eighth combat is against the spirit of pride, and of its character.

OUR eighth and last combat is against the spirit of pride, which evil, although it is the latest in our conflict with our faults and stands last on the list, yet in beginning and in the order of time is the first: an evil beast that is most savage and more dreadful than all the former ones, chiefly trying those who are perfect, and devouring with its dreadful bite those who have almost attained the consummation of virtue.

CHAPTER II.

How there are two kinds of pride.

AND of this pride there are two kinds: the one, that by which we said that the best of men and spiritually minded ones were troubled; the other, that which assaults even beginners and carnal persons. And though each kind of pride is excited with regard to both God and man by a dangerous elation, yet that first kind more particularly has to do with God; the second refers especially to men. Of the origin of this last and the remedies for it we will by God's help treat as far as possible in the latter part of this book. We now propose to say a few things about that former kind, by which, as I mentioned before, those who are perfect are especially tried.

CHAPTER III.

How pride is equally destructive of all virtues.

THERE is then no other fault which is so destructive of all virtues, and robs and despoils a man of all righteousness and holiness, as this evil of pride, which like some pestilential disease attacks the whole man, and, not content to damage one part or one limb only, injures the entire body by its deadly influence, and endeavours to cast down by a most fatal fall, and destroy those who were already at the top of the tree of the virtues. For every other fault is satisfied within its own bounds and limits, and though it clouds other virtues as well, yet it is in the main directed against one only, and specially attacks and assaults that. And so (to make my meaning clearer) gluttony, i.e., the appetites of the belly and the pleasures of the palate, is destructive of strict temperance: lust stains purity, anger destroys patience: so that sometimes a man who is in bondage to some one sin is not altogether wanting in other virtues: but being simply deprived of that one virtue which in the struggle yields to the vice which is its rival and opposed to it, can to some extent preserve his other virtues: but this one when once it has taken possession of some unfortunate soul, like some most brutal tyrant, when the lofty citadel of the virtues has been taken, utterly destroys and lays waste the whole city; and levelling with the ground of vices the once high walls of saintliness, and confusing them together, it allows no shadow of freedom henceforth to survive in the soul subject to it. And in proportion as it was originally the richer, so now will the yoke of servitude be the severer, through which by its cruel ravages it will strip the soul it has subdued of all its powers of virtue.

CHAPTER IV.

How by reason of pride Lucifer was turned from an archangel into a devil.

AND that we may understand the power of its awful tyranny we see that that angel who, for the greatness of his splendour and beauty was termed Lucifer, was cast out of heaven for no other sin but this, and, pierced with the dart of pride, was hurled down from his grand and exalted position as an angel into hell. If then pride of heart alone was enough to cast down from heaven to earth a power that was so great and adorned with the attributes of such might, the very greatness of his fall shows us with what care we who are surrounded by the weakness of the flesh ought to be on our guard. But we can learn how to avoid the most deadly poison of this evil if we trace out the origin and causes of his fall. For weakness can never be cured, nor the remedies for bad states of health be disclosed unless first their origin and causes are investigated by a wise scrutiny. For as he (viz., Lucifer) was endowed with divine splendour, and shone forth among the other higher powers by the bounty of his Maker, he believed that he had acquired the splendour of that wisdom and the beauty of those powers, with which he was graced by the gift of the Creator, by the might of his own nature, and not by the beneficence of His generosity. And on this account he was puffed up as if he stood in no need of divine assistance in order to continue in this state of purity, and esteemed himself to be like God, as if, like God, he had no need of any one, and trusting in the power of his own will, fancied that through it he could richly supply himself with everything which was necessary for the consummation of virtue or for the perpetuation of perfect bliss. This thought alone was the cause of his first fall. On account of which being forsaken by God, whom he fancied he no longer needed, he suddenly became unstable and tottering, and discovered the weakness of his own nature, and lost the blessedness which he had enjoyed by God's gift. And because he "loved the words of ruin," with which he had said, "I will ascend into heaven," and the "deceitful tongue," with which he had said of himself, "I will be like the Most High," [1] and of Adam and Eve, "Ye shall be as gods," therefore "shall God destroy him forever and pluck him out and remove him from his dwelling place and his root out of the land of the living." Then "the just," when they see his ruin, "shall fear, and shall laugh at him and say" (what may also be most justly aimed at those who trust that they can obtain the highest good without the protection and assistance of God): "Behold the man that made not God his helper, but trusted in the abundance of his riches, and prevailed in his vanity." [2]

CHAPTER V.

That incentives to all sins spring from pride.

THIS is the reason of the first fall, and the starting point of the original malady, which again insinuating itself into the first man, [3] through him who had already been destroyed by it, produced the weaknesses and materials of all faults. For while he believed that by the freedom of his will and by his own efforts he could obtain the glory of Deity, he actually lost that glory which he already possessed through the free gift of the Creator.

CHAPTER VI.

That the sin of pride is last in the actual order of the combat, but first in time and origin.

AND so it is most clearly established by instances and testimonies from Scripture that the mischief of pride, although it comes later in the order of the combat, is yet earlier in origin, and is the beginning of all sins and faults: nor is it (like the other vices) simply fatal to the virtue opposite to it (in this case, humility), but it is also at the same time destructive of all virtues: nor does it only tempt ordinary folk and small people, but chiefly those who already stand on the heights of valour. [4] For thus the prophet speaks of this spirit, "His meat is choice." [5] And so the blessed David, although he guarded the recesses of his heart with the utmost care, so that he dared to say to Him from whom the secrets of his conscience were not hid, "Lord, my heart is not exalted, nor are my eyes lofty: neither have I walked in great matters, nor in wonderful things above me. If I was not humbly minded;" [6] and again, "He that worketh pride shall not dwell in the midst of my house;" [7] yet, as he knew how hard is that watchfulness even for those that are perfect, he did not so presume on his own efforts, but prayed to God and implored His help, that he might escape unwounded by the darts of this foe, saying, "Let not the foot of pride come to me," [8] for he feared and dreaded falling into that which is said of the proud, viz., "God resisteth the proud;" [9] and again: "Every one that exalteth his heart is unclean before the Lord." [10]

CHAPTER VII.

That the evil of pride is so great that it rightly has even God Himself as its adversary.

How great is the evil of pride, that it rightly has no angel, nor other virtues opposed to it, but God Himself as its adversary! Since it should be noted that it is never said of those

---

1 Is. xiv. 13, 14.
2 Ps. li. (lii.) 6–9.
3 *Protoplastum* cf. Wisdom vii. 1; x. 1. where Adam is called πρωτόπλαστος. From these passages the term came to be commonly used as the designation of our first parents. So Clem. Alex. Strom. iii. 17: and in its Latin form it is found in the early translation of Irenæus. Hær. III. xxi. 20.

4 Cf. Milton's "last infirmity of noble minds." (Lycidas.)
5 Hab. i. 16 (LXX.).
6 Ps. cxxx. (cxxxi.) 1, 2.
7 Ps. c. (ci.) 1, 2.
8 Ps. xxxv. (xxxvi.) 1, 2.
9 S. James iv. 6.
10 Prov. xvi. 5 (LXX.).

who are entangled in other sins that they have God resisting them; I mean it is not said that God is opposed "to the gluttonous, fornicators, passionate, or covetous," but only "to the proud." For those sins react only on those who commit them, or seem to be committed against those who share in them, i.e., against other men; but this one has more properly to do with God, and therefore it is especially right that it should have Him opposed to it.

CHAPTER VIII.

How God has destroyed the pride of the devil by the virtue of humility, and various passages in proof of this.

AND so God, the Creator and Healer of all, knowing that pride is the cause and fountain head of evils, has been careful to heal opposites with opposites, that those things which were ruined by pride might be restored by humility. For the one says, "I will ascend into heaven;"[1] the other, "My soul was brought low even to the ground."[2] The one says, "And I will be like the most High;" the other, "Though He was in the form of God, yet He emptied Himself and took the form of a servant, and humbled Himself and became obedient unto death."[3] The one says, "I will exalt my throne above the stars of God;" the other, "Learn of me, for I am meek and lowly of heart."[4] The one says, "I know not the Lord and will not let Israel go;"[5] the other, "If I say that I know Him not, I shall be a liar like unto you: but I know Him, and keep His commandments."[6] The one says, "My rivers are mine and I made them:"[7] the other: "I can do nothing of myself, but my Father who abideth in me, He doeth the works."[8] The one says, "All the kingdoms of the world and the glory of them are mine, and to whomsoever I will, I give them;"[9] the other, "Though He were rich, yet He became poor, that we through His poverty might be made rich."[10] The one says, "As eggs are gathered together which are left, so have I gathered all the earth: and there was none that moved the wing or opened the mouth, or made the least noise;"[11] the other, "I am become like a solitary pelican; I watched and became as a sparrow alone upon the roof."[12] The one says, "I have dried up with the sole of my foot all the rivers shut up in banks;"[13] the other, "Cannot I ask my

Father, and He shall presently give me more than twelve legions of angels?"[14] If we look at the reason of our original fall, and the foundations of our salvation, and consider by whom and in what way the latter were laid and the former originated, we may learn, either through the fall of the devil, or through the example of Christ, how to avoid so terrible a death from pride.

CHAPTER IX.

How we too may overcome pride.

AND so we can escape the snare of this most evil spirit, if in the case of every virtue in which we feel that we make progress, we say these words of the Apostle: "Not I, but the grace of God with me," and "by the grace of God I am what I am;"[15] and "it is God that worketh in us both to will and to do of His good pleasure."[16] As the author of our salvation Himself also says: "If a man abide in me and I in him, the same beareth much fruit; for without me ye can do nothing."[17] And "Except the Lord build the house, they labour in vain that build it. Except the Lord keep the city, the watchman waketh but in vain." And "Vain is it for you to rise up before light."[18] For "it is not of him that willeth, nor of him that runneth, but of God that hath mercy."[19]

CHAPTER X.

How no one can obtain perfect virtue and the promised bliss by his own strength alone.

FOR the will and course of no one, however eager and anxious,[20] is sufficiently ready for him, while still enclosed in the flesh which warreth against the spirit, to reach so great a prize of perfection, and the palm of uprightness and purity, unless he is protected by the divine compassion, so that he is privileged to attain to that which he greatly desires and to which he runs. For "every good gift and every perfect gift is from above, and cometh down from the Father of lights."[21] "For what hast thou which thou didst not receive? But if thou hast received it, why dost thou glory as if thou hadst not received it?"[22]

---

[1] Is. xiv. 13.
[2] Ps. xliii. (xliv.) 25.
[3] Phil. ii. 6-8.
[4] S. Matt. xi. 29.
[5] Exod. v. 2.
[6] S. John viii. 55.
[7] Ezek. xxix. 3. (LXX.)
[8] S. John v. 30; xiv. 10.
[9] S. Luke iv. 6.
[10] 2 Cor. viii. 9.
[11] Is. x. 14.
[12] Ps. ci. (cii.) 7, 8.
[13] Is. xxxvii. 25.

[14] S. Matt. xxvi. 53.
[15] 1 Cor. xv. 10.
[16] Phil. ii. 13.
[17] S. John xv. 5.
[18] Ps. cxxvi. (cxxvii.) 1, 2.
[19] Rom. ix. 16.
[20] *Quamvis ferventis et cupientis* (Petschenig): *Quamvis volentis et currentis* (Gazæus).
[21] S. James i. 17.
[22] 1 Cor. iv. 7.

CHAPTER XI.

The case of the thief and of David, and of our call in order to illustrate the grace of God.

FOR if we recall that thief who was by reason of a single confession admitted into paradise,[1] we shall feel that he did not acquire such bliss by the merits of his life, but obtained it by the gift of a merciful God. Or if we bear in mind those two grievous and heinous sins of King David, blotted out by one word of penitence,[2] we shall see that neither here were the merits of his works sufficient to obtain pardon for so great a sin, but that the grace of God superabounded, as, when the opportunity for true penitence was taken, He removed the whole weight of sins through the full confession of but one word. If we consider also the beginning of the call and salvation of mankind, in which, as the Apostle says, we are saved not of ourselves, nor of our works, but by the gift and grace of God, we can clearly see how the whole of perfection is "not of him that willeth nor of him that runneth, but of God that hath mercy," who makes us victorious over our faults, without any merits of works and life on our part to outweigh them, or any effort of our will availing to scale the difficult heights of perfection, or to subdue the flesh which we have to use: since no tortures of this body, and no contrition of heart, can be sufficient for the acquisition of that true chastity of the inner man so as to be able to gain that great virtue of purity (which is innate in the angels alone and indigenous as it were to heaven) merely by human efforts, i.e., without the aid of God: for the performance of everything good flows from His grace, who by multiplying His bounty has granted such lasting bliss, and vast glory to our feeble will and short and petty course of life.

CHAPTER XII.

That no toil is worthy to be compared with the promised bliss.

FOR all the long years of this present life disappear when you have regard to the eternity of the future glory: and all our sorrows vanish away in the contemplation of that vast bliss, and like smoke melt away, and come to nothing, and like ashes are no more seen.

CHAPTER XIII.

The teaching of the elders on the method of acquiring purity.

WHEREFORE it is now time to produce, in the very words in which they hand it down, the opinion of the Fathers; viz., of those who have not painted the way of perfection and its character in high-sounding words, but rather, possessing it in deed and truth, and in the virtue of their spirit, have passed it on by their own experience and sure example. And so they say that no one can be altogether cleansed from carnal sins, unless he has realized that all his labours and efforts are insufficient for so great and perfect an end; and unless, taught, not by the system handed down to him, but by his feelings and virtues and his own experience, he recognizes that it can only be gained by the mercy and assistance of God. For in order to acquire such splendid and lofty prizes of purity and perfection, however great may be the efforts of fastings and vigils and readings and solitude and retirement applied to it, they will not be sufficient to secure it by the merits of the actual efforts and toil. For a man's own efforts and human exertions will never make up for the lack of the divine gift, unless it is granted by divine compassion in answer to his prayer.

CHAPTER XIV.

That the help of God is given to those who labour.[3]

NOR do I say this to cast a slight on human efforts, or in the endeavour to discourage any one from his purpose of working and doing his best. But clearly and most earnestly do I lay down, not giving my own opinion, but that of the elders, that perfection cannot possibly be gained without these, but that by these only without the grace of God nobody can ever attain it. For when we say that human efforts cannot of themselves secure it without the aid of God, we thus insist that God's mercy and grace are bestowed only upon those who labour and exert themselves, and are granted (to use the Apostle's expression) to them that "will" and "run," according to that which is sung in the person of God in the eighty-eighth Psalm: "I have laid help upon one that is mighty, and have exalted one chosen out of my people."[4] For we say, in accordance with

---

[1] Cf. S. Luke xxiii. 40. [2] Cf. 2 Sam. xii. 13.

[3] The language in this chapter is perilously near semi-Pelagianism, on which compare the Introduction p. 190, sq.
[4] Ps. lxxxviii. (lxxxix.) 20.

our Saviour's words, that it is given to them that ask, and opened to them that knock, and found by them that seek; [1] but that the asking, the seeking, and the knocking on our part are insufficient unless the mercy of God gives what we ask, and opens that at which we knock, and enables us to find that which we seek. For He is at hand to bestow all these things, if only the opportunity is given to Him by our good will. For He desires and looks for our perfection and salvation far more than we do ourselves. And the blessed David knew so well that by his own efforts he could not secure the increase of his work and labour, that he entreated with renewed prayers that he might obtain the "direction" of his work from the Lord, saying, "Direct thou the work of our hands over us; yea, the work of our hands do thou direct;" [2] and again: "Confirm, O God, what thou hast wrought in us." [3]

CHAPTER XV.

From whom we can learn the way of perfection.

AND so, if we wish in very deed and truth to attain to the crown of virtues, we ought to listen to those teachers and guides who, not dreaming with pompous declamations, but learning by act and experience, are able to teach us as well, and direct us likewise, and show us the road by which we may arrive at it by a most sure pathway; and who also testify that they have themselves reached it by faith rather than by any merits of their efforts. And further, the purity of heart that they have acquired has taught them this above all; viz., to recognize more and more that they are burdened with sin (for their compunction for their faults increases day by day in proportion as their purity of soul advances), and to sigh continually from the bottom of their heart because they see that they cannot possibly avoid the spots and blemishes of those faults which are ingrained in them through the countless triflings of the thoughts. And therefore they declared that they looked for the reward of the future life, not from the merits of their works, but from the mercy of the Lord, taking no credit to themselves for their great circumspection of heart in comparison with others, since they ascribed this not to their own exertions, but to divine grace; and without flattering themselves on account of the carelessness of those who are cold, and worse than they themselves are, they rather aimed at a lasting humility by fixing their gaze on those whom they knew to be really free from sin and already in the enjoyment of eternal bliss in the kingdom of heaven, and so by this consideration they avoided the downfall of pride, and at the same time always saw both what they were aiming at and what they had to grieve over: as they knew that they could not attain that purity of heart for which they yearned while weighed down by the burden of the flesh.

CHAPTER XVI.

That we cannot even make the effort to obtain perfection without the mercy and inspiration of God.

WE ought therefore, in accordance with their teaching and instruction, so to press towards it, and to be diligent in fastings, vigils, prayers, and contrition of heart and body, for fear lest all these things should be rendered useless by an attack of this malady. For we ought to believe not merely that we cannot secure this actual perfection by our own efforts and exertions, but also that we cannot perform those things which we practise for its sake, viz., our efforts and exertions and desires, without the assistance of the divine protection, and the grace of His inspiration, chastisement, and exhortation, which He ordinarily sheds abroad in our hearts either through the instrumentality of another, or in His own person coming to visit us.

CHAPTER XVII.

Various passages which clearly show that we cannot do anything which belongs to our salvation without the aid of God.

LASTLY, the Author of our salvation teaches us what we ought not merely to think, but also to acknowledge in everything that we do. "I can," He says, "of mine own self do nothing, but the Father which abideth in me, He doeth the works." [4] He says, speaking in the human nature which He had taken, [5] that He could do nothing of Himself; and shall we, who are dust and ashes, think that we have no need of God's help in what pertains to our salvation? And so let us learn in everything, as we feel our own weakness, and at the same time His help, to declare with the saints, "I was overturned that I might fall, but the Lord supported me. The Lord is my strength and my praise: and He is become my salvation." [6] And "Unless the Lord had helped me, my

---

[1] S. Matt. vii. 7.   [2] Ps. lxxxix. (xc.) 17.   [3] Ps. lxvii. (lxiii.) 29.

[4] S. John xiv. 10; v. 30.
[5] *Ex persona hominis assumpti.* See the note on Against Nestorius, I. v.
[6] Ps. cxvii. (cxviii.) 13, 14.

soul had almost dwelt in hell. If I said, My foot is moved: Thy mercy, O Lord, assisted me. According to the multitude of my sorrows in my heart, Thy comforts have given joy to my soul."[1] Seeing also that our heart is strengthened in the fear of the Lord, and in patience, let us say: "And the Lord became my protector; and He brought me forth into a large place."[2] And knowing that knowledge is increased by progress in work, let us say: "For thou lightest my lamp, O Lord: O my God, enlighten my darkness, for by Thee I shall be delivered from temptation, and through my God I shall go over a wall." Then, feeling that we have ourselves sought for courage and endurance, and are being directed with greater ease and without labour in the path of the virtues, let us say, "It is God who girded me with strength, and made my way perfect; who made my feet like hart's feet, and setteth me up on high: who teacheth my hands to war." And having also secured discretion, strengthened with which we can dash down our enemies, let us cry aloud to God: "Thy discipline hath set me up[3] unto the end, and Thy discipline the same shall teach me. Thou hast enlarged my steps under me, and my feet are not weakened." And because I am thus strengthened with Thy knowledge and power, I will boldly take up the words which follow, and will say, "I will pursue after my enemies and overtake them: and I will not turn again till they are consumed. I will break them, and they shall not be able to stand: they shall fall under my feet."[4] Again, mindful of our own infirmity, and of the fact that while still burdened with the weak flesh we cannot without His assistance overcome such bitter foes as our sins are, let us say, "Through Thee we will scatter our enemies:[5] and through Thy name we will despise them that rise up against us. For I will not trust in my bow: neither shall my sword save me. For Thou hast saved us from them that afflict us: and hast put them to shame that hate us."[6] But further: "Thou hast guided me with strength unto the battle, and hast subdued under me them that rose up against me. And Thou hast made mine enemies turn their backs upon me, and hast destroyed them that hated me."[7] And reflecting that with our own arms alone we cannot conquer, let us say, "Take hold of arms and shield: and rise up to help me. Bring out

the sword and stop the way against them that persecute me: say to my soul, I am thy salvation."[8] "And Thou hast made my arms like a brazen bow. And Thou hast given me the protection of Thy salvation: and Thy right hand hath held me up."[9] "For our fathers got not the possession of the land through their own sword: neither did their own arm save them: but Thy right hand and Thine arm and the light of Thy countenance because Thou wast pleased with them."[10] Lastly, as with anxious mind we regard all His benefits with thankfulness, let us cry to Him with the inmost feelings of our heart, for all these things, because we have fought, and have obtained from Him the light of knowledge, and self-control and discretion, and because He has furnished us with His own arms, and strengthened us with a girdle of virtue, and because He has made our enemies turn their backs upon us, and has given us the power of scattering them like the dust before the wind: "I will love Thee, O Lord my strength; the Lord is my stronghold, my refuge and my deliverer. My God is my helper, and in Him will I put my trust. My protector and the horn of my salvation, and my support. Praising I will call upon the name of the Lord; and I shall be saved from mine enemies."[11]

CHAPTER XVIII.

How we are protected by the grace of God not only in our natural condition, but also by His daily Providence.

NOT alone giving thanks to Him for that He has created us as reasonable beings, and endowed us with the power of free will, and blessed us with the grace of baptism, and granted to us the knowledge and aid of the law, but for these things as well, which are bestowed upon us by His daily providence; viz., that He delivers us from the craft of our enemies; that He works with us so that we can overcome the sins of the flesh, that, even without our knowing it, He shields us from dangers; that He protects us from falling into sin; that He helps us and enlightens us, so that we can understand and recognize the actual help which He gives us, (which some will have it is what is meant by the law);[12] that, when we are through His influence secretly struck with compunction for our sins and negligences, He visits us with His regard

---

[1] Ps. xciii. (xciv.) 17–19.
[2] Ps. xvii. (xviii.) 20 sq.
[3] *Erexit* (Petschenig). Gazæus reads *correxit*, with the Vulgate.
[4] Ps. xvii. (xviii.) 33 sq.
[5] Gazæus adds *cornu* after the Vulgate.
[6] Ps. xliii. (xliv.) 6–8.
[7] Ps. xvii. (xviii.) 40, 41.

[8] Ps. xxxiv. (xxxv.) 2–4.
[9] Ps. xvii. (xviii.) 35.
[10] Ps. xliii. (xliv.) 4, 5.
[11] Ps. xvii. (xviii.) 2–4.
[12] The allusion is to the Pelagians. Cf. S. Jerome Contra Pelag. I. c. ix.; and in Jerem. c. xxv.; and S. Augustine De Gratia Christi contra Pelag.

and chastens us to our soul's health; that even against our will we are sometimes drawn by Him to salvation; lastly that this very free will of ours, which is more readily inclined to sin, is turned by Him to a better purpose, and by His prompting and suggestion, bent towards the way of virtue.

CHAPTER XIX.

How this faith concerning the grace of God was delivered to us by the ancient Fathers.

THIS then is that humility towards God, this is that genuine faith of the ancient fathers which still remains intact among their successors. And to this faith, the apostolic virtues, which they so often showed, bear an undoubted witness, not only among us but also among infidels and unbelievers: for keeping in simplicity of heart the simple faith of the fishermen they did not receive it in a worldly spirit through dialectical syllogisms or the eloquence of a Cicero, but learnt by the experience of a pure life, and stainless actions, and by correcting their faults, and (to speak more truly) by visible proofs, that the character of perfection is to be found in that faith without which neither piety towards God, nor purification from sin, nor amendment of life, nor perfection of virtue can be secured.

CHAPTER XX.

Of one who for his blasphemy was given over to a most unclean spirit.

I KNEW one of the number of the brethren, whom I heartily wish I had never known; since afterwards he allowed himself to be saddled with the responsibilities of my order:[1] who confessed to a most admirable elder that he was attacked by a terrible sin of the flesh: for he was inflamed with an intolerable lust, with the unnatural desire of suffering rather than of committing a shameful act: then the other like a true spiritual physician, at once saw through the inward cause and origin of this evil. And, sighing deeply, said: "Never would the Lord have suffered you to be given over to so foul a spirit unless you had blasphemed against Him." And he, when this was discovered, at once fell at his feet on the ground, and, struck with the utmost astonishment, as if he saw the secrets of his heart laid bare by God, confessed that he had blasphemed with evil thoughts against the Son of God. Whence it is clear that one

who is possessed by the spirit of pride, or who has been guilty of blasphemy against God,— as one who offers a wrong to Him from whom the gift of purity must be looked for — is deprived of his uprightness and perfection, and does not deserve the sanctifying grace of chastity.

CHAPTER XXI.

The instance of Joash, King of Judah, showing what was the consequence of his pride.

SOME such thing we read of in the book of Chronicles. For Joash the king of Judah at the age of seven was summoned by Jehoiada the priest to the kingdom and by the witness of Scripture is commended for all his actions as long as the aforesaid priest lived. But hear what Scripture relates of him after Jehoiada's death, and how he was puffed up with pride and given over to a most disgraceful state. "But after the death of Jehoiada the princes went in and worshipped the king: and he was soothed by their services and hearkened unto them. And they forsook the temple of the Lord, the God of their fathers, and served groves and idols, and great wrath came upon Judah and Jerusalem because of this sin." And after a little: "When a year was come about, the army of Syria came up against him: and they came to Judah and Jerusalem, and killed all the princes of the people, and they sent all the spoils to the king to Damascus. And whereas there came a very small number of the Syrians, the Lord delivered into their hands an infinite multitude, because they had forsaken the Lord the God of their fathers: and on Joash they executed shameful judgments. And departing they left him in great diseases."[2] You see how the consequence of pride was that he was given over to shocking and filthy passions. For he who is puffed up with pride and has permitted himself to be worshipped as God, is (as the Apostle says) "given over to shameful passions and a reprobate mind to do those things which are not convenient."[3] And because, as Scripture says, "every one who exalts his heart is unclean before God,"[4] he who is puffed up with swelling pride of heart is given over to most shameful confusion to be deluded by it, that when thus humbled he may know that he is unclean through impurity of the flesh and knowledge of impure desires, — a thing which he had refused to recognize in the pride of his heart; and also that the shameful infection of the

---

[1] Viz., that of the priesthood.

[2] 2 Chr. xxiv. 17, 18; 23-25.
[3] Rom. i. 26, 28.
[4] Prov. xvi. 5 (LXX.).

flesh may disclose the hidden impurity of the heart, which he contracted through the sin of pride, and that through the patent pollution of his body he may be proved to be impure, who did not formerly see that he had become unclean through the pride of his spirit.

CHAPTER XXII

That every proud soul is subject to spiritual wickedness to be deceived by it.

AND this clearly shows that every soul of which the swellings of pride have taken possession, is given over to the Syrians of the soul,[1] i.e., to spiritual wickedness, and that it is entangled in the lusts of the flesh, that the soul being at last humbled by earthly faults, and carnally polluted, may recognize its uncleanness, though while it stood erect in the coldness of its heart, it could not understand that through pride of heart it was rendered unclean in the sight of God; and by this means being humbled, a man may get rid of his former coldness, and being cast down and confused with the shame of his fleshly lusts, may thenceforward hasten to betake himself the more eagerly towards fervour and warmth of spirit.

CHAPTER XXIII.

How perfection can only be attained through the virtue of humility.

AND so it is clearly shown that none can attain the end of perfection and purity, except through true humility, which he displays in the first instance to the brethren, and shows also to God in his inmost heart, believing that without His protection and aid extended to him at every instant, he cannot possibly obtain the perfection which he desires and to which he hastens so eagerly.

CHAPTER XXIV.

Who are attacked by spiritual and who by carnal pride.

THUS much let it suffice to have spoken, as far as, by God's help, our slender ability was able, concerning spiritual pride of which we have said that it attacks advanced Christians. And this kind of pride is not familiar to or experienced by most men, because the majority do not aim at attaining perfect purity of heart, so as to arrive at the stage of these

conflicts; nor have they secured any purification from the preceding faults of which we have here explained both the character and the remedies in separate books. But it generally attacks those only who have conquered the former faults and have already almost arrived at the top of the tree in respect of the virtues. And because our most crafty enemy has not been able to destroy them through a carnal fall, he endeavours to cast them down and overthrow them by a spiritual catastrophe, trying by this to rob them of the prizes of their ancient rewards secured as they were with great labour. But as for us, who are still entangled in earthly passions, he never deigns to tempt us in this fashion, but overthrows us by a coarser and what I called a carnal pride. And therefore I think it well, as I promised, to say a few things about this kind of pride by which we and men of our stamp are usually affected, and the minds especially of younger men and beginners are endangered.

CHAPTER XXV.

A description of carnal pride, and of the evils which it produces in the soul of a monk.

THIS carnal pride therefore, of which we spoke, when it has gained an entrance into the heart of a monk, which is but lukewarm, and has made a bad start in renouncing the world, does not suffer him to stoop from his former state of worldly haughtiness to the true humility of Christ, but first of all makes him disobedient and rough; then it does not let him be gentle and kindly; nor allows him to be on a level with and like his brethren: nor does it permit him to be stripped and deprived of his worldly goods, as God and our Saviour commands: and, though renunciation of the world is nothing but the mark of mortification and the cross, and cannot begin or rise from any other foundations, but these; viz., that a man should recognize that he is not merely spiritually dead to the deeds of this world, but also should realize daily that he must die in the body — it makes him on the contrary hope for a long life, and sets before him many lengthy infirmities, and covers him with shame and confusion. If when stripped of everything he has begun to be supported by the property of others and not his own, it persuades him that it is much better for food and clothing to be provided for him by his own rather than by another's means according to that text (which, as was before said,[2] those

---

[1] Intellectuales.

[2] See Book X. c. xviii.

who are rendered dense through such dulness and coldness of heart, cannot possibly understand.) "It is more blessed to give than to receive." [1]

CHAPTER XXVI.

That a man whose foundation is bad, sinks daily from bad to worse.

THOSE then who are possessed by such distrust of mind, and who through the devil's own want of faith fall away from that spark of faith, by which they seemed in the early days of their conversion to be enkindled, begin more anxiously to watch over the money which before they had begun to give away, and treasure it up with greater avarice, as men who cannot recover again what they have once wasted : or — what is still worse — take back what they had formerly cast away: or else (which is a third and most disgusting kind of sin), collect what they never before possessed, and thus are convicted of having gone no further in forsaking the world than merely to take the name and style of monk. With this beginning therefore, and on this bad and rotten foundation, it is a matter of course that the whole superstructure of faults must rise, nor can anything be built on such villanous foundations, except what will bring the wretched soul to the ground with a hopeless collapse.

CHAPTER XXVII.

A description of the faults which spring from the evil of pride.

THE mind then that is hardened by such feelings, and which begins with this miserable coldness is sure to go daily from bad to worse and to conclude its life with a more hideous end: and while it takes delight in its former desires, and is overcome, as the apostle says, by impious avarice (as he says of it "and covetousness, which is idolatry, or the worship of idols," and again "the love of money," says he, "is the root of all evils" [1]) can never admit into the heart the true and unfeigned humility of Christ, while the man boasts himself of his high birth, or is puffed up by his position in the world (which he has forsaken in body but not in mind) or is proud of his wealth which he retains to his own destruction; and because of this he is no longer content to endure the yoke of the monastery, or to be instructed by the teaching of any of the elders, and not only objects

to observe any rule of subjection or obedience, but will not even listen to teaching about perfection; and such dislike of spiritual talk grows up in his heart that if such a conversation should happen to arise, he cannot keep his eyes fixed on one spot, but his gaze wanders blankly about here and there, and his eyes shift hither and thither, as the custom is. Instead of wholesome coughs, he spits from a dry throat: he coughs on purpose without any need, he drums with his fingers, and twiddles them and scribbles like a man writing: and all his limbs fidget so that while the spiritual conversation is proceeding, you would think that he was sitting on thorns, and those very sharp ones, or in the midst of a mass of worms : and if the conversation turns in all simplicity on something which is for the good of the hearers, he thinks that it is brought forward for his especial benefit. And all the time that the examination of the spiritual life is proceeding, he is taken up with his own suspicious thoughts, and is not on the watch for something to take home for his good, but is anxiously seeking the reason why anything is said, or is quietly turning over in his mind, how he can raise objections to it, so that he cannot at all take in any of those things which are so admirably brought forward, or be done any good to by them. And so the result is that the spiritual conference is not merely of no use to him, but is positively injurious, and becomes to him an occasion of greater sin. For while he is conscience stricken and fancies that everything is being aimed at him he hardens himself more stubbornly in the obstinacy of his heart, and is more keenly affected by the stings of his wrath: then afterwards his voice is loud, his talk harsh, his answers bitter and noisy, his gait lordly and capricious; his tongue too ready, he is forward in conversation and no friend to silence except when he is nursing in his heart some bitterness against a brother, and his silence denotes not compunction or humility, but pride and wrath: so that one can hardly say which is the more objectionable in him, that unrestrained and boisterous merriment, or this dreadful and deadly solemnity. [3] For in the former we see inopportune chattering, light and frivolous laughter, unrestrained and undisciplined mirth. In the latter a silence that is full of wrath and deadly; and which simply arises from the desire to prolong as long as possible the rancorous feelings which are nourished in silence against some brother, and not from the wish to obtain from it the virtues of humility and patience.

---

[1] Acts xx. 35. [2] Col. iii. 5; 1 Tim. vi. 10. [3] *Serietas* (Petschenig) : *Taciturnitas* (Gazæus).

And as the man who is a victim to passion readily makes everybody else miserable and is ashamed to apologize to the brother whom he has wronged, so when the brother offers to do so to him, he rejects it with scorn. And not only is he not touched or softened by the advances of his brother; but is the rather made more angry because his brother anticipates him in humility. And that wholesome humiliation and apology, which generally puts an end to the devil's temptation, becomes to him an occasion of a worse outbreak.

CHAPTER XXVIII.

On the pride of a certain brother.

I HAVE heard while I have been in this district a thing which I shudder and am ashamed to recall; viz., that one of the juniors — when he was reproved by his Abbot because he had shown signs of throwing off the humility, of which he had made trial for a short time at his renunciation of the world, and of being puffed up with diabolical pride — most impertinently answered "Did I humiliate myself for a time on purpose to be always in subjection?" And at this wanton and wicked reply of his the elder was utterly aghast, and could say nothing, as if he had received this answer from old Lucifer himself and not from a man; so that he could not possibly utter a word against such impudence, but only let fall sighs and groans from his heart; turning over in silence in his mind that which is said of our Saviour: "Who being in the form of God humbled Himself and became obedient" — not, as the man said who was seized with a diabolical spirit of pride, "for a time," but " even to death." [1]

CHAPTER XXIX.

The signs by which you can recognize the presence of carnal pride in a soul.

AND to draw together briefly what has been said of this kind of pride, by collecting, as well as we can, some of its signs that we may somehow convey to those who are thirsting for instruction in perfection, an idea of its characteristics from the movements of the outward man: I think it well to unfold them in a few words that we may conveniently recognize the signs by which we can discern and detect it, that when the roots of this passion are laid bare and brought to the surface, and seen and

Phil. ii. 6, 8.

traced out with ocular demonstration, they may be the more easily plucked up and avoided. For only then will this most pestilent evil be altogether escaped, and if we do not begin too late in the day, when it has already got the mastery over us, to be on our guard against its dangerous heat and noxious influence, but if, recognizing its symptoms (so to speak) beforehand, we take precautions against it with wise and careful forethought. For, as we said before, you can tell a man's inward condition from his outward gait. By these signs, then, that carnal pride, of which we spoke earlier, is shown. To begin with, in conversation the man's voice is loud: in his silence there is bitterness: in his mirth his laughter is noisy and excessive: when he is serious he is unreasonably gloomy: in his answers there is rancour: he is too free with his tongue, his words tumbling out at random without being weighed. He is utterly lacking in patience, and without charity: impudent in offering insults to others, faint-hearted in bearing them himself: troublesome in the matter of obedience except where his own wishes and likings correspond with his duty: unforgiving in receiving admonition: weak in giving up his own wishes: very stubborn about yielding to those of others: always trying to compass his own ends, and never ready to give them up for others: and thus the result is that though he is incapable of giving sound advice, yet in everything he prefers his own opinion to that of the elders.

CHAPTER XXX.

How when a man has grown cold through pride he wants to be put to rule other people.

AND when a man whom pride has mastered has fallen through these stages of descent, he shudders at the discipline of the cœnobium, and — as if the companionship of the brethren hindered his perfection, and the sins of others impeded and interfered with his advance in patience and humility — he longs to take up his abode in a solitary cell; or else is eager to build a monastery and gather together some others to teach and instruct, as if he would do good to many more people, and make himself from being a bad disciple a still worse master. For when through this pride of heart a man has fallen into this most dangerous and injurious coldness, he can neither be a real monk nor a man of the world, and what is worse, promises to himself to gain perfection by means of this wretched state and manner of life of his.

CHAPTER XXXI.

How we can overcome pride and attain perfection.

WHEREFORE if we wish the summit of our building to be perfect and to rise well-pleasing to God, we should endeavour to lay its foundations not in accordance with the desires of our own lust, but according to the rules of evangelical strictness: which can only be the fear of God and humility, proceeding from kindness and simplicity of heart. But humility cannot possibly be acquired without giving up everything: and as long as a man is a stranger to this, he cannot possibly attain the virtue of obedience, or the strength of patience, or the serenity of kindness, or the perfection of love; without which things our hearts cannot possibly be a habitation for the Holy Spirit: as the Lord says through the prophet: "Upon whom shall My spirit rest, but on him that is humble and quiet and fears My words," or according to those copies which express the Hebrew accurately: "To whom shall I have respect, but to him that is poor and little and of a contrite spirit and that trembleth at My words?" [1]

CHAPTER XXXII.

How pride which is so destructive of all virtues can itself be destroyed by true humility.

WHEREFORE the Christian athlete who strives lawfully in the spiritual combat and desires to be crowned by the Lord, should endeavour by every means to destroy this most fierce beast, which is destructive of all virtues, knowing that as long as this remains in his breast he not only will never be free from all kinds of evils, but even if he seems to have any good qualities, will lose them by its malign influence. For no structure (so to speak) of virtue can possibly be raised in our soul unless first the foundations of true humility are

---

[1] Is. lxvi. 2. It is noteworthy that Cassian after giving a rendering which differs but slightly from that of the old Latin, as given in Sabbatier's great work, adds the version of "those copies which express the Hebrew accurately," and thus shows his acquaintance with Jerome's new translation which he quotes. He does the same thing again in the Conferences, XXIII. viii.; and On the Incarnation Against Nestorius IV. iii.; V. ii.; xv. Compare also Institutes VIII. xxi., and Conf. VIII. x., where he also betrays a knowledge of the Vulgate. As a general rule, however, his translations are taken from the old Latin, or possibly in some cases are made by him from the LXX.

laid in our heart, which being securely laid may be able to bear the weight of perfection and love upon them in such a way that, as we have said, we may first show to our brethren true humility from the very bottom of our heart, in nothing acquiescing in making them sad or in injuring them: and this we cannot possibly manage unless true self-denial, which consists in stripping and depriving ourselves of all our possessions, is implanted in us by the love of Christ. Next the yoke of obedience and subjection must be taken up in simplicity of heart without any pretence, so that, except for the commands of the Abbot, no will of our own is alive in us. But this can only be ensured in the case of one who considers himself not only dead to this world, but also unwise and a fool; and performs without any discussion whatever is enjoined him by his seniors, believing it to be divine and enjoined from heaven.

CHAPTER XXXIII.

Remedies against the evil of pride.

AND when men remain in this condition, there is no doubt that this quiet and secure state of humility will follow, so that considering ourselves inferior to every one else we shall bear everything offered to us, even if it is hurtful, and saddening, and damaging — with the utmost patience, as if it came from those who are our superiors. And these things we shall not only bear with the greatest ease, but we shall consider them trifling and mere nothings, if we constantly bear in mind the passion of our Lord and of all His Saints: considering that the injuries by which we are tried are so much less than theirs, as we are so far behind their merits and their lives: remembering also that we shall shortly depart out of this world, and soon by a speedy end to our life here become sharers of their lot. For considerations such as these are a sure end not only to pride but to all kinds of sins. Then, next after this we must keep a firm grasp of this same humility towards God: which we must so secure as not only to acknowledge that we cannot possibly perform anything connected with the attainment of perfect virtue without His assistance and grace, but also truly to believe that this very fact that we can understand this, is His own gift.

THE CONFERENCES OF JOHN CASSIAN.

PART I.

CONTAINING CONFERENCES I-X.

PREFACE.

THE obligation, which was promised to the blessed Pope Castor in the preface to those volumes which with God's help I composed in twelve books on the Institutes of the Cœnobia, and the remedies for the eight principal faults, has now been, as far as my feeble ability permitted, satisfied. I should certainly like to see what was the opinion fairly arrived at on this work both by his judgment and yours, whether, on a matter so profound and so lofty, and one which has never yet been made the subject of a treatise, we have produced anything worthy of your notice, and of the eager desire of all the holy brethren. But now as the aforesaid Bishop has left us and departed to Christ, meanwhile these ten Conferences of the grandest of the fathers, viz., the Anchorites who dwelt in the desert of Scete, which he, fired with an incomparable desire for saintliness, had bidden me write for him in the same style (not considering in the greatness of his affection, what a burden he placed on shoulders too weak to bear it) — these Conferences I have thought good to dedicate to you in particular, O blessed Pope, [1] Leontius, [2] and holy brother Helladius. [3] For one of you was united to him whom I have mentioned, by the ties of brotherhood, and the rank of the priesthood, and (what is more to the point) by fervour in sacred study, and so has an hereditary right to demand the debt due to his brother: while the other has ventured to follow the sublime customs of the Anchorites, not like some others, presumptuously on his own account, but seizing, at the inspiration of the Holy Ghost, on the right path of doctrine almost before he had been taught and choosing to learn not so much from his own ideas as from their traditions. Wherein just as I had anchored in the harbour of Silence, a wide sea opens out before me, so that I must venture to hand down for posterity some of the Institutes and teaching of these great men. For the bark of my slender abilities will be exposed to the dangers of a longer voyage on the deep, in proportion as the Anchorite's life is grander than that of the Cœnobium, and the contemplation of God, to which those inestimable men ever devoted themselves, more sublime than ordinary practical life. It is yours therefore to assist our efforts by your pious prayers for fear lest so sacred a subject that is to be treated in an untried but faithful manner, should be imperilled by us, or lest our simplicity should lose itself in the depths of the subject matter. Let us therefore pass from what is visible to the eye and the external mode of life of the monks, of which we treated in the former books, to the life of the inner man, which is hidden from view; and from the system of the canonical prayers, let our discourse mount to that continuance in unceasing prayer, which the Apostle enjoins, that whoever has through reading our former work already spiritually gained the name of Jacob by ousting his carnal faults, may now by the reception of the Institutes which are not mine but the fathers', mount by a pure insight to the merits and (so to speak) the dignity of Israel, and in the

---

[1] *Papa.* See note on the Preface to the Institutes.
[2] The see of which Leontius was Bishop is uncertain, possibly Fréjus.
[3] Helladius was afterwards raised to the Episcopate, but of what see is unknown. See the Preface to Conf. XVIII.

same way be taught what it is that he should observe on these lofty heights of perfection.[1] And so may your prayers gain from Him, Who has deemed us worthy both to see them and to learn from them and to dwell with them, that He will vouchsafe to grant us a perfect recollection of their teaching, and a ready tongue to tell it, that we may explain them as beautifully and as exactly as we received them from them and may succeed in setting before you the men themselves incorporated, as it were, in their own Institutes, and what is more to the point, speaking in the Latin tongue. Of this however we wish above all to advertise the reader of these Conferences as well as of our earlier works, that if there chances to be anything herein which by reason of his condition and the character of his profession, or owing to custom and the common mode of life seems to him either impossible or very difficult, he should measure it not by the limits of his own powers but by the worth and perfection of the speakers, whose zeal and purpose he should first consider, as they were truly dead to this worldly life, and so hampered by no feelings for their kinsmen according to the flesh, and by no ties of worldly occupations. Next let him bear in mind the character of the country in which they dwelt, how they lived in a vast desert, and were cut off from intercourse with all their fellow-men, and thus were able to have their minds enlightened, and to contemplate, and utter those things which perhaps will seem impossibilities to the uninitiated and uninstructed, because of their way of life and the commonplace character of their habits. But if any one wants to give a true opinion on this matter, and is anxious to try whether such perfection can be attained, let him first endeavour to make their purpose his own, with the same zeal and the same mode of life, and then in the end he will find that those things which used to seem beyond the powers of men, are not only possible, but really delightful. But now let us proceed at once to their Conferences and Institutes.

---

[1] The allusion is rather forced and strained. But Cassian means to say that those who have got the better of their carnal sins by perusing his former work, are already fit to be named Jacob (the supplanter), who got the better of his brother: and he hopes that this new work of his will give them such a view of God and insight into His dealings that they may be worthy to have their name changed, as Jacob's was, to Israel, which he takes to mean the man seeing God. Cf. the note on Against Nestorius, VII. ix. (intelligibilis here = spiritualis, cf. intellectualis. Conf. XII. xi., and elsewhere).

CASSIAN'S CONFERENCES.

FIRST CONFERENCE OF ABBOT MOSES.

CHAPTER I.

Of our stay in Scete, and that which we proposed to Abbot Moses.

WHEN I was in the desert of Scete, where are the most excellent monastic fathers and where all perfection flourishes, in company with the holy father Germanus (who had since the earliest days and commencement of our spiritual service been my closest companion both in the cœnobium and in the desert, so that to show the harmony of our friendship and aims, everybody would say that a single heart and soul existed in our two bodies), I sought out Abbot Moses,[1] who was eminent amid those splendid flowers, not only in practical but also in contemplative excellence, in my anxiety to be grounded by his instruction: and together we implored him to give us a discourse for our edification; not without tears, for we knew full well his determination never to consent to open the gate of perfection, except to those who desired it with all faithfulness, and sought it with all sorrow of heart; for fear lest if he showed it at random to those who cared nothing for it, or only desired it in a half-hearted way, by opening what is necessary, and what ought only to be discovered to those seeking perfection, to unworthy persons, and such as accepted it with scorn, he might appear to lay himself open either to the charge of bragging, or to the sin of betraying his trust; and at last being overcome by our prayers he thus began.

CHAPTER II.

Of the question of Abbot Moses, who asked what was the goal and what the end of the monk.

ALL the arts and sciences, said he, have some goal or mark; and end or aim of their own, on which the diligent pursuer of each art has his eye, and so endures all sorts of toils and dangers and losses, cheerfully and with equanimity, e.g., the farmer, shunning neither at one time the scorching heat of the sun, nor at another the frost and cold, cleaves the earth unweariedly, and again and again subjects the clods of his field to his ploughshare, while he keeps before him his goal; viz., by diligent labour to break it up small like fine sand, and to clear it of all briers, and free it from all weeds, as he believes that in no other way can he gain his ultimate end, which is to secure a good harvest, and a large crop; on which he can either live himself free from care, or can increase his possessions. Again, when his barn is well stocked he is quite ready to empty it, and with incessant labour to commit the seed to the crumbling furrow, thinking nothing of the present lessening of his stores in view of the future harvest. Those men too who are engaged in mercantile pursuits, have no dread of the uncertainties and chances of the ocean, and fear no risks, while an eager hope urges them forward to their aim of gain. Moreover those who are inflamed with the ambition of military life, while they look forward to their aim of honours and power take no notice of danger and destruction in their wanderings, and are not crushed by present losses and wars, while they are eager to obtain the end of some honour held out to them. And our profession too has its own goal and end, for which we undergo all sorts of toils not merely without weariness but actually with delight; on account of which the want of food in fasting is no trial to us, the weariness of our vigils becomes a delight; reading and constant meditation on the Scriptures does not pall upon us; and further incessant toil, and self-denial, and the privation of all things, and the horrors also of this vast desert have no terrors for us. And doubtless for this it was that you yourselves despised the love of

---

[1] On this Moses see the note on the Institutes, Book **X. xxv.**

kinsfolk, and scorned your fatherland, and the delights of this world, and passed through so many countries, in order that you might come to us, plain and simple folk as we are, living in this wretched state in the desert. Wherefore, said he, answer and tell me what is the goal and end, which incite you to endure all these things so cheerfully.

CHAPTER III.

Of our reply.

AND when he insisted on eliciting an opinion from us on this question, we replied that we endured all this for the sake of the kingdom of heaven.

CHAPTER IV.

Of Abbot Moses' question on the aforesaid statement.

To which he replied: Good, you have spoken cleverly of the (ultimate) end. But what should be our (immediate) goal or mark, by constantly sticking close to which we can gain our end, you ought first to know. And when we frankly confessed our ignorance, he proceeded: The first thing, as I said, in all the arts and sciences is to have some goal, i.e., a mark for the mind, and constant mental purpose, for unless a man keeps this before him with all diligence and persistence, he will never succeed in arriving at the ultimate aim and the gain which he desires. For, as I said, the farmer who has for his aim to live free from care and with plenty, while his crops are springing has this as his immediate object and goal; viz., to keep his field clear from all brambles, and weeds, and does not fancy that he can otherwise ensure wealth and a peaceful end, unless he first secures by some plan of work and hope that which he is anxious to obtain. The business man too does not lay aside the desire of procuring wares, by means of which he may more profitably amass riches, because he would desire gain to no purpose, unless he chose the road which leads to it: and those men who are anxious to be decorated with the honours of this world, first make up their minds to what duties and conditions they must devote themselves, that in the regular course of hope they may succeed in gaining the honours they desire. And so the end of our way of life is indeed the kingdom of God. But what is the (immediate) goal you must earnestly ask, for if it is not in the same way discovered by us, we shall strive and wear ourselves out to no purpose, because a

man who is travelling in a wrong direction, has all the trouble and gets none of the good of his journey. And when we stood gaping at this remark, the old man proceeded: The end of our profession indeed, as I said, is the kingdom of God or the kingdom of heaven: but the immediate aim or goal, is purity of heart, without which no one can gain that end: fixing our gaze then steadily on this goal, as if on a definite mark, let us direct our course as straight towards it as possible, and if our thoughts wander somewhat from this, let us revert to our gaze upon it, and check them accurately as by a sure standard, which will always bring back all our efforts to this one mark, and will show at once if our mind has wandered ever so little from the direction marked out for it.

CHAPTER V.

A comparison with a man who is trying to hit a mark.

As those, whose business it is to use weapons of war, whenever they want to show their skill in their art before a king of this world, try to shoot their arrows or darts into certain small targets which have the prizes painted on them; for they know that they cannot in any other way than by the line of their aim secure the end and the prize they hope for, which they will only then enjoy when they have been able to hit the mark set before them; but if it happens to be withdrawn from their sight, however much in their want of skill their aim may vainly deviate from the straight path, yet they cannot perceive that they have strayed from the direction of the intended straight line because they have no distinct mark to prove the skilfulness of their aim, or to show up its badness: and therefore while they shoot their missiles idly into space, they cannot see how they have gone wrong or how utterly at fault they are, since no mark is their accuser, showing how far they have gone astray from the right direction; nor can an unsteady look help them to correct and restore the straight line enjoined on them. So then the end indeed which we have set before us is, as the Apostle says, eternal life, as he declares, "having indeed your fruit unto holiness, and the end eternal life;"[1] but the immediate goal is purity of heart, which he not unfairly terms "sanctification," without which the afore-mentioned end cannot be gained; as if he had said in other words, having your immediate goal in purity of heart, but the end

---

1 Rom. vi. 22.

life eternal. Of which goal the same blessed Apostle teaches us, and significantly uses the very term, i.e., σκοπός, saying as follows, "Forgetting those things which are behind and reaching forward to those that are before, I press toward the mark, for the prize of the high calling of the Lord:" [1] which is more clearly put in Greek κατὰ σκοπὸν διώκω, i.e., "I press toward the mark," as if he said, "With this aim, with which I forget those things that are behind, i.e., the faults of earlier life, I strive to reach as the end the heavenly prize." Whatever then can help to guide us to this object; viz., purity of heart, we must follow with all our might, but whatever hinders us from it, we must shun as a dangerous and hurtful thing. For, for this we do and endure all things, for this we make light of our kinsfolk, our country, honours, riches, the delights of this world, and all kinds of pleasures, namely in order that we may retain a lasting purity of heart. And so when this object is set before us, we shall always direct our actions and thoughts straight towards the attainment of it; for if it be not constantly fixed before our eyes, it will not only make all our toils vain and useless, and force them to be endured to no purpose and without any reward, but it will also excite all kinds of thoughts opposed to one another. For the mind, which has no fixed point to which it may return, and on which it may chiefly fasten, is sure to rove about from hour to hour and minute to minute in all sorts of wandering thoughts, and from those things which come to it from outside, to be constantly changed into that state which first offers itself to it.

CHAPTER VI.

Of those who in renouncing the world, aim at perfection without love.

FOR hence it arises that in the case of some who have despised the greatest possessions of this world, and not only large sums of gold and silver, but also large properties, we have seen them afterwards disturbed and excited over a knife, or pencil, or pin, or pen. Whereas if they kept their gaze steadily fixed out of a pure heart they would certainly never allow such a thing to happen for trifles, while in order that they might not suffer it in the case of great and precious riches they chose rather to renounce them altogether. For often too some guard their books so jealously that they will not allow them to be even slightly moved or touched by any one else, and from this fact

they meet with occasions of impatience and death, which give them warning of the need of acquiring the requisite patience and love; and when they have given up all their wealth for the love of Christ, yet as they preserve their former disposition in the matter of trifles, and are sometimes quickly upset about them, they become in all points barren and unfruitful, as those who are without the charity of which the Apostle speaks: and this the blessed Apostle foresaw in spirit, and "though," says he, "I give all my goods to feed the poor, and give my body to be burned, but have not charity, it profiteth me nothing." [2] And from this it clearly follows that perfection is not arrived at simply by self-denial, and the giving up of all our goods, and the casting away of honours, unless there is that charity, the details of which the Apostle describes, which consists in purity of heart alone. For "not to be envious," "not to be puffed up, not to be angry, not to do any wrong, not to seek one's own, not to rejoice in iniquity, not to think evil," etc., what is all this except ever to offer to God a perfect and clean heart, and to keep it free from all disturbances?

CHAPTER VII.

How peace of mind should be sought.

EVERYTHING should be done and sought after by us for the sake of this. For this we must seek for solitude, for this we know that we ought to submit to fastings, vigils, toils, bodily nakedness, reading, and all other virtues that through them we may be enabled to prepare our heart and to keep it unharmed by all evil passions, and resting on these steps to mount to the perfection of charity, and with regard to these observances, if by accident we have been employed in some good and useful occupation and have been unable to carry out our customary discipline, we should not be overcome by vexation or anger, or passion, with the object of overcoming which, we were going to do that which we have omitted. For the gain from fasting will not balance the loss from anger, nor is the profit from reading so great as the harm which results from despising a brother. Those things which are of secondary importance, such as fastings, vigils, withdrawal from the world, meditation on Scripture, we ought to practise with a view to our main object, i.e., purity of heart, which is charity, and we ought not on their account to drive away this main virtue, for as long as it is still found in us intact and unharmed, we

---

[1] Phil. iii. 13, 14.   [2] 1 Cor. xiii. 3.

shall not be hurt if any of the things which are of secondary importance are necessarily omitted; since it will not be of the slightest use to have done everything, if this main reason of which we have spoken be removed, for the sake of which everything is to be done. For on this account one is anxious to secure and provide for one's self the implements for any branch of work, not simply to possess them to no purpose, nor as if one made the profit and advantage, which is looked for from them, to consist in the bare fact of possession but that by using them, one may effectually secure practical knowledge and the end of that particular art of which they are auxiliaries. Therefore fastings, vigils, meditation on the Scriptures, self-denial, and the abnegation of all possesions are not perfection, but aids to perfection: because the end of that science does not lie in these, but by means of these we arrive at the end. He then will practise these exercises to no purpose, who is contented with these as if they were the highest good, and has fixed the purpose of his heart simply on them, and does not extend his efforts towards reaching the end, on account of which these should be sought: for he possesses indeed the implements of his art, but is ignorant of the end, in which all that is valuable resides. Whatever then can disturb that purity and peace of mind — even though it may seem useful and valuable —should be shunned as really hurtful, for by this rule we shall succeed in escaping harm from mistakes and vagaries, and make straight for the desired end and reach it.

CHAPTER VIII.

Of the main effort towards the contemplation of heavenly things and an illustration from the case of Martha and Mary.

THIS then should be our main effort: and this steadfast purpose of heart we should constantly aspire after; viz., that the soul may ever cleave to God and to heavenly things. Whatever is alien to this, however great it may be, should be given the second place, or even treated as of no consequence, or perhaps as hurtful. We have an excellent illustration of this state of mind and condition in the gospel in the case of Martha and Mary: for when Martha was performing a service that was certainly a sacred one, since she was ministering to the Lord and His disciples, and Mary being intent only on spiritual instruction was clinging close to the feet of Jesus which she kissed and anointed with the ointment of a good confession, she is shown by the Lord to have chosen the better part, and one which should

not be taken away from her: for when Martha was toiling with pious care, and was cumbered about her service, seeing that of herself alone she was insufficient for such service she asks for the help of her sister from the Lord, saying: "Carest Thou not that my sister has left me to serve alone: bid her therefore that she help me"— certainly it was to no unworthy work, but to a praiseworthy service that she summoned her: and yet what does she hear from the Lord? "Martha, Martha, thou art anxious and troubled about many things: but few things are needful, or only one. Mary hath chosen the good part, which shall not be taken away from her."[1] You see then that the Lord makes the chief good consist in meditation, i.e., in divine contemplation: whence we see that all other virtues should be put in the second place, even though we admit that they are necessary, and useful, and excellent, because they are all performed for the sake of this one thing. For when the Lord says: "Thou art careful and troubled about many things, but few things are needful or only one," He makes the chief good consist not in practical work however praiseworthy and rich in fruits it may be, but in contemplation of Him, which indeed is simple and "but one"; declaring that "few things" are needful for perfect bliss, i.e., that contemplation which is first secured by reflecting on a few saints: from the contemplation of whom, he who has made some progress rises and attains by God's help to that which is termed "one thing," i.e., the consideration of God alone, so as to get beyond those actions and services of saints, and feed on the beauty and knowledge of God alone. "Mary" therefore "chose the good part, which shall not be taken away from her." And this must be more carefully considered. For when He says that Mary chose the good part, although He says nothing of Martha, and certainly does not appear to blame her, yet in praising the one, He implies that the other is inferior. Again when He says "which shall not be taken away from her" He shows that from the other her portion can be taken away (for a bodily ministry cannot last forever with a man), but teaches that this one's desire can never have an end.

CHAPTER IX.

A question how it is that the practice of virtue cannot remain with a man.

To which we, being deeply moved, replied what then? will the effort of fasting, dili-

---

[1] S. Luke x. 40-42. The reading which Cassian here follows is found in אBC,[2] but has not much Latin authority. It is however

gence in reading, works of mercy, justice, piety, and kindness, be taken away from us, and not continue with the doers of them, especially since the Lord Himself promises the reward of the kingdom of heaven to these works, when He says: "Come, ye blessed of My Father, inherit the kingdom prepared for you from the beginning of the world. For I was an hungred, and ye gave Me to eat; I was thirsty and ye gave Me to drink:" etc. [1] How then shall these works be taken away, which admit the doers of them into the kingdom of heaven?

CHAPTER X.

The answer that not the reward, but the doing of them will come to an end.

MOSES. I did not say that the reward for a good work would be taken away, as the Lord Himself says: "Whosoever shall give to one of the least of these, a cup of cold water only in the name of a disciple, verily I say unto you, he shall not lose his reward:" [2] but I maintain that the doing of a thing, which either bodily necessity, or the onslaught of the flesh, or the inequalities of this world, compel to be done, will be taken away. For diligence in reading, and self-denial in fasting, are usefully practised for purifying the heart and chastening the flesh in this life only, as long as "the flesh lusteth against the spirit," [3] and sometimes we see that even in this life they are taken away from those men who are worn out with excessive toil, or bodily infirmity or old age, and cannot be practised by them. How much more then will they come to an end hereafter, when "this corruptible shall have put on incorruption," [4] and the body which is now "a natural body" shall have risen "a spiritual body" [5] and the flesh shall have begun to be such that it no longer lusts against the spirit? And of this the blessed Apostle also clearly speaks, when he says that "bodily exercise is profitable for a little: but godliness" (by which he certainly means love) "is profitable for all things, having the promise of the life that now is and of that which is to come." [6] This clearly shows that what is said to be useful for a little, is not to be practised for all time, and cannot possibly by itself alone confer the highest state of perfection on the man who slaves at it. For the term "for a little" may mean either of the two things,

i.e., it may refer to the shortness of the time, because bodily exercise cannot possibly last on with man both in this life and in the world to come: or it may refer to the smallness of the profit which results from exercising the flesh, because bodily austerities produce some sort of beginnings of progress, but not the actual perfection of love, which has the promise of the life that now is and of that which is to come: and therefore we deem that the practice of the aforesaid works is needful, because without them we cannot climb the heights of love. For what you call works of religion and mercy are needful in this life while these inequalities and differences of conditions still prevail; but even here we should not look for them to be performed, unless such a large proportion of poor, needy, and sick folk abounded, which is brought about by the wickedness of men; viz., of those who have grasped and kept for their own use (without however using them) those things which were granted to all by the Creator of all alike. As long then as this inequality lasts in this world, this sort of work will be needful and useful to the man that practises it, as it brings to a good purpose and pious will the reward of an eternal inheritance: but it will come to an end in the life to come, where equality will reign, when there will be no longer inequality, on account of which these things must be done, but all men will pass from these manifold practical works to the love of God, and contemplation of heavenly things in continual purity of heart: to which those men who are urgent in devoting themselves to knowledge and purifying the heart, have chosen to give themselves up with all their might and main, betaking themselves, while they are still in the flesh, to that duty, in which they are to continue, when they have laid aside corruption, and when they come to that promise of the Lord the Saviour, which says "Blessed are the pure in heart for they shall see God." [7]

CHAPTER XI.

On the abiding character of love.

AND why do you wonder that those duties enumerated above will cease, when the holy Apostle tells us that even the higher gifts of the Holy Spirit will pass away: and points out that charity alone will abide without end, saying "whether there be prophecies, they shall fail; whether there be tongues, they shall cease: whether there be knowledge, it will

followed by Jerome Ep: ad Eustochium, xxii. 24, though the Vulgate has simply Porro unum est necessarium. For Mary as the type of the contemplative life, and Martha of the practical, compare S. Gregory the Great. Moralia VI. c. xxviii.

[1] S. Matt. xxv. 34, 35.   [3] Gal. v. 17.   [5] 1 Cor. xv. 44.
[2] S. Matt. x. 42.   [4] 1 Cor. xv. 53.   [6] 1 Tim. iv. 8.

[7] S. Matt. v. 8.

come to an end," but of this he says "Charity never faileth." For all gifts are given for a time as use and need require, but when the dispensation is ended they will without doubt presently pass away: but love will never be destroyed. For not only does it work usefully in us in this world; but also in that to come, when the burden of bodily needs is cast off, it will continue in far greater vigour and excellence, and will never be weakened by any defect, but by means of its perpetual incorruption will cling to God more intently and earnestly.[1]

CHAPTER XII.

A question on perseverance in spiritual contemplation.

GERMANUS. Who then, while he is burdened with our frail flesh, can be always so intent on this contemplation, as never to think about the arrival of a brother, or visiting the sick, or manual labour, or at least about showing kindness to strangers and visitors? And lastly, who is not interrupted by providing for the body, and looking after it? Or how and in what way can the mind cling to the invisible and incomprehensible God, this we should like to learn.

CHAPTER XIII.

The answer concerning the direction of the heart towards God, and concerning the kingdom of God and the kingdom of the devil.

MOSES. To cling to God continually, and as you say inseparably to hold fast to meditation on Him, is impossible for a man while still in this weak flesh of ours. But we ought to be aware on what we should have the purpose of our mind fixed, and to what goal we should ever recall the gaze of our soul: and when the mind can secure this it may rejoice; and grieve and sigh when it is withdrawn from this, and as often as it discovers itself to have fallen away from gazing on Him, it should admit that it has lapsed from the highest good, considering that even a momentary departure from gazing on Christ is fornication. And when our gaze has wandered ever so little from Him, let us turn the eyes of the soul back to Him, and recall our mental gaze as in a perfectly straight direction. For everything depends on the inward frame of mind, and when the devil has been expelled from this, and sins no longer reign in it, it follows that the kingdom of God is founded

in us, as the Evangelist says "The kingdom of God cometh not with observation, nor shall men say Lo here, or lo there: for verily I say unto you that the kingdom of God is within you."[2] But nothing else can be "within you," but knowledge or ignorance of truth, and delight either in vice or in virtue, through which we prepare a kingdom for the devil or for Christ in our heart: and of this kingdom the Apostle describes the character, when he says "For the kingdom of God is not meat and drink, but righteousness and peace and joy in the Holy Ghost."[3] And so if the kingdom of God is within us, and the actual kingdom of God is righteousness and peace and joy, then the man who abides in these is most certainly in the kingdom of God, and on the contrary those who live in unrighteousness, and discord, and the sorrow that worketh death, have their place in the kingdom of the devil, and in hell and death. For by these tokens the kingdom of God and the kingdom of the devil are distinguished: and in truth if lifting up our mental gaze on high we would consider that state in which the heavenly powers live on high, who are truly in the kingdom of God, what should we imagine it to be except perpetual and lasting joy? For what is so specially peculiar and appropriate to true blessedness as constant calm and eternal joy? And that you may be quite sure that this, which we say, is really so, not on my own authority but on that of the Lord, hear how very clearly He describes the character and condition of that world: "Behold," says He, "I create new heavens and a new earth: and the former things shall not be remembered nor come into mind. But ye shall be glad and rejoice forever in that which I create."[4] And again "joy and gladness shall be found therein: thanksgiving and the voice of praise, and there shall be month after month, and Sabbath after Sabbath."[5] And again: "they shall obtain joy and gladness; and sorrow and sighing shall flee away."[6] And if you want to know more definitely about that life and the city of the saints, hear what the voice of the Lord proclaims to the heavenly Jerusalem herself: "I will make," says He, "thine officers peace and thine overseers righteousness. Violence shall no more be heard in thy land, desolation nor destruction within thy borders. And salvation shall take possession of thy walls, and praise of thy gates. The sun shall be no more thy light by day, neither shall the brightness of the moon give light to thee: but the Lord shall be

---

[1] 1 Cor. xiii. 8.

[2] S. Luke xvii. 20, 21.   [4] Is. lxv. 17, 18.   [6] Is. xxxv. 10.
[3] Rom. xiv. 17.   [5] Is. li. 3; lxvi. 23.

thine everlasting light, and thy God thy glory. Thy sun shall no more go down, neither shall thy moon withdraw itself: but the Lord shall be thine everlasting light, and the days of thy mourning shall be ended:"[1] and therefore the holy Apostle does not say generally or without qualification that every joy is the kingdom of God, but markedly and emphatically that joy alone which is "in the Holy Ghost."[2] For he was perfectly aware of another detestable joy, of which we hear "the world shall rejoice,"[3] and "woe unto you that laugh, for ye shall mourn."[4] In fact the kingdom of heaven must be taken in a threefold sense, either that the heavens shall reign, i.e., the saints over other things subdued, according to this text, "Be thou over five cities, and thou over ten;"[5] and this which is said to the disciples: "Ye shall sit upon twelve thrones judging the twelve tribes of Israel:"[6] or that the heavens themselves shall begin to be reigned over by Christ, when "all things are subdued unto Him," and God begins to be "all in all:"[7] or else that the saints shall reign in heaven with the Lord.

CHAPTER XIV.

Of the continuance of the soul.

WHEREFORE every one while still existing in this body should already be aware that he must be committed to that state and office, of which he made himself a sharer and an adherent while in this life, nor should he doubt that in that eternal world he will be partner of him, whose servant and minister he chose to make himself here: according to that saying of our Lord which says "If any man serve Me, let him follow Me, and where I am, there shall My servant also be."[8] For as the kingdom of the devil is gained by consenting to sin, so the kingdom of God is attained by the practice of virtue in purity of heart and spiritual knowledge. But where the kingdom of God is, there most certainly eternal life is enjoyed, and where the kingdom of the devil is, there without doubt is death and the grave. And the man who is in this condition, cannot praise the Lord, according to the saying of the prophet which tells us: "The dead cannot praise Thee, O Lord; neither all they that go down into the grave (doubtless of sin). But we," says he, "who live (not forsooth to sin nor to this world but to God) will bless the Lord, from this time forth for evermore: for in death

no man remembereth God: but in the grave (of sin) who will confess to the Lord?"[9] i.e., no one will. For no man even though he were to call himself a Christian a thousand times over, or a monk, confesses God when he is sinning: no man who allows those things which the Lord hates, remembereth God, nor calls himself with any truth the servant of Him, whose commands he scorns with obstinate rashness: in which death the blessed Apostle declares that the widow is involved, who gives herself to pleasure, saying "a widow who giveth herself to pleasure is dead while she liveth."[10] There are then many who while still living in this body are dead, and lying in the grave cannot praise God; and on the contrary there are many who though they are dead in the body yet bless God in the spirit, and praise Him, according to this: "O ye spirits and souls of the righteous, bless ye the Lord:"[11] and "every spirit shall praise the Lord."[12] And in the Apocalypse the souls of them that are slain are not only said to praise God but to address Him also.[13] In the gospel too the Lord says with still greater clearness to the Sadducees: "Have ye not read that which was spoken by God, when He said to you: I am the God of Abraham, and the God of Isaac and the God of Jacob. He is not the God of the dead but of the living: for all do live unto Him."[14] Of whom also the Apostle says: "wherefore God is not ashamed to be called their God: for He hath prepared for them a city."[15] For that they are not idle after the separation from this body, and are not incapable of feeling, the parable in the gospel shows, which tells us of the beggar Lazarus and Dives clothed in purple, one of whom obtained a position of bliss, i.e., Abraham's bosom, the other is consumed with the dreadful heat of eternal fire.[16] But if you care too to understand the words spoken to the thief "To-day thou shalt be with Me in Paradise,"[17] what do they clearly show but that not only does their former intelligence continue with the souls, but also that in their changed condition they partake of some state which corresponds to their actions and deserts? For the Lord would certainly never have promised him this, if He had known that his soul after being separated from the flesh would either have been deprived of perception or have been resolved into nothing. For it was not his flesh but his soul which was to enter Paradise with Christ. At least we

---

[1] Is. lx. 17-20.
[2] Cf. Rom. xiv. 17.
[3] S. John xvi. 20.
[4] S. Luke vi. 25.

[5] S. Luke xix. 17, 19.
[6] S. Matt. xix. 28.
[7] 1 Cor. xv. 28
[8] S. John xii. 26.

[9] Ps. cxiii. 17, 18; vi. 6.
[10] 1 Tim. v. 6.
[11] Dan. iii. 86 (LXX).
[12] Ps. cl. 6.
[13] Cf. Rev. vi. 9, 10.

[14] S. Matt. xxii. 31, 32.
[15] Heb. xi. 16.
[16] Cf. S. Luke xvi. 19 sq.
[17] S. Luke xxiii. 43.

must avoid, and shun with the utmost horror, that wicked punctuation of the heretics, who, as they do not believe that Christ could be found in Paradise on the same day on which He descended into hell, thus punctuate "Verily, I say unto you to-day," and making a stop apply "thou shall be with Me in Paradise," in such a way that they imagine that this promise was not fulfilled at once after he departed from this life, but that it will be fulfilled after the resurrection,[1] as they do not understand what before the time of His resurrection He declared to the Jews, who fancied that He was hampered by human difficulties and weakness of the flesh as they were: "No man hath ascended into heaven, but He who came down from heaven, even the Son of man who is in heaven:"[2] by which He clearly shows that the souls of the departed are not only not deprived of their reason, but that they are not even without such feelings as hope and sorrow, joy and fear, and that they already are beginning to taste beforehand something of what is reserved for them at the last judgment, and that they are not as some unbelievers hold resolved into nothing after their departure from this life:[3] but that they live a more real life, and are still more earnest in waiting on the praises of God. And indeed to put aside for a little Scripture proofs, and to discuss, as far as our ability permits us, a little about the nature of the soul itself, is it not beyond the bounds of I will not say the folly, but the madness of all stupidity, even to have the slightest suspicion that the nobler part of man, in which as the blessed Apostle shows, the image and likeness of God consists,[4] will, when the burden of the body with which it is oppressed in this world is laid aside, become insensible, when, as it contains in itself all the power of reason, it makes the dumb and senseless material flesh sensible, by participation with it: especially when it follows, and the order of reason itself demands that when the mind has put off the grossness of the flesh with which it is now weighed down, it will restore its intellectual powers better than ever, and receive them in a purer and finer condition than it lost them. But so far did the blessed Apostle recognize that what we

say is true, that he actually wished to depart from this flesh; that by separation from it, he might be able to be joined more earnestly to the Lord; saying: "I desire to be dissolved and to be with Christ, which is far better, for while we are in the body we are absent from the Lord:" and therefore "we are bold and have our desire always to be absent from the body, and present with the Lord. Wherefore also we strive, whether absent or present, to be pleasing to Him;"[5] and he declares indeed that the continuance of the soul which is in the flesh is distance from the Lord, and absence from Christ, and trusts with entire faith that its separation and departure from this flesh involves presence with Christ. And again still more clearly the same Apostle speaks of this state of the souls as one that is very full of life: "But ye are come to Mount Sion, and the city of the living God, the heavenly Jerusalem, and to an innumerable company of angels, and the church of the first born, who are written in heaven, and the spirits of just men made perfect."[6] Of which spirits he speaks in another passage, "Furthermore we have had instructors of our flesh, and we reverenced them: shall we not much more be subject to the Father of spirits and live?"[7]

CHAPTER XV.

How we must meditate on God.

BUT the contemplation of God is gained in a variety of ways. For we not only discover God by admiring His incomprehensible essence, a thing which still lies hid in the hope of the promise, but we see Him through the greatness of His creation, and the consideration of His justice, and the aid of His daily providence: when with pure minds we contemplate what He has done with His saints in every generation, when with trembling heart we admire His power with which He governs, directs, and rules all things, or the vastness of His knowledge, and that eye of His from which no secrets of the heart can lie hid, when we consider the sand of the sea, and the number of the waves measured by Him and known to Him, when in our wonder we think that the drops of rain, the days and hours of the ages, and all things past and future are present to His knowledge; when we gaze in unbounded admiration on that ineffable mercy of His, which with unwearied patience endures countless sins which are

---

[1] The punctuation which Cassian here mentions only to reject, and which is rightly characterized by Alford as "worse than silly," is also mentioned by Theophylact. Com. in loc.
[2] S. John iii. 13.
[3] Augustine (De Hæres. c. lix.) speaks of "Seleuciani" or "Hermiani" as denying a visible Paradise, and a future resurrection; and again in c. lxxxiii. he speaks of some Arabian heretics, as teaching that the soul died and was dissolved (dissolvi) with the body, and that it would at the end of the world be revived and rise again. These were the heretics of whom Eusebius speaks in his Eccl. History Book VI. c. xxxvii., where he tells us that they were successfully refuted by Origen. It is probably to this last error that Cassian is here making allusion.
[4] Cf. I Cor. xi. 7; Col. iii. 10.

[5] Phil. i. 23 ; 2 Cor. v. 6.
[6] Heb. xii. 22, 13.
[7] *Ibid.*, ver. 9.

every moment being committed under His very eyes, or the call with which from no antecedent merits of ours, but by the free grace of His pity He receives us; or again the numberless opportunities of salvation which He grants to those whom He is going to adopt — that He made us be born in such a way as that from our very cradles His grace and the knowledge of His law might be given to us, that He Himself, overcoming our enemy in us simply for the pleasure of His good will, rewards us with eternal bliss and everlasting rewards, when lastly He undertook the dispensation of His Incarnation for our salvation, and extended the marvels of His sacraments[1] to all nations. But there are numberless other considerations of this sort, which arise in our minds according to the character of our life and the purity of our heart, by which God is either seen by pure eyes or embraced: which considerations certainly no one will preserve lastingly, if anything of carnal affections still survives in him, because "thou canst 'not," saith the Lord, "see My face: for no man shall see Me and live;"[2] viz., to this world and to earthly affections.

CHAPTER XVI.

A question on the changing character of the thoughts.

GERMANUS. How is it then, that even against our will, aye and without our knowledge idle thoughts steal upon us so subtilely and secretly that it is fearfully hard not merely to drive them away, but even to grasp and seize them? Can then a mind sometimes be found free from them, and never attacked by illusions of this kind?

CHAPTER XVII.

The answer what the mind can and what it cannot do with regard to the state of its thoughts.

MOSES. It is impossible for the mind not to be approached by thoughts, but it is in the power of every earnest man either to admit them or to reject them. As then their rising up does not entirely depend on ourselves, so the rejection or admission of them lies in our own power. But because we said that it is impossible for the mind not to be approached by thoughts, you must not lay everything to the charge of the assault, or to those spirits

---

[1] Mysteriorum.   [2] Exod. xxxiii. 20.

who strive to instil them into us, else there would not remain any free will in man, nor would efforts for our improvement be in our power: but it is, I say, to a great extent in our power to improve the character of our thoughts and to let either holy and spiritual thoughts or earthly ones grow up in our hearts. For for this purpose frequent reading and continual meditation on the Scriptures is employed that from thence an opportunity for spiritual recollection may be given to us, therefore the frequent singing of Psalms is used, that thence constant feelings of compunction may be provided, and earnest vigils and fasts and prayers, that the mind may be brought low and not mind earthly things, but contemplate things celestial, for if these things are dropped and carelessness creeps on us, the mind being hardened with the foulness of sin is sure to incline in a carnal direction and fall away.

CHAPTER XVIII.

Comparison of a soul and a millstone.

AND this movement of the heart is not unsuitably illustrated by the comparison of a mill wheel, which the headlong rush of water whirls round, with revolving impetus, and which can never stop its work so long as it is driven round by the action of the water: but it is in the power of the man who directs it, to decide whether he will have wheat or barley or darnel ground by it. That certainly must be crushed by it which is put into it by the man who has charge of that business. So then the mind also through the trials of the present life is driven about by the torrents of temptations pouring in upon it from all sides, and cannot be free from the flow of thoughts: but the character of the thoughts which it should either throw off or admit for itself, it will provide by the efforts of its own earnestness and diligence: for if, as we said, we constantly recur to meditation on the Holy Scriptures and raise our memory towards the recollection of spiritual things and the desire of perfection and the hope of future bliss, spiritual thoughts are sure to rise from this, and cause the mind to dwell on those things on which we have been meditating. But if we are overcome by sloth or carelessness and spend our time in idle gossip, or are entangled in the cares of this world and unnecessary anxieties, the result will be that a sort of species of tares will spring up, and afford an injurious occupation for our hearts, and as our

Lord and Saviour says, wherever the treasure of our works or purpose may be, there also our heart is sure to continue.[1]

CHAPTER XIX.

Of the three origins of our thoughts.

ABOVE all we ought at least to know that there are three origins of our thoughts, i.e., from God, from the devil, and from ourselves. They come from God when He vouchsafes to visit us with the illumination of the Holy Ghost, lifting us up to a higher state of progress, and where we have made but little progress, or through acting slothfully have been overcome, He chastens us with most salutary compunction, or when He discloses to us heavenly mysteries, or turns our purpose and will to better actions, as in the case where the king Ahasuerus, being chastened by the Lord, was prompted to ask for the books of the annals, by which he was reminded of the good deeds of Mordecai, and promoted him to a position of the highest honour and at once recalled his most cruel sentence concerning the slaughter of the Jews.[2] Or when the prophet says: "I will hearken what the Lord God will say in me."[3] Another too tells us "And an angel spoke, and said in me,"[4] or when the Son of God promised that He would come with His Father, and make His abode in us,[5] and "It is not ye that speak, but the Spirit of your Father which speaketh in you."[6] And the chosen vessel: "Ye seek a proof of Christ that speaketh in me."[7] But a whole range of thoughts springs from the devil, when he endeavours to destroy us either by the pleasures of sin or by secret attacks, in his crafty wiles deceitfully showing us evil as good, and transforming himself into an angel of light to us:[8] as when the evangelist tells us: "And when supper was ended, when the devil had already put it into the heart of Judas Iscariot, Simon's son, to betray"[9] the Lord: and again also "after the sop," he says, "Satan entered into him."[10] Peter also says to Ananias: "Why hath Satan tempted thine heart, to lie to the Holy Ghost?"[11] And that which we read in the gospel much earlier as predicted by Ecclesiastes: "If the spirit of the ruler rise up against thee, leave not thy place."[12] That too which is said to God

against Ahab in the third book of Kings, in the character of an unclean spirit: "I will go forth and will be a lying spirit in the mouth of all his prophets."[13] But they arise from ourselves, when in the course of nature we recollect what we are doing or have done or have heard. Of which the blessed David speaks: "I thought upon the ancient days, and had in mind the years from of old, and I meditated, by night I exercised myself with my heart, and searched out my spirit."[14] And again: "the Lord knoweth the thoughts of man, that they are vain:"[15] and "the thoughts of the righteous are judgments."[16] In the gospel too the Lord says to the Pharisees: "why do ye think evil in your hearts?"[17]

CHAPTER XX.

About discerning the thoughts, with an illustration from a good money-changer.

WE ought then carefully to notice this threefold order, and with a wise discretion to analyse the thoughts which arise in our hearts, tracking out their origin and cause and author in the first instance, that we may be able to consider how we ought to yield ourselves to them in accordance with the desert of those who suggest them, so that we may, as the Lord's command bids us, become good money-changers,[18] whose highest skill and whose training is to test what is perfectly pure gold and what is commonly termed *tested*,[19] or what is not sufficiently purified in the fire; and also with unerring skill not to be taken in by a common brass denarius, if by being coloured with bright gold it is made like some coin of great value; and not only shrewdly to recognize coins stamped with the heads of usurpers, but with a still shrewder skill to detect those which have the image of the right king, but are not properly made, and lastly to be careful by the test of the balance to see that they are not under proper weight. All of which

---

[1] Cf. S. Matt. vi. 21.
[2] Cf. Esth. vi. 1 sq.
[3] Ps. lxxxiv. (lxxxv.) 9.
[4] Zech. i. 14.
[5] Cf. S. John xiv. 23.
[6] S. Matt. x. 20.
[7] 2 Cor. xiii. 3.
[8] Cf. 2 Cor. xi. 4.
[9] S. John xiii. 2.
[10] *Ibid.*, ver. 27.
[11] Acts v. 3.
[12] Eccl. x. 4.

[13] 1 Kings xxii. 22.
[14] Ps. lxxvi. (lxxvii.) 6, 7. *Scobebam* (which Petschenig edits from the MSS.) = *scopebam*, which is found in the Gallican Psalter as in the old Latin in this passage. It is merely a Latinized form of σκοπεῖν.
[15] Ps. xciii. (xciv.) 11.
[16] Prov. xii. 5.
[17] S. Matt. ix. 4.
[18] *Ut efficiamur secundum præceptum Domini probabiles trapezitæ.* The saying to which Cassian here alludes, γίνεσθε τραπεξῖται δόκιμοι, is not found anywhere in the Gospels, but "is the most commonly quoted of all Apocryphal sayings, and seems to be genuine." Westcott, Introd. to the Gospels, p. 454. It is quoted among others by Origen in Joann. xix., and Jerome Ep. 152. See these and other reff. in Anger's Synopsis, p. 274; and cf. the note of Gazæus here.
[19] *Obrizum.* The word occurs in the Vulgate five times for "pure gold." See 2 Chr. iii. 5; Job xxviii. 15; xxxi. 24; Isa. xiii. 12; Dan. x. 5; and is akin to the Greek ὄβρυζον. Cf. Pliny Nat. Hist. xxxiii. c. 3, and Jerome De Nom. Hebr. s. v. Ophaz.

things the gospel saying, which uses this figure, shows us that we ought also to observe spiritually; first that whatever has found an entrance into our hearts, and whatever doctrine has been received by us, should be most carefully examined to see whether it has been purified by the divine and heavenly fire of the Holy Ghost, or whether it belongs to Jewish superstition, or whether it comes from the pride of a worldly philosophy and only externally makes a show of religion. And this we can do, if we carry out the Apostle's advice, "Believe not every spirit, but prove the spirits whether they are of God."[1] But by this kind those men also are deceived, who after having been professed as monks are enticed by the grace of style, and certain doctrines of philosophers, which at the first blush, owing to some pious meanings not out of harmony with religion, deceive as with the glitter of gold their hearers, whom they have superficially attracted, but render them poor and miserable for ever, like men deceived by false money made of copper: either bringing them back to the bustle of this world, or enticing them into the errors of heretics, and bombastic conceits: a thing which we read of as happening to Achan in the book of Joshua the son of Nun,[2] when he coveted a golden weight from the camp of the Philistines, and stole it, and was smitten with a curse and condemned to eternal death. In the second place we should be careful to see that no wrong interpretation fixed on to the pure gold of Scripture deceives us as to the value of the metal: by which means the devil in his craft tried to impose upon our Lord and Saviour as if He was a mere man, when by his malevolent interpretation he perverted what ought to be understood generally of all good men, and tried to fasten it specially on to Him, who had no need of the care of the angels: saying, "For He shall give His angels charge concerning Thee, to keep Thee in all Thy ways: and in their hands they shall bear Thee up, lest at any time Thou dash Thy foot against a stone,"[3] by a skilful assumption on his part giving a turn to the precious sayings of Scripture and twisting them into a dangerous sense, the very opposite of their true meaning, so as to offer to us the image and face of an usurper under cover of the gold colour which may deceive us. Or whether he tries to cheat us with counterfeits, for instance by urging that some work of piety should be taken up which as it does come from the true minds of the fathers, leads under the form of virtue to vice; and, deceiving us

either by immoderate or impossible fasts, or by too long vigils, or inordinate prayers, or unsuitable reading, brings us to a bad end. Or, when he persuades us to give ourselves up to mixing in the affairs of others, and to pious visits, by which he may drive us away from the spiritual cloisters of the monastery, and the secrecy of its friendly peacefulness, and suggests that we take on our shoulders the anxieties and cares of religious women who are in want, that when a monk is inextricably entangled in snares of this sort he may distract him with most injurious occupations and cares. Or else when he incites a man to desire the holy office of the clergy under the pretext of edifying many people, and the love of spiritual gain, by which to draw us away from the humility and strictness of our life. All of which things, although they are opposed to our salvation and to our profession, yet when covered with a sort of veil of compassion and religion, easily deceive those who are lacking in skill and care. For they imitate the coins of the true king, because they seem at first full of piety, but are not stamped by those who have the right to coin, i.e., the approved Catholic fathers, nor do they proceed from the head public office for receiving them, but are made by stealth and by the fraud of the devil, and palmed off upon the unskilful and ignorant not without serious harm. And even although they seem to be useful and needful at first, yet if afterwards they begin to interfere with the soundness of our profession, and as it were to weaken in some sense the whole body of our purpose, it is well that they should be cut off and cast away from us like a member which may be necessary, but yet offends us and which seems to perform the office of the right hand or foot. For it is better, without one member of a command, i.e., its working or result, to continue safe and sound in other parts, and to enter as weak into the kingdom of heaven rather than with the whole mass of commands to fall into some error which by an evil custom separates us from our strict rule and the system purposed and entered upon, and leads to such loss, that it will never outweigh the harm that will follow, but will cause all our past fruits and the whole body of our work to be burnt in hell fire.[4] Of which kind of illusions it is well said in the Proverbs: "There are ways which seem to be right to a man, but their latter end will come into the depths of hell,"[5] and again "An evil man is harmful when he attaches himself to a good man,"[6]

---

1 1 John iv. 1.
2 Cf. Josh. vii.
3 S. Matt. iv. 6; Ps. xc. 11, 12.

4 Cf. S. Matt. xviii. 8.
5 Prov xvi. 25 (LXX.).
6 Prov. xi. 15 (LXX.).

i.e., the devil deceives when he is covered with an appearance of sanctity: "but he hates the sound of the watchman,"[1] i.e., the power of discretion which comes from the words and warnings of the fathers.

CHAPTER XXI.

Of the illusion of Abbot John.

IN this manner we have heard that Abbot John who lived at Lycon,[2] was recently deceived. For when his body was exhausted and failing as he had put off taking food during a fast of two days, on the third day while he was on his way to take some refreshment the devil came in the shape of a filthy Ethiopian, and falling at his feet, cried "Pardon me because I appointed this labour for you." And so that great man, who was so perfect in the matter of discretion, understood that under pretence of an abstinence practised unsuitably, he was deceived by the craft of the devil, and engaged in a fast of such a character as to affect his worn out body with a weariness that was unnecessary, indeed that was harmful to the spirit; as he was deceived by a counterfeit coin, and, while he paid respect to the image of the true king upon it, was not sufficiently alive to the question whether it was rightly cut and stamped. But the last duty of this "good money-changer," which, as we mentioned before, concerns the examination of the weight, will be fulfilled, if whenever our thoughts suggest that anything is to be done, we scrupulously think it over, and, laying it in the scales of our breast, weigh it with the most exact balance, whether it be full of good for all, or heavy with the fear of God: or entire and sound in meaning; or whether it be light with human display or some conceit of novelty, or whether the pride of foolish vain glory has not diminished or lessened the weight of its merit. And so straightway weighing them in the public balance, i.e., testing them by the acts and proofs of the Apostles and Prophets let us hold them as it were entire and perfect and of full weight, or else with all care and diligence reject them as imperfect and counterfeit, and of insufficient weight.

CHAPTER XXII.

Of the fourfold method of discrimination.

THIS power of discriminating will then be necessary for us in the fourfold manner of which we have spoken; viz., first that the material does not escape our notice whether it be of true or of painted gold: secondly, that those thoughts which falsely promise works of religion should be rejected by us as forged and counterfeit coins, as they are those which are not rightly stamped, and which bear an untrue image of the king; and that we may be able in the same way to detect those which in the case of the precious gold of Scripture, by means of a false and heretical meaning, show the image not of the true king but of an usurper; and that we refuse those whose weight and value the rust of vanity has depreciated and not allowed to pass in the scales of the fathers, as coins that are too light, and are false and weigh too little; so that we may not incur that which we are warned by the Lord's command to avoid with all our power, and lose the value and reward of all our labour. "Lay not up for yourselves treasures on the earth, where rust and moth corrupt and where thieves break through and steal."[3] For whenever we do anything with a view to human glory we know that we are, as the Lord says, laying up for ourselves treasure on earth, and that consequently being as it were hidden in the ground and buried in the earth it must be destroyed by sundry demons or consumed by the biting rust of vain glory, or devoured by the moths of pride so as to contribute nothing to the use and profits of the man who has hidden it. We should then constantly search all the inner chambers of our hearts, and trace out the footsteps of whatever enters into them with the closest investigation lest haply some beast, if I may say so, relating to the understanding, either lion or dragon, passing through has furtively left the dangerous marks of his track, which will show to others the way of access into the secret recesses of the heart, owing to a carelessness about our thoughts. And so daily and hourly turning up the ground of our heart with the gospel plough, i.e., the constant recollection of the Lord's cross, we shall manage to stamp out or extirpate from our hearts the lairs of noxious beasts and the lurking places of poisonous serpents.

CHAPTER XXIII.

Of the discourse of the teacher in regard to the merits of his hearers.

AT this the old man seeing that we were astonished, and inflamed at the words of his discourse with an insatiable desire, stopped

---

1 Prov. xi. 15 (LXX.).
2 On this John of Lycon or Lycopolis see the note on Inst. IV. xxiii.

3 S. Matt. vi. 19.

his speech for a little in consequence of our admiration and earnestness, and presently added: Since your zeal, my sons, has led to so long a discussion, and a sort of fire supplies keener zest to our conference in proportion to your earnestness, as from this very thing I can clearly see that you are truly thirsting after teaching about perfection, I want still to say something to you on the excellence of discrimination and grace which rules and holds the field among all virtues, and not merely to prove its value and usefulness by daily instances of it, but also from former deliberations and opinions of the fathers. For I remember that frequently when men were asking me with sighs and tears for a discourse of this kind, and I myself was anxious to give them some teaching I could not possibly manage it, and not merely my thoughts but even my very power of speech failed me so that I could not find how to send them away with even some slight consolation. And by these signs we clearly see that the grace of the Lord inspires the speakers with words according to the deserts and zeal of the hearers. And because the very short night which is before us does not allow me to finish the discourse, let us the rather give it up to bodily rest, in which the whole of it will have to be spent, if a reasonable portion is refused, and let us reserve the complete scheme of the discourse for unbroken consideration on a future day or night. For it is right for the best counsellors on discretion to show the diligence of their minds in the first place in this, and to prove whether they are or can be possessors of it by this evidence and patience, so that in treating of that virtue which is the mother of moderation they may by no means fall into the vice which is opposite to it; viz.,

that of undue length, by their actions and deeds destroying the force of the system and nature which they recommend in word. In regard then to this most excellent discretion, on which we still propose to inquire, so far as the Lord gives us power, it may in the first instance be a good thing, when we are disputing about its excellence and the moderation which we know exists in it as the first of virtues, not to allow ourselves to exceed the due limit of the discussion and of our time.

And so with this the blessed Moses put a stop to our talk, and urged us, eager though we were and hanging on his lips, to go off to bed for a little, advising us to lie down on the same mats on which we were sitting, and to put our bundles[1] under our heads instead of pillows, as these being tied evenly to thicker leaves of papyrus collected in long and slender bundles, six feet apart, at one time provide the brethren when sitting at service with a very low seat instead of a footstool, at another time being put under their necks when they go to bed furnish a support for their heads, that is not too hard, but comfortable and just right. For which uses of the monks these things are considered especially fit and suitable not only because they are somewhat soft, and prepared at little cost of money and labour, as the papyrus grows everywhere along the banks of the Nile, but also because they are of a convenient stuff and light enough to be removed or fetched as need may require. And so at last at the bidding of the old man we settled ourselves down to sleep in deep stillness, both excited with delight at the conference we had held, and also buoyed up with hope of the promised discussion.

SECOND CONFERENCE OF ABBOT MOSES.

CHAPTER I.

Abbot Moses' introduction on the grace of discretion.

AND so when we had enjoyed our morning sleep, when to our delight the dawn of light again shone upon us, and we had begun to ask once more for his promised talk, the blessed Moses thus began: As I see you inflamed with such an eager desire, that I do not believe that that very short interval of quiet which I wanted to subtract from our spiritual conference and devote to bodily rest, has been of any use for the repose of your bodies, on

me too a greater anxiety presses when I take note of your zeal. For I must give the greater care and devotion in paying my debt, in proportion as I see that you ask for it the more earnestly, according to that saying: "When thou sittest to eat with a ruler consider diligently what is put before thee, and put forth thine hand, knowing that thou oughtest to prepare such things."[2] Wherefore as we are going

---

[1] Embrimium. The word is possibly of Egyptian origin. It occurs also in Cyril in Vita S. Euthymii Abbati, n. 90, and in Apophthegm, Patrum num. 7, and is possibly the same word as "Ebymium," which occurs in the Rule of Pachomius, c. xiv. See Ducange, *sub voce.*
[2] Prov. xxiii. 1, 2 (LXX.).

to speak of the excellent quality of discretion and the virtue of it, on which subject our discourse of last night had entered at the termination of our discussion, we think it desirable first to establish its excellence by the opinions of the fathers, that when it has been shown what our predecessors thought and said about it, then we may bring forward some ancient and modern shipwrecks and mischances of various people, who were destroyed and hopelessly ruined because they paid but little attention to it, and then as well as we can we must treat of its advantages and uses: after a discussion of which we shall know better how we ought to seek after it and practise it, by the consideration of the importance of its value and grace. For it is no ordinary virtue nor one which can be freely gained by merely human efforts, unless they are aided by the Divine blessing, for we read that this is also reckoned among the noblest gifts of the Spirit by the Apostle: "To one is given by the Spirit the word of wisdom, to another the word of knowledge by the same Spirit, to another faith by the same Spirit, to another the gift of healing by the same Spirit," and shortly after, "to another the discerning of spirits." Then after the complete catalogue of spiritual gifts he subjoins: "But all these worketh one and the selfsame Spirit, dividing to every man severally as He will."[1] You see then that the gift of discretion is no earthly thing and no slight matter, but the greatest prize of divine grace. And unless a monk has pursued it with all zeal, and secured a power of discerning with unerring judgment the spirits that rise up in him, he is sure to go wrong, as if in the darkness of night and dense blackness, and not merely to fall down dangerous pits and precipices, but also to make frequent mistakes in matters that are plain and straightforward.

CHAPTER II.

What discretion alone can give a monk; and a discourse of the blessed Antony on this subject.

AND so I remember that while I was still a boy, in the region of Thebaid, where the blessed Antony lived,[2] the elders came to him to inquire about perfection: and though the conference lasted from evening till morning, the greatest part of the night was taken up with this question. For it was discussed at great length what virtue or observance could preserve a monk always unharmed by the snares and deceits of the devil, and carry him forward on a sure and right path, and with firm step to the heights of perfection. And when each one gave his opinion according to the bent of his own mind, and some made it consist in zeal in fasting and vigils, because a soul that has been brought low by these, and so obtained purity of heart and body will be the more easily united to God, others in despising all things, as, if the mind were utterly deprived of them, it would come the more freely to God, as if henceforth there were no snares to entangle it: others thought that withdrawal from the world was the thing needful, i.e., solitude and the secrecy of the hermit's life; living in which a man may more readily commune with God, and cling more especially to Him; others laid down that the duties of charity, i.e., of kindness should be practised, because the Lord in the gospel promised more especially to give the kingdom to these; when He said "Come ye blessed of My Father, inherit the kingdom prepared for you from the foundation of the world. For I was an hungred and ye gave Me to eat, I was thirsty and ye gave Me to drink, etc.:"[3] and when in this fashion they declared that by means of different virtues a more certain approach to God could be secured, and the greater part of the night had been spent in this discussion, then at last the blessed Antony spoke and said: All these things which you have mentioned are indeed needful, and helpful to those who are thirsting for God, and desirous to approach Him. But countless accidents and the experience of many people will not allow us to make the most important of gifts consist in them. For often when men are most strict in fasting or in vigils, and nobly withdraw into solitude, and aim at depriving themselves of all their goods so absolutely that they do not suffer even a day's allowance of food or a single penny to remain to them, and when they fulfil all the duties of kindness with the utmost devotion, yet still we have seen them suddenly deceived, so that they could not bring the work they had entered upon to a suitable close, but brought their exalted fervour and praiseworthy manner of life to a terrible end. Wherefore we shall be able clearly to recognize what it is which mainly leads to God, if we trace out with greater care the reason of their downfall and deception. For when the works of the above mentioned virtues were abounding in them, discretion alone was wanting, and allowed them not to continue even to the end. Nor can any other reason for their falling off be discovered except that

---

[1] 1 Cor. xii. 8-11. [2] Cf. the note on the Institutes, V. iv. [3] S. Matt. xxv. 36, 35.

as they were not sufficiently instructed by their elders they could not obtain judgment and discretion, which passing by excess on either side, teaches a monk always to walk along the royal road, and does not suffer him to be puffed up on the right hand of virtue, i.e., from excess of zeal to transgress the bounds of due moderation in foolish presumption, nor allows him to be enamoured of slackness and turn aside to the vices on the left hand, i.e., under pretext of controlling the body, to grow slack with the opposite spirit of luke-warmness. For this is discretion, which is termed in the gospel the "eye," "and light of the body," according to the Saviour's saying: "The light of thy body is thine eye: but if thine eye be single, thy whole body will be full of light, but if thine eye be evil, thy whole body will be full of darkness:"[1] because as it discerns all the thoughts and actions of men, it sees and overlooks all things which should be done. But if in any man this is "evil," i.e., not fortified by sound judgment and knowledge, or deceived by some error and presumption, it will make our whole body "full of darkness," i.e., it will darken all our mental vision and our actions, as they will be involved in the darkness of vices and the gloom of disturbances. For, says He, "if the light which is in thee be darkness, how great will that darkness be!"[2] For no one can doubt that when the judgment of our heart goes wrong, and is overwhelmed by the night of ignorance, our thoughts and deeds, which are the result of deliberation and discretion, must be involved in the darkness of still greater sins.

CHAPTER III.

Of the error of Saul and of Ahab, by which they were deceived through lack of discretion.

LASTLY, the man who in the judgment of God was the first to be worthy of the kingdom of His people Israel, because he was lacking in this "eye" of discretion, was, as if his whole body were full of darkness, actually cast down from the kingdom while, being deceived by the darkness of this "light," and in error, he imagined that his own offerings were more acceptable to God than obedience to the command of Samuel, and met with an occasion of falling in that very matter in which he had hoped to propitiate the Divine Majesty.[3] And ignorance, I say, of this discretion led Ahab the king of Israel after a triumph and

splendid victory which had been granted to him by the favour of God to fancy that mercy on his part was better than the stern execution of the divine command, and, as it seemed to him, a cruel rule: and moved by this consideration, while he desired to temper a bloody victory with mercy, he was on account of his indiscriminating clemency rendered full of darkness in his whole body, and condemned irreversibly to death.[4]

CHAPTER IV.

What is said of the value of discretion in Holy Scripture.

SUCH is discretion, which is not only the "light of the body," but also called the sun by the Apostle, as it said "Let not the sun go down upon your wrath."[5] It is also called the guidance of our life: as it said "Those who have no guidance, fall like leaves."[6] It is most truly named counsel, without which the authority of Scripture allows us to do nothing, so that we are not even permitted to take that spiritual "wine which maketh glad the heart of man"[7] without its regulating control: as it is said "Do everything with counsel, drink thy wine with counsel,"[8] and again "like a city that has its walls destroyed and is not fenced in, so is a man who does anything without counsel."[9] And how injurious the absence of this is to a monk, the illustration and figure in the passage quoted shows, by comparing it to a city that is destroyed and without walls. Herein lies wisdom, herein lies intelligence and understanding without which our inward house cannot be built, nor can spiritual riches be gathered together, as it is said: "A house is built with wisdom, and again it is set up with intelligence. With understanding the storehouses are filled with all precious riches and good things."[10] This I say is "solid food," which can only be taken by those who are full grown and strong, as it is said: "But solid food is for full grown men, who by reason of use have their senses exercised to discern good and evil."[11] And it is shown to be useful and necessary for us, only in so far as it is in accordance with the word of God and its powers, as is said "For the word of God is quick and powerful, and sharper than any two-edged sword, and reaching even to the dividing asunder of soul and spirit, of both joints and marrow, and a dis-

---

[1] S. Matt. vi. 22, 23.   [2] S. Matt. vi. 22, 23.   [3] Cf. 1 Sam. xv.

[4] Cf. 1 Kings xx.
[5] Eph. iv. 26.
[6] Prov. xi. 14 (LXX.).
[7] Ps. ciii. (civ.) 15.
[8] Prov. xxxi. 3 (LXX.).
[9] Prov. xxv. 28 (LXX.).
[10] Prov. xxiv. 3, 4 (LXX.).
[11] Heb. v. 14.

cerner of the thoughts and intents of the heart:"[1] and by this it is clearly shown that no virtue can possibly be perfectly acquired or continue without the grace of discretion. And so by the judgment of the blessed Antony as well as of all others it has been laid down that it is discretion which leads a fearless monk by fixed stages to God, and preserves the virtues mentioned above continually intact, by means of which one may ascend with less weariness to the extreme summit' of perfection, and without which even those who toil most willingly cannot reach the heights of perfection. For discretion is the mother of all virtues, as well as their guardian and regulator.

CHAPTER V.

Of the death of the old man Heron.

AND to support this judgment delivered of old by the blessed Antony and the other fathers by a modern instance, as we promised to do, remember what you lately saw happen before your very eyes, I mean, how the old man Heron,[2] only a very few days ago was cast down by an illusion of the devil from the heights to the depths, a man whom we remember to have lived for fifty years in this desert and to have preserved a strict continence with especial severity, and who aimed at the secrecy of solitude with marvellous fervour beyond all those who dwell here. By what device then or by what method was he deluded by the deceiver after so many labours, and falling by a most grievous downfall struck with profound grief all those who live in this desert? Was it not because, having too little of the virtue of discretion he preferred to be guided by his own judgment rather than to obey the counsels and conference of the brethren and the regulations of the elders? Since he ever practised incessant abstinence and fasting with such severity, and persisted in the secrecy of solitude and a monastic cell so constantly that not even the observance of the Easter festival could ever persuade him to join in the feast with the brethren: when in accordance with the annual observance, all the brethren remained in the church and he alone would not join them for fear lest he might seem to relax in some degree from his purpose by taking only a little pulse. And deceived by this presumption he received with the utmost reverence an angel of Satan as an angel of light and with blind slavishness

obeyed his commands and cast himself down a well, so deep that the eye could not pierce its depths, nothing doubting of the promise of the angel who had assured him that the merits of his virtues and labours were such that he could not possibly run any risk. And that he might prove the truth of this most certainly by experimenting on his own safety, in the dead of night he was deluded enough to cast himself into the above mentioned well, to prove indeed the great merit of his virtue if he should come out thence unhurt. And when by great efforts on the part of the brethren he had been got out already almost dead, on the third day afterward he expired, and what was still worse, persisted in his obstinate delusion so that not even the experience of his death could persuade him that he had been deceived by the craft of devils. Wherefore in spite of the merits of his great labours and the number of years which he had spent in the desert those who with compassion and the greatest kindness pitied his end, could hardly obtain from Abbot Paphnutius[3] that he should not be reckoned among suicides, and be deemed unworthy of the memorial and oblation for those at rest.[4]

CHAPTER VI.

Of the destruction of two brethren for lack of discretion.

WHAT shall I say of those two brethren who lived beyond that desert of the Thebaiid where once the blessed Antony dwelt, and, not being sufficiently influenced by careful discrimination, when they were going through the vast and extended waste determined not to take any food with them, except such as the Lord Himself might provide for them. And when as they wandered through the deserts and were already fainting from hunger they were spied at a distance by the Mazices[5] (a race which is even more savage and ferocious than almost all wild tribes, for they are not driven to shed blood, as other tribes are, from desire of spoil but from simple ferocity of mind), and when these acting contrary to their natural ferocity, met them with bread, one of the two as discretion came to his aid, received it with delight and thankfulness as if it were offered to him by the Lord, thinking that the food

---

[1] Heb. iv. 12.
[2] Gazæus thinks that this is a different person from the man of the same name mentioned by Palladius, Hist. Laus. c. xxxii.

[3] On Paphnutius see the note on III. i.
[4] *Pausantium*, i.e., those at rest. The word is used for the departed in a similar way in the 6th Canon of the Council of Aurelia (Orleans) A.D. 511. "Quando recitantur pausantium nomina." And the phrase "Pausat in pace" is occasionally found in sepulchral inscriptions. Inscr. Boldetti Cimeter. p. 399; Inscr. Maff. Gall. Antiq. p. 55.
[5] *Mazices*: a people of Mauritania Cæsariensis, who joined in the revolt of Firmus, but submitted to Theodosius in 373. See Ammianus Marcellinus XXIX. v. § 17.

had been divinely provided for him, and that it was God's doing that those who always delighted in bloodshed had offered the staff of life to men who were already fainting and dying; but the other refused the food because it was offered to him by men and died of starvation. And though this sprang in the first instance from a persuasion that was blameworthy yet one of them by the help of discretion got the better of the idea which he had rashly and carelessly conceived, but the other persisting in his obstinate folly, and being utterly lacking in discretion, brought upon himself that death which the Lord would have averted, as he would not believe that it was owing to a Divine impulse that the fierce barbarians forgot their natural ferocity and offered them bread instead of a sword.

CHAPTER VII.

Of an illusion into which another fell for lack of discretion.

WHY also should I speak of one (whose name we had rather not mention as he is still alive), who for a long while received a devil in the brightness of an angelic form, and was often deceived by countless revelations from him and believed that he was a messenger of righteousness: for when these were granted, every night he provided a light in his cell without the need of any lamp. At last he was ordered by the devil to offer up to God his own son who was living with him in the monastery, in order that his merits might by this sacrifice be made equal to those of the patriarch Abraham. And he was so far seduced by his persuasion that he would really have committed the murder unless his son had seen him getting ready the knife and sharpening it with unusual care, and looking for the chains with which he meant to tie him up for the sacrifice when he was going to offer him up; and had fled away in terror with a presentiment of the coming crime.

CHAPTER VIII.

Of the fall and deception of a monk of Mesopotamia.

IT is a long business too to tell the story of the deception of that monk of Mesopotamia, who observed an abstinence that could be imitated by but few in that country, which he had practised for many years concealed in his cell, and at last was so deceived by revelations and dreams that came from the devil that after so many labours and good deeds, in

which he had surpassed all those who dwelt in the same parts, he actually relapsed miserably into Judaism and circumcision of the flesh. For when the devil by accustoming him to visions through the wish to entice him to believe a falsehood in the end, had like a messenger of truth revealed to him for a long while what was perfectly true, at length he showed him Christian folk together with the leaders of our religion and creed; viz. Apostles and Martyrs, in darkness and filth, and foul and disfigured with all squalor, and on the other hand the Jewish people with Moses, the patriarchs and prophets, dancing with all joy and shining with dazzling light; and so persuaded him that if he wanted to share their reward and bliss, he must at once submit to circumcision. And so none of these would have been so miserably deceived, if they had endeavoured to obtain a power of discretion. Thus the mischances and trials of many show how dangerous it is to be without the grace of discretion.

CHAPTER IX.

A question about the acquirement of true discretion.

To this Germanus: It has been fully and completely shown both by recent instances and by the decisions of the ancients how discretion is in some sense the fountain head and the root of all virtues. We want then to learn how it ought to be gained, or how we can tell whether it is genuine and from God, or whether it is spurious and from the devil: so that (to use the figure of that gospel parable which you discussed on a former occasion, in which we are bidden to become good money changers [1]) we may be able to see the figure of the true king stamped on the coin and to detect what is not stamped on coin that is current, and that, as you said in yesterday's talk using an ordinary expression, we may reject it as counterfeit, under the teaching of that skill which you treated of with sufficient fulness and detail, and showed ought to belong to the man who is spiritually a good money changer of the gospel. For of what good will it be to have recognized the value of that virtue and grace if we do not know how to seek for it and to gain it?

CHAPTER X.

The answer how true discretion may be gained.

THEN MOSES: True discretion, said he, is only secured by true humility. And of this

---

[1] Cf. I. xx.

humility the first proof is given by reserving everything (not only what you do but also what you think), for the scrutiny of the elders, so as not to trust at all in your own judgment but to acquiesce in their decisions in all points, and to acknowledge what ought to be considered good or bad by their traditions.[1] And this habit will not only teach a young man to walk in the right path through the true way of discretion, but will also keep him unhurt by all the crafts and deceits of the enemy. For a man cannot possibly be deceived, who lives not by his own judgment but according to the example of the elders, nor will our crafty foe be able to abuse the ignorance of one who is not accustomed from false modesty to conceal all the thoughts which rise in his heart, but either checks them or suffers them to remain, in accordance with the ripened judgment of the elders. For a wrong thought is enfeebled at the moment that it is discovered: and even before the sentence of discretion has been given, the foul serpent is by the power of confession dragged out, so to speak, from his dark under-ground cavern, and in some sense shown up and sent away in disgrace. For evil thoughts will hold sway in us just so long as they are hidden in the heart: and that you may gather still more effectually the power of this judgment I will tell you what Abbot Serapion did,[2] and what he used often to tell to the younger brethren for their edification.

CHAPTER XI.

The words of Abbot Serapion on the decline of thoughts that are exposed to others, and also on the danger of self-confidence.

WHILE, said he, I was still a lad, and stopping with Abbot Theonas,[3] this habit was forced upon me by the assaults of the enemy, that after I had supped with the old man at the ninth hour, I used every day secretly to hide a biscuit in my dress, which I would eat on the sly later on without his knowing it. And though I was constantly guilty of the theft with the consent of my will, and the want of restraint that springs from desire that has grown inveterate, yet when my unlawful desire was gratified I would come to myself and torment myself over the theft committed in a way that overbalanced the pleasure I had enjoyed in the eating. And when I was forced not without grief of heart to fulfil day after

day this most heavy task required of me, so to speak, by Pharaoh's taskmasters, instead of bricks, and could not escape from this cruel tyranny, and yet was ashamed to disclose my secret theft to the old man, it chanced by the will of God that I was delivered from the yoke of this voluntary captivity, when certain brethren had sought the old man's cell with the object of being instructed by him. And when after supper the spiritual conference had begun to be held, and the old man in answer to the questions which they had propounded was speaking about the sin of gluttony and the dominion of secret thoughts, and showing their nature and the awful power which they have so long as they are kept secret, I was overcome by the power of the discourse and was conscience stricken and terrified, as I thought that these things were mentioned by him because the Lord had revealed to the old man my bosom secrets; and first I was moved to secret sighs, and then my heart's compunction increased and I openly burst into sobs and tears, and produced from the folds of my dress which shared my theft and received it, the biscuit which I had carried off in my bad habit to eat on the sly; and I laid it in the midst and lying on the ground and begging for forgiveness confessed how I used to eat one every day in secret, and with copious tears implored them to intreat the Lord to free me from this dreadful slavery. Then the old man: "Have faith, my child," said he, "Without any words of mine, your confession frees you from this slavery. For you have today triumphed over your victorious adversary, by laying him low by your confession in a manner which more than makes up for the way in which you were overthrown by him through your former silence, as when, never confuting him with your own answer or that of another, you had allowed him to lord it over you, according to that saying of Solomon's: 'Because sentence is not speedily pronounced against the evil, the heart of the children of men is full within them to do evil:'[4] and therefore after this exposure of him that evil spirit will no longer be able to vex you, nor will that foul serpent henceforth make his lurking place in you, as he has been dragged out into light from the darkness by your life-giving confession." The old man had not finished speaking when lo! a burning lamp proceeding from the folds of my dress filled the cell with a sulphureous smell so that the pungency of the odour scarcely allowed us to stay there: and the old man resuming his admonition said Lo! the Lord

---

[1] Cf. what is said on this subject in the Institutes, Book IV. c. ix.
[2] Probably the author of Conference V., where see the note on c. i.
[3] See the note on Conf. xxi. i.

[4] Eccl. viii. 11 (LXX.).

has visibly confirmed to you the truth of my words, so that you can see with your eyes how he who was the author of His Passion has been driven out from your heart by your life-giving confession, and know that the enemy who has been exposed will certainly no longer find a home in you, as his expulsion is made manifest. And so, as the old man declared, said he, the sway of that diabolical tyranny over me has been destroyed by the power of this confession and stilled for ever, so that the enemy has never even tried to force upon me any more the recollection of this desire, nor have I ever felt myself seized with the passion of that furtive longing. And this meaning we see is neatly expressed in a figure in Ecclesiastes. "If" says he "a serpent bite without hissing there is no sufficiency for the charmer,"[1] showing that the bite of a serpent in silence is dangerous, i.e., if a suggestion or thought springing from the devil is not by means of confession shown to some charmer, I mean some spiritually minded person who knows how to heal the wound at once by charms from the Scripture, and to extract the deadly poison of the serpent from the heart, it will be impossible to help the sufferer who is already in danger and must soon die. In this way therefore we shall easily arrive at the knowledge of true discretion, so as by following the steps of the Elders never to do anything novel nor to decide anything by or on our own responsibility, but to walk in all things as we are taught by their tradition and upright life. And the man who is strengthened by this system will not only arrive at the perfect method of discretion, but also will remain perfectly safe from all the wiles of the enemy: for by no other fault does the devil drag down a monk so precipitately and lead him away to death, as when he persuades him to despise the counsel of the Elders and to rely on his own opinion and judgment: for if all the arts and contrivances discovered by man's ingenuity and those which are only useful for the conveniences of this temporary life, though they can be felt with the hand and seen with the eye, can yet not be understood by anyone without lessons from a teacher, how foolish it is to fancy that there is no need of an instructor in this one alone which is invisible and secret and can only be seen by the purest heart, a mistake in which brings about no mere temporary loss or one that can easily be repaired, but the destruction of the soul and everlasting death: for it is concerned with a daily and nightly conflict against no visible foes, but invisible and cruel ones, and a spiritual combat not against one or two only, but against countless hosts, failure in which is the more dangerous to all, in proportion as the foe is the fiercer and the attack the more secret. And therefore we should always follow the footsteps of the Elders with the utmost care, and bring to them everything which rises in our hearts, by removing the veil of shame.

CHAPTER XII.

A confession of the modesty which made us ashamed to reveal our thoughts to the elders.

GERMANUS: The ground of that hurtful modesty, through which we endeavour to hide bad thoughts, is especially owing to this reason; viz., that we have heard of a superior of the Elders in the region of Syria, as it was believed, who, when one of the brethren had laid bare his thoughts to him in a genuine confession, was afterwards extremely indignant and severely chid him for them. Whence it results that while we press them upon ourselves and are ashamed to make them known to the Elders, we cannot obtain the remedies that would heal them.

CHAPTER XIII.

The answer concerning the trampling down of shame, and the danger of one without contrition.

MOSES: Just as all young men are not alike in fervour of spirit nor equally instructed in learning and good morals, so too we cannot find that all old men are equally perfect and excellent. For the true riches of old men are not to be measured by grey hairs but by their diligence in youth and the rewards of their past labours. "For," says one, "the things that thou hast not gathered in thy youth, how shalt thou find them in thy old age?" "For venerable old age is not that of long time, nor counted by the number of years: but the understanding of a man is grey hairs, and a spotless life is old age."[2] And therefore we are not to follow in the steps or embrace the traditions and advice of every old man whose head is covered with grey hairs, and whose age is his sole claim to respect, but only of those whom we find to have distinguished themselves in youth in an approved and praiseworthy manner, and to have been trained up not on self-assurance but on the traditions of the Elders. For there are some,

---

[1] Eccl. x. 11 (LXX.).

[2] Ecclus. xxv. 5; Wisdom iv. 8, 9.

and unhappily they form the majority, who pass their old age in a lukewarmness which they contracted in youth, and in sloth, and so obtain authority not from the ripeness of their character but simply from the number of their years. Against whom that reproof of the Lord is specially aimed by the prophet: "Strangers have devoured his strength and he knew it not: yea, grey hairs also are spread about upon him, and he is ignorant of it."[1] These men, I say, are not pointed out as examples to youth from the uprightness of their lives, nor from the strictness of their profession, which would be worthy of praise and imitation, but simply from the number of their years; and so the subtle enemy uses their grey hairs to deceive the younger men, by a wrongful appeal to their authority, and endeavours in his cunning craftiness to upset and deceive by their example those who might have been urged into the way of perfection by their advice or that of others; and drags them down by means of their teaching and practice either into a baneful indifference, or into deadly despair. And as I want to give you an instance of this, I will tell you a fact which may supply us with some wholesome teaching, without giving the name of the actor, lest we might be guilty of something of the same kind as the man who published abroad the sins of the brother which had been disclosed to him. When this one, who was not the laziest of young men, had gone to an old man, whom we know very well, for the sake of the profit and health of his soul, and had candidly confessed that he was troubled by carnal appetites and the spirit of fornication, fancying that he would receive from the old man's words consolation for his efforts, and a cure for the wounds inflicted on him, the old man attacked him with the bitterest reproaches, and called him a miserable and disgraceful creature, and unworthy of the name of monk, while he could be affected by a sin and lust of this character, and instead of helping him so injured him by his reproaches that he dismissed him from his cell in a state of hopeless despair and deadly despondency. And when he, oppressed with such a sorrow, was plunged in deep thought, no longer how to cure his passion, but how to gratify his lust, the Abbot Apollos,[2] the most skilful of the Elders, met him, and seeing by his looks and gloominess his trouble and the

violence of the assault which he was secretly revolving in his heart, asked him the reason of this upset; and when he could not possibly answer the old man's gentle inquiry, the latter perceived more and more clearly that it was not without reason that he wanted to hide in silence the cause of a gloom so deep that he could not conceal it by his looks, and so began to ask him still more earnestly the reasons for his hidden grief. And by this he was forced to confess that he was on his way to a village to take a wife, and leave the monastery and return to the world, since, as the old man had told him, he could not be a monk, if he was unable to control the desires of the flesh and to cure his passion. And then the old man smoothed him down with kindly consolation, and told him that he himself was daily tried by the same pricks of desire and lust, and that therefore he ought not to give way to despair, nor be surprised at the violence of the attack of which he would get the better not so much by zealous efforts, as by the mercy and grace of the Lord; and he begged him to put off his intention just for one day, and having implored him to return to his cell, went as fast as he could to the monastery of the above mentioned old man — and when he had drawn near to him he stretched forth his hands and prayed with tears, and said "O Lord, who alone art the righteous judge and unseen Physician of secret strength and human weakness, turn the assault from the young man upon the old one, that he may learn to condescend to the weakness of sufferers, and to sympathize even in old age with the frailties of youth." And when he had ended his prayer with tears, he sees a filthy Ethiopian standing over against his cell and aiming fiery darts at him, with which he was straightway wounded, and came out of his cell and ran about hither and thither like a lunatic or a drunken man, and going in and out could no longer restrain himself in it, but began to hurry off in the same direction in which the young man had gone. And when Abbot Apollos saw him like a madman driven wild by the furies, he knew that the fiery dart of the devil which he had seen, had been fixed in his heart, and had by its intolerable heat wrought in him this mental aberration and confusion of the understanding; and so he came up to him and asked "Whither are you hurrying, or what has made you forget the gravity of years and disturbed you in this childish way, and made you hurry about so rapidly"? And when he owing to his guilty conscience and confused by this disgraceful excitement fancied that the lust of his heart was discovered, and, as

---

[1] Hos. vii. 9.

[2] Apollos or Apollonius was a most celebrated hermit of the fourth century, who finally became the head of a monastery of five hundred brethren in the Thebaid. Some account of him is given by Palladius (Hist. Laus. c. lii.) and Rufinus (Hist. Monach. c. vii.). Cf. also Sozomen III. xiv.; and VI. xx., whence we learn that his life was written by Timothy, Bishop of Alexandria. Cassian relates another story of him in XXIV. ix.

the secrets of his heart were known to the old man, did not venture to return any answer to his inquiries, "Return," said he, " to your cell, and at last recognize the fact that till now you have been ignored or despised by the devil, and not counted in the number of those with whom he is daily roused to fight and struggle against their efforts and earnestness, — you who could not — I will not say ward off, but not even postpone for one day, a single dart of his aimed at you after so many years spent in this profession of yours. And with this the Lord has suffered you to be wounded that you may at least learn in your old age to sympathize with infirmities to which you are a stranger, and may know from your own case and experience how to condescend to the frailties of the young, though when you received a young man troubled by an attack from the devil, you did not encourage him with any consolation, but gave him up in dejection and destructive despair into the hands of the enemy, to be, as far as you were concerned, miserably destroyed by him. But the enemy would certainly never have attacked him with so fierce an onslaught, with which he has up till now scorned to attack you, unless in his jealousy at the progress he was to make, he had endeavoured to get the better of that virtue which he saw lay in his disposition, and to destroy it with his fiery darts, as he knew without the shadow of a doubt that he was the stronger, since he deemed it worth his while to attack him with such vehemence. And so learn from your own experience to sympathize with those in trouble, and never to terrify with destructive despair those who are in danger, nor harden them with severe speeches, but rather restore them with gentle and kindly consolations, and as the wise Solomon says, "Spare not to deliver those who are led forth to death, and to redeem those who are to be slain,"[1] and after the example of our Saviour, break not the bruised reed, nor quench the smoking flax,[2] and ask of the Lord that grace, by means of which you yourself may faithfully learn both in deed and power to sing: "the Lord hath given me a learned tongue that I should know how to uphold by word him that is weary:"[3] for no one could bear the devices of the enemy, or extinguish or repress those carnal fires which burn with a sort of natural flame, unless God's grace assisted our weakness, or protected and supported it. And therefore, as the reason for this salutary incident is over, by which the Lord meant to set that young man free from dangerous desires

and to teach you something of the violence of their attack, and of the feeling of compassion, let us together implore Him in prayer, that He may be pleased to remove that scourge, which the Lord thought good to lay upon you for your good (for "He maketh sorry and cureth: he striketh and his hands heal. He humbleth and exalteth, he killeth and maketh alive: he bringeth down to the grave and bringeth up ")[4], and may extinguish with the abundant dew of His Spirit the fiery darts of the devil, which at my desire He allowed to wound you. And although the Lord removed this temptation at a single prayer of the old man with the same speed with which He had suffered it to come upon him, yet He showed by a clear proof that a man's faults when laid bare were not merely not to be scolded, but that the grief of one in trouble ought not to be lightly despised. And therefore never let the clumsiness or shallowness of one old man or of a few deter you and keep you back from that life-giving way, of which we spoke earlier, or from the tradition of the Elders, if our crafty enemy makes a wrongful use of their grey hairs in order to deceive younger men: but without any cloak of shame everything should be disclosed to the Elders, and remedies for wounds be faithfully received from them together with examples of life and conversation: from which we shall find like help and the same sort of result, if we try to do nothing at all on our own responsibility and judgment.

CHAPTER XIV.

Of the call of Samuel.

LASTLY so far has this opinion been shown to be pleasing to God that we see that this system not without reason finds a place in holy Scripture, so that the Lord would not of Himself instruct by the method of a Divine colloquy the lad Samuel, when chosen for judgment, but suffered him to run once or twice to the old man, and willed that one whom He was calling to converse with Him should be taught even by one who had offended God, as he was an old man, and preferred that he whom He had deemed worthy to be called by Him should be trained by the Elder in order to test the humility of him who was called to a Divine office, and to set an example to the younger men by the manner of his subjection.

---

[1] Prov. xxiv. 11. [2] Cf. S. Matt. xii. 20. [3] Is. l. 4. [4] Job v. 18; 1 Sam. ii. 6, 7.

CHAPTER XV.

Of the call of the Apostle Paul.

AND when Christ in His own Person called and addressed Paul, although He might have opened out to him at once the way of perfection, yet He chose rather to direct him to Ananias and commanded him to learn the way of truth from him, saying: "Arise and go into the city and there it shall be told thee what thou oughtest to do."[1] So He sends him to an older man, and thinks good to have him instructed by his teaching rather than His own, lest what might have been rightly done in the case of Paul might set a bad example of self-sufficiency, if each one were to persuade himself that he also ought in like manner to be trained by the government and teaching of God alone rather than by the instruction of the Elders. And this self-sufficiency the apostle himself teaches, not only by his letters but by his acts and deeds, ought to be shunned with all possible care, as he says that he went up to Jerusalem solely for this reason; viz., to communicate in a private and informal conference with his co-apostles and those who were before him that Gospel which he preached to the Gentiles, the grace of the Holy Spirit accompanying him with powerful signs and wonders: as he says "And I communicated with them the Gospel which I preach among the Gentiles lest perhaps I had run or should run in vain."[2] Who then is so self-sufficient and blind as to dare to trust in his own judgment and discretion when the chosen vessel confesses that he had need of conference with his fellow apostles. Whence we clearly see that the Lord does not Himself show the way of perfection to anyone who having the opportunity of learning depises the teaching and training of the Elders, paying no heed to that saying which ought most carefully to be observed: "Ask thy father and he will show it to thee: thine Elders and they will tell thee."[3]

CHAPTER XVI.

How to seek for discretion.

WE ought then with all our might to strive for the virtue of discretion by the power of humility, as it will keep us uninjured by either extreme, for there is an old saying ἀκρότητες ἰσότητες, i.e., extremes meet. For excess of fasting and gluttony come to the same thing, and an unlimited continuance of vigils is equally injurious to a monk as the torpor of a deep sleep: for when a man is weakened by excessive abstinence he is sure to return to that condition in which a man is kept through carelessness and negligence, so that we have often seen those who could not be deceived by gluttony, destroyed by excessive fasting and by reason of weakness liable to that passion which they had before overcome. Unreasonable vigils and nightly watchings have also been the ruin of some whom sleep could not get the better of: wherefore as the apostle says "with the arms of righteousness on the right hand and on the left,"[4] we pass on with due moderation, and walk between the two extremes, under the guidance of discretion, that we may not consent to be led away from the path of continence marked out for us, nor fall by undue carelessness into the pleasures of the palate and belly.

CHAPTER XVII.

On excessive fasts and vigils.

FOR I remember that I had so often resisted the desire for food, that having abstained from taking any for two or three days, my mind was not troubled even by the recollection of any eatables and also that sleep was by the assaults of the devil so far removed from my eyes, that for several days and nights I used to pray the Lord to grant a little sleep to my eyes; and then I felt that I was in greater peril from the want of food and sleep than from struggling against sloth and gluttony. And so as we ought to be careful not to fall into dangerous effeminacy through desire for bodily gratification, nor indulge ourselves with eating before the right time nor take too much, so also we ought to refresh ourselves with food and sleep at the proper time even if we dislike it. For the struggle in each case is caused by the devices of the enemy; and excessive abstinence is still more injurious to us than careless satiety: for from this latter the intervention of a healthy compunction will raise us to the right measure of strictness, and not from the former.

CHAPTER XVIII.

A question on the right measure of abstinence and refreshment.

GERMANUS: What then is the measure of abstinence by keeping which with even balance we shall succeed in passing unharmed between the two extremes?

---

[1] Acts ix. 6.   [2] Gal. ii. 2.   [3] Deut. xxxii. 7.   [4] 2 Cor. vi. 7.

CHAPTER XIX.

Of the best plan for our daily food.

MOSES: On this matter we are aware that there have been frequent discussions among our Elders. For in discussing the abstinence of some who supported their lives continually on nothing but beans or only on vegetables and fruits, they proposed to all of them to partake of bread alone, the right measure of which they fixed at two biscuits, so small that they assuredly scarcely weighed a pound.

CHAPTER XX.

An objection on the ease of that abstinence in which a man is sustained by two biscuits.

AND this we gladly embraced, and answered that we should scarcely consider this limit as abstinence, as we could not possibly reach it entirely.

CHAPTER XXI.

The answer concerning the value and measure of well-proved abstinence.

MOSES: If you want to test the force of this rule, keep to this limit continually, never departing from it by taking any cooked food even on Sunday or Saturday, or on the occasions of the arrival of any of the brethren; for the flesh, refreshed by these exceptions, is able not only to support itself through the rest of the week on a smaller quantity, but can also postpone all refreshment without difficulty, as it is sustained by the addition of that food which it has taken beyond the limit; while the man who has always been satisfied with the full amount of the above-mentioned measure will never be able to do this, nor to put off breaking his fast till the morrow. For I remember that our Elders (and I recollect that we ourselves also often had the same experience) found it so hard and difficult to practise this abstinence, and observed the rule laid down with such pain and hunger that it was almost against their will and with tears and lamentation that they set this limit to their meals.

CHAPTER XXII.

What is the usual limit both of abstinence and of partaking food.

BUT this is the usual limit of abstinence; viz., for everyone to allow himself food ac-

cording to the requirements of his strength or bodily frame or age, in such quantity as is required for the support of the flesh, and not for the satisfactory feeling of repletion. For on both sides a man will suffer the greatest injury, if having no fixed rule at one time he pinches his stomach with meagre food and fasts, and at another stuffs it by over-eating himself; for as the mind which is enfeebled for lack of food loses vigour in praying, while it is worn out with excessive weakness of the flesh and forced to doze, so again when weighed down with over-eating it cannot pour forth to God pure and free prayers: nor will it succeed in preserving uninterruptedly the purity of its chastity, while even on those days on which it seems to chastise the flesh with severer abstinence, it feeds the fire of carnal desire with the fuel of the food that it has already taken.

CHAPTER XXIII.

Quemadmodum abundantia umorum genitalium castigetur.[1]

NAM quod semel per escarum abundantiam concretus fuerit in medullis, necesse est egeri atque ab ipsa naturæ lege propelli, quæ exuberantiam cujuslibet umoris superflui velut noxiam sibi atque contrariam in semet ipsa residere non patitur ideoque rationabili semper et æquali est corpus nostrum parsimonia castigandum, ut si naturali hac necessitate commorantes in carne omnimodis carere non possumus, saltim rarius nos et non amplius quamtrina vice ista conluvione respersos totius anni cursus inveniat, quod tamen sine ullo pruritu quietus egerat sopor, non fallax imago index occultæ voluptatis eliciat.

Wherefore this is the moderate and even allowance and measure of abstinence, of which we spoke, which has the approval also of the judgment of the fathers; viz., that daily hunger should go hand in hand with our daily meals, preserving both body and soul in one and the same condition, and not allowing the mind either to faint through weariness from fasting, nor to be oppressed by over-eating, for it ends in such a sparing diet that sometimes a man neither notices nor remembers in the evening that he has broken his fast.

CHAPTER XXIV.

Of the difficulty of uniformity in eating; and of the gluttony of brother Benjamin.

AND so far is this not done without difficulty, that those who know nothing of perfect

---

[1] It has been thought best to leave the first part of the following chapter untranslated.

discretion would rather prolong their fasts for two days, and reserve for tomorrow what they should have eaten today, so that when they come to partake of food they may enjoy as much as they can desire. And you know that lastly your fellow citizen Benjamin most obstinately stuck to this: as he would not every day partake of his two biscuits, nor continually take his meagre fare with uniform self-discipline, but preferred always to continue his fasts for two days that when he came to eat he might fill his greedy stomach with a double portion, and by eating four biscuits enjoy a comfortable sense of repletion, and manage to fill his belly by means of a two days' fast. And you doubtless remember what sort of an end there was to the life of this man who obstinately and pertinaciously relied on his own judgment rather than on the traditions of the Elders, for he forsook the desert and returned back to the vain philosophy of this world and earthly vanities, and so confirmed the above mentioned opinion of the Elders by the example of his downfall, and by his destruction teaches a lesson that no one who trusts in his own opinion and judgment can possibly climb the heights of perfection, nor fail to be deceived by the dangerous wiles of the devil.

CHAPTER XXV.

A question how is it possible always to observe one and the same measure.

GERMANUS: How then can we observe this measure without ever breaking it? for sometimes at the ninth hour when the Station fast[1] is over, brethren come to see us and then we must either for their sakes add something to our fixed and customary portion, or certainly fail in that courtesy which we are told to show to everybody.

CHAPTER XXVI.

The answer-how we should not exceed the proper measure of food.

MOSES: Both duties must be observed in the same way and with equal care: for we ought most scrupulously to preserve the proper allowance of food for the sake of our

---

[1] On the *Statio* see the note on the Institutes V. xx.

abstinence, and in like manner out of charity to show courtesy and encouragement to any of the brethren who may arrive; because it is absolutely ridiculous when you offer food to a brother, nay, to Christ Himself, not to partake of it with him, but to make yourself a stranger to his repast. And so we shall keep clear of guilt on either hand if we observe this plan; viz., at the ninth hour to partake of one of the two biscuits which form our proper canonical allowance, and to keep back the other to the evening, in expectation of something like this, that if any of the brethren comes to see us we may partake of it with him, and so add nothing to our own customary allowance: and by this arrangement the arrival of our brother which ought to be a pleasure to us will cause us no inconvenience: since we shall show him the civilities which courtesy requires in such a way as to relax nothing of the strictness of our abstinence. But if no one should come, we may freely take this last biscuit as belonging to us according to our canonical rule, and by this frugality of ours as a single biscuit was taken at the ninth hour, our stomach will not be overloaded at eventide, a thing which is often the case with those who under the idea that they are observing a stricter abstinence put off all their repast till evening; for the fact that we have but recently taken food hinders our intellect from being bright and keen both in our evening and in our nocturnal prayers, and so at the ninth hour a convenient and suitable time has been allowed for food, in which a monk can refresh himself and so find that he is not only fresh and bright during his nocturnal vigils, but also perfectly ready for his evening prayers, as his food is already digested.

With such a banquet of two courses, as it were, the holy Moses feasted us, showing us not only the grace and power of discretion by his present learned speech, but also the method of renunciation and the end and aim of the monastic life by the discussion previously held; so as to make clearer than daylight what we had hitherto pursued simply with fervour of spirit and zeal for God but with closed eyes, and to make us feel how far we had up till then wandered from purity of heart and the straight line of our course, since the practice of all visible arts belonging to this life cannot possibly stand without an understanding of their aim, nor can it be taken in hand without a clear view of a definite end.

III.

CONFERNECE OF ABBOT PAPHNUTIUS.

ON THE THREE SORTS OF RENUNCIATIONS.

CHAPTER I.

Of the life and conduct of Abbot Paphnutius.

IN that choir of saints who shine like brilliant stars in the night of this world, we have seen the holy Paphnutius,[1] like some great luminary, shining with the brightness of knowledge. For he was a presbyter of our company, I mean of those whose abode was in the desert of Scete, where he lived to extreme old age, without ever moving from his cell, of which he had taken possession when still young, and which was five miles from the church, even to nearer districts; nor was he when worn out with years hindered by the distance from going to Church on Saturday or Sunday. But not wanting to return from thence empty handed he would lay on his shoulders a bucket of water to last him all the week, and carry it back to his cell, and even when he was past ninety would not suffer it to be fetched by the labour of younger men. He then from his earliest youth threw himself into the monastic discipline with such fervour that when he had spent only a short time in it, he was endowed with the virtue of submission, as well as the knowledge of all good qualities. For by the practice of humility and obedience he mortified all his desires, and by this stamped out all his faults and acquired every virtue which the monastic system and the teaching of the ancient fathers produces, and, inflamed with desire for still further advances, he was eager to penetrate into the recesses of the desert, so that, with no human companions to disturb him, he

might be more readily united to the Lord, to whom he longed to be inseparably joined, even while he still lived in the society of the brethren. And there once more in his excessive fervour he outstripped the virtues of the Anchorites, and in his eager desire for continual divine meditation avoided the sight of them: and he plunged into solitary places yet wilder and more inaccessible, and hid himself for a long while in them, so that, as the Anchorites themselves only with great difficulty caught a glimpse of him every now and then, the belief was that he enjoyed and delighted in the daily society of angels, and because of this remarkable characteristic of his[2] he was surnamed by them the Buffalo.

CHAPTER II.

Of the discourse of the same old man, and our reply to it.

As then we were anxious to learn from his teaching, we came in some agitation to his cell towards evening. And after a short silence he began to commend our undertaking, because we had left our homes, and had visited so many countries out of love for the Lord, and were endeavouring with all our might to endure want and the trials of the desert, and to imitate their severe life, which even those who had been born and bred in the same state of want and penury, could scarcely put up with; and we replied that we had come for his teaching and instruction in order that we might be to some extent initiated in the customs of so great a man, and in that perfection which we had known from many evidences to exist in him, not that we might be honoured by any commendations to which we had no right, or be puffed up with any elation of mind, (with which we were sometimes exercised in our own cells at the suggestion of our enemy) in consequence of any words of his. Wherefore we begged him rather to lay before us what would make us humble and contrite, and not what would flatter us and puff us up.

---

[1] Paphnutius. The name is not uncommon in the annals of the fourth century: (1) A Deacon who bore it suffered in the persecution of Diocletian; and (2) a Bishop of the same name, who had been a confessor, was mainly instrumental in preventing the rule of celibacy being forced on the clergy by the Council of Nicæa; (3) another was a prominent member of the Meletian schism; while (4) a fourth was present, as Bishop of Sais in Lower Egypt, at the Council of Alexandria in 362; and (5) the life of a fifth is given by Palladius (Hist. Laus. lxii.-lxv.) and Rufinus (Hist. Monach. c. xvi.). The one whom Cassian here mentions, surnamed the Buffalo, is apparently a different person from the last mentioned. Further details of his history are given in the Institutes IV. c. xxx. xxxi., and in Conference X. ii., iii. Cassian tells the interesting story of his share in the Anthropomorphite controversy, and the beneficial influence which he then exercised.

[2] i.e., his solitariness.

CHAPTER III.

The statement of Abbot Paphnutius on the three kinds of vocations, and the three sorts of renunciations.

THEN THE BLESSED PAPHNUTIUS: There are, said he, three kinds of vocations. And we know that there are three sorts of renunciations as well, which are necessary to a monk, whatever his vocation may be. And we ought diligently to examine first the reason for which we said that there were three kinds of vocations, that when we are sure that we are summoned to God's service in the first stage of our vocation, we may take care that our life is in harmony with the exalted height to which we are called, for it will be of no use to have made a good beginning if we do not show forth an end corresponding to it. But if we feel that only in the last resort have we been dragged away from a worldly life, then, as it appears that we rest on a less satisfactory beginning as regards religion, so must we proportionately make the more earnest endeavours to rouse ourselves with spiritual fervour to make a better end. It is well too on every ground for us to know secondly the manner of the threefold renunciations because we shall never be able to attain perfection, if we are ignorant of it or if we know it, but do not attempt to carry it out in act.

CHAPTER IV.

An explanation of the three callings.

To make clear therefore the main differences between these three kinds of calling, the first is from God, the second comes through man, the third is from compulsion. And a calling is from God whenever some inspiration has taken possession of our heart, and even while we are asleep stirs in us a desire for eternal life and salvation, and bids us follow God and cleave to His commandments with life-giving contrition: as we read in Holy Scripture that Abraham was called by the voice of the Lord from his native country, and all his dear relations, and his father's house; when the Lord said "Get thee out from thy country and from thy kinsfolk and from thy father's house."[1] And in this way we have heard that the blessed Antony also was called,[2] the occasion of whose con-

version was received from God alone. For on entering a church he there heard in the Gospel the Lord saying: "Whoever hateth not father and mother and children and wife and lands, yea and his own soul also, cannot be my disciple;" and "if thou wilt be perfect, go sell all that thou hast, and give to the poor, and thou shalt have treasure in heaven, and come, follow me:"[3] And with heartfelt contrition he took this charge of the Lord as if specially aimed at him, and at once gave up everything and followed Christ, without any incitement thereto from the advice and teaching of men. The second kind of calling is that which we said took place through man; viz., when we are stirred up by the example of some of the saints, and their advice, and thus inflamed with the desire of salvation: and by this we never forget that by the grace of the Lord we ourselves were summoned, as we were aroused by the advice and good example of the above-mentioned saint, to give ourselves up to this aim and calling; and in this way also we find in Holy Scripture that it was through Moses that the children of Israel were delivered from the Egyptian bondage. But the third kind of calling is that which comes from compulsion, when we have been involved in the riches and pleasures of this life, and temptations suddenly come upon us and either threaten us with peril of death, or smite us with the loss and confiscation of our goods, or strike us down with the death of those dear to us, and thus at length even against our will we are driven to turn to God whom we scorned to follow in the days of our wealth. And of this compulsory call we often find instances in Scripture, when we read that on account of their sins the children of Israel were given up by the Lord to their enemies; and that on account of their tyranny and savage cruelty they turned again, and cried to the Lord. And it says: "The Lord sent them a Saviour, called Ehud, the son of Gera, the son of Jemini, who used the left hand as well as the right:" and again we are told, "they cried unto the Lord, who raised them up a Saviour and delivered them, to wit, Othniel, the son of Kenaz, Caleb's younger brother."[4] And it is of such that the Psalm speaks: "When He slew them, then they sought Him: and they returned and came to Him early in the morning: and they remem-

---

[1] Gen. xii. 1.
[2] The story, to which allusion is here made, is given in the Vita Antonii of Athanasius. We are there told that six months after the death of his parents Antony, then a young man of eighteen, chanced to enter a church just as the gospel for the day was being read: and hearing the words, "If thou wilt be perfect," etc., he took them as

addressed specially to himself, and at once proceeded to act upon them, selling all that he had except a small portion which he reserved for his sister's maintenance. Shortly after he was struck by the words, "Take no thought for the morrow," which he heard in church, and acting upon this, made away with the little property which was left, committed his sister to the care of certain faithful virgins, and betook himself to the ascetic life.
[3] S. Luke xiv. 26; S. Matt. xix. 21.
[4] Judg. iii. 15, 9.

bered that God was their helper, and the most High God their redeemer." And again: "And they cried unto the Lord when they were troubled, and He delivered them out of their distress."[1]

CHAPTER V.

How the first of these calls is of no use to a sluggard, and the last is no hindrance to one who is in earnest.

OF these three calls then, although the two former may seem to rest on better principles, yet sometimes we find that even by the third grade, which seems the lowest and the coldest, men have been made perfect and most earnest in spirit, and have become like those who made an admirable beginning in approaching the Lord's service, and passed the rest of their lives also in most laudable fervour of spirit: and again we find that from the higher grade very many have grown cold, and often have come to a miserable end. And just as it was no hindrance to the former class that they seemed to be converted not of their own free will, but by force and compulsion, in as much as the loving kindness of the Lord secured for them the opportunity for repentance, so too to the latter it was of no avail that the early days of their conversion were so bright, because they were not careful to bring the remainder of their life to a suitable end. For in the case of Abbot Moses,[2] who lived in a spot in the wilderness called Calamus,[3] nothing was wanting to his merits and perfect bliss, in consequence of the fact that he was driven to flee to the monastery through fear of death, which was hanging over him because of a murder; for he made such use of his compulsory conversion that with ready zeal he turned it into a voluntary one and climbed the topmost heights of perfection. As also on the other hand; to very many, whose names I ought not to mention, it has been of no avail that they entered on the Lord's service with better beginning than this, as afterwards sloth and hardness of heart crept over them, and they fell into a dangerous state of torpor, and the bottomless pit of death, an instance of which we see clearly indicated in the call of the Apostles. For of what good was it to Judas that he had of his own free will embraced

the highest grade of the Apostolate in the same way in which Peter and the rest of the Apostles had been summoned, as he allowed the splendid beginning of his call to terminate in a ruinous end of cupidity and covetousness, and as a cruel murderer even rushed into the betrayal of the Lord? Or what hindrance was it to Paul that he was suddenly blinded, and seemed to be drawn against his will into the way of salvation, as afterwards he followed the Lord with complete fervour of soul, and having begun by compulsion completed it by a free and voluntary devotion, and terminated with a magnificent end a life that was rendered glorious by such great deeds? Everything therefore depends upon the end; in which one who was consecrated by a noble conversion at the outset may through carelessness turn out a failure, and one who was compelled by necessity to adopt the monastic life may through fear of God and earnestness be made perfect.

CHAPTER VI.

An account of the three sorts of renunciations.

WE must now speak of the renunciations, of which tradition and the authority of Holy Scripture show us three, and which every one of us ought with the utmost zeal to make complete. The first is that by which as far as the body is concerned we make light of all the wealth and goods of this world; the second, that by which we reject the fashions and vices and former affections of soul and flesh; the third, that by which we detach our soul from all present and visible things, and contemplate only things to come, and set our heart on what is invisible. And we read that the Lord charged Abraham to do all these three at once, when He said to him "Get thee out from thy country, and thy kinsfolk, and thy father's house."[4] First He said "from thy country," i.e., from the goods of this world, and earthly riches: secondly, "from thy kinsfolk," i.e., from this former life and habits and sins, which cling to us from our very birth and are joined to us as it were by ties of affinity and kinship: thirdly, "from thy father's house," i.e., from all the recollection of this world, which the sight of the eyes can afford. For of the two fathers, i.e., of the one who is to be forsaken, and of the one who is to be sought, David thus speaks in the person of God: "Hearken, O daughter, and consider, and incline thine ear: forget also thine own people and thy father's house:"[5] for the person

---

[1] Ps. lxxvii. (lxxviii.) 34, 35; cvi. (cvii.) 19.

[2] Moses. This Abbot is possibly a different person from the author of the first two Conferences, who had in his youth been a pupil of Antony; whereas the one here mentioned only took the monastic life out of fear of death on a charge of murder. He is mentioned again in Conferences VII. xxvi.; XIX. xi., and some account of him is given in Sozomen H.E. VI. xxix.

[3] Calamus, mentioned again in the Institutes X. xxiv. (where see note), and cf. Conf. VII. xxvi.; XXIV. iv.

[4] Gen. xii. 1.   [5] Ps. xliv. (xlv.) 11.

who says "Hearken, O daughter," is certainly a Father; and yet he bears witness that the one, whose house and people he urges should be forgotten, is none the less father of his daughter. And this happens when being dead with Christ to the rudiments of this world, we no longer, as the Apostle says, regard "the things which are seen, but those which are not seen, for the things which are not seen are eternal,"[1] and going forth in heart from this temporal and visible home, turn our eyes and heart towards that in which we are to remain for ever. And this we shall succeed in doing when, while we walk in the flesh, we are no longer at war with the Lord according to the flesh, proclaiming in deed and actions the truth of that saying of the blessed Apostle "Our conversation is in heaven."[2] To these three sorts of renunciations the three books of Solomon suitably correspond. For Proverbs answers to the first renunciation, as in it the desires for carnal things and earthly sins are repressed; to the second Ecclesiastes corresponds, as there everything which is done under the sun is declared to be vanity; to the third the Song of Songs, in which the soul soaring above all things visible, is actually joined to the word of God by the contemplation of heavenly things.

CHAPTER VII.

How we can attain perfection in each of these sorts of renunciations.

WHEREFORE it will not be of much advantage to us that we have made our first renunciation with the utmost devotion and faith, if we do not complete the second with the same zeal and ardour. And so when we have succeeded in this, we shall be able to arrive at the third as well, in which we go forth from the house of our former parent, (who, as we know well, was our father from our very birth, after the old man, when we were "by nature children of wrath, as others also,"[3]) and fix our whole mental gaze on things celestial. And of this father Scripture says to Jerusalem which had despised God the true Father, "Thy father was an Amorite, and thy mother a Hittite;"[4] and in the gospel we read "Ye are of your father the devil and the lusts of your father ye love to do."[5] And when we have left him, as we pass from things visible to things unseen we shall be able to say with the Apostle: "But we know that if our earthly house of this tabernacle is dissolved we have a habitation from God, a house not made with hands, eternal in the heavens,"[6]

and this also, which we quoted a little while ago: "But our conversation is in heaven, whence also we look for the Saviour, the Lord Jesus, who will reform the body of our low estate made like to the body of His glory,"[7] and this of the blessed David: "For I am a sojourner upon the earth," and "a stranger as all my fathers were;"[8] so that we may in accordance with the Lord's word be made like those of whom the Lord speaks to His Father in the gospel as follows: "They are not of the world, as I am not of the world,"[9] and again to the Apostles themselves: "If ye were of this world, the world would love its own: but because ye are not of this world, therefore the world hateth you."[10] Of this third renunciation then we shall succeed in reaching the perfection, whenever our soul is sullied by no stain of carnal coarseness, but, all such having been carefully eliminated, it has been freed from every earthly quality and desire, and by constant meditation on things Divine, and spiritual contemplation has so far passed on to things unseen, that in its earnest seeking after things above and things spiritual it no longer feels that it is prisoned in this fragile flesh, and bodily form, but is caught up into such an ecstasy as not only to hear no words with the outward ear, or to busy itself with gazing on the forms of things present, but not even to see things close at hand, or large objects straight before the very eyes. And of this no one can understand the truth and force, except one who has made trial of what has been said, under the teaching of experience; viz., one, the eyes of whose soul the Lord has turned away from all things present, so that he no longer considers them as things that will soon pass away, but as things that are already done with, and sees them vanish into nothing, like misty smoke; and like Enoch, "walking with God," and "translated" from human life and fashions, not "be found" amid the vanities of this life. And that this actually happened corporeally in the case of Enoch the book of Genesis thus tells us. "And Enoch walked with God, and was not found, for God translated him." And the Apostle also says: "By faith Enoch was translated that he should not see death," the death namely of which the Lord says in the gospel: "He that liveth and believeth in me shall not die eternally."[11] Wherefore, if we are anxious to attain true perfection, we ought to look to it that as we have outwardly with the body made light of parents, home, the riches and pleasures of the world, we may

---

[1] 2 Cor. iv. 18.
[2] Phil. iii. 20.
[3] Eph. ii. 3.
[4] Ezek. xvi. 3.
[5] S. John viii. 44.
[6] 2 Cor. v. 1.

[7] Phil. iii. 20, 21.
[8] Ps. cxviii. (cxix.) 19; Ps. xxxviii. (xxxix.) 13.
[9] S. John xvii. 16.
[10] S. John xv. 19.
[11] Gen. v. 24 (LXX.); Heb. xi. 5; S. John xi. 26.

also inwardly with the heart forsake all these things and never be drawn back by any desires to those things which we have forsaken, as those who were led up by Moses, though they did not literally go back, are yet said to have returned in heart to Egypt; viz., by forsaking God who had led them forth with such mighty signs, and by worshipping the idols of Egypt of which they had thought scorn, as Scripture says: "And in their hearts they turned back into Egypt, saying to Aaron: Make us gods to go before us,"[1] for we should fall into like condemnation with those who, while dwelling in the wilderness, after they had tasted manna from heaven, lusted after the filthy food of sins, and of mean baseness, and should seem together with them to murmur in the same way: "It was well with us in Egypt, when we sat over the flesh pots and ate the onions, and garlic, and cucumbers, and melons:"[2] A form of speech, which, although it referred primarily to that people, we yet see fulfilled today in our own case and mode of life: for everyone who after renouncing this world turns back to his old desires, and reverts to his former likings asserts in heart and act the very same thing that they did, and says "It was well with me in Egypt," and I am afraid that the number of these will be as large as that of the multitudes of backsliders of whom we read under Moses, for though they were reckoned as six hundred and three thousand armed men who came out of Egypt, of this number not more than two entered the land of promise. Wherefore we should be careful to take examples of goodness from those who are few and far between, because according to that figure of which we have spoken in the gospel "Many are called but few" are said to be "chosen."[3] A renunciation then in body alone, and a mere change of place from Egypt will not do us any good, if we do not succeed in achieving that renunciation in heart, which is far higher and more valuable. For of that mere bodily renunciation of which we have spoken the apostle declares as follows: "Though I bestow all my goods to feed the poor, and give my body to be burned, but have not charity, it profiteth me nothing."[4] And the blessed Apostle would never have said this had it not been that he foresaw by the spirit that some who had given all their goods to feed the poor would not be able to attain to evangelical perfection and the lofty heights of charity, because while pride or impatience ruled over their hearts they were not careful to purify themselves from their former

sins, and unrestrained habits, and on that account could never attain to that love of God which never faileth, and these, as they fall short in this second stage of renunciation, can still less reach that third stage which is most certainly far higher. But consider too in your minds with great care the fact that he did not simply say "If I bestow my goods." For it might perhaps be thought that he spoke of one who had not fulfilled the command of the gospel, but had kept back something for himself, as some half-hearted persons do. But he says "Though I bestow all my goods to feed the poor," i.e., even if my renunciation of those earthly riches be perfect. And to this renunciation he adds something still greater: "And though I give my body to be burned, but have not charity, I am nothing:" As if he had said in other words, though I bestow all my goods to feed the poor in accordance with that command in the gospel, where we are told "If thou wilt be perfect, go sell all that thou hast, and give to the poor, and thou shalt have treasure in heaven,"[5] renouncing them so as to keep back nothing at all for myself, and though to this distribution (of my goods) I should by the burning of my flesh add martyrdom so as to give up my body for Christ, and yet be impatient, or passionate or envious or proud, or excited by wrongs done by others, or seek what is mine, or indulge in evil thoughts, or not be ready and patient in bearing all that can be inflicted on me, this renunciation and the burning of the outer man will profit me nothing, while the inner man is still involved in the former sins, because, while in the fervour of the early days of my conversion I made light of the mere worldly substance, which is said to be not good or evil in itself but indifferent, I took no care to cast out in like manner the injurious powers of a bad heart, or to attain to that love of the Lord which is patient, which is "kind, which envieth not, is not puffed up, is not soon angry, dealeth not perversely, seeketh not her own, thinketh no evil," which "beareth all things, endureth all things,"[6] and which lastly never suffers him who follows after it to fall by the deceitfulness of sin.

CHAPTER VIII.

Of our very own possessions in which the beauty of the soul is seen or its foulness.

WE ought then to take the utmost care that our inner man as well may cast off and make

---

[1] Acts vii. 39, 40.
[2] Numb. xi. 18; Exod. xvi. 3; Numb. xi. 5.
[3] S. Matt. xxii. 14.
[4] 1 Cor. xiii. 3.
[5] S. Matt. xix. 21.   [6] 1 Cor. xiii. 4-7.

away with all those possessions of its sins, which it acquired in its former life: which as they continually cling to body and soul are our very own, and, unless we reject them and cut them off while we are still in the flesh, will not cease to accompany us after death. For as good qualities, or charity itself which is their source, may be gained in this world, and after the close of this life make the man who loves it lovely and glorious, so our faults transmit to that eternal remembrance a mind darkened and stained with foul colours. For the beauty or ugliness of the soul is the product of its virtues or its vices, the colour it takes from which either makes it so glorious, that it may well hear from the prophet "And the king shall have pleasure in thy beauty,"[1] or so black, and foul, and ugly, that it must surely acknowledge the stench of its shame, and say "My wounds stink and are corrupt because of my foolishness,"[2] and the Lord Himself says to it "Why is not the wound of the daughter of my people closed?"[3] And therefore these are our very own possessions, which continually remain with the soul, which no king and no enemy can either give or take away from us. These are our very own possessions which not even death itself can part from the soul, but by renouncing which we can attain to perfection, and by clinging to which we shall suffer the punishment of eternal death.

CHAPTER IX.

Of three sorts of possessions.

RICHES and possessions are taken in Holy Scripture in three different ways, i.e., as good, bad, and indifferent. Those are bad, of which it is said: "The rich have wanted and have suffered hunger,"[4] and "Woe unto you that are rich, for ye have received your consolation:"[5] and to have cast off these riches is the height of perfection; and a distinction which belongs to those poor who are commended in the gospel by the Lord's saying: "Blessed are the poor in spirit, for theirs is the kingdom of heaven;"[6] and in the Psalm: "This poor man cried, and the Lord heard him,"[7] and again: "The poor and needy shall praise thy name."[8] Those riches are good, to acquire which is the work of great virtue and merit, and the righteous possessor of which is praised by David who says "The

generation of the righteous shall be blessed: glory and riches are in his house, and his righteousness remaineth for ever:"[9] and again "the ransom of a man's life are his riches."[10] And of these riches it is said in the Apocalypse to him who has them not and to his shame is poor and naked: "I will begin," says he, "to vomit thee out of my mouth. Because thou sayest I am rich and wealthy and have need of nothing: and knowest not that thou art wretched and miserable and poor and blind and naked, I counsel thee to buy of me gold fire-tried, that thou mayest be made rich, and mayest be clothed in white garments, and that the shame of thy nakedness may not appear."[11] There are some also which are indifferent, i.e., which may be made either good or bad: for they are made either one or the other in accordance with the will and character of those who use them: of which the blessed Apostle says "Charge the rich of this world not to be high-minded nor to trust in the uncertainty of riches, but in God (who giveth us abundantly all things to enjoy), to do good, to give easily, to communicate to others, to lay up in store for themselves a good foundation that they may lay hold on the true life."[12] These are what the rich man in the gospel kept, and never distributed to the poor, — while the beggar Lazarus was lying at his gate and desiring to be fed with his crumbs; and so he was condemned to the unbearable flames and everlasting heat of hell-fire.[13]

CHAPTER X.

That none can become perfect merely through the first grade of renunciation.

IN leaving then these visible goods of the world we forsake not our own wealth, but that which is not ours, although we boast of it as either gained by our own exertions or inherited by us from our forefathers. For as I said nothing is our own, save this only which we possess with our heart, and which cleaves to our soul, and therefore cannot be taken away from us by any one. But Christ speaks in terms of censure of those visible riches, to those who clutch them as if they were their own, and refuse to share them with those in want. "If ye have not been faithful in what is another's, who will give to you what is your own?"[14] Plainly then it is not only daily

---

1 Ps. xliv. (xlv.) 12.
2 Ps. xxxvii. (xxxviii.) 6.
3 Jer. viii. 22.
4 Ps. xxxiii. (xxxiv.) 11.
5 S. Luke vi. 24.
6 S. Matt. v. 3.
7 Ps. xxxiii. (xxxiv.) 7.
8 Ps. lxxiii. (lxxiv.) 21.

9 Ps. cxi. (cxii.) 2, 3.
10 Prov. xiii. 8.
11 Rev. iii. 16-18.
12 1 Tim. vi. 17-19.
13 Cf. S. Luke xiv. 19 sq.
14 S. Luke xvi. 12.

experience which teaches us that these riches are not our own, but this saying of our Lord also, by the very title which it gives them. But concerning visible[1] and worthless riches Peter says to the Lord: "Lo, we have left all and followed thee. What shall we have therefore?"[2] when it is clear that they had left nothing but their miserable broken nets. And unless this expression "all" is understood to refer to that renunciation of sins, which is really great and important, we shall not find that the Apostles had left anything of any value, or that the Lord had any reason for bestowing on them the blessing of so great glory, that they were allowed to hear from Him that "in the regeneration, when the Son of Man shall sit on the throne of His glory, ye also shall sit upon twelve thrones judging the twelve tribes of Israel."[3] If then those, who have completely renounced their earthly and visible goods, cannot for sufficient reason attain to Apostolic charity, nor climb with readiness and vigour to that third stage of renunciation which is still higher and belongs to but few, what should those think of themselves, who do not even make that first step (which is very easy) a thorough one, but keep together with their old want of faith, their former sordid riches, and fancy that they can boast of the mere name of monks? The first renunciation then of which we spoke is of what is not our own, and therefore is not enough of itself to confer perfection on the renunciant, unless he advances to the second, which is really and truly a renunciation of what belongs to us. And when we have made sure of this by the expulsion of all our faults, we shall mount to the heights of the third renunciation also, whereby we rise above not merely all those things which are done in this world or specially belong to men, but even that whole universe around us which is esteemed so glorious, and shall with heart and soul look down upon it as subject to vanity and destined soon to pass away; as we look, as the Apostle says, "not on those things which are seen, but on those which are not seen: for the things that are seen, are temporal, and the things which are not seen are eternal;"[4] that so we may be found worthy to hear that highest utterance, which was spoken to Abraham: "and come into a land which I will show thee,"[5] which clearly shows that unless a man has made those three former renunciations with all earnest-

ness of mind, he cannot attain to this fourth, which is granted as a reward and privilege to one whose renunciation is perfect, that he may be found worthy to enter the land of promise which no longer bears for him the thorns and thistles of sins; which after all the passions have been driven out is acquired by purity of heart even in the body, and which no good deeds or exertions of man's efforts (can gain), but which the Lord Himself promises to show, saying "And come into the land which I will show to thee:" which clearly proves that the beginning of our salvation results from the call of the Lord, Who says "Get thee out from thy country," and that the completion of perfection and purity is His gift in the same way, as He says "And come into the land which I will show thee," i.e., not one you yourself can know or discover by your own efforts, but one which I will show not only to one who is ignorant of it, but even to one who is not looking for it. And from this we clearly gather that as we hasten to the way of salvation through being stirred up by the inspiration of the Lord, so too it is under the guidance of His direction and illumination that we attain to the perfection of the highest bliss.

CHAPTER XI.

A question on the free will of man and the grace of God.

GERMANUS: Where then is there room for free will, and how is it ascribed to our efforts that we are worthy of praise, if God both begins and ends everything in us which concerns our salvation?

CHAPTER XII.

The answer on the economy of Divine Grace, with free will still remaining in us.

PAPHNUTIUS: This would fairly influence us, if in every work and practice, the beginning and the end were everything, and there were no middle in between. And so as we know that God creates opportunities of salvation in various ways, it is in our power to make use of the opportunities granted to us by heaven more or less earnestly. For just as the offer came from God Who called him "get thee out of thy country," so the obedience was on the part of Abraham who went forth; and as the fact that the saying "Come into the land" was carried into action, was the work of him who obeyed, so the addition of the

---

[1] The MSS. vary between *visibilibus* and *invisibilibus*.
[2] S. Matt. xix. 27.
[3] *Ib.* ver. 28.
[4] 2 Cor. iv. 18.
[5] Gen. xii. 1.

words " which I will show thee " came from the grace of God Who commanded or promised it. But it is well for us to be sure that although we practise every virtue with unceasing efforts, yet with all our exertions and zeal we can never arrive at perfection, nor is mere human diligence and toil of itself sufficient to deserve to reach the splendid reward of bliss, unless we have secured it by means of the co-operation of the Lord, and His directing our heart to what is right. And so we ought every moment to pray and say with David " Order my steps in thy paths that my footsteps slip not : " [1] and " He hath set my feet upon a rock and ordered my goings : " [2] that He Who is the unseen ruler of the human heart may vouchsafe to turn to the desire of virtue that will of ours, which is more readily inclined to vice either through want of knowledge of what is good, or through the delights of passion. And we read this in a verse in which the prophet sings very plainly : " Being pushed I was overturned that I might fall," where the weakness of our free will is shown. And " the Lord sustained me : " [3] again this shows that the Lord's help is always joined to it, and by this, that we may not be altogether destroyed by our free will, when He sees that we have stumbled, He sustains and supports us, as it were by stretching out His hand. And again : " If I said my foot was moved ; " viz., from the slippery character of the will, " Thy mercy, O Lord, helped me." [4] Once more he joins on the help of God to his own weakness, as he confesses that it was not owing to his own efforts but to the mercy of God, that the foot of his faith was not moved. And again : " According to the multitude of the sorrows which I had in my heart," which sprang most certainly from my free will, " Thy comforts have refreshed my soul," [5] i.e., by coming through Thy inspiration into my heart, and laying open the view of future blessings which Thou hast prepared for them who labour in Thy name, they not only removed all anxiety from my heart, but actually conferred upon it the greatest delight. And again : " Had it not been that the Lord helped me, my soul had almost dwelt in hell." [6] He certainly shows that through the depravity of this free will he would have dwelt in hell, had he not been saved by the assistance and protection of the Lord. For " By the Lord," and not by free-will, " are a man's steps directed," and " although the righteous fall " at least by free will, " he shall not be cast away." And why ? because

" the Lord upholdeth him with His hand : " [7] and this is to say with the utmost clearness : None of the righteous are sufficient of themselves to acquire righteousness, unless every moment when they stumble and fall the Divine mercy supports them with His hands, that they may not utterly collapse and perish, when they have been cast down through the weakness of free will.

CHAPTER XIII.

That the ordering of our way comes from God.

AND truly the saints have never said that it was by their own efforts that they secured the direction of the way in which they walked in their course towards advance and perfection of virtue, but rather they prayed for it from the Lord, saying " Direct me in Thy truth," and "direct my way in thy sight." [8] But someone else declares that he discovered this very fact not only by faith, but also by experience, and as it were from the very nature of things : " I know, O Lord, that the way of man is not his : neither is it in a man to walk and to direct his steps." [9] And the Lord Himself says to Israel : " I will direct him like a green fir-tree : from Me is thy fruit found." [10]

CHAPTER XIV.

That knowledge of the law is given by the guidance and illumination of the Lord.

THE knowledge also of the law itself they daily endeavour to gain not by diligence in reading, but by the guidance and illumination of God as they say to Him : " Show me Thy ways, O Lord, and teach me Thy paths : " and "open Thou mine eyes : and I shall see the wondrous things of Thy law : " and " teach me to do Thy will, for Thou art my God ; " and again : " Who teacheth man knowledge." [11]

CHAPTER XV.

That the understanding, by means of which we can recognize God's commands, and the performance of a good will are both gifts from the Lord.

FURTHER the blessed David asks of the Lord that he may gain that very understanding, by which he can recognize God's com-

---

1 Ps. xvi. (xvii.) 5.
2 Ps. xxxix. (xl.) 3.
3 Ps. cxvii. (cxviii.) 13.
4 Ps. xciii. (xciv.) 18.
5 *Ib.* ver. 19.
6 *Ib.* ver. 17.
7 Ps. xxxvi. (xxxvii.) 23, 24.
8 Ps. xxiv. (xxv.) 5 ; vi. 9.
11 Ps. xxiv. (xxv.) 4 ; cxviii. (cxix.) 18 ; cxlii. (cxliii.) 10 ; xciii. (xciv.) 10.
9 Jer. x. 23.
10 Hos. xiv. 9.

mands which, he well knew, were written in the book of the law, and he says "I am Thy servant: O give me understanding that I may learn Thy commandments."[1] Certainly he was in possession of understanding, which had been granted to him by nature, and also had at his fingers' ends a knowledge of God's commands which were preserved in writing in the law: and still he prayed the Lord that he might learn this more thoroughly as he knew that what came to him by nature would never be sufficient for him, unless his understanding was enlightened by the Lord by a daily illumination from Him, to understand the law spiritually and to recognize His commands more clearly, as the "chosen vessel" also declares very plainly this which we are insisting on. "For it is God which worketh in you both to will and to do according to good will."[2] What could well be clearer than the assertion that both our good will and the completion of our work are fully wrought in us by the Lord? And again "For it is granted to you for Christ's sake, not only to believe in Him but also to suffer for Him."[3] Here also he declares that the beginning of our conversion and faith, and the endurance of suffering is a gift to us from the Lord. And David too, as he knows this, similarly prays that the same thing may be granted to him by God's mercy. "Strengthen, O God, that which Thou hast wrought in us:"[4] showing that it is not enough for the beginning of our salvation to be granted by the gift and grace of God, unless it has been continued and ended by the same pity and continual help from Him. For not free will but the Lord "looseth them that are bound." No strength of ours, but the Lord "raiseth them that are fallen:" no diligence in reading, but "the Lord enlightens the blind:" where the Greeks have κύριος σοφοῖ τυφλούς, i.e., "the Lord maketh wise the blind:" no care on our part, but "the Lord careth for the stranger :" no courage of ours, but "the Lord assists (or supports) all those who are down."[5] But this we say, not to slight our zeal and efforts and diligence, as if they were applied unnecessarily and foolishly, but that we may know that we cannot strive without the help of God, nor can our efforts be of any use in securing the great reward of purity, unless it has been granted to us by the assistance and mercy of the Lord: for "a horse is prepared for the day of battle: but help cometh from the

Lord,"[6] "for no man can prevail by strength."[7] We ought then always to sing with the blessed David: "My strength and my praise is" not my free will, but "the Lord, and He is become my salvation."[8] And the teacher of the Gentiles was not ignorant of this when he declared that he was made capable of the ministry of the New Testament not by his own merits or efforts but by the mercy of God. "Not," says he, "that we are capable of thinking anything of ourselves as of ourselves, but our sufficiency is of God," which can be put in less good Latin but more forcibly, "our capability is of God," and then there follows: "Who also made us capable ministers of the New Testament."[9]

CHAPTER XVI.

That faith itself must be given us by the Lord.

BUT so thoroughly did the Apostles realize that everything which concerns salvation was given them by the Lord, that they even asked that faith itself should be granted from the Lord, saying: "Add to us faith"[10] as they did not imagine that it could be gained by free will, but believed that it would be bestowed by the free gift of God. Lastly the Author of man's salvation teaches us how feeble and weak and insufficient our faith would be unless it were strengthened by the aid of the Lord, when He says to Peter "Simon, Simon, behold Satan hath desired to have you that he may sift you as wheat. But I have prayed to my Father that thy faith fail not."[11] And another finding that this was happening in his own case, and seeing that his faith was being driven by the waves of unbelief on the rocks which would cause a fearful shipwreck, asks of the same Lord an aid to his faith, saying "Lord, help mine unbelief."[12] So thoroughly then did those Apostles and men in the gospel realize that everything which is good is brought to perfection by the aid of the Lord, and not imagine that they could preserve their faith unharmed by their own strength or free will that they prayed that it might be helped or granted to them by the Lord. And if in Peter's case there was need of the Lord's help that it might not fail, who will be so presumptuous and blind as to fancy that he has no need of daily assistance from the Lord in order to preserve it? Especially

1 Ps. cxviii. (cxix.) 125.   3 Phil. i. 29.
2 Phil. ii. 13.   4 Ps. lxvii. (lxviii.) 29.
5 Ps. cxlv. (cxlvi.) 7, 8, 9; cxliv. (cxlv.) 16.

6 Prov. xxi. 31.   10 S. Luke xvii. 5.
7 1 Sam. ii. 9.   11 S. Luke xxii. 31, 32.
8 Ps. cxvii. (cxviii.) 14.   12 S. Mark ix. 23.
9 2 Cor. iii. 5, 6.

as the Lord Himself has made this clear in the gospel, saying: "As the branch cannot bear fruit of itself except it abide in the vine, so no more can ye, except ye abide in me." [1] And again: "for without me ye can do nothing." [2] How foolish and wicked then it is to attribute any good action to our own diligence and not to God's grace and assistance, is clearly shown by the Lord's saying, which lays down that no one can show forth the fruits of the Spirit without His inspiration and co-operation. For "every good gift and every perfect boon is from above, coming down from the Father of lights." [3] And Zechariah too says, "For whatever is·good is His, and what is excellent is from Him." [4] And so the blessed Apostle consistently says: "What hast thou which thou didst not receive? But if thou didst receive it, why boastest thou as if thou hadst not received it?" [5]

CHAPTER XVII.

That temperateness and the endurance of temptations must be given to us by the Lord.

AND that all the endurance, with which we can bear the temptations brought upon us, depends not so much on our own strength as on the mercy and guidance of God, the blessed Apostle thus declares: " No temptation hath come upon you but such as is common to man. But God is faithful, who will not suffer you to be tempted above that ye are able, but will with the temptation make also a way of escape, that ye may be able to bear it." [6] And that God fits and strengthens our souls for every good work, and worketh in us all those things which are pleasing to Him, the same Apostle teaches: "May the God of peace who brought out of darkness the great Shepherd of the sheep, Jesus Christ, in the blood of the everlasting Testament, fit you in all goodness, working in you what is well-pleasing in His sight." [7] And that the same thing may happen to the Thessalonians he prays as follows, saying: "Now our Lord Jesus Christ Himself and God our Father who hath loved us and hath given us everlasting consolation and good hope in grace, exhort your hearts, and confirm you in every good word and work." [8]

CHAPTER XVIII.

That the continual fear of God must be bestowed on us by the Lord.

AND lastly the prophet Jeremiah, speaking in the person of God, clearly testifies that even the fear of God, by which we can hold fast to Him, is shed upon us by the Lord: saying as follows: "And I will give them one heart, and one way, that they may fear Me all days: and that it may be well with them and with their children after them. And I will make an everlasting covenant with them and will not cease to do them good: and I will give My fear in their hearts that they may not revolt from Me." [9] Ezekiel also says: "And I will give them one heart, and will put a new spirit in their bowels: and I will take away the stony heart out of their flesh and will give them a heart of flesh: that they may walk in My commandments, and keep My judgments and do them: and that they may be My people, and I may be their God." [10]

CHAPTER XIX.

That the beginning of our good will and its completion comes from God.

AND this plainly teaches us that the beginning of our good will is given to us by the inspiration of the Lord, when He draws us towards the way of salvation either by His own act, or by the exhortations of some man, or by compulsion; and that the consummation of our good deeds is granted by Him in the same way: but that it is in our own power to follow up the encouragement and assistance of God with more or less zeal, and that accordingly we are rightly visited either with reward or with punishment, because we have been either careless or careful to correspond to His design and providential arrangement made for us with such kindly regard. And this is clearly and plainly described in Deuteronomy. "When," says he, " the Lord thy God shall have brought thee into the land which thou art going to possess, and shall have destroyed many nations before thee, the Hittite, and the Gergeshite, and the Amorite, the Canaanite, and the Perizzite, the Hivite, and the Jebusite, seven nations much more numerous than thou art and stronger than thou, and the Lord thy God shall have delivered them to thee, thou shalt utterly destroy them.

[1] S. John xv. 4.
[2] *Ib.* ver. 5.
[3] S. James i. 17.
[4] Zech. ix. 17 (LXX.).
[5] 1 Cor. iv. 7.
[6] 1 Cor. x. 13.
[7] Heb. xiii. 20, 21.
[8] 2 Thess. ii. 15, 16.
[9] Jerem. xxxii. 39, 40.
[10] Ezek. xi. 19, 20.

Thou shalt make no league with them. Neither shalt thou make marriage with them."[1] So then Scripture declares that it is the free gift of God that they are brought into the land of promise, that many nations are destroyed before them, that nations more numerous and mightier than the people of Israel are given up into their hands. But whether Israel utterly destroys them, or whether it preserves them alive and spares them, and whether or no it makes a league with them, and makes marriages with them or not, it declares lies in their own power. And by this testimony we can clearly see what we ought to ascribe to free will, and what to the design and daily assistance of the Lord, and that it belongs to divine grace to give us opportunities of salvation and prosperous undertakings and victory: but that it is ours to follow up the blessings which God gives us with earnestness or indifference. And this same fact we see is plainly taught in the healing of the blind men. For the fact that Jesus passed by them, was a free gift of Divine providence and condescension. But the fact that they cried out and said "Have mercy on us, Lord, thou son of David,"[2] was an act of their own faith and belief. That they received the sight of their eyes was a gift of Divine pity. But that after the reception of any blessing, the grace of God, and the use of free will both remain, the case of the ten lepers, who were all healed alike, shows us. For when one of them through goodness of will returned thanks, the Lord looking for the nine, and praising the one, showed that He was ever anxious to help even those who were unmindful of His kindness. For even this is a gift of His visitation; viz., that he receives and commends the grateful one, and looks for and censures those who are thankless.

CHAPTER XX.

That nothing can be done in this world without God.

But it is right for us to hold with unswerving faith that nothing whatever is done in this world without God. For we must acknowledge that everything is done either by His will or by His permission, i.e., we must believe that whatever is good is carried out by the will of God and by His aid, and whatever is the reverse is done by His permission, when the Divine Protection is withdrawn from us for our sins and the hardness of our hearts, and suffers the devil and the shameful passions

of the body to lord it over us. And the words of the Apostle most assuredly teach us this, when he says: "For this cause God delivered them up to shameful passions:" and again: "Because they did not like to have God in their knowledge, God delivered them up to a reprobate sense, to do those things which are not convenient."[3] And the Lord Himself says by the prophet: "But My people did not hear My voice and Israel did not obey me: Wherefore I gave them up unto their own hearts' lusts. They shall walk after their own inventions."[4]

CHAPTER XXI.

An objection on the power of free will.

Germanus: This passage very clearly shows the freedom of the will, where it is said "If My people would have hearkened unto Me," and elsewhere "But My people would not hear My voice."[5] For when He says "If they would have heard" He shows that the decision to yield or not to yield lay in their own power. How then is it true that our salvation does not depend upon ourselves, if God Himself has given us the power either to hearken or not to hearken?

CHAPTER XXII.

The answer; viz., that our free will always has need of the help of the Lord.

Paphnutius: You have shrewdly enough noticed how it is said "If they would have hearkened to Me:" but have not sufficiently considered either who it is who speaks to one who does or does not hearken; or what follows: "I should soon have put down their enemies, and laid My hand on those that trouble them."[6] Let no one then try by a false interpretation to twist that which we brought forward to prove that nothing can be done without the Lord, nor take it in support of free will, in such a way as to try to take away from man the grace of God and His daily oversight, through this test: "But My people did not hear My voice," and again: "If My people would have hearkened unto Me, and if Israel would have walked in My ways, etc.:" but let him consider that just as the power of free will is evidenced by the disobedience of the people, so the daily over-

---

[1] Deut. vii. 1–3.　　[2] S. Matt. xx. 31.

[3] Rom. i. 26, 28.　　[5] Ps. lxxx. (lxxxi.) 12, 13.
[4] Ps. lxxx. (lxxxi.) 12, 13.　　[6] *Ib.* ver. 15.

sight of God who declares and admonishes him is also shown. For where He says "If My people would have hearkened unto Me" He clearly implies that He had spoken to them before. And this the Lord was wont to do not only by means of the written law, but also by daily exhortations, as this which is given by Isaiah: "All day long have I stretched forth My hands to a disobedient and gain-saying people."[1] Both points then can be supported from this passage, where it says: "If My people would have hearkened, and if Israel had walked in My ways, I should soon have put down their enemies, and laid My hand on those that trouble them." For just as free will is shown by the disobedience of the people, so the government of God and His assistance is made clear by the beginning and end of the verse, where He implies that He had spoken to them before, and that afterwards He would put down their enemies, if they would have hearkened unto Him. For we have no wish to do away with man's free will by what we have said, but only to establish the fact that the assistance and grace of God are necessary to it every day and hour. When he had instructed us with this discourse Abbot Paphnutius dismissed us from his cell before midnight in a state of contrition rather than of liveliness; insisting on this as the chief lesson in his discourse; viz., that when we fancied that by making perfect the first renunciation (which we were endeavouring to do with all our powers), we could climb the heights of perfection, we should make the discovery that we had not yet even begun to dream of the heights to which a monk can rise, since after we had learnt some few things about the second renunciation, we should find out that we had not before this even heard a word of the third stage, in which all perfection is comprised, and which in many ways far exceeds these lower ones.

IV.

CONFERENCE OF ABBOT DANIEL.

ON THE LUST OF THE FLESH AND OF THE SPIRIT.

CHAPTER I.

Of the life of Abbot Daniel.

AMONG the other heroes of Christian philosophy we also knew Abbot Daniel, who was not only the equal of those who dwelt in the desert of Scete in every sort of virtue, but was specially marked by the grace of humility. This man on account of his purity and gentleness, though in age the junior of most, was preferred to the office of the diaconate by the blessed Paphnutius, presbyter in the same desert: for the blessed Paphnutius was so delighted with his excellent qualities, that, as he knew that he was his equal in virtue and grace of life, he was anxious also to make him his equal in the order of the priesthood. And since he could not bear that he should remain any longer in an inferior office, and was also anxious to provide a worthy successor to himself in his lifetime, he promoted him to the dignity of the priesthood.[2] He however relinquished nothing of his former customary humility, and when the other was present, never took upon himself anything from his advance to a higher order, but when Abbot Paphnutius was offering spiritual sacrifices, ever continued to act as a deacon in the office of his former ministry. However, the blessed Paphnutius though so great a saint as to possess the grace of foreknowledge in many matters, yet in this case was disappointed of his hope of the succession and the choice he had made, for he himself passed to God no long time after him whom he had prepared as his successor.

---

[1] Is. lxv. 2.
[2] Nothing further appears to be known of Daniel than what is here told us by Cassian. There has been some discussion as to the action of Paphnutius in having him raised to the priesthood, as Cassian here narrates. Was Paphnutius really a bishop, or is it a case of presbyterian orders, or do Cassian's expressions merely mean that Paphnutius procured his ordination first to the Diaconate and then to the Priesthood? Probably the latter, for (1) all the evidence goes to show that presbyters had not the power of ordination; and (2) there are many instances, in which it is said even of the laity that they "ordained" men to the ministry when all that can possibly be meant is that they "procured their ordination:" further (3) it will be noticed that it is not even said that Paphnutius ordained Daniel, but merely that he "promoted" him to the priesthood; an expression which might equally well be used of nomination as of actual ordination. See the subject discussed in Bingham's Antiquities, Book II. c. iii. § 7, and C. Gore's "Church and the Ministry," p. 374.

CHAPTER II.

An investigation of the origin of a sudden change of feeling from inexpressible joy to extreme dejection of mind.

So then we asked this blessed Daniel why it was that as we sat in the cells we were sometimes filled with the utmost gladness of heart, together with inexpressible delight and abundance of the holiest feelings, so that I will not say *speech*, but even *feeling* could not follow it, and pure prayers were readily breathed, and the mind being filled with spiritual fruits, praying to God even in sleep could feel that its petitions rose lightly and powerfully to God: and again, why it was that for no reason we were suddenly filled with the utmost grief, and weighed down with unreasonable depression, so that we not only felt as if we ourselves were overcome with such feelings, but also our cell grew dreadful, reading palled upon us, aye and our very prayers were offered up unsteadily and vaguely, and almost as if we were intoxicated: so that while we were groaning and endeavouring to restore ourselves to our former disposition, our mind was unable to do this, and the more earnestly it sought to fix again its gaze upon God, so was it the more vehemently carried away to wandering thoughts by shifting aberrations and so utterly deprived of all spiritual fruits, as not to be capable of being roused from this deadly slumber even by the desire of the kingdom of heaven, or by the fear of hell held out to it. To this he replied.

CHAPTER III.

His answer to the question raised.

A THREEFOLD account of this mental dryness of which you speak has been given by the Elders. For it comes either from carelessness on our part, or from the assaults of the devil, or from the permission and allowance of the Lord. From carelessness on our part, when through our own faults, coldness has come upon us, and we have behaved carelessly and hastily, and owing to slothful idleness have fed on bad thoughts, and so make the ground of our heart bring forth thorns and thistles; which spring up in it, and consequently make us sterile, and powerless as regards all spiritual fruit and meditation. From the assaults of the devil when, sometimes, while we are actually intent on good desires, our enemy with crafty subtilty makes his way into our heart, and without our knowledge and against our will we are drawn away from the best intentions.

CHAPTER IV.

How there is a twofold reason for the permission and allowance of God.

BUT for God's permission and allowance there is a twofold reason. First, that being for a short time forsaken by the Lord, and observing with all humility the weakness of our own heart, we may not be puffed up on account of the previous purity of heart, granted to us by His visitation; and that by proving that when we are forsaken by Him we cannot possibly recover our former state of purity and delight by any groanings and efforts of our own, we may also learn that our previous gladness of heart resulted not from our own earnestness but from His gift, and that for the present time it must be sought once more from His grace and enlightenment. But a second reason for this allowance, is to prove our perseverance, and steadfastness of mind, and real desires, and to show in us, with what purpose of heart, or earnestness in prayer we seek for the return of the Holy Spirit, when He leaves us, and also in order that when we discover with what efforts we must seek for that spiritual gladness — when once it is lost — and the joy of purity, we may learn to preserve it more carefully, when once it is secured, and to hold it with firmer grasp. For men are generally more careless about keeping whatever they think can be easily replaced.

CHAPTER V.

How our efforts and exertions are of no use without God's help.

AND by this it is clearly shown that God's grace and mercy always work in us what is good, and that when it forsakes us, the efforts of the worker are useless, and that however earnestly a man may strive, he cannot regain his former condition without His help, and that this saying is constantly fulfilled in our case: that it is "not of him that willeth or runneth but of God which hath mercy."[1] And this grace on the other hand sometimes does not refuse to visit with that holy inspiration of which you spoke, and with an abundance of spiritual thoughts, even the careless and indifferent; but inspires the unworthy, arouses the slumberers, and enlightens those who are blinded by ignorance, and mercifully reproves us and chastens us, shedding itself abroad in our hearts, that thus we may be stirred by the compunction which He excites, and impelled

---

1 Rom. ix. 16.

to rise from the sleep of sloth. Lastly we are often filled by His sudden visitation with sweet odours, beyond the power of human composition — so that the soul is ravished with these delights, and caught up, as it were, into an ecstasy of spirit, and becòmes oblivious of the fact that it is still in the flesh.

CHAPTER VI.

How it is sometimes to our advantage to be left by God.

BUT the blessed David recognizes that sometimes this departure of which we have spoken, and (as it were) desertion by God may be to some extent to our advantage, so that he was unwilling to pray, not that he might not be absolutely forsaken by God in anything (for he was aware that this would have been disadvantageous both to himself and to human nature in its course towards perfection) but he rather entreated that it might be in measure and degree, saying "Forsake me not utterly"[1] as if to say in other words: I know that thou dost forsake thy saints to their advantage, in order to prove them, for in no other way could they be tempted by the devil, unless they were for a little forsaken by Thee. And therefore I ask not that Thou shouldest never forsake me, for it would not be well for me not to feel my weakness and say "It is good for me that Thou hast brought me low"[2] nor to have no opportunity of fighting. And this I certainly should not have, if the Divine protection shielded me incessantly and unbrokenly. For the devil will not dare to attack me while supported by Thy defence, as he brings both against me and Thee this objection and complaint, which he ever slanderously brings against Thy champions, "Does Job serve God for nought? Hast not Thou made a fence for him and his house and all his substance round about?"[3] But I rather entreat that Thou forsake me not utterly — what the Greeks call ἕως σφόδρα, i.e., too much. For, first, as it is advantageous to me for Thee to forsake me a little, that the steadfastness of my love may be tried, so it is dangerous if Thou suffer me to be forsaken excessively in proportion to my faults and what I deserve, since no power of man, if in temptation it is forsaken for too long a time by Thine aid, can endure by its own steadfastness, and not forthwith give in to the power of the enemy's side, unless Thou Thyself, as Thou knowest the strength of man, and moderatest his struggles, "Suffer us not to be tempted

above that we are able, but makest with the temptation a way of escape that we may be able to bear it."[4] And something of this sort we read in the book of Judges was mystically designed in the matter of the extermination of the spiritual nations which were opposed to Israel: "These are the nations, which the Lord left that by them He might instruct Israel, that they might learn to fight with their enemies," and again shortly after: "And the Lord left them that He might try Israel by them, whether they would hear the commandments of the Lord, which He had commanded their fathers by the hand of Moses, or not."[5] And this conflict God reserved for Israel, not from envy of their peace, or from a wish to hurt them, but because He knew that it would be good for them that while they were always oppressed by the attacks of those nations they might not cease to feel themselves in need of the aid of the Lord, and for this reason might ever continue to meditate on Him and invoke His aid, and not grow careless through lazy ease, and lose the habit of resisting, and the practice of virtue. For again and again, men whom adversity could not overcome, have been cast down by freedom from care and by prosperity.

CHAPTER VII.

Of the value of the conflict which the Apostle makes to consist in the strife between the flesh and the spirit.

THIS conflict too we read in the Apostle has for our good been placed in our members: "For the flesh lusteth against the spirit: and the spirit against the flesh. But these two are opposed to each other so that ye should not do what ye would."[6] You have here too a contest as it were implanted in our bodies, by the action and arrangement of the Lord. For when a thing exists in everybody universally and without the slightest exception, what else can you think about it except that it belongs to the substance of human nature, since the fall of the first man, as it were naturally: and when a thing is found to be congenital with everybody, and to grow with their growth, how can we help believing that it was implanted by the will of the Lord, not to injure them but to help them? But the reason of this conflict; viz., of flesh and spirit, he tells us is this: "that ye should not do what ye would." And so, if we fulfil what God arranged that we should not fulfil, i.e., that we should not do what we liked, how can we help

---

[1] Ps. cxviii. (cxix.) 8.　　[2] *Ib.* ver. 71.　　[3] Job i. 9, 10.　　[4] 1 Cor. x. 13.　　[5] Judg. iii. 1-4.　　[6] Gal. v. 17.

believing that it is bad for us? And this conflict implanted in us by the arrangement of the Creator is in a way useful to us, and calls and urges us on to a higher state: and if it ceased, most surely there would ensue on the other hand a peace that is fraught with danger.

CHAPTER VIII.

A question, how it is that in the Apostle's chapter, after he has spoken of the lusts of the flesh and spirit opposing one another, he adds a third thing; viz., man's will.

GERMANUS: Although some glimmer of the sense now seems clear to us, yet as we cannot thoroughly grasp the Apostle's meaning, we want you to explain this more clearly to us. For the existence of three things seems to be indicated here: first, the struggle of the flesh against the spirit, secondly the desire of the spirit against the flesh, and thirdly our own free will, which seems to be placed between the two, and of which it is said: "Ye should not do what ye will." And on this subject, though as I said we can gather some hints, from what you have explained of the meaning, yet — since this conference gives the opportunity — we are anxious to have it more fully explained to us.

CHAPTER IX.

The answer on the understanding of one who asks rightly.

DANIEL: It belongs to the understanding to discern the distinctions and the drift of questions; and it is a main part of knowledge to understand how ignorant you are. Wherefore it is said that "if a fool asks questions, it will be accounted wisdom,"[1] because, although one who asks questions is ignorant of the answer to the question raised, yet as he wisely asks, and learns what he does not know, this very fact will be counted as wisdom in him, because he wisely discovers what he was ignorant of. According then to this division of yours, it seems that in this passage the Apostle mentions three things, the lust of the flesh against the spirit, and of the spirit against the flesh, the mutual struggle of which against each other appears to have this as its cause and reason; viz., "that," says he, "we should not do what we would." There remains then a fourth case, which you have overlooked; viz., that we should do what we would not. Now then, we must first discover

the meaning of those two desires, i.e., of the flesh and spirit, and so next learn to discuss our free will, which is placed between the two, and then lastly in the same way we can see what cannot belong to our free will.

CHAPTER X.

That the word flesh is not used with one single meaning only.

WE find that the word flesh is used in holy Scripture with many different meanings: for sometimes it stands for the whole man, i.e., for that which consists of body and soul, as here "And the Word was made flesh,"[2] and "All flesh shall see the salvation of our God."[3] Sometimes it stands for sinful and carnal men, as here "My spirit shall not remain in those men, because they are flesh."[4] Sometimes it is used for sins themselves, as here: "But ye are not in the flesh but in the spirit,"[5] and again "Flesh and blood shall not inherit the kingdom of God:" lastly there follows, "Neither shall corruption inherit incorruption."[6] Sometimes it stands for consanguinity and relationship, as here: "Behold we are thy bone and thy flesh,"[7] and the Apostle says: "If by any means I may provoke to emulation them who are my flesh, and save some of them."[8] We must therefore inquire in which of these four meanings we ought to take the word flesh in this place, for it is clear that it cannot possibly stand as in the passage where it is said "The Word was made flesh," and "All flesh shall see the salvation of God." Neither can it have the same meaning as where it is said "My Spirit shall not remain in those men because they are flesh," because the word flesh is not used here as it is there where it stands simply for a sinful man — when he says "The flesh lusteth against the spirit and the spirit against the flesh."[9] Nor is he speaking of things material, but of realities which in one and the same man struggle either at the same time or separately, with the shifting and changing of time.

CHAPTER XI.

What the Apostle means by flesh in this passage, and what the lust of the flesh is.

WHEREFORE in this passage we ought to take "flesh" as meaning not man, i.e., his ma-

---

[1] Prov. xvii. 28. (LXX.).

[2] S. John i. 14.
[3] S. Luke iii. 6.
[4] Gen. vi. 3.
[5] Rom. viii. 9.

[6] 1 Cor. xv. 50.
[7] 2 Sam. v. 1.
[8] Rom. xi. 14.
[9] Gal. v. 17.

terial substance, but the carnal will and evil desires, just as " spirit " does not mean anything material, but the good and spiritual desires of the soul: a meaning which the blessed Apostle has clearly given just before, where he begins: "But I say, walk in the spirit, and ye shall not fulfil the desires of the flesh; for the flesh lusteth against the spirit and the spirit against the flesh: but these are contrary the one to the other, that ye may not do what ye would." And since these two; viz., the desires of the flesh and of the spirit co-exist in one and the same man, there arises an internal warfare daily carried on within us, while the lust of the flesh which rushes blindly towards sin, revels in those delights which are connected with present ease. And on the other hand the desire of the spirit is opposed to these, and wishes to be entirely absorbed in spiritual efforts, so that it actually wants to be rid of even the necessary uses of the flesh, longing to be so constantly taken up with these things as to desire to have no share of anxiety about the weakness of the flesh. The flesh delights in wantonness and lust: the spirit does not even tolerate natural desires. The one wants to have plenty of sleep, and to be satiated with food: the other is nourished with vigils and fasting, so as to be unwilling even to admit of sleep and food for the needful purposes of life. The one longs to be enriched with plenty of everything, the other is satisfied even without the possession of a daily supply of scanty food. The one seeks to look sleek by means of baths, and to be surrounded every day by crowds of flatterers, the other delights in dirt and filth, and the solitude of the inaccessible desert, and dreads the approach of all mortal men. The one lives on the esteem and applause of men, the other glories in injuries offered to it, and in persecutions.

CHAPTER XII.

What is our free will, which stands in between the lust of the flesh and the spirit.

BETWEEN these two desires then the free will of the soul stands in an intermediate position somewhat worthy of blame, and neither delights in the excesses of sin, nor acquiesces in the sorrows of virtue. Seeking to restrain itself from carnal passions in such a way as not nevertheless to be willing to undergo the requisite suffering, and wanting to secure bodily chastity without chastising the flesh, and to acquire purity of heart without the exertion of vigils, and to abound in

spiritual virtues together with carnal ease, and to attain the grace of patience without the irritation of contradiction, and to practise the humility of Christ without the loss of worldly honour, to aim at the simplicity of religion in conjunction with worldly ambition, to serve Christ not without the praise and favour of men, to profess the strictness which truth demands without giving the slightest offence to anybody: in a word, it is anxious to pursue future blessings in such a way as not to lose present ones. And this free will would never lead us to attain true perfection, but would plunge us into a most miserable condition of lukewarmness, and make us like those who are rebuked by the Lord's remonstrance in the Apocalypse: "I know thy works, that thou art neither hot nor cold. I would that thou wert hot or cold. But now thou art lukewarm, and I will forthwith spue thee out of my mouth;"[1] were it not that these contentions which rise up on both sides disturb and destroy this condition of lukewarmness. For when we give in to this free will of ours and want to let ourselves go in the direction of this slackness, at once the desires of the flesh start up, and injure us with their sinful passions, and do not suffer us to continue in that state of purity in which we delight, and allure us to that cold and thorny path of pleasure which we have to dread. Again, if inflamed with fervour of spirit, we want to root out the works of the flesh, and without any regard to human weakness try to raise ourselves altogether to excessive efforts after virtue, the frailty of the flesh comes in, and recalls us and restrains us from that over excess of spirit which is bad for us: and so the result is that as these two desires are contradicting each other in a struggle of this kind, the soul's free will, which does not like either to give itself up entirely to carnal desires, nor to throw itself into the exertions which virtue calls for, is tempered as it were by a fair balance, while this struggle between the two hinders that more dangerous free will of the soul, and makes a sort of equitable balance in the scales of our body, which marks out the limits of flesh and spirit most accurately, and does not allow the mind inflamed with fervour of spirit to sway to the right hand, nor the flesh to incline through the pricks of sin, to the left. And while this struggle goes on day after day in us to our profit, we are driven most beneficially to come to that fourth stage which we do not like, so as to gain purity of heart not by ease and carelessness, but by constant efforts and

---

1 Rev. iii. 15, 16.

contrition of spirit; to retain our chastity of the flesh by prolonged fastings, hunger, thirst, and watchfulness; to acquire purpose of heart by reading, vigils, constant prayer and the wretchedness of solitude; to preserve patience by the endurance of tribulation; to serve our Maker in the midst of blasphemies and abounding insults ; to follow after truth if need be amid the hatred of the world and its enmity; and while, with such a struggle going on in our body, we are secured from slothful carelessness, and incited to that effort which is against the grain, and to the desire for virtue, our proper balance is admirably secured, and on one side the languid choice of our free will is tempered by fervour of spirit, and on the other the frigid coldness of the flesh is moderated by a gentle warmth, and while the desire of the spirit does not allow the mind to be dragged into unbridled licence, neither does the weakness of the flesh allow the spirit to be drawn on to unreasonable aspirations after holiness, lest in the one case incentives to all kinds of sins might arise, or in the other the earliest of all sins might lift its head and wound us with a yet more fatal dart of pride : but a due equilibrium will result from this struggle, and open to us a safe and secure path of virtue between the two, and teach the soldier of Christ ever to walk on the King's highway. And thus the result will be that when, in consequence of the lukewarmness arising from this sluggish will of which we have spoken, the mind has been more easily entangled in carnal desires, it is checked by the desire of the spirit, which by no means acquiesces in earthly sins; and again, if through over much feeling our spirit has been carried in unbounded fervour and towards ill-considered and impossible heights, it is recalled by the weakness of the flesh to sounder considerations and rising above the lukewarm condition of our free will with due proportion and even course proceeds along the way of perfection. Something of this sort we hear that the Lord ordained in the case of the building of that tower in the book of Genesis, where a confusion of tongues suddenly sprang up, and put a stop to the blasphemous and wicked attempts of men. For there would have remained there in opposition to God, aye and against the interest of those who had begun to assail His Divine Majesty, an agreement boding no good, unless by God's providence the difference of languages, raising disturbances among them, had forced them because of the variations of their words to go on to a better condition, and a happy and valuable discord had recalled to salvation those whom a ruin-

ous union had driven to destruction, as when divisions arose they began to experience human weakness of which when puffed up by their wicked plots they had hitherto known nothing.

CHAPTER XIII.

Of the advantage of the delay which results from the struggle between flesh and spirit.

BUT from the differences which this conflict causes, there arises a delay that is so far advantageous to us, and from this struggle an adjournment that is for our good, so that while through the resistance of the material body we are hindered from carrying out those things which we have wickedly conceived with our minds, we are sometimes recalled to a better mind either by penitence springing up, or by some better thoughts which usually come to us when delay in carrying out things, and time for reflection intervene. Lastly, those who, as we know, are not prevented from carrying out the desires of their free will by any hindrances of the flesh, I mean devils and spiritual wickednesses, these, since they have fallen from a higher and angelical state, we see are in a worse plight than men, in as much as (owing to the fact that opportunity is always present to gratify their desires) they are not delayed from irrevocably performing whatever evil they have imagined because as their mind is quick to conceive it, so their substance is ready and free to carry it out; and while a short and easy method is given them of doing what they wish, no salutary second thoughts come in to amend their wicked intention.

CHAPTER XIV.

Of the incurable depravity of spiritual wickednesses.

FOR a spiritual substance and one that is not tied to any material flesh has no excuse for an evil thought which arises within, and also shuts out forgiveness for its sin, because it is not harassed as we are by incentives of the flesh without, to sin, but is simply inflamed by the fault of a perverse will. And therefore its sin is without forgiveness and its weakness without remedy. For as it falls through the allurements of no earthly matter, so it can find no pardon or place for repentance. And from this we can clearly gather that this struggle which arises in us of the flesh and spirit against each other is not merely harmless, but actually extremely useful to us.

CHAPTER XV.

Of the value of the lust of the flesh against the spirit in our case.

To begin with, because it is an immediate reproof of our sloth and carelessness, and like some energetic schoolmaster who never allows us to deviate from the line of strict discipline, and if our carelessness has ever so little exceeded the limits of due gravity which become it, it immediately excites us by the stimulus of desire, and chides us and recalls us to due moderation. Secondly, because, in the matter of chastity and perfect purity, when by God's grace we see that we have been for some time kept from carnal pollution, in order that we may not imagine that we can no longer be disturbed by the motions of the flesh and thereby be elated and puffed up in our secret hearts as if we no longer bore about the corruption of the flesh, it humbles and checks us, and reminds us by its pricks that we are but men.[1] For as we ordinarily fall without much thought into other kinds of sins and those worse and more harmful, and are not so easily ashamed of committing them, so in this particular one the conscience is especially humbled, and by means of this illusion it is stung by the recollection of passions that have been neglected, as it sees clearly that it is rendered unclean by natural emotions, of which it knew nothing while it was still more unclean through spiritual sins; and so coming back at once to the cure of its former sluggishness, it is warned both that it ought not to trust in the attainments of purity in the past, which it sees to be lost by ever so small a falling away from the Lord, and also that it cannot attain the gift of this purity except by God's grace alone, since actual experience somehow or other teaches us that if we are anxious to reach abiding perfection of heart we must constantly endeavour to obtain the virtue of humility.

CHAPTER XVI.

Of the excitements of the flesh, without the humiliation of which we should fall more grievously.

To the fact then that the pride which results from this purity would be more dangerous than all sins and wickednesses, and that we should on that account gain no reward for any height of perfect chastity, we may call as witnesses those powers of which we spoke before, which since it is believed that they

[1] *Suo nos rursum quamvis quieto ac simplici visitans fluxu.*

experience no such fleshly lusts, were cast down from their high and heavenly estate in everlasting destruction simply from pride of heart. And so we should be altogether hopelessly lukewarm, since we should have no warning of carelessness on our part implanted either in our body or in our mind, nor should we ever strive to reach the glow of perfection, or even keep to strict frugality and abstinence, were it not that this excitement of the flesh springs up and humbles us and baffles us and makes us keen and anxious about purifying ourselves from spiritual sins.

CHAPTER XVII.

Of the lukewarmness of eunuchs.

LASTLY, on this account in those who are Eunuchs, we often detect the existence of this lukewarmness of mind, because, as they are so to speak free from the needs of the flesh, they fancy that they have no need either of the trouble of bodily abstinence, or of contrition of heart; and being rendered slack by this freedom from anxiety, they make no efforts either truly to seek or to acquire perfection of heart or even purity from spiritual faults. And this condition which is the result of their state in the flesh, becomes natural, which is altogether a worse state. For he who passes from the state of coldness to that of lukewarmness is branded by the Lord's words as still more hateful.

CHAPTER XVIII.

The question what is the difference between the carnal and natural man.

GERMANUS: You have, it seems to us, very clearly shown the value of the struggle which is raised between the flesh and spirit, so that we can believe that it can in a sort of way be grasped by us; and therefore we want to have this also explained to us in the same way; viz., what is the difference between the carnal and the natural man, or how the natural man can be worse than the carnal.

CHAPTER XIX.

The answer concerning the threefold condition of souls.

DANIEL: There are, according to the statements of Scripture, three kinds of souls; the first is the carnal, the second the natural, and the third the spiritual: which we find are thus described by the Apostle. For of the carnal he says: "I gave you milk to drink, not meat: for you were not able as yet. But neither indeed are you now able; for you are yet carnal." And again: "For whereas there is among you envying and contention, are you not carnal?"[1] Concerning the natural he also speaks as follows: "But the natural man perceiveth not the things that are of the spirit of God; for it is foolishness to him." But concerning the spiritual: "But the spiritual man judgeth all things: and he himself is judged by no man."[2] And again "You who are spiritual instruct such ones in the spirit of meekness."[3] And so, though at our renunciation we ceased to be carnal, i.e., we began to separate ourselves from intercourse with those in the world, and to have nothing to do with open pollution of the flesh, we must still be careful to strive with all our might to attain forthwith a spiritual condition, lest haply we flatter ourselves because we seem as far as the outer man is concerned to have renounced this world and got rid of the defilement of carnal fornication, as if by this we had reached the heights of perfection; and thence become careless and indifferent about purifying ourselves from other affections, and so being kept back between these two, become unable to reach the stage of spiritual advancement; either because we think that it is amply sufficient for our perfection if we seem to separate ourselves, as regards the outward man, from intercourse with this world and from its pleasure, or because we are free from corruption and carnal intercourse, and thus we find ourselves in that lukewarm condition which is considered the worst of all, and discover that we are spued out of the mouth of the Lord, in accordance with these words of His: "I would that thou wert hot or cold. But now thou art lukewarm and I will begin to spue thee out of My mouth."[4] And not without good reason does the Lord declare that those whom he has previously received in the bowels of His love, and who have become shamefully lukewarm, shall be spued out and rejected from His bosom: in as much as, though they might have yielded Him some health-giving subsistence, they preferred to be torn away from His heart: thus becoming far worse than those who had never found their way into the Lord's mouth as food, just as we turn away with loathing from that which nausea compels us to bring up. For whatever is cold is warmed when received into

the mouth and is received with satisfaction and good results. But whatever has been once rejected owing to its miserable lukewarmness, we cannot — I will not say touch with the lips — but even look on from a distance without the greatest disgust. Rightly then is he said to be worse, because the carnal man, i.e., the worldly man and the heathen, is more readily brought to saving conversion and to the heights of perfection than one who has been professed as a monk, but has not, as his rule directs, laid hold on the way of perfection, and so has once for all drawn back from that fire of spiritual fervour. For the former is at last broken down by the sins of the flesh, and acknowledges his uncleanness, and in his compunction hastens from carnal pollution to the fountain of true cleansing, and the heights of perfection, and in his horror at that cold state of infidelity in which he finds himself, he is kindled with the fire of the spirit and flies the more readily to perfection. For one who has, as we said, once started with a lukewarm beginning, and has begun to abuse the name of monk, and who has not laid hold on the way of this profession with the humility and fervour that he ought, when once he is infected by this miserable plague, and is as it were unstrung by it, can no longer of himself discern what is perfect nor learn from the admonitions of another. For he says in his heart that which the Lord tells us: "Because I am rich and wealthy and want nothing;" and so this which follows is at once applied to him: "But thou art wretched, and miserable, and poor, and blind, and naked:"[5] and he is so far in a worse condition than a worldly man, because he has no idea that he is wretched or blind or naked or requires cleansing, or needs to be directed and taught by any one; and on this account he receives no sound advice as he does not realise that he is weighted with the name of monk, and is lowered in the judgment of all, whereas, though everybody believes him to be a saint and regards him as a servant of God, he must hereafter be subjected to a stricter judgment and punishment. Lastly, why should we any longer linger over those things which we have sufficiently discovered and proved by experience? We have often seen those who were cold and carnal, i.e., worldly men and heathen, attain spiritual warmth: but lukewarm and "natural" men never. And these too we read in the prophet are hated of the Lord, so that a charge is given to spiritual and learned men to desist from warning and teaching them, and not to sow the seed of the

---

[1] 1 Cor. iii. 2, 3.   [3] Gal. vi. 1.
[2] 1 Cor. ii. 14, 15.   [4] Rev. iii. 15, 16.   [5] Rev. iii. 17.

life-giving word in ground that is barren and unfruitful and choked by noxious thorns; but that they should scorn this, and rather cultivate fallow ground, i.e., that they should transfer all their care and teaching, and their zeal in the life-giving word to pagans and worldly men: as we thus read: "Thus saith the Lord to the men of Judah and inhabitants of Jerusalem: break up your fallow ground, and sow not among thorns."[1]

CHAPTER XX.

Of those who renounce the world but ill.

IN the last place I am ashamed to say how we find that a large number have made their renunciation in such a way that we find that they have altered nothing of their former sins and habits, but only their state of life and worldly garb. For they are eager in amassing wealth which they never had before, or else do not give up that which they had, or which is still sadder, they actually strive to augment it under this excuse; viz., that they assert that it is right that they should always support with it their relations or the brethren, or they hoard it under pretence of starting congregations which they imagine that they can preside over as Abbots. But if only they would sincerely seek after the way of perfection, they would rather endeavour with all their might and main to attain to this: viz., that they might strip themselves not only of their wealth but of all their former likings and occupations, and place themselves unreservedly and entirely under the guidance of the Elders so as to have no anxiety not merely about others, but even about themselves. But on the contrary we find that while they are eager to be set over their brethren, they are never subject to their Elders themselves, and, with pride for their starting point, while they are quite ready to teach others they take no trouble to learn themselves or to practise what they are to teach: and so it is sure to end in their becoming, as the Saviour said, "blind leaders of the blind" so that "both fall into the ditch."[2] And this pride though there is only one kind of it, yet takes a twofold form. One form continually puts on the appearance of seriousness and gravity, the other breaks out with unbridled freedom into silly giggling and laughing. The former delights in not talking: the latter thinks it hard to be kept to the restraint of silence, and has no scruples about talking freely on matters that are unsuitable and foolish, while it is ashamed to be thought inferior to or less well informed than others. The one on account of pride seeks clerical office, the other looks down upon it, since it fancies that it is unsuitable or beneath its former dignity and life and the deserts of its birth. And which of these two should be accounted the worse each man must consider and decide for himself. At any rate the kind of disobedience is one and the same, if a man breaks the Elder's commands whether it be owing to zeal in work, or to love of ease: and it is as hurtful to upset the rules of the monastery for the sake of sleep, as it is for the sake of vigilance, and it is just the same to transgress the Abbot's orders in order to read, as it is to slight them in order to sleep: nor is there any difference in the incentive to pride if you neglect a brother, whether it is because of your fast or because of your breakfast: except that those faults which seem to show themselves under the guise of virtues and in the form of spirituality are worse and less likely to be cured than those which arise openly and from carnal pleasures. For these latter, like sicknesses which are perfectly plain and visible, are grappled with and cured, while the former, since they are covered under the cloak of virtue, remain uncured, and cause their victims to fall into a more dangerous and deadly state of ill health.

CHAPTER XXI.

Of those who having made light of great things busy themselves about trifles.

FOR how can we show how absurd it is that we see that some men after their first enthusiasm of renunciation in which they forsook their estates and vast wealth and the service of the world, and betook themselves to the monasteries, are still earnestly devoted to those things which cannot altogether be cut off, and which we cannot do without in this state of life, even though they are small and trifling things; so that in their case the anxiety about these trifles is greater than their love of all their property. And it certainly will not profit them much that they have disregarded greater riches and property, if they have only transferred their affections (on account of which they were to make light of them) to small and trifling things. For the sin of covetousness and avarice of which they cannot be guilty in the matter of really valuable things, they retain with regard to commoner matters, and so show that they have

---

[1] Jerem. iv. 3.   [2] Cf. S. Matt. xv. 14.

not got rid of their former greed but only changed its object. For if they are too careful about their mats, baskets, blankets, books, and other trifles such as these, the same passion holds them captive as before. And they actually guard and defend their rights over them so jealously as to get angry with their brethren about them, and, what is worse, they are not ashamed to quarrel over them. And being still troubled by the bad effects of their former covetousness, they are not content to possess those things which the needs and requirements of the body compel a monk to have, according to the common number and measure, but here too they show the greediness of their heart, as they try to have those things which they are obliged to use, better got up than the others; or, exceeding all due bounds, keep as their special and peculiar property and guard from the touch of others that which ought to belong to all the brethren alike. As if the difference of metals, and not the passion of covetousness was what mattered; and as if it was wrong to be angry about big things, while one might innocently be about trifling matters: and as if we had not given up all our precious things just in order that we might learn more readily to think nothing about trifles! For what difference does it make whether one gives way to covetousness in the matter of large and splendid things, or in the matter of the merest trifles, except that we ought to think a man so far worse if he has made light of great things and then is a slave to little things? And so that sort of renunciation of the world does not attain perfection of heart, because though it ranks as poverty it still keeps the mind of wealth.

V.

CONFERENCE OF ABBOT SERAPION.

ON THE EIGHT PRINCIPAL FAULTS.

CHAPTER I.

Our arrival at Abbot Serapion's cell, and inquiry on the different kinds of faults and the way to overcome them.

IN that assembly of Ancients and Elders was a man named Serapion,[1] especially endowed with the grace of discretion, whose Conference I think it is worth while to set down in writing. For when we entreated him to discourse of the way to overcome our faults, so that their origin and cause might be made clearer to us, he thus began.

CHAPTER II.

Abbot Serapion's enumeration of eight principal faults.

THERE are eight principal faults which attack mankind ; viz., first gastrimargia, which means gluttony, secondly fornication, thirdly philargyria, i.e., avarice or the love of money, fourthly anger, fifthly dejection, sixthly acedia, i.e., listlessness or low spirits, seventhly cenodoxia, i.e., boasting or vain glory; and eighthly pride.

CHAPTER III.

Of the two classes of faults and their fourfold manner of acting on us.

OF these faults then there are two classes. For they are either natural to us as gluttony, or arise outside of nature as covetousness. But their manner of acting on us is fourfold. For some cannot be consummated without an act on the part of the flesh, as gluttony and fornication, while some can be completed without any bodily act, as pride and vainglory. Some find the reasons for their being excited outside us, as covetousness and anger; others are aroused by internal feelings, as accidie [2] and dejection.

CHAPTER IV.

A review of the passions of gluttony and fornication and their remedies.

AND to make this clearer not only by a short discussion to the best of my ability, but by

---

1 Serapion when young was a pupil of Theonas, and an anecdote of his youthful indulgence in good things in secret has been already told in Conference II. c. xi. Another story of him is given in XVIII. xi. One of this name is mentioned by Palladius in the Lausiac History, c. lxxvi., and by Rufinus in the History of the Monks, c. xviii., where we are told that he lived at Arsinöe, and that he had ten thousand monks subject to his rule; a number which Sozomen also gives (H. E. VI. xxviii.). It is, however, doubtful whether this Serapion of Arsinöe is the person whose Conference Cassian here gives. Gazet identifies, Tillemont distinguishes the two. Jerome, it should be noticed, speaks in Ep. cviii. (Epitaphium Paulæ) as if there was not only one of this name famous among the monks of Egypt at that time.

2 For this word see the note on the Institutes V. i.

Scripture proof as well, gluttony and fornication, though they exist in us naturally (for sometimes they spring up without any incitement from the mind, and simply at the motion and allurement of the flesh) yet if they are to be consummated, must find an external object, and thus take effect only through bodily acts. For "every man is tempted of his own lust. Then lust when it has conceived beareth sin, and sin when it is consummated begets death."[1] For the first Adam could not have fallen a victim to gluttony unless he had had material food at hand, and had used it wrongly, nor could the second Adam be tempted without the enticement of some object, when it was said to Him: "If Thou art the Son of God, command that these stones be made bread."[2] And it is clear to everybody that fornication also is only completed by a bodily act, as God says of this spirit to the blessed Job: "And his force is in his loins, and his strength in the navel of his belly."[3] And so these two faults in particular, which are carried into effect by the aid of the flesh, especially require bodily abstinence as well as spiritual care of the soul; since the determination of the mind is not in itself enough to resist their attacks (as is sometimes the case with anger or gloominess or the other passions, which an effort of the mind alone can overcome without any mortification of the flesh); but bodily chastisement must be used as well, and be carried out by means of fasting and vigils and acts of contrition; and to this must be added change of scene, because since these sins are the results of faults of both mind and body, so they can only be overcome by the united efforts of both. And although the blessed Apostle says generally that all faults are carnal, since he enumerates enmities and anger and heresies among other works of the flesh,[4] yet in order to cure them and to discover their nature more exactly we make a twofold division of them: for we call some of them carnal, and some spiritual. And those we call carnal, which specially have to do with pampering the appetites of the flesh, and with which it is so charmed and satisfied, that sometimes it excites the mind when at rest and even drags it against its will to consent to its desire. Of which the blessed Apostle says: "In which also we all walked in time past in the desires of our flesh, fulfilling the will of the flesh and of our thoughts, and were by nature children of wrath even as the rest."[5] But we call those spiritual which spring only from the impulse of the mind and

not merely contribute no pleasure to the flesh, but actually bring on it a weakness that is harmful to it, and only feed a diseased mind with the food of a most miserable pleasure. And therefore these need a single medicine for the heart: but those which are carnal can only be cured, as we said, by a double remedy. Whence it is extremely useful for those who aspire to purity, to begin by withdrawing from themselves the material which feeds these carnal passions, through which opportunity for or recollection of these same desires can arise in a soul that is still affected by the evil. For a complicated disease needs a complicated remedy. For from the body the object and material which would allure it must be withdrawn, for fear lest the lust should endeavour to break out into act; and before the mind we should no less carefully place diligent meditation on Scripture and watchful anxiety and the withdrawal into solitude, lest it should give birth to desire even in thought. But as regards other faults intercourse with our fellows is no obstacle, or rather it is of the greatest possible use, to those who truly desire to get rid of them, because in mixing with others they more often meet with rebuke, and while they are more frequently provoked the existence of the faults is made evident, and so they are cured with speedy remedies.

CHAPTER V.

How our Lord alone was tempted without sin.

AND so our Lord Jesus Christ, though declared by the Apostle's word to have been tempted in all points like as we are, is yet said to have been "without sin,"[6] i.e., without the infection of this appetite, as He knew nothing of incitements of carnal lust, with which we are sure to be troubled even against our will and without our knowledge;[7] for the archangel thus describes the manner of His conception: "The Holy Ghost shall come upon thee and the power of the Most High

---

1 S. James i. 14, 15.
2 S. Matt. iv. 3.
3 Job xl. 16.

4 Cf. Gal. v. 19.
5 Eph. ii. 3.

---

6 Heb. iv. 15.
7 The following from D. Mozley's profound work on the Augustinian Theory of Predestination may serve to illustrate the remarks in the text: "Scripture says that our Lord was in all points tempted like as we are. But the Church has not considered it consistent with piety to interpret this text to mean that our Lord had the same direct propension to sin that we have, or that which is called by divines concupiscence. Such direct appetite for what is sinful is the characteristic of our fallen and corrupt nature; and our Lord did not assume a corrupt, but a sound humanity. Indeed, concupiscence, even prior to and independent of its gratification, has of itself the nature of sin; and therefore could not belong to a perfect Being. Our Lord had all the passions and affections that legitimately belong to man; which passions and affections, tending as they do in their own natures to become inordinate, constituted of themselves a state of trial; but the Church has regarded our Lord's trial as consisting in preserving ordinate affections from becoming inordinate, rather than in restraining desire proximate to sin from gratification" (p. 97).

shall overshadow thee: therefore that which shall be born of thee shall be called holy, the Son of God." [1]

CHAPTER VI.

Of the manner of the temptation in which our Lord was attacked by the devil.

FOR it was right that He who was in possession of the perfect image and likeness of God should be Himself tempted through those passions, through which Adam also was tempted while he still retained the image of God unbroken, that is, through gluttony, vainglory, pride; and not through those in which he was by his own fault entangled and involved after the transgression of the commandment, when the image and likeness of God was marred. For it was gluttony through which he took the fruit of the forbidden tree, vainglory through which it was said "Your eyes shall be opened," and pride through which it was said "Ye shall be as gods, knowing good and evil." [2] With these three sins then we read that the Lord our Saviour was also tempted; with gluttony when the devil said to Him: "Command these stones that they be made bread:" with vainglory: "If Thou art the Son of God cast Thyself down:" with pride, when he showed him all the kingdoms of the world and the glory of them and said: "All this will I give to Thee if Thou wilt fall down and worship me:" [3] in order that He might by His example teach us how we ought to vanquish the tempter when we are attacked on the same lines of temptation as He was. And so both the former and the latter are spoken of as Adam; the one being the first for destruction and death, and the other the first for resurrection and life. Through the one the whole race of mankind is brought into condemnation, through the other the whole race of mankind is set free. The one was fashioned out of raw and unformed earth, the other was born of the Virgin Mary. In His case then though it was fitting that He should undergo temptation, yet it was not necessary that He should fail under it. Nor could He who had vanquished gluttony be tempted by fornication, which springs from superfluity and gluttony as its root, with which even the first Adam would not have been destroyed unless before its birth he had been deceived by the wiles of the devil and fallen a victim to passion. And therefore the Son of God is not said absolutely to have come "in the flesh of sin," but "in the likeness of the flesh of sin," because though His was true flesh and He ate and drank and slept, and truly received the prints of the nails, there was in Him no true sin inherited from the fall, but only what was something like it. For He had no experience of the fiery darts of carnal lust, which in our case arise even against our will, from the constitution of our natures, but He took upon Him something like this, by sharing in our nature. For as He truly fulfilled every function which belongs to us, and bore all human infirmities, He has consequently been considered to have been subject to this feeling also, that He might appear through these infirmities to bear in His own flesh the state even of this fault and sin. Lastly the devil only tempted Him to those sins, by which he had deceived the first Adam, inferring that He as man would similarly be deceived in other matters if he found that He was overcome by those temptations by which he had overthrown His predecessor. But as he was overthrown in the first encounter he was not able to bring upon Him the second infirmity which had shot up as from the root of the first fault. For he saw that He had not even admitted anything from which this infirmity might take its rise, and it was idle to hope for the fruit of sin from Him, as he saw that He in no sort of way received into Himself seeds or roots of it. Yet according to Luke, who places last that temptation in which he uses the words "If Thou art the Son of God, cast Thyself down," [4] we can understand this of the feeling of pride, so that that earlier one, which Matthew places third, in which, as Luke the evangelist says, the devil showed Him all the kingdoms of the world in a moment of time and promised them to Him, may be taken of the feeling of covetousness, because after His victory over gluttony, he did not venture to tempt Him to fornication, but passed on to covetousness, which he knew to be the root of all evils, [5] and when again vanquished in this, he did not dare attack Him with any of those sins which follow, which, as he knew full well, spring from this as a root and source ; and so he passed on to the last passion; viz., pride, by which he knew that those who are perfect and have overcome all other sins, can be affected, and owing to which he remembered that he himself in his character of Lucifer, and many others too, had fallen from their heavenly estate, without temptation from any of the preceding passions. In this order then which we have mentioned, which is the one given by the evangelist Luke,

---

1 S. Luke i. 35.   2 Gen. iii. 5.   3 *Imaginarium.*   4 S. Luke iv. 9.   5 1 Tim. vi. 10.

there is an exact agreement between the allurements and forms of the temptations by which that most crafty foe attacked both the first and the second Adam. For to the one he said "Your eyes shall be opened;" to the other "he showed all the kingdoms of the world and the glory of them." In the one case he said "Ye shall be as gods;" in the other, "If Thou art the Son of God." [1]

CHAPTER VII.

How vainglory and pride can be consummated without any assistance from the body.

AND to go on in the order which we proposed, with our account of the way in which the other passions act (our analysis of which was obliged to be interrupted by this account of gluttony and of the Lord's temptation) vainglory and pride can be consummated even without the slightest assistance from the body. For in what way do those passions need any action of the flesh, which bring ample destruction on the soul they take captive simply by its assent and wish to gain praise and glory from men? Or what act on the part of the body was there in that pride of old in the case of the above mentioned Lucifer; as he only conceived it in his heart and mind, as the prophet tells us: "Who saidst in thine heart: I will ascend into heaven, I will set my throne above the stars of God. I will ascend above the heights of the clouds, I will be like the most High." [2] And just as he had no one to stir him up to this pride, so his thoughts alone were the authors of the sin when complete and of his eternal fall; especially as no exercise of the dominion at which he aimed followed.

CHAPTER VIII.

Of covetousness, which is something outside our nature, and of the difference between it and those faults which are natural to us.

COVETOUSNESS and anger, although they are not of the same character (for the former is something outside our nature, while the latter seems to have as it were its seed plot within us) yet they spring up in the same way, as in most instances they find the reasons for their being stirred in something outside of us. For often men who are still rather weak complain that they have fallen into these sins through irritation and the instigation of others, and are plunged headlong into the

passions of anger and covetousness by the provocation of other people. But that covetousness is something outside our nature, we can clearly see from this; viz., that it is proved not to have its first starting point inside us, nor does it originate in what contributes to keeping body and soul together, and to the existence of life. For it is plain that nothing belongs to the actual needs and necessities of our common life except our daily meat and drink: but everything else, with whatever zeal and care we preserve it, is shown to be something distinct from the wants of man by the needs of life itself. And so this temptation, as being something outside our nature, only attacks those monks who are but lukewarm and built on a bad foundation, whereas those which are natural to us do not cease from troubling even the best of monks and those who dwell in solitude. And so far is this shown to be true, that we find that there are some nations who are altogether free from this passion of covetousness, because they have never by use and custom received into themselves this fault and infirmity. And we believe that the old world before the flood was for long ages ignorant of the madness of this desire. And in the case of each one of us who makes his renunciation of the world a thorough one, we know that it is extirpated without any difficulty, if, that is, a man gives up all his property, and seeks the monastic discipline in such a way as not to allow himself to keep a single farthing. And we can find thousands of men to bear witness to this, who in a single moment have given up all their property, and have so thoroughly eradicated this passion as not to be in the slightest degree troubled by it afterwards, though all their life long they have to fight against gluttony, and cannot be safe from it without striving with the utmost watchfulness of heart and bodily abstinence.

CHAPTER IX.

How dejection and accidie generally arise without any external provocation, as in the case of other faults. [3]

DEJECTION and accidie generally arise without any external provocation, like those others of which we have been speaking: for we are well aware that they often harass solitaries, and those who have settled themselves in the desert without any intercourse with

---

[1] Cf. Gen. iii. 5 with S. Matt. iv. 6, 8.   [2] Is. xiv. 13, 14.

[3] Such is the heading which Gazet gives. Petschenig edits "De ira atque tristitia, quod inter accedentia vitia plerumque [non] inveniantur;" where "non" is his own insertion, and as he frankly tells us, the heading does not suit the chapter.

other men, and this in the most distressing way. And the truth of this any one who has lived in the desert and made trial of the conflicts of the inner man, can easily prove by experience.

CHAPTER X.

How six of these faults are related, and the two which differ from them are akin to one another.

Of these eight faults then, although they are different in their origin and in their way of affecting us, yet the six former; viz., gluttony, fornication, covetousness, anger, dejection, accidie, have a sort of connexion with each other, and are, so to speak, linked together in a chain, so that any excess of the one forms a starting point for the next. For from superfluity of gluttony fornication is sure to spring, and from fornication covetousness, 'from covetousness anger, from anger, dejection, and from dejection, accidie. And so we must fight against them in the same way, and with the same methods: and having overcome one, we ought always to enter the lists against the next. For a tall and spreading tree of a noxious kind will the more easily be made to wither if the roots on which it depends have first been laid bare or cut; and a pond of water which is dangerous will be dried up at once if the spring and flowing channel which produce it are carefully stopped up. Wherefore in order to overcome accidie, you must first get the better of dejection: in order to get rid of dejection, anger must first be expelled: in order to quell anger, covetousness must be trampled under foot: in order to root out covetousness, fornication must be checked: and in order to destroy fornication, you must chastise the sin of gluttony. But the two remaining faults; viz., vainglory and pride, are connected together in a somewhat similar way as the others of which we have spoken, so that the growth of the one makes a starting point for the other (for superfluity of vainglory produces an incentive to pride); but they are altogether different from the six former faults, and are not joined in the same category with them, since not only is there no opportunity given for them to spring up from these, but they are actually aroused in an entirely different way and manner. For when these others have been eradicated these latter flourish the more vigorously, and from the death of the others they shoot forth and grow up all the stronger: and therefore we are attacked by these two faults in quite a different way. For we fall into each one of those six faults at the moment when we have been overcome by the ones that went before them; but into these two we are in danger of falling when we have proved victorious, and above all after some splendid triumph. In the cases then of all faults just as they spring up from the growth of those that go before them, so are they eradicated by getting rid of the earlier ones. And in this way in order that pride may be driven out vainglory must be stifled, and so if we always overcome the earlier ones, the later ones will be checked; and through the extermination of those that lead the way, the rest of our passions will die down without difficulty. And though these eight faults of which we have spoken are connected and joined together in the way which we have shown, yet they may be more exactly divided into four groups and sub-divisions. For to gluttony fornication is linked by a special tie: to covetousness anger, to dejection accidie, and to vainglory pride is closely allied.

CHAPTER XI.

Of the origin and character of each of these faults.

And now, to speak about each kind of fault separately: of gluttony there are three sorts: (1) that which drives a monk to eat before the proper and stated times; (2) that which cares about filling the belly and gorging it with all kinds of food, and (3) that which is on the lookout for dainties and delicacies. And these three sorts give a monk no little trouble, unless he tries to free himself from all of them with the same care and scrupulousness. For just as one should never venture to break one's fast before the right time so we must utterly avoid all greediness in eating, and the choice and dainty preparation of our food: for from these three causes different but extremely dangerous conditions of the soul arise. For from the first there springs up dislike of the monastery, and thence there grows up disgust and intolerance of the life there, and this is sure to be soon followed by withdrawal and speedy departure from it. By the second there are kindled the fiery darts of luxury and lasciviousness. The third also weaves the entangling meshes of covetousness for the nets of its prisoners, and ever hinders monks from following the perfect self-abnegation of Christ. And when there are traces of this passion in us we can recognize them by this; viz., if we are kept to dine by one of the brethren we are not content to eat our food with the relish which he has prepared and offers to us, but take the unpardonable liberty of asking to have something else poured over it or added to it, a thing which we should never do for three reasons: (1) because the monastic mind ought always to be accustomed to practise endurance and abstinence, and like the Apostle, to learn to be content in whatever state he is.[1] For one who is upset by taking an unsavoury morsel once and in a way, and who cannot even for a short time overcome the delicacy of his appetite will never succeed in curbing the secret and more important desires of the body; (2) because it sometimes happens that at the time our host is out of that particular thing which we ask for, and we make him feel ashamed of the wants and bareness of his table, by exposing his poverty which he would rather was only known to God; (3) because sometimes other people do not care about the relish which we ask for, and so it turns out that we are annoying most of them while intent on satisfying the desires of our own palate. And on this account we must by all means avoid such a liberty. Of fornication there are three sorts: (1) that which is accomplished by sexual intercourse; (2) that which takes place without touching a woman, for which we read that Onan the son of the patriarch Judah was smitten by the Lord; and which is termed by Scripture uncleanness: of which the Apostle says: "But I say to the unmarried and to widows, that it is good for them if they abide even as I. But if they do not contain let them marry: for it is better to marry than to burn;"[2] (3) that which is conceived in heart and mind, of which the Lord says in the gospel: "Whosoever looketh on a woman to lust after her hath already committed adultery with her in his heart."[3] And these three kinds the blessed Apostle tells us must be stamped out in one and the same way. "Mortify," says he, "your members which are upon the earth, fornication, uncleanness, lust, etc."[4] And again of two of them he says to the Ephesians: "Let fornication and uncleanness be not so much as named among you:" and once more: "But know this that no fornicator or unclean person, or covetous person who is an idolater hath inheritance in the kingdom of Christ and of God."[5] And just as these three must be avoided by us with equal care, so they one and all shut us out and exclude us equally from the kingdom of Christ. Of covetousness there are three kinds: (1) That which hinders

renunciants from allowing themselves to be stripped of their goods and property; (2) that which draws us to resume with excessive eagerness the possession of those things which we have given away and distributed to the poor; (3) that which leads a man to covet and procure what he never previously possessed. Of anger there are three kinds: one which rages within, which is called in Greek θυμός; another which breaks out in word and deed and action, which they term ὀργή: of which the Apostle speaks, saying "But now do ye lay aside all anger and indignation;"[6] the third, which is not like those in boiling over and being done with in an hour, but which lasts for days and long periods, which is called μῆνις. And all these three must be condemned by us with equal horror. Of dejection there are two kinds: one, that which springs up when anger has died down, or is the result of some loss we have incurred or of some purpose which has been hindered and interfered with; the other, that which comes from unreasonable anxiety of mind or from despair. Of accidie there are two kinds: one of which sends those affected by it to sleep; while the other makes them forsake their cell and flee away. Of vainglory, although it takes various forms and shapes, and is divided into different classes, yet there are two main kinds: (1) when we are puffed up about carnal things and things visible, and (2) when we are inflamed with the desire of vain praise for things spiritual and unseen.

CHAPTER XII.

How vainglory may be useful to us.

But in one matter vainglory is found to be a useful thing for beginners. I mean by those who are still troubled by carnal sins, as for instance, if, when they are troubled by the spirit of fornication, they formed an idea of the dignity of the priesthood, or of reputation among all men, by which they may be thought saints and immaculate: and so with these considerations they repel the unclean suggestions of lust, as deeming them base and at least unworthy of their rank and reputation; and so by means of a smaller evil they overcome a greater one. For it is better for a man to be troubled by the sin of vainglory than for him to fall into the desire for fornication, from which he either cannot recover at all or only with great difficulty after he has fallen.

---

[1] Cf. Phil. iv. 11.
[2] 1 Cor. vii. 8, 9.
[3] S. Matt. v. 28.
[4] Col. iii. 5.
[5] Eph. v. 3–5.
[6] Col. iii. 8.

And this thought is admirably expressed by one of the prophets speaking in the person of God, and saying: "For My name's sake I will remove My wrath afar off: and with My praise I will bridle thee lest thou shouldest perish,"[1] i.e., while you are enchained by the praises of vainglory, you cannot possibly rush on into the depths of hell, or plunge irrevocably into the commission of deadly sins. Nor need we wonder that this passion has the power of checking anyone from rushing into the sin of fornication, since it has been again and again proved by many examples that when once a man has been affected by its poison and plague, it makes him utterly indefatigable, so that he scarcely feels a fast of even two or three days. And we have often known some who are living in this desert, confessing that when their home was in the monasteries of Syria they could without difficulty go for five days without food, while now they are so overcome with hunger even by the third hour, that they can scarcely keep on their daily fast to the ninth hour. And on this subject there is a very neat answer of Abbot Macarius[2] to one who asked him why he was troubled with hunger as early as the third hour in the desert, when in the monastery he had often scorned food for a whole week, without feeling hungry. "Because," said he, "here there is nobody to see your fast, and feed and support you with his praise of you: but there you grew fat on the notice of others and the food of vainglory." And of the way in which, as we said, the sin of fornication is prevented by an attack of vainglory, there is an excellent and significant figure in the book of Kings, where, when the children of Israel had been taken captive by Necho, King of Egypt, Nebuchadnezzar, King of Assyria, came up and brought them back from the borders of Egypt to their own country, not indeed meaning to restore them to their former liberty and their native land, but meaning to carry them off to his own land and to transport them to a still more distant country than the land of Egypt in which they had been prisoners. And this illustration exactly applies to the case before us. For though there is less harm in yielding to the sin of vainglory than to fornication, yet it is more difficult to escape from the dominion of vainglory. For somehow or other the prisoner who is carried off to a greater distance, will have more difficulty in returning to his native land and the freedom of his fathers, and the prophet's rebuke will be deservedly aimed at him: "Wherefore art thou grown old in a strange country?"[3] since

a man is rightly said to have grown old in a strange country, if he has not broken up the ground of his faults. Of pride there are two kinds: (1) carnal, and (2) spiritual, which is the worse. For it especially attacks those who are seen to have made progress in some good qualities.

CHAPTER XIII.

Of the different ways in which all these faults assault us.

ALTHOUGH then these eight faults trouble all sorts of men, yet they do not attack them all in the same way. For in one man the spirit of fornication holds the chief place: wrath rides rough shod over another: over another vainglory claims dominion: in another pride holds the field: and though it is clear that we are all attacked by all of them, yet the difficulties come to each of us in very different ways and manners.

CHAPTER XIV.

Of the struggle into which we must enter against our faults, when they attack us.

WHEREFORE we must enter the lists against these faults in such a way that every one should discover his besetting sin, and direct his main attack against it, directing all his care and watchfulness of mind to guard against its assault, directing against it daily the weapons of fasting, and at all times hurling against it the constant darts of sighs and groanings from the heart, and employing against it the labours of vigils and the meditation of the heart, and further pouring forth to God constant tears and prayers and continually and expressly praying to be delivered from its attack. For it is impossible for a man to win a triumph over any kind of passion, unless he has first clearly understood that he cannot possibly gain the victory in the struggle with it by his own strength and efforts, although in order that he may be rendered pure he must night and day persist in the utmost care and watchfulness. And even when he feels that he has got rid of this fault, he should still search the inmost recesses of his heart with the same purpose, and single out the worst fault which he can see among those still there, and bring all the forces of the Spirit to bear against it in particular, and

---

[1] Is. xlviii. 9. [2] Cf. note on the Institutes V. xli. [3] Baruch iii. 11.

so by always overcoming the stronger passions, he will gain a quick and easy victory over the rest, because by a course of triumphs the soul is made more vigorous, and the fact that the next conflict is with weaker passion insures him a readier success in the struggle: as is generally the case with those who are wont to face all kinds of wild beasts in the presence of the kings of this world, out of consideration for the rewards — a kind of spectacle which is generally called "pancarpus." [1] Such men, I say, direct their first assault against whatever beasts they see to be the strongest and fiercest, and when they have despatched these, then they can more easily lay low the remaining ones, which are not so terrible and powerful. So too, by always overcoming the stronger passions, as weaker ones take their place, a perfect victory will be secured for us without any risk. Nor need we imagine that if any one grapples with *one* fault in particular, and seems too careless about guarding against the attacks of others, he will be easily wounded by a sudden assault, for this cannot possibly happen. For where a man is anxious to cleanse his heart, and has steeled his heart's purpose against the attack of any one fault, it is impossible for him not to have a general dread of all other faults as well, and take similar care of them. For if a man renders himself unworthy of the prize of purity by contaminating himself with other faults, how can he possibly succeed in gaining the victory over that one passion from which he is longing to be freed? But when the main purpose of our heart has singled out one passion as the special object of its attack, we shall pray about it more earnestly, and with special anxiety and fervour shall entreat that we may be more especially on our guard against it and so succeed in gaining a speedy victory. For the giver of the law himself teaches us that we ought to follow this plan in our conflicts and not to trust in our own power; as he says: "Thou shalt not fear them because the Lord thy God is in the midst of thee, a God mighty and terrible: He will consume these nations in thy sight by little and little and by degrees. Thou wilt not be able to destroy them altogether: lest perhaps the beasts of the earth should increase upon thee. But the Lord thy God shall deliver them in thy sight; and shall slay them until they be utterly destroyed." [2]

CHAPTER XV.

How we can do nothing against our faults without the help of God, and how we should not be puffed up by victories over them.

AND that we ought not to be puffed up by victories over them he likewise charges us; saying, "Lest after thou hast eaten and art filled, hast built goodly houses and dwelt in them, and shalt have herds of oxen and flocks of sheep, and plenty of gold and of silver, and of all things, thy heart be lifted up and thou remember not the Lord thy God, who brought thee out of the land of Egypt, out of the house of bondage; and was thy leader in the great and terrible wilderness." [3] Solomon also says in Proverbs: "When thine enemy shall fall be not glad, and in his ruin be not lifted up, lest the Lord see it and it displease Him, and He turn away His wrath from him," [4] i.e., lest He see thy pride of heart, and cease from attacking him, and thou begin to be forsaken by Him and so once more to be troubled by that passion which by God's grace thou hadst previously overcome. For the prophet would not have prayed in these words, "Deliver not up to beasts, O Lord, the soul that confesseth to Thee," [5] unless he had known that because of their pride of heart some were given over again to those faults which they had overcome, in order that they might be humbled. Wherefore it is well for us both to be certified by actual experience, and also to be instructed by countless passages of Scripture, that we cannot possibly overcome such mighty foes in our own strength, and unless supported by the aid of God alone; and that we ought always to refer the whole of our victory each day to God Himself, as the Lord Himself also gives us instruction by Moses on this very point: "Say not in thine heart when the Lord thy God shall have destroyed them in thy sight: For my righteousness hath the Lord brought me in to possess this land, whereas these nations are destroyed for their wickedness. For it is not for thy righteousness, and the uprightness of thine heart, that thou shalt go in to possess their lands: but because they have done wickedly they are destroyed at thy coming in." [6] I ask what could be said clearer in opposition to that impious notion and impertinence of ours, in which we want to ascribe everything that we do to our own free will and our own exertions? "Say not," he tells us, "in thine heart, when the Lord thy God shall have destroyed them in thy sight: For my

---

[1] *Pancarpus* (πάγκαρπος). The word was originally applied to an offering of all kinds of fruit. Cf. Tertullian ad Valent. xii. It is also used in the general sense "of all sorts" by Augustine, Adv. Secund. xxiii. Cassian here speaks as if it had become the popular name for the conflicts of gladiators with all kinds of beasts, though there is apparently no other authority for this.
[2] Deut. vii. 21–23.

[3] Deut. viii. 12–15.   [5] Ps. lxxiii. (lxxiv.) 19.
[4] Prov. xxiv. 17, 18 (LXX.).   [6] Deut. ix. 4, 5.

righteousness the Lord hath brought me in to possess this land." To those who have their eyes opened and their ears ready to hearken does not this plainly say: When your struggle with carnal faults has gone well for you, and you see that you are free from the filth of them, and from the fashions of this world, do not be puffed up by the success of the conflict and victory and ascribe it to your own power and wisdom, nor fancy that you have gained the victory over spiritual wickedness and carnal sins through your own exertions and energy, and free will? For there is no doubt that in all this you could not possibly have succeeded, unless you had been fortified and protected by the help of the Lord.

CHAPTER XVI.

Of the meaning of the seven nations of whose lands Israel took possession, and the reason why they are sometimes spoken of as "seven," and sometimes as "many."

THESE are the seven nations whose lands the Lord promised to give to the children of Israel when they came out of Egypt. And everything which, as the Apostle says, happened to them "in a figure"[1] we ought to take as written for our correction. For so we read: "When the Lord thy God shall have brought thee into the land, which thou art going in to possess, and shall have destroyed many nations before thee, the Hittite, and the Girgashites, and the Amorite, the Canaanite, and the Perizzite, and the Hivite, and the Jebusite, seven nations much more numerous than thou art and much stronger than thou: and the Lord thy God shall have delivered them to thee, thou shalt utterly destroy them."[2] And the reason that they are said to be much more numerous, is that faults are many more in number than virtues and so in the list of them the nations are reckoned as seven in number, but when the attack upon them is spoken of they are set down without their number being given, for thus we read "And shall have destroyed many nations before thee." For the race of carnal passions which springs from this sevenfold incentive and root of sin, is more numerous than that of Israel. For thence spring up murders, strifes, heresies, thefts, false witness, blasphemy, surfeiting, drunkenness, back-biting, buffoonery, filthy conversation, lies, perjury, foolish talking, scurrility, restlessness, greediness, bitterness, clamour, wrath, contempt, murmuring, temptation, despair, and many other

faults, which it would take too long to describe. And if we are inclined to think these small matters, let us hear what the Apostle thought about them, and what was his opinion of them: "Neither murmur ye," says he, "as some of them murmured, and were destroyed of the destroyer:" and of temptation: "Neither let us tempt Christ as some of them tempted and perished by the serpents."[3] Of backbiting: "Love not backbiting lest thou be rooted out."[4] And of despair: "Who despairing have given themselves up to lasciviousness unto the working of all error, in uncleanness."[5] And that clamour is condemned as well as anger and indignation and blasphemy, the words of the same Apostle teach us as clearly as possible when he thus charges us: "Let all bitterness, and anger, and indignation, and clamour, and blasphemy be put away from you with all malice,"[6] and many more things like these. And though these are far more numerous than the virtues are, yet if those eight principal sins, from which we know that these naturally proceed, are first overcome, all these at once sink down, and are destroyed together with them with a lasting destruction. For from gluttony proceed surfeiting and drunkenness. From fornication filthy conversation, scurrility, buffoonery and foolish talking. From covetousness, lying, deceit, theft, perjury, the desire of filthy lucre, false witness, violence, inhumanity, and greed. From anger, murders, clamour and indignation. From dejection, rancor, cowardice, bitterness, despair. From accidie, laziness, sleepiness, rudeness, restlessness, wandering about, instability both of mind and body, chattering, inquisitiveness. From vainglory, contention, heresies, boasting and confidence in novelties. From pride, contempt, envy, disobedience, blasphemy, murmuring, backbiting. And that all these plagues are stronger than we, we can tell very plainly from the way in which they attack us. For the delight in carnal passions wars more powerfully in our members than does the desire for virtue, which is only gained with the greatest contrition of heart and body. But if you will only gaze with the eyes of the spirit on those countless hosts of our foes, which the Apostle enumerates where he says: "For we wrestle not against flesh and blood, but against principalities, against powers, against the world-rulers of this darkness, against spiritual wickedness in heavenly places,"[7] and this which we find of the right-

---

[1] Cf. 1 Cor. x. 6.   [2] Deut. vii. 1, 2.

[3] 1 Cor. x. 9, 10.   [6] Eph. iv. 31.
[4] Prov. xx. 13 (LXX.).   [7] *Ibid.*, iv. 12.
[5] Eph. iv. 19.

eous man in the nineteenth Psalm: "A thousand shall fall beside thee and ten thousand at thy right hand,"[1] then you will clearly see that they are far more numerous and more powerful than are we, carnal and earthly creatures as we are, while to them is given a substance which is spiritual and incorporeal.

CHAPTER XVII.

A question with regard to the comparison of seven nations with eight faults.

GERMANUS: How then is it that there are *eight* faults which assault us, when Moses reckons the nations opposed to the people of Israel as *seven*, and how is it well for us to take possession of the territory of our faults?

CHAPTER XVIII.

The answer how the number of eight nations is made up in accordance with the eight faults.

SERAPION: Everybody is perfectly agreed that there are eight principal faults which affect a monk. And all of them are not included in the figure of the nations for this reason, because in Deuteronomy Moses, or rather the Lord through him, was speaking to those who had already gone forth from Egypt and been set free from one most powerful nation, I mean that of the Egyptians. And we find that this figure holds good also in our case, as when we have got clear of the snares of this world we are found to be free from gluttony, i.e., the sin of the belly and palate; and like them we have a conflict against these seven remaining nations, without taking account at all of the one which has been already overcome. And the land of this nation was not given to Israel for a possession, but the command of the Lord ordained that they should at once forsake it and go forth from it. And for this cause our fasts ought to be made moderate, that there may be no need for us through excessive abstinence, which results from weakness of the flesh and infirmity, to return again to the land of Egypt, i.e., to our former greed and carnal lust which we forsook when we made our renunciation of this world. And this has happened in a figure, in those who after having gone forth into the desert of virtue again hanker after the flesh pots over which they sat in Egypt.

CHAPTER XIX.

The reason why one nation is to be forsaken, while seven are commanded to be destroyed.

BUT the reason why that nation in which the children of Israel were born, was bidden not to be utterly destroyed but only to have its land forsaken, while it was commanded that these seven nations were to be completely destroyed, is this: because however great may be the ardour of spirit, inspired by which we have entered on the desert of virtues, yet we cannot possibly free ourselves entirely from the neighbourhood of gluttony or from its service and, so to speak, from daily intercourse with it. For the liking for delicacies and dainties will live on as something natural and innate in us, even though we take pains to cut off all superfluous appetites and desires, which, as they cannot be altogether destroyed, ought to be shunned and avoided. For of these we read "Take no care for the flesh with its desires."[2] While then we still retain the feeling for this care, which we are bidden not altogether to cut off, but to keep without its desires, it is clear that we do not destroy the Egyptian nation but separate ourselves in a sort of way from it, not thinking anything about luxuries and delicate feasts, but, as the Apostle says, being "content with our daily food and clothing."[3] And this is commanded in a figure in the law, in this way: "Thou shalt not abhor the Egyptian, because thou wast a stranger in his land."[4] For necessary food is not refused to the body without danger to it and sinfulness in the soul. But of those seven troublesome faults we must in every possible way root out the affections from the inmost recesses of our souls. For of them we read: "Let all bitterness and anger and indignation and clamour and blasphemy be put away from you with all malice:" and again: "But fornication and all uncleanness and covetousness let it not so much as be named among you, or obscenity or foolish talking or scurrility."[5] We can then cut out the roots of these faults which are grafted into our nature from without while we cannot possibly cut off occasions of gluttony. For however far we have advanced, we cannot help being what we were born. And that this is so we can show not only from the lives of little people like ourselves but from the lives and customs of all who have attained perfection, who even when they have

---

[1] Ps. xc. (xci.) 7.

[2] Rom. xiii. 14.
[3] Cf. 1 Tim. vi. 8.
[4] Deut. xxiii. 7.
[5] Eph. iv. 31; v. 3, 4.

got rid of incentives to all other passions, and are retiring to the desert with perfect fervour of spirit and bodily abnegation, yet still cannot do without thought for their daily meal and the preparation of their food from year to year.

CHAPTER XX.

Of the nature of gluttony, which may be illustrated by the simile of the eagle.

AN admirable illustration of this passion, with which a monk, however spiritual and excellent, is sure to be hampered, is found in the simile of the eagle. For this bird when in its flight on high it has soared above the highest clouds, and has withdrawn itself from the eyes of all mortals and from the face of the whole earth, is yet compelled by the needs of the belly to drop down and descend to the earth and feed upon carrion and dead bodies. And this clearly shows that the spirit of gluttony cannot be altogether extirpated like all other faults, nor be entirely destroyed like them, but that we can only hold down and check by the power of the mind all incentives to it and all superfluous appetites.

CHAPTER XXI.

Of the lasting character of gluttony as described to some philosophers.

FOR the nature of this fault was admirably expressed under cover of the following puzzle by one of the Elders in a discussion with some philosophers, who thought that they might chaff him like a country bumpkin because of his Christian simplicity. "My father," said he, "left me in the clutches of a great many creditors. All the others I have paid in full, and have freed myself from all their pressing claims; but one I cannot satisfy even by a daily payment." And when they could not see the meaning of the puzzle, and urgently begged him to explain it: "I was," said he, "in my natural condition, encompassed by a great many faults. But when God inspired me with the longing to be free, I renounced this world, and at the same time gave up all my property which I had inherited from my father, and so I satisfied them all like pressing creditors, and freed myself entirely from them. But I was never able altogether to get rid of the incentives to gluttony. For though I reduce the quantity of food which I take to the smallest possible amount, yet I cannot avoid the force of its daily solicitations, but must be perpetually

'dunned' by it, and be making as it were interminable payments by continually satisfying it, and pay never ending toll at its demand." Then they declared that this man, whom they had till now despised as a booby and a country bumpkin, had thoroughly grasped the first principles of philosophy, i.e., training in ethics, and they marvelled that he could by the light of nature have learnt that which no schooling in this world could have taught him, while they themselves with all their efforts and long course of training had not learnt this. This is enough on gluttony in particular. Now let us return to the discourse in which we had begun to consider the general relation of our faults to each other.

CHAPTER XXII.

How it was that God foretold to Abraham that Israel would have to drive out ten nations.

WHEN the Lord was speaking with Abraham about the future (a point which you did not ask about) we find that He did not enumerate seven nations, but ten, whose land He promised to give to his seed.[1] And this number is plainly made up by adding idolatry, and blasphemy, to whose dominion, before the knowledge of God and the grace of Baptism, both the irreligious hosts of the Gentiles and blasphemous ones of the Jews were subject, while they dwelt in a spiritual Egypt. But when a man has made his renunciation and come forth from thence, and having by God's grace conquered gluttony, has come into the spiritual wilderness, then he is free from the attacks of these three, and will only have to wage war against those seven which Moses enumerates.

CHAPTER XXIII.

How it is useful for us to take possession of their lands.

BUT the fact that we are bidden for our good to take possession of the countries of those most wicked nations, may be understood in this way. Each fault has its own especial corner in the heart, which it claims for itself in the recesses of the soul, and drives out Israel, i.e., the contemplation of holy and heavenly things, and never ceases to oppose them. For virtues cannot possibly live side by side with faults. "For what participation hath righteousness with unrighteousness? Or what fellowship hath light with darkness?"[2] But as

---

[1] Cf. Gen. xv. 18–21.   [2] 2 Cor. vi. 14.

soon as these faults have been overcome by the people of Israel, i.e., by those virtues which war against them, then at once the place in our heart which the spirit of concupiscence and fornication had occupied, will be filled by chastity. That which wrath had held, will be claimed by patience. That which had been occupied by a sorrow that worketh death, will be taken by a godly sorrow and one full of joy. That which had been wasted by accidie, will at once be tilled by courage. That which pride had trodden down will be ennobled by humility: and so when each of these faults has been expelled, their places (that is the tendency towards them) will be filled by the opposite virtues which are aptly termed the children of Israel, that is, of the soul that seeth God:[1] and when these have expelled all passions from the heart we may believe that they have recovered their own possessions rather than invaded those of others.

CHAPTER XXIV.

How the lands from which the Canaanites were expelled, had been assigned to the seed of Shem.

FOR, as an ancient tradition tells us,[2] these same lands of the Canaanites into which the children of Israel were brought, had been formerly allotted to the children of Shem at the division of the world, and afterward the descendants of Ham wickedly invading them with force and violence took possession of them. And in this the righteous judgment of God is shown, as He expelled from the land of others those who had wrongfully taken possession of them, and restored to those others the ancient property of their fathers which had been assigned to their ancestors at the division of the world. And we can perfectly well see that this figure holds good in our own case. For by nature God's will assigned the possession of our heart not to vices but to virtues, which, after the fall of Adam were driven out from their own country by the sins which grew up, i.e., by the Canaanites; and so when by God's grace they are by our efforts and labour restored again to it, we may hold that they have not occupied the territory of another, but rather have recovered their own country.

CHAPTER XXV.

Different passages of Scripture on the meaning of the eight faults.

AND in reference to these eight faults we also have the following in the gospel: "But when the unclean spirit is gone out from a man, he walketh through dry places seeking rest and findeth none. Then he saith, I will return to my house from whence I came out: and coming he findeth it empty, swept, and garnished: then he goeth and taketh seven other spirits worse than himself, and they enter in and dwell there: and the last state of that man is made worse than the first."[3] Lo, just as in the former passages we read of seven nations besides that of the Egyptians from which the children of Israel had gone forth, so here too seven unclean spirits are said to return beside that one which we first hear of as going forth from the man. And of this sevenfold incentive of sins Solomon gives the following account in Proverbs: "If thine enemy speak loud to thee, do not agree to him because there are seven mischiefs in his heart;"[4] i.e., if the spirit of gluttony is overcome and begins to flatter you with having humiliated it, asking in a sort of way that you would relax something of the fervour with which you began, and yield to it something beyond what the due limits of abstinence, and measure of strict severity would allow, do not you be overcome by its submission, nor return in fancied security from its assaults, as you seem to have become for a time freed from carnal desires, to your previous state of carelessness or former liking for good things. For through this the spirit whom you have vanquished is saying "I will return to my house from whence I came out," and forthwith the seven spirits of sins which proceed from it will prove to you more injurious than that passion which in the first instance you overcame, and will presently drag you down to worse kinds of sins.

CHAPTER XXVI.

How when we have got the better of the passion of gluttony we must take pains to gain all the other virtues.

WHEREFORE while we are practising fasting and abstinence, we must be careful when we have got the better of the passion of gluttony never to allow our mind to remain empty of the virtues of which we stand in need; but

---

[1] Cf. the note on "Against Nestorius" VII. ix.
[2] The "ancient tradition" to which Cassian here alludes is given in the Clementine Recognitions I. xxix., xxx.; and in Epiphanius "Heresies," c. lxvi. § 83, *sq.*, where it is given as an answer to the Manichæan objection against the cruelty and injustice of the extermination of the Canaanites by the Israelites.

[3] S. Matt. xii. 43–45.   [4] Prov. xxvi. 25. (lxx.).

we should the more earnestly fill the inmost recesses of our heart with them for fear lest the spirit of concupiscence should return and find us empty and void of them, and should not be content to secure an entrance there for himself alone, but should bring in with him into our heart this sevenfold incentive of sins and make our last state worse than the first. For the soul which boasts that it has renounced this world with the eight faults that hold sway over it, will afterwards be fouler and more unclean and visited with severer punishments, than it was when formerly it was at home in the world, when it had taken upon itself neither the rules nor the name of monk. For these seven spirits are said to be worse than the first which went forth, for this reason; because the love of good things, i.e., gluttony would not be in itself harmful, were it not that it opened the door to other passions; viz, to fornication, covetousness, anger, dejection, and pride, which are clearly hurtful in themselves to the soul, and domineering over it. And therefore a man will never be able to gain perfect purity, if he hopes to secure it by means of abstinence alone, i.e., bodily fasting, unless he knows that he ought to practise it for this reason that when the flesh is brought low by means of fasting, he may with greater ease enter the lists against other faults, as the flesh has not been habituated to gluttony and surfeiting.

CHAPTER XXVII.

That our battles are not fought with our faults in the same order as that in which they stand in the list.

But you must know that our battles are not all fought in the same order, because, as we mentioned that the attacks are not always made on us in the same way, each one of us ought also to begin the battle with due regard to the character of the attack which is especially made on him so that one man will have to fight his first battle against the fault which stands third on the list, another against that which is fourth or fifth. And in proportion as faults hold sway over us, and the character of their attack may demand, so we too ought to regulate the order of our conflict, in such a way that the happy result of a victory and triumph succeeding may insure our attainment of purity of heart and complete perfection.

Thus far did Abbot Serapion discourse to us of the nature of the eight principal faults, and so clearly did he expound the different sorts of passions which are latent within us — the origin and connexion of which, though we were daily tormented by them, we could never before thoroughly understand and perceive — that we seemed almost to see them spread out before our eyes as in a mirror.

VI.

CONFERENCE OF ABBOT THEODORE.[1]

ON THE DEATH OF THE SAINTS.

CHAPTER I.

Description of the wilderness, and the question about the death of the saints.

In the district of Palestine near the village of Tekoa which had the honour of producing the prophet Amos,[2] there is a vast desert which stretches far and wide as far as Arabia and the dead sea, into which the streams of Jordan enter and are lost, and where are the ashes of Sodom. In this district there lived

for a long while monks of the most perfect life and holiness, who were suddenly destroyed by an incursion of Saracen robbers:[3] whose bodies we knew were seized upon with the greatest veneration[4] both by the Bishops of the neighbourhood and by the whole populace

---

[1] This Abbot Theodore is probably the same person as the one mentioned in the Institutes, Book V. cc. xxxiii.-xxxv. ; but nothing further is known of him, and there is no reason for identifying him with any of the other monks of this name of the fourth century.
[2] Cf. Amos i. 1.

[3] Saraceni (Σαρακηνοί): a name given by the classical geographers to a tribe of Arabia Felix, famous for its predatory propensities. Jerome speaks of the " mons et desertum Saracenorum quod vocatur Pharan " (Liber de situ et nominibus sub voce Choreb) and elsewhere describes their predatory habits (Liber Heb. Quæst in Genesim) " Saracenos vagos . . . qui universas gentes . . . incursant." By the seventh century the name had become a merely general term equivalent to Arab, and was accordingly adopted and applied indifferently to all the followers of Mohammed by the writers of the middle ages (cf. the Dictionary of Greek and Roman Geography, sub voce).
[4] There is no mention of these martyrs in the so-called Martyrologium Hieronymianum, but they are commemorated on May 28, in the Roman Martyrology.

of Arabia, and deposited among the relics of the martyrs, so that swarms of people from two towns met, and made terrible war upon each other, and in their struggle actually came to blows for the possession of the holy spoil, while they strove among themselves with pious zeal as to which of them had the better claim to bury them and keep their relics — the one party boasting of their vicinity to the place of their abode, the other of the fact that they were near the place of their birth. But we were upset by this and being disturbed either on our own account or on account of some of the brethren who were in no small degree scandalized at it, inquired why men of such illustrious merits and of so great virtues should be thus slain by robbers, and why the Lord permitted such a crime to be committed against his servants, so as to give up into the hands of wicked men those who were the admiration of everybody: and so in our grief we came to the holy Theodore, a man who excelled in practical common sense. For he was living in Cellæ,[1] a place that lies between Nitria and Scete, and is five miles distant from the monasteries of Nitria, and cut off by eighty intervening miles of desert from the wilderness of Scete where we were living. And when we had made our complaint to him about the death of the men mentioned above, and expressed our surprise at the great patience of God, because He suffered men of such worth to be killed in this way, so that those who ought to be able by the weight of their sanctity to deliver others from trials of this kind, could not save themselves from the hands of wicked men (and asked) why it was that God allowed so great a crime to be committed against his servants, then the blessed Theodore replied.

CHAPTER II.

Abbot Theodore's answer to the question proposed to him.

THIS question often exercises the minds of those who have not much faith or knowledge, and imagine that the prizes and rewards of the saints (which are not given in this world, but laid up for the future) are bestowed in the short space of this mortal life. But we whose hope in Christ is not only in this life, for fear lest, as the Apostle says, we should be "of all men most miserable "[2] (because as we receive none of the promises in this world we should for our unbelief lose them also in that to come) ought not wrongly to follow their ideas, lest through ignorance of the true real explanation, we should hesitate and tremble and fail in temptation, if we find ourselves given up to such men; and should ascribe to God injustice or carelessness about the affairs of mankind — a thing which it is almost a sin to mention — because He does not protect in their temptations men who are living an upright and holy life, nor requite good men with good things and evil men with evil things in this world; and so we should deserve to fall under the condemnation of those whom the prophet Zephaniah rebukes, saying "who say in their hearts the Lord will not do good, nor will He do evil:"[3] or at least be found among those of whom we are told that they blaspheme God with such complaints as this: "Every one that doeth evil is good in the sight of the Lord, and such please Him: for surely where is the God of judgment?"[4] Adding further that blasphemy which is described in the same way in what follows: "He laboureth in vain that serveth God, and what profit is it that we have kept His ordinances, and walked sorrowful before the Lord? Wherefore now we call the proud happy, for they that work wickedness are enriched, and they have tempted God, and are preserved."[5] Wherefore that we may avoid this ignorance which is the root and cause of this most deadly error, we ought in the first place to know what is really good, and what is bad, and so finally if we grasp the true scriptural meaning of these words, and not the false popular one, we shall escape being deceived by the errors of unbelievers.

CHAPTER III.

Of the three kinds of things there are in the world; viz., good, bad, and indifferent.

ALTOGETHER there are three kinds of things in the world; viz., good, bad, and indifferent. And so we ought to know what is properly good, and what is bad, and what is indifferent, that our faith may be supported by true knowledge and stand firm in all temptations. We must then believe that in things which

---

[1] Cellæ, which was, according to the passage before us, between the deserts of Scete and Nitria, apparently derived its name from the cells of the monks who congregated there. This at least is the explanation of the name given by Sozomen (H. E. VI. xxxi.) who speaks of a region called κελλία, throughout which numerous little dwellings (οἰκήματα) are dispersed, whence it obtains its name. Sozomen also speaks (c. xxix.) of Macarius as priest of Cellæ, a fact which gives some ground for conjecturing that Cellæ may be identified with Dair Abu Makâr, one of the four monasteries still existing in the deserts of Nitria and Scete, probably founded by the saint whose name it bears (Macarius). See A. J. Butler's "Coptic Churches of Egypt," vol. i. c. vii.

[2] 1 Cor. xv. 19.   [4] Mal. ii. 17.
[3] Zeph. i. 12.   [5] Mal. iii. 14, 15.

are merely human there is no real good except virtue of soul alone, which leads us with unfeigned faith to things divine, and makes us constantly adhere to that unchanging good. And on the other hand we ought not to call anything bad, except sin alone, which separates us from the good God, and unites us to the evil devil. But those things are indifferent which can be appropriated to either side according to the fancy or wish of their owner, as for instance riches, power, honour, bodily strength, good health, beauty, life itself, and death, poverty, bodily infirmities, injuries, and other things of the same sort, which can contribute either to good or to evil as the character and fancy of their owner directs. For riches are often serviceable for our good, as the Apostle says, who charges "the rich of this world to be ready to give, to distribute to the needy, to lay up in store for themselves a good foundation against the time to come, that" by this means "they may lay hold on the true life."[1] And according to the gospel they are a good thing for those who "make to themselves friends of the unrighteous mammon."[2] And again, they can be drawn in the direction of what is bad when they are amassed only for the sake of hoarding them or for a life of luxury, and are not employed to meet the wants of the poor. And that power also and honour and bodily strength and good health are indifferent and available for either (good or bad) can easily be shown from the fact that many of the Old Testament saints enjoyed all these things and were in positions of great wealth and the highest honour, and blessed with bodily strength, and yet are known to have been most acceptable to God. And on the contrary those who have wrongfully abused these things and perverted them for their own purposes are not without good reason punished or destroyed, as the Book of Kings shows us has often happened. And that even life and death are in themselves indifferent the birth of S. John and of Judas proves. For in the case of the one his life was so profitable to himself that we are told that his birth brought joy to others also, as we read "And many shall rejoice at his birth; "[3] but of the life of the other it is said: "It were good for that man if he had never been born."[4] Further it is said of the death of John and of all saints "Right dear in the sight of the Lord is the death of His saints: "[5] but of that of Judas and men like him "The death of the wicked is very evil."[6] And how useful bodily

sickness sometimes may be the blessing on Lazarus, the beggar who was full of sores, shows us. For Scripture makes mention of no other good qualities or deserts of his, but it was for this fact alone; viz., that he endured want and bodily sickness with the utmost patience, that he was deemed worthy of the blessed lot of a place in Abraham's bosom.[7] And with regard to want and persecution and injuries which everybody thinks to be bad, how useful and necessary they are is clearly proved by this fact; viz., that the saints not only never tried to avoid them, but actually either sought them with all their powers or bravely endured them, and thus became the friends of God, and obtained the reward of eternal life, as the blessed Apostle chants: "For which cause I delight myself in my infirmities, in reproaches, in necessities, in persecutions, in distresses for Christ. For when I am weak, then I am strong, for power is made perfect in infirmity."[8] And therefore those who are exalted with the greatest riches and honours and powers of this world, should not be deemed to have secured their chief good out of them (for this is shown to consist only in virtue) but only something indifferent, because just as to good men who use them well and properly they will be found to be useful and convenient (for they afford them opportunities for good works and fruits which shall endure to eternal life), so to those who wrongfully abuse their wealth, they are useless and out of place, and furnish occasions of sin and death.

CHAPTER IV.

How evil cannot be forced on any one by another against his will.

PRESERVING then these distinctions clear and fixed, and knowing that there is nothing good except virtue alone, and nothing bad except sin alone and separation from God, let us now carefully consider whether God ever allows evil to be forced on his saints either by Himself or by some one else. And you will certainly find that this never happens. For another can never possibly force the evil of sin upon anyone, who does not consent and who resists, but only on one who admits it into himself through sloth and the corrupt desire of his heart. Finally, when the devil having exhausted all his wicked devices had tried to force upon the blessed Job this evil of sin, and had not only stripped him of all his worldly goods, but also after that terrible and

---

[1] 1 Tim. vi. 17-19.
[2] S. Luke xvi. 9.
[3] S. Luke i. 14.
[4] S. Matt. xxvi. 24.
[5] Ps. cxv. 6 (cxvi. 15).
[6] Ps. xxxiii. (xxxiv.) 32.
[7] Cf. S. Luke xvi. 20.
[8] 2 Cor. xii. 9, 10.

utterly unlooked for calamity of bereavement through the death of his seven children, had heaped upon him dreadful wounds and intolerable tortures from the crown of his head to the sole of his foot, he tried in vain to fasten on him the stain of sin, because he remained steadfast through it all, never brought himself to consent to blasphemy.

CHAPTER V.

An objection, how God Himself can be said to create evil.

GERMANUS: We often read in holy Scripture that God has created evil or brought it upon men, as is this passage: "There is none beside Me. I am the Lord, and there is none else: I form the light and create darkness, I make peace, and create evil." [1] And again: "Shall there be evil in a city which the Lord hath not done?" [2]

CHAPTER VI.

The answer to the question proposed.

THEODORE: Sometimes holy Scripture is wont by an improper use of terms to use "evils" for "affliction;" not that these are properly and in their nature evils, but because they are imagined to be evils by those on whom they are brought for their good. For when divine judgment is reasoning with men it must speak with the language and feelings of men. For when a doctor for the sake of health with good reason either cuts or cauterizes those who are suffering from the inflammation of ulcers, it is considered an evil by those who have to bear it. Nor are the spur and the whip pleasant to a restive horse. Moreover all chastisement seems at the moment to be a bitter thing to those who are chastised, as the Apostle says: "Now all chastisement for the present indeed seemeth not to bring with it joy but sorrow; but afterwards it will yield to them that are exercised by it most peaceable fruits of righteousness," and "whom the Lord loveth He chasteneth, and scourgeth every son whom He receiveth: for what son is there whom the father doth not correct?" [3] And so evils are sometimes wont to stand for afflictions, as where we read: "And God repented of the evil which He had said that He would do to them and

He did it not." [4] And again: "For Thou, Lord, are gracious and merciful, patient and very merciful and ready to repent of the evil," [5] i.e., of the sufferings and losses which Thou art forced to bring upon us as the reward of our sins. And another prophet, knowing that these are profitable to some men, and certainly not through any jealousy of their safety, but with an eye to their good, prays thus: "Add evils to them, O Lord, add evils to the haughty ones of the earth;" [6] and the Lord Himself says "Lo, I will bring evils upon them," [7] i.e., sorrows, and losses, with which they shall for the present be chastened for their soul's health, and so shall be at length driven to return and hasten back to Me whom in their prosperity they scorned. And so that these are originally evil we cannot possibly assert: for to many they conduce to their good and offer the occasions of eternal bliss, and therefore (to return to the question raised) all those things, which are thought to be brought upon us as evils by our enemies or by any other people, should not be counted as evils, but as things indifferent. For in the end they will not be what he thinks, who brought them upon us in his rage and fury, but what *he* makes them who endures them. And so when death has been brought upon a saint, we ought not to think that an evil has happened to him but a thing indifferent; which is an evil to a wicked man, while to the good it is rest and freedom from evils. "For death is rest to a man whose way is hidden." [8] And so a good man does not suffer any loss from it, because he suffers nothing strange, but by the crime of an enemy he only receives (and not without the reward of eternal life) that which would have happened to him in the course of nature, and pays the debt of man's death, which must be paid by an inevitable law, with the interest of a most fruitful passion, and the recompense of a great reward.

CHAPTER VII.

A question whether the man who causes the death of a good man is guilty, if the good man is the gainer by his death.

GERMANUS: Well then, if a good man does not only suffer no evil by being killed, but actually gains a reward from his suffering, how can we accuse the man who has done him no harm but good by killing him?

---

[1] Is. xlv. 6, 7. [2] Amos iii. 6. [3] Heb. xii. 6-11.

[4] Jonah iii. 10 (LXX.). [7] Jer. xi. 11.
[5] Joel ii. 13 (LXX.). [8] Job iii. 23 (LXX.).
[6] Is. xxvi. 15 (LXX.).

CHAPTER VIII.

The answer to the foregoing question.

THEODORE: We are talking about the actual qualities of things good and bad, and what we call indifferent; and not about the characters of the men who do these things. Nor ought any bad or wicked man to go unpunished because his evil deed was not able to do harm to a good man. For the endurance and goodness of a righteous man are of no profit to the man who is the cause of his death or suffering, but only to him who patiently endures what is inflicted on him. And so the one is justly punished for his savage cruelty, because he meant to injure him, while the other nevertheless suffers no evil, because in the goodness of his heart he patiently endures his temptation and sufferings, and so causes all those things, which were inflicted upon him with evil. intent, to turn out to his advantage, and to conduce to the bliss of eternal life.

CHAPTER IX.

The case of Job who was tempted by the devil; and of the Lord who was betrayed by Judas: and how prosperity as well as adversity is advantageous to a good man.

FOR the patience of Job did not bring any gain to the devil, through making him a better man by his temptations, but only to Job himself who endured them bravely; nor was Judas granted freedom from eternal punishment, because his act of betrayal contributed to the salvation of mankind. For we must not regard the result of the deed, but the purpose of the doer. Wherefore we should always cling to this assertion; viz., that evil cannot be brought upon a man by another, unless a man has admitted it by his sloth or feebleness of heart: as the blessed Apostle confirms this opinion of ours in a verse of Scripture: "But we know that all things work together for good to them that love God."[1] But by saying "All things work together for good," he includes everything alike, not only things fortunate, but also those which seem to be misfortunes: through which the Apostle tells us in another place that he himself has passed, when he says: "By the armour of righteousness on the right hand and on the left," i.e., "Through honour and dishonour, through evil report and good

report, as deceivers and yet true, as sorrowful but always rejoicing, as needy and yet enriching many:"[2] All those things then which are considered fortunate, and are called those "on the right hand," which the holy Apostle designates by the terms honour and good report; and those too which are counted misfortunes, which he clearly means by dishonour and evil report, and which he describes as "on the left hand," become to the perfect man "the armour of righteousness," if when they are brought upon him, he bears them bravely, because, as he fights with these, and uses those very weapons with which he seems to be attacked, and is protected by them as by bow and sword and stout shield against those who bring these things upon him, he secures the advantage of his patience and goodness, and obtains a grand triumph of steadfastness by means of those very weapons of his enemies which are hurled against him to kill him; and if only he is not elated by success or cast down by failure, but ever marches straightforward on the king's highway, and does not swerve from that state of tranquillity as it were to the right hand, when joy overcomes him, nor let himself be driven so to speak to the left hand, when misfortunes overwhelm him, and sorrow holds sway. For "Much peace have they that love Thy law, and to them there is no stumbling block."[3] But of those who shift about according to the character and changes of the several chances which happen to them, we read: "But a fool will change like the moon."[4] For just as it is said of men who are perfect and wise: "To them that love God all things work together for good,"[5] so of those who are weak and foolish it is declared that "everything is against a foolish man,"[6] for he gets no profit out of prosperity, nor does adversity make him any better. For it requires as much goodness to bear sorrows bravely, as to be moderate in prosperity: and it is quite certain that one who fails in one of these, will not bear up under the other. But a man can be more easily overcome by prosperity than by misfortunes: for these sometimes restrain men against their will and make them humble and through most salutary sorrow cause them to sin less, and make them better: while prosperity puffs up the mind with soothing but most pernicious 'flatteries and when men are secure in the prospect of their happiness dashes them to the ground with a still greater destruction.

---

[1] Rom. viii. 28.

[2] 2 Cor. vi. 7-10.
[3] Ps. cxviii. (cxix.) 165.
[4] Ecclus. xxvii. 11.
[5] Rom. viii. 28.
[6] Prov. xiv. 7 (LXX.).

CHAPTER X.

Of the excellence of the perfect man who is figuratively
spoken of as ambidextrous.

THOSE are they then who are figurately
spoken of in holy Scripture as ἀμφοτεροδέξιον,
i.e., ambidextrous, as Ehud is described in
the book of Judges "who used either hand as
the right[1] hand." And this power we also
can spiritually acquire, if by making a right
and proper use of those things which are fortunate, and which seem to be "on the right
hand," as well as of those which are unfortunate and as we call it "on the left hand," we
make them both belong to the right side, so
that whatever turns up proves in our case, to
use the words of the Apostle, "the armour of
righteousness." For we see that the inner
man consists of two parts, and if I may be
allowed the expression, two hands, nor can
any of the saints do without that which we
call the left hand: but by means of it the perfection of virtue is shown, where a man by
skilful use can turn both hands into right
hands. And in order to make our meaning
clearer, the saint has for his right hand his
spiritual achievements, in which he is found
when with fervent spirit he gets the better of
his desires and passions, when he is free from
all attacks of the devil, and without any effort
or difficulty rejects and cuts off all carnal sins,
when he is exalted above the earth and regards
all things present and earthly as light smoke
or vain shadows, and scorns them as what is
about to vanish away, when with an overflowing heart he not only longs most intensely
for the future but actually sees it the more
clearly, when he is more effectually fed on
spiritual contemplations, when he sees heavenly mysteries more brightly laid open to
him, when he pours forth his prayers to God
with greater purity and readiness, when he is
so inflamed with fervour of spirit as to pass
with the utmost readiness of soul to things
invisible and eternal, so as scarcely to believe
that he any longer remains in the flesh. He
has also a left hand, when he is entangled in
the toils of temptation, when he is inflamed
with the heat of desire for carnal lusts, when
he is set on fire by emotion towards rage and
anger, when he is overcome by being puffed
up with pride or vainglory, when he is oppressed by a sorrow that worketh death, when
he is shaken to pieces by the contrivances and
attacks of accidie, and when he has lost all
spiritual warmth, and grows indifferent with
a sort of lukewarmness and unreasonable grief

so that not only is he forsaken by good and
kindling thoughts, but acually Psalms, prayer,
reading, and retirement in his cell all pall
upon him, and all virtuous exercises seem by
an intolerable and horrible loathing to have
lost their savour. And when a monk is
troubled in this way, then he knows that he
is attacked "on the left hand." Anyone therefore who is not at all puffed up through the
aid of vainglory by any of those things on
the right hand which we have mentioned, and
who struggles manfully against those on the
left hand, and does not yield to despair and
give in, but rather on the other hand seizes
the armour of patience to practise himself in
virtue — this man can use both hands as right
hands, and in each action he proves triumphant and carries off the prize of victory from
that condition on the left hand as well as that
on the right. Such, we read, was the reward
which the blessed Job obtained who was certainly crowned (for a victory) on the right
hand, when he was the father of seven sons
and walked as a rich and wealthy man, and
yet offered daily sacrifices to the Lord for their
purification, in his anxiety that they might
prove acceptable and dear to God rather than
to himself, when his gates stood open to every
stranger, when he was "feet to lame and eyes
to blind,"[2] when the shoulders of the suffering were kept warm by the wool of his sheep,
when he was a father to orphans and a husband
to widows, when he did not even in his heart
rejoice at the fall of his enemy. And again
it was the same man who with still greater
virtue triumphed over adversity on the left
hand, when deprived in one moment of his
seven sons he was not as a father overcome
with bitter grief but as a true servant of God
rejoiced in the will of his Creator. When
instead of being a wealthy man he became
poor, naked instead of rich, pining away
instead of strong, despised and contemptible
instead of famous and honourable, and yet
preserved his fortitude of mind unshaken,
when, lastly, bereft of all his wealth and substance he took up his abode on the dunghill,
and like some stern executioner of his own
body scraped with a potsherd the matter that
broke out, and plunging his fingers deep into
his wounds dragged out on every side masses
of worms from his limbs. And in all this he
never fell into despair and blasphemy, nor
murmured at all against his Creator. Moreover also so little was he overcome by such a
weight of bitter temptations that the cloak
which out of all his former property remained
to cover his body, and which alone could be

---

[1] Judg. iii. 15, where the LXX. has ἀμφοτεροδέξιον.

[2] Job xxix. 15.

saved from destruction by the devil because he was clothed with it, he rent and cast off, and covered with it his nakedness which he voluntarily endured, which the terrible robber had brought upon him. The hair of his head too, which was the only thing left untouched out of all the remains of his former glory, he shaved and cast to his tormentor, and cutting off even that which his savage foe had left to him he exulted over him and mocked him with that celestial cry of his: "If we have received good at the hand of the Lord, should we not also receive evil? Naked came I out of my mother's womb, and naked shall I return thither. The Lord gave and the Lord hath taken away; as it hath pleased the Lord, so is it done; blessed be the name of the Lord." [1] I should also with good reason call Joseph ambidextrous, as in prosperity he was very dear to his father, affectionate to his brethren, acceptable to God; and in adversity was chaste, and faithful to the Lord, in prison most kind to the prisoners, forgetful of wrongs, generous to his enemies; and to his brethren who were envious of him and as far as lay in their powers, his murderers, he proved not only affectionate but actually munificent. These men then and those who are like them are rightly termed ἀμφοτεροδέξιον, i.e., ambidextrous. For they can use either hand as the right hand, and passing through those things which the Apostle enumerates can fairly say: "Through the armour of righteousness on the right hand and on the left, through honour and dishonour, through evil report and good report etc." And of this right and left hand Solomon speaks as follows in the Song of songs, in the person of the bride: "His left hand is under my head, and his right hand shall embrace me." [2] And while this passage shows that both are useful, yet it puts one under the head, because misfortunes ought to be subject to the control of the heart, since they are only useful for this; viz., to train us for a time and discipline us for our salvation and make us perfect in the matter of patience. But the right hand she hopes will ever cling to her to cherish her and hold her fast in the blessed embrace of the Bridegroom, and unite her to him indissolubly. We shall then be ambidextrous, when neither abundance nor want affects us, and when the former does not entice us to the luxury of a dangerous carelessness, while the latter does not draw us to despair, and complaining; but when, giving thanks to God in either case alike, we gain one and the same advantage out of good and bad fortune. And such that truly ambidextrous man, the teacher of the Gentiles, testifies that he himself was, when he says: "For I have learnt in whatsoever state I am, to be content therewith. I know both how to be brought low and I know how to abound: everywhere and in all things I am instructed both to be full and to be hungry, both to abound and to suffer need. I can do all things in Him which strengtheneth me." [3]

CHAPTER XI.

Of the two kinds of trials, which come upon us in a threefold way.

WELL then, though we say that trial is twofold, i.e., in prosperity and in adversity, yet you must know that all men are tried in three different ways. Often for their probation, sometimes for their improvement, and in some cases because their sins deserve it. For their probation indeed, as we read that the blessed Abraham and Job and many of the saints endured countless tribulations; or this which is said to the people in Deuteronomy by Moses: "And thou shalt remember all the way through which the Lord thy God hath brought thee for forty years through the desert, to afflict thee and to prove thee, and that the things that were in thy heart might be made known, whether thou wouldst keep His Commandments or no:" [4] and this which we find in the Psalms: "I proved thee at the waters of strife." [5] To Job also: "Thinkest thou that I have spoken for any other cause than that thou mightest be seen to be righteous?" [6] But for improvement, when God chastens his righteous ones for some small and venial sins, or to raise them to a higher state of purity, and delivers them over to various trials, that He may purge away all their unclean thoughts, and, to use the prophet's word, the "dross," which he sees to have collected in their secret parts, and may thus transmit them like pure gold, to the judgment to come, as He allows nothing to remain in them for the fire of judgment to discover when hereafter it searches them with penal torments according to this saying: "Many are the tribulations of the righteous." [7] And: "My son, neglect not the discipline of the Lord, neither be thou wearied whilst thou art rebuked by Him. For whom the Lord loveth He chastiseth, and scourgeth every son whom He receiveth. For what son is there whom the father doth not correct? But if ye are without chastisement, whereof all are partakers, then are ye bastards, and

---

[1] Job ii. 10; i. 21. [2] Cant. ii. 6.

[3] Phil. iv. 11–13. [6] Job xl. 3 (LXX.).
[4] Deut. viii. 2. [7] Ps. xxxiii. (xxxiv.) 19.
[5] Ps. lxxx. (lxxxi.) 7.

not sons."[1] And in the Apocalypse: "Those whom I love, I reprove and chasten."[2] To whom under the figure of Jerusalem the following words are spoken by Jeremiah, in the person of God: "For I will utterly consume all the nations among which I scattered thee: but I will not utterly consume thee: but I will chastise thee in judgment, that thou mayest not seem to thyself innocent."[3] And for this life-giving cleansing David prays when he says: "Prove me, O Lord, and try me; turn my reins and my heart."[4] Isaiah also, well knowing the value of this trial, says "O Lord, correct us but with judgment: not in Thine anger."[5] And again: "I will give thanks to thee, O Lord, for thou wast angry with me: Thy wrath is turned away, and Thou hast comforted me."[6] But as a punishment for sins, the blows of trial are inflicted, as where the Lord threatens that He will send plagues upon the people of Israel: "I will send the teeth of beasts upon them, with the fury of creatures that trail upon the ground:"[7] and "In vain have I struck your children: they have not received correction."[8] In the Psalms also: "Many are the scourges of the sinners:"[9] and in the gospel: "Behold thou art made whole: now sin no more, lest a worse thing happen unto thee."[10] We find, it is true, a fourth way also in which we know on the authority of Scripture that some sufferings are brought upon us simply for the manifestation of the glory of God and His works, according to these words of the gospel: "Neither did this man sin nor his parents, but that the works of God might be manifested in him:"[11] and again: "This sickness is not unto death, but for the glory of God that the Son of God may be glorified by it."[12] There are also other sorts of vengeance, with which some who have overpassed the bounds of wickedness are smitten in this life, as we read that Dathan and Abiram or Korah were punished, or above all, those of whom the Apostle speaks: "Wherefore God gave them up to vile passions and a reprobate mind:"[13] and this must be counted worse than all other punishments. For of these the Psalmist says: "They are not in the labours of men; neither shall they be scourged like other men."[14] For they

are not worthy of being healed by the visitation of the Lord which gives life, and by plagues in this world, as "in despair they have given themselves over to lasciviousness, unto the working of all error unto uncleanness,"[15] and as by hardening their hearts, and by growing accustomed and used to sin they have got beyond cleansing in this brief life and punishment in the present world: men, who are thus reproved by the holy word of the prophet: "I destroyed some of you, as God destroyed Sodom and Gomorrah, and you were as a firebrand plucked out of the burning: yet you returned not to Me, saith the Lord,"[16] and Jeremiah: "I have killed and destroyed thy people, and yet they are not returned from their ways."[17] And again: "Thou hast smitten them and they have not grieved: Thou hast bruised them and they refused to receive correction: they have made their faces harder than the rock, they have refused to return."[18] And the prophet seeing that all the remedies of this life will have been applied in vain for their healing, and already as it were despairing of their life, declares: "The bellows have failed in the fire, the founder hath melted in vain: for their wicked deeds are not consumed. Call them reprobate silver, for the Lord hath rejected them."[19] And the Lord thus laments that to no purpose has He applied this salutary cleansing by fire to those who are hardened in their sins, in the person of Jerusalem crusted all over with the rust of her sins, when He says: "set it empty upon burning coals, that it may be hot, and the brass thereof may be melted; and let the filth of it be melted in the midst thereof. Great pains have been taken, and the great rust thereof is not gone out, no not even by fire. Thy uncleanness is execrable: because I desired to cleanse thee, and thou art not cleansed from thy filthiness."[20] Wherefore like a skilful physician, who has tried all saving cures, and sees there is no remedy left which can be applied to their disease, the Lord is in a manner overcome by their iniquities and is obliged to desist from that kindly chastisement of His, and so denounces them saying: "I will no longer be angry with thee, and thy jealousy has departed from thee."[21] But of others, whose heart has not grown hard by continuance in sin, and who do not stand in need of that most severe and (if I may so call it) caustic remedy, but for whose salvation the instruction of the life-giving word is suffi-

---

[1] Heb. xii. 5–8.
[2] Rev. iii. 19.
[3] Jer. xxx. 11.
[4] Ps. xxv. (xxvi.) 2.
[5] The passage is not from Isaiah, but from Jer. x. 24.
[6] Is. xii. 1.
[7] Deut. xxxii. 24.
[8] Jer. ii. 30.
[9] Ps. xxxi. (xxxii.) 10.
[10] S. John v. 14.
[11] S. John ix. 3.
[12] S. John xi. 4.
[13] Rom. i. 26, 28.
[14] Ps. lxxii. (lxxiii.) 5.

[15] Eph. iv. 19.
[16] Amos iv. 11.
[17] Jer. xv. 7.
[18] Jer. v. 3.
[19] Jer. vi. 29, 30.
[20] Ezek. xxiv. 11–13.
[21] Ezek. xvi. 42.

cient — of them it is said: "I will improve them by hearing of their suffering."[1] We are well aware that there are other reasons also of the punishment and vengeance which is inflicted on those who have sinned grievously — not to expiate their crimes, nor wipe out the deserts of their sins, but that the living may be put in fear and amend their lives. And these we plainly see were inflicted on Jeroboam the son of Nebat, and Baasha the son of Ahiah, and Ahab and Jezebel, when the Divine reproof thus declares: "Behold, I will bring evil upon thee, and will cut down thy posterity, and will kill of Ahab every male, and him that is shut up and the last in Israel. And I will make thy house like the house of Jeroboam the son of Nebat and like the house of Baasha the son of Ahiah: for that which thou hast done to provoke Me to anger, and for making Israel to sin. The dogs also shall eat Jezebel in the field of Jezreel. If Ahab die in the city, the dogs shall eat him: but if he die in the field the birds of the air shall eat him,"[2] and this which is threatened as the greatest threat of all: "Thy dead body shall not be brought to the sepulchre of thy fathers."[3] It was not that this short and momentary punishment would suffice to purge away the blasphemous inventions of him who first made the golden calves and led to the lasting sin of the people, and their wicked separation from the Lord, — or the countless and disgraceful profanities of those others, but it was that by their example the fear of those punishments which they dreaded might fall on others also, who, as they thought little of the future or even disbelieved in it altogether, would only be moved by consideration of things present; and that owing to this proof of His severity they might acknowledge that there is no lack of care for the affairs of men, and for their daily doings, in the majesty of God on high, and so through that which they greatly feared might the more clearly see in God the rewarder of all their deeds. We find, it is true, that even for lighter faults some men have received the same sentence of death in this world, as that with which those men were punished who, as we said before, were the authors of a blasphemous falling away: as happened in the case of the man who gathered sticks on the Sabbath,[4] and in that of Ananias and Sapphira, who through the sin of unbelief kept back some portion of their goods: not that the guilt of their sins was equal, but because they were the first found out in a new kind of transgression, and

so it was right that as they had given to others an example of sin, so also they should give them an example of punishment and of fear, that anyone, who should attempt to copy them, might know that (even if his punishment were postponed in this life) he would be punished in the same way that they were at the trial of the judgment hereafter. And, since in our desire to run through the different kinds of trials and punishments we seem to have wandered somewhat from our subject, on which we were saying that the perfect man will always remain steadfast in either kind of trial, now let us return to it once more.

CHAPTER XII.

How the upright man ought to be like a stamp not of wax but of hard steel.

AND so the mind of the upright man ought not to be like wax or any other soft material which always yields to the shape of what presses on it, and is stamped with its form and impress and keeps it until it takes another shape by having another seal stamped upon it; and so it results that it never retains its own form but is turned and twisted about to correspond to whatever is pressed upon it. But he should rather be like some stamp of hard steel, that the mind may always keep its proper form and shape inviolate, and may stamp and imprint on everything which occurs to it the marks of its own condition, while upon it itself nothing that happens can leave any mark.

CHAPTER XIII.

A question whether the mind can constantly continue in one and the same condition.

GERMANUS: But can our mind constantly preserve its condition unaltered, and always continue in the same state?

CHAPTER XIV.

The answer to the point raised by the questioner.

THEODORE: It is needful that one must either, as the Apostle says, "be renewed in the spirit of the mind,"[5] and daily advance by "pressing forward to those things which are before,"[6] or, if one neglects to do this, the sure result will be to go back, and become

---

[1] Hos. vii. 12 (LXX.).
[2] 1 Kings xxi. 21-24.
[3] 1 Kings xiii. 22.
[4] Cf. Numb. xv. 32.
[5] Eph. iv. 23.
[6] Phil. iii. 13.

worse and worse. And therefore the mind cannot possibly remain in one and the same state. Just as when a man, by pulling hard, is trying to force a boat against the stream of a strong current he must either stem the rush of the torrent by the force of his arms, and so mount to what is higher up, or letting his hands slacken be whirled headlong down stream. Wherefore it will be a clear proof of our failure if we find that we have gained nothing more, nor should we doubt but that we have altogether gone back, whenever we find that we have not advanced upwards, because, as I said, the mind of man cannot possibly continue in the same condition, nor so long as he is in the flesh will any of the saints ever reach the height of all virtues, so that they continue unalterable. For something must either be added to them or taken away from them, and in no creature can there be such perfection, as not to be subject to the feeling of change; as we read in the book of Job: "What is man that he should be without spot, and he that is born of a woman that he should appear just? Behold among His saints none is unchangeable, and the heavens are not pure in His sight."[1] For we confess that God only is unchangeable, who alone is thus addressed by the prayer of the holy prophet "But Thou art the same,"[2] and who says of Himself "I am God, and I change not,"[3] because He alone is by nature always good, always full and perfect, and one to whom nothing can ever be added, or from whom nothing can be taken away. And so we ought always with incessant care and anxiety to give ourselves up to the acquirement of virtue, and constantly to occupy ourselves with the practice of it, lest, if we cease to go forward, the result should immediately be a going back. For, as we said, the mind cannot continue in one and the same condition, I mean without receiving addition to or diminution of its good qualities. For to fail to gain new ones, is to lose them, because when the desire of making progress ceases, there the danger of going back is present.

CHAPTER XV.

How one loses by going away from one's cell.

AND so we ought always to remain shut up in our cell. For whenever a man has strayed from it and returns fresh to it and begins again to live there he will be upset and dis-turbed. For if he has let it go he cannot without difficulty and pains recover that fixed purpose of mind, which he had gained when he remained in his cell; and as through this he has gone back, he will not think anything of the advance which he has missed, and which he would have secured if he had not allowed himself to leave his cell, but he will rather congratulate himself if he finds that he has regained that condition from which he fell away. For just as time once lost and gone cannot any more be recovered, so neither can those advantages which have been missed be restored: for whatever earnest purpose of the mind there may be afterwards, it will be the profit of the day then present, and the gain that belongs to the time that then is, and will not make up for the gain that has been once for all lost.

CHAPTER XVI.

How even celestial powers above are capable of change.

BUT that even the powers above are, as we said, subject to change is shown by those who fell from their ranks through the fault of a corrupt will. Wherefore we ought not to think that the nature of those is unchangeable, who remain in the blessed condition in which they were created, simply because they were not in like manner led astray to choose the worse part. For it is one thing to have a nature incapable of change, and another thing for a man through the efforts of his virtue, and by guarding what is good through the grace of the unchangeable God, to be kept from change. For everything that is secured or preserved by care, can also be lost by carelessness. And so we read: "Call no man blessed before his death,"[4] because so long as a man is still engaged in the struggle, and if I may use the expression, still wrestling — even though he generally conquers and carries off many prizes of victory, — yet he can never be free from fear, and from the suspicion of an uncertain issue. And therefore God alone is called unchangeable and good, as His goodness is not the result of effort, but a natural possession, and so He cannot be anything but good. No virtue then can be acquired by man without the possibility of change, but in order that when it once exists it may be continually preserved, it must be watched over with the same care and diligence with which it was acquired.

---

[1] Job xv. 14, 15. [2] Ps. ci. (cii.) 27. [3] Mal. iii. 6. [4] Ecclus. xi. 30.

CHAPTER XVII.

That no one is dashed to the ground by a sudden fall.

BUT we must not imagine that anyone slips and comes to grief by a sudden fall, but that he falls by a hopeless collapse either from being deceived by beginning his training badly, or from the good qualities of his soul failing through a long course of carelessness of mind, and so his faults gaining ground upon him little by little. For "loss goeth before destruction, and an evil thought before a fall,"[1] just as no house ever falls to the ground by a sudden collapse, but only when there is some flaw of long standing in the foundation, or when by long continued neglect of its inmates, what was at first only a little drip finds its way through, and so the protecting walls are by degrees ruined, and in consequence of long standing neglect the gap becomes larger, and break away, and in time the drenching storm and rain pours in like a river: for "by slothfulness a building is cast down, and through the weakness of hands the house shall drop through,"[2] And that the same thing happens spiritually to the soul the same Solomon thus tells us in other words, when he says: "water dripping drives a man out of the house on a stormy day."[4] Elegantly then does he compare carelessness of mind to a roof, and to tiles that have not been looked after, through which in the first instance only very slight drippings (so to speak) of the passions make their way to the soul: but if these are not heeded, as being but small and trifling, then the beams of virtues will decay and be carried away by a great tempest of sins, through which "on a stormy day," i.e., in the time of temptation, the devil's attack will assail us, and the soul will be driven forth from the abode of virtue, in which, as long as it preserved all watchful diligence, it had remained as in a house that belonged to it.

And so when we had heard this, we were so immensely delighted with our spiritual repast, that the mental pleasure with which we were filled by this conference outweighed the sorrow which we had experienced before from the death of the saints. For not only were we instructed in things about which we had been puzzled, but we also learnt from the raising of that question some things, which our understanding had been too small for us to ask about.

CONFERENCE VII.

FIRST CONFERENCE OF ABBOT SERENUS.

ON INCONSTANCY OF MIND, AND SPIRITUAL WICKEDNESS.

CHAPTER I.

On the chastity of Abbot Serenus.[3]

As we desire to introduce to earnest minds the Abbot Serenus, a man of the greatest holiness and continence, and one who answers like a mirror to his name, whom we admired above all others with peculiar veneration, we think that we only carry out our desire by the attempt to insert his conferences in our book. To this man beyond all other virtues, which shone forth not merely in his actions and manners, but by God's grace in his very look as well, there was granted by a special blessing the gift of continence, so that he never felt himself disturbed even by natural incitements even in sleep. And how it was that by the assistance of God's grace he attained such wondrous purity of the flesh, as it seems beyond the conditions of human nature, I think that I ought first of all to explain.

CHAPTER II.

The question of the aforesaid old man on the state of our thoughts.

THIS man then in his prayers by day and night, and in fasts and vigils unweariedly entreated for inward chastity of heart and soul, and seeing that he had obtained what he wished and prayed for, and that all the passions of carnal concupiscence in his heart were dead, was roused as it were by the sweetest taste of purity, and inflamed by his zeal for

---

[1] Prov. xvi. 18 (LXX.).
[2] Eccl. x. 18 (LXX.).
[3] Very little is known of Serenus but what is here told. Cf. the Vitæ Patrum, c. l.

[4] Prov. xxvii. 15 (LXX.).

chastity towards a yet more ardent desire, and began to apply himself to stricter fasts and prayers that the mortification of this passion which by God's grace had been granted to his inner man, might be extended also so as to include external purity, to such an extent that he might no longer be affected by any simple and natural movement, such as is excited even in children and infants. And by the experience of the gift he had obtained, which he knew he had secured by no merit of his labours, but by the grace of God, he was the more ardently stimulated to obtain this also in like manner, as he believed that God could much more easily tear up by the roots this incitement of the flesh, (which even by man's art and skill is sometimes destroyed by potions and remedies or by the use of the knife) since He had of His own free gift conferred that purity of spirit which is a still greater thing, and which cannot be acquired by human efforts and exertions. And when with unceasing supplications and tears he was applying himself unweariedly to the petition he had commenced, there came to him an angel in a vision by night, and seemed to open his belly, and to remove from his bowels a sort of fiery fleshly humour, and to cast it away, and restore everything to its place as before; and "lo" he said, "the incitements of your flesh are removed, and you may be sure that you have this day obtained that lasting purity of body for which you have faithfully asked." It will be enough thus briefly to have told this of the grace of God which was granted to this famous man in a special way. But I deem it unnecessary to say anything of those virtues which he possessed in common with other good men, for fear lest that particular narrative on this man's name might seem to deprive others of that which is specially mentioned of him. Him therefore, as we were inflamed with the greatest eagerness for conference with and instruction from him, we arranged to visit in Lent; and when he had very quietly inquired of us of the character of our thoughts and the state of our inner man, and what help we had got towards its purity from our long stay in the desert, we approached him with these complaints:

CHAPTER III.

Our answer on the fickle character of our thoughts.

THE time spent here, and the dwelling in solitude, and meditation, through which you think that we ought to have attained perfection of the inner man, has only done this for us; viz., teach us that which we are unable to be, without making us what we are trying to be. Nor do we feel that by this knowledge we have acquired any fixed steadfastness of the purity which we long for, or any strength and firmness; but only an increase of confusion and shame: for though our meditation in all our discipline aims at this in our daily studies, and endeavours from trembling beginnings to reach a sure and unwavering skill, and to begin to know something of what originally it knew but vaguely or was altogether ignorant of, and by advancing by sure steps (so to speak) towards the condition of that discipline, to habituate itself perfectly to it without any difficulty, I find on the contrary that while I am struggling in this desire for purity, I have only got far enough to know what I cannot be. And hence I feel that nothing but trouble results to me from all this contrition of heart, so that matter for tears is never wanting, and yet I do not cease to be what I ought not to be. And so what is the good of having learnt what is best, if it cannot be attained even when known? for when we have been feeling that the aim of our heart was directed towards what we purposed, insensibly the mind returns to its previous wandering thoughts and slips back with a more violent rush, and is taken up with daily distractions and incessantly drawn away by numberless things that take it captive, so that we almost despair of the improvement which we long for, and all these observances seem useless. Since the mind which every moment wanders off vaguely, when it is brought back to the fear of God or spiritual contemplation, before it is established in it, darts off and strays; and when we have been roused and have discovered that it has wandered from the purpose set before it, and want to recall it to the meditation from which it has strayed, and to bind it fast with the firmest purpose of heart, as if with chains, while we are making the attempt it slips away from the inmost recesses of the heart swifter than a snake. Wherefore we being inflamed by daily exercises of this kind, and yet not seeing that we gain from them any strength and stability in heart are overcome and in despair driven to this opinion; viz., to believe that it is from no fault of our own but from a fault of our nature that these wanderings of mind are found in mankind.

CHAPTER IV.

The discourse of the old man on the state of the soul and its excellence.

SERENUS: It is dangerous to jump to a conclusion and lay down the law hastily on the nature of anything before you have properly discussed the subject and considered its true character. Nor should you, looking only at your own weakness, hazard a conjecture instead of pronouncing a judgment based on the character and value of the practice itself, and others' experience of it. For if anyone, who was ignorant of swimming but knew that the weight of his body could not be supported by water, wished from the proof which his inexperience afforded, to lay down that no one composed of solid flesh could possibly be supported on the liquid element, we ought not therefore to think his opinion a true one, which he seemed to bring forward in accordance with his own experience, since this can be shown to be not merely not impossible but actually extremely easily done by others, by the clearest proofs and ocular demonstration. And so the νοῦς, i.e., the mind, is defined as ἀεικίνητος καὶ πολυκίνητος, i.e., ever shifting and very shifting: as it is thus described in the so called wisdom of Solomon in other words: καὶ γεῶδες σκῆνος βρίθει νοῦν πολυφρόντιδα, i.e., "And the earthly tabernacle weigheth down the mind that museth on many things."[1] This then in accordance with its nature can never remain idle, but unless provision is made where it may exercise its motions and have what will continually occupy it, it must by its own fickleness wander about and stray over all kinds of things until, accustomed by long practice and daily use — in which you say that you have toiled without result — it tries and learns what food for the memory it ought to prepare, toward which it may bring back its unwearied flight and acquire strength for remaining, and thus may succeed in driving away the hostile suggestion of the enemy by which it is distracted, and in persisting in that state and condition which it yearns for. We ought not then to ascribe this wandering inclination of our heart either to human nature or to God its Creator. For it is a true statement of Scripture, that "God made man upright; but they themselves found out many thoughts"[2] The character of these then depends on us ourselves, for it says "a good thought comes near to those that know it, but a prudent man will find it."[3] For where any-

thing is subject to our prudence and industry so that it can be found out, there if it is *not* found out, we ought certainly to set it down to our own laziness or carelessness and not to the fault of our nature. And with this meaning the Psalmist also is in agreement, when he says: "Blessed is the man whose help is from Thee: in his heart he hath disposed his ascents."[4] You see then that it lies in our power to dispose in our hearts either *ascents,* i.e., thoughts that belong to God, or *descents;* viz., those that sink down to carnal and earthly things. And if this was not in our power the Lord would not have rebuked the Pharisees, saying "Why do ye think evil in your hearts?"[5] nor wou. He have given this charge by the prophet, saying: "Take away the evil of your thoughts from mine eyes;" and "How long shall wicked thoughts remain in you?"[6] Nor would the character of them as of our works be taken into consideration in the day of judgment in our case as the Lord threatens by Isaiah: "Lo, I come to gather together their works and thoughts together with all nations and tongues;"[7] nor would it be right that we should be condemned or defended by their evidence in that terrible and dreadful examination, as the blessed Apostle says: "Their thoughts between themselves accusing or also defending one another, in the day when God shall judge the secrets of men according to my gospel."[8]

CHAPTER V.

On the perfection of the soul, as drawn from the comparison of the Centurion in the gospel.

OF this perfect mind then there is an excellent figure drawn in the case of the centurion in the gospel; whose virtue and consistency, owing to which he was not led away by the rush of thoughts, but in accordance with his own judgment either admitted such as were good, or easily drove away those of the opposite character, are described in this tropical form: "For I also am a man under authority, having soldiers under me: and I say to this man, Go, and he goeth; and to another, Come, and he cometh; and to my servant, Do this, and he doeth it."[9] If then we too strive manfully against disturbances and sins and can bring them under our own control and discretion, and fight and destroy the passions in our flesh, and bring under the sway of reason

---

[1] Wisdom ix. 15. [2] Eccl. vii. 29 (LXX.).
[3] Prov. xix. 7 (LXX.).

[4] Ps. lxxxiii. (lxxxiv.) 6. [7] Is. lxvi. 18.
[5] S. Matt. ix. 4. [8] Rom. ii. 15, 16.
[6] Is. i. 16; Jer. iv. 14. [9] S. Matt. viii. 9.

the swarm of our thoughts, and drive back from our breast the terrible hosts of the powers opposed to us by the life-giving standard of the Lord's cross, we shall in reward for such triumphs be promoted to the rank of that centurion spiritually understood, who, as we read in Exodus, was mystically pointed to by Moses: "Appoint for thee rulers of thousands, and of hundreds, and of fifties and of tens."[1] And so we too when raised to the height of this dignity shall have the same right and power to command, so that we shall not be carried away by thoughts against our will, but shall be able to continue in and cling to those which spiritually delight us, commanding the evil suggestions to depart, and they will depart, while to good ones we shall say "Come," and they will come: and to our servant also, i.e., the body we shall in like manner enjoin what belongs to chastity and continence, and it will serve us without any gainsaying, no longer arousing in us the hostile incitements of concupiscence, but showing all subservience to the spirit. And what is the character of the arms of this centurion, and for what use in battle they are, hear the blessed Apostle declaring: "The arms," he says, "of our warfare are not carnal, but mighty to God." He tells us their character; viz., that they are not carnal or weak, but spiritual and mighty to God. Then he next suggests in what struggles they are to be used: "Unto the pulling down of fortifications, purging the thoughts, and every height that exalteth itself against the knowledge of God, and bringing into captivity every understanding unto the obedience of Christ, and having in readiness to avenge all disobedience, when your obedience shall be first fulfilled."[2] And since though useful, it yet belongs to another time to run through these one by one, I only want you to see the different sorts of these arms and their characteristics, as we also ought always to walk with them girt upon us if we mean to fight the Lord's battles and to serve among the centurions of the gospel. "Take," he says "the shield of faith, wherewith ye may be able to quench all the fiery darts of the evil one."[3] Faith then is that which intercepts the flaming darts of lust, and destroys them by the fear of future judgment, and belief in the heavenly kingdom. "And the breastplate," he says, "of charity."[4] This indeed is that which going round the vital parts of the breast and protecting what is exposed

to the deadly wounds of swelling thoughts, keeps off the blows opposed to it, and does not allow the darts of the devil to penetrate to our inner man. For it "endureth all things, suffereth all things, beareth all things."[5] "And for an helmet the hope of salvation."[6] The helmet is what protects the head. As then Christ is our head, we ought always in all temptations and persecutions to protect it with the hope of future good things to come, and especially to keep faith in Him whole and undefiled. For it is possible for one who has lost other parts of the body, weak as he may be, still to survive: but even a short time of living is extended to no one without a head. "And the sword of the Spirit which is the word of God."[7] For it is "sharper than any two-edged sword, and piercing even to the dividing of soul and spirit, and of the joints and marrow, and is a discerner of the thoughts and intents of the heart:"[8] as it divides and cuts off whatever carnal and earthly things it may find in us. And whosoever is protected by these arms will ever be defended from the weapons and ravages of his foes, and will not be led away bound in the chains of his spoilers, a captive and a prisoner, to the hostile land of vain thoughts, nor hear the words of the prophet: "Why art thou grown old in a strange country?"[9] But he will stand like a triumphant conqueror in the land of thoughts which he has chosen. Would you understand too the strength and courage of this centurion, by which he bears these arms of which we spoke before as not carnal but mighty to God? Hear of the selection by which the King himself marks and approves brave men when he summons them to the spiritual combat. "Let," says He, "the weak say that I am strong;" and: "Let him who is the sufferer become a warrior."[10] You see then that none but sufferers and weak people can fight the Lord's battles, weak indeed with that weakness, founded on which that centurion of ours in the gospel said with confidence: "For when I am weak, then am I strong," and again, "for strength is made perfect in weakness."[11] Of which weakness one of the prophets says: "And he that is weak among them shall be as the house of David.[12] For the patient sufferer shall fight these wars, with that patience of which it is said "patience is necessary for you that doing the will of God you may receive the reward."[13]

---

[1] Exod. viii. 21.
[2] 1 Cor. x. 4-6.
[3] Eph. vi. 16.
[4] 1 Thess. v. 8.
[5] 1 Cor. xiii. 7.
[6] 1 Thess. v. 8.
[7] Eph. vi. 17.
[8] Heb. iv. 12.
[9] Baruch iii. 11.
[10] Joel ii. 10, 11 (LXX.).
[11] 2 Cor. xii. 9, 10.
[12] Zech. xii. 8.
[13] Heb. x. 36.

CHAPTER VI.

Of perseverance as regards care of the thoughts.

BUT we shall find out by our own experience that we can and ought to cling to the Lord if we have our wills mortified and the desires of this world cut off, and we shall be taught by the authority of those who in converse with the Lord say in all confidence: "My soul hath stuck close to Thee;" and: "I have stuck unto Thy testimonies, O Lord;" and: "It is good for me to stick fast to God;" and: "He who cleaveth to the Lord, is one spirit."[1] We ought not then to be wearied out by these wanderings of mind and relax from our fervour: for "he that tilleth his ground shall be filled with bread: but he that followeth idleness shall be filled with poverty."[2] Nor should we be drawn away from being intent on this watchfulness through a dangerous despair, for "in every one who is anxious there is abundance, for he who is pleasant and free from grief will be in want;" and again: "a man in grief labours for himself, and forcibly brings about his own destruction."[3] Moreover also: "the kingdom of heaven suffereth violence and the violent take it by force,"[4] for no virtue is acquired without effort, nor can anyone attain to that mental stability which he desires without great sorrow of heart, for "man is born to trouble,"[5] and in order that he may be able to attain to "the perfect man, the measure of the stature of the fulness of Christ"[6] he must ever be on the watch with still greater intentness, and toil with ceaseless carefulness. But to the fulness of this measure no one will ever attain, but one who has considered it beforehand and been trained to it now and has had some foretaste of it while still in this world, and being marked a most precious member of Christ, has possessed in the flesh an earnest of that "joint"[7] by which he can be united to His body: desiring one thing alone, thirsting for but one thing, ever bringing not only his acts but even his thoughts to bear on one thing alone; viz., that he may even now keep as an earnest that which is said of the blessed life of the saints hereafter; viz., that "God may be" to him "all in all."[8]

CHAPTER VII.

A question on the roving tendency of the mind and the attacks of spiritual wickedness.

GERMANUS: Perhaps this tendency of the mind to rove might to some extent be checked were it not that so great a swarm of enemies surrounded it, and ceaselessly urged it toward what it has no wish for, or rather whither the roving character of its own nature drives it. And since such numberless foes, and those so powerful and terrible, surround it, we should not fancy that it was possible for them to be withstood especially by this weak flesh of ours, were we not encouraged to this view by your words as if by oracles from heaven.

CHAPTER VIII.

The answer on the help of God and the power of free will.

SERENUS: No one who has experienced the conflicts of the inner man, can doubt that our foes are continually lying in wait for us. But we mean that they oppose our progress in such a way that we can think of them as only *inciting* to evil things and not *forcing*. But no one could altogether avoid whatever sin they were inclined to imprint upon our hearts, if a strong impulse was present to force (evil) upon us, just as it is to suggest it. Wherefore as there is in them ample power of inciting, so in us there is a supply of power of rejection, and of liberty of acquiescing. But if we are afraid of their power and assaults, we may also claim the protection and assistance of God against them, of which we read: "For greater is He who is in us than he who is in this world:"[9] and His aid fights on our side with much greater power than their hosts fight against us; for God is not only the suggester of what is good, but the maintainer and insister of it, so that sometimes He draws us towards salvation even against our will and without our knowing it. It follows then that no one can be deceived by the devil but one who has chosen to yield to him the consent of his own will: as Ecclesiastes clearly puts it in these words: "For since there is no gainsaying by those who do evil speedily, therefore the heart of the children of men is filled within them to do evil."[10] It is therefore clear that each man goes wrong from this; viz., that when evil thoughts assault him he does not immediately meet them with refusal and contradiction, for it says: "resist him, and he will flee from you."[11]

---

[1] Ps. xlii. (lxiii.) 9; cxviii. (cxix.) 31; lxxi. (lxxiii) 28; 1 Cor. vi. 17.
[2] Prov. xxviii. 19.
[3] Prov. xiv. 23; xvi. 26 (LXX.).
[4] S. Matt. xi. 12.
[5] Job v. 7.
[6] Eph. iv. 13.
[7] *Ibid.*
[8] 1 Cor. xv. 28.

[9] 1 John iv. 4.   [10] Eccl. viii. 11 (LXX.).   [11] S. James iv. 7.

CHAPTER IX.

A question on the union of the soul with devils.

GERMANUS: What, I pray you, is that indiscriminate and common union of the soul with those evil spirits, by which it is possible for them to be (I will not say joined with but) united to it in such a way that they can imperceptibly talk with it, and find their way into it and suggest to it whatever they want, and incite it to whatever they like, and look into and see its thoughts and movements; and the result is so close a union between them and the soul that it is almost impossible without God's grace to distinguish between what results from their instigation, and what from our free will.

CHAPTER X.

The answer how unclean spirits are united with human souls.

SERENUS: It is no wonder that spirit can be imperceptibly joined with spirit, and exercise an unseen power of persuasion toward what is allowed to it. For there is between them (just as between men) some sort of similarity and kinship of substance, since the description which is given of the nature of the soul, applies equally well to their substance. But it is impossible for spirits to be implanted in spirits inwardly or united with them in such a way that one can hold the other; for this is the true prerogative of Deity alone, which is the only simple and incorporeal nature.

CHAPTER XI.

An objection whether unclean spirits can be present in or united with the souls of those whom they have filled.

GERMANUS: To this idea we think that what we see happen in the case of those possessed is sufficiently opposed, when they say and do what they know not under the influence of the spirits. How then are we to refuse to believe that their souls are not united to those spirits, when we see them made their instruments, and (forsaking their natural condition) yielding to their movements and moods, in such a way that they give expression no longer to their own words and actions and wishes, but to those of the demons?

CHAPTER XII.

The answer how it is that unclean spirits can lord it over those possessed.

SERENUS: What you speak of as taking place in the case of demoniacs is not opposed to our assertion; viz., that those possessed by unclean spirits say and do what they do not want to, and are forced to utter what they know not; for it is perfectly clear that they are not subject to the entrance of the spirits all in the same way: for some are affected by them in such a way as to have not the slightest conception of what they do and say, while others know and afterwards recollect it. But we must not imagine that this is done by the infusion of the spirit in such a way that it penetrates into the actual substance of the soul and, being as it were united to it and somehow clothed with it, utters words and sayings through the mouth of the sufferer. For we ought not to believe that this can possibly be done by them. For we can clearly see that this results from no loss of the soul but from weakness of the body, when the unclean spirit seizes on those members in which the vigour of the soul resides, and laying on them an enormous and intolerable weight overwhelms it with foulest darkness, and interferes with its intellectual powers: as we see sometimes happen also from the fault of wine and fever or excessive cold, and other indispositions affecting men from without; and it was this which the devil was forbidden to attempt to inflict on the blessed Job, though he had received power over his flesh, when the Lord commanded him saying: "Lo, I give him into thine hands: only preserve his soul,"[1] i.e., do not weaken the seat of his soul and make him mad, and overpower the understanding and wisdom of what remains, by smothering the ruling power in his heart with your weight.

CHAPTER XIII.

How spirit cannot be penetrated by spirit, and how God alone is incorporeal.

FOR even if spirit is mingled with this crass and solid matter; viz., flesh (as very easily happens), should we therefore believe that it can be united to the soul, which is in like manner spirit, in such a way as to make it also receptive in the same way of its own nature: a thing which is possible to the

[1] Job ii. 6 (LXX.).

Trinity alone, which is so capable of pervading every intellectual nature, that it cannot only embrace and surround it but even insert itself into it and, incorporeal though it is, be infused into a body? For though we maintain that some spiritual natures exist, such as angels, archangels and the other powers, and indeed our own souls and the thin air, yet we ought certainly not to consider them incorporeal. For they have in their own fashion a body in which they exist, though it is much finer than our bodies are, in accordance with the Apostle's words when he says: "And there are bodies celestial, and bodies terrestrial:" and again: "It is sown a natural body, it is raised a spiritual body;" [1] from which it is clearly gathered that there is nothing incorporeal but God alone, and therefore it is only by Him that all spiritual and intellectual substances can be pervaded, because He alone is whole and everywhere and in all things, in such a way as to behold and see the thoughts of men and their inner movements and all the recesses of the soul; since it was of Him alone that the blessed Apostle spoke when he said: "For the word of God is quick and powerful and sharper than any two-edged sword, and piercing even to the dividing of soul and spirit and of the joints and marrow; and is a discerner of the thoughts and intents of the heart; and there is no creature invisible in His sight, but all things are naked and open to His eyes." [2] And the blessed David says: "Who fashioneth their hearts one by one;" and again: "For He knoweth the secrets of the heart;" [3] and Job too: "Thou who alone knowest the hearts of men." [4]

CHAPTER XIV.

An objection, as to how we ought to believe that devils see into the thoughts of men.

GERMANUS: In this way, which you describe, those spirits cannot possibly see into our thoughts. But we think it utterly absurd to hold such an opinion, when Scripture says: "If the spirit of him that hath power ascend upon thee;" [5] and again: "When the devil had put it into the heart of Simon Iscariot to betray the Lord." [6] How then can we believe that our thoughts are not open to them, when we feel that for the most part they spring up and are nursed by their suggestions and instigation?

CHAPTER XV.

The answer what devils can and what they cannot do in regard to the thoughts of men.

SERENUS: Nobody doubts that unclean spirits can influence the character of our thoughts, but this is by affecting them from without by sensible influences, i.e., either from our inclinations or from our words, and those likings to which they see that we are especially disposed. But they cannot possibly come near to those which have not yet come forth from the inmost recesses of the soul. And the thoughts too, which they suggest, whether they are actually or in a kind of way embraced, are discovered by them not from the nature of the soul itself, i.e., that inner inclination which lies concealed so to speak in the very marrow, but from motions and signs given by the outward man, as for example, when they suggest gluttony, if they have seen a monk raising his eyes anxiously to the window or to the sun, or inquiring eagerly what o'clock it is, they know that he has admitted the feeling of greediness. If when they suggest fornication they find him calmly submitting to the attack of lust, or see him perturbed in body, or at any rate not groaning as he ought under the wantonness of an impure suggestion, they know that the dart of lust is already fixed in his very soul. If they stir up incitements to grief, or anger, or rage, they can tell whether they have taken root in the heart by the movements of the body, and visible disturbances, when, for instance, they have noticed him either groaning silently, or panting with indignation or changing colour; and so they cunningly discover the fault to which he is given over. For they know that every one of us is enticed in a regular way by that one, to the incitement of which they see, by a sort of assenting motion of the body, that he has yielded his consent and agreement. And it is no wonder that this is discovered by those powers of the air, when we see that even clever men can often discover the state of the inner man from his mien and look and external bearing. How much more surely then can this be discovered by those who as being of a spiritual nature are certainly much more subtle and cleverer than men.

CHAPTER XVI.

An illustration showing how we are taught that unclean spirits know the thoughts of men.

FOR just as some thieves are in the habit of examining the concealed treasures of the

---

[1] 1 Cor. xv. 40, 44.
[2] Heb. iv. 12, 13.
[3] Ps. xxxii. (xxxiii.) 15 ; xliii. (xliv.) 22.
[4] 2 Chron. vi. 30.
[5] Eccl. x. 4.
[6] S. John xiii. 2.

men in those houses which they mean to rob, and in the dark shades of night sprinkle with careful hands little grains of sand and discover the hidden treasures which they cannot see by the tinkling sound with which they answer to the fall of the sand, and so arrive at certain knowledge of each thing and metal, which betrays itself in a way by the voice elicited from it; so these too, in order to explore the treasures of our heart, scatter over us the sand of certain evil suggestions, and when they see some bodily affection arise corresponding to their character, they recognize as if by a sort of tinkling sound proceeding from the inmost recesses, what it is that is stored up in the secret chamber of the inner man.

CHAPTER XVII.

On the fact that not every devil has the power of suggesting every passion to men.

BUT we ought to know this, that not all devils can implant all the passions in men, but that certain spirits brood over each sin, and that some gloat over uncleanness and filthy lusts, others over blasphemy, others are more particularly devoted to anger and wrath, others thrive on gloominess, others are pacified with vainglory and pride; and each one implants in the hearts of men that sin, in which he himself revels, and they cannot implant their special vices all at one time, but in turn, according as the opportunity of time or place, or a man, who is open to their suggestions, excites them.

CHAPTER XVIII.

A question whether among the devils there is any order observed in the attack, or system in its changes.

GERMANUS: Must we then believe that wickedness is arranged and so to speak systematized among them in such a way that there is some order in the changes observed by them, and a regular plan of attack carried out, though it is clear that method and system can only exist among good and upright men, as Scripture says: "Thou shalt seek wisdom among the ungodly and shalt not find it;" and: "our enemies are senseless;" and this: "There is neither wisdom, nor courage, nor counsel among the ungodly."[1]

---

[1] Prov. xiv. 6; Deut. xxxii. 31; Prov. xxi. 30 (LXX.).

CHAPTER XIX.

The answer how far an agreement exists among devils about the attack and its changes.

SERENUS: It is a true assertion that there is no lasting concord among bad men, and that perfect harmony cannot exist even in regard to those particular faults which have attractions for them all in common. For, as you have said, it can never be that system and discipline are preserved among undisciplined things. But in some matters, where community of interests, and necessity enforces it, or participation in some gain recommends it, they must arrange for some agreement for the time being. And we see very clearly that this is so in the case of this war of spiritual wickedness; so that not only do they observe times and changes among themselves, but actually are known specially to occupy some particular spots and to haunt them persistently: for since they must make their attacks through certain fixed temptations and well defined sins, and at particular times, we clearly infer from this that no one can at one and at the same time be deluded by the emptiness of vainglory and inflamed by the lust of fornication, nor at one and the same time be puffed up by the outrageous haughtiness of spiritual pride, and subject to the humiliation of carnal gluttony. Nor can anyone be overcome by silly giggling and laughter and at the same time be excited by the stings of anger, or at any rate filled with the pains of gnawing grief: but all the spirits must one by one advance to attack the soul, in such a way that when one has been vanquished and retreated, he must make way for another spirit to attack it still more vehemently, or if he has come forth victorious, he will none the less hand it over to be deceived by another.

CHAPTER XX.

Of the fact that opposite powers are not of the same boldness, and that the occasions of temptation are not under their control.

WE ought also not to be ignorant of this, that they have not all the same fierceness and energy, nor indeed the same boldness and malice, and that with beginners and feeble folk only the weaker spirits join battle, and when these spiritual wickednesses are beaten, then gradually the assaults of stronger ones are made against the athlete of Christ. For in proportion to a man's strength and progress, is the difficulty of the struggle made greater: for none of the saints could possibly be equal to the endurance of the malice of so many and so great foes, or meet their attacks, or even bear their cruelty and savagery, were it not that the merciful judge of our contest, and president of the games, Christ Himself, equalized the strength of the combatants, and repelled and checked their excessive attacks, and made with the temptation a way of escape as well that we might be able to bear it.[1]

CHAPTER XXI.

Of the fact that devils struggle with men not without effort on their part.

But our belief is that they undertake this struggle not without effort on their part. For in their conflict they themselves have some sort of anxiety and depression, and especially when they are matched with stronger rivals, i.e., saints and perfect men. Otherwise no contest or struggle, but only a simple deception of men, and one free from anxiety on their part would be assigned to them. And how then would the Apostle's words stand, where he says: "We wrestle not against flesh and blood, but against principalities, against powers, against world-rulers of this darkness, against spiritual wickedness in heavenly places;" and this too: "So fight I, not as one that beateth the air;" and again: "I have fought a good fight"?[2] For where it is spoken of as a fight, and conflict, and battle, there must be effort and exertion and anxiety on both sides, and equally there must either be in store for them chagrin and confusion for their failure, or delight consequent upon their victory. But where one fights with ease and security against another who struggles with great effort, and in order to overthrow his rival makes use of his will alone as his strength, there it ought not to be called a battle, struggle, or strife, but a sort of unfair and unreasonable assault and attack. But they certainly have to labour, and when they attack men, exert themselves in no lesser degree in order to secure from each one that victory which they want to obtain, and there is hurled back upon them the same confusion which was awaiting us had we been worsted by them; as it is said: "The head of their compassing me about, the labour of their own lips shall overwhelm them;" and: "His sorrow shall be turned on his own head;" and again: "Let the snare which he knoweth not come upon him, and let the net which he hath hidden catch him, and into that very snare let him fall;"[3] viz., that which he contrived for the de-

ception of men. They then themselves also come to grief, and as they damage us so are they also in like manner damaged by us, nor when they are worsted do they depart without confusion, and seeing these defeats of theirs and their struggles, one who had good eyes in his inner man, seeing also that they gloated over the downfall and mischances of individuals, and fearing lest his own case might furnish them with this kind of delight, prayed to the Lord saying: "Lighten mine eyes that I sleep not in death: lest mine enemy say, I have prevailed against him. They that trouble me will rejoice if I be moved;" and: "O My God, let them not rejoice over me; let them not say in their hearts, Aha, Aha, our very wish; neither let them say, we have devoured him;" and: "They gnashed their teeth upon me. Lord, how long wilt Thou look on this?" for: "he lieth in wait secretly as a lion in his den: he lieth in wait to ravish the poor;" and: "He seeketh from God his meat."[4] And again when all their efforts are exhausted, and they have failed to secure our deception, they must "be confounded and blush" at the failure of their efforts, "who seek our souls to destroy them: and let them be covered with shame and confusion who imagine evil against us."[5] Jeremiah also says: "Let them be confounded, and let not me be confounded: let them be afraid, and let not me be afraid: bring upon them the fury of Thy wrath, and with a double destruction destroy them."[6] For no one can doubt that when they are vanquished by us they will be destroyed with a double destruction: first, because while men are seeking after holiness, they, though they possessed it, lost it, and became the cause of man's ruin; secondly, because being spiritual existences, they have been vanquished by carnal and earthly ones. Each one then of the saints when he looks on the destruction of his foes and his own triumphs, exclaims with delight: "I will follow after mine enemies and overtake them: and I will not turn until they are destroyed. I will break them and they shall not be able to stand: they shall fall under my feet,"[7] and in his prayers against them the same prophet says: "Judge thou, O Lord, them that wrong me: overthrow them that fight against me. Take hold of arms and shield: and rise up to help me. Bring out the sword and shut up the way against them that persecute me: say to my soul, I am thy salvation."[8] And when by

---

[1] 1 Cor. x. 13. [2] Eph. vi. 12; 1 Cor. ix. 26; 2 Tim. iv. 7.
[3] Ps. cxxxix. (cxl.) 1^c vii. 17; xxxiv. (xxxv.) 8.

[4] Ps. xii. (xiii.) 4, 5; xxxiv. (xxxv.) 24, 28; 16, 17; ix. (x.) 9; ciii. (civ.) 21.
[5] Ps. xxxix. (xl.) 15; xxxiv. (xxxv.) 26; xxxix. (xl.), 15.
[6] Jer. xvii. 18.   [7] Ps. xvii. (xviii.) 38, 39.
[8] Ps. xxiv. (xxxv.) 1-3.

subduing and destroying all our passions we have vanquished these, we shall then be permitted to hear those words of blessing: "Thy hand shall be exalted over thine enemies, and all thine enemies shall perish." [1] And so when we read or chant all these and such like passages found in holy writ, unless we take them as written against those spiritual wickednesses which lie in wait for us night and day, we shall not only fail to draw from them any edification to make us gentle and patient, but shall actually meet with some dreadful consequence and one that is quite contrary to evangelical perfection. For we shall not only not be taught to pray for or to love our enemies, but actually shall be stirred up to hate them with an implacable hatred, and to curse them and incessantly to pour forth prayers against them. And it is terribly wrong and blasphemous to think that these words were uttered in such a spirit by holy men and friends of God, on whom before the coming of Christ the law was not imposed for the very reason that they went beyond its commands, and chose rather to obey the precepts of the gospel and to aim at apostolical perfection, though they lived before the dispensation of the time.

CHAPTER XXII.

On the fact that the power to hurt does not depend upon the will of the devils.

But that they have not the power of hurting any man is shown in a very clear way by the instance of the blessed Job, where the enemy did not venture to try him beyond what was allowed to him by the Divine permission; and it is evidenced by the confession of the same spirits contained in the records of the gospel, where they say: "If Thou cast us out, suffer us to go into the herd of swine." [2] And far more must we hold that they cannot of their own free will enter into any one of men who are created in the image of God, if they have not power to enter into dumb and unclean animals without the permission of God. But no one — I will not say of the younger men, whom we see living most steadfastly in this desert, but even of those who are perfect — could live alone in the desert, surrounded by such swarms of foes of this kind, if they had unlimited power and freedom to hurt and tempt us: and still more clearly is this supported by the words of our Lord and Saviour, which in the lowliness of the manhood He had assumed, He uttered to Pilate, when He

said: "Thou couldest have no power against Me at all, unless it were given thee from above." [3]

CHAPTER XXIII.

Of the diminished power of the devils.

But we have thoroughly discovered both by our own experience and by the testimony of the Elders that the devils have not now the same power as they had formerly during the early days of the anchorites, when yet there were only a few monks living in the desert. For such was their fierceness that it was witn difficulty that a few very steadfast men, and those advanced in years were able to endure a life of solitude. Since in the actual monasteries where eight or ten men used to live, their violence attacked them so and their assaults were experienced so frequently, and so visibly, that they did not dare all to go to bed at once by night, but took turns and while some snatched a little sleep, others kept watch and devoted themselves to Psalms and prayer and reading. And when the wants of nature compelled them to sleep, they awoke the others, and committed to them in like manner the duty of keeping watch over those who were going to bed. Whence we cannot doubt that one of two things has brought about this result not only in the case of us who seem to be fairly strong from the experience which our age gives us, but also in the case of younger men as well. For either the malice of the devils has been beaten back by the power of the cross penetrating even to the desert, and by its grace which shines everywhere; or else our carelessness makes them relax something of their first onslaught, as they scorn to attack us with the same energy with which they formerly raged against those most admirable soldiers of Christ; and by this deceit and ceasing from open attacks they do us still more damage. For we see that some have fallen into so sluggish a condition that they have to be coaxed by too gentle exhortations for fear lest they should forsake their cells and fall into more dangerous troubles, and wander and stray about and be entangled in what I would call grosser sins; and it is thought that a great thing is got from them if they can even with some listlessness remain in the desert, and the Elders often say to them as a great relief: Stop in your cells, and eat and drink and sleep as much as you like, [4] if only you will stay in them always.

---

[1] Micah v. 9.   [2] S. Matt. viii. 31.

[3] S. John xix. 11.
[4] So centuries later it is told of a Jesuit father that when one wanted to relax the strictness of his fast, he replied, " Eat an ox, but be a Christian."

CHAPTER XXIV.

Of the way in which the devils prepare for themselves an entrance into the bodies of those whom they are going to possess.

IT is clear then that unclean spirits cannot make their way into those whose bodies they are going to seize upon, in any other way than by first taking possession of their minds and thoughts. And when they have robbed them of fear and the recollection of God and spiritual meditation, they boldly advance upon them, as if they were dispossessed of all protection and Divine safeguard, and could easily be bound, and then take up their dwelling in them as if in a possession given over to them.

CHAPTER XXV.

On the fact that those men are more wretched who are possessed by sins than those who are possessed by devils.

ALTHOUGH it is a fact that those men are more grievously and severely troubled, who, while they seem to be very little affected by them in the body, are yet possessed in spirit in a far worse way, as they are entangled in their sins and lusts. For as the Apostle says: "Of whom a man is overcome, of him he is also the servant." Only that in this respect they are more dangerously ill, because though they are their slaves, yet they do not know that they are assaulted by them, and under their dominion. But we know that even saintly men have been given over in the flesh to Satan and to great afflictions for some very slight faults, since the Divine mercy will not suffer the very least spot or stain to be found in them on the day of judgment, and purges away in this world every spot of their filth, as the prophet, or rather God Himself says, in order that He may commit them to eternity as gold or silver refined and needing no penal purification. "And," says He, "I will clean purge away thy dross, and I will take away all thy tin; and after this thou shalt be called the city of the just, a faithful city." And again: "Like as silver and gold are tried in the furnace, so the Lord chooseth the hearts;" And again: "The fire tries gold and silver; but man is tried in the furnace of humiliation;" and this also: "For whom the Lord loveth He chasteneth, and scourgeth every son whom He receiveth."[1]

CHAPTER XXVI.

Of the death of the prophet who was led astray, and of the infirmity of the Abbot Paul, with which he was visited for the sake of his cleansing.

AND we see clear instance of this in the case of that prophet and man of God in the third book of Kings, who was straightway destroyed by a lion for a single fault of disobedience, in which he was implicated not of set purpose nor by the fault of his own will but by the enticement of another, as the Scripture speaks thus of him: "It is the man of God, who was disobedient to the mouth of the Lord, and the Lord delivered him to the lion, and it tare him according to the word of the Lord, which He spake."[2] In which case the punishment of the present offence and carelessness together with the reward of his righteousness, for which the Lord gave over his prophet in this world to the destroyer, are shown by the moderation and abstinence of the beast of prey, as that most savage creature did not dare even to taste the carcass that was given over to him. And of the same thing a very clear and plain proof has been given in our own days in the case of the Abbots Paul and Moses who lived in a spot in this desert called Calamus,[3] for the former had formerly dwelt in the wilderness which is hard by the city of Panephysis,[4] which we know had only recently been made a wilderness by an inundation of salt water; which whenever the north wind blew, was driven from the marshes and spreading over the adjacent fields covered the face of the whole district, so as to make the ancient villages, which on this very account had been deserted by all their inhabitants, look like islands. Here, then, the Abbot Paul had made such progress in purity of heart in the stillness and silence of the desert, that he did not suffer, I will not say a woman's face, but even the clothes of one of that sex to appear in his sight. For when as he was going to the cell of one of the Elders together with Abbot Archebius[5] who lived in the same desert, by accident a woman met him, he was so disgusted at meeting her that he dropped the business of his friendly visit which he had taken in hand and dashed back again to his own monastery with greater speed than a man would flee from the face of a lion or terrible dragon; so that he was not moved even by the shouts and prayers of the aforesaid Abbot Archebius who called him back to

---

[1] Is. i. 25, 26; Prov. xvii. 3 (LXX.); Ecclus. ii. 5; Heb. xii. 6.

[2] 1 Kings xiii. 26.   [4] Cf. on the Institutes IV. xxx.
[3] Cf. on the Institutes X. xxiv.   [5] On Archebius cf. the note on XI. ii.

go on with the journey they had undertaken to ask the old man what they had proposed to do. But though this was done in his eagerness for chastity and desire for purity, yet because it was done not according to knowledge, and because the observance of discipline, and the methods of proper strictness were overstrained, for he imagined that not merely familiarity with a woman (which is the real harm,) but even the very form of that sex was to be execrated, he was forthwith overtaken by such a punishment that his whole body was struck with paralysis, and none of his limbs were able to perform their proper functions, since not merely his hands and feet, but even the movements of the tongue, which enables us to frame our words, (were affected) and his very ears lost the sense of hearing, so that there was left in him nothing more of his manhood than an immovable and insensible figure. But he was reduced to such a condition that the utmost care of men was unable to minister to his infirmity, but only the tender service of women could attend to his wants: for when he was taken to a convent of holy virgins, food and drink, which he could not ask for even by signs, were brought to him by female attendants, and for the performance of all that nature required he was ministered to by the same service for nearly four years, i.e., to the end of his life. And though he was affected by such weakness of all his members that none of his limbs retained their keen power of motion and feeling, nevertheless such grace of goodness proceeded from him that when sick persons were anointed with the oil which had touched what should be called his corpse rather than his body, they were instantly healed of all diseases, so that as regards his own malady it was made clearly and plainly evident even to unbelievers that the infirmity of all his limbs was caused by the providence and love of the Lord, and that the grace of these healings was granted by the power of the Holy Ghost as a witness of his purity and a manifestation of his merits.

CHAPTER XXVII.

On the temptation of Abbot Moses.

BUT the second person whom we mentioned as living in this desert, although he was also a remarkable and striking man, yet, in order to punish a single word, to which in a dispute with Abbot Macarius,[1] he had given utterance

somewhat too sharply, as he was anticipated in some opinion, he was instantly delivered to so dreadful a demon that he filled his mouth with filth[2] which he supplied, and the Lord showed by the quickness of his cure, and the author of his healing, that He had brought this scourge upon him to purify him, that there might not remain in him any stain from his momentary error: for as soon as Abbot Macarius committed himself to prayer, quicker than a word the evil spirit fled away from him and departed.

CHAPTER XXVIII.

How we ought not to despise those who are delivered up to unclean spirits.

FROM which it plainly results that we ought not to hate or despise those whom we see to be delivered up to various temptations or to those spirits of evil, because we ought firmly to hold these two points: first, that none of them can be tempted at all by them without God's permission, and secondly that all things which are brought upon us by God, whether they seem to us at the present time to be sad or joyful, are inflicted for our advantage as by a most kind father and most compassionate physician, and that therefore men are, as it were, given into the charge of schoolmasters, and humbled in order that when they depart out of this world they may be removed in a state of greater purity to the other life, or have a lighter punishment inflicted on them, as they have been, as the Apostle says, delivered over at the present time " to Satan for the destruction of the flesh that the spirit may be saved in the day of the Lord Jesus."[3]

CHAPTER XXIX.

An objection, asking why those who are tormented by unclean spirits are separated from the Lord's communion.

GERMANUS: And how is it that we see them not only scorned and shunned by everybody, but actually always kept away from the Lord's communion in our provinces, in accordance with these words of the gospel: "Give not that which is holy to the dogs, neither cast your pearls before swine;"[4] while you tell us that somehow we ought to hold that the humiliation of this temptation is brought upon them with a view to their purification and profit?

---

[1] On Macarius see the note on the Institutes V. xli.   [2] *Humanas egestiones.*   [3] 1 Cor. v. 5.   [4] S. Matt. vii. 6.

CHAPTER XXX.

The answer to the question raised.

SERENUS: If we had this knowledge or rather faith, of which I treated above; viz., to believe that all things were brought about by God, and ordered for the good of our souls, we should not only never despise them, but rather pray without ceasing for them as our own members, and sympathize with them with all our hearts and the fullest affection (for "when one member suffers, all the members suffer with it"[1]), as we know that we cannot possibly be perfected without them inasmuch as they are members of us, just as we read that our predecessors could not attain the fulness of promise without us, as the Apostle speaks of them as follows: "And these all being approved by the testimony of faith, received not the promise, God providing some better thing for us that they should not be perfected without us."[2] But we never remember that holy communion was forbidden them; nay rather if it were possible, they thought that it ought to be given to them *daily;* nor indeed according to the words of the gospel which you incongruously apply in this sense "Give not that which is holy to dogs,"[3] ought we to believe that holy communion becomes food for the demon, and not a purification and safeguard of body and soul; for when it is received by a man it, so to speak, burns out and puts to flight the spirit which has its seat in his members or is trying to lurk in them. For in this way we have lately seen Abbot Andronicus and many others cured. For the enemy will more and more abuse the man who is possessed, if he sees him cut off from the heavenly medicine, and will tempt him more often and more fearfully, as he sees him removed the further from this spiritual remedy.[4]

CHAPTER XXXI.

On the fact that those men are more to be pitied to whom it is not given to be subjected to those temporal temptations.

BUT we ought to consider those men truly wretched and miserable in whose case, although they defile themselves with all kinds of sins and wickedness, yet not only is there no visible sign of the devil's possession shown in them, nor is any temptation propor-

tionate to their actions, nor any scourge of punishment brought to bear upon them. For they are vouchsafed no swift and immediate remedy in this world, whose "hardness and impenitent heart," being too much for punishment in this life, "heapeth up for itself wrath and indignation in the day of wrath and revelation of the righteous judgment of God," "where their worm dieth not, and their fire is not quenched."[5] Against whom the prophet as if perplexed at the affliction of the saints, when he sees them subject to various losses and temptations, and on the other hand sees sinners not only passing through the course of this world without any scourge of humiliation, but even rejoicing in great riches, and the utmost prosperity in everything, inflamed with uncontrollable indignation and fervour of spirit, exclaims: "But as for me, my feet had almost gone, my treadings had well nigh slipped. For I was grieved at the wicked, when I saw the peace of sinners. For there is no regard to their death, nor is there strength in their stripes. They are not in the labour of men, neither shall they be scourged like other men,"[6] since hereafter they shall be punished with the devils, to whom in this world it was not vouchsafed to be scourged in the lot and discipline of sons, together with men. Jeremiah also, when conversing with God on this prosperity of sinners, although he never professes to doubt about the justice of God, as he says "for Thou art just, O Lord, if I dispute with Thee," yet in his inquiry as to the reasons of this inequality, proceeds to say: "But yet I will speak what is just to Thee. Why doth the way of the wicked prosper? Why is it well with all them that transgress and do wickedly? Thou hast planted them and they have taken root: they prosper and bring forth fruit. Thou art near in their mouth and far from their reins."[7] And when the Lord mourns for their destruction by the prophet, and anxiously directs doctors and physicians to heal them, and in a manner urges them on to a similar lamentation and says: "Babylon is suddenly fallen: she is destroyed. Howl for her: take balm for her pain, if so she may be healed;" then, in their despair, the angels, to whom is entrusted the care of man's salvation, make reply; or at any rate the prophet in the person of the Apostles and spiritual men and doctors who see the hardness of their soul, and their impenitent heart: "We have healed Babylon: but she is not cured. Let us forsake her, and let us go every man to his own land because her judgment hath reached even to

---

1 1 Cor. xii. 26.　2 Heb. xi. 39, 40.　3 S. Matt. vii. 6.
4 The question whether the Holy Communion should ever be given to those possessed is discussed by S. Thomas Aquinas, in the Summa III. Q. lxxx. Art. 9, and answered in the affirmative, the authorities quoted in its favour being this passage from Cassian, and the third Canon of the 1st Council of Orange (A.D. 441).

5 Rom. ii. 5; Is. lxvi. 24.　6 Ps. lxxii. (lxxiii.) 2-5.　7 Jer. xii. 1, 2.

the heavens, and is lifted up to the clouds."[1] Of their desperate feebleness then Isaiah speaks in the Person of God to Jerusalem: "From the sole of the foot unto the top of the head there is no soundness therein: wounds and bruises and swelling sores: they are not bound up nor dressed nor fermented with oil."[2]

CHAPTER XXXII.

Of the different desires and wishes which exist in the powers of the air.

BUT it is clearly proved that there exist in unclean spirits as many desires as there are in men. For some of them, which are commonly called Plani,[3] are shown to be so seductive and sportive that, when they have taken continual possession of certain places or roads, they delight themselves not indeed with tormenting the passers by whom they can deceive, but, contenting themselves merely with laughing at them and mocking them, try to tire them out rather than to injure them: while some spend the night merely by harmlessly taking possession of men, though others are such slaves to fury and ferocity that they are not simply content with hurting the bodies of those, of whom they have taken possession, by tearing them in a dreadful manner, but actually are eager to rush upon those who are passing by at a distance, and to attack them with most savage slaughter: like those described in the gospel, for fear of whom no man dared to pass by that way. And there is no doubt that these and such as these in their insatiable fury delight in wars and bloodshed. Others we find affect the hearts of those whom they have seized with empty pride, (and these are commonly called Bacucei[4]) so that they stretch themselves up beyond their proper height and at one time puff themselves up with arrogance and pomposity, and at another time condescend in an ordinary and bland manner, to a state of calmness and affability: and as they fancy that they are great people and the wonder of everybody, at one time show by bowing their body that they are worshipping higher powers, while at another time they think that they are worshipped by others, and so go through all those movements which express true service either proudly or humbly. Others we find are not only keen for lies, but also inspire men with blasphemies. And of this we ourselves can

testify as we have heard a demon openly confessing that he had proclaimed a wicked and impious doctrine by the mouths of Arius and Eunomius. And the same thing we read that one of them openly proclaimed in the fourth book of Kings: "I will go forth," he said, "and will be a lying spirit in the mouth of all his prophets."[5] On which the Apostle, when reproving those who are deceived by them, adds as follows: "giving heed to seducing spirits and doctrines of devils speaking lies in hypocrisy."[6] And that there are other kinds of devils which are deaf and dumb the gospels testify. And that some spirits incite to lust and wantonness the prophet maintains saying: "The spirit of fornication deceived them and they went astray from their God."[7] In the same way the authority of Scripture teaches us that there are demons of the night and of the day and of the noonday:[8] But it would take too long to search through the whole of Scripture and run through the different kinds of them, as they are termed by the prophets onocentaurs, satyrs, sirens, witches, howlers, ostriches, urchins; and asps and basilisks in the Psalms; and are called lions, dragons, scorpions in the gospel, and are named by the Apostle the prince of this world, rulers of this darkness, and spirits of wickedness.[9] And all these names we ought not to take as given at random or hap-hazard, but as alluding to their fierceness and madness under the sign of those wild beasts which are more or less harmful and dangerous among us, and by comparing them to the poisonous wickedness or power which among other beasts or serpents, some pre-eminence in evil confers on them, they are called by their names, in such a way that to one is assigned the name of lion because of the fury of his rage and the madness of his anger, to another that of basilisk because of his deadly poison, which kills a person before it is perceived, and to another that of onocentaur or urchin or ostrich because of his sluggish malice.

CHAPTER XXXIII.

A question as to the origin of such differences in powers of evil in the sky.

GERMANUS: We certainly do not doubt that those orders which the Apostle enumerates refer to them: "For we wrestle not against flesh and blood, but against principalities,

---

[1] Jer. li. 8, 9.   [2] Is. i. 6.
[3] "Πλάνοι," "Seducers," if the reading be correct: but some MSS. have "Fauni."
[4] The origin of this term is obscure.

[5] 1 Kings xxii. 22.   [7] Hos. iv. 12.
[6] 1 Tim. iv. 1, 2.   [8] Ps. xc. (xci.) 5, 6.
[9] Cf. Is. xiii. 21, 22; xxxiv. 13, 15; Ps. xc. (xci.) 13; S. Luke x. 19; S. John xiv. 30. Eph. vi. 12.

against powers, against the world-rulers of this darkness, against spirits of wickedness in heavenly places:"[1] but we want to know whence comes such a difference between them, or how such grades of wickedness exist? Were they created for this, to meet with these orders of evil, and in some way to serve this wickedness?

CHAPTER XXXIV.

The postponement of the answer to the question raised.

SERENUS: Although your proposals would rob us of our whole night's rest, so that we should not notice the approach of the rising dawn, and should be tempted greedily to prolong our conference till sunrise, yet since the solving of the question raised, if we began to trace it out, would launch us on a wide and deep sea of questions, which the shortness of the time at our disposal would not permit us to traverse, I think it will be more convenient to reserve it for consideration another night, when by the raising of this question I shall receive from your very ready converse some spiritual joy and richer fruit, and we shall be able if the Holy Spirit grants us a prosperous breeze to penetrate more freely into the intricacies of the questions raised. Wherefore let us enjoy a little sleep, and so shake off the drowsiness that steals over our eyes, as the dawn approaches, and then we will go together to church, for the observance of Sunday bids us do this, and after service will come back, and as you wish, discuss with redoubled delight what the Lord may have given to us for our common improvement.

VIII.

THE SECOND CONFERENCE OF ABBOT SERENUS.

ON PRINCIPALITIES.

CHAPTER I.

Of the hospitality of Abbot Serenus.

WHEN we had finished the duties of the day, and the congregation had been dismissed from Church we returned to the old man's cell, and enjoyed a most sumptuous repast. For instead of the sauce which with a few drops of oil spread over it was usually set on the table for his daily meal, he mixed a little decoction and poured over it a somewhat more liberal allowance of oil than usual; for each of them when he is going to partake of his daily repast, pours those drops of oil on, not that he may receive any enjoyment from the taste of it (for so limited is the supply that it is hardly enough I will not say to line the passage of his throat and jaws, but even to pass down it) but that using it, he may keep down the pride of his heart (which is certain to creep in stealthily and surely if his abstinence is any stricter) and the incitements to vainglory, for as his abstinence is practised with the greater secrecy, and is carried on without anyone to see it, so much the more subtly does it never cease to tempt the man who conceals it. Then he set before us table salt, and three olives each: after which he produced a basket containing parched vetches which they call trogalia,[2] from which we each took five grains, two prunes and a fig apiece. For it is considered wrong for anyone to exceed that amount in that desert. And when we had finished this repast and had begun to ask him again for his promised solution of the question, "Let us hear," said the old man, "your question, the consideration. of which we postponed till the present time."

CHAPTER II.

Statements on the different kinds of spiritual wickednesses.

THEN GERMANUS: We want to know what is the origin of the great variety of hostile powers opposed to men, and the difference between them, which the blessed Apostle sums up as follows: "We wrestle not against flesh and blood, but against principalities, against powers, against the world-rulers of this darkness, against spiritual wickedness in hea-

---

[1] Eph. vi. 12.

[2] Cf. Horace, De Arte Poetica, l. 249.

venly places:"[1] and again: "Neither angels nor principalities nor powers nor any other creature, can separate us from the love of God which is in Christ Jesus our Lord."[2] Whence then arises the enmity of all this malice jealous of us? Are we to believe that those powers were created by the Lord for this; viz., to fight against men in these grades and orders?

CHAPTER III.

The answer on the many kinds of food provided in holy Scripture.

SERENUS: The authority of holy Scripture says on those points on which it would inform us some things so plainly and clearly even to those who are utterly void of understanding, that not only are they not veiled in the obscurity of any hidden meaning, but do not even require the help of any explanation, but carry their meaning and sense on the surface of the words and letters: but some things are so concealed and involved in mysteries as to offer us an immense field for skill and care in the discussion and explanation of them. And it is clear that God has so ordered it for many reasons: first for fear lest the holy mysteries, if they were covered by no veil of spiritual meaning, should be exposed equally to the knowledge and understanding of everybody, i.e., the profane as well as the faithful, and thus there might be no difference in the matter of goodness and prudence between the lazy and the earnest: next that among those who are indeed of the household of faith, while immense differences of intellectual power open out before them, there might be the opportunity of reproving the slothfulness of the idle, and of proving the keenness and diligence of the earnest. And so holy Scripture is fitly compared to a rich and fertile field, which, while bearing and producing much which is good for man's food without being cooked by fire, produces some things which are found to be unsuitable for man's use or even harmful unless they have lost all the roughness of their raw condition by being tempered and softened down by the heat of fire. But some are naturally fit for use in both states, so that even when uncooked they are not unpleasant from their raw condition, but still are rendered more palatable by being cooked and heated by fire. Many more things too are produced only fit for the food of irrational creatures, and cattle, and wild animals and birds, but utterly useless as food for men, which while still in their rough state without being in any way touched by fire, conduce to the health and life of cattle. And we can clearly see that the same system holds good in that most fruitful garden of the Scriptures of the Spirit, in which some things shine forth clear and bright in their literal sense, in such a way that while they have no need of any higher interpretation, they furnish abundant food and nourishment in the simple sound of the words, to the hearers: as in this passage: "Hear, O Israel, the Lord thy God is one Lord;" and: "Thou shalt love the Lord thy God with all thy heart, and with all thy soul, and with all thy strength."[3] But there are some which, unless they are weakened down by an allegorical interpretation, and softened by the trial of the fire of the spirit cannot become wholesome food for the inner man without injury and loss to him; and damage rather than profit will accrue to him from receiving them: as with this passage: " But let your loins be girded up and your lights burning;" and: " whosoever has no sword, let him sell his coat and buy himself a sword;" and: "whosoever taketh not up his cross and followeth after Me is not worthy of Me;"[4] a passage which some most earnest monks, having "indeed a zeal for God, but not according to knowledge"[5] understood literally, and so made themselves wooden crosses, and carried them about constantly on their shoulders, and so were the cause not of edification but of ridicule on the part of all who saw them. But some are capable of being taken suitable and properly in both ways, i.e., the historical and allegorical, so that either explanation furnishes a healing draught to the soul; as this passage: "If any one shall smite thee on the right cheek, turn to him the other also;" and: "when they persecute you in one city, flee to another;" and: "if thou wilt be perfect, go, sell all that thou hast and give to the poor, and thou shalt have treasure in heaven, and come follow Me."[6] It produces indeed "grass for the cattle" also, (and of this food all the fields of Scripture are full); viz., plain and simple narratives of history, by which simple folk, and those who are incapable of perfect and sound understanding (of whom it is said "Thou, Lord, wilt save both man and beast")[7] may be made stronger and more vigorous for their hard work and the labour of actual life, in accordance with the state and measure of their capacity.

---

[1] Eph. vi. 12.   [2] Rom. viii. 38, 39.

[3] Deut. vi. 4, 5.   [4] S. Luke xii. 35; xxii. 36; S. Matt. x. 38.
[5] Rom. x. 2. [6] S. Matt. v. 39; x. 23; xix. 21. [7] Ps. xxxv. (xxxvi.) 7.

CHAPTER IV.

Of the double sense in which Holy Scripture may be taken.

WHEREFORE on those passages which are brought forward with a clear explanation we also can constantly lay down the meaning and boldly state our own opinions. But those which the Holy Spirit, reserving for our meditation and exercise, has inserted in holy Scripture with veiled meaning, wishing some of them to be gathered from various proofs and conjectures, ought to be step by step and carefully brought together, so that their assertions and proofs may be arranged by the discretion of the man who is arguing or supporting them. For sometimes when a difference of opinion is expressed on one and the same subject, either view may be considered reasonable and be held without injury to the faith either firmly, or doubtfully, i.e., in such a way that neither is full belief nor absolute rejection accorded to it, and the second view need not interfere with the former, if neither of them is found to be opposed to the faith: as in this case: where Elias came in the person of John,[1] and is again to be the precursor of the Lord's Advent: and in the matter of the "Abomination of desolation" which "stood in the holy place," by means of that idol of Jupiter which, as we read, was placed in the temple in Jerusalem, and which is again to stand in the Church through the coming of Antichrist,[2] and all those things which follow in the gospel, which we take as having been fulfilled before the captivity of Jerusalem and still to be fulfilled at the end of this world. In which matters neither view is opposed to the other, nor does the first interpretation interfere with the second.

CHAPTER V.

Of the fact that the question suggested ought to be included among those things to be held in a neutral or doubtful way.

AND therefore since the question raised by us, does not seem to have been sufficiently or often ventilated among men, and is not clear to most people, and from this fact what we bring forward may perhaps appear to some to be doubtful, we ought to regulate our own view (since it does not interfere with faith in the Trinity) so that it may be included among those things which are to be held doubtfully; although they rest not on mere opinions such as are usually given to guesses and conjectures, but on clear Scripture proof.

CHAPTER VI

Of the fact that nothing is created evil by God.

GOD forbid that we should admit that God has created anything which is substantially evil, as Scripture says "everything that God had made was very good."[3] For if they were created by God such as they are now, or made for this purpose; viz., to occupy these positions of malice, and ever to be ready for the deception and ruin of men, we should in opposition to the view of the above quoted Scripture slander God as the Creator and author of evil, as having Himself formed utterly evil wills and natures, creating them for this very purpose; viz., that they might ever persist in their wickedness and never pass over to the feeling of a good will. The following reason then of this diversity is what we received from the tradition of the fathers, being drawn from the fount of Holy Scripture.

CHAPTER VII.

Of the origin of principalities or powers.

NONE of the faithful question the fact that before the formation of this visible creation God made spiritual and celestial powers, in order that owing to the very fact that they knew that they had been formed out of nothing by the goodness of the Creator for such glory and bliss, they might render to Him continual thanks and ceaselessly continue to praise Him. For neither should we imagine that God for the first time began to originate His creation and work with the formation of this world, as if in those countless ages beforehand He had taken no thought of Providence and the divine ordering of things, and as if we could believe that having none towards whom to show the blessings of His goodness, He had been solitary, and a stranger to all bountifulness; a thing which is too poor and unsuitable to fancy of that boundless and eternal and incomprehensible Majesty; as the Lord Himself says of these powers: "When the stars were made together, all my angels praised Me with a loud voice."[4] Those then who were present at the creation of the stars, are most clearly proved to have been created before that "beginning" in which it is said that heaven and earth were made, inasmuch as they are said with loud voices and admiration to have praised the Creator because of all those visible creatures which, as they saw,

---

[1] Cf. S. Matt. xi. 14.
[2] See Dan. ix. 27; 2 Macc. vi. 2; S. Matt. xxiv. 15 *sq.*

[3] Gen. i. 31.　　[4] Job xxxviii. 7 (LXX.).

proceeded forth from nothing. Before then that beginning in time which is spoken of by Moses, and which according to the historic and Jewish interpretation denotes the age of this world (without prejudice to *our* interpretation, according to which we explain that the "beginning," of all things is Christ, in whom the Father created all things, as it is said "All things were made by him, and without Him was not anything made,")[1] before, I say, that beginning of Genesis in time there is no question that God had already created all those powers and heavenly virtues; which the Apostle enumerates in order and thus describes: "For in Christ were created all things both in heaven and on earth, visible and invisible, whether they be angels or archangels, whether they be thrones or dominions, whether they be principalities or powers. All things were made by Him and in Him."[2]

CHAPTER VIII.

Of the fall of the devil and the angels.

AND so we are clearly shown that out of that number of them some of the leaders fell, by the lamentations of Ezekiel and Isaiah, in which we know that the prince of Tyre or that Lucifer who rose in the morning is lamented with a doleful plaint: and of him the Lord speaks as follows to Ezekiel: "Son of man, take up a lamentation over the prince of Tyre, and say to him: Thus saith the Lord God: Thou wast the seal of resemblance, full of wisdom, perfect in beauty. Thou wast in the pleasures of the paradise of God: every precious stone was thy covering: the sardius, the topaz and the jasper, the chrysolyte and the onyx and the beryl, the sapphire and the carbuncle and the emerald: gold the work of thy beauty, and thy pipes were prepared in the day that thou wast created. Thou wast a cherub stretched out and protecting, and I set thee in the holy mountain of God, thou hast walked in the midst of the stones of fire. Thou wast perfect in thy ways from the day of thy creation, until iniquity was found in thee. By the multitude of thy merchandise thy inner parts were filled with iniquity and thou hast sinned; and I cast thee out from the mountain of God, and destroyed thee, O covering cherub, out of the midst of the stones of fire. And thy heart was lifted up with thy beauty: thou hast lost thy wisdom in thy beauty, I have cast thee to the ground: I have set thee before the face of kings, that they

might behold thee. Thou hast defiled thy sanctuaries by the multitude of thy iniquities and by the iniquity of thy traffic."[3] Isaiah also says of another: "How art thou fallen from heaven, O Lucifer, who didst rise in the morning? how art thou fallen to the ground, that didst wound the nations? and thou saidst in thine heart, I will ascend into heaven, I will exalt my throne above the stars of God, I will sit in the mountain of the covenant, in the sides of the north. I will ascend above the heights of the clouds. I will be like the Most High."[4] But Holy Scripture relates that these fell not alone from that summit of their station in bliss, as it tells us that the dragon dragged down together with himself the third part of the stars.[5] One of the Apostles too says still more plainly: "But the angels who kept not their first estate, but left their own dwelling, He hath reserved in everlasting chains under darkness to the judgment of the great day."[6] This too which is said to us: "But ye shall die like men and fall like one of the princes,"[7] what does it imply but that many princes have fallen? And by these testimonies we can gather the reason for this diversity; viz., either that they still retain those differences of rank (which adverse powers are said to possess, after the manner of holy and heavenly virtues) from the station of their former rank in which they were severally created, or else that, though themselves cast down from heavenly places, yet, as a reward for that wickedness of theirs in which they have graduated in evil, they claim in perversity these grades and titles of rank among themselves, by way of copying those virtues which have stood firm there.

CHAPTER IX.

An objection stating that the fall of the devil took its origin from the deception of God.

GERMANUS: Up till now we used to believe that the reason and commencement of the ruin and fall of the devil, in which he was cast out from his heavenly estate, was more particularly envy, when in his spiteful subtlety he deceived Adam and Eve.

CHAPTER X.

The answer about the beginning of the devil's fall.

SERENUS: The passage in Genesis shows that that was not the beginning of his fall and

---

[1] S. John i. 3.   [2] Col. i. 16.

[3] Ezek. xxviii. 11-18.   [4] Is. xiv. 12-14.   [5] Cf. Rev. xii. 4.
[6] Ep. of S. Jude, ver. 6.   [7] Ps. lxxxi. (lxxx.) 7.

ruin, as before their deception it takes the view that he had already been branded with the ignominy of the name of the serpent, where it says: "But the serpent was wiser" or as the Hebrew copies express it, "more subtle than all the beasts of the earth, which the Lord God had made."[1] You see then that he had fallen away from his angelic holiness even before he deceived the first man, so that he not only deserved to be stamped with the ignominy of this title, but actually excelled all other beasts of the earth in the subterfuges of wickedness. For Holy Scripture would not have designated a good angel by such a term, nor would it say of those who were still continuing in that state of bliss: "But the serpent was wiser than all the beasts of the earth." For this title could not possibly be applied I say not to Gabriel or Michael, but it would not even be suitable to any good man. And so the title of serpent and the comparison to beasts most clearly suggests not the dignity of an angel but the infamy of an apostate. Finally the occasion of the envy and seduction, which led him to deceive man, arose from the ground of his previous fall, in that he saw that man, who had but recently been formed out of the dust of the ground, was to be called to that glory, from which he remembered that he himself, while still one of the princes, had fallen. And so that first fall of his, which was due to pride, and which obtained for him the name of the serpent, was followed by a second owing to envy: and as this one found him still in the possession of something upright so that he could enjoy some interchange of conference and counsel with man, by the Lord's sentence he was very properly cast down to the lowest depth, that he might no longer walk as before erect, and looking up on high, but should cleave to the ground and creep along, and be brought low upon his belly and feed upon the earthly food and works of sins, and henceforward proclaim his secret hostility, and put between himself and man an enmity that is to our advantage, and a discord that is to our profit, so that while men are on their guard against him as a dangerous enemy, he can no longer injure them by a deceptive show of friendship.

CHAPTER XI.

The punishment of the deceiver and the deceived.

BUT we ought in this matter, in order that we may shun evil counsels, to learn a special

lesson from the fact that though the author of the deception was visited with a fitting punishment and condemnation, yet still the one who was led astray did not go scot free from punishment, although it was somewhat lighter than that of him who was the author of the deception. And this we see was very plainly expressed. For Adam who was deceived, or rather (to use the Apostle's words) "was *not* deceived" but, acquiescing in the wishes of her who was deceived, seems to have come to yield a consent that was deadly, is only condemned to labour and the sweat of his brow, which is assigned to him not by means of a curse upon himself, but by means of a curse upon the ground, and its barrenness. But the woman, who persuaded him to this, is visited with an increase of anguish, and pains and sorrow, and also given over to the yoke of perpetual subjection. But the serpent who was the first to incite them to this offence, is punished by a lasting curse. Wherefore we should with the utmost care and circumspection be on our guard against evil counsels, for as they bring punishment upon their authors, so too they do not suffer those who are deceived by them to go free from guilt and punishment.

CHAPTER XII.

Of the crowd of the devils, and the disturbance which they always raise in our atmosphere.

BUT the atmosphere which extends between heaven and earth is ever filled with a thick crowd of spirits, which do not fly about in it quietly or idly, so that most fortunately the divine providence has withdrawn them from human sight. For through fear of their attacks, or horror at the forms, into which they transform and turn themselves at will, men would either be driven out of their wits by an insufferable dread, and faint away, from inability to look on such things with bodily eyes, or else would daily grow worse and worse, and be corrupted by their constant example and by imitating them, and thus there would arise a sort of dangerous familiarity and deadly intercourse between men and the unclean powers of the air, whereas those crimes which are now committed among men, are concealed either by walls and enclosures or by distance and space, or by some shame and confusion: but if they could always look on them with open face, they would be stimulated to a greater pitch of insanity, as there would not be a single moment in which they would see them desist from their

[1] Gen. iii. 1.

wickedness, since no bodily weariness, or occupation in business or care for their daily food (as in our case) forces them sometimes even against their will to desist from the purposes they have begun to carry out.

CHAPTER XIII.

Of the fact that opposing powers turn the attack, which they aim at men, even against each other.

FOR it is quite clear that they aim these attacks, with which they assault men, even against each other, for in like manner they do not cease to promote with unwearied strife the discords and struggles which they have undertaken for some peoples because of a sort of innate love of wickedness which they have: and this we read of as being very clearly set forth in the vision of Daniel the prophet, where the angel Gabriel speaks as follows: "Fear not, Daniel: for from the first day that thou didst set thy heart to understand, to afflict thyself in the sight of thy God, thy words have been heard: and I am come for thy words. But the prince of the kingdom of the Persians resisted me one and twenty days: and behold Michael one of the chief princes came to help me, and I remained there by the king of the Persians. But I am come to teach thee what things shall befall thy people in the latter days."[1] And we cannot possibly doubt that this prince of the kingdom of the Persians was a hostile power, which favoured the nation of the Persians an enemy of God's people; for in order to hinder the good which it saw would result from the solution of the question for which the prophet prayed the Lord, by the archangel, in its jealousy it opposed itself to prevent the saving comfort of the angel from reaching Daniel too speedily, and from strengthening the people of God, over which the archangel Gabriel was: and the latter said that even then, owing to the fierceness of his assaults, he would not have been able to come to him, had not Michael the archangel come to help him, and met the prince of the kingdom of the Persians, and joined battle with him, and intervened, and defended him from his attack, and so enabled him to come to instruct the prophet after twenty-one days. And a little later on it says: "And the angel said: Dost thou know wherefore I am come to thee? And now I will return to fight against the prince of the Persians. For when I went forth, there appeared the prince of the Greeks coming. But I will tell thee what is written

down in the Scriptures of truth: and none is my helper in all these things but Michael your prince."[2] And again: "At that time shall Michael rise up, the great prince, who standeth for the children of thy people."[3] So then we read that in the same way another was called the prince of the Greeks, who since he was patron of that nation which was subject to him seems to have been opposed to the nation of the Persians as well as to the people of Israel. From which we clearly see that antagonistic powers raise against each other those quarrels of nations, and conflicts and dissensions, which they show among themselves at their instigation, and that they either exult at their victories or are cast down at their defeats, and thus cannot live in harmony among themselves, while each of them is always striving with restless jealousy on behalf of those whom he presides over, against the patron of some other nation.

CHAPTER XIV.

How it is that spiritual wickednesses obtained the names of powers or principalities.

WE can then see clear reasons, in addition to those ideas which we expounded above, why they are called principalities or powers; viz., because they rule and preside over different nations, and at least hold sway over inferior spirits and demons, of which the gospels give us evidence by their own confession that there exist legions. For they could not be called lords unless they had some over whom to exercise the sway of lordship; nor could they be called powers or principalities, unless there were some over whom they could claim power: and this we find pointed out very clearly in the gospel by the Pharisees in their blasphemy: "He casteth out devils by Beelzebub the prince of the devils,"[4] for we find that they are also called "rulers of darkness,"[5] and that one of them is styled "the prince of this world."[6] But the blessed Apostle declares that hereafter, when all things shall be subdued to Christ, these orders shall be destroyed, saying: "When He shall have delivered up the kingdom to God even the Father, when He shall have destroyed all principalities and powers and dominions."[7] And this certainly can only take place if they are removed from the sway of those over whom we know that powers and dominions and principalities take charge in this world.

---

[1] Dan. x. 12-14.

[2] Dan. x. 20, 21. [4] S. Luke xi. 15. [6] S. John xiv. 30.
[3] Dan. xii. 1. [5] Eph. vi. 12. [7] 1 Cor. xv. 24.

CHAPTER XV.

Of the fact that it is not without reason that the names of angels and archangels are given to holy and heavenly powers.

FOR no one doubts that not without cause or reason are the same titles of rank assigned to the better sort, and that they are names of office and of worth or dignity, for it is plain that they are termed angels, i.e., messengers from their office of bearing messages, and the appropriateness of the name teaches that they are "archangels" because they preside over angels, "dominions" because they hold dominion over certain persons, and "principalities" because they have some to be princes over, and "thrones" because they are so near to God and so privy and close to Him that the Divine Majesty specially rests in them as in a Divine throne, and in a way reclines surely on them.

CHAPTER XVI.

Of the subjection of the devils, which they show to their own princes, as seen in a brother's victim.

BUT that unclean spirits are ruled over by worse powers and are subject to them we not only find from those passages of Scripture, recorded in the gospels when the Pharisees maligned the Lord, and He answered "If I by Beelzebub the prince of the devils cast out devils,"[1] but we are also taught this by clear visions and many experiences of the saints, for when one of our brethren was making a journey in this desert, as day was now declining he found a cave and stopped there meaning to say his evening office in it, and there midnight passed while he was still singing the Psalms. And when after he had finished his office he sat down a little before refreshing his wearied body, on a sudden he began to see innumerable troops of demons gathering together on all sides, who came forward in an immense crowd, and a long line, some preceding and others following their prince; who at length arrived, being taller and more dreadful to look at than all the others; and, a throne having been placed, he sat down as on some lofty tribunal, and began to investigate by a searching examination the actions of each one of them; and those who said that they had not yet been able to circumvent their rivals, he commanded to be driven out of his sight with shame and ignominy as idle and slothful, rebuking them with angry wrath for the waste of so much time, and for their

labour thrown away: but those who reported that they had deceived those assigned to them, he dismissed before all with the highest praise amidst the exultation and applause of all, as most brave warriors, and most renowned as an example to all the rest: and when in this number some most evil spirit had presented himself, in delight at having to relate some magnificent triumph, he mentioned the name of a very well known monk, and declared that after having incessantly attacked him for fifteen years, he had at last got the better of him, so as to destroy him that very same night by the sin of fornication, for that he had not only impelled him to commit adultery with some consecrated maid, but had actually persuaded him to keep her and marry her. And when there arose shouts of joy at this narrative, he was extolled with the highest praise by the prince of darkness, and departed crowned with great honours. And so when at break of day the whole swarm of demons had vanished from his eyes, the brother being doubtful about the assertion of the unclean spirit, and rather thinking that he had desired to entice him by an ancient customary deceit, and to brand an innocent brother with the crime of incest, being mindful of those words of the gospel; viz., that "he abode not in the truth because there is no truth in him. When he speaketh a lie, he speaketh of his own, for he is a liar, and its father,"[2] he made his way to Pelusium, where he knew that the man lived, whom the evil spirit declared to be destroyed: for the brother was very well known to him, and when he had asked him, he found that on the same night on which that foul demon had announced his downfall to his company and prince, he had left his former monastery, and sought the town, and had gone astray by a wretched fall with the girl mentioned.

CHAPTER XVII.

Of the fact that two angels always cling to every man.

FOR Holy Scripture bears witness that two angels, a good and a bad one, cling to each one of us. And of the good ones the Saviour says: "Do not despise one of these little ones; for I say unto you that their angels in heaven do always behold the face of thy Father which is in heaven:"[3] and this also: "the angel of the Lord shall encamp round about them that fear Him, and deliver them."[4] Moreover this also which is said in

---

[1] S. Luke xi. 19.

[2] S. John viii. 44.   [3] S. Matt. xviii. 10.   [4] Ps. xxxiii. (xxxiv.) 8.

the Acts of the Apostles, of Peter, that "it is his angel." [1] But of both sorts the book of the Shepherd teaches us very fully. [2] But if we consider about him who attacked the blessed Job we shall clearly learn that it was he who always plotted against him but never could entice him to sin, and that therefore he asked for power from the Lord, as he was worsted not by his (Job's) virtue but by the Lord's protection which ever shielded him. Of Judas also it is said: "And let the devil stand at his right hand." [3]

CHAPTER XVIII.

Of the degrees of wickedness which exist in hostile spirits, as shown in the case of two philosophers.

BUT of the difference that there is between demons we have learnt a great deal by means of those two philosophers who formerly by acts of magic had oftentimes great experience both of their laziness and of their courage and savage wickedness. For these looking down on the blessed Antony as a boor and rustic, and wanting, if they could not injure him any further, at least to drive him from his cell by illusions of magic and the devices of demons, despatched against him most foul spirits. for they were impelled to this attack upon him by the sting of jealousy because enormous crowds came daily to him as the servant of God. And when these most savage demons did not even venture to approach him as he was now signing his breast and forehead with the sign of the cross, and, now devoting himself to prayer and supplication, they returned without any result to those who had directed them; and these again sent against him others more desperate in wickedness, and when these too had spent their strength in vain, and returned without having accomplished anything, and others still more powerful were nevertheless told off against the victorious soldier of Christ, and could prevail nothing against him, all these great plots of theirs devised with all the arts of magic were only useful in proving the great value that there is in the profession of Christians, so that those fierce and powerful shadows, which they thought would veil the sun and moon if they were directed towards them, could not only not injure him, but not even draw him forth from his monastery for a single instant.

CHAPTER XIX.

Of the fact that devils cannot prevail at all against men unless they have first secured possession of their minds.

AND when in their astonishment at this they came straight to Abbot Antony and disclosed the extent of their attacks and the reason of them and their plots, they dissembled their jealousy and asked that they might forthwith be made Christians. But when he had asked of them the day when the assault was made, he declared that at that time he had been afflicted with the most bitter pangs of thought. And by this experience the blessed Antony proved and established the opinion which we expressed yesterday in our Conference, that demons cannot possibly find an entrance into the mind or body of anyone, nor have they the power of overwhelming the soul of anyone, unless they have first deprived it of all holy thoughts, and made it empty and free from spiritual meditation. But you must know that unclean spirits are obedient to men in two ways. For either they are by divine grace and power subject to the holiness of the faithful, or they are captivated by the sacrifices of sinners, and certain charms, and are flattered by them as their worshippers. And the Pharisees too were led astray by this notion and fancied that by this device even the Lord the Saviour gave commands to devils, and said "By Beelzebub the prince of the devils He casteth out devils," in accordance with that plan by which they knew that their own magicians and enchanters — by invoking his name and offering sacrifices, with which they know he is pleased and delighted — have as his servants power even over the devils who are subject to him.

CHAPTER XX.

A question about the fallen angels who are said in Genesis to have had intercourse with the daughters of men.

GERMANUS: Since a passage of Genesis was a little while ago by the providence of God brought forward in our midst, and happily reminded us that we can now conveniently ask about a point which we have always longed to learn, we want to know what view we ought to take about those fallen angels who are said to have had intercourse with the daughters of men, and whether such a thing can literally

---

[1] Acts xii. 15.
[2] The reference is to the Pastor or Shepherd of Hermas, a work of the second century. The passage to which Cassian alludes is found in Book II. Commandm. vi.; where it is said that "there are two angels with a man, one of righteousness and the other of iniquity," and suggestions are given how to recognize each of them and to distinguish the suggestions of the one from those of the other. The passage is also alluded to by Origen, De Principiis, Book III. c. ii. and Hom. xxxv. in (Lucam); and Cassian refers to it again in Conf. XIII. c. xii.
[3] Ps. cviii. (cix.) 6.

take place with a spiritual nature. And also with regard to this passage of the gospel which you quoted of the devil a little while back, "for he is a liar and his father,"[1] we should like in the same way to hear who is to be understood by "his father."

CHAPTER XXI.

The answer to the question raised.

SERENUS: You have propounded two not unimportant questions, to which I will reply, to the best of my ability, in the order in which you have raised them. We cannot possibly believe that spiritual existences can have carnal intercourse with women. But if this could ever have literally happened how is it that it does not now also sometimes take place, and that we do not see some in the same way born of women by the agency of demons without intercourse with men? especially when it is clear that they delight in the pollution of lust, which they would certainly prefer to bring about through their own agency rather than through that of men, if they could possibly manage it, as Ecclesiastes declares: "What is it that hath been? The same that is. And what is it that hath been done? The same that is done. And there is nothing new that can be said under the sun, so that a man can say: Behold this is new; for it hath already been in the ages which were before us."[2] But the question raised may be resolved in this way. After the death of righteous Abel, in order that the whole human race might not spring from a wicked fratricide, Seth was born in the place of his brother who was slain, to take the place of his brother not only as regards posterity, but also as regards justice and goodness. And his offspring, following the example of their father's goodness, always remained separate from intercourse with and the society of their kindred descended from the wicked Cain, as the difference of the genealogy very clearly tells us, where it says: "Adam begat Seth, Seth begat Enos, Enos begat Cainan, but Cainan begat Mahalaleel, but Mahalaleel begat Jared, Jared begat Enoch, Enoch begat Methuselah, Methuselah begat Lamech, Lamech begat Noah."[3] And the genealogy of Cain is given separately as follows: "Cain begat Enoch, Enoch begat

Cainan, Cainan begat Mahalaleel, Mahalaleel begat Methuselah, Methuselah begat Lamech, Lamech begat Jabal and Jubal."[4] And so the line which sprang from the seed of righteous Seth always mixed with its own kith and kin, and continued for a long while in the holiness of its fathers and ancestors, untouched by the blasphemies and the wickedness of an evil offspring, which had implanted in it a seed of sin as it were transmitted by its ancestors. As long then as there continued that separation of the lines between them, the seed of Seth, as it sprang from an excellent root, was by reason of its sanctity termed "angels of God," or as some copies have it "sons of God;"[5] and on the contrary the others by reason of their own and their fathers' wickedness and their earthly deeds were termed "children of men." Though then there was up to this time that holy and salutary separation between them, yet after this the sons of Seth who were the sons of God saw the daughters of those who were born of the line of Cain, and inflamed with the desire for their beauty took to themselves from them wives who taught their husbands the wickedness of their fathers, and at once led them astray from their innate holiness and the single-mindedness of their forefathers. To whom this saying applies with sufficient accuracy: "I have said: Ye are Gods, and ye are all the children of the Most High. But ye shall die like men, and fall like one of the princes;"[6] who fell away from that true study of natural philosophy, handed down to them by their ancestors, which the first man who forthwith traced out the study of all nature, could clearly attain to, and transmit to his descendants on sure grounds, inasmuch as he had seen the infancy of this world, while still as it were tender and throbbing and unorganized; and as there was in him not only such fulness of wisdom, but also the grace of prophecy given by the Divine inspiration, so that while he was still an untaught inhabitant of this world he gave names to all living creatures, and not only knew about the fury and poison of all kinds of beasts and serpents, but also distinguished between the virtues of plants and trees and the natures of stones, and the changes of seasons of which he had as yet no experience, so that he could well say: "The Lord

---

[1] S. John viii. 44. We find from Augustine (Tract. xxiv. in Johan.) that the Manichees interpreted this text as implying that the devil had a father, translating it "For he is a liar, and so is his father." Augustine himself explains it as Abbot Serenus does below in c. xxv.; viz., that the devil is not only a liar himself but the parent of lies.
[2] Eccl. i. 9, 10.   [3] Gen. v. 4-30.

[4] Gen. iv. 17-21.
[5] In Gen. vi. 2 the MSS. of the LXX. fluctuate between ἄγγελοι τοῦ θεοῦ and υἱοὶ τοῦ θεοῦ. The interpretation of the passage which Cassian here rejects is adopted by Philo and Josephus, the book of Enoch, and several of the early fathers, including Justin Martyr, Tertullian, Clement of Alexandria, Lactantius and others. The explanation, which Cassian here gives, taking the "sons of God" of the Sethites, and the "daughters of men" of the line of Cain, is apparently first found in Julius Africanus (οἱ ἀπὸ τοῦ Σὴθ δίκαιοι), and is adopted among others by Augustine, De Civitate Dei, Book XV. xxiii., where the passage is fully discussed.
[6] Ps. lxxxi. (lxxxii.) 6, 7.

hath given me the true knowledge of the things that are, to know the disposition of the whole world, and the virtues of the elements, the beginning and the ending and the midst of times, the alterations of their courses and the changes of their seasons, the revolutions of the year and the disposition of the stars, the natures of living creatures and the rage of wild beasts, the force of winds, and the reasonings of men, the diversities of plants and the virtues of roots, and all such things as are hid and open I have learnt."[1] This knowledge then of all nature the seed of Seth received through successive generations, handed down from the fathers, so long as it remained separate from the wicked line, and as it had received it in holiness, so it made use of it to promote the glory of God and the needs of everyday life. But when it had been mingled with the evil generation, it drew aside at the suggestion of devils to profane and harmful uses what it had innocently learnt, and audaciously taught by it the curious arts of wizards and enchantments and magical superstitions, teaching its posterity to forsake the holy worship of the Divinity and to honour and worship either the elements or fire or the demons of the air. How it was then that this knowledge of curious arts of which we have spoken, did not perish in the deluge, but became known to the ages that followed, should, I think, be briefly explained, as the occasion of this discussion suggests, although the answer to the question raised scarcely requires it. And so, as ancient traditions tell us, Ham the son of Noah, who had been taught these superstitions and wicked and profane arts, as he knew that he could not possibly bring any handbook on these subjects into the ark, into which he was to enter with his good father and holy brothers, inscribed these nefarious arts and profane devices on plates of various metals which could not be destroyed by the flood of waters, and on hard rocks, and when the flood was over he hunted for them with the same inquisitiveness with which he had concealed them, and so transmitted to his descendants a seedbed of profanity and perpetual sin. In this way then that common notion, according to which men believe that angels delivered to men enchantments and diverse arts, is in truth fulfilled. From these sons of Seth then and daughters of Cain, as we have said, there were born still worse children who became mighty hunters, violent and most fierce men who were termed giants by reason of the size of their bodies and their cruelty and wickedness. For these first began to harass their neighbours

and to practise pillaging among men, getting their living rather by rapine than by being contented with the sweat and labour of toil, and their wickedness increased to such a pitch that the world could only be purified by the flood and deluge. So then when the sons of Seth at the instigation of their lust had transgressed that command which had been for a long while kept by a natural instinct from the beginning of the world, it was needful that it should afterwards be restored by the letter of the law: "Thou shalt not give thy daughter to his son to wife, nor shalt thou take a wife of his daughters to thy son; for they shall seduce your hearts to depart from your God, and to follow their gods and serve them."[2]

CHAPTER XXII.

An objection, as to how an unlawful intermingling with the daughters of Cain could be charged against the line of Seth before the prohibition of the law.

GERMANUS: If that command had been given to them, then the sin of breaking it might fairly have been brought against them for their audacity in so marrying. But since the observance of that separation had not yet been established by any rule, how could that intermingling of races be counted wrong in them, as it had not been forbidden by any command? For a law does not ordinarily forbid crimes that are past, but those that are future.

CHAPTER XXIII.

The answer, that by the law of nature men were from the beginning liable to judgment and punishment.

SERENUS: God at man's creation implanted in him naturally complete knowledge of the law, and if this had been kept by man, as at the beginning, according to the Lord's purposes, there would not have been any need for another law to be given, which He afterwards proclaimed in writing: for it were superfluous for an external remedy to be offered, where an internal one was still implanted and vigorous. But since this had been, as we have said, utterly corrupted by freedom and the opportunity of sinning, the severe restrictions of the law of Moses were added as the executor and vindicator of this (earlier law) and to use the expressions of Scripture, as its helper, that through fear of immediate punishment men might be kept from altogether losing the good of natural

---

[1] Wis. vii. 17-21.

[2] Deut. viii. 3; Exod. xxxiv. 16: cf. 1 Kings xi. 2.

knowledge, according to the word of the prophet who says "He gave the law to help them:"[1] and it is also described by the Apostle as having been given as a school-master[2] to little children, as it instructs and guards them to prevent them from departing through sheer forgetfulness from the teaching in which they had been instructed by the light of nature: for that the complete knowledge of the law was implanted in man at his first creation, is clearly proved from this; viz., that we know that before the law, aye, and even before the flood, all holy men observed the commands of the law without having the letter to read. For how could Abel, without the command of the law, have known that he ought to offer to God a sacrifice of the first-lings of his flock and of the fat thereof,[3] unless he had been taught by the law which was naturally implanted in him? How could Noah have distinguished what animals were clean and what were unclean,[4] when the command-ment of the law had not yet made a distinc-tion, unless he had been taught by a natural knowledge? Whence did Enoch learn how to "walk with God,"[5] having never acquired any light of the law from another? Where had Shem and Japheth read "Thou shalt not uncover the nakedness of thy father," so that they went backwards and covered the shame of their father?[6] How was Abraham taught to abstain from the spoils of the enemy which were offered to him, that he might not receive any recompense for his toil, or to pay to the priest Melchizedec the tithes which are ordered by the law of Moses?[7] How was it too that the same Abraham and Lot also humbly offered to passers by and strangers offices of kindness and the washing of their feet, while yet the Evangelic command had not shone forth?[8] Whence did Job obtain such earnest-ness of faith, such purity of chastity, such knowledge of humility, gentleness, pity and kindness, as we now see shown not even by those who know the gospels by heart? Which of the saints do we read of as not having observed some commandment of the law before the giving of the law? Which of them failed to keep this: "Hear, O Israel, the Lord thy God is one Lord?"[9] Which of them did not fulfil this: "Thou shalt not make to thyself any graven image, nor the likeness of anything which is in heaven or in the earth or under the earth?" Which of them did not observe this: "Honour thy father and thy mother," or what follows in the Decalogue: "Thou shalt

do no murder; Thou shalt not commit adul-tery; Thou shalt not steal; Thou shalt not bear false witness; Thou shalt not covet thy neighbour's wife,"[10] and many other things be-sides, in which they anticipated the commands not only of the law but even of the gospel?

CHAPTER XXIV.

Of the fact that they were justly punished, who sinned before the flood.

AND so then we see that from the beginning God created everything perfect, nor would there have been need for anything to have been added to His original arrangement — as if it were shortsighted and imperfect — if everything had continued in that state and condition in which it had been created by Him. And therefore in the case of those who sinned before the law and even before the flood we see that God visited them with a righteous judgment, because they deserved to be punished without any excuse, for having transgressed the law of nature; nor should we fall into the blasphemous slanders of those who are ignorant of this reason, and so depre-ciate the God of the Old Testament, and run down our faith, and say with a sneer: Why then did it please your God to will to promul-gate the law after so many thousand years, while He suffered such long ages to pass with-out any law? But if He afterwards discovered something better, then it appears that at the beginning of the world His wisdom was infe-rior and poorer, and that afterwards as if taught by experience He began to provide for some-thing better, and to amend and improve His original arrangements. A thing which cer-tainly cannot happen to the infinite foreknow-ledge of God, nor can these assertions be made about Him by the mad folly of heretics with-out grievous blasphemy, as Ecclesiastes says: "I have learnt that all the words which God hath made from the beginning shall continue forever: nothing can be added to them, and nothing can be taken away from them,"[11] and therefore "the law is not made for the righteous, but for the unrighteous, and insubordinate, for the ungodly and sinners, for the wicked and profane."[12] For as they had the sound and complete system of natural laws implanted in them they had no need of this external law in addition, and one committed to writing, and what was given as an aid to that natural law. From which we infer by the clearest of reason-ings that that law committed to writing need not have been given at the beginning (for it was

[1] Is. viii. 20 (LXX.).
[2] Cf. Gal. iii. 24.
[3] Gen. iv. 4.
[4] Gen. vii. 2.
[5] Gen. v. 22.
[6] Gen. ix. 23; Lev. xviii. 7.
[7] Gen. xiv. 20, 22.
[8] Gen. xviii., xix.; cf. S. John xiii. 34.
[9] Deut. vi. 4.
[10] Exod. xx. 4-17. [11] Eccl. iii. 14. (LXX.). [12] 1 Tim. i-9.

unnecessary for this to be done while the natural law still remained, and was not utterly violated) nor could evangelical perfection have been granted before the law had been kept. For they could not have listened to this saying: "If a man strikes thee on the right cheek, turn to him the other also," [1] who were not content to avenge wrongs done to them with the even justice of the *lex talionis*, but repaid a very slight touch with deadly kicks and wounds with weapons, and for a single truth sought to take the life of those who had struck them. Nor could it be said to them, "love your enemies," [2] among whom it was considered a great thing and most important if they loved their friends, but avoided their enemies and dissented from them only in hatred without being eager to oppress and kill them.

CHAPTER XXV.

How this that is said of the devil in the gospel is to be understood; viz., that "he is a liar, and his father."

BUT as for this which disturbed you about the devil, that "he is a liar and his father," [3] as if it seemed that he and his father were pronounced by the Lord to be liars, it is sufficiently ridiculous to imagine this even cursorily. For as we said a little while ago spirit does not beget spirit just as soul cannot procreate soul, though we do not doubt that the compacting of flesh is formed from man's seed, as the Apostle clearly distinguishes in the case of both substances ; viz., flesh and spirit, what should be ascribed to whom as its author, and says: "Moreover we have had fathers of our flesh for instructors, and we reverenced them: shall we not much more be in subjection to the Father of spirits and live?" [4] What could show more clearly than this distinction, that he laid down that men were the fathers of our flesh, but always taught that God alone was the Father of souls. Although even in the actual compacting of this body a ministerial office alone must be attributed to men, but the chief part of its formation to God the Creator of all, as David says: "Thy hands have made me and fashioned me:" [5] And the blessed Job: "Hast thou not milked me as milk, and curdled me as cheese? Thou hast put me together with bones and sinews;" [6] and the Lord to Jeremiah: "Before I formed thee in the womb, I knew thee." [7] But Ecclesiastes very clearly and accurately gathers the nature of either substance, and its begin-

ning, by an examination of the rise and commencement, from which each originated, and by a consideration of the end to which each is tending, and decides also of the division of this body and soul, and discourses as follows: "Before the dust returns to the earth as it was, and the spirit returns unto God who gave it." [8] But what could be said with greater plainness than that he declares that the matter of the flesh which he styled dust, because it springs from the seed of man, and seems to be sown by his ministration, must, as it was taken from the earth, again return to the earth, while he points out that the spirit which is not begotten by intercourse between the sexes, but belongs to God alone in a special way, returns to its creator? And this also is clearly implied in that breathing by God, through which Adam in the first instance received his life. And so from these passages we clearly infer that no one can be called the Father of spirits but God alone, who makes them out of nothing whenever He pleases, while men can only be termed the fathers of our flesh. So then the devil also in as much as he was created a spirit or an angel and good, had no one as his Father but God his Maker. But when he had become puffed up by pride and had said in his heart: "I will ascend above the heights of the clouds, I will be like the Most High," [9] he became a liar, and "abode not in the truth;" [10] but brought forth a lie from his own storehouse of wickedness and so became not only a liar, but also the father of the actual lie, by which when he promised Divinity to man and said "Ye shall be as gods," [11] he abode not in the truth, but from the beginning became a murderer, both by bringing Adam into a state of mortality, and by slaying Abel by the hand of his brother at his suggestion. But already the approach of dawn is bringing to a close our discussion, which has occupied nearly two whole nights, and our brief and simple words have drawn our bark of this Conference from the deep sea of questions to a safe harbour of silence, in which deep indeed, as the breath of the Divine Spirit drives us further in, so is there ever opened out a wider and boundless space reaching beyond the sight of our eye, and, as Solomon says, "It will become much further from us than it was, and a great depth; who shall find it out?" [12] Wherefore let us pray the Lord that both His fear and His love, which cannot fail, may continue steadfast in us, and make us wise in all things, and ever shield us unharmed, from the darts

---

[1] S. Matt. v. 39.
[2] *Ib.* ver. 44.
[3] S. John viii. 44.

[4] Heb. xii. 9.
[5] Ps. cxviii. (cxix.) 73.

[6] Job x. 10, 11.
[7] Jer. i. 5.

[8] Eccl. xii. 7.
[9] Is. xiv. 14.

[10] S. John viii 44.
[11] Gen. iii. 5.

[12] Eccl. vii. 25.

of the devil. For with these guards it is impossible for anyone to fall into the snares of death. But there is this difference between the perfect and imperfect, that in the case of the former love is steadfast, and so to speak riper and lasts more abidingly and so makes them persevere in holiness more steadfastly and more easily, while in the case of the latter its position is weaker and it more easily grows cold, and so quickly and more frequently allows them to be entangled in the snares of sin. And when we heard this, the words of this Conference so fired us that when we went away from the old man's cell we longed with a keener ardour of soul than when we first came, for the fulfilment of his teaching.

IX.

THE FIRST CONFERENCE OF ABBOT ISAAC.

ON PRAYER.

CHAPTER I.

Introduction to the Conference.

WHAT was promised in the second book of the Institutes[1] on continual and unceasing perseverance in prayer, shall be by the Lord's help fulfilled by the Conferences of this Elder, whom we will now bring forward; viz., Abbot Isaac:[2] and when these have been propounded I think that I shall have satisfied the commands of Pope Castor of blessed memory, and your wishes, O blessed Pope Leontius and holy brother Helladius, and the length of the book in its earlier part may be excused, though, in spite of our endeavour not only to compress what had to be told into a brief discourse, but also to pass over very many points in silence, it has been extended to a greater length than we intended. For having commenced with a full discourse on various regulations which we have thought it well to curtail for the sake of brevity, at the close the blessed Isaac spoke these words.

CHAPTER II.

The words of Abbot Isaac on the nature of prayer.

THE aim of every monk and the perfection of his heart tends to continual and unbroken perseverance in prayer, and, as far as it is allowed to human frailty, strives to acquire an immovable tranquillity of mind and a perpetual purity, for the sake of which we seek unweariedly and constantly to practise all bodily labours as well as contrition of spirit. And there is between these two a sort of reciprocal and inseparable union. For just as the crown of the building of all virtues is the perfection of prayer, so unless everything has been united and compacted by this as its crown, it cannot possibly continue strong and stable. For lasting and continual calmness in prayer, of which we are speaking, cannot be secured or consummated without them, so neither can those virtues which lay its foundations be fully gained without persistence in it. And so we shall not be able either to treat properly of the effect of prayer, or in a rapid discourse to penetrate to its main end, which is acquired by labouring at all virtues, unless first all those things which for its sake must be either rejected or secured, are singly enumerated and discussed, and, as the Parable in the gospel teaches,[3] whatever concerns the building of that spiritual and most lofty tower, is reckoned up and carefully considered beforehand. But yet these things when prepared will be of no use nor allow the lofty height of perfection to be properly placed upon them unless a clearance of all faults be first undertaken, and the decayed and dead rubbish of the passions be dug up, and the strong foundations of simplicity and humility be laid on the solid and (so to speak) living soil of our breast, or rather on that rock of the gospel,[4] and by being built in this way this tower of spiritual virtues will rise, and be able to stand unmoved, and be raised to the utmost heights of heaven in full assurance of its stability. For if it rests

---

[1] See the Institutes Book II. c. ix.
[2] Isaac was, as we gather from c. xxxi., a disciple of St. Antony, and is mentioned by Palladius Dial. de vita Chrysost. There are also a few stories of him in the Apophegmata Patrum (Migne, Vol. lxv. p. 223); and see the Dictionary of Christian Biography, Vol. iii. p. 294.

[3] Cf. S. Luke xiv. 28.   [4] Cf. S. Luke vi. 48.

on such foundations, then though heavy storms of passions break over it, though mighty torrents of persecutions beat against it like a battering ram, though a furious tempest of spiritual foes dash against it and attack it, yet not only will no ruin overtake it, but the onslaught will not injure it even in the slightest degree.

CHAPTER III.

How pure and sincere prayer can be gained.

AND therefore in order that prayer may be offered up with that earnestness and purity with which it ought to be, we must by all means observe these rules. First all anxiety about carnal things must be entirely got rid of; next we must leave no room for not merely the care but even the recollection of any business affairs, and in like manner also must lay aside all backbitings, vain and incessant chattering, and buffoonery; anger above all, and disturbing moroseness must be entirely destroyed, and the deadly taint of carnal lust and covetousness be torn up by the roots. And so when these and such like faults which are also visible to the eyes of men, are entirely removed and cut off, and when such a purification and cleansing, as we spoke of, has first taken place, which is brought about by pure simplicity and innocence, then first there must be laid the secure foundations of a deep humility, which may be able to support a tower that shall reach the sky; and next the spiritual structure of the virtues must be built up upon them, and the soul kept free from all conversation and from roving thoughts that thus it may by little and little begin to rise to the contemplation of God and to spiritual insight. For whatever our mind has been thinking of before the hour of prayer, is sure to occur to us while we are praying through the activity of the memory. Wherefore what we want to find ourselves like while we are praying, that we ought to prepare ourselves to be before the time for prayer. For the mind in prayer is formed by its previous condition, and when we are applying ourselves to prayer the images of the same actions and words and thoughts will dance before our eyes, and make us either angry, as in our previous condition, or gloomy, or recall our former lust and business, or make us shake with foolish laughter (which I am ashamed to speak of) at some silly joke, or smile at some action, or fly back to our previous conversation. And therefore if we do not want anything to haunt us while we are praying, we should be careful before our prayer, to exclude it from the shrine of our heart, that we may thus fulfill the Apostle's injunction: "Pray without ceasing;" and: "In every place lifting up holy hands without wrath or disputing." [1] For otherwise we shall not be able to carry out that charge unless our mind, purified from all stains of sin, and given over to virtue as to its natural good, feed on the continual contemplation of Almighty God.

CHAPTER IV.

Of the lightness of the soul which may be compared to a wing or feather.

FOR the nature of the soul is not inaptly compared to a very fine feather or very light wing, which, if it has not been damaged or affected by being spoilt by any moisture falling on it from without, is borne aloft almost naturally to the heights of heaven by the lightness of its nature, and the aid of the slightest breath: but if it is weighted by any moisture falling upon it and penetrating into it, it will not only not be carried away by its natural lightness into any aerial flights but will actually be borne down to the depths of earth by the weight of the moisture it has received. So also our soul, if it is not weighted with faults that touch it, and the cares of this world, or damaged by the moisture of injurious lusts, will be raised as it were by the natural blessing of its own purity and borne aloft to the heights by the light breath of spiritual meditation; and leaving things low and earthly will be transported to those that are heavenly and invisible. Wherefore we are well warned by the Lord's command: "Take heed that your hearts be not weighed down by surfeiting and drunkenness and the cares of this world." [2] And therefore if we want our prayers to reach not only the sky, but what is beyond the sky, let us be careful to reduce our soul, purged from all earthly faults and purified from every stain, to its natural lightness, that so our prayer may rise to God unchecked by the weight of any sin.

CHAPTER V.

Of the ways in which our soul is weighed down.

BUT we should notice the ways in which the Lord points out that the soul is weighed down: for He did not mention adultery, or fornication, or murder, or blasphemy, or rapine, which everybody knows to be deadly and

---

[1] 1 Thess. v. 17; 1 Tim. ii. 8.   [2] S. Luke xxi. 34.

damnable, but surfeiting and drunkenness, and the cares or anxieties of this world: which men of this world are so far from avoiding or considering damnable that actually some who (I am ashamed to say) call themselves monks entangle themselves in these very occupations as if they were harmless or useful. And though these three things, when literally given way to weigh down the soul, and separate it from God, and bear it down to things earthly, yet it is very easy to avoid them, especially for us who are separated by so great a distance from all converse with this world, and who do not on any occasion have anything to do with those visible cares and drunkenness and surfeiting. But there is another surfeiting which is no less dangerous, and a spiritual drunkenness which it is harder to avoid, and a care and anxiety of this world, which often ensnares us even after the perfect renunciation of all our goods, and abstinence from wine and all feastings and even when we are living in solitude — and of such the prophet says: "Awake, ye that are drunk but not with wine;"[1] and another: "Be astonished and wonder and stagger: be drunk and not with wine: be moved, but not with drunkenness."[2] And of this drunkenness the wine must consequently be what the prophet calls "the fury of dragons": and from what root the wine comes you may hear: "From the vineyard of Sodom," he says, "is their vine, and their branches from Gomorrha." Would you also know about the fruit of that vine and the seed of that branch? "Their grape is a grape of gall, theirs is a cluster of bitterness"[3] for unless we are altogether cleansed from all faults and abstaining from the surfeit of all passions, our heart will without drunkenness from wine and excess of any feasting be weighed down by a drunkenness and surfeiting that is still more dangerous. For that worldly cares can sometimes fall on us who mix with no actions of this world, is clearly shown according to the rule of the Elders, who have laid down that anything which goes beyond the necessities of daily food, and the unavoidable needs of the flesh, belongs to worldly cares and anxieties, as for example if, when a job bringing in a penny would satisfy the needs of our body, we try to extend it by a longer toil and work in order to get twopence or threepence; and when a covering of two tunics would be enough for our use both by night and day, we manage to become the owners of three or four, or when a hut containing one or two cells would be sufficient, in the pride of worldly ambition and greatness we build four or five cells, and

these splendidly decorated, and larger than our needs required, thus showing the passion of worldly lusts whenever we can.

CHAPTER VI.

Of the vision which a certain Elder saw concerning the restless work of a brother.

AND that this is not done without the prompting of devils we are taught by the surest proofs, for when one very highly esteemed Elder was passing by the cell of a certain brother who was suffering from this mental disease of which we have spoken, as he was restlessly toiling in his daily occupations in building and repairing what was unnecessary, he watched him from a distance breaking a very hard stone with a heavy hammer, and saw a certain Ethiopian standing over him and together with him striking the blows of the hammer with joined and clasped hands, and urging him on with fiery incitements to diligence in the work: and so he stood still for a long while in astonishment at the force of the fierce demon and the deceitfulness of such an illusion. For when the brother was worn out and tired and wanted to rest and put an end to his toil, he was stimulated by the spirit's prompting and urged on to resume his hammer again and not to cease from devoting himself to the work which he had begun, so that being unweariedly supported by his incitements he did not feel the harm that so great labour was doing him. At last then the old man, disgusted at such a horrid mystification by a demon, turned aside to the brother's cell and saluted him, and asked "what work is it, brother, that you are doing?" and he replied: "We are working at this awfully hard stone, and we can hardly break it at all." Whereupon the Elder replied: "You were right in saying 'we can,' for you were not alone, when you were striking it, but there was another with you whom you did not see, who was standing over you not so much to help you as urge you on with all his force." And thus the fact that the disease of worldly vanity has not got hold of our hearts, will be proved by no mere abstinence from those affairs which even if we want to engage in, we cannot carry out, nor by the despising of those matters which if we pursued them would make us remarkable in the front rank among spiritual persons as well as among worldly men, but only when we reject with inflexible firmness of mind whatever ministers to our power and seems to be veiled in a show of right. And in reality these things which seem trivial

---

[1] Joel i. 5. [2] Is. xxix. 9. [3] Deut. xxxii. 32, 33.

and of no consequence, and which we see to be permitted indifferently by those who belong to our calling, none the less by their character affect the soul than those more important things, which according to their condition usually intoxicate the senses of worldly people and which do not allow[1] a monk to lay aside earthly impurities and aspire to God, on whom his attention should ever be fixed; for in his case even a slight separation from that highest good must be regarded as present death and most dangerous destruction. And when the soul has been established in such a peaceful condition, and has been freed from the meshes of all carnal desires, and the purpose of the heart has been steadily fixed on that which is the only highest good, he will then fulfil this Apostolic precept: "Pray without ceasing;" and: "in every place lifting up holy hands without wrath and disputing:"[2] for when by this purity (if we can say so) the thoughts of the soul are engrossed, and are re-fashioned out of their earthly condition to bear a spiritual and angelic likeness, whatever it receives, whatever it takes in hand, whatever it does, the prayer will be perfectly pure and sincere.

CHAPTER VII.

A question how it is that it is harder work to preserve than to originate good thoughts.

GERMANUS: If only we could keep as a lasting possession those spiritual thoughts in the same way and with the same ease with which we generally conceive their germs! for when they have been conceived in our hearts either through the recollection of the Scriptures or by the memory of some spiritual actions, or by gazing upon heavenly mysteries, they vanish all too soon and disappear by a sort of unnoticed flight. And when our soul has discovered some other occasions for spiritual emotions, different ones again crowd in upon us, and those which we had grasped are scattered, and lightly fly away so that the mind retaining no persistency, and keeping of its own power no firm hand over holy thoughts, must be thought, even when it does seem to retain them for a while, to have conceived them at random and not of set purpose. For how can we think that their rise should be ascribed to our own will, if they do not last and remain with us? But that we may not owing to the consideration of this question

wander any further from the plan of the discourse we had commenced, or delay any longer the explanation promised of the nature of prayer, we will keep this for its own time, and ask to be informed at once of the character of prayer, especially as the blessed Apostle exhorts us at no time to cease from it, saying "Pray without ceasing." And so we want to be taught first of its character, i.e., how prayer ought *always* to be offered up, and then how we can secure this, whatever it is, and practise it without ceasing. For that it cannot be done by any light purpose of heart both daily experience and the explanation of your holiness show us, as you have laid it down that the aim of a monk, and the height of all perfection consist in the consummation of prayer.

CHAPTER VIII.

Of the different characters of prayer.

ISAAC: I imagine that all kinds of prayers cannot be grasped without great purity of heart and soul and the illumination of the Holy Spirit. For there are as many of them as there can be conditions and characters produced in one soul or rather in all souls. And so although we know that owing to our dulness of heart we cannot see all kinds of prayers, yet we will try to relate them in some order, as far as our slender experience enables us to succeed. For according to the degree of the purity to which each soul attains, and the character of the state in which it is sunk owing to what happens to it, or is by its own efforts renewing itself, its very prayers will each moment be altered: and therefore it is quite clear that no one can always offer up uniform prayers. For every one prays in one way when he is brisk, in another when he is oppressed with a weight of sadness or despair, in another when he is invigorated by spiritual achievements, in another when cast down by the burden of attacks, in another when he is asking pardon for his sins, in another when he asks to obtain grace or some virtue or else prays for the destruction of some sin, in another when he is pricked to the heart by the thought of hell and the fear of future judgment, in another when he is aglow with the hope and desire of good things to come, in another when he is taken up with affairs and dangers, in another when he is in peace and security, in another when he is enlightened by the revelation of heavenly mysteries, and in another when he is depressed by a sense of barrenness in virtues and dryness in feeling.

---

[1] *Sinentes,* though the reading of almost all MSS. must be an error either of the author or of a copyist for *sinentia.*

[2] 1 Thess. v. 17; 1 Tim. ii. 8.

CHAPTER IX.

Of the fourfold nature of prayer.

AND therefore, when we have laid this down with regard to the character of prayer, although not so fully as the importance of the subject requires, but as fully as the exigencies of time permit, and at any rate as our slender abilities admit, and our dulness of heart enables us, — a still greater difficulty now awaits us; viz., to expound one by one the different kinds of prayer, which the Apostle divides in a fourfold manner, when he says as follows: "I exhort therefore first of all that supplications, prayers, intercessions, thanksgivings be made."[1] And we cannot possibly doubt that this division was not idly made by the Apostle. And to begin with we must investigate what is meant by supplication, by prayer, by intercession, and by thanksgiving. Next we must inquire whether these four kinds are to be taken in hand by him who prays all at once, i.e., are they all to be joined together in every prayer,— or whether they are to be offered up in turns and one by one, as, for instance, ought at one time supplications, at another prayers, at another intercessions, and at another thanksgivings to be offered, or should one man present to God supplications, another prayers, another intercessions, another thanksgivings, in accordance with that measure of age, to which each soul is advancing by earnestness of purpose?

CHAPTER X.

Of the order of the different kinds laid down with regard to the character of prayer.

AND so to begin with we must consider the actual force of the names and words, and discuss what is the difference between prayer and supplication and intercession; then in like manner we must investigate whether they are to be offered separately or all together; and in the third place must examine whether the particular order which is thus arranged by the Apostle's authority has anything further to teach the hearer, or whether the distinction simply is to be taken, and it should be considered that they were arranged by him indifferently in such a way: a thing which seems to me utterly absurd. For one must not believe that the Holy Spirit uttered anything casually or without reason through the Apostle. And so we will, as the Lord grants us, consider them in the same order in which we began.

CHAPTER XI.

Of Supplications.

"I EXHORT therefore first of all that supplications be made." Supplication is an imploring or petition concerning sins, in which one who is sorry for his present or past deeds asks for pardon.

CHAPTER XII.

Of Prayer.

PRAYERS are those by which we offer or vow something to God, what the Greeks call εὐχή, i.e., a vow. For where we read in Greek ἱὰς ἐυχάς μου τῷ κυρίῳ ἀποδώσω, in Latin we read: "I will pay my vows unto the Lord;"[2] where according to the exact force of the words it may be thus represented: "I will pay my prayers unto the Lord." And this which we find in Ecclesiastes: "If thou vowest a vow unto the Lord do not delay to pay it," is written in Greek likewise: ἐὰν ἐὐξη ἐυχὴν τῷ κυρίῳ, i.e., "If thou prayest a prayer unto the Lord, do not delay to pay it,"[3] which will be fulfilled in this way by each one of us. We pray, when we renounce this world and promise that being dead to all worldly actions and the life of this world we will serve the Lord with full purpose of heart. We pray when we promise that despising secular honours and scorning earthly riches we will cleave to the Lord in all sorrow of heart and humility of spirit. We pray when we promise that we will ever maintain the most perfect purity of body and steadfast patience, or when we vow that we will utterly root out of our heart the roots of anger or of sorrow that worketh death. And if, enervated by sloth and returning to our former sins we fail to do this we shall be guilty as regards our prayers and vows, and these words will apply to us: "It is better not to vow, than to vow and not to pay," which can be rendered in accordance with the Greek: "It is better for thee not to pray than to pray and not to pay."[4]

CHAPTER XIII.

Of Intercession.

IN the third place stand intercessions, which we are wont to offer up for others also, while we are filled with fervour of spirit, making request either for those dear to us or

---

[1] 1 Tim. ii. 1.   [2] Ps. cxv. 4 (cxvi. 14).   [3] Eccl. v. 3.   [4] *Ibid.* ver. 4.

for the peace of the whole world, and to use the Apostle's own phrase, we pray "for all men, for kings and all that are in authority."[1]

CHAPTER XIV.

Of Thanksgiving.

THEN in the fourth place there stand thanksgivings which the mind in ineffable transports offers up to God, either when it recalls God's past benefits or when it contemplates His present ones, or when it looks forward to those great ones in the future which God has prepared for them that love Him. And with this purpose too sometimes we are wont to pour forth richer prayers, while, as we gaze with pure eyes on those rewards of the saints which are laid up in store hereafter, our spirit is stimulated to offer up unspeakable thanks to God with boundless joy.

CHAPTER XV.

Whether these four kinds of prayers are necessary for everyone to offer all at once or separately and in turns.

AND of these four kinds, although sometimes occasions arise for richer and fuller prayers (for from the class of supplications which arises from sorrow for sin, and from the kind of prayer which flows from confidence in our offerings and the performance of our vows in accordance with a pure conscience, and from the intercession which proceeds from fervour of love, and from the thanksgiving which is born of the consideration of God's blessings and His greatness and goodness, we know that oftentimes there proceed most fervent and ardent prayers so that it is clear that all these kinds of prayer of which we have spoken are found to be useful and needful for all men, so that in one and the same man his changing feelings will give utterance to pure and fervent petitions now of supplications, now of prayers, now of intercessions) yet the first seems to belong more especially to beginners, who are still troubled by the stings and recollection of their sins; the second to those who have already attained some loftiness of mind in their spiritual progress and the quest of virtue; the third to those who fulfil the completion of their vows by their works, and are so stimulated to intercede for others also through the consideration of their weakness, and the earnestness of their love; the fourth to those who have

already torn from their hearts the guilty thorns of conscience, and thus being now free from care can contemplate with a pure mind the beneficence of God and His compassions, which He has either granted in the past, or is giving in the present, or preparing for the future, and thus are borne onward with fervent hearts to that ardent prayer which cannot be embraced or expressed by the mouth of men. Sometimes however the mind which is advancing to that perfect state of purity and which is already beginning to be established in it, will take in all these at one and the same time, and like some incomprehensible and all-devouring flame, dart through them all and offer up to God inexpressible prayers of the purest force, which the Spirit Itself, intervening with groanings that cannot be uttered, while we ourselves understand not, pours forth to God, grasping at that hour and ineffably pouring forth in its supplications things so great that they cannot be uttered with the mouth nor even at any other time be recollected by the mind. And thence it comes that in whatever degree any one stands, he is found sometimes to offer up pure and devout prayers; as even in that first and lowly station which has to do with the recollection of future judgment, he who still remains under the punishment of terror and the fear of judgment is so smitten with sorrow for the time being that he is filled with no less keenness of spirit from the richness of his supplications than he who through the purity of his heart gazes on and considers the blessings of God and is overcome with ineffable joy and delight. For, as the Lord Himself says, he begins to love the more, who knows that he has been forgiven the more.[2]

CHAPTER XVI.

Of the kinds of prayer to which we ought to direct ourselves.

YET we ought by advancing in life and attaining to virtue to aim rather at those kinds of prayer which are poured forth either from the contemplation of the good things to come or from fervour of love, or which at least, to speak more humbly and in accordance with the measure of beginners, arise for the acquirement of some virtue or the extinction of some fault. For otherwise we shall not possibly attain to those sublimer kinds of supplication of which we spoke, unless our mind has been little by little and by degrees raised through the regular course of those intercessions.

---

[1] 1 Tim. ii, 1, 2.

[2] Cf. S. Luke vii. 47.

CHAPTER XVII.

How the four kinds of supplication were originated by the Lord.

THESE four kinds of supplication the Lord Himself by His own example vouchsafed to originate for us, so that in this too He might fulfil that which was said of Him: "which Jesus began both to do and to teach."[1] For He made use of the class of *supplication* when He said: "Father, if it be possible, let this cup pass from me;" or this which is chanted in His Person in the Psalm: "My God, My God, look upon Me, why hast Thou forsaken me,"[2] and others like it. It is *prayer* where He says: "I have magnified Thee upon the earth, I have finished the work which Thou gavest Me to do," and this: "And for their sakes I sanctify Myself that they also may be sanctified in the truth."[3] It is *intercession* when He says: "Father, those whom Thou hast given me, I will that they also may be with Me that they may see My glory which Thou hast given Me;" or at any rate when He says: "Father, forgive them for they know not what they do."[4] It is *thanksgiving* when He says: "I confess to Thee, Father, Lord of heaven and earth, that Thou hast hid these things from the wise and prudent, and hast revealed them unto babes. Even so, Father, for so it seemed good in Thy sight:" or at least when He says: "Father, I thank Thee that Thou hast heard Me. But I knew that Thou hearest Me always."[5] But though our Lord made a distinction between these four kinds of prayers as to be offered separately and one by one according to the scheme which we know of, yet that they can all be embraced in a perfect prayer at one and the same time He showed by His own example in that prayer which at the close of S. John's gospel we read that He offered up with such fulness. From the words of which (as it is too long to repeat it all) the careful inquirer can discover by the order of the passage that this is so. And the Apostle also in his Epistle to the Philippians has expressed the same meaning, by putting these four kinds of prayers in a slightly different order, and has shown that they ought sometimes to be offered together in the fervour of a single prayer, saying as follows: "But in everything by prayer and supplication with thanksgiving let your requests be made known unto God."[6] And by this he wanted us

especially to understand that in prayer and supplication thanksgiving ought to be mingled with our requests.

CHAPTER XVIII.

Of the Lord's Prayer.

AND so there follows after these different kinds of supplication a still more sublime and exalted condition which is brought about by the contemplation of God alone and by fervent love, by which the mind, transporting and flinging itself into love for Him, addresses God most familiarly as its own Father with a piety of its own. And that we ought earnestly to seek after this condition the formula of the Lord's prayer teaches us, saying "Our Father." When then we confess with our own mouths that the God and Lord of the universe is our Father, we profess forthwith that we have been called from our condition as slaves to the adoption of sons, adding next "Which art in heaven," that, by shunning with the utmost horror all lingering in this present life, which we pass upon this earth as a pilgrimage, and what separates us by a great distance from our Father, we may the rather hasten with all eagerness to that country where we confess that our Father dwells, and may not allow anything of this kind, which would make us unworthy of this our profession and the dignity of an adoption of this kind, and so deprive us as a disgrace to our Father's inheritance, and make us incur the wrath of His justice and severity. To which state and condition of sonship when we have advanced, we shall forthwith be inflamed with the piety which belongs to good sons, so that we shall bend all our energies to the advance not of our own profit, but of our Father's glory, saying to Him: "Hallowed be Thy name," testifying that our desire and our joy is His glory, becoming imitators of Him who said: "He who speaketh of himself, seeketh his own glory. But He who seeks the glory of Him who sent Him, the same is true and there is no unrighteousness in Him."[7] Finally the chosen vessel being filled with this feeling wished that he could be anathema from Christ[8] if only the people belonging to Him might be increased and multiplied, and the salvation of the whole nation of Israel accrue to the glory of His Father; for with all assurance could he wish to die for Christ as he knew that no one perished for life. And again he says: "We

---

[1] Acts i. 1.
[2] S. Matt. xxvi. 39; Ps. xxi. (xxii.) 2.
[3] S. John xvii. 4, 19.
[4] *Ib.* 24; S. Luke xxiii. 34.
[5] S. Matt. xi. 25, 26; S. John xi. 41, 42.
[6] Phil. iv. 6.

[7] S. John vii. 18.　　[8] Cf. Rom. ix. 3.

rejoice when we are weak but ye are strong." [1] And what wonder if the chosen vessel wished to be anathema from Christ for the sake of Christ's glory and the conversion of His own brethren and the privilege of the nation, when the prophet Micah wished that he might be a liar and a stranger to the inspiration of the Holy Ghost, if only the people of the Jews might escape those plagues and the going forth into captivity which he had announced in his prophecy, saying: "Would that I were not a man that hath the Spirit, and that I rather spoke a lie;" [2] — to pass over that wish of the Lawgiver, who did not refuse to die together with his brethren who were doomed to death, saying: "I beseech Thee, O Lord; this people hath sinned a heinous sin; either forgive them this trespass, or if Thou do not, blot me out of Thy book which Thou hast written." [3] But where it is said "Hallowed be Thy name," it may also be very fairly taken in this way: "The hallowing of God is our perfection." And so when we say to Him "Hallowed be Thy name" we say in other words, make us, O Father, such that we may be able both to understand and take in what the hallowing of Thee is, or at any rate that Thou mayest be seen to be hallowed in our spiritual converse. And this is effectually fulfilled in our case when "men see our good works, and glorify our Father which is in heaven." [4]

CHAPTER XIX.

Of the clause "Thy kingdom come."

THE second petition of the pure heart desires that the kingdom of its Father may come at once; viz., either that whereby Christ reigns day by day in the saints (which comes to pass when the devil's rule is cast out of our hearts by the destruction of foul sins, and God begins to hold sway over us by the sweet odour of virtues, and, fornication being overcome, charity reigns in our hearts together with tranquillity, when rage is conquered; and humility, when pride is trampled under foot) or else that which is promised in due time to all who are perfect, and to all the sons of God, when it will be said to them by Christ: "Come ye blessed of My Father, inherit the kingdom prepared for you from the foundation of the world;" [5] (as the heart) with fixed and steadfast gaze, so to speak, yearns and longs for it and says to Him "Thy

kingdom come." For it knows by the witness of its own conscience that when He shall appear, it will presently share His lot. For no guilty person would dare either to say or to wish for this, for no one would want to face the tribunal of the Judge, who knew that at His coming he would forthwith receive not the prize or reward of his merits but only punishment.

CHAPTER XX.

Of the clause "Thy will be done."

THE third petition is that of sons: "Thy will be done as in heaven so on earth." There can now be no grander prayer than to wish that earthly things may be made equal with things heavenly: for what else is it to say "Thy will be done as in heaven so on earth," than to ask that men may be like angels and that as God's will is ever fulfilled by them in heaven, so also all those who are on earth may do not their own but His will? This too no one could say from the heart but only one who believed that God disposes for our good all things which are seen, whether fortunate or unfortunate, and that He is more careful and provident for our good and salvation than we ourselves are for ourselves. Or at any rate it may be taken in this way: The will of God is the salvation of all men, according to these words of the blessed Paul: "Who willeth all men to be saved and to come to the knowledge of the truth." [6] Of which will also the prophet Isaiah says in the Person of God the Father: "And all Thy will shall be done." [7] When we say then "Thy will be done as in heaven so on earth," we pray in other words for this; viz., that as those who are in heaven, so also may all those who dwell on earth be saved, O Father, by the knowledge of Thee.

CHAPTER XXI.

Of our supersubstantial or daily bread.

NEXT: "Give us this day our bread which is ἐπιούσιον," i.e., "supersubstantial," which another Evangelist calls "daily." [8] The former indicates the quality of its nobility and substance, in virtue of which it is above all

---

[1] 2 Cor. xiii. 9.   [4] S. Matt. v. 16.
[2] Micah ii. 11.   [5] S. Matt. xxv. 34.
[3] Exod. xxxii. 31. 32.

[6] Tim, ii. 4.   [7] Is. xlvi. 10.
[8] Here Cassian is relying entirely on Jerome's revised text of the Latin, which has *supersubstantialis* in S. Matt. vi. 11, as the rendering of ἐπιούσιος but translates the same word by *quotidianum* in the parallel passage in S. Luke xi. 3. It is curious that Cassian should have been thus misled, with his knowledge of Greek, as well as his acquaintance with the old Latin version which has *quotidianum* in both gospels. Cf Bishop Lightfoot "On a Fresh Revision of the New Testament," p. 219.

substances and the loftiness of its grandeur and holiness exceeds all creatures, while the latter intimates the purpose of its use and value. For where it says "daily" it shows that without it we cannot live a spiritual life for a single day. Where it says "today" it shows that it must be received daily and that yesterday's supply of it is not enough, but that it must be given to us today also in like manner. And our daily need of it suggests to us that we ought at all times to offer up this prayer, because there is no day on which we have no need to strengthen the heart of our inner man, by eating and receiving it, although the expression used, "today" may be taken to apply to his present life, i.e., while we are living in this world supply us with this bread. For we know that it will be given to those who deserve it by Thee hereafter, but we ask that Thou wouldest grant it to us today, because unless it has been vouchsafed to a man to receive it in this life he will never be partaker of it in that.

CHAPTER XXII.

Of the clause : " Forgive us our debts, etc."

"AND forgive us our debts as we also forgive our debtors." O unspeakable mercy of God, which has not only given us a form of prayer and taught us a system of life acceptable to Him, and by the requirements of the form given, in which He charged us always to pray, has torn up the roots of both anger and sorrow, but also gives to those who pray an opportunity and reveals to them a way by which they may move a merciful and kindly judgment of God to be pronounced over them and which somehow gives us a power by which we can moderate the sentence of our Judge, drawing Him to forgive our offences by the example of our forgiveness: when we say to Him: "Forgive us as we also forgive." And so without anxiety and in confidence from this prayer a man may ask for pardon of his own offences, if he has been forgiving towards his own debtors, and not towards those of his Lord. For some of us, which is very bad, are inclined to show ourselves calm and most merciful in regard to those things which are done to God's detriment, however great the crimes may be, but to be found most hard and inexorable exactors of debts to ourselves even in the case of the most trifling wrongs. Whoever then does not from his heart forgive his brother who has offended him, by this prayer calls down upon himself not forgiveness but

condemnation, and by his own profession asks that he himself may be judged more severely, saying: Forgive me as I also have forgiven. And if he is repaid according to his own request, what else will follow but that he will be punished after his own example with implacable wrath and a sentence that cannot be remitted? And so if we want to be judged mercifully, we ought also to be merciful towards those who have sinned against us. For only so much will be remitted to us, as we have remitted to those who have injured us however spitefully. And some dreading this, when this prayer is chanted by all the people in church, silently omit this clause, for fear lest they may seem by their own utterance to bind themselves rather than to excuse themselves, as they do not understand that it is in vain that they try to offer these quibbles to the Judge of all men, who has willed to show us beforehand how He will judge His suppliants. For as He does not wish to be found harsh and inexorable towards them, He has marked out the manner of His judgment, that just as we desire to be judged by Him, so we should also judge our brethren, if they have wronged us in anything, for "he shall have judgment without mercy who hath shown no mercy."[1]

CHAPTER XXIII.

Of the clause : " Lead us not into temptation."

NEXT there follows: "And lead us not into temptation," on which there arises no unimportant question, for if we pray that we may not be suffered to be tempted, how then will our power of endurance be proved, according to this text: "Every one who is not tempted is not proved;"[2] and again: "Blessed is the man that endureth temptation?"[3] The clause then, "Lead us not into temptation," does not mean this; viz., do not permit us ever to be tempted, but do not permit us when we fall into temptation to be overcome. For Job was tempted, but was not led into temptation. For he did not ascribe folly to God nor blasphemy, nor with impious mouth did he yield to that wish of the tempter toward which he was drawn. Abraham was tempted, Joseph was tempted, but neither of them was led into temptation for neither of them yielded his consent to the tempter. Next there follows: "But deliver us from evil," i.e., do not suffer us to be tempted by the devil above that we

---

[1] S. James ii. 13.　　[2] Ecclus. xxxiv. 11.　　[3] S. James i. 12.

are able, but "make with the temptation a way also of escape that we may be able to bear it." [1]

CHAPTER XXIV.

How we ought not to ask for other things, except only those which are contained in the limits of the Lord's Prayer.

YOU see then what is the method and form of prayer proposed to us by the Judge Himself, who is to be prayed to by it, a form in which there is contained no petition for riches, no thought of honours, no request for power and might, no mention of bodily health and of temporal life. For He who is the Author of Eternity would have men ask of Him nothing uncertain, nothing paltry, and nothing temporal. And so a man will offer the greatest insult to His Majesty and Bounty, if he leaves on one side these eternal petitions and chooses rather to ask of Him something transitory and uncertain; and will also incur the indignation rather than the propitiation of the Judge by the pettiness of his prayer.

CHAPTER XXV.

Of the character of the sublimer prayer.

THIS prayer then though it seems to contain all the fulness of perfection, as being what was originated and appointed by the Lord's own authority, yet lifts those to whom it belongs to that still higher condition of which we spoke above, and carries them on by a loftier stage to that ardent prayer which is known and tried by but very few, and which to speak more truly is ineffable; which transcends all human thoughts, and is distinguished, I will not say by any sound of the voice, but by no movement of the tongue, or utterance of words, but which the mind enlightened by the infusion of that heavenly light describes in no human and confined language, but pours forth richly as from a copious fountain in an accumulation of thoughts, and ineffably utters to God, expressing in the shortest possible space of time such great things that the mind when it returns to its usual condition cannot easily utter or relate. And this condition our Lord also similarly prefigured by the form of those supplications which, when he retired alone in the mountain He is said to have poured forth in silence, and when being in an agony of prayer He shed forth even drops of blood, as an example of a purpose which it is hard to imitate.

CHAPTER XXVI.

Of the different causes of conviction.

BUT who is able, with whatever experience he may be endowed, to give a sufficient account of the varieties and reasons and grounds of conviction, by which the mind is inflamed and set on fire and incited to pure and most fervent prayers? And of these we will now by way of specimen set forth a few, as far as we can by God's enlightenment recollect them. For sometimes a verse of any one of the Psalms gives us an occasion of ardent prayer while we are singing. Sometimes the harmonious modulation of a brother's voice stirs up the minds of dullards to intense supplication. We know also that the enunciation and the reverence of the chanter adds greatly to the fervour of those who stand by. Moreover the exhortation of a perfect man, and a spiritual conference has often raised the affections of those present to the richest prayer. We know too that by the death of a brother or some one dear to us, we are no less carried away to full conviction. The recollection also of our coldness and carelessness has sometimes aroused in us a healthful fervour of spirit. And in this way no one can doubt that numberless opportunities are not wanting, by which through God's grace the coldness and sleepiness of our minds can be shaken off.

CHAPTER XXVII.

Of the different sorts of conviction.

BUT how and in what way those very convictions are produced from the inmost recesses of the soul it is no less difficult to trace out. For often through some inexpressible delight and keenness of spirit the fruit of a most salutary conviction arises so that it actually breaks forth into shouts owing to the greatness of its incontrollable joy; and the delight of the heart and greatness of exultation makes itself heard even in the cell of a neighbour. But sometimes the mind hides itself in complete silence within the secrets of a profound quiet, so that the amazement of a sudden illumination chokes all sounds of words and the overawed spirit either keeps all its feelings to itself or loses [2] them and pours forth its desires

---

[1] 1 Cor. x. 13.

[2] Petschenig's text reads "amittat." v. l. emittat.

to God with groanings that cannot be uttered. But sometimes it is filled with such overwhelming conviction and grief that it cannot express it except by floods of tears.

CHAPTER XXVIII.

A question about the fact that a plentiful supply of tears is not in our own power.

GERMANUS: My own poor self indeed is not altogether ignorant of this feeling of conviction. For often when tears arise at the recollection of my faults, I have been by the Lord's visitation so refreshed by this ineffable joy which you describe that the greatness of the joy has assured me that I ought not to despair of their forgiveness. Than which state of mind I think there is nothing more sublime if only it could be recalled at our own will. For sometimes when I am desirous to stir myself up with all my power to the same conviction and tears, and place before my eyes all my faults and sins, I am unable to bring back that copiousness of tears, and so my eyes are dry and hard like some hardest flint, so that not a single tear trickles from them. And so in proportion as I congratulate myself on that copiousness of tears, just so do I mourn that I cannot bring it back again whenever I wish.

CHAPTER XXIX.

The answer on the varieties of conviction which spring from tears.

ISAAC: Not every kind of shedding of tears is produced by one feeling or one virtue. For in one way does that weeping originate which is caused by the pricks of our sins smiting our heart, of which we read: "I have laboured in my groanings, every night I will wash my bed ; I will water my couch with my tears." [1] And again : "Let tears run down like a torrent day and night: give thyself no rest, and let not the apple of thine eye cease." [2] In another, that which arises from the contemplation of eternal good things and the desire of that future glory, owing to which even richer wellsprings of tears burst forth from uncontrollable delights and boundless exultation, while our soul is athirst for the mighty Living God, saying, "When shall I come and appear before the presence of God? My tears have been my meat day and night," [3] declaring with daily crying and lamentation: "Woe is me that my sojourning is prolonged;" and: "Too long

hath my soul been a sojourner." [4] In another way do the tears flow forth, which without any conscience of deadly sin, yet still proceed from the fear of hell and the recollection of that terrible judgment, with the terror of which the prophet was smitten and prayed to God, saying : "Enter not into judgment with Thy servant, for in Thy sight shall no man living be justified." [5] There is too another kind of tears, which are caused not by knowledge of one's self but by the hardness and sins of others ; whereby Samuel is described as having wept for Saul, and both the Lord in the gospel and Jeremiah in former days for the city of Jerusalem, the latter thus saying : "Oh, that my head were water and mine eyes a fountain of tears ! And I will weep day and night for the slain of the daughter of my people." [6] Or also such as were those tears of which we hear in the hundred and first Psalm : "For I have eaten ashes for my bread, and mingled my cup with weeping." [7] And these were certainly not caused by the same feeling as those which arise in the sixth Psalm from the person of the penitent, but were due to the anxieties of this life and its distresses and losses, by which the righteous who are living in this world are oppressed. And this is clearly shown not only by the words of the Psalm itself, but also by its title, which runs as follows in the character of that poor person of whom it is said in the gospel that "blessed are the poor in spirit, for theirs is the kingdom of heaven :" [8] "A prayer of the poor when he was in distress and poured forth his prayer to God." [9]

CHAPTER XXX.

How tears ought not to be squeezed out, when they do not flow spontaneously.

FROM these tears those are vastly different which are squeezed out from dry eyes while the heart is hard : and although we cannot believe that these are altogether fruitless (for the attempt to shed them is made with a good intention, especially by those who have not yet been able to attain to perfect knowledge or to be thoroughly cleansed from the stains of past or present sins), yet certainly the flow of tears ought not to be thus forced out by those who have already advanced to the love of virtue, nor should the weeping of the outward man be with great labour attempted, as even if it is produced it will never attain the rich copiousness of spontaneous tears. For it will rather

---

[1] Ps. vi. 7.   [2] Lam. ii. 18.   [3] Ps. xii. (xliii.) 3, 4.

[4] Ps. cix. (cxix.) 5, 6.   [6] Jer. ix. 1.   [8] S. Matt. v. 3.
[5] Ps. cxlii. (cxliii.) 2.   [7] Ps. ci. (cii.) 10.   [9] Ps. ci. (cii.) 1.

cast down the soul of the suppliant by his endeavours, and humiliate him, and plunge him in human affairs and draw him away from the celestial heights, wherein the awed mind of one who prays should be steadfastly fixed, and will force it to relax its hold on its prayers and grow sick from barren and forced tears.

CHAPTER XXXI.

The opinion of Abbot Antony on the condition of prayer.

AND that you may see the character of true prayer I will give you not my own opinion but that of the blessed Antony: whom we have known sometimes to have been so persistent in prayer that often as he was praying in a transport of mind, when the sunrise began to appear, we have heard him in the fervour of his spirit declaiming: Why do you hinder me, O sun, who art arising for this very purpose; viz., to withdraw me from the brightness of this true light? And his also is this heavenly and more than human utterance on the end of prayer: That is not, said he, a perfect prayer, wherein a monk understands himself and the words which he prays. And if we too, as far as our slender ability allows, may venture to add anything to this splendid utterance, we will bring forward the marks of prayer which are heard from the Lord, as far as we have tried them.

CHAPTER XXXII.

Of the proof of prayer being heard.

WHEN, while we are praying, no hesitation intervenes and breaks down the confidence of our petition by a sort of despair, but we feel that by pouring forth our prayer we have obtained what we are asking for, we have no doubt that our prayers have effectually reached God. For so far will one be heard and obtain an answer, as he believes that he is regarded by God, and that God can grant it. For this saying of our Lord cannot be retracted: "Whatsoever ye ask when ye pray, believe that you shall receive, and they shall come to you." [1]

CHAPTER XXXIII.

An objection that the confidence of being thus heard as described belongs only to saints.

GERMANUS: We certainly believe that this confidence of being heard flows from purity of conscience, but for us, whose heart is still smitten by the pricks of sins, how can we have it, as we have no merits to plead for us, whereby we might confidently presume that our prayers would be heard?

CHAPTER XXXIV.

Answer on the different reasons for prayer being heard.

ISAAC: That there are different reasons for prayer being heard in accordance with the varied and changing condition of souls the words of the gospels and of the prophets teach us. For you have the fruits of an answer pointed out by our Lord's words in the case of the agreement of two persons; as it is said: "If two of you shall agree upon earth touching anything for which they shall ask, it shall be done for them of my Father which is in heaven." [2] You have another in the fulness of faith, which is compared to a grain of mustard-seed. "For," He says, "if you have faith as a grain of mustard seed, ye shall say unto this mountain: Be thou removed, and it shall be removed; and nothing shall be impossible to you." [3] You have it in continuance in prayer, which the Lord's words call, by reason of unwearied perseverance in petitioning, importunity: "For, verily, I say unto you that if not because of his friendship, yet because of his importunity he will rise and give him as much as he needs." [4] You have it in the fruits of almsgiving: "Shut up alms in the heart of the poor and it shall pray for thee in the time of tribulation." [5] You have it in the purifying of life and in works of mercy, as it is said: "Loose the bands of wickedness, undo the bundles that oppress;" and after a few words in which the barrenness of an unfruitful fast is rebuked, "then," he says, "thou shalt call and the Lord shall hear thee; thou shalt cry, and He shall say, Here am I." [6] Sometimes also excess of trouble causes it to be heard, as it is said: "When I was in trouble I called unto the Lord, and He heard me;" [7] and again: "Afflict not the stranger for if he crieth unto Me, I will hear him, for I am merciful." [8] You see then in how many ways the gift of an answer may be obtained, so that no one need be crushed by the despair of his conscience for securing those things which are salutary and eternal. For if in contemplating our wretchedness I admit that we are utterly destitute of all those virtues which we mentioned above, and that we have neither that laudable agreement of two persons, nor that faith which

---

[1] S. Mark xi. 24.

[2] S. Matt. xviii. 19. [5] Ecclus. xxix. 15. [7] Ps. cxix. (cxx.) 1.
[3] S. Matt. xvii. 19. [6] Is. lviii. 6, 9. [8] Exod. xxii. 21, 27.
[4] S. Luke xi. 8.

is compared to a grain of mustard seed, nor those works of piety which the prophet describes, surely we cannot be without that importunity which He supplies to all who desire it, owing to which alone the Lord promises that He will give whatever He has been prayed to give. And therefore we ought without unbelieving hesitation to persevere, and not to have the least doubt that by continuing in them we shall obtain all those things which we have asked according to the mind of God. For the Lord, in His desire to grant what is heavenly and eternal, urges us to constrain Him as it were by our importunity, as He not only does not despise or reject the importunate, but actually welcomes and praises them, and most graciously promises to grant whatever they have perseveringly hoped for; saying, "Ask and ye shall receive: seek and ye shall find: knock and it shall be opened unto you. For every one that asketh receiveth, and he that seeketh findeth, and to him that knocketh it shall be opened;"[1] and again: "All things whatsoever ye shall ask in prayer believing ye shall receive, and nothing shall be impossible to you."[2] And therefore even if all the grounds for being heard which we have mentioned are altogether wanting, at any rate the earnestness of importunity may animate us, as this is placed in the power of any one who wills without the difficulties of any merits or labours. But let not any suppliant doubt that he certainly will *not* be heard, so long as he doubts whether he is heard. But that this also shall be sought from the Lord unweariedly, we are taught by the example of the blessed Daniel, as, though he was heard from the first day on which he began to pray, he only obtained the result of his petition after one and twenty days.[3] Wherefore we also ought not to grow slack in the earnestness of the prayers we have begun, if we fancy that the answer comes but slowly, for fear lest perhaps the gift of the answer be in God's providence delayed, or the angel, who was to bring the Divine blessing to us, may when he comes forth from the Presence of the Almighty be hindered by the resistance of the devil, as it is certain that he cannot transmit and bring to us the desired boon, if he finds that we slack off from the earnestness of the petition made. And this would certainly have happened to the above mentioned prophet unless he had with incomparable steadfastness prolonged and persevered in his prayers until the twenty-first day. Let us then not be at all cast down by despair from the confidence of this faith of ours, even when we fancy that we are far from having obtained what we prayed for, and let us not have any doubts about the Lord's promise where He says: "All things, whatsoever ye shall ask in prayer believing, ye shall receive."[4] For it is well for us to consider this saying of the blessed Evangelist John, by which the ambiguity of this question is clearly solved: "This is," he says, "the confidence which we have in Him, that whatsoever we ask according to His will, He heareth us."[5] He bids us then have a full and undoubting confidence of the answer only in those things which are not for our own advantage or for temporal comforts, but are in conformity to the Lord's will. And we are also taught to put this into our prayers by the Lord's Prayer, where we say "Thy will be done," — *Thine* not ours. For if we also remember these words of the Apostle that "we know not what to pray for as we ought"[6] we shall see that we sometimes ask for things opposed to our salvation and that we are most providentially refused our requests by Him who sees what is good for us with greater right and truth than we can. And it is clear that this also happened to the teacher of the Gentiles when he prayed that the messenger of Satan who had been for his good allowed by the Lord's will to buffet him, might be removed, saying: "For which I besought the Lord thrice that He might depart from me. And He said unto me, My grace is sufficient for thee, for strength is made perfect in weakness."[7] And this feeling even our Lord expressed when He prayed in the character[8] of man which He had taken, that He might give us a form of prayer as other things also by His example; saying thus: "Father, if it be possible, let this cup pass from me: nevertheless not as I will but as Thou wilt,"[9] though certainly His will was not discordant with His Father's will, "For He had come to save what was lost and to give His life a ransom for many;"[10] as He Himself says: "No man taketh my life from Me, but I lay it down of Myself. I have power to lay it down and I have power to take it again."[11] In which character there is in the thirty-ninth Psalm the following sung by the blessed David, of the Unity of will which He ever maintained with the Father: "To do Thy will: O My God, I am willing."[12] For even if we read of the Father: "For God so loved the world that He gave His only begotten

---

[1] S. Luke xi. 9, 10. [2] S. Matt. xxi. 22; xvii. 20. [3] Cf. Dan. x. 2 sq.

[4] S. Matt. xxi. 22.
[5] 1 John v. 16.
[6] Rom. viii. 26.
[7] 2 Cor. xii. 8, 9.
[8] *Ex persona hominis assumpti.* The language is scarcely accurate, but it must be remembered that the Conferences were written before the rise of the Nestorian heresy had shown the need of exactness of expression on the subject of the Incarnation. Compare the note on "Against Nestorius," Book III. c. iii.
[9] S. Matt. xxvi. 39.
[10] S. Matt. xviii. 11; xx. 28.
[11] S. John x. 18.
[12] Ps. xxxix. (xl.) 9.

Son," [1] we find none the less of the Son : "Who gave Himself for our sins." [2]   And as it is said of the One : " Who spared not His own Son, but gave Him for all of us," [3] so it is written of the other : " He was offered because He Himself, willed it." [4]   And it is shown that the will of the Father and of the Son is in all things one, so that even in the actual mystery of the Lord's resurrection we are taught that there was no discord of operation. For just as the blessed Apostle declares that the Father brought about the resurrection of His body, saying : " And God the Father, who raised Him from the dead," [5] so also the Son testifies that He Himself will raise again the Temple of His body, saying : " Destroy this temple, and in three days I will raise it up again." [6]   And therefore we being instructed by all these examples of our Lord which have been enumerated ought to end our supplications also with the same prayer, and always to subjoin this clause to all our petitions : " Nevertheless not as I will, but as Thou wilt." [7]   But it is clear enough that one who does not [8] pray with attention of mind cannot observe that threefold reverence [9] which is usually practised in the assemblies of the brethren at the close of service.

CHAPTER XXXV.

Of prayer to be offered within the chamber and with the door shut.

BEFORE all things however we ought most carefully to observe the Evangelic precept, which tells us to enter into our chamber and shut the door and pray to our Father, which may be fulfilled by us as follows : We pray within our chamber, when removing our hearts inwardly from the din of all thoughts and anxieties, we disclose our prayers in secret and in closest intercourse to the Lord.   We pray with closed doors when with closed lips and complete silence we pray to the searcher not of words but of hearts.   We pray in secret when from the heart and fervent mind we disclose our petitions to God alone, so that no hostile powers are even able to discover the character of our petition.   Wherefore we

should pray in complete silence, not only to avoid distracting the brethren standing near by our whispers or louder utterances, and disturbing the thoughts of those who are praying, but also that the purport of our petition may be concealed from our enemies who are especially on the watch against us while we are praying.   For so we shall fulfil this injunction : " Keep the doors of thy mouth from her who sleepeth in thy bosom." [10]

CHAPTER XXXVI.

Of the value of short and silent prayer.

WHEREFORE we ought to pray often but briefly, lest if we are long about it our crafty foe may succeed in implanting something in our heart. For that is the true sacrifice, as "the sacrifice of God is a broken spirit."   This is the salutary offering, these are pure drink offerings, that is the " sacrifice of righteousness," the " sacrifice of praise," these are true and fat victims, " holocausts full of marrow," which are offered by contrite and humble hearts, and which those who practise this control and fervour of spirit, of which we have spoken, with effectual power can sing : " Let my prayer be set forth in Thy sight as the incense : let the lifting up of my hands be an evening sacrifice." [11]   But the approach of the right hour and of night warns us that we ought with fitting devotion to do this very thing, of which, as our slender ability allowed, we seem to have propounded a great deal, and to have prolonged our conference considerably, though we believe that we have discoursed very little when the magnificence and difficulty of the subject are taken into account.

With these words of the holy Isaac we were dazzled rather than satisfied, and after evening service had been held, rested our limbs for a short time, and intending at the first dawn again to return under promise of a fuller discussion departed, rejoicing over the acquisition of these precepts as well as over the assurance of his promises.   Since we felt that though the excellence of prayer had been shown to us, still we had not yet understood from his discourse its nature, and the power by which continuance in it might be gained and kept.

---

[1] 1 John iii. 16.   [3] Rom. viii. 32.   [5] Gal. i. 1.
[2] Gal. i. 4.   [4] Is. liii. 7. (Lat.)   [6] S. John ii. 19.
[7] S. Matt. xxvi. 39.
[8] " Non" though wanting in most MSS. must be read in the text.
[9] Reading " curvationis " with Petschenig : the text of Gazæus has " orationis."

[10] Micah vii. 5.
[11] Ps. l. (li.) 19, 21; xlix. (l.) 23; lxv. (lxvi.) 15; cxl. (cxli.) 2.

X.

THE SECOND CONFERENCE OF ABBOT ISAAC.

ON PRAYER.

CHAPTER I.

Introduction.

AMONG the sublime customs of the anchorites which by God's help have been set forth although in plain and unadorned style, the course of our narration compels us to insert and find a place for something, which may seem so to speak to cause a blemish on a fair body: although I have no doubt that by it no small instruction on the image of Almighty God of which we read in Genesis will be conferred on some of the simpler sort, especially when the grounds are considered of a doctrine so important that men cannot be ignorant of it without terrible blasphemy and serious harm to the Catholic faith.

CHAPTER II.

Of the custom which is kept up in the Province of Egypt for signifying the time of Easter.

IN the country of Egypt this custom is by ancient tradition observed that — when Epiphany is past, which the priests of that province regard as the time, both of our Lord's baptism and also of His birth in the flesh, and so celebrate the commemoration of either mystery not separately as in the Western provinces but on the single festival of this day,[1] — letters are sent from the Bishop of Alexandria through all the Churches of Egypt, by which the beginning of Lent, and the day of Easter are pointed out not only in all the cities but also in all the monasteries.[2] In accordance then with this custom, a very few days after the previous conference had been held with Abbot Isaac, there arrived the festal letters of Theophilus [3] the Bishop of the aforesaid city, in which together with the announcement of Easter he considered as well the foolish heresy of the Anthropomorphites [4] at great length, and abundantly refuted it. And this was received by almost all the body of monks residing in the whole province of Egypt with such bitterness owing to their simplicity and error, that the greater part of the Elders decreed that on the contrary the aforesaid Bishop ought to be abhorred by the whole body of the brethren as tainted with heresy of the worst kind, because he seemed to impugn the teaching of holy Scripture by the denial that Almighty God was formed in the fashion of a human

---

[1] The observance of Epiphany can be traced back in the Christian Church to the second century, and, as Cassian tells us here, in the East (in which its observance apparently originated) it was in the first instance a double festival, commemorating both the Nativity and the Baptism of our Lord. From the East its observance passed over to the West, where however the Nativity was already observed as a separate festival, and hence the *special* reference of Epiphany was somewhat altered, and the manifestation to the Magi was coupled with that at the Baptism: hence the plural *Epiphaniorum dies*. Meanwhile, as the West adopted the observance of this festival from the East, so the East followed the West in observing a separate feast of the Nativity. Cassian's words show us that when he wrote the two festivals were both observed separately in the West, though apparently *not* yet (to the best of his belief) in the East, but the language of a homily by S. Chrysostom (Vol. ii. p. 354 Ed. Montfaucon) delivered in A.D. 386 shows that the separation of the two festivals had already begun at Antioch, and all the evidence goes to show that "the Western plan was being gradually adopted in the period which we may roughly define as the last quarter of the 4th and the first quarter of the 5th century." Dictionary of Christian Antiquities, Vol. i. p. 361. See further Origines du Culte Chrétien, par L'Abbé Duchesne, p. 247 *sq*.

[2] The ". Festal letters " (ἑορταστικαὶ ἐπιστολαί, Euşeb. VII. xx., xxi.) were delivered by the Bishop of Alexandria as Homilies, and then put into the form of an Epistle and sent round to all the churches of Egypt ; and, according to some late writers, to the Bishops of all the principal sees, in accordance with a decision of the Council of Nicæa, in order to inform them of the right day on which Easter should be celebrated. Cassian here speaks of them as sent immediately after Epiphany, and this was certainly the time at which the announcement of the date of Easter was made in the West shortly after his day (so the Council of Orleans, Canon i., A.D. 541); that of Braga A.D. 572, Canon ix. ; and that of Auxerre A.D. 572, Canon ii.), but there is ample evidence in the Festal letters both of S. Athanasius and of S. Cyril that at Alexandria the homilies were preached on the previous Easter, and it is difficult to resist the inference that Cassian's memory is here at fault as to the exact time at which the incident related really occurred, and that he is transferring to Egypt the custom with which he was familiar in the West, assigning to the festival of Epiphany what really must have taken place at Easter.

[3] Theophilus succeeded Timothy as Bishop of Alexandria in the summer of 385. The festal letters of which Cassian here speaks were issued by him in the year 399.

[4] The Anthropomorphite heresy, into which the monks of Egypt had fallen, "supposed that God possesses eyes, a face, and hands and other members of a bodily organization." It arose from taking too literally those passages of the Old Testament in which God is spoken of in human terms, out of condescension to man's limited powers of grasping the Divine nature and appears historically to have been a recoil from the allegorism of Origen and others of the Alexandrian school. The Festal letter of Theophilus in which he condemned these views, and maintained the incorporeal nature of God is no longer extant, but is alluded to also by Sozomen, H. E. VIII. xi., where an account is given of the Origenistic controversy, of which it was the occasion, and out of which Theophilus came so badly. On the heresy see also Epiphanius, Hær. lxx.; Augustine, Hær. l. and lxxvi.; and Theodoret, H. E. IV. x.

figure, though Scripture teaches with perfect clearness that Adam was created in His image. Lastly this letter was rejected also by those who were living in the desert of Scete and who excelled all who were in the monasteries of Egypt, in perfection and in knowledge, so that except Abbot Paphnutius the presbyter of our congregation, not one of the other presbyters, who presided over the other three churches in the same desert, would suffer it to be even read or repeated at all in their meetings.

CHAPTER III.

Of Abbot Sarapion and the heresy of the Anthropomorphites into which he fell in the error of simplicity.

AMONG those then who were caught by this mistaken notion was one named Sarapion, a man of long-standing strictness of life, and one who was altogether perfect in actual discipline, whose ignorance with regard to the view of the doctrine first mentioned was so far a stumbling block to all who held the true faith, as he himself outstripped almost all the monks both in the merits of his life and in the length of time (he had been there). And when this man could not be brought back to the way of the right faith by many exhortations of the holy presbyter Paphnutius, because this view seemed to him a novelty, and one that was not ever known to or handed down by his predecessors, it chanced that a certain deacon, a man of very great learning, named Photinus, arrived from the region of Cappadocia with the desire of visiting the brethren living in the same desert : whom the blessed Paphnutius received with the warmest welcome, and in order to confirm the faith which had been stated in the letters of the aforesaid Bishop, placed him in the midst and asked him before all the brethren how the Catholic Churches throughout the East interpreted the passage in Genesis where it says " Let us make man after our image and likeness." [1] And when he explained that the image and likeness of God was taken by all the leaders of the churches not according to the base sound of the letters, but spiritually, and supported this very fully and by many passages of Scripture, and showed that nothing of this sort could happen to that infinite and incomprehensible and invisible glory, so that it could be comprised in a human form and likeness, since its nature is incorporeal and uncompounded and

simple, and what can neither be apprehended by the eyes nor conceived by the mind, at length the old man was shaken by the numerous and very weighty assertions of this most learned man, and was drawn to the faith of the Catholic tradition. And when both Abbot Paphnutius and all of us were filled with intense delight at his adhesion, for this reason ; viz., that the Lord had not permitted a man of such age and crowned with such virtues, and one who erred only from ignorance and rustic simplicity, to wander from the path of the right faith up to the very last, and when we arose to give thanks, and were all together offering up our prayers to the Lord, the old man was so bewildered in mind during his prayer because he felt that the Anthropomorphic image of the Godhead which he used to set before himself in prayer, was banished from his heart, that on a sudden he burst into a flood of bitter tears and continual sobs, and cast himself down on the ground and exclaimed with strong groanings : " Alas ! wretched man that I am ! they have taken away my God from me, and I have now none to lay hold of ; and whom to worship and address I know not." By which scene we were terribly disturbed, and moreover with the effect of the former Conference still remaining in our hearts, we returned to Abbot Isaac, whom when we saw close at hand, we addressed with these words.

CHAPTER IV.

Of our return to Abbot Isaac and question concerning the error into which the aforesaid old man had fallen.

ALTHOUGH even besides the fresh matter which has lately arisen, our delight in the former conference which was held on the character of prayer would summon us to postpone everything else and return to your holiness, yet this grievous error of Abbot Sarapion, conceived, as we fancy, by the craft of most vile demons, adds somewhat to this desire of ours. For it is no small despair by which we are cast down when we consider that through the fault of this ignorance he has not only utterly lost all those labours which he has performed in so praiseworthy a manner for fifty years in this desert, but has also incurred the risk of eternal death. And so we want first to know why and wherefore so grievous an error has crept into him. And next we should like to be taught how we can arrive at that condition in prayer, of which you discoursed some time back not only fully but splendidly. For that admirable Con-

[1] Gen. i. 26.

ference has had this effect upon us, that it has only dazzled our minds and has not shown us how to perform or secure it.

CHAPTER V.

The answer on the heresy described above.

ISAAC: We need not be surprised that a really simple man who had never received any instruction on the substance and nature of the Godhead could still be entangled and deceived by an error of simplicity and the habit of a long-standing mistake, and (to speak more truly) continue in the original error which is brought about, not as you suppose by a new illusion of the demons, but by the ignorance of the ancient heathen world, while in accordance with the custom of that erroneous notion, by which they used to worship devils formed in the figure of men, they even now think that the incomprehensible and ineffable glory of the true Deity should be worshipped under the limitations of some figure, as they believe that they can grasp and hold nothing if they have not some image set before them, which they can continually address while they are at their devotions, and which they can carry about in their mind and have always fixed before their eyes. And against this mistake of theirs this text may be used : " And they changed the glory of the incorruptible God into the likeness of the image of corruptible man." [1] Jeremiah also says: " My people have changed their glory for an idol." [2] Which error although by this its origin, of which we have spoken, it is en-grained in the notions of some, yet none the less is it contracted in the hearts also of those who have never been stained with the superstition of the heathen world, under the colour of this passage where it is said " Let us make man after our image and our likeness," [3] ignorance and simplicity being its authors, so that actu-ally there has arisen owing to this hateful interpretation a heresy called that of the An-thropomorphites, which maintains with obsti-nate perverseness that the infinite and simple substance of the Godhead is fashioned in our lineaments and human configuration. Which however any one who has been taught the Catholic doctrine will abhor as heathenish blas-phemy, and so will arrive at that perfectly pure condition in prayer which will not only not con-nect with its prayers any figure of the Godhead or bodily lineaments (which it is a sin even to speak of), but will not even allow in itself even the memory of a name, or the appearance of an action, or an outline of any character.

CHAPTER VI.

Of the reasons why Jesus Christ appears to each one of us either in His humility or in His glorified condition.

FOR according to the measure of its purity, as I said in the former Conference, each mind is both raised and moulded in its prayer, if it forsakes the consideration of earthly and material things so far as the condition of its purity may carry it forward, and enable it with the inner eyes of the soul to see Jesus either still in His humility and in the flesh, or glori-fied and coming in the glory of His Majesty : for those cannot see Jesus coming in His Kingdom who are still kept back in a sort of state of Jewish weakness, and cannot say with the Apostle : " And if we have known Christ after the flesh, yet now we know Him so no more ; " [4] but only those can look with purest eyes on His Godhead, who rise with Him from low and earthly works and thoughts and go apart in the lofty mountain of solitude which is free from the disturbance of all earthly thoughts and troubles, and secure from the interference of all sins, and being exalted by pure faith and the heights of virtue reveals the glory of His Face and the image of His splendour to those who are able to look on Him with pure eyes of the soul. But Jesus is seen as well by those who live in towns and villages and hamlets, i.e., who are occupied in practical affairs and works, but not with the same brightness with which He appeared to those who can go up with Him into the afore-said mount of virtues, i.e., Peter, James, and John. For so in solitude He appeared to Moses and spoke with Elias. And as our Lord wished to establish this and to leave us examples of perfect purity, although He Himself, the very fount of inviolable sanctity, had no need of external help and the assistance of soli-tude in order to secure it (for the fulness of purity could not be soiled by any stain from crowds, nor could He be contaminated by in-tercourse with men, who cleanses and sanctifies all things that are polluted) yet still He retired into the mountain alone to pray, thus teach-ing us by the example of His retirement that if we too wish to approach God with a pure and spotless affection of heart, we should also retire from all the disturbance and confusion of crowds, so that while still living in the body we may manage in some degree to adapt ourselves to some likeness of that bliss which is promised hereafter to the saints, and that " God may be" to us " all in all." [5]

---

[1] Rom. i. 23.   [2] Jer. ii. 11.   [3] Gen. i. 26.   [4] 2 Cor. v. 16.   [5] 1 Cor. xv. 28.

CHAPTER VII.

What constitutes our end and perfect bliss.

FOR then will be perfectly fulfilled in our case that prayer of our Saviour in which He prayed for His disciples to the Father saying : " that the love wherewith Thou lovedst Me may be in them and they in us ; " and again : " that they all may be one as Thou, Father, in Me and I in Thee, that they also may be one in us," [1] when that perfect love of God, wherewith " He first loved us " [2] has passed into the feelings of our heart as well, by the fulfilment of this prayer of the Lord which we believe cannot possibly be ineffectual. And this will come to pass when God shall be all our love, and every desire and wish and effort, every thought of ours, and all our life and words and breath, and that unity which already exists between the Father and the Son, and the Son and the Father, has been shed abroad in our hearts and minds, so that as He loves us with a pure and unfeigned and indissoluble love, so we also may be joined to Him by a lasting and inseparable affection, since we are so united to Him that whatever we breathe or think, or speak is God, since, as I say, we attain to that end of which we spoke before, which the same Lord in His prayer hopes may be fulfilled in us : " that they all may be one as we are one, I in them and Thou in Me, that they also may be made perfect in one ; " and again : " Father, those whom Thou hast given Me, I will that where I am, they may also be with Me." [3] This then ought to be the destination of the solitary, this should be all his aim that it may be vouchsafed to him to possess even in the body an image of future bliss, and that he may begin in this world to have a foretaste of a sort of earnest of that celestial life and glory. This, I say, is the end of all perfection, that the mind purged from all carnal desires may daily be lifted towards spiritual things, until the whole life and all the thoughts of the heart become one continuous prayer.

CHAPTER VIII.

A question on the training in perfection by which we can arrive at perpetual recollection of God.

GERMANUS : The extent of our bewilderment at our wondering awe at the former Conference, because of which we came back again, increases still more. For in proportion as by the incitements of this teaching we are fired with the desire of perfect bliss, so do we fall back into greater despair, as we know not how to seek or obtain training for such lofty heights. Wherefore we entreat that you will patiently allow us (for it must perhaps be set forth and unfolded with a good deal of talk) to explain what while sitting in the cell we had begun to revolve in a lengthy meditation, although we know that your holiness is not at all troubled by the infirmities of the weak, which even for this reason should be openly set forth, that what is out of place in them may receive correction. Our notion then is that the perfection of any art or system of training must begin with some simple rudiments, and grow accustomed first to somewhat easy and tender beginnings, so that being nourished and trained little by little by a sort of reasonable milk, it may grow up and so by degrees and step by step mount up from the lowest depths to the heights : and when by these means it has entered on the plainer principles and so to speak passed the gates of the entrance of the profession, it will consequently arrive without difficulty at the inmost shrine and lofty heights of perfection. For how could any boy manage to pronounce the simplest union of syllables unless he had first carefully learnt the letters of the alphabet ? Or how can any one learn to read quickly, who is still unfit to connect together short and simple sentences ? But by what means will one who is ill instructed in the science of grammar attain eloquence in rhetoric or the knowledge of philosophy ? Wherefore for this highest learning also, by which we are taught even to cleave to God, I have no doubt that there are some foundations of the system, which must first be firmly laid and afterwards the towering heights of perfection may be placed and raised upon them. And we have a slight idea that these are its first principles ; viz., that we should first learn by what meditations God may be grasped and contemplated, and next that we should manage to keep a very firm hold of this topic whatever it is which we do not doubt is the height of all perfection. And therefore we want you to show us some material for this recollection, by which we may conceive and ever keep the idea of God in the mind, so that by always keeping it before our eyes, when we find that we have dropped away from Him, we may at once be able to recover ourselves and return thither and may succeed in laying hold of it again without any delay from wandering around the subject and searching for it. For it happens that when we have wandered away from our spiritual speculations and have come back to ourselves as if waking from

---

[1] S. John xvii. 26, 21.   [2] I John iv. 16.   [3] S. John xvii. 22-24.

a deadly sleep, and, being thoroughly roused, look for the subject matter, by which we may be able to revive that spiritual recollection which has been destroyed, we are hindered by the delay of the actual search before we find it, and are once more drawn aside from our endeavour, and before the spiritual insight is brought about, the purpose of heart which had been conceived, has disappeared. And this trouble is certain to happen to us for this reason because we do not keep something special firmly set before our eyes like some principle to which the wandering thoughts may be recalled after many digressions and varied excursions ; and, if I may use the expression, after long storms enter a quiet haven. And so it comes to pass that as the mind is constantly hindered by this want of knowledge and difficulty, and is always tossed about vaguely, and as if intoxicated, among various matters, and cannot even retain firm hold for any length of time of anything spiritual which has occurred to it by chance rather than of set purpose : while, as it is always receiving one thing after another, it does not notice either their beginning and origin or even their end.

CHAPTER IX.

The answer on the efficacy of understanding, which is gained by experience.

ISAAC : Your minute and subtle inquiry affords an indication of purity being very nearly reached. For no one would be able even to make inquiries on these matters, — I will not say to look within and discriminate, — except one who had been urged to sound the depths of such questions by careful and effectual diligence of mind, and watchful anxiety, and one whom the constant aim after a well controlled life had taught by practical experience to attempt the entrance to this purity and to knock at its doors. And therefore as I see you, I will not say, standing before the doors of that true prayer of which we have been speaking, but touching its inner chambers and inward parts as it were with the hands of experience, and already laying hold of some parts of it, I do not think that I shall find any difficulty in introducing you now within what I may call its hall, for you to roam about its recesses, as the Lord may direct; nor do I think that you will be hindered from investigating what is to be shown you by any obstacles or difficulties. For he is next door to understanding who carefully recognizes what he ought to ask about, nor is he far from knowledge, who begins to understand how

ignorant he is. And therefore I am not afraid of the charge of betraying secrets, and of levity, if I divulge what when speaking in my former discourse on the perfection of prayer I had kept back from discussing, as I think that its force was to be explained to us who are occupied with this subject and interest even without the aid of my words, by the grace of God.

CHAPTER X.

Of the method of continual prayer.

WHEREFORE in accordance with that system, which you admirably compared to teaching children (who can only take in the first lessons on the alphabet and recognize the shapes of the letters, and trace out their characters with a steady hand if they have, by means of some copies and shapes carefully impressed on wax, got accustomed to express their figures, by constantly looking at them and imitating them daily), we must give you also the form of this spiritual contemplation, on which you may always fix your gaze with the utmost steadiness, and both learn to consider it to your profit in unbroken continuance, and also manage by the practice of it and by meditation to climb to a still loftier insight. This formula then shall be proposed to you of this system, which you want, and of prayer, which every monk in his progress towards continual recollection of God, is accustomed to ponder, ceaselessly revolving it in his heart, having got rid of all kinds of other thoughts ; for he cannot possibly keep his hold over it unless he has freed himself from all bodily cares and anxieties. And as this was delivered to us by a few of those who were left of the oldest fathers, so it is only divulged by us to a very few and to those who are really keen. And so for keeping up continual recollection of God this pious formula is to be ever set before you. "O God, make speed to save me : O Lord, make haste to help me," [1] for this verse has not unreasonably been picked out from the whole of Scripture for this purpose. For it embraces all the feelings which can be implanted in human nature, and can be fitly and satisfactorily adapted to every condition, and all assaults. Since it contains an invocation of God against every danger, it contains humble and pious confession, it contains the watchfulness of anxiety and continual fear, it contains the thought of one's own weakness, confidence in the answer, and the assurance of a present and ever ready help.

---

[1] Ps. lxix. (lxx.) 2. It is not improbable that this chapter suggested to S. Benedict the use of these words as the opening versicle of the hour services, a position which it has ever since occupied in the West. See the Rule of S. Benedict, cc. ix., xvii., and xviii.

For one who is constantly calling on his protector, is certain that He is always at hand. It contains the glow of love and charity, it contains a view of the plots, and a dread of the enemies, from which one, who sees himself day and night hemmed in by them, confesses that he cannot be set free without the aid of his defender. This verse is an impregnable wall for all who are labouring under the attacks of demons, as well as impenetrable coat of mail and a strong shield. It does not suffer those who are in a state of moroseness and anxiety of mind, or depressed by sadness or all kinds of thoughts to despair of saving remedies, as it shows that He, who is invoked, is ever looking on at our struggles and is not far from His suppliants. It warns us whose lot is spiritual success and delight of heart that we ought not to be at all elated or puffed up by our happy condition, which it assures us cannot last without God as our protector, while it implores Him not only always but even speedily to help us. This verse, I say, will be found helpful and useful to every one of us in whatever condition we may be. For one who always and in all matters wants to be helped, shows that he needs the assistance of God not only in sorrowful or hard matters but also equally in prosperous and happy ones, that he may be delivered from the one and also made to continue in the other, as he knows that in both of them human weakness is unable to endure without His assistance. I am affected by the passion of gluttony. I ask for food of which the desert knows nothing, and in the squalid desert there are wafted to me odours of royal dainties, and I find that even against my will I am drawn to long for them. I must at once say: "O God, make speed to save me: O Lord, make haste to help me." I am incited to anticipate the hour fixed for supper, or I am trying with great sorrow of heart to keep to the limits of the right and regular meagre fare. I must cry out with groans: "O God, make speed to save me: O Lord, make haste to help me." Weakness of the stomach hinders me when wanting severer fasts, on account of the assaults of the flesh, or dryness of the belly and constipation frightens me. In order that effect may be given to my wishes, or else that the fire of carnal lust may be quenched without the remedy of a stricter fast, I must pray: "O God, make speed to save me: O Lord, make haste to help me." When I come to supper, at the bidding of the proper hour I loathe taking food and am prevented from eating anything to satisfy the requirements of nature: I must cry with a sigh: "O God, make speed to save me: O Lord, make haste to help me." When I want for the sake of steadfastness of heart to apply myself

to reading a headache interferes and stops me, and at the third hour sleep glues my head to the sacred page, and I am forced either to overstep or to anticipate the time assigned to rest; and finally an overpowering desire to sleep forces me to cut short the canonical rule for service in the Psalms: in the same way I must cry out: "O God, make speed to save me: O Lord, make haste to help me." Sleep is withdrawn from my eyes, and for many nights I find myself wearied out with sleeplessness caused by the devil, and all repose and rest by night is kept away from my eyelids; I must sigh and pray: "O God, make speed to save me: O Lord, make haste to help me." While I am still in the midst of a struggle with sin suddenly an irritation of the flesh affects me and tries by a pleasant sensation to draw me to consent while in my sleep. In order that a raging fire from without may not burn up the fragrant blossoms of chastity, I must cry out: "O God, make speed to save me: O Lord, make haste to help me." I feel that the incentive to lust is removed, and that the heat of passion has died away in my members: In order that this good condition acquired, or rather that this grace of God may continue still longer or forever with me, I must earnestly say: "O God, make speed to save me: O Lord, make haste to help me." I am disturbed by the pangs of anger, covetousness, gloominess, and driven to disturb the peaceful state in which I was, and which was dear to me: In order that I may not be carried away by raging passion into the bitterness of gall, I must cry out with deep groans: "O God, make speed to save me: O Lord, make haste to help me." I am tried by being puffed up by accidie, vainglory, and pride, and my mind with subtle thoughts flatters itself somewhat on account of the coldness and carelessness of others: In order that this dangerous suggestion of the enemy may not get the mastery over me, I must pray with all contrition of heart: "O God, make speed to save me: O Lord, make haste to help me." I have gained the grace of humility and simplicity, and by continually mortifying my spirit have got rid of the swellings of pride: In order that the "foot of pride" may not again "come against me," and "the hand of the sinner disturb me,"[1] and that I may not be more seriously damaged by elation at my success, I must cry with all my might, "O God, make speed to save me: O Lord, make haste to help me." I am on fire with innumerable and various wanderings of soul and shiftiness of heart, and cannot collect my scattered thoughts, nor can I even pour forth my prayer without interruption and images

---

[1] Ps. xxxv. (xxxvi.) 12.

of vain figures, and the recollection of conversations and actions, and I feel myself tied down by such dryness and barrenness that I feel I cannot give birth to any offspring in the shape of spiritual ideas : In order that it may be vouchsafed to me to be set free from this wretched state of mind, from which I cannot extricate myself by any number of sighs and groans, I must full surely cry out: "O God, make speed to save me : O Lord, make haste to help me." Again, I feel that by the visitation of the Holy Spirit I have gained purpose of soul, steadfastness of thought, keenness of heart, together with an ineffable joy and transport of mind, and in the exuberance of spiritual feelings I have perceived by a sudden illumination from the Lord an abounding revelation of most holy ideas which were formerly altogether hidden from me : In order that it may be vouchsafed to me to linger for a longer time in them I must often and anxiously exclaim : " O God, make speed to save me : O Lord, make haste to help me." Encompassed by nightly horrors of devils I am agitated, and am disturbed by the appearances of unclean spirits, my very hope of life and salvation is withdrawn by the horror of fear. Flying to the safe refuge of this verse, I will cry out with all my might : " O God, make speed to save me : O Lord, make haste to help me.' Again, when I have been restored by the Lord's consolation, and, cheered by His coming, feel myself encompassed as if by countless thousands of angels, so that all of a sudden I can venture to seek the conflict and provoke a battle with those whom a while ago I dreaded worse than death, and whose touch or even approach I felt with a shudder both of mind and body: In order that the vigour of this courage may, by God's grace, continue in me still longer, I must cry out with all my powers: "O God, make speed to save me: O Lord, make haste to help me." We must then ceaselessly and continuously pour forth the prayer of this verse, in adversity that we may be delivered, in prosperity that we may be preserved and not puffed up. Let the thought of this verse, I tell you, be conned over in your breast without ceasing. Whatever work you are doing, or office you are holding, or journey you are going, do not cease to chant this. When you are going to bed, or eating, and in the last necessities of nature, think on this. This thought in your heart may be to you a saving formula, and not only keep you unharmed by all attacks of devils, but also purify you from all faults and earthly stains, and lead you to that invisible and celestial contemplation, and carry you on to that ineffable glow of prayer, of which so few have any experience. Let sleep come upon you still considering this verse, till having been moulded by the constant use of it, you grow accustomed to repeat it even in your sleep. When you wake let it be the first thing to come into your mind, let it anticipate all your waking thoughts, let it when you rise from your bed send you down on your knees, and thence send you forth to all your work and business, and let it follow you about all day long. This you should think about, according to the Lawgiver's charge, " at home and walking forth on a journey," [1] sleeping and waking. This you should write on the threshold and door of your mouth, this you should place on the walls of your house and in the recesses of your heart so that when you fall on your knees in prayer this may be your chant as you kneel, and when you rise up from it to go forth to all the necessary business of life it may be your constant prayer as you stand.

CHAPTER XI.

Of the perfection of prayer to which we can rise by the system described.

THIS, this is the formula which the mind should unceasingly cling to until, strengthened by the constant use of it and by continual meditation, it casts off and rejects the rich and full material of all manner of thoughts and restricts itself to the poverty of this one verse, and so arrives with ready ease at that beatitude of the gospel, which holds the first place among the other beatitudes : for He says " Blessed are the poor in spirit, for theirs is the kingdom of heaven." [2] And so one who becomes grandly poor by a poverty of this sort will fulfil this saying of the prophet : " The poor and needy shall praise the name of the Lord." [3] And indeed what greater or holier poverty can there be than that of one who knowing that he has no defence and no strength of his own, asks for daily help from another's bounty, and as he is aware that every single moment his life and substance depend on Divine assistance, professes himself not without reason the Lord's bedesman, and cries to Him daily in prayer : " But I am poor and needy : the Lord helpeth me." [4] And so by the illumination of God Himself he mounts to that manifold knowledge of Him and begins henceforward to be nourished on sublimer and still more sacred mysteries, in accordance with these words of the prophet : " The high hills are a refuge for the stags, the rocks for the

[1] Deut. vi. 7.
[2] S. Matt. v. 3.
[3] Ps. lxxiii. (lxxiv.) 21.
[4] Ps. xxxix (xl) 17 (LXX.).

hedgehogs," [1] which is very fairly applied in the sense we have given, because whosoever continues in simplicity and innocence is not injurious or offensive to any one, but being content with his own simple condition endeavours simply to defend himself from being spoiled by his foes, and becomes a sort of spiritual hedgehog and is protected by the continual shield of that rock of the gospel, i.e., being sheltered by the recollection of the Lord's passion and by ceaseless meditation on the verse given above he escapes the snares of his opposing enemies. And of these spiritual hedgehogs we read in Proverbs as follows: "And the hedgehogs are a feeble folk, who have made their homes in the rocks." [2] And indeed what is feebler than a Christian, what is weaker than a monk, who is not only not permitted any vengeance for wrongs done to him but is actually not allowed to suffer even a slight and silent feeling of irritation to spring up within? But whoever advances from this condition and not only secures the simplicity of innocence, but is also shielded by the virtue of discretion, becomes an exterminator of deadly serpents, and has Satan crushed beneath his feet, and by his quickness of mind answers to the figure of the reasonable stag, this man will feed on the mountains of the prophets and Apostles, i.e., on their highest and loftiest mysteries. And thriving on this pasture continually, he will take in to himself all the thoughts of the Psalms and will begin to sing them in such a way that he will utter them with the deepest emotion of heart not as if they were the compositions of the Psalmist, but rather as if they were his own utterances and his very own prayer; and will certainly take them as aimed at himself, and will recognize that their words were not only fulfilled formerly by or in the person of the prophet, but that they are fulfilled and carried out daily in his own case. For then the Holy Scriptures lie open to us with greater clearness and as it were their very veins and marrow are exposed, when our experience not only perceives but actually anticipates their meaning, and the sense of the words is revealed to us not by an exposition of them but by practical proof. For if we have experience of the very state of mind in which each Psalm was sung and written, we become like their authors and anticipate the meaning rather than follow it, i.e., gathering the force of the words before we really know them, we remember what has happened to us, and what is happening in daily assaults when the thoughts of them come over us, and while we sing them we call to mind all that

our carelessness has brought upon us, or our earnestness has secured, or Divine Providence has granted or the promptings of the foe have deprived us of, or slippery and subtle forgetfulness has carried off, or human weakness has brought about, or thoughtless ignorance has cheated us of. For all these feelings we find expressed in the Psalms so that by seeing whatever happens as in a very clear mirror we understand it better, and so instructed by our feelings as our teachers we lay hold of it as something not merely heard but actually seen, and, as if it were not committed to memory, but implanted in the very nature of things, we are affected from the very bottom of the heart, so that we get at its meaning not by reading the text but by experience anticipating it. And so our mind will reach that incorruptible prayer to which in our former treatise, as the Lord vouchsafed to grant, the scheme of our Conference mounted, and this is not merely not engaged in gazing on any image, but is actually distinguished by the use of no words or utterances; but with the purpose of the mind all on fire, is produced through ecstasy of heart by some unaccountable keenness of spirit, and the mind being thus affected without the aid of the senses or any visible material pours it forth to God with groanings and sighs that cannot be uttered.

CHAPTER XII.

A question as to how spiritual thoughts can be retained without losing them.

GERMANUS: We think that you have described to us not only the system of this spiritual discipline for which we asked, but perfection itself; and this with great clearness and openness. For what can be more perfect and sublime than for the recollection of God to be embraced in so brief a meditation, and for it, dwelling on a single verse, to escape from all the limitations of things visible, and to comprise in one short word the thoughts of all our prayers. And therefore we beg you to explain to us one thing which still remains; viz., how we can keep firm hold of this verse which you have given us as a formula, in such a way that, as we have been by God's grace set free from the trifles of worldly thoughts, so we may also keep a steady grasp on all spiritual ones.

CHAPTER XIII.

On the lightness of thoughts.

FOR when the mind has taken in the meaning of a passage in any Psalm, this insensibly slips

---

[1] Ps. ciii. (civ.) 18. [2] Prov. xxx. 26 (LXX.).

away from it, and ignorantly and thoughtlessly it passes on to a text of some other Scripture. And when it has begun to consider this with itself, while it is still not thoroughly explored, the recollection of some other passage springs up, and shuts out the consideration of the former subject. From this too it is transferred to some other, by the entrance of some fresh consideration, and the soul always turns about from Psalm to Psalm and jumps from a passage in the Gospels to read one in the Epistles, and from this passes on to the prophetic writings, and thence is carried to some spiritual history, and so it wanders about vaguely and uncertainly through the whole body of the Scriptures, unable, as it may choose, either to reject or keep hold of anything, or to finish anything by fully considering and examining it, and so becomes only a toucher or taster of spiritual meanings, not an author and possessor of them. And so the mind, as it is always light and wandering, is distracted even in time of service by all sorts of things, as if it were intoxicated, and does not perform any office properly. For instance, while it is praying, it is recalling some Psalm or passage of Scripture. While it is chanting, it is thinking about something else besides what the text of the Psalm itself contains. When it repeats a passage of Scripture, it is thinking about something that has to be done, or remembering something that has been done. And in this way it takes in and rejects nothing in a disciplined and proper way, and seems to be driven about by random incursions, without the power either of retaining what it likes or lingering over it. It is then well for us before everything else to know how we can properly perform these spiritual offices, and keep firm hold of this particular verse which you have given us as a formula, so that the rise and fall of our feelings may not be in a state of fluctuation from their own lightness, but may lie under our own control.

CHAPTER XIV.

The answer how we can gain stability of heart or of thoughts.

ISAAC: Although, in our former discussion on the character of prayer, enough was, as I

think, said on this subject, yet as you want it repeated to you again, I will give you a brief instruction on steadfastness of heart. There are three things which make a shifting heart steadfast, watchings, meditation, and prayer, diligence in which and constant attention will produce steadfast firmness of mind. But this cannot be secured in any other way unless all cares and anxieties of this present life have been first got rid of by indefatigable persistence in work dedicated not to covetousness but to the sacred uses of the monastery, that we may thus be able to fulfil the Apostle's command: "Pray without ceasing."[1] For he prays *too little*, who is accustomed only to pray at the times when he bends his knees. But he *never* prays, who even while on his bended knees is distracted by all kinds of wanderings of heart. And therefore what we would be found when at our prayers, that we ought to be before the time of prayer. For at the time of its prayers the mind cannot help being affected by its previous condition, and while it is praying, will be either transported to things heavenly, or dragged down to earthly things by those thoughts in which it had been lingering before prayer.

Thus far did Abbot Isaac carry on his Second Conference on the character of Prayer to us astonished hearers; whose instruction on the consideration of that verse quoted above (which he gave as a sort of outline for beginners to hold) we greatly admired, and wished to follow very closely, as we fancied that it would be a short and easy method; but we have found it even harder to observe than that system of ours by which we used formerly to wander here and there in varied meditations through the whole body of the Scriptures without being tied by any chains of perseverance. It is then certain that no one is kept away from perfection of heart by not being able to read, nor is rustic simplicity any hindrance to the possession of purity of heart and mind, which lies close at hand for all, if only they will by constant meditation on this verse keep the thoughts of the mind safe and sound towards God.

---

[1] 1 Thess. v. 17.

THE SECOND PART OF THE CONFERENCES
OF JOHN CASSIAN.

PREFACE.

ALTHOUGH many of the saints who are taught by your example can scarcely emulate the greatness of your perfection, with which you shine like great luminaries with marvellous brightness in this world, yet still you, O holy brothers Honoratus and Eucherius,[1] are so stirred by the great glory of those splendid men from whom we received the first principles of monasticism, that one of you, presiding as he does over a large monastery of the brethren, is hoping that his congregation, which learns a lesson from the daily sight of your saintly life, may be instructed in the precepts of those fathers, while the other has been anxious to make his way to Egypt to be edified by the sight of these in the flesh, that he might leave this province that is frozen as it were with the cold of Gaul, and like some pure turtle dove fly to those lands on which the sun of righteousness looks and to which it approaches nearest, and which abound with the ripe fruits of virtues. As a matter of course the greatness of my love wrings this from me; viz., that considering the desire of the one and the labour of the other, I should not decline the danger and peril of writing, if only to the one there may be added authority among his children, and from the other may be removed the necessity for so risky a journey. Further since neither the Institutes of the cœnobia which we wrote to the best of our ability in twelve books for Bishop Castor of blessed memory, nor the ten Conferences of the fathers living in the desert of Scete, which we composed somehow or other at the bidding of Saints Helladius and Leontius the Bishops,[2] were able to satisfy your faith and zeal, now in order that the reason for our journey may be also known, I have thought that seven Conferences of the three fathers whom we first saw living in another desert, might be written in the same style and dedicated to you, in which whatever has been in our previous works perhaps obscurely explained or even omitted on the subject of perfection, may be supplied. But if even this is not enough to satisfy the holy thirst of your desires, seven other Conferences, which are to be sent to the holy brethren living in the islands of the Stœchades,[3] will, I fancy, satisfy your wants and your ardour.

---

[1] On Honoratus and Eucherius, see the Introduction, p. 189.   [2] Cf The Preface to Conference I.
[3] A group of islands off the coast of France opposite Marseilles; mentioned by Pliny, H. N. III. V., now known as *Les Isles d'Hieres*.

THE SECOND PART OF THE CONFERENCES OF JOHN CASSIAN.

XI.

THE FIRST CONFERENCE OF ABBOT CHÆREMON.

ON PERFECTION.

CHAPTER I.

Description of the town of Thennesus.

WHEN we were living in a monastery in Syria after our first infancy in the faith, and when after we had grown somewhat we had begun to long for some greater grace of perfection, we determined straightway to seek Egypt and penetrating even to the remotest desert of the Thebaid,[1] to visit very many of the saints, whose glory and fame had spread abroad everywhere, with the wish if not to emulate them at any rate to know them. And so we came by a very lengthy voyage to a town of Egypt named Thennesus,[2] whose inhabitants are so surrounded either by the sea or by salt lakes that they devote themselves to business alone and get their wealth and substance by naval commerce as the land fails them, so that indeed when they want to build houses, there is no soil sufficient for this, unless it is brought by boat from a distance.

CHAPTER II.

Of Bishop Archebius.

AND when we arrived there, God gratified our wishes, and had brought about the arrival of that most blessed and excellent man Bishop Archbius,[3] who had been carried off from the assembly of anchorites and given as Bishop to the town of Panephysis,[4] and who kept all his life long to his purpose of solitude with such strictness that he relaxed nothing of the character of his former humility, nor flattered himself on the honour that had been added to him (for he vowed that he had not been summoned to that office as fit for it, but complained that he had been expelled from the monastic system as unworthy of it because though he had spent thirty-seven years in it he had never been able to arrive at the purity so high a profession demands); he then when he had received us kindly and most graciously in the aforesaid Thennesus whither the business of electing a Bishop there had brought him, as soon as he heard of our wish and desire to inquire of the holy fathers even in still more remote parts of Egypt: "Come," said he, "see in the meanwhile the old men who live not far from our monastery, the length of whose service is shown by their bent bodies, as their holiness shines forth in their appearance, so that even the mere sight of them will give a great lesson to those who see them: and from them you can learn not so much by their words as by the actual example of their holy life, what I grieve that I have lost, and having lost cannot give to you. But I think that my poverty will be somewhat lessened by this zeal of mine, if when you are seeking that pearl of the Gospel which I have not, I at least provide where you can conveniently procure it.'

---

[1] It is very doubtful whether Cassian ever carried out the intention, of which he here speaks, of visiting the Thebaid. So far as we can trace the course of his wanderings, he does not seem to have penetrated farther into Egypt than the desert of Scete.

[2] Thennesus, a town at the Tanitic mouth of the Nile near Lake Menzaleh. For the description of the neighbouring country compare Conference VII. c. xxvi.

[3] Archebius has already been mentioned in Conference VII. xxvi.; and in the Institutes V. xxxvii., xxxviii., two stories are told illustrative of his kindness and goodness of disposition; but he is not known to us from any other source except Cassian's writings.

[4] For the situation of Panephysis, see the note on the Institutes, Book IV. c. xxx.

CHAPTER III.

Description of the desert where Chæremon, Nesteros, and Joseph lived.

AND so he took his staff and scrip, as is there the custom for all monks starting on a journey, and himself led us as guide of our road to his own city, i.e., Panephysis, the lands of which and indeed the greater part of the neighbouring region (formerly an extremely rich one since from it, as report says, everything was supplied for the royal table), had been covered by the sea which was disturbed by a sudden earthquake and overflowed its banks, and so (almost all the villages being in ruins) covered what were formerly rich lands with salt marshes, so that you might think that what is spiritually sung in the psalm was a literal prophecy of that region. "He hath turned rivers into a wilderness; and the springs of waters into a thirsty land: a fruitful land into saltness for the wickedness of them that dwell therein."[1] In these districts then many towns perched in this way on the higher hills were deserted by their inhabitants and turned by the inundation into islands, and these afforded the desired solitude to the holy anchorites, among whom three old men; viz., Chæremon, Nesteros and Joseph, stood out as anchorites of the longest standing.

CHAPTER IV.

Of Abbot Chæremon and his excuse about the teaching which we asked for.

AND so the blessed Archebius thought it best to take us first to Chæremon,[2] because he was nearer to his monastery, and because he was more advanced than the other two in age: for he had passed the hundredth year of his life, vigorous only in spirit, but with his back bowed with age and constant prayer, so that, as if he were once more in his childhood he crawled with his hands hanging down and resting on the ground. Gazing then at one and the same time on this man's wonderful face and on his walk (for though all his limbs had already failed and were dead yet he had lost none of the severity of his previous strictness) when we humbly asked for the word and doctrine, and declared that longing for spiritual instruction was the only reason for our coming, he sighed deeply and said: What doctrine can I teach you, I in whom the feebleness of age has relaxed my former strictness, as it has also

destroyed my confidence in speaking? For how could I presume to teach what I do not do, or instruct another in what I know I now practise but feebly and coldly? Wherefore I do not allow any of the younger men to live with me now that I am of such an advanced age, lest the other's strictness should be relaxed owing to my example. For the authority of a teacher will never be strong unless he fixes it in the heart of his hearer by the actual performance of his duty.

CHAPTER V.

Of our answer to his excuse.

AT this we were overwhelmed with no slight confusion and replied as follows: Although both the difficulty of the place and the solitary life itself, which even a robust youth could scarcely put up with, ought to be sufficient to teach us everything (and indeed without your saying anything they *do* teach and impress us a very great deal) yet still we ask you to lay aside your silence for a little and in a more worthy manner implant in us those principles by which we may be able to embrace, not so much by imitating it as by admiring it, that goodness which we see in you. For even if our coldness is known to you, and does not deserve to obtain what we are asking for, yet at least the trouble of so long a journey ought to be repaid by it, as we made haste to come here after our first beginning in the monastery of Bethlehem, owing to a longing for your instruction, and a yearning for our own good.

CHAPTER VI.

Abbot Chæremon's statement that faults can be overcome in three ways.

THEN the blessed CHÆREMON: There are, said he, three things which enable men to control their faults; viz., either the fear of hell or of laws even now imposed; or the hope and desire of the kingdom of heaven; or a liking for goodness itself and the love of virtue. For then we read that the fear of evil loathes contamination: "The fear of the Lord hateth evil."[3] Hope also shuts out the assaults of all faults: for "all who hope in Him shall not fail."[4] Love also fears no destruction from sins, for "love never faileth;"[5] and again: "love covers a multitude of sins."[6] And therefore the blessed Apostle confines the whole

---

[1] Ps. cvi. (cvii.) 33 *sq.*
[2] Chæremon is perhaps the same person of whom a short account is given in the Lausiac History of Palladius, c. xcii.

[3] Prov. viii. 13.
[4] Ps. xxxiii. (xxxiv.) 23.

[5] 1 Cor. xiii. 8.
[6] 1 Pet. iv. 8.

sum of salvation in the attainment of those three virtues, saying "Now abideth faith, hope, love, these three." [1] For faith is what makes us shun the stains of sin from fear of future judgment and punishment; hope is what withdraws our mind from present things, and despises all bodily pleasures from its expectation of heavenly rewards; love is what inflames us with keenness of heart for the love of Christ and the fruit of spiritual goodness, and makes us hate with a perfect hatred whatever is opposed to these. And these three things although they all seem to aim at one and the same end (for they incite us to abstain from things unlawful) yet they differ from each other greatly in the degrees of their excellence. For the two former belong properly to those men who in their aim at goodness have not yet acquired the love of virtue, and the third belongs specially to God and to those who have received into themselves the image and likeness of God. For He alone does the things that are good, with no fear and no thanks or reward to stir Him up, but simply from the love of goodness. For, as Solomon says, "The Lord hath made all things for Himself." [2] For under cover of His own goodness He bestows all the fulness of good things on the worthy and the unworthy because He cannot be wearied by wrongs, nor be moved by passions at the sins of men, as He ever remains perfect goodness and unchangeable in His nature.

CHAPTER VII.

By what steps we can ascend to the heights of love and what permanence there is in it.

IF then any one is aiming at perfection, from that first stage of fear which we rightly termed servile (of which it is said: "When ye have done all things say: we are unprofitable servants," [3]) he should by advancing a step mount to the higher path of hope — which is compared not to a slave but to a hireling, because it looks for the payment of its recompense, and as if it were free from care concerning absolution of its sins and fear of punishment, and conscious of its own good works, though it seems to look for the promised reward, yet it cannot attain to that love of a son who, trusting in his father's kindness and liberality, has no doubt that all that the father has is his, to which also that prodigal who together with his father's substance had lost the very name of son, did not venture to aspire, when he said: "I am no more worthy to be called thy son;" for after those husks which the swine ate, satisfaction from which was denied to him, i. e., the disgusting food of sin, as he "came to himself," and was overcome by a salutary fear, he already began to loathe the uncleanness of the swine, and to dread the punishment of gnawing hunger, and as if he had already been made a servant, desires the condition of a hireling and thinks about the remuneration, and says: "How many hired servants of my father have abundance of bread, and I perish here with hunger. I will then return to my father and will say unto him, 'Father I have sinned against heaven and before thee, and am no more worthy to be called thy son: make me as one of thy hired servants.'" [4] But those words of humble penitence his father who ran to meet him received with greater affection than that with which they were spoken, and was not content to allow him lesser things, but passing through the two stages without delay restored him to his former dignity of sonship. We also ought forthwith to hasten on that by means of the indissoluble grace of love we may mount to that third stage of sonship, which believes that all that the father has is its own, and so we may be counted worthy to receive the image and likeness of our heavenly Father, and be able to say after the likeness of the true son: "All that the Father hath is mine." [5] Which also the blessed Apostle declares of us, saying: "All things are yours, whether Paul or Apollos or Cephas, or the world, or life, or death, or things present, or things to come; all are yours." [6] And to this likeness the commands of our Saviour also summon us: "Be ye," says He, "perfect, even as your Father in heaven is perfect." [7] For in these persons sometimes the love of goodness is found to be interrupted, when the vigour of the soul is relaxed by some coldness or joy or delight, and so loses either the fear of hell for the time, or the desire of future blessings. And there is indeed in these a stage leading to some advance, which affects us so that when from fear of punishment or from hope of reward we begin to avoid sin we are enabled to pass on to the stage of love, for "fear," says one, "is not in love, but perfect love casteth out fear: for fear hath torment, but he who fears is not perfect in love. We therefore love because God first loved us." [8] We can then only ascend to that true perfection when, as He first loved us for the grace of nothing but our salvation, we also have loved Him for the sake of nothing but His own love alone. Wherefore we must do our best to mount with

---

[1] 1 Cor. xiii. 13. [2] Prov. xvi. 4. [3] S. Luke xvii. 10.

[4] S. Luke xv. 17-19. [6] 1 Cor. iii. 22. [8] 1 John iv. 18, 19.
[5] S. John xvi. 15. [7] St. Matt v. 48.

perfect ardour of mind from this fear to hope, from hope to the love of God, and the love of the virtues themselves, that as we steadily pass on to the love of goodness itself, we may, as far as it is possible for human nature, keep firm hold of what is good.

CHAPTER VIII.

How greatly those excel who depart from sin through the feeling of love.

FOR there is a great difference between one who puts out the fire of sin within him by fear of hell or hope of future reward, and one who from the feeling of divine love has a horror of sin itself and of uncleanness, and keeps hold of the virtue of purity simply from the love and longing for purity, and looks for no reward from a promise for the future, but, delighted with the knowledge of good things present, does everything not from regard to punishment but from delight in virtue. For this condition can neither abuse an opportunity to sin when all human witnesses are absent, nor be corrupted by the secret allurements of thoughts, while, keeping in its very marrow the love of virtue itself, it not only does not admit into the heart anything that is opposed to it, but actually hates it with the utmost horror. For it is one thing for a man in his delight at some present good to hate the stains of sins and of the flesh, and another thing to check unlawful desires by contemplating the future reward; and it is one thing to fear present loss and another to dread future punishment. Lastly it is a much greater thing to be unwilling to forsake good for good's own sake, than it is to withhold consent from evil for fear of evil. For in the former case the good is voluntary, but in the latter it is constrained and as it were violently forced out of a reluctant party either by fear of punishment or by greed of reward. For one who abstains from the allurements of sin owing to fear, will whenever the obstacle of fear is removed, once more return to what he loves and thus will not continually acquire any stability in good, nor will he ever rest free from attacks because he will not secure the sure and lasting peace of chastity. For where there is the disturbance of warfare there cannot help being the danger of wounds. For one who is in the midst of the conflict, even though he is a warrior and by fighting bravely inflicts frequent and deadly wounds on his foes, must still sometimes be pierced by the point of the enemy's sword. But one who has defeated the attack of sins and is now in the enjoyment of the security of peace, and has passed on to the love of virtue itself, will keep this condition of good continually, as he is entirely wrapped up in it, because he believes that nothing can be worse than the loss of his inmost chastity. For he deems nothing dearer or more precious than present purity, to whom a dangerous departure from virtue or a poisonous stain of sin is a grievous punishment. To such an one, I say, neither will regard for the presence of another add anything to his goodness nor will solitude take anything away from it : but as always and everywhere he bears about with him his conscience as a judge not only of his actions but also of his thoughts, he will especially try to please it, as he knows that it cannot be cheated nor deceived, and that he cannot escape it.

CHAPTER IX.

That love not only makes sons out of servants, but also bestows the image and likeness of God.

AND if to anyone relying on the help of God and not on his own efforts, it has been vouchsafed to acquire this state, from the condition of a servant, wherein is fear, and from a mercenary greed of hope, whereby there is sought not so much the good of the donor as the recompense of reward, he will begin to pass on to the adoption of sons, where there is no longer fear, nor greed, but that love which never faileth continually endures. Of which fear and love the Lord in chiding some shows what is befitting for each one : " A son knoweth his own father, and a servant feareth his lord : And if I be a Father, where is My honour : and if I be a Lord, where is my fear ? " [1] For one who is a servant must needs fear because "if knowing his lord's will he has done things worthy of stripes, he shall be beaten with many stripes." [2] Whoever then by this love has attained the image and likeness of God, will now delight in goodness for the pleasure of goodness itself, and having somehow a like feeling of patience and gentleness will henceforth be angered by no faults of sinners, but in his compassion and sympathy will rather ask for pardon for their infirmities, and, remembering that for so long he himself was tried by the stings of similar passions till by the Lord's mercy he was saved, will feel that, as he was saved from carnal attacks not by the teaching of his own exertions but by God's protection, not anger but pity ought to be shown to those who go astray; and with full peace of mind will he sing to God

---

[1] Mal i. 6.   [2] S. Luke xii. 47.

the following verse: "Thou hast broken my chains. I will offer to Thee the sacrifice of praise;" and: "except the Lord had helped me, my soul had almost dwelt in hell."[1] And while he continues in this humility of mind he will be able even to fulfil this Evangelic command of perfection: "Love your enemies, do good to them that hate you, and pray for them that persecute you and slander you."[2] And so it will be vouchsafed to us to attain that reward which is subjoined, whereby we shall not only bear the image and likeness of God, but shall even be called sons: "that ye may be," says He, "sons of your Father which is in heaven, Who maketh His sun to rise on the good and evil, and sends rain on the just and on the unjust:"[3] and this feeling the blessed John knew that he had attained when he said: "that we may have confidence in the day of judgment, because as He is so are we also in this world."[4] For in what can a weak and fragile human nature be like Him, except in always showing a calm love in its heart towards the good and evil, the just and the unjust, in imitation of God, and by doing good for the love of goodness itself, arriving at that true adoption of the sons of God, of which also the blessed Apostle speaks as follows: "Every one that is born of God doeth not sin, for His seed is in him, and he cannot sin, because he is born of God;" and again: "We know that every one who is born of God sinneth not, but his birth of God preserves him, and the wicked one toucheth him not?"[5] And this must be understood not of all kinds of sins, but only of mortal sins: and if any one will not extricate and cleanse himself from these, for him the aforesaid Apostle tells us in another place that we ought not even to pray, saying: "If a man knows his brother to be sinning a sin not unto death, let him ask, and He will give him life for them that sin not unto death. There is a sin unto death: I do not say that he should ask for it."[6] But of those which he says are not unto death, from which even those who serve Christ faithfully cannot, with whatever care they keep themselves, be free, of these he says: "If we say that we have no sin we deceive ourselves and the truth is not in us;" and again: "If we say that we have not sinned, we make Him a liar, and His word is not in us."[7] For it is an impossibility for any one of the saints not to fall into those trivial faults which are committed by word, and thought, and ignorance, and forgetfulness, and necessity, and will, and surprise: which though quite different from that sin which is said to

be unto death, still cannot be free from fault and blame.

CHAPTER X.

How it is the perfection of love to pray for one's enemies and by what signs we may recognize a mind that is not yet purified.

WHEN then any one has acquired this love of goodness of which we have been speaking, and the imitation of God, then he will be endowed with the Lord's heart of compassion, and will pray also for his persecutors, saying in like manner: "Father, forgive them, for they know not what they do."[8] But it is a clear sign of a soul that is not yet thoroughly purged from the dregs of sin, not to sorrow with a feeling of pity at the offences of others, but to keep to the rigid censure of the judge: for how will he be able to obtain perfection of heart, who is without that by which, as the Apostle has pointed out, the full requirements of the law can be fulfilled, saying: "Bear one another's burdens and so fulfil the law of Christ,"[9] and who has not that virtue of love, which "is not grieved, is not puffed up, thinketh no evil," which "endureth all things, beareth all things."[10] For "a righteous man pitieth the life of his beasts: but the heart of the ungodly is without pity."[11] And so a monk is quite certain to fall into the same sins which he condemns in another with merciless and inhuman severity, for "a stern king will fall into misfortunes," and "one who stops his ears so as not to hear the weak, shall himself cry, and there shall be none to hear him."[12]

CHAPTER XI.

A question why he has called the feeling of fear and hope imperfect.

GERMANUS: You have indeed spoken powerfully and grandly of the perfect love of God. But still this fact disturbs us; viz., that while you were exalting it with such praise, you said that the fear of God and the hope of eternal reward were imperfect, though the prophet seems to have thought quite differently about them, where he said: "Fear the Lord, all ye His saints, for they that fear Him lack nothing."[13] And again in the matter of observing God's righteous acts he admits that he has done them from consideration of the reward, saying: "I have inclined my heart to do thy righteous acts forever, for the reward."[14] And the Apostle says: "By faith Moses when he

1 Ps. cxv. 7, 8 (cxvi. 16, 17); xciii. (xciv.) 17.   6 Ib. ver. 16.
2 S. Matt. v. 44.   4 1 John iv. 17.   7 1 John i. 8, 10.
3 Ib. 45.   5 1 John iii. 9; v. 18.

8 S. Luke xxiii. 34.   12 Prov. xiii. 17; xxi. 13.
9 Gal. vi. 2.   13 Ps. xxxiii. (xxxiv.) 10.
10 1 Cor. xiii. 4-7.   14 Ps. cxviii. (cxix.) 112.
11 Prov. xii. 10 (LXX.).

was grown up, denied himself to be the son of Pharaoh's daughter; choosing rather to be afflicted with the people of God than to have the pleasure of sin for a season, esteeming the reproach of Christ greater riches than the treasure of the Egyptians; for he looked unto the reward."[1] How then can we think that they are imperfect, if the blessed David boasted that he did the righteous acts of God in hope of a recompense, and the giver of the Law is said to have looked for a future reward and so to have despised the adoption to royal dignity, and to have preferred the most terrible affliction to the treasures of the Egyptians?

CHAPTER XII.

The answer on the different kinds of perfection.

CHÆREMON: In accordance with the condition and measure of every mind Holy Scripture summons our free wills to different grades of perfection. For no uniform crown of perfection can be offered to all men, because all have not the same virtue, or purpose, or fervour, and so the Divine Word has in some way appointed different ranks and different measures of perfection itself. And that this is so the variety of beatitudes in the gospel clearly shows. For though they are called blessed, whose is the kingdom of heaven, and blessed are they who shall possess the earth, and blessed are they who shall receive their consolation, and blessed are they who shall be filled, yet we believe that there is a great difference between the habitations of the kingdom of heaven, and the possession of the earth, whatever it be, and also between the reception of consolation and the fulness and satisfaction of righteousness; and that there is a great distinction between those who shall obtain mercy, and those who shall be deemed worthy to enjoy the most glorious vision of God. "For there is one glory of the sun, and another glory of the moon, and another glory of the stars: for star differeth from star in glory, so also is the resurrection of the dead."[2] While therefore in accordance with this rule holy Scripture praises those who fear God, and says "Blessed are all they that fear the Lord,"[3] and promises them for this a full measure of bliss, yet it says again: "There is no fear in love, but perfect love casteth out fear: for fear hath torment. But he that feareth is not yet perfect in love."[4] And again, though it is a grand thing to serve God, and it is said:

"Serve the Lord in fear;" and: "It is a great thing for thee to be called My servant;" and: "Blessed is that servant whom his Lord, when He cometh, shall find so doing,"[5] yet it is said to the Apostles: "I no longer call you servants, for the servant knoweth not what his Lord doeth: but I call you friends, for all things whatsoever I have heard from my Father, I have made known unto you."[6] And once more: "Ye are My friends, if ye do whatever I command you."[7] You see then that there are different stages of perfection, and that we are called by the Lord from high things to still higher in such a way that he who has become blessed and perfect in the fear of God, going as it is written "from strength to strength,"[8] and from one perfection to another, i.e., mounting with keenness of soul from fear to hope, is summoned in the end to that still more blessed stage, which· is love, and he who has been "a faithful and wise servant"[9] will pass to the companionship of friendship and to the adoption of sons. So then our saying also must be understood according to this meaning: not that we say that the consideration of that enduring punishment or of that blessed recompense which is promised to the saints is of no value, but because, though they are useful and introduce those who pursue them to the first beginning of blessedness, yet again love, wherein is already fuller confidence, and a lasting joy, will remove them from servile fear and mercenary hope to the love of God, and carry them on to the adoption of sons, and somehow make them from being perfect still more perfect. For the Saviour says that in His Father's house are "many mansions,"[10] and although all the stars seem to be in the sky, yet there is a mighty difference between the brightness of the sun and of the moon, and between that of the morning star and the rest of the stars. And therefore the blessed Apostle prefers it not only above fear and hope but also above all gifts which are counted great and wonderful, and shows the way of love still more excellent than all. For when after finishing his list of spiritual gifts of virtues he wanted to describe its members, he began as follows: "And yet I show unto you a still more excellent way. Though I speak with the tongues of men and angels, and though I have the gift of prophecy and know all mysteries and all knowledge, and though I have all faith so that I can remove mountains, and though I bestow all my goods to feed the poor, and give my body to be burned,

---

[1] Heb. xi. 24–26.
[2] 1 Cor. xv. 41, 42.
[3] Ps. cxxvii. (cxxviii.) 1.
[4] 1 John iv. 18.
[5] Ps. ii. 11; Is. xlix. 6; S. Matt. xxiv. 46.
[6] S. John xv. 14, 15.
[7] S. John xv. 13.
[8] Ps. lxxxiii. (lxxxiv.) 8.
[9] S. Matt. xxiv. 45.
[10] S. John xiv. 2.

but have not love, it profiteth me nothing." You see then that nothing more precious, nothing more perfect, nothing more sublime, and, if I may say so, nothing more enduring can be found than love. For "whether there be prophecies, they shall fail, whether there be tongues, they shall cease, whether there be knowledge, it shall be destroyed," but "love never faileth," [1] and without it not only those most excellent kinds of gifts, but even the glory of martyrdom itself will fail.

CHAPTER XIII.

Of the fear which is the outcome of the greatest love.

WHOEVER then has been established in this perfect love is sure to mount by a higher stage to that still more sublime fear belonging to love, which is the outcome of no dread of punishment or greed of reward, but of the greatest love; whereby a son fears with earnest affection a most indulgent father, or a brother fears his brother, a friend his friend, or a wife her husband, while there is no dread of his blows or reproaches, but only of a slight injury to his love, and while in every word as well as act there is ever care taken by anxious affection lest the warmth of his love should cool in the very slightest degree towards the object of it. And one of the prophets has finely described the grandeur of this fear, saying : "Wisdom and knowledge are the riches of salvation : the fear of the Lord is his treasure." [2] He could not describe with greater clearness the worth and value of that fear than by saying that the riches of our salvation, which consist in true wisdom and knowledge of God, can only be preserved by the fear of the Lord. To this fear then not sinners but saints are invited by the prophetic word where the Psalmist says : " O fear the Lord, all ye His Saints: for they that fear Him lack nothing." [3] For where a man fears the Lord with this fear, it is certain that nothing is lacking to his perfection. For it was clearly of that other penal fear that the Apostle John said that " He who feareth is not made perfect in love, for fear hath punishment." [4] There is then a great difference between this fear, to which nothing is lacking, which is the treasure of wisdom and knowledge, and that imperfect fear which is called "the beginning of wisdom," [5] and which has in it punishment and so is expelled from the hearts of those who are perfect by the incoming of the fulness of love. For " there is no

fear in love, but perfect love casteth out fear." [6] And in truth if the beginning of wisdom consists in fear, what will its perfection be except in the love of Christ which, as it contains in it the fear which belongs to perfect love, is called not the beginning but the treasure of wisdom and knowledge? And therefore there is a twofold stage of fear. The one for beginners, i.e., for those who are still subject to the yoke and to servile terror; of which we read : "And the servant shall fear his Lord ;" [7] and in the gospel : " I no longer call you servants, for the servant knoweth not what his Lord doeth ; " and therefore " the servant," He tells us, " abideth not in the house for ever, but the Son abideth for ever." [8] For He is instructing us to pass on from that penal fear to the fullest freedom of love, and the confidence of the friends and sons of God. Finally the blessed Apostle, who had by the power of the Lord's love already passed through the servile stage of fear, scorns lower things and declares that he has been enriched with good things by the Lord, "for God hath not given us," he says, "a spirit of fear, but of power and of love and of a sound mind." [9] Those also who are inflamed with a perfect love of their heavenly Father, and whom the Divine adoption has already made sons instead of servants, he addresses in these words : " For ye have not received the spirit of bondage again to fear, but ye received the spirit of adoption, whereby we cry, Abba, Father." [10] It is of this fear too, that the prophet spoke when he would describe that sevenfold spirit, which according to the mystery of the Incarnation, full surely descended on the God man : [11] " And there shall rest upon Him the Spirit of the Lord : the Spirit of wisdom and of understanding, the Spirit of counsel and of might, the Spirit of knowledge and of true godliness," and in the last place he adds as something special these words : " And the Spirit of the fear of the Lord shall fill Him." [12] Where we must in the first place notice carefully that he does not say " and there shall rest upon Him the Spirit of fear," as he said in the earlier cases, but he says " there shall fill Him the Spirit of the fear of the Lord." For such is the greatness of its richness that when once it has seized on a man by its power, it takes possession not of a portion but of his whole mind. And not without good reason. For as it is closely joined to that love which " never faileth," it not only fills the man, but takes a lasting and inseparable

1 1 Cor. xii. 31; xiii. 1-8. 3 Ps. xxxiii. (xxxiv.) 10. 5 Ps. cx. (cxi.) 10.
2 Is. xxxiii. 6.   4 1 John iv. 18.

6 1 John iv. 18.   8 S. John xv. 15; viii. 35.
7 Mal. i. 6 (LXX.).   9 2 Tim. i. 7.
10 Rom. viii. 15.
11 Homo Dominicus. See the note on Against Nestorius, V. v.
12 Is. xi. 2, 3.

and continual possession of him in whom it has begun, and is not lessened by any allurements of temporal joy or delights, as is sometimes the case with that fear which is cast out. This then is the fear belonging to perfection, with which we are told that the God-man,[1] who came not only to redeem mankind, but also to give us a pattern of perfection and example of goodness, was filled. For the true Son of God " who did no sin neither was guile found in His mouth," [2] could not feel that servile fear of punishment.

CHAPTER XIV.

A question about complete chastity.

GERMANUS : Now that you have finished your discourse on perfect chastity, we want also to ask somewhat more freely about the end of chastity. For we do not doubt that those lofty heights of love, by which, as you have hitherto explained, we mount to the image and likeness of God, cannot possibly exist without perfect purity. But we should like to know whether a lasting grant of it can be secured so that no incitement to lust may ever disturb the serenity of our heart, and that thus we may be enabled to pass the time of our sojourneying in the flesh free from this carnal passion, so as never to be inflamed by the fire of excitement.

CHAPTER XV.

The postponement of the explanation which is asked for.

CHÆREMON : It is indeed a sign of the utmost blessedness and of singular goodness both continually to learn and to teach that love by which we cling to the Lord, so that meditation on Him may, as the Psalmist says, occupy all the days and nights of our life,[3] and may support our soul, which insatiably hungers and thirsts after righteousness, by continually chewing the cud of this heavenly food. But we must also, in accordance with the kindly forethought of our Saviour, make some provision for the food of the body, that we faint not by the way,[4] for " the spirit indeed is willing, but the flesh is weak." [5] And this we must now secure by taking a little food, so that after supper, the mind may be rendered more attentive for the careful tracing out of what you want.

XII.

THE SECOND CONFERENCE OF ABBOT CHÆREMON.

ON CHASTITY.

Not translated.

XIII.

THE THIRD CONFERENCE OF ABBOT CHÆREMON.

ON THE PROTECTION OF GOD.[6]

CHAPTER I.

Introduction.

WHEN after a short sleep we returned for morning service and were waiting for the old man, Abbot Germanus was troubled by great scruples because in the previous discussion, the force of which had inspired us with the utmost longing for this chastity which was till now unknown to us, the blessed old man had by the addition of a single sentence broken down the claims of man's exertions, adding that man even though he strive with all his

---

[1] *Homo Dominicus.* [3] Cf. Ps. i. 2. [5] S. Matt. xxvi. 41.
[2] 1 Pet. ii 22. [4] Cf. S. Matt. xv. 32.

[6] On the Semi-Pelagianism of this Conference and the erroneous passages from it extracted by Prosper, see the Introduction, p. 190, *sq.*

might for a good result, yet cannot become master of what is good unless he has acquired it simply by the gift of Divine bounty and not by the efforts of his own toil. While then we were puzzling over this question the blessed Chæremon arrived at the cell, and as he saw that we were whispering together about something, he cut the service of prayers and Psalms shorter than usual, and asked us what was the matter.

CHAPTER II.

A question why the merit of good deeds may not be ascribed to the exertions of the man who does them.

THEN GERMANUS: As we are almost shut out, so to speak, by the greatness of that splendid virtue, which was described in last night's discussion, from believing in the possibility of it, so, if you will pardon my saying so, it seems to us absurd for the reward of our efforts, i.e., perfect chastity, which is gained by the earnestness of one's own toil, not to be ascribed chiefly to the exertions of the man who makes the effort. For it is foolish, if, when for example, we see a husbandman taking the utmost pains over the cultivation of the ground, we do not ascribe the fruits to his exertions.

CHAPTER III.

The answer that without God's help not only perfect chastity but all good of every kind cannot be performed.

CHÆREMON: By this very instance which you bring forward we can still more clearly prove that the exertions of the worker can do nothing without God's aid. For neither can the husbandman, when he has spent the utmost pains in cultivating the ground, forthwith ascribe the produce of the crops and the rich fruits to his own exertions, as he finds that these are often in vain unless opportune rains and a quiet and calm winter aids them, so that we have often seen fruits already ripe and set and thoroughly matured snatched as it were from the hands of those who were grasping them; and their continuous and earnest efforts were of no use to the workers because they were not under the guidance of the Lord's assistance. As then the Divine goodness does not grant these rich crops to idle husbandmen who do not till their fields by frequent ploughing, so also toil all night long is of no use to the workers unless the mercy of the Lord prospers it. But herein human pride should never try to put itself on a level with the grace of God or to intermingle

itself with it, so as to fancy that its own efforts were the cause of Divine bounty, or to boast that a very plentiful crop of fruits was an answer to the merits of its own exertions. For a man should consider and with a most careful scrutiny weigh the fact that he could not by his own strength apply those very efforts which he has earnestly used in his desire for wealth, unless the Lord's protection and pity had given him strength for the performance of all agricultural labours; and that his own will and strength would have been powerless unless Divine compassion had supplied the means for the completion of them, as they sometimes fail either from too much or from too little rain. For when vigour has been granted by the Lord to the oxen, and bodily health and the power to do all the work, and prosperity in undertakings, still a man must pray lest there come to him, as Scripture says, "a heaven of brass and an earth of iron," and "the cankerworm eat what the locust hath left, and the palmerworm eat what the cankerworm hath left, and the mildew destroys what the palmerworm hath left."[1] Nor is it only in this that the efforts of the husbandman in his work need God's help, unless it also averts unlooked for accidents by which, even when the field is rich with the expected fruitful crops, not only is the man deprived of what he has vainly hoped and looked for, but actually loses the abundant fruits which he has already gathered and stored up in the threshing floor or in the barn. From which we clearly infer that the initiative not only of our actions but also of good thoughts comes from God, who inspires us with a good will to begin with, and supplies us with the opportunity of carrying out what we rightly desire: for "every good gift and every perfect gift cometh down from above, from the Father of lights,"[2] who both begins what is good, and continues it and completes it in us, as the Apostle says: "But He who giveth seed to the sower will both provide bread to eat and will multiply your seed and make the fruits of your righteousness to increase."[3] But it is for us, humbly to follow day by day the grace of God which is drawing us, or else if we resist with "a stiff neck," and (to use the words of Scripture) "uncircumcised ears,"[4] we shall deserve to hear the words of Jeremiah: ".Shall he that falleth, not rise again? and he that is turned away, shall he not turn again? Why then is this people in Jerusalem turned away with a stubborn revolting? They have stiffened their necks and refused to return."[5]

---

[1] Deut. xxviii. 23; Joel i. 4. [3] 2 Cor. ix. 10. [5] Jer. viii. 4, 5.
[2] S. James i. 17. [4] Acts vii. 51.

CHAPTER IV.

An objection, asking how the Gentiles can be said to have chastity without the grace of God.

GERMANUS: To this explanation, the excellence of which we cannot hastily disprove, it seems a difficulty that it tends to destroy free will. For as we see that many of the heathen to whom the assistance of Divine grace has certainly not been vouchsafed, are eminent not only in the virtues of frugality and patience, but (which is more remarkable) in that of chastity, how can we think that the freedom of their will is taken captive and that these virtues are granted to them by God's gift, especially as in following after the wisdom of this world, and in their utter ignorance not only of God's grace but even of the existence of the true God, as we have known Him by the course of our reading and the teaching of others — they are said to have gained the most perfect purity of chastity by their own efforts and exertions.

CHAPTER V.

The answer on the imaginary chastity of the philosophers.

CHÆREMON: I am pleased that, though you are fired with the greatest longing to know the truth, yet you bring forward some foolish points, as by your raising these objections the value of the Catholic faith may seem better established, and if I may use the expression, more thoroughly explored. For what wise man would make such contradictory statements as yesterday to maintain that the heavenly purity of chastity could not possibly even by God's grace be bestowed on any mortals, and now to hold that it was obtained even by the heathen by their own strength? But as you have certainly, as I said, made these objections from the desire of getting at the truth, consider what we hold on these points. First we certainly must not think that the philosophers attained such chastity of soul as is required of us, on whom it is enjoined that not fornication only, but uncleanness be not so much as named among us. But they had a sort of μερική, i.e., some particle of chastity; viz., continence of the flesh, by which they could restrain their lust from carnal intercourse: but this internal purity of mind and continual purity of body they could not attain, I will not say, in act, but even in thought. Finally Socrates, the most famous of them all, as they themselves esteem him, was not ashamed to profess this of himself. For when one who judged a man's character by his looks (ψυσιογνώμων) looked at him, and said ὄμματα παιδ

ἐραστοῦ, i.e., "the eyes of a corrupter of boys," and his scholars rushed at him, and brought him to their master and wanted to avenge the insult, it is said that he checked their indignation with these words: παύσασθε, ἐταῖροι · εἰμὶ γάρ, ἐπέχω δέ, i.e., Stop, my friends, for I am, but I restrain myself. It is then quite clearly shown not only by our assertions but actually by their own admissions that it was only the performance of indecent acts, i.e., the disgrace of intercourse, that was by force of necessity checked by them, and that the desire and delight in this passion was not shut out from their hearts. But with what horror must one bring forward this saying of Diogenes? For a thing which the philosophers of this world were not ashamed to bring forward as something remarkable, cannot be spoken or heard by us without shame: for to one to be punished for the crime of adultery they relate that he said τὸ δωρεὰν πωλούμενον θανάτῳ μὴ ἀγόραζε, i.e., you should not buy with your death what is sold for nothing.[1] It is clear then that they did not recognize the virtue of the true chastity which we seek for, and so it is quite certain that our circumcision which is in the spirit cannot be acquired save only by the gift of God, and that it belongs only to those who serve God with full contrition of their spirit.

CHAPTER VI.

That without the grace of God we cannot make any diligent efforts.

AND therefore though in many things, indeed in everything, it can be shown that men always have need of God's help, and that human weakness cannot accomplish anything that has to do with salvation by itself alone, i.e., without the aid of God, yet in nothing is this more clearly shown than in the acquisition and preservation of chastity. For as the discussion on the difficulty of its perfection is put off for so long, let us meanwhile discourse briefly on the instruments of it. Who, I ask, could, however fervent he might be in spirit, relying on his own strength with no praise from men endure the squalor of the desert, and I will not say the daily lack but the supply of dry bread? Who without the Lord's consolation, could put up with the continual thirst for water, or deprive his human eyes of that sweet and delicious morning sleep, and regularly compress his whole time of rest and repose into the limits of four hours? Who would be sufficient without God's grace to give continual attendance to reading and constant earnestness in work, receiving no advantage of

---

[1] The source of these stories of Socrates and Diogenes has not been traced.

present gain ? And all these matters, as we cannot desire them continuously without divine inspiration, so in no respect whatever can we perform them without His help. And that we may ensure that these things are not only proved to us by the teaching of experience, but also made still clearer by sure proof and arguments, does not some weakness intervene in the case of many things which we wish usefully to perform, and though the full keenness of our desire and the perfection of our will be not wanting, yet interfere with the wish we have conceived, so that there is no carrying out of our purpose, unless the power to perform it has been granted by the mercy of the Lord, so that, although there are countless swarms of people who are anxious to stick faithfully to the pursuit of virtue, you can scarcely find any who are able to carry it out and endure it, to say nothing of the fact that, even when no weakness at all hinders us, the opportunity for doing everything that we wish does not lie in our own power. For it is not in our power to secure the silence of solitude and severe fasts and undisturbed study even when we could use such opportunities, but by a chapter of accidents we are often very much against our will kept away from the salutary ordinances so that we have to pray to the Lord for opportunities of place or time in which to practise them. And it is clear that the ability for these is not sufficient for us unless there be also granted to us by the Lord an opportunity of doing what we are capable of (as the Apostle also says : " For we wanted to come to you once and again, but Satan hindered us "[1]), so that sometimes we find for our advantage we are called away from these spiritual exercises in order that while without our own consent the regularity of our routine is broken and we yield something to weakness of the flesh, we may even against our will be brought to a salutary patience. Of which providential arrangement of God the blessed Apostle says something similar : " For which I besought the Lord thrice that it might depart from me. And He said to me : My grace is sufficient for thee : for my strength is made perfect in weakness : " and again : " For we know not what to pray for as we ought." [2]

CHAPTER VII.

Of the main purpose of God and His daily Providence.

FOR the purpose of God whereby He made man not to perish but to live for ever, stands immovable. And when His goodness sees in

us even the very smallest spark of good will shining forth, which He Himself has struck as it were out of the hard flints of our hearts, He fans and fosters it and nurses it with His breath, as He " willeth all men to be saved and to come to the knowledge of the truth," for as He says, " it is not the will of your Father which is in heaven that one of these little ones should perish," and again it says : " Neither will God have a soul to perish, but recalleth," meaning that he that is cast off should not altogether perish.[3] For He is true, and lieth not when He lays down with an oath : " As I live, saith the Lord God, for I will not the death of a sinner, but that he should turn from his way and live." [4] For if He willeth not that one of His little ones should perish, how can we imagine without grievous blasphemy that He does not generally will *all* men, but only *some* instead of *all* to be saved ? Those then who perish, perish against His will, as He testifies against each one of them day by day : " Turn from your evil ways, and why will ye die, O house of Israel ? " [5] And again : " How often would I have gathered thy children together as a hen gathereth her chickens under her wings, and ye would not ; " and : " Wherefore is this people in Jerusalem turned away with a stubborn revolting ? They have hardened their faces and refused to return." [6] The grace of Christ then is at hand every day, which, while it " willeth all men to be saved and to come to the knowledge of the truth," calleth all without any exception, saying : " Come unto Me, all ye that labour and are heavy laden, and I will refresh you." [7] But if He calls not all generally but only some, it follows that not all are heavy laden either with original or actual sin, and that this saying is not a true one : " For all have sinned and come short of the glory of God ; " nor can we believe that " death passed on all men." [8] And so far do all who perish, perish against the will of God, that God cannot be said to have made death, as Scripture itself testifies : " For God made not death, neither rejoiceth in the destruction of the living." [9] And hence it comes that for the most part when instead of good things we ask for the opposite, our prayer is either heard but tardily or not at all ; and again the Lord vouchsafes to bring upon us even against our will, like some most beneficent physician, for our good what we think is opposed to it, and sometimes He delays and hinders our injurious purposes and deadly attempts from having their

---

[1] 1 Thess. ii. 18.   [2] 2 Cor. xii. 8, 9 ; Rom. viii. 26.

[3] 1 Tim. ii. 4; S. Matt. xviii. 14; 2 Sam. xiv. 14.
[4] Ezek. xxxiii. 11.   [7] S. Matt. xi. 28.
[5] Ib.   [8] Rom. iii. 23 ; v. 12.
[6] S. Matt. xxiii. 37; Jer. viii. 5.   [9] Wisdom i. 13.

horrible effects, and, while we are rushing headlong towards death, draws us back to salvation, and rescues us without our knowing it from the jaws of hell.

CHAPTER VIII.

Of the grace of God and the freedom of the will.

AND this care of His and providence with regard to us the Divine word has finely described by the prophet Hosea under the figure of Jerusalem as an harlot, and inclining with disgraceful eagerness to the worship of idols, where when she says : " I will go after my lovers, who give me my bread, and my water, and my wool, and my flax, and my oil, and my drink ; " the Divine consideration replies having regard to her salvation and not to her wishes : " Behold I will hedge up thy way with thorns, and I will stop it up with a wall, and she shall not find her paths. And she shall follow after her lovers, and shall not overtake them : and she shall seek them, and shall not find them, and shall say : I will return to my first husband, because it was better with me then than now." [1] And again our obstinacy, and scorn, with which we in our rebellious spirit disdain Him when He urges us to a salutary return, is described in the following comparison : He says : " And I said thou shalt call Me Father, and shalt not cease to walk after Me. But as a woman that despiseth her lover, so hath the house of Israel despised Me, saith the Lord." [2] Aptly then, as He has compared Jerusalem to an adulteress forsaking her husband, He compares His own love and persevering goodness to a man who is dying of love for a woman. For the goodness and love of God, which He ever shows to mankind, — since it is overcome by no injuries so as to cease from caring for our salvation, or be driven from His first intention, as if vanquished by our iniquities, — could not be more fitly described by any comparison than the case of a man inflamed with most ardent love for a woman, who is consumed by a more burning passion for her, the more he sees that he is slighted and despised by her. The Divine protection then is inseparably present with us, and so great is the kindness of the Creator towards His creatures, that His Providence not only accompanies it, but actually constantly precedes it, as the prophet experienced and plainly confessed, saying : " My God will prevent me with His mercy." [3] And when He sees in us some beginnings of a good

will, He at once enlightens it and strengthens it and urges it on towards salvation, increasing that which He Himself implanted or which He sees to have arisen from our own efforts. For He says " Before they cry, I will hear them : While they are still speaking I will hear them ; " and again : " As soon as He hears the voice of thy crying, He will answer thee." [4] And in His goodness, not only does He inspire us with holy desires, but actually creates occasions for life and opportunities for good results, and shows to those in error the direction of the way of salvation.

CHAPTER IX.

Of the power of our good will, and the grace of God.

WHENCE human reason cannot easily decide how the Lord gives to those that ask, is found by those that seek, and opens to those that knock, and on the other hand is found by those that sought Him not, appears openly among those who asked not for Him, and all the day long stretches forth His hands to an unbelieving and gainsaying people, calls those who resist and stand afar off, draws men against their will to salvation, takes away from those who want to sin the faculty of carrying out their desire, in His goodness stands in the way of those who are rushing into wickedness. But who can easily see how it is that the completion of our salvation is assigned to our own will, of which it is said: " If ye be willing, and hearken unto Me, ye shall eat the good things of the land," [5] and how it is " not of him that willeth or runneth, but of God that hath mercy?" [6] What too is this, that God " will render to every man according to his works ; " [7] and " it is God who worketh in you both to will and to do, of His good pleasure ; " [8] and " this is not of yourselves but it is the gift of God : not of works, that no man may boast ? " [9] What is this too which is said : " Draw near to the Lord, and He will draw near to you," [10] and what He says elsewhere : " No man cometh unto Me except the Father who sent Me draw Him ? " [11] What is it that we find : " Make straight paths for your feet and direct your ways," [12] and what is it that we say in our prayers : " Direct my way in Thy sight," and " establish my goings in Thy paths, that my footsteps be not moved ? " [13] What is it again that we are admonished: " Make you a new heart and a new spirit," [14] and what is this which is promised to us : " I will

---

[1] Hosea ii. 5-7.   [2] Jer. iii. 19, 20.   [3] Ps. lviii. (lix.) 11.

[4] Is. lxv. 24 ; xxx. 19.   [8] Phil. ii. 13.   [12] Prov. iv. 26 (LXX.).
[5] Is. i. 19.   [9] Eph. ii. 8, 9.   [13] Ps. v. 9; xvi. (xvii.) 5.
[6] Rom. ix. 16.   [10] S. James iv. 8.   [14] Ezek. xviii 31.
[7] Rom. ii. 6.   [11] S. John vi. 44.

give them one heart and will put a new spirit within them : " and " I will take away the stony heart from their flesh and will give them an heart of flesh that they may walk in Thy statutes and keep My judgments ? " [1] What is it that the Lord commands, where He says : " Wash thine heart of iniquity, O Jerusalem, that thou mayest be saved," [2] and what is it that the prophet asks for from the Lord, when he says " Create in me a clean heart, O God," and again : " Thou shalt wash me, and I shall be whiter than snow ? " [3] What is it that is said to us : " Enlighten yourselves with the light of knowledge ; " [4] and this which is said of God : " Who teacheth man knowledge ; " [5] and : " the Lord enlightens the blind," [6] or at any rate this, which we say in our prayers with the prophet : " Lighten mine eyes that I sleep not in death," [7] unless in all these there is a declaration of the grace of God and the freedom of our will, because even of his own motion a man can be led to the quest of virtue, but always stands in need of the help of the Lord ? For neither does anyone enjoy good health whenever he will, nor is he at his own will and pleasure set free from disease and sickness. But what good is it to have desired the blessing of health, unless God, who grants us the enjoyments of life itself, grant also vigorous and sound health ? But that it may be still clearer that through the excellence of nature which is granted by the goodness of the Creator, sometimes the first beginnings of a good will arise, which however cannot attain to the complete performance of what is good unless it is guided by the Lord, the Apostle bears witness and says : " For to will is present with me, but to perform what is good I find not." [8]

CHAPTER X.

On the weakness of free will.

FOR Holy Scripture supports the freedom of the will where it says : " Keep thy heart with all diligence," [9] but the Apostle indicates its weakness by saying " The Lord keep your hearts and minds in Christ Jesus." [10] David asserts the power of free will, where he says " I have inclined my heart to do Thy righteous acts," [11] but the same man in like manner teaches us its weakness, by praying and saying, " Incline my heart unto Thy testimonies and not to covetousness : " [12] Solomon also : " The Lord incline our hearts unto Himself

that we may walk in all His ways and keep His commandments, and ordinances and judgments." [13] The Psalmist denotes the power of our will, where he says : " Keep thy tongue from evil, and thy lips that they speak no guile," [14] our prayer testifies to its weakness, when we say : " O Lord, set a watch before my mouth, and keep the door of my lips." [15] The importance of our will is maintained by the Lord, when we find " Break the chains of thy neck, O captive daughter of Zion : " [16] of its weakness the prophet sings, when he says : " The Lord looseth them that are bound : " and " Thou hast broken my chains : To Thee will I offer the sacrifice of praise." [17] We hear in the gospel the Lord summoning us to come speedily to Him by our free will : " Come unto Me all ye that labour and are heavy laden, and I will refresh you," [18] but the same Lord testifies to its weakness, by saying : " No man can come unto Me except the Father which sent Me draw him." [19] The Apostle indicates our free will by saying : " So run that ye may obtain : " [20] but to its weakness John Baptist bears witness where he says : " No man can receive anything of himself, except it be given him from above." [21] We are commanded to keep our souls with all care, when the Prophet says : " Keep your souls," [22] but by the same spirit another Prophet proclaims : " Except the Lord keep the city, the watchman waketh but in vain." [23] The Apostle writing to the Philippians, to show that their will is free, says " Work out your own salvation with fear and trembling," but to point out its weakness, he adds : " For it is God that worketh in you both to will and to do of His good pleasure." [24]

CHAPTER XI.

Whether the grace of God precedes or follows our good will.

AND so these are somehow mixed up and indiscriminately confused, so that among many persons, which depends on the other is involved in great questionings, i.e., does God have compassion upon us because we have shown the beginning of a good will, or does the beginning of a good will follow because God has had compassion upon us ? For many believing each of these and asserting them more widely than is right are entangled in all kinds of opposite errors. For if we say that the beginning of free will is in our own power, what

[1] Ezek. i. 19, 20.
[2] Jer. iv. 14.
[3] Ps. l. (li.) 12, 9.
[4] Hos. x. 12 (LXX.).
[5] Ps. xciii. (xciv.) 10.
[6] Ps. cxlv. (cxlvi.) 8.
[7] Ps. xii. (xiii.) 4.
[8] Rom. vii. 18.
[9] Prov. iv. 23.
[10] Phil. iv. 7.
[11] Ps. cxviii. (cxix.) 112.
[12] Ib. ver 36.
[13] 1 Kings viii. 58.
[14] Ps. xxxiii. (xxxiv.) 14.
[15] Ps. cxl. (cxli.) 3.
[16] Is. lii. 2.
[17] Ps. cxlv (cxlvi.) 7 ; cxv. (cxvi.) 16, 17.
[18] S. Matt. xi. 28.
[19] S. John vi. 44.
[20] 1 Cor. ix. 24.
[21] S. John iii. 27.
[22] Jer. xvii. 21.
[23] Ps. cxxvi. (cxxvii.) 1.
[24] Phil. ii. 12, 13.

about Paul the persecutor, what about Matthew the publican, of whom the one was drawn to salvation while eager for bloodshed and the punishment of the innocent, the other for violence and rapine ? But if we say that the beginning of our free will is always due to the inspiration of the grace of God, what about the faith of Zaccheus, or what are we to say of the goodness of the thief on the cross, who by their own desires brought violence to bear on the kingdom of heaven and so prevented the special leadings of their vocation ? But if we attribute the performance of virtuous acts, and the execution of God's commands to our own will, how do we pray : " Strengthen, O God, what Thou hast wrought in us ; " and " The work of our hands stablish Thou upon us ? " [1] We know that Balaam was brought to curse Israel, but we see that when he wished to curse he was not permitted to. Abimelech is preserved from touching Rebecca and so sinning against God. Joseph is sold by the envy of his brethren, in order to bring about the descent of the children of Israel into Egypt, and that while they were contemplating the death of their brother provision might be made for them against the famine to come : as Joseph shows when he makes himself known to his brethren and says : " Fear not, neither let it be grievous unto you that ye sold me into these parts : for for your salvation God sent me before you ; " and below : " For God sent me before that ye might be preserved upon the earth and might have food whereby to live. Not by your design was I sent but by the will of God, who has made me a father to Pharaoh and lord of all his house, and chief over all the land of Egypt." And when his brethren were alarmed after the death of his father, he removed their suspicions and terror by saying : " Fear not: Can ye resist the will of God ? You imagined evil against me but God turned it into good, that He might exalt me, as ye see at the present time, that He might save much people." [2] And that this was brought about providentially the blessed David likewise declared saying in the hundred and fourth Psalm : " And He called for a dearth upon the land : and brake all the staff of bread. He sent a man before them : Joseph was sold for a slave." [3] These two then ; viz., the grace of God and free will seem opposed to each other, but really are in harmony, and we gather from the system of goodness that we ought to have both alike, lest if we withdraw one of them from man, we may seem to have broken the rule of the Church's

faith : for when God sees us inclined to will what is good, He meets, guides, and strengthens us : for " At the voice of thy cry, as soon as He shall hear, He will answer thee ; " and : " Call upon Me," He says, " in the day of tribulation and I will deliver thee, and thou shalt glorify Me." [4] And again, if He finds that we are unwilling or have grown cold, He stirs our hearts with salutary exhortations, by which a good will is either renewed or formed in us.

CHAPTER XII.

That a good will should not always be attributed to grace, nor always to man himself.

FOR we should not hold that God made man such that he can never will or be capable of what is good : or else He has not granted him a free will, if He has suffered him only to will or be capable of evil, but neither to will or be capable of what is good of himself. And, in this case how will that first statement of the Lord made about men after the fall stand : " Behold, Adam is become as one of us, knowing good and evil ? " [5] For we cannot think that before, he was such as to be altogether ignorant of good. Otherwise we should have to admit that he was formed like some irrational and insensate beast : which is sufficiently absurd and altogether alien from the Catholic faith. Moreover as the wisest Solomon says : " God made man upright," i.e., always to enjoy the knowledge of good only, " But they have sought out many imaginations," [6] for they came, as has been said, to know good and evil. Adam therefore after the fall conceived a knowledge of evil which he had not previously, but did not lose the knowledge of good which he had before. Finally the Apostle's words very clearly show that mankind did not lose after the fall of Adam the knowledge of good : as he says : " For when the Gentiles, which have not the law, do by nature the things of the law, these, though they have not the law, are a law to themselves, as they show the work of the law written in their hearts, their conscience bearing witness to these, and their thoughts within them either accusing or else excusing them, in the day in which God shall judge the secrets of men." [7] And with the same meaning the Lord rebukes by the prophet the unnatural but freely chosen blindness of the Jews, which they by their obstinacy brought upon themselves, saying : " Hear ye deaf, and ye blind, behold that you may see.

---

[1] Ps. lxvii. (lxviii.) 29; lxxxix. (xc.) 17.
[2] Gen. xlv. 5-8; l. 19, 20.   [3] Ps. civ. (cv). 16, 17.
[4] Is. xxx. 19; Ps. xlix. (l.) 15.   [6] Eccl. vii. 29 (LXX.).
[5] Gen. iii. 22.   [7] Rom. ii. 14-16.

Who is deaf but My servant? and blind, but he to whom I have sent My messengers?"[1] And that no one might ascribe this blindness of theirs to nature instead of to their own will, elsewhere He says: "Bring forth the people that are blind and have eyes: that are deaf and have ears;" and again: "having eyes, but ye see not; and ears, but ye hear not."[2] The Lord also says in the gospel: "Because seeing they see not, and hearing they hear not neither do they understand."[3] And in them is fulfilled the prophecy of Isaiah which says: "Hearing ye shall hear and shall not understand: and seeing ye shall see and shall not see. For the heart of this people is waxed fat, and their ears are dull of hearing: and they have closed their eyes, lest they should see with their eyes and hear with their ears and understand with their heart, and be turned and I should heal them."[4] Finally in order to denote that the possibility of good was in them, in chiding the Pharisees, He says: "But why of your own selves do ye not judge what is right?"[5] And this he certainly would not have said to them, unless He knew that by their natural judgment they could discern what was fair. Wherefore we must take care not to refer all the merits of the saints to the Lord in such a way as to ascribe nothing but what is evil and perverse to human nature: in doing which we are confuted by the evidence of the most wise Solomon, or rather of the Lord Himself, Whose words these are; for when the building of the Temple was finished and he was praying, he spoke as follows: "And David my father would have built a house to the name of the Lord God of Israel: and the Lord said to David my father: Whereas thou hast thought in thine heart to build a house to My name, thou hast well done in having this same thing in thy mind. Nevertheless thou shalt not build a house to My name."[6] This thought then and this purpose of king David, are we to call it good and from God or bad and from man? For if that thought was good and from God, why did He by whom it was inspired refuse that it should be carried into effect? But if it is bad and from man, why is it praised by the Lord? It remains then that we must take it as good and from man. And in the same way we can take our own thoughts today. For it was not given only to David to think what is good of himself, nor is it denied to us naturally to think or imagine anything that is good. It cannot then be doubted that there are by nature some seeds of goodness in every soul implanted by the kindness of the Creator: but unless these are quickened by the assis-

tance of God, they will not be able to attain to an increase of perfection, for, as the blessed Apostle says: "Neither is he that planteth anything nor he that watereth, but God that giveth the increase."[7] But that freedom of the will is to some degree in a man's own power is very clearly taught in the book termed the Pastor,[8] where two angels are said to be attached to each one of us, i.e., a good and a bad one, while it lies at a man's own option to choose which to follow. And therefore the will always remains free in man, and can either neglect or delight in the grace of God. For the Apostle would not have commanded saying: "Work out your own salvation with fear and trembling," had he not known that it could be advanced or neglected by us. But that men might not fancy that they had no need of Divine aid for the work of Salvation, he subjoins: "For it is God that worketh in you both to will and to do, of His good pleasure."[9] And therefore he warns Timothy and says: "Neglect not the grace of God which is in thee;" and again: "For which cause I exhort thee to stir up the grace of God which is in thee"[10] Hence also in writing to the Corinthians he exhorts and warns them not through their unfruitful works to show themselves unworthy of the grace of God, saying: "And we helping, exhort you that ye receive not the grace of God in vain:"[11] for the reception of saving grace was of no profit to Simon doubtless because he had received it in vain; for he would not obey the command of the blessed Peter who said: "Repent of thine iniquity, and pray God if haply the thoughts of thine heart may be forgiven thee; for I perceive that thou art in the gall of bitterness and the bonds of iniquity."[12] It prevents therefore the will of man, for it is said: "My God will prevent me with His mercy;"[13] and again when God waits and for our good delays, that He may put our desires to the test, our will precedes, for it is said: "And in the morning my prayer shall prevent Thee;" and again: "I prevented the dawning of the day and cried;" and: "Mine eyes have prevented the morning."[14] For He calls and invites us, when He says: "All the day long I stretched forth My hands to a disobedient and gainsaying people;"[15] and He is invited by us when we say to Him: "All the day long I have stretched forth My hands unto Thee"[16] He waits for us, when it is said by the prophet: "Wherefore the Lord waiteth to have compassion upon

---

[1] Is. xlii. 18, 19. [3] S. Matt. xiii. 13. [5] S. Luke xii. 57.
[2] Is. xliii. 8; Jer. v. 21. [4] Is. vi. 9, 10. [6] 1 Kings viii. 17-19.

[7] 1 Cor. iii. 7.
[8] Cf. Conf. VIII. c. xvii.
[9] Phil. ii. 12; 13.
[10] 1 Tim. iv. 14; 2 Tim. i. 6.
[11] 2 Cor. vi. 1.
[12] Acts viii. 22, 23.
[13] Ps. lviii. (lix.) 11.
[14] Ps. lxxxvii. (lxxxviii.) 14; cxviii. (cxix.) 147, 148.
[15] Rom. x. 21.
[16] Ps. lxxxvii. (lxxxviii.) 10.

us;"[1] and He is waited for by us, when we say: "I waited patiently for the Lord, and He inclined unto me;" and: "I have waited for thy salvation, O Lord."[2] He strengthens us when He says: "And I have chastised them, and strengthened their arms; and they have imagined evil against me;"[3] and He exhorts us to strengthen ourselves when He says: "Strengthen ye the weak hands, and make strong the feeble knees."[4] Jesus cries: "If any man thirst let him come unto Me and drink;"[5] the prophet also cries to Him: "I have laboured with crying, my jaws are become hoarse: mine eyes have failed, whilst I hope in my God."[6] The Lord seeks us, when He says: "I sought and there was no man. I called, and there was none to answer;"[7] and He Himself is sought by the bride who mourns with tears: "I sought on my bed by night Him whom my soul loved: I sought Him and found Him not; I called Him, and He gave me no answer."[8]

CHAPTER XIII.

How human efforts cannot be set against the grace of God.

AND so the grace of God always co-operates with our will for its advantage, and in all things assists, protects, and defends it, in such a way as sometimes even to require and look for some efforts of good will from it that it may not appear to confer its gifts on one who is asleep or relaxed in sluggish ease, as it seeks opportunities to show that as the torpor of man's sluggishness is shaken off its bounty is not unreasonable, when it bestows it on account of some desire and efforts to gain it. And none the less does God's grace continue to be free grace while in return for some small and trivial efforts it bestows with priceless bounty such glory of immortality, and such gifts of eternal bliss. For because the faith of the thief on the cross came as the first thing, no one would say that therefore the blessed abode of Paradise was not promised to him as a free gift, nor could we hold that it was the penitence of King David's single word which he uttered: "I have sinned against the Lord," and not rather the mercy of God which removed those two grievous sins of his, so that it was vouchsafed to him to hear from the prophet Nathan: "The Lord also hath put away thine iniquity: thou shalt not die."[9] The fact then that he added murder to adultery, was certainly due to free will: but that he was reproved by the prophet, this was the grace of Divine Compassion. Again it was his own doing that he was humbled and acknowledged his guilt; but that in a very short interval of time he was granted pardon for such sins, this was the gift of the merciful Lord. And what shall we say of this brief confession and of the incomparable infinity of Divine reward, when it is easy to see what the blessed Apostle, as he fixes his gaze on the greatness of future remuneration, announced on those countless persecutions of his? "for," says he, "our light affliction which is but for a moment worketh in us a far more exceeding and eternal weight of glory,"[10] of which elsewhere he constantly affirms, saying that "the sufferings of this present time are not worthy to be compared with the future glory which shall be revealed in us."[11] However much then human weakness may strive, it cannot come up to the future reward, nor by its efforts so take off from Divine grace that it should not always remain a free gift. And therefore the aforesaid teacher of the Gentiles, though he bears his witness that he had obtained the grade of the Apostolate by the grace of God, saying: "By the grace of God I am what I am," yet also declares that he himself had corresponded to Divine Grace, where he says: "And His Grace in me was not in vain; but I laboured more abundantly than they all: and yet not I, but the Grace of God with me."[12] For when he says: "I laboured," he shows the effort of his own will; when he says: "yet not I, but the grace of God," he points out the value of Divine protection; when he says: "with me," he affirms that it co-operates with him when he was not idle or careless, but working and making an effort.

CHAPTER XIV.

How God makes trial of the strength of man's will by means of his temptations.

AND this too we read that the Divine righteousness provided for in the case of Job His well tried athlete, when the devil had challenged him to single combat. For if he had advanced against his foe, not with his own strength, but solely with the protection of God's grace; and, supported only by Divine aid without any virtue of patience on his own part, had borne that manifold weight of temptations and losses, contrived with all the cruelty of his foe, how would the devil have repeated with some justice

---

[1] Is. xxx. 18.
[2] Ps. xxxix. (xl.) 2; cxviii. (cxix.) 166.
[3] Hosea vii. 15.
[4] Is. xxxv. 3.
[5] S. John vii. 37.
[6] Ps. lxviii. (lxix.) 4.
[7] Cant. v. 6.
[8] Cant. iii. 1.
[9] 2 Sam. xii. 13.
[10] 2 Cor. iv. 17.
[11] Rom. viii. 18.
[12] 1 Cor. xv. 10.

that slanderous speech which he had previously uttered: "Doth Job serve God for nought? Hast Thou not hedged him in, and all his substance round about? but take away thine hand," i.e., allow him to fight with me in his own strength, "and he will curse Thee to Thy face."[1] But as after the struggle the slanderous foe dare not give vent to any such murmur as this, he admitted that he was vanquished by his strength and not by that of God; although too we must not hold that the grace of God was altogether wanting to him, which gave to the tempter a power of tempting in proportion to that which it knew that he had of resisting, without protecting him from his attacks in such a way as to leave no room for human virtue, but only providing for this; viz., that the most fierce foe should not drive him out of his mind and overwhelm him when weakened, with unequal thoughts and in an unfair contest. But that the Lord is sometimes wont to tempt our faith that it may be made stronger and more glorious, we are taught by the example of the centurion in the gospel, in whose case though the Lord knew that He would cure his servant by the power of His word, yet He chose to offer His bodily presence, saying: "I will come and heal him:" but when the centurion overcame this offer of His by the ardour of still more fervent faith, and said: "Lord, I am not worthy that Thou shouldest come under my roof: but speak the word only and my servant shall be healed," the Lord marvelled at him and praised him, and put him before all those of the people of Israel who had believed, saying: "Verily, I say unto you, I have not found so great faith in Israel."[2] For there would have been no ground for praise or merit, if Christ had only preferred in him what He Himself had given. And this searching trial of faith we read that the Divine righteousness brought about also in the case of the grandest of the patriarchs; where it is said: "And it came to pass after these things that God did tempt Abraham."[3] For the Divine righteousness wished to try not that faith with which the Lord had inspired him, but that which when called and enlightened by the Lord he could show forth by his own free will. Wherefore the firmness of his faith was not without reason proved, and when the grace of God, which had for a while left him to prove him, came to his aid, it was said: "Lay not thine hand on the lad, and do nothing unto him: for now I know that thou fearest the Lord, and for my sake hast not spared thy beloved son."[4] And that this kind of temptation can befall us, for the sake of proving us, is suffi-

ciently clearly foretold by the giver of the Law in Deuteronomy: "If there rise in the midst of you a prophet or one that saith he hath seen a dream, and foretell a sign and wonder; and that come to pass which he spoke, and he say to thee: Let us go and serve strange gods which ye know not, thou shalt not hear the words of that prophet or dreamer; for the Lord your God surely trieth thee, whether thou lovest Him with all thine heart, and keepest His Commandments, or no."[5] What then follows? When God has permitted that prophet or dreamer to arise, must we hold that He will protect those whose faith He is purposing to try, in such a way as to leave no place for their own free will, where they can fight with the tempter with their own strength? And why is it necessary for them even to be tried if He knows them to be so weak and feeble as not to be able by their own power to resist the tempter? But certainly the Divine righteousness would not have permitted them to be tempted, unless it knew that there was within them an equal power of resistance, by which they could by an equitable judgment be found in either result either guilty or worthy of praise. To the same effect also is this which the Apostle says: "Therefore let him that thinketh he standeth, take heed lest he fall. There hath no temptation taken you but such as is common to man. But God is faithful, who will not suffer you to be tempted above that ye are able, but will with the temptation make also a way of escape that ye may be able to bear it."[6] For when he says "Let him that standeth take heed lest he fall" he sets free will on its guard, as he certainly knew that, after grace had been received, it could either stand by its exertions or fall through carelessness. But when he adds: "there hath no temptation taken you but what is common to man" he chides their weakness and the frailty of their heart that is not yet strengthened, as they could not yet resist the attacks of the hosts of spiritual wickedness, against which he knew that he and those who were perfect daily fought; of which also he says to the Ephesians: "For we wrestle not against flesh and blood, but against principalities, against powers, against the world-rulers of this darkness, against spiritual wickedness in heavenly places."[7] But when he subjoins: "But God is faithful who will not suffer you to be tempted above that ye are able," he certainly is not hoping that the Lord will not suffer them to be tempted, but that they may not be tempted above what they are able to bear. For the one shows the power of man's will,

---

[1] Job i. 9–11.
[2] S. Matt. viii. 7–10.
[3] Gen. xxii. 1.   [4] Ib. ver. 12.
[5] Deut. xiii. 1–3.   [6] 1 Cor. x. 12, 13.   [7] Eph. vi. 12.

the other denotes the grace of the Lord who moderates the violence of temptations. In all these phrases then there is proof that Divine grace ever stirs up the will of man, not so as to protect and defend it in all things in such a way as to cause it not to fight by its own efforts against its spiritual adversaries, the victor over whom may set it down to God's grace, and the vanquished to his own weakness, and thus learn that his hope is always not in his own courage but in the Divine assistance, and that he must ever fly to his Protector. And to prove this not by our own conjecture but by still clearer passages of Holy Scripture let us consider what we read in Joshuah the son of Nun : " The Lord," it says, " left these nations and would not destroy them, that by them He might try Israel, whether they would keep the commandments of the Lord their God, and that they might learn to fight with their enemies." [1] And if we may illustrate the incomparable mercy of our Creator from something earthly, not as being equal in kindness, but as an illustration of mercy : if a tender and anxious nurse carries an infant in her bosom for a long time in order sometime to teach it to walk, and first allows it to crawl, then supports it that by the aid of her right hand it may lean on its alternate steps, presently leaves it for a little and if she sees it tottering at all, catches hold of it, and grabs at it when falling, when down picks it up, and either shields it from a fall, or allows it to fall lightly, and sets it up again after a tumble, but when she has brought it up to boyhood or the strength of youth or early manhood, lays upon it some burdens or labours by which it may be not overwhelmed but exercised, and allows it to vie with those of its own age ; how much more does the heavenly Father of all know whom to carry in the bosom of His grace, whom to train to virtue in His sight by the exercise of free will, and yet He helps him in his efforts, hears him when he calls, leaves him not when he seeks Him, and sometimes snatches him from peril even without his knowing it.

CHAPTER XV.

Of the manifold grace of men's calls.

AND by this it is clearly shown that God's " judgments are inscrutable and His ways past finding out," [2] by which He draws mankind to salvation. And this too we can prove by the instances of calls in the gospels. For He chose Andrew and Peter and the rest of the

apostles by the free compassion of His grace when they were thinking nothing of their healing and salvation. Zacchæus, when in his faithfulness he was struggling to see the Lord, and making up for his littleness of stature by the height of the sycamore tree, He not only received, but actually honoured by the blessing of His dwelling with him. Paul even against his will and resisting He drew to Him. Another He charged to cleave to Him so closely that when he asked for the shortest possible delay in order to bury his father He did not grant it. To Cornelius when constantly attending to prayers and alms the way of salvation was shown by way of recompense, and by the visitation of an angel he was bidden to summon Peter, and learn from him the words of salvation, whereby he might be saved with all his. And so the manifold wisdom of God grants with manifold and inscrutable kindness salvation to men ; and imparts to each one according to his capacity the grace of His bounty, so that He wills to grant His healing not according to the uniform power of His Majesty but according to the measure of the faith in which He finds each one, or as He Himself has imparted it to each one. For when one believed that for the cure of his leprosy the will of Christ alone was sufficient He healed him by the simple consent of His will, saying : " I will, be thou clean." [3] When another prayed that He would come and raise his dead daughter by laying His hands on her, He entered his house as he had hoped, and granted what was asked of Him. When another believed that what was essential for his salvation depended on His command, and answered : " Speak the word only, and my servant shall be healed," [4] He restored to their former strength the limbs that were relaxed, by the power of a word, saying : " Go thy way, and as thou hast believed so be it unto thee." [5] To others hoping for restoration from the touch of His hem, He granted rich gifts of healing. To some, when asked, He bestowed remedies for their diseases. To others He afforded the means of healing unasked : others He urged on to hope, saying : " Willest thou to be made whole ? " [6] to others when they were without hope He brought help spontaneously. The desires of some He searched out before satisfying their wants, saying : " What will ye that I should do for you ? " [7] To another who knew not the way to obtain what he desired, He showed it in His kindness, saying : " If thou believest thou shalt see the glory of God." [8] Among some so richly did He pour

---

[1] Judg. iii. 1, 2 ; ii. 22.　　　[2] Rom. xi. 33.

[3] S. Matt. viii. 3.　[5] Ib. ver. 13.　[7] S. Matt. xx. 32.
[4] Ib. ver. 8.　[6] S. John v. 6.　[8] S. John xi. 40.

forth the mighty works of His cures that of them the Evangelist says : "And He healed all their sick." [1] But among others the unfathomable depth of Christ's beneficence was so stopped up, that it was said : "And Jesus could do there no mighty works because of their unbelief." [2] And so the bounty of God is actually shaped according to the capacity of man's faith, so that to one it is said : "According to thy faith be it unto thee : " [3] and to another : "Go thy way, and as thou hast believed so be it unto thee ; " [4] to another "Be it unto thee according as thou wilt," [5] and again to another : "Thy faith hath made thee whole." [6]

CHAPTER XVI.

Of the grace of God; to the effect that it transcends the narrow limits of human faith.

BUT let no one imagine that we have brought forward these instances to try to make out that the chief share in our salvation rests with our faith, according to the profane notion of some who attribute everything to free will and lay down that the grace of God is dispensed in accordance with the desert of each man : but we plainly assert our unconditional opinion that the grace of God is superabounding, and sometimes overflows the narrow limits of man's lack of faith. And this, as we remember, happened in the case of the ruler in the gospel, who, as he believed that it was an easier thing for his son to be cured when sick than to be raised when dead, implored the Lord to come at once, saying : "Lord, come down ere my child die ; " and though Christ reproved his lack of faith with these words : "Except ye see signs and wonders ye will not believe," yet He did not manifest the grace of His Divinity in proportion to the weakness of his faith, nor did He expel the deadly disease of the fever by His bodily presence, as the man believed he would, but by the word of His power, saying : "Go thy way, thy son liveth." [7] And we read also that the Lord poured forth this superabundance of grace in the case of the cure of the paralytic, when, though he only asked for the healing of the weakness by which his body was enervated, He first brought health to the soul by saying : "Son, be of good cheer, thy sins be forgiven thee." After which, when the scribes did not believe that He could forgive men's sins, in order to confound their incredulity, He set free by the power of His word the man's limb, and put an end to his disease of paralysis, by saying :

"Why think ye evil in your hearts ? Whether is easier to say, thy sins be forgiven thee, or to say, arise and walk ? But that ye may know that the Son of man hath power on earth to forgive sins, then saith He to the sick of the palsy : Arise, take up thy bed, and go unto thine house." [8] And in the same way in the case of the man who had been lying for thirty-eight years near the edge of the pool, and hoping for a cure from the moving of the water, He showed the princely character of His bounty unasked. For when in His wish to arouse him for the saving remedy, He had said to him : "willest thou to be made whole," and when the man complained of his lack of human assistance and said : "I have no man to put me into the pool when the water is troubled," the Lord in His pity granted pardon to his unbelief and ignorance, and restored him to his former health, not in the way which he expected, but in the way which He Himself willed, saying : "Arise, take up thy bed and go unto thine house." [9] And what wonder if these acts are told of the Lord's power, when Divine grace has actually wrought similar works by means of His servants ! For when Peter and John were entering the temple, when the man who was lame from his mother's womb and had no idea how to walk, asked an alms, they gave him not the miserable coppers which the sick man asked for, but the power to walk, and when he was only expecting the smallest of gifts to console him, enriched him with the prize of unlooked for health, as Peter said : "Silver and gold have I none : but such as I have, give I unto thee. In the name of Jesus Christ of Nazareth, rise up and walk." [10]

CHAPTER XVII.

Of the inscrutable providence of God.

By those instances then which we have brought forward from the gospel records we can very clearly perceive that God brings salvation to mankind in diverse and innumerable methods and inscrutable ways, and that He stirs up the course of some, who are already wanting it, and thirsting for it, to greater zeal, while He forces some even against their will, and resisting. And that at one time He gives his assistance for the fulfilment of those things which he sees that we desire for our good, while at another time He puts into us the very beginnings of holy desire, and grants both the commencement of a good work and perseverance in it. Hence it comes that in our

---

1 S. Matt. xiv. 14.
2 S. Mark vi. 5, 6.
3 S. Matt. ix. 29.
4 S. Matt. viii. 13.
5 S. Matt. xv. 28.
6 S. Luke xviii. 42.
7 S. John iv. 48–50.

8 S. Matt. ix. 2–6.
9 S. John v. 6–8.
10 Acts iii. 6.

prayers we proclaim God as not only our Protector and Saviour, but actually as our Helper and Sponsor. For whereas He first calls us to Him, and while we are still ignorant and unwilling, draws us towards salvation, He is our Protector and Saviour, but whereas when we are already striving, He is wont to bring us help, and to receive and defend those who fly to Him for refuge, He is termed our Sponsor and Refuge. Finally the blessed Apostle when revolving in his mind this manifold bounty of God's providence, as he sees that he has fallen into some vast and boundless ocean of God's goodness, exclaims: "O the depth of the riches of the wisdom and knowledge of God! How inscrutable are the judgments of God and His ways past finding out! For who hath known the mind of the Lord?"[1] Whoever then imagines that he can by human reason fathom the depths of that inconceivable abyss, will be trying to explain away the astonishment at that knowledge, at which that great and mighty teacher of the gentiles was awed. For if a man thinks that he can either conceive in his mind or discuss exhaustively the dispensation of God whereby He works salvation in men, he certainly impugns the truth of the Apostle's words and asserts with profane audacity that His judgments can be scrutinized, and His ways searched out. This providence and love of God therefore, which the Lord in His unwearied goodness vouchsafes to show us, He compares to the tenderest heart of a kind mother, as He wishes to express it by a figure of human affection, and finds in His creatures no such feeling of love, to which he could better compare it. And He uses this example, because nothing dearer can be found in human nature, saying: "Can a mother forget her child, that she should not have compassion on the son of her womb?" But not content with this comparison He at once goes beyond it, and subjoins these words: "And though she may forget, yet will not I forget thee."[2]

CHAPTER XVIII.

The decision of the fathers that free will is not equal to save a man.

AND from this it is clearly gathered by those who, led not by chattering words but by experience, measure the magnitude of grace, and the paltry limits of man's will, that "the race is not to the swift nor the battle to the strong, nor food to the wise, nor riches to

the prudent, nor grace to the learned," but that "all these worketh that one and the selfsame Spirit, dividing to every man severally as He will."[3] And therefore it is proved by no doubtful faith but by experience which can (so to speak) be laid hold of, that God the Father of all things worketh indifferently all things in all, as the Apostle says, like some most kind father and most benign physician; and that now He puts into us the very beginnings of salvation, and gives to each the zeal of his free will; and now grants the carrying out of the work, and the perfecting of goodness; and now saves men, even against their will and without their knowledge, from ruin that is close at hand, and a headlong fall; and now affords them occasions and opportunities of salvation, and wards off headlong and violent attacks from purposes that would bring death; and assists some who are already willing and running, while He draws others who are unwilling and resisting, and forces them to a good will. But that, when we do not always resist or remain persistently unwilling, everything is granted to us by God, and that the main share in our salvation is to be ascribed not to the merit of our own works but to heavenly grace, we are thus taught by the words of the Lord Himself: "And you shall remember your ways and all your wicked doings with which you have been defiled; and you shall be displeased with yourselves in your own sight for all your wicked deeds which you have committed. And you shall know that I am the Lord, when I shall have done well by you for My own name's sake, not according to your evil ways, nor according to your wicked deeds, O house of Israel."[4] And therefore it is laid down by all the Catholic fathers who have taught perfection of heart not by empty disputes of words, but in deed and act, that the first stage in the Divine gift is for each man to be inflamed with the desire of everything that is good, but in such a way that the choice of free will is open to either side: and that the second stage in Divine grace is for the aforesaid practices of virtue to be able to be performed, but in such a way that the possibilities of the will are not destroyed: the third stage also belongs to the gifts of God, so that it may be held by the persistence of the goodness already acquired, and in such a way that the liberty may not be surrendered and experience bondage. For the God of all must be held to work in all, so as to incite, protect, and strengthen, but not to take away the freedom of the will which He Himself has once given. If however any more subtle

---

[1] Rom. xi. 33, 34.   [2] Is. xlix. 15.   [3] Eccl. ix. 11 (LXX.); 1 Cor. xii. 11.   [4] Ezek. xx. 43, 44.

inference of man's argumentation and reasoning seems opposed to this interpretation, it should be avoided rather than brought forward to the destruction of the faith (for we gain not faith from understanding, but understanding from faith, as it is written: " Except ye believe, ye will not understand " [1]) for how God works all things in us and yet everything can be ascribed to free will, cannot be fully grasped by the mind and reason of man.

Strengthened by this food the blessed Chæremon prevented us from feeling the toil of so difficult a journey.

XIV.

THE FIRST CONFERENCE OF ABBOT NESTEROS.

ON SPIRITUAL KNOWLEDGE.

CHAPTER I.

The words of Abbot Nesteros on the knowledge of the religious.

THE order of our promise and course demands that there should follow the instruction of Abbot Nesteros,[2] a man of excellence in all points and of the greatest knowledge: who when he had seen that we had committed some parts of Holy Scripture to memory and desired to understand them, addressed us in these words. There are indeed many different kinds of knowledge in this world, since there is as great a variety of them as there is of the arts and sciences. But, while all are either utterly useless or only useful for the good of this present life, there is yet none which has not its own system and method for learning it, by which it can be grasped by those who seek it. If then those arts are guided by certain special rules for their publication, how much more does the system and expression of our religion, which tends to the contemplation of the secrets of invisible mysteries, and seeks no present gain but the reward of an eternal recompense, depend on a fixed order and scheme. And the knowledge of this is twofold: first, πραϰτιϰή, i. e., practical, which is brought about by an improvement of morals and purification from faults: secondly, θεωρητιϰή, which consists in the contemplation of things Divine and the knowledge of most sacred thoughts.

CHAPTER II.

On grasping the knowledge of spiritual things.

WHOEVER then would arrive at this theoretical knowledge must first pursue practical knowledge with all his might and main. For this practical knowledge can be acquired without theoretical, but theoretical cannot possibly be gained without practical. For there are certain stages, so distinct, and arranged in such a way that man's humility may be able to mount on high; and if these follow each other in turn in the order of which we have spoken, man can attain to a height to which he could not fly, if the first step were wanting. In vain then does one strive for the vision of God, who does not shun the stains of sins: " For the spirit of God hates deception, and dwells not in a body subject to sins." [3]

CHAPTER III.

How practical perfection depends on a double system.

BUT this practical perfection depends on a double system; for its first method is to know the nature of all faults and the manner of their cure. Its second, to discover the order of the virtues, and form our mind by their perfection so that it may be obedient to them, not as if it were forced and subject to some fierce sway, but as if it delighted in its natural good, and throve upon it, and mounted by that steep and narrow way with real pleasure. For in what way will one, who has neither succeeded in understanding the nature of his own faults, nor tried to eradicate them, be able to gain an understanding of virtues, which is the second stage of practical training, or the mysteries of spiritual and heavenly things, which exist in the higher stage of theoretical knowledge? For it will necessarily be maintained that he

---

[1] Is. vii. 9.
[2] Nesteros. In the Vitæ Patrum there are some stories of one or two of this name (for it is not quite clear whether they are distinct persons or one and the same to whom the stories refer). One was known as ὁ μέγας, and was a friend of St. Antony, and is supposed by some to be the same whose Conferences Cassian here relates, but nothing certain is known of him. [3] Wisdom i. 4, 5.

cannot advance to more lofty heights who has not surmounted the lower ones, and much less will he be able to grasp those things that are without, who has not succeeded in understanding what is within his comprehension. But you should know that we must make an effort with a twofold purpose in our exertion ; both for the expulsion of vice, and for the attainment of virtue. And this we do not gather from our own conjecture, but are taught by the words of Him who alone knows the strength and method of His work : " Behold," He says : " I have set thee this day over the nations and over kingdoms, to root up, and to pull down, and to waste, and to destroy, and to build, and to plant. " [1] He points out that for getting rid of noxious things four things are requisite ; viz., to root up, to pull down, to waste, and to destroy : but for the performance of what is good, and the acquisition of what pertains to righteousness only to build and to plant. Whence it is perfectly evident that it is a harder thing to tear up and eradicate the inveterate passions of body and soul than to introduce and plant spiritual virtues.

CHAPTER IV.

How practical life is distributed among many different professions and interests.

THIS practical life then, which as has been said rests on a double system, is distributed among many different professions and interests. For some make it their whole purpose to aim at the secrecy of an anchorite, and purity of heart, as we know that in the past Elijah and Elisha, and in our own day the blessed Antony and others who followed with the same object, were joined most closely to God by the silence of solitude. Some have given all their efforts and interests towards the system of the brethren and the watchful care of the cœnobium ; as we remember that recently Abbot John, who presided over a big monastery in the neighbourhood of the city Thmuis,[2] and some other men of like merits were eminent with the signs of Apostles. Some are pleased with the kindly service of the guest house and reception, by which in the past the patriarch Abraham and Lot pleased the Lord, and recently the blessed Macarius,[3] a man of singular courtesy and

patience who presided over the guest house at Alexandria in such a way as to be considered inferior to none of those who aimed at the retirement of the desert. Some choose the care of the sick, others devote themselves to intercession, which is offered up for the oppressed and afflicted, or give themselves up to teaching, or give alms to the poor, and flourish among men of excellence and renown, by reason of their love and goodness.

CHAPTER V.

On perseverance in the line that has been chosen.

WHEREFORE it is good and profitable for each one to endeavour with all his might and main to attain perfection in the work that has been begun, according to the line which he has chosen as the grace which he has received ; and while he praises and admires the virtues of others, not to swerve from his own line which he has once for all chosen, as he knows that, as the Apostle says, the body of the Church indeed is one, but the members many, and that it has " gifts differing according to the grace which is given us, whether prophecy, according to the proportion of the faith, whether ministry, in ministering, or he that teacheth, in doctrine, or he that exhorteth in exhortation, he that giveth, in simplicity, he that ruleth, with carefulness, he that showeth mercy, with cheerfulness." [4] For no members can claim the offices of other members, because the eyes cannot perform the duties of the hands, nor the nostrils of the ears. And so not all are Apostles, not all prophets, not all doctors, not all have the gifts of healing, not all speak with tongues, not all interpret.[5]

CHAPTER VI.

How the weak are easily moved.

For those who are not yet settled in the line which they have taken up are often, when they hear some praised for different interests and virtues, so excited by the praise of them that they try forthwith to imitate their method : and in this human weakness is sure to expend its efforts to no purpose. For it is an impossibility for one and the same man to excel at once in all those good deeds which I enumerated above. And if anyone is anxious equally to affect them all, he is quite sure to come to this ; viz., that while he pursues them all, he will not thoroughly

---

[1] Jer. i. 10.
[2] It is doubtful whether this is the same John who was mentioned in the Institutes V. xxviii. and to whom the xixth Conference is assigned. Thmuis is the coptic Thmoui, a little to the south of the Mendesian branch of the Nile. See Rawlinson's note to Herod. ii. c. 166 and cf. Ptolemy IV. v. § 51.
[3] On the two Macarii see the note on the Institutes V. xli.

[4] Rom. xii. 4-8.   [5] Cf. 1 Cor. xii. 28.

succeed in any one, and will lose more than he will gain from this changing and shifting about. For in many ways men advance towards God, and so each man should complete that one which he has once fixed upon, never changing the course of his purpose, so that he may be perfect in whatever line of life his may be.

CHAPTER VII.

An instance of chastity which teaches us that all men should not be emulous of all things.

For apart from that loss, which we have said that a monk incurs who wants in light-mindedness to pass from one pursuit to another, there is a risk of death that is hence incurred, because at times things which are rightly done by some are wrongly taken by others as an example, and things which turned out well for some, are found to be injurious to others. For, to give an instance, it is as if one wished to imitate the good deed of that man, which Abbot John is wont to bring forward, not for the sake of imitating him but simply out of admiration for him ; for one came to the aforesaid old man in a secular dress and when he had brought him some of the first fruits of his crops, he found some one there possessed by a most fierce devil. And this one though he scorned the adjurations and commands of Abbot John, and vowed that he would never at his bidding leave the body which he had occupied, yet was terrified at the coming of this other, and departed with a most humble utterance of his name. And the old man marvelled not a little at his so evident grace and was the more astonished at him because he saw that he had on a secular dress ; and so began carefully to ask of him the manner of his life and pursuit. And when he said that he was living in the world and bound by the ties of marriage, the blessed John, considering in his mind the greatness of his virtue and grace, searched out still more carefully what his manner of life might be. He declared that he was a countryman, and that he sought his food by the daily toil of his hands, and was not conscious of anything good about him except that he never went forth to his work in the fields in the morning nor came home in the evening without having returned thanks in Church for the food of his daily life, to God Who gave it ; and that he had never used any of his crops without having first offered to God their first fruits and tithes ; and that he had never driven his oxen over the bounds of another's harvest without having first muzzled them that his neighbour might not sustain the slightest loss through his carelessness. And

when these things did not seem to Abbot John sufficient to procure such grace as that with which he saw that he was endowed, and he inquired of him and investigated what it was which could be connected with the merits of such grace, he was induced by respect for such anxious inquiries to confess that, when he wanted to be professed as a monk, he had been compelled by force and his parents' command, twelve years before to take a wife, who, without any body to that day being aware of it, was kept by him as a virgin in the place of a sister. And when the old man heard this, he was so overcome with admiration that he announced publicly in his presence that it was not without good reason that the devil who had scorned him himself, could not endure the presence of this man, whose virtue he himself, not only in the ardour of youth, but even now, would not dare to aim at without risk of his chastity. And though Abbot John would tell this story with the utmost admiration, yet he never advised any monk to try this plan as he knew that many things which are rightly done by some involved others who imitate them in great danger, and that that cannot be tried by all, which the Lord bestowed upon a few by a special gift.

CHAPTER VIII.

Of spiritual knowledge.

But to return to the explanation of the knowledge from which our discourse took its rise. Thus, as we said above, *practical* knowledge is distributed among many subjects and interests, but *theoretical* is divided into two parts, i.e., the historical interpretation and the spiritual sense. Whence also Solomon when he had summed up the manifold grace of the Church, added: "for all who are with her are clothed with double garments." [1] But of spiritual knowledge there are three kinds, tropological, allegorical, anagogical,[2] of which we read as follows in Proverbs: "But do you describe these things to yourself in three ways according

---

[1] Prov. xxxi. 21 (LXX.).

[2] The meaning of the four senses of Scripture here spoken of ; viz., the historical, tropological, allegorical, and anagogical, is well summed up in these lines :

> Litera, gesta docet ; quid credas, allegoria ;
> Moralis, quid agas ; quo tendas anagogia.

Or, as the lines are sometimes given :

> Litera scripta docet ; quod credas, allegoria ;
> Quod speres, anagoge : quid agas, tropologia.

Both Origen and Jerome had spoken of the threefold sense of Scripture, referring to the LXX. rendering of Proverbs xxii. 20 (which Cassian quotes below) : but in general the Latin Fathers, and the Schoolmen after them, separated the third of Origen's senses ; viz., the spiritual, into two, the allegorical and the anagogical : and so the " fourfold " sense became the established method of interpretation in the West.

to the largeness of your heart." [1] And so the history embraces the knowledge of things past and visible, as it is repeated in this way by the Apostle : " For it is written that Abraham had two sons, the one by a bondwoman, the other by a free : but he who was of the bondwoman was born after the flesh, but he who was of the free was by promise." But to the allegory belongs what follows, for what actually happened is said to have prefigured the form of some mystery : " For these," says he, " are the two covenants, the one from Mount Sinai, which gendereth into bondage, which is Agar. For Sinai is a mountain in Arabia, which is compared to Jerusalem which now is, and is in bondage with her children." But the anagogical sense rises from spiritual mysteries even to still more sublime and sacred secrets of heaven, and is subjoined by the Apostle in these words : " But Jerusalem which is above is free, which is the mother of us. For it is written, Rejoice, thou barren that bearest not, break forth and cry, thou that travailest not, for many are the children of the desolate more than of her that hath an husband." [2] The tropological sense is the moral explanation which has to do with improvement of life and practical teaching, as if we were to understand by these two covenants practical and theoretical instruction, or at any rate as if we were to want to take Jerusalem or Sion as the soul of man, according to this : " Praise the Lord, O Jerusalem : praise thy God, O Sion." [3] And so these four previously mentioned figures coalesce, if we desire, in one subject, so that one and the same Jerusalem can be taken in four senses : historically, as the city of the Jews ; allegorically as the Church of Christ, anagogically as the heavenly city of God " which is the mother of us all," tropologically, as the soul of man, which is frequently subject to praise or blame from the Lord under this title. Of these four kinds of interpretation the blessed Apostle speaks as follows : " But now, brethren, if I come to you speaking with tongues what shall I profit you unless I speak to you either by revelation or by knowledge or by prophecy or by doctrine ? " [4] For "revelation" belongs to allegory whereby what is concealed under the historical narrative is revealed in its spiritual sense and interpretation, as for instance if we tried to expound how "all our fathers were under the cloud and were all baptized unto Moses in the cloud and in the sea," and how they "all ate the same spiritual meat and drank the same spiritual drink from the rock that followed them. But the rock was Christ." [5] And this explanation where there is a comparison of the figure of the body and blood of Christ which we receive daily, contains the allegorical sense. But the knowledge, which is in the same way mentioned by the Apostle, is tropological, as by it we can by a careful study see of all things that have to do with practical discernment whether they are useful and good, as in this case, when we are told to judge of our own selves "whether it is fitting for a woman to pray to God with her head uncovered." [6] And this system, as has been said, contains the moral meaning. So " prophecy " which the Apostle puts in the third place, alludes to the anagogical sense by which the words are applied to things future and invisible, as here : " But we would not have you ignorant, brethren, concerning those that sleep : that ye be not sorry as others also who have no hope. For if we believe that Christ died and rose again, even so them also which sleep in Jesus will God bring with Him. For this we say to you by the word of God, that we which are alive at the coming of the Lord shall not prevent those that sleep in Christ, for the Lord Himself shall descend from heaven with a shout, with the voice of the archangel and with the trump of God ; and the dead in Christ shall rise first." [7] In which kind of exhortation the figure of anagogé is brought forward. But " doctrine " unfolds the simple course of historical exposition, under which is contained no more secret sense, but what is declared by the very words : as in this passage : " For I delivered unto you first of all what I also received, how that Christ died for our sins according to the Scriptures, and that He was buried, and that He rose again on the third day, and that he was seen of Cephas ; " [8] and : " God sent His Son, made of a woman, made under the law, to redeem them that were under the law ; " [9] or this : " Hear, O Israel, the Lord the God is one Lord." [10]

CHAPTER IX.

How from practical knowledge we must proceed to spiritual.

WHEREFORE if you are anxious to attain to the light of spiritual knowledge, not wrongly for an idle boast but for the sake of being made better men, you are first inflamed with the longing for that blessedness, of which we read : " blessed are the pure in heart for they shall see God," [11] that you may also attain to that of which the angel said to Daniel : " But they that are learned shall shine as the splendor of the firmament : and they that turn many to righteousness as the stars for ever

---

[1] Prov. xxii. 20 (LXX.).
[2] Gal. iv. 22-27.
[3] Ps. cxlvii. 12.
[4] 1 Cor. xiv. 6.
[5] 1 Cor. x. 1-4.
[6] 1 Cor. xi. 13.
[7] 1 Thess. iv. 12-15.
[8] 1 Cor. xv. 3-5.
[9] Gal. iv. 4, 5.
[10] Deut. vi. 4.
[11] S. Matt. v. 8.

and ever;" and in another prophet: "Enlighten yourselves with the light of knowledge while there is time."[1] And so keeping up that diligence in reading, which I see that you have, endeavour with all eagerness to gain in the first place a thorough grasp of practical, i.e., ethical knowledge. For without this that theoretical purity of which we have spoken cannot be obtained, which those only, who are perfected not by the words of others who teach them, but by the excellence of their own actions, can after much expenditure of effort and toil attain as a reward for it. For as they gain their knowledge not from meditation on the law but from the fruit of their labour, they sing with the Psalmist: "From Thy commandments I have understanding;" and having overcome all their passions, they say with confidence: "I will sing, and I will understand in the undefiled way."[2] For he who is striving in an undefiled way in the course of a pure heart, as he sings the Psalm, understands the words which are chanted. And therefore if you would prepare in your heart a holy tabernacle of spiritual knowledge, purge yourselves from the stain of all sins, and rid yourselves of the cares of this world. For it is an impossibility for the soul which is taken up even to a small extent with worldly troubles, to gain the gift of knowledge or to become an author of spiritual interpretation, and diligent in reading holy things. Be careful therefore in the first place, and especially you, John, as your more youthful age requires you the rather to be careful about what I am going to say — that you may enjoin absolute silence on your lips, in order that your zeal for reading and the efforts of your purpose may not be destroyed by vain pride. For this is the first practical step towards learning, to receive the regulations and opinions of all the Elders with an earnest heart, and with lips that are dumb; and diligently to lay them up in your heart, and endeavour rather to perform than to teach them. For from teaching, the dangerous arrogance of vainglory, but from performing, the fruit of spiritual knowledge will flourish. And so you should never venture to say anything in the conference of the Elders unless some ignorance that might be injurious, or a matter which it is important to know leads you to ask a question; as some who are puffed up with vainglory, pretend that they ask, in order really to show off the knowledge which they perfectly possess. For it is an impossibility for one, who takes to the pursuit of reading with the purpose of gaining the praise of men, to be rewarded with the gift of true knowledge. For one who is bound by the chain of this passion, is sure to be also in bondage to other faults, and especially to that of pride: and so if he is baffled by his encounter with practical and ethical knowledge, he will certainly not attain that spiritual knowledge which springs from it. Be then in all things "swift to hear, but slow to speak,"[3] lest there come upon you that which is noted by Solomon: "If thou seest a man who is quick to speak, know that there is more hope of a fool than of him;[4] and do not presume to teach any one in words what you have not already performed in deed. For our Lord taught us by His own example that we ought to keep to this order, as of Him it is said: "what Jesus began to do and to teach."[5] Take care then that you do not rush into teaching before doing, and so be reckoned among the number of those of whom the Lord speaks in the gospel to the disciples: "What they say unto you, that observe and do, but not after their words: for they say and do not. But they bind heavy burdens and grievous to be borne, and lay them on men's shoulders; but they themselves will not move them with one of their fingers."[6] For if he who shall "break one of these commands, and shall teach men so, shall be called least in the kingdom of heaven,"[7] it follows that one who has dared to despise many and greater commands and to teach men so, shall certainly be considered not least in the kingdom of heaven, but greatest in the punishment of hell. And therefore you must be careful not to be led on to teach by the example of those who have attained some skill in discussion and readiness in speech and because they can discourse on what they please elegantly and fully, are imagined to possess spiritual knowledge, by those who do not know how to distinguish its real force and character. For it is one thing to have a ready tongue and elegant language, and quite another to penetrate into the very heart and marrow of heavenly utterances and to gaze with pure eye of the soul on profound and hidden mysteries; for this can be gained by no learning of man's, nor condition of this world, only by purity of soul, by means of the illumination of the Holy Ghost.

CHAPTER X.

How to embrace the system of true knowledge.

YOU must then, if you want to get at the true knowledge of the Scriptures, endeavour

---

[1] Dan. xii. 3; Hos. x. 12. [2] Ps. cxviii. (cxix.) 104; c. (ci.) 1, 2.

[3] S. James i. 19. [5] Acts i. 1. [7] S. Matt. v. 19.
[4] Prov. xxix. 20 (lxx.). [6] S. Matt. xxiii. 3, 4.

first to secure steadfast humility of heart, to carry you on by the perfection of love not to the knowledge which puffeth up, but to that which enlightens. For it is an impossibility for an impure mind to gain the gift of spiritual knowledge. And therefore with every possible care avoid this, lest through your zeal for reading there arise in you not the light of knowledge nor the lasting glory which is promised through the light that comes from learning but only the instruments of your destruction from vain arrogance. Next you must by all means strive to get rid of all anxiety and worldly thoughts, and give yourself over assiduously or rather continuously, to sacred reading, until continual meditation fills your heart, and fashions you so to speak after its own likeness, making of it, in a way, an ark of the testimony,[1] which has within it two tables of stone, i.e., the constant assurance of the two testaments ;[2] and a golden pot, i.e., a pure and undefiled memory which preserves by a constant tenacity the manna stored up in it, i.e., the enduring and heavenly sweetness of the spiritual sense and the bread of angels ; moreover also the rod of Aaron, i.e., the saving standard of Jesus Christ our true High Priest, that ever buds with the freshness of immortal memory. For this is the rod which after it had been cut from the root of Jesse, died and flourished again with a more vigorous life. But all these are guarded by two Cherubim, i.e., the fulness of historical and spiritual knowledge. For the Cherubim mean a multitude of knowledge : and these continually protect the mercy seat of God, i.e., the peace of your heart, and overshadow it from all the assaults of spiritual wickedness. And so your soul will be carried forward not only to the ark of the Divine Covenant, but also to the priestly kingdom, and owing to its unbroken love of purity being as it were engrossed in spiritual studies, will fulfil the command given to the priests, enjoined as follows by the giver of the Law : " And he shall not go forth from the sanctuary, lest he pollute the Sanctuary of God," [3] i.e., his heart, in which the Lord promised that he would ever dwell, saying : " I will dwell in them and will walk among them." [4] Wherefore the whole series of the Holy Scriptures should be diligently committed to memory and ceaselessly repeated. For this continual meditation will bring us a twofold fruit : first, that while the attention of the mind is taken up in reading and preparing the lessons it cannot possibly be taken captive in any snares of bad thoughts : next that those things which were conned over and frequently repeated and which while we were trying to commit them to memory we could not understand as the mind was at that time taken up, we can afterward see more clearly, when we are free from the distraction of all acts and visions, and especially when we reflect on them in silence in our meditation by night. So that when we are at rest, and as it were plunged in the stupor of sleep, there is revealed to us the understanding of the most secret meanings, of which in our waking hours we had not the remotest conception.

CHAPTER XI.

Of the manifold meaning of the Holy Scriptures.

BUT as the renewal of our soul grows by means of this study, Scripture also will begin to put on a new face, and the beauty of the holier meanings will somehow grow with our growth. For their form is adapted to the capacity of man's understanding, and will appear earthly to carnal people, and divine to spiritual ones, so that those to whom it formerly appeared to be involved in thick clouds, cannot apprehend its subtleties nor endure its light. But to make this which we are aiming at somewhat clearer by an instance, it will be enough to produce a single passage of the law, by which we can prove that all the heavenly commands as well are applied to men in accordance with the measure of our state. For it is written in the law : " Thou shalt not commit adultery." [5] This is rightly observed according to the simple meaning of the letter, by a man who is still in bondage to foul passions. But by one who has already forsaken these dirty acts and impure affections, it must be observed in the spirit, so that he may forsake not only the worship of idols but also all heathen superstitions and the observance of auguries and omens and all signs and days and times, or at any rate that he be not entangled in the conjectures of words and names which destroy the simplicity of our faith. For by fornication of this kind we read that Jerusalem was defiled, as she committed adultery " on every high hill and under every green tree," [6] whom also the Lord rebuked by the prophet, saying : " Let now the astrologers stand and save thee, they that gazed at the stars and counted the months, that from them they might tell the things that shall come to thee," [7] of which fornication elsewhere also

---

[1] Cf Heb. ix. 4, 5.
[2] Instrumentum is a favourite word with Tertullian, who uses it more than once of the two Testaments, e.g., Apol. xix. ; and, Against Marcion iv. where he speaks of the " Two Instruments, or, as it is usual to speak, of the Two Testaments."
[3] Lev. xxi. 12.   [4] 2 Cor. v. 16.

[5] Exod. xx. 14.   [6] Jer. iii. 6.   [7] Is. xlvii. 13.

the Lord says in rebuking them : "The spirit of fornication deceived them, and they went a whoring from their God." [1] But one who has forsaken both these kinds of fornication, will have a third kind to avoid, which is contained in the superstitions of the law and of Judaism; of which the Apostle says: "Ye observe days and months and times and years;" and again: "Touch not, taste not, handle not." [2] And there is no doubt that this is said of the superstitions of the law, into which one who has fallen has certainly gone a whoring from Christ, and is not worthy to hear this from the Apostle : "For I have espoused you to one husband, to exhibit you as a chaste virgin to Christ." [3] But this that follows will be directed to him by the words of the same Apostle : "But I am afraid lest as the serpent by his cunning deceived Eve, so your minds should be corrupted and fall from the simplicity which is in Christ Jesus." [4] But if one has escaped the uncleanness even of this fornication there will still be a fourth, which is committed by adulterous intercourse with heretical teaching. Of which too the blessed Apostle speaks : "I know that after my departure grievous wolves shall enter in among you, not sparing the flock, and of yourselves also shall arise men speaking perverse things so as to lead astray the disciples after them." [5] But if a man has succeeded in avoiding even this, let him beware lest he fall by a more subtle sin into the guilt of fornication. I mean that which consists in wandering thoughts, because every thought which is not only shameful but even idle, and departing in however small a degree from God is regarded by the perfect man as the foulest fornication.

CHAPTER XII.

A question how we can attain to forgetfulness of the cares of this world.

Upon this I was at first moved by a secret emotion, and then groaned deeply and said, All these things which you have set forth so fully have affected me with still greater despair than that which I had previously endured: as besides those general captivities of the soul whereby I doubt not that weak people are smitten from without, a special hindrance to salvation is added by that knowledge of literature which I seem already to have in some slight measure attained, in which the efforts of my tutor, or my attention to continual reading have so weakened me that now my mind is

filled with those songs of the poets so that even at the hour of prayer it is thinking about those trifling fables, and the stories of battles with which from its earliest infancy it was stored by its childish lessons: and when singing Psalms or asking forgiveness of sins either some wanton recollection of the poems intrudes itself or the images of heroes fighting presents itself before the eyes, and an imagination of such phantoms is always tricking me and does not suffer my soul to aspire to an insight into things above, so that this cannot be got rid of by my daily lamentations.

CHAPTER XIII.

Of the method by which we can remove the dross from our memory.

Nesteros : From this very fact, from which there springs up for you the utmost despair of your purification, a speedy and effectual remedy may arise if only you will transfer to the reading of and meditation upon the writings of the Spirit, the same diligence and earnestness which you say that you showed in those secular studies of yours. For your mind is sure to be taken up with those poems until it is gaining with the same zeal and assiduity other matters for it to reflect upon, and is in labour with spiritual and divine things instead of unprofitable earthly ones. But when these are thoroughly and entirely conceived and it has been nourished upon them, then by degrees the former thoughts can be expelled and utterly got rid of. For the mind of man cannot be emptied of all thoughts, and so as long as it is not taken up with spiritual interests, is sure to be occupied with what it learnt long since. For as long as it has nothing to recur to and exercise itself upon unweariedly, it is sure to fall back upon what it learnt in childhood, and ever to think about what it took in by long use and meditation. In order then that this spiritual knowledge may be strengthened in you with a lasting steadfastness, and that you may not enjoy it only for a time like those who just touch it not by their own exertions but at the recital of another, and, if I may use the expression, perceive its scent in the air ; but that it may be laid up in your heart, and deeply noted in it, and thoroughly seen and handled, it is well for you to use the utmost care in securing that, even if perhaps you hear things that you know very well produced in the Conference, you do not regard them in a scornful and disdainful way because you already know them, but that you lay them to your heart with the same eagerness,

---

[1] Hos. iv. 12.
[2] Gal. iv. 10 ; Col. ii. 21.
[3] 2 Cor. xi. 2.
[4] *Ib.* ver. 3.
[5] Acts xx. 29, 30.

with which the words of salvation which we are longing for ought to be constantly poured into our ears or should ever proceed from our lips. For although the narration of holy things be often repeated, yet in a mind that feels a thirst for true knowledge the satiety will never create disgust, but as it receives it every day as if it were something new and what it wanted, however often it may have taken it in, it will so much the more eagerly either hear or speak, and from the repetition of these things will gain confirmation of the knowledge it already possesses, rather than weariness of any sort from the frequent Conference. For it is a sure sign of a mind that is cold and proud, if it receives with disdain and carelessness the medicine of the words of salvation, although it be offered with the zeal of excessive persistence. For " a soul that is full jeers at honeycomb : but to a soul that is in want even little things appear sweet." [1] And so if these things have been carefully taken in and stored up in the recesses of the soul and stamped with the seal of silence, afterwards like some sweet scented wine that maketh glad the heart of man, they will, when mellowed by the antiquity of the thoughts and by long-standing patience, be brought forth from the jar of your heart with great fragrance, and like some perennial fountain will flow abundantly from the veins of experience and irrigating channels of virtue and will pour forth copious streams as if from some deep well in your heart. For that will happen in your case, which is spoken in Proverbs to one who has achieved this in his work : " Drink waters from your own cisterns and from the fount of your own wells. Let waters from your own fountain flow in abundance for you, but let your waters pass through into your streets." [2] And according to the prophet Isaiah : " Thou shalt be like a watered garden, and like a fountain of water whose waters shall not fail. And the places that have been desolate for ages shall be built in thee ; thou shalt raise up the foundations of generation and generation ; and thou shalt be called the repairer of the fences, turning the paths into rest." [3] And that blessedness shall come upon thee which the same prophet promises : " And the Lord will not cause thy teacher to flee away from thee any more, and thine eyes shall see thy teacher. And thine ears shall hear the word of one admonishing thee behind thy back : This is the way, walk ye in it, and go not aside either to the right hand or to the left.' [4] And so it will come to pass that not only every purpose and thought of your heart, but also all the wanderings and rovings of your imagination will become to you a holy and unceasing pondering of the Divine law.

CHAPTER XIV.

How an unclean soul can neither give nor receive spiritual knowledge.

BUT it is, as we have already said, impossible for a novice either to understand or to teach this. For if one is incapable of receiving it how can he be fit to pass it on to another ? But if he has had the audacity to teach anything on these matters, most certainly his words will be idle and useless and only reach the ears of his hearers, without being able to touch their hearts, uttered as they were in sheer idleness and unfruitful vanity, for they do not proceed from the treasure of a good conscience, but from the empty impertinence of boastfulness. For it is impossible for an impure soul (however earnestly it may devote itself to reading) to obtain spiritual knowledge. For no one pours any rich ointment or fine honey or any precious liquid into a dirty and stinking vessel. For a jar that has once been filled with foul odours spoils the sweetest myrrh more readily than it receives any sweetness or grace from it, for what is pure is corrupted much more quickly than what is corrupt is purified. And so the vessel of our bosom unless it has first been purified from all the foul stains of sin will not be worthy to receive that blessed ointment of which it is said by the prophet : " Like the ointment upon the head, which ran down upon the beard of Aaron, which ran down upon the edge of his garment," [5] nor will it keep undefiled that spiritual knowledge and the words of Scripture which are " sweeter than honey and the honeycomb." [6] " For what share hath righteousness with iniquity ? or what agreement hath light with darkness ? or what concord has Christ with Belial ? " [7]

CHAPTER XV.

An objection owing to the fact that many impure persons have knowledge while saints have not.

GERMANUS : This assertion does not seem to us founded on truth, or based on solid reasoning. For if it is clear that all who either never receive the faith of Christ at all or who corrupt it by the wicked sin of heresy, are of unclean hearts, how is it that many Jews and heretics, and Catholics also who are entangled

---

[1] Prov. xxvii. 7.
[2] Prov. v. 15, 16.
[3] Is. lviii. 11, 12.
[4] Is. xxx. 20, 21.

[5] Ps. cxxxii. (cxxxiii.) 2. [6] Ps. xviii. (xix.) 11. [7] 2 Cor. vi. 14, 15.

in various sins, have acquired perfect knowledge of the Scriptures and boast of the greatness of their spiritual learning, and on the other hand countless swarms of saintly men, whose heart has been purified from all stain of sin, are content with the piety of simple faith and know nothing of the mysteries of a deeper knowledge? How then will that opinion stand, which attributes spiritual knowledge solely to purity of heart?

CHAPTER XVI.

The answer to the effect that bad men cannot possess true knowledge.

NESTEROS: One who does not carefully weigh every word of the opinions uttered cannot rightly discover the value of the assertion. For we said to begin with that men of this sort only possess skill in disputation and ornaments of speech; but cannot penetrate to the very heart of Scripture and the mysteries of its spiritual meanings. For true knowledge is only acquired by true worshippers of God; and certainly this people does not possess it to whom it is said: "Hear, O, foolish people, thou who hast no heart: ye who having eyes see not, and having ears, hear not." And again: "Because thou hast rejected knowledge, I also will reject thee from acting as My priest."[1] For as it is said that in Christ "all the treasures of wisdom and knowledge are hid,"[2] how can we hold that he who has scorned to find Christ, or, when He is found, blasphemes Him with impious lips, or at least defiles the Catholic faith by his impure deeds, has acquired spiritual knowledge? "For the Spirit of God will avoid deception, and dwelleth not in a body that is subject to sin."[3] There is then no way of arriving at spiritual knowledge but this which one of the prophets has finely described: "Sow to yourselves for righteousness: reap the hope of life. Enlighten yourselves with the light of knowledge."[4] First then we must sow for righteousness, i.e., by works of righteousness we must extend practical perfection; next we must reap the hope of life, i.e., by the expulsion of carnal sins must gather the fruits of spiritual virtues; and so we shall succeed in enlightening ourselves with the light of knowledge. And the Psalmist also sees that this system ought to be followed, when he says: "Blessed are they that are undefiled in the way: who walk in the law of the Lord. Blessed are they that seek His tes-

timonies."[5] For he does not say in the first place: "Blessed are they that seek His testimonies," and afterwards add: "Blessed are they that are undefiled in the way;" but he begins by saying: "Blessed are they that are undefiled in the way;" and by this clearly shows that no one can properly come to seek God's testimonies unless he first walks undefiled in the way of Christ by his practical life. Those therefore whom you mentioned do not possess that knowledge which the impure cannot attain, but ψευδώνυμον, i.e., what is falsely so-called, of which the blessed Apostle speaks: "O Timothy, keep that which is committed to thee, avoiding profane novelties of words, and oppositions of the knowledge that is falsely so called;"[6] which is in the Greek τὰς ἀντιθέσεις τῆς ψευδωνύμου γνώσεως. Of those then who seem to acquire some show of knowledge or of those who while they devote themselves diligently to reading the sacred volume and to committing the Scriptures to memory, yet forsake not carnal sins, it is well said in Proverbs: "Like as a golden ring in a swine's snout so is the beauty of an evil-disposed woman."[7] For what does it profit a man to gain the ornaments of heavenly eloquence and the most precious beauty of the Scriptures if by clinging to filthy deeds and thoughts he destroys it by burying it in the foulest ground, or defiles it by the dirty wallowing of his own lusts? For the result will be that that which is an ornament to those who rightly use it, is not only unable to adorn them, but actually becomes dirty by the increased filth and mud. For "from the mouth of a sinner praise is not comely;"[8] as to him it is said by the prophet: "Wherefore dost thou declare My righteous acts, and takest My covenant in thy lips?"[9] of souls like this, who never possess in any lasting fashion the fear of the Lord of which it is said: "the fear of the Lord is instruction and wisdom,"[10] and yet try to get at the meaning of Scripture by continual meditation on them, it is appropriately asked in Proverbs: "What use are riches to a fool? For a senseless man cannot possess wisdom."[11] But so far is this true and spiritual knowledge removed from that worldly erudition, which is defiled by the stains of carnal sins, that we know that it has sometimes flourished most grandly in some who were without eloquence and almost illiterate. And this is very clearly shown by the case of the Apostles and many holy men, who did not spread themselves out with an empty show of leaves, but were bowed down by the weight of the true fruits of spiritual

---

[1] Jer. v. 21; Hos. iv. 6. [3] Wisd. i. 4, 5.
[2] Col. ii. 3. [4] Hos. x. 12.

[5] Ps. cxviii. (cxix.) 1, 2. [8] Ecclus. xv. 9. [10] Prov. xv. 33.
[6] 1 Tim. vi. 20. [9] Ps. xlix. (l.) 16. [11] Prov. xvii. 16.
[7] Prov. xi. 22.

knowledge: of whom it is written in the Acts of the Apostles: "But when they saw the boldness of Peter and John, and perceived that they were ignorant and unlearned men, they were astonished." [1] And therefore if you are anxious to attain to that never-failing fragrance, you must first strive with all your might to obtain from the Lord the purity of chastity. For no one, in whom the love of carnal passions and especially of fornication still holds sway, can acquire spiritual knowledge. For "in a good heart wisdom will rest;" and: "He that feareth the Lord shall find knowledge with righteousness." [2] But that we must attain to spiritual knowledge in the order of which we have already spoken, we are taught also by the blessed Apostle. For when he wanted not merely to draw up a list of all his own virtues, but rather to describe their order, that he might explain which follows what, and which gives birth to what, after some others he proceeds as follows: "In watchings, in fastings, in chastity, in knowledge, in long suffering, in gentleness, in the Holy Ghost, in love unfeigned." [3] And by this enumeration of virtues he evidently meant to teach us that we must come from watchings and fastings to chastity, from chastity to knowledge, from knowledge to long suffering, from long suffering to gentleness, from gentleness to the Holy Ghost, from the Holy Ghost to the rewards of love unfeigned. When then by this system and in this order you too have come to spiritual knowledge, you will certainly have, as we said, not barren or idle learning but what is vigorous and fruitful; and the seed of the word of salvation which has been committed by you to the hearts of your hearers, will be watered by the plentiful showers of the Holy Ghost that will follow; and, according to this that the prophet promised, "the rain will be given to your seed, wherever you shall sow in the land, and the bread of the corn of the land shall be most plentiful and fat." [4]

CHAPTER XVII.

To whom the method of perfection should be laid open.

TAKE care too, when your riper age leads you to teach, lest you be led astray by the love of vainglory, and teach at random to the most impure persons these things which you have learnt not so much by reading as by the effects of experience, and so incur what

Solomon, that wisest of men, denounced: "Attach not a wicked man to the pastures of the just, and be not led astray by the fulness of the belly," for "delicacies are not good for a fool, nor is there room for wisdom where sense is wanting: for folly is the more led on, because a stubborn servant is not improved by words, for even though he understands, he will not obey." And "Do not say anything in the ears of an imprudent man, lest haply he mock at thy wise speeches." [5] And "give not that which is holy to dogs, neither cast ye your pearls before swine, lest haply they trample them under foot and turn again and rend you." [6] It is right then to hide the mysteries of spiritual meanings from men of this sort, that you may effectually sing: "Thy words have I hid within my heart: that I should not sin against Thee." [7] But you will perhaps say: And to whom are the mysteries of Holy Scripture to be dispensed? Solomon, the wisest of men, shall teach you: "Give, says he, strong drink to those who are in sorrow, and give wine to drink, to those who are in pain, that they may forget their poverty, and remember their pain no more," [8] i.e., to those who in consequence of the punishment of their past actions are oppressed with grief and sorrow, supply richly the joys of spiritual knowledge like "wine that maketh glad the heart of man," [9] and restore them with the strong drink of the word of salvation, lest haply they be plunged in continual sorrow and a despair that brings death, and so those who are of this sort be "swallowed up in overmuch sorrow." [10] But of those who remain in coldness and carelessness, and are smitten by no sorrow of heart we read as follows: "For one who is kindly and without sorrow, shall be in want." [11] With all possible care therefore avoid being puffed up with the love of vainglory, and so failing to become a partaker with him whom the prophet praises, "who hath not given his money upon usury." [12] For every one who, from love of the praise of men dispenses the words of God, of which it is said "the words of the Lord are pure words, as silver tried by the fire, purged from the earth, refined seven times," [13] puts out his money upon usury, and will deserve for this not merely no reward, but rather punishment. For for this reason he chose to use up his Lord's money that *he* might be the gainer from a temporal profit, and not that the Lord, as it is written, might "when He comes, receive His own with usury." [14]

---

[1] Acts iv. 13.
[2] Prov. xiv. 33 ; Ecclus. xxxii. 20.
[3] 2 Cor. vi. 5, 6.
[4] Is. xxx. 23.

[5] Prov. xxiv. 15 ; xix. 10 ; xviii. 2 ; xxix. 19 ; xxiii. 9 (LXX.).
[6] S. Matt. vii. 6.   [9] Ps. ciii. (civ.) 15.   [12] Ps. xiv. (xv.) 5.
[7] Ps. cxviii. (cxix.) 11.   [10] 2 Cor. ii. 7.   [13] Ps. xi. (xii.) 7.
[8] Prov. xxxi. 6, 7.   [11] Prov. xiv. 23.   [14] S. Matt. xxv. 27.

CHAPTER XVIII.

Of the reasons for which spiritual learning is unfruitful.

BUT it is certain that for two reasons the teaching of spiritual things is ineffectual. For either the teacher is commending what he has no experience of, and is trying with empty-sounding words to instruct his hearer, or else the hearer is a bad man and full of faults and cannot receive in his hard heart the holy and saving doctrine of the spiritual man; and of these it is said by the prophet: "For the heart of this people is blinded, and their ears are dull of hearing and their eyes have they closed: lest at any time they should see with their eyes and hear with their ears, and understand with their heart and be converted and I should heal them." [1]

CHAPTER XIX.

How often even those who are not worthy can receive the grace of the saving word.

BUT sometimes in the lavish generosity of God in His Providence, "Who willeth all men to be saved and to come to the knowledge of the truth," [3] it is granted that one who has not shown himself by an irreproachable life to be worthy of the preaching of the gospel attains the grace of spiritual teaching for the good of many. But by what means the gifts of healing are granted by the Lord for the expulsion of devils it follows that we must in a similar discussion explain, which as we are going to rise for supper we will keep for the evening, because that is always more effectually grasped by the heart which is taken in by degrees and without excessive bodily efforts.

XV.

THE SECOND CONFERENCE OF ABBOT NESTEROS.

ON DIVINE GIFTS.

CHAPTER I.

Discourse of Abbot Nesteros on the threefold system of gifts.

AFTER evening service we sat down together on the mats as usual ready for the promised narration: and when we had kept silence for some little time out of reverence for the Elder, he anticipated the silence of our respect by such words as these. The previous order of our discourse had brought us to the exposition of the system of spiritual gifts, which we have learnt from the tradition of the Elders is a threefold one. The first indeed is for the sake of healing, when the grace of signs accompanies certain elect and righteous men on account of the merits of their holiness, as it is clear that the apostles and many of the saints wrought signs and wonders in accordance with the authority of the Lord Who says: "Heal the sick, raise the dead, cleanse the lepers, cast out devils: freely ye have received, freely give." [2] The second when for the edification of the church or on account of the faith of those who bring their sick, or of those who

are to be cured, the virtue of health proceeds even from sinners and men unworthy of it. Of whom the Saviour says in the gospel: "Many shall say to Me in that day, Lord, Lord, have we not prophesied in Thy name, and in Thy name cast out devils, and in Thy name done many mighty works? And then I will confess to them, I never knew you: Depart from Me, ye workers of iniquity." [4] And on the other hand, if the faith of those who bring them or of the sick is wanting, it prevents those on whom the gifts of healing are conferred from exercising their powers of healing. On which subject Luke the Evangelist says: "And Jesus could not there do any mighty work because of their unbelief." [5] Whence also the Lord Himself says: "Many lepers were in Israel in the days of Elisha the prophet, and none of them was cleansed but Naaman the Syrian." [6] The third method of healing is copied by the deceit and contrivance of devils, that, when a man who is enslaved to evident sins is out of admiration for his miracles regarded as a saint and a servant of God, men may be persuaded

---

[1] Is. vi. 10.   [2] S. Matt. x. 8.

[3] 1 Tim. ii. 4.   [5] S. Mark vi. 5, 6.
[4] S. Matt. vii. 22, 23.   [6] S. Luke iv. 27.

to copy his sins and thus an opening being made for cavilling, the sanctity of religion may be brought into disgrace, or else that he, who believes that he possesses the gift of healing, may be puffed up by pride of heart and so fall more grievously. Hence it is that invoking the names of those, who, as they know, have no merits of holiness or any spiritual fruits, they pretend that by their merits they are disturbed and made to flee from the bodies they have possessed. Of which it says in Deuteronomy: "If there rise up in the midst of thee a prophet, or one who says that he has seen a dream, and declare a sign and a wonder, and that which he hath spoken cometh to pass, and he say to thee: Let us go and follow after other gods whom thou knowest not, and let us serve them: thou shalt not hear the words of that prophet or of that dreamer, for the Lord thy God is tempting thee that it may appear whether thou lovest Him or not, with all thy heart and with all thy soul."[1] And in the gospel it says: "There shall arise false Christs and false prophets, and shall give great signs and wonders, so that, if it were possible, even the elect should be led astray."[2]

CHAPTER II.

Wherein one ought to admire the saints.

WHEREFORE we never ought to admire those who affect these things, for these powers, but rather to look whether they are perfect in driving out all sins, and amending their ways, for this is granted to each man not for the faith of some other, or for a variety of reasons, but for his own earnestness, by the action of God's grace. For this is practical knowledge which is termed by another name by the Apostle; viz., love, and is by the authority of the Apostle preferred to all tongues of men and of angels, and to full assurance of faith which can even remove mountains, and to all knowledge, and prophecy, and to the distribution of all one's goods, and finally to the glory of martyrdom itself. For when he had enumerated all kinds of gifts and had said: "To one is given by the Spirit the word of wisdom, to another the word of knowledge, to another faith, to another the gift of healing, to another the working of miracles, etc.:"[3] when he was going to speak about love notice how in a few words he put it before all gifts: "And

yet," he says, "I show unto you a still more excellent way."[4] By which it is clearly shown that the height of perfection and blessedness does not consist in the performance of those wonderful works but in the purity of love. And this not without good reason. For all those things are to pass away and be destroyed, but love is to abide for ever. And so we have never found that those works and signs were affected by our fathers: nay, rather when they did possess them by the grace of the Holy Spirit they would never use them, unless perhaps extreme and unavoidable necessity drove them to do so.

CHAPTER III.

Of a dead man raised to life by Abbot Macarius.

As also we remember that a dead man was raised to life by Abbot Macarius who was the first to find a home in the desert of Scete.[5] For when a certain heretic who followed the error of Eunomius was trying by dialectic subtlety to destroy the simplicity of the Catholic faith, and had already deceived a large number of men, the blessed Macarius was asked by some Catholics, who were terribly disturbed by the horror of such an upset, to set free the simple folk of all Egypt from the peril of infidelity, and came for this purpose. And when the heretic had approached him with his dialectic art, and wanted to drag him away in his ignorance to the thorns of Aristotle, the blessed Macarius put a stop to his chatter with apostolic brevity, saying: "the kingdom of God is not in word but in power."[6] Let us go therefore to the tombs, and let us invoke the name of the Lord over the first dead man we find, and let us, as it is written, "show our faith by our works,"[7] that by His testimony the manifest proofs of a right faith may be shown, and we may prove the clear truth not by an empty discussion of words but by the power of miracles and that judgment which cannot be deceived. And when he heard this the heretic was overwhelmed with shame before the people who were present, and pretended for the moment that he consented to the terms proposed, and promised that he would come on the morrow, but the next day when they were

---

[1] Deut. xiii. 1-3.   [2] S. Matt. xxiv. 24.   [3] 1 Cor. xii. 8-10.

[4] 1 Cor. xii. 31.
[5] This was the "Egyptian," not the "Alexandrian" Macarius. See the note on the Institutes, V. xli. The story is also given by Rufinus, History of the Monks, c. xxviii.; as well as Sozomen, H. E. III. xiv., and by both of these writers is expressly ascribed to the Egyptian Macarius.
[6] 1 Cor. iv. 20.   [7] Cf. S. James ii. 14.

all in expectation who had come together with greater eagerness to the appointed place, owing to their desire for the spectacle, he was terrified by the consciousness of his want of faith, and fled away, and at once escaped out of all Egypt. And when the blessed Macarius had waited together with the people till the ninth hour, and saw that he had owing to his guilty conscience avoided him, he took the people, who had been perverted by him and went to the tombs determined upon. Now in Egypt the overflow of the river Nile has introduced this custom that, since the whole breadth of that country is covered for no small part of the year by the regular flood of waters like a great sea so that there is no means of getting about except by a passage in boats, the bodies of the dead are embalmed and stored away in cells an good height up. For the soil of that land being damp from the continual moisture prevents them from burying them. For if it receives any bodies buried in it, it is forced by the excessive inundations to cast them forth on its surface. When then the blessed Macarius had taken up his position by a most ancient corpse, he said "O man, if that heretic and son of perdition had come hither with me, and, while he was standing by, I had exclaimed and invoked the name of Christ my God, say in the presence of these who were almost perverted by his fraud, whether you would have arisen." Then he arose and replied with words of assent. And then Abbot Macarius asked him what he had formerly been when he enjoyed life here, or in what age of men he had lived, or if he had then known the name of Christ, and he replied that he had lived under kings of most ancient date, and declared that in those days he had never heard the name of Christ. To whom once more Abbot Macarius: "Sleep," said he, "in peace with the others in your own order, to be roused again by Christ in the end." All this power then and grace of his which was in him would perhaps have always been hidden, unless the needs of the whole province which was endangered, and his entire devotion to Christ, and unfeigned love, had forced him to perform this miracle. And certainly it was not the ostentation of glory but the love of Christ and the good of all the people that wrung from him the performance of it. As the passage in the book of Kings shows us that the blessed Elijah also did, who asked that fire might descend from heaven on the sacrifices laid on the pyre, for this reason that he might set free the faith of the whole people which was endangered by the tricks of the false prophets.

CHAPTER IV.

Of the miracle which Abbot Abraham wrought on the breasts of a woman.

WHY also need I mention the acts of Abbot Abraham,[1] who was surnamed ἁπλοῦς, i.e., the simple, from the simplicity of his life and his innocence. This man when he had gone from the desert to Egypt for the harvest in the season of Quinquagesima[2] was pestered with tears and prayers by a woman who brought her little child, already pining away and half dead from lack of milk; he gave her a cup of water to drink signed with the sign of the cross; and when she had drunk it at once most marvellously her breasts that had been till then utterly dry flowed with a copious abundance of milk.

CHAPTER V.

Of the cure of a lame man which the same saint wrought.

OR when the same man as he went to a village was surrounded by mocking crowds, who sneered at him and showed him a man who was for many years deprived of the power of walking from a contracted knee, and crawled from a weakness of long standing, they tempted him and said, "Show us, father Abraham, if you are the servant of God, and restore this man to his former health, that we may believe that the name of Christ, whom you worship, is not vain." Then he at once invoked the name of Christ, and stooped down and laid hold of the man's withered foot and pulled it. And immediately at his touch the dried and bent knee was straightened, and he got back the use of his legs, which he had forgotten how to use in his long years of weakness, and went away rejoicing.

CHAPTER VI.

How the merits of each man should not be judged by his miracles.

AND so these men gave no credit to themselves for their power of working such wonders, because they confessed that they were done not by their own merits but by the compassion of the Lord and with the words of the Apostle they refused the human hon-

---

[1] Possibly the same person as the author of Conference xxiv., but nothing further appears to be known of him.
[2] i.e., the fifty days from Easter to Whitsuntide; cf. the note on the Institutes, II. xviii.

our offered out of admiration for their miracles: "Men and brethren, why marvel ye at this, or why look ye on us as though by our own power or holiness we had caused this man to walk."[1] Nor did they think that any one should be renowned for the gifts and marvels of God, but rather for the fruits of his own good deeds, which are brought about by the efforts of his mind and the power of his works. For often, as was said above, men of corrupt minds, reprobate concerning the truth, both cast out devils and perform the greatest miracles in the name of the Lord. Of whom when the Apostles complained and said: "Master, we saw one casting out devils in Thy name, and we forbade him because he followeth not with us," though for the present Christ replied to them "Forbid him not, for he that is not against you is for you,"[2] still when they say at the end: "Lord, Lord, have we not in Thy name prophesied, and in Thy name cast out devils, and in Thy name done many mighty works?" He testifies that then He will answer: "I never knew you: depart from me, ye workers of iniquity."[3] And therefore He actually warns those, to whom He Himself has given this glory of miracles and mighty works because of their holiness, that they be not puffed up by them, saying: "Rejoice not because the devils are subject to you, but rejoice rather because your names are written in heaven."[4]

CHAPTER VII.

How the excellence of gifts consists not in miracles but in humility.

FINALLY the Author Himself of all miracles and mighty works, when He called His disciples to learn His teaching, clearly showed what those true and specially chosen followers ought chiefly to learn from Him, saying: "Come and learn of Me," not chiefly to cast out devils by the power of heaven, not to cleanse the lepers, not to give sight to the blind, not to raise the dead: for even though I do these things by some of My servants, yet man's estate cannot insert itself into the praises of God, nor can a minister and servant gather hereby any portion for himself there where is the glory of Deity alone. But do ye, says He, learn this of Me, "for I am meek and lowly of heart."[5] For this it is which it is possible for all men generally to learn and practise, but the working of miracles and signs is not always necessary, nor good

for all, nor granted to all. Humility therefore is the mistress of all virtues, it is the surest foundation of the heavenly building, it is the special and splendid gift of the Saviour. For he can perform all the miracles which Christ wrought, without danger of being puffed up, who follows the gentle Lord not in the grandeur of His miracles, but in the virtues of patience and humility. But he who aims at commanding unclean spirits, or bestowing gifts of healing, or showing some wonderful miracle to the people, even though when he is showing off he invokes the name of Christ, yet he is far from Christ, because in his pride of heart he does not follow his humble Teacher. For when He was returning to the Father, He prepared, so to speak, His will and left this to His disciples: "A new commandment," said He, "give I unto you that ye love one another; as I have loved you, so do ye also love one another:" and at once He subjoined: "By this shall all men know that ye are My disciples, if ye have love to one another."[6] He says not: "if ye do signs and miracles in the same way," but: "if ye have love to one another;" and this it is certain that none but the meek and humble can keep. Wherefore our predecessors never reckoned those as good monks or free from the fault of vainglory, who professed themselves exorcists among men, and proclaimed with boastful ostentation among admiring crowds the grace which they had either obtained or which they claimed. But in vain, for "he who trusteth in lies feedeth the winds: and the same runneth after birds that fly away."[7] For without doubt that will happen to them which we find in Proverbs: "As the winds and clouds and rain are very clear so are these who boast of a fictitious gift."[8] And so if any one does any of these things in our presence, he ought to meet with commendation from us not from admiration of his miracles, but from the beauty of his life, nor should we ask whether the devils are subject to him, but whether he possesses those features of love which the Apostle describes.

CHAPTER VIII.

How it is more wonderful to have cast out one's faults from one's self than devils from another.

AND in truth it is a greater miracle to root out from one's own flesh the incentives to wantonness than to cast out unclean spirits from the bodies of others, and it is a grander sign to restrain the fierce passions of anger

---

by the virtue of patience than to command the powers of the air, and it is a greater thing to have shut out the devouring pangs of gloominess from one's own heart than to have expelled the sickness of another and the fever of his body.   Finally it is in many ways a grander virtue and a more splendid achievement to cure the weaknesses of one's own soul than those of the body of another.   For just as the soul is higher than the flesh, so is its salvation of more importance, and as its nature is more precious and excellent, so is its destruction more grievous and dangerous.

CHAPTER IX.

How uprightness of life is of more importance than the working of miracles.

AND of those cures it was said to the blessed Apostles: "Rejoice not that the devils are subject to you"[1]   For this was wrought not by their own power, but by the might of the name invoked.   And therefore they are warned not to presume to claim for themselves any blessedness or glory on this account as it was done simply by the power and might of God, but only on account of the inward purity of their life and heart, for which it was vouchsafed to them to have their names written in heaven.

CHAPTER X.

A revelation on the trial of perfect chastity.

AND to prove this that we have said both by the testimony of the ancients and divine oracles, we had better bring forward in his own words and experience what the blessed Paphnutius[2] felt on the subject of admiration of miracles and the grace of purity, or rather what he learnt from the revelation of an angel.   For this man had been famous for many years for his signal strictness so that he fancied that he was completely free from the snares of carnal concupiscence because he felt himself superior to all the attacks of the demons with whom he had fought openly and for a long while; and when some holy men had come to him, he was preparing for them a porridge of lentiles which they call Athera,[3] and his hand, as it happened, was

burnt in the oven, by a flame that darted up. And when this happened he was much mortified and began silently to consider with himself, and ask why was not the fire at peace with me, when my more serious contests with demons have ceased? or how will that unquenchable fire which searches out the deserts of all pass me by in that dread day of judgment, and fail to detain me, if this trivial temporal fire from without has not spared me? And as he was troubled by thoughts of this kind and vexation a sudden sleep overcame him and an angel of the Lord came to him and said: "Paphnutius, why are you vexed because that earthly fire is not yet at peace with you, while there still remains in your members some disturbance of carnal motions that is not completely removed?   For as long as the roots of this flourish within you, they will not suffer that material fire to be at peace with you.   And certainly you could not feel it harmless unless you found by such proofs as these that all these internal motions within you were destroyed.   Go, take a naked and most beautiful virgin, and if while you hold her you find that the peace of your heart remains steadfast, and that carnal heat is still and quiet within you, then the touch of this visible flame also shall pass over you gently and without harming you as it did over the three children in Babylon."   And so the Elder was impressed by this revelation and did not try the dangers of the experiment divinely shown to him, but asked his own conscience and examined the purity of his heart; and, guessing that the weight of purity was not yet sufficient to outweigh the force of this trial, it is no wonder, said he, if when the battles with unclean spirits come upon me, I still feel the flames of the fire, which I used to think of less importance than the savage attacks of demons, still raging against me.   Since it is a greater virtue and a grander grace to extinguish the inward lust of the flesh than by the sign of the Lord[4] and the power of the might of the Most High to subdue the wicked demons which rush upon one from without, or to drive them by invoking the Divine name from the bodies which they have possessed. So far Abbot Nesteros, finishing the account of the true working of the gifts of grace accompanied us to the cell of the Elder Joseph which was nearly six miles distant from his, as we were eager for instruction in his doctrine.

---

[1] S. Luke x. 20.   [2] Cf. the note on Conferences III. i.
[3] *Athera*.   This is noticed by Pliny (Hist. Nat. xxii. 25, 57, §121) as the Egyptian name for a decoction made from grain.

e., the sign of the cross.

XVI.

THE FIRST CONFERENCE OF ABBOT JOSEPH.

ON FRIENDSHIP.

CHAPTER I.

What Abbot Joseph asked us in the first instance.

THE blessed Joseph,[1] whose instructions and precepts are now to be set forth, and who was one of the three whom we mentioned in the first Conference,[2] belonged to a most illustrious family, and was the chief man of his city in Egypt, which was named Thmuis,[3] and so was carefully trained in the eloquence of Greece as well as Egypt, so that he could talk admirably with us or with those who were utterly ignorant of Egyptian, not as the others did through an interpreter, but in his own person. And when he found that we were anxious for instruction from him, he first inquired whether we were own brothers, and when he heard that we were united in a tie of spiritual and not carnal brotherhood, and that from the first commencement of our renunciation of the world we had always been joined together in an unbroken bond as well in our travels, which we had both undertaken for the sake of spiritual service, as also in the pursuits of the monastery, he began his discourse as follows.

CHAPTER II.

Discourse of the same elder on the untrustworthy sort of friendship.

THERE are many kinds of friendship and companionship which unite men in very different ways in the bonds of love. For some a previous recommendation makes to enter upon an intercourse first of acquaintance and afterwards even of friendship. In the case of others some bargain or an agreement to give and take something has joined them in the bonds of love. Others a similarity and union of business or science or art or study has united

in the chain of friendship, by which even fierce souls become kindly disposed to each other, so that those, who in forests and mountains delight in robbery and revel in human bloodshed, embrace and cherish the partners of their crimes. But there is another kind of love, where the union is from the instincts of nature and the laws of consanguinity, whereby those of the same tribe, wives and parents, and brothers and children are naturally preferred to others, a thing which we find is the case not only with mankind but with all birds and beasts. For at the prompting of a natural instinct they protect and defend their offspring and their young ones so that often they are not afraid to expose themselves to danger and death for their sakes. Indeed those kinds of beasts and serpents and birds, which are cut off and separated from all others by their intolerable ferocity or deadly poison, as basilisks, unicorns and vultures, though by their very look they are said to be dangerous to every one, yet among themselves they remain peaceful and harmless owing to community of origin and fellow-feeling. But we see that all these kinds of love of which we have spoken, as they are common both to the good and bad, and to beasts and serpents, certainly cannot last for ever. For often separation of place interrupts and breaks them off, as well as forgetfulness from lapse of time, and the transaction of affairs and business and words. For as they are generally due to different kinds of connexions either of gain, or desires, or kinship, or business, so when any occasion for separation intervenes they are broken off.

CHAPTER III.

How friendship is indissoluble.

AMONG all these then there is one kind of love which is indissoluble, where the union is owing not to the favour of a recommendation, or some great kindness or gifts, or the reason

---

[1] Nothing further appears to be known of this Joseph than what Cassian here states.
[2] viz., the *first* of the Second Part of the Conferences, i.e., Conference XI. [3] See on Conference XIV. c. iv.

of some bargain, or the necessities of nature, but simply to similarity of virtue. This, I say, is what is broken by no chances, what no interval of time or space can sever or destroy, and what even death itself cannot part. This is true and unbroken love which grows by means of the double perfection and goodness of friends, and which, when once its bonds have been entered, no difference of liking and no disturbing opposition of wishes can sever. But we have known many set on this purpose, who though they had been joined together in companionship out of their burning love for Christ, yet could not maintain it continually and unbrokenly, because although they relied on a good beginning for their friendship, yet they did not with one and the same zeal maintain the purpose on which they had entered, and so there was between them a sort of love only for a while, for it was not maintained by the goodness of both alike, but by the patience of the one party, and so although it is held to by the one with unwearied heroism, yet it is sure to be broken by the pettiness of the other. For the infirmities of those who are somewhat cold in seeking the healthy condition of perfection, however patiently they may be borne by the strong, are yet not put up with by those who are weaker themselves. For they have implanted within them causes of disturbance which do not allow them to be at ease, just as those, who are affected by bodily weakness, generally impute the delicacy of their stomach and weak health to the carelessness of their cooks and servants, and however carefully their attendants may serve them, yet nevertheless they ascribe the grounds of their upset to those who are in good health, as they do not see that they are really due to the failure of their own health. Wherefore this, as we said, is the sure and indissoluble union of friendship, where the tie consists only in likeness in goodness. For "the Lord maketh men to be of one mind in an house."[1] And therefore love can only continue undisturbed in those in whom there is but one purpose and mind to will and to refuse the same things. And if you also wish to keep this unbroken, you must be careful that having first got rid of your faults, you mortify your own desires, and with united zeal and purpose diligently fulfil that in which the prophet specially delights: "Behold how good and joyful a thing it is for brethren to dwell together in unity."[2] Which should be taken of unity of spirit rather than of place. For it is of no use for those who differ in character and purpose to be united in one dwelling, nor is it an hindrance

for those who are grounded on equal goodness to be separated by distance of place. For with God the union of character, not of place, joins brethren together in a common dwelling, nor can unruffled peace ever be maintained where difference of will appears.

CHAPTER IV.

A question whether anything that is really useful should be performed even against a brother's wish.

GERMANUS: What then? If when one party wants to do something which he sees is useful and profitable according to the mind of God, the other does not give his consent, ought it to be performed even against the wish of the brother, or should it be thrown on one side as he wants?

CHAPTER V.

The answer, how a lasting friendship can only exist among those who are perfect.

JOSEPH: For this reason we said that the full and perfect grace of friendship can only last among those who are perfect and of equal goodness, whose likemindedness and common purpose allows them either never, or at any rate hardly ever, to disagree, or to differ in those matters which concern their progress in the spiritual life. But if they begin to get hot with eager disputes, it is clear that they have never been at one in accordance with the rule which we gave above. But because no one can start from perfection except one who has begun from the very foundation, and your inquiring is not with regard to its greatness, but as to how you can attain to it, I think it well to explain to you, in a few words, the rule for it and the sort of path along which your steps should be directed, that you may be able more easily to secure the blessing of patience and peace.

CHAPTER VI.

By what means union can be preserved unbroken.

THE first foundation then, of true friendship consists in contempt for worldly substance and scorn for all things that we possess. For it is utterly wrong and unjustifiable if, after the vanity of the world and all that is in it has been renounced, whatever miserable furniture remains is more regarded than what is most valuable; viz., the love of a brother.

---

[1] Ps. lxvii. (lxviii.) 7. [2] Ps. cxxxii. (cxxxiii.) 1.

The second is for each man so to prune his own wishes that he may not imagine himself to be a wise and experienced person, and so prefer his own opinions to those of his neighbour. The third is for him to recognize that everything, even what he deems useful and necessary, must come after the blessing of love and peace. The fourth for him to realize that he should never be angry for any reason good or bad. The fifth for him to try to cure any wrath which a brother may have conceived against him however unreasonably, in the same way that he would cure his own, knowing that the vexation of another is equally bad for him, as if he himself were stirred against another, unless he removes it, to the best of his ability, from his brother's mind. The last is what is undoubtedly generally decisive in regard to all faults; viz., that he should realize daily that he is to pass away from this world; as the realization of this not only permits no vexation to linger in the heart, but also represses all the motions of lusts and sins of all kinds. Whoever then has got hold of this, can neither suffer nor be the cause of bitter wrath and discord. But when this fails, as soon as he who is jealous of love has little by little infused the poison of vexation in the hearts of friends, it is certain that owing to frequent quarrels love will gradually grow cool, and at sometime or other he will part the hearts of the lovers, that have been for a long while exasperated. For if one is walking along the course previously marked out, how can he ever differ from his friend, for if he claims nothing for himself, he entirely cuts off the first cause of quarrel (which generally springs from trivial things and most unimportant matters), as he observes to the best of his power what we read in the Acts of the Apostles on the unity of believers: "But the multitude of believers was of one heart and soul; neither did any of them say that any of the things which he possessed was his own, but they had all things common."[1] Then how can any seeds of discussion arise from him who serves not his own but his brother's will, and becomes a follower of his Lord and Master, who speaking in the character[2] of man which He had taken, said: "I am not come to do Mine own will, but the will of Him that sent Me?"[3] But how can he arouse any incitement to contention, who has determined to trust not so much to his own judgment as to his brother's decision, on his own intelligence and meaning, in accordance with his will either approving or disapproving his discoveries, and fulfilling in the humility of a pious heart these words from the Gospel: "Nevertheless, not as I will, but as Thou wilt."[4] Or in what way will he admit anything which grieves the brother, who thinks that nothing is more precious than the blessing of peace, and never forgets these words of the Lord: "By this shall all men know that ye are My disciples, that ye love one another;"[5] for by this, as by a special mark, Christ willed that the flock of His sheep should be known in this world, and be separated from all others by this stamp, so to speak? But on what grounds will he endure either to admit the rancour of vexation in himself or for it to remain in another, if his firm decision is that there cannot be any good ground for anger, as it is dangerous and wrong, and that when his brother is angry with him he cannot pray, in just the same way as when he himself is angry with his brother, as he ever keeps in an humble heart these words of our Lord and Saviour: "If thou bring thy gift to the altar and there remember that thy brother hath aught against thee, leave there thy gift at the altar, and go thy way; first be reconciled to thy brother, and then come and offer thy gift."[6] For it will be of no use for you to declare that you are not angry, and to believe that you are fulfilling the command which says: "Let not the sun go down upon thy wrath;" and: "Whosoever is angry with his brother, shall be in danger of the judgment,"[7] if you are with obstinate heart disregarding the vexation of another which you could smooth down by kindness on your part. For in the same way you will be punished for violating the Lord's command. For He who said that you should not be angry with another, said also that you should not disregard the vexations of another, for it makes no difference in the sight of God, "Who willeth all men to be saved,"[8] whether you destroy yourself or someone else. Since the death of any one is equally a loss to God, and at the same time it is equally a gain to him to whom all destruction is delightful, whether it is acquired by your death or by the death of your brother. Lastly, how can he retain even the least vexation with his brother, who realizes daily that he is presently to depart from this world?

CHAPTER VII.

How nothing should be put before love, or after anger.

As then nothing should be put before love, so on the other hand nothing should be put

---

[1] Acts iv. 32.   [2] *Ex persona.* See note on VIII. xxxv.
[3] S. John vi. 38.

[4] S. Matt. xxvi. 39.   [7] Eph. iv. 26; S. Matt. v. 22.
[5] S. John xiii. 35.   [8] 1 Tim. ii. 4.
[6] S. Matt. v. 23, 24.

below rage and anger. For all things, however useful and necessary they seem, should yet be disregarded that disturbing anger may be avoided, and all things even which we think are unfortunate should be undertaken and endured that the calm of love and peace may be preserved unimpaired, because we should reckon nothing more damaging than anger and vexation, and nothing more advantageous than love.

CHAPTER VIII.

On what grounds a dispute can arise among spiritual persons.

FOR as our enemy separates brethren who are still weak and carnal by a sudden burst of rage on account of some trifling and earthly matter, so he sows the seeds of discord even between spiritual persons, on the ground of some difference of thoughts, from which certainly those contentions and strifes about words, which the Apostle condemns, for the most part arise: whereby consequently our spiteful and malignant enemy sows discord between brethren who were of one mind. For these words of wise Solomon are true: "Contention breeds hatred: but friendship will be a defence to all who do not strive."[1]

CHAPTER IX.

How to get rid even of spiritual grounds of discord.

WHEREFORE for the preservation of lasting and unbroken love, it is of no use to have removed the first ground of discord, which generally arises from frail and earthly things, or to have disregarded all carnal things, and to have permitted to our brethren an unrestricted share in everything which our needs require, unless too we cut off in like manner the second, which generally arises under the guise of spiritual feelings; and unless we gain in everything humble thoughts and harmonious wills.

CHAPTER X.

On the best tests of truth.

FOR I remember, that when my youthful age suggested to me to cling to a partner, thoughts of this sort often mingled with our

moral training and the Holy Scriptures, so that we fancied that nothing could be truer or more reasonable: but when we came together and began to produce our ideas, in the general discussion which was held, some things were first noted by the others as false and dangerous, and then presently were condemned and pronounced by common consent to be injurious; though before they had seemed to shine as if with a light infused by the devil, so that they would easily have caused discord, had not the charge of the Elders, observed like some divine oracle, restrained us from all strife, that charge; namely, whereby it was ordered by them almost with the force of a law, that neither of us should trust to his own judgments more than his brother's, if he wanted never to be deceived by the craft of the devil.

CHAPTER XI.

How it is impossible for one who trusts to his own judgment to escape being deceived by the devil's illusions.

FOR often it has been proved that what the Apostle says really takes place. "For Satan himself transforms himself into an angel of light,"[2] so that he deceitfully sheds abroad a confusing and foul obscuration of the thoughts instead of the true light of knowledge. And unless these thoughts are received in a humble and gentle heart, and kept for the consideration of some more experienced brother or approved Elder, and when thoroughly sifted by their judgment, either rejected or admitted by us, we shall be sure to venerate in our thoughts an angel of darkness instead of an angel of light, and be smitten with a grievous destruction: an injury which it is impossible for any one to avoid who trusts in his own judgment, unless he becomes a lover and follower of true humility and with all contrition of heart fulfils what the Apostle chiefly prays for: "If then there be any consolation in Christ, if any comfort of love, if any bowels of compassion, fulfil ye my joy, that you be of one mind, having the same love, being of one accord, doing nothing by contention, neither by vainglory; but in humility each esteeming others better than themselves;" and this: "in honour preferring one another,"[3] that each may think more of the knowledge and holiness of his partner, and hold that the better part of true discretion is to be found in the judgment of another rather than in his own.

---

[1] Prov. x. 12.   [2] 2 Cor. xi. 14.   [3] Phil. ii. 1-3; Rom. xii. 10.

CHAPTER XII.

Why inferiors should not be despised in Conference.

FOR it often happens either by an illusion of the devil or by the occurrence of a human mistake (by which every man in this life is liable to be deceived) that sometimes one who is keener in intellect and more learned, gets some wrong notion in his head, while he who is duller in wits and of less worth, conceives the matter better and more truly. And therefore no one, however learned he may be, should persuade himself in his empty vanity that he cannot require conference with another. For even if no deception of the devil blinds his judgment, yet he cannot avoid the noxious snares of pride and conceit. For who can arrogate this to himself without great danger, when the chosen vessel in whom, as he maintained, Christ Himself spoke, declares that he went up to Jerusalem simply and solely for this reason, that he might in a secret discussion confer with his fellow-Apostles on the gospel which he preached to the gentiles by the revelation and co-operation of the Lord? By which fact we are shown that we ought not only by these precepts to preserve unanimity and harmony, but that we need not fear any crafts of the devil opposing us, or snares of his illusions.

CHAPTER XIII.

How love does not only belong to God but is God.

FINALLY so highly is the virtue of love extolled that the blessed Apostle John declares that it not only belongs to God but that it is God, saying: "God is love: he therefore that abideth in love, abideth in God, and God in him."[1] For so far do we see that it is divine, that we find that what the Apostle says is plainly a living truth in us: "For the love of God is shed abroad in our hearts by the Holy Ghost Who dwelleth in us."[2] For it is the same thing as if he said that God is shed abroad in our hearts by the Holy Ghost Who dwelleth in us: who also, when we know not what we should pray for, "makes intercession for us with groanings that cannot be uttered: But He that searcheth the hearts knoweth what the Spirit desireth, for He asketh for the saints according to God."[3]

CHAPTER XIV.

On the different grades of love.

IT is possible then for all to show that love which is called ἀγάπη, of which the blessed Apostle says: "While therefore we have time, let us do good unto all men, but specially to them that are of the household of faith."[4] And this should be shown to all men in general to such an extent that we are actually commanded by our Lord to yield it to our enemies, for He says: "Love your enemies."[5] But διάθεσις, i.e., affection is shown to but a few and those who are united to us by kindred dispositions or by a tie of goodness; though indeed affection seems to have many degrees of difference. For in one way we love our parents, in another our wives, in another our brothers, in another our children, and there is a wide difference in regard to the claims of these feelings of affection, nor is the love of parents towards their children always equal. As is shown by the case of the patriarch Jacob, who, though he was the father of twelve sons and loved them all with a father's love, yet loved Joseph with a deeper affection, as Scripture clearly shows: "But his brethren envied him, because his father loved him;"[6] evidently not that that good man his father failed in greatly loving the rest of his children, but that in his affection he clung to this one, because he was a type of the Lord, more tenderly and indulgently. This also, we read, was very clearly shown in the case of John the Evangelist, where these words are used of him: "that disciple whom Jesus loved,"[7] though certainly He embraced all the other eleven, whom He had chosen in the same way, with His special love, as this He shows also by the witness of the gospel, where He says: "As I have loved you, so do ye also love one another;" of whom elsewhere also it is said: "Loving His own who were in the world, He loved them even to the end."[8] But this love of one in particular did not indicate any coldness in love for the rest of the disciples, but only a fuller and more abundant love towards the one, which his prerogative of virginity and the purity of his flesh bestowed upon him. And therefore it is marked by exceptional treatment, as being something more sublime, because no hateful comparison with others, but a richer grace of superabundant love singled it out. Something of this sort too we have in the character of the bride in the Song of Songs, where she says: "Set in order love in me."[9] For this

---

[1] 1 John iv. 16.   [2] Rom. v. 5.   [3] Rom. viii. 26, 27.

[4] Gal. vi. 10.   [6] Gen. xxxvii. 4.   [8] Ib. ver. 34, 1.
[5] S. Matt. v. 44.   [7] S. John xiii. 23.   [9] Cant. ii. 4.

is true love set in order, which, while it hates no one, yet loves some still more by reason of their deserving it, and which, while it loves all in general, singles out for itself some from those, whom it may embrace with a special affection, and again among those, who are the special and chief objects of its love, singles out some who are preferred to others in affection.

CHAPTER XV.

Of those who only increase their own or their brother's grievances by hiding them.

On the other hand we know (and O! would that we did not know) some of the brethren who are so hard and obstinate, that when they know that their own feelings are aroused against their brother, or that their brother's are against them, in order to conceal their vexation of mind, which is caused by indignation at the grievance of one or the other, go apart from those whom they ought to smooth down by humbly making up to them and talking with them; and begin to sing some verses of the Psalms. And these while they fancy that they are softening the bitter thoughts which have arisen in their heart, increase by their insolent conduct what they could have got rid of at once if they had been willing to show more care and humility, for a well-timed expression of regret would cure their own feelings and soften their brother's heart. For by that plan they nourish and cherish the sin of meanness or rather of pride, instead of stamping out all inducement to quarrelling, and they forget the charge of the Lord which says: "Whosoever is angry with his brother, is in danger of the judgment;" and: "if thou remember that thy brother hath aught against thee, leave there thy gift before the altar, and go thy way, first be reconciled to thy brother, and then come and offer thy gift." [1]

CHAPTER XVI.

How it is that, if our brother has any grudge against us, the gifts of our prayers are rejected by the Lord.

So far therefore is our Lord anxious that we should not disregard the vexation of another that He does not accept our offerings if our brother has anything against us, i.e., He does not allow prayers to be offered by us to Him until by speedy amends we remove from his (our brother's) mind the vexation which he whether rightly or wrongly feels.

For He does not say: "if thy brother hath a true ground for complaint against thee leave thy gift at the altar, and go thy way, first be reconciled to him;" but He says: "if thou remember that thy brother hath aught against thee," i.e., if there be anything however trivial or small, owing to which your brother's anger is roused against you, and this comes back to your recollection by a sudden remembrance, you must know that you ought not to offer the spiritual gift of your prayers until by kindly amends you have removed from your brother's heart the vexation arising from whatever cause. If then the words of the Gospel bid us make satisfaction to those who are angry for past and utterly trivial grounds of quarrel, and those which have arisen from the slightest causes, what will become of us wretches who with obstinate hypocrisy disregard more recent grounds of offence, and those of the utmost importance, and due to our own faults; and being puffed up with the devil's own pride, as we are ashamed to humble ourselves, deny that we are the cause of our brother's vexation and in a spirit of rebellion disdaining to be subject to the Lord's commands, contend that they never ought to be observed and never can be fulfilled? And so it comes to pass that as we make up our minds that He has commanded things which are impossible and unsuitable, we become, to use the Apostle's expression, "not doers but judges of the law." [2]

CHAPTER XVII.

Of those who hold that patience should be shown to worldly people rather than to the brethren.

This too should be bitterly lamented; namely, that some of the brethren, when angered by some reproachful words, if they are besieged by the prayers of some one else who wants to smooth them down, when they hear that vexation ought not to be admitted or retained against a brother, according to what is written: "Whoever is angry with his brother is in danger of the judgment;" and: "Let not the sun go down upon your wrath," [3] instantly assert that if a heathen or one living in the world had said or done this, it rightly ought to be endured. But who could stand a brother who was accessory to so great a fault, or gave utterance to so insolent a reproach with his lips! As if patience were to be shown only to unbelievers and blasphemers, and not to all in general, or as if anger should be reckoned as bad when it is against

---

[1] S. Matt. v. 22–24. [2] S. James iv. 11. [3] Eph. iv. 26.

a heathen, but good when it is against a brother; whereas certainly the obstinate rage of an angry soul brings about the same injury to one's self whoever may be the subject against whom it is aroused. But how terribly obstinate, aye and senseless is it for them, owing to the stupidity of their dull mind, not to be able to discern the meaning of these words, for it is not said: "Every one who is angry with a stranger shall be in danger of the judgment," which might perhaps according to their interpretation except those who are partners of our faith and life, but the word of the Gospel most significantly expresses it by saying: "Every one who is angry with his brother, shall be in danger of the judgment." And so though we ought according to the rule of truth to regard every man as a brother, yet in this passage one of the faithful and a partaker of our mode of life is denoted by the title of brother rather than a heathen.

CHAPTER XVIII.

Of those who pretend to patience but excite their brethren to anger by their silence.

But what sort of a thing is this, that sometimes we fancy that we are patient because when provoked we scorn to answer, but by sullen silence or scornful motions and gestures so mock at our angry brothers that by our silent looks we provoke them to anger more than angry reproaches would have excited them, meanwhile thinking that we are in no way guilty before God, because we have let nothing fall from our lips which could brand us or condemn us in the judgment of men. As if in the sight of God mere words, and not mainly the will was called in fault, and as if only the actual deed of sin, and not also the wish and purpose, was reckoned as wrong ; or as if it would be asked in the judgment only what each one had done and not what he also purposed to do. For it is not only the character of the anger roused, but also the purpose of the man who provokes it which is bad, and therefore the true scrutiny of our judge will ask, not how the quarrel was stirred up but by whose fault it arose: for the purpose of the sin, and not the way in which the fault is committed must be taken into account. For what does it matter whether a man kills a brother with a sword by himself, or drives him to death by some fraud, when it is clear that he is killed by his wiles and crime? As if it were enough not to have pushed a blind man down with one's own hand, though he is equally guilty who scorned to save him, when it was in his power, when

fallen and on the point of tumbling into the ditch: or as if he alone were guilty who had caught a man with the hand, and not also the one who had prepared and set the trap for him, or who would not set him free when he might have done so. So then it is of no good to hold one's tongue, if we impose silence upon ourselves for this reason that by our silence we may do what would have been done by an outcry on our part, simulating certain gestures by which he whom we ought to have cured, may be made still more angry, while we are commended for all this, to his loss and damage: as if a man were not for this very reason the more guilty, because he tried to get glory for himself out of his brother's fall. For such a silence will be equally bad for both because while it increases the vexation in the heart of another, so it prevents it from being removed from one's own: and against such persons the prophet's curse is with good reason directed: "Woe to him that giveth drink to his friend, and presenteth his gall, and maketh him drunk, that he may behold his nakedness. He is filled with shame instead of glory."[1] And this too which is said of such people by another: "For every brother will utterly supplant, and every friend will walk deceitfully. And a man shall mock his brother, and they will not speak the truth, for they have bent their tongue like a bow for lies and not for truth."[2] But often a feigned patience excites to anger more keenly than words, and, a spiteful silence exceeds the most awful insults in words, and the wounds of enemies are more easily borne than the deceitful blandishment of mockers, of which it is well said by the prophet: "Their words are smoother than oil, and yet they are darts:" and elsewhere "the words of the crafty are soft: but they smite within the belly:" to which this also may be finely applied: "With the mouth he speaks peace to his friend, but secretly he layeth snares for him;" with which however the deceiver is rather deceived, for "if a man prepares a net before his friend, it surrounds his own feet;" and: "if a man digs a pit for his neighbour, he shall fall into it himself."[3] Lastly when a great multitude had come with swords and staves to take the Lord, none of the murderers of the author of our life stood forth as more cruel than he who advanced before them all with a counterfeit respect and salutation and offered a kiss of feigned love; to whom the Lord said: "Judas, betrayest thou the Son of man with a kiss?"[4] i.e., the bitter-

---

[1] Hab. ii. 15, 16.　　　　　[2] Jer. ix. 4, 5.
[3] Ps. liv. (lv.) 22; Prov. xxvi. 22; Jer. ix. 8; Prov. xxix. 5; xxvi. 27.
[4] S. Luke xxii. 48.

ness of thy persecution and hatred has taken as a cloke this which expresses the sweetness of true love. More openly too and more energetically does He emphasize the force of this grief by the prophet, saying: "For if mine enemy had cursed me, I would have borne it: and if he who hated me had spoken great things against me, I would have hid myself from him. But it was thou, a man of one mind, my guide, and my familiar friend: who didst take sweet meats together with me: in the house of God we walked with consent." [1]

CHAPTER XIX.

Of those who fast out of rage.

THERE is too another evil sort of vexation which would not be worth mentioning were it not that we know it is allowed by some of the brethren who, when they have been vexed or enraged actually abstain persistently from food, so that (a thing which we cannot mention without shame) those who when they are calm declare that they cannot possibly put off their refreshment to the sixth or at most the ninth hour, when they are filled with vexation and rage do not feel fasts even for two days, and support themselves, when exhausted by such abstinence, by a surfeit of anger. Wherein they are plainly guilty of the sin of sacrilege, as out of the devil's own rage they endure fasts which ought specially to be offered to God alone out of desire for humiliation of heart and purification from sin: which is much the same as if they were to offer prayers and sacrifices not to God but to devils, and so be worthy of hearing this rebuke of Moses: "They sacrificed to devils and not to God ; to gods whom they knew not." [2]

CHAPTER XX.

Of the feigned patience of some who offer the other cheek to be smitten.

WE are not ignorant also of another kind of insanity, which we find in some of the brethren under colour of a counterfeit patience, as in this case it is not enough to have stirred up quarrels unless they incite them with irritating words so as to get themselves smitten, and when they have been touched by the slightest blow, at once they offer another part of their body to be smitten, as if in this way they could fulfil to perfection that command which says: "If a man smite thee on

the right cheek, offer him the other also;" [3] while they totally ignore the meaning and purpose of the passage. For they fancy that they are practising evangelical patience through the sin of anger, for the utter eradication of which not only was the exchange of retaliation and the irritation of strife forbidden, but the command was actually given us to mitigate the wrath of the striker by the endurance of a double wrong.

CHAPTER XXI.

A question how if we obey the commands of Christ we can fail of evangelical perfection.

GERMANUS: How can we blame one who satisfies the command of the Gospel and not only does not retaliate, but is actually prepared to have a double wrong offered to him?

CHAPTER XXII.

The answer that Christ looks not only at the action but also at the will.

JOSEPH: As was said a little before, we must look not only at the thing which is done, but also at the character of the mind and the purpose of the doer. And therefore if you weigh with a careful scrutiny of heart what is done by each man and consider with what mind it is done or from what feeling it proceeds, you will see that the virtue of patience and gentleness cannot possibly be fulfilled in the opposite spirit, i.e., that of impatience and rage. Since our Lord and Saviour, when giving us a thorough lesson on the virtue of patience and gentleness (i.e., teaching us not only to profess it with our lips, but to store it up in the inmost recesses of the soul) gave us this summary of evangelical perfection, saying: "If any one smites thee on thy right cheek, offer him the other also" [4] (doubtless the "right" cheek is mentioned, as another "right" cheek cannot be found except in the face of the inner man, so to speak), as by this He desires entirely to remove all incitement to anger from the deepest recesses of the soul, i.e., that if your external right cheek has received a blow from the striker, the inner man also humbly consenting may offer its right cheek to be smitten, sympathizing with the suffering of the outward man, and in a way submitting and subjecting its own body to wrong from the striker, that the inner man may not even silently be

---

[1] Ps. liv. (lv.) 13–15.   [2] Deut. xxxii. 17.   [3] S. Matt. v. 39.   [4] Ibid.

disturbed in itself at the blows of the outward man. You see then that they are very far from evangelical perfection, which teaches that patience must be maintained, not in words, but in inward tranquillity of heart, and which bids us preserve it whatever evil happens, that we may not only keep ourselves always from disturbing anger, but also by submitting to their injuries compel those, who are disturbed by their own fault, to become calm, when they have had their fill of blows; and so overcome their rage by our gentleness. And so also we shall fulfil these words of the Apostle: "Be not overcome of evil, but overcome evil with good."[1] And it is quite clear that this cannot be fulfilled by those who utter words of gentleness and humility in such a spirit and rage that they not only fail to lessen the fire of wrath which has been kindled, but rather make it blaze up the more fiercely both in their own feelings and in those of their enraged brother. But these, even if they could in some way keep calm and quiet themselves, would yet not bear any fruits of righteousness, while they claim the glory of patience on their part by their neighbour's loss, and are thus altogether removed from that Apostolic love which "Seeketh not her own,"[2] but the things of others. For it does not so desire riches in such a way as to make profit for itself out of one's neighbour's loss, nor does it wish to gain anything if it involves the spoiling of another.

CHAPTER XXIII.

How he is the strong and vigorous man, who yields to the will of another.

BUT you must certainly know that in general he plays a stronger part who subjects his own will to his brother's, than he who is found to be the more pertinacious in defending and clinging to his own decisions. For the former by bearing and putting up with his neighbour gains the character of being strong and vigorous, while the latter gains that of being weak and sickly, who must be pampered and petted so that sometimes for the sake of his peace and quiet it is a good thing to relax something even in necessary matters. And indeed in this he need not fancy that he has lost anything of his own perfection, though by yielding he has given up something of his intended strictness, but on the contrary he may be sure that he has gained much more by his virtue of long-suffering and patience. For this is the Apostle's command: "Ye who are strong should bear the infirmities of the weak;" and: "Bear ye

one another's burdens, and so fulfil the law of Christ."[3] For a weak man will never support a weak man, nor can one who is suffering in the same way, bear or cure one in feeble health, but one who is himself not subject to infirmity brings remedies to one in weak health. For it is rightly said to him: "Physician, heal thyself."[4]

CHAPTER XXIV.

How the weak are harmful and cannot bear wrongs.

WE must note too the fact that the nature of the weak is always such that they are quick and ready to offer reproaches and sow the seeds of quarrels, while they themselves cannot bear to be touched by the shadow of the very slightest wrong, and while they are riding roughshod over us and flinging about wanton charges, they are not able to bear even the slightest and most trivial ones themselves. And so according to the aforesaid opinion of the Elders love cannot last firm and unbroken except among men of the same purpose and goodness. For at some time or other it is sure to be broken, however carefully it may be guarded by one of them.

CHAPTER XXV.

A question how he can be strong who does not always support the weak.

GERMANUS: How then can the patience of a perfect man be worthy of praise if it cannot always bear the weak?

CHAPTER XXVI.

The answer that the weak does not always allow himself to be borne.

JOSEPH: I did not say that the virtue and endurance of one who is strong and robust would be overcome, but that the miserable condition of the weak, encouraged by the tolerance of the perfect, and daily growing worse, is sure to give rise to reasons on account of which he himself ought no longer to be borne; or else with a shrewd suspicion that the patience of his neighbour shows up and sets off his own impatience at some time or other he chooses to make off rather than always to be borne by the magnanimity of the other. This then we think should be above all else observed by those who want to keep the affec-

---

[1] Rom. xii. 21.   [2] 1 Cor. xiii. 5.   [3] Rom. xv. 1; Gal. vi. 2.   [4] S. Luke iv. 23.

tion of their companions unimpaired; viz., that first of all when provoked by any wrongs, a monk should keep not only his lips but even the depth of his breast unmoved: but if he finds that they are even slightly disturbed, let him keep himself in by entire silence, and diligently observe what the Psalmist speaks of: "I was troubled and spake nothing;" and: "I said I will take heed to thy ways that I offend not with my tongue. I have set a guard to my mouth, when the sinner stood against me. I was dumb and was humbled, and kept silence from good things;"[1] and he should not pay any heed to his present state, nor give vent to what his violent rage suggests and his exasperated mind expresses at the moment, but should dwell on the grace of past love or look forward in his mind to the renewal and restoration of peace, and contemplate it even in the very hour of rage, as if it were sure presently to return. And while he is reserving himself for the delight of harmony soon to come, he will not feel the bitterness of the present quarrel and will easily make such answers that, when love is restored, he will not be able to accuse himself as guilty or be blamed by the other; and thus he will fulfil these words of the prophet: "In wrath remember mercy."[2]

CHAPTER XXVII.

How anger should be repressed.

WE ought then to restrain every movement of anger and moderate it under the direction of discretion, that we may not by blind rage be hurried into that which is condemned by Solomon: "The wicked man expends all his anger, but the wise man dispenses it bit by bit,"[3] i.e., a fool is inflamed by the passion of his anger to avenge himself; but a wise man, by the ripeness of his counsel and moderation little by little diminishes it, and gets rid of it. Something of the same kind too is this which is said by the Apostle: "Not avenging yourselves, dearly beloved: but give place to wrath,"[4] i.e., do not under the compulsion of wrath proceed to vengeance, but give place to wrath, i.e., do not let your hearts be confined in the straits of impatience and cowardice so that, when a fierce storm of passion rises, you cannot endure it; but be ye enlarged in your hearts, receiving the adverse waves of anger in the wide gulf of that love which "suffereth all things, beareth all

things;"[5] and so your mind will be enlarged with wide long-suffering and patience, and will have within it safe recesses of counsel, in which the foul smoke of anger will be received and be diffused and forthwith vanish away; or else the passage may be taken in this way: we give place to wrath, as often as we yield with humble and tranquil mind to the passion of another, and bow to the impatience of the passionate, as if we admitted that we deserved any kind of wrong. But those who twist the meaning of the perfection of which the Apostle speaks so as to make out that those give place to anger, who go away from a man in a rage, seem to me not to cut off but rather to foment the incitement to quarrelling, for unless a neighbour's wrath is overcome at once by amends being humbly made, a man provokes rather than avoids it by his flight. And there is something like this that Solomon says: "Be not hasty in thy spirit to be wroth, for anger reposes in the bosom of fools;" and: "Be not quick to rush into a quarrel, lest thou repent thereof at the last."[6] For he does not blame a hasty exhibition of quarrelling and anger in such a way as to praise a tardy one. In the same way too must this be taken: "A fool declares his anger in the very same hour, but a prudent man hides his shame."[7] For he does not lay it down that a shameful outburst of anger ought to be hidden by wise men in such a way that while he blames a speedy outburst of anger he fails to forbid a tardy one, as certainly, if owing to human weakness it does burst forth, he means that it should be hidden for this reason, that while for the moment it is wisely covered up, it may be destroyed forever. For the nature of anger is such that when it is given room it languishes and perishes, but if openly exhibited, it burns more and more. The hearts then should be enlarged and opened wide, lest they be confined in the narrow straits of cowardice, and be filled with the swelling surge of wrath, and so we become unable to receive what the prophet calls the "exceeding broad" commandment of God in our narrow heart, or to say with the prophet: "I have run the way of thy commandments for thou hast enlarged my heart."[8] For that long-suffering is wisdom we are taught by very clear passages of Scripture: for "a man who is long-suffering is great in prudence; but a coward is very foolish."[9] And therefore Scripture says of him who to his credit asked the gift of wisdom from the Lord: "God gave Solomon wisdom and prudence

1 Ps. lxxvi. (lxxvii.) 5; xxxviii. (xxxix.) 2, 3. 3 Prov. xxix. 11.   5 1 Cor. xiii. 7.   7 Prov. xii. 16.   9 Prov. xiv. 29.
2 Hab. iii. 2.   4 Rom. xii. 19.   6 Eccl. vii. 9; Prov. xxv. 8.   8 Ps. cxviii. (cxix.) 32.

exceeding much, and largeness of heart as the sand of the sea for multitude." [1]

CHAPTER XXVIII.

How friendships entered upon by conspiracy cannot be lasting ones.

THIS too has been often proved by many experiments; viz., that those who entered the bonds of friendship from a beginning of conspiracy, cannot possibly preserve their harmony unbroken; either because they tried to keep it not out of their desire for perfection nor because of the sway of Apostolic love, but out of earthly love, and because of their wants and the bonds of their agreement; or else because that most crafty foe of ours hurries them on the more speedily to break the chains of their friendship in order that he may make them breakers of their oath. This opinion then of the most prudent men is most certainly established; viz., that true harmony and undivided union can only exist among those whose life is pure, and who are men of the same goodness and purpose.

Thus much the blessed Joseph discoursed in his spiritual talk on friendship, and fired us with a more ardent desire to preserve the love of our fellowship as a lasting one.

XVII.

THE SECOND CONFERENCE OF ABBOT JOSEPH.

ON MAKING PROMISES.

CHAPTER I.

Of the vigils which we endured.

WHEN then the previous Conference was ended, and the intervening silence of night as well, as we had been conducted by the holy Abbot Joseph to a separate cell for the sake of quiet, but had passed the whole night without sleep (since owing to his words a fire was raging in our hearts), we came forth from the cell and retired about a hundred yards from it and sat down in a secluded spot. And so as an opportunity was given by the shades of night for secret and familiar converse together, as we sat there Abbot Germanus groaned heavily.

CHAPTER II.

Of the anxiety of Abbot Germanus at the recollection of our promise.

WHAT are we doing? said he. For we see that we are involved in a great difficulty and are in an evil plight, as reason itself and the life of the saints is effectually teaching us what is the best thing for our progress in the spiritual life, and yet our promise given to the Elders does not allow us to choose what is helpful. For we might, by the examples of such great men, be formed for a more perfect life and aim, were it not that the terms of our promise compelled us to return at once to the monastery. But if we return thither, we shall never get another chance of coming here again. But if we stay here and choose to carry out our wishes, what becomes of the faith of the oath which we are aware that we gave to our Elders promising a speedy return; that we might be allowed to make a hasty round of the monasteries and saints of this province? And when in this state of tumult we could not make up our minds what we ought to decide on the state of our salvation we simply testified by our groans the hard fate of our condition, upbraiding the audacity of our impudence, and yet hating the shame which was natural to us, weighed down by which we could not in any other way resist the prayers of those who kept us back against our profit and purpose, except by the promise of a speedy return, as we wept indeed that we laboured under the fault of that shame, of which it is said "There is a shame that bringeth sin." [2]

CHAPTER III.

My ideas on this subject.

THEN I replied: The counsel or rather the authority of the Elder to whom we ought to

---

[1] 1 Kings iv. 29.

[2] Prov. xxvi. 11.

refer our anxieties would make a short way out of our difficulties, and whatever is decided by his verdict, may, like a divine and heavenly reply, put an end to all our troubles. And we need not have any doubt of what is given to us by the Lord through the lips of this Elder, both for the sake of his merits and for our own faith. For by His gift believers have often obtained saving counsel from unworthy people, and unbelievers from saints, as the Lord grants this either on account of the merit of those who answer, or on account of the faith of those who ask advice. And so the holy Abbot Germanus caught eagerly at these words as if I had uttered them not of myself but at the prompting of the Lord, and when we had waited a little for the coming of the Elder and the approaching hour of the nocturnal service, after we had welcomed him with the usual greeting and finished reciting the right number of Psalms and prayers, we sat down again as usual on the same mats on which we had settled ourselves to sleep.

CHAPTER IV.

Abbot Joseph's question and our answer on the origin of our anxiety.

THEN the venerable Joseph saw that we were in rather low spirits, and, guessing that this was not the case without reason, addressed us in these words of the patriarch Joseph: "Why are your faces sad today?"[1] to whom we answered: We are not like those bond slaves of Pharaoh who have seen a dream and there is none to interpret it, but I admit that we have passed a sleepless night and there is no one to lighten the weight of our troubles unless the Lord may remove them by your wisdom. Then he, who recalled the excellence of the patriarch both by his merits and name, said: Does not the cure of man's perplexities come from the Lord? Let them be brought forward: for the Divine Compassion is able to give a remedy for them by means of our advice according to your faith.

CHAPTER V.

The explanation of Abbot Germanus why we wanted to stay in Egypt, and were drawn back to Syria.

TO THIS GERMANUS: We used to think, said he, that we should go back to our monastery abundantly filled not only with spiritual joy but also with what is profitable by the sight of your holiness, and that after our return we should follow, though with but a feeble rivalry, what we had learnt from your teaching. For this our love for our Elders led us to promise them, while we fancied that we could in some degree follow in that monastery your sublime life and doctrine. Wherefore as we thought that by this means all joy would be bestowed upon us, so on the other hand we are overwhelmed with intolerable grief, as we find that we cannot possibly obtain in this way what we know to be good for us. On both sides then we are now hemmed in. For if we want to keep our promise which we made in the presence of all the brethren in the cave where our Lord Himself shone forth from His chamber in the Virgin's womb,[2] and which He Himself witnessed, we shall incur the greatest loss in our spiritual life. But if we ignore our promise and stay in this district, and choose to consider that oath of ours as of less importance than our perfection, we are afraid of the awful dangers of falsehood and perjury. But not even by this plan can we lighten our burdens; viz., by fulfilling the terms of our oath by a very hasty return, and then coming back again as quickly as possible to these parts. For although even a small delay is dangerous and hurtful for those who are aiming at goodness and advance in spiritual things, yet still we would keep our faith and promise, though by an unwilling return, were it not that we felt sure that we should be so tightly bound down both by the authority and also by the love of the Elders, that we should henceforth have no opportunity at all to come back again to this place.

CHAPTER VI.

Abbot Joseph's question whether we got more good in Egypt than in Syria.

To this the blessed Joseph, after a short silence: Are you sure, said he, that you can get more profit in spiritual matters in this country?

CHAPTER VII.

The answer on the difference of customs in the two countries.

GERMANUS: Although we ought to be *most* grateful for the teaching of those men who taught us from our youth up to attempt great things, and, by giving us a taste of their excellence, implanted in our hearts a splendid thirst for perfection, yet if any reliance is to

---

[1] Gen. xl. 7.

[2] Compare on the Institutes IV. c. xxxi.

be placed on our judgment, we cannot draw any comparison between these customs and those which we learnt there, so as to hold our tongues about the inimitable purity of your life, which we believe is granted to you not only owing to the concentration of your mind and aim, but also owing to the aid and assistance of the place itself. Wherefore we do not doubt that for the following of your grand perfection this instruction which is given to us is not enough by itself, unless we have also the help of the life, and a long course of instruction somewhat dissolves the coldness of our heart by daily training.

CHAPTER VIII.

How those who are perfect ought not to make any promises absolutely, and whether decisions can be reversed without sin.

JOSEPH: It is good indeed and right and altogether in accordance with our profession, for us effectually to perform what we decided to do in the case of any promise. Wherefore a monk ought not to make any promise hastily, lest he may be forced to do what he incautiously promised, or if he is kept back by consideration of a sounder view, appear as a breaker of his promise. But because at the present moment our purpose is to treat not so much of a state of health as of the cure of sickness we must with salutary counsel consider not what you ought to have done in the first instance, but how you can escape from the rocks of this perilous shipwreck. When then no chains impede us and no conditions restrict us, in the case of a comparison of good things, if a choice is proposed, that which is most advantageous should be preferred: but when some detriment and loss stands in the way, in a comparison of things to our hurt, that should be sought which exposes us to the smallest loss. Further, as your assertion shows, when your heedless promise has brought you to this state that in either case some serious loss and inconvenience must result to you, the will in choosing should incline to that side which involves a loss that is more tolerable, or can be more easily made up for by the remedy of making amends. If then you think that you will get more good for your spirit by staying here than what accrued to you from your life in that monastery, and that the terms of your promise cannot be fulfilled without the loss of great good, it is better for you to undergo the loss from a falsehood and an unfulfilled promise (as it is done once for all, and need not any

longer be repeated or be the cause of other sins) than for you to incur that loss, through which you say that your state of life would become colder, and which would affect you with a daily and unceasing injury. For a careless promise is changed in such a way that it may be pardoned or indeed praised, if it is turned into a better path, nor need we take it as a failure in consistency, but as a correction of rashness, whenever a promise that was faulty is corrected. And all this may be proved by most certain witness from Scripture, that for many the fulfilment of their promise has led to death, and on the other hand that for many it has been good and profitable to have refused it.

CHAPTER IX.

How it is often better to break one's engagements than to fulfil them.

AND both these points are very clearly shown by the cases of S. Peter the Apostle and Herod. For the former, because he departed from his expressed determination which he had as it were confirmed with an oath saying "Thou shalt never wash my feet," [1] gained an immortal partnership with Christ, whereas he would certainly have been cut off from the grace of this blessedness, if he had clung obstinately to his word. But the latter, by clinging to the pledge of his ill-considered oath, became the bloody murderer of the Lord's forerunner, and through the vain fear of perjury plunged himself into condemnation and the punishment of everlasting death. In everything then we must consider the end, and must according to it direct our course and aim, and if when some wiser counsel supervenes, we see it diverging to the worse part, it is better to discard the unsuitable arrangement, and to come to a better mind rather than to cling obstinately to our engagements and so become involved in worse sins.

CHAPTER X.

Our question about our fear of the oath which we gave in the monastery in Syria.

GERMANUS: In so far as it concerns our desire, which we undertook to carry out for the sake of spiritual profit, we were hoping to be edified by continual intercourse with you. For if we were to return to our monastery it is certain that we should not only fail of so sublime a purpose, but that we should also

---

[1] S. John xiii. 8.

suffer grievous loss from the mediocrity of the manner of life there.   But that command of the gospel frightens us terribly: "Let your speech be yea, yea, nay, nay: but whatsoever is more than these, is from the evil one."[1] For we hold that we cannot compensate for transgressing so important a command by any righteousness, nor can that finally turn out well which has once been started with a bad beginning.

CHAPTER XI.

The answer that we must take into account the purpose of the doer rather than the execution of the business.

JOSEPH: In every case, as we said, we must look not at the progress of the work but at the intention of the worker, nor must we inquire to begin with what a man has done, but with what purpose, so that we may find that some have been condemned for those deeds from which good has afterwards arisen, and on the other hand that some have arrived by means of acts in themselves reprehensible at the height of righteousness.   And in the case of the former the good result of their actions was of no avail to them as they took the matter in and with an evil purpose, and wanted to bring about — not the good which actually resulted, but something of the opposite character; nor was the bad beginning injurious to the latter, as he put up with the necessity of a blameworthy start, not out of disregard for God, or with the purpose of doing wrong, but with an eye to a needful and holy end.

CHAPTER XII.

How a fortunate issue will be of no avail to evil doers, while bad deeds will not injure good men.

AND that we may make these statements clear by instances from Holy Scripture, what could be brought about that was more salutary and more to the good of the whole world, than the saving remedy of the Lord's Passion? And yet it was not only of no advantage, but was actually to the disadvantage of the traitor by whose means it is shown to have been brought about, so that it is absolutely said of him: "It were good for that man if he had never been born."[2]   For the fruits of his labour will not be repaid to him according to the actual result, but according to what he wanted to do, and believed that he would

accomplish.   And again, what could there be more culpable than craft and deceit shown even to a stranger, not to mention one's brother and father?   And yet the patriarch Jacob not only met with no condemnation or blame for such things but was actually dowered with the everlasting heritage of the blessing.   And not without reason, for the last mentioned desired the blessing destined for the first-born not out of a greedy desire for present gain but because of his faith in everlasting sanctification; while the former (Judas) delivered the Redeemer of all to death, not for the sake of man's salvation, but from the sin of covetousness.   And therefore in each case the fruits of their action are reckoned according to the intention of the mind and purpose of the will, according to which the object of the one was not to work fraud, nor was that of the other to work salvation.   For justly is there repayment to each man as the recompense of reward, for what he conceived in the first instance in his mind, and not for what resulted from it either well or badly, against the wish of the worker. And so the most just Judge regarded him who ventured on such a falsehood as excusable and indeed worthy of praise, because without it he could not secure the blessing of the first-born; and that should not be reckoned as a sin, which arose from desire of the blessing. Otherwise the aforesaid patriarch would have been not only unfair to his brother, but also a cheat of his father and a blasphemer, if there had been any other way by which he could secure the gift of that blessing, and he had preferred to follow this which would damage and injure his brother.   You see then that with God the inquiry is not into the carrying out of the act, but into the purpose of the mind.   With this preparation then for a return to the question proposed (for which all this has been premised) I want you first to tell me for what reason you bound yourselves in the fetters of that promise.

CHAPTER XIII.

Our answer as to the reason which demanded an oath from us.

GERMANUS: The first reason, as we said, was that we were afraid of vexing our Elders and resisting their orders; the second was that we very foolishly believed that, if we had learnt from you anything perfect or splendid to hear or look at, when we returned to the monastery, we should be able to perform it.

---

[1] S. Matt. v. 37.   [2] S. Matt. xxvi. 24.

CHAPTER XIV.

The discourse of the Elder showing how the plan of action may be changed without fault provided that one keeps to the carrying out of a good intention.

JOSEPH: As we premised, the intent of the mind brings a man either reward or condemnation, according to this passage: "Their thoughts between themselves accusing or also defending one another, in the day when God shall judge the secrets of men;" and this too: "But I am coming to gather together their works and thoughts together with all nations and tongues." [1] Wherefore it was, as I see, from a desire for perfection that you bound yourselves with the chain of these oaths, as you then thought that by this plan it could be gained, while now that a riper judgment has supervened, you see that you cannot by this means scale its heights. And so any departure from that arrangement, which may seem to have happened, will be no hindrance, if only no change in that first purpose follows. For a change of instrument does not imply a desertion of the work, nor does the choice of a shorter and more direct road argue laziness on the path of the traveller. And so in this matter an improvement in a short-sighted arrangement is not to be reckoned a breach of a spiritual promise. For whatever is done out of the love of God and desire for goodness, which has "promise of the life that now is and of that which is to come," [2] even though it may appear to commence with a hard and adverse beginning, is most worthy, not only of no blame, but actually of praise. And therefore the breaking of a careless promise will be no hindrance, if in every case the end, i.e., the proposed aim at goodness, be maintained. For we do all for this reason, that we may be able to show to God a clean heart, and if the attainment of this is considered to be easier in this country the alteration of the agreement extracted from you will be no hindrance to you, if only the perfection of that purity for the sake of which your promise was originally made, be the sooner secured according to the Lord's will.

CHAPTER XV.

A question whether it can be without sin that our knowledge affords to weak brethren an opportunity for lying.

GERMANUS: As far as the force of the words which have been reasonably and carefully considered, is concerned, our scruple about our promise would have easily been removed from us were it not that we were terribly alarmed lest by this example an opportunity for lying might be offered to certain weaker brethren, if they knew that the faith of an agreement could be in any way lawfully broken, whereas this very thing is forbidden in such vigorous and threatening terms by the prophet when he says: "Thou shalt destroy all those who utter a lie;" and: "the mouth that speaketh a lie, shall slay the soul." [3]

CHAPTER XVI.

The answer that Scripture truth is not to be altered on account of an offence given to the weak.

JOSEPH: Occasions and opportunities for destroying themselves cannot possibly be wanting to those who are on the road to ruin, or rather who are anxious to destroy themselves; nor are those passages of Scripture to be rejected and altogether torn out of the volume, by which the perversity of heretics is encouraged, or the unbelief of the Jews increased, or the pride of heathen wisdom offended; but surely they are to be piously believed, and firmly held, and preached according to the rule of truth. And therefore we should not, because of another's unbelief, reject the οἰκονομίας, i.e., the "economy" of the prophets and saints which Scripture relates, lest while we are thinking that we ought to condescend to their infirmities, we stain ourselves with the sin not only of lying but of sacrilege. But, as we said, we ought to admit these according to the letter, and explain how they were rightly done. But for those who are wrongly disposed, the opening for lies will not be blocked up by this means, if we are trying either altogether to deny or to explain away by allegorical interpretations the truth of those things which we are going to bring forward or have already brought forward. For how will the authority of these passages injure them if their corrupt will is alone sufficient to lead them to sin?

CHAPTER XVII.

How the saints have profitably employed a lie like hellebore.

AND so we ought to regard a lie and to employ it as if its nature were that of hellebore; which is useful if taken when some deadly disease is threatening, but if taken without being required by some great danger is the cause of immediate death. For so also we

---

[1] Rom. ii. 15, 16; Is. lxvi. 18.　　[2] 1 Tim. iv. 8.　　[3] Ps. v. 7; Wisd. i. 11.

read that holy men and those most approved by God employed lying, so as not only to incur no guilt of sin from it, but even to attain the greatest goodness; and if deceit could confer glory on them, what on the other hand would the truth have brought them but condemnation? Just as Rahab, of whom Scripture gives a record not only of no good deed but actually of unchastity, yet simply for the lie, by means of which she preferred to hide the spies instead of betraying them, had it vouchsafed to her to be joined with the people of God in everlasting blessing. But if she had preferred to speak the truth and to regard the safety of the citizens, there is no doubt that she and all her house would not have escaped the coming destruction, nor would it have been vouchsafed to her to be inserted in the progenitors of our Lord's nativity,[1] and reckoned in the list of the patriarchs, and through her descendants that followed, to become the mother of the Saviour of all. Again Dalila, who to provide for the safety of her fellow citizens betrayed the truth she had discovered, obtained in exchange eternal destruction, and has left to all men nothing but the memory of her sin. When then any grave danger hangs on confession of the truth, then we must take to lying as a refuge, yet in such a way as to be for our salvation troubled by the guilt of a humbled conscience. But where there is no call of the utmost necessity present, there a lie should be most carefully avoided as if it were something deadly: just as we said of a cup of hellebore which is indeed useful if it is only taken in the last resort when a deadly and inevitable disease is threatening, while if it is taken when the body is in a state of sound and rude health, its deadly properties at once go to find out the vital parts. And this was clearly shown of Rahab of Jericho, and the patriarch Jacob; the former of whom could only escape death by means of this remedy, while the latter could not secure the blessing of the first-born without it. For God is not only the Judge and inspector of our words and actions, but He also looks into their purpose and aim. And if He sees that anything has been done or promised by some one for the sake of eternal salvation and shows insight into Divine contemplation, even though it may appear to men to be hard and unfair, yet He looks at the inner goodness of the heart and regards the desire of the will rather than the actual words spoken, because He must take into account the aim of the work and the disposition of the doer, whereby, as was said

above, one man may be justified by means of a lie, while another may be guilty of a sin of everlasting death by telling the truth. To which end the patriarch Jacob also had regard when he was not afraid to imitate the hairy appearance of his brother's body by wrapping himself up in skins, and to his credit acquiesced in his mother's instigation of a lie for this object. For he saw that in this way there would be bestowed on him greater gains of blessing and righteousness than by keeping to the path of simplicity: for he did not doubt that the stain of this lie would at once be washed away by the flood of the paternal blessing, and would speedily be dissolved like a little cloud by the breath of the Holy Spirit; and that richer rewards of merit would be bestowed on him by means of this dissimulation which he put on than by means of the truth, which was natural to him.

CHAPTER XVIII.

An objection that only those men employed lies with impunity, who lived under the law.

GERMANUS: It is no wonder that these schemes were properly employed in the Old Testament, and that some holy men laudably or at any rate venially told lies, as we see that many worse things were permitted to them owing to the rude character of the times. For why should we wonder that when the blessed David was fleeing from Saul, in answer to the inquiry of Abimelech the priest who said: "Why art thou alone, and is no man with thee?" he replied as follows: "The king hath commanded me a business, and said, Let no man know the thing for which thou art sent by me, for I have appointed my servants to such and such a place;" and again: "Hast thou here at hand a spear or a sword, for I brought not my own sword nor my own weapon with me, for the king's business required haste;" or this, when he was brought to Achish king of Gath, and feigned himself mad and frantic, "and changed his countenance before them, and slipped down between their hands; and stumbled against the doors of the gate and his spittle ran down on his beard;"[2] when they were even allowed to enjoy crowds of wives and concubines, and no sin was on this account imputed to them, and when moreover they often shed the blood of their enemies with their own hand, and this was thought not only worthy of no blame, but actually praiseworthy? And all these things

---

[1] Cf. S. Matt. i. 5.

[2] 1 Sam. xxi. 1, 2, 8, 13.

we see by the light of the gospel are utterly forbidden, so that not one of them can be done without great sin and guilt. And in the same way we hold that no lie can be employed by any one, I will not say rightly, but not even venially, however it may be covered with the colour of piety, as the Lord says: "Let your speech be yea, yea, nay, nay: but whatsoever is more than these is of the evil one;" and the Apostle also agrees with this: "And lie not one to another."[1]

CHAPTER XIX.

The answer, that leave to lie, which was not even granted under the old Covenant, has rightly been taken by many.

JOSEPH: All liberty in the matter of wives and many concubines, as the end of time is approaching and the multiplying of the human race completed, ought rightly to be cut off by evangelical perfection, as being no longer necessary. For up to the coming of Christ it was well that the blessing of the original sentence should be in full vigour, whereby it was said: "Increase and multiply, and fill the earth."[2] And therefore it was quite right that from the root of human fecundity which happily flourished in the synagogue, in accordance with that dispensation of the times, the buds of angelical virginity should spring, and the fragrant flowers of continence be produced in the Church. But that lying was even then condemned the text of the whole Old Testament clearly shows, as it says: "Thou shall destroy all them that speak lies;" and again: "The bread of lying is sweet to a man, but afterwards his mouth is filled with gravel;" and the Giver of the law himself says: "Thou shalt avoid a lie."[3] But we said that it was then properly employed as a last resort when some need or plan of salvation was linked on to it, on account of which it ought not to be condemned. As is the case, which you mentioned, of king David when in his flight from the unjust persecution of Saul, to Abimelech the priest he used lying words, not with the object of getting any gain nor with the desire to injure anybody, but simply to save himself from that most iniquitous persecution; inasmuch as he would not stain his hands with the blood of the hostile king, so often delivered up to him by God; as he said: "The Lord be merciful to me that I may do no such thing to my master the Lord's anointed, as to lay my hand upon him, because he is the Lord's anointed."[4] And

therefore these plans which we hear that holy men under the old covenant adopted either from the will of God, or for the prefiguring of spiritual mysteries or for the salvation of some people, we too cannot refuse altogether, when necessity constrains us, as we see that even apostles did not avoid them, where the consideration of something profitable required them: which in the meanwhile we will for a time postpone, while we first discuss those instances which we propose still to bring forward from the Old Testament, and afterwards we shall more suitably introduce them so as more readily to prove that good and holy men, both in the Old and in the New Testament, were entirely at one with each other in these contrivances. For what shall we say of that pious fraud of Hushai to Absalom for the salvation of king David, which though uttered with all appearance of good-will by the deceiver and cheat, and opposed to the good of him who asked advice, is yet commended by the authority of Holy Scripture, which says: "But by the will of the Lord the profitable counsel of Ahithophel was defeated that the Lord might bring evil upon Absalom?"[5] Nor could that be blamed which was done for the right side with a right purpose and pious intent, and was planned for the salvation and victory of one whose piety was pleasing to God, by a holy dissimulation. What too shall we say of the deed of that woman, who received the men who had been sent to king David by the aforesaid Hushai, and hid them in a well, and spread a cloth over its mouth, and pretended that she was drying pearl-barley, and said "They passed on after tasting a little water";[6] and by this invention saved them from the hands of their pursuers? Wherefore answer me, I pray you, and say what you would have done, if any similar situation had arisen for you, living now under the gospel; would you prefer to hide them with a similar falsehood, saying in the same way: "They passed on after tasting a little water," and thus fulfil the command: "Deliver those who are being led to death, and spare not to redeem those who are being killed;"[7] or by speaking the truth, would you have given up those in hiding to the men who would kill them? And what then becomes of the Apostle's words: "Let no man seek his own but the things of another;" and: "Love seeketh not her own, but the things of others;" and of himself he says: "I seek not mine own good but the good of many that they may be saved?"[8] For if we seek our own,

---

1 S. Matt. v. 37; Col. iii. 9.　　　2 Gen. i. 28.　　　5 2 Sam. xvii. 14.　　　7 Prov. xxiv. 11.
3 Ps. v. 7; Prov. xx. 17; Exod. xxiii. 7.　　4 1 Sam. xxiv. 7.　　6 2 Ib. ver. 20.　　8 1 Cor. x. 24; xiii. 5; 1 Cor. x. 33.

and want obstinately to keep what is good for ourselves, we must even in urgent cases of this sort speak the truth, and so become guilty of the death of another: but if we prefer what is for another's advantage to our own good, and satisfy the demands of the Apostle, we shall certainly have to put up with the necessity of lying. And therefore we shall not be able to keep a perfect heart of love, or to seek, as Apostolic perfection requires, the things of others, unless we relax a little in those things which concern the strictness and perfection of our own lives, and choose to condescend with ready affection to what is useful to others, and so with the Apostle become weak to the weak, that we may be able to gain the weak.

CHAPTER XX.

How even Apostles thought that a lie was often useful and the truth injurious.

INSTRUCTED by which examples, the blessed Apostle James also, and all the chief princes of the primitive Church urged the Apostle Paul in consequence of the weakness of feeble persons to condescend to a fictitious arrangement and insisted on his purifying himself according to the requirements of the law, and shaving his head and paying his vows, as they thought that the present harm which would come from this hypocrisy was of no account, but had regard rather to the gain which would result from his still continued preaching. For the gain to the Apostle Paul from his strictness would not have counterbalanced the loss to all nations from his speedy death. And this would certainly have been then incurred by the whole Church unless this good and salutary hypocrisy had preserved him for the preaching of the Gospel. For then we may rightly and pardonably acquiesce in the wrong of a lie, when, as we said, a greater harm depends on telling the truth, and when the good which results to us from speaking the truth cannot counterbalance the harm which will be caused by it. And elsewhere the blessed Apostle testifies in other words that he himself always observed this disposition; for when he says: "To the Jews I became as a Jew that I might gain the Jews; to those who were under the law as being under the law, though not myself under the law, that I might gain those who were under the law; to those who were without law, I became as without law, though I was not without the law of God but under the law of Christ, that I might gain those who were

without law; to the weak I became weak, that I might gain the weak: I became all things to all men, that I might save all;"[1] what does he show but that according to the weakness and the capacity of those who were being instructed he always lowered himself and relaxed something of the vigour of perfection, and did not cling to what his own strict life might seem to demand, but rather preferred that which the good of the weak might require? And that we may trace these matters out more carefully and recount one by one the glories of the good deeds of the Apostles, some one may ask how the blessed Apostle can be proved to have suited himself to all men in all things. When did he to the Jews become as a Jew? Certainly in the case where, while he still kept in his inmost heart the opinion which he had maintained to the Galatians saying: "Behold, I, Paul, say unto you that if ye be circumcised Christ shall profit you nothing,"[2] yet by circumcising Timothy he adopted a shadow as it were of Jewish superstition. And again, where did he become to those under the law, as under the law? There certainly where James and all the Elders of the Church, fearing lest he might be attacked by the multitude of Jewish believers, or rather of Judaizing Christians, who had received the faith of Christ in such a way as still to be bound by the rites of legal ceremonies, came to his rescue in his difficulty with this counsel and advice, and said: "Thou seest, brother, how many thousands there are among the Jews, who have believed, and they are all zealots for the law. But they have heard of thee that thou teachest those Jews who are among the Gentiles to depart from Moses, saying that they ought not to circumcise their children;" and below: "Do therefore this that we say unto thee: we have four men who have a vow on them. These take and sanctify thyself with them and bestow on them, that they may shave their heads; and all will know that the things which they have heard of thee are false, but that thou thyself also walkest keeping the law."[3] And so for the good of those who were under the law, he trode under foot for a while the strict view which he had expressed: "For I through the law am dead unto the law that I may live unto God;"[4] and was driven to shave his head, and be purified according to the law and pay his vows after the Mosaic rites in the Temple. Do you ask also where for the good of those who were utterly ignorant of the law of God, he himself became as if without law? Read

---

[1] 1 Cor. ix. 20–22.
[2] Gal. v. 2.
[3] Acts xxi. 20–24.
[4] Gal. ii. 19.

the introduction to his sermon at Athens where heathen wickedness was flourishing: "As I passed by," he says, "I saw your idols and an altar on which was written: To the unknown God;" and when he had thus started from their superstition, as if he himself also had been without law, under the cloke of that profane inscription he introduced the faith of Christ, saying: "What therefore ye ignorantly worship, that declare I unto you." And after a little, as if he had known nothing whatever of the Divine law, he chose to bring forward a verse of a heathen poet rather than a saying of Moses or Christ, saying: "As some also of your own poets have said: for we are also His offspring." And when he had thus approached them with their own authorities, which they could not reject, thus confirming the truth by things false, he added and said: "Since then we are the offspring of God we ought not to think that the Godhead is like to gold or silver or stone sculptured by the art and device of man."[1] But to the weak he became weak, when, by way of permission, not of command, he allowed those who could not contain themselves to return together again,[2] or when he fed the Corinthians with milk and not with meat, and says that he was with them in weakness and fear and much trembling.[3] But he became all things to all men that he might save all, when he says: "He that eateth let him not despise him that eateth not, and let not him that eateth not judge him that eateth:" and: "He that giveth his virgin in marriage doeth well, and he that giveth her not in marriage doeth better;" and elsewhere: "Who," says he, "is weak, and I am not weak? Who is offended, and I burn not?" and in this way he fulfilled what he had commanded the Corinthians to do when he said: "Be ye without offence to Jews and Greeks and the Church of Christ, as I also please all men in all things, not seeking mine own profit but that of the many, that they may be saved."[4] For it had certainly been profitable not to circumcise Timothy, not to shave his head, not to undergo Jewish purification, not to practice going barefoot,[5] not to pay legal vows; but he did all these things because he did not seek his own profit but that of the many. And although this was done with the full consideration of God, yet it was not free from dissimulation. For one who through the law of

Christ was dead to the law that he might live to God, and who had made and treated that righteousness of the law in which he had lived blameless, as dung, that he might gain Christ, could not with true fervour of heart offer what belonged to the law; nor is it right to believe that he who had said: "For if I again rebuild what I have destroyed, I make myself a transgressor,"[6] would himself fall into what he had condemned. And to such an extent is account taken, not so much of the actual thing which is done as of the disposition of the doer, that on the other hand truth is sometimes found to have injured some, and a lie to have done them good. For when Saul was grumbling to his servants about David's flight, and saying: "Will the son of Jesse give you all fields and vineyards, and make you all tribunes and centurions: that all of you have conspired against me, and there is no one to inform me," did Doeg the Edomite say anything but the truth, when he told him: "I saw the son of Jesse in Nob, with Abimelech the son of Ahitub the priest, who consulted the Lord for him, and gave him victuals, and gave him also the sword of Goliath the Philistine?"[7] For which true story he deserved to be rooted up out of the land of the living, and it is said of him by the prophet: "Wherefore God shall destroy thee forever, and pluck thee up and tear thee out of thy tabernacle, and thy root from the land of the living:"[8] He then for showing the truth is forever plucked and rooted up out of that land in which the harlot Rahab with her family is planted for her lie: just as also we remember that Samson most injuriously betrayed to his wicked wife the truth which he had hidden for a long time by a lie, and therefore the truth so inconsiderately disclosed was the cause of his own deception, because he had neglected to keep the command of the prophet: "Keep the doors of thy mouth from her that sleepeth in thy bosom."[9]

CHAPTER XXI.

Whether secret abstinence ought to be made known, without telling a lie about it, to those who ask, and whether what has once been declined may be taken in hand.

AND to bring forward some instances from our unavoidable and almost daily wants which with all our care we can never so guard against as not to be driven to incur them whether with or against our will: what, I ask you, is to be done when, while we are proposing to put off our supper, a brother comes and asks us if we have had it: is our fast to

---

[1] Acts xvii. 23, 29. [2] Cf. 1 Cor. vii. 5. [3] Cf. 1 Cor. iii. 2; ii. 3.
[4] Rom. xiv. 3; 1 Cor. viii. 38; 2 Cor. xi. 29; 1 Cor. x. 32, 33.
[5] *Nudipedalia non exercere.* The expression is also used by Jerome of S. Paul's purification in Jerusalem (in Gal. Book II. c. iv.), though there is nothing in the account in the Acts about his going barefoot. Compare also Jerome against Jovinian, Book I. c. viii., and for the word, in connexion with the rites of the Christian Church, see Tertullian Apologeticum, c. xl.

[6] Gal. ii. 18.   [8] Ps. li. (lii.) 7.
[7] 1 Sam. xxii. 7-10.   [9] Micah ii. 7.

be concealed, and the good act of abstinence hidden, or is it to be proclaimed by telling the truth? If we conceal it, to satisfy the Lord's command which says: "Thou shalt not appear unto men to fast but unto thy Father Who is in secret;" and again: "Let not thy left hand know what thy right hand doeth,"[1] we must at once tell a lie. If we make manifest the good act of abstinence, the word of the gospel rightly discourages us: "Verily I say unto you, they have their reward."[2] But what if any one has refused with determination a cup offered to him by some brother, denying altogether that he will take what the other, rejoicing at his arrival, begs and intreats him to receive? Is it right that he should force himself to yield to his brother who goes on his knees and bows himself to the ground, and who thinks that he can only show his loving heart by this service, or should he obstinately cling to his own word and intention?

CHAPTER XXII.

An objection, that abstinence ought to be concealed, but that things that have been declined should not be received.

GERMANUS: In the former instance we think there can be no doubt that it is better for our abstinence to be hidden than for it to be displayed to the inquirers, and in cases of this sort we also admit that a lie is unavoidable. But in the second there is no need for us to tell a lie, first because we can refuse what is offered by the service of a brother in such a way as to bind ourselves in no bond of determination, and next because when we once refuse we can keep our opinion unchanged.

CHAPTER XXIII.

The answer that obstinacy in this decision is unreasonable.

JOSEPH: There is no doubt that these are the decisions of those monasteries in which the infancy of your renunciation was, as you tell us, trained, as their leaders are accustomed to prefer their own will to their brother's supper, and most obstinately stick to what they have once intended. But our Elders, to whose faith the signs of Apostolical powers have borne witness, and who have treated everything with judgment and discretion of spirit rather than with stiff obstinacy of mind, have laid down that those men who give in to the infirmities of others, receive

much richer fruits than those who persist in their determinations, and have declared that it is a better deed to conceal abstinence, as was said, by this needful and humble lie, rather than to display it with a proud show of truth.

CHAPTER XXIV.

How Abbot Piamun chose to hide his abstinence.

FINALLY Abbot Piamun[3] after twenty-five years did not hesitate to receive some grapes and wine offered to him by a certain brother, and at once preferred, against his rule, to taste what was brought him rather than to display his abstinence which was a secret from everybody. For if we would also bear in mind what we remember that our Elders always did, who used to conceal the marvels of their own good deeds, and their own acts, which they were obliged to bring forward in Conference for the instruction of the juniors, under cover of other persons, what else can we consider them but an open lie? And O that we too had anything worthy which we could bring forward for stirring up the faith of the juniors! Certainly we should have no scruples in following their fictions of that kind. For it is better under the colour of a figure like that to tell a lie than for the sake of maintaining that unreasonable truthfulness either hide in ill-advised silence what might be edifying to the hearers, or run into the display of an objectionable vanity by telling them truthfully in our own character. And the teacher of the Gentiles clearly teaches us the same lesson by his teaching, as he chose to bring forward the great revelations made to him, under the character of some one else, saying: "I know a man in Christ, whether in the body or out of the body I cannot tell, God knoweth, caught up even unto the third heaven: and I know such a man, that he was caught up into paradise and heard unspeakable words, which it is not lawful for man to utter."[4]

CHAPTER XXV.

The evidence of Scripture on changes of determination.

IT is impossible for us briefly to run through everything. For who could count up almost all the patriarchs and numberless saints, some of whom for the preservation of life, others out of desire for a blessing, others out of pity, others to conceal some secret, others out of zeal for God, others in searching for the

---

[1] S. Matt. vi. 18, 3.   [2] *Ib.* ver. 2.   [3] On Piamun see the note on XVIII. i.   [4] 2 Cor. xii. 2–4.

truth, became, so to speak, patrons of lying? And as all cannot be enumerated, so all ought not to be altogether passed over. For piety forced the blessed Joseph to raise a false charge against his brethren even with an oath by the life of the king, saying: "Ye are spies: to see the nakedness of the land are ye come;" and below: "send," says he, "one of you, and bring your brothers hither: but ye shall be kept here until your words are made manifest whether ye speak the truth or no: but if not, by the life of Pharaoh, ye are spies."[1] For if he had not out of pity alarmed them by this lie, he would not have been able to see again his father and his brother, nor to preserve them in their great danger of starvation, nor to free the conscience of his brethren from the guilt of selling him. The act then of striking his brethren with fear by means of a lie was not so reprehensible as was it a holy and laudable act to urge his enemies and seekers to a salutary penitence by means of a feigned danger. Finally when they were weighed down by the odium of the very serious accusation, they were conscience-stricken not at the charge falsely raised against them, but at the thought of their earlier crime, and said to one another: "We suffer this rightly because we sinned against our brother, in that we saw the anguish of his soul when he asked us and we did not hearken to him: wherefore all this trouble hath come upon us."[2] And this confession, we think, expiated by most salutary humility their terrible sin not only against their brother, against whom they had sinned with wicked cruelty, but also against God. What about Solomon, who in his first judgment manifested the gift of wisdom, which he had received of God, only by making use of falsehood? For in order to get at the truth which was hidden by the woman's lie, even he used the help of a lie most cunningly invented, saying: "Bring me a sword and divide the living child into two parts, and give the one half to the one and the other half to the other." And when this pretended cruelty stirred the heart of the true mother, but was received with approval by her who was not the true mother, then at last by this most sagacious discovery of the truth he pronounced the judgment which every one has felt to have been inspired by God, saying: "Give her the living child and slay it not: she is the mother of it."[3] Further we are more fully taught by other passages of Scripture as well that we neither can nor should carry out everything which we determine either with peace or disturbance of mind, as we often

hear that holy men and angels and even Almighty God Himself have changed what they had decided upon. For the blessed David determined and confirmed it by an oath, saying: "May God do so and add more to the foes of David if I leave of all that belong unto Nabal until the morning a single male." And presently when Abigail his wife interceded and intreated for him, he gave up his threats, lightened the sentence, and preferred to be regarded as a breaker of his word rather than to keep his pledged oath by cruelly executing it, saying: "As the Lord liveth, if thou hadst not quickly come to meet me there had not been left to Nabal by the morning light a single male."[4] And as we do not hold that his readiness to take a rash oath (which resulted from his anger and disturbance of mind) ought to be copied by us, so we do think that the pardon and revision of his determination is to be followed. The "chosen vessel," in writing to the Corinthians, promises unconditionally to return, saying: "But I will come to you when I pass through Macedonia: for I will pass through Macedonia. But I will stay or even pass the winter with you that you may conduct me whithersoever I shall go. For I do not want only to see you in passing: for I hope to stay with you for some time."[5] And this fact he remembers in the Second Epistle, thus: "And in this confidence I was minded first to come unto you, that ye might receive a second favour, and by you to pass into Macedonia and again to come to you from Macedonia and by you be conducted to Judæa." But a better plan suggested itself and he plainly admits that he is not going to fulfil what he had promised. "When then," says he, "I purposed this, did I use light-mindedness? or the things that I think, do I think after the flesh, that there should be with me yea, yea, and nay, nay?" Lastly, he declares even with the affirmation of an oath, why it was that he preferred to put on one side his pledged word rather than by his presence to bring a burden and grief to his disciples: "But I call God to witness against my soul that it was to spare you that I came not as far as Corinth. For I determined this with myself that I would not come unto you in sorrow."[6] Though when the angels had refused to enter the house of Lot at Sodom, saying to him: "We will not enter but will remain in the street," they were presently forced by his prayers to change their determination, as Scripture subjoins: "And Lot constrained them, and they turned in to him."[7] And

---

[1] Gen. xlii. 9, 16. [2] Ib. ver. 21. [3] 1 Kings iii. 24-27.

[4] 1 Sam. xxv. 22, 34. [6] 2 Cor. i. 15-17, 23; ii. 1.
[5] 1 Cor. xvi. 5, 7. [7] Gen. xix. 2, 3.

certainly if they knew that they would turn in to him, they refused his request with a sham excuse: but if their excuse was a real one, then they are clearly shown to have changed their mind. And certainly we hold that the Holy Spirit inserted this in the sacred volume for no other reason but to teach us by their examples that we ought not to cling obstinately to our own determinations, but to subject them to our will, and so to keep our judgment free from all the chains of law that it may be ready to follow the call of good counsel in any direction, and may not delay or refuse to pass without any delay to whatever a sound discretion may find to be the better choice. And to rise to still higher instances, when king Hezekiah was lying on his bed and afflicted with grievous sickness the prophet Isaiah addressed him in the person of God, and said: "Thus saith the Lord: set thine house in order for thou shalt die and not live. And Hezekiah," it says, "turned his face to the wall and prayed to the Lord and said: I beseech thee, O Lord, remember how I have walked before Thee in truth and with a perfect heart, and how I have done what was right in Thy sight. And Hezekiah wept sore." After which it was again said to him: "Go, return, and speak to Hezekiah king of Judah, saying: Thus saith the Lord God of David thy father: I have heard thy prayer, I have seen thy tears: and behold, I will add to thy days fifteen years: and I will deliver thee out of the hand of the king of the Assyrians, and I will defend this city for thy sake and for my servant David's sake." [1] What can be clearer than this proof that out of consideration for mercy and goodness the Lord would rather break His word and instead of the pre-arranged limit of death extend the life of him who prayed, for fifteen years, rather than be found inexorable because of His unchangeable decree? In the same way too the Divine sentence says to the men of Nineveh: "Yet three days, and Nineveh shall be overthrown;" [2] and presently this stern and abrupt sentence is softened by their penitence and fasting, and is turned to the side of mercy with goodness that is easy to be intreated. But if any one maintains that the Lord had threatened the destruction of their city (while He foreknew that they would be converted) for this reason, that He might incite them to a salutary penitence, it follows that those who are set over their brethren may, if need arises, without any blame for telling lies, threaten those who need improvement with severer treatment than they are really going to inflict. But if one says that God revoked that severe sentence in consideration of their penitence, according to what he says by Ezekiel: "If I say to the wicked, Thou shalt surely die: and he becomes penitent for his sin, and doeth judgment and justice, he shall surely live, he shall not die;" [3] we are similarly taught that we ought not obstinately to stick to our determination, but that we should with gentle pity soften down the threats which necessity called forth. And that we may not fancy that the Lord granted this specially to the Ninevites, He continually affirms by Jeremiah that He will do the same in general towards all, and promises that without delay He will change His sentence in accordance with our deserts; saying: "I will suddenly speak against a nation and against a kingdom to root out and to pull down and to destroy it. If that nation repent of the evil, which I have spoken against it, I also will repent of the evil which I thought to do to them. And I will suddenly speak of a nation and a kingdom, to build up and to plant it. If it shall do evil in My sight, that it obey not My voice: I will repent of the good that I thought to do to it." To Ezekiel also: "Leave out not a word, if so be they will hearken and be converted every one from his evil way: that I may repent Me of the evil that I thought to do to them for the wickedness of their doings." [4] And by these passages it is declared that we ought not obstinately to stick to our decisions, but to modify them with reason and judgment, and that better courses should always be adopted and preferred, and that we should turn without any delay to that course which is considered the more profitable. For this above all that invaluable sentence teaches us, because though each man's end is known beforehand to Him before his birth, yet somehow He so orders all things by a plan and method for all, and with regard to man's disposition, that He decides on everything not by the mere exercise of His power, nor according to the ineffable knowledge which His Prescience possesses, but according to the present actions of men, and rejects or draws to Himself each one, and daily either grants or withholds His grace. And that this is so the election of Saul also shows us, of whose miserable end the foreknowledge of God certainly could not be ignorant, and yet He chose him out of so many thousands of Israel and anointed him king, rewarding the then existing merits of his life, and not considering the sin of his coming fall, so that after he became

---

[1] 2 Kings xx. 1–6.   [2] Jonah iii. 4 (LXX.).   Ezek. xxxiii. 14, 15.   [4] Jer. xviii. 7, 10 ; xxvi. 2, 3.

reprobate, God complains almost in human terms and, with man's feelings, as if He repented of his choice, saying: "It repenteth Me that I have appointed Saul king: for he hath forsaken Me, and hath not performed My words;" and again: "But Samuel was grieved for Saul because the Lord repented that He had made Saul king over Israel."[1] Finally this that He afterwards executed, that the Lord also declares by the prophet Ezekiel that He will by His daily judgment do with all men, saying: "Yea, if I shall say to the righteous that he shall surely live, and he trusting in his righteousness commit iniquity: all his righteousness shall be forgotten, and in his iniquity which he hath committed, in the same he shall die. And if I shall say to the wicked: Thou shalt surely die; and if he repent of his sin and do judgment and righteousness, and if that wicked man restore the pledge and render what he hath robbed, and walk in the commandments of life, and do no righteous thing, he shall surely live, he shall not die. None of his sins which he hath committed shall be imputed unto him."[2] Finally, when the Lord would for their speedy fall, turn away His merciful countenance from the people, whom He had chosen out of all nations, the giver of the law interposes on their behalf and cries out: "I beseech Thee, O Lord, this people have sinned a great sin; they have made for themselves gods of gold; and now if Thou forgivest their sin, forgive it; but if not, blot me out of Thy book which Thou hast written. To whom the Lord answered: If any man hath sinned before Me, I will blot him out of My book."[3] David also, when complaining in prophetic spirit of Judas and the Lord's persecutors, says: "Let them be blotted out of the book of the living;" and because they did not deserve to come to saving penitence because of the guilt of their great sin, he subjoins: "And let them not be written among the righteous."[4] Finally in the case of Judas himself the meaning of the prophetic curse was clearly fulfilled, for when his deadly sin was completed, he killed himself by hanging, that he might not after his name was blotted out be converted and repent and deserve to be once more written among the righteous in heaven. We must therefore not doubt that at the time when he was chosen by Christ and obtained a place in the Apostolate, the name of Judas was written in the book of the living, and that he heard as well as the rest the words: "Rejoice not because the devils are subject unto you, but rejoice because your names are written in heaven."[5]

But because he was corrupted by the plague of covetousness and had his name struck out from that heavenly list, it is suitably said of him and of men like him by the prophet: "O Lord, let all those that forsake Thee be confounded. Let them that depart from Thee be written in the earth, because they have forsaken the Lord, the vein of living waters." And elsewhere: "They shall not be in the counsel of My people, nor shall they be written in the writing of the house of Israel, neither shall they enter into the land of Israel."[6]

CHAPTER XXVI.

How saintly men cannot be hard and obstinate.

NOR must we omit the value of that command because even if we have bound ourselves by some oath under the influence of anger or some other passion, (a thing which ought never to be done by a monk) still the case for each side should be weighed by a thorough judgment of the mind, and the course on which we have determined should be compared to that which we are urged to adopt, and we should without hesitation adopt that which on the occurrence of sounder considerations is decided to be the best. For it is better to put our promise on one side than to undergo the loss of something good and more desirable. Finally we never remember that venerable and approved fathers were hard and unyielding in decisions of this sort, but as wax under the influence of heat, so they were modified by reason, and when sounder counsels prevailed, did not hesitate to give in to the better side. But those whom we have seen obstinately clinging to their determinations we have always set down as unreasonable and wanting in judgment.

CHAPTER XXVII.

A question whether the saying: "I have sworn and am purposed" is opposed to the view given above.

GERMANUS: So far as this consideration is concerned which has been clearly and fully treated of, a monk ought never to determine anything for fear lest he turn out a breaker of his word or else obstinate. And what then can we make of this saying of the Psalmist: "I have sworn and am purposed to keep Thy righteous judgments?"[7] What is "to swear and purpose" except to keep one's determinations fixedly?

---

[1] I Sam. xv. 11, 35.   [3] Exod. xxxii. 31–33.   [5] S. Luke x. 20.
[2] Ezek. xxxiii. 13–16.   [4] Ps. lxviii. (lxix.) 29.

[6] Jer. xvii. 13; Ezek. xiii. 9.   [7] Ps. cxviii. (cxix.) 106.

CHAPTER XXVIII.

The answer telling in what cases the determination is to be kept fixedly, and in what cases it may be broken if need be.

JOSEPH: We do not lay this down with regard to those fundamental commands, without which our salvation cannot in any way exist, but with regard to those which we can either relax or hold fast to without endangering our state, as for instance, an unbroken and strict fast, or total abstinence from wine or oil, or entire prohibition to leave one's cell, or incessant attention to reading and meditation, all of which can be practised at pleasure, without damage to our profession and purpose, and, if need be, can be given up without blame. But we must most resolutely make up our minds to observe those fundamental commands, and not even, if need arise, to avoid death in their cause, with regard to which we must immovably assert: "I have sworn and am purposed." And this should be done for the preservation of love, for which all things else should be disregarded lest the beauty and perfection of its calm should suffer a stain. In the same way we must swear for the purity of our chastity, and we ought to do the same for faith, and sobriety and justice, to all of which we must cling with unchangeable persistence, and to forsake which even for a little is worthy of blame. But in the case of those bodily exercises, which are said to be profitable for a little,[1] we must, as we said, decide in such a way that, if there occurs any more decided opportunity for a good act, which would lead us to relax them, we need not be bound by any rule about them, but may give them up and freely adopt what is more useful. For in the case of those bodily exercises, if they are dropped for a time, there is no danger: but to have given up these others even for a moment is deadly.

CHAPTER XXIX.

How we ought to do those things which are to be kept secret.

YOU must also provide with the same care that if by chance some word has slipped out of your mouth which you want to be a secret, no injunction to secrecy may trouble the hearer. For it will be more likely to be unheeded if it is let pass carelessly and simply, because the brother, whoever he is, will not be tormented with such a temptation to divulge it, as he will take it as something trivial dropped in casual conversation, and as what is for this very reason of less account, because it was not committed to the hearer's mind with a strict injunction to silence. For even if you bind his faith by exacting an oath from him, you need not doubt that it will very soon be divulged; for a fiercer assault of the devil's power will be made upon him, both to annoy and betray you, and to make him break his oath as quickly as possible.

CHAPTER XXX.

That no determination should be made on those things which concern the needs of the common life.

AND therefore a monk ought not hastily to make any promise on those things which merely concern bodily exercise, for fear lest he may stir up the enemy still more to attack what he is keeping as it were under the observance of the law, and so he may be more readily compelled to break it. Since every one who lives under the grace of liberty, and sets himself a law, thereby binds himself in a dangerous slavery, so that if by chance necessity constrains him to do what he might have ventured on lawfully, and indeed laudably and with thanksgiving, he is forced to act as a transgressor, and to fall into sin: "for where there is no law there is no transgression."[2]

By this instruction and the teaching of the blessed Joseph we were confirmed as by a Divine oracle and made up our minds to stop in Egypt. But though henceforward we were but a little anxious about our promise, yet when seven years were over we were very glad to fulfil it. For we hastened to our monastery, at a time when we were confident of obtaining permission to return to the desert, and first paid our respects properly to our Elders; next we revived the former love in their minds as out of the ardour of their love they had not been at all softened by our very frequent letters to satisfy them, and in the last place, we entirely removed the sting of our broken promise and returned to the recesses of the desert of Scete, as they themselves forwarded us with joy.

This learning and doctrine of the illustrious fathers, our ignorance, O holy brother, has to the best of its ability made plain to you. And if perhaps our clumsy style has confused it instead of setting it in order, I trust that the blame which our clumsiness deserves will not interfere with the praise due to these grand

---

[1] Cf. 1 Tim. iv. 8.

[2] Rom. iv. 15.

men. Since it seemed to us a safer course in the sight of our Judge to state even in unadorned style this splendid doctrine rather than to hold our tongues about it, since if he considers the grandeur of the thoughts, the fact that the awkwardness of our style annoys him, need not be prejudicial to the profit of the reader, and for our part we are more anxious about its usefulness than its being praised.

This at least I charge all those into whose hand this little book may fall; viz., that they must know that whatever in it pleases them belongs to the fathers, and whatever they dislike is all our own.[1]

---

[1] In this last chapter Cassian certainly makes his own the sentiments of Abbot Joseph on the permissibility of lying; and is therefore not unreasonably attacked for the teaching of this Conference by Prosper. "Contra Collatorem," c. ix.

THE THIRD PART OF THE CONFERENCES OF JOHN CASSIAN.

PREFACE.

WHEN by the help of the grace of Christ I had published ten Conferences of the Fathers, which were composed at the urgent request of the most blessed Helladius and Leontius, I dedicated·seven others to Honoratus a Bishop blessed in name as well as merits, and also to that holy servant of Christ, Eucherius. The same number also I have thought good to dedicate now to you, O holy brothers, Jovinianus, Minervius, Leontius, and Theodore.[1] Since the last named of you founded that holy and splendid monastic rule in the province of Gaul, with the strictness of ancient virtue, while the rest of you by your instructions have stirred up monks not only before all to seek the common life of the cœnobia, but even to thirst eagerly for the sublime life of the anchorite. For those Conferences of the best of the fathers are arranged with such care, and so carefully considered in all respects, that they are suited to both modes of life whereby you have made not only the countries of the West, but even the isles to flourish with great crowds of brethren; i.e., I mean that not only those who still remain in congregations with praiseworthy subjection to rule, but those also who retire to no great distance from your monasteries, and try to carry out the rule of anchorites, may be more fully instructed, according as the nature of the place and the character of their condition may require. And to this your previous efforts and labours have especially contributed this, that, as they are already prepared and practised in these exercises, they can more readily receive the precepts and institutes of the Elders, and receiving into their cells the authors of the Conferences together with the actual volumes of the Conferences and talking with them after a fashion by daily questions and answers, they may not be left to their own resources to find that way which is difficult and almost unknown in this country, but full of danger even there where well-worn paths and numberless instances of those who have gone before are not wanting, but may rather learn to follow the rule of the anchorite's life taught by their examples, whom ancient tradition and industry and long experience have thoroughly instructed.

---

[1] See the introduction p. 189.

THE THIRD PART OF THE CONFERENCES OF JOHN CASSIAN.

XVIII.

CONFERENCE OF ABBOT PIAMUN.

ON THE THREE SORTS OF MONKS.

CHAPTER I.

How we came to Diolcos and were received by Abbot Piamun.[1]

AFTER visiting and conversing with those three Elders, whose Conferences we have at the instance of our brother Eucherius tried to describe, as we were still more ardently desirous to seek out the further parts of Egypt, in which a larger and more perfect company of saints dwelt, we came — urged not so much by the necessities of our journey as by the desire of visiting the saints who were dwelling there — to a village named Diolcos,[2] lying on one of the seven mouths of the river Nile. For when we heard of very many and very celebrated monasteries founded by the ancient fathers, like most eager merchants, at once we undertook the journey on an uncertain quest, urged on by the hope of greater gain. And when we wandered about there for some long time and fixed our curious eyes on those mountains of virtue conspicuous for their lofty height, the gaze of those around first singled out Abbot Piamun, the senior of all the anchorites living there and their presbyter, as if he were some tall lighthouse. For he was set on the top of a high mountain like that city in the gospel,[3] and at once shed his light on our faces, whose virtues and miracles, which were wrought by him under our very

eyes, Divine Grace thus bearing witness to his excellence, if we are not to exceed the plan and limits of this volume, we feel we must pass over in silence. For we promised to commit to memory what we could recollect, not of the miracles of God, but of the institutes and pursuits of the saints, so as to supply our readers merely with necessary instruction for the perfect life, and not with matter for idle and useless admiration without any correction of their faults. And so when Abbot Piamun had received us with welcome, and had refreshed us with becoming kindness, as he understood that we were not of the same country, he first asked us anxiously whence or why we had visited Egypt, and when he discovered that we had come thither from a monastery in Syria out of desire for perfection he began as follows : —

CHAPTER II.

The words of Abbot Piamun, how monks who were novices ought to be taught by the example of their elders.

WHATEVER man, my children, is desirous to attain skill in any art, unless he gives himself up with the utmost pains and carefulness to the study of that system which he is anxious to learn, and observes the rules and orders of the best masters of that work or science, is indulging in a vain hope to reach by idle wishes any similarity to those whose pains and diligence he avoids copying. For we know that some have come from your country to these parts, only to go round the monasteries for the sake of getting to know the brethren, not meaning to adopt the rules and

---

[1] Piamun, who has been already spoken of in XVII. xxiv., is also mentioned by Rufinus (History of the Monks, c. xxxii.), Palladius (the Lausiac History, clxxii.), and Sozomen (H. E. VI. xxix.), all of whom tell, with slight variations, the same story, how that one day while he was officiating at the altar, he saw an angel writing down the names of some of the brethren, and passing by the names of others, all of whom Piamun on subsequent inquiry found to have been guilty of some grievous sin.

[2] On Diolcos see on the Institutes V. xxxvi.

[3] Cf. S. Matt. v. 14.

regulations, for the sake of which they travelled hither, nor to retire to the cells and aim at carrying out in action what they had learnt by sight or by teaching. And these people retained their character and pursuits to which they had grown accustomed, and, as is thrown in their teeth by some, are held to have changed their country not for the sake of their profit, but owing to the need of escaping want. For in the obstinacy of their stubborn mind, they not only could learn nothing, but actually would not stay any longer in these parts. For if they changed neither their method of fasting, nor their scheme of Psalms, nor even the fashion of their garments, what else could we think that they were after in this country, except only the supply of their victuals.

CHAPTER III.

How the juniors ought not to discuss the orders of the seniors.

WHEREFORE if, as we believe, the cause of God has drawn you to try to copy our knowledge, you must utterly ignore all the rules by which your early beginnings were trained, and must with all humility follow whatever you see our Elders do or teach. And do not be troubled or drawn away and diverted from imitating it, even if for the moment the cause or reason of any deed or action is not clear to you, because if men have good and simple ideas on all things and are anxious faithfully to copy whatever they see taught or done by their Elders, instead of discussing it, then the knowledge of all things will follow through experience of the work. But he will never enter into the reason of the truth, who begins to learn by discussion, because as the enemy sees that he trusts to his own judgment rather than to that of the fathers' he easily urges him on so far till those things which are especially useful and helpful seem to him unnecessary or injurious, and the crafty foe so plays upon his presumption, that by obstinately clinging to his own opinion he persuades himself that only that is holy, which he himself in his pig-headed error thinks to be good and right.

CHAPTER IV.

Of the three sorts of monks which there are in Egypt.

WHEREFORE you should first hear how or whence the system and beginning of our order took its rise. For only then can a man at all effectually be trained in any art he may wish,

and be urged on to practise it diligently, when he has learnt the glory of its authors and founders. There are three kinds of monks in Egypt, of which two are admirable, the third is a poor sort of thing and by all means to be avoided. The first is that of the *cœnobites*, who live together in a congregation and are governed by the direction of a single Elder: and of this kind there is the largest number of monks dwelling throughout the whole of Egypt. The second is that of the *anchorites*, who were first trained in the cœnobium and then being made perfect in practical life chose the recesses of the desert: and in this order we also hope to gain a place. The third is the reprehensible one of the *Sarabaites*.[1] And of these we will discourse more fully one by one in order. Of these three orders then you ought, as we said, first to know about the founders. For at once from this there may arise either a hatred for the order which is to be avoided, or a longing for that which is to be followed, because each way is sure to carry the man who follows it, to that end which its author and discoverer has reached.

CHAPTER V.

Of the founders who originated the order of cœnobites.

AND so the system of cœnobites took its rise in the days of the preaching of the Apostles. For such was all that multitude of believers in Jerusalem, which is thus described in the Acts of the Apostles: "But the multitude of believers was of one heart and one soul, neither said any of them that any of the things which he possessed was his own, but they had all things common. They sold their possessions and property and divided them to all, as any man had need." And again: "For neither was there any among them that lacked; for as many as possessed fields or houses, sold them and brought the price of the things that they sold and laid them before the feet of the Apostles: and distribution was made to every man as he had need."[2] The whole Church, I say, was then such as now are those few who can be found with difficulty in cœnobia. But when at the death of the Apostles the multitude of believers began to wax cold, and especially that multitude which had come to the faith of Christ from diverse foreign nations, from whom the Apostles out of consideration for the infancy of their faith and their ingrained heathen habits, required nothing more than that they should " abstain

---

[1] See the note on c. vii.   [2] Acts iv. 32; ii. 45; iv. 34, 35.

from things sacrificed to idols and from fornication, and from things strangled, and from blood,"[1] and so that liberty which was conceded to the Gentiles because of the weakness of their newly-born faith, had by degrees begun to mar the perfection of that Church which existed at Jerusalem, and the fervour of that early faith cooled down owing to the daily increasing number both of natives and foreigners, and not only those who had accepted the faith of Christ, but even those who were the leaders of the Church relaxed somewhat of that strictness. For some fancying that what they saw permitted to the Gentiles because of their weakness, was also allowable for themselves, thought that they would suffer no loss if they followed the faith and confession of Christ keeping their property and possessions. But those who still maintained the fervour of the apostles, mindful of that former perfection left their cities and intercourse with those who thought that carelessness and a laxer life was permissible to themselves and the Church of God, and began to live in rural and more sequestered spots, and there, in private and on their own account, to practise those things which they had learnt to have been ordered by the apostles throughout the whole body of the Church in general: and so that whole system of which we have spoken grew up from those disciples who had separated themselves from the evil that was spreading. And these, as by degrees time went on, were separated from the great mass of believers and because they abstained from marriage and cut themselves off from intercourse with their kinsmen and the life of this world, were termed monks or solitaries from the strictness of their lonely and solitary life. Whence it followed that from their common life they were called cœnobites and their cells and lodgings cœnobia. That then alone was the earliest kind of monks, which is first not only in time but also in grace, and which continued unbroken for a very long period up to the time of Abbot Paul and Antony; and even to this day we see its traces remaining in strict cœnobia

CHAPTER VI.

Of the system of the Anchorites and its beginning.

Out of this number of the perfect, and, if I may use the expression, this most fruitful root of saints, were produced afterwards the

flowers and fruits of the anchorites as well. And of this order we have heard that the originators were those whom we mentioned just now; viz., Saint Paul[2] and Antony, men who frequented the recesses of the desert, not as some from faintheartedness, and the evil of impatience, but from a desire for loftier heights of perfection and divine contemplation, although the former of them is said to have found his way to the desert by reason of necessity, while during the time of persecution he was avoiding the plots of his neighbours. So then there sprang from that system of which we have spoken another sort of perfection, whose followers are rightly termed anchorites; i.e., withdrawers, because, being by no means satisfied with that victory whereby they had trodden under foot the hidden snares of the devil, while still living among men, they were eager to fight with the devils in open conflict, and a straightforward battle, and so feared not to penetrate the vast recesses of the desert, imitating, to wit, John the Baptist, who passed all his life in the desert, and Elijah and Elisha and those of whom the Apostle speaks as follows: "They wandered about in sheepskins and goatskins, being in want, distressed, afflicted, of whom the world was not worthy, wandering in deserts, in mountains and in dens and in caves of the earth." Of whom too the Lord speaks figuratively to Job: "But who hath sent out the wild ass free, and who hath loosed his bands? To whom I have given the wilderness for an house, and a barren land for his dwelling. He scorneth the multitude of the city and heareth not the cry of the driver; he looketh round about the mountains of his pasture, and seeketh for every green thing." In the Psalms also: "Let now the redeemed of the Lord say, those whom He hath redeemed from the hand of the enemy;" and after a little: "They wandered in a wilderness in a place without water: they found not the way of a city of habitation. They were hungry and thirsty: their soul fainted in them. And they cried unto the Lord in their trouble and He delivered them out of their distress;" whom Jeremiah too describes as follows: "Blessed is the man that hath borne the yoke from his youth. He shall sit solitary and hold his peace because he hath taken it up upon himself," and there sing in heart and deed these words of the Psalmist:

---

[1] Acts xv. 29.

[2] Paul was from very early days celebrated as the first of the anchorites. Indeed S. Jerome, who wrote his life (Works, Vol. ii. p. 13 ed. Migne) calls him "auctor vitæ monasticæ" (Ep. xxii. ad Eustochium). He is said to have fled to the Thebaid from the terrors of the Decian persecution, and to have died there in extreme old age. Antony has already been several times mentioned by Cassian. See the Institutes V. iv.: Conference II. ii.; III. iv., etc.

"I am become like a pelican in the wilderness. I watched and am become like a sparrow alone upon the house-top."[1]

CHAPTER VII.

Of the origin of the Sarabaites and their mode of life.

AND while the Christian religion was rejoicing in these two orders of monks though this system had begun by degrees to deteriorate, there arose afterwards that disgusting and unfaithful kind of monks; or rather, that baleful plant revived and sprang up again which when it first shot up in the persons of Ananias and Sapphira in the early Church was cut off by the severity of the Apostle Peter — a kind which among monks has been for a long while considered detestable and execrable, and which was adopted by no one any more, so long as there remained stamped on the memory of the faithful the dread of that very severe sentence, in which the blessed Apostle not merely refused to allow the aforesaid originators of the novel crime to be cured by penitence or any amends, but actually destroyed that most dangerous germ by their speedy death. When then that precedent, which was punished with Apostolical severity in the case of Ananias and Sapphira had by degrees faded from the minds of some, owing to long carelessness and forgetfulness from lapse of time, there arose the race of Sarabaites, who owing to the fact that they have broken away from the congregations of the cœnobites and each look after their own affairs, are rightly named in the Egyptian language Sarabaites,[2] and these spring from the number of those, whom we have mentioned, who wanted to imitate rather than truly to aim at Evangelical perfection, urged thereto by rivalry or by the praises of those who preferred the complete poverty of Christ to all manner of riches. These then while in their feeble mind they make a pretence of the greatest goodness and are forced by necessity to join this order, while they are anxious to be reckoned by the name of monks without emulating their pursuits, in no sort

of way practise discipline, or are subject to the will of the Elders, or, taught by their traditions, learn to govern their own wills or take up and properly learn any rule of sound discretion; but making their renunciation only as a public profession, i.e., before the face of men, either continue in their homes devoted to the same occupations as before, though dignified by this title, or building cells for themselves and calling them monasteries remain in them perfectly free and their own masters, never submitting to the precepts of the gospel, which forbid them to be busied with any anxiety for the day's food, or troubles about domestic matters: commands which those alone fulfil with no unbelieving doubt, who have freed themselves from all the goods of this world and subjected themselves to the superiors of the cœnobia so that they cannot admit that they are at all their own masters. But those who, as we said, shirk the severity of the monastery, and live two or three together in their cells, not satisfied to be under the charge and rule of an Abbot, but arranging chiefly for this; viz., that they may get rid of the yoke of the Elders and have liberty to carry out their wishes and go and wander where they will, and do what they like, these men are more taken up both day and night in daily business than those who live in the cœnobia, but not with the same faith and purpose. For these Sarabaites do it not to submit the fruits of their labours to the will of the steward, but to procure money to lay by. And see what a difference there is between them. For the others think nothing of the morrow, and offer to God the most acceptable fruits of their toil: while these extend their faithless anxiety not only to the morrow, but even to the space of many years. and so fancy that God is either false or impotent as He either could not or would not grant them the promised supply of food and clothing. The one seek this in all their prayers; viz., that they may gain ἀκτημοσύνην, i.e., the deprivation of all things, and lasting poverty: the other that they may secure a rich quantity of all sorts of supplies. The one eagerly strive to go beyond the fixed rule of daily work that whatever is not wanted for the sacred purposes of the monastery, may be distributed at the will of the Abbot either among the prisons, or in the guest-chamber or in the infirmary or to the poor; the others that whatever the day's gorge leaves over, may be useful for extravagant wants or else laid by through the sin of covetousness. Lastly, if we grant that what has been collected by them with no good design, may be disposed of in better ways than we have men-

---

[1] Heb. xi. 37, 38; Job xxxix. 5-8; Ps. cvi. (cvii.) 2, 4-6; Lam. iii. 27, 28; Ps. ci. (cii.) 7, 8.

[2] Sarabaites, this third sort of monks, whom Cassian here paints in such dark colours, are spoken of by S. Jerome (Ep. xxii. ad Eustochium) under the name of Remoboth. The origin of both names is obscure, but Jerome and Cassian are quite at one in their scorn for these pretended monks. S. Benedict begins his monastic rule by describing the four kinds of monks, cœnobites, anchorites, sarabaites, and a fourth class to which he gives the name of "gyrovagi," i.e., wandering monks; these must be those of whom Cassian speaks below in c. viii. without giving them any definite name. See further Bingham, Antiquities VII. ii., and the Dictionary of Christian Antiquities, Art. Sarabaites.

tioned, yet not even thus do they rise to the merits of goodness and perfection. For the others bring in such returns to the monastery, and daily report to them, and continue in such humility and subjection that they are deprived of their rights over what they gain by their own efforts, just as they are of their rights over themselves, as they constantly renew the fervour of their original act of renunciation, while they daily deprive themselves of the fruits of their labours: but these are puffed up by the fact that they are bestowing something on the poor, and daily fall headlong into sin. The one party are by patience and the strictness whereby they continue devoutly in the order which they have once embraced, so as never to fulfil their own will, crucified daily to this world and made living martyrs; the others are cast down into hell by the lukewarmness of their purpose. These two sorts of monks then vie with each other in almost equal numbers in this province; but in other provinces, which the need of the Catholic faith compelled me to visit, we have found that this third class of Sarabaites flourishes and is almost the only one, since in the time of Lucius who was a Bishop of Arian misbelief[1] in the reign of Valens, while we carried alms[2] to our brethren; viz., those from Egypt and the Thebaid, who had been consigned to the mines of Pontus and Armenia[3] for their steadfastness in the Catholic faith, though we found the system of cœnobia in some cities few and far between, yet we never made out that even the name of anchorites was heard among them.

CHAPTER VIII.

Of a fourth sort of monks.

THERE is however another and a fourth kind, which we have lately seen springing up among those who flatter themselves with the appearance and form of anchorites, and who in their early days seem in a brief fervour to seek the perfection of the cœnobium, but presently cool off, and, as they dislike to put an end to their former habits and faults, and

are not satisfied to bear the yoke of humility and patience any longer, and scorn to be in subjection to the rule of the Elders, look out for separate cells and want to remain by themselves alone, that as they are provoked by nobody they may be regarded by men as patient, gentle, and humble: and, this arrangement, or rather this lukewarmness never suffers those, of whom it has once got hold, to approach to perfection. For in this way their faults are not merely not rooted up, but actually grow worse, while they are excited by no one, like some deadly and internal poison which the more it is concealed, so much the more deeply does it creep in and cause an incurable disease to the sick person. For out of respect for each man's own cell no one ventures to reprove the faults of a solitary, which he would rather have ignored than cured. Moreover virtues are created not by hiding faults but by driving them out.

CHAPTER IX.

A question as to what is the difference between a cœnobium and a monastery.

GERMANUS: Is there any distinction between a cœnobium and a monastery, or is the same thing meant by either name?

CHAPTER X.

The answer.

PIAMUN: Although many people indifferently speak of monasteries instead of cœnobia, yet there is this difference, that monastery is the title of the dwelling, and means nothing more than the place, i.e., the habitation of monks, while cœnobium describes the character of the life and its system: and monastery may mean the dwelling of a single monk, while a cœnobium cannot be spoken of except where dwells a united community of a large number of men living together. They are however termed monasteries in which groups of Sarabaites live.

CHAPTER XI.

Of true humility, and how Abbot Serapion exposed the mock humility of a certain man.

WHEREFORE as I see that you have learnt the first principles of this life from the best sort of monks, i.e., that starting from the excellent school of the cœnobium you are aim-

---

[1] Lucius took the lead of the Arian party at Alexandria after the murder of George of Cappadocia in 361, and was put forward by his party as the candidate for the see which they regarded as vacant. In 373, after the death of Athanasius, he was forced upon the reluctant Church of Alexandria by the Arian Emperor Valens, and according to Gregory Nazianzen a fresh persecution of the orthodox party at once began; and to this it is that Piamun alludes in the text.

[2] *Diaconia.* The word is used again by Cassian for almsgiving in Conf. XXI. i., viii., ix., and cf. Gregory the Great, Ep. xxii., and compare εἰς διακονίαν in Acts xi. 29.

[3] To work in the mines was a punishment to which the Confessors were frequently subjected in the time of persecution: Cf. the prayer in the Liturgy of S. Mark that God would have mercy on those in prison, or in the mines, etc. *Hammond's Liturgies*, p. 181.

ing at the lofty heights of the anchorite's rule, you should with genuine feeling of heart pursue the virtue of humility and patience, which I doubt not that you learnt there; and not feign it, as some do, by mock humility in words, or by an artificial and unnecessary readiness for some duties of the body. And this sham humility Abbot Serapion[1] once laughed to scorn most capitally. For when one had come to him making a great display of his lowliness by his dress and words, and the old man urged him, after his custom, to "collect the prayer"[2] he would not consent to his request, but debasing himself declared that he was involved in such crimes that he did not deserve even to breathe the air which is common to all, and refusing even the use of the mat preferred to sit down on the bare ground. But when he had shown still less inclination for the washing of the feet, then Abbot Serapion, when supper was finished, and the customary Conference gave him an opportunity, began kindly and gently to urge him not to roam with shifty lightmindedness over the whole world, idly and vaguely, especially as he was young and strong, but to keep to his cell in accordance with the rule of the Elders, and to elect to be supported by his own efforts rather than by the bounty of others; which even the Apostle Paul would not allow, and though when he was labouring in the cause of the gospel this provision might rightly have been made for him, yet he preferred to work night and day, to provide daily food for himself and for those who were ministering to him and could not do the work with their own hands. Whereupon the other was filled with such vexation and disgust that he could not hide by his looks the annoyance which he felt in his heart. To whom the Elder: Thus far, my son, you have loaded yourself with the weight of all kinds of crimes, not fearing lest by the confession of such awful sins you bring a reproach upon your reputation; how is it then, I pray, that now, at our simple admonition, which involved no reproof, but simply showed a feeling for your edification and love, I see that you are moved with such disgust that you cannot hide it by your looks, or conceal it by an appearance of calmness? Perhaps while you were humiliating yourself, you were hoping to hear from our lips this saying: "The righteous man is the accuser of himself in the opening of his discourse?"[3] Further, true humility of heart must be preserved, which comes not from an affected humbling of body and in word, but from an

inward humbling of the soul: and this will only then shine forth with clear evidences of patience when a man does not boast about sins, which nobody will believe, but, when another insolently accuses him of them, thinks nothing of it, and when with gentle equanimity of spirit he puts up with wrongs offered to him.

CHAPTER XII.

A question how true patience can be gained.

GERMANUS: We should like to know how that calmness can be secured and maintained, that, as when silence is enjoined on us we shut the door of our mouth, and lay an embargo on speech, so also we may be able to preserve gentleness of heart, which sometimes even when the tongue is restrained loses its state of calmness within: and for this reason we think that the blessing of gentleness can only be preserved by one in a remote cell and solitary dwelling.

CHAPTER XIII.

The answer.

PIAMUN: True patience and tranquillity is neither gained nor retained without profound humility of heart: and if it has sprung from this source, there will be no need either of the good offices of the cell or of the refuge of the desert. For it will seek no external support from anything, if it has the internal support of the virtue of humility, its mother and its guardian. But if we are disturbed when attacked by anyone it is clear that the foundations of humility have not been securely laid in us, and therefore at the outbreak even of a small storm, our whole edifice is shaken and ruinously disturbed. For patience would not be worthy of praise and admiration if it only preserved its purposed tranquillity when attacked by no darts of enemies, but it is grand and glorious because when the storms of temptation beat upon it, it remains unmoved. For wherein it is believed that a man is annoyed and hurt by adversity, therein is he strengthened the more; and he is therein the more exercised, wherein he is thought to be annoyed. For everybody knows that patience gets its name from the passions and endurance, and so it is clear that no one can be called patient but one who bears without annoyance all the indignities offered to him, and so it is not without reason that he is praised by Solomon: "Better is the patient

---

[1] On Serapion see the note on Conf. V. i.
[2] Orationem Colligere. See the notes on the Institutes III. vii.
[3] Prov. xviii. 17.

man than the strong, and he who restrains his anger than he who takes a city;" and again: "For a long-suffering man is mighty in prudence, but a faint-hearted man is very foolish."[1] When then anyone is overcome by a wrong, and blazes up in a fire of anger, we should not hold that the bitterness of the insult offered to him is the *cause* of his sin, but rather the *manifestation* of secret weakness, in accordance with the parable of our Lord and Saviour which He spoke about the two houses,[2] one of which was founded upon a rock, and the other upon the sand, on both of which He says that the tempest of rain and waters and storm beat equally: but that one which was founded on the solid rock felt no harm at all from the violence of the shock, while that which was built on the shifting and moving sand at once collapsed. And it certainly appears that it fell, not because it was struck by the rush of the storms and torrents, but because it was imprudently built upon the sand. For a saint does not differ from a sinner in this, that he is not himself tempted in the same way, but because he is not worsted even by a great assault, while the other is overcome even by a slight temptation. For the fortitude of any good man would not, as we said, be worthy of praise, if his victory was gained without his being tempted, as most certainly there is no room for victory where there is no struggle and conflict: for "Blessed is the man that endureth temptation, for when he has been proved he shall receive the crown of life which God hath promised to them that love Him."[3] According to the Apostle Paul also "Strength is made perfect" not in ease and delights but "in weakness." "For behold," says He, "I have made thee this day a fortified city, and a pillar of iron, and a wall of brass, over all the land, to the kings of Judah, and to the princes thereof, and to the priests thereof, and to all the people of the land. And they shall fight against thee, and shall not prevail: for I am with thee, saith the Lord, to deliver thee."[4]

CHAPTER XIV.

Of the example of patience given by a certain religious woman.

OF this patience then I want to give you at least two examples: one of a certain religious woman, who aimed at the virtue of patience so eagerly that she not only did not avoid the assaults of temptation, but actually made for herself occasions of trouble that she might not cease to be tried more often. For this woman as she was living at Alexandria and was born of no mean ancestors, and was serving the Lord religiously in the house which had been left to her by her parents, came to Athanasius the Bishop, of blessed memory, and entreated him to give her some other widow to support, who was being provided for at the expense of the Church. And, to give her petition in her own words: "Give me," she said, "one of the sisters to look after." When then the Bishop had commended the woman's purpose because he saw that she was very ready for a work of a mercy, he ordered a widow to be chosen out of the whole number, who was preferred to all the rest for the goodness of her character, and her grave and well-regulated life, for fear lest her wish to be liberal might be overcome by the fault of the recipient of her bounty, and she who sought gain out of the poor might be disgusted at her bad character and so suffer an injury to her faith. And when the woman was brought home, she ministered to her with all kinds of service, and found out her excellent modesty and gentleness, and saw that every minute she was honoured by thanks from her for her kind offices, and so after a few days she came back to the aforesaid Bishop, and said: I asked you to bid that a woman be given to me for me to support and to serve with obedient complaisance. And when he, not yet understanding the woman's object and desire, thought that her petition had been neglected by the deceitfulness of the superior, and inquired not without some anger in his mind, what was the reason of the delay, at once he discovered that a widow who was better than all the rest had been assigned to her, and so he secretly gave orders that the one who was the worst of all should be given to her, the one, I mean, who surpassed in anger and quarrelling and wine-bibbing and talkativeness all who were under the power of these faults. And when she was only too easily found and given to her, she began to keep her at home, and to minister to her with the same care as to the former widow, or even more attentively, and this was all the thanks which she got from her for her services; viz., to be constantly tried by unworthy wrongs and continually annoyed by her by reproaches and upbraiding, as she complained of her, and chid her with spiteful and disparaging remarks, because she had asked for her from the Bishop not for her refreshment but rather for her torment and annoyance, and had taken her away from rest to labour instead of from labour to rest. When then her continual re-

---

[1] Prov. xvi. 32 ; xiv. 29.
[2] Cf. S. Matt. vii. 24, 59.
[3] S. James i. 12.
[4] 2 Cor. xii. 9 ; Jer. i. 18, 19.

proaches broke out so far that the wanton woman did not restrain herself from laying hands on her, the other only redoubled her services in still humbler offices, and learnt to overcome the vixen not by resisting her, but by subjecting herself still more humbly, so that, when provoked by all kinds of indignities, she might smooth down the madness of the shrew by gentleness and kindness. And when she had been thoroughly strengthened by these exercises, and had attained the perfect virtue of the patience she had longed for, she came to the aforesaid Bishop to thank him for his decision and choice as well as for the blessing of her exercise, because he had at last as she wished provided her with a most worthy mistress for her patience, strengthened daily by whose constant annoyance as by some oil for wrestling, she had arrived at complete patience of mind; and, at last, said she, you have given me one to support, for the former one rather honoured and refreshed me by her services. This may be sufficient to have told about the female sex, that by this tale we may not only be edified, but even confounded, as *we* cannot maintain our patience unless we are like wild beasts removed in caves and cells.

CHAPTER XV.

Of the example of patience given by Abbot Paphnutius.

Now let us give the other instance of Abbot Paphnutius, who always remained so zealously in the recesses of that renowned and far-famed desert of Scete, in which he is now Presbyter, so that the rest of the anchorites gave him the name of Bubalis,[1] because he always delighted in dwelling in the desert as if with a sort of innate liking. And so as even in boyhood he was so good and full of grace that even the renowned and great men of that time admired his gravity and steadfast constancy, and although he was younger in age, yet put him on a level with the Elders out of regard for his virtues, and thought fit to admit him to their order, the same envy, which formerly excited the minds of his brethren against the patriarch Joseph, inflamed one out of the number of his brethren with a burning and consuming jealousy. And this man wanting to mar his beauty by some blemish or spot, hit on this kind of devilry, so as to seize an opportunity when Paphnutius had left his cell to go to Church on Sunday: and secretly entering his cell he slyly hid his

own book among the boughs which he used to weave of palm branches, and, secure of his well-planned trick, himself went off as if with a pure and clean conscience to Church. And when the whole service was ended as usual, in the presence of all the brethren he brought his complaint to S. Isidore[2] who was Presbyter of this desert before this same Paphnutius, and declared that his book had been stolen from his cell. And when his complaint had so disturbed the minds of all the brethren, and more especially of the Presbyter, so that they knew not what first to suspect or think, as all were overcome with the utmost astonishment at so new and unheard of a crime, such as no one remembered ever to have been committed in that desert before that time, and which has never happened since, he who had brought forward the matter as the accuser urged that they should all be kept in Church and certain selected men be sent to search the cells of the brethren one by one. And when this had been entrusted to three of the Elders by the Presbyter, they turned over the bed-chambers of them all, and at last found the book hidden in the cell of Paphnutius among the boughs of the palms which they call σειρά, just as the plotter had hidden it. And when the inquisitors at once brought it back to the Church and produced it before all, Paphnutius, although he was perfectly clear in the sincerity of his conscience, yet like one who acknowledged the guilt of thieving, gave himself up entirely to make amends and humbly asked for a plan of repentance, as he was so careful of his shame and modesty (and feared) lest if he tried to remove the stain of the theft by words, he might further be branded as a liar, as no one would believe anything but what had been found out. And when he had immediately left the Church not cast down in mind but rather trusting to the judgment of God, he continually shed tears at his prayers, and fasted thrice as often as before, and prostrated himself in the sight of men with all humility of mind. But when he had thus submitted himself with all contrition of flesh and spirit for almost a fortnight, so that he came early on the morning of Saturday and Sunday not to receive the Holy Communion[3] but to prostrate himself on the threshold of the Church and humbly ask for pardon, He, Who is the witness of all secret things and knows them, suffered him to be no

---

[1] i.e., the Buffalo. On Paphnutius see the note on Conf. III.

[2] Gazet thinks that this Isidore is the same person as the one mentioned in the Lausiac History c. i.; and Sozomen VI. xxviii., but doubts whether he is identical with the person of the same name mentioned in Rufinus: History of the Monks c. xvii., Sozomen VIII. xii., and Socrates VI. ix.

[3] On the Saturday and Sunday celebration of the Holy Communion in Egypt compare the Institutes III. ii. In Gaul it was apparently received daily: Institutes VI. viii.

longer tried by Himself or defamed by others. For what the author of the crime, the wicked thief of his own property, the cunning defamer of another's credit, had done with no man there as a witness, that He made known by means of the devil who was himself the instigator of the sin. For possessed by a most fierce demon, he made known all the craft of his secret plot, and the same man who had conceived the accusation and the cheat betrayed it. But he was so long and grievously vexed by that unclean spirit that he could not even be restored by the prayers of the saints living there, who by means of divine gifts can command the devils, nor could the special grace of the Presbyter Isidore himself cast out from him his cruel tormenter, though by the Lord's bounty such power was given him that no one who was possessed was ever brought to his doors without being at once healed; for Christ was reserving this glory for the young Paphnutius, that the man should be cleansed only by the prayers of him against whom he had plotted, and that the jealous enemy should receive pardon for his offence and an end of his present punishment, only by proclaiming his name, from whose credit he had thought that he could detract. He then in his early youth already gave these signs of his future character, and even in his boyish years sketched the lines of that perfection which was to grow up in mature age. If then we want to attain to his height of virtue, we must lay the same foundation to begin with.

CHAPTER XVI.

On the perfection of patience.

A TWOFOLD reason however led me to relate this fact, first that we may weigh this steadfastness and constancy of the man, and as we are attacked by less serious wiles of the enemy, may the better secure a greater feeling of calmness and patience, secondly that we may with resolute decision hold that we cannot be safe from the storms of temptation and assaults of the devil if we make all the protection for our patience and all our confidence consist not in the strength of our inner man but in the doors of our cell or the recesses of the desert, and companionship of the saints, or the safeguard of anything else outside us. For unless our mind is strengthened by the power of His protection Who says in the gospel "the kingdom of God is within you," [1] in vain do we fancy that we can defeat the plots of our airy foe by the aid of men who

are living with us, or that we can avoid them by distance of place, or exclude them by the protection of walls. For though none of these things was wanting to Saint Paphnutius yet the tempter did not fail to find a way of access against him to attack him; nor did the encircling walls, or the solitude of the desert or the merits of all those saints in the congregation repulse that most foul spirit. But because the holy servant of God had fixed the hope of his heart not on those external things but on Him Who is the judge of all secrets, he could not be moved even by the machinations of such an assault as that. On the other hand did not the man whom envy had hurried into so grievous a sin enjoy the benefit of solitude and the protection of a retired dwelling, and intercourse with the blessed Abbot and Presbyter Isidore and other saints? And yet because the storm raised by the devil found him upon the sand, it not only drove in his house but actually overturned it. We need not then seek for our peace in externals, nor fancy that another person's patience can be of any use to the faults of our impatience. For just as "the kingdom of God is within you," so "a man's foes are they of his own household." [2] For no one is more my enemy than my own heart which is truly the one of my household closest to me. And therefore if we are careful, we cannot possibly be injured by intestine enemies. For where those of our own household are not opposed to us, there also the kingdom of God is secured in peace of heart. For if you diligently investigate the matter, I cannot be injured by any man however spiteful, if I do not fight against myself with warlike heart. But if I am injured, the fault is not owing to the other's attack, but to my own impatience. For as strong and solid food is good for a man in good health, so it is bad for a sick one. But it cannot hurt the man who takes it, unless the weakness of its recipient gives it its power to hurt. If then any similar temptation ever arises among brethren, we need never be shaken out of the even tenor of our ways and give an opening to the blasphemous snarls of men living in the world, nor wonder that some bad and detestable men have secretly found their way into the number of the saints, because so long as we are trodden down and trampled in the threshing floor of this world, the chaff which is destined for eternal fire is quite sure to be mingled with the choicest of the wheat. Finally if we bear in mind that Satan was chosen among the angels, and Judas among the apostles, and Nicholas the

---

[1] S. Luke xvii. 21.

[2] S. Matt. x. 36.

author of a detestable heresy among the deacons, it will be no wonder that the basest of men are found among the ranks of the saints. For although some maintain that this Nicholas was not the same man who was chosen for the work of the ministry by the Apostles,[1] nevertheless they cannot deny that he was of the number of the disciples, all of whom were clearly of such a character and so perfect as those few whom we can now with difficulty discover in the cœnobia. Let us then bring forward not the fall of the above-mentioned brother, who fell in the desert with so grievous a collapse, nor that horrible stain which he afterwards wiped out by the copious tears of his penitence, but the example of the blessed Paphnutius; and let us not be destroyed by the ruin of the former, whose ingrained sin of envy was increased and made worse by his affected piety, but let us imitate with all our might the humility of the latter, which in his case was no sudden production of the quiet of the desert, but had been gained among men, and was consummated and perfected by solitude. However you should know that the evil of envy is harder to be cured than other faults, for I should almost say that a man whom it has once tainted with the mischief of its poison is without a remedy. For it is the plague of which it is figuratively said by the prophet: "Behold I will send among you serpents, basilisks, against which there is no charm: and they shall bite you."[2] Rightly then are the stings of envy compared by the prophet to the deadly poison of basilisks, as by it the first author of all poisons and their chief perished and died. For he slew himself before him of whom he was envious, and destroyed himself before that he poured forth the poison of death against man: for "by the envy of the devil death entered into the world: they therefore who are on his side follow him."[3] For just as he who was the first to be corrupted by the plague of that evil, admitted no remedy of penitence, nor any healing plaster, so those also who have given themselves up to be smitten by the same pricks, exclude all the aid of the sacred charmer, because as they are tormented not by the faults but by the prosperity of those of whom they are jealous, they are ashamed to display the real truth and look out for some external unnecessary and trifling causes of

offence: and of these, because they are altogether false, vain is the hope of cure, while the deadly poison which they will not produce is lurking in their veins. Of which the wisest of men has fitly said: "If a serpent bite without hissing, there is no supply for the charmer."[4] For those are silent bites, to which alone the medicine of the wise is no succour. For that evil is so far incurable that it is made worse by attentions, it is increased by services, is irritated by presents, because as the same Solomon says: "envy endures nothing."[5] For just in proportion as another has made progress in humble submission or in the virtue of patience or in the merit of munificence, so is a man excited by worse pricks of envy, because he desires nothing less than the ruin or death of the man whom he envies. Lastly no submission on the part of their harmless brother could soften the envy of the eleven patriarchs, so that Scripture relates of them: "But his brothers envied him because his father loved him, and they could not speak peaceably unto him"[6] until their jealousy, which would not listen to any entreaties on the part of their obedient and submissive brother, desired his death, and would scarcely be satisfied with the sin of selling a brother. It is plain then that envy is worse than all faults, and harder to get rid of, as it is inflamed by those remedies by which the others are destroyed. For, for example, a man who is grieved by a loss that has been caused to him, is healed by a liberal compensation: one who is sore owing to a wrong done to him, is appeased by humble satisfaction being made. What can you do with one who is the more offended by the very fact that he sees you humbler and kinder, who is not aroused to anger by any greed which can be appeased by a bribe; or by any injurious attack or love of vengeance, which is overcome by obsequious services; but is only irritated by another's success and happiness? But who is there who in order to satisfy one who envies him, would wish to fall from his good fortune, or to lose his prosperity or to be involved in some calamity? Wherefore we must constantly implore the divine aid, to which nothing is impossible, in order that the serpent may not by a single bite of this evil destroy whatever is flourishing in us, and animated as it were by the life and quickening power of the Holy Ghost. For the other poisons of serpents, i.e., carnal sins and faults, in which human frailty is easily entangled and from which it is as easily purified, show some traces of their wounds

---

[1] As Cassian here implies, considerable doubt exists whether the Nicholas from whom the sect of the Nicolaitans (Rev. ii. 15) derive their name was the same person as Nicholas the last of the seven "deacons" mentioned in Acts vi. 5. According to Irenæus (Hær. I. xxvi.) the Nicolaitans themselves claimed him as their founder, and the claim is allowed by Hippolytus (Philos. vii. § 36), Epiphanius (Hær. I. ii. §25), and other writers of the fourth century. Clement of Alexandria however disputes the claim (Strom. III. iv. and cf. Euseb. H. E. III. xxix.), as does Theodoret (Hær. Tab. iii. 1).
[2] Jer. viii. 17.　　　[3] Wisd. ii. 24, 25.

[4] Eccl. x. 2.　　　[5] Prov. xxvii. 4.　　　[6] Gen. xxxvii. 4.

in the flesh, whereby although the earthly body is most dangerously inflamed, yet if any charmer well skilled in divine incantations applies a cure and antidote or the remedy of words of salvation, the poisonous evil does not reach to the everlasting death of the soul. But the poison of envy as if emitted by the basilisk, destroys the very life of religion and faith, even before the wound is perceived in the body. For he does not raise himself up against men, but, in his blasphemy, against God, who carps at nothing in his brother except his felicity, and so blames no fault of man, but simply the judgment of God. This then is that "root of bitterness springing up"[1] which raises itself to heaven and tends to reproaching the very Author Who bestows good things on man. Nor shall anyone be disturbed because God threatens to send "serpents, basilisks,"[2] to bite those by whose crimes He is offended. For although it is certain that God cannot be the author of envy, yet it is fair and worthy of the divine judgment that, while good gifts are bestowed on the humble and refused to the proud and reprobate, those who, as the Apostle says, deserve to be given over "to a reprobate mind,"[5] should be smitten and consumed by envy sent as it were by Him, according to this passage: "They have provoked me to jealousy by them that are no gods: and I will provoke them to jealousy by them that are no nation."[6]

By this discourse the blessed Piamun excited still more keenly our desire in which we had begun to be promoted from the infant school of the cœnobium to the second standard of the anchorites' life. For it was under his instruction that we made our first start in solitary living, the knowledge of which we afterwards followed up more thoroughly in Scete.

XIX.

CONFERENCE OF ABBOT JOHN.

ON THE AIM OF THE CŒNOBITE AND HERMIT.

CHAPTER I.

Of the cœnobium of Abbot Paul and the patience of a certain brother.

AFTER only a few days we made our way once more with great alacrity, drawn by the desire for further instruction, to the cœnobium of Abbot Paul, where though a greater number than two hundred of the brethren dwell there, yet, in honour of the festival which was then being held, an enormous collection of monks from other cœnobia had come there as well: for the anniversary of the death[3] of a former Abbot who had presided over the same monastery was being solemnly kept. And we have mentioned this assembly for this reason that we may briefly treat of the patience of a certain brother, which was remarkable for immovable gentleness on his part in the presence of all this congregation. For though the object of this work has regard to another person; viz., that we may produce the utterances of Abbot John[4] who left the desert and submitted himself to that cœnobium with the utmost goodness and humility, yet we think it not at all absurd to relate without any unnecessary verbiage, what we think is most instructive to those who are eager for goodness. And so when the whole body of the monks was seated in separate parties of twelve, in the large open court, when one of the brethren had been rather slow in fetching and bringing in a dish, the aforesaid Abbot Paul, who was busily hurrying about among the troops of brethren who were serving, saw it and struck him such a blow before them all on his open palm that the sound of the hand which was struck actually reached the ears of those whose backs were turned nd who were sitting some way off. But the youth of remarkable patience received it with such calmness of mind that not only did he let no word fall from his mouth or give the slightest sign of murmuring by the silent movements of his lips, but actually did not change colour in the slightest degree or (lose) the modest and peaceful look about his mouth.

---

[1] Heb. xii. 15. [2] Jer. viii. 17.
[3] *Depositio.* A word frequently used for the day of the death (or burial) in Calendars and Martyrologies.
[4] On this Abbot John compare the note on the Institutes V. xxviii.

[5] Rom. i. 28. [6] Deut. xxxii. 21.

And this fact struck with astonishment not merely us, who had lately come from a monastery of Syria and had not learnt the blessing of this patience by such clear examples, but all those as well who were not without experience of such earnestness, so that by it a great lesson was taught even to those who were well advanced, because even if this paternal correction had not disturbed his patience, neither did the presence of so great a number bring the slightest sign of colour to his cheeks.

CHAPTER II.

Of Abbot John's humility and our question.

IN this cœnobium then we found a very old man named John, whose words and humility we think ought certainly not to be passed over in silence as in them he excelled all the saints, as we know that he was especially vigorous in this perfection, which though it is the mother of all virtues and the surest foundation of the whole spiritual superstructure, yet is altogether a stranger to our system. Wherefore it is no wonder that we cannot attain to the height of those men, as we cannot stand the training of the cœnobium I will not say up to old age, but are scarcely content to endure the yoke of subjection for a couple of years, and at once escape to enjoy a dangerous liberty, while even for that short time we seem to be subject to the rule of the Elder not according to any strict rule, but as our free will directs. When then we had seen this old man in Abbot Paul's cœnobium, we were struck, first by his age and the grace with which the man was endowed, and with looks fixed on the ground began to entreat him to vouchsafe to explain to us why he had forsaken the freedom of the desert and that exalted profession, in which his fame and celebrity had raised him above others who had adopted the same life, and why he had chosen to enter under the yoke of the cœnobium. He said that as he was unequal to the system of the anchorites and unworthy of the heights of such perfection, he had gone back to the infant school, that he might learn to carry out the lessons taught there, according as the life demanded. And when our entreaties were not satisfied and we refused to take this humble answer, at last he began as follows.

CHAPTER III.

Abbot John's answer why he had left the desert.

THE system of the anchorites, which you are surprised at my leaving, I not only neither re-

ject nor refuse, but rather embrace and regard with the utmost veneration: in which system, and after I had passed thirty years living in a cœnobium, I rejoice that I have also spent twenty more, so that I can never be accused of sloth among those who tried it in a half-hearted way. But because its purity, of which I had had some slight experience, was sometimes soiled by the presence of anxiety about carnal matters, it seemed better to return to the cœnobium to secure a readier attainment of an easier aim undertaken, and less danger from venturing on the higher life of the humble solitary.[1] For it is better to seem earnest with smaller promises than careless in larger ones. And therefore if possibly I bring forward anything somewhat arrogantly and indeed somewhat too freely, I beg that you will not think it due to the sin of boasting but rather to my desire for your edification; and that, as I think that, when you ask so earnestly, nothing of the truth should be kept back from you, you will set it down to love rather than to boasting. For I think that some instruction may be given to you if I lay aside my humility, and simply lay bare the whole truth about my aim. For I trust that I shall not incur any reproach of vainglory from you because of the freedom of my words, nor any charge of falsehood from my conscience because of any suppression of the truth.

CHAPTER IV.

Of the excellence which the aforesaid old man showed in the system of the anchorites.

IF then anyone else delights in the recesses of the desert and would forget all human intercourse and say with Jeremiah: "I have not desired the day of man: Thou knowest,"[2] I confess that by the blessing of God's grace, I also secured or at any rate tried to secure this. And so by the kind gift of the Lord I remember that I was often caught up into such an ecstasy as to forget that I was clothed with the burden of a weak body, and my soul on a sudden forgot all external notions and entirely cut itself off from all material objects, so that neither my eyes nor ears performed their proper functions. And my soul was so filled with divine meditations

---

[1] The true reading, as given by Petschenig, appears to be the following: *Et minus de præsumptæ sublimioris professionis humilitate periculum.* It is probably on account of its difficulty that *humilitate* has been altered into *difficultate*, as in the text of Gazet (the two *humilitate difficultate* are found together in some MSS.) But the fact appears to be that *humilitas* is here used for the life of an anchorite, as in Conference XXIV. ix., where Abbot Abraham uses the expression *districtionem hujus humilitatis.* The word is also used in a somewhat similar sense in Conf. I. xx. and XI. ii.
[2] Jer. xvii. 16.

and spiritual contemplations that often in the evening I did not know whether I had taken any food and on the next day was very doubtful whether I had broken my fast yesterday. For which reason, a supply of food for seven days, i.e., seven sets of biscuits were set apart in a sort of hand-basket,[1] and laid by on Saturday, that there might be no doubt when supper had been omitted; and by this plan another mistake also from forgetfulness was obviated, for when the number of cakes was finished it showed that the course of the week was over, and that the services of the same day had come round, and that the festival and holy day and services of the congregation could not escape the notice of the solitary. But even if that ecstasy of mind of which we have spoken should happen to interfere with this arrangement, yet still the method of the days' work would show the number of the days and check the mistake. And to pass over in silence the other advantages of the desert (for it is not our business to treat of their number and quantity, but rather of the aim of solitude and the cœnobium) I will the rather briefly explain the reasons why I preferred to leave it, which you also wanted to know, and will in a concise discourse glance at all those fruits of solitude which I mentioned, and show to what greater advantages on the other side they ought to be held inferior.

CHAPTER V.

Of the advantages of the desert.

So long then as owing to the fewness of those who were then living in the desert, a greater freedom was afforded to us in a wider expanse of the wilderness, so long as in the seclusion of larger retreats we were caught up to those celestial ecstasies, and were not overwhelmed by a great quantity of brethren to visit us, and thus owing to the necessity of showing hospitality overburdened in our thoughts by the distractions of great cares, I frequented with insatiable desire and all my heart the peaceful retreats of the desert and that life which can only be compared to the bliss of the angels. But when, as I said, a larger number of the brethren began to seek a dwelling in that desert, and by cramping the freedom of the vast wilderness, not only caused that fire of divine contemplation to grow cold, but also entangled the mind in many ways in the chains of carnal matters, I determined to carry out my purpose in this

system rather than to grow cold in that sublime mode of life, by providing for carnal wants; so that, if that liberty and those spiritual ecstasies are denied me, yet as all care for the morrow is avoided, I may console myself by fulfilling the precept of the gospel, and what I lose in sublimity of contemplation, may be made up to me by submission and obedience. For it is a wretched thing for a man to profess to learn any art or pursuit, and never to arrive at perfection in it.

CHAPTER VI.

Of the conveniences of the cœnobium.

WHEREFORE I will briefly explain what advantages I now enjoy in this manner of life. *You* must consider my words and judge whether those advantages of the desert outweigh these comforts, and by this you will also be able to prove whether I chose to be cramped within the narrow limits of the cœnobium from dislike or from desire of that purity of the solitary life. In this life then there is no providing for the day's work, no distractions of buying and selling, no unavoidable care for the year's food, no anxiety about bodily things, by which one has to get ready what is necessary not only for one's own wants but also for those of any number of visitors, finally no conceit from the praise of men, which is worse than all these things and sometimes in the sight of God does away with the good of even great efforts in the desert. But, to pass over those waves of spiritual pride and the deadly peril of vainglory in the life of the anchorite, let us return to this general burden which affects everybody, i.e., the ordinary anxiety in providing food, which has so far exceeded I say not the measure of that ancient strictness which altogether did without oil, but is beginning not to be content even with the relaxation of our own time according to which the requirements of all the supply of food for a year were satisfied by the preparation of a single pint of oil and a modius of lentils prepared for the use of visitors; but now the needful supply of food is scarcely met by two or three times that amount. And to such an extent has the force of this dangerous relaxation grown among some that, when they mix vinegar and sauce, they do not add that single drop of oil, which our predecessors who followed the rules of the desert with greater powers of abstinence, were accustomed to pour in simply for the sake of avoiding vainglory,[1] but they

---

[1] *In prochirio id est admanuensi sporta.*

[1] Cf. Conference VIII.

break an Egyptian cheese for luxury and pour over it more oil than is required, and so take, under a single pleasant relish, two sorts of food which differ in their special flavour, each of which ought singly to be a pleasant refreshment at different times for a monk. To such a pitch however has this ὑλικὴ κτῆσις, i.e., acquisition of material things grown, that actually under pretence of hospitality and welcoming guests anchorites have begun to keep a blanket in their cells — a thing which I cannot mention without shame — to omit those things by which the mind that is awed by and intent on spiritual meditation is more especially hampered; viz., the concourse of brethren, the duties of receiving the coming and speeding the parting guest, visits to each other and the endless worry of various confabulations and occupations, the expectation of which owing to the continuous character of these customary interruptions keeps the mind on the stretch even during the time when these bothers seem to cease. And so the result is that the freedom of the anchorite's life is so hindered by these ties that it can never rise to that ineffable keenness of heart, and thus loses the fruits of its hermit life. And if this is now denied to me while I am living in the congregation and among others, at least there is no lack of peace of mind and tranquillity of heart that is freed from all business. And unless this is ready at hand for those also who live in the desert, they will indeed have to undergo the labours of the anchorite's life, but will lose its fruits which can only be gained in peaceful stability of mind. Finally even if there is any diminution of my purity of heart while I am living in the cœnobium, I shall be satisfied by keeping in exchange that one precept of the Gospel, which certainly cannot be less esteemed than all those fruits of the desert; I mean that I should take no thought for the morrow, and submitting myself completely to the Abbot seem in some degree to emulate Him of whom it is said: "He humbled Himself, and became obedient unto death;" and so be able humbly to make use of His words: "For I came not to do mine own will, but the will of the Father which sent me." [1]

CHAPTER VII.

A question on the fruits of the cœnobium and the desert.

GERMANUS: Since it is evident that you have not, like so many, just touched the mere outskirts of each mode of life, but have ascended to the very heights, we should like to know what is the end of the cœnobite's life and what the end of the hermit's. For no one can doubt that no man can discourse with greater fulness or fidelity, on these subjects than one who, taught by long use and experience, has followed them both, and so can by veracious teaching show us their value and aim.

CHAPTER VIII.

The answer to the question proposed.

JOHN: I should absolutely maintain that one and the same man could not attain perfection in both lives unless I was hindered by the example of some few. And since it is no small matter to find a man who is perfect in either of them, it is clear how much harder and I had almost said impossible it is for a man to be thoroughly efficient in both. And if this has ever happened, it cannot come under any general rule. For a general rule must be based not on exceptional instances, i.e., on the experience of a very few, but on what is within the power of the many or rather of all. But what is attained to here and there by but one or two, and is beyond the capacity of ordinary goodness, must be kept out of general rules as something permitted outside the condition and nature of human weakness, and should be brought forward as a miracle rather than as an example. Wherefore I will, as my slender ability allows, briefly intimate what you want to know. The aim indeed of the cœnobite is to mortify and crucify all his desires and, according to that salutary command of evangelic perfection, to take no thought for the morrow. And it is perfectly clear that this perfection cannot be attained by any except a cœnobite, such a man as the prophet Isaiah describes and blesses and praises as follows: "If thou turn away thy foot from the Sabbath, from doing thy own will in my holy day, and glorify Him, while thou dost not thine own ways, and thine own will is not found to speak a word: then shalt thou be delighted in the Lord, and I will lift thee up above the high places of the earth, and will feed thee with the inheritance of Jacob thy father. For the mouth of the Lord hath spoken it." [2] But the perfection for a hermit is to have his mind freed from all earthly things, and to unite it, as far as human frailty allows, with Christ: and such a man the prophet Jeremiah describes when he says: "Blessed is the man who hath borne the

---

[1] Phil. ii. 8; S. John vi. 38.

[2] Is. lviii. 13, 14.

yoke from his youth. He shall sit solitary and hold his peace, because he hath taken it upon himself;" the Psalmist also: "I am become like a pelican in the desert. I watched and became as a sparrow alone upon the housetop."[1] To this aim then, which we have described as that of either life, unless each of them attains, in vain does the one adopt the system of the cœnobium, and the other of the hermitage: for neither of them will get the good of his method of life.

CHAPTER IX.

Of true and complete perfection.

But this is $\mu\epsilon\rho\iota\kappa\dot\eta$, i.e., no thorough and altogether complete perfection, but only a partial one. Perfection then is very rare and granted by God's gift to but a very few. For he is truly and not partially perfect who with equal imperturbability can put up with the squalor of the wilderness in the desert, as well as the infirmities of the brethren in the cœnobium. And so it is hard to find one who is perfect in both lives, because the anchorite cannot thoroughly acquire $\dot\alpha\kappa\tau\eta\mu o\sigma\acute\nu\eta$, i.e., a disregard for and stripping oneself of material things, nor the cœnobite purity in contemplation, although we know that Abbot Moses and Paphnutius and the two Macarii[2] were masters of both in perfection. And so they were perfect in either life, and while they withdrew further than all the dwellers in the desert and delighted themselves unceasingly in the retirement of the wilderness, and as far as in them lay never sought intercourse with other men, yet they put up with the presence and the infirmities of those who came to them so that when a large number of the brethren came to them for the sake of seeing them and profiting by it, they endured this almost continuous trouble of receiving them with imperturbable patience, and men fancied that all the days of their life they had neither learnt nor practised anything but how to show common civility to those who came, so that it was a puzzle to all to say in which life their zeal was mainly shown, i.e., whether their greatness adapted itself more remarkably to the purity of the hermitage or to the common life.

CHAPTER X.

Of those who while still imperfect retire into the desert.

But some are sometimes so tantalized by the silence of the desert lasting all through the day that they altogether dread intercourse with men, and, when they have even for a little while broken through their habit of retirement owing to the accident of a visit from some of the brethren, boil over with marked vexation of mind, and show clear signs of annoyance. And this especially happens in the case of those who have betaken themselves to the solitary life without a well-matured purpose and without being thoroughly trained in the cœnobium, as these men are always imperfect and easily upset, and incline to one side or the other, as the gales of trouble may drive them. For as they boil over impatiently at intercourse or conversation with the brethren, so while they are living in solitude they cannot stand the vastness of that silence which they themselves have courted, inasmuch as they themselves do not even know the reason why solitude ought to be wanted and sought for, but imagine that the value and the main part of this life consist in this; viz., in avoiding intercourse with the brethren and simply shunning and loathing the sight of a man.

CHAPTER XI.

A question how to cure those who have hastily left the congregation of the cœnobium.

Germanus: By what treatment can any help be given to us or to others who are thus weak and only up to this; who had received but little instruction in the system of the cœnobium when we began to aspire to dwell in solitude before we had got rid of our faults; or by what means shall we be able to acquire the constancy of an imperturbable mind, and immovable steadfastness of patience; we who all too soon gave up the common life in the cœnobium, and forsook the schools and training ground for these exercises, in which our principles ought first to have been thoroughly schooled and perfected? How then can we now while we are living alone gain perfection in long-suffering and patience; or how can conscience, that searcher out of inward motives, discover whether these virtues exist in us or are wanting, so that because we are severed from intercourse with men, and not irritated by any of their provocations, we may not be deceived by false notions, and fancy that we have gained that imperturbable peace of mind?

---

[1] Lam. iii. 27, 28; Ps. ci. (cii.) 7, 8.
[2] Moses, Paphnutius, and the two Macarii have all been men-

tioned frequently before. On Moses (to whom the first two Conferences are assigned) see the note on the Institutes X. xxv.; on Paphnutius see on Conference III. i.; and on the two Macarii, the Institutes V. xli.

CHAPTER XII.

The answer telling how a solitary can discover his faults.

JOHN: To those who are really seeking relief, healing remedies from the true Physician of souls will certainly not be wanting; and to those above all will they be given who do not disregard their ill-condition (either because they despair of it, or because they do not care about it), nor hide the danger they are in from their wound, nor in their wanton heart reject the remedy of penitence, but with an humble and yet careful heart flee to the heavenly Physician for the diseases they have contracted from ignorance or error or necessity. And so we ought to know that if we retire to solitude or secret places, without our faults being first cured, their operation is but repressed, while the power of feeling them is not extinguished. For the root of all sins not having been eradicated is still lying hid in us, or rather creeping up, and that it is still alive we can tell by these signs. For instance, if, when we are living in solitude we receive the approach of some brethren, or any very slight tarrying on their part, with any anxiety or fretfulness of mind, we should recognize that an incentive to the most hasty impatience is still existing in us. But if when we are hoping for the coming of a brother, and from some cause he perhaps delays a little, our mental indignation either silently blames his slowness, and annoyance at this inconvenient waiting disturbs our mind, the examination of our conscience will show that the sin of anger and vexation is plainly still remaining in us. Again, if when a brother asks for our book to read, or for some other article to use, his request annoys us, or a refusal on our part disgusts him, there can be no doubt that we are still entangled in the meshes of avarice or covetousness. But if a sudden thought or a passage of Holy Scripture brings up the recollection of a woman and we feel that we are at all attracted towards her, we should know that the fire of fornication is not yet extinguished in us. But if on a comparison of our own strictness with the laxity of another even the slightest conceit tries our mind, it is clear that we are affected with the dreadful plague of pride. When then we detect these signs of faults in our heart, we should clearly recognize that it is only the opportunity and not the passion of sin of which we are deprived. And certainly these passions, if at any time we were to mingle in the ordinary life of men, would at once start up from their lurking places in our thoughts and prove that they did not then for the first time come into exist-

ence when they broke out, but that they were then at last made public, because they had been long lying hid. And so even a solitary can detect by sure signs that the roots of each fault are still implanted in him, if he tries not to show his purity to men, but to maintain it inviolate in His sight, from whom no secrets of the heart can be hid.

CHAPTER XIII.

A question how a man can be cured who has entered on solitude without having his faults eradicated.

GERMANUS: We very clearly and plainly see the proofs by which the signs of infirmities are inferred, and the method of discerning diseases, i.e., how the faults which are concealed in us can be detected: for our every day experience and the daily motions of our thoughts show us all these as they have been stated. It remains then that as the proofs and causes of our maladies have been exposed to us in a most clear way so their remedies and cures may also be shown. For no one can doubt that one who has first discovered the grounds and beginnings of ailments, with the approving witness of the conscience of those affected, can best discourse on their remedies. And so though the teaching of your holiness has laid bare the secrets of our wounds whereby we venture to have some hope of a remedy, because so clear a diagnosis of the disease gives promise of the hope of a cure, yet because, as you say, the first elements of salvation are acquired in the cœnobium, and men cannot be in a sound condition in solitude, unless they have first been healed by the medicine of the cœnobium, we have fallen again into a dangerous state of despair lest as we left the cœnobium in an imperfect condition we may not now that we are in the desert succeed in becoming perfect.

CHAPTER XIV.

The answer on their remedies.

JOHN: For those who are anxious for the cure of their ailments a saving remedy is sure not to be wanting, and therefore remedies should be sought by the same means that the signs of each fault are discovered. For as we have said that the faults of men's ordinary life are not wanting to solitaries, so we do not deny that all zeal for virtue, and all the means of healing are at the disposal of all those who are cut off from men's ordinary life. When then anyone discovers by those signs which we described above, that he is attacked by outbreaks of impatience or anger, he should always practise himself in the opposite and contrary things, and by setting before himself all sorts of injuries and wrongs, as if offered to him by somebody else, accustom his mind to submit with perfect humility to everything that wickedness can bring upon him; and by often representing to himself all kinds of rough and intolerable things, continually consider with all sorrow of heart with what gentleness he ought to meet them. And, by thus looking at the sufferings of all the saints, or indeed at those 'of the Lord Himself, he will admit that the various reproaches as well as punishments are less than he deserves, and prepare himself to endure all kinds of griefs. And when occasionally he has been recalled by some invitation to the assembly of the brethren — a thing which cannot but happen every now and then even to the strictest inmates of the desert, — if he finds that his mind is silently disturbed even for trifles, he should like some stern censor of his secret emotions charge himself with all those various hard wrongs, to the perfect endurance of which he was training himself by his daily meditations, and blaming and chiding himself as follows, say: My good man, are you the fellow who while training yourself in the practising ground of solitude, ventured most determinedly to think that you would get the better of all bad qualities, and who just now, when you were representing to yourself not only all sorts of bitter reproaches, but also intolerable punishments, fancied that you were pretty strong and able to stand against all storms? How is it that that unconquered patience of yours is upset by the first trial even of a light word? How is it that even a gentle breeze has shaken that house of yours which you fancied was built so strongly on the solid rock? Where is that which you announced when during a time of peace you were in your foolish confidence longing for war? "I am ready, and am not troubled;" and this which you used often to say with the prophet: "Prove me, O Lord, and try me: search out my reins and my heart;" and: "prove me, O Lord, and know my heart: question me and know my paths; and see if there be any way of wickedness in me."[1] How has a tiny ghost of an enemy frightened your grand preparations for war? With such reproaches and remorse a man should condemn himself and not allow the sudden temptation which has upset him to go unpunished, but by chastising his flesh with a severer

penalty of fasting and vigils; and, by punishing his sin of lightness of mind by continual pains of self-restraint, he should while living in solitude consume in this fire of practice what he ought to have thoroughly driven out in the life of the cœnobium. This at any rate we must firmly and resolutely hold to in order to secure a lasting and unbroken patience; viz., that for us, to whom by the Divine law not merely vengeance for, but even the recollection of injuries is forbidden, it is not permissible to be roused to anger because of some loss or annoyance. For what greater injury can happen to the soul than for it, owing to some sudden blindness from rage, to lose the brightness of the true and eternal light and to fail of the sight of Him "Who is meek and lowly of heart?"[2] What I ask could be more dangerous or awkward than for a man to lose his power of judging of goodness, and his standard and rule of true discernment, and for one in his sober senses to do what even a drunken man, and a fool would not be pardoned for doing? One then who carefully considers these and other injuries of the same kind, will readily endure and disregard not only all kinds of losses, but also whatever wrongs and punishments can be inflicted by the cruellest of men, as he will hold that there is nothing more damaging than anger, nor more valuable than peace of mind and unbroken purity of heart, for the sake of which we should think nothing of the advantages not merely of carnal matters but also of those things which appear to be spiritual, if they cannot be gained or done without some disturbance of this tranquillity.

CHAPTER XV.

A question whether chastity ought to be ascertained just as the other feelings.

GERMANUS: As the cure for other ailments, viz., anger, vexation, and impatience, has been shown to consist in opposing to them their contraries, so also we should like to learn what sort of treatment we ought to use against the spirit of fornication: I mean, whether the fire of lust can be quenched by the representation, as in those other cases, of greater inducements and things to excite it: because not merely to increase the incentives to lust within us, but even to touch them with a passing look of the mind, we believe to be utterly fatal to chastity.

1 Ps. cxviii. (cxix.) 60; xxv. (xxvi.) 2; cxxxviii. (cxxxix.) 23, 24.　　2 S. Matt. xi. 29.

CHAPTER XVI.

The answer giving the proofs by which it can be recognized.

JOHN: Your shrewd question has anticipated the subject, which even if you had said nothing must have arisen from our discourse, and therefore I do not doubt that it will be effectually grasped by your minds, since indeed your sharp wits have outstripped our instruction. For the puzzle of any question is easily removed, when the inquiry anticipates the answer, and is the first to travel along the road which it is to follow. And so to the treatment of those faults of which we have spoken above, intercourse with other men is not merely no hindrance, but a considerable help, for the more often that the outbursts of their impatience are exposed, the more thorough is the sorrow and compunction which they bring on those who have failed, and the speedier is the recovery of health which they confer on those who struggle against them. Wherefore even when we are living in solitude, though the incentive to irritation and matter for it cannot arise from men, yet we ought of set purpose to meditate on incitements to it, that as we are fighting against it with a continual struggle in our thoughts a speedier cure for it may be found for us. But against the spirit of fornication the system is different, and the method an altered one. For as we must deprive the body of opportunities of lust, and contact with flesh, so we must deprive the mind of the recollection of it. For it is sufficiently dangerous for bosoms that are still weak and infirm even to tolerate the slight-est recollection of this passion, in such a way that sometimes at the remembrance of holy women, or in reading a story in Holy Scripture a stimulus of dangerous excitement is aroused. For which reason our Elders used deliberately to omit passages of this kind when any of the juniors were present. However for those who are perfect and established in the feelings of chastity there can be no lack of proofs by which they may examine themselves, and establish their perfect uprightness of heart by the uncorrupted judgment of their own conscience. There will then be for the man who is thoroughly established a similar test even in regard to this passion, so that one who is sure that he has altogether exterminated the roots of this evil may for the sake of ascertaining his chastity, call up some picture as with a lascivious mind. But it is by no means proper for such a test to be attempted by those who are still weak (for to them it will be dangerous rather than useful), ut conjunctionem femineam et palpationem quodammodo teneram atque mollissimam corde pertractent. Cum ergo perfecta quis virtute fundatus ad illecebram blandissimorum tactuum, quos cogitando confinxerit, nullum mentis assensum, nullam commotionem carnis in se deprehenderit exagitatam, he will have a very sure proof of his purity, so that training himself to this steadfast purity he will not only possess the blessing of chastity and freedom from defilement in his heart, but even if he is obliged to touch the body of a woman, he will be horrified at it.

With this Abbot John brought his Conference to an end, as he saw that it was just time for the refreshment of the ninth hour.

XX.

CONFERENCE OF ABBOT PINUFIUS.

ON THE END OF PENITENCE AND THE MARKS OF SATISFACTION.

CHAPTER I.

Of the humility of Abbot Pinufius, and of his hiding-place.

Now that I am going to relate the precepts of that excellent and remarkable man, Abbot Pinufius, on the end of penitence, I fancy that I can dispose of a very large part of my material, if out of consideration lest I weary my reader, I here pass over in silence the praise of his humility, which I touched on in a brief discourse in the fourth book of the Institutes,[1] which was entitled "Of the rules to be observed by renuncants," especially as many who have no knowledge of that work, may happen to read this, and then all the authority

---

[1] Cf. Institutes IV. c. xxx., xxxi. Nothing further is known of Pinufius than what we gather from these passages of Cassian.

of the utterances will be weakened if there is no account of the virtues of the speaker. For this man when he was presiding as Abbot and Presbyter over a large cœnobium not far from Panephysis, a city, as was there said, of Egypt, and when all that province had praised him to the skies for his virtues and miracles, so that he already seemed to himself to have received the reward of his labours in the remuneration of the praise of men, as he was afraid lest the emptiness of popular favour, which he especially disliked, might interfere with the fruits of an eternal reward, he secretly fled from his monastery and made his way to the furthest recesses of the monks of Tabennæ,[1] where he chose not the solitude of the desert, not that freedom from care of which the life of one alone affords, which even those who are imperfect and who cannot endure the effort which obedience requires in the cœnobium, sometimes seek after with proud presumption, but he chose to submit himself to a most famous monastery. Where, however, that he might not be betrayed by any signs of his dress, he clothed himself in a secular garb, and lay before the doors with tears, as is the custom there, for many days, and clinging to the knees of all after being daily repulsed by those who to test his purpose said that now in extreme old age he was seeking this holy life not in sincerity, but driven by the lack of food, at last he obtained admission, and there he was told off to help a young brother who had been given the charge of a garden, and when he not only fulfilled with such marvellous and holy humility everything which his chief ordered him or which the care of the work entrusted to him demanded, but also performed in stealthy labour by night certain necessary offices which were avoided by the rest out of disgust for them, so that when morning dawned, all the congregation was delighted at such useful works but knew not their author; and when he had passed nearly three years there rejoicing in the labours, which he had desired, but to which he was so unfairly subjected, it happened that a certain brother known to him came there from the same parts of Egypt from which he himself had come. And this man for a time hesitated because the meanness of his clothes and of his office prevented him from readily recognizing him at once, but after looking very closely at him, fell at his feet, and first astonished all the brethren, and afterwards, when he betrayed his name, which the fame of his special sanctity had made known to them also, he smote them with sorrow and com-

punction because they had told off a man of his virtues and a priest to such mean offices. But he, shedding copious tears, and charging the serious accident of his betrayal to the envy of the devil, was brought in honourable custody by his brethren surrounding him to the monastery; and after that he had stayed there for a short time, he was once more troubled by the respect shown to his dignity and rank, and stealthily embarked on board ship and sailed to the Palestinian province of Syria, where he was received as a beginner and a novice in the house of that monastery in which we were living, and was charged by the Abbot to stop in our cell. But not even there could his virtues and merits long remain secret. For he was discovered and betrayed in the same way, and brought back to his own monastery with the utmost honour and respect.

CHAPTER II.

Of our coming to him.

WHEN then after no long time a desire for holy instruction had urged us also to visit Egypt, we sought him out with the utmost eagerness and devotion and were welcomed by him with such kindness and courtesy that he actually honoured us, as former sharers of the same cell with him, with a lodging in his own cell which he had built in the furthest corner of his garden. And there when in the presence of all the brethren at service he had delivered to one of the brethren who was submitting to the rule of the monastery sufficiently difficult and elevated precepts, which as we said, I summarized as briefly as I could in the fourth book of the Institutes, the heights of a true renunciation seemed to us so unattainable and so marvellous that we did not think that such humble folks as we could ever scale them. And therefore, cast down in despair, and not concealing in our looks the inner bitterness of our thoughts, we came back to the blessed old man with a tolerably anxious heart: and when he at once asked the reason why we were so sad, Abbot Germanus groaned deeply and replied as follows.

CHAPTER III.

A question on the end of penitence and the marks of satisfaction.

As your grand and splendid exposition of a doctrine new to us has opened out to us a more difficult road to the most glorious re-

---

[1] On Tabennæ or Tabenna see the note on the Institutes IV. i.

nunciation, and has removed the scales from our eyes, and shown to us its summit raised in the heavens, so are we proportionately cast down with a greater weight of despair. Since, when we measure its vastness against our puny strength, and compare the excessively humble character of our ignorance with the boundless height of virtue shown to us, we feel that we are so small that we not only cannot attain to it, but that we are sure to fall short in what we have. For as we are weighed down by the burden of excessive despair, we fall away somehow from the lowest depths to still lower ones. Accordingly there is one and only one support which can provide a cure for our wounds; viz., for us to learn something of the end of penitence and especially of the marks of satisfaction, that we may feel sure of the forgiveness of past sins, and so be spurred on to scale the heights of the perfection described above.

CHAPTER IV.

The answer on the humility shown by our request.

PINUFIUS: I am indeed delighted at the very plentiful fruits of your humility, which indeed I saw with no indifferent concern, when I was formerly received in the habitation of that cell of yours, and I am very glad that you welcome with such respect the charge given by us, the least of all Christians, and the words that I have taken the liberty of saying so that if I am not mistaken you carry them out as soon as ever they are spoken by us; and though, as I remember, the importance of the words scarcely deserves the efforts you bestow on them, yet you so conceal the merits of your virtue, as if no breath ever reached you of those things which you are daily practising. But because this fact is worthy of the highest praise; viz., that you declare that those institutes of the saints are still unknown to you as if you were still beginners we will, as briefly as possible, summarize what you so eagerly ask of us. For we must even beyond our powers and ability, obey the commands of such old friends as you. And so on the value and appeasing power of penitence many have published a great deal, not only in words but also in writing, showing how useful it is, how strong, and full of grace, so that when God is offended by our past sins, and on the point of inflicting a most just punishment for such offences, it somehow, if it is not wrong to say so, stops Him, and, if I may so say, stays the right hand of the Avenger even against His will. But I have

no doubt that all this is well known to you, either from your natural wisdom, or from your unwearied study of Holy Scripture, so that from this the first shoots, so to speak, of your conversion sprang up. Finally, you are anxious not about the character of penitence but about its end, and the marks of satisfaction, and so by a very shrewd question ask what has been left out by others.

CHAPTER V.

Of the method of penitence and the proof of pardon.

WHEREFORE in order to satisfy as briefly and shortly as possible, your desire and question, the full and perfect description of penitence is, never again to yield to those sins for which we do penance, or for which our conscience is pricked. But the proof of satisfaction and pardon is for us to have expelled the love of them from our hearts. For each one may be sure that he is not yet free from his former sins as long as any image of those sins which he has committed or of others like them dances before his eyes, and I will not say a delight in — but the recollection of — them haunts his inmost soul while he is devoting himself to satisfaction for them and to tears. And so one who is on the watch to make satisfaction may then feel sure that he is free from his sins and that he has obtained pardon for past faults, when he never feels that his heart is stirred by the allurements and imaginations of these same sins. Wherefore the truest test of penitence and witness of pardon is found in our own conscience, which even before the day of judgment and of knowledge, while we are still in the flesh, discloses our acquittal from guilt, and reveals the end of satisfaction and the grace of forgiveness. And that what has been said may be more significantly expressed, then only should we believe that the stains of past sins are forgiven us, when the desires for present delights as well as the passions have been expelled from our heart.

CHAPTER VI.

A question whether our sins ought to be remembered out of contrition of heart.

GERMANUS: And whence can there be aroused in us this holy and salutary contrition from humiliation, which is described as follows in the person of the penitent: "I have acknowledged my sin, and mine unrighteousness have I not hid. I said: I will acknowledge against myself mine unrighteousness to the Lord," so that we may be able effectually to say also what follows: "And Thou forgavest the iniquity of my heart;"[1] or how, when we kneel in prayer shall we be able to stir ourselves up to tears of confession, by which we may be able to obtain pardon for our offences, according to these words: "Every night will I wash my bed: I will water my couch with tears;"[2] if we expel from our hearts all recollection of our faults, though on the contrary we are bidden carefully to preserve the remembrance of them, as the Lord says: "And thine iniquities I will not remember: but do thou recollect them?"[3] Wherefore not only when I am at work, but also when I am at prayer I try of set purpose to recall to my mind the recollection of my sins, that I may be more effectually inclined to true humility and contrition of heart, and venture to say with the prophet: "Look upon my humility and my labour: and forgive me all my sins."[4]

CHAPTER VII.

The answer showing how far we ought to preserve the recollection of previous actions.

PINUFIUS: Your question, as has been already said above, was not raised with regard to the character of penitence, but with regard to its end, and the marks of satisfaction: to which, as I think, a fair and pertinent reply has been given. But what you have said as to the remembrance of sins is sufficiently useful and needful to men who are still doing penance, that they may with constant smiting of the breast say: "For I acknowledge my wickedness: and my sin is ever before me;" and this too: "And I will think for my sin."[5] While then we do penance, and are still grieved by the recollection of faulty actions, the shower of tears which is caused by the confession of our faults is sure to quench the fire of our conscience. But when, while a man is still in this state of humility of heart and contrition of spirit and continuing to labour and to weep, the remembrance of these things fades away, and the thorns of conscience are by God's grace extracted from his inmost heart, then it is clear that he has attained to the end of satisfaction and the reward of pardon, and that he is purged from the stain of the sins he has committed. To which state of forgetfulness we can only attain by the obliteration of our former sins and likings, and by perfect and complete purity of heart. And this most certainly will not be attained by any of those who from sloth or carelessness have failed to purge out their faults, but only by one who by constantly continuing to groan and sigh sorrowfully has removed every spot of his former stains, and by the goodness of his heart and his labour has proclaimed to the Lord: "I have acknowledged my sin, and mine unrighteousness have I not hid;" and: "My tears have been my meat day and night;" so that in the end it may be vouchsafed to him to hear these words: "Let thy voice cease from weeping, and thine eyes from tears: for there is a reward for thy labour, saith the Lord;"[6] and these words also may be uttered of him by the voice of the Lord: "I have blotted out as a cloud thine iniquities, and as a mist thy sins:" and again: "I even I am He that blotteth out thine iniquities for mine own sake, and thine offences I will no longer remember;"[7] and so, when he is freed from the "cords of his sins," by which "everyone is bound,"[8] he will with all thanksgiving sing to the Lord: "Thou hast broken my chains: I will offer to thee the sacrifice of praise."[9]

CHAPTER VIII.

Of the various fruits of penitence.

FOR after that grace of baptism which is common to all, and that most precious gift of martyrdom which is gained by being washed in blood, there are many fruits of penitence by which we can succeed in expiating our sins. For eternal salvation is not only promised to the bare fact of penitence, of which the blessed Apostle Peter says: "Repent and be converted that your sins may be forgiven;" and John the Baptist and the Lord Himself: "Repent ye, for the kingdom of heaven is at hand:"[10] but also by the affection of love is the weight of our sins overwhelmed: for "charity covers a multitude of sins."[11] In the same way also by the fruits of almsgiving a remedy is provided for our wounds, because "As water extinguishes fire, so does almsgiving extinguish sin."[12] So also by the shedding of tears is gained the washing away of offences, for "Every night I will wash my bed: I will water my couch with tears." Finally to show that they are not shed in vain, he adds: "Depart from me all ye that

---

[1] Ps. xxxi. (xxxii.) 5, 6.   [4] Ps. xxiv. (xxv.) 18.
[2] Ps. vi. 7.   [5] Ps. l. (li.) 5; xxxvii. (xxxviii.) 19.
[3] Is. xliii. 25, 26.

[6] Ps. xxxi. (xxxii.) 5; xli. (xlii.) 4; Jer. xxxi. 16.
[7] Is. xliv. 22; xliii. 25.   [10] Acts iii. 19; S. Matt. iii. 2.
[8] Prov. v. 22.   [11] 1 Pet. iv. 8.
[9] Ps. cxv. 16, 17.   [12] Ecclus. iii. 33.

work iniquity, for the Lord hath heard the voice of my weeping." [1] Moreover by means of confession of sins, their absolution is granted: for "I said: I will confess against myself my sin to the Lord: and Thou forgavest the iniquity of my heart;" and again: "Declare thine iniquities first, that thou mayest be justified." [2] By afflicting the heart and body also is forgiveness of sins committed in like manner obtained, for he says: "Look on my humility and my labour, and forgive me all my sins;" and more especially by amendment of life: "Take away," he says, "the evil of your thoughts from mine eyes. Cease to do evil, learn to do well. Seek judgment, relieve the oppressed: judge the orphan, defend the widow. And come, reason with Me, saith the Lord: and though your sins were as scarlet, yet shall they be as white as snow, though they were red as crimson, they shall be as white as wool." [3] Sometimes too the pardon of our sins is obtained by the intercession of the saints, for "if a man knows his brother to sin a sin not unto death, he asks, and He will give to him his life, for him that sinneth not unto death;" and again: "Is any sick among you? Let him send for the Elders of the Church and they shall pray over him, anointing him with oil in the name of the Lord. And the prayer of faith shall save the sick, and the Lord will raise him up, and if he be in sins, they shall be forgiven him." [4] Sometimes too by the virtue of compassion and faith the stains of sin are removed, according to this passage: "By compassion and faith sins are purged away." [5] And often by the conversion and salvation of those who are saved by our warnings and preaching: "For he who converts a sinner from the error of his way, shall save his soul from death, and cover a multitude of sins." [6] Moreover by pardon and forgiveness on our part we obtain pardon of our sins: "For if ye forgive men their offences, your heavenly Father will also forgive you your sins." [7] You see then what great means of obtaining mercy the compassion of our Saviour has laid open to us, so that no one when longing for salvation need be crushed by despair, as he sees himself called to life by so many remedies. For if you plead that owing to weakness of the flesh you cannot get rid of your sins by fasting, and you cannot say: "My knees are weak from fasting, and my flesh is changed for oil; for I have eaten ashes for my bread, and mingled my drink with weeping," [8] then atone for them by profuse almsgiving. If you have nothing that you can give to the needy (although the claims of want and poverty exclude none from this office, since the two mites of the widow are ranked higher than the splendid gifts of the rich, and the Lord promises that He will give a reward for a cup of cold water), at least you can purge them away by amendment of life. But if you cannot secure perfection in goodness by the eradication of all your faults, you can show a pious anxiety for the good and salvation of another. But if you complain that you are not equal to this service, you can cover your sins by the affection of love. And if in this also some sluggishness of mind makes you weak, at least you should submissively with a feeling of humility entreat for remedies for your wounds by the prayers and intercession of the saints. Finally who is there who cannot humbly say: "I have acknowledged my sin: and mine unrighteousness have I not hid;" so that by this confession he may be able also to add this: "And Thou forgavest the iniquity of my heart." [9] But if shame holds you back, and you blush to reveal them before men, you should not cease to confess them with constant supplication to Him from Whom they cannot be hid, and to say to Him: "I acknowledge mine iniquity, and my sin is ever before me. Against Thee only have I sinned, and have done evil before Thee;" [10] as He is wont to heal them without any publication which brings shame, and to forgive sins without any reproaching. And further besides that ready and sure aid the Divine condescension has afforded us another also that is still easier, and has entrusted the possession of the remedy to our own will, so that we can infer from our own feelings the forgiveness of our offences, when we say to Him: "Forgive us our debts as we also forgive our debtors." [11] Whoever then desires to obtain forgiveness of his sins, should study to fit himself for it by these means. Let not the stubbornness of an obdurate heart turn away any from the saving remedy and the fount of so much goodness, because even if we have done all these things, they will not be able to expiate our offences, unless they are blotted out by the goodness and mercy of the Lord, who when He sees the service of pious efforts offered by us with a humble heart, supports our small and puny efforts with the utmost bounty, and says: "I even I am He that blotteth out thine iniquities for Mine own sake, and I will remember thy sins no more." [12] Whoever then is aiming

---

[1] Ps. vi. 7, 9.　　[2] Ps. xxxi. (xxxii.) 5; Is. xliii. 26.
[3] Ps. xxiv. (xxv.) 18; Is. i. 16–18.　　[6] S. James v. 20.
[4] 1 John v. 16; S. James v. 14, 15.　　[7] S. Matt. vi. 14.
[5] Prov. xv. 27.　　[8] Ps. cviii. (cix.) 24; ci. (cii.) 10.

[9] Ps. xxxi. (xxxii.) 5.　　[11] S. Matt. vi. 12.
[10] Ps. l. (li.) 5, 6.　　[12] Is. xliii. 25.

at this condition, which we have mentioned, will seek the grace of satisfaction by daily fasting and mortification of heart and body, for, as it is written, "Without shedding of blood there is no remission;"[1] and this not without good reason. For "flesh and blood cannot inherit the kingdom of God."[2] And therefore one who would withhold "the sword of the spirit which is the word of God"[3] from this shedding of blood certainly comes under the lash of that curse of Jeremiah's; for "Cursed," says he, "is he who withholds his sword from blood."[4] For this is the sword, which for our good sheds that bad blood whereby the material of our sins lives; and cuts off and pares away everything carnal and earthly which it finds to have grown up in the members of our soul; and makes men die to sin and live to God, and flourish with spiritual virtues. And so he will begin to weep no more at the recollection of former sins, but at the hope of what is to come, and, thinking less of past evils than of good things to come, will shed tears not from sorrow at his sins, but from delight in that eternal joy, and "forgetting those things which are behind," i.e., carnal sins, will press on "to those before,"[5] i.e., to spiritual gifts and virtues.

CHAPTER IX.

How valuable to the perfect is the forgetfulness of sin.

But with regard to this that you said a little way back; viz., that you of set purpose go over the recollections of past sins, this ought certainly not to be done, nay, if it forcibly surprises you, it must be at once expelled. For it greatly hinders the soul from the contemplation of purity, and especially in the case of one who is living in solitude, as it entangles him in the stains of this world and swamps him in foul sins. For while you are recalling those things which you did through ignorance or wantonness in accordance with the prince of this world, though I grant you that while you are engaged in these thoughts no delight in them steals in, yet at least the mere taint of the ancient filthiness is sure to corrupt your soul with its foul stink, and to shut out the spiritual fragrance of goodness, i.e., the odour of a sweet savour. When then the recollection of past sins comes over your mind, you must recoil from it just as an honest and upright man runs away if he is sought out in public by an immodest and wanton woman

either by words or by embraces. And certainly unless he at once withdraws himself from contact with her, and if he allows himself to linger the very least in impure talk, even if he refuses his consent to the shameful pleasures, yet he cannot avoid the brand of infamy and scorn in the judgment of all the passers by. So then we also, if by noxious recollections we are led to thoughts of this kind, ought at once to desist from dwelling upon them and to fulfil what we are commanded by Solomon: "But go forth," says he, "do not linger in her place, nor fix thine eye on her;"[6] lest if the angels see us taken up with unclean and foul thoughts, they may not be able to say to us in passing by: "The blessing of the Lord be upon you."[7] For it is impossible for the soul to continue in good thoughts, when the main part of the heart is taken up with foul and earthly considerations. For this saying of Solomon's is true: "When thine eyes look on a strange woman, then shall thy mouth speak wickedly, and thou shalt lie as it were in the midst of the sea, and as a pilot in a great storm. But thou shalt say: They have beaten me, but I felt no pain; and they mocked me, but I felt not."[8] So then we should forsake not only all foul but even all earthly thoughts and ever raise the desires of our soul to heavenly things, in accordance with this saying of our Saviour: "For where I am," He says, "there also shall My servant be."[9] For it often happens that when anyone out of pity is in thought going over his own falls or those of other faulty persons, he is affected by the delight and assent to this most subtle attack, and that which was undertaken and started with a show of goodness ends with a filthy and damaging termination, for "there are ways which appear to men to be right, but the ends thereof will come to the depths of hell."[10]

CHAPTER X.

How the recollection of our sins should be avoided.

Wherefore we must endeavour to rouse ourselves to this praiseworthy contrition, by aiming at virtue and by the desire for the kingdom of heaven rather than by dangerous recollections of sins, for a man is sure to be suffocated by the pestilential smells of the sewer as long as he chooses to stand over it or to stir its filth.

---

[1] Heb. ix. 22.   [3] Eph. vi. 17.   [5] Phil. iii. 13.   [6] Prov. ix. 18.   [8] Prov. xxiii. 33-35.   [10] Prov. xvi. 25.
[2] 1 Cor. xv. 50.   [4] Jer. xlviii. 10.   [7] Ps. cxxviii. (cxxix.) 8.   [9] S. John xii. 26.

CHAPTER XI.

Of the marks of satisfaction, and the removal of past sins.

BUT we know, as we have often said, that then only have we made satisfaction for past sins, when the very motions and feelings, through which we were guilty of what we have to sorrow for, have been eradicated from our hearts. But no one should fancy that he can secure this, unless he has first with all the fervour of his spirit cut off the opportunities and occasions, owing to which he fell into those sins; as for instance, if through dangerous familiarity with a woman he has fallen into fornication or adultery, he must take the utmost pains to avoid even looking on one; or if he has been overcome by too much wine and over-eating, he should chastise with the utmost severity his craving for immoderate food. And again if he has been led astray by the desire for and love of money, and has fallen into perjury or theft or murder or blasphemy, he should cut off the occasion for avarice, which has allured and deceived him. If he is driven by the passion of pride into the sin of anger, he should with all the virtue of humility, remove the incentive to arrogance. And so, in order that each single sin may be destroyed, the occasion and opportunity by which or for which it was committed should be first got rid of. For by this curative treatment we can certainly attain to forgetfulness of the sins we have committed.

CHAPTER XII.

Wherein we must do penance for a time only; and wherein it can have no end.

BUT that description of the forgetfulness spoken of only has to do with capital offences, which are also condemned by the mosaic law, the inclination to which is destroyed and put an end to by a good life, and so also the penance for them has an end. But for those small offences in which, as it is written, "the righteous falls seven times and will rise again,"[1] penitence will never cease. For either through ignorance, or forgetfulness, or thought, or word, or surprise, or necessity, or weakness of the flesh, or defilement in a dream, we often fall every day either against our will or voluntarily; offences for which David also prays the Lord, and asks for purification and pardon, and says: "Who can understand sins? from my secret ones cleanse me; and from those of others spare Thy servant;" and the Apostle: "For the good which I would I do not, and the evil which I would not, that I do." For which also the same man exclaims with a sigh: "O wretched man that I am! who shall deliver me from the body of this death?"[2] For we slip into these so easily as it were by a law of nature, that however carefully and guardedly we are on the lookout against them, we cannot altogether avoid them. Since it was of these that one of the disciples, whom Jesus loved, declared and laid down absolutely saying: "If we say that we have no sin we deceive ourselves, and His word is not in us."[3] Further for a man who is anxious to reach the heights of perfection it will not greatly help him to have arrived at the end of penitence, i.e., to restrain himself from unlawful acts, unless he has always urged himself forward in unwearied course to those virtues whereby we come to the signs of satisfaction. For it will not be enough for a man to have kept himself clear from those foul stains of sins which the Lord hates, unless he has also secured by purity of heart and perfect Apostolical love that sweet fragrance of virtue in which the Lord delights. Thus far Abbot Pinufius discoursed on the marks of satisfaction and the end of penitence. And although he pressed us with anxious love to decide to stay in his coenobium, yet when he could not retain us, as we were incited by the fame of the desert of Scete, he sent us on our way.

---

[1] Prov. xxiv. 16.   [2] Ps. xviii. (xix.)   Rom. vii. 19, 24.
[3] 1 John i. 8, 10.

XXI.

THE FIRST CONFERENCE OF ABBOT THEONAS.

ON THE RELAXATION DURING THE FIFTY DAYS.[1]

CHAPTER I.

How Theonas came to Abbot John.

BEFORE we begin to set forth the words of this Conference held with that excellent man Abbot Theonas,[2] I think it well to describe in a brief discourse the origin of his conversion, because from this the reader will be able to see more clearly both the excellence and the grace of the man. He then while still very young was by the desire and command of his parents joined in the tie of marriage, for as with pious anxiety they were careful about his chastity, and were afraid of a critical fall at a dangerous age, they thought that the passions of youth might be anticipated by the remedy of a lawful marriage. When then he had lived for five years with a wife, he came to Abbot John, who was then for his marvellous sanctity chosen to preside over the administration of the alms.[3] For it is not anyone who likes who is of his own wish or ambition promoted to this office, but only he whom the congregation of all the Elders considers from the advantage of his age and the witness of his faith and virtues to be more excellent than, and superior to, all others. To this blessed John then the aforesaid young man had come in the eagerness of his pious devotion, bringing gifts of piety among other owners who were eager to offer tithes and firstfruits of their substance to the old man I mentioned,[4] and when the old man saw them pouring in upon him with many gifts, and was anxious to make some recompense in return for their offerings, he began, as the Apostle says, to sow spiritual things to them whose carnal gifts he was reaping.[5] And finally thus began his word of exhortation.

CHAPTER II.

The exhortation of Abbot John to Theonas and the others who had come together with him.

I AM indeed delighted, my children, with the duteous liberality of your gifts; and your devout offering, the disposal of which is entrusted to me, I gratefully accept, because you are offering your firstfruits and tithes for the good and use of the needy, as a sacrifice to the Lord, of a sweet smelling savour, in the belief that by the offering of them, the abundance of your fruits and all your substance, from which you have taken away these for the Lord, will be richly blessed, and that you yourselves will according to the faith of His command be endowed even in this world with manifold richness in all good things: "Honour the Lord from thy righteous labours, and offer to Him of the fruits of thy righteousness; that thy garners may be full of abundance of wheat, and thy vats may overflow with wine."[6] And as you are faithfully carrying out this service, you may know that you have fulfilled the righteousness of the old law, under which those who then lived if they transgressed it inevitably incurred guilt, while if they fulfilled it they could not attain to a pitch of perfection.

CHAPTER III.

Of the offering of tithes and firstfruits.

FOR indeed by the Lord's command tithes were consecrated to the service of the Levites, but oblations and firstfruits for the priests.[7] But this was the law of the firstfruits; viz.,

---

[1] On *Quinquagesima* see the note on the Institutes II. vi.
[2] Nothing further is known of this Theonas than what Cassian here tells us: he is clearly a different person from the one mentioned by Rufinus, Hist. Mon. c. vi. Cf. Palladius, Lausiac History, c. l.
[3] *Diaconia.* Cf. the note on XVIII. vii.
[4] This is noteworthy as being the earliest instance on record of the payment of tithes to a monastery. The language of the Conference, it will be noted, shows that they were not regarded as legally due or in any way compulsory, but as a free-will offering on the part of the faithful. Cf. Bingham, Antiquities, Book VII. ciii. § 19; and the Dictionary of Christian Antiquities, Vol. ii. p. 1964.

[5] Cf. 1 Cor. ix. 11.
[6] Prov. iii. 9, 10.
[7] Cf. Numb. xviii. 26; v. 9, 10.

that the fiftieth part of fruits or animals should be given for the service of the temple and the priests: and this proportion some who were faithlessly indifferent diminished, while those who were very religious increased it, so that the one gave only the sixtieth part, and the other gave the fortieth part of their fruits. For the righteous, for whom the law is not enacted, are thus shown to be not under the law, as they try not only to fulfil but even to exceed the righteousness of the law, and their devotion is greater than the legal requirement, as it goes beyond the observance of precepts and adds to what is due of its own free will.

CHAPTER IV.

How Abraham, David, and other saints went beyond the requirement of the law.

FOR so we read that Abraham went beyond the requirement of the law which was afterwards to be given, when after his victory over the four kings, he would not touch any of the spoils of Sodom, which were fairly due to him as the conqueror, and which indeed the king himself, whose spoils he had rescued, offered him; and with an oath by the Divine name he exclaimed: "I lift up my hand to the Lord Most High, who made heaven and earth, that I will not take from a thread to a shoe's latchet of all that is thine."[1] So we know that David went beyond the requirement of the law, as, though Moses commanded that vengeance should be taken on enemies,[2] he not only did not do this, but actually embraced his persecutors with love, and piously entreated the Lord for them, and wept bitterly and avenged them when they were slain. So we are sure that Elijah and Jeremiah were not under the law, as though they might without blame have taken advantage of lawful matrimony, yet they preferred to remain virgins. So we read that Elisha and others of the same mode of life went beyond the commands of Moses, as of them the Apostle speaks as follows: "They went about in sheepskins and in goatskins, they were oppressed, afflicted, in want, of whom the world was not worthy, they wandered about in deserts and in mountains, and in caves and in dens of the earth."[3] What shall I say of the sons of Jonadab the son of Rechab, of whom we are told that, when at the Lord's bidding the prophet Jeremiah offered them wine, they replied: "We drink no wine: for Jonadab the son of Rechab, our father, commanded us, saying: Ye shall drink no wine, ye and your sons forever: and ye shall build no house,

nor sow any seed, nor plant vineyards nor possess them: but ye shall dwell in tents all your days"? Wherefore also they were permitted to hear from the same prophet these words: "Thus saith the Lord God of hosts, the God of Israel: there shall not fail a man from the stock of Jonadab the son of Rechab to stand in My sight all the days;"[4] as all of them were not satisfied with merely offering tithes of their possessions, but actually refused property, and offered the rather to God themselves and their souls, for which no redemption can be made by man, as the Lord testifies in the gospel: "For what shall a man give in exchange for his own soul?"[5]

CHAPTER V.

How those who live under the grace of the Gospel ought to go beyond the requirement of the law.

WHEREFORE we ought to know that we from whom the requirements of the law are no longer exacted, but in whose ears the word of the gospel daily sounds: "If thou wilt be perfect, go and sell all that thou hast and give to the poor, and thou shalt have treasure in heaven, and come follow Me,"[6] when we offer to God tithes of our substance, are still in a way ground down beneath the burden of the law, and not able to rise to those heights of the gospel, those who conform to which are recompensed not only by blessings in this present life, but also by future rewards. For the law promises to those who obey it no rewards of the kingdom of heaven, but only solaces in this life, saying: "The man that doeth these things shall live in them."[7] But the Lord says to His disciples: "Blessed are the poor in spirit, for theirs is the kingdom of heaven;" and: "Everyone that leaveth house or brothers or sisters or father or mother or wife or children or field for My name's sake, shall receive an hundredfold, and shall inherit eternal life."[8] And this with good reason. For it is not so praiseworthy for us to abstain from forbidden as from lawful things, and not to use these last out of reverence for Him, Who has permitted us to use them because of our weakness. And so if even those who, faithfully offering tithes of their fruits, are obedient to the more ancient precepts of the Lord, cannot yet climb the heights of the gospel, you can see very clearly how far short of it those fall who do not even do this. For how can those men be partakers of the grace of the gospel who disregard the

---

[1] Gen. xiv. 22, 23. [2] Cf. Exod. xxi. 24. [3] Heb. xi. 37, 38.

[4] Jer. xxxv. 6, 7, 19. [6] S. Matt. xix. 21. [8] S. Matt. v. 3; xix. 29.
[5] S. Matt. xvi. 25. [7] Lev. xviii. 5.

fulfilment even of the lighter commands of the law, to the easy character of which the weighty words of the giver of the law bear testimony, as a curse is actually invoked on those who do not fulfil them; for it says: "Cursed is everyone that does not continue in all things that are written in the book of the law to do them."[1] But here on account of the superiority and excellence of the commandments it is said: "He that can receive it, let him receive it."[2] There the forcible compulsion of the lawgiver shows the easy character of the precepts; for he says: "I call heaven and earth to record against you this day, that if ye do not keep the commandments of the Lord your God ye shall perish from off the face of the earth."[3] Here the grandeur of sublime commands is shown by the very fact that He does not *order*, but *exhorts*, saying: "if thou wilt be perfect go" and do this or that. There Moses lays a burden that cannot be refused on those who are unwilling: here Paul meets with counsels those who are willing and eager for perfection. For that was not to be enjoined as a general charge, nor to be required, if I may so say, as a regular rule from all, which could not be secured by all, owing to its wonderful and lofty nature; but by counsels all are rather stimulated to grace, that those who are great may deservedly be crowned by the perfection of their virtues, while those who are small, and not able to come up to "the measure of the stature of the fulness of Christ,"[4] although they seem to be lost to sight and hidden as it were by the brightness of larger stars, may yet be free from the darkness of the curses which are in the law, and not adjudged to suffer present evils or visited with eternal punishment. Christ therefore does not constrain anyone, by the compulsion of a command, to those lofty heights of goodness, but stimulates them by the power of free will, and urges them on by wise counsels and the desire of perfection. For where there is a command, there is duty, and consequently punishment. But those who keep those things to which they are driven by the severity of the law established escape the punishment with which they were threatened, instead of obtaining rewards and a recompense.

CHAPTER VI.

How the grace of the gospel supports the weak so that they can obtain pardon, as it secures to the perfect the kingdom of God.

AND as the word of the gospel raises those that are strong to sublime and lofty heights,

so it suffers not the weak to be dragged down to the depths, for it secures to the perfect the fulness of blessing, and brings to those who are overcome through weakness pardon. For the law placed those who fulfilled its commands in a sort of middle state between what they deserved in either case, severing them from the condemnation due to transgressors, as it also kept them away from the glory of the perfect. But how wretched and miserable this is, you can see from comparing the state of this present life, in which it is considered a very poor thing for a man to sweat and labour only to avoid being regarded as guilty among good men, not also to be esteemed rich and honourable and renowned.

CHAPTER VII.

How it lies in our own power to choose whether to remain under the grace of the gospel or under the terror of the law.

WHEREFORE it lies today in our own power whether we choose to live under the grace of the gospel or under the terrors of the law: for each man must incline to one side or the other in accordance with the character of his actions, for either the grace of Christ welcomes those who go beyond the law, or else the law keeps its hold over the weaker ones as those who are its debtors and within its clutches. For one who is guilty as regards the precepts of the law will never be able to attain to the perfection of the gospel, even though he idly boasts that he is a Christian and freed by the Lord's grace: for we must not only regard as still under the law the man who refuses to fulfil what the law enjoins, but the man as well who is satisfied with the mere observance of what the law commands, and who never brings forth fruits worthy of his vocation and the grace of Christ, where it is not said: "Thou shalt offer to the Lord thy God thy tithes and firstfruits;" but: "Go and sell all that thou hast and give to the poor, and come follow Me;"[5] where, owing to the grandeur of perfection, to the request of the disciple there is not granted even the very short space of an hour in which to bury his father,[6] as the offices of human charity are outweighed by the virtue of Divine love.

CHAPTER VIII.

How Theonas exhorted his wife that she too should make her renunciation.

AND when he had heard this the blessed Theonas was fired with an uncontrollable

---

[1] Deut. xxvii. 26. [3] Deut. iv. 26.
[2] S. Matt. xix. 12. [4] Eph. iv. 13.

[5] Exod. xxii. 29; S. Matt. xix. 21. [6] Cf. S. Matt. viii. 21, *sq.*

desire for the perfection of the gospel, and, committed, as it were, the seed of the word, which he had received in a fruitful heart, to the deep and broken furrows of his bosom, as he was greatly humiliated and conscience-stricken because the old man had said not only that he had failed to attain to the perfection of the gospel, but also that he had scarcely fulfilled the commands of the law; since though he was accustomed every year to pay the tithes of his fruits as alms, yet he mourned that he had never even heard of the law of the firstfruits; and even if he had in the same way fulfilled this, he humbly confessed that still he would in the old man's view have been very far from the perfection of the gospel. And so he returned home sad and filled with that sorrow which worketh repentance unto salvation,[1] and of his own will and determination turns all his wife's care and anxiety of mind towards salvation; and began to stir her up to the same eager desire with which he himself had been inflamed, with the same sort of exhortations, and with tears day and night to urge her that together they might serve God in sanctity and chastity, telling her that their conversion to a better life ought not to be deferred because a vain hope in their youth would be no argument against the inevitableness of a sudden death, which carries off boys and youths and young persons equally with old men.

CHAPTER IX.

How he fled to a monastery when his wife would not consent.

AND when his wife was hard and would not consent to him as he constantly persisted with entreaties of this kind, but said that as she was in the flower of her age she could not altogether do without the solace of her husband, and further that supposing she was deserted by him and fell into sin, the guilt would rather be his who had broken the bonds of wedlock: to this he, when he had for a long while urged the condition of human nature (which being so weak and uncertain, it would be dangerous for it to be any longer mixed up with carnal desires and works), added the assertion that it was not right for anyone to cut himself off from that virtue to which he had learnt that he ought by all means to cleave, and that it was more dangerous to disregard goodness when discovered, than to fail to love it before it was discovered; further that he was already involved in the guilt of a fall if when he had discovered such grand and heavenly bless-

ings he had preferred earthly and mean ones. Further that the grandeur of perfection was open to every age and either sex, and that all the members of the Church were urged to scale the heights of heavenly goodness when the Apostle said: "So run that ye may obtain;"[2] nor should those who were ready and eager for it hang back because of the delays of the slow and dawdlers, as it is better for the sluggards to be urged on by those running before than for those who are doing their best to be hampered by the slothful. Further that he had determined and made up his mind to renounce the world and to die to the world that he might live to God, and that if he could not attain this happiness; viz., to pass with his wife into union with Christ, he would rather be saved even with the loss of one member, and enter into the kingdom of heaven as one maimed rather than be condemned with his body whole. But he also added and spoke as follows: If Moses suffered wives to be divorced for the hardness of their hearts, why should not Christ allow this for the desire of chastity, especially when the same Lord among those other affections; viz., for fathers and mothers and children (all due regard to which not only the law but He Himself also charged to be shown, yet for His name's sake and for the desire of perfection He decreed that they should not simply be disregarded but actually hated) — to these, I say, He joined also the mention of wives, saying: "And everyone that hath left house, or brethren or sisters or father or mother or wife or children for My name's sake, shall receive an hundredfold and shall inherit eternal life."[3] So far then is He from allowing anything to be set against that perfection which He is proclaiming, that He actually enjoins that the ties to father and mother should be broken and disregarded out of love for Him, though according to the Apostle it is the first commandment with promise; viz., "Honour thy father and thy mother, which is the first commandment with promise, that it may be well with thee and that thy days may be long upon earth."[4] And as the word of the gospel condemns those who break the chains of matrimony where there has been no sin of adultery, so it clearly promises a reward of an hundredfold to those who have cast off a carnal yoke out of love for Christ and the desire for chastity. Wherefore if it can be brought about that you may listen to reason and be turned together with me to this most desirable choice; viz., that we should together serve the Lord and escape the pains of hell, I will not refuse the affection of marriage,

---

[1] Cf. 2 Cor. vii. 10.

[2] 1 Cor. ix. 24. [3] S. Matt. xix. 29. [4] Eph. vi. 2, 3.

nay I will embrace it with a still greater love. For I acknowledge and honour my helpmeet assigned to me by the word of the Lord, and I do not refuse to be joined to her in an unbroken tie of love in Christ, nor do I separate from me what the Lord joined to me by the law of the original condition,[1] if only you yourself will be what your Maker meant you to be. But if you will not be a helpmeet, but prefer to make yourself a deceiver and an assistance not to me but to the adversary, and fancy that the sacrament of matrimony was granted to you for this reason that you may deprive yourself of this salvation which is offered to you, and also hold me back from following the Saviour as a disciple, then I will resolutely lay hold on the words which were uttered by the lips of Abbot John, or rather of Christ Himself, so that no carnal affection may be able to tear me away from spiritual blessings, for He says: "He that hateth not father and mother and children and brothers and sisters and wife and lands, yea and his own soul also, cannot be My disciple."[2] When then by these and such like words the woman's purpose was not moved and she persisted in the same obstinate hardness, If, said the blessed Theonas, I cannot drag you away from death, neither shall you separate me from Christ: but it is safer for me to be divorced from a human person than from God. And so by the aid of God's grace he at once set about the execution of his purpose and suffered not the ardour of his desire to grow cool through any delay. For at once he stripped himself of all his worldly goods, and fled to a monastery, where in a very short time he was so famous for the splendour of his sanctity and humility that when John of blessed memory departed this life to the Lord, and the holy Elias, a man who was no less great than his predecessor, had likewise died, Theonas was chosen by the judgment of all as the third to succeed them in the administration of the almsgiving.

CHAPTER X.

An explanation that we may not appear to recommend separation from wives.

But let no one imagine that we have invented this for the sake of encouraging divorce, as we not only in no way condemn marriage, but also, following the words of the Apostle, say: "Marriage is honourable in all, and the bed undefiled,"[3] but it was in order faithfully to show the reader the origin of the conversion by which this great man was dedicated to God. And I ask the reader kindly to allow that, whether he likes this or no, in either case I am free from blame, and to give the praise or blame for this act to its real author. But as for me, as I have not put forward an opinion of my own on this matter, but have given a simple narration of the history of the facts, it is fair that as I claim no praise from those who approve of what was done, so I should not be attacked by the hatred of those who disapprove of it. Let every man therefore, as we said, have his own opinion on the matter. But I advise him to restrain his censure in considering it, lest he come to fancy that he is more just and holy than the Divine judgment, whereby the signs even of Apostolic virtue were conferred upon him (viz., Theonas), not to mention the opinion of such great fathers by whom it is clear that his action was not only not blamed, but even so far praised that in the election to the office of almoner they preferred him to splendid and most excellent men. And I fancy that the judgment of so many spiritual men, uttered with God as its author, was not wrong, as it was, as was said above, confirmed by such wonderful signs.

CHAPTER XI.

An inquiry why in Egypt they do not fast during all the fifty days (of Easter) nor bend their knees in prayer.

But it is now time to follow out the plan of the promised discourse. So then when Abbot Theonas had come to visit us in our cell during Eastertide[4] after Evensong was over we sat for a little while on the ground and began diligently to consider why they were so very careful that no one should during the whole fifty days either bend his knees in prayer[5] or venture to fast till the ninth hour, and we made our inquiry the more earnestly because we had never seen this custom so carefully observed in the monasteries of Syria.

CHAPTER XII.

The answer on the nature of things good, bad, and indifferent.

To this Abbot Theonas thus began his reply. It is indeed right for us, even when we can-

---

[1] Cf. Gen. ii. 18.   [2] S. Luke xiv. 26.   [3] Heb. xiii. 4.

[4] Quinquagesima.
[5] The 20th Canon of the Council of Nicæa (A.D. 325) alludes to diversities of custom with regard to posture for prayer on Sundays and from Easter to Pentecost, and ordered that for the future prayer should be made standing at these times. Cassian's language in the text would seem to show that in his day the Canon in question, though kept in Egypt, was not strictly observed in Palestine, but that the ancient diversity of customs still to some extent prevailed.

not see the reason, to yield to the authority of the fathers and to a custom of our predecessors that has been continued through so many years down to our own time, and to observe it, as handed down from antiquity, with constant care and reverence. But since you want to know the reasons and grounds for this, receive in few words what we have heard as handed down by our Elders on this subject. But before we bring forward the authority of Holy Scripture, we will, if you please, say a little about the nature and character of the fast, that afterwards the authority of Holy Scripture may support our words. The Divine Wisdom has pointed out in Ecclesiastes that for everything, i.e., for all things happy or those which are considered unfortunate and unhappy, there is a right time: saying: "For all things there is a time, and a time for everything under the heaven. A time to bring forth and a time to die; a time to plant and a time to pull down what is planted; a time to kill and a time to heal; a time to destroy and a time to build; a time to weep and a time to laugh; a time to mourn and a time to dance; a time to cast away stones and a time to gather stones; a time to embrace and a time to refrain from embracing; a time to get and a time to lose; a time to keep and a time to send away; a time to scatter and a time to collect; a time to be silent and a time to speak; a time to love and a time to hate; a time for war and a time for peace;" and below: "For there is a time," it says, "for everything and for every deed."[1] None therefore of these things does it lay down as always good, but only when any of them are fittingly done and at the right time, so that these very things which at one time, when done at the right moment, turn out well, if they are ventured on at a wrong or unsuitable time, are found to be useless or harmful; only excepting those things which are in their own nature good or bad, and which cannot ever be made the opposite, as, e.g., justice, prudence, fortitude, temperance and the rest of the virtues, or on the other hand, those faults, the description of which cannot possibly be altered or fall under the other head. But those things which can sometimes turn out with either result, so that, in accordance with the character of those who use them, they are found to be either good or bad, these we consider to be not absolutely in their own natures useful or injurious, but only so in accordance with the mind of the doer, and the suitableness of the time.

CHAPTER XIII.

What kind of good fasting is.

WHEREFORE we must now inquire what we ought to hold about the state of fasting, whether we meant that it was good in the same sort of way as justice, prudence, fortitude and temperance, which cannot possibly be made anything else, or whether it is something indifferent which sometimes is useful when done, and may be sometimes omitted without condemnation; and which sometimes it is wrong to do, and sometimes laudable to omit. For if we hold fasting to be included in that list of virtues, so that abstinence from food is placed among those things which are good in themselves, then certainly the partaking of food will be bad and wrong. For whatever is the opposite of that which is in its own nature good, must certainly be held to be in its own nature bad. But this the authority of Holy Scripture does not allow to us to lay down. For if we fast with such thoughts and intentions, so as to think that we fall into sin by taking food, we shall not only gain no advantage by our abstinence but shall actually contract grievous guilt and fall into the sin of impiety, as the Apostle says: "Abstaining from meats which God has created to be received with thanksgiving by the faithful and those who know the truth. For every creature of God is good, and nothing to be refused if it is partaken of with thanksgiving." For "if a man thinks that a thing is common, to him it is common."[2] And therefore we never read that anyone is condemned simply for taking food, but only when something was joined with it or followed afterwards, for which he deserved condemnation.

CHAPTER XIV.

How fasting is not good in its own nature.

AND so that it is a thing indifferent is very clearly shown from this also; viz., because as it brings justification when observed, so it does not bring condemnation when it is broken in upon; unless perhaps the transgression of a command rather than the partaking of food brings punishment. But in the case of a thing that is good in its own nature, no time should be without it, in such a way as that a man may do without it, for if it ceases, the man who is careless about it is sure to fall into

---

[1] Eccl. iii. 1–8, 17.

[2] 1 Tim. iv. 3, 4; Rom. xiv. 14.

mischief. Nor again is any time given for what is bad in its own nature, because what is hurtful cannot help hurting, if it is indulged in, nor can it ever be made of a praiseworthy character. And further it is clear that these things, for which we see conditions and times appointed, and which sanctify, when observed without corrupting us when they are neglected, are things indifferent, as, e.g., marriage, agriculture, riches, retirement into the desert, vigils, reading and meditation on Holy Scripture and fasting itself, from which our discussion took its rise. All of which things the Divine precepts and the authority of Holy Scripture decreed should not be so incessantly aimed at, or so constantly observed, as for it to be wrong for them to be for a time intermitted. For anything that is absolutely commanded brings death if it be not fulfilled: but whatever things we are urged to rather than commanded, when done are useful, when left undone bring no punishment. And therefore in the case of all or some of these things our predecessors commanded us either to do them with consideration, or to observe them carefully with regard to the reason, place, manner, and time, because if any of them are done suitably, it is fit and convenient, but if incongruously, then it becomes foolish and hurtful. And if at the coming of a brother, in whose person he ought to refresh Christ with courtesy and to embrace him with a most kindly welcome, a man should choose to observe a strict fast, would he not rather be guilty of incivility than gain the praise or reward of devoutness? or if when the failure or weakness of the flesh requires the strength to be restored by the partaking of food, a man will not consent to relax the rigour of his abstinence, is he not to be regarded as a cruel murderer of his own body rather than as one who is careful for his salvation? So too when a festival season permits a suitable indulgence in food and a necessarily liberal repast, if a man will resolutely cling to the strict observance of a fast he must be considered as not religious so much as boorish and unreasonable. But to those men also will these things be found bad, who are on the lookout for the praises of men by their fasts, and by a foolish show of paleness gain credit for sanctity, of whom the word of the Gospel tells us that they have received their reward in this life, and whose fast the Lord execrates by the prophet. In whose person he first objected to himself and said: "Wherefore have we fasted and Thou hast not regarded: wherefore have we humbled our souls, and Thou hast not known it?" and then at once he answered and explained the reasons why

they did not deserve to be heard: "Behold," he says, "in the days of your fast your own will is found and you exact of all your debtors. Behold you fast for debates and strife, and strike with the fist wickedly. Do not fast as ye have done unto this day, to make your cry to be heard on high. Is this such a fast as I have chosen, for a man to afflict his soul for a day? Is it this, to wind his head about like a circle, and to spread sackcloth and ashes? Will ye call this a fast and a day acceptable to the Lord?" Then he proceeds to teach how the abstinence of one who fasts may become acceptable, and clearly lays down that fasting cannot be good of itself alone, but only when it has the following reasons which are added: "Is not this," he says, "the fast that I have chosen? Loose the bands of wickedness, undo the bundles that oppress, let them that are broken go free, and break asunder every burden. Deal thy bread to the hungry, and bring the needy and the harbourless into thine house: and when thou shalt see one naked cover him, and despise not thine own flesh. Then shalt thy light break forth as the morning and thy health shall speedily arise, and thy righteousness shall go before thy face and the glory of the Lord shall gather thee up. Then shalt thou call, and the Lord shall hear: thou shalt cry, and He shall say, Here am I."[1] You see then that fasting is certainly not considered by the Lord as a thing that is good in its own nature, because it becomes good and well-pleasing to God not by itself but by other works, and again from the surrounding circumstances it may be regarded as not merely vain but actually hateful, as the Lord says: "When they fast I will not hear their prayers."[2]

CHAPTER XV.

How a thing that is good in its own nature ought not to be done for the sake of some lesser good.

FOR we ought not to practise pity, patience and love, and the precepts of the virtues mentioned above, wherein there is what is good in its own nature, for the sake of fasting, but rather fasting for the sake of them. For our endeavour must be that those virtues which are really good may be gained by fasting, not that the practice of those virtues may lead to fasting as its end. For this then the affliction of the flesh is useful, for this the remedy of abstinence must be employed; viz., that by it we may succeed in attaining to love, wherein there is what is good without change,

----

[1] Isa. lviii. 3–9.   [2] Jer. xiv. 12.

and continually with no exception of time. For medicines, and the goldsmith's art, and the systems of other arts which there are in this world are not employed for the sake of the instruments which belong to the particular work; but rather the implements are prepared for the practice of the art. And as they are useful for those who understand them, so they are useless to those who are ignorant of the system of the art in question; and as they are a great help to those who rely on their aid for doing their work, so they cannot be of the smallest use to those who do not know for what purpose they were made, and are contented simply with the possession of them; because they make all their value consist in the mere having of them, and not in the performance of work. That then is in its own nature the best thing, for the sake of which things indifferent are done, but the very chiefest good is done not for the sake of anything else but because of its own intrinsic goodness.

CHAPTER XVI.

How what is good in its own nature can be distinguished from other things that are good.

AND this may be distinguished from those other things which we have termed indifferent, in these ways: if a thing is good in itself and not by reason of something else: if it is useful for its own sake, and not for the sake of something else: if it is unchangeably and at all times good, and always keeps its character and can never become anything different: if its removal or cessation cannot fail to produce the greatest harm: if that which is its opposite is in the same way evil in its own nature, and can never be turned into anything good. And these descriptions by which the nature of things that are good in themselves can be distinguished, cannot possibly be applied to fasting, for it is not good of itself, nor useful for its own sake because it is wisely used for the acquisition of purity of heart and body, that the pricks of the flesh being dulled the soul may be pacified and reconciled to its Creator, nor is it unchangeably and at all times good, because often we are not injured by its intermission, and indeed sometimes if it is unreasonably practised it becomes injurious. Nor is that which seems its opposite evil in its own nature, i.e., the partaking of food, which is naturally agreeable, which cannot be regarded as evil, unless intemperance and luxury or some other faults are the result; "For not that which entereth into the mouth, defileth a man, but that which cometh

out of the mouth, that defileth a man."[1] And so a man disparages what is good in its own nature, and does not treat it properly or without sin, if he does it not for its own sake but for the sake of something else, for everything else should be done for the sake of it, but it should be sought for its own sake alone.

CHAPTER XVII.

Of the reason for fasting and its value.

So then let us constantly remember this description of the character of fasting, and always aim at it with all the powers of the soul, in such a way as to recognize that then only is it suitable for us if in it we preserve regard for time, its character and degree, and this not so as to set the end of our hope upon it, but so that by it we may succeed in attaining to purity of heart and Apostolical love. Therefore from this it is clear that fasting, for which not only are there special seasons appointed at which it should be practised or relaxed, but conditions and rules also laid down, is not good in its own nature, but something indifferent. But those things which are either enjoined as good by the authority of a precept, or are forbidden as bad, are never subject to any exceptions of time in such a way that sometimes we should do what is forbidden or omit what is commanded. For there is no limit set to justice, patience, soberness, modesty, love, nor on the other hand is a licence ever granted for injustice, impatience, wrath, immodesty, envy, and pride.

CHAPTER XVIII.

How fasting is not always suitable.

WHEREFORE as we have premised this on the conditions of fasting, it seems well to subjoin the authority of Holy Scripture, by which it will be more clearly proved that fasting neither can nor should be always observed. In the Gospel when the Pharisees were fasting together with the disciples of John the Baptist, as the Apostles, as friends and companions of the heavenly Bridegroom, were not yet keeping the observance of a fast, the disciples of John (who thought that they acquired perfect righteousness by their fasts, as they were followers of that grand preacher of repentance who afforded a pattern to all the people by his own example, as he not only refused the differ-

---

[1] S. Matt. xv. 11.

ent kinds of food which are supplied for man's use, but actually altogether did without eating the bread which is common to all) complained to the Lord and said: "Why do we and the Pharisees fast oft but thy disciples fast not?" to whom the Lord in His reply plainly showed that fasting is not suitable or necessary at all times, when any festival season or opportunity for love intervenes and permits an indulgence in food, saying: "Can the children of the bridegroom mourn while the bridegroom is with them? But the days will come when the bridegroom shall be taken away from them; and then shall they fast;"[1] words which although they were spoken before the resurrection of His Body, yet specially point to the season of Eastertide, in which after His resurrection for forty days He ate with His disciples, and their joy in His daily Presence did not allow them to fast.

CHAPTER XIX.

A question why we break the fast all through Eastertide.

GERMANUS: Why then do we relax the rigour of our abstinence in our meals all through the fifty days, whereas Christ only remained with His disciples for forty days after His resurrection?

CHAPTER XX.

The answer.

YOUR pertinent question deserves to be told the perfect true reason. After the Ascension of our Saviour which took place on the fortieth day after His Resurrection, the apostles returned from the Mount of Olives, on which He had suffered them to see Him when He was returning to the Father, as the book of the Acts of the Apostles also testifies, and entered Jerusalem and are said to have waited ten days for the coming of the Holy Ghost, and when these were fulfilled on the fiftieth day they received Him with joy. And thus in this way the number of this festival was clearly made up, which as we read was figuratively foreshadowed also in the Old Testament, where when seven weeks were fulfilled the bread of the firstfruits was ordered to be offered by the priests to the Lord:[2] and this was indeed shown to be offered to the Lord by the preaching of the Apostles which they are said on that day to have addressed to the people; the true bread of the firstfruits, which

when produced from the instruction of a new doctrine, consecrated the firstfruits of the Jews as a Christian people to the Lord, five thousand men being filled with the gifts of the food. And therefore these ten days are to be kept with equal solemnity and joy as the previous forty. And the tradition about this festival, transmitted to us by Apostolic men, should be kept with the same uniformity. For therefore on those days they do not bow their knees in prayer, because the bending of the knees is a sign of penitence and mourning. Wherefore also during these days we observe in all things the same solemnities as on Sunday, on which day our predecessors taught that men ought not to fast nor to bow the knee, out of reverence for the Lord's Resurrection.

CHAPTER XXI.

A question whether the relaxation of the fast is not prejudicial to the chastity of the body.

GERMANUS: Can the flesh, attracted by the unwonted luxuries of so long a festival fail to produce something thorny from the incentives to sin although they have been cut down? or can the soul weighed down by the consumption of unaccustomed feasts fail to mitigate the rigour of its rule over its servant the body, especially when in our case our mature age can excite our subject members to a speedy revolt, if we venture to take our usual food in larger quantities, or unaccustomed food more freely than usual?

CHAPTER XXII.

The answer on the way to keep control over abstinence.

THEONAS: If we weigh everything that we do, by a reasonable judgment of the mind, and on the purity of our heart always consult not the opinions of other people but our own conscience, that interval for refreshment is sure not to interfere with our proper strictness, if only, as was said, our pure mind impartially considers the right limits of indulgence and abstinence, and fairly checks excess in either, and with real discrimination discerns whether the weight of the delicacies is a burden upon our spirits, or whether too much austerity in abstaining weighs down the other side, i.e., that of the body, and either depresses or raises that side which it sees to be raised or weighed down. For our Lord would have nothing done to His honour and glory without being tempered by judgment, for "the honour of a

---

[1] S. Matt. ix. 14, 15.　　[2] Cf. Deut. xvi. 9.

king loveth judgment,"[1] and therefore Solomon, the wisest of men, urges us not to let our judgment incline to either side, saying: "Honour God with thy righteous labours and offer to Him of the fruits of thy righteousness."[2] For we have residing in our conscience an uncorrupt and true judge who sometimes, when all are wrong, is the only person not deceived as to the state of our purity. And so with all care and pains we should preserve a constant purpose in our circumspect heart for fear lest if the judgment of our discretion goes wrong, we may be fired with the desire for an ill-considered abstinence, or allured by the wish for an excessive relaxation, and so weigh the substance of our strength in the tongue of an unfair balance; but we should place in one of the scales our purity of soul, and in the other our bodily strength, and weigh them both in the true judgment of conscience, so that we may not perversely incline the scale of fairness to either side, either to undue strictness or to excessive relaxation, from the preponderating desire for one or the other, and so have this said to us by reason of excessive strictness or relaxation: "If thou offerest rightly, but dost not divide rightly, hast thou not sinned?"[3] For those offerings of fasts, which we thoughtlessly extort by violently tearing our bowels, and fancy that we rightly offer to the Lord, these He execrates who "loves mercy and judgment," saying: "I the Lord love judgment, but I hate robbery in a burnt offering."[4] Those also who take the main part of their offerings, i.e., their offices and actions, to benefit the flesh for their own use, but leave the remains of them and a tiny portion for the Lord, these the Divine Word thus condemns as fraudulent workmen: "Cursed is he that doeth the work of the Lord fraudulently."[5] It is not then without reason that the Lord reproves him who thus deceives himself by unfair considerations, saying: "But vain are the children of men: the children of men are liars upon the balances that they may deceive."[6] And therefore the blessed Apostle warns us to keep hold of the reins of discretion and not to be attracted by excess and swerve to either side, saying: "Your reasonable service."[7] And the giver of the law similarly forbids the same thing, saying: "Let the balance be just and the weights equal, the bushel just and the sextarius equal,"[8] and Solomon also gives a like opinion on this matter: "Great and small weights and double measures are both unclean before the Lord, and one who uses them shall be hindered in his contrivances."[9] Further not only in the way in which we have said, but also in this must we strive not to have unfair weights in our hearts, nor double measures in the storehouse of our conscience, i.e., not to overwhelm those, to whom we are to preach the word of the Lord, with precepts that are too strict and heavier than we ourselves can bear, while we take for granted that for ourselves those things which have to do with the rule of strictness are to be softened by a freer allowance of relaxation. For when we do this, what is it but to weigh and measure the goods and fruits of the Lord's commands in a double weight and measure? For if we dispense them in one way to ourselves and in another to our brethren, we are rightly blamed by the Lord because we have unfair balances and double measures, in accordance with the saying of Solomon which tells us that "A double weight is an abomination to the Lord, and a deceitful balance is not good in His sight."[10] In this way also we plainly incur the guilt of using a deceitful weight and a double measure, if out of the desire for the praise of men, we make a show before the brethren of greater strictness than what we practice in private in our own cells, trying to appear more abstinent and holier in the sight of men than in the sight of God, an evil which we should not only avoid but actually loathe. But meanwhile as we have wandered some way from the question before us, let us return to the point from which we started.

CHAPTER XXIII.

Of the time and measure of refreshment.

So then we should keep the observance of the days mentioned in such a way that the relaxation allowed may be useful rather than harmful to the good of body and soul, because the joy of any festival cannot blunt the pricks of the flesh, nor can that fierce enemy of ours be pacified by regard for days. In order then that the observance of the customs appointed for festival seasons may be kept and that the most salutary rule of abstinence be not at all exceeded it is enough for us to allow the permitted relaxation to go so far, as for us out of regard for the festival season to take the food, which ought to be taken at the ninth hour, a little earlier; viz., at the sixth hour,

[1] Ps. xcviii. (xcix.) 4.
[2] Prov. iii. 9.
[3] Gen. iv. 7 (xxx.).
[4] Ps. xxxii. (xxxiii.) 5; Isa. lxi. 8.
[5] Jer. xlviii. 10.
[6] Ps. lxi. (lxii.) 10.
[7] Rom. xii. 1.
[8] Lev. xix. 36.
[9] Prov. xx. 10, 11.
[10] Ib. 23.

but with this condition, that the regular allowance and character of the food be not altered, for fear lest the purity of body and uprightness of soul which has been gained by the abstinence of Lent be lost by the relaxation of Easter-tide, and it profit us nothing to have acquired by our fast what a careless satiety causes us presently to lose, especially as the well-known cunning of our enemy assaults the stronghold of our purity then chiefly when he sees that our guard over it is somewhat relaxed at the celebration of some festival. Wherefore we must most vigilantly look out that the vigour of our soul be never enervated by seductive flatteries, and we lose not the purity of our chastity, gained, as was said, by the continuous efforts of Lent, by the repose and carelessness of Eastertide. And therefore no addition at all should be made to the quality or the quantity of the food, but even on the highest festivals we should similarly abstain from those foods, by abstinence from which we preserve our uprightness on common days, that the joy of the festival may not excite in us a most deadly conflict of carnal desires, and so be turned to grief, and put an end to that most excellent festival of the heart, which exults in the joy of purity; and after a brief show of carnal joy we begin to mourn our lost purity of heart with a lasting sorrow of repentance. Moreover we should strive that this warning of the prophetic exhortation may not be uttered against us to no purpose: "Celebrate, O Judah, thy festivals, and pay thy vows." [1] For if the occurrence of festival days does not interfere with the continuity of our abstinence, we shall continually enjoy spiritual festivals and so, when we cease from servile work, "there shall be month after month and Sabbath after Sabbath." [2]

CHAPTER XXIV.

A question on the different ways of keeping Lent.

GERMANUS: What is the reason why Lent is kept for six weeks, while in some countries a possibly more earnest care for religion seems to have added a seventh week as well, though neither number when you subtract Sunday and Saturday, gives the total of forty days? For only six and thirty days are included in these weeks. [3]

CHAPTER XXV.

The answer to the effect that the fast of Lent has reference to the tithe of the year.

THEONAS: Although the pious simplicity of some folks would put aside a question on this subject, yet because you are more scrupulous in your examination of those things which another would consider unworthy to be asked about, and want to know the whole truth of this observance of ours and the secret of it, you shall have a very clear reason for this also, that you may still more plainly be convinced that our predecessors taught nothing unreasonable. By the law of Moses the command propounded to all the people generally was this: "Thou shalt offer to the Lord thy God thy tithes and firstfruits." [4] And so, while we are commanded to offer tithes of our substance and all our fruits, it is much more needful for us to offer tithes of our life and ordinary employments and actions, which certainly is clearly arranged for in the calculation of Lent. For the tithe of the number of all the days included in the revolving circle of the year is thirty-six days and a half. But in seven weeks, if Sundays and Saturdays are subtracted, there remain thirty-five days assigned for fasting. But by the addition of Easter Eve when the Saturday's fast is prolonged to the cock-crowing at the dawn of Easter Day, not only is the number of thirty-six days made up, but in regard to the tithe of the five days which seemed to be over, if the bit of the night which was added be taken into account nothing will be wanting to the whole sum.

CHAPTER XXVI.

How we ought also to offer our firstfruits to the Lord.

BUT what shall I say of the firstfruits which surely are given daily by all who serve Christ

---

[1] Nah. i. 15.   [2] Isa. lxvi. 23.
[3] On the different uses in regard to the Lenten fast Socrates (H. E. V. xxii.) writes as follows: "Those at Rome fast three successive weeks before Easter, excepting Saturdays and Sundays. The Illyrians, Achaians, and Alexandrians observe a fast of six weeks, which they call the forty days' fast. Others commencing their fast from the seventh week before Easter, and fasting for fifteen days by intervals, yet call that time the forty days' fast." There are difficulties in the way of accepting the statement about the custom at Rome (see below), but the great variety of customs is fully confirmed by Sozomen (H. E. VII. xix.): "In some churches the time before Easter, which is called Quadragesima, and is devoted by the people to fasting, is made to consist of six weeks: and this is the case in Illyria, and the western regions, in Libya, throughout Egypt, and in Palestine: whereas it is made to comprise seven weeks at Constantinople, and in the neighbouring provinces as far as Phœnicia. In some churches the people fast three alternate weeks during the space of six or seven weeks; whereas in others they fast continuously during the three weeks immediately preceding the festival." The statement here made with regard to the West is true except as regards Milan, where Saturday was kept (as in the East) as a festival: while for the Constantinopolitan practice Chrysostom (Hom. xi. in Gen. § 2) confirms what Sozomen says: while Cassian's language in the text bears witness to the fact that both Egypt and Palestine agreed with the Roman practice. In either case, whether the fast began seven or six weeks before Easter, the number of days observed in the fast was the same; Saturdays (with the exception of Easter Eve which was always regarded as a fast) being excluded in the former case, while they were all included in the latter. Cf. below, c. xxvi.   [4] Exod. xxii. 29.

faithfully? For when men waking from sleep and arising with renewed activity after their rest, before they take in any impulse or thought in their heart, or admit any recollection or consideration of business consecrate their first and earliest thoughts as divine offerings, what are they doing indeed but rendering the firstfruits of their produce through the High Priest Jesus Christ for the enjoyment of this life and a figure of the daily resurrection? And also when roused from sleep in the same way they offer to God a sacrifice of joy and invoke Him with the first motion of their tongue and celebrate His name and praise, and throwing open, the first thing, the door of their lips to sing hymns to Him they offer to God the offices of their mouth; and to Him also in the same way they bring the earliest offerings of their hands and steps, when they rise from bed and stand in prayer and before they use the services of their limbs for their own purposes, take to themselves nothing of their services, but for His glory advance their steps, and set them in His praise and so render the first fruits of all their movements by stretching forth the hands, bending the knees, and prostrating the whole body. For in no other way can we fulfil that of which we sing in the Psalm: "I prevented the dawning of the day and cried;" and: "Mine eyes to Thee have prevented the morning that I might meditate on Thy words;" and: "In the morning shall my prayer prevent Thee;"[1] unless after our rest in sleep when, as we said above, we are restored as from darkness and death to this light, we have the courage not to begin by taking any of all the services both of mind and body for our own uses. For there is no other morning which the prophet "prevented," or which in the same way we ought to prevent, except either ourselves, i. e., our occupations and feelings and earthly cares, without which we cannot exist — or the most subtle suggestions of the adversary, which he tries to suggest to us, while still resting and overcome with sleep, by the phantoms of vain dreams, with which, when we presently awake, he will fill our minds and occupy us, that he may be the first to seize and carry off the spoils of our firstfruits. Wherefore we must take the utmost care (if we want to fulfil in act the meaning of the above quoted verse) that an anxious watchfulness takes regard of our first and earliest morning thoughts, that they may not be defiled beforehand being hastily taken possession of by our jealous adversary, and thus he may make our firstfruits to be rejected

by the Lord as worthless and common. And if he is not prevented by us with watchful circumspection of mind, he will not lay aside his habit of miserably anticipating us nor cease day after day to prevent us by his wiles. And therefore if we want to offer firstfruits that are acceptable and well pleasing to God of the fruits of our mind, we ought to spend no ordinary care to keep all the senses of our body, especially during the hours of the morning, as a sacred holocaust to the Lord pure and undefiled in all things. And this kind of devotion many even of those who live in the world observe with the utmost care, as they rise before it is light or very early, and do not at all mix in the ordinary and necessary business of this world before hastening to church and striving to consecrate in the sight of God the firstfruits of all their actions and doings.

CHAPTER XXVII.

Why Lent is kept by very many with a different number of days.

FURTHER, as for what you say; viz., that in some countries Lent is kept in different ways, i. e., for six or seven weeks, it is but one system and the same manner of the fast that is preserved by the different observance of the weeks. For those who think one ought to fast also on the Saturday, have determined on the observance of six weeks. They therefore fast for six days out of the seven, and this being six times repeated makes up the six and thirty days. It is therefore, as we said, but one system and the same manner of the fast, although there seems to be a difference in the number of the weeks.

CHAPTER XXVIII.

Why it is called Quadragesima, when the fast is only kept for thirty-six days.

BUT further, as man's carelessness dropped out of sight the reason of this, this season when, as was said, the tithes of the year are offered by fasts for thirty-six days and a half, was called Quadragesima,[2] a name which per-

---

[1] Ps. cxviii. (cxix.) 147, 148; lxxxvii. (lxxxviii.) 14.

[2] Cassian here gives three suggestions why the fast of thirty-six days' duration was called Quadragesima. (1) As roughly corresponding to the forty days fast of Moses, Elijah, and the Lord Himself; (2) because "forty" is the number associated with a time of probation in Scripture; and (3) because of the analogy of a legal tribute of "Quadragesima" paid to the Sovereign. It is certainly a curious and difficult question why the name Quadragesima should have been so universally applied to the fast, when there is no evidence of its having been kept for forty days till sometime after the date of Gregory the Great, when Ash Wednesday and the three following days were prefixed to the six weeks expressly for the purpose of making up the number forty. The *name* however, had as we

haps they thought ought to be given to it for this reason; viz., that it is said that Moses and Elijah and our Lord Jesus Christ Himself fasted for forty days. To the mystery of which number are not unsuitably applied those forty years in which Israel dwelt in the wilderness, and in like manner the forty stations which they are said to have passed through with a mystic meaning. Or perhaps the tithe was properly given the name of Quadragesima from the use of the custom-house. For so that state tax is commonly called, from which the same proportion of the increment is assigned for the king's use, as the legal tribute of Quadragesima, which is required of us by the King of all the ages for the use of our life. At any rate, although this has nothing to do with the question raised, yet I think that I ought not to omit the fact that very often our elders used to testify that especially on these days the whole body of monks was attacked according to the ancient custom of the people opposed to them, and was more vehemently urged to forsake their homes, for this reason, because in accordance with this figure, whereby the Egyptians formerly oppressed the children of Israel with grievous afflictions, so now also the spiritual Egyptians try to bow down the true Israel, i.e., the monastic folk, with hard and vile tasks, lest by means of that peace which is dear to God, we should forsake the land of Egypt, and for our good cross to the desert of virtues, so that Pharaoh rages against us and says: "They are idle and therefore they cry saying: Let us go and sacrifice to the Lord our God. Let them be oppressed with labours, and be harassed in their works, and they shall not be harassed by vain words." [1] For certainly their folly imagines that the holy sacrifice of the Lord, which is only offered in the desert of a pure heart, is the height of folly, for "religion is an abomination to a sinner." [2]

CHAPTER XXIX.

How those who are perfect go beyond the fixed rule of Lent.

By this law of Lent then the man who is upright and perfect is not restrained nor is he content with merely submitting to that paltry rule which the heads of the church have estab-

lished for those who all the year round are involved in pleasure or business, that they may be bound by this legal requirement and forced at any rate during these days to find time for the Lord, and dedicate to Him the tithe of the days of their life, all of which they would have consumed as their profits. But the righteous, for whom the law is not appointed, and who devote to spiritual duties not a small part; viz., the tenth, but the whole time of their life, because they are free from the burden of tithes according to law, for this reason, if any worthy and pious occasion happening to them constrains them, are ready to relax their station fast [3] without any hesitation. For in their case it is no paltry tithe that is diminished, as they offer all that they have to the Lord equally with themselves. And this certainly a man could not do without being guilty of a grievous wrong, who, offering nothing of his own free will to God, is forced to pay his tithes by the stern compulsion of the law which takes no excuse. Wherefore it is clearly established that the servant of the law cannot be perfect, who only shuns those things which are forbidden and does those things which are commanded, but that those are really perfect who do not take advantage even of those things which the law allows. And in this way, though it is said of the Mosaic law that "the law brought nothing to perfection," [4] we read that some of the saints in the Old Testament were perfect because they went beyond the commands of the law and lived under the perfection of the Gospel: "Knowing that the law is not appointed for the righteous but for the unrighteous and disobedient, for the ungodly and sinners, for the wicked and defiled, etc." [5]

CHAPTER XXX.

Of the origin and beginning of Lent.

Howbeit you should know that as long as the primitive church retained its perfection unbroken, this observance of Lent did not exist. For they were not bound by the requirements of this order, or by any legal enactments, nor confined in the very narrow limits of the fast, as the fast embraced equally the whole year round. But when the multitude of believers began day by day to decline from that apostolic fervour, and to look after their own wealth, and not to portion it out for the good of all the faithful in accordance with

see from Socrates, Sozomen, Cassian himself, and many other writers, existed long before this; and on the whole it appears probable that it originated in none of the reasons given above by Cassian, but that in the first instance it was connected "with the period during which our Lord yielded to the power of death, which was estimated at *forty hours*; viz., from noon on Friday till 4 A.M. on Sunday." See Dictionary of Christian Antiquities, Vol. ii. p. 973; and cf. Irenæus Ep. ad Victor. in Euseb. V. xxiv.; and Tertullian De Orat. c. 18; and De Jejuniis c. ii. and xiii.
[1] Exod. v. 8, 9.   [2] Ecclus. l. 24.

[3] *Statio.* Cf Note on the Institutes V. xxiv.
[4] Heb. vii. 19.   [5] i Tim. i. 9, 10.

the arrangement of the apostles, but having an eye to their own private expenses, tried not only to keep it but actually to increase it, not content with following the example of Ananias and Sapphira, then it seemed good to all the priests that men who were hampered by worldly cares, and almost ignorant, if I may say so, of abstinence and contrition, should be recalled to the pious duty by a fast canonically enjoined, and be constrained by the necessity of paying the legal tithes, as this certainly would be good for the weak brethren and could not do any harm to the perfect who were living under the grace of the gospel and by their voluntary devotion going beyond the law, so as to succeed in attaining to the blessedness which the Apostle speaks of: "For sin shall not have dominion over you; for ye are not under the law but under grace." [1] For of a truth sin cannot exercise dominion over one who lives faithfully under the liberty of grace.

CHAPTER XXXI.

A question, how we ought to understand the Apostle's words: "Sin shall not have dominion over you."

GERMANUS: Because this saying of the Apostle, which promises freedom from care not only to monks but to all Christians in general, cannot lead us wrong, it seems to us somewhat obscure. For whereas he maintains that all those who believe the gospel are at liberty and free from the yoke and dominion of sin, how is it that the dominion of sin holds vigorous sway over almost all the baptized, in accordance with the Lord's words, where He says: "Every one that doeth sin is the servant of sin"? [2]

CHAPTER XXXII.

The answer on the difference between grace and the commands of the law.

THEONAS: Your inquiry once more raises before us a question of no small extent. The explanation of which though I know that it cannot be taught to or understood by the inexperienced, yet as far as I can, I will try to set forth in words and briefly to explain, if only your minds will follow up and act upon what we say. For whatever is known not by teaching but by experience, just as it cannot be taught by one without experience, so neither can it be grasped or taken in by the mind of

one who has not laid the foundation by a similar study and training. And therefore I think it necessary for us first to inquire somewhat carefully what is the purpose or meaning of the law, and what is the system and perfection of grace, that from this we may succeed in understanding the dominion of sin and how to drive it out. And so the law chiefly commands men to seek the bonds of wedlock, saying: "Blessed is he that hath seed in Sion and an household in Jerusalem;" [3] and: "Cursed is the barren that hath not borne." [4] On the other hand grace invites us to the purity of perpetual chastity, and the undefiled state of blessed virginity, saying: "Blessed are the barren, and the breasts which have not given suck;" and: "he that hateth not father and mother and wife cannot be my disciple;" and this of the Apostle: "It remaineth that they that have wives be as though they had them not." [5] The law says: "Thou shalt not delay to offer thy tithes and firstfruits ;" grace says: "If thou wilt be perfect, go and sell all that thou hast and give to the poor." [6] The law forbids not retaliation for wrongs and vengeance for injuries, saying: "An eye for an eye and a tooth for a tooth." Grace would have our patience proved by the injuries and blows offered to us being redoubled, and bids us be ready to endure twice as much damage; saying: "If a man strike thee on one cheek, offer him the other also; and to him who will contend with thee at the law and take away thy coat, give him thy cloak also." [7] The one decrees that we should hate our enemies, the other that we should love them so that it holds that even for them we ought always to pray to God.

CHAPTER XXXIII.

Of the fact that the precepts of the gospel are milder than those of the law.

WHOEVER therefore climbs this height of evangelical perfection, is at once raised by the merits of such virtue above every law, and disregarding as trivial all that is commanded by Moses, recognizes that he is only subject to the grace of the Saviour, by whose aid he knows that he attained to that most exalted condition. Therefore sin has no dominion over him, "because the love of God, which is shed abroad in our hearts by the Holy Ghost which is given to us," [8] shuts out all

---

[1] Rom. vi. 14. [2] S. John viii. 34.

[3] Isa. xxxi. 9 (lxx.). [4] Cf. Job xxiv. 21.
[5] S. Luke xxiii. 29; xiv. 26; 1 Cor. vii. 29.
[6] Exod. xxii. 29; S. Matt. xix. 21.
[7] Exod. xxi. 24; S. Matt. v. 39, 40. [8] Rom. v. 5.

care for everything else, and can neither desire what is forbidden, or disregard what is commanded, as its whole aim and all its desire is ever fixed on divine love, and to such an extent is it not caught by the delights of worthless things, that it actually does not take advantage of those things which are permitted. But under the law, where lawful marriages are observed, although the rovings of wantonness are restrained, and bound down to one woman alone, yet the pricks of carnal lust cannot help being vigorous; and it is hard for the fire, for which fuel is expressly supplied, to be thus shut in within prearranged limits, so as not to spread further and burn up anything it touches. As even if this objection occurs to it that it is not allowed to be kindled beyond these limits, yet even while it is kept in check, it is on fire because the will itself is in fault, and its habit of carnal intercourse hurries it into too speedy excesses of adultery. But those whom the grace of the Saviour has fired with the holy love of chastity, so consume all the thorns of carnal desires in the fire of the Lord's love, that no dying embers of sin interfere with the coldness of their purity. The servants of the law then from the use of lawful things fall away to unlawful; the partakers of grace while they disregard lawful things know nothing of unlawful ones. But as sin is alive in one who loves marriage, so is it also in one who is satisfied with merely paying his tithes and firstfruits. For, while he is dawdling or careless, he is sure to sin in regard to either their quality or quantity, or the daily distribution of them. For as he is commanded unweariedly to minister to those in want of what is his, although he may dispense it with the fullest faith and devotion, yet it is hard for him not to fall often into the snares of sin. But over those who have not set at naught the counsel of the Lord, but who, disposing of all their property to the poor, take up their cross and follow the bestower of grace, sin can have no dominion. For no faithless anxiety for getting food will annoy him who piously distributes and disperses his wealth already consecrated to Christ and no longer regarded as his own; nor will any grudging hesitation take away from the cheerfulness of his almsgiving, because without any thought of his own needs or fear of his own food running short he is distributing what has once for all been completely offered to God, and is no longer regarded as his own, as he is sure that when he has succeeded in stripping himself as he desires, he will be fed by God much more than the birds of the air. On the other hand he who retains his goods

of this world, or, bound by the rules of the old law, distributes the tithe of his produce, and his firstfruits, or a portion of his income, although he may to a considerable degree quench the fire of his sins by this dew of almsgiving, yet, however generously he gives away his wealth, it is impossible for him altogether to rid himself of the dominion of sin, unless perhaps by the grace of the Saviour, together with his substance he gets rid of all love of possessing. In the same way he cannot fail to be subject to the bloody sway of sin, whoever chooses to pull out, as the law commands, an eye for an eye, a tooth for a tooth, or to hate his enemy, for while he desires by retaliation in exchange to avenge an injury done to himself, and while he cherishes bitter hatred against an enemy, he is sure always to be inflamed with the passion of anger and rage. But whoever lives under the light of the grace of the gospel, and overcomes evil by not resisting it, but by bearing it, and does not hesitate of his own free will to give to one who smites his right cheek, the other also, and to one who wants to raise a lawsuit against him for his coat, gives his cloak also, and who loves his enemies, and prays for those who slander him, this man has broken the yoke of sin and burst its chains. For he is not living under the law, which does not destroy the seeds of sin (whence not without reason the Apostle says of it: "There is a setting aside of the former commandment because of the weakness and unprofitableness thereof: for the law brought nothing to perfection;" and the Lord says by the prophet: "And I gave them commands that were not good, and ordinances, whereby they could not live"[1]), but under grace which does not merely lop off the boughs of wickedness, but actually tears up the very roots of an evil will.

CHAPTER XXXIV.

How a man can be shown to be under grace.

WHOEVER then strives to reach the perfection of evangelical teaching, this man living under grace is not oppressed by the dominion of sin, for to be under grace is to do those things which grace commands. But whoever will not submit himself to the complete requirements of evangelical perfection, must not remain ignorant that, although he seems to be baptized and to be a monk, yet he is not under grace, but is still shackled by the chains of the law, and weighed down by the burden of sin. For it is the aim of Him, who by the

---

[1] Heb. vii. 18, 19; Ezek. xx. 25.

grace of adoption accepts all those by whom He has been received, not to destroy but to build upon, not to abolish but to fulfil the Mosaic requirements. But some knowing nothing about this, and disregarding the splendid counsels and exhortations of Christ, are so emancipated by the carelessness of a freedom too hastily assumed, that they not only fail to carry out the commands of Christ as if they were too hard, but actually scorn as antiquated, the commands given to them as beginners and children by the law of Moses, saying in this dangerous freedom of theirs that which the Apostle execrates: "We have sinned, because we are not under the law but under grace."[1] He then who is neither under grace, because he has never climbed the heights of the Lord's teaching, nor under the law, because he has not accepted even those small commands of the law, this man, ground down beneath a twofold rule of sin, fancies that he has received the grace of Christ, simply and solely for this, that by this dangerous liberty of his he may make himself none of His, and falls into that state, which the Apostle Peter warns us to avoid, saying: "Act as free, and not having your liberty as a cloak of wickedness." The blessed Apostle Paul also says: "For ye, brethren, were called to liberty," i.e., that ye might be free from the dominion of sin, "only use not your liberty for an occasion of the flesh,"[2] i.e., believe that the doing away with the commands of the law is a licence to sin. But this liberty, the Apostle Paul teaches us is nowhere but where the Lord is dwelling, for he says: "The Lord is the Spirit, but where the Spirit of the Lord is there is liberty."[3] Wherefore I know not whether I could express and explain the meaning of the blessed Apostle, as those know how, who have experience; one thing I do know, that it is very clearly revealed even without anyone's explanation to all those who have perfectly acquired πρακτική, i.e., practical training. For they will need no effort to understand in discussion what they have already learnt by practice.

CHAPTER XXXV.

A question, why sometimes when we are fasting more strictly than usual, we are troubled by carnal desires more keenly than usual.

GERMANUS: You have very clearly explained a most difficult question, and one which, as we think, is unknown to many. Wherefore we pray you to add this also for our good, and

carefully to expound why sometimes when we are fasting more strictly than usual, and are exhausted and worn out, severer bodily struggles are excited. For often on waking from sleep, when we have discovered that we have been defiled[4] we are so dejected in heart that we do not even venture faithfully to rise even for prayer.

CHAPTER XXXVI.

The answer, telling that this question should be reserved for a future Conference.

THEONAS: Your zeal indeed, whereby you desire to reach the way of perfection, not for a moment only but fully and perfectly, urges us to continue this discussion unweariedly. For you are anxiously inquiring not about external chastity or outward circumcision, but about that which is secret, as you know that complete perfection does not consist in this visible continence of the flesh which can be attained either by constraint, or by hypocrisy even by unbelievers, but in that voluntary and invisible purity of heart, which the blessed Apostle describes as follows: "For he is not a Jew which is so outwardly, nor is that circumcision which is outward in the flesh, but he is a Jew which is one inwardly, and the circumcision is that of the heart, in the spirit not in the letter, whose praise is not of men but of God,"[5] who alone searches the secrets of the heart. But because it is not possible for your wish to be fully satisfied (as the short space of the night that is left is not enough for the investigation of this most difficult question,) I think it well to postpone it for a while. For these matters, as they should be propounded by us quietly and with an heart entirely free from all bustling thoughts, so should they be received into your minds; for just as the inquiry ought to be undertaken for the sake of our common purity, so they cannot be learnt or acquired by one who is without the gift of uprightness. For we do not ask what arguments of empty words, but what the inward faith of the conscience and the greater force of truth can persuade. And therefore with regard to the knowledge and teaching of this purification nothing can be brought forward except by one who has had experience of it, nor can anything be committed except to one who is a most eager and very earnest lover of the truth itself, who does not hope to attain it by asking questions with mere vain words, but by striving with all his might and main, with no wish for useless chattering but with the desire to purify himself internally.

---

[1] Rom. vi. 15. [2] 1 Pet. ii. 16; Gal. v. 13. [3] 2 Cor. iii. 17.

[4] Cum deprehenderimus nos sordidi liquoris contagius pertulisse.
[5] Rom. ii. 28, 29.

XXII.

THE SECOND CONFERENCE OF ABBOT THEONAS.

ON NOCTURNAL ILLUSIONS.

This Conference is omitted.

XXIII.

THE THIRD CONFERENCE OF ABBOT THEONAS.

ON SINLESSNESS.

CHAPTER I.

Discourse of Abbot Theonas on the Apostle's words : " For I
do not the good which I would."

AT the return of light therefore, as the old
man was forced by our intense urgency to investigate the depths of the Apostle's subject,
he spoke as follows: As for the passages by
which you try to prove that the Apostle Paul
spoke not in his own person but in that of
sinners: "For I do not the good that I would,
but the evil which I hate, that I do;" or
this: "But if I do that which I would not, it
is no longer I that do it but sin that dwelleth
in me;" or what follows: "For I delight in
the law of God after the inner man, but I see
another law in my members opposing the law
of my mind, and bringing me into captivity
to the law of sin which is in my members;"[1]
these passages on the contrary plainly show
that they cannot possibly fit the person of
sinners, but that what is said can only apply
to those that are perfect, and that it only suits
the chastity of those who follow the good
example of the Apostles. Else how could
these words apply to the person of sinners:
"For I do not the good which I would, but
the evil which I hate that I do"? or even
this: "But if I do what I would not it is no
longer I that do it but sin that dwelleth in
me"? For what sinner defiles himself unwil-

lingly by adulteries and fornication? Who
against his will prepares plots against his
neighbour? Who is driven by unavoidable
necessity to oppress a man by false witness or
cheat him by theft, or covet the goods of
another or shed his blood? Nay rather, as
Scripture says, "Mankind is diligently inclined to wickedness from his youth."[2] For
to such an extent are all inflamed by the love
of sin and desire to carry out what they like,
that they actually look out with watchful care
for an opportunity of committing wickedness
and are afraid of being too slow to enjoy
their lusts, and glory in their shame and the
mass of their crimes, as the Apostle says in
censure,[3] and seek credit for themselves out
of their own confusion, of whom also the
prophet Jeremiah maintains that they commit
their flagitious crimes not only not unwillingly nor with ease of heart and body, but
with laborious efforts to such an extent that
they come to toil to carry them out, so that
they are prevented even by the hindrance of
arduous difficulty from their deadly quest of
sin; as he says: "They have laboured to do
wickedly."[4] Who also will say that this
applies to sinners: "And so with the mind I
myself serve the law of God, but with the
flesh the law of sin," as it is plain that they
serve God neither with the mind nor the
flesh? Or how can those who sin with the
body serve God with the mind, when the flesh

---

[1] Rom. vii. 18, *sq.*   [2] Gen. viii. 21.   [3] Cf. Phil. iii. 19.   [4] Jer. ix. 5.

receives the incitement to sin from the heart, and the Creator of either nature Himself declares that the fount and spring of sin flows from the latter, saying: "From the heart proceed evil thoughts, adulteries, fornications, thefts, false witness, etc."[1] Wherefore it is clearly shown that this cannot in any way be taken of the person of sinners, who not only do not hate, but actually love what is evil and are so far from serving God with either the mind or the flesh that they sin with the mind before they do with the flesh, and before they carry out the pleasures of the body are overcome by sin in their mind and thoughts.

CHAPTER II.

How the Apostle completed many good actions.

IT remains therefore for us to measure its meaning and drift from the inmost feelings of the speaker, and to discuss what the blessed Apostle called good, and what he pronounced by comparison evil, not by the bare meaning of the words, but with the same insight which he showed, and to investigate his meaning with due regard to the worth and goodness of the speaker. For then we shall be able to understand the words, which were uttered by God's inspiration, in accordance with his purpose and wish, when we weigh the position and character of those by whom they were spoken, and are ourselves clothed with the same feelings (not in words but by experience), in accordance with the character of which most certainly all the thoughts are conceived and opinions uttered. Wherefore let us carefully consider what was in the main that good which the Apostle could not do when he would. For we know that there are many good things which we cannot deny that the blessed Apostle and all men as good as he either have by nature, or acquire by grace. For chastity is good, continence is praiseworthy, prudence is to be admired, kindness is liberal, sobriety is careful, temperance is modest, pity is kind, justice is holy: all of which we cannot doubt existed fully and in perfection in the Apostle Paul and his companions, so that they taught religion by the lesson of their virtues rather than their words. What if they were always consumed with the constant care of all the churches and watchful anxiety? How great a good is this pity, what perfection it is to burn for them that are offended, to be weak with the weak![2] If then the Apostle abounded with such good things, we cannot recognize what that good was, in the perfection of which the Apostle was lacking, unless we have advanced to that state of mind in which he was speaking. And so all those virtues which we say that he possessed, though they are like most splendid and precious gems, yet when they are compared with that most beautiful and unique pearl which the merchant in the gospel sought and wanted to acquire by selling all that he possessed, so does their value seem poor and trifling, so that if they are without hesitation got rid of, the possession of one good thing alone will enrich the man who sells countless good things.

CHAPTER III.

What is really the good which the Apostle testifies that he could not perform.

WHAT then is that one thing which is so incomparably above those great and innumerable good things, that, while they are all scorned and rejected, it alone should be acquired? Doubtless it is that truly good part, the grand and lasting character of which is thus described by the Lord, when Mary disregarded the duties of hospitality and courtesy and chose it: "Martha, Martha, thou art careful and troubled about many things: but there is but need of but few things or even of one only. Mary hath chosen the good part which shall not be taken away from her."[3] Contemplation then, i.e., meditation on God, is the one thing, the value of which all the merits of our righteous acts, all our aims at virtue, come short of. And all those things which we said existed in the Apostle Paul, were not only good and useful, but even great and splendid. But as, for example, the metal of alloy which is considered of some use and worth, becomes worthless when silver is taken into account, and again the value of silver disappears in comparison with gold, and gold itself is disregarded when compared with precious stones, and yet a quantity of precious stones however splendid are outdone by the brightness of a single pearl, so all those merits of holiness, although they are not merely good and useful for the present life, but also secure the gift of eternity, yet if they are compared with the merit of Divine contemplation, will be considered trifling and so to speak, fit to be sold. And to support this illustration by the authority of Scripture, does not Scripture declare of all things in general which were created by God, and say: "And behold everything that God had made was very good;" and again: "And things that

---

[1] S. Matt. xv. 19.　　　[2] Cf. 2 Cor. xi. 29.　　　[3] S. Luke x. 41, 42. Cf. the note on I. viii.

God hath made are all good in their season"?[1] These things then which in the present time are termed not simply and solely good, but emphatically "very good" (for they are really convenient for us while living in this world, either for purposes of life, or for remedies for the body, or by reason of some unknown usefulness, or else they are indeed "very good," because they enable us "to see the invisible things of God from the creatures of the world, being understood by the things that are made, even His eternal power and Godhead,"[2] from this great and orderly arrangement of the fabric of the world; and to contemplate them from the existence of everything in it), yet none of these things will keep the name of good if they are regarded in the light of that world to come, where no variation of good things, and no loss of true blessedness need be feared. The bliss of which world is thus described: "The light of the moon shall be as the light of the sun, and the light of the sun shall be sevenfold as the light of seven days."[3] These things then which are great and wondrous to be gazed on, and marvellous, will at once appear as vanity if they are compared with the future promises from faith; as David says: "They all shall wax old as a garment, and as a vesture shall Thou change them, and they shall be changed. But Thou art the same, and Thy years shall not fail."[4] Because then there is nothing of itself enduring, nothing unchangeable, nothing good but Deity alone, while every creature, to obtain the blessing of eternity and immutability, aims at this not by its own nature but by participation of its Creator, and His grace, they cannot maintain their character for goodness when compared with their Creator.

CHAPTER IV.

How man's goodness and righteousness are not good if compared with the goodness and righteousness of God.

But if we want also to establish the force of this opinion by still clearer proofs, is it not the case that while we read of many things as called good in the gospel, as a good tree, and good treasure, and a good man, and a good servant, for He says: "A good tree cannot bring forth evil fruit;" and: "a good man out of the good treasure of his heart brings forth good things;" and: "Well done, good and faithful servant;"[5] and certainly there can be no doubt that none of these are good in themselves, yet if we take into consideration the goodness of God, none of them will be called good, as the Lord says: "None is good save God alone"?[6] In whose sight even the apostles themselves, who in the excellence of their calling in many ways went beyond the goodness of mankind, are said to be evil, as the Lord thus speaks to them: "If ye then being evil know how to give good gifts to your children, how much more shall your Father which is in heaven give good things to them that ask Him."[7] Finally as our goodness turns to badness in the eyes of the Highest so also our righteousness when set against the Divine righteousness is considered like a menstruous cloth, as Isaiah the prophet says: "All your righteousness is like a menstruous cloth."[8] And to produce something still plainer, even the vital precepts of the law itself, which are said to have been "given by angels by the the hand of a mediator," and of which the same Apostle says: "So the law indeed is holy and the commandment is holy and just and good,"[9] when they are compared with the perfection of the gospel are pronounced anything but good by the Divine oracle: for He says: "And I gave them precepts that were not good, and ordinances whereby they should not live in them."[10] The Apostle also affirms that the glory of the law is so dimmed by the light of the New Testament that he declares that in comparison with the splendour of the gospel it is not to be considered glorious, saying: "For even that which was glorious was not glorified by reason of the glory that excelleth."[11] And Scripture keeps up this comparison on the other side also, i.e., in weighing the merits of sinners, so that in comparison with the wicked it justifies those who have sinned less, saying: "Sodom is justified above thee;" and again: "For what hath thy sister Sodom sinned?" and: "The rebellious Israel hath justified her soul in comparison of the treacherous Judah."[12] So then the merits of all the virtues, which I enumerated above, though in themselves they are good and precious, yet become dim in comparison of the brightness of contemplation. For they greatly hinder and retard the saints who are taken up with earthly aims even at good works, from the contemplation of that sublime good.

CHAPTER V.

How no one can be continually intent upon that highest good.

For who, when "delivering the poor from the hand of them that are too strong for him,

---

[1] Gen. i. 31; Ecclus. xxxix. 16.
[2] Rom. i. 20.
[3] Isa. xxx. 26.
[4] Ps. ci. (cii.) 27, 28.
[5] S. Matt. vii. 18; xii. 35; xxv. 21.
[6] S. Luke xviii. 19.
[7] S. Matt. vii. 11.
[8] Isa. lxiv. 6.
[9] Gal. iii. 19; Rom. vii. 12.
[10] Ezek. xx. 25.
[11] 2 Cor. iii. 10.
[12] Ezek. xvi. 52, 49; Jer. iii. 11.

and the needy and the poor from them that strip him," who when "breaking the jaws of the wicked and snatching their prey from between their teeth,"[1] can with a calm mind regard the glory of the Divine Majesty during the actual work of intervention? Who when ministering support to the poor, or when receiving with benevolent kindness the crowds that come to him, can at the very moment when he is with anxious mind perplexed for the wants of his brethren, contemplate the vastness of the bliss on high, and while he is shaken by the troubles and cares of the present life look forward to the state of the world to come with an heart raised above the stains of earth? Whence the blessed David when laying down that this alone is good for man, longs to cling constantly to God, and says: " It is good for me to cling to God, and to put my hope in the Lord."[2] And Ecclesiastes also declares that this cannot be done without fault by any of the saints, and says: "For there is not a righteous man upon earth, that doeth good and sinneth not."[3] For who, even if he be the chief of all righteous and holy men, can we ever think could, while bound in the chains of this life, so acquire this chief good, as never to cease from divine contemplation, or be thought to be drawn away by earthly thoughts even for a short time from Him Who alone is good? Who ever takes no care for food, none for clothing or other carnal things, or when anxious about receiving the brethren, or change of place, or building his cell, has never desired the aid of man's assistance, nor when harassed by scarcity and want has incurred this sentence of reproof from the Lord: " Be not anxious for your life what ye shall eat, nor for your body what ye shall put on "?[4] Further we confidently assert that even the Apostle Paul himself who surpassed in the number of his sufferings the toils of all the saints, could not possibly fulfil this, as he himself testifies to the disciples in the Acts of the Apostles: " Ye yourselves know that these hands have ministered to my needs, and to the needs of those who were with me," or when in writing in the Thessalonians he testifies that he " worked in labour and weariness night and day."[5] And although for this there were great rewards for his merits prepared, yet his mind, however holy and sublime it might be, could not help being sometimes drawn away from that heavenly contemplation by its attention to earthly labours. Further, when he saw himself enriched with such practical fruits, and on the

other hand considered in his heart the good of meditation, and weighed as it were in one scale the profit of all these labours and in the other the delights of divine contemplation, when for a long time he had corrected the balance in his breast, while the vast rewards for his labours delighted him on one side, and on the other the desire for unity with and the inseparable companionship of Christ inclined him to depart this life, at last in his perplexity he cries out and says: "What I shall choose I know not. For I am in a strait betwixt two, having a desire to depart and to be with Christ, for it were much better: but to abide in the flesh is more necessary for your sakes."[6] Though then in many ways he preferred this excellent good to all the fruits of his preaching, yet he submits himself in consideration of love, without which none can gain the Lord; and for their sakes, whom hitherto he had soothed with milk as nourishment from the breasts of the gospel, does not refuse to be parted from Christ, which is bad for himself though useful for others. For he is driven to choose this the rather by that excessive goodness of his whereby for the salvation of his brethren he is ready, were it possible, to incur even the last evil of an Anathema. "For I could wish," he says, "that I myself were Anathema from Christ for my brethren's sake, who are my kinsmen according to the flesh, who are Israelites,"[7] i.e., I could wish to be subject not only to temporal, but even to perpetual punishment, if only all men, were it possible, might enjoy the fellowship of Christ: for I am sure that the salvation of all would be better for Christ and for me than my own. That then the Apostle might perfectly gain this chief good, i.e., to enjoy the vision of God and to be joined continually to Christ, he was ready to be parted from this body, which as it is feeble and hindered by the many requirements of its frailties cannot help separating from union with Christ: for it is impossible for the mind, that is harassed by such frequent cares, and hampered by such various and tiresome troubles, always to enjoy the Divine vision. For what aim of the saints can be so persistent, what purpose can be so high that that crafty plotter does not sometimes destroy it? Who has frequented the recesses of the desert and shunned intercourse with all men in such a way that he never trips by unnecessary thoughts, and by looking on things or being occupied in earthly actions falls away from that contemplation of God, which truly alone is good? Who ever could preserve such fervour of spirit

---

[1] Ps. xxxiv. (xxxv.) 10; Job xxix. 17. [4] S. Matt. vi. 23.
[2] Ps. lxxii. (lxxiii.) 28.　　　　　　[5] Acts xx. 34; 2 Thess. iii. 8.
[3] Eccl. vii. 21.

[6] Phil. i. 22-24.　　　　[7] Rom. ix. 3, 4.

as not sometimes to pass by roving thoughts from his attention to prayer, and fall away suddenly from heavenly to earthly things? Which of us (to pass over other times of wandering) even at the very moment when he raises his soul in prayer to God on high, does not fall into a sort of stupor, and even against his will offend by that very thing from which he hoped for pardon of his sins? Who, I ask, is so alert and vigilant as never, while he is singing a Psalm to God, to allow his mind to wander from the meaning of Scripture? Who is so intimate with and closely joined to God, as to congratulate himself on having carried out for a single day that rule of the Apostle's, whereby he bids us pray without ceasing? [1] And though all these things may seem to some, who are involved in grosser sins, to be trivial and altogether foreign to sin, yet to those who know the value of perfection a quantity even of very small matters becomes most serious.

CHAPTER VI.

How those who think that they are without sin are like purblind people.

As if we were to suppose that two men, one of whom was clear sighted with perfect vision, and the other, one whose eyesight was obscured by dimness of vision, had together entered some great house that was filled with a quantity of bundles, instruments, and vessels, would not he, whose dullness of vision prevented his seeing everything, assert that there was nothing there but chests, beds, benches, tables, and whatever met the fingers of one who felt them rather than the eyes of one who saw them, while on the other hand would not the other, who searched out what was hidden with clear and bright eyes, declare that there were there many most minute articles, and what could scarcely be counted; which if they were ever gathered up into a single pile, would by their number equal or perhaps exceed the size of those few things which the other had felt. So then even saints, and, if we may so say, men who *see*, whose aim is the utmost perfection, cleverly detect in themselves even those things which the gaze of our mind being as it were darkened cannot see, and condemn them very severely, to such an extent that those who have not, as it seems to our carelessness, dimmed the whiteness of their body, which is as it were like snow, with even the slightest spot of sin, seem to themselves to be covered with many stains, if, I will not

say any evil or vain thoughts creep into the doors of their mind, but even the recollection of a Psalm which has to be said takes off the attention of the kneeler at the time for prayer. For if, say they, when we ask some great man, I will not say for our life and salvation, but for some advantage and profit, we fasten all our attention of mind and body upon him, and hang with trembling expectation on his nod, with no slight dread lest haply some foolish or unsuitable word may turn aside the pity of our hearer, and then too, when we are standing in the forum or in the courts of earthly judges, with our opponent standing over against us, if in the midst of the prosecution and trial any coughing, or spitting, or laughing, or yawning, or sleep overtakes us, with what malice will our ever watchful opponent stir up the severity of the judge to our damage: how much more, when we entreat Him who knows all secrets, should we, by reason of our imminent danger of everlasting death, plead with earnest and anxious prayer for the kindness of the judge, especially as on the other side there stands one who is both our crafty seducer and our accuser! And not without reason will he be bound by no light sin, but by a grievous fault of wickedness, who, when he pours forth his prayer to God, departs at once from His sight as if from the eyes of one who neither sees nor hears, and follows the vanity of wicked thoughts. But they who cover the eyes of their heart with a thick veil of their sins, and as the Saviour says, "Seeing see not and hearing hear not nor understand," [2] hardly regard in the inmost recesses of their breast even those faults which are great and deadly, and cannot with clear eyes look at any deceitful thoughts, nor even those vague and secret desires which strike the mind with slight and subtle suggestions, nor the captivities of their soul, but always wandering among impure thoughts they know not how to be sorry when they are distracted from that meditation which is so special, nor can they grieve that they have lost anything as while they lay open their mind to the entrance of any thought as they please, they have nothing set before them to hold to as the main thing or to desire in every way.

CHAPTER VII.

How those who maintain that a man can be without sin are charged with a twofold error.

THE reason however which drives us into this error is that, as we are utterly ignorant

---

[1] Cf. 1 Thess. v. 17.   [2] S. Matt. xiii. 13.

of the virtue of being without sin,[1] we fancy that we cannot contract any guilt from those idle and random vagaries of our thoughts, but being rendered stupid by dullness and as it were smitten with blindness we can see nothing in ourselves but capital offences, and think that we have only to keep clear of those things which are condemned also by the severity of secular laws, and if we find that even for a short time we are free from these we at once imagine that there is no sin at all in us. Accordingly we are distinguished from the number of those who see, because we do not see the many small stains, which are crowded together in us, and are not smitten with saving contrition, if the malady of vexation overtakes our thoughts, nor are we sorry that we are struck by the suggestions of vainglory, nor do we weep over our prayers offered up so tardily and coldly, nor consider it a fault if while we are singing or praying, something else besides the actual prayer or Psalm fills our thoughts, nor are we horrified because we do not blush to conceive many things which we are ashamed to speak or do before men, in our heart, which, as we know, lies open to the Divine gaze; nor do we purge away the pollution of filthy dreams with copious ablutions of our tears, nor grieve that in the pious act of almsgiving when we are assisting the needs of the brethren, or ministering support to the poor, the brightness of our cheerfulness is clouded over by a stingy delay, nor do we think that we are affected by any loss when we forget God and think about things that are temporal and corrupt, so that these words of Solomon fairly apply to us: "They smite me but I have not grieved, and they have mocked me, but I knew it not."[2]

CHAPTER VIII.

How it is given to but few to understand what sin is.

THOSE on the other hand who make the sum of all their joy and delight and bliss consist in the contemplation of divine and spiritual things alone, if they are unwillingly withdrawn from them even for a short time by thoughts that force themselves upon them, punish this as if it were a kind of sacrilege in them, and avenge it by immediate chastisement, and in their grief that they have preferred some worthless creature (to which their mental gaze was turned aside) to their Creator, charge themselves with the guilt (I had almost said) of impiety, and although they turn

the eyes of their heart with the utmost speed to behold the brightness of the Divine Glory, yet they cannot tolerate even for a very short time the darkness of carnal thoughts, and execrate whatever keeps back their soul's gaze from the true light. Finally when the blessed Apostle John would instill this feeling into everybody he says: "Little children, love not the world, neither the things which are in the world. If any man love the world, the love of God is not in him: for everything that is in the world is the lust of the flesh and the lust of the eyes and the pride of life, which is not of the Father but of the world. And the world perisheth and the lust thereof: but he that doeth the will of God abideth forever."[3] The saints therefore scorn all those things on which the world exists, but it is impossible for them never to be carried away to them by a brief aberration of thoughts, and even now no man, except our Lord and Saviour, can keep his naturally wandering mind always fixed on the contemplation of God so as never to be carried away from it through the love of something in this world; as Scripture says: "Even the stars are not clean in His sight," and again: "If He puts no trust in His saints, and findeth iniquity in His angels," or as the more correct translation has it: "Behold among His saints none is unchangeable, and the heavens are not pure in His sight."[4]

CHAPTER IX.

Of the care with which a monk should preserve the recollection of God.

I SHOULD say then that the saints who keep a firm hold of the recollection of God and are borne along, as it were, with their steps suspended on a line stretched out on high, may be rightly compared to rope dancers, commonly called funambuli, who risk all their safety and life on the path of that very narrow rope, with no doubt that they will immediately meet with a most dreadful death if their foot swerves or trips in the very slightest degree, or goes over the line of the course in which alone is safety. And while with marvellous skill they ply their airy steps through space, if they keep not their steps to that all too narrow path with careful and anxious regulation, the earth which is the natural base and the most solid and safest foundation for all, becomes to them an immediate and clear danger, not because its nature is changed, but because they fall headlong upon it by the

---

[1] *Anamarteti id est impeccantæ.*   [2] Prov. xxiii. 35.   [3] 1 John ii. 15-17.   [4] Job xxv. 5; xv. 15.

weight of their bodies. So also that un-wearied goodness of God and His unchanging nature[1] hurts no one indeed, but we ourselves by falling from on high and tending to the depths are the authors of our own death, or rather the very fall becomes death to the faller. For it says: "Woe to them for they have departed from Me: they shall be wasted because they have transgressed against Me;" and again: "Woe to them when I shall depart from them." For "thine own wickedness shall reprove thee, and thy apostasy shall re-buke thee. Know thou and see that it is an evil and a bitter thing for thee to have left the Lord thy God;" for "every man is bound by the cords of his sins."[2] To whom this rebuke is aptly directed by the Lord: "Be-hold," He says, "all you that kindle a fire, encompassed with flames, walk ye in the light of your fire and in the flames which you have kindled;" and again: "He that kindleth ini-quity, shall perish by it."[3]

CHAPTER X.

How those who are on the way to perfection are truly humble, and feel that they always stand in need of God's grace.

WHEN then holy men feel that they are op-pressed by the weight of earthly thoughts and fall away from their loftiness of mind, and that they are led away against their will or rather without knowing it, into the law of sin and death, and (to pass over other matters) are kept back by those actions which I described above, which are good and right though earthly, from the vision of God; they have something to groan over constantly to the Lord; they have something for which indeed to humble themselves, and in their contrition to profess themselves not in words only but in heart, sinners; and for this, while they continually ask of the Lord's grace pardon for everything that day by day they commit when overcome by the weakness of the flesh, they should shed without ceasing true tears of penitence; as they see that being involved even to the very end of their life in the very same troubles, with continual sorrow for which they are tried, they cannot even offer their prayers without ha-rassing thoughts. So then as they know by ex-perience that through the hindrance of the burden of the flesh they cannot by human strength reach the desired end, nor be united according to their heart's desire with that chief and highest good, but that they are led away from the vision of it captive to worldly

things, they betake themselves to the grace of God, "Who justifieth the ungodly,"[4] and cry out with the Apostle: "O wretched man that I am! Who shall deliver me from the body of this death? Thanks be to God through our Lord Jesus Christ."[5] For they feel that they cannot perform the good that they would, but are ever falling into the evil which they would not, and which they hate, i.e., wandering thoughts and care for carnal things.

CHAPTER XI.

Explanation of the phrase: "For I delight in the law of God after the inner man," etc.

AND they "delight" indeed "in the law of God after the inner man," which soars above all visible things and ever strives to be united to God alone, but they "see another law in their members," i.e., implanted in their na-tural human condition, which "resisting the law of their mind,"[6] brings their thoughts into captivity to the forcible law of sin, com-pelling them to forsake that chief good and submit to earthly notions, which though they may appear necessary and useful when they are taken up in the interests of some religious want, yet when they are set against that good which fascinates the gaze of all the saints, are seen by them to be bad and such as should be avoided, because by them in some way or other and for a short time they are drawn away from the joy of that perfect bliss. For the law of sin is really what the fall of its first father brought on mankind by that fault of his, against which there was uttered this sen-tence by the most just Judge: "Cursed is the ground in thy works; thorns and thistles shall it bring forth to thee, and in the sweat of thy brow shalt thou eat bread."[7] This, I say, is the law, implanted in the members of all mor-tals, which resists the law of our mind and keeps it back from the vision of God, and which, as the earth is cursed in our works after the knowledge of good and evil, begins to pro-duce the thorns and thistles of thoughts, by the sharp pricks of which the natural seeds of vir-tues are choked, so that without the sweat of our brow we cannot eat our bread which "cometh down from heaven," and which "strengtheneth man's heart."[8] The whole human race in general therefore is without exception subject to this law. For there is no one, however saintly, who does not take the

[1] *Substantia.* [2] Hos. vii. 13; ix. 12; Jer. ii. 19; Prov. v. 22.
[3] Isa. l. 11; Prov. xix. 9.

[4] Rom. iv. 5. [7] Gen. iii. 17, 19.
[5] Rom. vii. 24, 25. [8] S. John vi. 33; Ps. ciii. (civ.) 15.
[6] *Ib.* vii. 22, 23.

bread mentioned above with the sweat of his brow and anxious efforts of his heart. But many rich men, as we see, are fed on that common bread without any sweat of their brow.

CHAPTER XII.

Of this also: "But we know that the law is spiritual," etc.

AND this law the Apostle also calls spiritual saying: "But we know that the law is spiritual, but I am carnal, sold under sin."[1] For this law is spiritual which bids us eat in the sweat of our brow that "true bread which cometh down from heaven"[2] but that sale under sin makes us carnal. What, I ask, or whose is that sin? Doubtless Adam's, by whose fall, and, if I may so say, ruinous transaction and fraudulent bargain we were sold. For when he was led astray by the persuasion of the serpent he brought all his descendants under the yoke of perpetual bondage, as they were alienated by taking the forbidden food. For this custom is generally observed between the buyer and seller, that one who wants to make himself over to the power of another, receives from his buyer a price for the loss of his liberty, and his consignment to perpetual slavery. And we can very plainly see that this took place between Adam and the serpent. For by eating of the forbidden tree he received from the serpent the price of his liberty, and gave up his natural freedom and chose to give himself up to perpetual slavery to him from whom he had obtained the deadly price of the forbidden fruit; and thenceforth he was bound by this condition and not without reason subjected all the offspring of his posterity to perpetual service to him whose slave he had become. For what can any marriage in slavery produce but slaves? What then? Did that cunning and crafty buyer take away the rights of ownership from the true and lawful lord? Not so. For neither did he overcome all God's property by the craft of a single act of deception so that the true lord lost his rights of ownership, who though the buyer himself was a rebel and a renegade, yet oppressed him with the yoke of slavery; but because the Creator had endowed all reasonable creatures with free will, he would not restore to their natural liberty against their will those who contrary to right had sold themselves by the sin of greedy lust. Since anything that is contrary to goodness and fairness is abhorrent to Him who is the Author of justice and piety. For

it would have been wrong for Him to have recalled the blessing of freedom granted, unfair for Him to have by His power oppressed man who was free, and by taking him captive, not to have allowed him to exercise the prerogative of the freedom he had received, as He was reserving his salvation for future ages, that in due season the fulness of the appointed time might be fulfilled. For it was right that his offspring should remain under the ancient conditions for so long a time, until by the price of His own blood the grace of the Lord redeemed them from their original chains and set them free in the primeval state of liberty, though He was able even then to save them, but would not, because equity forbade Him to break the terms of His own decree. Would you know the reason for your being sold? Hear thy Redeemer Himself proclaiming openly by Isaiah the prophet: "What is this bill of the divorce of your mother with which I have put her away? Or who is My creditor to whom I sold you? Behold you are sold for your iniquities and for your wicked deeds have I put your mother away." Would you also plainly see why when you were consigned to the yoke of slavery He would not redeem you by the might of His own power? Hear what He added to the former passage, and how He charges the same servants of sin with the reason for their voluntary sale. "Is My hand shortened and become little that I cannot redeem, or is there no strength in Me to deliver?"[3] But what it is which is always standing in the way of His most powerful pity the same prophet shows when he says: "Behold the hand of the Lord is not shortened that it cannot save, neither is His ear heavy that it cannot hear: But your iniquities have divided between you and your God and your sins have hid His face from you that He should not hear."[4]

CHAPTER XIII.

Of this also: "But I know that in me, that is in my flesh, dwelleth no good thing."

BECAUSE then the original curse of God has made us carnal and condemned us to thorns and thistles, and our father has sold us by that unhappy bargain so that we cannot do the good that we would, while we are torn away from the recollection of God Most High and forced to think on what belongs to human weakness, while burning with the love of purity, we are often even against our will

---

[1] Rom. vii. 14.   [2] S. John vi. 33.   [3] Isa. l. 1, 2.   [4] Isa. lix. 1, 2.

troubled by natural desires, which we would rather know nothing about; we know that in our flesh there dwelleth no good thing[1] viz., the perpetual and lasting peace of this meditation of which we have spoken; but there is brought about in our case that miserable and wretched divorce, that when with the mind we want to serve the law of God, since we never want to remove our gaze from the Divine brightness, yet surrounded as we are by carnal darkness we are forced by a kind of law of sin to tear ourselves away from the good which we know, as we fall away from that lofty height of mind to earthly cares and thoughts, to which the law of sin, i.e., the sentence of God, which the first delinquent received, has not without reason condemned us. And hence it is that the blessed Apostle, though he openly admits that he and all saints are bound by the constraint of this sin, yet boldly asserts that none of them will be condemned for this, saying: "There is therefore now no condemnation to them that are in Christ Jesus: for the law of the spirit of life in Christ Jesus hath set me free from the law of sin and death,"[2] i.e., the grace of Christ day by day frees all his saints from this law of sin and death, under which they are constantly reluctantly obliged to come, whenever they pray to the Lord for the forgiveness of their trespasses. You see then that it was in the person not of sinners but of those who are really saints and perfect, that the blessed Apostle gave utterance to this saying: "For I do not the good that I would, but the evil which I hate, that I do;" and: "I see another law in my members resisting the law of my mind and bringing me captive to the law of sin which is in my members."[3]

CHAPTER XIV.

An objection, that the saying: "For I do not the good that I would," etc., applies to the persons neither of unbelievers nor of saints.

GERMANUS: We say that this does not apply to the persons either of those who are involved in capital offences, or of an Apostle and those who have advanced to his measure, but we think that it ought properly to be taken of those who after receiving the grace of God and the knowledge of the truth, are anxious to keep themselves from carnal sins but, as ancient custom like a natural law rules most forcibly in their members, they are carried away to the ingrained lust of their passions. For the custom and frequency of sinning be-

comes like a natural law, which, implanted in the man's weak members, leads the feelings of the soul that is not yet instructed in all the pursuits of virtue, but is still, if I may say so, of an uninstructed and tender chastity, captive to sin and subjecting them by an ancient law to death, brings them under the yoke of sin that rules over them, not suffering them to obtain the good of purity which they love, but rather forcing them to do the evil which they hate.

CHAPTER XV.

The answer to the objection raised.

THEONAS: Your notion does not come to much; as you yourselves have actually now begun to maintain that this cannot possibly stand in the person of those who are out and out sinners, but that it properly applies to those who are trying to keep themselves clear from carnal sins. And since you have already separated these from the number of sinners, it follows that you must shortly admit them into the ranks of the faithful and holy. For what kinds of sin do you say that those can commit, from which, if they are involved in them after the grace of baptism, they can be freed by the daily grace of Christ? or of what body of death are we to think that the Apostle said: "Who shall deliver me from the body of this death? Thanks be to God through Jesus Christ our Lord"?[4] Is it not clear, as truth compels you yourselves also to admit, that it is spoken not of those members of capital crimes, by which the wages of eternal death are gained; viz., murder, fornication, adultery, drunkenness, thefts and robberies, but of that body before mentioned, which the daily grace of Christ assists? For whoever after baptism and the knowledge of God falls into that death, must know that he will either have to be cleansed, not by the daily grace of Christ, i.e., an easy forgiveness, which our Lord when at any moment He is prayed to, is wont to grant to our errors, but by a life-long affliction of penitence and penal sorrow, or else will be hereafter consigned to the punishment of eternal fire for them, as the same Apostle thus declares: "Be not deceived: neither fornicators, nor idolaters, nor adulterers, nor effeminate, nor defilers of themselves with mankind, nor thieves, nor covetous persons, nor drunkards, nor railers, nor extortioners shall possess the kingdom of God."[5] Or what is that law warring in our members

---

[1] Cf. Rom. vii. 18. [2] Rom. viii. 1, 2. [3] Rom. vii. 19.   [4] Rom. vii. 24, 25.   [5] 1 Cor. vi. 9, 10.

which resists the law of our mind, and when it has led us resisting but captives to the law of sin and death, and has made us serve it with the flesh, nevertheless suffers us to serve the law of God with the mind? For I do not suppose that this law of sin denotes crimes or can be taken of the offences mentioned above, of which if a man is guilty he does not serve the law of God with the mind, from which law he must first have departed in heart before he is guilty of any of them with the flesh. For what is it to serve the law of sin, but to do what is commanded by sin? What sort of sin then is it to which so great holiness and perfection feels that it is captive, and yet doubts not that it will be freed from it by the grace of Christ, saying: "O wretched man that I am! Who shall deliver me from the body of this death? Thanks be to God through Jesus Christ our Lord"? What law, I ask, will you maintain to be implanted in our members, which, withdrawing us from the law of God and bringing us into captivity to the law of sin, could make us wretched rather than guilty so that we should not be consigned to eternal punishment, but still as it were sigh for the unbroken joys of bliss, and, seeking for a helper who shall restore us to it, exclaim with the Apostle: ' O wretched man that I am! Who shall deliver me from the body of this death?'" For what is it to be led captive to the law of sin but to continue to perform and commit sin? Or what other chief good can be given which the saints cannot fulfil, except that in comparison with which, as we said above, everything else is not good? Indeed we know that many things in this world are good, and chiefly, modesty, continence, sobriety, humility, justice, mercy, temperance, piety: but all of these things fail to come up to that chief good, and can be done I say not by apostles, but even by ordinary folk; and, those by whom they are not done, are either chastised with eternal punishment, or are set free by great exertions, as was said above, of penitence, and not by the daily grace of Christ. It remains then for us to admit that this saying of the Apostle is rightly applied only to the persons of saints, who day after day falling under this law, which we described, of sin not of crimes, are secure of their salvation and not precipitated into wicked deeds, but, as has often been said, are drawn away from the contemplation of God to the misery of bodily thoughts, and are often deprived of the blessing of that true bliss. For if they felt that by this law of their members they were bound daily to crimes, they would complain of the loss not of happiness but of innocence, and the Apostle Paul would not say:

"O wretched man that I am," but "Impure," or "Wicked man that I am," and he would wish to be rid not of the body of this death, i.e., this mortal state, but of the crimes and misdeeds of this flesh. But because by reason of his state of human frailty he felt that he was captive, i.e., led away to carnal cares and anxieties which the law of sin and death causes, he groans over this law of sin under which against his will he had fallen, and at once has recourse to Christ and is saved by the present redemption of His grace. Whatever of anxiety therefore that law of sin, which naturally produces the thorns and thistles of mortal thoughts and cares, has caused to spring up in the ground of the Apostle's breast, that the law of grace at once plucks up. "For the law," says he, "of the spirit of life in Christ Jesus hath set me free from the law of sin and death." [1]

CHAPTER XVI.

What is the body of sin.

This then is that body of death from which we cannot escape, pent in which those who are perfect, who have tasted "how gracious the Lord is," [2] daily feel with the prophet "how bad for himself and bitter it is for a man to depart from the Lord his God." [3] This is the body of death which restrains us from the heavenly vision and drags us back to earthly things, which causes men while singing Psalms and kneeling in prayer to have their thoughts filled with human figures, or conversations, or business, or unnecessary actions. This is the body of death, owing to which those, who would emulate the sanctity of angels, and who long to cling continually to God, yet are unable to arrive at the perfection of this good, because the body of death stands in their way, but they do the evil that they would not, i.e., they are dragged down in their minds even to the things which have nothing to do with their advance and perfection in virtue. Finally that the blessed Apostle might clearly denote that he said this of saintly and perfect men, and those like himself, he in a way points with his finger to himself and at once proceeds: "And so I myself," i.e, I who say this, lay bare the secrets of my own not another's conscience. This mode of speech at any rate the Apostle is familiarly accustomed to use, whenever he wants to point specially to himself, as here : "I, Paul, myself beseech you by the mildness and modesty of Christ;" and again: "except that I myself was not burdensome to you;" and once more: "But be it so: I myself did not burden you;" and elsewhere: "I, Paul, myself say unto you: if ye be circumcised Christ shall profit you nothing;" and to the Romans: "For I could wish that I myself were Anathema from Christ for my brethren." [1] But it cannot unreasonably be taken in this way, that "And so I myself" is expressly said with emphasis, i.e., I whom you know to be an Apostle of Christ, whom you venerate with the utmost respect, whom you believe to be of the highest character and perfect, and one in whom Christ speaks, though with the mind I serve the law of God, yet with the flesh I confess that I serve the law of sin, i.e., by the occupations of my human condition I am sometimes dragged down from heavenly to earthly things and the height of my mind is brought down to the level of care for humble matters. And by this law of sin I find that at every moment I am so taken captive that although I persist in my immovable longing around the law of God, yet in no way can I escape the power of this captivity, unless I always fly to the grace of the Saviour.

CHAPTER XVII.

How all the saints have confessed with truth that they were unclean and sinful.

AND therefore with daily sighs all the saints grieve over this weakness of their nature and while they search into their shifting thoughts and the secrets and inmost recesses of their conscience, cry out in entreaty: "Enter not into judgment with Thy servant, for in Thy sight shall no man living be justified;" and this: "Who will boast that he hath a chaste heart? or who will have confidence that he is pure from sin?" and again: "There is not a righteous man upon earth that doeth good and sinneth not;" and this also: "Who knoweth his faults?" [2] And so they have recognized that man's righteousness is weak and imperfect and always needs God's mercy, so that one of those whose iniquities and sins God purged away with the live coal of His word sent from the altar, after that marvellous vision of God, after his view of the Seraphim on high and the revelation of heavenly mysteries, said: "Woe is me! for I am a man of unclean lips, and I dwell in the midst of a people of unclean lips." [3] And I fancy that

perhaps even then he would not have felt the uncleanness of his lips, unless it had been given him to recognize the true and complete purity of perfection by the vision of God, at the sight of Whom he suddenly became aware of his own uncleanness, of which he had previously been ignorant. For when he says: "Woe is me! for I am a man of unclean lips," he shows that his confession that follows refers to his own lips, and not to the uncleanness of the people: "and I dwell in the midst of a people of unclean lips." But even when in his prayer he confesses the uncleanness of all sinners, he embraces in his general supplication not only the mass of the wicked but also of the good, saying: "Behold Thou art angry, and we have sinned: in them we have been always, and we shall be saved. We are all become as one unclean, and all our righteousnesses' as filthy rags." [4] What, I ask, could be clearer than this saying, in which the prophet includes not one only but all our righteousnesses and, looking round on all things that are considered unclean and disgusting, because he could find nothing in the life of men fouler or more unclean, chose to compare them to filthy rags. In vain then is the sharpness of a nagging objection raised against this perfectly clear truth, as a little while back you said: "If no one is without sin, then no one is holy; and if no one is holy, then no one will be saved." [5] For the puzzle of this question can be solved by the prophet's testimony. "Behold," he says, "Thou art angry and we have sinned," i.e., when Thou didst reject our pride of heart or our carelessness, and deprive us of Thine aid, at once the abyss of our sins swallowed us up, as if one should say to the bright substance of the sun: Behold thou hast set, and at once murky darkness covered us. And yet though he here says that the saints have sinned, and have not only sinned but also have always remained in their sins, he does not altogether despair of salvation but adds: "In them we have been always, and we shall be saved." This saying: "Behold Thou art angry and we have sinned," I will compare to that one of the Apostle's: "O wretched man that I am! Who shall deliver me from the body of this death?" Again this that the prophet subjoins: "In them we have been always, and we shall be saved," corresponds to the following words of the Apostle: "Thanks be to God through Jesus Christ our Lord." In the same way also this passage of the same prophet: "Woe is me! for I am a man of unclean lips and I dwell in the midst of a people of

---

[1] 2 Cor. x. 1; xii. 13, 16; Gal. v. 2; Rom. ix. 3.
[2] Ps. cxlii. (cxliii.) 2; Prov. xx. 9; Eccl. vii. 21; Ps. xviii. (xix.) 13.   [3] Isa. vi. 5.   [4] Isa. lxiv. 5, 6.   [5] Cf. XXII. viii.

unclean lips," seems to agree with the words quoted above: "O wretched man that I am! Who shall deliver me from the body of this death?" And what follows in the prophet: "And behold there flew to me one of the Seraphim, having in his hand a coal (or stone) which he had taken with the tongs from off the altar. And he touched my mouth and said: Lo, with this I have touched thy lips, and thine iniquity is taken away and thy sin is purged," [1] is just what seems to have fallen from the mouth of Paul, who says: "Thanks be to God through Jesus Christ our Lord." You see then how all the saints with truth confess not so much in the person of the people as in their own that they are sinners, and yet by no means despair of their salvation, but look for full justification (which they do not hope that they cannot obtain by virtue of the state of human frailty) from the grace and mercy of the Lord.

CHAPTER XVIII.

That even good and holy men are not without sin.

But that no one however holy is in this life free from trespasses and sin, we are told also by the teaching of the Saviour, who gave His disciples the form of the perfect prayer; and among those other sublime and sacred commands, which as they were only given to the saints and perfect cannot apply to the wicked and unbelievers, He bade this to be inserted: "And forgive us our debts as we also forgive our debtors." [2] If then this is offered as a true prayer and by saints, as we ought without the shadow of a doubt to believe, who can be found so obstinate and impudent, so puffed up with the pride of the devil's own rage, as to maintain that he is without sin, and not only to think himself greater than apostles, but also to charge the Saviour Himself with ignorance or folly, as if He either did not know that some men could be free from debts, or was idly teaching those whom He knew to stand in no need of the remedy of that prayer? But since all the saints who altogether keep the commands of their King, say every day "Forgive us our debts," if they speak the truth, there is indeed no one free from sin, but if they speak falsely, it is equally true that they are not free from the sin of falsehood. Wherefore also that most wise Ecclesiastes reviewing in his mind all the actions and purposes of men declares without any exception: "that there is not a righteous man upon earth, that doeth good and sinneth not," [3] i.e., no one ever could or ever will be found on this earth so holy, so diligent, so earnest as to be able continually to cling to that true and unique good, and not day after day to feel that he is drawn aside from it and fails. But still though he maintains that he cannot be free from wrong doing, yet none the less we must not deny that he is righteous.

CHAPER XIX.

How even in the hour of prayer it is almost impossible to avoid sin.

Whoever then ascribes sinlessness to human nature must fight against no idle words but the witness and proof of his conscience which is on our side, and then only should maintain that he is without sin, when he finds that he is not torn away from this highest good: nay rather, whoever considering his own conscience, to say no more, finds that he has celebrated even one single service without the distraction of a single word or deed or thought, may say that he is without sin. Further because we admit that the discursive lightness of the human mind cannot get rid of these idle and empty things, we thus consequently confess with truth that we are not without sin. For with whatever care a man tries to keep his heart, he can never, owing to the resistance of the nature of the flesh, keep it according to the desire of his spirit. For however far the human mind may have advanced and progressed towards a finer purity of contemplation, so much the more will it see itself to be unclean, as it were in the mirror of its purity, because while the soul raises itself for a loftier vision and as it looks forth yearns for greater things than it performs, it is sure always to despise as inferior and worthless the things in which it is mixed up. Since a keener sight notices more; and a blameless life produces greater sorrow when found fault with; and amendment of life, and earnest striving after goodness multiplies groans and sighs. For no one can rest content with that stage to which he has advanced, and however much a man may be purified in mind, so much the more does he see himself to be foul, and find grounds for humiliation rather than for pride, and, however swiftly he may climb to greater heights, so much more does he see above him whither he is tending. Finally that chosen Apostle "whom Jesus loved," [4] who lay on His bosom, uttered this saying as if from the heart of the Lord:

---

[1] Isa. vi. 6, 7.   [2] S. Matt. vi. 12.   [3] Eccl. vii. 21.   [4] S. John xiii. 23.

"If we say that we have no sin we deceive ourselves and the truth is not in us." [1] And so if when we say that we have no sin, we have not the truth, that is Christ, in us, what good do we do except to prove ourselves by this very profession, criminals and wicked among sinners?

CHAPTER XX.

From whom we can learn the destruction of sin and perfection of goodness.

LASTLY if you would like to investigate more thoroughly whether it is possible for human nature to attain sinlessness, from whom can we more clearly learn this than from those who "have crucified the flesh with its faults and lusts," and to whom "the world is really crucified"? [2] Who though they have not only utterly eradicated all faults from their hearts, but also are trying to shut out even the thought and recollection of sin, yet still day after day faithfully maintain that they cannot even for a single hour be free from spot of sin.

CHAPTER XXI.

That although we acknowledge that we cannot be without sin, yet still we ought not to suspend ourselves from the Lord's Communion.

YET we ought not to suspend ourselves from the Lord's Communion because we confess ourselves sinners, but should more and more eagerly hasten to it for the healing of our soul, and purifying of our spirit, and seek the rather a remedy for our wounds with humility of mind and faith, as considering ourselves unworthy to receive so great grace. Otherwise we cannot worthily receive the Communion even once a year, as some do, who live in monasteries and so regard the dignity and holiness and value of the heavenly sacraments, as to think that none but saints and spotless persons should venture to receive them, and not rather that they would make us saints and pure by taking them. And these thereby fall into greater presumption and arrogance than what they seem to themselves to avoid, because at the time when they do receive them, they consider that they are worthy to receive them. But it is much better to receive them every Sunday for the healing of our infirmities, with that humility of heart, whereby we believe and confess that we can never touch those holy mysteries worthily, than to be puffed up by a foolish persuasion of heart, and believe that at the year's end we are worthy to receive them. Wherefore that we may be able to grasp this and hold it fruitfully, let us the more earnestly implore the Lord's mercy to help us to perform this, which is learnt not like other human arts, by some previous verbal explanation, but rather by experience and action leading the way; and which also unless it is often considered and hammered out in the Conferences of spiritual persons, and anxiously sifted by daily experience and trial of it, will either become obsolete through carelessness or perish by idle forgetfulness.

XXIV.

CONFERENCE OF ABBOT ABRAHAM.

ON MORTIFICATION.

CHAPTER I.

How we laid bare the secrets of our thoughts to Abbot Abraham.

THIS twenty-fourth Conference of Abbot Abraham [3] is by the favour of Christ produced, which concludes the traditions and decisions of all the Elders; and when by the aid of your prayers it has been finished, as the number mystically corresponds to that of the four and twenty Elders who are said in the holy Apocalypse [2] to offer their crowns to the Lamb, we think that we shall have paid the debt of all our promises. And henceforth if these four and twenty Elders of ours have been crowned with any glory for the sake of their teaching, they shall with bowed heads offer it to the Lamb who was slain for the salvation of the world: for He it was Who vouschafed

---

[1] 1 John i. 8.   [2] Gal. v. 24; vi. 14.   [3] Cf. the note on XV. iv.   [4] Rev. iv. 4.

for the honour of His name to grant to them such exalted feelings and to us whatever words were needful to set forth such profound thoughts. And the merits of His gift must be referred to the Author of all good, to whom the more is owed, as the more is paid. Therefore with anxious confession we laid before this Abraham the impulse of our thoughts, whereby we were urged by daily perplexities of our mind to return to our country and revisit our kinsfolk. For from this the greatest reason for our desire sprang, because we remembered that our kinsfolk were endowed with such piety and goodness that we felt sure that they would never interfere with our purpose, and we constantly reflected, that we should gain more good out of their earnestness, and should be hampered by no cares about bodily matters, and no trouble in providing food, as they would gladly minister abundantly to the supply of all our wants, and besides this we were feeding our souls on the hope of empty joys, as we thought that we should gain the greatest good from the conversion[1] of many, who were to be turned to the way of salvation by our example and instructions. Then besides this the very spot, where was the ancestral possession of our forefathers, and the delightful pleasantness of the neighbourhood was painted before our eyes, how pleasantly and suitably it stretched away to the desert, so that the recesses of the woods would not only delight the heart of a monk, but would also furnish him with a plentiful supply of food.[2] And when we explained all this to the aforesaid old man, in a straightforward way, according to the faith of our consience, and showed by our copious tears that we could no longer resist the violence of the impulse, unless the grace of God came to our rescue by the healing which he could give, he waited for a long time in silence and at last sighed deeply and said:

CHAPTER II.

How the old man exposed our errors.

THE feebleness of your ideas shows that you have not yet renounced worldly desires nor mortified your former lusts. For as the wandering character of your desires testifies to the sloth of your heart, this pilgrimage and absence from your kinsfolk, which you ought rather to endure with your heart, you *do* endure only with the flesh. For all these things would have been buried and altogether driven out of your hearts, if you had got hold of the right method of renunciation, and the main reason for the solitude in which we dwell. And so I see that you are labouring under that infirmity of sluggishness, which is thus described in Proverbs: "Every sluggard is always desiring something;" and again: "Desires kill the slothful."[3] For in our case too these supplies of worldly conveniences, which you have described, would not be wanting, if we believed that they were appropriate to our calling, or thought that we could get out of those delights and pleasures as much profit as that which is gained from this squalor of the country and bodily affliction. Nor are we so deprived of the solace of our kinsfolk, that those who delight to support us with their substance should fail us, were it not that this saying of the Saviour meets us and excludes everything that contributes to the support of this flesh, as He says: "He who doth not leave (or hate) father and mother and children and brethren cannot be My disciple."[4] But if we were altogether deprived of the protection of our parents, the services of the princes of this world would not be wanting, as they would most thankfully rejoice to minister to our necessities with prompt liberality. And supported by their bounty, we should be free from the care of preparing food, were it not that this curse of the prophet terribly frightened us. For "Cursed," he says, "is the man that putteth his hope in man;" and: "Put not your trust in princes."[5] We should also at any rate place our cells on the banks of the river Nile and have water at our very doors, so as not to be obliged to carry it on our necks for four miles, were it not that the blessed Apostle rendered us indefatigable in enduring this labour, and cheered us by his words, saying: "Every one shall receive his own reward according to his labour."[6] Nor are we ignorant that there are even in our country some pleasant recesses, where plenty of fruits, and pleasant gardens, and fertile ground would furnish the food we need with the slightest bodily efforts on our part, were it not that we were afraid lest that reproach might apply to us, which is directed against the rich man in the gospel: "Because thou hast received thy consolation in this life."[7] But as we despise all these things and scorn them together with all the pleasures of this world, we delight only in this squalor, and prefer to all luxuries this dreadful and vast desert, and cannot compare any riches of a fertile soil to these

---

[1] Petschenig's text reads *conversione*, others *conversatione*.
[2] On the bearing of this passage on the question of Cassian's nationality see the Introd., p. 183.

[3] Prov. xiii. 4; xxi. 25.
[4] S. Luke xiv. 26.
[5] Jer. xvii. 5; Ps. cxlv. (cxlvi.) 2.

[6] 1 Cor. iii. 8.
[7] S. Luke xvi. 25.

barren sands, as we pursue no temporal gains of this body, but the eternal rewards of the spirit. For it is but little for a monk to have once made his renunciation, i.e., in the early days of his conversion to have disregarded the present world, unless he continues to renounce it daily. For to the very end of this life we must with the prophet say this: "And I have not desired the day of man, Thou knowest."[1] Wherefore also the Lord says in the gospel: "If any man will come after Me, let him deny himself and take up his cross daily and follow Me."[2]

CHAPTER III.

Of the character of the districts which anchorites ought to seek.

AND therefore by him who is exercising anxious care over the purity of his inner man, those districts should be sought, which do not by their fruitfulness and fertility invite his mind to the trouble of cultivating them, nor drive him forth from his fixed and immovable position in his cell, and force him to go forth to some work in the open air, and so, his thoughts being as it were poured forth openly, scatter to the winds all his concentration of mind and all the keenness of his vision of his aim. And this cannot be guarded against or seen by anyone at all however careful and watchful, except one who continually keeps his body and soul shut up and enclosed in walls, that, like a splendid fisherman, looking out for food for himself by the apostolic art, he may eagerly and without moving catch the swarms of thoughts swimming in the calm depths of his heart, and surveying with curious eye the depths as from a high rock, may sagaciously and cunningly decide what he ought to lure to himself by his saving hook, and what he can neglect and reject as bad and nasty fishes.

CHAPTER IV.

What sorts of work should be chosen by solitaries.

EVERYONE therefore who constantly perseveres in this watchfulness will effectually fulfil what is very plainly expressed by the prophet Habakkuk: "I will stand upon my watch, and ascend upon the rock, and will look out to see what He shall say to me, and what I may answer to Him that reproveth me."[3] And how difficult and tiresome this is, is very clearly shown by the experience of those who live in the desert of Calamus or Porphy-

rion.[4] For though they are separated from all the cities and dwellings of men by a longer stretch of desert than the wilderness of Scete (since by penetrating seven or eight days' journey into the recesses of the vast wilderness, they scarcely arrive at their hiding places and cells) yet because there they are devoted to agriculture and not in the least confined to the cloister, whenever they come to these squalid districts in which we are living, or to Scete, they are annoyed by such harassing thoughts and such anxiety of mind that, as if they were beginners and men who had never given the slightest attention to the exercises of solitude, they cannot endure the life of the cells and the peace and quietness of them, and are at once driven forth and obliged to leave them, as if they were inexperienced and novices. For they have not learnt to still the motions of the inner man, and to quell the tempests of their thoughts by anxious care and persevering efforts, as, toiling day after day in work in the open air, they are moving about all day long in empty space, not only in the flesh but also in heart; and pour forth their thoughts openly as the body moves hither and thither. And therefore they do not notice the folly of their mind in longing for many things, nor can they put a check upon its vague discursiveness; and as they cannot bear sorrow of spirit they think that the fact of a continuance of silence is unendurable, and those who are never tired by hard work in the country, are beaten by silence and worn out by the length of their rest.

CHAPTER V.

That anxiety of heart is made worse rather than better by restlessness of body.

NOR is it wonderful if one who lives in a cell, having his thoughts collected together as it were in a narrow cloister, is oppressed by a multitude of anxieties, which break out with the man himself from the confinement of the dwelling, and at once dash here and there like wild horses. But while they are now roaming at large from their stalls, for the moment some short and sad solace is enjoyed: but when, after the body has returned to its own cell, the whole troop of thoughts retires again to its proper home, the habit of chronic licence gives rise to worse pangs. Those then who are unable and ignorant how to struggle against the promptings of their own fancies, when they are harassed in their cell, by accidie attacking their bosom more violently

---

[1] Jer. xvii. 16. [2] S. Luke ix. 23. [3] Hab. ii. 1. (LXX.). [4] Cf. Institutes X. xxiv.

than usual, if they relax their strict rule and allow themselves the liberty of going out oftener, will arouse a worse plague against themselves by means of this which they fancy is a remedy: just as men fancy that they can check the violence of an inward fever by a draught of the coldest water, though it is a fact that by it its fire is inflamed rather than quenched, as a far worse attack follows after the momentary alleviation.

CHAPTER VI.

A comparison showing how a monk ought to keep guard over his thoughts.

WHEREFORE a monk's whole attention should thus be fixed on one point, and the rise and circle of all his thoughts be vigorously restricted to it; viz., to the recollection of God, as when a man, who is anxious to raise on high a vault of a round arch, must constantly draw a line round from its exact centre, and in accordance with the sure standard it gives discover by the laws of building all the evenness and roundness required. But if anyone tries to finish it without ascertaining its centre — though with the utmost confidence in his art and ability, it is impossible for him to keep the circumference even, without any error, or to find out simply by looking at it how much he has taken off by his mistake from the beauty of real roundness, unless he always has recourse to that test of truth and by its decision corrects the inner and outer edge of his work, and so finishes the large and lofty pile to the exact point.[1] So also our mind, unless by working round the love of the Lord alone as an immovably fixed centre, through all the circumstances of our works and contrivances, it either fits or rejects the character of all our thoughts by the excellent compasses, if I may so say, of love, will never by excellent skill build up the structure of that spiritual edifice of which Paul is the architect, nor possess that beautiful house, which the blessed, David desired in his heart to show to the Lord and said: "I have loved the beauty of Thine house and the place of the dwelling of Thy glory;"[2] but will without foresight raise in his heart a house that is not beautiful, and that is unworthy of the Holy Ghost, one that will presently fall, and so will receive no glory from the reception of the blessed Inhabitant, but will be miserably destroyed by the fall of his building.

CHAPTER VII.

A question why the neighbourhood of our kinsfolk is considered to interfere with us, whereas it does not interfere in the case of those living in Egypt.

GERMANUS: It is a very useful and needful rule that is given for the kind of works that can be done within the cells. For we have often proved the value of this not only by the example of your holiness, based on the imitation of the virtues of the apostles, but also by our own experience. But it is not sufficiently clear why we ought so thoroughly to avoid the neighbourhood of our kinsfolk, which you did not reject altogether. For if we see you, blamelessly walking in all the way of perfection, and not only dwelling in your own country but some of you having not even retired far from their own village, why should that which does not hurt you be considered bad for us?

CHAPTER VIII.

The answer that all things are not suitable for all men.

ABRAHAM: Sometimes we see bad precedents taken from good things. For if a man ventures to do the same thing as another, but not with the same mind and purpose, or not with equal goodness, he will immediately fall into the snares of deception and death through the very things from which others gain the fruit of eternal life: As that strong armed lad matched with the warlike giant in the combat would certainly have found, if he had been clad in the heavy armour of Saul fit only for men; and that by which one of stronger age would have laid low countless hosts of foes, would only have brought certain danger to the stripling, had he not with prudent discretion chosen the sort of weapons suitable to his youth, and armed himself against his foul foe not with breastplate and shield, with which he saw that others were equipped, but with those weapons with which he was able to fight. Wherefore it is right for each one of us first to consider carefully the measure of his powers and in accordance with its limits, to choose what system he pleases, because though all are good, yet all things cannot be fit for all men. For we do not assert that because the anchorite's life is good, it is therefore suited for everybody: for by many it is felt to be not only useless, but even injurious. Nor because we are right in taking up the system of the coenobium and the pious and praiseworthy care of the brethren, do we therefore consider that it ought to be followed by everybody. So also the fruits of the care of

---

[1] *Unius puncti lege.*   [2] Ps. xxv. (xxvi.) 8.

strangers are very plentiful, but this cannot be taken up by everybody without loss of patience. Further, the systems of your country and of this must first be weighed against each other; and then the powers of men gathered from the constant occurrence of their virtues or vices must be severally weighed in the opposite scales. For it may happen that what is difficult or impossible for a man of one nation in the case of others is somehow turned by ingrained habit into nature: just as some nations, separated by a wide difference of region, can bear tremendous force of cold or heat of the sun without any covering of the body, which certainly others who have no experience of that inclement sky, could not possibly endure, however strong they may be. So also do you who with the utmost efforts of mind and body are trying in this district to get the better of the nature of your country in many respects, diligently consider whether in those regions which, as report says, are frozen, and bound by the cold of excessive unbelief, you could endure this nakedness, if I may so term it. For to us the fact that our holy life is of long standing has almost naturally imparted this fortitude in our purpose, and if we see that you are our equals in virtue and constancy, you in like manner need not shun the neighbourhood of your kinsfolk and brethren.

CHAPTER IX.

That those need not fear the neighbourhood of their kinsfolk, who can emulate the mortification of Abbot Apollos.

BUT that you may be able fairly to measure the amount of your strength by a certain test of strictness I will point out to you what was done by a certain old man; viz., Abbot Apollos[1] that if your secret scrutiny of your heart decides that you are not behind this man in purpose and goodness, you may venture on remaining in your country and living near your kinsfolk without detriment to your purpose or injury to your mode of life, and be sure that neither the feeling of nearness nor your love for the district can interfere with the strictness of this humble lot,[2] which not only your own will but the needs also of your pilgrimage enforce upon you in this country. When then his own brother had come to this old man, whom we have mentioned, in the dead of night, begging him to come out for a little while from his monastery, to help him to rescue an ox, which as he sadly complained had stuck in the mire of a swamp a little way off, because he could not possibly rescue it

alone, Abbot Apollos stolidly replied to his entreaties: "Why did you not ask our younger brother who was nearer to you as you passed by than I?" and when the other, thinking that he had forgotten the death of his brother who had been long ago buried, and that he was almost weak in his mind from excessive abstinence and continual solitude, replied: "How could I summon one who died fifteen years ago?" Abbot Apollos said: "Don't you know that I too have been dead to this world for twenty years, and that I can't from my tomb in this cell give you any assistance in what belongs to the affairs of this present life? And Christ is so far from allowing me ever so little to relax my purpose of mortification on which I have entered, for extricating your ox, that He did not even permit the very shortest intermission of it for my father's funeral, which would have been undertaken much more readily properly and piously." And so do ye now search out the secrets of your breast and carefully consider whether you also can continually preserve such strictness of mind with regard to your kinsfolk, and when you find that you are like him in this mortification of soul, then at last you may know that in the same way the neighbourhood of your kinsfolk and brothers will not hurt you, when, I mean, you hold that though they are very close to you, you are dead to them, in such a way that you suffer neither them to be benefited by your assistance, nor yourselves to be relaxed by duties towards them.

CHAPTER X.

A question whether it is bad for a monk to have his wants supplied by his kinsfolk.

GERMANUS: On this subject you have certainly left no room for any further uncertainty. For we are sure that we cannot possibly keep up our present wretched garb, or our daily going barefoot in their neighbourhood, and that there we should not even procure with the same labour what is necessary for our sustenance, as here we are actually obliged to fetch our water on our necks for three miles. For shame on our part as well as on theirs would not in the least allow us to do this before them. However how will it hurt our plan of life if we are altogether set free from anxiety on the score of preparing our food, by being supplied by them with all things, and so give ourselves up simply to reading and prayer, that by the removal of that labour with which we are now distracted we may devote ourselves more earnestly to spiritual interests alone?

---

[1] Cf. the note on II. xiii.   [2] Cf. the note on XIX. iii.

CHAPTER XI.

The answer stating what Saint Antony laid down on this matter.

ABRAHAM: I will not give you my own opinion against this, but that of the blessed Antony, whereby he confounded the laziness of a certain brother (overcome by this lukewarmness which you describe) in such a way as also to cut the knot of your subject. For when one came as I said to the aforesaid old man, and said that the Anchorite system was not at all to be admired, declaring that it required greater virtue for a man to practise what belongs to perfection living among men rather than in the desert, the blessed Antony asked where he lived himself, and when he said that he lived close to his relations, and boasted that by their provision he was set free from all care and anxiety of daily work, and gave himself up ceaselessly and solely to reading and prayer without any distraction of spirit, once more the blessed Antony said: "Tell me, my good friend, whether you grieve with their griefs and misfortunes, and in the same way rejoice in their good fortune?" He confessed that he shared in them both. To whom the old man: "You should know," said he, "that in the world to come also you will be judged in the lot of those with whom in this life you have been affected by sharing in their gain or loss, or joy or sorrow." And not satisfied with this statement the blessed Antony entered on a still wider field of discussion, saying: "This mode of life and this most lukewarm condition not only strike you with that damage of which I spoke (though you do not feel it now, when somehow you say in accordance with that saying in Proverbs: 'They strike me but I am not grieved: and they mocked me but I knew it not;' or this that is said in the Prophet: 'And strangers have devoured his strength, but he himself knew it not'[1]), because day after day they ceaselessly drag down your mind to earthly things, and change it in accordance with the variations of chance; but also because they defraud you of the fruits of your hands and the due reward of your own exertions, as they do not suffer you to be supported by what these supply, or to procure your daily food for yourself with your own hands, according to the rule of the blessed Apostle, as he when giving his last charge to the heads of the Church of Ephesus, asserts that though he was occupied with the sacred duties of preaching the gospel yet he provided not only for himself, but

also for those who were prevented by necessary duties with regard to his ministry, saying: 'Ye yourselves know that these hands have ministered to my necessities and to the necessities of those who were with me.' But to show that he did this as a pattern to be useful to us he says elsewhere: 'We were not idle among you; neither did we eat any man's bread for nothing, but in labour and in toil we worked night and day lest we should be chargeable to any of you. Not as if we had not power; but that we might give ourselves a pattern unto you, to imitate us."[2]

CHAPTER XII.

Of the value of work and the harm of idleness.

AND so though we also might have the protection of our kinsfolk, yet we have preferred this abstinence to all riches, and have chosen to procure our daily bodily sustenance by our own exertions rather than rely on the sure provision made by our relations, having less inclination for idle meditation on holy Scripture of which you have spoken, and that fruitless attendance to reading than to this laborious poverty. And certainly we should most gladly pursue the former, if the authority of the apostles had taught us by their examples that it was better for us, or the rules of the Elders had laid it down for our good. But you must know that you are affected by this no less than by that harm of which I spoke above, because though your body may be sound and lusty, yet you are supported by another's contributions, a thing which properly belongs only to the feeble. For certainly the whole human race, except only that class of monks, who live in accordance with the Apostle's command by the daily labours of their own hands, looks for the charity of another's compassion. Wherefore it is clear that not only those who boast that they themselves are supported either by the wealth of their relations or the labours of their servants or the produce of their farms, but also the kings of this world are supported by charity. This at any rate is embraced in the definition of our predecessors, who have laid down that anything that is taken for the requirements of daily food which has not been procured and prepared by the labour of our own hands, ought to be referred to| charity, as the Apostle teaches, who altogether forbids the help of another's bounty to the idle and says: "If a man does not work, neither let him eat."[3] These words

---

[1] Prov. xxiii. 35 (LXX.); Hos. vii. 9.   [2] Acts xx. 34; 2 Thess. iii. 7, 9.   [3] 2 Thess. iii. 10.

the blessed Antony used against some one, and instructed us also by the example of his teaching, to shun the pernicious allurements of our relations and of all who provide the needful charity for our food as well as the delights of a pleasant home, and to prefer to all the wealth of this world sandy wastes horrid with the barrenness of nature, and districts overwhelmed by living incrustations, and for that reason subject to no control or dominion of man, so that we should not only avoid the society of men for the sake of a pathless waste, but also that the character of a fruitful soil may never entice us to the distractions of cultivating it, whereby the mind would be recalled from the chief service of the heart, and rendered useless for spiritual aims.

CHAPTER XIII.

A story of a barber's payments, introduced for the sake of recognizing the devil's illusions.

FOR as you hope that you can save others also, and are eager to return to your country with the hope of greater gain, hear also on this subject a story of Abbot Macarius, very neatly and prettily invented, which he also gave to a man in a tumult of similar desires, to cure him by a most appropriate story. "There was," said he, "in a certain city a very clever barber, who used to shave everybody for three pence and by getting this poor and wretched sum for his work, out of this same amount used to procure what was required for his daily food, and after having taken all care of his body, used every day to put a hundred pence into his pocket. But while he was diligently amassing this gain, he heard that in a city a long way off each man paid the barber a shilling as his pay. And when he found this out, 'how long,' said he, 'shall I be satisfied with this beggary, so as to get with my labour a pay of three pence, when by going thither I might amass riches by a large gain of shillings?' And so at once taking with him the implements of his art, and using up in the expense all that he had got together and saved during a long time, he made his way with great difficulty to that most lucrative city. And there on the day of his arrival, he received from everyone the pay for his labour in accordance with what he had heard, and at eventide seeing that he had gained a large number of shillings he went in delight to the butcher's to buy the food he wanted for his supper. And when he began to purchase it for a large sum of shillings he spent on a

tiny bit of meat all the shillings that he had gained, and did not take home a surplus of even a single penny. And when he saw that his gains were thus used up every day so that he not only failed to put by anything but could scarcely get what he required for his daily food, he thought over the matter with himself and said: 'I will go back to my city, and once more seek those very moderate profits, from which, when all my bodily wants were satisfied, a daily surplus gave a growing sum to support my old age; which, though it seemed small and trifling, yet by being constantly increased was amounting to no slight sum. In fact that gain of coppers was more profitable to me than is this nominal one of shillings from which not only is there nothing over to be laid by, but the necessities of my daily food are scarcely met.'" And therefore it is better for us with unbroken continuance to aim at this very slender profit in the desert, from which no secular cares, no worldly distractions, no pride of vainglory and vanity can detract, and which the pressure of no daily wants can lessen (for "a small thing that the righteous hath is better than great riches of the ungodly"[1]) rather than to pursue those larger profits which even if they are procured by the most valuable conversion of many, are yet absorbed by the claims of secular life and the daily leakage of distractions. For, as Solomon says, "Better is a single handful with rest than both hands full with labour and vexation of mind."[2] And in these allusions and inconveniences all that are at all weak are sure to be entangled, as while they are even doubtful of their own salvation, and themselves stand in need of the teaching and instruction of others, they are incited by the devil's tricks to convert and guide others, and as, even if they succeed in gaining any advantage from the conversion of some, they waste by their impatience and rude manners whatever they have gained. For that will happen to them which is described by the prophet Haggai: "And he that gathereth riches, putteth them into a bag with holes."[3] For indeed a man puts his gains into a bag with holes, if he loses by want of self control and daily distractions of mind whatever he appears to gain by the conversion of others. And so it results that while they fancy that they can make larger profits by the instruction of others, they are actually deprived of their own improvement. For "There are who make themselves out rich though possessing nothing, and there are who humble themselves amid great riches;" and: "Better is a

---

[1] Ps. xxxvi. (xxxvii.) 16.   [2] Eccl. iv. 6.   [3] Hag. i. 6.

man who serves himself in a humble station than one who gains honour for himself and wanteth bread."[1]

CHAPTER XIV.

A question how such wrong notions can creep into us.

GERMANUS: Very aptly has your discussion shown the error of these illusions by this illustration: but we should like in the same way to be taught its origin and how to cure it, and we are equally anxious to learn how this deception has taken hold of us. For everybody must see that no one at all can apply remedies to ill health except one who has already diagnosed the actual origin of the disease.

CHAPTER XV.

The answer on the threefold movement of the soul.

ABRAHAM: Of all faults there is one source and origin, but different names are assigned to the passions and corruptions in accordance with the character of that part, or member, if I may so call it, which has been injuriously affected in the soul: As is sometimes also shown by the case of bodily diseases, in which though the cause is one and the same, yet there is a division into different kinds of maladies in accordance with the nature of the member affected. For when the violence of a noxious moisture has seized on the body's citadel, i.e., the head, it brings about a feeling of headache, but when it affects the ears or eyes, it passes into the malady of earache or ophthalmia: when it spreads to the joints and the extremities of the hands it is called the gout in the joints or hands; but when it descends to the extremities of the feet, its name is changed and it is termed podagra: and the noxious moisture which is originally one and the same is described by as many names as there are separate members which it affects. In the same way to pass from visible to invisible things, we should hold that the tendency to each fault exists in the parts and, if I may use the expression, members of our soul. And, as some very wise men have laid down that its powers are threefold, either what is λογικόν, i.e., reasonable, or θυμικόν, i.e., irascible, or ἐπιθυμητικόν, i.e., subject to desire, is sure to be troubled by some assault. When then the force of noxious passion takes possession of anyone by reason of these feelings, the name of the fault is given to it in accordance with the part affected. For if the plague of sin has infested its rational parts, it will produce the sins of vainglory, conceit, envy, pride, presumption, strife, heresy. If it has wounded the irascible feelings, it will give birth to rage, impatience, sulkiness, accidie, pusillanimity and cruelty. If it has affected that part which is subject to desire, it will be the parent of gluttony, fornication, covetousness, avarice, and noxious and earthly desires.

CHAPTER XVI.

That the rational part of our soul is corrupt.

AND therefore if you want to discover the source and origin of this fault, you must recognize that the rational part of your mind and soul is corrupt, that part namely from which the faults of presumption and vainglory for the most part spring. Further this first member, so to speak, of your soul must be healed by the judgment of a right discretion and the virtue of humility, as when it is injured, while you fancy that you can not only still scale the heights of perfection but actually teach others, and hold that you are capable and sufficient to instruct others, through the pride of vainglory you are carried away by these vain rovings, which your confession discloses. And these you will then be able to get rid of without difficulty, if you are established as I said in the humility of true discretion and learn with sorrow of heart how hard and difficult a thing it is for each of us to save his soul, and admit with the inmost feelings of your heart that you are not only far removed from that pride of teaching, but that you are actually still in need of the help of a teacher.

CHAPTER XVII.

How the weaker part of the soul is the first to yield to the devil's temptations.

YOU should then apply to this member or part of the soul which we have described as particularly wounded, the remedy of true humility: for as, so far as appears, it is weaker than the other powers of the soul in you, it is sure to be the first to yield to the assaults of the devil. As when some injuries come upon us, which are caused either by toil laid upon us or by a bad atmosphere, it is generally the case in the bodies of men that those which are the weaker are the first to give in and yield to those chances, and when the disease has more particularly laid hold

---

[1] Prov. xiii. 7; xii. 9.

of them, it affects the sound parts of the body also with the same mischief, so also, when the pestilent blast of sin breathes over us the soul of each one of us is sure to be tempted above all by that passion, in the case of which its feebler and weaker portion does not make so stubborn a resistance to the powerful attacks of the foe, and to run the risk of being taken captive by those, in the case of which a careless watch opens an easier way to betrayal. For so Balaam[1] gathered that God's people could be by a sure method deceived, when he advised, that in that quarter, wherein he knew that the children of Israel were weak, the dangerous snares should be set for them, as he had no doubt that when a supply of women was offered to them, they would at once fall and be destroyed by fornication, because he was aware that the parts of their souls which were subject to desire were corrupted. So then the spiritual wickednesses tempt with crafty malice each one of us, by particularly laying insidious snares for those affections of the soul, in which they have seen that it is weak, as for instance, if they see that the reasonable parts of our soul are affected, they try to deceive us in the same way that the Scripture tells us that king Ahab was deceived by those Syrians, who said: "We know that the kings of Israel are merciful: And so let us put sackcloth upon our loins, and ropes round our heads, and go out to the king of Israel, and say to him: Thy servant Benhadad saith: I pray thee, let my soul live." And thereby he was affected by no true goodness, but by the empty praise of his clemency, and said: "If he still liveth, he is my brother;" and after this fashion they can deceive us also by the error of that reasonable part, and make us incur the displeasure of God owing to that from which we were hoping that we might gain a reward and receive the recompense of goodness, and to us too the same rebuke may be addressed: "Because thou hast let go from thy hand a man who was worthy of death, thy life shall be for his life, and thy people for his people."[2] Or when the unclean spirit says: "I will go forth, and will be a lying spirit in the mouth of all his prophets,"[3] he certainly spread the nets of deception by means of the reasonable feeling which he knew to be exposed to his deadly wiles. And this also the same spirit expected in the case of our Lord, when he tempted Him in these three affections of the soul, wherein he knew that all mankind had been taken captive, but gained nothing by his crafty wiles. For he approached that portion of his mind which was subject to desire, when he said: "Command that these stones be made bread;" the part subject to wrath, when he tried to incite Him to seek the power of the present life and the kingdoms of this world; the reasonable part when he said: "If Thou art the Son of God cast Thyself down from hence."[4] And in these his deception availed nothing for this reason because he found that there was nothing damaged in Him, in accordance with the supposition which he had formed from a false idea. Wherefore no part of His soul yielded when tempted by the wiles of the foe, "For lo," He saith, "the prince of this world cometh and shall find nothing in Me."[5]

CHAPTER XVIII.

A question whether we should be drawn back to our country by a proper desire for greater silence.

GERMANUS: Among other kinds of illusions and mistakes on our part, which by the vain promise of spiritual advantages have fired us with a longing for our country (as your holiness has discovered by the keen insight of your mind), this stands out as the principal reason, that sometimes we are beset by our brethren and cannot possibly continue in unbroken solitude and continual silence, as we should like. And by this the course and measure of our daily abstinence, which we always want to maintain undisturbed for the chastening of our body, is sure to be interfered with on the arrival of some of the brethren. And this we certainly feel would never happen in our own country, where it is impossible to find anyone, or scarcely anyone who adopts this manner of life.

CHAPTER XIX.

The answer on the devil's illusion, because he promises us the peace of a vaster solitude.

ABRAHAM: Never to be resorted to by men at all is a sign of an unreasonable and ill-considered strictness, or rather of the greatest coldness. For if a man walks in this way, on which he has entered, with too slow steps, and lives according to the former man, it is right that none — I say not of the saints — but of any men should visit him. But you, if you are inflamed with true and perfect love of our Lord, and follow God, who indeed is love, with entire fervour of spirit, are sure to be

---

[1] Cf. Numb. xxiv. [2] 1 Kings xx. 31, 32, 42. [3] 1 Kings xxii. 22. [4] S. Matt. iv. 3, 6. [5] S. John xiv. 30.

resorted to by men, to whatever inaccessible spot you may flee, and, in proportion as the ardour of divine love brings you nearer to God, so will a larger concourse of saintly brethren flock to you. For, as the Lord says, "A city set on an hill cannot be hid,"[1] because "them that love Me," saith the Lord, "will I honour, and they that despise Me shall be contemned."[2] But you ought to know that this is the subtlest device of the devil, this is his best concealed pitfall, into which he precipitates some wretched and heedless persons, so that, while he is promising them greater things, he takes away the requisite advantages of their daily profit, by persuading them that more remote and vaster deserts should be sought, and by portraying them in their heart as if they were sown with marvellous delights. And further some unknown and non-existent spots, he feigns to be well-known and suitable and already given over to our power and able to be secured without any difficulty. The men also of that country he feigns to be docile and followers of the way of salvation, that, while he is promising richer fruits for the soul there, he may craftily destroy our present profits. For when owing to this vain hope each one separates himself from living together with the Elders and has been deprived of all those things that he idly imagined in his heart, he rises as it were from a most profound slumber, and when awake will find nothing of those things of which he had dreamed. And so as he is hampered by larger requirements for this life and inextricable snares, the devil will not even allow him to aspire to those things which he had once promised himself, and as he is liable no longer to those rare and spiritual visits of the brethren which he had formerly avoided, but to daily interruptions from worldly folk, he will never suffer him to return even to the moderate quiet and system of the anchorite's life.

CHAPTER XX.

How useful is relaxation on the arrival of brethren.

THAT most refreshing interlude also of relaxation and courtesy, which sometimes is wont to intervene because of the arrival of brethren, although it may seem to us tiresome and what we ought to avoid, yet how useful it is and good for our bodies as well as our souls you must patiently hear in few words. It often happens I say not to novices and weak persons but even to those of the greatest

experience and perfection, that unless the strain and tension of their mind is lessened by the relaxation of some changes, they fall either into coldness of spirit, or at any rate into a most dangerous state of bodily health. And therefore when there occur even frequent visits from the brethren they should not only be patiently put up with, but even gratefully welcomed by those who are wise and perfect; first because they stimulate us always to desire with greater eagerness the retirement of the desert (for somehow while they are thought to impede our progress, they really maintain it unwearied and unbroken, and if it was never hindered by any obstacles, it would not endure to the end with unswerving perseverance), next because they give us the opportunity of refreshing the body, together with the advantages of kindness, and at the same time with a most delightful relaxation of the body confer on us greater advantage than those which we should have gained by the weariness which results from abstinence. On which matter I will briefly give a most apt illustration handed down in an old story.

CHAPTER XXI.

How the Evangelist John is said to have shown the value of relaxation.

IT is said that the blessed John, while he was gently stroking a partridge with his hands suddenly saw a philosopher approaching him in the garb of a hunter, who was astonished that a man of so great fame and reputation should demean himself to such paltry and trivial amusements, and said: "Can you be that John, whose great and famous reputation attracted me also with the greatest desire for your acquaintance? Why then do you occupy yourself with such poor amusements?" To whom the blessed John: "What is it," said he, "that you are carrying in your hand?" The other replied: "a bow." "And why," said he, "do you not always carry it everywhere bent?" To whom the other replied: "It would not do, for the force of its stiffness would be relaxed by its being continually bent, and it would be lessened and destroyed, and when the time came for it to send stouter arrows after some beast, its stiffness would be lost by the excessive and continuous strain, and it would be impossible for the more powerful bolts to be shot." "And, my lad," said the blessed John, "do not let this slight and short relaxation of my mind disturb you, as unless it sometimes relieved and relaxed the rigour of its purpose by some recreation, the spirit would lose its spring owing to the unbroken strain, and would be unable when need required, implicitly to follow what was right."[1]

CHAPTER XXII.

A question how we ought to understand what the gospel says: "My yoke is easy and My burden is light."

GERMANUS: As you have given us a remedy for all delusions, and by God's grace all the wiles of the devil by which we were harassed, have been exposed by your teaching, we beg that you will also explain to us this that is said in the gospel: "My yoke is easy, and My burden is light."[2] For it seems tolerably opposed to that saying of the prophet where it is said: "For the sake of the words of Thy lips I kept hard ways;" while even the Apostle says: "All who will live godly in Christ suffer persecutions."[3] But whatever is hard and fraught with persecutions cannot be easy and light.

CHAPTER XXIII.

The answer with the explanation of the saying.

ABRAHAM: We can prove by the easy teaching of our own experience that our Lord and Saviour's saying is perfectly true, if we approach the way of perfection properly and in accordance with Christ's will, and mortifying all our desires, and cutting off injurious likings, not only allow nothing to remain with us of this world's goods (whereby our adversary would find at his pleasure opportunities of destroying and damaging us) but actually recognize that we are not our own masters, and truly make our own the Apostle's words: "I live, yet not I, but Christ liveth in me."[4] For what can be burdensome, or hard to one who has embraced with his whole heart the yoke of Christ, who is established in true humility and ever fixes his eye on the Lord's sufferings and rejoices in all the wrongs that are offered to him, saying: "For which cause I please myself in my infirmities, in reproaches, in necessities, in persecutions, in distresses, for Christ: for when I am weak, then am I strong"?[5] By what loss of any common thing, I ask, will he be injured, who boasts of perfect renunciation, and voluntarily rejects for Christ's sake all the pomp of this world, and considers all and every of its desires as dung, so that he may gain Christ, and by continual meditation on this command of the gospel, scorns and gets rid of agitation at every loss: "For what shall it profit a man if he gain the whole world, but lose his own soul? Or what shall a man give in exchange for his soul?"[6] For the loss of what will he be vexed, who recognizes that everything that can be taken away from others is not their own, and proclaims with unconquered valour: "We brought nothing into this world: it is certain that we cannot carry anything out"?[7] By the needs of what want will his courage be overcome, who knows how to do without "scrip for the way, money for the purse,"[8] and, like the Apostle, glories "in many fasts, in hunger and thirst, in cold and nakedness"?[9] What effort, or what hard command of an Elder can disturb the peace of his bosom, who has no will of his own, and not only patiently but even gratefully accepts what is commanded him, and after the example of our Saviour, seeks to do not his own will, but the Father's, as He says Himself to His Father: "Nevertheless not as I will, but as Thou wilt"?[10] By what wrongs also, by what persecution will he be frightened, nay, what punishment can fail to be delightful to him, who always rejoices together with apostles in stripes, and longs to be counted worthy to suffer shame for the name of Christ?

CHAPTER XXIV.

Why the Lord's yoke is felt grievous and His burden heavy.

BUT the fact that to us on the contrary the yoke of Christ seems neither light nor easy, must be rightly ascribed to our perverseness, as we are cast down by unbelief and want of faith, and fight with foolish obstinacy against His command, or rather advice, who says: "If thou wilt be perfect, go sell (or get rid of) all that thou hast, and come follow Me,"[11] for we keep the substance of our worldly goods. And as the devil holds our soul fast in the toils of these, what remains but that, when he wants to sever us from spiritual delights, he should vex us by diminishing these and depriving us of them, contriving by his crafty wiles that when the sweetness of His yoke and lightness of His burden have become grievous to us through the evil of a corrupt desire, and when we are caught in the chains of that very property and substance, which we kept for our comfort and solace, he may

---

[1] The story is quoted by S. Francis de Sales, The Devout Life, and by Dean Goulbourn, Personal Religion, Part III. c. x.
[2] S. Matt. xi. 30.
[3] Ps. xvi. (xvii.) 4; 2 Tim. iii. 12.
[4] Gal. ii. 20.
[5] 2 Cor. xii. 10.
[6] S. Matt. xvi. 26.
[7] 1 Tim. vi. 7.
[8] S. Matt. x. 9, 10.
[9] 2 Cor. xi. 27.
[10] S. Matt. xxvi. 39.
[11] S. Matt. xix. 21.

always torment us with the scourges of worldly cares, extorting from us ourselves that wherewith we are tortured? For "Each one is bound by the cords of his own sins," and hears from the prophet: "Behold all you that kindle a fire, encompassed with flames, walk in the light of your fire, and in the flames which you have kindled." Since, as Solomon is witness, "Each man shall thereby be punished, whereby he has sinned." [1] For the very pleasures which we enjoy become a torment to us, and the delights and enjoyments of this flesh, turn like executioners upon their originator, because one who is supported by his former wealth and property is sure not to admit perfect humility of heart, not entire mortification of dangerous pleasures. But where all these implements of goodness give their aid, there all the trials of this present life, and whatever losses the enemy can contrive, are endured not only with the utmost patience, but with real pleasure, and again when they are wanting so dangerous a pride springs up that we are actually wounded by the deadly strokes of impatience at the slightest reproach, and it may be said to us by the prophet Jeremiah: "And now what hast thou to do in the way of Egypt, to drink the troubled water? And what hast thou to do with the way of the Assyrians, to drink the water of the river? Thy own wickedness shall reprove thee, and thy apostasy shall rebuke thee. Know thou and see that it is an evil and a bitter thing for thee to have left the Lord thy God, and that My fear is not with thee, saith the Lord." [2] How then is it that the wondrous sweetness of the Lord's yoke is felt to be bitter, but because the bitterness of our dislike injures it? How is it that the exceeding lightness of the Divine burden becomes heavy, but because in our obstinate presumption we despise Him by whom it was borne, especially as Scripture itself plainly testifies to this very thing saying: "For if they would walk in right paths, they would certainly have found the paths of righteousness smooth"? [3] It is plain, I say, that it is we, who make rough with the nasty and hard stones of our desires the right and smooth paths of the Lord; who most foolishly forsake the royal road made stony with the flints of apostles and prophets, and trodden down by the footsteps of all the saints and of the Lord Himself, and seek trackless and thorny places, and, blinded by the allurements of present delights, tear our way with torn legs and our wedding garment rent, through dark paths, overrun with the briars of sins, so as not only to be pierced

by the sharp thorns of the brambles but actually laid low by the bites of deadly serpents and scorpions lurking there. For "there are thorns and thistles in wrong ways, but he that feareth the Lord shall keep himself from them." [4] Of such also the Lord says elsewhere by the prophet: "My people have forgotten, sacrificing in vain, and stumbling in their ways, in ancient paths, to walk in them in a way not trodden." [5] For according to Solomon's saying: "The ways of those who do not work are strewn with thorns, but the ways of the lusty are trodden down." [6] And thus wandering from the king's highway, they can never arrive at that metropolis, whither our course should ever be directed without swerving. And this also Ecclesiastes has pretty significantly expressed saying: "The labour of fools wearies those who know not how to go to the city;" viz., that "heavenly Jerusalem, which is the mother of us all." [7] But whoever truly gives up this world and takes upon him Christ's yoke and learns of Him, and is trained in the daily practice of suffering wrong, for He is "meek and lowly of heart," [8] will ever remain undisturbed by all temptations, and "all things will work together for good to him." [9] For as the prophet Obadiah says the words of God are "good to him that walketh uprightly;" and again: "For the ways of the Lord are right, and the just shall walk in them; but the transgressors shall fall in them." [10]

CHAPTER XXV.

Of the good which an attack of temptation brings about.

AND so by the struggle with temptation the kindly grace of the Saviour bestows on us larger rewards of praise than if it had taken away from us all need of conflict. For it is a mark of a loftier and grander virtue to remain ever unmoved when hemmed in by persecutions and trials, and to stand faithfully and courageously at the ramparts of God, and in the attacks of men, girt as it were with the arms of unconquered virtue, to triumph gloriously over impatience and somehow to gain strength out of weakness, for "strength is made perfect in weakness." "For behold I have made thee," saith the Lord, "a pillar of iron and a wall of brass, over all the land, to the kings of Judah, and the princes and the

---

[1] Prov. v. 22; Isa. l. 11; Wisd. xi. 17.
[2] Jer. ii. 18, 19.   [3] Prov. ii. 20.

[4] Prov. xxii. 5.
[5] Jer. xviii. 15.
[6] Prov. xv. 19.
[7] Eccl. x. 15 (LXX.); Gal. iv. 26.
[8] S. Matt. xi. 29.
[9] Rom. viii. 28.
[10] Micah ii. 7; Hos. xiv. 10.

priests thereof, and all the people of the land. And they shall fight against thee and shall not prevail: for I am with thee to deliver thee, saith the Lord."[1] Therefore according to the plain teaching of the Lord the king's highway is easy and smooth, though it may be felt as hard and rough: for those who piously and faithfully serve Him, when they have taken upon them the yoke of the Lord, and have learnt of Him, that He is meek and lowly of heart, at once somehow or other lay aside the burden of earthly passions, and find no labour but rest for their souls, by the gift of the Lord, as He Himself testifies by Jeremiah the prophet, saying: "Stand ye on the ways and see, and ask for the old paths, which is the good way, and walk ye in it: and you shall find refreshment for your souls." For to them at once "the crooked shall become straight and the rough ways plain;" and they shall "taste and see that the Lord is gracious,"[2] and when they hear Christ proclaiming in the gospel: "Come unto Me all ye that labour and are heavy laden, and I will refresh you," they will lay aside the burden of their sins, and realize what follows: "For My yoke is easy, and My burden is light."[3] The way of the Lord then has refreshment if it is kept to according to His law. But it is we who by troublesome distractions bring sorrows and troubles upon ourselves, while we try even with the utmost exertion and difficulty to follow the crooked and perverse ways of this world. But when in this way we have made the Lord's yoke heavy and hard to us, we at once complain in a blasphemous spirit of the hardness and roughness of the yoke itself or of Christ who lays it upon us, in accordance with this passage: "The folly of man corrupteth his ways, but he blames God in his heart;"[4] and as Haggai the prophet says, when we say that "the way of the Lord is not right" the reply is aptly made to us by the Lord: "Is not My way right? Are not your ways rather crooked?"[5] And indeed if you will compare the sweet scented flower of virginity, and tender purity of chastity to the foul and fetid sloughs of lust, the calm and security of monks to the dangers and losses in which the men of this world are involved, the peace of our poverty to the gnawing vexations and anxious cares of riches, in which they are night and day consumed not without the utmost peril to life, then you will prove that the yoke of Christ is most easy and His burden most light.

CHAPTER XXVI.

How the promise of an hundredfold in this life is made to those whose renunciation is perfect.

FURTHER also that recompense of reward, wherein the Lord promises an hundredfold in this life to those whose renunciation is perfect, and says: "And everyone that hath left house or brethren or sisters or father or mother or wife or children or lands for My name's sake, shall receive an hundredfold in the present time and shall inherit eternal life,"[6] is rightly and truly taken in the same sense without any disturbance of faith. For many taking occasion by this saying, insist with crass intelligence that these things will be given carnally in the millennium, though they must certainly admit that that age, which they say will be after the resurrection cannot possibly be understood as present. It is then more credible and much clearer that one, who at the persuasion of Christ has made light of any worldly affections or goods, receives from the brethren and partners of his life, who are joined to him by a spiritual tie, even in this life a love which is an hundred times better: since it is certain that among parents and children and brothers, wives and relations, where either the tie is merely formed by intercourse, or the bond of union by the claims of relationship, the love is tolerably short lived and easily broken. Finally even good and duteous children when they have grown up, are sometimes shut out by their parents from their homes and property, and sometimes for a really good reason the tie of matrimony is severed, and a quarrelsome division destroys the property of brothers. Monks alone maintain a lasting union in intimacy, and possess all things in common, as they hold that everything that belongs to their brethren is their own, and that everything which is their own is their brethren's. If then the grace of our love is compared to those affections where the bond of union is a carnal love, certainly it is an hundred times sweeter and finer. There will indeed also be gained from conjugal continence a pleasure that is an hundred times greater than that which arises from the union of the sexes. And instead of that joy, which a man experiences from the possession of a single field or house, he will enjoy a delight in riches a hundred times greater, if he passes over to the adoption of sons of God, and possesses as his own all things which belong to the eternal Father, and asserts in heart and soul after the fash-

---

[1] Jer. i. 18, 19. [2] Jer. vi. 16; Isa. xl. 4; Ps. xxxiii. (xxxiv.) 9.
[3] S. Matt. xi. 28-30. [5] Ezek. xviii. 25 (LXX.).
[4] Prov. xix. 3 (LXX.).

[6] S. Matt. xix. 29.

ion of that true Son: "All things that the Father hath are mine;"[1] and if no longer tried by that criminal anxiety in distractions and cares, but free from care and glad at heart, he succeeds everywhere to his own, hearing daily the announcement made to him by the Apostle: "For all things are yours, whether the world, or things present, or things to come;" and by Solomon: "The faithful man has a whole world of riches."[2] You have then that recompense of an hundredfold brought out by the greatness of the value, and the difference of the character that cannot be estimated. For if for a fixed weight of brass or iron or some still commoner metal, one had given in exchange the same weight only in gold, he would appear to have given much more than an hundredfold. And so when for the scorn of delights and earthly affections there is made a recompense of spiritual joy and the gladness of a most precious love, even if the actual amount be the same, yet it is an hundred times better and grander. And to make this plainer by frequent repetition: I used formerly to have a wife in the lustful passion of desire: I now have one in honourable sanctification and the true love of Christ. The woman is but one, but the value of the love has increased an hundredfold. But if instead of distrusting anger and wrath you have regard to constant gentleness and patience, instead of the stress of anxiety and trouble, peace and freedom from care, instead of the fruitless and criminal vexation of this world the salutary fruits of sorrow, instead of the vanity of temporal joy the richness of spiritual delights, you will see in the change of these feelings a recompense of an hundred-fold. And if we compare with the short-lived and fleeting pleasure of each sin the benefits of the opposite virtues the increased delights will prove that these are an hundred times better. For in counting on your fingers you transfer the number of an hundred from the left hand to the right and though you seem to keep the same arrangement of the fingers yet there is a great increase in the amount of the quantity.[3] For the result will be that we who seemed to bear the form of the goats on the left hand, will be removed and gain the reward of the sheep on the right hand. Now let us pass on to consider the nature of those things which Christ gives back to us in this world for our scorn of worldly advantages, more particularly according to

the Gospel of Mark who says: "There is no man who hath left house or brethren or sisters or mother or children or lands for My sake and the gospel's sake, who shall not receive an hundred times as much now in this time: houses and brethren and sisters and mothers and children and lands, with persecutions, and in the world to come life eternal."[4] For he who for the sake of Christ's name disregards the love of a single father or mother or child, and gives himself over to the purest love of all who serve Christ, will receive an hundred times the amount of brethren and kinsfolk; since instead of but one he will begin to have so many fathers and brethren bound to him by a still more fervent and admirable affection. He also will be enriched with an increased possession of lands, who has given up a single house for the love of Christ, and possesses countless homes in monasteries as his own, to whatever part of the world he may retire, as to his own house. For how can he fail to receive an hundred-fold, and, if it is not wrong to add somewhat to our Lord's words, more than an hundred-fold, who gives up the faithless and compulsory service of ten or twenty slaves and relies on the spontaneous attendance of so many noble and free born men? And that this is so you could prove by your own experience, as since you have each left but one father and mother and home, you have gained without any effort or care, in any part of the world to which you have come, countless fathers and mothers and brethren, as well as houses and lands and most faithful servants, who receive you as their masters, and welcome, and respect, and take care of you with the utmost attention. But, I say that deservedly and confidently will the saints enjoy this service, if they have first submitted themselves and everything they have by a voluntary offering for the service of the brethren. For, as the Lord says, they will freely receive back that which they themselves have bestowed on others. But if a man has not first offered this with true humility to his companions, how can he calmly endure to have it offered to him by others, when he knows that he is burdened rather than helped by their services, because he prefers to receive attention from the brethren rather than to give it to them? But all these things he will receive not with careless slackness and a lazy delight, but, in accordance with the Lord's word, "with persecutions," i.e., with the pressure of this world, and terrible distress from his passions, because, as the wise man testifies: "He who is easy going and without trouble shall come

---

[1] S. John xvi. 15.   [2] 1 Cor. iii. 22; Prov. xvii. 6 (LXX.).
[3] The passage alludes to the practice of counting on the fingers, in which all the tens up to ninety were reckoned on the fingers of the *left* hand, but with the number of a hundred the reckoning began with the same arrangement of the fingers, on the *right* hand. S. Jerome has a similar allusion to the practice in his work against Jovinian I. i. and compare also Juvenal Satire. X. l. 247, 248.

[4] S. Mark x. 29, 30.

to want."[1] For not the slothful, or the careless, or the delicate, or the tender take the kingdom of heaven by force, but the violent. Who then are the violent? Surely they are those who show a splendid violence not to others, but to their own soul, who by a laudable force deprive it of all delights in things present, and are declared by the Lord's mouth to be splendid plunderers, and by rapine of this kind, violently seize upon the kingdom of heaven. For, as the Lord says, "The kingdom of heaven suffereth violence and the violent take it by force."[2] Those are certainly worthy of praise as violent, who do violence to their own destruction, for, "A man," as it is written, "that is in sorrow laboureth for himself and does violence to his own destruction."[3] For our destruction is delight in this present life, and to speak more definitely, the performance of our own likes and desires, as, if a man withdraws these from his soul and mortifies them, he straightway does glorious and valuable violence to his own destruction, provided that he refuses to it the pleasantest of its wishes which the Divine word often rebukes by the prophet, saying: "For in the days of your fast your own will is found;" and again: "If thou turn away thy foot from the Sabbath, to do thy will on My holy day, and glorify him, while thou dost not thy own ways, and thy own will is not found, to speak a word." And the great blessedness that is promised to him is at once added by the prophet. "Then," he says, "shalt thou be delighted in the Lord, and I will lift thee up above the high places of the earth, and will feed thee with the inheritance of Jacob thy father. For the mouth of the Lord hath spoken it."[4] And therefore our Lord and Saviour, to give us an example of giving up our own wills, says: "I came not to do My own will, but the will of Him that sent Me;" and again: "Not as I will, but as Thou wilt."[5] And this good quality those men in particular show who live in the cœnobia and are governed by the rule of the Elders, who do nothing of their own choice, but their will depends upon the will of the Abbot. Finally to bring this discussion to a close, I ask you, do not those who faithfully serve Christ, most clearly receive grace an hundredfold in this, while for His name's sake they are honoured by the greatest princes, and though they do not look for the praise of men, yet become venerated in the trials of persecution

whose humble condition would perhaps have been looked down upon even by common folk, either because of their obscure birth, or because of their condition as slaves, if they had continued in their life in the world? But because of the service of Christ no one will venture to raise a calumny against their state of nobility, or to fling in their teeth the obscurity of their origin. Nay rather, through the very opprobrium of a humble condition by which others are shamed and confounded, the servants of Christ are more splendidly ennobled, as we can clearly show by the case of Abbot John who lives in the desert which borders on the town of Lycus. For he sprang from obscure parents, but owing to the name of Christ has become so well known to almost all mankind that the very lords of creation, who hold the reins of this world and of empire, and are a terror to all powers and kings, venerate him as their lord, and from distant countries seek his advice, and entrust to his prayers and merits the crown of their empire, and the state of safety, and the fortunes of war.[6]

In such terms the blessed Abraham discoursed on the origin of and remedy for our illusion, and exposed to our eyes the crafty thoughts which the devil had originated and suggested, and kindled in us the desire of true mortification, wherewith we hope that many also may be inflamed, even though all these things have been written in a somewhat simple style. For though the dying embers of our words cover up the glowing thoughts of the greatest fathers, yet we hope that in the case of very many who try to remove the embers of our words and to fan into a flame the hidden thoughts, their coldness will be turned into heat. But, O holy brethren, I have not indeed been so puffed up by the spirit of presumption as to give forth to you this fire (which the Lord came to send upon the earth, and which He eagerly longs to kindle[7]) in order that by the application of this warmth I might set on fire your purpose which is already at a white heat, but in order that your authority with your children might be greater, if in addition the precepts of the greatest and most ancient fathers support what you are teaching not by the dead sound of words but by your living example. It only remains that I who have been till now tossed about by a most dangerous tempest, should be wafted to the safe harbour of silence by the spiritual gales of your prayers.

---

[1] Prov. xiv. 23 (LXX.).
[2] S. Matt. xi. 12.
[3] Prov. xiv. 26 (LXX.).
[4] Isa. lviii. 3, 13, 14.
[5] S. John vi. 38; S. Matt. xxvi. 39.

---

[6] Cf. the note on the Institutes IV. xxiii. [7] Cf. S. Luke xii. 49.

THE SEVEN BOOKS OF JOHN CASSIAN

ON THE

INCARNATION OF THE LORD, AGAINST NESTORIUS.

PREFACE.

WHEN I had now finished the books of Spiritual Conferences, the merit of which consists in the thoughts expressed rather than in the language used (since my rude utterances were unequal to the deep thoughts of the saints), I had contemplated and almost determined on taking refuge in silence (as I was ashamed of having exposed my ignorance) that I might as far as possible make up for my audacity in speaking by modestly holding my tongue for the future. But you have overcome my determination and purpose by your commendable earnestness and most urgent affection, my dear Leo, my esteemed and highly regarded friend, ornament that you are of the Roman Church and sacred ministry,[1] as you drag me forth from the obscurity of the silence on which I had determined, into a public court which I may well dread, and oblige me to undertake new labours while I am still blushing for my past ones. And though I was unequal to lesser tasks, you compel me to match myself with greater ones. For even in those trifling works, in which of our small ability we offered some small offering to the Lord, I would never have attempted to do or apply myself to anything unless I had been led to it by Episcopal command. And so through you there has been an increase of importance both of our subject and of our language. For whereas before we spoke, when bidden, of the business of the Lord, you now require us to speak of the actual Incarnation and glory of the Lord Himself. And so we who were formerly brought as it were into the holy place of the temple by priestly hands, now penetrate under your guidance and protection, so to speak, into the holy of holies. Great is the honour but most perilous the undertaking,[2] because the prize of the holy sanctuary and the divine reward can only be secured by a victory over our foe. And so you require and charge us to raise our feeble hands against a fresh heresy and a new enemy of the faith,[3] and that we should take our stand, so to speak, against the awful open-mouthed gapings of the deadly serpent, that at my summons the power of prophecy and the divine force of the gospel word may destroy the dragon now rising up with sinuous course against the Churches of God. I obey your intreaty: I yield to your command: for I had rather trust in my own matters to you than to myself, especially as the love of Jesus Christ my Lord commands me this as well as you, for He Himself gives me this charge in your person. For in this matter you are more concerned than I am, as your judgment stands in peril rather than my duty. For in my case, whether I prove equal to what you have commanded me or no, the very fact of my obedience and humility will be in some degree an excuse for me; if indeed I might not urge that there is more value in my obedience, if there is less that I can do. For we easily comply with any one's orders, out of our abundance: but his is a great and wonderful work, whose desires exceed his powers. Yours then is this work and business, and yours it is to be ashamed of it. Pray and intreat that your choice may not be discredited by my clumsiness; and that, supposing we do not answer the expectations which you have formed of us, you may not seem to have been wrong in commanding out of an ill-considered determination, while I was right in yielding, owing to the claims of obedience.

---

[1] *Mi Leo, veneranda ac suscipienda caritas mea, Romanæ ecclesiæ ac divini ministerii decus* (Pętschenig). Gennadius (De Vir. Illust. c. lxi.) tells us of Cassian, that "finally at the request of Leo, then archdeacon of Rome and afterwards Bishop, he wrote seven books against Nestorius on the Incarnation of the Lord, and thus brought to a close his literary labours at Marseilles, as well as his life, in the reign of Theodosius and Valentinian. The date of the work must have been A.D. 430, shortly before the Council of Ephesus.

[2] *Professio* (Petschenig): *Progressio* (Gazæus).

[3] Nestorius had been consecrated Bishop of Constantinople in A.D. 428, and very shortly afterwards joined Anastasius in the denial that God could be born of a woman, and developed the heresy associated with his name.

THE SEVEN BOOKS OF JOHN CASSIAN

ON THE

INCARNATION OF THE LORD, AGAINST NESTORIUS.

BOOK I.

CHAPTER I.

The heresy compared to the hydra of the poets.[1]

THE tales of poets tell us that of old the hydra when its heads were cut off gained by its injuries, and sprang up more abundantly: so that owing to a miracle of a strange and unheard-of kind, its loss proved a kind of gain to the monster which was thus increased by death, while that extraordinary fecundity doubled everything which the knife of the executioner cut off, until the man who was eagerly seeking its destruction, toiling and sweating, and finding his efforts so often baffled by useless labours, added to the courage of battle the arts of craft, and by the application of fire, as they tell us, cut off with a fiery sword the manifold offspring of that monstrous body; and so when the inward parts were thus burnt, by cauterizing the rebellious throbbings of that ghastly fecundity, at length those prodigious births were brought to an end. Thus also heresies in the churches bear some likeness to that hydra which the poets' imagination invented; for *they* too hiss against us with deadly tongues; and *they* too cast forth their deadly poison, and spring up again when their heads are cut off. But because the medicine should not be wanting when the disease revives, and because the remedy should be the more speedy as the sickness is the more dangerous, our Lord God is able to bring to pass that that may be a truth in the church's warfare, which Gentile fictions imagined of the death of the hydra, and that the fiery sword of the Holy Spirit may cauterize the inward parts of that most dangerous birth, in the new heresy to be put down, so that at last its monstrous fecundity may cease to answer to its dying throbs.

CHAPTER II.

Description of the different heretical monsters which spring from one another.

FOR these shoots of an unnatural seed are no new thing in the churches. The harvest of the Lord's field has always had to put up with burrs and briars, and in it the shoots of choking tares have constantly sprung up. For hence have arisen the Ebionites, Sabellians, Arians, as well as Eunomians and Macedonians, and Photinians and Apollinarians, and all the other tares of the churches, and thistles which destroy the fruits of good faith. And of these the earliest was Ebion,[2] who while over-anxious about asserting our Lord's humanity[3] robbed it of its union with Divinity. But after him the schism of Sabellius burst forth out of reaction against the above mentioned heresy, and as he declared that there was no distinction between the Father, Son and Holy Ghost, he impiously confounded, as far as was possible, the Persons, and failed to distinguish the holy and ineffable Trinity. Next after him whom we have mentioned there followed the blasphemy of Arian perversity, which, in order to avoid the appearance of confounding the Sacred Persons, declared that there were different and

---

[1] Petschenig's text gives no titles to the chapters in this work. They are added here from the text of Gazæus.

[2] The earliest writer to allude to an "Ebion" as the supposed founder of the Ebionites is Tertullian (Præscriptio c. xxxiii.). He is followed in this by Epiphanius (I. xxx.); Rufinus (In Symb. Apost. c. xxxix.), and others; but the existence of such a person is more than doubtful, and the name is now generally believed to have been derived from the Hebrew "Ebhion"=poor.

[3] Incarnatio.

dissimilar substances in the Trinity. But after him in time though like him in wickedness came Eunomius, who, though allowing that the Persons of the Holy Trinity were divine and like [1] each other, yet insisted that they were separate from each other; and so while admitting their likeness denied their equality. Macedonius also blaspheming against the Holy Ghost with unpardonable wickedness, while allowing that the Father and the Son were of one substance, termed the Holy Ghost a creature, and so sinned against the entire Divinity, because no injury can be offered to anything in the Trinity without affecting the entire Trinity. But Photinus, though allowing that Jesus who was born of the Virgin was God, yet erred in his notion that His Godhead began with the beginning of His manhood; [2] while Apollinaris through inaccurately conceiving the union of God and man wrongly believed that He was without a human soul. For it is as bad an error to add to our Lord Jesus Christ what does not belong to Him as to rob Him of that which is His. For where He is spoken of otherwise than as He is — even though it seems to add to His glory — yet it is an offence. And so one after another out of reaction against heresies they give rise to heresies, and all teach things different from each other, but equally opposed to the faith. And just lately also, i.e., in our own days, we saw a most poisonous heresy spring up from the greatest city of the Belgæ, [3] and though there was no doubt about its error, yet there was a doubt about its name, because it arose

with a fresh head from the old stock of the Ebionites, and so it is still a question whether it ought to be called old or new. For it was new as far as its upholders were concerned; but old in the character of its errors. Indeed it blasphemously taught that our Lord Jesus Christ was born as a mere man, and maintained that the fact that He afterwards obtained the glory and power of the Godhead resulted from His human worth and not from His Divine nature; and by this it taught that He had not always His Divinity by the right of His very own Divine nature which belonged to Him, but that He obtained it afterwards as a reward for His labours and sufferings. Whereas then it blasphemously taught that our Lord and Saviour was not God at His birth, but was subsequently taken into the Godhead, it was indeed bordering on this heresy which has now sprung up, and is as it were its first cousin and akin to it, and, harmonizing both with Ebionism and these new ones, came in point of time between them, and was linked with them both in point of wickedness. And although there are some others like those which we have mentioned yet it would take too long to describe them all. Nor have we now undertaken to enumerate those that are dead and gone, but to refute those which are novel.

CHAPTER III.

He describes the pestilent error of the Pelagian.

AT any rate we think that this fact ought not to be omitted, which was special and peculiar to that heresy mentioned above which sprang from the error of Pelagius; viz., that in saying that Jesus Christ had lived as a mere man without any stain of sin, they actually went so far as to declare that men could also be without sin if they liked. For they imagined that it followed that if Jesus Christ being a mere man was without sin, all men also could without the help of God be whatever He as a mere man without participating in the Godhead, could be. And so they made out that there was no difference between any man and our Lord Jesus Christ, as any man could by effort and striving obtain just the same as Christ had obtained by His earnestness and efforts. Whence it resulted that they broke out into a more grievous and unnatural madness, and said that our Lord Jesus Christ had come into this world not to bring redemption to mankind but to give an example of good works, to wit, that men, by following His teaching, and by

---

[1] Cassian's statement here is scarcely accurate, as Eunomius is best known from his bold assertion that the Son was *unlike* (ἀνόμοιον) to the Father.

[2] Photinus, the pupil of Marcellus of Ancyra, appears to have taught a form of Sabellianism, teaching that Christ Himself, the Son of God, had not existed from all eternity but only from the time when He became the Son of God and Christ; viz., at the Incarnation.

[3] *Et maxima Belgarum urbe* (Petschenig). Gazæus edits: *Et maxime Beligarum urbe.* The city must be Trêves, and the allusion is to the heresy of Leporius, which was an outcome of Pelagianism. Leporius was apparently a native of Trêves, who propagated Pelagian views in Gaul, ascribing his virtues to his own free will and his own strength; and going to far greater lengths than his master in that he connected this doctrine of human sufficiency with heretical views on the Incarnation; thus combining Pelagianism with what was practically Nestorianism, teaching that Jesus was a mere man who had used His free will so well as to have lived without sin, and had only been made Christ in virtue of His Baptism, whereby the Divine and Human were associated so as virtually to make two Christs. He taught further that the only object of His coming into the world was to exhibit to mankind an example of virtue; and that if they chose to profit by it they also might be without sin. For these errors he was rebuked by Cassian and others in Gaul, and on his refusal to abandon them was formally censured by Proculus Bishop of Marseilles and Cylinnius (Bishop of Fréjus?). He then left Gaul and came to Africa, where he was convinced by Augustine of the erroneous character of his teaching, and under his influence signed a recantation, which was perhaps drawn up by Augustine himself, and from which Cassian quotes below (c. v.). This recantation was read in the Church of Carthage, and subscribed by four bishops as witnesses (including Augustine). It was then sent to the Gallican Bishops accompanied by a letter from the four attesting bishops (Epp. August. no. ccxxix.) commending the treatment which Leporius had previously received, but recommending him once more to their favour as having retracted his errors. See further Fleury H. E. Book XXIV. c. xlix. and Dictionary of Christian Biography, Art. Leporius.

walking along the same path of virtue, might arrive at the same reward of virtue: thus destroying, as far as they could, all the good of His sacred advent and all the grace of Divine redemption, as they declared that men could by their own lives obtain just that which God had wrought by dying for man's salvation. They added as well that our Lord and Saviour became the Christ after His Baptism, and God after His Resurrection, tracing the former to the mystery of His anointing, the latter to the merits of His Passion. Whence this new author [1] of a heresy that is not new, who declares that our Lord and Saviour was born a mere man, observes that he says exactly the same thing which the Pelagians said before him, and allows that it follows from his error that as he asserts that our Lord Jesus Christ lived as a mere man entirely without sin, so he must maintain in his blasphemy that all men can of themselves be without sin, nor would he admit that our Lord's redemption was a thing needful for His example, since men can (as they say) reach the heavenly kingdom by their own exertions. Nor is there any doubt about this, as the thing itself shows us. For hence it comes that he encourages the complaints of the Pelagians by his intervention, and introduces their case into his writings, because he cleverly or (to speak more truly) cunningly patronizes them and by his wicked liking for them recommends their mischievous teaching which is akin to his own, for he is well aware that he is of the same opinion and of the same spirit, and therefore is distressed that a heresy akin to his own has been cast out of the church, as he knows that it is entirely allied to his own in wickedness.

CHAPTER IV.

Leporius together with some others recants his Pelagianism.

BUT still as those who were the outcome of this stock of pestilent thorns have already by the Divine help and goodness been healed, we should also now pray to our Lord God that as in some points that older heresy and this new one are akin to each other, He would grant a like happy ending to those which had a like bad beginning. For Leporius, then a monk, now a presbyter, who followed the teaching or rather the evil deeds of Pelagius, as we said above, and was among the earliest and greatest champions of the aforesaid heresy in Gaul, was admonished by

us and corrected by God, and so nobly condemned his former erroneous persuasion that his amendment was almost as much a matter for congratulation as is the unimpaired faith of many. For it is the best thing never to fall into error: the second best thing to make a good repudiation of it. He then coming to himself confessed his mistake with grief but without shame not only in Africa, where he was then and is now, [2] but also gave to all the cities of Gaul penitent letters containing his confession and grief; in order that his return to the faith might be made known where his deviation from it had been first published, and that those who had formerly been witnesses of his error might also afterwards be witnesses of his amendment.

CHAPTER V.

By the case of Leporius he establishes the fact that an open sin ought to be expiated by an open confession; and also teaches from his words what is the right view to be held on the Incarnation.

AND from his confession or rather lamentation we have thought it well to quote some part, for two reasons: that their recantation might be a testimony to us, and an example to those who are weak, and that they might not be ashamed to follow in their amendment, the men whom they were not ashamed to follow in their error ; and that they might be cured by a like remedy as they suffered from a like disease. He then acknowledging the perverseness of his views, and seeing the light of faith, wrote to the Gallican Bishops, and thus began: [3] "I scarcely know, O my most venerable lords and blessed priests, what first to accuse myself of, and what first to excuse myself for. Clumsiness and pride and foolish ignorance together with wrong notions, zeal combined with indiscretion, and (to speak truly) a weak faith which was gradually failing, all these were admitted by me and flourished to such an extent that I am ashamed of having yielded to such and so many sins, while

---

[1] Nestorius.

[2] The after history of Leporius appears to have been this. Having come under Augustine's influence, he was persuaded by him to give up all his property, and renounce the temporal care of a monastery which he had previously founded in a garden at Hippo; where also he had begun to build a *xenodochium* or house of refuge for strangers, partly at his own expense, and partly out of the alms of the faithful. He also at Augustine's suggestion, built a church in memory of the "eight martyrs" (see Aug. Serm. 356). This complete renunciation of the world must have taken place about 425; and in the following year we find that he was present at the election of Eraclius to succeed Augustine (Aug. Ep. 213); but subsequent to this nothing is known of his history except that he was still living when Cassian wrote. It is right to mention that doubts have been raised by Tillemont whether the presbyter of Hippo is identical with the quondam heretic, but on scarcely sufficient grounds.

[3] The recantation of Leporius may be found in the Bibliotheca Maxima Patrum. vol. vii. p. 14; Labbe, Concilia, ii. p. 1678; and Migne Patrol. Lat. xxxi. p. 1221.

at the same time I am profoundly thankful for having been able to cast them out of my soul." And after a little he adds: "If then, not understanding this power of God, and wise in our conceits and opinions, from fear lest God should seem to act a part that was beneath Him, we suppose that a man was born in conjunction with God, in such a way that we ascribe to God alone what belongs to God separately, and attribute to man alone what belongs to man separately, we clearly add a fourth Person to the Trinity and out of the one God the Son begin to make not one but two Christs; from which may our Lord and God Jesus Christ Himself preserve us. Therefore we confess that our Lord and God Jesus Christ the only Son of God, who for His own sake[1] was begotten of the Father before all worlds, when in time He was for our sakes[1] made man of the Holy Ghost and the ever-virgin Mary, was God at His birth; and while we confess the two substances of the flesh and the Word,[2] we always acknowledge with pious belief and faith one and the same Person to be indivisibly God and man; and we say that from the time when He took upon Him flesh all that belonged to God was given to man, as all that belonged to man was joined to God.[3] And in this sense ' the Word was made flesh: '[4] not that He began by any conversion or change to be what He was not, but that by the Divine 'economy' the Word of the Father never left the Father,[5] and yet vouchsafed to become truly man, and the Only Begotten was incarnate through that hidden mystery which He alone understands (for it is ours to *believe:* His to *understand*). And thus God ' the Word' Himself receiving everything that belongs to man, is made man, and the manhood[6] which is assumed, receiving everything that belongs to God cannot but be God; but whereas He is said to be incarnate and unmixed, we must not hold that there is any

diminution of His substance: for God knows how to communicate Himself without suffering any corruption, and yet truly to communicate Himself. He knows how to receive into Himself without Himself being increased thereby, just as He knows how to impart Himself in such a way as Himself to suffer no loss. We should not then in our feeble minds make guesses, in accordance with visible proofs and experiments, from the case of creatures which are equal, and which mutually enter into each other, nor think that God and man are mixed together, and that out of 'such a fusion of flesh and the Word (i.e., the Godhead and manhood) some sort of body is produced. God forbid that we should imagine that the two natures being in a way moulded together should become one substance. For a mixture of this sort is destructive of both parts. For God, who contains and is not Himself contained, who enters into things and is not Himself entered into, who fills things and is not Himself filled, who is everywhere at once in His completeness and is diffused everywhere, communicates Himself graciously to human nature by the infusion of His power." And after a little: "Therefore the God-man, Jesus Christ, the Son of God, is truly born for us of the Holy Ghost and the ever-virgin Mary. And so in the two natures the Word and Flesh become one, so that while each substance continues naturally perfect in itself, what is Divine imparteth without suffering any loss, to the humanity, and what is human participates in the Divine; nor is there one person God, and another person man, but the same person is God who is also man: and again the man who is also God is called and indeed is Jesus Christ the only Son of God; and so we must always take care and believe so as not to deny that our Lord Jesus Christ, the Son of God, Very God (whom we confess as existing ever with the Father and equal to the Father before all worlds) became from the moment when He took flesh the God-man. Nor may we imagine that gradually as time went on He became God, and that He was in one condition before the resurrection and in another after it, but that He was always of the same fulness and power." And again a little later on: "But because the Word of God[7] vouchsafed to come down upon manhood by assuming manhood, and manhood was taken up into the Word by being assumed by God, God the Word in His completeness became complete man. For it was not God the Father who was made man, nor the Holy Ghost, but the Only Be-

---

[1] *Sibi . . . nobis.*

[2] *Caro* and *Verbum* when used in this way stand for the Humanity and the Divinity of Christ.

[3] The meaning of course is not that the manhood was endowed with the properties of Deity, or conversely the Deity with the properties of Humanity, but simply that *two whole and perfect natures* were joined together in the one Person.

[4] S. John i. 14.

[5] This phrase gives some countenance to the idea that the recantation was actually drawn up by Augustine, as the thought which it contains is a favorite one with him, as excluding any notion that Christ ever for one moment ceased to be God. See Serm. 184. "Intelligerent . . . Eum . . . in homine ad nos venisse et a Patre non recessisse." 186 "manens quod erat." Similar language is used by S. Leo, Serm. 18. c. 5. In Natio. 2. c. 2. and S. Thomas Aquinas in the well-known Sacramental hymn "Verbum supernum prodiens, Nec Patris linquens dexteram." Cf. Bright's S. Leo on the Incarnation, p. 220.

[6] *Homo* is here used as frequently by Augustine and other early writers for "Manhood," and not an "individual man." In this way it was freely used till the Nestorian Controversy, after which it went out of favour as capable of a Nestorian interpretation, and gave place to "humanitas" or "humana natura," when the manhood of Christ was spoken of. See the Church Quarterly Review, vol. xviii. p. 10; and Bright's S. Leo on the Incarnation, p. 165.

[7] *Verbum Dei* (Petschenig) *Verbum Deus* (Gazæus).

gotten of the Father; and so we must hold that there is one Person of the Flesh and the Word: so as faithfully and without any doubt to believe that one and the same Son of God, who can never be divided, existing in two natures [1] (who was also spoken of as a "giant" [2]) in the days of His Flesh truly took upon Him all that belongs to man, and ever truly had as His own what belongs to God: since even though [3] He was crucified in weakness, yet He liveth by the power of God."

CHAPTER VI.

The united doctrine of the Catholics is to be received as the orthodox faith.

THIS confession of his therefore, which was the faith of all Catholics was approved of by all the Bishops of Africa, [4] whence he wrote, and by all those of Gaul, to whom he wrote. Nor has there ever been anyone who quarrelled with this faith, without being guilty of unbelief: for to deny what is right and proved is to confess what is wrong. The agreement of all ought then to be in itself already sufficient to confute heresy: for the authority of all shows undoubted truth, and a perfect reason results where no one disputes it: so that if a man endeavours to hold opinions contrary to these, we should

in the first instance rather condemn his perverseness than listen to his assertions, for one who impugns the judgment of all announces beforehand his own condemnation, and a man who disturbs what has been determined by all, is not even given a hearing. For when the truth has once for all been established by all men, whatever arises contrary to it is by this very fact to be recognized at once as falsehood, because it differs from the truth. And thus it is agreed that this alone is sufficient to condemn a man; viz., that he differs from the judgment of truth. But still as an explanation of a system does no harm to the system, and truth always shines brighter when thoroughly ventilated, and as it is better that those who are wrong should be set right by discussion rather than condemned by severe censures, we should cure, as far as we can with the Divine assistance, this old heresy appearing in the persons of new heretics, that when through God's mercy they have recovered their health, their cure may bear testimony to our holy faith instead of their condemnation proving an instance of just severity. Only may the Truth indeed be present at our discussion and discourse concerning it, and assist our human weakness with that goodness with which God vouchsafed to come to men, as for this purpose above all He willed to be born on earth and among men; viz., that there might be no more room for falsehood.

BOOK II.

CHAPTER I.

How the errors of later heretics have been condemned and refuted in the persons of their authors and originators.

As we began by setting down in the first book some things by which we showed that our new heretic is but an offshoot from ancient stocks of heresy, the due condemnation of the earlier heretics ought to be enough to secure a

sentence of due condemnation for him. For as he has the same roots and grows up out of the same fallow [5] he has already been amply condemned in the persons of his predecessors, especially as those who went wrong immediately before these men very properly condemned the very thing which these men are now asserting, [6] so that the examples of their own party ought to be amply sufficient for them in both directions; viz., that of those who were restored and that of those who were condemned. For if they are capable of amendment they have their remedy set forth in the correction of their own party. If they are incapable of it they receive their sentence in the condemna-

---

[1] Substantiæ.
[2] The allusion is to Ps. xviii. (xix.) 5, where the Latin (Gallican Psalter) has "Exultavit, ut gigas, ad currendam viam." The mystical interpretation which takes the words as referring to Christ is not uncommon. So in a hymn "De Adventu Domini" (Mone. Vol. i. p. 43) we have the verse, "Procedit a thalamo suo Pudoris aula regia Geminæ gigas substantiæ, Alacris ut currat viam," and in another "De natali Domini" (p. 58) "Ut gigas egreditur ad currendam viam."
[3] Etsi (Petschenig) Et sic (Gazæus).
[4] The attesting Bishops who subscribed his recantation as witnesses were Aurelius of Carthage; Augustine of Hippo Regius; Florentius of the other Hippo; and Secundinus of Megarmita.

[5] Scrobibus (Petschenig): The text of Gazæus has enoribus.
[6] The allusion is to the recantation of Leporius and his companions. They were the immediate predecessors of Nestorius, and Cassian means to say that their recantation of their error ought to have been an example for Nestorius to follow.

tion of their own folk. But that we may not be thought to have prejudged the case against them instead of fairly judging it, we will produce their actual pestilent assertions, or rather I should say their blasphemous folly: taking "above all the shield of faith, and the sword of the Spirit which is the Word of God,"[1] that when the head of the old serpent rises once more, the same sword of the Divine Word which formerly severed it in the case of those ancient dragons may even now cut it off in the persons of these new serpents. For since the error of these is the same as that of those former ones, the decapitation of those ought to be counted as the decapitation of these; and as the serpents revive and emit pestilent blasts against the Lord's church, and cause some to fail through their hissing, we must on account of these new diseases add a fresh remedy to those older cures, so that even if what has already been done prove insufficient to heal[2] the malady, what we are now doing may be adequate to restore those who are suffering from it.

CHAPTER II.

Proof that the Virgin Mother of God was not only Christotocos but also Theotocos, and that Christ is truly God.

AND so you say, O heretic, whoever you may be, who deny that God was born of the Virgin, that Mary the Mother of our Lord Jesus Christ ought not to be called Theotocos, i.e., Mother of God, but Christotocos, i.e., only the Mother of Christ, not of God.[3] For no one, you say, brings forth what is anterior in time. And of this utterly foolish argument whereby you think that the birth of God can be understood by carnal minds, and fancy that the mystery of His Majesty can be accounted for by human reasoning, we will, if God permits, say something later on.[4] In the meanwhile we will now prove by Divine testimonies that Christ is God, and that Mary is the Mother of God. Hear then how the

angel of God speaks to the shepherds of the birth of God. "There is born," he says, "to you this day in the city of David a Saviour who is Christ the Lord."[5] In order that you may not take Christ for a mere man, he adds the name of Lord and Saviour, on purpose that you may have no doubt that He whom you acknowledge as Saviour is God, and that (as the office of saving belongs only to Divine power) you may not question that He is of Divine power, in whom you have learnt that the power to save resides. But perhaps this is not enough to convince your unbelief, as the angel of the Lord termed Him Lord and Saviour rather than God or the Son of God, as you certainly most wickedly deny Him to be God, whom you acknowledge to be Saviour. Hear then what the archangel Gabriel announces to the Virgin Mary. "The Holy Ghost," he says, "shall come upon thee, and the power of the Most High shall overshadow thee: therefore also that holy thing which shall be born of thee shall be called the Son of God."[6] Do you see how, when he is going to point out the nativity of God, he first speaks of a work of Divinity. For "the Holy Ghost," he says, "shall come upon thee, and the power of the Most High shall overshadow thee." Admirably did the angel speak, and explain the majesty of the Divine work by the Divine character of his words. For the Holy Ghost sanctified the Virgin's womb, and breathed into it by the power of His Divinity, and thus imparted and communicated Himself to human nature; and made His own what was before foreign to Him, taking it to Himself by His own power and majesty.[7] And lest the weakness of human nature should not be able to bear the entrance of Divinity the power of the Most High strengthened the ever to be honoured Virgin, so that it supported her bodily weakness by embracing it with overshadowing protection, and human weakness was not insufficient for the consummation of the ineffable mystery of the holy conception, since it was supported by the Divine overshadowing. "Therefore," he says, "the Holy Ghost shall come upon thee, and the power of the Most High shall overshadow thee." If only a mere man was to be born of a pure virgin why should there be such careful mention of the Divine Advent? Why such intervention of Divinity itself? Certainly if only a man was to be born from man, and flesh from flesh, a command alone might have done it, or the Divine will. For if the will of God alone, and His command

---

[1] Eph. vi. 16-17.
[2] *Curationem* (Petschenig): *Damnationem* (Gazæus).
[3] The Nestorian controversy was originated by a sermon of Anastasius a follower of Theodore of Mopsuestia, whom Nestorius brought with him to Constantinople as his chaplain on his appointment as Archbishop, A.D. 428. This man, preaching in the presence of the archbishop, said: "Let no one call Mary Theotocos; for Mary was but a woman, and it is impossible that God should be born of a woman." In the controversy which was immediately excited by these words Nestorius at once took the part of his chaplain and preached a course of sermons in maintenance of his views; refusing to the Blessed Virgin the title of Theotocos, while admitting that she might be termed Christotocos. See Socrates H. E. Book VII. c. xxxii. Evagrius H. E. Book I. c. ii. and Vincentius Lirinensis Book I. c. xvii. The sermons are still partially existing in the writings of Marius Mercator: and in the second of them the title Χριστοτόκος is admitted. Cf. Hefele's Councils Book IX. c. i. (Vol. iii. Eng. Transl. p. 12 *sq.*).
[4] The subject is dealt with in Book IV. c. ii.; VII. c. ii. *sq.*

[5] S. Luke ii. 11.   [6] S. Luke i. 35.
[7] On the conception by the Holy Ghost compare Pearson on the Creed. Article III. c. ii.

sufficed to fashion the heavens, form the earth, create the sea, thrones, and seats, and angels, and archangels, and principalities, and powers, and in a word to create all the armies of heaven, and those countless thousands of thousands of the Divine hosts ("For He spake and they were made, He commanded and they were created"[1]), why was it that *that* was insufficient for the creation of (according to you) a single man, which was sufficient for the production of all things divine, and that the power and majesty of God did not entrust *that* with the birth of a single infant, which had availed to fashion all things earthly and heavenly? But certainly the reason why all those works were performed by the command of God, but the nativity was only accomplished by His coming was because God could not be conceived by man unless He allowed it, nor be born unless He Himself entered in; and therefore the archangel pointed out that that sacred majesty would come upon the Virgin, I mean that as so great an event could not be brought about by human appointment, he announced that there would be present at the conception the glory of Him who was to be born.[2] And so the Word, the Son, descended: the majesty of the Holy Ghost was present: the power of the Father was overshadowing; that in the mystery of the holy conception the whole Trinity might cooperate. "Therefore," he says, "also that holy thing which shall be born of thee shall be called the Son of God." Admirably does he add "Therefore," in order to show that this would *therefore* follow *because* that had gone before; and that *because* God had come upon her at the conception *therefore* God would be present at the birth. And when the maiden understood not, he gave a reason for this great thing, saying: "Because the Holy Spirit shall come upon thee, and because the power of the Most High shall overshadow thee, therefore also that holy thing which shall be born shall be called the Son of God;" that is to say: That thou mayest not be ignorant of the provision for so great a work, and the mystery of this great secret, the majesty of God shall therefore come upon thee completely; because the Son of God shall be born of thee. What further doubt can there be about this? or what is there further to be said? He said that God would come upon her; that the Son of God would be born. Ask now, if you like, how the Son of God can help being God, or how she who brought forth God can fail to be

Theotocos, i.e., the Mother of God? This alone ought to be enough for you; aye this ought to be amply sufficient for you.

CHAPTER III.

Follows up the same argument with passages from the Old Testament.

BUT as there is an abundant supply of witnesses to the holy nativity; viz., all that has been on this account written, to bear witness to it, let us examine in some slight degree an announcement about God even in the Old Testament, that you may know that the fact that the birth of God was to be from a virgin was not only then announced when it actually came to pass, but had been foretold from the very beginning of the world, that, as the event to be brought about was ineffable, incredulity of the fact when actually present might be removed by its having been previously announced while still future. And so the prophet Isaiah says: "Behold a virgin shall conceive and bear a Son, and they shall call his name Emmanuel, which is interpreted God with us."[3] What room is there here for doubt, you incredulous person?[4] The prophet said that a virgin should conceive: a virgin *has* conceived: that a Son should be born: a Son *has* been born: that He should be called God: He *is* called God. For He is called by that name as being of that nature. Therefore when the Spirit of God said that He should be called God, He proved that He is without the Spirit of God who makes himself a stranger to all fellowship with the Divine title. "Behold then," he says, "a virgin shall conceive and bear a Son, and they shall call His name Emmanuel, which is interpreted God with us." But here is a point on which it is possible that your shuffling incredulity may fasten; viz., by saying that this which the prophet declared He should be called referred not to the glory of His Divinity, but to the name by which He should be addressed. But what are we to do because Christ is never spoken of by this name in the gospels, though the Spirit of God cannot be said to have spoken falsely through the prophet? How is it then? Surely that we should understand that that prophecy then foretold the name of His Divine nature and not of His humanity. For since in His manhood united to the Godhead[5] He received another name

---

[1] Ps. xxxii. (xxxiii.) 9.
[2] Petschenig's text is as follows: *Videlicet ut, quia agi tanta res per humanum officium non valebat, ipsius ad futuram diceret majestatem in conceptu, qui erat futurus in partu;* while Gazæus reads *deceret* for *diceret*.

[3] Isa. vii. 14. [4] *Incredule* (Petschenig). *Incredulæ* (Gazæus).
[5] Here is an instance of language which the mature judgment of the Church has rejected, as experience showed how it was capable of being pressed into the service of heresy. *Homo unitus Deo*, in Cassian's mouth evidently means the *manhood joined to the God-*

in the gospel, it is certainly clear that *this* name belonged to His humanity, *that* to His Divinity. But let us proceed further and summon other true witnesses to establish the truth: For where we are speaking about the Godhead, the Divinity cannot be better established than by His own witnesses. So then the same prophet says elsewhere: "For unto us a Son is born: unto us a child is given; and the government shall be upon His shoulder; and His name shall be called the angel of great counsel, God the mighty, the Father of the world to come, the Prince of peace."[1] Just as above the prophet had expressly said that He should be called Emmanuel, so here he says that He should be called "the angel of great counsel, and God the mighty, and the Father of the world to come and the prince of peace" (although we certainly never read that He was called by these names in the gospel): of course that we may understand that these are not terms belonging to His human, but to His Divine nature; and that the name used in the gospel belonged to the manhood which He took upon Him,[2] and this one to His innate power. And because God was to be born in human form, these names were so distributed in the sacred economy, that to the manhood a human name was given and to the Divinity a Divine one. Therefore he says: "He shall be called the angel of great counsel, God the mighty, the Father of the world to come, the prince of peace." Not, O heretic, whoever you may be, not that here the prophet, full as he was of the Holy Spirit, followed your example and compared Him who was born to a molten image and a figure fashioned without sense.[3] For "a Son," he says, "is born to us, a Child is given to us; and the government shall be upon his shoulder; and His name shall be called the angel of great counsel, God the

mighty." And that you may not imagine Him whom He announced as God[4] to be other than Him who was born in the flesh, he adds a term referring to His birth, saying: "A child is born to us: a son is given to us." Do you see how many titles the prophet used to make clear the reality of His birth in the body? for he called Him both Son and child on purpose that the manner of the child which was born might be more clearly shown by a name referring to His infancy; and the Holy Spirit foreseeing without doubt this perversity of blasphemous heretics, showed to the whole world that it was God who was born, by the very terms and words used; that even if a heretic was determined to utter blashemy, he might not find any loophole for his blasphemy. Therefore he says: "A Son is born to us; a child is given to us; and the government shall be upon His shoulder; and His name shall be called the angel of great counsel, God the mighty, the Father of the world to come, the prince of peace." He teaches that this child which was born is both prince of peace and Father of the world to come and God the mighty. What room is there then for shuffling? This child which is born cannot be severed from God who is born in Him, for he called Him, whom he spoke of as born, Father of the world to come; Him whom he called a child, he foretold as God the mighty. What is it, O heretic? Whither will you betake yourself? Every place is hedged and shut in: there is no possibility of getting out of it. There is nothing for it but that you should at length be obliged to confess the mistake which you *would* not understand. But not content with these passages which are indeed enough let us inquire what the Holy Ghost said through another prophet. "Shall a man," says he, "pierce his God, for you are piercing me?"[5] In order that the subject of the prophecy might be still clearer the prophet foretells what he proclaimed of the Lord's passion as if from the mouth of Him of whom he was speaking. "Shall a man pierce his God, for you are piercing me?" Does not our Lord God, I ask, seem to have said this when He was led to the Cross? Why indeed do you not acknowledge Me as your Redeemer? Why are ye ignorant of God clothed in flesh for you? Are you

---

head, but the words might easily be taken as implying that *a man* was united to God, i.e., that there were in the Incarnation two persons, one assuming and the other assumed, which was the essence of Nestorianism. Compare above, the note on *Homo* to Book I. c. v.

[1] Isa. ix. 6 where in the LXX. B reads ὅτι παιδίον ἐγεννήθη ἡμῖν, υἱὸς καὶ ἐδόθη ἡμῖν, οὗ ἡ ἀρχὴ ἐγενήθη ἐπὶ τοῦ ὤμου αὐτοῦ, καὶ καλεῖται τὸ ὄνομα αὐτοῦ Μεγάλης Βουλῆς ἄγγελος ἄξω γὰρ κ. τ. λ. To this, however, א and A add after ἄγγελος, θαυμαστὸς σύμβουλος · Θεὸς (our Θεὸς A) ἰσχυρὸς 'ἐξουσιαστὴς ἄρχων εἰρήνης πατὴρ τοῦ μέλλοντος αἰῶνος and hence in the main comes the old Latin version, which Cassian here follows. Jerome's version has Parvulus enim natus est nobis et filius datus est nobis; et factus est principatus super humerum ejus: et vocabitur nomen ejus admirabilis consiliarius Deus fortis pater futuri sæculi princeps pacis. The Hebrew has nothing directly corresponding to the "angel of great counsel," which seems to be intended as a paraphrase of "Wonderful Counsellor" (Cf. Judg. xiii. 18), while "Father of the world to come" is an interpretation of the Hebrew "Father of eternity."

[2] *Suscepti hominis.* Cf. the line in the Te Deum, which originally ran "Tu ad liberandum mundum suscepisti hominem: non horruisti virginis uterum."

[3] See the language of Nestorius himself quoted below in Book VII. c. vi. and cf. V. iii.

[4] The text of Gazæus omits *Deus.*

[5] Malachi iii. 8. Jerome's rendering is almost identical "Si affiget homo Deum, quia vos configitis me; " where the Douay version strangely departs from the literal sense of the word and renders vaguely "afflict." It is clear however that it was intended to be understood literally, as it is here taken by Cassian as a direct prophecy of the Crucifixion. The LXX. has πτερνιεῖ. The Hebrew word, which is only found again in Prov. xxii. 23, appears to mean "defraud."

preparing death for your Saviour? Are you leading forth to death the Author of life? I am your God whom ye are lifting up: your God whom ye are crucifying. What mistake, I ask, is here or what madness is it? "Shall a man pierce his God, for you are piercing me?" Do you see how exactly the words describe what was actually done? Could you ask for anything more express or clearer? Do you see how sacred testimonies follow our Incarnate Lord Jesus Christ from the very cradle to the Cross which He bore, as here you can see that He whom elsewhere you read of as God when born in the flesh was God when pierced on the cross? And so there, where His birth was treated of, He is spoken of by the prophet as God: and here where His crucifixion is concerned, He is most clearly named God; that the taking upon Him of manhood might not in any point prejudice the dignity of His Divinity, nor the humiliation of His body and the shame of the passion affect the glory of His majesty; for His condescension to so lowly a birth and His generous goodness in enduring his passion ought to increase our love and devotion to Him; since it is certainly a great and monstrous sin if, the more He lavishes love upon us, the less He is honoured by us.

CHAPTER IV.

He produces testimonies to the same doctrine from the Apostle Paul.

BUT passing over these things which cannot possibly be unfolded because there would be no limit to the telling of them, as the blessings which he gives are without stint, it is time for us to consult the Apostle Paul, the stoutest and clearest witness to Him, for he can tell us everything about God in the most trustworthy way because God always spoke from his breast. He then, the chosen teacher of the nations, who was sent to destroy the errors of Gentile superstition, bears his witness in the following way to the grace and coming of our Lord God: "The grace," he says, "of God and our Saviour appeared unto all men, instructing us that denying ungodliness and worldly desires we should live soberly and justly and godly in this world, looking for the blessed hope and coming of the glory of the great God and our Saviour Jesus Christ."[1] He says that "there appeared the grace of God our Saviour." Admirably does he use a word suited to show the arrival of a new grace and birth; for by saying "there appeared," he indicated the approach of a new grace and birth, for thenceforward the gift of a new grace began to appear, from the moment when God appeared as born in the world. Thus by using the right word, and one exactly suitable, he shows the light of this new grace almost as if he pointed to it with his finger. For that is most properly said to *appear*, which is shown by sudden light manifesting it. Just as we read in the gospel that the star *appeared* to the wise men in the East:[2] and in Exodus: "There *appeared*," he says, "to Moses an angel in a flame of fire in the bush:"[3] for in all these and in the case of other visions in the Holy Scripture, Scripture determined that this word in particular should be used, that it might speak of that as "appearing," which shone forth with unwonted light. So then the Apostle also, well knowing the coming of the heavenly grace, which appeared at the approach of the holy nativity, indicated it by using a term applied to a bright appearance; expressly in order to say that it *appeared*, as it shone with the splendour of a new light. "There appeared" then "the grace of God our Saviour." Surely you cannot raise any quibble about the ambiguity of the names in this place, so as to say that "Christ" is one and "God" another, or to divide "the Saviour" from the glory of His name, and separate "the Lord" from the Divinity? Lo, here the vessel[4] of God speaks from God, and testifies by the clearest statement that the grace of God appeared from Mary. And in order that you may not deny that God appeared from Mary, he at once adds the name of Saviour, on purpose that you may believe that He who is born of Mary is God, whom you cannot deny to have been born a Saviour, in accordance with this passage: "For to you is born to-day a Saviour."[5] O excellent teacher of the Gentiles truly given by God to them, for he knew that this wild heretical folly would arise, which would turn to controversial uses the names of God, and would not hesitate to slander God from His own titles; and so just in order that the heretic might not separate the title of Saviour from the Divinity he put first the name of God, that the name of God standing first might claim as His all the names which followed, and that no one might imagine that in what followed Christ was spoken of as a mere man, as by the very first word used he had

---

[1] Titus ii. 11–13.
[2] S. Matt. ii. 2, 7.
[3] Exod. iii. 2.
[4] *Vas Dei* (Petschenig): Gazæus has *Vis Dei*.
[5] S. Luke ii. 11.

taught that He was God. "Looking," says the same Apostle, "for the blessed hope and coming of the glory of the great God and our Saviour Jesus Christ." Certainly that teacher of divine wisdom saw that plain and simple teaching would not in itself be sufficient to meet the crafty wiles of the devil's cunning, unless he fortified the holy preaching of the faith with a protection of extreme care. And so although he had used the name of God the Saviour up above, he here adds "Jesus Christ," in case you might think that the mere name of Saviour was not enough to indicate to you our Lord Jesus Christ, and might fail to understand that the God, whom you acknowledge as God the Saviour, is the same Jesus Christ. What then does he say? He says: "Looking for the blessed hope and coming of the glory of the great God and our Saviour Jesus Christ." Nothing is here wanting as regards the titles of our Lord, and you see here God, and the Saviour, and Jesus, and Christ. But when you see all these, you see that they all belong to God. For you have heard of Him as God, but as Saviour as well. You have heard of Him as God, but as Jesus as well. You have heard of Him as God, but as Christ as well. That which the Divinity has joined and united together cannot be separated by this diversity of titles; for whichever you may seek for of them all, you will find it there. The Saviour is God, Jesus is God, Christ is God. In all of this which you hear, though the titles used are many, yet they belong to one Person in power. For whereas the Saviour is God, and Jesus is God, and Christ is God, it is easy to see that all these, though different appellations, are united as regards the Majesty. And when you hear quite plainly that one and the same Person is called God in each case, you can surely clearly see that in all these cases there is but one God spoken of. And so you cannot any longer seek to make out a distinction of power from the different names given to the Lord, or to make a difference of Person owing to variety of titles. You cannot say: Christ was born of Mary, but God was not; for an Apostle declares that God was. You cannot say that Jesus was born of Mary, but God was not; for an Apostle testifies that God was. You cannot say: the Saviour was born, but God was not; for an Apostle supports the fact that God was. There is no way of escape for you. Whichever of the titles of the Lord you may take, He is God, of whom you speak. You have nothing to say: nothing to assert: nothing to invent in your wicked falsehood. You can in impious un-

belief refuse to believe: you have nothing to deny in the matter of your blasphemy.

CHAPTER V.

From the gifts of Divine grace which we receive through Christ he infers that He is truly God.

ALTHOUGH we began to speak some time back on this Divine grace of our Lord and Saviour, I want to say somewhat more on the same subject from the Holy Scriptures. We read in the Acts of the Apostles that the Apostle James [1] thus refuted those who thought that when they received the gospel they ought still to bear the yoke of the old Law: "Why," said he, "do ye tempt God, to put a yoke upon the necks of the disciples which neither our fathers nor we have been able to bear. But by the grace of our Lord Jesus Christ we believe to be saved in like manner as they also." [2] The Apostle certainly speaks of the gift of this grace as given by Jesus Christ. Answer me now, if you please: do you think that this grace which is given for the salvation of all men, is given by man or by God? If you say, By man, Paul, God's own vessel, will cry out against you, saying: "There appeared the grace of God our Saviour." [3] He teaches that this grace is the result of a Divine gift, and not of human weakness. And even if the sacred testimony was not sufficient, the truth of the matter itself would bear its witness, because fragile earthly things cannot possibly furnish a thing of lasting and immortal value; nor can anyone give to another that in which he himself is lacking, nor supply a sufficiency of that, from the want of which he admits that he himself is suffering. You cannot then help admitting that the grace comes from God. It is God then who has given it. But it has been given by our Lord Jesus Christ. Therefore the Lord Jesus Christ is God. But if He be, as He certainly is, God: then she who bore God is Theotocos, i.e., the mother of God. Unless perhaps you want to take refuge in so utterly absurd and blasphemous a contradiction as to deny that she from whom God was born is the mother of God, while you cannot deny that He who was born is God. But, however, let us see what the gospel of God thinks about this same grace of our Lord: "Grace and truth," it says, "came by Jesus Christ." [4] If

---

[1] *Jacobum.* So Petschenig, after his authority. It is however an error on Cassian's part, as the words quoted were spoken not by S. James, but by S. Peter. (The text of Gazæus reads apparently with no authority *Petrum.*)
[2] Acts xv. 10, 11.   [3] Titus ii. 11.   [4] S. John i. 17.

Christ is a mere man, how did these come by Christ? Whence was there in Him Divine power if, as you say, there was in Him only the nature of man? Whence comes heavenly largesse, if His is earthly poverty? For no one can give what he has not already. As then Christ gave Divine grace, He already had that which He gave. Nor can anyone endure a diversity of things that are so utterly different from each other, as at one and the same time to suffer the wants of a poor man, and also to show the munificence of a bounteous one. And so the Apostle Paul, knowing that all the treasures of heavenly riches are found in Christ, rightly writes to the Churches: "The grace of our Lord Jesus Christ be with you."[1] For though he had already often enough taught that God is the same as Christ, and that all the glory of Deity resides in Him, and that all the fulness of the Godhead dwelleth in Him bodily, yet here he is certainly right in praying for the grace of Christ alone, without adding the word God: for while he had often taught that the grace of God is the same as the grace of Christ, he now most perfectly prays only for the grace of Christ, for he knows that in the grace of Christ is contained the whole grace of God. Therefore he says: "The grace of our Lord Jesus Christ be with you." If Jesus Christ was a mere man, then in his wish that the grace of Christ might be given to the Churches he was wishing that the grace of a man might be given; and by saying: "The grace of Christ be with you" he meant: the grace of a man be with you, the grace of flesh be with you, the grace of bodily weakness, the grace of human frailty! Or why did he ever even mention the word grace, if his wish was for the grace of a man? For there was no reason for wishing, if that was not in existence which was wished for; nor ought he to have prayed that there might be bestowed on them the grace of one who, according to you, did not possess the reality of that grace for which he was wishing. And so you see that it is utterly absurd and ridiculous — or rather not a thing to laugh at but to cry over, for what is a matter for laughter to some frivolous persons becomes a matter for crying to pious and faithful souls, for they shed tears of charity for the folly of your unbelief, and weep pious tears at the folly of another's impiety. Let us then recover ourselves for a while and take our breath, for this idea is not only without wisdom but also without the Spirit, as it is certainly wanting in spiritual wisdom and has nothing to do with the Spirit of salvation.

CHAPTER VI.

That the power of bestowing Divine grace did not come to Christ in the course of time, but was innate in Him from His very birth.

BUT perhaps you will say that this grace of our Lord Jesus Christ, of which the Apostle writes, was not born with Him, but was afterwards infused into Him by the descent of Divinity upon Him, since you say that the man Jesus Christ our Lord (whom you call a mere man) was not born with God, but afterwards was assumed by God:[2] and that through this grace was given to the man at the same time that Divinity was given to Him. Nor do we say anything else than that Divine grace descended with the Divinity, for the Divine grace of God is in a way a bestowal of actual Divinity and a gift of a liberal supply of graces. Perhaps then it may be thought that the difference between us is one of time rather than of what is essential, since the Divinity which we say was born with Jesus Christ you say was afterwards infused into Him. But the fact is that if you deny that Divinity was born with the Lord you cannot afterwards make a confession according to the faith; for it is an impossibility for one and the same thing to be partly impious and also to turn out partly pious, and for the same thing partly to belong to faith and partly to misbelief. To begin with then I ask you this: Do you say that our Lord Jesus Christ, who was born of the Virgin Mary is only the Son of man, or that He is the Son of God as well? For we, I mean all who hold the Catholic faith, all of us, I say, believe and are sure and know and confess that He is both, i.e., that He is Son of man because born of a woman and Son of God because conceived of Divinity. Do you then admit that He is both, i.e., Son of God and Son of man, or do you say that He is Son of man only? If Son of man only then there cry out against you apostles and prophets, aye and the Holy Ghost Himself, by whom the conception was brought about. That most shameless mouth of yours is stopped by all the witnesses of the Divine decrees: it is stopped by sacred writings and holy witnesses: aye and it is stopped by the very gospel of God as if by a Divine hand. And that mighty Gabriel who in the case of Zacharias restrained the voice of unbelief by the power of his word, much more strongly condemned in your case the voice of

[2] Nestorius maintained that "that which was formed in the womb of Mary was not God Himself . . . but because God dwells in him whom He has assumed, therefore also He who is assumed is called God because of Him who assumes Him. And it is not God who has suffered, but God was united with the crucified flesh." (Fragm. in Marius Mercator p. 789 sq. (ed. Migne).) Thus he made out that in Christ were two Persons, one assuming and the other assumed.

blasphemy and sin, by his own lips, saying to the Virgin Mary, the mother of God: "The Holy Ghost shall come upon thee, and the power of the Most High shall overshadow thee: therefore also that holy thing which shall be born of thee shall be called the Son of God."[1] Do you see how Jesus Christ is first proclaimed to be the Son of God that according to the flesh He might become the Son of man? For when the Virgin Mary was to bring forth the Lord she conceived owing to the descent of the Holy Spirit upon her and the co-operation of the power of the Most High. And from this you can see that the origin of our Lord and Saviour must come from thence, whence His conception came; and since He was born owing to the descent of the fulness of Divinity in its completeness upon the Virgin, He could not be the Son of man unless He had first been the Son of God; and so the angel when sent to announce His nativity and sacred birth, when he had already spoken of the mystery of His conception added a word expressive of His birth, saying: "Therefore also that holy thing which shall be born of thee shall be called the Son of God [i.e., He shall be called the Son of Him from whom He was begotten].[2] Jesus Christ is therefore the Son of God, because He was begotten of God and conceived of God. But if He is the Son of God, then most certainly He is God: but if He is God, then He is not lacking in the grace of God. Nor indeed was He ever lacking in that of which He is Himself the maker. For grace and truth were made by Jesus Christ.

CHAPTER VII.

How in Christ the Divinity, Majesty, Might and Power have existed in perfection from eternity, and will continue.

THEREFORE all grace, power, might, Divinity, aye, and the fulness of actual Divinity and glory have ever existed together with Him and in Him, whether in heaven or in earth or in the womb or at His birth. Nothing that is proper to God was ever wanting to God. For the Godhead was ever present with God, no where and at no time severed from Him. For everywhere God is present in His completeness and in His perfection. He suffers no division or change or diminution; for nothing can be either added to God or taken away from Him, for He is subject to no diminution of Divinity, as to no increase of It. He was the same Person then on earth who was also in heaven: the same Person in His low estate who was also in the highest: the same Person in the littleness of manhood as in the glory of the Godhead. And so the Apostle was right in speaking of the grace of Christ when He meant the grace of God. For Christ was. everything that God is. At the very time of His conception as man there came all the power of God, all the fulness of the Godhead; for thence came all the perfection of the Godhead, whence was His origin. Nor was that Human nature of His[3] ever without the Deity as it received from Deity the very fact of its existence. And so, to begin with, whether you like it or no, you cannot deny this; viz., that the Lord Jesus Christ is the Son of God, especially as the archangel declares in the gospels: "That holy thing which shall be born of thee shall be called the Son of God." But when this is established then remember that whatever you read of Christ you read of the Son of God: whatever you read of the Lord or Jesus belongs to the Son of God. And so when you recognize a title of Divinity in all these terms which you hear uttered, as you see that in each case you ought to understand that the Son of God is meant, prove to me, if you like, how you can separate the Godhead from the Son of God.

BOOK III.

CHAPTER I.

That Christ, who is God and man in the unity of Person, sprang from Israel and the Virgin Mary according to the flesh.

THAT divine teacher of the Churches when in writing to the Romans he was reproving or rather lamenting the unbelief of the Jews, i.e., of his own brethren, made use of these words: "I wished myself," said he, "to be accursed from Christ, for my brethren, who are my kinsmen according to the flesh, who are Israelites, to whom belongeth the adoption as of children, and the glory, and the testaments, and the giving of the law, and the ser-

---

[1] S. Luke i. 35.
[2] There is some doubt whether the words enclosed in brackets form part of the genuine text. Petschenig brackets them, as wanting in some MSS.

[3] Hom. ille.

vice of God, and the promises: whose are the fathers, of whom is Christ according to the flesh, who is over all things, God blessed for ever." [1] O, the love of that most faithful Apostle, and most kindly kinsman! who in his infinite charity wished to die — as a kinsman for his relations, and as a master for his disciples. And what then was the reason why he wished to die? Only one; viz., that they might live. But in what did their life consist? Simply in this, as he himself says, that they might recognize a Divine Christ born according to the flesh, of their own flesh. And therefore the Apostle grieved the more, because those who ought to have loved Him the more as sprung from their own stock, failed to understand that He was born of Israel. "Of whom," said he, "is Christ according to the flesh, who is over all things, God blessed for ever." Clearly he lays down that from them according to the flesh, was born that Christ who is over all, God blessed for ever. You certainly cannot deny that Christ was born from them according to the flesh. But the same Person, who was born from them, is God. How can you get round this? How can you shuffle out of it? The Apostle says that Christ who was born of Israel according to the flesh, is God. Teach us, if you can, at what time He did not exist. "Of whom," he says, "is Christ according to the flesh, who is over all, God." You see that because the Apostle has united and joined together these, "God" cannot possibly be separated from "Christ." For just as the Apostle declares that Christ is of them, so he asserts that God is in Christ. You must either deny both of these statements, or you must accept both. Christ is said to be born of them according to the flesh: but the same Person is declared by the Apostle to be "God in Christ." Whence also he says elsewhere: "For God was in Christ, reconciling the world to Himself." [2] It is absolutely impossible to separate one from the other. Either deny that Christ sprang from them, or admit that there was born of the virgin God in Christ, "who is," as he says, "over all, God blessed for ever."

CHAPTER II.

The title of God is given in one sense to Christ, and in another to men.

THE name of God would for the faithful be amply sufficient to denote the glory of His Divinity, but by adding "over all, God

blessed," he excludes a blasphemous and perverse interpretation of it, for fear that some evil-disposed person to depreciate His absolute Divinity might quote the fact that the word God is sometimes applied by grace in the Divine economy temporarily to men, and thus apply it to God by unworthy comparisons, as where God says to Moses: "I have given thee as a God to Pharaoh," [3] or in this passage: "I said ye are Gods," [4] where it clearly has the force of a title given by condescension. For as it says "I said," it is not a name showing power, so much as a title given by the speaker. But that passage also, where it says: "I have given thee as a God to Pharaoh," shows the power of the giver rather than the Divinity of him who receives the title. For when it says: "I have given," it thereby certainly indicates the power of God, who gave, and not the Divine nature, in the person of the recipient. But when it is said of our God and Lord Jesus Christ, "who is over all, God blessed for ever," the fact is at once proved by the words, and the meaning of the words shown by the name given: because in the case of the Son of God the name of God does not denote an adoption by favour, but what is truly and really His nature.

CHAPTER III.

He explains the apostle's saying: "If from henceforth we know no man according to the flesh," etc.

AND so the same Apostle says: "From henceforth we know no man according to the flesh, and if we have known Christ according to the flesh, yet now we know Him so no longer." [5] Admirably consistent are all the writings of the sacred word with each other, and in every portion of them: even where they do not correspond in the *form* of the words, yet they agree in the drift and substance. As where he says: "And if we have known Christ according to the flesh, yet now we know Him so no longer." For the witness of the passage before us confirms that quoted above, in which he said: "Of whom is Christ according to the flesh, who is over all, God blessed for ever." For there he writes: "Of whom is Christ according to the flesh;" and here: "if we have known Christ according to the flesh." There: "who is over all, God blessed for ever;" and here: "yet now we no longer know Christ according to the flesh." The look of the words is different, but their force and drift is the same. For it is the same Person whom he

---

[1] Rom. ix. 3-5.   [2] 2 Cor. v. 19.   [3] Exod. vii. 1.   [4] Ps. lxxxi. (lxxxii.) 6.   [5] 2 Cor. v. 16.

there declares to be God over all born according to the flesh, whom he here asserts that he no longer knows according to the flesh. And plainly for this reason; viz., because Him whom he had known as born in the flesh, he acknowledges as God for ever; and therefore says that he knows him not after the flesh, because He is over all, God blessed for ever; and the phrase there: "who is over all God," answers to this: "we no longer know Christ according to the flesh;" and this phrase: "we no longer know Christ according to the flesh" implies this: "who is God blessed for ever." [1] The declaration of Apostolic teaching then somehow rises, as it were to greater heights, and though it is self-consistent throughout, yet it supports the mystery of the perfect faith, with a still more express statement, and says: "And though we have known Christ according to the flesh, yet now we know Him so no longer," i.e., as formerly we knew Him as man as well as God, yet now only as God. For when the frailty of flesh comes to an end, we no longer know anything in Him except the power of Divinity, for all that is in Him is the power of Divine Majesty, where the weakness of human infirmity has ceased to exist. In this passage then he has thoroughly expounded the whole mystery of the Incarnation, and of His perfect Divinity. For where he says: "And if we have known Christ according to the flesh," he speaks of the mystery of God born in flesh. But by adding "yet now we know Him so no longer," he manifests His power when weakness is laid aside. And thus that knowledge of the flesh has to do with His humanity, and that ignorance, with the glory of His Divinity. For to say "we have known Christ according to the flesh:" means "as long as that which was known, existed. Now we no longer know it, after it has ceased to exist. For the nature of flesh has been transformed into a spiritual substance: and that which formerly belonged to the manhood, has all become God's. And therefore we no longer know Christ according to the flesh, because when bodily infirmity has been absorbed by Divine Majesty,[2] nothing remains in that Sacred Body, from which weakness of the flesh can be known in it. And thus whatever had formerly belonged to a twofold substance, has become attached to a single Power. Since there is no sort of doubt that Christ, who was crucified through human weakness lives entirely through the glory of His Divinity.

CHAPTER IV.

From the Epistle to the Galatians he brings forward a passage to show that the weakness of the flesh in Christ was absorbed by His Divinity.

THE Apostle indeed declares this in the whole body of his writings, and admirably says in writing to the Galatians: "Paul an Apostle not of men, neither by man, but by Jesus Christ and God the Father." [3] You see how thoroughly consistent he is with himself in the former and the present passage. For there he says : "Now we no longer know Christ according to the flesh." Here he says: "Not of men, neither by man, but by Jesus Christ." It is clear that his doctrine is the same here as in the former passage. For where he says that he is not sent by man, he implies: "We have not known Christ according to the flesh:" and so I am "not sent by man" but "by Christ;" [4] for if I am sent by Christ, I am not sent by man but by God. For there is no longer room for the name of man, in Him whom Divinity claims entirely for itself. And so when he had said that he was sent "not of men, neither by man, but by Jesus Christ," he rightly added: "And God the Father," thus showing that he was sent by God the Father and God the Son; in whom owing to the mystery of the sacred and ineffable generation there are two Persons (He who begets, and He who is begotten), but there is but one single Power of God who is the sender. And so in saying that he was sent by God the Father and God the Son, he shows that the Persons are two in number, but he also teaches that their Power is One in sending.

CHAPTER V.

As it is blasphemy to pare away the Divinity of Christ, so also is it blasphemous to deny that He is true man.

BUT he says "by Jesus Christ, and God the Father, who raised Him from the dead."

---

[1] Petschenig's text reads as follows: *Ac per hoc et illud ibi; Qui est super omnia Deus, hoc dicit: non novimus, jam Christum secundum carnem, et hic: non novimus jam Christum secundum carnem, hoc ait: Qui est Deus benedictus in sæcula.* That of Gazæus has: *Ac per hoc et illud ibi qui est super omnia Deus: et hoc dicit, non novimus jam Christum secundum carnem: Quia est Deus benedictus in sæcula.*

[2] The language used in the text by Cassian is scarcely defensible. The whole tenour of the treatise shows clearly enough that his *meaning* is orthodox enough, and that he fully recognizes that the Human nature of Christ is still existing (See especially c. vi.): but the *language* used comes perilously near to Eutychianism, and might be taken to imply that the human nature had been absorbed in the Divine. Again in Book V. c. vii. he speaks of the Son of man "united to the Son of God" (Cf. also c. viii.) language which taken by itself might seem to sanction Nestorianism, the very heresy against which Cassian himself is writing. These instances of inaccurate language, which a later writer would have carefully avoided, serve to show one great service which heresies did to the Church in making Churchmen write λογικώτερον. Cf. Dorner, Doctrine of the Person of Christ, Vol. i. p. 458 (E. T.).

[3] Gal. i. 1.   [4] *Christum* (Petschenig): *Jesum* (Gazæus).

That renowned and admirable teacher, knowing that our Lord Jesus Christ must be preached as true man, as well as true God, always declares the glory of the Divine in Him, in such a way as not to lose hold of the confession of the Incarnation: plainly excluding the phantasm of Marcion, by a real Incarnation, and the poverty of the Ebionite, by Divinity: lest through one or other of these wicked blasphemies it might be believed that our Lord Jesus Christ was either altogether man without God, or God without man. Excellently then did the Apostle, when declaring that He was sent by God the Son as well as by God the Father, add at once a confession of the Lord's Incarnation, by saying: "Who raised Him from the dead:" clearly teaching that it was a real body of the Incarnate God, which was raised from the dead: in accordance with this: "And though we have known Christ according to the flesh," excellently adding: "Yet now we know Him so no longer." For he says that he knows this in Him according to the flesh; viz., that He was raised from the dead; but that he knows Him no longer according to the flesh inasmuch as when the weakness of the flesh is at an end, he knows that He exists in the Power of God only. Surely he is a faithful and satisfactory witness of our Lord's Divinity which had to be proclaimed, who at his first call was smitten from heaven itself, and did not merely believe in his heart the glory of our Lord Jesus Christ, who was raised from the dead, but actually established its truth by the evidence of his bodily eyes.

CHAPTER VI.

He shows from the appearance of Christ vouchsafed to the Apostle when persecuting the Church, the existence of both natures in Him.

WHEREFORE also, when arguing before King Agrippa and others of the world's judges, he speaks as follows: "When I was going to Damascus with authority and permission of the chief priests, at midday, O king, I saw in the way a light from heaven above the brightness of the sun, shining round about me and all those that were with me. And when we were all fallen down to the ground, I heard a voice saying unto me in the Hebrew tongue, Saul, Saul, why persecutest thou Me? It is hard for thee to kick against the goad. And I said, Who art Thou, Lord? And the Lord said to me: I am Jesus of Nazareth, whom thou persecutest."[1] You see how truly

the Apostle said that he no longer knew according to the flesh one whom he had seen in such splendour and majesty. For when as he lay prostrate he saw the splendour of that divine light which he was unable to endure, there followed this voice: "Saul, Saul, why persecutest thou Me?" And when he asked who it might be, the Lord answers and clearly points out His Personality: "I am Jesus of Nazareth, whom thou persecutest." Now then, you heretic, I ask you, I summon you. Do you believe what the Apostle says of himself, or do you not believe it? Or if you think that unimportant, do you believe what the Lord says of Himself or do you not believe it? If you do believe it, there is an end of the matter: for you cannot help believing what we believe. For we, like the Apostle, even if we have known Christ according to the flesh, yet know Him so no longer. *We* do not heap insults on Christ. *We* do not separate the flesh from the Divinity; and all that is in Christ *we* believe is in God. If then you believe the same that we believe you must acknowledge the same mysteries of the faith. But if you differ from us, if you refuse to believe the Churches, the Apostle, aye and God's own testimony about Himself, show us in this vision which the Apostle saw, how much is flesh, and how much God. For I cannot here separate one from the other. I see the ineffable light, I see the inexpressible splendour, I see the radiance that human weakness cannot endure, and beyond what mortal eyes can bear, the glory of God shining with inconceivable light.[2] What room is there here for division and separation? In the voice we hear Jesus, in the majesty we see God. How can we help believing that in one and the same (Personal) substance God and Jesus exist. But I should like to have a few more words with you on this subject. Tell me, I pray you, if there appeared to you in your present persecution of the Catholic faith that same vision which then appeared to the Apostle in his ignorance, if when you were not expecting it and were off your guard, that radiance shone round about you, and the glory of that boundless light smote you in your terror and confusion, and you lay prostrate in darkness of body and soul; which the unlimited and indescribable terror of your heart increased,[3] — tell me, I intreat you; When the dread of immediate death was pressing on you, and the terror of the glory that threatened you from above, weighed you down, and you

---

[1] Acts xxvi. 12-15.

[2] *Inæstimabili majestatem Dei luce fulgentem* (Petschenig): Gazæus edits *Inæstimabilem majestatem, Dei luce fulgentem.*

[3] *Quas tibi immensas et ineffabilis pavor mentis augeret* (Petschenig): Gazæus has *Quas tibi immensas et ineffabiles angustias pavor mentis augeret?*

heard as well in your bewilderment of mind those words which your sin so well deserves: "Saul, Saul, why persecutest thou Me?" and to your inquiry who it was the answer was given from heaven: "I am Jesus of Nazareth, whom thou persecutest," what would you say? "I do not know, I do not yet fully believe. I want to think over it with myself a little longer, who I think that Thou art, who speakest from heaven, who overwhelmest me with the brightness of Thy Divinity: whose voice I hear and whose splendour I cannot bear. I must consider of this matter, whether I ought to believe Thee or not: whether Thou art Christ or God. If Thou art God alone whether it is in Christ. If Thou art Christ alone, whether it is in God. I want this distinction to be carefully observed, and thoroughly considered, what we should believe that Thou art, and what we should judge Thee to be. For I don't want any of my offices to be wasted. As if I were to regard Thee as a man, and yet pay to Thee some Divine honours." If then you were lying on the ground, as the Apostle Paul was then lying, and overwhelmed with the brightness of the Divine light, were at your last gasp, perhaps you would say this, and prate with all this silly chattering. But what shall we make of the fact that another course commended itself to the Apostle; and when he had fallen down, trembling and half dead, he did not think that he ought any longer to conceal his belief, or to deliberate; it was enough for him that he was taught by inexpressible arguments to know that He whom he had ignorantly fancied to be a man, was God. He did not conceal his belief, he made no delay. He did not any longer protract his erroneous ideas by deliberating and disbelieving, but as soon as he heard from heaven the name of Jesus his Lord, he replied in a voice, subdued like that of a servant, tremulous like that of one scourged, and full of fervour like that of one converted, "What shall I do, Lord?" And so at once for his ready and earnest faith, it was granted to him that He should never be without His presence whom he had faithfully believed: and that He, to whom he had passed in heart, should Himself pass into his heart: as the Apostle himself says of himself: "Do you seek a proof of Christ that speaketh in me?"[1]

CHAPTER VII.

He shows once more by other passages of the Apostle that Christ is God.

I WANT you to tell me, you heretic, whether in this passage He who, as the Apostle tells us, speaks in him, is man or God. If He is man, how can another's body speak in his heart? If God, then Christ is not a man but God; for since Christ spoke in the Apostle, and only God could speak in him, therefore a Divine Christ spoke in him. And so you see that there is nothing to be said here, that no division or separation can be made between Christ and God: because complete Divinity was in Christ, and Christ was completely in God. No division or severing of the two can here be admitted. There is only one simple, pious, and sound confession to be made; viz., to adore, love, and worship Christ as God. But do you want to understand more fully and thoroughly that there is no separation to be made between God and Christ, and that we must hold that God is altogether one with Christ? Hear what the Apostle says to the Corinthians: "For we must all be manifested before the judgment seat of Christ, that every one may receive the proper things of the body, according as he hath done, whether it be good or evil."[2] But in another passage, in writing to the Romans he says: "We shall all stand before the judgment seat of God: for it is written: As I live, saith the Lord, every knee shall bow to me, and every tongue shall confess to God."[3] You see then that the judgment seat of God is the same as that of Christ; understand then without any doubt that Christ is God; and when you see that the substance of God and Christ is altogether inseparable, admit also that the Person cannot be severed. Unless forsooth because the Apostle in one Epistle said that we should be manifested before the judgment seat of Christ, and in another before that of God, you invent two judgment seats, and fancy that some will be judged by Christ and others by God. But this is foolish and wild, and madder than a madman's utterances. Acknowledge then the Lord of all, the God of the universe, acknowledge the judgment seat of God in the judgment seat of Christ. Love life, love your salvation, love Him by whom you were created. Fear Him by whom you are to be judged. For whether you will or no, you have to be manifested before the judgment seat of Christ, and laying aside wicked blasphemy and the childish talk of unbelieving words, though you think that the judgment seat of God is different from that of Christ, you will come before the judgment seat of Christ, and will find by evidence that there is no gainsaying, that the judgment seat of God is indeed the same as that of Christ, and that in Christ the Son of God, there is all the glory of God the Son, and the power of God the

---

[1] 2 Cor. xiii. 3.   [2] 2 Cor. v. 10.   [3] Rom. xiv. 10, 11.

Father. "For the Father judgeth no man, but hath committed all judgment to the Son, that all men may honour the Son as they honour the Father." [1] For whoever denies the Father denies the Son also. "Whosoever denieth the Son, the same hath not the Father: he that confesseth the Son, hath the Father also." [2] And so you should learn that the glory of the Father and the Son is inseparable, and their majesty is inseparable also; and that the Son cannot be honoured without the Father, nor the Father without the Son. But no man can honour God and the Son of God except in Christ the only-begotten Son of God. For it is impossible for a man to have the Spirit of God who is to be honoured except in the Spirit of Christ, as the Apostle says: "But ye are not in the flesh, but in the Spirit, if so be that the Spirit of God dwell in you. But if any man have not the Spirit of Christ, he is none of His." [3] And again: "Who shall lay anything to the charge of God's elect? It is God that justifieth. Who is he that condemneth? It is Christ Jesus who died, yea rather who rose again." [4] You see then now, even against your will, that there is absolutely no difference between the Spirit of God and the Spirit of Christ, or between the judgment of God and the judgment of Christ. Choose then which you will — for one of the two must happen — either acknowledge in faith that Christ is God, or admit that God is in Christ at your condemnation.

CHAPTER VIII.

When confessing the Divinity of Christ we ought not to pass over in silence the confession of the cross.

BUT let us see what else follows. In writing to the church of Corinth, he whom we spoke of above, the instructor of all the churches viz. Paul, speaks thus: "The Jews," says he, "seek signs, and the Greeks ask for wisdom. But we preach Christ crucified, to the Jews a stumbling-block, to the Gentiles foolishness: but to them that are saved, both Jews and Greeks, Christ the power of God and the wisdom of God." [5] O most powerful teacher of the faith, who even in this passage, when teaching the Church thought it not enough to speak of Christ as God without adding that He was crucified on purpose that for the sake of the open and solid teaching of the faith he might proclaim Him, whom he called the crucified, to be the wisdom of God. He then employed no subtilty or circumlocution, nor did he when· he preached the gospel of the Lord blush at the mention of the cross of Christ. And though it was a stumbling-block to the Jews, and foolishness to the Gentiles to hear of God as born, God in bodily form, God suffering, God crucified, yet he did not weaken the force of his pious utterance because of the wickedness of the offence of the Jews: nor did he lessen the vigour of his faith because of the unbelief and the foolishness of others: but openly, persistently, and boldly proclaimed that He, whom a mother [6] had borne, whom men had slain, the spear had pierced, the cross had stretched — was "the power and wisdom of God, to the Jews a stumbling-block, and to the Gentiles foolishness." But still that which was to some a stumbling-block and foolishness, was to others the power and wisdom of God. For as the persons differed, so was there a difference of their thoughts: and what a man who was void of sound understanding, and incapable of true good, foolishly denied in unbelief, that a wise faith could feel in its inmost soul to be holy and life giving.

CHAPTER IX.

How the Apostle's preaching was rejected by Jews and Gentiles because it confessed that the crucified Christ was God.

TELL me then, you heretic, you enemy of all men, but of yourself above all — to whom the cross of our Lord Jesus Christ is an offence as with the Jews, and foolishness as with the Gentiles, you who reject the mysteries of true salvation, with the stumbling of the former, and are foolish with the stubbornness of the others, why was the preaching of the Apostle Paul foolishness to the pagans, and a stumbling-block to the Jews? Surely it would never have offended men, if he had taught that Christ was, as you maintain He is, a mere man? For who would think that His birth, passion, cross, and death were incredible or a difficulty? Or what would there have been novel or strange about the preaching of Paul, if he had said that a merely human Christ suffered that which human nature daily endures among men everywhere? But it was surely this that the foolishness of the Gentiles could not receive, and the unbelief of the Jews rejected; viz., that the Apostle declared that Christ whom they, like you, fancied to be a mere man, was God. This it certainly was which the thoughts of these wicked men rejected, which the ears of the faithless could not endure; viz., that the

---

[1] S. John v. 22, 23.   [3] Rom. viii. 9.   [5] 1 Cor. i. 22–24.
[2] 1 John ii. 23.   [4] Ibid. ver. 33, 34.

[6] Mater (Petschenig): Caro (Gazæus).

birth of God should be proclaimed in the man Jesus Christ, that the passion of God should be asserted, and the cross of God proclaimed. This it was which was a difficulty: this was what was incredible; for that was incredible to the hearing of men, which had never been heard of as happening to the Divine nature. And so you are quite secure, with such an announcement and teaching as yours, that your preaching will never be either foolishness to the Gentiles or a stumbling-block to the Jews. You will never be crucified with Peter by Jews and Gentiles, nor stoned with James, nor beheaded with Paul. For there is nothing in your preaching to offend them. You maintain that a mere man was born, a mere man suffered. You need not be afraid of their troubling you with persecution, for you are helping them by your preaching.

CHAPTER X.

How the apostle maintains that Christ is the power of God and the wisdom of God.

But let us see something more on the subject. Christ then, according to the Apostle, is the power of God and the wisdom of God. What have you to say to this? How can you get out of it? There is no place for you to escape and fly to. Christ is the wisdom of God and the power of God. He, I say, whom the Jews attacked, the Gentiles mocked, whom you yourself together with them are persecuting,—He, I say, who is foolishness to the heathen, and a stumbling-block to the Jews, and both to you, He, I say, is the power of God and the wisdom of God. What is there that you can do? Shut your ears, forsooth, so as not to hear? This the Jews did also when the Apostle was preaching. Do what you will, Christ is in heaven, and in God, and with Him, and in Him in the heavens above in whom also He was here below: you can no longer persecute Him with the Jews. But you do the one thing that you can. You persecute Him in the faith, you persecute Him in the church, you persecute Him with the arms of a wicked belief, you persecute Him with the sword of false doctrine. Perhaps you do rather more than the Jews of old did. You now persecute Christ, after even those who did persecute Him, have believed. But perhaps you think that the sin is less because you can no longer lay hands on Him. No less grievous, I tell you, no less grievous to Him is that persecution, in which sinful men persecute Him in the persons of His followers. But the mention of the Lord's cross

offends you. It always offended the Jews as well. You shudder at hearing that God suffered: the Gentiles in their error mocked at this also. I ask you then, in what point do you differ from them, since you both agree in this frowardness? But for my part I not only do not water down this preaching of the holy cross, this preaching of the Lord's passion, but as far as my wishes and powers go I emphasise it. For I will declare that He who was crucified is not only the power and wisdom of God, than which there is nothing greater, but actually Lord of absolute Divinity and glory. And this the rather, because this assertion of mine is the doctrine of God, as the Apostle says: "We speak wisdom among them that are perfect: but the wisdom not of this world, nor of the rulers of this world who are brought to nought; but we speak the hidden wisdom of God in a mystery, which God ordained before the world, unto our glory: which none of the princes of this world knew: for if they had known it, they would never have crucified the Lord of glory. But as it is written: that eye hath not seen, nor ear heard, neither hath it entered into the heart of man, what God hath prepared for them that love Him." [1] You see what great matters the Apostle's discourse comprises in how small a compass. He says that he speaks wisdom, but a wisdom which only those that are perfect can know, and which the prudent of this world cannot know. For he says that this is the wisdom of God, which is hidden in a Divine mystery, and predestined before all worlds for the glory of the saints: and that therefore it is only known to those who savour of God; while the princes of this world are utterly ignorant of it. But he adds the reason, to establish both points that he had mentioned, saying: "For if they had known it, they would never have crucified the Lord of glory. But it is written, that eye hath not seen, nor ear hath heard, neither hath it entered into the heart of man, what God hath prepared for them that love Him." You see then how the wisdom of God, hidden in a mystery, and predestined before all worlds, was unknown to those who crucified the Lord of glory, and known by those who received it. And well does he say that the wisdom of God was hidden in a mystery, for never yet could the eye of any man see, or the ear hear, or the heart imagine this; viz., that the Lord of glory should be born of a virgin and come in the flesh, and suffer all kinds of punishment, and shameful passion. But with regard to these gifts of God, as there is no one who—since

---

[1] 1 Cor. i. 6–9.

they were hidden in a mystery — could ever of himself understand them, so blessed is he who has grasped them when they are revealed. Thus all who have failed to grasp them must be reckoned among the princes of this world, and those who have grasped them among God's wise ones. He then does not grasp it who denies God born in the flesh; therefore you also do not grasp it, as you deny this. But do what you will, deny as impiously as you like, we the rather believe the Apostle. But why should I say the Apostle? the rather do we believe God. For through the Apostle we believe Him, whom we know to have spoken by the Apostle. The Divine word says that the ord of glory was crucified by the princes of the world. You deny it. They also who crucified Him denied that it was God whom they were crucifying. They then who confess Him have their portion with the Apostle who confessed Him. You are sure to have your lot with His persecutors. What is there then that can be replied to this? The Apostle says that the Lord of glory was crucified. Alter this if you can. Separate now, if you please, Jesus from God. At least you cannot deny that Christ was crucified by the Jews. But it was the Lord of glory who was crucified. Therefore you must either deny that Christ was nailed to the cross, or you must admit that God was nailed to it.

CHAPTER XI.

He supports the same doctrine by proofs from the gospel.

BUT perhaps it is a difficulty to you that all this time I am chiefly using the witness of the Apostle Paul alone. He is good enough for me, whom God chose, nor do I blush to call as the witness to my faith, the man whom God willed to be the teacher of the whole world. But to yield to your wishes, as perhaps you fancy that I have no other proofs to use, hear the perfect mystery of man's salvation and eternal bliss, which Martha proclaims in the gospel. For what does she say? "Of a truth, Lord, I have believed that Thou art the Christ, the Son of the living God, who art come into this world."[1] Learn the true faith from a woman. Learn the confession of eternal hope. Yet you have a splendid consolation: you need not blush to be taught the mystery of salvation by her, whose testimony God did not refuse to accept.

[1] S. John xi. 27.

CHAPTER XII.

He proves from the renowned confession of the blessed Peter that Christ is God.

BUT if you prefer the authority of a greater person (although you ought not to slight the authority of any one of either sex, on whom the confession of the mystery confers weight — for whatever may be a person's condition, or however humble his position, yet the value of his faith is not thereby diminished) let us interrogate no beginner or untaught schoolboy, nor a woman whose faith might perhaps appear to be but rudimentary; but that greatest of disciples among disciples, and of teachers among teachers, who presided and ruled over the Roman Church, and held the chief place[2] in the priesthood as he did in the faith. Tell us then, tell us, we pray, O Peter, thou chief of Apostles, tell us how the Churches ought to believe in God. For it is right that you should teach us, as you were taught by the Lord, and that you should open to us the gate, of which you received the key. Shut out all those who try to overthrow the heavenly house: and those who are endeavouring to enter by secret holes and unlawful approaches: as it is clear that none can enter the gate of the kingdom save one to whom the key bestowed on the Churches is revealed by you. Tell us then how we ought to believe in Jesus Christ and to confess our common Lord. You will surely reply without hesitation: "Why do you consult me as to the way in which the Lord should be confessed, when you have before you my own confession of Him? Read the gospel, and you will not want me myself, when you have got my confession. Nay, you have got me myself when you have my confession; for though I have no weight apart from my confession, yet the actual confession adds weight to my person." Tell us then, O Evangelist, tell us the confession: tell us the faith of the chief Apostle: did he confess that Jesus was only a man, or God? did he say that there was nothing but flesh in Him, or did he proclaim Him the Son of God? When then the Lord Jesus Christ asked whom the disciples believed and confessed Him to be, Peter, the first of the Apostles, replied — one in the name of all—for the answer of one was to the same effect as the faith of them all. But it was fitting that he should first give the answer, that the order of the answer might correspond to the degree of honour: and that he might outstrip them in confession, as he outstripped them in age. What then does he

[2] *Principatus.*

say? "Thou art," he says, "the Christ the Son of the living God."[1] I am obliged, you heretic, to make use of a plain and simple question to confute you. Tell me, I pray, who was He, to whom Peter gave that answer? You cannot deny that it was the Christ. I ask then, what do you call Christ? man or God? Man certainly without any doubt: for hence springs the whole of your heresy, because you deny that Christ is the Son of God. And so too you say that Mary is Christotocos, but not Theotocos, because she was the mother of Christ, not of God. Therefore you maintain that Christ is only a man, and not God, and so that He is the Son of man not of God. What then does Peter reply to this? "Thou art," he says, "the Christ, the Son of the living God." That Christ whom you declare to be only the Son of man, he testifies to be the Son of God. Whom would you like us to believe? you or Peter? I imagine that you are not so shameless as to venture to prefer your own opinion to that of the first of the Apostles. And yet what is there that you would not venture on? or how can you help scorning the Apostle, if you can deny God? "Thou art then," he says, "the Christ, the Son of the living God." Is there anything puzzling or obscure in this? It is nothing but a plain and open confession: he proclaims Christ to be the Son of God. Perhaps you will deny that the words were spoken: but the Evangelist testifies that they were. Or do you say that the Apostle told a lie? But it is an awful lie to accuse an Apostle of lying. Or perhaps you will maintain that the words were spoken of some other Christ? But this is a novel kind of monstrous fabrication. What then is left for you? One thing indeed; viz., that since what is written is read, and what is read is true, you should finally be driven by force and compulsion (as you cannot assert its falsehood) to desist from impugning its truth.

CHAPTER XIII.

The confession of the blessed Peter receives a testimony to its truth from Christ Himself.

BUT still, as I have made use of the testimony of the chief Apostle, in which he openly confessed the Lord Jesus Christ as God, let us see how He whom he confessed approved of his confession; for of far more value than the Apostle's words is the fact that God Himself commended his utterance. When then the Apostle said: "Thou art the Christ

the Son of the living God," what was the answer of our Lord and Saviour? "Blessed art thou," said He, "Simon Barjonah, for flesh and blood hath not revealed it unto thee but the Spirit of My Father which is in heaven." If you do not like to use the testimony of the Apostle use that of God. For by commending what was said God added His own authority to the Apostle's utterance, so that although the utterance came from the lips of the Apostle, yet God who approved of it made it His own. "Blessed art thou," said He, "Simon Barjonah, for flesh and blood hath not revealed it unto thee, but the Spirit of My Father which is in heaven." Thus in the words of the Apostle you have the testimony of the Holy Spirit and of the Son who was present and of God the Father. What more can you want, or what comes up to this? The Son commended: the Father was present: the Holy Ghost revealed. The utterance of the Apostle thus gives the testimony of the entire Godhead: for this utterance must necessarily have the authority of Him from whose prompting it proceeds. "Blessed then art thou," said He, "Simon Barjonah, for flesh and blood hath not revealed it unto thee, but the Spirit of My Father which is in heaven." If then flesh and blood did not reveal this to Peter or inspire him, you must at last see who inspires you. If the Spirit of God taught him who confessed that Christ was God, you see how you are taught by the spirit of the devil if you can deny it.

CHAPTER XIV.

How the confession of the blessed Peter is the faith of the whole Church.

BUT what are the other words which follow that saying of the Lord's, with which He commends Peter? "And I," said He, "say unto thee, that thou art Peter and upon this rock I will build My Church." Do you see how the saying of Peter is the faith of the Church? He then must of course be outside the Church, who does not hold the faith of the Church. "And to thee," saith the Lord, "I will give the keys of the kingdom of heaven." This faith deserved heaven: this faith received the keys of the heavenly kingdom. See what awaits you. You cannot enter the gate to which this key belongs, if you have denied the faith of this key. "And the gate," He adds, "of hell shall not prevail against thee." The gates of hell are the belief or rather the misbelief of heretics. For widely as hell is separated from heaven, so widely is he who denies from him who confessed that Christ is God. "Whatsoever," He proceeds, "thou shalt bind on earth, shalt be bound in heaven, and whatsoever thou shalt loose on earth, shalt be loosed also in heaven." The perfect faith of the Apostle somehow is given the power of Deity, that what it should bind or loose on earth, might be bound or loosed in heaven. For you then, who come against the Apostle's faith, as you see that already you are bound on earth, it only remains that you should know that you are bound also in heaven. But it would take too long to go into details which are so numerous as to make a long and wearisome story, even if they are related with brevity and conciseness.

CHAPTER XV.

St. Thomas also confessed the same faith as Peter after the Lord's resurrection.

BUT I want still to add one more testimony from an Apostle for you: that you may see how what followed after the passion corresponded with what went before it. When then the Lord appeared in the midst of His disciples when the doors were shut, and wished to make clear to the Apostles the reality of His body, when the Apostle Thomas felt His flesh and handled His side and examined His wounds — what was it that he declared, when he was convinced of the reality of the body shown to him? "My Lord," he said, "and my God." [1] Did he say what you say, that it was a man and not God? Christ and not Divinity? He surely touched the body of his Lord and answered that He was God. Did he make any separation between man and God? or did he call that flesh Theotocos, to use your expression, i.e., that which received Divinity? or did he, after the fashion of your blasphemy, declare that He whom he touched was to be honoured not for His own sake, but for the sake of Him whom He had received into Himself? But perhaps God's Apostle knew nothing of that subtle separation of yours, and had no experience of the fine distinctions of your judgment, as he was a rude countryman, ignorant of the dialectic art, and of the method of philosophic disputation; for whom the Lord's teaching was amply sufficient, and as he was one who knew nothing whatever except what he learnt from the instruction of the Lord! And so his words contain heavenly doctrine; his faith is a Divine lesson. He had never learnt to separate, as

you do, the Lord from His body: and had no idea how to rend God asunder from Himself. He was holy, straightforward, upright: filled with practical innocence, unalloyed faith, and pure knowledge: having a simple understanding joined with prudence, a wisdom entirely free from all evil, together with perfect simplicity: ignorant of any corruption, and free from all heretical perversity, and as one who had experienced in himself the force of the Divine lesson, he held fast everything which he had learnt. And so he — countryman and ignorant fellow as you fancy him — shuts you up with a brief answer, and destroys your position with a few words of his. What then did the Apostle Thomas touch when he drew near to handle his God? Certainly it was Christ without any doubt. But what did he exclaim? "My Lord," he said, "and my God." Now, if you can, separate Christ from God, and change this saying, if you are able to. Make use of all dialectic art — all the prudence of this world, and that foolish wisdom which consists in wordy subtlety. Turn yourself about in every direction, and draw in your horns. Do whatever you can with ingenuity and art. Say what you like, and do what you like; you cannot possibly get out of this without confessing that what the Apostle touched was God. And indeed, if the thing can possibly be done, perhaps you will want to alter the statement of the gospel story, so that we may not read that the Apostle Thomas touched the body of the Lord, or that he called Christ Lord and God. But it is absolutely impossible to alter what is written in the gospel of God. For "heaven and earth shall pass away, but the words" of God "shall not pass away." [2] For lo, even now he who then bore his witness, the Apostle Thomas, proclaims to you: "Jesus whom I touched is God. It is God whose limbs I handled. I did not feel what was incorporeal, not handle what was intangible: I touched not a Spirit with my hand, so that it might be believed that I said of it alone 'It is God.' For 'a spirit,' as my Lord Himself said, 'hath not flesh and bones.' [3] I touched the body of my Lord. I handled flesh and bones. I put my fingers into the prints of the wounds: and I declared of Christ my Lord, whom I had handled: 'My Lord and my God.' For I know not how to make a separation between Christ and God, and I cannot insert blasphemous distinctions between Jesus and God, or rend my Lord asunder from Himself. Away from me, whoever is of a different opinion, and whoever says anything different. I know not that

---

[1] S. John xx. 28.   [2] S. Matt. xxiv. 35.   [3] S. Luke xxiv. 39.

Christ is other than God. This faith I held together with my fellow apostles: this I delivered to the Churches: this I preached to the Gentiles: this I proclaim to thee also, Christ is God, Christ is God. A sound mind imagines nothing else: a sound faith says nothing else. The Deity cannot be parted from Itself. And since whatever is Christ is God, there can be found in God none other but God."

CHAPTER XVI.

He brings forward the witness of God the Father to the Divinity of the Son.

WHAT do you say now, you heretic? Are these evidences of the faith, aye and of all your unbelief, enough for you: or would you like some more to be added to them? but what can be added after Prophets and Apostles? unless perhaps — as the Jews once demanded — you too might ask for a sign to be given you from heaven? But if you ask this, we must give you the same answer which was formerly given to them: "An evil and adulterous generation seeketh after a sign. And no sign shall be given to it, but the sign of the prophet Jonah."[1] And indeed this sign would be enough for you as for the Jews who crucified Him, that you might be taught to believe in the Lord God by this alone, through which even those who had persecuted Him, came to believe. But as we have mentioned a sign from heaven, I will show you a sign from heaven: and one of such a character that even the devils have never gainsaid it: while, constrained by the demands of truth, though they saw Jesus in bodily form, they yet cried out that He was God, as indeed He was. What then does the Evangelist say of the Lord Jesus Christ? "When He was baptized," he says, "straightway He went up out of the water. And lo, the heavens were opened to Him, and He saw the Spirit descending like a dove, and coming upon Him. And behold, a voice from heaven, saying: This is My beloved Son, in whom I am well pleased."[2] What do you say to this, you heretic? Do you dislike the words spoken, or the Person of the Speaker? The meaning of the utterance at any rate needs no explanation: nor does the worth of the Speaker need the commendation of words. It is God the Father who spoke. What He said is clear enough. Surely you cannot make so shameless and blasphemous an assertion as to say that God the Father is

not to be believed concerning the only begotten Son of God? "This," He then says, "is My beloved Son in whom I am well pleased." But perhaps you will try to maintain that this is madness, and that this was said of the Word and not of Christ. Tell me then who was it who was baptized? The Word or Christ? Flesh or Spirit? You cannot possibly deny that it was Christ. That man then, born of man and of God, conceived by the descent of the Holy Spirit upon the Virgin, and by the overshadowing of the Power of the Most High, and thus the Son of man and of God, He it was, as you cannot deny, who was baptized. If then it was He who was baptized, it was He also who was named, for certainly the Person who was baptized was the one named. "This," said He, "is My beloved Son, in whom I am well pleased." Could anything be said with greater significance or clearness? Christ was baptized. Christ went up out of the water. When Christ was baptized the heavens were opened. For Christ's sake the dove descended upon Christ, the Holy Spirit was present in a bodily form. The Father addressed Christ. If you venture to deny that this was spoken of Christ, the only thing is for you to maintain that Christ was not baptized, that the Spirit did not descend, and that the Father did not speak. But the truth itself is urgent and weighs you down so that even if you will not confess it, yet you cannot deny it. For what says the Evangelist? "When He was baptized, straightway He went up out of the water." Who was baptized? Most certainly Christ. "And behold," he says, "the heavens were opened to Him." To whom, forsooth, save to Him who was baptized? Most certainly to Christ. "And He saw the Spirit of God descending like a dove and coming upon Him." Who saw? Christ indeed. Upon whom did It descend? Most certainly upon Christ. "And a voice came from heaven, saying" — of whom? Of Christ indeed: for what follows? "This is My beloved Son, in whom I am well pleased." In order that it might be made clear on whose account all this happened, there followed the voice, saying: "This is My beloved Son," as if to say: This is He on whose account all this took place. For this is My Son: on His account the heavens were opened: on His account My Spirit came: on His account My voice was heard. For this is My Son. In saying then "This is My Son" whom did He so designate? Certainly Him whom the dove touched. And whom did the dove touch? Christ indeed. Therefore Christ is the Son of God. My promise is fulfilled, I fancy. Do you see

---

[1] S. Matt. xvi. 4.   [2] S. Matt. iii. 16, 17.

then now, O heretic, a sign given you from heaven; and not one only, but many and special ones? For there is one in the opening of heaven, another in the descent of the Spirit, a third in the voice of the Father. All of which most clearly show that Christ is God, for the laying open of the heavens indicates that He is God, and the descent of the Holy Spirit upon Him supports His Divinity, and the address of the Father confirms it. For heaven would not have been opened except in honour of its Lord: nor would the Holy Ghost have descended in a bodily form except upon the Son of God: nor would the Father have declared Him to be the Son, had he not been truly such; especially with such tokens of a Divine birth, as not merely to confirm the truth of the right faith, but also to exclude the wickedness of guilty and erroneous belief. For when the Father had expressly and pointedly said with the inexpressible majesty of a Divine utterance, "This is My Son," He added also what follows — I mean, "My beloved, in whom I am well pleased." As He had already declared Him by the prophet to be God the Mighty and God the Great, so when He says here, "My beloved Son in whom I am well pleased," He adds further to the name of His own Son the title also of His beloved Son, in whom He is well pleased: that the addition of the titles might denote the special properties of the Divine nature; and that that might specially redound to the glory of the Son of God, which had never happened to any man. And so just as in the case of our Lord Jesus Christ these special and unique things happened; viz., that the heavens were opened, that in the sight of all God the Father touched Him in a sort of way, through the coming and presence of the dove, and pointed almost with His finger to Him saying, "This is My Son;" so this too is special and unique in His case; viz., that He is specially beloved, and is specially named as well-pleasing to the Father, in order that these special accompaniments might mark the special import of His nature, and that the special character of His names might support the special position of the only begotten Son, which the honour of the signs previously given had already confirmed. But here comes the end of this book. For this saying of God the Father can neither be added to, nor equalled by any words of men. For us God the Father Himself is a sufficiently satisfactory witness concerning our Lord Jesus Christ, when He says "This is My Son." If you think that it is possible for these utterances of God the Father to be gainsaid, then you are forced to contradict Him, who by the clearest possible announcement caused Him to be acknowledged as His Son by the whole world.

BOOK IV.

CHAPTER I.

That Christ was before the Incarnation God from everlasting.

As we have finished three books with the most certain and the most valuable witnesses, whose truth is substantiated not only by human but also by Divine evidences, they would abundantly suffice to prove our case by Divine authority, especially as the Divine authority of the case itself would be enough for this. But still as the whole mass of the sacred Scriptures is full of these evidences, and where there are so many witnesses, there are so many opinions to be urged — nay where Holy Scripture itself gives its witness so to speak with one Divine mouth — we have thought it well to add some others still, not from any need of confirmation, but because of the supply of material at our disposal; so that anything which might be unnecessary for purposes of defence, might be useful by way of ornamentation. Therefore since in the earlier books we proved the Divinity of our Lord Jesus Christ while He was in the flesh by the evidence not only of prophets and apostles, but of evangelists and angels as well, let us now show that He who was born in the flesh was God even before His Incarnation; that you may understand by the harmony and concord of the evidences from the sacred Scriptures, that you ought to believe that at His birth in the body He was both God and man, who before His birth was only God, and that He who after He had been brought forth by the Virgin in the body was God, was before His birth from the Virgin, God the Word. Learn then first of all from the Apostle the teacher of the whole world, that He who is without beginning, God, the Son of God, became the Son of man at the end of the world, i.e., in the fulness of the times. For he says: "But when the fulness of the times was come, God sent His Son, made of a woman, made under the law." [1] Tell me then, before the Lord Jesus Christ was born of His mother Mary, had God a Son or had He not? You cannot deny that He had, for never yet was there either a son without a father, or a father without a son: because as a son is so called with reference to a father, so is a father so named with reference to a son.

CHAPTER II.

He infers from what he has said that the Virgin Mary gave birth to a Son who had pre-existed and was greater than she herself was.

You see then that when the Apostle says that God sent His Son, it was His own Son, to use the actual words of the Apostle, "His own Son" that God sent. For, since He sent His own Son, it was not some one else's Son that He sent, nor could He send Him at all if He who was sent had no existence. He sent then, he says, "His own Son, made of a woman." Therefore because He sent Him, He sent one who existed: and because He sent His own, it certainly was not another's but His own whom He sent. What then becomes of that argument of yours drawn from this world's subtleties? No one ever yet gave birth to one who had already existed before. For had not the Lord a pre-existence before Mary? Was not the Son of God existent before the daughter of man? In a word did not God Himself exist before man — since certainly there is no man who is not from God. You see then that I do not merely say that Mary gave birth to one who had existed before her, not only, I say, one who had existed before her, but one who was the author of her being, and that in giving birth to her Creator, she became the mother of Him who gave her being: because it was as simple for God to bring about birth for Himself as for man, and as easy for Him to arrange that He Himself should be born of mankind, as that a man should be born. For the power of God is not limited in regard to His own Person, as if what was allowable to Him in the case of all others, was not allowable in His own case, and as if He who in the Divine nature could do all things as God, was yet unable in His own Person to become God in man. Setting aside then and rejecting your foolish and feeble and dull arguments from earthly things, we ought merely to put credence in straightforward evidence and the naked truth, and to adapt our faith to those witnesses of God alone, whom God sent,

and in whose person He Himself, so to speak, preached. For it is right to believe Him in a matter concerning knowledge of Himself, as everything that we know of Him comes from Him Himself, for God could not possibly be known of men, unless He Himself gave us the knowledge of Himself. And so it is right that we should believe everything of Him that we know, from whom comes everything that we know, for if we do not believe Him from whom our knowledge comes, the result will be that we shall know nothing at all, since we refuse to believe Him, through whom our knowledge comes.

CHAPTER III.

He proves from the Epistle to the Romans the eternal Divinity of Christ.

And so as it is clear from the above testimony that God sent His own Son, and that He who was ever the Son of God became the Son of man, let us see whether the same Apostle gives any other testimony of the same sort elsewhere, that the truth which is already clear enough in itself, may be rendered still more clear by the light of a twofold testimony. So then the same Apostle says: "God sent His own Son in the likeness of sinful flesh." [2] You see that the Apostle certainly did not use these words by chance or at random, as he repeated what he had already said once — for indeed there could not be found in him chance or want of consideration as the fulness of Divine counsel and speech had taken up its abode in him. What then does he say? "God sent His own Son in the likeness of sinful flesh." He says the same thing again and repeats it, saying, "God sent His own Son." Oh renowned and excellent teacher! for knowing that in this is contained the whole mystery [3] of the Catholic faith, in order that it might be believed that the Lord was born in the flesh and that the Son of God was sent into this world, again and again he makes the same proclamation saying, "God sent His own Son." Nor need we wonder that he who was specially sent to preach the coming of God, made this announcement, since even before the law, the giver of the law himself proclaimed it, saying: "I beseech Thee, O Lord, provide another whom Thou mayest send," or as it stands still more clearly in the Hebrew text: "I beseech Thee, O Lord, send whom Thou wilt send." [4] It is clear that the holy prophet,

---

[1] Gal. iv. 4.

[2] Rom. viii. 3.   [3] *Sacramentum.*
[4] Exod. iv. 13. Where the LXX. has Δέομαι, κύριε, προχείρισαι δυνάμενον ἄλλον ὃν ἀποστελεῖς, which was followed by the old Latin. Jerome however rendered the passage correctly from the Hebrew: "obsecro, Domine, mitte quem misurus es." Cf. the note on the Institutes, XII. xxxi.

feeling in himself a yearning for the whole human race, prayed as it were with the voices of all mankind to God the Father that He would send as speedily as possible Him who was to be sent by the Father for the redemption and salvation of all men, when he said, " I beseech Thee, O Lord, send whom Thou wilt send." "God," he therefore says, "sent His own Son in the likeness of sinful flesh." Full well, when he says that He was sent in the flesh, does he exclude for Him sin of the flesh : for he says "God sent His own Son in the likeness of the flesh of sin," in order that we may know that though the flesh was truly taken, yet there was no true sin, and that, as far as the body is concerned, we should understand that there was reality ; as far as sin is concerned, only the likeness of sin. For though all flesh is sinful, yet He had flesh without sin, and had in Himself the likeness of sinful flesh, while He was in the flesh . but He was free from what was truly sin, because He was without sin : and therefore he says : "God sent His own Son in the likeness of sinful flesh."

CHAPTER IV.

He brings forward other testimonies to the same view.

If you would know how admirably the Apostle preached this, hear how this utterance was put into his mouth ; as if from the mouth of God Himself, as the Lord says : " For God sent not His Son into the world to judge the world, but that the world might be saved through Him." [1] For lo, as you see, the Lord Himself affirms that He was sent by God the Father to save mankind. But if you think that it ought to be shown still more clearly, what Son God sent to save men, — though God's own and only begotten can only be one, and when God is said to have sent His Son, He is certainly shown to have sent His only begotten Son, — yet hear the prophet David pointing out with the utmost clearness Him who was sent for the salvation of Men. "He sent," said he, "His Word and healed them." [2] Can you twist this so as to refer it to the flesh as if you could say that a mere man was sent by God to heal mankind ? You certainly cannot, for the prophet David and all the holy Scriptures would cry out against you, saying, "He sent His Word and healed them." You see then, that the Word was sent to heal men, for though healing was given through Christ, yet the Word of God was in Christ, and healed all things through Christ : and so

since Christ and the Word were united in the mystery of the Incarnation, Christ and the Word of God became one Son of God in either substance. And when the Apostle John was anxious to state this clearly, he said " God sent His Son to be the Saviour of the world." [3] Do you see how he joined together God and man in an union that cannot be severed ? For Christ who was born of Mary is without the slightest doubt called Saviour, as it is said, "For to you is born this day a Saviour, which is Christ the Lord." [4] But here he calls the very Word of God, which was sent, a Saviour, saying : " God sent his Son to be the Saviour of the world."

CHAPTER V.

How in virtue of the hypostatic union of the two natures in Christ the Word is rightly termed the Saviour, or incarnate man, and the Son of God.

And so it is clear that through the mystery of the Word of God joined to man, the Word, which was sent to save men, can be termed Saviour, and the Saviour, who was born in the flesh, can through union with the Word be called the Son of God ; and so through the indifferent use of either title, since God is joined to man, whatever is God and man, can be termed altogether God. [5] And so the same Apostle well adds the words : "Whoever believeth that Jesus is the Son of God, God abideth in him, and the love of God is perfected in him." [6] He tells us that *he* believes, and declares that *he* is filled with divine love, who believes that Jesus is the Son of God. But he testifies that the Word of God is the Son of God, and thus means us fully to understand that the only begotten Word of God, and Jesus Christ the Son of God are one and the same Person. But do you want to be told more fully that, — though Christ according to the flesh was truly born as man of man, — yet in virtue of the ineffable unity of the mystery, by which man was joined to God, there is no separation between Christ and the Word ? Hear the gospel of the Lord, or rather hear the Lord

---

[1] S. John iii. 17.   [2] Ps. cvi. (cvii.) 20.

[3] 1 John iv. 14.   [4] S. Luke ii. 11.
[5] Cf. Hooker Eccl : Polity., Book V. c. liii. § 4. " A kind of mutual commutation there is whereby those concrete names, *God* and *man*, when we speak of Christ, do take interchangeably one another's room, so that for truth of speech it skilleth not whether we say that the Son of God hath created the world, and the Son of man by His death hath saved it, or else that the Son of man did create, and the Son of God die to save the world. Howbeit as oft as we attribute to God what the manhood of Christ claimeth, or to man what His Deity hath right unto, we understand by the name of God and the name of man neither the one nor the other nature, but the whole person of Christ, in whom both natures are." The technical phrase by which this interchange of names is described is the Communicatio idiomatum, and in Greek ἀντίδοσις. Cf. Pearson on the Creed, Art. IV. c. i.
[6] 1 John iv. 12.

Himself saying of Himself:[1] "This," says He, "is life eternal, that they may know Thee, the only true God, and Jesus Christ whom Thou hast sent."[2] You heard above that the Word of God was sent to heal mankind: here you are told that He who was sent is Jesus Christ. Separate this, if you can, — though you see that so great is the unity of Christ and the Word, that it was not merely that Christ was united with the Word, but that in virtue of the actual unity [of Person] Christ may even be said to be the Word.

CHAPTER VI.

That there is in Christ but one Hypostasis (i.e., Personal self).

BUT perhaps you think it a trifle to make this clear: not because it fails in clearness, but because the obscurity of unbelief always causes obscurity even in what is clear. Hear then how the Apostle sums up in a few words this whole mystery of the Lord's unity [of Person]. "Our one Lord Jesus Christ," he says, "by whom are all things."[3] O good Jesus, what weight there is in Thy words! For Thine they are, when spoken of Thee by Thine own. See how much is embraced in the few words of this saying of the Apostle's. "One Lord," says he, "Jesus Christ, by whom are all things." Did he make use of any circumlocution in order to proclaim the truth of this great mystery?[4] or did he make a long story of that which he wanted us to grasp? "Our one Lord," he says, "Jesus Christ, by whom are all things." In a plain and short phrase he taught the secret of this great mystery, through this confidence by which he realized that in what refers to God his statements had no need of lengthened arguments, and that the Divinity added faith to his utterances. For the demonstration of facts is enough to confirm what is said, whenever the proof rests on the authority of the speaker. There is then, he says, "one Lord Jesus Christ, by whom are all things." Notice how you read the same thing of the Word of the Father, which you read of Christ. For the gospel tells us that "All things were made by Him, and without Him was not anything made."[5] The Apostle says, "By Christ are all things:" the gospel says, "By the Word are all things." Do these sacred utterances contradict each other? Most certainly not. But by Christ, by whom the Apostle said that all

things were created, and by the Word, by whom the Evangelist relates that all things were made, we are meant to understand one and the same Person. Hear, I tell you, what the Word of God, Himself God, has said of Himself. "No man," he saith, "hath ascended into heaven, save He who came down from heaven, even the Son of man, who is in heaven."[6] And again He says: "If ye shall see the Son of man ascending where He was before."[7] He said that the Son of man was in heaven: He asserted that the Son of man had come down from heaven. What does it mean? Why are you muttering? Deny it, if you can. But do you ask the reason of what is said? However I do not give it you. God has said this. God has spoken this to me: His Word is the best reason. I get rid of arguments and discussions. The Person of the Speaker alone is enough to make me believe. I may not debate about the trustworthiness of what is said, nor discuss it. Why should I question whether what God has said is true, since I ought not to doubt that what God says is true. "No man," He says, "hath ascended into heaven, save He who came down from heaven, even the Son of man, who is in heaven." Certainly the Word of the Father was ever in heaven: and how did He assert that the Son of man was ever in heaven? You are then to understand that He showed that He who was ever the Son of God was also the Son of man: when He asserted that He, who had but recently appeared as the Son of man, was ever in heaven. To this points still more that other passage in which He testifies that the same Son of man; viz., the Word of God who, as He said, came down from heaven, even at the time when He was speaking on earth, was in heaven. For "no man," He said, "hath ascended into heaven, save He who came down from heaven, even the Son of man who is in heaven." Who, I pray you, is this who is speaking? Assuredly it is Christ. But where was He at the moment when He spoke? Assuredly on earth. And how can He assert that He came down from heaven when He was born, and that He was in heaven when He was speaking, or say that He is the same Son of man, when certainly no one but God can come down from heaven, and when He speaks on earth, and certainly cannot be in heaven except through the Infinite nature of God? Consider then this at last, and note that the Son of man is the same Person as the Word of God: for He is the Son of man since He is truly born of man, and the Word of God, since He who speaks on earth abideth

---

[1] *De se dicentem* (Petschenig): Gazæus reads *descendentem*.
[2] S. John xvii. 3.
[3] 1 Cor. viii. 6.
[4] *Tanti mysterii sacramentum.*
[5] S. John i. 3.
[6] S. John iii. 13.
[7] S. John vi. 63.

ever in heaven. And so when He truly terms Himself the Son of man, it refers to His human birth, while the fact that He never departs from heaven, refers to the Infinite character of His Divine nature. And so the Apostle's teaching is admirably in accordance with those sacred words: ("for He that descended," says He, "is the same that ascended also above all heavens, that He might fill all things,"[1]) when He says that He that descended is the same that ascended. But none can descend from heaven except the Word of God: who certainly "being in the form of God, emptied Himself, taking the form of a servant, being made in the likeness of men, and being found in fashion as a man, He humbled Himself, and became obedient unto death, even the death of the Cross."[2] Thus the Word of God descended from heaven: but the Son of man ascended. But He says that the same Person ascended and descended. Thus you see that the Son of man is the same Person as the Word of God.

CHAPTER VII.

He returns to the former subject, in order to show against the Nestorians that those things are said of the man, which belong to the Divine nature as it were of a Person of Divine nature, and conversely that those things are said of God, which belong to the human nature as it were of a Person of human nature, because there is in Christ but one and a single Personal self.

AND so following the guidance of the sacred word we may now say fearlessly and unhesitatingly that the Son of man came down from heaven, and that the Lord of Glory was crucified: because in virtue of the mystery of the Incarnation, the Son of God became Son of man, and the Lord of Glory was crucified in (the nature of) the Son of man.[3] What more is there need of? It would take too long to go into details: for time would fail me, were I to try to examine and explain everything which could be brought to bear on this subject. For one who wished to do this would have to study and read the whole Bible. For what is there which does not bear on this,

when all Scripture was written with reference to this? We must then say — as far as can be said — some things briefly and cursorily, and enumerate rather than explain them, and sacrifice some to save the rest, as for this reason it would certainly be well hurriedly to run through some points, lest one should be obliged[4] to pass over almost everything in silence. The Saviour then in the gospel says that "the Son of man is come to save what was lost."[5] And the Apostle says: "This is a faithful saying and worthy of all acceptation; that Christ Jesus came into the world to save sinners, of whom I am chief."[6] But the Evangelist John also says: "He came unto his own, and His own received Him not."[7] You see then that Scripture says in one place that the Son of man, in another Jesus Christ, in another the Word of God came into the world. And so we must hold that the difference is one of title not of fact, and that under the appearance of different names there is but one Power [or Person]. For though at one time we are told that the Son of man, and at another that the Son of God came into the world, but one Person is meant under both names.

CHAPTER VIII.

How this interchange of titles does not interfere with His Divine power.

FOR certainly when the evangelist says that He came into the world by whom the world itself was made, and that He was made the Son of man, who is as God the creator of the world, it makes no difference what particular title is used, as God in all cases is meant. For His condescension and will do not interfere with His Divinity, since they the rather prove His Divinity, because whatever He willed came to pass. Therefore also because He willed it, He came into the world; and because He willed it, He was born a man; and because He willed it, He was termed the Son of man. For just as there are so many words, so are they powers belonging to God. The variety of names in Him does not take anything away from the efficacy of His power. Whatever may be the names given Him, in all cases it is one and the same Person. Though there may be some variety in the appearance of His titles, yet there is but a single Divine Person (Majestas) meant by all the names.

---

[1] Eph. iv. 10. [2] Phil. ii. 6–8.
[3] See Hooker as above (V. liii. 4) "When the Apostle saith of the Jews that they crucified the Lord of Glory, and when the Son of man being on earth affirmeth that the Son of man was in heaven at the same instant, there is in these two speeches that mutual circulation before mentioned. In the one, there is attributed to God or the Lord of Glory death, whereof Divine nature is not capable; in the other ubiquity unto man which human nature admitteth not. Therefore by the Lord of Glory we must needs understand the whole person of Christ, who being Lord of Glory, was indeed crucified, but not in that nature for which he is termed the Lord of Glory. In like manner by the Son of man the whole person of Christ must necessarily be meant, who being man upon earth, filled heaven with his glorious presence, but not according to that nature for which the title of man is given Him."

[4] *Ne necesse sit* (Petschenig). [6] 1 Tim. i. 15.
[5] S. Luke xix. 10. [7] S. John i. 11.

CHAPTER IX.

He corroborates this statement by the authority of the old prophets.

But since up to this point we have made use more particularly of the witness, comparatively new, of evangelists and apostles, now let us bring forward the testimony of the old prophets, intermingling at times new things with old, that everybody may see that the holy Scriptures proclaim as it were with one mouth that Christ was to come in the flesh, with a body of His own complete. And so that far-famed and renowned prophet as richly endowed with God's gifts as with his testimony, to whom alone it was given to be sanctified before His birth,[1] Jeremiah, says, "This is our Lord, and there shall no other be accounted of in comparison with Him. He found out all the way of knowledge and gave it to Jacob His servant and Israel His beloved. Afterwards He was seen upon earth and conversed with men."[2] "This is," then, he says, "our God." You see how the prophet points to God as it were with his hand, and indicates Him as it were with his finger. "This is," he says, "our God." Tell me then, who was it that the prophet showed by these signs and tokens to be God? Surely it was not the Father? For what need was there that He should be pointed out, whom all believed that they knew? For even then the Jews were not ignorant of God, for they were living under God's law. But he was clearly aiming at this, that they might come to know the Son of God as God. And so excellently did the Prophet say that He who had found out all knowledge, i.e., had given the law, was to be seen upon earth, i.e., was to come in the flesh, in order that, as the Jews did not doubt that He who had given the law was God, they might recognize that He who was to come in the flesh was God, especially since they heard that He, in whom they believed as God the giver of the law, was to be seen among men by taking upon Him manhood, as He Himself promises His own advent by the prophet: "For I myself that spoke, behold I am here."[3] "There shall then," says the Scriptures, "be no other accounted of in comparison of Him." Beautifully does the prophet here foresee false teaching, and so exclude the interpretations of heretical perverseness. "There shall no other be accounted of in comparison of Him." For He is alone begotten to be God of God: at whose bidding the completion of the universe followed: whose will is the beginning of things: whose empire is the fabric of the world: who spake all things, and they came to pass: commanded all things, and they were created. He then alone it is who spake to the patriarchs, dwelt in the prophets, was conceived by the Spirit, born of the Virgin Mary, appeared in the world, lived among men, fastened to the wood of the cross the handwriting of our offences, triumphed in Himself,[4] slew by His death the powers that were at enmity and hostile to us; and gave to all men belief in the resurrection, and by the glory of His body put an end to the corruption of man's flesh. You see then that all these belong to the Lord Jesus Christ alone: and therefore no other shall be accounted of in comparison with Him, for He alone is God begotten of God in this glory and unique blessedness. This then is what the prophet's teaching was aiming at; viz., that He might be known by all men to be the only begotten Son of God the Father, and that when they heard that no other was accounted of as God in comparison with the Son, they might confess that there was but one God in the Persons of the Father and the Son. "After this," he said, "He was seen upon earth and conversed with men." You see how plainly this points to the advent and nativity of the Lord. For surely the Father — of whom we read that He can only be seen in the Son — was not seen upon earth, nor born in the flesh, nor conversed with men? Most certainly not. You see then that all this is spoken of the Son of God. For since the prophet said that God should be seen upon earth, and no other but the Son was seen upon earth, it is clear that the prophet said this only of Him, of whom facts afterwards proved that it was spoken. For when He said that God should be seen, He could not say this truly, except of Him who was indeed afterwards seen. But enough of this. Now let us turn to another point. "The labour of Egypt," says the prophet Isaiah, "and the merchandise of Ethiopia and of the Sabæans, men of stature, shall come over to thee and shall be thy servants. They shall walk after thee, bound with manacles, and they shall worship thee, and they shall make supplication to thee: for in thee is God, and there is no God beside thee. For thou

---

[1] Cf. Jer. i. 5.

[2] The passage comes not from Jeremiah, but from Baruch (iii. 36–38). It is also quoted as from Jeremiah by Augustine (c. Faustin. xii. c. 43): and in the LXX. version the book of Baruch is placed among the works of Jeremiah, e.g., In both the Vatican and Alexandrine MSS. they stand in the following order: (1) Jeremiah, (2) Baruch, (3) Lamentations, (4) the Epistle of Jeremy (Baruch c. vi. in A.V.). The passage which Cassian here quotes is constantly appealed to by both Greek and Latin Fathers, as a prophecy of the Incarnation. See e.g. S. Augustine (l.c.) S. Chrysost. "Ecloga" Hom. xxxiv. Rufinus in. Symb. § 5.

[3] Isa. lii. 6.

[4] Cf. Col. ii. 14, 15.

art our God and we knew thee not, O God of Israel the Saviour." [1] How wonderfully consistent the Holy Scriptures always are! For the first mentioned prophet said, "This is our God," and this one says, "Thou art our God." In the one there is the teaching of Divinity, in the other the confession of men. The one exhibits the character of the Master teaching, the other that of the people confessing. For consider now the prophet Jeremiah daily teaching, as he does, in the church, and saying of the Lord Jesus Christ, "This is our God," what else could the whole Church reply, as it does, than what the other prophet said to the Lord Jesus, "Thou art our God." So that full well could the mention of their past ignorance be joined to their present acknowledgment, in the words of the people: "Thou art our God, and we knew thee not." For well can these who, in times past being taken up with the superstitions of devils did not know God, yet when now converted to the faith say, "Thou art our God, and we knew thee not."

CHAPTER X.

He proves Christ's Divinity from the blasphemy of Judaizing Jews as well as from the confession of converts to the faith of Christ.

BUT if you would like to have this proved to you rather from representatives of the Jews, consider the Jewish people when after their unhappy ignorance and wicked persecution they were converted, and acknowledged God here and there, and see whether they could not rightly say, "Thou art our God, and we knew Thee not." But I will add something else, to prove it to you not only from those Jews who confess Him, but also from those who deny Him. For ask those Jews who still continue in their state of unbelief whether they know or believe in God. They will certainly confess that they both know and believe in Him. But on the other hand ask them whether they believe in the Son of God. They will at once deny and begin to blaspheme against Him. You see then that the Prophet said this of Him of whom the Jews have always been ignorant, and whom now they know not; and not of Him whom they imagine that they believe in and confess. And so full well can those, who after having been in ignorance come out of Judaism to the faith, say, "Thou art our God, and we knew Thee not." For rightly do those, who after having been ignorant come to believe, say that they knew not Him in whom up to this time they have not believed, and whom they strive not to

know. For it is clear that those who after their previous ignorance come to confess Him, say that formerly they knew Him not, whom up to this time they have ignorantly denied.

CHAPTER XI.

He returns to the prophecy of Isaiah.

"THE labour," says he, "of Egypt, and the merchandize of Ethiopia, and the Sabæans, men of stature shall come over to thee." No one can doubt that in these names of different nations is signified the coming of the nations who were to believe. But you cannot deny that the nations have come over to Christ, for since the name of Christianity has arisen, they have come over to the Lord Jesus Christ not only in faith but actually in name. For since they are called what they really are, that which was the work of faith becomes the token by which they are named. "They shall," he says, "come over to thee and shall be thine: they shall walk after thee bound with manacles." As there are chains of coercion, so too there are chains of love, as the Lord says: "I drew them with chains of love." [2] For indeed great are these chains, and chains of ineffable love, for those who are bound with them rejoice in their fetters. Do you want to know whether this is true? Hear how the Apostle Paul exults and rejoices in his chains, when he says: "I therefore a prisoner in the Lord beseech you." [3] And again: "I beseech thee, whereas thou art such an one as Paul the aged, and now a prisoner also of Jesus Christ." [4] You see how he rejoiced in the dignity of his chains, by the example of which he actually stirred up others. But there can be no doubt that where there is single-minded love of the Lord, there is also single-minded delight in chains worn for the Lord's sake: as it is written: "But the multitude of the believers was of one heart and one soul." [5] "And they shall worship thee," he says, "and shall make supplication to thee: for in thee is God, and there is no God beside thee." The Apostle clearly explains the prophet's words, when he says that "God was in Christ reconciling the world to Himself." [6] "In Thee then," he says, "is God and there is no God beside thee." When the prophet says "In Thee is God," most admirably does he point not merely to Him who was visible, but to Him who was in what was visible, distinguishing the indweller from Him in whom He dwelt, by pointing out the two natures, not by denying the unity (of Person).

[1] Isa. xiv. 14, 15.

[2] Hosea xi. 4.   [4] Philemon, ver. 9.   [6] 2 Cor. v. 19.
[3] Eph. iv. 1.   [5] Acts iv. 32.

CHAPTER XII.

How the title of Saviour is given to Christ in one sense, and to men in another.

"Thou," he says, "art our God, and we knew Thee not, O God of Israel the Saviour." Although holy Scripture has already shown by many and clear tokens, who is here spoken of, yet it has most plainly pointed to the name of Christ by using the name of Saviour: for surely the Saviour is the same as Christ, as the angel says: "For to you is born this day a Saviour who is Christ the Lord."[1] For everybody knows that in Hebrew "Jesus" means "Saviour," as the angel announced to the holy Virgin Mary, saying: "And thou shalt call His name Jesus, for He it is that shall save His people from their sins."[2] And that you may not say that He is termed Saviour in the same sense as the title is given to others ("And the Lord raised up to them a Saviour, Othniel the Son of Kenaz,"[3] and again, "the Lord raised up to them a Saviour, Ehud the son of Gera"[4]), he added: "for He it is that shall save His people from their sins." But it does not lie in the power of a man to redeem his people from the captivity of sin, — a thing which is only possible for Him of whom it is said, "Behold the Lamb of God, which taketh away the sin of the world."[5] For the others saved a people not their own but God's, and not from their sins, but from their enemies.

CHAPTER XIII.

He explains who are those in whose person the Prophet Isaiah says: "Thou art our God, and we knew Thee not."

"Thou art then," he says, "our God, and we knew Thee not, O God of Israel the Saviour." Who do you imagine chiefly say this; and in whose mouths are such words specially suitable, Jews or Gentiles? If you say Jews: certainly the Jews did not know Christ, as it is said, "But Israel hath not known Me, My people have not considered;"[6] and, "The world was made by Him, and the world knew Him not. He came unto His own, and His own received Him not."[7] But if you say Gentiles, it is clear that the Gentile world was given over to idols, and knew not Christ, though it knew not the Father any more; but still if it has now come to know Him, it is only through Christ. You see then that whether the believing people belong to the Jews or the Gentiles, in either case they can truly say for themselves: "Thou art our God, and we knew Thee not, O God of Israel the Saviour." For the Gentiles who formerly worshipped idols knew not God; and the Jews who denied the Lord, knew not the Son of God. And thus both truly say of Christ: "Thou art our God and we knew Thee not." For those who did not believe in God were as ignorant of Him as those who denied the Son of God. If therefore Christ is to be believed in, as the truth declares, as the Deity asserts, as indeed Christ Himself declares, who is both, why are you miserably trying in your madness to interpose between God and Christ? Why do you seek to divide His body from the Son of God, and try to separate God from Himself? You are severing what is one, and dividing what is joined together. Believe the Word of God concerning God: for you cannot possibly make a better confession of God's Divinity than by confessing with your voice that which God teaches about Himself. For you must know that, as the Prophet says, "the Lord Himself is God, who found out all the way of knowledge; who was seen upon earth and conversed with men."[8] He brought the light of faith into the world. He showed the light of salvation. "For God is the Lord, and hath given us light."[9] Then believe Him, and love Him, and confess Him. For since, as it is written, "Every knee shall bow to Him, of things in heaven, and things on earth, and things under the earth, and every tongue shall confess that Jesus Christ is Lord in the glory of God the Father,"[10] whether you will or no, you cannot deny that Jesus Christ is Lord in the glory of God the Father. For this is the crowning virtue of a perfect confession, to acknowledge that Jesus Christ is ever Lord and God in the glory of God the Father.

BOOK V.

CHAPTER I.

He vehemently inveighs against the error of the Pelagians, who declared that Christ was a mere man.

We said in the first book that that heresy which copies and follows the lead of Pelagianism, strives and contends in every way to make it believed that the Lord Jesus Christ, the Son of God, when born of the Virgin was only a mere man; and that having afterwards taken the path of virtue He merited by His holy and pious life to be counted worthy for this

---

[1] S. Luke ii. 11.
[2] S. Matt. i. 21.
[3] Judges iii. 9.
[4] *Ib.* ver. 15.
[5] S. John i. 29.
[6] Isa. i. 3.
[7] S. John i. 11.
[8] Baruch iii. 37, 38.
[9] Ps. cxvii. (cviii.) 27.
[10] Phil. ii. 10, 11.

holiness of His life that the Divine Majesty should unite Itself to Him: and thus by cutting off altogether from Him the honour of His sacred origin, it only left to Him the selection on account of His merits.[1] And their aim and endeavour was this; viz., that, by bringing Him down to the level of common men, and making Him one of the common herd, they might assert that all men could by their good life and deeds secure whatever He had secured by His good life.[2] A most dangerous and deadly assertion indeed, which takes away what truly belongs to God, and holds out false promises to men; and which should be condemned for abominable lies on both sides, since it attacks God with wicked blasphemy, and gives to men the hope of a false assurance. A most perverse and wicked assertion as it gives to men what does not belong to them, and takes away from God what is His. And so of this dangerous and deadly evil this new heresy which has recently sprung up,[3] is in a way stirring and reviving the embers, and raising a fresh flame from its ancient ashes: by asserting that our Lord Jesus Christ was born a mere man. And so why is there any need for us to ask whether its consequences are dangerous, as in its fountain head it is utterly wrong. It is unnecessary to examine what it is like in its issues, as in its commencement it leaves us no reason for examination. For what object is there in inquiring whether like the earlier heresy, it holds out the same promises to man, if (which is the most awful sin) it takes away the same things from God? So that it would be almost wrong, when we see what it begins like, to ask what there is to follow; as if some possible way might appear in the sequel, in which a man who denies God, could prove that he was not irreligious. The new heresy then, as we have already many times declared, says that the Lord Jesus Christ was born of the Virgin Mary, only a mere man: and so that Mary should be called Christotocos not Theotocos, because she was the mother of Christ, not of God. And further to this blasphemous statement it adds arguments that are as wicked as they are foolish, saying, " No one ever gave birth to one who was before her."

[1] See above Book I. cc. ii. iii.
[2] See below Book VI. c. xiv. For the twofold error of Pelagianism cf. a striking article on " Theodore of Mopsuestia and Modern Thought " in the Church Quarterly Review, vol. i. See esp. p. 135; where, speaking of Pelagianism, the writer says: " As the hypostatic union was denied, lest it should derogate from the ethical completeness of Christ, so the efficacious working of grace must be explained away lest it should derogate from the moral dignity of Christians. The divine and human elements must be kept as jealously apart in the moral life of the members as in the person of the Head of the Church. In the ultimate analysis it must be proved that the initial movement in every good action came from the human will itself, though when this was allowed, the grace of God might receive, by an exact process of assessment, its due share of credit for the result."
[3] Viz., Nestorianism.

As if the birth of the only begotten of God, predicted by prophets, announced since the beginning of the world, could be dealt with or measured by human reasons. Or did the Virgin Mary, O you heretic, whoever you are, who slander her for her childbearing — bring about and consummate that which came to pass, by her own strength, so that in a matter and event of so great importance, human weakness can be brought as an objection? And so if there was anything in this great event which was the work of man, look for human arguments. But if everything, which was done, was due to the power of God, why should you consider what is impossible with men, when you see that it is the work of Divine power? But of this more anon. Now let us follow up the subject we began to treat of some little way back; that everybody may know that you are trying to fan the flame in the ashes of Pelagianism, and to revive the embers by breathing out fresh blasphemy.

CHAPTER II.

That the doctrine of Nestorius is closely connected with the error of the Pelagians.

YOU say then that Christ was born a mere man. But certainly this was asserted by that wicked heresy of Pelagius, as we clearly showed in the first book; viz., that Christ was born a mere man. You add besides, that Jesus Christ the Lord of all should be termed a form that received God (Θεοδόχος), i.e., not God, but the receiver of God, so that your view is that He is to be honoured not for His own sake because He is God, but because He receives God into Himself. But clearly this also was asserted by that heresy of which I spoke before; viz., that Christ was not to be worshipped for His own sake because He was God, but because owing to His good and pious actions He won this; viz., to have God dwelling in Him. You see then that you are belching out the poison of Pelagianism, and hissing with the very spirit of Pelagianism. Whence it comes that you seem rather to have been already judged, than to have now to undergo judgment, for since your error is one and the same, you must be believed to fall under the same condemnation: not to mention for the present that you compare the Lord to a statue of the Emperor, and break out into such wicked and blasphemous impieties that you seem in this madness of yours to surpass even Pelagius himself, who surpassed almost every one else in impiety.

CHAPTER III.

How this participation in Divinity which the Pelagians and Nestorians attribute to Christ, is common to all holy men.

You say then that Christ should be termed a form which received God (Θεοδόχος), i.e., that He should be revered not for His own sake because He is God, but because He received God within Him. And so in this way you make out that there is no difference between Him and all other holy men: for all holy men have certainly had God within them. For we know well that God was in the patriarchs, and that He spoke in the prophets. In a word we believe that, I do not say apostles and martyrs, but, all the saints and servants of God have within them the Spirit of God, according to this: "Ye are the temple of the living God: as God said, For I will dwell in them."[1] And again: "Know ye not that ye are the temple of God, and the Spirit of God dwelleth in you?"[2] And thus we are all receivers of God (Θεοδόχοι); and in this way you say that all the saints are only like Christ, and equal to God. But away with such a wicked and abominable heresy as that the Creator should be compared to His creatures, the Lord to His servants, the God of things earthly and heavenly, to earthly frailty: and out of His very kindnesses this wrong be done to Him; viz., that He who honours man by dwelling in him should therefore be said to be only the same as man.

CHAPTER IV.

What the difference is between Christ and the saints.

Moreover there is between Him and all the saints the same difference that there is between a dwelling and one who dwells in it, for certainly it is the doing of the dweller not the dwelling, if it is inhabited, for on him it depends both to build the house and to occupy it. I mean, that he can choose, if he will, to make it a dwelling, and when he has made it, to live in it. "Or do you seek a proof," says the Apostle, "of Christ speaking in me?"[3] And elsewhere, "Know ye not that Jesus Christ is in you except ye be reprobate?"[4] And again: "in the inner man, that Christ may dwell in your hearts by faith."[5] Do you not see what a difference there is between the Apostle's doctrine and your blasphemies? You say that God dwells in Christ as in a man. He testifies that Christ Himself dwells in men: which certainly, as you admit,

flesh and blood cannot do; so that He is shown to be God, from the very fact from which you deny Him to be God. For since you cannot deny that He who dwells in man is God, it follows that we must believe that He, whom we know to dwell in men, is most decidedly God. All, then, whether patriarchs, or prophets, or apostles, or martyrs, or saints, had every one of them God within him, and were all made sons of God and were all receivers of God (Θεοδόχοι), but in a very different and distinct way. For all who believe in God are sons of God by adoption: but the only begotten alone is Son by nature: who was begotten of His Father, not of any material substance, for all things, and the substance of all things exist through the only begotten Son of God — and not out of nothing, because He is from the Father: not like a birth, for there is nothing in God that is void or mutable, but in an ineffable and incomprehensible manner God the Father, wherein He Himself was ingenerate, begat his only begotten Son; and so from the Most High, Ingenerate, and Eternal Father proceeds the Most High, Only Begotten, and Eternal Son. Who must be considered the same Person in the flesh as He is in the Spirit: and must be held to be the same Person in the body as He is in glory, for when He was about to be born in the flesh,[6] He made no division or separation within Himself, as if some portion of Him was born while another portion was not born: or as if some portion of Divinity afterwards came upon Him, which had not been in Him at His birth from the Virgin. For according to the Apostle, "all the fulness of the Godhead dwelleth in Christ bodily."[7] Not that It dwells in Him at times, and at times dwells not; nor that It was there at a later date, and not an earlier one: otherwise we are entangled in that impious heresy of Pelagius, so as to say that from a fixed moment God dwelt in Christ, and that He then came upon Him; when He had won by His life and conversation this; viz., that the power of the Godhead should dwell in Him. These things then belong to men, to men, I say, not to God, — that as far as human weakness can, they should humble themselves to God, be subject to God, make themselves dwellings for God, and by their faith and piety win this, to have God as their guest and indweller. For in proportion as anyone is fit for God's gift, so does the Divine grace reward him: in proportion as a man seems worthy of

---

[1] 2 Cor. vi. 16.   [3] 2 Cor. xiii. 3.   [5] Eph. iii. 16, 17.
[2] 1 Cor. iii. 16.   [4] *Ib.* ver. 5.

[6] *Idem credendus in corpore qui creditur in majestate, quia nasciturus in carne non divisionem*, etc., (Petschenig): Gazæus reads *Idem credendus in majestate quia nasciturus in carne. Non divisionem*, etc.
[7] Col. ii. 9.

God, so does he enjoy God's presence, according to the Lord's promise: "If any man love Me, he will keep My word; and I and My Father will come to him and make Our abode with Him."[1] But very different is the case as regards Christ; in whom all the fulness of the Godhead dwelleth bodily: for He has within Him the fulness of the Godhead so that He gives to all of His fulness, and He — as the fulness of the Godhead dwells in Him — Himself dwells in each of the saints in proportion as He deems them worthy of His Presence, and gives of His fulness to all, yet in such a way that He Himself continues in all that fulness, — who even when He was on earth in the flesh, yet was present in the hearts of all the saints, and filled the heaven, the earth, the sea, aye and the whole universe with His infinite power and majesty; and yet was so complete in Himself that the whole world could not contain Him. For however great and inexpressible whatever is made may be, yet there are no things so boundless and infinite as to be able to contain the Creator Himself.

CHAPTER V.

That before His birth in time Christ was always called God by the prophets.

He it is then of whom the Prophet says: "For in Thee is God, and there is no God beside Thee. For Thou art our God and we knew Thee not, O God of Israel the Saviour."[2] Who "afterwards appeared on earth and conversed with men."[3] Of whom and in whose Person the Prophet David also speaks: "From my mother's womb Thou art my God:"[4] showing clearly that He who was Lord and man[5] was never separate from God: in whom even in the Virgin's womb the fulness of the Godhead dwelt. As elsewhere the same Prophet says: "Truth has sprung from the earth

and righteousness hath looked down from heaven,"[6] that we may know that when the Son of God looked down from heaven (i.e., came and descended), righteousness was born of the flesh of the Virgin, no phantasm of a body, but the Truth: for He is the Truth, according to His own witness of Truth: "I am the Truth and the life."[7] And so as we have proved in the earlier books that this Truth; viz., the Lord Jesus Christ, was God when born of the Virgin, let us now do as we determined to do in the book before this, and show that He who was to be born of the Virgin, was always declared to be God beforehand. And so the prophet Isaiah says, "Cease ye from the man whose breath is in his nostrils, for it is He in whom he is reputed to be;" or as it is more exactly and clearly in the Hebrew: "for he is reputed high."[8] But by saying "cease ye," a term which deprecates violence, he admirably denotes the disturbance of persecution. "Cease ye," he says, "from the man whose breath is in his nostrils, for he is reputed high." Does he not in one and the same sentence speak of the taking upon Him of the manhood, and the truth of His Godhead? "Cease ye," he says, "from the man whose breath is in his nostrils, for he is reputed high." Does he not, I ask you, seem plainly to address the Lord's persecutors, and to say, "Cease ye from the man" whom ye are persecuting, for this man is God: and though He appears in the lowliness of human flesh, yet He still continues in the high estate of Divine glory? But by saying "Cease ye from the man whose breath is in his nostrils," he admirably showed His manhood, by the clearest tokens of a human body, and this fearlessly and confidently, as one who would as urgently assert the truth of His humanity as that of His Godhead, for this is the true and Catholic faith, to believe that the Lord Jesus Christ possessed the substance of a true body just as He possessed a true and perfect Divinity. Unless possibly you think that anything can be made out of the fact that he uses the word "High" instead of "God"; whereas it is the habit of holy Scripture to put "High" for "God," as where the prophet says: "the Most High uttered His voice and the earth was moved,"[9] and "Thou alone art Most High over all the earth."[10] Isaiah too, who says this: "The High and lofty one who inhabiteth eternity":[11] where we are clearly to understand that as he there puts Most High without adding the name of God, so here too he speaks of God by the name of Most High. So then,

[1] S. John xiv. 23.   [3] Baruch iii. 37.
[2] Isa. xlv. 14, 15.   [4] Ps. xxi. (xxii.) 11.
[5] *Dominicus Homo*, literally "the Lordly man." The same title is used again by Cassian in Book VI. cc. xxi., xxii., and in the Conferences XI. xiii. It is however an instance of a title which the mature judgment of the Church has rejected as savouring of an heretical interpretation. We learn from Gregory Nazianzen (Orat. 51) that the Greek equivalent of the title ὁ κυριακὸς ἄνθρωπος, was a favourite term with the Apollinarians, as it might be taken to favour their view that the Divinity supplied the place of a human soul in Christ. It is however freely used by Epiphanius in his Anchoratus, and is also found in the exposition of faith assigned to Athanasius (Migne. Pat. Græc. xxv. p. 197). And Augustine himself actually uses the title Dominicus Homo in his treatise on the Sermon on the Mount, Book II. c. vi., though he afterwards retracted the term, see "Retract," Book I. c. xx. "Non video utrum recte dicatur *Homo Dominicus*, qui est mediator Dei et hominum, homo Christus Jesus, cum sit utique Dominus: Dominicus antem homo quis in ejus sancta familia non potest dici? Et hoc quidem ut dicerem, apud quosdam legi tractores catholicos divinorum eloquiorum. Sed ubicunque hoc dici, dixisse me nollem. Postea quippe vidi non esse dicendum, quamvis nonnulla possit ratione defendi." The question is discussed by S. Thomas, whether the title is rightly applied to Christ and decided by him in the negative. Summa III. Q. vi. art. 3.

[6] Ps. lxxxiv. (lxxxv.) 12.   [7] S. John xiv. 6.
[8] Isa. ii. 22. Cf. the note on the Institutes xii. xxxi.
[9] Ps. xlv. (xlvi.) 7.   [10] Ps. lxxxii. (lxxxiii.) 19.   [11] Isa. lvii. 15.

since the Divine word spoken by the prophet clearly announced beforehand that the Lord Jesus Christ would be both God and man, let us now see whether the New Testament corresponds to and harmonizes with the testimony of the Old.

CHAPTER VI.

He illustrates the same doctrine by passages from the New Testament.

"THAT," says the Apostle John, "which was from the beginning, which we have heard, which we have seen with our eyes, which we have looked upon, and our hands have handled, of the word of the life: for the life was manifested: and we have seen, and do bear witness, and declare unto you the life eternal, which was with the Father, and hath appeared unto us."[1] You see how the old testimonies are confirmed by fresh ones, and the support of the new preaching is given to the ancient prophecy. Isaiah said: "Cease ye from the man whose breath is in his nostrils for he is reputed high." But John says: "That which was from the beginning, which we have seen with our eyes, which we have looked upon, and our hands have handled." The former said that as man He would be persecuted by the Jews: the latter declared that as man He was handled by men's hands. The one predicted that He whom he announced as man, would be God Most High: the other asserts that He whom he showed to have been handled by men, was ever God in the beginning. It is then as clear as possible that they both showed the Lord Jesus Christ to be both God and man; and that the same Person was afterwards man who had always been God, and thus He was God and man, because God Himself became man. That then, he says, "which was from the beginning, which we have heard, which we have seen with our eyes, which we have looked upon, and our hands have handled of the word of life; and the life was manifested, and we have seen, and do bear witness, and declare unto you the life eternal which was with the Father, and hath appeared unto us." You see the number of proofs and ways, very different and numerous, in which that Apostle so well beloved and so devoted to God, indicates the mystery of the Divine Incarnation. In the first instance he testifies that He, who ever was in the beginning, was seen in the flesh. Lest in case it might not seem sufficient for unbelievers that he had spoken of Him as seen and heard, he supports it by saying that He was handled,

i.e., touched and felt by his own hands and by those of others. Admirably indeed by showing how He took flesh, does he shut out the view of the Marcionites and the error of the Manichees, so that no one may think that a phantom appeared to men, since an apostle has declared that a true body was handled by him. Then he adds "the word of life: and the life was manifested," and that he saw it, announced it, and proclaimed it: thus at the same time carrying out the duties of the faith and striking the unbelievers with terror, that while he declares that he proclaims Him, he may bring home the danger in which he stands, to the man who will not listen. "We declare to you," he says, "the life eternal which was with the Father, and hath appeared to us." He teaches that that which was ever with the Father appeared to men: and that which was ever in the beginning, was seen of men: and that which was the Word of life without beginning, was handled by men's hands. You see the number and variety, the particularity and the clearness of the ways in which he unfolds the mystery of the flesh joined to God, in such a way that no one could speak at all of either without acknowledging both. As the Apostle himself clearly says elsewhere: "For Jesus Christ is the same yesterday, and to-day, and for ever."[2] This is what he said in the passage given above: "That which was from the beginning, our hands have handled." Not that a spirit can in its own nature be handled: but that the Word made flesh was in a sense handled in the manhood with which it was joined. And so Jesus is "the same yesterday and to-day": i.e., the same Person before the commencement of the world, as in the flesh; the same in the past as in the present, the same also for ever, for He is the same through all the ages, as before all the ages. And all this is the Lord Jesus Christ.

CHAPTER VII.

He shows again from the union in Christ of two natures in one Person that what belongs to the Divine nature may rightly be ascribed to man, and what belongs to the human nature to God.

AND how was it the same Person before the origin of the world, who was but recently born? Because it was the same Person, who was recently born in human nature, who was God before the rise of all things. And so the name of Christ includes everything that the name of God does; for so close is the union between Christ and God that no one, when he uses the name of Christ can help speaking of God un-

---

[1] 1 John i. 1, 2.   [2] Heb. xiii. 8.

der the name of Christ, nor, when he speaks of God, can he help speaking of Christ under the name of God. And as through the glory of His holy nativity the mystery of each substance is joined together in Him, whatever was in existence — I mean both human and Divine — all is regarded as God. And hence the Apostle Paul seeing with unveiled eyes of faith the whole mystery of the ineffable glory in Christ, spoke as follows, in inviting the peoples who were ignorant of God's goodness to give thanksgiving to God: "Giving thanks to the Father, who hath made us worthy to be partakers of the lot of the saints in light, who hath delivered us from the power of darkness, and hath translated us into the kingdom of the Son of His love, in whom we have redemption through His blood, the remission of sins; who is the image of the invisible God, the first-born of every creature: for in Him were all things created in heaven and on earth, visible and invisible, whether thrones or dominations, or powers: all things were created by Him and in Him. And He is before all, and by Him all things consist. And He is the head of the body the Church, who is the beginning, the first-born from the dead; that in all things He may hold the primacy. Because it pleased the Father that in Him should all fulness dwell; and through Him to reconcile all things unto Himself, making peace through the blood of His cross, both as to the things on earth, and the things that are in heaven." [1] Surely this does not need the aid of any further explanation, as it is so fully and clearly expressed that in itself it contains not merely the substance of the faith, but a clear exposition of it. For he bids us give thanks to the Father: and adds a weighty reason for thus giving thanks; viz., because He hath made us worthy to be partakers with the saints, and hath delivered us from the power of darkness, hath translated us unto the kingdom of the Son of His love, in whom we have redemption and remission of sins: who is the image of the invisible God, the first-born of every creature; for in Him and through Him were all things created; of which He is both the Creator and the ruler: and what follows after this? " He is," he says, " the head of the body the Church: who is the beginning, the first-born from the dead." Scripture speaks of the resurrection as a birth: because as birth is the beginning of life, so resurrection gives birth unto life. Whence also the resurrection is actually spoken of as regeneration, according to the words of the Lord: " Verily I say unto you, that ye which have followed me, in the regeneration when

the Son of man shall sit on the throne of His glory, ye also shall sit upon twelve thrones, judging the twelve tribes of Israel." [2] Therefore he calls Him the first-born from the dead, whom he had previously declared to be the invisible Son and image of God. But who is the image of the invisible God, except the only-begotten, the Word of God? And how can we say that He rose from the dead, who is termed the image and word of the invisible God? And what is it that follows afterwards? " That in all things He may hold the primacy: for it pleased the Father that in Him should all fulness dwell, and by Him to reconcile all things to Himself, making peace through the blood of His cross, both as to things on earth and the things that are in heaven." Surely the Creator of all things has no need of the primacy in all things? Nor He who made them, of the primacy of those things which were made by Him? And how can we say of the Word, that it pleased God that all fulness should dwell in Him who was the first-born from the dead, when He was Himself the only-begotten Son of God and the Word of God, before the origin of all things, and had within Him the invisible Father, and so first had within Him all fulness, that He might Himself be the fulness of all things? And what next? " Bringing all things to peace through the blood of His cross, both things on earth, and the things which are in heaven." Certainly he has made it as clear as possible of whom he was speaking, when he called Him the first-born from the dead. For are all things reconciled and brought into peace through the blood of the Word or Spirit? Most certainly not. For no sort of passion can happen to nature that is impassible, nor can the blood of any but a man be shed, nor any but a man die: and yet the same Person who is spoken of in the following verses as dead, was above called the image of the invisible God. How then can this be? Because the apostles took every possible precaution that it might not be thought that there was any division in Christ, or that the Son of God being joined to a Son of man, might come by wild interpretations to be made into two Persons, and thus He who is in Himself but one might by wrongful and wicked notions of ours, be made into a double Person in one nature. And so most excellently and admirably does the apostle's preaching pass from the only begotten Son of God to the Son of man united to the Son of God, that the exposition of the doctrine might follow the actual course of the things that happened. And so he continues with an unbroken connexion, and

---

[1] Col. i. 12–20.

[2] S. Matt. xix. 28.

makes as it were a sort of bridge, that without any gap or separation you might find at the end of time Him whom we read of as in the beginning of the world; and that you might not by admitting some division and erroneous separation imagine that the Son of God was one person in the flesh and another in the Spirit; when the teaching of the apostle had so linked together God and man through the mystery of His birth in the body, so as to show that it was the same Person reconciling to Himself all things on the Cross, who had been proclaimed the image of the invisible God before the foundation of the world.

CHAPTER VIII.

He confirms the judgment of the Apostle by the authority of the Lord.

AND though this is the saying of an Apostle, yet it is the very doctrine of the Lord. For the same Person says this to Christians by His Apostle, who had Himself said something very like it to Jews in the gospel, when He said: "But now ye seek to kill me, a man, who have spoken the truth to you, which I heard of God: for I am not come of Myself, but He sent me."[1] He clearly shows that He is both God and man: man, in that He says that He is a man: God, in that He affirms that He was sent. For He must have been with Him from whom He came: and He came from Him, from whom He said that He was sent. Whence it comes that when the Jews said to Him, "Thou art not yet fifty years old and hast Thou seen Abraham?" He replied in words that exactly suit His eternity and glory, saying, "Verily, verily, I say unto you, Before Abraham came into being, I am."[2] I ask then, whose saying do you think this is? Certainly it is Christ's without any doubt. And how could He who had been but recently born, say that He was before Abraham? Simply owing to the Word of God, with which He was entirely united, so that all might understand the closeness of the union of Christ and God: since whatever God said in Christ, that in its fulness the unity of the Divinity claimed for Himself. But conscious of His own eternity, He rightly then when in the body, replied to the Jews, with the very words which He had formerly spoken to Moses in the Spirit. For here He says, "Before Abraham came into being, I am." But to Moses He says, "I am that I am."[3] He

certainly announced the eternity of His Divine nature with marvellous grandeur of language, for nothing can be spoken so worthily of God, as that He should be said ever to *be*. For "to be" admits of no beginning in the past or end in the future. And so this is very clearly spoken of the nature of the eternal God, as it exactly describes His eternity. And this the Lord Jesus Christ Himself, when He was speaking of Abraham, showed by the difference of terms used, saying, "Before Abraham came into being I am." Of Abraham he said, "Before he came into being:" Of Himself, "I am," for it belongs to things temporal to come into being: to *be* belongs to eternity. And so "to come into being" He assigns to human transitoriness: but "to be" to His own nature. And all this was found in Christ who, by virtue of the mystery of the manhood and Divinity joined together in Him who ever "was," could say that He already "was."

CHAPTER IX.

Since those marvellous works which from the days of Moses were shown to the children of Israel are attributed to Christ, it follows that He must have existed long before His birth in time.

AND when the Apostle wanted to make this clear and patent to everybody he spoke as follows, saying that, "Jesus having saved the people out of the land of Egypt afterward destroyed them that believed not."[4] But elsewhere too we read: "Neither let us tempt Christ, as some of them tempted, and were destroyed by serpents."[5] Peter also the chief of the apostles says: "And now why tempt ye God to put a yoke upon the neck of the disciples, which neither our fathers nor we have been able to bear. But we believe that we shall be saved by the grace of our Lord Jesus Christ even as they were."[6] We know most certainly that the people of God were delivered from Egypt, and led dryshod through mighty tracts of water, and preserved in the vast desert wastes, by none but God alone; as it is written: "The Lord alone did lead them, and there was no strange God among them."[7] And how can an Apostle declare in so many and such clear passages that the people of the Jews were delivered from Egypt by *Jesus*, and that *Christ* was at that time tempted by the Jews in the wilderness, saying, "Neither let us tempt Christ, as some

---

[1] S. John viii. 40, 42.   [2] *Ibid.* ver. 58.   [3] Exod. iii. 14.

[4] S. Jude, ver. 5.   [6] Acts xv. 10, 11.
[5] 1 Cor. x. 9.   [7] Deut. xxxii. 12.

of them tempted, and were destroyed of the serpents?" And further the blessed Apostle Peter says of all the saints who lived under the law of the Old Covenant that they were saved by the grace of our Lord Jesus Christ. Get out then, and wriggle out of this if you can — whoever you are — you who rage with vapid mouth and a spirit of blasphemy, and think that there is no difference at all between Adam and Christ; and you who deny that He was God before His birth of the Virgin, show clearly how you can prove that He was not God before His body came into existence. For lo, an Apostle says that the people were saved out of the land of Egypt by Jesus: and that Christ was tempted by unbelievers in the wilderness: and that our fathers, i.e., the patriarchs and prophets, were saved by the grace of our Lord Jesus Christ. Deny it if you can. I shall not be surprised if you manage to deny what we all read, as you have already denied what we all believe. Know then that even then it was Christ in God who led the people out of Egypt, and it was Christ in God who was tempted by the people who tempted, and it was Christ in God who saved all the righteous men by His lavish grace: for through the oneness of the mystery (of the Incarnation) the terms God and Christ so pass into each other, that whatever God did, that we may say that Christ did; and whatever afterwards Christ bore, we may say that God bore. And so when the prophet said, "There shall no new God be in thee, neither shalt thou worship any other God," [1] he announced it with the same meaning and in the same spirit as that with which the Apostle said that Christ was the leader of the people of Israel out of Egypt; to show that He who was born of the Virgin as man, was even through the unity of the mystery still in God. Otherwise, unless we believe this, we must either believe with the heretics that Christ is not God, or against the teaching of the prophet hold that He is a new God. But may it be far from the Catholic people of God, to seem either to differ from the prophet or to agree with heretics: or perchance the people who should be blessed may be involved in a curse, and be charged with putting their hope in man. For whoever declares that the Lord Jesus Christ was at His birth a mere man, is doubly liable to the curse, whether he believes in Him or not. For if he believes, "Cursed is he who puts his hope in man." [2] But if he does not believe, none the less is he still cursed, because though not believing in man, he still has altogether denied God.

CHAPTER X.

He explains what it means to confess, and what it means to dissolve Jesus.

FOR this it is which John, the man so dear to God, foresaw from the Lord's own revelation to him and so spoke of Him, who was speaking in him. "Every spirit," he says, "which confesseth Jesus come in the flesh is of God, and every spirit that dissolveth Jesus is not of God: and this is the spirit of Antichrist, of whom you have heard already, and he is now already in the world." [3] O the marvellous and singular goodness of God, who like a most careful and skilful physician, foretold beforehand the diseases that should come upon His Church, and when He showed the mischief beforehand, gave in showing it, a remedy for it: that all men when they saw the evil approaching, might at once flee as far as possible from that which they already knew to be imminent. And so Saint John says, "Every spirit that dissolveth Jesus is not of God; and this is the spirit of Antichrist." Do you recognize him, O you heretic? Do you recognize that it is plainly and markedly spoken of you? For no one thus dissolves Jesus but he who does not confess that He is God. For since in this consists all the faith and all the worship of the Church; viz., to confess that Jesus is very God; who can more dissolve His glory and worship than one who denies the existence in Him of all that we all worship? Take then, I beseech you, take care lest any one may even term you Antichrist. Do you think that I am reviling and cursing? What I am saying is not my own idea: for lo, the Evangelist says, "Every one that dissolveth Jesus is not of God; and this is Antichrist." If you do not dissolve Jesus, and deny God, no one may call you Antichrist. But if you deny it why do you accuse any one for calling you Antichrist? While you are denying it, I declare you have said it of yourself. Would you like to know whether this is true? Tell me, when Jesus was born of a Virgin, what do you make Him to be — man or God? If God only, you certainly dissolve Jesus, as you deny that in Him manhood was joined to Divinity. But if you say He was man, none the less do you dissolve Him, as you blasphemously say that a mere

[3] 1 S. John iv. 2, 3. It will be noticed that Cassian quotes this passage with the reading "Qui solvit Jesum," where the Greek has ὁ μὴ ὁμολογεῖ τὸν Ἰησοῦν. Λύει is found in no Greek MS., uncial or cursive, and the only Greek authority for it is that of Socrates, who says it was the reading in "the old copies." "Qui solvit" was probably an early gloss, current in very early days in the West, being found in Tertullian (adv. Marc. v. 16; De Jejun: i.) and in all Latin MSS. whether of the Vetus or Vulgate (with a single exception), and finally becoming universal in the Fathers of the Western Church. Cf. Westcott on the Epp. of S. John, p. 156, sq.

man (as you will have it) was born. Unless perhaps you think that you do not dissolve Jesus, you who deny Him to be God, you who would certainly dissolve Him even if you did not deny[1] that man was born together with God. But possibly you would like this to be made clearer by examples. You shall have them in both directions. The Manichees are outside the Church, who declare that Jesus was God alone: and the Ebionites, who say that he was a mere man. For both of them deny and dissolve Jesus: the one by saying that He is only man, the other by saying that He is only God. For though their opinions were the opposite of each other, yet the blasphemy of these diverse opinions is much the same, except that if any distinction can be drawn between the magnitude of the evils, your blasphemy which asserts that He is a mere man is worse than that which says that He is only God: for though both are wrong, yet it is more insulting to take away from the Lord what is Divine than what is human. This then alone is the Catholic and the true faith; viz., to believe that as the Lord Jesus Christ is God so also is He man; and that as He is man so also is He God. "Every one who dissolves Jesus is not of God." But to dissolve Him is to try to rend asunder what is united in Jesus; and to sever what is but one and indivisible. But what is it in Jesus that is united and but one? Certainly the manhood and the Godhead. He then dissolves Jesus who severs these and rends them asunder. Otherwise, if he does not rend them asunder and sever them, he does not dissolve Jesus: But if he rends them asunder he certainly dissolves Him.[2]

CHAPTER XI.

The mystery of the Lord's Incarnation clearly implies the Divinity of Christ.

AND so to every man who breaks out into this mad blasphemy, the Lord Jesus in the gospel Himself repeats what He said to the Pharisees, and declares: "What God hath joined together, let not man put asunder."[3] For although where it was originally spoken by God it seems to be in answer to another matter, yet the deep wisdom of God which was speaking not more of carnal than of spiritual things, would have this to be taken of that subject indeed, but even more of this: for

when the Jews of that day believed with you that Jesus was only a man without Divinity, and the Lord was asked a question about the union in marriage, in His teaching He not only referred to it, but to this also: though consulted about matters of less importance His answer applied to greater and deeper matters, when he said, "What God hath joined together, let not man put asunder," i.e., Do not sever what God hath joined together in My Person. Let not human wickedness sever that which the Divine Glory hath united in Me. But if you want to be told more fully that this is so, hear the Apostle talking about these very subjects of which the Saviour was then teaching, for he, as a teacher sent from God that his weak-minded hearers might be able to take in his teaching, expounded those very subjects which God had proclaimed in a mystery. For when he was discussing the subject of carnal union, on which the Saviour had been asked a question in the gospel, he repeated those very passages from the old Law on which He had dwelt, on purpose that they might see that as he was using the same authorities he was expounding the same subject: besides which, that nothing may seem to be wanting to his case, he adds the mention of carnal union, and puts in the names of husband and wife whom he exhorts to love one another: "Husbands, love your wives even as Christ also loved the Church." And again: "So also ought men to love their wives even as their own bodies. He that loveth his wife loveth himself. For no man ever hated his own flesh, but nourisheth and cherisheth it, as Christ also doth the Church, for we are members of His body."[4] You see how by adding to the mention of man and wife the mention of Christ and the Church, he leads all from taking it carnally to understand it in a spiritual sense. For when he had said all this, he added those passages which the Lord had applied in the Gospel, saying: "For this cause shall a man leave his father and his mother, and shall cleave unto his wife, and they twain shall be one flesh." And after this with special emphasis he adds: "This is a great mystery." He certainly altogether cuts off and gets rid of any carnal interpretation, by saying that it is a Divine mystery. And what did he add after this? "But I am speaking of Christ and the Church." That is to say: "But that is a great mystery. But I am speaking of Christ and the Church," i.e., since perhaps at the present time all cannot grasp that, they may at least grasp this, which is not at variance with it, nor different from it,

---

[1] *Non negares* (Petschenig). Gazæus has *denegares*.
[2] The last sentences are placed in brackets by Petschenig.
[3] S. Matt. xix. 6.

[4] Eph. v. 25-30.

because both refer to Christ. But because they cannot grasp those more profound truths, let them at least take in these easier ones, that by making a commencement by grasping what lies on the surface, they may come to the deeper truths, and that the acquisition of a somewhat simple matter may open the way in time to what is more profound.

CHAPTER XII.

He explains more fully what the mystery is which is signified under the name of the man and wife.

WHAT then is that great mystery which is signified under the name of the man and his wife? Let us ask the Apostle himself, who elsewhere to teach the same thing uses words of the same force, saying: "And evidently great is the mystery of godliness, which was manifested in the flesh, justified in the Spirit, seen of angels, preached to the Gentiles, believed on in the world, received up in glory." [1] What then is that great mystery which was manifested in the flesh? Clearly it was God born of the flesh, God seen in bodily form: who was openly received up in glory just as He was openly manifested in the flesh. This then is the great mystery, of which he says: "For this cause shall a man leave his father and mother, and shall cleave to his wife; and they two shall be one flesh." Who then were the two in one flesh? God and the soul, for in the one flesh of man which is joined to God are present God and the soul, as the Lord Himself says: "No man can take My life (anima) away from Me. But I lay it down of Myself. I have power to lay it down, and I have power to take it again." [2] You see then in this, three; viz., God, the flesh, and the soul. It is God who speaks: the flesh in which He speaks: the soul of which He speaks. Is He therefore that man of whom the prophet says: "A brother cannot redeem, nor shall a man redeem"? [3] Who, as it was said, "ascended up where He was before," [4] and of whom we read: "No man hath ascended into heaven, but He who came down from heaven, even the Son of man who is in heaven." [5] For this cause, I say, He has left his father and mother, i.e., God from whom He was begotten and that

"Jerusalem which is the mother of us all," [6] and has cleaved to human flesh, as to his wife. And therefore he expressly says in the case of the father "a man shall leave *his* father," but in the case of the mother he does not say "his," but simply says "mother:" because she was not so much his mother, as the mother of all believers, i.e., of all of us. And He was joined to his wife, for just as man and wife make but one body, so the glory of Divinity and the flesh of man are united and the two, viz., God and the soul, become one flesh. For just as that flesh had God as an indweller in it, so also had it the soul within it dwelling with God. This then is that great mystery, to search out which our admiration for the Apostle summons us, and God's own exhortation bids us: and it is one not foreign to Christ and His Church, as he says, "But I am speaking of Christ and the Church." Because the flesh of the Church is the flesh of Christ, and in the flesh of Christ there is present God and the soul: and so the same person is present in Christ as in the Church, because the mystery which we believe in the flesh of Christ, is contained also by faith in the Church.

CHAPTER XIII.

Of the longing with which the old patriarchs desired to see the revelation of that mystery.

THIS mystery then, which was manifested in the flesh and appeared in the world, and was preached to the Gentiles, many of the saints of old longed to see in the flesh, as they foresaw it in the spirit. For "Verily," saith the Lord, "I say unto you that many prophets and righteous men have desired to see the things which ye see, and have not seen them; and to hear the things which ye hear and have not heard them." [7] And so the prophet Isaiah says: "O that Thou, Lord, would rend the heavens and come down," [8] and David too: "O Lord, bow the heavens and come down." [9] Moses also says: "Show me Thyself that I may see Thee plainly." [10] No one ever approached nearer to God speaking out of the clouds, and to the very presence of His glory than Moses who received the law. And if no one ever saw more closely into God than he did, why did he ask for a still clearer vision, saying, "Show me Thyself that I may see Thee plainly"? Simply because he prayed that this

---

[1] 1 Tim. iii. 16. *Quod manifestum in carne.* The true reading is pretty certainly ὅς, see Westcott and Hort, Greek Testament, vol. ii., p. 132. The neuter ὅ is found in D. and in many Latin Fathers, as well as the Vulgate.
[2] S. John x. 18.
[3] Ps. xlviii. (xlix.). 8.
[4] Cf. S. John vi. 62.
[5] S. John iii. 13.

[6] Gal. iv. 26.
[7] S. Matt. xiii. 17.
[8] Isa. lxiv. 1.
[9] Ps. xciii. (cxliv). 5.
[10] Exod. xxxiii. 13.

might happen which the apostle tells us in almost the same words actually did happen; viz., that the Lord might be openly manifested in the flesh, might openly appear to the world, openly be received up in glory; and that at last the saints might with their very bodily eyes see all those things which with spiritual sight they had foreseen.

CHAPTER XIV.

He refutes the wicked and blasphemous notion of the heretics who said that God dwelt and spoke in Christ as in an instrument or a statue.

OTHERWISE, as the heretics say, God would be in the Lord Jesus Christ as in a statue or in an instrument, i.e., He would dwell as it were in a man and speak as it were through a man, and it would not be He who dwelt and spoke as God of Himself and in His own body: and certainly He had already thus dwelt in the saints and spoken in the persons of the saints. In those men too, of whom I spoke above, who had prayed for His advent, He had thus dwelt and spoken. And what need was there for all these to ask for what they already possessed, if they were seeking for what they had previously received? Or why should they long to see with their eyes what they were keeping in their hearts, especially as it is better for a man to have the same thing within himself than to see it outside? Or if God was to dwell in Christ in the same way as in all the saints, why should all the saints long to see Christ rather than themselves? And if they were only to see the same thing in Jesus Christ, which they themselves possessed, why should they not much rather prefer to have this in themselves than to see it in another? But you are wrong, you wretched madman, "not understanding," as the Apostle says, "what you say and whereof you affirm":[1] for all the prophets and all the saints received from God some portion of the Divine Spirit as they were able to bear it. But in Christ "all the fulness of the Godhead" dwelt and "dwells bodily." And therefore they all fall far short of His fulness, from whose fulness they receive something: for the fact that they are filled is the gift of Christ: because they would all certainly be empty, were He not the fulness of all.

---

[1] 1 Tim. i. 7.

CHAPTER XV.

What the prayers of the saints for the coming of Messiah contained; and what was the nature of that longing of theirs.

THIS then all the saints wished for: for this they prayed. This they longed to see with their eyes in proportion as they were wise in heart and mind. And so the prophet Isaiah says: "O that Thou wouldst rend the heavens and come down."[2] But Habakkuk too declaring the same thing which the other was wishing for, says: "When the years draw nigh, Thou wilt show Thyself: at the coming of the times Thou wilt be manifested: God will come from Teman," or "God will come from the south."[3] David also: "God will clearly come:" and again: "Thou that sittest above the Cherubim, show Thyself."[4] Some declared His advent which He presented to the world: others prayed for it. Some in different forms but all with equal longing: understanding up to a certain point how great a thing they were praying for, that God dwelling in God, and continuing in the form and bosom of God, might "empty Himself,"[5] and take the form of a servant and submit Himself to endure all the bitterness and insults of the passion, and undergo punishment for His goodness, and what is hardest, and the most disgraceful thing of all, meet with death at the hands of those very persons for whom He would die. All the saints then understanding this up to a certain point — up to a certain point, I say, for how vast it is none can understand — with concordant voice and (so to speak) by mutual consent all prayed for the advent of God: for indeed they knew that the hope of all men lay therein, and that the salvation of all was bound up in this, because no one could loose the prisoners except one who was Himself free from chains: no one could release sinners, save one Himself without sin: for no one can in any case set free anyone, unless he is himself free in that particular, in which another is freed by him. And so when death had passed on all, all were wanting in life, that, dying in Adam, they might live in Christ. For though there were many saints, many elect and even friends of God, yet none could ever of themselves be saved, had they not been saved by the advent of the Lord and His redemption.

---

[2] Isa. lxiv. 1.
[3] Hab. iii. 2, 3, where the Old Latin has "Theman," and the Vulgate "Austro."
[4] Ps. xlix. (l.) 3; lxxix. (lxxx.) 2.   [5] Phil. ii. 7.

BOOK VI.

CHAPTER I.

From the miracle of the feeding of the multitude from five barley loaves and two fishes he shows the majesty of Divine Power.

WE read in the gospel that when five loaves were at the Lord's bidding brought to Him, an immense number of God's people were fed with them. But *how* this was done it is impossible to explain, or to understand or to imagine. So great and so incomprehensible is the might of Divine Power, that though we are perfectly assured of the *fact*, yet we are unable to understand the *manner* of the fact. For first one would have to comprehend how so small a number of loaves could be sufficient, I will not say for them to eat and be filled, but even to be divided and set before them, when there were many more thousands of men than there were loaves; and almost more companies than there could be fragments of the whole number of loaves. The plentiful supply then was the creation of the word of the Lord. The work grew in the doing of it. And though what was visible was but little; yet what was given to them became more than could be reckoned. There is then no room for conjecture, for human speculation, or imagination. The only thing in such a case is that like faithful and wise men we should acknowledge that, however great and incomprehensible are the things which are done by God, even if they are altogether beyond our comprehension, we must recognize that nothing is impossible with God. But of these unspeakable acts of Divine Power, we will, as the subject demands it, speaks more fully later on, because it exactly corresponds to the ineffable miracles of His Holy Nativity.

CHAPTER II.

The author adapts the mystery of the number seven (made up of the five loaves and two fishes) to his own work.

MEANWHILE as we have alluded to the five loaves, I think it will not be out of place to make a comparison of the five books which we have already composed. For as they are equal in number, so they are not dissimilar in character. For as the loaves were of barley, so these books may (as far as my ability is concerned) be fairly termed " of barley," although they are enriched with passages from Holy Scripture, and contain life-giving treasures in contemptible surroundings. And even in this point they are not unlike those loaves, for though they were poor things to look at, yet they proved to be rich in blessing : and so these books, though, as far as my powers are concerned, they are worthless, yet they are valuable from the sacred matter which is mingled with them : and though they appear outwardly worthless like barley owing to my words, yet within they have the savour of the bread of life owing to the testimonies from the Lord Himself. It remains that, after His example, they may, by the gift of Divine grace, furnish life-giving food from countless seeds. And as those loaves supplied bodily strength to those who ate them, so may these give spiritual vigour to those who read them. But as then the Lord, from whom this gift comes as did that, by means of that food provided that they might be filled and so should not faint by the way, so now is He able to bring it about that by means of this men may be filled and not err (from the faith). But still because there, where a countless host of God's people was fed with a mighty gift, though there was very little for them to eat, we read that to those five loaves there were added two fishes, it is fitting that we too, who are anxious to give to all God's people who are following, the nourishment of a spiritual repast, should add to those five books corresponding to the five loaves, two more books corresponding to the two fishes : praying and beseeching Thee, O Lord, that Thou wilt look on our efforts and prayers, and grant a prosperous issue to our pious undertaking. And since we, out of our love and obedience, desire to make the number of our books correspond to the number of loaves and fishes, do Thou grant the virtue of Thy Benediction upon them ; and, as Thou dost bless [1] this little work of ours with a gospel number, so mayest Thou fill up the number with the fruit of the gospel, and grant that this may be for holy and saving food to all the people of Thy Church, of every age and sex. And if there are some who are affected by the deadly breath of that poisonous serpent, and in an unhealthy state of soul and spirit have caught a pestilential disease in their feeble dispositions, give to them all the vigour of health, and entire soundness of faith, that by granting to them all, by means of these writings of ours, the saving care of Thy gift — just as

---

[1] *Muneraris,* (Petschenig) : Gazæus reads *numeraris.*

that food in the gospel was completely sanctified by Thee, so that by eating it those hungry souls were strengthened, — so mayest Thou bid languid souls to be healed by these.

CHAPTER III.

He refutes his opponent by the testimony of the Council of Antioch.

THEREFORE since we have, as I fancy, already in all the former books with the weight of sacred testimonies, given a complete answer to the heretic who denies God, now let us come to the faith of the Creed of Antioch and its value. For as he [1] was himself baptized and regenerated in this, he ought to be confuted by his own profession, and (so to speak) to be crushed beneath the weight of his own arms, for this is the method, that as he is already convicted by the evidence of holy Scripture, so now he may be convicted by evidence out of his own mouth. Nor will there be any need to bring anything else to bear against him when he has clearly and plainly convicted himself. The text then and the faith of the Creed of Antioch is this.[2] " I believe in one and the only true God, the Father Almighty, Maker of all things visible and invisible. And in one Lord Jesus Christ, His only begotten Son, and the first-born of every creature, begotten of Him before all worlds, and not made: Very God of Very God, Being of one substance with the Father: By whom both the worlds were framed, and all things were made. Who for us came, and was born of the Virgin Mary, and was crucified under Pontius Pilate and was buried: and

the third day He rose again according to the Scripture: and ascended into heaven, and shall come again to judge the quick and the dead," etc.[3] In the Creed which gives the faith of all the Churches, I should like to know which you would rather follow, the authority of men or of God ? Though I would not press hardly or unkindly upon you, but give the opportunity of choosing whichever alternative you please, that accepting one, I may deny the other: for I will grant you and yield to you either of them. And what do I grant, I ask ? I will force you to one or other even against your will. For you ought, if you like, to understand of your own free will that one or other of these is in the Creed: if you don't like it, you must be forced against your will to see it. For, as you know, a Creed (Symbolum) gets its name from being a " collection."[4] For what is called in Greek σίμβολος is termed in Latin "Collatio." But it is therefore a collection (collatio) because when the faith of the whole Catholic law was collected together by the apostles of the Lord, all those matters which are spread over the whole body of the sacred writings with immense fulness of detail, were collected together in sum in the matchless brevity of the Creed, according to to the Apostle's words : " Completing His word, and cutting it short in righteousness : because a short word shall the Lord make upon the earth." [5] This then is the " short word " which the Lord made, collecting together in few words the faith of both of His Testaments, and including in a few brief clauses the drift of all the Scriptures, building up His own out of His own, and giving the force of the whole law in a most compen-

---

[1] Nestorius, who had belonged to the monastery of St. Euprepius near the gate of Antioch before his elevation to the see of Constantinople.

[2] This creed is plainly given by Cassian as the baptismal formula of the Church of Antioch ; and with it agrees almost verbally a fragment of the Creed preserved in a *Contestatio* comparing Nestorius to Paul of Samosata (A.D. 429, or 430) which is said by Leontius to have been the work of Eusebius afterward Bishop of Dorylæum. The form is especially interesting as showing that the Creed of Antioch, in common with several other Eastern Creeds, underwent revision, probably about the middle of the fourth century, from the desire to enrich the local creed with Nicene phraseology. The insertions which are obviously due to the Creed of Nicæa are : non factum, Deum verum ex Deo vero, homoousion patri, or as they would run in the original οὐ ποιηθέντα, Θεὸν ἀληθινὸν ἐκ Θεοῦ ἀληθινοῦ, ὁμοούσιον τῷ Πατρι, and it has been suggested that they were probably introduced at the Synod held at Antioch under Meletius in 363. Similar forms of local creeds thus enlarged by the adoption of Nicene phraseology are (1) that of Jerusalem as given by Cyril in his Catechetical Lectures, (2) the Creed of Cappadocia, (3) that of Mesopotamia, and (4) the " Creed of Charisius " preserved in the Acts of the Council of Ephesus (Mansi IV. 1348). On all of these see Dr. Hort's " Two Dissertations," p. 110 *sq.*

Another interesting feature in the Creed as given by Cassian is that it was in the singular " Credo," *I believe ;* whereas the Eastern Creeds are almost all in the plural πιστεύομεν. That however which is found in the Apostolical Constitutions (VII. xli.) has the singular πιστεύω καὶ βαπτίζομαι, and therefore it is possible that Cassian may have preserved the original form here. It is however more probable that the singular Credo is due to a reminiscence of the form current in the Western church, which has influenced the translation. See further Hahn's Bibliothek des Symbole p. 64 *sq.*

[3] Cassian nowhere quotes the last section of the Creed of Antioch, as it did not concern the question at issue. A few clauses of it may however be recovered from S. Chrysostom's Homilies (In 1 Cor. Hom. xl. § 2); viz., καὶ εἰς ἁμαρτιῶν ἄφεσιν καὶ εἰς νεκρῶν ἀνάστασιν καὶ εἰς ζωὴν αἰώνιον.

[4] *Symbolus,* or more commonly and correctly Symbolum (= σύμβολον) is the general name for the creed in the ancient church, met with from the days of Cyprian (who uses it more than once, e.g., Ep. lxix.) onwards. In the account which Cassian gives in the text of the origin of the name he is certainly copying Rufinus (whose exposition of the Apostles' Creed is directly quoted by him below in Book VII. c. xxvii.). The passage which Cassian evidently has in his mind is the following: " Moreover for many and excellent reasons they determined that it should be called Symbolum. For ' Symbolum ' in Greek may mean both *Indicium* (a token) and *collatio* (a collection), that is, that which several bring together into one ; for the apostles effected this in these sentences by bringing together into one what each thought good. . . . Therefore being about to depart to preach, the apostles appointed that token of their unanimity and faith." (Ruf. De Symb. § 2). Cf. also § 1. " In these words there is truly discovered the prophecy which says : ' Completing His work and cutting it short in righteousness, because a short word will the Lord make upon the earth.' " This explanation, however, of the origin of the term labours under the fatal mistake of confusing two distinct Greek words συμβολή a " collection," and σύμβολον a " watchword : " and the true explanation of the word is probably that which Rufinus gives as an alternative, which gives it the meaning of " watchword." It was the watchword of the Christian soldier, carefully and jealously guarded by him, as that by which he could himself be distinguished from heretics, and that for which he could challenge others of whose orthodoxy he might be in doubt.

[5] Rom. ix. 28.

dious and brief formula. Providing in this, like a most tender father, for the carelessness and ignorance of some of his children, that no mind however simple and ignorant might have any trouble over what could so easily be retained in the memory.

CHAPTER IV.

How the Creed has authority Divine as well as human.

You see then that the Creed has the authority of God: for "a short word will the Lord make upon the earth." But perhaps you want the authority of men: nor is that wanting, for God made it by means of men. For as He fashioned the whole body of the sacred Scriptures by means of the patriarchs and more particularly his own prophets, so He formed the Creed by means of His apostles and priests. And whatever He enlarged on in these (in Scripture) with copious and abundant material, He here embraced in a most complete and compendious form by means of His own servants. There is nothing wanting then in the Creed; because as it was formed from the Scriptures of God by the apostles of God, it has in it all the authority it can possibly have, whether of men or of God: Although too that which was made by men, must be accounted God's work, for we should not look on it so much as their work, by whose instrumentality it was made, but rather as His, who was the actual maker. "I believe," then, says the Creed, "in one true and only God, the Father Almighty, Maker of all things visible and invisible; and in one Lord Jesus Christ, His only begotten Son, and the first-born of every creature; Begotten of Him before all worlds, and not made; Very God of Very God, being of one substance with the Father; by whom both the worlds were framed and all things were made; who for us came, and was born of the Virgin Mary; and was crucified under Pontius Pilate, and was buried. And the third day He rose again according to the Scriptures; and ascended into heaven: and shall come again to judge the quick and the dead," etc.

CHAPTER V.

He proceeds against his opponent with the choicest arguments, and shows that we ought to hold fast to the religion which we have received from our fathers.

If you were an assertor of the Arian or Sabellian heresy, and did not use your own creed, I would still confute you by the authority of the holy Scriptures; I would confute you by the words of the law itself; I would refute you by the truth of the Creed which has been approved throughout the whole world. I would say that, even if you were void of sense and understanding, yet still you ought at least to follow universal consent: and not to make more of the perverse view of a few wicked men than of the faith of all the Churches: which as it was established by Christ, and handed down by the apostles ought to be regarded as nothing but the voice of the authority of God, which is certainly in possession of the voice and mind of God. And what then if I were to deal with you in this way? What would you say? What would you answer? Would it not, I adjure you, be this: viz., that you had not been trained up and taught in this way: that something different had been delivered to you by your parents, and masters, and teachers. That you did not hear this in the meeting place of your father's teaching, nor in the Church of your Baptism: finally that the text and words of the Creed delivered and taught to you contained something different. That in it you were baptized and regenerated. You would say that you would hold fast this which you had received, and that you would live in that Creed in which you learnt that you were regenerated. When you said this, would you not, I pray, fancy that you were using a very strong shield even against the truth? And indeed it would be no unreasonable defence, even in a bad business, and one which would give no bad excuse for error, if it did not unite obstinacy with error. For if you held this, which you had received from your childhood, we should try to amend and correct your present error, rather than be severe in punishing your past fault: Whereas now, as you were born in a Catholic city, instructed in the Catholic faith, and regenerated with Catholic Baptism, how can I deal with you as with an Arian or Sabellian? Would that you were one! I should grieve less had you been brought up in what was wrong, instead of having fallen away from what was right: had you never received the faith, instead of having lost it: had you been an old heretic instead of a fresh apostate, for you would have brought less scandal and harm on the whole Church; finally it would have been a less bitter sorrow, and less injurious example had you been able to try the Church as a layman rather than a priest. Therefore, as I said above, if you had been a follower and assertor of Sabellianism or Arianism or any heresy you please, you might shelter yourself under the example of your parents, the teaching of your instructors, the company of those about you, the faith of your creed. I ask, O you heretic, nothing unfair, and nothing hard. As you have been brought up in the Catholic faith, do that which you would do for a wrong belief. Hold fast to the teaching of your parents. Hold fast the faith of the Church : hold fast the truth of the Creed : hold fast the salvation of baptism. What sort of a wonder — what sort of a monster are you? You will not do for yourself what others have done for their errors. But we have launched out far enough : and out of love for a city that is connected with us,[1] have yielded to our grief as to a strong wind, and while we were anxious to make way, have overshot the mark of our proper course.

CHAPTER VI.

Once more he challenges him to the profession of the Creed of Antioch.

THE Creed then, O you heretic, of which we gave the text above, though it is that of all the churches (for the faith of all is but one) is yet specially that of the city and Church of Antioch, i.e., of that Church in which you were brought up, instructed, and regenerated. The faith of this Creed brought you to the fountain of life, to saving regeneration, to the grace of the Eucharist, to the Communion of the Lord: And what more ! Alas for the grievous and mournful complaint ! Even to the ministerial office, the height of the presbyterate, the dignity of the priesthood. Do you, you wretched madman, think that this is a light or trivial matter? Do you not see what you have done? Into what a depth you have plunged yourself? In losing the faith of the Creed, you have lost everything that you were. For the mysteries of the priesthood and of your salvation rested on the truth of the Creed. Can you possibly deny that? I say that you have denied your very self. But perhaps you think that you cannot deny yourself. Let us look at the text of the Creed; that if you say what you used to do, you may not be refuted, but if you say things widely different and contrary, you may not look to be confuted by me, as you have condemned yourself already. For if you now maintain something else than what is in the Creed and what you formerly maintained yourself, how can you help ascribing your punishment to nobody but yourself, when you see that the opinion of everybody else about you

is the same as your own? "I believe," the Creed says, "in one God, the Father Almighty, Maker of all things visible and invisible; and in the Lord Jesus Christ, His only begotten Son, the first-born of every creature; Begotten of Him before all worlds, and not made." It is well that you should first reply to this : Do you confess this of Jesus Christ the Son of God, or do you deny it? If you confess it, everything is right enough. But if not, how do you now deny what you yourself formerly confessed? Choose then which you will : Of two things one must follow; viz., that that same confession of yours, if it still holds good, should alone set you free, or if you deny it, be the first to condemn you. For you said in the Creed : "I believe in one Lord Jesus Christ His only begotten Son, and the first-born of every creature." If the Lord Jesus Christ is the only begotten, and the first-born of every creature, then by our own confession He is certainly God. For no other is the only begotten and first-born of every creature but the only begotten Son of God: as He is the first-born of the creatures, so He is also God the Creator of all. And how can you say that He was a mere man at His birth from the Virgin, whom you confessed to be God before the world. Next the Creed says : "Begotten of the Father before all worlds, and not made." This Creed was uttered by you. You said by your Creed, that Jesus Christ was begotten before the worlds of God the Father, and not made. Does the Creed say anything about those phantasms, of which you now rave? Did you yourself say anything about them? Where is the statue? Where that instrument of yours, I pray? For God forbid that this should be another's and not yours. Where is it that you assert that the Lord Jesus Christ is like a statue, and so you think that He ought to be worshipped not because He is God, but because He is the image of God; and out of the Lord of glory you make an instrument, and blasphemously say that He ought to be adored not for His own sake, but for the sake of Him who (as it were) breathes in Him and sounds through Him? You said in the Creed that the Lord Jesus Christ was begotten of the Father before all worlds, and not made : and this certainly belongs to none but the only begotten Son of God : that His birth should not be a creation, and that He could be said simply to be begotten, not made : for it is contrary to the nature of things and to His honour that the Creator of all should be believed to be a creature : and that He, the author of all things that have a commencement, should Himself have a beginning, as all things began from Him. And so we say that He was begotten

---

[1] Viz., Constantinople, where Nestorius was Bishop and where Cassian himself had been ordained deacon by S. Chrysostom, as he tells us below in Book VII. c. xxxi., where he returns to the subject of his love for the city of his ordination, and interest in it.

not made: for His generation was unique and no ordinary creation. And since He is God, begotten of God, the Godhead of Him who is begotten must have everything complete which the majesty of Him who begat has.

CHAPTER VII.

He continues the same line of argument drawn from the Creed of Antioch.

BUT there follows in the Creed: "Very God of Very God; Being of one substance with the Father; by whom both the worlds were framed, and all things were made." And when you said all this, remember that you said it all of the Lord Jesus Christ. For you find stated in the Creed: that you believe in the Lord Jesus Christ, the only begotten Son of God, and the first-born of every creature: and after this and other clauses: "Very God of Very God, Being of one substance with the Father; by whom also the worlds were framed." How then can the same Person be God and not God; God and a statue; God and an instrument? These do not harmonize, you heretic, in any one Person, nor do they fit together, so that you can, when you like, call Him God; and when you like, consider the same Person a creation. You said in the Creed, "Very God." Now you say: "a mere man." How can these things fit together and harmonize so that one and the same Person may be the greatest Power, and utter weakness: the Highest glory, and mere mortality? These things do not meet together in one and the same Lord. So that severing Him for worship and for degradation, on one side, you may do Him honour as you like, and on the other, you may injure Him as you like. You said in the Creed when you received the Sacrament of true Salvation: "the Lord Jesus Christ, Very God of Very God, Being of one substance with the Father, Creator of the worlds, Maker of all things." Where are you alas! Where is your former self? Where is that faith of yours? Where that confession? How have you fallen back and become a monstrosity and a prodigy? What folly, what madness was your ruin? You turned the God of all power and might into inanimate material and a lifeless creation: Your faith has certainly grown in time, in age, and in the priesthood. You are worse as an old man than formerly as a child: worse now as a veteran than as a tyro: worse as a Bishop than you were as a novice: nor were you ever a learner after you had begun to be a teacher.

CHAPTER VIII.

How it can be said that Christ came and was born of a Virgin.

BUT let us look at the remainder which follows. As then the Creed says: "The Lord Jesus Christ, Very God of Very God, Being of one substance with the Father; By whom both the worlds were framed, and all things were made," it immediately subjoins in closest connexion the following, and says: "Who for us came and was born of the Virgin Mary." He then, who is Very God, who is of one substance with the Father, who is the Maker of all things, He, I repeat, came into the world and was born of the Virgin Mary; as the Apostle Paul says: "But when the fulness of the times was come, God sent forth His Son, made of a woman, made under the law."[1] You see how the mysteries of the Creed correspond with the Holy Scriptures. The Apostle declares that the Son of God was "sent from the Father:" The Creed affirms that He "came." For it certainly follows that our faith should confess that He has "come," whom the Apostle had taught us to be sent. Then the Apostle says: "Made of a woman:" The Creed, "born of Mary." And so you see that there speaks through the Creed the Scripture itself, from which the Creed acknowledges that it is itself derived. But when the Apostle says, "made of a woman," he rightly enough uses "made" for "born," after the manner of Holy Scripture in which "made" stands for "born:" as in this passage: "Instead of thy fathers there are made to thee sons:"[2] or this: "Before Abraham was made, I am;"[3] where we certainly see clearly that He meant "Before he was born, I am:" alluding to the fact of his birth under the term "was made," because whatever does not need to be made has the very reality of creation. "Who," it then says, "for us came and was born of the Virgin Mary." If a mere man was born of Mary, how can it be said that He "came"? For no one "comes" but He who has it in Him to be able to come. But in the case of one who had not yet received His existence, how could He have it in Him to come. You see then how by the word "coming" it is shown that He who came was already in existence: for He only had the power to come, to whom there could be the opportunity of coming, from the fact that He was already existing. But a mere man was certainly not in existence before he was conceived, and so had not in himself the power

---

[1] Gal. iv. 4.   [2] Ps. xliv. (xlv.) 17   [3] S. John viii. 58.

to come. It is clear then that it was God who came: to whom it belongs in each case both to *be*, and to *come*. For certainly He *came* because He *was*, and He ever *was*, because He could ever *come*.

CHAPTER IX.

Again he convicts his opponent of deadly heresy by his own confession.

BUT why are we arguing about words, when the facts are clear enough? and seeking for a determination of the matter from the terms of the Creed, when the Creed itself deals with the question. Let us repeat the confession of the Creed, and of you yourself (for yours it is as well as the Creed's, for you made it yours by confessing it), that you may see that you have departed not only from the Creed but from yourself. "I believe" then, says the Creed, "In one only true God, the Father Almighty, Maker of all things visible and invisible: And in the Lord Jesus Christ, His only begotten Son, and the first-born of every creature: Begotten of Him before all worlds and not made; Very God of Very God; Being of one substance with the Father; By whom both the worlds were framed, and all things were made. Who for us came, and was born of the Virgin Mary." "For us" then the Creed says, our Lord Jesus Christ "came and was born of the Virgin Mary, and was crucified under Pontius Pilate; and was buried, and rose again according to the Scriptures." The Churches are not ashamed to confess this: the Apostles were not ashamed to preach it. You yourself, you, I say, whose every utterance is now blasphemy, you who now deny everything, you did not deny all these truths: that God was born; that God suffered, that God rose again. And what next? Whither have you fallen? What have you become? To what are you reduced? What do you say? What are you vomiting forth? What, as one says, even mad Orestes himself would swear to be the words of a madman.[1] For what is it that you say? "Who then is the Son of God who was born of the Christotocos? As for instance if we were to say I believe in God the Word, the only Son of God, begotten of His Father, Being of one substance with the Father, who came down and was buried, would not our ears be shocked at the sound? God dead?" And again: "Can it possibly be, you say, that He who was begotten before all worlds, should be born a second time; and be God?" If all these things cannot possibly be, how is it that the Creed of the Churches

says that they did happen? How is it that you yourself said that they did? For let us compare what you now say with what you formerly said. Once you said: "I believe in God the Father Almighty; and in Jesus Christ His Son, Very God of Very God; Being of one substance with the Father; who for us came and was born of the Virgin Mary; and was crucified under Pontius Pilate; and was buried." But now what is it that you say? "If we should say: I believe in God the Word, the only Son of God, Begotten of His Father; Being of one substance with the Father, who came down and was buried, would not our ears be shocked at the sound?" The bitterness indeed and blasphemy of your words might drive us to a furious and ferocious attack in answer; but we must somewhat curb the reins of our pious sorrow.

CHAPTER X.

He inveighs against him because though he has forsaken the Catholic religion, he nevertheless presumes to teach in the Church, to sacrifice, and to give decisions.

I APPEAL then to you, to you yourself, I say. Tell me, I pray, if any Jew or pagan denied the Creed of the Catholic faith, should you think that we ought to listen to him? Most certainly not. What if a heretic or an apostate does the same? Still less should we listen to him, for it is worse for a man to forsake the truth which he has known, than to deny it without ever having known it. We see then two men in you: a Catholic and an apostate: first a Catholic, afterwards an apostate. Determine for yourself which you think we ought to follow: for you cannot press the claims of the one in yourself without condemning the other. Do you say then that it is your former self which is to be condemned: and that you condemn the Catholic Creed, and the confession and faith of all men? And what then? O shameful deed! O wretched grief! What are you doing in the Catholic Church, you preventer of Catholics? Why is it that you, who have denied the faith of the people, are still polluting the meetings of the people: And above all venture to stand at the altar, to mount the pulpit, and show your impudent and treacherous face to God's people — to occupy the Bishop's throne, to exercise the priesthood, to set yourself up as a teacher? To teach the Christians what? Not to believe in Christ: to deny that He in whose Divine temple they are, is God.[2] And after all this, O folly! O

---

[1] Persius Sat. iii. l. 116 . . . "quod ipse non sani esse hominis non sanus juret Orestes."

[2] Petschenig's text is as follows: *Ut quid doceas Christianos? Christum non credere, cum ipsum in cujus Dei templo sint Deum negare.* Gazæus edits: *Ut quid doces Christianos, Christum non credens? Cum ipsum, in cujus Dei templo sunt, Deum neges.*

madness! you fancy that you are a teacher and a Bishop, while (O wretched blindness) you are denying His Divinity, His Divinity (I repeat it) whose priest you claim to be. But we are carried away by our grief. What then says the Creed? or what did you yourself say in the Creed? Surely "the Lord Jesus Christ, Very God of Very God; Being of one substance with the Father; By whom the worlds were created and all things made:" and that this same Person "for us came and was born of the Virgin Mary." Since then you said that God was born of Mary, how can you deny that Mary was the mother of God? Since you said that God came, how can you deny that He is God who has come? You said in the Creed: "I believe in Jesus Christ the Son of God: I believe in Very God of Very God, of one substance with the Father: who for us came and was born of the Virgin Mary; and was crucified under Pontius Pilate; and was buried." But now you say: "If we should say, I believe in God the Word, the only Son of God, Begotten of the Father, of one substance with the Father; who came and was buried, would not our ears be shocked at the sound?" Do you see then how you are utterly destroying and stamping out the whole faith of the Catholic Creed and the Catholic mystery? "O Sin, O monstrosity, to be driven away," as one says,[1] "to the utmost parts of the earth:" for this is more truly said of you, that you may forsooth go into that solitude where you will not be able to find anyone to ruin. You think then that the faith of our salvation, and the mystery of the Church's hope is a shock to your ears and hearing. And how was it that formerly when you were hastening to be baptized, you heard these mysteries with unharmed ears? How was it that when the teachers of the church were instructing you your ears were not damaged? You certainly at that time did your duty without any double shock to your mouth and ears; when you repeated what you heard from others, and as the speaker yourself heard yourself speaking. Where then were these injuries to your ears? Where these shocks to your hearing? Why did you not contradict and cry out against it? But indeed you are at your will and fancy, when you please, a disciple; and when you please, the Church's enemy: when you please a Catholic, and when you please an apostate. A worthy leader indeed, to draw Churches after you, to whatever side you attach yourself; to make your will the law of our life, and to change mankind as you yourself change, that, as you will

not be what all others are, they may be what you want![2] A splendid authority indeed, that because you are not now what you used to be, the world must cease to be what it formerly was!

CHAPTER XI.

He removes the silent objection of heretics who want to recant the profession of their faith made in childhood.

BUT perhaps you say that you were a baby when you were regenerated, and so were not then able to think or to contradict. It is true: that your infancy *did* prevent you from contradicting, when if you had been a man you would have died for contradicting. For what if when in that most faithful and devout Church of Christ the priest delivered the Creed[3] to the Catechumen and the attesting people, you had tried to hold your tongue at any point, or to contradict? Perhaps you would have been heard, and not sent forth at once like some new kind of monster or prodigy as a plague to be expelled. Not because that most earnest and religious people of God has any wish to be stained with the blood of even the worst of men: but because especially in great cities the people inflamed with the love of God cannot restrain the ardour of their faith when they see anyone rise up against their God. But be it so. As a baby, if it be so, you could not contradict and deny the Creed. Why did you hold your tongue when you were older and stronger. At any rate you grew up, and became a man, and were placed in the ministry of the Church. Through all these years, through all the steps of office and dignity, did you never understand the faith which you taught so long before? At any rate you knew that you were His deacon and priest. If the rule of salvation was a difficulty to you, why did you undertake the honour of that, of which you disliked the faith? But indeed you were a far sighted and simply devout man, who

---

[1] Cicero in Verr. Act. II. Book I. xv. 40.

[2] *Ut, quia tu esse nolis quod omnes sint, omnes sint, quod tu velis* (Petschenig). Gazæus has: *Et quia tu esse nolis quod omnes sunt, quod tu velis:* a text which he confesses must be corrupt.
[3] The reference is the ceremony known as the *Traditio Symboli,* which is thus described by Professor Lumby: "The practice of the early church in the admission of converts to baptism seems to have been of this nature. For some period previous to their baptism (the usual seasons for which were Easter and Pentecost) the candidates for admission thereto were trained in the doctrines of the faith by the presbyters. A few days before they were to be baptized (the number of days varying at different periods) the Creed was delivered to them accompanied with a sermon. This ceremony was known as *Traditio Symboli,* the delivery of the Creed. At the time of Baptism each candidate was interrogated upon the articles of the Creed which he had received, and was to return an answer in the words which had been given to him. This was known as *Redditio Symboli,* the repetition of the Creed, and Baptism was the only occasion on which the Creed was introduced into any public service of the Church." History of the Creeds, pp. 11, 12.

wished so to balance yourself between the two, as to maintain both your wicked blasphemy, and the honour of Catholicity!

CHAPTER XII.

Christ crucified is an offence and foolishness to those who declare that He was a mere man.

THE shock then to your hearing and ears is that God was born, and God suffered. And where is that saying of yours, O Apostle Paul: "But we preach Christ crucified, to the Jews indeed a stumbling block, but to the Gentiles foolishness: but to them that are called, both Jews and Greeks, Christ the Power of God and the Wisdom of God."[1] What is the Wisdom and Power of God? Certainly it is God. But he preaches Christ who was crucified, as the Power and Wisdom of God. If then Christ is without any doubt the Wisdom of God, He is therefore without any doubt God. "We," then, he says, "preach Christ crucified, to the Jews indeed a stumbling block, but to the Gentiles foolishness." And so the Lord's cross, which was foolishness to the Gentiles and a stumbling block to the Jews is both together to you. Nor indeed is there any greater foolishness than not to believe, or any greater stumbling block than to refuse to listen. Their ears were wounded then by the preaching and the passion of God, just as yours are wounded now. They thought as you think that this shocked their ears. And hence it was that when the Apostle was preaching Christ as God, at the name of our God and Lord Jesus Christ, they stopped the ears in their head, as you stop the ears of your understanding. The sin of both of you in this matter might seem to be equal, were it not that your fault is the greater, because they denied Him, in whom the passion still showed the manhood,[2] while you deny Him, whom the resurrection has already proved to be God. And so they were persecuting Him on the earth, whom you are persecuting even in heaven. And not only so, but this is more cruel and wicked, because *they* denied Him in ignorance, *you* deny Him after having received the faith: *they* not knowing the Lord, *you* when you have confessed Him as God: *they* under cover of zeal for the law, *you* under the cloke of your Bishopric: *they* denied Him to whom they thought that they were strangers, *you* deny Him whose priest you are. O unworthy act, and one never heard of before! You persecute and attack the very One, whose office you are still holding.

CHAPTER XIII.

He replies to the objection in which they say that the child born[3] ought to be of one substance with the mother.

BUT indeed in your deceit and blasphemy you use a grand argument for denying and attacking the Lord God, when you say that "the child born ought to be of one substance with the mother."[4] I do not entirely admit it, and maintain that in the matter of the birth of God it would not be observed; for the birth was not so much the work of her who bore Him as of her Son, and He was born as He willed, whose doing it was that He was born. Next, if you say that the child born ought to be of one substance with the parent, I affirm that the Lord Jesus Christ was of one substance with His Father, and also with His mother. For in accordance with the difference of the Persons He showed a likeness to each parent. For according to His Divinity He was of one substance with the Father: but according to the flesh He was of one substance with His mother. Not that it was one Person who was of one substance with the Father, and another who was of one substance with His mother, but because the same Lord Jesus Christ, both born as man, and also being God, had in Him the properties of each parent, and in that He was man He showed a likeness to His human mother, and in that He was God He possessed the very nature of God the Father.

CHARTER XIV.

He compares this erroneous view with the teaching of the Pelagians.

OTHERWISE if Christ who was born of Mary is not the same Person as He who is of God, you certainly make two Christs; after the manner of that abominable error of Pelagius, which in asserting that a mere man was born of the Virgin, said that He was the teacher rather than the redeemer of mankind; for He did not bring to men redemption of life but only an example of how to live, i.e., that by following Him men should do the same sort of things and so come to a similar state. Your blasphemy then has but one source, and the root of the errors is one and the same. They maintain that a mere man was born of Mary: you maintain the same. They sever the Son of man from the Son of God: you do the same. They say that the Saviour was made the Christ by His baptism: you say that in baptism He became the Temple of God.

---

[1] 1 Cor. i. 23, 24.   [2] *Homo.*   [3] *Nativitas.*   [4] *Homoousios parenti debet esse nativitas.*

They do not deny that He became God after His Passion : you deny Him even after His ascension. In one point only therefore your perverseness goes beyond theirs, for they seem to blaspheme the Lord on earth, and you even in heaven. We do not deny that you have beaten and outstripped those whom you are copying. They at last cease to deny God ; you never do. Although theirs must not altogether be deemed a true confession, as they only allow the glory of Divinity to the Saviour after His Passion, and while they deny that He was God before this, only confess it afterwards : for, as it seems to me, one who denies some part in regard to God, denies Him altogether : and one who does not confess that He ever existed, denies Him forever. Just as you also, even if you were to admit that now in the heavens the Lord Jesus Christ, who was born of the Virgin Mary, is God, would not truly confess Him unless you admitted that He was always God. But indeed you do not want in any point to change or vary your opinion. For you assert that He whom you speak of as born a mere man, is still at the present time not God. O novel and marvellous blasphemy, though with the heretics you assert Him to be man, you do not with the heretics confess Him to be God !

CHAPTER XV.

He shows that those who patronize this false teaching acknowledge two Christs.

But still, I had begun to say, that as you certainly make out two Christs this very matter must be illustrated and made clear. Tell me, I pray you, you who sever Christ from the Son of God, how can you confess in the Creed that Christ was begotten of God ? For you say : "I believe in God the Father, and in Jesus Christ His Son." Here then you have Jesus Christ the Son of God : but you say that it was not the same Son of God who was born of Mary. Therefore there is one Christ of God, and another of Mary. In your view then there are two Christs. For, though in the Creed you do not deny Christ, you say that the Christ of Mary is another than the one whom you confess in the Creed. But perhaps you say that Christ was not begotten of God : how then do you say in the Creed : "I believe in Jesus Christ the Son of God ?" You must then either deny the Creed or confess that Christ is the Son of God. But if you confess in the Creed that Christ is the Son of God, you must also confess that the same Christ, the Son of God, is of Mary. Or if you make out another Christ of Mary, you certainly make the blasphemous assertion that there are two Christs.

CHAPTER XVI.

He shows further that this teaching is destructive of the confession of the Trinity.

But still even if your obstinacy and dishonesty are not restrained by this faith of the Creed, are you not, I ask you, overwhelmed by an appeal to reason and the light of truth ? Tell me, I ask, whoever you are, O you heretic — At least there is a Trinity, in which we believe, and which we confess : Father and Son and Holy Ghost. Of the Glory of the Father and the Spirit there is no question. You are slandering the Son, because you say that it was not the same Person who was born of Mary, as He who was begotten of God the Father. Tell me then : if you do not deny that the only Son of God was begotten of God, whom do you make out that He is who was born of Mary ? You say "a mere man," according to that which He Himself said : "That which is born of the flesh, is flesh." [1] But He cannot be called a mere man who was begotten not after the law of human creation alone. "For that which is conceived in her," said the angel, "is of the Holy Ghost." [2] And this even you dare not deny, though you deny almost all the mysteries of salvation. Since then He was born of the Holy Ghost, and cannot be termed a mere man, as He was conceived by the inspiration of God, if it is not He who, as the Apostle says, "emptied Himself by taking the form of a servant," and "the word was made flesh," and "humbled Himself by becoming obedient unto death," and "who for our sakes, though He was rich, became poor," [3] tell me, then, who He is, who was born of the Holy Ghost, and was conceived by the overshadowing of God ? You say that He is certainly a different Person. Then there are two Persons; viz., the one, who was begotten of God the Father in heaven ; and the other who was conceived of Mary, by the inspiration of God. And thus there is a fourth Person whom you introduce, and whom (though in words you term Him a mere man) you assert actually not to have been a mere man, since you allow (not however as you ought) that He is to be honoured, worshipped, and adored. Since then the Son of God who was begotten of the Father is certainly to be worshipped, and He who was conceived of Mary by the Holy Ghost is to

---

[1] St. John iii. 6.   [2] S. Matt. i. 20.
[3] Phil. ii. 7, 8; S. John i. 14; 2 Cor. viii. 9.

be worshipped, you make two Persons to be honoured and venerated, whom you so far sever from each other, as to venerate each with an honour special and peculiar to Him. And thus you see that by denying and by severing from Himself the Son of God, you destroy, as far as you can, the whole mystery of the divinity. For while you are endeavouring to introduce a fourth Person into the Trinity,[1] you see that you have utterly denied the whole Trinity.

CHAPTER XVII.

Those who are under an error in one point of the Catholic religion, lose the whole faith, and all the value of the faith.

AND since this is so, in denying that Jesus Christ the Son of God is one, you have denied everything. For the scheme of the mysteries of the Church and the Catholic faith is such that one who denies one portion of the Sacred Mystery cannot confess the other. For all parts of it are so bound up and united together that one cannot stand without the other, and if a man denies one point out of the whole number, it is of no use for him to believe all the others. And so if you deny that the Lord Jesus Christ is God, the result is that in denying the Son of God you deny the Father also. For as St. John says: "He who hath not the Son hath not the Father; but he who hath the Son hath the Father also."[2] By denying then Him who was begotten you deny also Him who begat. By denying also that the Son of God was born in the flesh, you are led also to deny that He was born in the Spirit, for it is the same Person who was born in the flesh who was first born in the Spirit. If you do not believe that He was born in the flesh, the result is that you do not believe that He suffered. If you do not believe in His Passion what remains for you but to deny His resurrection? For faith in one raised springs out of faith in one dead. Nor can the reference to the resurrection keep its place, unless belief in His death has first preceded it. By denying then his Passion and Death, you deny also his resurrection from hell.[3] It follows certainly that you deny His ascension also, for there cannot be the ascension without the resurrection. And if we do not believe that He rose again, we cannot either believe that He ascended: as the Apostle says, "For He that descended is the same also that ascended."[4] Thus, so far as you are concerned, the Lord Jesus Christ did not rise from hell, nor ascend into heaven, nor sit at the right hand of God the Father, nor will He come at that day of judgment which we look for, nor will He judge the quick and the dead.

CHAPTER XVIII.

He directs his discourse upon his antagonist with whom he is disputing, and begs him to return to his senses. The sacrament of reconciliation is necessary for the lapsed for their salvation.

AND so, you wretched, insane, obstinate creature, you see that you have utterly upset the whole faith of the Creed, and all that is valuable in our hope and the mysteries. And yet you still dare to remain in the Church: and imagine that you are a priest, though you have denied everything by which you came to be a priest. Return then to the right way, and recover your former mind, return to your senses if you ever had any. Come to yourself, if there ever was in you a self to which you can come back. Acknowledge the sacraments of your salvation, by which you were initiated and regenerated. They are of no less use to you now than they were then; for they can now regenerate you by penance, as they then gave you birth through the Font. Hold fast the full scheme of the Creed. Hold the entire truth of the faith. Believe in God the Father: believe in God the Son: in one who begat and one who was begotten, the Lord of all, Jesus Christ; Being of one substance with the Father; Begotten in His divinity; born in the flesh: of twofold birth, yet of but one glory; who Himself creator of all things, was begotten of the Father, and was afterwards born of the Virgin.

CHAPTER XIX.

That the birth of Christ in time diminished nothing of the glory and power of His Deity.

FOR the fact that He came of the flesh and in the flesh, has reference to His birth, and involves no diminution in Him: and He was simply born, not changed for the worse.[5] For though, still remaining in the form of God, He took upon Him the form of a servant, yet the weakness of His human constitution had no effect on His nature as God: but while the power of His Deity remained whole and unimpaired, all that took place in His human flesh was an advancement of His manhood and no diminution of His glory. For when God was born in human flesh, He was not born in human flesh in such a way as not to remain

---

[1] Cf. Augustine, Tr. 78 in Joan.
[2] 1 John ii. 23.
[3] ab inferis.
[4] Eph. iv. 10.
[5] Demutatus.

Divine in Himself, but so that, while the Godhead remained as before, God might become man. And so Martha while she saw with her bodily eyes the man, confessed Him by spiritual sight to be God, saying, "Yea, Lord, I have believed that Thou art the Christ the Son of the living God, who art come into the world." [1] So Peter, owing to the Holy Spirit's revelation, while externally he beheld the Son of man, yet proclaimed Him to be the Son of God, saying, "Thou art the Christ, the Son of the living God." [2] So Thomas when he touched the flesh, believed that he had touched God, saying, "My Lord and my God." [3] For they all confessed but one Christ, so as not to make Him two. Do you therefore believe Him; and so believe that Jesus Christ the Lord of all, both only Begotten and first-born, is both Creator of all things and Preserver of men; and that the same Person is first the framer of the whole world, and afterwards redeemer of mankind? Who still remaining with the Father and in the Father, Being of one substance with the Father, did (as the Apostle says), "Take the form of a servant, and humble Himself even unto death, the death of the Cross:" [4] and (as the Creed says) "was born of the Virgin Mary, crucified under Pontius Pilate, and was buried. And the third day He rose again according to the Scriptures; and ascended into heaven; and shall come again to judge both the quick and the dead." This is our faith; this is our salvation: to believe that our God and Lord Jesus Christ is one and the same before all things and after all things. For, as it is written, "Jesus Christ is yesterday and today and the same for ever." [5] For "yesterday" signifies all time past, wherein, before the beginning, He was begotten of the Father. "Today" covers the time of this world, in which He was again born of the Virgin, suffered, and rose again. But by the expression the same "for ever" is denoted the whole boundless eternity to come.

CHAPTER XX.

He shows from what has been said that we do not mean that God was mortal or of flesh before the worlds, although Christ, who is God from eternity and was made man in time, is but one Person.

BUT perhaps you will say: If I admit that the same Person was in the end of time born of a Virgin, who was begotten before all things of God the Father, I shall imply that before the beginning of the world God was in the flesh, as I say that He was afterwards

man, who was always God: and so I shall say that that man who was afterwards born, had always existed. I do not want you to be confused by this blind ignorance, and these obscure misconceptions, so as to fancy that I am maintaining that the manhood [6] which was born of Mary had existed before the beginning of things, or asserting that God was always in a bodily form before the commencement of the world. I do not say, I repeat it, I do not say that the manhood was in God before it was born: but that God was afterwards born in the manhood. For that flesh which was born of the flesh of the Virgin had not always existed: but God who always was, came in the flesh of man of the flesh of the Virgin. For "the Word was made flesh," and did not manifest flesh together with Himself: but in the glory of Divinity joined Himself to human flesh. For tell me when or where the Word was made flesh, or where He emptied Himself by taking the form of a servant: or where He became poor, though He was rich? Where but in the holy womb of the Virgin, where at His Incarnation, the Word of God is said to have been made flesh, at His birth He truly took the form of a servant; and when He is in human nature nailed to the Cross, He became poor, and was made poor in His sufferings in the flesh, though He was rich in His Divine glory? Otherwise if, as you say, at some later period the Deity entered into Him as into one of the Prophets and saints, then "the Word was made flesh" in those men also in whom He vouchsafed to dwell: then in each one of them He emptied Himself and took upon Him the form of a servant. And thus there is nothing new or unique in Christ. Neither His conception, nor His birth nor His death had anything special or miraculous about it.

CHAPTER XXI.

The authority of Holy Scripture teaches that Christ existed from all eternity.

AND yet to return to what we said before, though all these things are so, as we have stated: how do we read that Jesus Christ (whom you assert to be a mere man) was ever existing even before His birth of a Virgin, and how is He proclaimed by prophets and apostles as God even before the worlds? As Paul says: "One Lord Jesus, through whom are all things." [7] And elsewhere he says: "For in Christ were created all things in heaven and on earth, both visible and invisible." [8] The

---

[1] S. John xi. 27.   [3] S. John xx. 28.   [5] Heb. xiii. 8.
[2] S. Matt. xvi. 16.   [4] Phil. ii. 7, 8.

[6] *Hominem.*   [7] 1 Cor. viii. 6.   [8] Col. i. 16.

Creed too, which is framed both by human and Divine authority, says: "I believe in God the Father, and in the Lord Jesus Christ, His Son." And after other clauses: "Very God of Very God; by whom both the worlds were framed and all things were made." And further: "Who for us came and was born of the Virgin Mary, and was crucified, and was buried."

CHAPTER XXII.

The hypostatic union enables us to ascribe to God what belongs to the flesh in Christ.

How then is Christ (whom you term a mere man) proclaimed in Holy Scripture to be God without beginning, if by our own confession the Lord's manhood[1] did not exist before His birth and conception of a Virgin? And how can we read of so close a union of man and God, as to make it appear that man was ever co-eternal with God, and that afterwards God suffered with man: whereas we cannot believe that man can be without beginning or that God can suffer? It is this which we established in our previous writings; viz., that God being joined to manhood,[2] i.e., to His own body, does not allow any separation to be made in men's thoughts between man and God. Nor will He permit anyone to hold that there is one Person of the Son of man, and another Person of the Son of God. But in all the holy Scriptures He joins together and as it were incorporates in the Godhead, the Lord's manhood,[3] so that no one can sever man from God in time, nor God from man at His Passion. For if you regard Him in time, you will find that the Son of man is ever with the Son of God. If you take note of His Passion, you will find that the Son of God is ever with the Son of man, and that Christ the Son of man and the Son of God is so one and indivisible, that, in the language of holy Scripture, the man cannot be severed in time from God, nor God from man at His Passion. Hence comes this: "No man hath ascended into heaven, but He who came down from heaven, even the Son of man who is in heaven."[4] Where the Son of God while He was speaking on earth testified that the Son of man was in heaven: and testified that the same Son of man, who, He said, would ascend into heaven, had previously come down from heaven. And this: "What and if ye shall see the Son of man ascend up where He was before,"[5] where He gives the name of Him who

was born of man, but affirms that He ever was up on high. And the Apostle also, when considering what happened in time, says that all things were made by Christ. For he says, "There is one Lord Jesus Christ, by whom are all things."[6] But when speaking of His Passion, he shows that the Lord of glory was crucified. "For if," he says, "they had known, they would never have crucified the Lord of glory."[7] And so too the Creed speaking of the only and first-begotten Lord Jesus Christ, "Very God of Very God, Being of one substance with the Father, and the Maker of all things," affirms that He was born of the Virgin and crucified and afterwards buried. Thus joining in one body (as it were) the Son of God and of man, and uniting God and man, so that there can be no severance either in time or at the Passion, since the Lord Jesus Christ is shown to be one and the same Person, both as God through all eternity, and as man through the endurance of His Passion; and though we cannot say that man is without beginning or that God is passible, yet in the one Person of the Lord Jesus Christ we can speak of man as eternal, and of God as dead. You see then that Christ means the whole Person, and that the name represents both natures, for both man and God are born, and so it takes in the whole Person so that when this name is used we see that no part is left out. There was not then before the birth of a Virgin the same eternity belonging in the past to the manhood as to the Divinity, but because Divinity was united to manhood in the womb of the Virgin, it follows that when we use the name of Christ one cannot be spoken of without the other.

CHAPTER XXIII.

That the figure Synecdoche, in which the part stands for the whole, is very familiar to the Holy Scripture.

WHATEVER then you say of the Lord Jesus Christ, you say of the whole person, and in mentioning the Son of God you mention the Son of man, and in mentioning the Son of man you mention the Son of God: by the grammatical trope synecdoche in which you understand the whole from the parts, and a part is put for the whole: and the holy Scriptures certainly show this, as in them the Lord often uses this trope, and teaches in this way about others and would have us understand about Himself in the same way. For sometimes days, and things, and men, and times are de-

---

[1] *Dominicus homo*, see above on V. v.
[2] *Homini.*
[3] *Dominicus homo.*
[4] S. John iii. 13.
[5] S. John vi. 63.

[6] 1 Cor. viii. 6.
[7] 1 Cor. ii. 8. See the note on IV. vii.

noted in holy Scripture in no other fashion. As in this case where God declares that Israel shall serve the Egyptians for four hundred years, and says to Abraham: "Know thou that thy seed shall be a stranger in a land not theirs, and they shall bring them under bondage and afflict them four hundred years." [1] Whereas if you take into account the whole time after that God spoke, they are more than four hundred: but if you only reckon the time in which they were in slavery, they are less. And in giving this period indeed, unless you understand it in this way, we must think that the Word of God lied (and away with such a thought from Christian minds!). But since from the time of the Divine utterance, the whole period of their lives amounted to more than four hundred years, and their bondage endured for not nearly four hundred, you must understand that the part is to be taken for the whole, or the whole for the part. There is also a similar way of representing days and nights, where, when in the case of either division of time one day is meant, either period is shown by a portion of a single period. And indeed in this way the difficulty about the time of our Lord's Passion is cleared up: for whereas the Lord prophesied that after the model of the prophet Jonah, the Son of man would be three days and three nights in the heart of the earth,[2] and whereas after the sixth day of the week on which He was crucified, He was only in hell [3] for one day and two nights, how can we show the truth of the Divine words? Surely by the trope of Synecdoche, i.e., because to the day on which He was crucified the previous night belongs, and to the night on which He rose again, the coming day; and so when there is added the night which preceded the day belonging to it, and the day which followed the night belonging to it, we see that

there is nothing lacking to the whole period of time, which is made up of its portions. The holy Scriptures abound in such instances of ways of speaking: but it would take too long to relate them all. For so when the Psalm says, "What is a man that Thou art mindful of Him," [4] from the part we understand the whole, as while only one man is mentioned the whole human race is meant. So also where Ahab sinned we are told that the people sinned. Where — though all are mentioned, a part is to be understood from the whole. John also the Lord's forerunner says: "After me cometh a man who is preferred before me for He was before me." [5] How then does He mean that He would come after Him, whom He shows to be before Him? For if this is understood of a man who was afterwards born, how was he before him? But if it is taken of the Word how is it, "a *man* cometh after me?" Except that in the one Lord Jesus Christ is shown both the posteriority of the manhood and the precedence of the Godhead. And so the result is that one and the same Lord was before him and came after him: for according to the flesh He was posterior in time to John; and according to His Deity was before all men. And so he, when he named that man, denoted both the manhood and the Word, for as the Lord Jesus Christ the Son of God was complete in both manhood and Divinity [6] in mentioning one of these natures in Him he denoted the whole person. And what need is there of anything further? I think that the day would fail me if I were to try to collect or to tell everything that could be said on this subject. And what we have already said is enough, at any rate on this part of the subject, both for the exposition of the Creed, and for the requirements of our case, and for the limits of our book.

BOOK VII.

CHAPTER I.

As he is going to reply to the slanders of his opponents he implores the aid of Divine grace to teach a prayer to be used by those who undertake to dispute with heretics.

As it happens to those who having escaped the perils of the sea, are in terror of the sands that stretch before the harbour, or the rocks that line the shore, so it is in my case that, — as I have kept to the last some of the slanders

of the heretics, — although I have reached the limit of the work which I set myself, yet I am beginning to dread the close, which I had longed to reach. But, as the Prophet says, "The Lord is my helper; I will not fear what man can do to me," [7] so we will not fear the pitfalls which crafty heretics have dug in front of us, nor the paths thickly strewn with horrid thorns. For as they make our road difficult but do not close it, there is before us the

[1] Gen. xv. 13. [2] S. Matt. xii. 40. [3] *Apud inferos.*
[4] Ps. viii. 5. [5] S. John i. 15. [6] Verbi. [7] Ps. cxvii. (cxviii.) 6.

trouble of clearing them away, rather than the fear of not being able to do so. For when, as we are walking feebly along the right road, they come in our way, and frighten the walkers rather than hurt them, our work and business has more to do in clearing them away, than to fear from the difficulty of this: And so, laying our hands upon that monstrous head of the deadly serpent, and longing to lay hold of all the limbs that are entangled in the huge folds and coils of his body, again and again do we pray to Thee, O Lord Jesus, to whom we have ever prayed, that Thou wouldst give us words by opening our mouth "to the pulling down of strongholds, destroying counsels, and every height that exalteth itself against the knowledge of God, and bringing into captivity every understanding unto Thine obedience:"[1] for he is indeed free, who has begun to be led captive by Thee. Do Thou then be present to this work of thine, and to those of Thine who are striving for Thee above the measure of their strength. Grant us to bruise the gaping mouths of this new serpent, and its neck that swells with deadly poison, O Thou who makest the feet of believers to tread unharmed on serpents and scorpions, and to go upon the adder and basilisk, to tread under foot the lion and the dragon.[2] And grant that through the fearless boldness of steadfast innocence, the sucking child may play on the hole of the asp, and the weaned child thrust his hand into the den of the basilisk.[3] Grant then to us also that we may thrust our hands unharmed into the den of this monstrous and most wicked basilisk; and if it has in any holes, i.e., in the human heart, a lurking or resting place, or has laid its eggs there, or left a trace of its slimy course, do Thou remove from them all the foul and deadly pollution of this most noxious serpent. Take away the uncleanness their blasphemy has brought on them, and purify with the fan of Thy sacred cleansing[4] the souls that are plunged in stinking mud, so that the "dens of thieves" may become "houses of prayer:"[5] and that in those which are now, as is written, the dwellings where hedgehogs and monsters,[6] and satyrs, and all kinds of strange creatures dwell, there the gifts of Thy Holy Spirit, namely the beauty of faith and holiness may shine forth. And as once Thou didst destroy idolatry and cast out images, and make shrines of virtue out of the temples of devils, and let into the dens of serpents and scorpions the rays of shining light, and make out of the dens of error and shame the homes of beauty

and splendour, so do Thou pour upon all whose eyes the darkness of heretical obstinacy has blinded, the light of Thy compassion and truth, that they may at length with clear and unveiled sight behold the great and life-giving mystery of Thine Incarnation, and so come to know Thee to have been born as Very man of that sacred womb of a pure Virgin, and yet to acknowledge that Thou wast always Very God.

CHAPTER II.

He meets the objection taken from these words: No one gave birth to one who had existed before her.

AND before I begin to speak of those things of which I have given no foretaste in the earlier books, I think it right to try to carry out what I have already promised, that when I have thoroughly redeemed my pledge, I may begin to speak more freely of what has not been touched upon, after having satisfied my promise. So then that new serpent, in order to destroy the faith of the holy nativity, hisses out against the Church of God and says: "No one ever gives birth to one older than herself." To begin with then I think that you know neither what you say nor where you get it from. For if you knew or understood where you got it from, you would never regard the nativity of the only begotten of God in the light of human fancies, nor would you try to settle by merely human propositions, about Him who was born without His conception originating from man: nor would you bring human impossibilities as objections against Divine Omnipotence if you knew that with God nothing was impossible. No one then, you say, gives birth to one older than herself. Tell me then, I pray, of what cases are you speaking, for the nature of what creatures do you think that you can lay down rules? Do you suppose that you can fix laws for men or beasts or birds or cattle? Those (and others of the same kind) are the things of which such assertions can be made. For none of them is able to produce one older than itself; for what has already been produced cannot return to it again so as to be born again by a new creation. And so no one can bear one older than herself, as no one can beget one older than himself: for the opportunity of bearing only results where there is the possibility of begetting. Do you then imagine that in reference to the nativity of Almighty God regard must be had to the same considerations as in the birth of earthly creatures? And do you bring the nature of man's conditions as a difficulty in the case of Him who is Himself the

---

[1] 2 Cor. x. 4, 5.   [2] Cf. S. Luke x. 19; Ps. xc. (xci.) 13.
[3] Isa. xi. 8.   [4] Cf. Mal. iii. 2, 3.   [5] S. Matt. xxi. 13.
[6] Onocentauri: the allusion is to Is. xxxiv. 14, 15. Cf. Jerome in Esaiam, Bk. X.

author of nature? You see then that, as I said above, you know not whence or of whom you are talking, as you are comparing creatures to the Creator; and in order to calculate the power of God are drawing an instance from those things which would never have existed at all, but that the very fact of their existence comes from God. God then came as He would, when He would, and of her whom He would. Neither time nor person, nor the manner of men, nor the custom of creatures was any difficulty with Him; for the law of the creatures could not stand in the way of Him who is Himself the Creator of them all. And whatever He would have possible was ready to His hand, for the power of willing it was His. Do you want to know how far the omnipotence of God extends, and how great it is? I believe that the Lord could do that even in the case of His creatures which you do not believe that He could do in His own case. For all living creatures which now bear things younger than themselves could, if only God gave the word, bear things much older than themselves. For even food and drink, if it were God's will, could be turned into the foetus and offspring: and even water, which has been flowing from the beginning of things, and which all living creatures use, could, if God gave the word, be made a body in the womb, and have birth given to it. For who can set a limit to divine works, or circumscribe Divine Providence? or who (to use the words of Scripture) can say to Him "What doest thou?"[1] If you deny that God can do all things, then deny, that, when God was born, one older than Mary could be born of her. But if there is nothing impossible with God, why do you bring as an objection against His coming an impossibility, when you know that for Him nothing is impossible in anything?

CHAPTER III.

He replies to the cavil that the one who is born must be of one substance with the one who bears.

THE second blasphemous slander or slanderous blasphemy of your heresy is when you say that the one who is born must be of one substance with the one who bears. It is not very different from the previous one, for it differs from it in terms rather than in fact and reality. For when we are treating of the birth of God, you maintain that one of greater power could not be born of Mary just as above you maintain than one older could not be begotten. And so you may take it that the same answer

may be given to this as to what you said before: or you may conceive that the answer given to this assertion, which you are now making, applies to that also. You say then that the one who is born must be of one substance with the one who bears. If this refers to earthly creatures, it is most certainly the case. But if it refers to the birth of God, why in the case of His birth do you regard precedents from nature? for appointments are subject to Him who appointed them, and not the appointer to His appointments. But would you like to know more fully how these slanders of yours are not only wicked but foolish, and the idle talk of one who does not in the least see the omnipotence of God? Tell me, I pray, you who think that like things can only be produced from like things, whence was the origin of that unaccountable host of quails in the wilderness of old time to feed the children of Israel, for nowhere do we read that they had been previously born of mother birds, but that they were brought up and came suddenly. Again whence came that heavenly food which for forty years fell on the camp of the Hebrews? Did manna produce manna? But these refer to ancient miracles. And what of more recent ones? With a few loaves and small fishes the Lord Jesus Christ fed countless hosts of the people that followed Him, and not once only. The reason that they were satisfied lay not in the food: for a secret and unseen cause satisfied the hungry folk, especially as there was much more left when they were filled than there had been set before them when they were hungry. And how was all this brought about that when those who ate were satisfied, the food itself was multiplied by an extraordinary increase? We read that in Galilee wine was produced from water. Tell me how what was of one nature produced something of an altogether different substance from its own quality? Especially when (which exactly applies to the birth of the Lord) it was the production of a nobler substance from what was inferior to it? Tell me then how from mere water there could be produced rich and splendid wine? How was it that one thing was drawn out, another poured in? Was the cistern a well of such a nature as to change the water drawn from it into the best wine? Or did the character of the vessels or the diligence of the servants effect this? Most certainly neither of these. And how is it that the *manner* of the fact is not understood by the thoughts of the heart, though the *truth* of the fact is firmly held by the conscience? In the gospel clay was placed on the eyes of a blind man and when it was washed off[2] eyes

---

[1] Isa. xlv. 9; Rom. ix. 20.

[2] *Abluto eo* (Petschenig): *Ab luto eo* (Gazæus).

were produced. Had water the power of giving birth to eyes, or clay of creating light? Certainly not, especially as water could be of no use to a blind man, and clay would actually hinder the sight of those who could see. And how was it that a thing that itself in its own nature was injurious, became the means of restoring health; and that what was ordinarily hurtful to sound people, was then made the instrument of healing? You say that the power of God brought it about, and the remedy of God caused it, and that all these things of which we have been speaking were simply brought about by Divine Omnipotence; which is able to fashion new things from unwonted material, and to make serviceable things out of their opposites, and to change what belongs to the realm of things impossible and impracticable into possibilities and actual performances.

CHAPTER IV.

How God has shown His Omnipotence in His birth in time as well as in everything else.

CONFESS then the same truth in respect of the actual nativity of the Lord, as in respect of everything else. Believe that God was born when He would, for you do not deny that He could do what He would; unless possibly you think that that power which belonged to Him for all other things was deficient as regards Himself, and that His Omnipotence though proceeding from Him and penetrating all things, was insufficient to bring about His own nativity. In the case of the Lord's nativity you bring this as an objection against me: No one gives birth to one who is anterior in time: and in regard of the birth which Almighty God underwent you say that the one who is born ought to be of one substance with the one who bears; as if you had to do with human laws as in the case of any ordinary man, to whom you might bring the impossibility as an objection, as you include him in the weakness of earthly things. You say that for all men there are common conditions of birth, and but one law of generation; and that a thing could not possibly happen to one man only out of the whole of humanity, which God has forbidden to happen to all. You do not understand of whom you are speaking; nor do you see of whom you are talking; for He is the Author of all conditions, and the very Law of all natures, through whom exists whatever man can do, and whatever man cannot do: for He certainly has laid down the limits of both; viz., how far his powers should extend, and the bounds beyond which his weak-

ness should not advance. How wildly then do you bring human impossibilities as an objection in the case of Him, who possesses all powers and possibilities. If you estimate the Person of the Lord by earthly weaknesses, and measure God's Omnipotence by human rules, you will most certainly fail to find anything which seems appropriate to God as concerns the sufferings of His Body. For if it can seem to you unreasonable that Mary could give birth to God who was anterior to her, how will it seem reasonable that God was crucified by men? And yet the same God who was crucified Himself predicted: "Shall a man afflict God, for you afflict Me?"[1] If then we cannot think that the Lord was born of a Virgin because He who was born was anterior to her who bore Him, how can we believe that God had blood? And yet it was said to the Ephesian elders: "Feed the Church of God which He has purchased with His own Blood."[2] Finally how can we think that the Author of life was Himself deprived of life: And yet Peter says: "Ye have killed the Author of life."[3] No one who is set on earth can be in heaven: and how does the Lord Himself say: "The Son of man who is in heaven"?[4] If then you think that God was not born of a Virgin because the one who is born must be of one substance with the one who bears, how will you believe that different things can be produced from different natures? Thus according to you the wind did not suddenly bring the quails, nor did the manna fall, nor was water turned into wine nor were many thousands of men fed with a few loaves, nor did the blind man receive his sight after the clay had been put on him. But if all these things seem incredible and contrary to nature, unless we believe that they were wrought by God, why should you deny in the matter of His nativity, what you admit in the matter of His works? Or was He unable to contribute to His own nativity and advent what He did not refuse for the succour and profit of men?

CHAPTER V.

He shows by proofs drawn from nature itself, that the law which his opponents lay down; viz., that the one born ought to be of one substance with the one who bears, fails to hold good in many cases.

IT would be tedious and almost childish to speak further on this subject. But still in order to refute that folly and madness of yours, in which you maintain that the one born ought to be of one substance with the one who

---

[1] Mal. iii. 8.   [2] Acts xx. 28.   [3] Acts iii. 15.   [4] S. John iii. 13.

bears, i.e., that nothing can produce something of a different nature to itself, I will bring forward some instances of earthly things, to convince you that many creatures are produced from things of a different nature. Not that it is possible or right to make any comparison in such a case as this: but that you may not doubt the possibility of that happening in the case of the holy Nativity, which as you see takes place in these frail earthly things. Bees, tiniest of creatures though they are, are yet so clever and cunning that we read that they can be produced and spring from things of an entirely different nature. For as they are creatures of marvellous intelligence, and well endowed not merely with sense but with foresight, they are produced from the gathered flowers of plants. What greater instance do you think can be produced and quoted? Living creatures are produced from inanimate: sensate from insensate.[1] What artificer, what architect was there? Who formed their bodies? Who breathed in their souls? Who gave them articulate sounds by which to converse with each other? Who fashioned and arranged these harmonies of their feet, the cunning of their mouths, the neatness of their wings? Their powers, wrath, foresight, movements, calmness, harmony, differences, wars, peace, arrangements, contrivances, business, government, all those things indeed which they have in common with men — from whose teaching, or whose gift did they receive them? from whose implanting or instruction? Did they gain this through generation? or learn it in their mother's womb or from her flesh? They never were in the womb, and had no experience of generation. It was only that flowers which they culled were brought into the hive; and from this by a marvellous contrivance bees issued forth.[2] Then the womb of the mother imparted nothing to the offspring: nor are bees produced from bees. They are but their artificers, not their authors. From the blossoms of plants living creatures proceed. What is there akin in plants and animals? I fancy then that you see who is the contriver of those things. Go now and inquire whether the Lord could bring about that in the case of His own nativity, which you see that He procured in the case of these tiniest of creatures. Perhaps it is needless after this to add anything further. But still let us add in support of the argument what may not be necessary to prove the point. We see how the air

is suddenly darkened, and the earth filled with locusts. Show me their seed — their birth — their mothers. For, as you see, they proceed thence, whence they have their birth. Assert in all these cases that the one who is born must be of one substance with the one who bears. And in these assertions you will be shown to be as silly, as you are wild in your denial of the Nativity of the Lord. And what next? Do even *you* think that we must go on any further? But still we will add something else. There is no doubt that basilisks are produced from the eggs of the birds which in Egypt they call the Ibis. What is there of kindred or relationship between a bird and a serpent? Why is the thing born not of one substance with that which bears it? And yet those who bear are not the authors of all these things, nor do those who are born understand them: but they result from secret causes, and from some inexplicable and manifold law of nature which produces them. And you are bringing as objections to His Nativity your petty assertions from earthly notions, while you cannot explain the origin of those things, which are produced by His bidding and command, whose will does everything, whose sway causes everything: whom nothing can oppose or resist; and whose will is sufficient for everything which can possibly be done.

CHAPTER VI.

He refutes another argument of Nestorius, in which he tried to make out that Christ was like Adam in every point.

BUT since we cannot (as we should much prefer) ignore them, it is now time to expose the rest of your more subtle and insidious blasphemies that at least they may not deceive ignorant folk. In one of your pestilent treatises you have maintained and said that "Since man is the image of the Divine nature, and the devil dragged this down and shattered it, God grieved over His image, as an Emperor over his statue, and repairs the shattered image: and formed without generation a nature from the Virgin, like that of Adam who was born without generation; and raises up man's nature by means of man: for as by man came death, so also by man came the resurrection of the dead." They tell us that some poisoners have a custom of mixing honey with the poison in the cups which they prepare; that the injurious ingredient may be concealed by the sweet: and while a man is charmed with the sweetness of the honey, he may be destroyed by the deadly poison. So then, when you say that man is the image of the Divine nature, and that the devil dragged

---

[1] *Ex inanimis animalia, ex insensibilibus sensibilia nascuntur* (Petschenig). The text of Gazæus has *ex atomis animalia nascuntur*.

[2] Cf. Virgil's Georgics IV. Rufinus, on the Apostle's Creed (c. xi.) gives the same illustration of the Incarnation, and cf. with the passage in the text S. Basil Hom. in Hexaem, IX. ii.

this down and shattered it, and that God grieved over His image as an Emperor over his statue, you smear (so to speak) the lips of the cup with something sweet like honey, that men may drain the cup offered to them, and not perceive its deadliness, while they taste what is alluring. You put forward God's name, in order to speak falsehoods in the name of religion. You set holy things in the front, in order to persuade men of what is untrue: and by means of your confession of God you contrive to deny Him whom you are confessing. For who is there who does not see whither you are going? What you are contriving? You say indeed that God grieved over His image as an Emperor over his statue, and repaired the shattered image, and formed without generation a nature from the Virgin, like that of Adam who was born without generation, and raises up man's nature by man, for as by man came death, so also by man came the resurrection of the dead. So then with all your earnestness, with all your professions, you crafty plotter, you have managed by your smooth assertions, by naming God in the forefront, to come down to a (mere) man in the conclusion: and in the end you degrade Him to the condition of a mere man, from whom under colour of humility you have already taken away the glory of God. You say then that the Divine goodness has restored the image of God which the devil shattered and destroyed, for you say that He restores the shattered image. Now with what craft you say that He restores the shattered image: in order to persuade us that there was nothing more in Him, in whom the image is restored, than there was in the actual image, of which the restoration was brought about. And thus you make out that the Lord is only the same as Adam was: that the restorer of the image is nothing more than the actual destructible image. Finally in what follows you show what you are aiming and driving at, when you say that He formed without generation a nature from the Virgin like that of Adam, who was born without generation, and raises up man's nature by man. You maintain that the Lord Jesus Christ was in all respects like Adam: that the one was without generation, and the other without generation: the one a mere man, and the other a mere man. And thus you see that you have carefully guarded and provided against our thinking of the Lord Jesus Christ as in any way greater or better than Adam: since you have compared them together by the same standard, so that you would think that you detracted something from Adam's perfection, if you added anything more to Christ.

CHAPTER VII.

Heretics usually cover their doctrines with a cloak of holy Scripture.

"FOR as," you say, "by man came death, so by man came also the resurrection of the dead." Do you actually try to prove your wrong and impious notion by the witness of the Apostle? And do you bring the "chosen vessel" into disgrace by mixing him up with your wicked ideas? I mean, that, as you cannot understand the author of your Salvation, therefore the Apostle must be made out to have denied God. And yet, if you wanted to make use of Apostolic witnesses, why did you rest contented with one, and pass over all the others in silence? and why did you not at once add this: "Paul, an Apostle not of men neither by man, but by Jesus Christ:"[1] or this: "We speak wisdom among the perfect:" and presently: "Whom none," says he, "of the princes of this world knew; for had they known, they would not have crucified the Lord of glory."[2] Or this: "For in Him dwelleth all the fulness of the Godhead bodily."[3] And: "One Lord Jesus Christ through whom are all things."[4] Or do you partly agree, and partly disagree with the Apostle, and only receive him so far as in consequence of the Incarnation[5] he names Christ man, and repudiate him where he speaks of Him as God? For Paul does not deny that Jesus is man, but still he confesses that that man is God: and declares that to mankind the resurrection came by man in such a way that he shows that in that man God arose. For see whether he declares that He who rose was God, as he bears his witness that He who was crucified was the Lord of glory.

CHAPTER VIII.

The heretics attribute to Christ only the shadow of Divinity, and so assert that he is to be worshipped together with God but not as God.

BUT still in order to avoid thinking of the Lord Jesus as one of the whole mass of people, you have given to Him some glory, by attributing to Him honour as a saint, but not Deity as true man and true God. For what do you say? "God brought about the Lord's Incarnation. Let us honour the form of the Theodochos[6] together with God, as one form of Godhead, as a figure that cannot be severed from the Divine link, as an image of the un-

---

[1] Gal. i. 1.   [3] Col. ii. 9.   [5] *Dispensatio.*
[2] 1 Cor. ii. 6, 8. [4] 1 Cor. viii. 6.   [6] Cf. V. ii.

seen God." Above you said that Adam was the image of God, here you call Christ the image: the one you speak of as a statue, and the other also as a statue. But I suppose we ought for God's honour to be grateful to you, because you grant that the form of the Theodochos should be worshipped together with God: in which you wrong Him rather than honour Him. For in this you do not attribute to the Lord Jesus Christ the glory of Deity, but you deny it. By a subtle and wicked art you say that He is to be worshipped together with God in order that you may not have to confess that He is God, and by the very statement in which you seem deceitfully to join Him with God, you really sever Him from God. For when you blasphemously say that He is certainly not to be adored as God, but to be worshipped together with God, you thus grant to Him an union of nearness to Divinity, in order to get rid of the truth of His Divinity. Oh, you most wicked and crafty enemy of God, you want to perpetrate the crime of denying God under pretext of confessing Him. You say: Let us worship Him as a figure that cannot be severed from the Divine will, as an image of the unseen God. It is I suppose, then, owing to His kind acts that our Lord Jesus Christ has obtained among us honour as Creator and Redeemer. If then we were redeemed by Him from eternal destruction, in calling our Redeemer a figure we are endeavouring indeed to respond to His kindness and goodness, by a worthy service and a worthy allegiance, if we try to get rid of that glory which He did not refuse to bring low for our sakes.

CHAPTER IX.

How those are wrong who say that the birth of Christ was a secret, since it was clearly shown even to the patriarch Jacob.

BUT I suppose you excuse the degradation offered to the Lord by means of a subordinate honour, by the words "as the image of the secret God." By the fact that you term Him an image you compare Him to man's estate. In speaking of Him as the image of the secret God, you detract from the honour plainly due to Him. For "God," says David, " shall plainly come ; our God, and shall not keep silence."[1] And He surely came and did not keep silence, who before that He in His own person uttered anything after His birth, made known His advent by both earthly and heavenly witnesses alike, while the star points Him out, the magi

adore Him, and angels declare Him. What more do you want? His voice was yet silent on earth, and His glory was already crying aloud in heaven. Do you say then that God was and is secret in Him? But this was not the announcement of the Prophets, of the Patriarchs, aye and of the whole Law. For they did not say that He would be secret, whose coming they all foretold. You err in your wretched blindness, seeking grounds for blasphemy and not finding them. You say that He was secret even after His advent. I maintain that He was not secret even before His advent. For did the mystery of God to be born of a Virgin escape the knowledge of that celebrated Patriarch on whom the vision of God present with him conferred a title, whereby from the name of Supplanter he rose to the name of Israel? Who, when from the struggle with the man who wrestled with him he understood the mystery of the Incarnation yet to come, said, " I have seen God face to face, and my life is preserved."[2] What, I pray you, had he seen, for him to believe that he had seen God? Did God manifest Himself to him in the midst of thunder and lightning? or when the heavens were opened, did the dazzling face of the Deity show itself to him? Most certainly not: but rather on the contrary he saw a man and acknowledged a God. O truly worthy of the name he received, as with the eyes of the soul rather than of the body he earned the honour of a title given by God! He saw a human form wrestling with him, and declared that he saw God. He certainly knew that that human form was indeed God: for in that form in which God then appeared, in the selfsame form He was in very truth afterwards to come. Although why should we be surprised that so great a patriarch unhesitatingly believed what God Himself so plainly showed in His own Person to him, when he said, " I have seen God face to face and my life is preserved." How did God show to him so much of the presence of Deity, that he could say that the face of God was shown to him? For it seems that only a man had appeared to him, whom he had actually beaten in the struggle. But God was certainly bringing this about by precursory signs, that there might not be any one to disbelieve

[2] Gen. xxxii. 30.
The name Israel was in the 4th and 5th centuries commonly explained to mean the "man seeing God" as if it came from אִישׁ, רָאָה, and אֵל. S. Jerome (Quæst. in Genesim c. xxxii. ver. 27, 28) rejects this interpretation as forced, and prefers " a Prince with God." Hence the rendering in the A.V. " For as a prince hast thou power with God and with men and hast prevailed." This however is now generally rejected, and the right interpretation of the name appears to be " He who striveth with God." Cf. R. V. " For thou hast striven with God and with men, and hast prevailed." Cf. the Conferences, Pref. and V. xxiii. XII. xi.

that God was born of man, when already long before the Patriarch had seen God in human form.

CHAPTER X.

He collects more witnesses of the same fact.

BUT why am I lingering so long over one instance, as if many were wanting? For even then how could the fact that God was to come in the flesh escape the knowledge of men, when the Prophet said openly as if to all mankind of Him: "Behold your God;" and elsewhere: "Behold our God." And this: "God the mighty, the Father of the world to come, the Prince of Peace;" and: "of His kingdom there shall be no end." [1] But also when He had already come, could the fact of His having come escape the knowledge of those who openly confessed that He had come? Was Peter ignorant of the coming of God, when he said, "Thou art the Christ, the Son of the living God?" [2] Did not Martha know what she was saying or whom she believed in, when she said, "Yea, Lord, I have believed that Thou art the Christ, the Son of the living God, who art come into this world?" [3] And all those men, who sought from Him the cure of their sicknesses, or the restoration of their limbs, or the life of their dead, did they ask these things from man's weakness, or from God's omnipotence?

CHAPTER XI.

How the devil was forced by many reasons to the view that Christ was God.

FINALLY as for the devil himself, when he was tempting Him with every show of allurements, and every art of his wickedness, what was it that in his ignorance he suspected, or wanted to find out by tempting Him? Or what so greatly moved him, that he sought God under the humble form of man? Had he learned that by previous proofs? Or had he known of anyone who came as God in man's body? Most certainly not. But it was by the mighty evidence of signs, by mighty results of actions, by the words of the Truth Himself that he was driven to suspect and examine into this matter: inasmuch as he had already once heard from John: "Behold the Lamb of God, behold Him who taketh away the sin of the world." [4] And again from the same person: "I have need to be baptized of Thee, and comest Thou to me?" [5] The dove also which came down from heaven and stopped over the

Lord's head had made itself a clear and open proof of a God who declared Himself. The voice too which was sent from God not in riddles or figures had moved him, when it said: "Thou art My beloved Son, in Thee I am well pleased." [6] And though he saw a man outwardly in Jesus, yet he was searching for the Son of God, when he said: "If Thou art the Son of God, command that these stones be made bread." [7] Did the contemplation of the man drive away the devil's suspicions of His Divinity, so that owing to the fact that he saw a man, he did not believe that He could be God? Most certainly not. But what does he say? "If Thou art the Son of God, command that these stones be made bread." Certainly he had no doubt about the possibility of that, the existence of which he was examining into. His anxiety was about its truth. There was no security as to its impossibility.

CHAPTER XII.

He compares this notion and reasonable suspicion of the devil with the obstinate and inflexible idea of his opponents, and shows that this last is worse and more blasphemous than the former.

BUT he certainly knew that the Lord Jesus Christ was born of Mary: he knew that He was wrapped in swaddling clothes and laid in a manger: that His childhood was that of a poor person at the commencement of His human life; and His infancy without the proper accessories of cradles: further he did not doubt that He had true flesh, and was born a true man. And why did this seem to him not enough for him to be secure in? Why did he believe that He could not be God, whom he knew to be very man? Learn then, you wretched madman, learn, you lunatic, you cruel sinner, learn, I pray, even from the devil, to lessen your blasphemy. He said: "If Thou art the Son of God." You say: "Thou art not the Son of God." You deny what he asked about. No one was ever yet found but you, to outdo the devil in blasphemy. That which he confessed to be possible in the case of the Lord, you do not believe to have been possible.

CHAPTER XIII.

How the devil always retained this notion of Christ's Divinity (because of His secret working which he experienced) even up to His Cross and Death.

BUT perhaps he afterwards ceased and rested, and when his temptations were van-

---

[1] Isa. xl. 9; xxv. 9; ix. 6, 7. [3] S. John xi. 27. [5] S. Matt. iii. 14.
[2] S. Matt. xvi. 16. [4] S. John i. 29.

[6] S. Matt. iii. 17. [7] S. Luke iv. 3.

quished laid aside his suspicion because he found no result? Nay, it rather remained always in him, and even up to the very cross of the Lord the suspicion lasted in him and was increased by peculiar terrors. What need is there of anything further? Not even then did he cease to think of Him as the Son of God, after that he knew that such licence was granted to His persecutors against Him. But the crafty foe saw even in the midst of His bodily sufferings the signs of Divinity, and though he would have much preferred Him to be a (mere) man, was yet forced to suspect that He was God: for though he would have preferred to believe what he wanted, yet he was driven by surest proofs to that which he feared. And no wonder: for although he beheld Him spitted on, and scourged, and disgraced, and led to the Cross, yet he saw Divine powers abounding even in the midst of the indignities and wrongs; when the veil of the temple is rent, when the sun hides itself, the day is darkened, and all things feel the effects of the Passion: all things even, which know not God, acknowledge the work of Deity. And therefore the devil seeing this, and trembling, tried in every way to arrive at the knowledge of His Godhead, even at the very death of the manhood, saying in the person of those who crucified Him: "If He be the Son of God, let Him come down now from the Cross, and we will believe Him."[1] He certainly perceived that by His bodily Passion our Lord God was working out the redemption of man's salvation, and also that by it he was being destroyed and subdued, while we were being redeemed and saved. And so the enemy of mankind wanted by every means and every wile to defeat that which he knew was being done for the redemption of all men. "If," he says, "He be the Son of God, let Him come down now from the Cross and we will believe Him:" on purpose that the Lord might be moved by the reproach of the words, and destroy the mystery, while He avenged the wrong. You see then that the Lord even when hanging on the Cross was termed the Son of God. You see that they suspect the fact to which they refer. And so do you learn, as I said above, even from His persecutors, even from the devil, to believe on the Son of God. Who ever came up to the unbelief of the devil? Who went beyond it? *He* suspected that He was the Son of God even when He endured death. *You* deny it even when He has risen. *He* suspected that He was God, from whom He hid Himself. *You*, to whom He has proved it, deny it.

CHAPTER XIV.

He shows how heretics pervert holy Scripture, by replying to the argument drawn from the Apostle's words, "Without father, without mother," etc.: Heb. vii.

You then make use of the holy Scriptures against God, and try to bring His own witnesses against Him. But how? Truly so as to become a false accuser not only of God, but of the evidences themselves. Nor indeed is it wonderful that, as you cannot do what you want, you only do what you can: as you cannot turn the sacred witnesses against God, you do what you can, and pervert them. For you say: Then Paul tells a lie, when he says of Christ: "Without mother, without genealogy."[2] I ask you, of whom do you think that Paul said this? Of the Son and Word of God, or of the Christ, whom you separate from the Son of God, and blasphemously assert to be a mere man? If of the Christ, whom you maintain to be a mere man, how could a man be born without a mother and without a genealogy on the mother's side? But if of the Word of God and Son of God — what can we make of it, when the same Apostle, your own witness, as you impiously imagine, testifies in the same place and by the same witness, that He whom you assert to be without mother, was also without father; saying, "Without father, without mother, without genealogy"? It follows then that if you use the Apostle's witness, since you assert that the Son of God was "without mother," you must also be guilty of the blasphemy that He was "without father." You see then in what a downfall of impiety you have landed yourself, in your eagerness for your perversity and wickedness, so that, while you say that the Son of God had not a mother, you must also deny Him a Father — a thing which no one yet since the world began, except perhaps a madman, ever did. And this, whether with greater wickedness or folly, I hardly know; for what is more foolish and silly than to give the name of Son and to try to keep back the name of Father? But you say I don't keep it back, I don't deny it. And what madness then drove you to quote that passage, where, while you say that He had no mother, you must seem also to deny to Him a Father? For as in the same passage He is said to be without mother and also without father, it follows that if it can be understood that there He is without mother, in the same way in which we understand that He is without mother, we must also believe that He is without father. But that hasty craze for deny-

---

ing God did not see this; and when it quoted mutilated, what was written entire, it failed to see that the shameless and palpable lie could be refuted by laying open the contents of the sacred volume. O foolish blasphemy, and madness! which, while it failed to see what it ought to follow, had not the wit to see even what could be read: as if, because it could get rid of its own intelligence, it could get rid of the power of reading from everybody else, or as if everybody would lose their eyes in their heads for reading, because it had lost the eyes of the mind. Hear then, you heretic, the passage you have garbled: hear in full and completely, what you quoted mutilated and hacked about. The Apostle wants to make clear to every one the twofold birth of God — and in order to show how the Lord was born in the Godhead and in flesh, he says, "Without father, without mother:" for the one belongs to the birth of Divinity, the other to that of the flesh. For as He was begotten in His Divine nature "without mother," so He is in the body "without father:" and so though He is neither without father nor without mother, we must believe in Him "without father and without mother." For if you regard Him as He is begotten of the Father, He is without mother: if, as born of His mother, He is without father. And so in each of these births He has one: in both together He is without each: for the birth of Divinity had no need of mother, and for the birth of His body, He was Himself sufficient, without a father. Therefore says the Apostle "Without mother, without genealogy."

CHAPTER XV.

How Christ could be said by the Apostle to be without genealogy.

How does he say that the Lord was "without genealogy," when the Gospel of the Evangelist Matthew begins with the Saviour's genealogy, saying: "The book of the generations of Jesus Christ, the Son of David, the Son of Abraham"?[1] Therefore according to the Evangelist He has a genealogy, and according to the Apostle, He has not: for according to the Evangelist, He has it on the mother's side, according to the Apostle He has not, as He springs from the Father. And so the Apostle well says: "Without father, without mother, without genealogy:" and where he lays down that He was begotten without mother, there also he records that He was without genealogy. And thus as regards both the nativities of

the Lord, the writings of the Evangelist and of the Apostle agree together. For according to the Evangelist He has a genealogy "without father," when born in the flesh: and according to the Apostle, the Lord has not, when begotten in His Divine nature "without mother;" as Isaiah says: "But who shall declare His generation?"[2]

CHAPTER XVI.

He shows that like the devil when tempting Christ, the heretics garble and pervert holy Scripture.

WHY then, you heretic, did you not in this way quote the whole and entire passage which you had read? So you see that the Apostle laid down that the Lord was "without mother" in the same way in which he laid down that He was born "without father:" that we might know that He is "without mother" in the same way in which we understand Him to be "without father." And as it is impossible to believe Him to be altogether "without father," so we cannot understand that He is altogether "without mother." Why then, you heretic, did you not in this way quote what you had read in the Apostle, entire and unmutilated? But you insert part, and omit part; and garble the words of truth in order that you may be able to build up your false notions by your wicked act. I see who was your master. We must believe that you had *his* instruction, whose example you are following. For so the devil in the gospel when tempting the Lord said: "If Thou art the Son of God, cast Thyself down. For it is written that He shall give His angels charge concerning Thee to keep Thee in all Thy ways."[3] And when he had said this, he left out the context and what belongs to it; viz., "Thou shalt walk upon the asp and the basilisk: and thou shalt trample under foot the lion and the dragon."[4] Surely he cunningly quoted the previous verse and left out the latter: for he quoted the one to deceive Him: he held his tongue about the latter to avoid condemning himself. For he knew that he himself was signified by the asp and basilisk, the lion and dragon in the Prophet's words. So then you also bring forward a part and omit a part; and quote the one to deceive; and omit the other for fear lest if you were to quote the whole, you might condemn your own deception. But it is now time to pass on to further matters, for by dwelling too long on particular points, as we are led to do by the desire of giving a full answer, we exceed the limits even of a longish book.

---

[1] S. Matt. i. 1.   [2] Isa. liii. 8.   [3] S. Luke iv. 9, 10.   [4] Ps. xc. (xci.) 13.

CHAPTER XVII.

That the glory and honour of Christ is not to be ascribed to the Holy Ghost in such a way as to deny that it proceeds from Christ Himself, as if all that excellency, which was in Him, was another's and proceeded from another source.

You say then in another discussion, nay rather in another blasphemy of yours, "and He separated[1] the Spirit from the Divine nature Who created His humanity. For Scripture says that that which was born of Mary is of the Holy Ghost.[2] Who also filled with righteousness (justitia) that which was created: for it says 'He appeared in the flesh, was justified in the Spirit.'[3] Again: Who made Him also to be feared by the devils: 'For I,' He says, 'by the Spirit of God cast out devils.'[4] Who also made His flesh a temple. 'For I saw His spirit descending like a dove and abiding upon Him.'[5] Again: Who granted to Him His ascension into Heaven. For it says, "Giving a commandment to the apostles whom He had chosen, by the Holy Ghost He was taken up."[6] Finally that it was He who granted such glory to Christ." The whole of your blasphemy then consists in this: that Christ had nothing of Himself: nor did He, a mere man, as you say, receive anything from the Word, i.e., the Son of God; but everything in Him was the gift of the Spirit. If then we can show that all that which you refer to the Spirit, is His own, what remains but that we prove that He whom you therefore would have taken to be a man, because as you say everything which He has is another's, is therefore God, because everything which He has is His own? And indeed we will prove this not only by discussion and argument, but by the voice of Divinity Itself: for nothing testifies of God better than things divine. And because nothing knows itself better than the very glory of God, we believe nothing on the subject of God with greater right than those writings in which God Himself is His own witness. First then, as to this that you say that the Holy Spirit created His humanity; we might take it simply, if we could acknowledge that you had not brought it forward in the interests of unbelief. For neither do we deny that the flesh of the Lord was conceived by the Holy Ghost: but we assert that the body was conceived by the co-operation of the Holy Ghost in such a way that we can say that His Humanity[7] was created for Himself by the Son of God, as the Holy Spirit Itself says in holy Scripture, testifying that "Wisdom hath builded for Itself a house."[8] You see

then that that which was conceived by the Holy Ghost was built and perfected by the Son of God: not that the work of the Son of God is one thing, and the work of the Holy Ghost another: but that through the unity of the Godhead and glory the operation of the Spirit is the building of the Son of God; and the building of the Son of God is the co-operation of the Holy Ghost. And so we read not only that the Holy Ghost came upon the Virgin, but also that the power of the Most High overshadowed the Virgin; that since Wisdom Itself is the fulness of the Godhead, no one might doubt that when Wisdom built Itself a house all the fulness of the Godhead was present. But the wretched hardness of your blasphemy, while it tries to sever Christ from the Son of God, fails to see that it is entirely severing the nature of the Godhead from Itself. Unless perhaps you believe that the house is therefore built for Him by the Holy Ghost because He Himself was insufficient and incapable of building for Himself an house. But it is as absurd as it is wild, to believe that He, whom we believe to have created the whole universe of things heavenly and earthly by His will, was unable to build for Himself a body: especially as the power of the Holy Ghost is His power, and the Divinity and Glory of the Trinity are so united and inseparable, that we cannot think of anything at all in One Person of the Trinity, which can be separated from the fulness of the Godhead. Therefore when this is laid down and grasped; viz., that according to the faith of holy Scripture, when the Holy Ghost came upon (the Virgin) and the power of the Most High overshadowed her, Wisdom builded Itself an house; the rest of the slanders of your blasphemy come to nothing. For neither is it doubtful that He made all things by Himself and in Himself, in whose name and faith, the faith even of believers can do anything. For neither did He need the aid of another, as neither have they needed it, who have trusted in His power. And so as for your assertions that He was justified by the Spirit, and that the Spirit made Him to be feared by the devils, and that His flesh became the temple of the Holy Ghost, and that He was taken up by the Spirit into heaven, they are all blasphemous and wild: not because we are to believe that in all these things which He Himself did, the unity and co-operation of the Spirit was wanting — since the Godhead is never wanting to Itself, and the power of the Trinity was ever present in the Saviour's works — but because you will have it that the Holy Ghost gave assistance to the Lord Jesus Christ as if He had been feeble and powerless; and that He granted those

---

[1] *Separavit* (Petschenig). [4] S. Luke xi. 20. [7] *Hominem suum.*
[2] S. Matt. i. 20. [5] S. John i. 32. [8] Prov. ix. 1.
[3] 1 Tim. iii. 16. [6] Acts i. 2.

things to Him, which He was unable to procure for Himself. Learn then from sacred witnesses to believe God, and not to mingle falsehood with truth: for the subject does not admit it, and common sense abhors the idea of mingling the notions of the spirit of the devil with the witnesses that are Divine.

CHAPTER XVIII.

How we are to understand the Apostle's words: " He appeared in the flesh, was justified in the Spirit," etc.

For to begin with this assertion of yours that the Spirit filled with righteousness (justitia) what was created, and your attempts to prove this by the evidence of the Apostle, where he says that " He appeared in the flesh, was justified in the Spirit," you make each statement in an unsound sense and wild spirit. For you make this assertion; viz., that you will have it that He was filled with righteousness by the Spirit, in order to show how He was void of righteousness, as you assert that the being filled with it was given to Him. And as for your use of the evidence of the Apostle on this matter, you garble the arrangement and meaning of the sacred passage. For the Apostle's statement is not as you have quoted it, mutilated and spoilt. For what says the Apostle? "And evidently great is the mystery of Godliness, which was manifested in the flesh, was justified in the Spirit." [1] You see then that the Apostle declared that the mystery or sacrament of Godliness was justified. For he was not so forgetful of his own words and teaching as to say that He was void of righteousness, whom he had always proclaimed as righteousness, saying: "Who was made unto us righteousness and sanctification and redemption." [2] Elsewhere also he says: " But ye were washed, but ye were justified, but ye were sanctified in the name of our Lord Jesus Christ." [3] How far then from Him was it to need being filled with righteousness, as He Himself filled all things with righteousness, and for His glory to be without righteousness, whose very name justifies all things. You see then how foolish and wild are your blasphemies, since you are trying to take away from our Lord what is ever shed forth by Him upon all believers in such a way that still in its continuous supply it is never diminished.

CHAPTER XIX.

That it was not only the Spirit, but Christ Himself also who made Him to be feared.

You say too that the Spirit made Him to be feared by the devils. To reject and refute which, even though the horrible character of the utterance is enough, we will still add some instances. Tell me, I pray, you who say that the fact that the devils feared Him was not His own doing but another's, and who will have it that this was not His own power but a gift, how was it that even His name had that power, of which He Himself was, according to you, void? How was it that in His name devils were cast out, sick persons were cured, dead men were raised? For the Apostle Peter says to that lame man who was sitting at the beautiful gate of the Temple: " In the name of Jesus Christ arise and walk." [4] And again in the city of Joppa to the man who had been lying on his bed paralysed for eight years he says, " Æneas, may the Lord Jesus Christ heal thee: arise and make thy bed for thyself." [5] Paul too says to the pythonical spirit: " I charge thee in the name of Jesus Christ come out of her," and the devil came out of her. [6] But understand from this how utterly alien this weakness was from our Lord: for I do not call even those weak, whom He by His name made strong, since we never heard of any devil or infirmity able to resist any of the apostles since the Lord's resurrection. How then did the Spirit make Him to be feared, who made others to be feared? Or was He in Himself weak, whose faith even through the instrumentality of others reigned over all things? Finally those men who received power from God, never used that power as if it were their own: but referred the power to Him from whom they received it: for the power itself could never have any force except through the name of Him who gave it. And so both the apostles and all the servants of God never did any thing in their own name, but in the name and invocation of Christ: for the power itself derived its force from the same source as its origin, and could not be given through the instrumentality of the ministers, unless it had come from the Author. You then — who say that the Lord was the same as one of His servants (for as the apostles had nothing but what they received from their Lord, so you make out that the Lord Himself had nothing

---

[1] 1 Tim. iii. 16. [2] 1 Cor. i. 30. [3] 1 Cor. vi. 11. [4] Acts iii. 6. [5] Acts ix. 34. [6] Acts xvi. 18.

but what He received from the Spirit; and thus you make out that everything that He had, He had not as Lord, but had received it as a servant), do you tell me then, how it was that He used this power as His own and not as something which He had received? For what do we read of Him? He says to the paralytic: "Arise, take up thy bed, and go. to thine house."[1] And again to a father who pleads on behalf of his child, He says: "Go thy way: thy son liveth."[2] And where an only son of his mother was being carried forth for burial, "Young man," He says, "I say unto thee, Arise."[3] Did He then, like those who received power from God, ask that power might be given to Him for performing these things by the invocation of the Divine Name? Why did He not Himself work by the name of the Spirit, just as the apostles wrought by His Name? Finally, what does the gospel itself state about Him? It says: "He was teaching them as one that had authority, and not like the Scribes and Pharisees."[4] Or do you make out that He was so proud and haughty as to put to the credit of His own might the power which (according to you) He had received from God? But what do we make of the fact that the power never submitted to His servants, except through the name of its author, and could have no efficacy if the actor claimed any of it as his own?

CHAPTER XX.

He tries by stronger and weightier arguments to destroy that notion.

BUT why are we so long dealing with your wild blasphemy, with arguments that are plain indeed but still slight? Let us hear God Himself speaking to His disciples: "Heal the sick, raise the dead, cleanse the lepers, cast out devils."[5] And again: "In My name," He says, "ye shall cast out devils."[6] Had He any need of Another's name for the exercise of His power, who made His own name to be a power? But what is still added? "Behold," He says, "I have given you power to tread upon serpents and scorpions and upon all the power of the enemy."[7] He Himself says that He was gentle, as indeed He was, and humble in heart. And how was it that as regards the greatest possible power, He commanded others

to work in His own name, if He Himself worked in Another's name? Or did He give to others, as if it were His own, what He Himself, according to you, did not possess, unless He received it from Another? But tell me, which of the saints receiving power from God, so worked? Or would not Peter have been thought a lunatic, or John a madman, or Paul out of his mind, if they had said to any sick folk: "In our name arise;" or to the lame: "In our name walk;" or to the dead: "In our name live;" or this to some: "We give you power to tread upon serpents and scorpions and upon all the power of the enemy"? You see then from this your madness: for just as these words are mad if they spring from man's assurance, so are you utterly mad if you do not see that they come from Divine power. For you must admit one of two alternatives; either that man could possess and give Divine power, or at any rate if no man can do this, that He who could do it, was God. For no one can grant of His liberality Divine power, except Him who possesses it by nature.

CHAPTER XXI.

That it must be ascribed equally to Christ and the Holy Ghost that His flesh and Humanity became the temple of God.

BUT there follows in your blasphemy that His flesh was made a temple of the Holy Ghost, for this reason, that John has said: "For I saw the Spirit descending from heaven and abiding upon Him."[8] For you try to support even this wild statement of yours by Scriptural authority: wherefore let us see whether this sacred authority has said that which you say. "For I saw," it says, "the Spirit descending like a dove, and abiding upon Him." Discern here, if you can, which is the more powerful, which greater, which more to be honoured? He who descended, or He to whom the descent was made? He who brought down the honour, or He to whom the honour was brought? Where do you find in this passage that the Spirit made His flesh a temple? or wherein does it lessen the honour of God, if God Himself descended to show God to mankind? For certainly we ought not to think that He is less whose high estate was pointed out, than He who pointed out His high estate. But away with the thought of believing or making any separation in the Godhead: for one and the same Godhead

---

[1] S. Matt. ix. 6.   [4] S. Matt. vii. 29.   [6] S. Mark xvi. 17.
[2] S. John iv. 50.   [5] S. Matt. x. 8.   [7] S. Luke x. 19.
[3] S. Luke vii. 14.

[8] S. John i. 32.

and equal power shut out altogether the wicked notion of inequality. And so in this matter, where there is the Person of the Father and of the Son and of the Holy Ghost, and where it is the Son of God to whom the descent is made, the Spirit who descends, the Father who gives His witness, no one had more honour, and no one received any slight, but it all redounds equally to the fulness of the Godhead, for each Person of the Trinity contains within Himself the glory of the whole Trinity. And so nothing further needs to be said, except only to show the rise and origin of your blasphemy. For thorns and thistles springing up from the roots produce shoots of their own nature, and from their character show their origin. So then you also, a thorny offshoot of the Pelagian heresy, show in germ just the same that your father is said to have had in the root. For he[1] (as Leporius his follower said) declared that our Lord was made the Christ by His baptism : you say that at His baptism He was made the temple of God by the Spirit. The words are not altogether identical : but the wrong-headedness is altogether the same.

CHAPTER XXII.

That the raising up of Christ into heaven is not to be ascribed to the Spirit alone.

But you add this also to those impieties of yours mentioned above ; viz., that the Spirit granted to the Lord His ascension into heaven : showing by this blasphemous notion of yours that you believe that the Lord Jesus Christ was so weak and powerless that had not the Spirit raised Him up to heaven, you fancy that He would still at this day have been on earth. But to prove this assertion you bring forward a passage of Scripture : for you say " Giving commands to the apostles whom He had chosen, by the Holy Ghost He was raised up."[2] What am I to call you? What am I to think of you who by corrupting the sacred writings contrive that their evidences should not have the force of evidences? A new kind of audacity, which strives by its impious arguments to manage that truth may seem to confirm falsehood. For the Acts of the Apostles does not say what you make out. For what says the Scripture? " What Jesus began to do and to teach until the day in which giving charge to the apostles whom He

had chosen by the Holy Ghost, He was taken up." Which is an instance of Hyperbaton, and must be understood in this way : what Jesus began to do and to teach until the day in which he was taken up, giving charge to the apostles whom He had chosen by the Holy Ghost ; so that we ought not perhaps to have to give you any further answer in this matter than that of the passage itself, for the entire passage ought to be sufficient for the full truth, if the mutilation of it was available for your falsehood. But still, you, who think that our Lord Jesus Christ could not have ascended into heaven, unless He had been raised up by the Spirit ; tell me how is it that He Himself says " No one hath ascended into heaven but He who came down from heaven, even the Son of man who is in heaven "?[3] Confess then how foolish and absurd your notion is that He could not ascend into heaven, who is said, although He had descended into earth, never to have been absent from heaven : and say whether to leave the regions below and ascend into heaven was possible for Him to whom it was easy when still on earth, ever to continue in heaven. But what is that which He Himself says : " I ascend unto my Father."[4] Did He imply that in this ascension there would be the intervention of Another's help, who by the very fact that He said He would ascend, shows the efficacy of His own power? David also says of the Ascension of the Lord : " God ascended with a merry noise, the Lord with the sound of the trumpet : "[5] He clearly explained the glory of Him who ascends by the power of the ascension.

CHAPTER XXIII.

He continues the same argument to show that Christ had no need of another's glory as He had a glory of His own.

But to end let us see the addition with which you sum up your preceding blasphemies. Your words are, " Who gave such[6] glory to Christ?" You name glory in order to degrade Him. For by the assertion that the Lord was endowed with glory, in saying that He received it you blasphemously imply that He stood in need of it. For your perverse notion suggests that the generosity of the giver shows the need of the receiver. O miserable impiety of yours! and where is that which Divinity itself once foretold of the Lord Jesus Christ ascending into heaven? Saying: " Lift up your heads, and the King of glory

---

[1] *Ille enim ;* viz., Pelagius. This appears to be the true reading, though one MS. followed by Gazæus has *Leporius ille enim ;* a reading which would involve the supposition that there were two persons of the name of Leporius, master and scholar.
[2] Acts i. 2.

[3] S. John iii. 13.   [5] Ps. xlvi. (xlvii.) 6.
[4] S. John xx. 17.   [6] *Tantam* Petschenig. *Tamen* Gazæus.

shall come in."[1] And when He (after the fashion of Divine utterances) had made answer to Himself as if in the character of an inquirer: "Who is the King of glory?" at once He adds: "The Lord strong and mighty, the Lord mighty in battle:" showing under the figure of a battle fought, the victory of the Lord in His triumph. Then when, to complete the exposition of it, He had repeated the words of the utterance quoted above, He showed by the following conclusion the majesty of the Lord as He entered heaven, saying "The Lord of hosts, He is the King of glory." On purpose that the fact of His taking a body might not interfere with the glory of His mighty Divinity, He taught that the same Person was Lord of hosts and King of heavenly glory, whom He had previously proclaimed Victor in the battle below. Go now[2] and say that the glory was given to the Lord, when both prophecy has said that He was the King of glory, and He Himself also has testified of Himself as follows: "When the Son of man shall come in His glory."[3] Refute it, if you can, and contradict this; viz., that whereas He testifies that He has glory of His own, you say that He has received Another's. Although we maintain that He has His own glory, in such a way that we do not deny that His very property of glory is common to Him with the Father and the Holy Ghost. For whatever God possesses belongs to the Godhead: and the kingdom of glory belongs to the Son of God in such a way that it is not kept back from belonging to the entire Godhead.

CHAPTER XXIV.

He supports this doctrine by the authority of the blessed Hilary.

BUT it is quite time to finish the book, aye and the whole work, if I may however add the sayings of a few saintly men and illustrious priests, to support by the faith of the present day what we have already proved by the authority of holy Scripture. Hilary, a man endowed with all virtues and graces, and famous for his life as well as for his eloquence, who also, as a teacher of the churches and a priest, advanced not only by his own merits but also by the progress of others, and remained so steadfast during the storms of persecution that through the fortitude of his unconquered faith

he attained the dignity of being a Confessor,[4] —he testifies in the First book on the faith that the Lord Jesus Christ, Very God of Very God, was both begotten before the world, and afterwards born as man. Again in the Second book: "One only Begotten God grew in the womb of the holy Virgin into the form of a human body; He who contains all things, and in whose power all things are, is brought forth according to the law of human birth." Again in the same book: "An angel is witness that He who is born is God with us." Again in the Tenth book: "We have taught the mystery of God born as man by the birth from the Virgin." Again in the same book: "For when God was born as man, He was not born on purpose not to remain God."[5] Again in the same writer's preface to his exposition of the gospel according to Matthew:[6] "For to begin with it was needful for us that for our sakes the only Begotten God should be known to be born as man." Again in what follows: "that besides being God, He should be born as man, which He was not yet." Again in the same place: "Then this third matter was fitting: that as God was born as man in the world" etc.: Here are a few passages out of any number. But still you see even from these which we have quoted, how clearly and plainly he asserts that God was born of Mary. And where then is this saying of yours: "The creature could not bring forth the Creator: and that which is born of the flesh, is flesh." It would take too long to quote passages bearing on this point from each separate writer. I must try to enumerate them rather than to explain them: for they will sufficiently explain themselves.

CHAPTER XXV.

He shows that Ambrose agrees with S. Hilary.

AMBROSE, that illustrious priest of God, who never leaving the Lord's hand, ever shone like a jewel upon the finger of God, thus speaks in his book to the Virgins: "My brother is white and ruddy.[7] White because He is the glory of the Father: ruddy because He was born of the Virgin. But remember that in Him the tokens of Divinity are of longer standing than the mysteries of the body. For He did not

---

[1] Ps. xxiii. (xxiv.) 7.
[2] *I nunc* Petschenig. The text is however doubtful. One MS. reading *In hunc*, and another *jam nunc*.
[3] S. Matt. xxv. 31.

[4] S. Hilary of Poictiers (*ob.* A.D. 368). The reference is of course to his banishment to Phrygia by the Emperor Constantius in 356, because of his resolute defence of the Nicene faith against Arianism.
[5] De Trinitate II. xxv., xxvii.; X. vii.
[6] This Preface to Hilary's work on S. Matthew is now lost, though the commentary itself still exists. See Opera S. Hilarii Pictav: (Verona, 1730). Vol. i. 658.
[7] Cf. Cant. v. 10 (LXX.).

begin to exist from the Virgin, but He who was already in existence, came into the Virgin."[1] Again on Christmas Day: "See the miracle of the mother of the Lord: A Virgin conceived, a Virgin brought forth. She was a Virgin when she conceived, a Virgin when with child, a Virgin after the birth. As is said in Ezekiel: "And the gate was shut and not opened, because the Lord passed through it."[2] A splendid Virginity, and wondrous fruitfulness! The Lord of the world is born: and there are no cries from her who brought Him forth. The womb is left empty, and a true child is born, and yet the Virginity is not destroyed. It was right that when God was born the power of chastity should become greater, and that her purity should not be violated by the going forth of Him who had come to heal what was corrupt."[3] Again in his exposition of the gospel according to Luke he says that "one was especially chosen, to bring forth God, who was espoused to an husband."[4] He certainly declares that God was born of the Virgin. He calls Mary the mother of God. And where is that awful and execrable utterance of yours asking how can she be the mother of one of a different nature from her own. But if she is called mother by them, it is the human nature which was born not the Godhead. So, that illustrious teacher of the faith says both that she who bare Him was human, and that He who was born is God: and yet that this is no reason for unbelief, but only a miracle of faith.

CHAPTER XXVI.

He adds to the foregoing the testimony of S. Jerome.

JEROME, the Teacher of the Catholics, whose writings shine like divine lamps throughout the whole world, says in his book to Eustochium: "The Son of God for our salvation was made the Son of man. He waits ten months in the womb to be born: and He, in whose hand the world is held, is contained in a narrow manger."[5] Again in his commentary on Isaiah: "For the Lord of hosts, who is the King of glory, Himself descended into the Virgin's womb, and entered in and went forth from the East Gate which is ever shut."[6] Of whom Gabriel says to the Virgin: "The Holy Ghost shall come upon thee, and the power of the Most High shall overshadow

thee. Wherefore that holy thing which shall be born of thee shall be called the Son of God." And in Proverbs: "Wisdom hath builded herself an house."[7] Compare this if you please with your doctrine or rather your blasphemy, in which you assert that God is the Creator of the months, and was not an offspring of months. For lo, Jerome, a man of the greatest knowledge and also of the most pure and approved doctrine testifies almost in the very words in which you deny that the Son of God was an offspring of months, that He was an offspring of months. For he says that He waits ten months in the womb to be born. But perhaps the authority of this man seems a mere nothing to you. You may take it that every one says the same and in the same words, for whoever does not deny that the Son of God is the offspring of the Virgin, admits that He is the offspring of months.

CHAPTER XXVII.

To the foregoing he adds Rufinus and the blessed Augustine.

RUFINUS also, a Christian philosopher, with no mean place among Ecclesiastical Doctors testifies as follows of the Lord's Nativity in his Exposition of the Creed. "For the Son of God," he says, "is born of a Virgin, not chiefly allied to the flesh alone, but generated in the soul which is the medium between the flesh and God."[8] Does he witness obscurely that God was born of man? Augustine the priest[9] of Hippo Regiensis says: "That men might be born of God, God was first born of them: for Christ is God. And Christ when born of men only required a mother on earth, because He always had a Father in heaven, being born of God through whom we are made, and also born of a woman, through whom we might be re-created."[10] Again, in this place: "And the Word was made flesh and dwelt among us. Why then need you wonder that men are born of God? Notice how God Himself was born of men." Again in his Epistle to Volusianus: "But Moses himself and the rest of the prophets most truly prophesied of Christ the Lord, and gave Him great glory: they declared that He would come not as one like themselves, nor merely greater in the same sort of power of working miracles, but clearly as the Lord God of all, and as made man for men. Who therefore Himself also willed to do such things as they

---

[1] S. Ambrose. De Virg. Lib. i. xlvi.   [2] Ezek. xliv. 2.
[3] These words are not found in any extant writing of S. Ambrose, but something very like them occurs in S. Augustine's Sixth Sermon in Natali Domini.
[4] In Lucam II. i.   [5] Ep. xxii. Ad Eustochium.
[6] Cf. Ezek. xliv. 2.

[7] Book III. c. vii.   [8] Rufinus in Symb. c. xiii.
[9] There is no authority for the reading of Cuyck and Gazæus "*Magnus Sacerdos.*" On the coldness with which Augustine is here spoken of see the Introduction, p. 191. Note.
[10] August. Tract. II. in Johan. xv.

did to prevent the absurdity of His not doing Himself those things which He did through them. But still it was right also for Him to do something special; viz., to be born of a Virgin, to rise from the dead, to ascend into heaven. And if anyone thinks that this is too little for God, I know not what more he can look for.[1]

CHAPTER XXVIII.

As he is going to produce the testimony of Greek or Eastern Bishops, he brings forward in the first place S. Gregory Nazianzen.

BUT perhaps because those whom we have enumerated came from different parts of the world, their authority may seem to you less valuable. An absurd thing, indeed, because faith is not interfered with by place, and we have to consider *what* a man is, not *where*: especially since religion unites all together, and those who are in the one faith may be also known to be in the one body. But still we will bring forward for you some, whom you cannot despise, even from the East. Gregory, that most grand light of knowledge and doctrine, who though he has been for some time dead, yet still lives in authority and faith, and though he has been for some time removed in the body from the Churches, yet has not forsaken them in word and authority. "When then," he says, "God had come forth from the Virgin, in that human nature which He had taken, as He existed in one out of two which are the opposite of each other; viz., flesh and spirit, the one is taken into God, the other exalts into the grace of Deity.[2] O new and unheard of intermingling! O marvellous and exquisite union! He who was, came to be, and the Creator is created: and He who is infinite is embraced by the soul which is the medium between God and the flesh: and He who makes all rich, is made poor." Again he says of the Epiphany: "But what happens? What is done concerning us and for us? There is brought about some new and unheard of change of natures and God is made man." Again in this passage:[3] "The Son of God began to be also the Son of man, not being changed from what He was, for He is un-

changeable, but taking to Himself what He was not: for He is pitiful so that He, who could not be embraced, can now be embraced." You see how grandly and nobly he asserts the majesty of His Godhead so that He may bring in the condescension of the Incarnation: for that admirable teacher of the faith knew well that of all the blessings which God granted to us at His coming into the world this was the chief, without diminishing in any way His glory. For whatever God gave to man, ought to increase the love of Him in us, and not to lessen the honour which we give to Him.

CHAPTER XXIX.

In the next place he puts the authority of S. Athanasius.

ATHANASIUS also, priest of the city of Alexandria, a splendid instance of constancy and virtue, whom the storm of heretical persecution tested without crushing him: whose life was always like a clear glass, and who had almost obtained the reward of martyrdom before attaining the dignity of confessorship: Let us see what was his view of the Lord Jesus Christ and the mother of the Lord. "This then," he says, "is the mind and stamp of Holy Scripture, as we have often said; viz., that in one and the same Saviour two things have to be understood: (1) that He was ever God, and is Son, Word, and Light, and Wisdom of the Father, and (2) that afterwards for our sakes He took flesh of the Virgin Mary the Theotocos, and was made man."[4] Again after some other matter: "Many then were saints and clean from sin: Jeremiah also was sanctified from the womb, and John, while still in the womb leapt for joy at the voice of Mary the Theotocos."[5] He certainly says that God, the Son of God, who (to declare the faith of all in his words) is "the Word, and Light and Wisdom of the Father," took flesh for our sakes; and therefore he calls the Virgin Mary Theotocos, because she was the Mother of God.

CHAPTER XXX.

He adds also S. John Chrysostom.

As for John the glory of the Episcopate of Constantinople, whose holy life obtained

---

[1] Ep. cxxxvii. c. 4.

[2] *Aliud in Deum adsumitur, aliud in Deitatis gratiam præstat.* So Petschenig edits. The text of Gazæus has *aliud Deitatis gratia præstat.*

[3] Greg. Nazianz. Oratio xxxviii. The Greek of the passage which Cassian translates is as follows: προελθὼν δὲ Θεὸς μετὰ τῆς προσλήψεως ἐν ἐκ δύο τῶν ἐναντίων, σαρκὸς καὶ πνεύματος· ὧν τὸ μὲν ἐθέωσε τὸ δὲ ἐθεώθη, ὦ τῆς καινῆς μίξεως, ὦ τῆς παραδόξου κράσεως, ὁ ὢν γίνεται καὶ ὁ ἄκτιστος κτίζεται καὶ ὁ ἀχώρητος χωρεῖται διὰ μέσης ψυχῆς νοερᾶς μεσιτευούσης θεότητι καὶ σαρκὸς παχύτητι, καὶ ὁ πλουτίζων πτωχεύει. Oratio xxxix. Τί γίνεται καὶ τί τὸ μέγα περὶ ἡμᾶς μυστήριον; καινοτομοῦνται φύσεις καὶ Θεὸς ἄνθρωπος γίνεται . . . καὶ ὁ υἱὸς τοῦ Θεοῦ δέχεται καὶ υἱὸς ἀνθρώπου γενέσθαι τε καὶ κληθῆναι, οὐχ ὃ ἦν μεταβαλών, ἄτρεπτον γὰρ, ἀλλ᾽ ὃ οὐκ ἦν προσλαβών, φιλάνθρωπος γάρ, ἵνα χωρηθῇ ὁ ἀχώρητος.

[4] See the orations against the Arians IV. The Greek is as follows: Σκοπὸς τοίνυν οὗτος καὶ χαρακτὴρ τῆς γραφῆς, ὡς πολλάκις εἴπομεν, διπλῆν εἶναι τὴν περὶ τοῦ σωτῆρος ἀπαγγελίαν ἐν αὐτῇ, ὅτι τε ἀεὶ Θεὸς ἦν καὶ ἔστιν ὁ υἱός, λόγος ὢν καὶ ἀπαύγασμα καὶ σοφία τοῦ πατρος, καὶ ὅτι ὕστερον δι᾽ ἡμᾶς σάρκα λαβὼν ἐκ παρθένου τῆς θεοτόκου Μαρίας ἄνθρωπος γέγονεν.

[5] *Ibid.* πολλοὶ γοῦν ἅγιοι γεγόνασι καὶ καθαροὶ πάσης ἁμαρτίας· Ἱερεμίας δὲ καὶ ἐκ κοιλίας ἡγιάσθη καὶ Ἰωάννης ἔτι κυοφορούμενος ἐσκίρτησεν ἐν ἀγαλλιάσει ἐπὶ τῇ φωνῇ τῆς Θεοτόκου Μαρίας.

the reward of martyrdom without any show of Gentile persecution, hear what he thought and taught on the Incarnation of the Son of God: "And Him," he says, "whom if He had come in unveiled Deity neither the heaven nor the earth nor the sea nor any other creature could have contained, the pure womb of a Virgin bore."[1] This man's faith and doctrine then, even if you ignore that of others, you ought to follow and hold, as out of love and affection for him the pious people chose you as their Bishop. For when it took you for its priest from the Church of Antioch, from which it had formerly chosen him, it believed that it would receive in you all that it had lost in him.[2] Did not, I ask you, all these things almost with prophetic spirit say all these things in order to confound your blasphemies. For you declare that our Lord and Saviour Christ is not God: they declare that Christ the Lord is Very God. You blasphemously assert that Mary is Christotocos not Theotocos: they do not deny that she is Christotocos, while they acknowledge her as Theotocos. Not merely the substance but the words also are opposed to your blasphemies: that we may clearly see that an impregnable bulwark was formerly prepared by God against your blasphemies, to break on the wall of truth ready prepared, the force of the heretical attack which was at some time or other to come. And you, O you most wicked and shameless contaminator of an illustrious city, you disastrous and deadly plague of a Catholic and holy people, do you dare to stand and teach in the Church of God, and with your wild and blasphemous words slander the priests of an ever unbroken faith and Catholic confession, and say that the people of the city of Constantinople are in error through the fault of their earlier teachers? Are you then the corrector of former Bishops, the accuser of ancient priests, are you better than Gregory, more approved than Nectarius, greater than John,[3] and all the other Bishops of Eastern cities who, though not of the same renown as those whom I have enumerated, were yet of the same faith? which, as far as the matter in hand is concerned, is enough:

---

[1] The passage has not been identified with any now extant in the writings of S. Chrysostom.
[2] S. Chrysostom had been taken from Antioch for the Bishopric of Constantinople: and after the death of Sisinnius in 426, as there was so much rivalry and party spirit displayed at Constantinople, the Emperor determined that none of that Church should fill the vacant see, but sent for Nestorius from Antioch, where he had already gained a great reputation for eloquence (cf. Socrates H. E. VII. xxix.). It is to the fact that both S. Chrysostom and Nestorius came from the same city that Cassian alludes in the text.
[3] The reference is to Gregory Nazianzen, Bishop of Constantinople from 379 to 381 when he retired in the interests of peace; to Nectarius who was chosen to succeed him, and occupied the post from 381 to 397; and to his successor, S. John Chrysostom, 397 to 404.

for when it is a question of the faith, all are as good as the best in so far as they agree with the best.

CHAPTER XXXI.

He bemoans the unhappy lot of Constantinople owing to the misfortune which has overtaken it from that heretic; and at the same time he urges the citizens to stand fast in the ancient Catholic and ancestral faith.

WHEREFORE I also, humble and insignificant as I am in name as in desert, and although I cannot claim a place as Teacher among those illustrious Bishops of Constantinople, yet venture to claim the zeal and enthusiasm of a disciple. For I was admitted into the sacred ministry by the Bishop John, of blessed memory, and offered to God, and even though I am absent in body yet I am still there in heart: and though by actual presence I no longer mix with that most dear and honourable people of God, yet I am still joined to them in spirit. And hence it comes that condoling and sympathizing with them, I broke out just now into the utterance of our common grief and sorrow, and in my weakness cried out (which was all that I could do) by means of the dolorous lamentation of my works, as if for my own limbs and members: for if as the Apostle says, when the smaller part of the body is grieved, the greater part grieves and sympathizes with it,[4] how much more should the smaller part sympathize when the greater part is grieved? It is indeed utterly inhuman for the smaller parts not to feel the sufferings of the greater in one and the same body, if the greater feel those of the smaller. Wherefore I pray and beseech you, you who live within the circuit of Constantinople, and who are my fellow-citizens through the love of my country, and my brothers through the unity of the faith; separate yourselves from that ravening wolf who (as it is written) devours the people of God, as if they were bread.[5] Touch not, taste not anything of his, for all those things lead to death. Come out from the midst of him and be ye separate and touch not the unclean thing. Remember your ancient teachers, and your priests; Gregory whose fame was spread through the world, Nectarius renowned for holiness, John a marvel of faith and purity. John, I say; that John who like John the Evangelist was indeed a disciple of Jesus and an Apostle; and so to speak ever reclined on the breast and heart of the Lord. Remember him, I say. Follow him. Think of his purity, his faith, his doctrine, and holiness. Remem-

---

[4] Cf. 1 Cor. xii. 26.
[5] Ps. xiii. (xiv.) 4; Col. ii. 21, 23; 2 Cor. vi. 17.

ber him ever as your teacher and nurse, in whose bosom and embraces you as it were grew up. Who was the teacher in common both of you and of me: whose disciples and pupils we are. Read his writings. Hold fast his instruction. Embrace his faith and merits. For though to attain this is a hard and magnificent thing: yet even to follow is beautiful and sublime. For in the highest matters, not merely the attainment, but even the attempt to copy is worthy of praise. For scarcely anyone entirely misses all parts in that to which he is trying to climb and reach. He then should ever be in your minds and almost in your sight: he should live in your hearts and in your thoughts. He would himself commend to you this that I have written, for it was he who taught me what I have written: and so do not think of this as mine, so much as his: for the stream comes from the spring, and whatever you think belongs to the disciple, ought all to be referred to the honour of the master. But, beyond and above all I pray with all my heart and voice, to Thee, O God the Father of our Lord Jesus Christ, that Thou wouldest fill with the gift of Thy love whatever we have written by Thy bounteous grace. And because, as the Lord our God Thine Only Begotten Son Himself taught us, Thou hast so loved this world as to send Thine Only Begotten Son to save the world, grant to Thy people whom Thou hast redeemed that in the Incarnation of Thine Only Begotten Son they may perceive both Thy gift and His love: and that all may understand the truth that for us Thine Only Begotten, our Lord God, was born and suffered and rose again, and may so love it that the condescension of His glory may increase our love: and let not His Humility lead to a diminution of His honour in the hearts of all men, but let it ever produce an increase of love: and may we all rightly and wisely comprehend the blessings of His Sacred Compassion, so as to see that we owe the more to God, in proportion as for our sakes God humbled Himself yet lower.

INDICES.

SULPITIUS SEVERUS.

INDEX OF SUBJECTS.

Abraham, 71.

Ambrose, St., on baptism, 5.

Angels, 71.

Antichrist, the coming of, 15; battle with Nero about the rule of the earth, 45; the ten plagues at his coming, 112.

Arianism, in Illyria and Gaul, 7; origin, spread, definition, and history, 113; infiltration in the catholic church after the council of Nice, intrigues, violence, 114; Valens, the condemnation of Athanasius, 115; Liberius and Hilarius exiled, homo-ousion and homoi-ousion, Osius of Spain, the Gallic bishops at Ariminum, 116, the synod of Seleucia in the East, 117; victory of the Arians, 118; final overthrow of Arianism, 119.

Athanasius, 114.

Auxentius, 7.

Avenger and Defensor, 8.

Avitianus, 47, 49.

Baptism, in its relation to regeneration, 5; dying without baptism, 8.

Bishops, appointment of, 8; "summus sacerdos," 17; St. Martin's episcopal throne, 38; his miraculous power greater while a monk than when a bishop, 39.

Christ, the birth, life, and crucifixion of, 110.

Chronology, 56, 71, 72, 77, 106.

Clarus, 15, 20.

Claudia, the sister of Sulpitius, 55, 58.

Creation of the world, the number of days not given, but the number of years, 71.

Cross, The true, 113.

Daniel, 97.

David, 87 et seq.

Day of Judgment approaching, The, 14.

Demons, 42, 48, 49, 53, 110.

Devil, The, and St. Martin, 14;

Clarus, Anatolius, and the devil's garment, 15; tempts St. Martin, 16.

Dialogue I., between Postumianus, returning from the East, Sulpitius, and a Gallic friend, concerning the virtues of the monks of the East, 24; visit to Cyrene; the presbyter's hut, the church; comparison between Cyrene and Gaul; refusal of gold coins, acceptance of pieces of clothing, 25; visit to Alexandria, strife between the bishops and the monks about the writings of Origen, 26; visit to Bethlehem; Hieronymus; his attack on the Gallic monks, 27; visit to Thebais; the monks of the Desert and their abbot, 28; comparison with the monks of Gaul, 29; the hermit and his ox, 30; the hermit and the wolf, 30; the anchorite and the lioness, 31; the anchorite and the ibex, 32; the recluse of Mount Sinai, 32; the monasteries along the Nile and the principle of monastic life; obedience, 32; examples of obedience, 32; recluses caught by vanity and spurious righteousness, and punished therefor, 33; eulogy of the book of Sulpitius on St. Martin; eulogy of the monarchism of the East, and transition to the eulogy of St. Martin, 34.

Dialogue II., between the same interlocutors concerning the virtues of St. Martin, 37; clothing the shivering man, 37; restores Evanthius and the poisoned bag, 38; is beaten by the soldiers but stops their conveyance, 39; preaches to the Carmites and restores the widow's dead son, 40; forces an entrance to Valentinian, 40; in intercourse with the palace, 41; the cow with the demon on its back, 42; the

hunted hare, 43; sayings, 43; the soldier and his wife, 43; virgins and women, 44; conversation with Agnes, Thecla, and Mary, 45; synod of Memausus; Nero and Antichrist, 45.

Dialogue III., continuation of Dialogue II., 46. A great number of people rush to the place but are not admitted, as it is not proper for the merely curious to mix with the truly pious, 46; St. Martin as a Western compeer of the Eastern saints, 46; the dumb girl of Carmites, 46; blessed oil, 47; Avitianus, 47, 49; manner of exorcising demons, 48; the village of the Senones, 49; the idol-temple of the Ambatienses, 49; various miracles, 50; Priscillian and Ithacius, 50; the ordination of Felix, 52; the Egyptian merchant, Lycontius, and other miracles, 52; "If Christ bore with Judas why should not I bear with Brichio?" 53.

Esther and Judith, 102.

Felix, 52, 54.

Fish at Easter, 50.

Gnosticism appears in Spain, 119; its origin in the East, spread, and invasion in the West, 120.

Helena, 113.

Herod, 110.

Idols and idolatry among the Gauls, 49; among the Hebrews, 84.

Israel in Egypt, 75.

Ithacius, 50, 120.

Jerome in Bethlehem; his attack on the Gallic monks, 27.

Jerusalem, 91; destruction, 111; the Jews forbidden to approach the city, 112; magnificently rebuilt by the Christians, 113.

623

INDEX OF TEXTS.

VINCENT OF LERINS.

INDEX OF SUBJECTS.

INDEX OF TEXTS.

JOHN CASSIAN.

INDEX OF SUBJECTS.

Abel replaced by Seth and his seed, 383.

Abraham, Egyptian abbot, consulted by Germanus and Cassian, 186; quoted from, 188; works miraculous cures, 447; his Conference on mortification, 531 sq.

Accidie, Acedia, 233, 266 sq., 339, 343-4, 533; akin to dejection, 266, 342, 533; injures the soul, 267 sq.; description of, 267 sq., 533; how to be cured, 268 sq., 275, 342 sq., 350, 533; of two kinds, 344.

Adam called πρωτόπλαστος 281; an example of sin, 340; had knowledge by divine inspiration, 383; how tempted and fell, 379; sacrificed his liberty, 526; moral results of his transgression, 519 sq.; not a complete figure of Christ, 607-8; first restored in the Second, 340.

Alleluia, ending a psalm, 207, 210.

Alms, a duty and privilege, 503.

Altar reproached by Nestorius' presence, 596.

Ambidextrous, applied spiritually, 356-7.

Ambrose, Bishop of Milan, his teaching on the Incarnation, 617.

Ammon organised monasticism in Lower Egypt, 186.

Ananias and Sapphira, 252, 256, 257, 482, 516.

Anastasius, Nestorius' chaplain, 190, 556; follower of Theodore of Mopsuestia, 556; preaches against Theotokos, 190, 556; originates Nestorianism, 190, 549, 556.

Anchorites in Egypt, 184, 293, 319, 477, 480 sq., 523; visited by Cassian and Germanus, 184; originated by St. Antony and St. Paul, and why so called, 481; their aim, 185, 293, 319, 477, 484, 490, 492; their humility and patience, 484, 490; preferred by Cassian, 185, 480, 523; have a grander life than the Cœnobites, 293, 481, 490, 523; how they are trained, 480, 490, 523; the best districts for them, 523.

Andronicus, abbot, cured of a Possession, 373.

Angelic powers created by God, 377, 381; His purpose in creating, 377; two to each person, 381.

Anger, its evils, 257, 342, 367, 451 sq., 459, 485; its better side, 258; examples against, 259; against ourselves is valuable, 260; as spoken of God, 258; its implacable form as revenge, 260, 261; cured by reconciliation, 261, 386, 452, 457, 459; as cured by the Gospel, 263, 350, 386; "with excuse" considered, 363, 452; of three kinds, 344; destroys friendship, 452, 453, 459; to be repressed, 459, 485; to be rooted out by a monk, 257 sq., 339, 343, 350, 452.

Anger's Synopsis, 304.

Anthropomorphic language accounted for, 258-9.

Anthropomorphites and their teaching, 187, 188, 258, 401, 403; the heresy and controversy, 319, 401 sq.

Antidosis, its definition, 375.

Antioch, creed of, 592, 593, 596; used against Nestorius, 594-6.

Antiphona, 205, 208, 217.

Antiphonal singing, 205, 217.

Antony, hermit in the Thebaid, 186, 234, 308, 310; founder of monasticism, 234, 243, 481; his sayings to the monks, 234; his fastings, 243; how he became an ascetic, 320; bequeathed his sheepskin to Athanasius, 203; originated the anchorites, 481; his opinion on prayer and its conditions, 398; and on self-help for a monk, 536; was tempted by the devils, 382.

Apollinarians, 551-2; taught that Jesus had no human soul, 552.

Apollonius, Apollos, abbot in the Thebaid, 314, 335.

Appear, its Scriptural force, 559.

Arcadius, Bishop in Gaul, 192.

Archebius, anchorite, Bishop in Egypt, 184, 245, 246, 371, 415; assists Cassian, 184, 246, 415; gives his cell to Cassian, and builds

others, 186, 246; earned money to clear off his mother's debts, 246; was Bishop of Panephysis, 415.

Arians and Arianism, 551, 552, 593.

Ascension of Christ by His own power, 616, 617.

Ash-Wednesday, 514.

Athanasius quoted, 401; teaches the Incarnation, 619.

Athlete in Christ, 237 sq., 263.

Augustine, Bishop of Hippo Regius, teaches the Incarnation, 618; developed predestinarianism, 190-3; his teaching one-sided, 193; how related to Pelagianism, 190, 191; not valued by Cassian, 191, 618; restored Leporius, 552-5; date of his death, 192.

Augustinianism, 190-3.

Aurelian of Arles, his rule, 224.

Auxerre, Council of, 401.

Auxonius, Bishop in Gaul, 192.

Avarice a principal fault, 339.

Babel and the confusion of tongues, 335.

Bad things, discussed, 352 sq.

Baptism, the grace of, 527.

Barber, Abbot Macarius' story of, 537.

Basil, Bishop of Cæsarea, 254; aided monasticism, 200, 212; his rule, 213, 217, 219, 224, 274; a saying of his, 254.

Basilisk said to be from the Ibis' egg, 607.

Bees, used in illustration, 607.

Benedict of Nursia, organiser of monastic system, 189, 194, 243; his rule, 194, 205, 209, 215, 216, 218, 219, 220, 221, 222, 224, 225, 232, 243, 274, 405, 482.

Bethlehem, monastery at, 184, 185, 230; received Cassian and Germanus, 185.

Bibliotheca Maxima Patrum, 553.

Bingham quoted, 217, 330, 482, 503.

Birth, the new, through the font, 593 sq., 600.

Bishops, why disliked by the Egyptian monks, 401.

Blessed oil, 244.

Braga, Council of, 401.

INDEX OF TEXTS.